TRADE IN GOODS

The GATT and the Other WTO Agreements Regulating Trade in Goods

PETROS C. MAVROIDIS

OXFORD

UNIVERSITY PRESS

OXFORD

UNIVERSITY PRESS

Great Clarendon Street, Oxford, OX2 6DP,
United Kingdom

Oxford University Press is a department of the University of Oxford.
It furthers the University's objective of excellence in research, scholarship,
and education by publishing worldwide. Oxford is a registered trade mark of
Oxford University Press in the UK and in certain other countries

Published in the United States of America by Oxford University Press
198 Madison Avenue, New York, NY 10016, United States of America

British Library Cataloguing in Publication Data
Data available

ISBN 978–0–19–965748–3 (hbk)
ISBN 978–0–19–968975–0 (pbk)

Printed in Great Britain on acid-free paper by
CPI Group (UK) Ltd, Croydon, CR0 4YY

For Meritas always

FOREWORD

I thought the time had come to write the second edition of my book while reading Lawrence Durrell's classic, *Bitter Lemons* (1957). In that book, he refers to a Greek saying, mainly used in Cyprus, namely 'no spark in last year's ashes'. The rich case law and some new agreements that saw the light of the day after 2007 when the first edition came out made me think that the book was slowly becoming *dépassé par les événements*. Reading it once again cover to cover, I was persuaded that I could have written it in a clearer, more systematic manner. Consistently reminded of Schumpeter's perennial gale of creative (hopefully) destruction, I realized that, whatever spark was there, I did not manage to honour it in my first effort. I hope I have come closer this time, although I think I took Schumpeter's creative-destruction parabola a bit too literally.

Working on this second edition of *Trade in Goods* made me realize first and foremost how much I have changed my mind on a number of issues where I thought I was more or less on safe ground. I would not exaggerate, I think, if I were to say that this volume has been almost totally rewritten. The process also made me realize how many inaccuracies existed in the first edition, for which I apologize. I cannot claim that all is perfect in this second edition, but I can state that I have eliminated a lot of embarrassing mistakes. I take some comfort in George Bernard Shaw's maxim, 'those who cannot change their mind cannot change anything'.

I tried to provide a book that I hoped would make people think about the intellectual validity of the various legal propositions. In this vein, while insisting on the law as it is, I use the work of many people I admire in order to ask questions regarding the soundness of the approach followed so far and also show some possible avenues for the future.

I have kept the instruments-based approach that I followed in the first edition of the book. In my view, law is man-made, it does not pre-date us, and it exists to the extent we want it to exist. Law is not necessarily justice. World Trade Organization (WTO) law is a contract signed by 157 trading nations nowadays who agreed to limit their sovereignty by disciplining instruments affecting trade (and thus, to pursue trade liberalization). A number of natural questions arise, such as why not pursue trade liberalization irrespective of an agreement etc., which we discuss in the first chapter. Once, however, the intellectual case for an agreement to liberalize trade is made, I ask what is the legal disciplining of instruments committed to this endeavour? It has become a commonplace to refer to feasible contracting as 'incomplete contracting': the original contract will be completed through renegotiation and adjudication, and in the case of the WTO, mainly through the latter. WTO adjudicators cannot complete the contract as they deem appropriate: their 'agency' contract requires from them certain conduct. Throughout this volume, consequently, I look at the law as 'completed' through case law and ask the question whether the final outcome is reasonable. If my response to this question is affirmative, I leave it there, but in the opposite case I ask the additional question whether the source of my dissatisfaction lies in the interpretation of the contract or in the contract itself. In the former case, I have tried to point to avenues which, in my view, could help WTO adjudicators reach coherent judgments in the future, whereas in the latter I leave it to the WTO framers to rethink the usefulness of specific agreements they have entered into.

The focus of the book has shifted: I spend more time discussing everything included in the first edition, but have added lots of new material as well: Chapter 1 is dedicated to the question of 'why the GATT?' Chapters 2–5 discuss the GATT, the disciplining of trade- and domestic instruments, and the lawful deviations from assumed obligations respectively. In Chapter 6, I discuss the various agreements dealing with customs procedures (such as customs valuation, import licensing, etc.). Chapters 7–9 concern the various contingent protection instruments, such as antidumping, countervailing, and safeguards. In Chapter 10, I shift focus and review the 'new generation' agreements dealing with domestic instruments, such as the agreement on Technical Barriers to Trade, and the Agreement on Sanitary and Phyto-sanitary Measures. Chapter 11 includes a discussion of the two sectoral agreements, the Agreement on Agriculture, and the Agreement on Textiles and Clothing. Chapter 12 is dedicated to plurilateral agreements dealing with trade in goods, such as the Agreement on Government Procurement. Transparency is the subject-matter of Chapter 13, whereas the final chapter sets out some conclusions. It is evident that my desire was to rebalance the first edition and spend as much time on agreements dealing with trade in goods as on the GATT, thus doing justice to the title of this volume. For various reasons, ranging from the intellectual appeal of the 'new generation' agreements to the use of non-GATT agreements dealing with trade in goods, I felt a similar rebalancing was necessary.

Kyle Bagwell, Bill Davey, Diwakar Dixit, Aris Georgopoulos, Andrea Mastromatteo, Suja Rishikesh, Michele Ruta, Kamal Saggi, Erik Wijkstrom read chapters of the book, corrected my numerous mistakes, and gave me most valuable comments.

Writing the second edition also made me realize my huge intellectual debt to the people I have been working with over the years: Henrik Horn has been a fellow traveller for almost two decades by now and this book is as much his (assuming he wants to get credit for it) as it is mine. The group that I have been working with at the American Law Institute (ALI), Kyle Bagwell, Gene Grossman, Bob Staiger, and Alan Sykes, has emerged as the hothouse where my understanding of everything I discuss here has blossomed. Under this umbrella, I also had the luck to work with Alan Sykes and Doug Irwin on *The Genesis of the GATT*, a volume we published in 2008, and this led me to appreciate the negotiating record of the GATT, the heart of this volume. Doug's approach to the historical record has been a major influence ever since in all my work. I guess I will never thank Lance Liebman enough for putting this group together.

I have been very fortunate to belong to the Columbia Law School Faculty for some years where I have had the chance to interact with many Faculty members and especially with George Bermann, Mike Gerrard, Merit Janow, Ben Liebman, Katharina Pistor, Mark Wu (now at Harvard Law School). Teaching WTO over the years with Jagdish Bhagwati has been a privilege, for Jagdish has been at the forefront of discussions regarding international trade for decades. He has very generously shared the wealth of his knowledge with me and influenced my thinking on all issues discussed in this volume. Thanks to the generous support of my Dean, David Schizer, I had the good fortune to be in a position to bring many experts to New York who spent time, taught, and interacted with my students and me: Chad Bown, Marc Busch, Steve Charnovitz, Bill Davey, Claus-Dieter Ehlermann, Bill Ethier, Caroline Freund, Bernard Hoekman, Gary Horlick, Rob Howse, Patrick Messerlin, Damien Neven, Tom Prusa, Kamal Saggi, André Sapir, Terry Stewart, Joel Trachtman, Joseph Weiler, Alan Winters, Jan Wouters have been regular visitors. Terry has also helped me a lot, sharing his work with me and providing me with archival documents that I would have never unearthed myself. My 'computer gurus', in New York, Angay Vijayakumar, Erik 'Blue' Espenberg, Frantz Merine, Tan 'Sleepy Tiger' Truong, and Willer 'Butterfingers' Ciprian, were there for me any time (and there were many such occasions) whenever I presented them with a problem to be resolved as a matter of extreme urgency. Alex 'Sasho' Shneyderman deserves particular mention, for his decision to move to Switzerland also meant more time on the phone with me on software-related issues.

At the European University Institute (EUI), I benefited from discussion with Carlo-Maria Cantore, David Kleimann, Juan Jorge Piernas Lopez, Boris Rigod, and Luca Rubini.

At the WTO, Rohini Acharya, Cato Adrian, Marc Auboin, Marc Bacchetta, Willie Chatsika, Dixit Diwakar, Lessie Doré, Alejandro Gamboa, Eki Kim, Mark Koulen, Patrick Allison Low, Gabrielle Marceau, Juan-Alberto Marchetti, Andrea Mastromatteo, Wolf Meier-Ewert, Julie Pain, Maria Pereyra, Roy Santana, and Erik Wijkstrom never tired of responding to my ever increasing number of questions. Edwini Kessie treated each and every one of my requests as a matter of life and death and promptly responded to my numerous queries. My dear friend Harsha Vardana Singh, his many duties notwithstanding, still found time to discuss issues with me and point me to various precious sources. Luigi Stendardo, the WTO librarian, always made time for my 'urgent' requests and responded to my multiple queries regarding old books and negotiating archives. Rhian-Mary

Wood-Richards went studiously through the whole manuscript, and made sure that many of the mistakes of the first edition would not be repeated.

Mark Sanctuary and the ENTWINED group he put together provided me with the much appreciated opportunity to work with Henrik and many others on trade and climate change issues. This part of my work has been a catalyst in my thinking regarding the disciplining of domestic instruments at the WTO level.

I was fortunate to work with co-authors with substantial expertise in their field and learnt a lot as a consequence: Bernard Hoekman, Juan Alberto Marchetti, Aditya Mattoo, Patrick Messerlin, David Palmeter, Tom Prusa, André Sapir, Jasper 'Tijnte' Wauters shared with me their expertise in various fields of trade integration.

Teaching WTO law at Columbia Law School over the years has been a blessing, not only because of my association there with Kyle Bagwell, Jagdish Bhagwati, and Ben Liebman, but equally importantly because of the quality of our students there, who have helped me through their interventions to rethink all the issues discussed in this volume. There are dozens that deserve to be mentioned here and I hope they understand that lack of specific mention of their names does not mean that I do not appreciate their input. In naming Mariel Fernandez, Jessica Fjeld, David Garfinkel, Eric Jay, Andrew Joyce, and Cecilia Wang, who took a short, intensive course with me while I was working on this volume, I would like to thank all of them.

My wife, Suja Rishikesh-Mavroidis, and our daughters, Meera, Riya, and Tara, have shown remarkable understanding while I was spending hours in the basement of our house working on this manuscript, and provided me with much-needed perspective when the hours in the basement became too long. This book is for them, as is all my work.

This book has been written in different parts of the world (mostly in Switzerland, our home) and I am grateful to various people for the hospitality I have benefited from while working on it. The book was completed, in the loving company of my family and my in-laws, in Trivandrum (Thiruvananthapuram), a port city where people from different cultures and origins trade goods on a daily basis. I could not dream of a more fitting background.

Petros C. Mavroidis
Trivandrum, India
27 December 2011

PREFACE TO THE PAPERBACK EDITION

To state that the WTO is at a crossroads is probably a good candidate for the 'understatement of the year'. For various good as well as bad reasons, we have ended up in the current mess where a compass is urgently needed in order to plan the next moves. What is undeniable is that we observe more and more a disjoint between the aspirations of the business community, on the one hand, and the agenda of WTO negotiators on the other. Equally, if not more, disturbing, is the fact that preferential trade agreements, with their more flexible and adjustable structure seem to be in a better position to respond to requests by the stakeholders, and this, along with other factors of course, probably explains their proliferation.

This is not to suggest that the multilateral trading system as we know it is condemned to oblivion. It is definitely challenged but, in principle, it has a card, a strong card to play: other things equal, bilateral deals increase transaction costs (more than multilateral deals do). And then there are all the positive external effects stemming from a healthy WTO which could serve as an institution signaling cooperation in other areas of international relations as well.

It is my hope that this volume will help the readership understand the nuts and bolts of the world trading system, the rationale for the legal arsenal that has been put into place, as well as the manner in which it has been interpreted and understood in practice. It is my belief that unless the trade community delves into its intricacies, it will not properly understand its shortcomings, and might risk repeating the mistakes of the past. If this volume makes a small contribution in this perspective, I will consider that the aims of this book have been accomplished.

One substantive change does need to be noted, with reference to the discussion of 'Less Favourable Treatment' on p289. In its report on *US-Clove Cigarettes*, the Appellate Body complicated matters even more. We read in footnote 372:

> We disagree with the United States to the extent that it suggests that *Dominican Republic – Import and Sale of Cigarettes* stands for the proposition that, under Article III:4, panels should inquire further whether "the detrimental effect is unrelated to the foreign origin of the product"...In *Thailand – Cigarettes (Philippines)*, the Appellate Body further clarified that for a finding of less favourable treatment under Article III:4 "there must be in every case a genuine relationship between the measure at issue and its adverse impact on competitive opportunities for imported versus like domestic products to support a finding that imported products are treated less favourably"...The Appellate Body eschewed an additional inquiry as to whether such detrimental impact was related to the foreign origin of the products or explained by other factors or circumstances.

This probably means that if a genuine and substantial relationship between the measure and the adverse impact on competitive opportunities has been established there is no need to also show that the intent was to disfavour imports. Only future practice though, will clarify an admittedly unclear pronouncement.

Petros C. Mavroidis
June 2013

CONTENTS—SUMMARY

CONTENTS—DETAILED

TABLE OF CASES

Please note this table makes use of short titles of GATT Panel, WTO Panel, and AB Reports. Full report titles and citations can be found in the Tables in Chapter 3.

GATT PANEL, WTO PANEL AND AB REPORTS

EUROPE

NAFTA

USA

TABLE OF CONVENTIONS, INSTRUMENTS, AND LEGISLATION

NATIONAL LEGISLATION

LIST OF ABBREVIATIONS

AAC	Average Avoidable Cost
AB	Appellate Body
ACP	Africa, Caribbean, Pacific
ACTE	Approvals Committee for Technical Equipment
ACWL	Advisory Centre for WTO Law
AD	Antidumping
ADICMA	Association of Industrial Producers of Leather, Leather Manufactures and Related Products
ADP	WTO Committee on Antidumping Practices
AG	Agriculture
AGOA	Africa Growth and Opportunity Act
AIDCP	Agreement on International Dolphin Conservation Program
ALCM	Apple Leafcurling Midge
ALI	American Law Institute
AMS	Aggregate Measurement of Support
ASATAP	Applied So As To Afford Protection
ASP	American Selling Price
ATC	Agreement on Textiles and Clothing
AVC	Average Variable Cost
BDV	Brussels Definition of Value
BIA	Best Information Available
BCI	Business Confidential Information
BoP	Balance of Payments
BPOA	Brussels Programme for Action for the LDCs
BRIC	Brazil, Russia, India, China
BRICS	Brazil, Russia, India, China, South Africa
BTA	Border Tax Adjustment
BTN	Brussels Convention on Nomenclature for the Classification of Goods in Customs Tariffs
C-20	Committee of Twenty (of the IMF)
CA	Civil Aircraft
CAA	US Clean Air Act of 1990
CACM	Central American Common Market
CAFC	US Court of Appeals for the Federal Circuit
CAFTA	Central American Free Trade Agreement
CAP	Common Agricultural Policy
CARICOM	Caribbean Community and Common Market
CAT	Convention against Torture
CCC	Customs Cooperation Council
CCCN	Customs Cooperation Council Nomenclature

CCCMC	Chinese Chamber of Commerce of Metals, Minerals & Chemicals Importers & Exporters
CDSOA	Continued Dumping and Subsidies Offset Act
CEA	Council of Economic Advisors (US)
CEN	Committee for Standardization
CENELEC	European Committee for Electrotechnical Standardization
CFC	Common Fund for Commodities
CG18	Consultative Group of Eighteen
CIF	Cost Insurance Freight
CITES	Convention on International Trade of Endangered Species
COCOM	Coordinating Committee for Multilateral Export Controls
CRC	Convention on Rights of the Child
CRN	Central Registry of Notifications
CRS	Creditor Reporting System
CRTA	Committee on Regional Trade Agreements
CTD	Committee on Trade and Development
CTG	Council for Trade in Goods
CTS	Consolidated Tariff Schedules
CU	Customs Union
CV	Customs Valuation
CVD	Countervailing Duty
DCS	Directly Competitive or Substitutable
DDA	Doha Development Agenda
DFQF	Duty-Free and Quota-Free
DG	Director-General
DISC	Domestic International Sales Corporations
DOC	Department of Commerce
DR	Designated Representative
DRAM	Dynamic Random Access Memory
DSB	Dispute Settlement Body
DSU	Dispute Settlement Understanding
EAEC	Eurasian Economic Community
EBA	Everything But Arms
EC	European Communities
EC-CARIFORUM	Caribbean Forum
ECJ	European Court of Justice
ECOSOC	UN Economic and Social Council
ECSC	European Coal and Steel Community
ECT	Treaty Establishing the European Community
EFSA	European Food Safety Authority
EIF	Enhanced Integrated Framework
EMS	Equivalent Measurement of Support
ENP	European Neighbourhood Policy
EP	Export Price
EPA	US Environmental Protection Agency (EPA)
ESTO	European Scientific Technology Observatory
ETSI	European Telecommunications Standards Institute
EU	European Union

EVI	Economic Vulnerability Index
FANs	Friends of Antidumping Negotiations
FAO	Food and Agriculture Organization
FBTAMS	Final Bound Total AMS
FCC	Federal Communications Commission
FCN	Friendship, Commerce and Navigation
FDA	Food and Drugs Authority
FDI	Foreign Direct Investment
FIRA	Foreign Investment Review Act
FOB	Free on Board
FOREX	Foreign Exchange Contract
FRUS	Federal Register of the United States
FSC	Foreign Sales Corporation
FTA	Free Trade Area
GAAP	Generally Accepted Accounting Principles
GATS	General Agreement on Trade in Services
GATT	General Agreement on Tariffs and Trade
GCC	Gulf Cooperation Council
GDP	Gross Domestic Product
GIR	General Interpretative Rule
GMO	Genetically Modified Organism
GN	Geneva Nomenclature
GNP	Gross National Product
GPA	Government Procurement Agreement
GSP	Generalized System of Preferences
HAI	Human Assets Index
HHI	Herfindahl-Hirschman Index
HS	Harmonized System
HSEN	Harmonized System Explanatory Note
HWP	Harmonization Work Programme
IA	Investigating Authority
IASB	International Accounting Standards Board
IAWG	Inter-Agency Working Group
IBM	International Arrangement Regarding Bovine Meat
ICA	International Commodity Agreement
ICAC	International Cotton Advisory Committee
ICB	International Commodity Bodies
ICC	International Chamber of Commerce
ICCO	International Cocoa Organization
ICCPR	International Covenant on Civil and Political Rights
ICITO	Interim Commission for the International Trade Centre
ICJ	International Court of Justice
ICO	International Coffee Organization
ICSG	International Copper Study Group
IDA	International Dairy Arrangement
IDB	Integrated Database
IEC	International Electrotechnical Commission
IF	Integrated Framework

IFIA	International Federation of Inspection Agencies
IFSC	Integrated Framework Steering Committee
IGC	International Grains Council
IGE	Informal Group of Experts
IJSG	International Jute Study Group
ILA	Import Licensing Agreement
ILAC	International Laboratory Accreditation Cooperation
ILC	International Law Commission
ILO	International Labour Organization
ILZSG	International Lead and Zinc Study Group
IMF	International Monetary Fund
INR	Initial Negotiating Right
INSG	International Nickel Study Group
IOOC	International Olive Oil Council
IRSG	International Rubber Study Group
ISG	International Study Group
ISO	International Organization for Standardization
ISO	International Sugar Organization
IT	Information Technology
IT	Individual Treatment
ITA	Information Technology Agreement
ITC	International Trade Centre
ITC	International Trade Commission
ITCB	International Textiles and Clothing Bureau
ITLOS	International Tribunal of the Law of the Sea
ITO	International Trade Organization
ITTO	International Tropical Timber Organization
JEFCA	Joint FAO/WHO Committee for Food Additives
JITAP	Joint Integrated Technical Assistance Programme
LAN	Local Area Network
LCD	Liquid Crystal Display
LDCs	Least Developed Countries
LFT	Less Favourable Treatment
LTA	Long-Term Cotton Arrangement
LTFV	Less Than Fair Value
MAI	Multilateral Agreement on Investment
MAS	Mutually Agreed Solution
MERCOSUR	Mercado del Sur
MET	Market Economy Test
METI	Ministry of Economy, Trade and Industry
MFA	Multi-fibre Arrangement
MFN	Most Favoured Nation
MIGA	Multilateral Investment Guarantee Agency
MITI	Ministry of Trade and Investment
MRA	Mutual Recognition Agreement
NAFTA	North Atlantic Free Trade Area
NAMA	Non-agricultural Market Access
NGO	Non-governmental Organization

NME	Non-market Economies
NSS	Notification Submission System
NT	National Treatment
NTB	Non-tariff Barrier
NTM	Non-tariff Measure
NV	Normal Value
NVC	Non-violation Complaint
OCD	Ordinary Customs Duty
ODC	Other Duties and Charges
OECD	Organisation for Economic Co-operation and Development
OIE	Organisation International des Epizooties
OMA	Orderly Marketing Arrangement
OMB	Office of Management and Budget
OPEC	Organization of the Petroleum Exporting Countries
ORRC	Other Restrictive Regulations of Commerce
PFC	Production Flexibility Contract
PGE	Permanent Group of Experts
POI	Period of Investigation
PPA	Protocol of Provisional Application
PPM	Production Process Method
PSE	Producer Subsidy Equivalent
PSI	Pre-shipment Inspection
PSI	Principal Supplier Interest
PTA	Preferential Trade Agreement
QFTI	Qualified Foreign Trade Income
QR	Quantitative Restriction
RBPs	Restrictive Business Practices
R&D	Research and Development
ROO	Rules of Origin
RPT	Reasonable Period of Time
RTAA	Reciprocal Trade Agreements Act
SACU	South African Customs Union
SAT	Substantially All Trade
SCM	Subsidies and Countervailing Measures
SDoC	Supplier's Declaration of Conformity
SDRs	Special Drawing Rights
SG	Safeguards
SG&A	Selling, General and Administrative Expenses
SGS	Société Générale de Surveillance
SI	Substantial Interest
SOCB	State Owned Commercial Bank
SOE	State Owned Enterprise
SP	Special Products
SPS	Sanitary and Phyto-sanitary Measures
SSG	Special Safeguard Provision
SSM	Special Safeguard Mechanism
STA	Short-Term Cotton Arrangement
STC	Specific Trade Concern

STDF	Standards and Trade Development Facility
STE	State Trading Enterprise
TBT	Technical Barriers to Trade
TDM	Temporary Defence Mechanism
TEC	Transatlantic Economic Council
TED	Turtle-Excluding Device
TFEU	Treaty on the Functioning of the European Union
TMB	Textiles Monitoring Body
TNC	Trade Negotiating Committee
TPA	Trade Promotion Authority
TPRB	Trade Policy Review Body
TPRM	Trade Policy Review Mechanism
TRIMs	Trade Related Investment Measures
TRIPs	Trade Related Intellectual Property Rights
TRQ	Tariff Quota
TRTA	Trade-Related Technical Assistance
TSB	Textiles Surveillance Body
UN	United Nations
UNCITRAL	United Nations Commission for International Trade Law
UNCLOS	United Nations Convention on the Law of the Sea
UNCTAD	United Nations Conference on Trade and Development
UNDP	United Nations Development Programme
UNIDO	UN Industrial Development Organization
UNLK	UN Layout Key
URM	Usual Marketing Requirement
VAT	Value Added Tax
VCLT	Vienna Convention on the Law of Treaties
VER	Voluntary Export Restraint
VIEs	Voluntary Import Expansions
VRA	Voluntary Restraint Agreement
WA	Weighted Average
WAN	Wide Area Network
WB	World Bank
WCO	World Customs Organization
WHO	World Health Organization
WP	Working Party
WTO	World Trade Organization
WWII	World War II

For the rational study of law the black letter man may be the man of the present, but the man of the future is the man of statistic, and master of economics.

Oliver Wendell Holmes, Jr.

(*The Path of Law*, Harcourt, Brace and Company: New York, 1920, p.187)

Man in his elemental state is a peasant with a possessive love of his own turf; a mercantilist who favors exports over imports; a Populist who distrusts banks, especially foreign banks; a monopolist who abhors competition; a xenophobe who feels threatened by strangers and foreigners, and above all, a child who wants to have his cake and eat it too, in this case to have the benefits of foreign investments but not the costs. In international economics we are inclined to patronize these views as juvenile and regard our task in education as extirpating some or all of them, particularly intuitive mercantilism and love of monopoly. I would argue, however, that most people, even those taught at length in international economics, retain their antipathy to intrusion by foreigners.

Charles P. Kindleberger

(*Multinational Excursions*, MIT Press: Cambridge, Mass., 1984, p. 39)

1

FROM GATT TO THE WTO

1. Why the GATT?

1.1 We Need to Act before the Vested Interests Get their Vests on

Adlai Stevenson is reported to have said that trade is quite boring, and that its greatest need was for fresh clichés.[1] Viewed from the perspective of a statesman, this is probably a wise statement: trade talks until recently, with the emergence of the anti-globalization movement, would not make the headlines the way other events do. This was probably even more the case when the General Agreement on Tariffs and Trade (GATT) was created amidst other towering achievements in the post-World War II era, such as the advent of the United Nations (UN), the World Bank (WB), and the International Monetary Fund (IMF). The GATT came lame into life before its institutional umbrella, the International Trade Organization (ITO); the ITO, the 'big' project, never saw the light of the day. The reputed US statesman was not out of tune when one takes all of this into account.

---

[1] See Aaronson (1999).

1

The ITO was intended to serve as the institutional foundation to administer the Havana Charter, an international agreement designed to regulate trade in goods, and GATT was supposed to be part of it.[2] Two important worldwide negotiations took place right before the end of World War II (WWII): the San Francisco conference that signalled the advent of the UN,[3] which was intended to be the overarching international organization to help avoid another world war, without however addressing comprehensively the underlying reasons for conflict; at the risk of vulgarizing, the UN system was designed as a multilateral response to unilateral aggression. The Bretton Woods conference, which took place in the homonymous city on the other side of the North American continent, aimed to fill this gap and address the causes for aggression: in this vein, providing technical assistance to address development-related issues, and financing development policies were meant to be the international community's response;[4] this was the intended role of the World Bank, and the International Monetary Fund.[5]

There was no formal negotiation during the Bretton Woods conference of a 'commercial' leg that would complement the WB and the IMF, although some informal discussions pointed to this direction.[6] Remarkably, as Dam (2004) explains, in developed countries such as the US, as late as 1916 the majority of US congressmen considered tariffs to be a domestic issue. Similar views would not lend support of course to an international negotiation on trade liberalization. A notable exception among them was Cordell Hull, a genuine free-trader whose role in bringing the GATT around we will be discussing in more detail *infra*. Hull saw the international dimension in setting tariffs and firmly believed that trade 'dovetailed with peace': when deciding on them consequently, countries should, in his view, be mindful of the effect that trade policies have on world peace.[7]

The formal negotiation of the ITO started in 1946, but its origins, as we will see *infra*, predate both the UN and the Bretton Woods conferences. A handful of remarkable personalities participated directly or indirectly in the negotiation of the

---

[2] Dam (1970), Gardner (1956), Hoekman and Kostecki (2009), Hudec (1975), Jackson (1969), Matsushita et al. (2006), Trebilcock and Howse (2005), Van den Bossche (2005), Wilcox (1949), and Zeiler (1999).

[3] The UN, or a form of it, was of course in place before the end of WWII, but nations wanted to signal the beginning of a new era and celebrated its advent in 1945 at the end of WWII; see Plesch (2011).

[4] Henry Cabot Lodge used to say that the UN system was designed to avoid hell, but it was no guarantee of heaven.

[5] The IMF was inspired, but did not correspond exactly to, Keynes's idea for a Clearing Union, which was aimed at ensuring that countries ran neither deficits nor surpluses; Eichengreen (2011).

[6] Jackson (1969). Diebold (1993, p. 335) mentions that at the time it was common to refer to the ITO as 'the third leg of the Bretton Woods stool'. In his classic study, Musgrave (1959) suggested that government activity had three functions: achieving macro-stabilization, income redistribution, and efficient resource allocation. In a way, the Bretton Woods system complemented by the ITO corresponds to this idea, the IMF stabilizing, the WB aiming to ensure equity, and the ITO efficient resource allocation.

[7] Hull (1948, pp. 81ff).

2

GATT: Will Clayton and Harry Hawkins from the United States (US); James Meade (Nobel Prize in Economics, 1977) and Lionel Robbins (Professor of Economics at the London School of Economics) from the United Kingdom (UK); Norman Robertson from Canada; and Alexandre Kojève (philosopher) from France. John Maynard Keynes passed away in 1946 following the Bretton Woods conference and did not have the chance to leave his mark on this negotiation. These statesmen produced a text dealing with highly complicated issues that has managed to withstand the test of time for almost 65 years now.

The negotiation is very much a shared initiative by the US and UK bureaucracies, although they did not see eye to eye on all issues involved in the negotiation. Still, they both felt that they shared responsibility towards establishing a liberal trade order that would complement the new international architecture. Having been chosen by Roosevelt to serve as Secretary of State, Hull was uniquely positioned to pursue his belief that freer trade[8] might lead to economic and political conditions that would be more favourable to peace. Hull had to fight an uphill battle inside the US administration, where many economic nationalists were opposed to freer trade, fearing that it might eviscerate New Deal policies such as government price support for farm products. The goal he set was not free trade in the sense of zero tariffs, then an inconceivable objective, but simply to reduce excessive tariffs and allow some additional growth in foreign trade.[9] Non-discrimination was a key component of his vision for trade liberalization and, to achieve this, Hull believed that he had to do away with the UK 'imperial preferences' which were openly discriminatory: goods originating in the Commonwealth would be traded in the UK on more favourable terms than goods originating in non-Commonwealth countries. Hull believed that absence of discrimination in world trade relations should be seen as part of the US contribution to world peace, but was also mindful of the trade impact of the imperial preferences; he went so far as to refer to them when testifying before the US Congress in 1940 as:

> the greatest injury, in a commercial way, that has been inflicted on this country since I have been in public life.[10]

In 1938, the US and the UK signed a reciprocal trade agreement, but the results were limited, as the agreement failed to put a dent in Britain's system of imperial preferences. The agreement went into effect in January 1939 but was rendered moot a few months later when the UK adopted extensive controls on imports with its entry into WWII in September of that year.

The US efforts to extract a better deal from the UK were revived thanks to the Lend-Lease programme. US Congress passed the Lend Lease Act in March 1941,

---

[8] In neither the ITO nor the GATT was there any mention of *free trade*: the term was politically untouchable at the time; Diebold (1993) at p. 336.

[9] What follows in this subsection draws on Irwin et al. (2008).

[10] Quoted in Gardner (1956) at p. 19.

and through this, the US government could transfer billions of dollars worth of equipment and supplies to the UK (initially, and later to other allies as well); instead of compensation, the UK was required to provide a benefit which the US President deemed satisfactory. In this vein, the US decided to extract foreign policy promises from the UK and require a commitment to participate in a new world economic framework. In August 1941, Churchill presented to President Roosevelt a first draft of the Atlantic Charter that included the pledge that the two countries would

> strive to bring about a fair and equitable distribution of essential produce . . . between the nations of the world.[11]

The final version of the Atlantic Charter read:

> Fourth, they will endeavor, with due respect for their existing obligations, to further the enjoyment by all States, great or small, victor or vanquished, of access, on equal terms, to the trade and to the raw materials of the world which are needed for their economic prosperity.[12]

Those sympathetic to this idea were increasingly vocal: James Meade (1942), then working for the UK administration, highlighted several features of a possible multilateral trade convention. In his view, an International Commercial Union should be established, and it should have three essential characteristics:

(a) membership open to all states willing to carry out the obligations of membership;
(b) no preferences or discrimination (with an exception for imperial preferences) among the participants, and
(c) a commitment to remove altogether certain protective devices against the commerce of other members of the Union and to reduce to a defined maximum the degree of protection which they would afford to their own home producers against the produce of other members of the Union.

This draft impressed UK administrators in high positions who requested and obtained Meade's move to the Trade Department to work with them on the upcoming trade negotiation.

The scene was thus set for the upcoming transatlantic negotiation: the imperial preferences would have to give way to non-discriminatory trade; the consideration for this concession would have to be negotiated; and of course the question arose who else (besides the US and UK) should participate in the negotiation.

The enactment of the US Reciprocal Trade Agreements Act (RTAA) in 1934 greatly facilitated this process. Irwin (2005, pp. 204ff) states that the RTAA

> fundamentally changed US trade politics by shifting tariff authority from Congress, which proved very responsive to domestic import-competing industries, to the

---

[11] Quoted in Wilson (1991) at p. 164.
[12] Quoted in Irwin et al. (2008) at p. 17.

executive branch, which was more apt to consider the national interest and use tariff negotiations in the service of foreign policy objectives.

The RTAA, however, was met with a lot of scepticism in some quarters. The prevailing view at the time, as Aaronson (1999) reports, was that trade protectionism protected US jobs. RTAA was thus portrayed as a mere temporary measure, and not as a permanent feature in the US legal arsenal. Be it as it may, the UK and the US decided to go ahead and negotiate a trade agreement. Two questions figured prominently on their agenda at this stage: who should participate, and what would the ambit of the agreement be?

There were some informal talks with 'natural' candidates to participate in the upcoming negotiation: one of them, Canada, favoured a 'nucleus' approach, whereby only 'like-minded' countries would participate; this meant that only countries of the so-called 'Western bloc' would be included, and the door would be closed to NMEs (non-market economies).[13] This position had the obvious merit of facilitating the negotiation, but the obvious weakness of restricting trade liberalization to a small subset of all countries. It carried the day in the end with few concessions, as the group that was invited to negotiate the multilateral trade agreement consisted of: Australia, Belgium, Brazil, Canada, Chile, China, Cuba, Czechoslovakia, France, India, Lebanon, Luxembourg, Netherlands, New Zealand, Norway, Union of South Africa, Union of Soviet Socialist Republics (USSR), United Kingdom, United States. The USSR nonetheless declined the invitation to participate.[14] There was no doubt as to the basis of the negotiation: the US had prepared a document (called the Suggested Charter) which was based on the Atlantic Charter and reflected a substantial part of Meade's ideas.

From August to October 1946, US State Department officials travelled to Canada, Cuba, Brazil, Chile, New Zealand, Australia, South Africa, India, and China to brief them on the Suggested Charter and get their reaction. Irwin et al. (2008) report negative reactions: Brazil was lukewarm; India questioned the compatibility of non-discriminatory trade in a world formed by countries with asymmetric bargaining power; Australian officials believed the draft failed to give sufficient emphasis to efforts to expand domestic demand.[15] Canada was reported to be the most supportive, while the UK criticized the draft charter only to the extent that it differed from its own, December 1945 Proposals.[16] One State Department document summarized the reactions in this way:

---

[13] Irwin et al. (2008) discuss this issue in detail.

[14] During the negotiation, Czechoslovakia was undergoing the change to NME and various documents attest to the difficulties stemming from this change; Irwin et al. (2008).

[15] DAFP 10, 174–6.

[16] After reading the draft US charter in September 1946, Meade (1990, p. 327) wrote: 'A grand sign of the intention, at least of the Truman Administration, really to take this all seriously; and I personally confess that I am rather glad to hear that they propose next week to publish the whole draft charter, though the official view here is that this is dangerous since it will frighten off a number

A definite different opinion is to be found in the less-developed countries (Australia, New Zealand, India, China, Cuba, Brazil, and Chile) with regard to the reduction of trade barriers. These countries, deeply concerned with the problem of industrialization and full employment, want to use restrictive measures to protect their infant industries. In general, they remain unimpressed with our contention that subsidies offer the least objectionable method for this purpose. They point out that, while tariffs and subsidies both amount to charges on their economies, the very real difficulties in raising the revenue to pay subsidies make the latter impractical for them. The Cubans are reluctant to give up their preferential position in the US market, as are the New Zealanders in the UK. The British, however, are willing to negotiate on preferences if convinced of the sincerity of the US intention to lower substantially our tariff wall, as a defense against which the Empire preferential system was developed. A major point of difficulty will be faced in connection with our cartel provisions. The Dutch, the Czechs and the Belgians are not willing to concede that all cartels are bad. They would be willing to have the Charter state that certain practices may have undesirable effects, but they object to having the burden of proof put on those engaging in cartel arrangements, as our draft Charter now provides.[17]

The will to negotiate was nevertheless present. Against this background, the negotiation was launched following the establishment of a Preparatory Committee for the ITO in 1946.[18] The ambit of the negotiation was quite vast: the ITO was definitely designed to be a far-reaching agreement dealing with both state and private barriers to trade liberalization and opening up for discussion issues such as social dumping and domestic employment policies.[19] The GATT was one of the Chapters coming under the aegis of this endeavour and designed to address state barriers to trade liberalization only. The Preparatory Committee held three meetings, in London (1946), in New York (1947), and in Geneva (1947). Negotiators realized already at the London meeting that the ITO endeavour was quite formidable: the sheer number of issues on the table made the negotiation a cumbersome and delicate exercise. Countries were slowly becoming more aware of the amount of sovereignty that they would be transferring to the international plane as a result of their accession to the ITO, and were worried about it. The GATT, conversely, seemed a more 'attainable' target since it was both confined to disciplining few instruments and keeping important regulatory choices within the exclusive domain of state sovereignty. Moreover, trading nations could realize the gains from disciplining trade-obstructing instruments and, thus, delaying the advent of the GATT solely because of the uncertainty surrounding the wider ITO negotiation emerged as an unwarranted option. As a result, negotiators decided in London to bifurcate the two agendas, and negotiate the GATT on a separate (from the ITO) track.

---

of countries. On the contrary, I believe now that anything which brings it all nearer to finality is to the good.'

[17] FRUS 1946, I, 1349.

[18] The full name of this body was the Preparatory Committee for the UN Conference on Trade and Employment.

[19] Charnovitz (1995), Drache (2003).

But there were other reasons as well arguing in favour of a speedy negotiation. Diebold (1993, p. 336) attributes to Will Clayton—a southern businessman who established a cotton brokerage firm, moved from the Commerce Department to the State Department in 1944, where he served first as Assistant Secretary and then Under Secretary of State for Economic Affairs, and eventually became the Head of the US delegation in the Geneva talks (1947)—the following phrase:

... we need to act before the vested interests get their vests on.[20]

The decision to bifurcate is also probably due to the awareness that a negotiation that would drag on forever might become an impossible negotiation in the end. On the other hand, the GATT would be the first step in the direction of the ITO; assuming it carried out its promises, the GATT, it was believed, would help bring about the ITO. To borrow again from Diebold (1993), the GATT was regareded as an 'advance instalment' that could be folded into the ITO later on.

The GATT, as we know it, was essentially negotiated in London and in Lake Success, New York, a village in northwest Long Island which had also been the temporary headquarters of the UN: between January and February 1947, state representatives held the second meeting of the Preparatory Committee there.[21] Whereas no reservations were allowed in the final text, reservations were quite appropriate during the drafting stage.[22] The negotiations on the GATT text were complemented by negotiations on tariff reductions: between April and October 1947 the state representatives, negotiating under the institutional umbrella of the Preparatory Committee, conducted a round of tariff negotiations at the European office of the UN in Geneva, Switzerland. In effect, this was the very first round of multilateral trade negotiations.[23] The outcome of these negotiations, together with the document negotiated at Lake Success, constituted the Geneva Final Act, which included the Protocol of Provisional Application (PPA). Under the terms of the PPA, the governments that participated in the negotiations undertook to fully apply Part I of the GATT (dealing with tariff concessions and the most-favoured-nation (MFN) clause),[24] and Part III of the GATT (containing provisions dealing

---

[20] Diebold must be right. In his foreword to Wilcox (1949), Clayton stated at pp. vii–viii: '... we might have decided to postpone our proposals until things got back to normal. But we knew, if we did so, that nations might set up a whole series of new restrictions that the world might never succeed in bringing down'.

[21] Penrose (1953, pp. 12ff, and 90ff) highlights the role that some eminent economists, such as James Meade, and Lionel Robbins, played in drafting the GATT. The final text was drafted by John Leddy, a US public official who had also been trained in economics.

[22] See §2 of the Drafting Committee of the Preparatory Committee of the UN Conference on Trade and Employment, Draft GATT, E/PC/T/C.6/85 of 15 February 1947.

[23] See 55 UNTS 187 (1947). 45,000 tariff concessions were negotiated, that is, roughly $10 billion worth of trade, see Drache (2003).

[24] The UK still managed to 'grandfather' its imperial preferences by virtue of Art. I.2 GATT: the term 'grandfathering' suggests in GATT-speak that pre-existing legislation trumps obligations assumed under the GATT.

with administrative issues). The same governments further undertook to apply Part II of the GATT (the heart of the GATT, covering national treatment, antidumping, subsidies, safeguards, balance of payments, prohibition of quantitative restrictions, general exceptions to the obligations assumed, and dispute settlement) 'to the fullest extent not inconsistent with existing legislation'.[25] The application of Part II only to the extent consistent with existing (domestic) legislation is what became known as 'grandfathering' of inconsistent legislation (with the GATT) obligations.[26] It was agreed that similar inconsistencies would be tolerated on a temporary basis only:

> Part II of this Agreement shall be suspended on the day on which the Havana Charter comes into force.

The GATT entered into force on 1 January 1948 by virtue of the PPA. Its original 23 members were: Australia, Belgium, Brazil, Burma, Canada, Ceylon, Chile, Republic of China, Cuba, Czechoslovak Republic, France, India, Lebanon, Luxembourg, Netherlands, New Zealand, Norway, Pakistan, Southern Rhodesia, Syria, South Africa, the United Kingdom, and the United States. The entry into force of the GATT was provisional. As explained in Jackson (1969), the GATT could have entered into force on a permanent basis, once a given number of countries representing a high percentage of international trade had agreed to do so. It was decided, nevertheless, not to proceed in this way in order to avoid creating discrepancies between those who had accepted the GATT on a provisional basis, and those who would be accepting it permanently.

The GATT entered into force independently of the ITO: the adoption of the Havana Charter, which would signal the advent of the ITO, was expected to occur within a fairly short period following the entry into force of the GATT, and the plan was that the GATT would come under the aegis of the ITO. In the meantime, the legal relationship between the GATT and the ITO was governed by Art. XXIX GATT: this provision imposed on the GATT-signatories a best endeavours obligation to behave in an ITO-consistent manner as well, with respect to the obligations included in the Chapters of the Havana Charter mentioned in Art. XXIX.1 GATT. Since the Havana Charter never came into force, the GATT was provisionally applied for 47 years pending the advent of the ITO. The successful conclusion of the Uruguay round negotiations and the consequential advent of the World Trade Organization (WTO) signalled the definitive end of the ITO project.

---

[25] See UNTS 308, 1 (a) and (b) (1947).

[26] A good example is the US countervailing duty law which did not require a determination of material injury as required by Art. VI GATT. The US agreed to include such a requirement for signatories to the so-called 1979 Tokyo round Subsidies Code, and for other countries that entered into comparable bilateral agreements with the US.

1.2 What Did Negotiators Have in Mind?

Trade liberalization can serve different purposes; it is not as if one can hit only one bird with this stone. In Lewis Carroll's oft-quoted passage from *Alice in Wonderland*, Alice asks 'where do we go from here?', only to get the response 'it depends where you want to go'. 'Why the GATT?' is the question a wondering Alice would ask the framers of the GATT.

The natural place to raise this question is in the historical account of the GATT, that is, the (official and unofficial) records of the negotiation. There are two revelation mechanisms so to speak, a national and a multilateral: under the former, one could extend research to a wide range of possible sources, ranging from official constitutional records to unofficial representations; the preparatory work of the GATT exhausts the multilateral sources. Researching into national sources is, of course, informative about national perceptions but not necessarily about common intentions: any time, for example, we observe variance between a nationally defined objective and the end result of the international negotiation, we can legitimately cast doubt on the validity of the national intention to act as an explanatory variable for the common understanding. We also do not know much about the national positions of the original participants, apart from the positions of the UK and the US. There are few works on the negotiating positions of the remaining original GATT signatories and they all point to the same conclusion: the GATT was, for all practical purposes, a transatlantic bargain. Hart (2002), for example, offers a very comprehensive account of Canada's priorities. His main conclusions are that Canada essentially played second fiddle to the UK and US negotiators who monopolized the negotiations, and was quite happy with the introduction of MFN, which was perceived as a means to curtail the dominance of the then two superpowers.[27] Capling (2001) discusses the Australian participation, and concludes that it did not heavily influence the negotiated outcome. In Capling's account, Australia was largely preoccupied with sectoral negotiations, and even threatened to walk out of the negotiating room when the US initially refused to reduce its duties on wool and wool products.

The overwhelming majority of historical accounts focus on the US and UK negotiating positions and the literature is unanimous regarding the influence that the two had in shaping the original GATT. Irwin (1996 and 2005) delves into the US constitutional process. He aptly describes the context in which US trade policy was being shaped in order to describe the goals sought by the US administration. The US was coming out of the era of the Great Depression and the Smoot-Hawley Tariff Act,[28] under which high tariffs had been imposed on a wide series of products. The US had practised high tariffs a few years before the enactment of

---

[27] Hart (2002, pp. 133ff).

[28] On this, Irwin (2011). Reed Smoot was a Republican Senator from Utah, whereas Willis Hawley, a Republican member of the House of Representatives from Oregon and Chairman of the

Smoot-Hawley as well, but the effects were not as dramatic: by the time the Fordney-McCumber tariff of 1922 had been implemented, the US economy was growing rapidly and European exports were growing at a steady pace. By contrast, when the Smoot-Hawley Tariff Act was enacted and implemented, the US economy was contracting and European exports suffered as a result. We quote from Irwin (2011, p. 151):

> The United States' move to erect even higher trade barriers on top of that imposed in 1922 sharpened European resentment at American policy. With Smoot-Hawley, the United States seemed to be signalling that its economic policies would become more isolationist. For this reason, the European response to the passage of the Smoot-Hawley tariff 'was disapproval-immediate, undisguised, and unanimous'. As Percy Bidwell (1932, p. 395) noted: 'There was a common note in the chorus of protests, however much they may have differed in expression, namely the conviction that the new American duties constituted a serious menace to the economic progress of western Europe'.

Canada first, and then Western European states imposed retaliatory tariffs. The negative impact of Smoot-Hawley did not stop here: anti-US feelings rose in Cuba as well and a blatantly anti-American government was installed as a result.[29] Discriminatory tariffs against the US certainly fuelled Hull's belief that the GATT should be an instrument to abolish discriminatory treatment on trade issues. The US administration was looking for a reduction in the role of the state, taking the view that trade would be safer in private hands,[30] and, in Irwin's account, for product-by-product tariff reductions.[31]

The UK attitude was quite different: it sought tariff reductions, but also the maintenance of its imperial preferences, which would allow it to trade with its Commonwealth partners on preferential basis. The UK government, largely influenced by the thinking of John Maynard Keynes who was acting as policy adviser, believed that it would have less to offer as consideration for US across-the-board tariff reductions, if it had already unilaterally removed its imperial preferences: thus, keeping imperial preferences in place for as long as it could would provide the UK negotiators with an important bargaining chip;. imperial preferences were the quid pro quo for US non-discriminatory tariff reductions.[32]

The two delegations had a different approach to the issue of state trading, cartels, and quotas: Miller (2000) explains that the UK delegation, in favour of a

---

House Ways and Means Committee from 1928 to 1931. Smoot was an apostle in the Mormon Church and was known as the 'apostle for protection'; see Irwin (2011) at p. 44.

[29] Irwin (2011) at pp. 150ff discusses in detail all reactions to Smoot-Hawley.

[30] Miller (2000) agrees. So do Gardner (1956), Jackson (1969), Dam (1970), and Zeiler (1999).

[31] In a separate study, Irwin (2011) makes a very strong case to the effect that the Smoot-Hawley Tariff Act was hardly responsible for the Great Depression. It did nevertheless provoke retaliation against the US by a host of nations.

[32] Miller (2000).

strong role for government in the post-WWII era, insisted on allowing for quotas for balance of payments (BoP) reasons. In Miller's (2000) account, the pragmatic, government-friendly attitude of the UK delegation found friends around the table and this explains the regulation of preferences (which were not eliminated but grandfathered as we will see *infra*), quotas (which were allowed for BoP reasons), state trading (which could legitimately persist, provided that it operated on non-discriminatory terms), and cartels (that were not disallowed) in the final GATT text.[33]

So much for their differences, but there was, of course, a substantial overlap between them as well. The British were not opposed to the idea of creating a trade institution, which they also viewed as a means to curtail US dominance. Both governments shared the belief that trade expansion was an appropriate means to fight the unemployment that crippled the US economy in the pre-New Deal era and was looming all over Europe in the aftermath of WWII.[34] It should come as no surprise that a specific provision in an earlier GATT draft was dedicated to this issue.[35] However, whereas the US delegates viewed opening of trade as an antidote, the UK government had a more cautious approach on this issue: arguably influenced by Keynes's thinking, the UK delegates did not deny that trade could indeed be beneficial on this score; they seemed to privilege nevertheless short-term macroeconomic solutions to addressing unemployment. In the dominant UK view, a drop in tariffs would not in and of itself help achieve the GATT objective to end unemployment; wealthy domestic markets (with little, if any, unemployment) would in turn drive trade expansion.[36]

So how did all these positions converge at the negotiating table? It is important to note here that the UK and the US, their differences on certain issues

---

[33] The provisions on cartels (restrictive business practices, RBPs) were included in Chapter V of the ITO Charter. The non-advent of the latter meant that the only legal relevance of this provision was through the rather innocuous Art. XXIX of the GATT reflected *supra*.

[34] Gardner (1956) underscores this point. Modern research casts doubt on the usefulness of trade instruments to solve unemployment problems; see, inter alia, Krugman (1995), and Dewatripont et al. (1999). Jansen and Lee (2007) offer a survey of the most recent empirical literature on this score which questions some of the orthodoxies of the past.

[35] Art. XVI of the New York Draft, entitled Maintenance of Domestic Employment, recognized the right of every government to aim to achieve full employment, and imposed an obligation on states striving for full employment to avoid creating balance of payment problems for their trading partners. According to the companion provision (Art. XVII), governments which aimed at promoting the establishment or reconstruction of particular industries would be free to do so, provided that they negotiated a settlement with the affected states; see UN Economic and Social Council Doc. E/PC/T/C.6/85 of 15 February 1947.

[36] This is very much a Keynesian view. Keynes cared a lot about short-run effects and tended to pay less attention to the long run: a drop in tariffs could, for example, in the short run lead to domestic unemployment, and such effects preoccupied him. It was he, after all, who famously used to say 'in the long run we are all dead'. One should not, however, overestimate his influence on the drafting of the GATT. Keynes passed away in 1946 before the actual negotiating process had meaningfully started and the UK position was more influenced by the views of Meade and Robbins, who definitely had a more favourable attitude towards trade liberalization; Irwin et al. (2008).

notwithstanding, were the only participants that had a view about the whole endeavour, the kind of trade agreement they were looking for, whereas other participants were preoccupied with narrower trade interests. And the US and the UK agreed on one thing: the GATT should come into being anyway, and it should be about tariff commitments necessary to avoid tariff volatility (and the ensuing uncertainty with regard to transaction costs); they further agreed that there was need to add the necessary legal arsenal to ensure that the value of tariff commitments would not be circumvented through subsequent unilateral actions, that is, through domestic policies applicable to both imported as well as domestic goods. Following the bifurcation between the GATT and the ITO negotiation, it became clear that the GATT would remain a negative integration contract, whereby domestic policies (e.g. public health, tax policies etc.) would be decided in a sovereign manner by each and every signatory, while respecting an obligation not to discriminate. If at all, the place to discuss the need, assuming one could agree that it existed, to move to common policies would be the ITO.[37] It bears repetition that the study of negotiating documents and indeed the nature of the negotiating process itself suggests that the heart of the GATT is the tariff bargain, and the rest of the Agreement is supporting mechanisms necessary to ensure that the value of tariff promises would not be undermined through subsequent unilateral action; the text of the GATT supports this view:

(a) Arts. I, II, XXVIII, XXVIIIbis all deal in a detailed manner with tariffs, whereas only one provision (Art. III GATT) deals with all domestic instruments;

(b) It was agreed that the function of Art. III GATT would be akin to an insurance policy to guarantee that the value of tariff promises would not be undone through subsequent unilateral action.[38] There was general dissatisfaction with some of the terms used in this provision but negotiators spent no extra time fine-tuning them, having satisfied themselves that what mattered was the function of this provision and having agreed to reopen similar issues at the ITO negotiation;[39]

(c) It is also clear that, assuming a reasonable understanding of the term 'protection'—an elusive concept, alas—trading partners, upon accession to the GATT, would be in a position to protect their domestic producers only

---

[37] Moreover, as Irwin (2005) suggests, prior to the late 1940s, at least in the US, there was no generally held view that the government was responsible for maintaining full employment, and for avoiding recessions. The Council of Economic Advisors (CEA), established by the US Employment Act of 1946, was a watershed: the government was explicitly assuming responsibility for macroeconomic management. The preamble is broad, and thus unhelpful when it comes to using it as a compass that will help us orientate the various GATT instruments, but it does reflect a new view of the government's role, and thus, very much the mindset of the founding fathers.

[38] Irwin et al. (2008) cite numerous documents to this effect.

[39] Ibid. The authors refer, for example, to the dissatisfaction regarding the chosen term 'like products' and the decision to renegotiate this term in the context of the ITO negotiation.

through tariffs. All other instruments affecting trade would have to be used in a non-discriminatory (non-protectionist) manner, or not used at all (e.g. import and export quantitative restrictions);

(d) The consequence of the above is that, assuming the insurance policy described above fulfilled its intended function, trading nations would have an incentive to continue exchanging tariff concessions.

Baldwin (1970) has provided the most persuasive explanation of the structure of the GATT, arguing that negotiators rationally focused on tariff barriers which constituted the main market access impediment at the time and, because of their sheer size (Smoot-Hawley), were hiding the relevance of non-tariff barriers (NTBs).[40] He called this a 'draining of the swamp' effect, that is, the impact of NTBs would be better appreciated only when tariffs were out of place.

Annexure 10 of the London Draft[41] deals with the manner in which tariff liberalization would occur: negotiations should take place under strict reciprocity[42] (in the sense, that countries should not be expecting one-way preferences), and following the 'principal supplier rule'. Where does MFN play in all this? MFN was of course costly to those with substantial bargaining power, and to none more so than the US: this is probably why, before the GATT/ITO negotiations, the US government did not practise widespread MFN in its trade relations, and instead, practised conditional MFN.[43] In negotiating the GATT/ITO, the US fought for widespread MFN, thus providing those with little bargaining power with a sizeable gift: to automatically and unconditionally profit from the tariff promises that those with substantial bargaining power could extract from their trading partners. For Hull it was the duty of the US as leader to behave in this way and thus to contribute to peace, the long-term objective that GATT should be after all pursuing.

In a nutshell, the negotiating record reveals that the UK and the US wanted to constrain each other's behaviour, believing that, through the GATT, they would be establishing non-discriminatory trade relations around the world, an ingredient of world peace. That much should be undisputed. We will return to a more detailed discussion regarding the specific GATT disciplines, the GATT approach to reach its objective of trade liberalization, following a

---

[40] An official US document (Committee on Finance, United States Finance, Summary and Analysis of HR 10710—The Trade Reform Act of 1973, 26 February 1974, US Government Printing Office, Washington, DC, 1974) states (at p. 1) that it was the view of the US Subcommittee on International Trade that the focus would shift on NTBs only after the conclusion of the Kennedy round. 'NTBs' carries a negative undertone, in that regulatory interventions are equated to 'barriers'. Staiger (2011) and others use the term non-tariff measures (NTMs), a more neutral term to convey the same point. Yet, its shortcomings notwithstanding, we privilege the use of the term 'NTBs' throughout this volume, which is the term most widely used.

[41] E/PC/T/33.

[42] On the origin of reciprocity in the GATT negotiations, see Irwin (2002).

[43] Hawkins (1951, pp. 81ff); Miller (2000, pp. 10ff).

brief detour into economic theory and a discussion of how economists understand the rationale for trade agreements. After all, the GATT pursues economic objectives and its shaping was influenced by the ideas of eminent economists who, as argued above, directly participated in its negotiation.

1.3 Economic Theory

Economists will, usually, ask the following questions:

(a) are there gains from trade liberalization?
(b) if yes, why are countries not pursuing trade liberalization anyway, that is, in the absence of a written commitment (agreement) to do so?

Assuming a positive response to (a) above, it is the response to (b) that will take us close to the response to the question: what is the rationale for trade agreements? One will be hard-pressed to find economists arguing that there are no gains from trade liberalization. Indeed, as explained in numerous writings from Smith's classic, *The Wealth of Nations*, onwards, all nations have an advantage in producing particular goods, and gains from trade result from specialization. The modern understanding of international trade theory is, to a large extent, still based on the notion of comparative advantage, as developed by Ricardo.[44] Graham (1948) insisted that trade took place between firms, and the fact that they were in different states was irrelevant as long as economic policy was appropriate. But states may differentiate between firms, through tariffs, embargos, exchange rates etc.; hence, the need for an agreement. The so-called new trade theory has strengthened the case for trade liberalization by explaining that there are gains even when homogeneous countries open up to trade, because of the inherent advantages of specialization (which allows large-scale production). Krugman (1979) developed a monopolistic competition model, explaining why similar countries gain from trading with each other, and why a significant part of that trade may take place within the same industries. Some producers, however, will lose, and governments might wish to protect such producers through the use of safeguards. Two assumptions are crucial to Krugman's model: increasing returns to scale (economies of scale) and consumers' love of variety.[45] There is tension between the two assumptions: consumers' love of variety favours the existence of many small firms; the organization of production in large firms is key to exploiting economies of scale.

---

[44] Economic historians have long quarrelled over whether the law of comparative advantage should be attributed to Ricardo or to Torrens (1815). There are dozens of writings regarding the law of comparative advantage and its limits. Deardorff (1980), in a very elegant piece, relaxes the rigidity of many propositions that had been previously presented, and presents a model where the law of comparative advantage holds for an appropriate average rather than for each individual commodity itself. For a clear explanation of the gains from trade, see Krugman and Wells (2005) and Helpman (2011).

[45] Subsequent research, notably by Broda et al. (2008), has empirically confirmed that there are sizeable gains in increased varieties.

Krugman built the two opposite tensions in a single model, whereby producers have a monopoly over a variety of the product they produce and can, thus, set their prices unilaterally; because the varieties are, to some extent, substitutes for one another, each firm continues to face competition from other firms. Trade opening means that consumers will have access to more varieties, but they will also become more price-sensitive. As a result, some firms will go out of business, but the gains from trade opening will outweigh such losses: there will be a scale effect, since companies now sell in more than one country and can thus exploit economies of scale; there will be a love of variety effect, since consumers now have access to more products; and there will be a pro-competitive effect, since consumers will now pay a lower price.[46] This much is not in dispute.[47]

The next question is: why then does not trade liberalization take place unilaterally? Why, in other words, do we need the GATT (and now the WTO) in order to do what we would have been anyway doing (even without the GATT)?

Economists have not always seen eye to eye on this latter question. Indeed, according to standard economic reasoning, GATT should not exist, and so any attempt to offer an economic interpretation of GATT was doomed to failure. In this vein, Krugman (1991) noted (pp. 25ff):

> There is no generally accepted label for the theoretical underpinnings of the GATT. I like to refer to it as 'GATT-think'—a simple set of principles that is entirely consistent, explains most of what goes on in negotiations, but makes no sense in terms of economics . . . The reason why GATT-think works is, instead, that it captures some basic realities of the political process.

Krugman, again in 1997, stated (p. 113):

> If economists ruled the world, there would be no need for a World Trade Organization. The economist's case for free trade is essentially a unilateral case: a country

---

[46] In subsequent research, Krugman (1980) shows that, for example, if trade is costly, production may be concentrated in the larger market (the home country effect); Ethier (1982) provides a variant with trade in intermediate goods. The new trade theory does not aim to explain trade based on endowments, as is, for example, the case in a Hecksher-Ohlin model (which does not dispute the law of comparative advantage as long as comparative advantage is measured by relative autarky prices), and starts with the pioneering work of Balassa (1966). It was Balassa (1966), studying the European integration process, who observed that reduction in tariffs across the participants in the process led to intra-industry specialization and that in this scenario 'the welfare effects of an increased exchange of consumer goods may now consist largely of improvements in the efficiency of exchange (the satisfaction of consumer wants) whereas specialization in narrower ranges of machinery and intermediate products will permit the exploitation of economies of scale through the lengthening of production runs' (p. 472). Balassa contested the 'orthodox' view at the time, arguing that tariff reductions would lead to inter-industry specialization only in the case of standardized products; he thus opened the door to the subsequent research on 'gains from variety'. For an excellent discussion of Balassa's many contributions in this field, see Sapir (2011). Grubel and Lloyd (1975) developed the famous Grubel-Lloyd Index, which is a measure of the importance of intra-industry trade within a given industry.

[47] More recently, the new new trade theory allows for firm heterogeneity: low productivity firms will exit the market and resources will be reallocated within the same sector to expanding (exporting) high productivity firms; see Melitz (2003) and the survey by Helpman (2006).

serves its own interests by pursuing free trade regardless of what other countries may do. Or, as Frederic Bastiat put it, it makes no more sense to be protectionist because other countries have tariffs than it would to block up our harbours because other countries have rocky coasts. So, if our theories really held sway, there would be no need for treaties: global free trade would emerge spontaneously from the unrestricted pursuit of national interests.[48]

This view is not shared by all. Two theories have been advanced to offer a rationale for the GATT (and now the WTO): the commitment theory and the terms of trade theory. Briefly, the former rests on the idea that an international agreement is necessary for trading nations that want to lock in policies and avoid future pressure from domestic lobbies (that is, it is a response to domestic political economy concerns); the latter leans on the concept that, since governments for good reasons might have no incentive to unilaterally liberalize, an international agreement is necessary in order to 'internalize' all externalities stemming from unilateral definition of protection (that is, it is a response to an international, not a domestic, concern, namely, cost-shifting by other trading nations when they unilaterally design their trade policies).

Commitment theory has been developed in various research papers. The focus of this approach is the relationship between government and its private sector: a government will choose its trade policy and will commit it to an international agreement signed to this effect; the private sector will act accordingly. The gain for the government is that investment decisions are forestalled; it will lose, however, contributions by the various lobbies.[49] There are many good arguments in support of this view: for a government facing unpopular (for some segments of society) choices, the argument 'I have tied my hands to the mast'[50] is an easy way out that minimizes the political costs associated with such unpopular choices.[51] On this understanding, national governments will use GATT as an excuse for unpopular choices. In other words, to deter pressure from lobbies, a government might be willing to 'tie' its policies to the GATT mast.[52]

---

[48] In a footnote to this quote, Krugman acknowledges that large countries might have an incentive to limit imports and exports by imposing tariffs, but goes on to state that 'this optimal tariff argument, however, plays almost no role in real world disputes over trade policy'.

[49] Bagwell and Staiger (2002, pp. 32–4).

[50] Irwin (1996), Maggi (1999), and Maggi and Rodriguez-Clare (1998) all discuss the time-inconsistency issue, that is, how by committing to an international regime, governments avoid acting inconsistently over time (assuming, of course, that the regime itself does not change either). Compare Downs and Rocke (1997).

[51] Economic theory distinguishes between Pareto and Kaldor-Hicks efficiency. Trade liberalization is Kaldor-Hicks efficient, that is, while overall society gains from market opening, some of its segments (domestic producers facing foreign competition) might (and often do) lose. Overall, however, that is, when the losses are measured against the gains of other segments of society (users of cheaper inputs, consumers), society will, in the usual case, benefit.

[52] Tumlir (1985); Maggi and Rodriguez-Clare (1998); Staiger and Tabellini (1987) and (1999); Tang and Wei (2009).

Since it is the will to reduce the importance of political economy-type considerations that drives this theory, the subject-matter of the commitment matters. Now what do domestic (producers') lobbies care about? They would critically be driven by the motto 'exports are good, imports are bad'. So what they would typically care about would be flexibility when making tariff concessions, the possibility of reneging on the commitment when necessary, etc. This is precisely what governments would like to buy insurance against: they would ideally like to make inflexible tariff commitments.

Commitment theory suffers from serious weaknesses. First, contrary to the terms of trade theory discussed *infra*, consideration is not an issue: highly asymmetric commitments could very well be the end result since the extent of commitment is not a function of an international negotiation aiming to preserve the value of an international transaction; it is the relationship of governments with their own domestic lobbies that defines the extent of commitment. One thing is for sure: no international negotiation is required for the content of commitment to be decided.

Second, and a natural consequence of the first point, the placing of the commitment is also immaterial: all trading nations need is a safe box where they can lock in their domestic policies. Naturally, this should be the national constitution, or something equivalent. The terms of trade theory, in stark contrast here, requires the conclusion of an international agreement, since it is the behaviour of foreign sovereigns and not of domestic lobbies that is being addressed. Srinivasan (2005), in this vein, casts doubt on the validity of the theory, since, in his view, there is no need for an international commitment when the source of the distortion is domestic.

Third, enforcement could be a serious issue in the commitment scenario: both the terms of trade and the commitment theories rely on enforcement. Do foreigners though have similar incentives to pursue deviators in the commitment and the terms of trade stories? It is submitted that incentives to enforce are asymmetric across the two agreements: in the commitment story, governments would rather place their commitments in international agreements, and rely on someone else enforcing them, thus avoiding blame for opting for unpopular choices and the ensuing political cost; but foreigners might be totally uninterested in enforcing commitments except where non-enforcement entails negative welfare implications for them. In other words, enforcement will occur because of the cost-shifting that takes place and the resulting deterioration in welfare terms of the situation for foreigners, and not because a commitment has been entered into to lock in specific behaviour. Enforcement in the terms of trade story, on the other hand, relies on foreigners' incentive to ensure that the terms of trade between goods of interest to them and goods of interest to the other party remain intact: in this explanation of trade agreements, the incentive to enforce is stronger. Consequently, there are good reasons to doubt the validity of this approach as explanation for the original

GATT, which was a tariff bargain with auxiliary commitments aimed at ensuring that the value of the tariff bargain would be preserved.

Commitment theory is of limited value in explaining the original tariff bargain, but may be of more relevance in explaining why some trading nations are in favour of legal institutions of the WTO (as opposed to the GATT) such as the WTO Agreement on Subsidies and Countervailing Measures,[53] accessions to the WTO (during the Uruguay round), and especially recent (post-Uruguay round) accessions to the WTO, that is, the part of the negotiation that does not rely on strict reciprocity. From the Tokyo round onwards, all instruments of contingent protection have been steadily undergoing a process akin to 'tightening of the screws': typically, the discretion of the investigating authority in charge of say an antidumping investigation will be eviscerated through the passage of the new agreement at the end of every negotiating round. The advent of the TRIPs (Trade Related Intellectual Property Rights) Agreement in 1995 meant that WTO Members no longer have any discretion when choosing their basic policies with respect to protection of certain intellectual property rights. And, to cap it all, after 1995, it has been essentially non-market economies (NMEs) that have acceded to the multilateral system. The WTO is quite different from the GATT: not only does the contract now cover more policy space than ever before (because of the advent of TRIPs and GATS),[54] but, through their Protocol of Accession, NMEs often agree to adopt policies that incumbents (WTO Members) do not have to observe ('WTO +' obligations in WTO-speak).[55] It bears repeating, to avoid misunderstandings: commitment theory might help explain why governments might have an incentive to lock in behaviour with respect to similar instruments, not why an agreement will eventually be signed.

The terms of trade theory differs from the commitment theory, in that it traces the rationale for trade agreements not in domestic distortions but in international externalities. Critically, it is the manner in which similar externalities 'travel' that is at the heart of this approach: through the price mechanism and the ensuing terms of trade between two goods. Bagwell (2008) traces this theory to the work of early and mid-nineteenth century economists such as Mill and Torrens. Harry Johnson (1953–4) is credited with its elegant formalization, and the theory has recently

---

[53] We will refer to the work of Brou and Ruta (2011), and Potipiti (2006) on this score in Chapter 6: these papers, as we will try to show, make a good case for commitments on subsidies, but not for international negotiations that would lead to similar commitments.

[54] GATS stands for General Agreement on Trade in Services.

[55] There is a flip side here: small countries often making concessions in areas other than tariffs—say in intellectual property rights or investment protection—might support the terms of trade theory to some degree, since they do not have much to give in terms of tariff concessions if such concessions do not affect world prices. But in terms of protection of intellectual property rights and investment, their policies can have a large effect on rents earned by foreign firms in their markets. This is how they get tariff concessions from large countries. This is of course the flip side of letting small countries retaliate by means other than tariffs since tariff retaliation is often not in their interest. See Tang and Wei (2009).

found an advocate in the scholarship of Bagwell and Staiger (2002), who take the pre-existing analysis a number of steps further, and use it to interpret the various GATT institutions in a context of perfect as well as imperfect competition.

The starting point is that it is simply not the case that unilateral trade liberalization is the first-best instrument for all: countries that can influence the terms of trade have a strong incentive to set tariffs and influence to their advantage the terms under which particular goods are being traded on the world stage; optimal tariff theory suggests that governments behaving in accordance with their self-interest should not necessarily abolish tariffs unilaterally.[56] Hence, tariffs can and do occur for good reasons. Unilateral setting of tariffs can, however, lead to terms of trade externalities: a country setting tariffs will choose its tariff rates by calculating the welfare implications for its domestic producers and consumers only. It will also, nevertheless, be imposing an externality on foreign producers of the product or commodity affected by the tariffs, which in all likelihood will not be internalized.[57] Consequently, unilateral tariff-setting can spiral into a Prisoner's Dilemma,[58] where countries behave in a non-cooperative manner and impose externalities on each other. In other words, in this vein, absent a trade agreement, different countries will not behave cooperatively. A trade agreement is the means to internalize these externalities and accordingly, a means to escape from the Prisoner's Dilemma. Through international negotiations, trading partners will aim at reducing tariffs to the politically optimum level (that is, to the levels which governments would choose were they not motivated by the terms of trade implications of their trade policies). In this vein, reciprocity is the driving force.

In other words, the idea here is that (some) trading nations, by using trade instruments, can reduce the relative world price of the goods they import in terms of the goods they export. Since many nations might have the power to influence terms of trade in particular markets, if they all behave in this way, the result would be a suboptimal total volume of trade and it is through trade agreements that trade would be expanded back to its 'normal' level through reciprocal tariff negotiations.

---

[56] Krugman's (1991) quoted paper, summarizes GATT-think in three sentences: (a) exports are good; (b) imports are bad; (c) other things equal, an equal increase in imports and exports is good. In Krugman's explanation, there is not enough empirical evidence to support optimal tariff theory; a government needs to be mercantilist to behave in the manner he describes. In a series of papers, Bagwell and Staiger have since explained why a politically motivated government, and probably a government that wants to affect terms of trade to its own advantage, could behave in a similar manner; Broda et al. (2008) provided the empirical support Krugman was looking for. Compare Kindleberger (1984) and (1986).

[57] Absent extraordinary circumstances, the country setting the tariff level will have little incentive to internalize this externality. In Bagwell and Staiger's terminology, such will not be a politically optimum tariff, that is, a tariff which takes adequately into consideration the interests of domestic producers and consumers, but imposes no external effect on foreign producers. One can of course take issue with the terminology here: since the (negative) effect on foreign producers travels through the price mechanism, one should not speak of an externality. This is, however, pure semantics.

[58] Fudenberg and Tirole (1991, pp. 9–10 and 110–12) provide an explanation of the Prisoner's Dilemma and how one gets out of it by changing the payoffs. See also Axelrod (1984).

At first, this approach was dismissed in essence because the prevailing view was that it rested on the rather weak foundation that trading nations choose their policies without thinking at all in terms of domestic political economy, that is, disregarding lobbies' pressure. Its appeal in recent years is largely due to the fact that Bagwell and Staiger in a series of papers demonstrated that the theory holds irrespective of the political motivations of governments. In their reformulation, the theory rests on only two key assumptions: *ceteris paribus*, a government preference is such that it suffers a welfare loss when its terms of trade deteriorate; second, assuming a country is large, an increase in an import tariff results in a terms of trade gain for the importing country,[59] and a terms of trade loss for the exporting country.[60] Both assumptions are of course quite reasonable.

Bagwell and Staiger (2002) point to the actual design of the main GATT features to make the point that their theory offers a satisfactory explanation of the GATT as we know it, and not of *any* trade agreement: using terms of trade as their workhorse, they have published a series of papers explaining key GATT institutions, such as MFN, renegotiation of duties, safeguards, in this prism. In the words of Staiger, one of the proponents of this theory (2011, p. 12):

> According to the terms-of-trade theory of trade agreements, the purpose of a trade agreement is to give foreign exporters a 'voice' in the tariff choices of their trading partners, so that through negotiations they can make their trading partners responsive to the costs that these trading partners impose on foreign exporters when making their tariff choices. And in accomplishing this, a trade agreement then naturally leads to lower tariffs and an expansion of market access to internationally efficient levels.

A number of voices have been raised against the power of this theory to explain the GATT: Ethier (2004) has taken issue with the terms of trade theory: first, he has argued that trade agreements like the GATT do not in fact prevent countries from influencing the terms of trade. For instance, the GATT does not include

---

[59] Indeed, the classic work of Edgeworth (1894) and Bickerdike (1907) suggests that as long as a foreign country's offer curve is not perfectly elastic, a country can gain from a tariff (the offer curve shows the quantity of one product that an agent will export for each quantity of another product that it will import). Countries with large import markets will be in a position to affect terms of trade in a more meaningful manner (than small import markets) and thus will have more to gain through tariff imposition. Economists have viewed the arguments on optimal tariff with considerable scepticism: Krugman and Obstfeld (1997) observe that at any rate this argument is of little practical importance since small countries (which constitute the majority of the WTO membership) cannot affect terms of trade anyway. Feenstra (2004) further noted that there was little empirical knowledge about the elasticity of foreign export supply. Empirical evidence came first from the work of Broda et al. (2008). In this paper, the authors show that countries that are not members of the WTO systematically set higher tariffs on goods that are supplied inelastically. This paper supplies considerable empirical evidence for the optimal tariff theory.

[60] By relying on these two assumptions only, as Bagwell and Staiger (2002) have elegantly shown, the terms of trade theory is robust to a wide range of government preference specifications, including specifications that allow for political motivations and constraints. The authors examine the political economy of the whole endeavour in which governments have an enlarged (and probably more realistic) objective function so as to include political considerations.

disciplines on export taxes (duties); second, in his view, the terms of trade theory does not explain why small countries, which cannot affect the terms of trade, participate in trade agreements. Ethier bases his first point on the fact that the GATT does not include a provision as elaborate as Art. II that would be applicable to export taxes. This does not mean, however, that export taxes cannot be negotiated and bound. In fact, the GATT treats import and export duties symmetrically, in that they are not disallowed but can be disciplined.[61] The presumption behind the second point is that developing countries cannot affect the terms of trade at all.[62] There is no empirical evidence on this score, other than the work of Broda et al. (2008), which nonetheless refers to a different time period. Assuming the presumption is correct, this is a valid criticism which, we should add, does not bring into question the terms of trade as an explanation for those who can influence terms of trade. It is probably the case that, as with MFN, this is the influence that Cordell Hull has had on the shaping of the GATT, that is, to negotiate fiercely with the UK (in a scenario similar to terms of trade), but to allow those with lesser bargaining power to benefit from the outcome of negotiation.

A similar critique can be raised by shifting the focus of the analysis to domestic instruments: terms of trade can be affected through domestic instruments as well, and terms of trade theory is taking the first steps to explaining how its insights can find application in this context as well. As Horn et al. (2010) recognize, however, there are substantial negotiating costs when it comes to contracting domestic instruments, and this probably explains why the GATT does not reproduce the contracting formula of trade instruments in this respect. Under the circumstances, that is, in the absence of contracting each and every domestic instrument in the GATT, reciprocity, a central concept in terms of trade, becomes difficult to prove, if not entirely elusive.

Regan (2006) has offered a different critique, arguing that terms of trade manipulation does not happen simply because there is market power. In his view, terms of trade manipulation is a sophisticated policy which should not be assumed light-heartedly. The models that economists use are two countries–two goods models. And, indeed, there is nothing that makes it mathematically impossible to extrapolate the results to a world with many countries and many goods.

---

[61] Export duties are not widely used, probably for political economy reasons, since export lobbies might (at least in the short run) object to their use. There are, nevertheless, increasingly instances of commitments on export duties both at the multilateral (Annex 6 of the China Protocol of Accession) and at the bilateral level (Morocco in its free trade agreement with the US agreed not to impose export taxes on phosphates, a commodity where Morocco accounts for a sizeable percentage of the world production).

[62] There is no mystery about why small (developing or otherwise) countries would want to join GATT, as they would enjoy a terms of trade benefit from gaining access to the reduced tariffs of large countries like the US. The more interesting question is why large countries would want small countries to join GATT, given that the tariff reduction by a small country offers no terms of trade gain to other members. It is in this spirit that we address the question.

The issue nonetheless is whether trade delegates as we know them can perform very complicated analyses and be clear about the terms of trade of all their countries' exports and imports and do the same for each WTO participant. This sounds too demanding probably, but at the same time, having a rough idea about terms of trade is probably all that is realistically required.[63]

Others have argued that the terms of trade theory does not explain some important legal institutions like antidumping. But this was never the intention of the theory: its purpose was to explain the core issues, the heart of the GATT. Indeed, the GATT could have existed without antidumping, with the safeguards clause alone.[64]

The terms of trade theory, its limitations notwithstanding, is the more attractive theory explaining the GATT, in that it traces the rationale for the GATT to the desire to curb foreign behaviour that can have negative external effects beyond national borders. In a world which in Friedman's (2005) inimitable expression becomes increasingly 'flat', the need to constrain unilateral behaviour increases as well. True, externalities do not have to travel through the price mechanism and this is addressed in the more recent work by Bagwell and Staiger. At the end of the day, it is market access that is being inhibited as a result of the manipulation of terms of trade. There could be other externalities that travel outside the price mechanism but so far no one has made a persuasive case for it.[65]

Finally, there are those who take the view that adherence to the GATT/WTO does not matter at all. Rose (2004) is credited with this view, arguing that there is not much evidence that the GATT/WTO has contributed to trade liberalization; in his view, nations would have behaved more or less in the same way even in the absence of an institutional framework such as the GATT/WTO. A series of papers have responded persuasively. First, Subramanian and Wei (2007) have shown that there are sizeable effects for developed countries' trade, but maybe not so for developing countries' trade, but this is so because the latter have not liberalized at

---

[63] In the same paper, Regan (2006) has forcefully argued that the very purpose of the GATT (and the WTO) is to counter-attack protectionism. In this view, absent the GATT, trading nations will have an incentive to continue protecting domestic producers. His view is not the classic commitment story: in his story, there is a divide between government and country preferences. Trade agreements aim to bridge this gap and make governments act in accordance with the country interest. Hence, in his story, the game is not between government and the private sector. There is, however, an important overlap: both in the commitment and the protectionism stories, the role of trade agreement is essentially to address a domestic problem and not an international externality. The problem with this explanation for the GATT is that it remains unclear why governments would negotiate such an agreement in the first place, unless their true aim was to maximize social welfare (in which case, the country–government divide does not exist).

[64] Still, there are various terms of trade-based theories of safeguards, such as Martin and Vergote (2008), that provide possible explanations for antidumping.

[65] Ossa (2011), for example, explains the role of the GATT in dealing with the production relocation effect of trade policy: focusing on the major players in recent negotiations, the author finds that the production relocation effect implies non-cooperative tariffs as well as moderate gains from negotiations.

all (or did so to a limited extent). On their calculations, the WTO has had a strong positive impact on trade, amounting to 120 per cent additional world trade (or $8 trillion in 2000 alone).[66] Second, as stated above, Broda et al. (2008) found evidence of optimal tariffs when checking tariffs of WTO Members before accession to the WTO: the larger the market, the higher the tariff in specific goods. Finally, Bagwell and Staiger (2011a) check the tariff concessions made by countries that have acceded to the WTO and find that little countries make little concessions, whereas big countries make big ones and that concessions are greater where pre-negotiation import volumes are greater, as predicted by the theory. They find strong and robust support for the central predictions of the terms of trade theory in the observed pattern of negotiated tariff cuts. In short, the GATT/WTO does matter.[67]

There is hardly any historical support in favour of the commitment theory. There is, on the other hand, some historical support for the view that it was international externalities and not domestic problems that should be addressed by a trade agreement.

Knowledge about the identity of the negotiating partners (who negotiated with whom the tariff treatment of particular commodities), the level of agreed tariff cuts, and the change in trade volumes would provide definitive confirmation that it was all about terms of trade. The negotiating history of the GATT is, at the moment of writing, partly accessible to the public, and partly not. Unfortunately, the latter part covers the negotiation of the first tariff bargain, the negotiation in Geneva from April–July 1947. Alas, we are still in the dark on this score.

There is some indirect evidence though, the probative value of which is debatable. Meade, writing on customs unions, mentions (1955, pp. 64–5):

> ... the larger the trading area which is negotiating as a single unit the better the commercial policy treatment which it can hope to exact in its bargains from other countries, and the better therefore its terms of trade with the rest of the world are likely to be.

Meade was of course one of the key UK negotiators of the original GATT, and the discussion here applies as much to customs unions as it does to single entities: the point is that bargaining power does matter. Moreover, several GATT institutions indirectly support the view that terms of trade was indeed what (some) negotiators had in mind: the focus on principal suppliers and reciprocal concessions hints that the arrangement was indeed focused on unravelling the damage done to the volume of trade by non-cooperative tariffs. The renegotiation of schedules also lends extra support to this thesis, since this instrument addresses the need for rebalancing of concessions following a deviation from the originally agreed level.

---

[66] See also Irwin (2005).

[67] The sheer volume of legal obligations entered into and the need to explain the obligations to users of the system is probably the best explanation for why the agreement was made in writing.

Drache (2003) reports that, at their 1941 meeting in Newfoundland, Churchill and Roosevelt held the view that international beggar-thy-neighbour policies must be addressed in the post-World War II era within the framework of a (trade) institution: the terms of trade theory of course sees the rationale for the agreement in the need to curb behaviour by trading partners that have effects beyond national borders. Borrowing from Will Clayton again:

> The world will be a better place to live in if nations, instead of taking unilateral actions, without regard to the interests of others, will adopt and follow common principles and enter into consultation when interests come into conflict. And this, throughout the entire range of trade relationships, is what the signatories of the *Charter* will agree to do. Each will surrender some part of its freedom to take action that might prove harmful to others and each will thus gain the assurance that others will not take action harmful to it.[68]

This is not conclusive evidence, but it does point to the direction of the terms of trade, in the sense that the rationale for the GATT was the disciplining of the behaviour of trading partners and not the 'domestication' of lobbies at home. The various instruments employed to achieve trade liberalization (reciprocal tariff liberalization; negotiations on tariff concessions based on the principal-supplier rule, where those with bargaining power would participate) lend support to this thesis. The GATT, it seems, was conceived as an agreement aimed at curbing unilateralism.[69]

What is the reason for opting for a formal agreement? If the GATT thus explained represents an equilibrium from which deviations are suboptimal, why put it down on paper? Trading nations would behave in this way anyway. The case for a formal agreement is supported by the sheer amount of information that went into the GATT contract: the complexity of the subject-matter does not facilitate collusive behaviour through tacit cooperation.[70] The GATT is magnificent in its simplicity, yet it covers a lot of ground and one should not rationally expect that all trading nations will always behave in a GATT-conforming manner even in the absence of a document that they can use as compass. The agreement is also needed in order to explain to economic operators what their governments have agreed to do and what not. The need for formalism has been intensified over the years as new agreements were added to the old ones, and as the membership grew from the original 23 to the current 157.

---

[68] Wilcox (1949) at pp. ix–x. This passage supports the view that what Clayton had in mind when referring to 'vested interests' was not an agreement to resolve domestic issues (something akin to what the commitment theory suggests), but an agreement to resolve international external effects stemming from unilateral definition of trade policies.

[69] There is international relations literature that views the creation of the GATT as a shield aimed at advancing political goals: Eichengreen (2006), for example, views the GATT as the continuation of the Bretton Woods regime which establishes a liberal order and thus, curbs Soviet expansionism. Compare Irwin (1996, 1998b).

[70] Compare Schelling (1960).

2. The GATT in the GATT Era: An Agreement and an Institution

2.1 The GATT Recipe for Trade Liberalization

The GATT framers can be credited with a remarkable document that has with-stood the test of time for 60 years. The GATT could be briefly described as follows:

(a) Since both trade (tariffs, quotas) and domestic instruments (that is, instruments affecting both domestic as well as foreign goods, such as environmental, public health, tax policies etc.) can affect trade, the disciplining of both sets of instruments is necessary, otherwise any obligations imposed could be easily circumvented;[71]

(b) Trading nations that signed the GATT negotiate the level of tariffs to be imposed on imported products; let us call such tariffs, default tariffs. Such tariffs serve as ceilings (or bindings, in GATT-speak) and GATT signatories cannot impose higher tariffs than what they promised to their trading partners (Art. II GATT). Through bindings, tariff volatility is impossible beyond the agreed cap, and thus, unpredictability as to transaction costs is severely tamed. GATT signatories can increase their duties above the bound level only if they follow the multilateral process established in Art. XXVIII GATT;

(c) Irrespective of whether tariffs have been bound or not, GATT signatories are required to apply their tariff protection in a non-discriminatory manner (Art. I GATT). This is the very essence of the MFN clause. Importantly, GATT signatories cannot treat non-GATT signatories better than those who have signed the GATT. MFN is thus the carrot that will induce outsiders to join the GATT: acceding countries know that their products will receive, in principle, the best possible treatment in the markets of GATT incumbents.[72] Exceptions to MFN have been included in the GATT: for example, members of a preferential trade agreement (PTA), that is, a customs union (CU) or a free trade area (FTA), can have recourse to preferential rates (Art. XXIV GATT);

(d) GATT signatories cannot apply import and/or export quotas (Art. XI GATT);

(e) GATT signatories can legitimately have recourse to contingent protection, and thus add to their default tariffs, if their trading partners practise unfair trade (dumping, subsidization) and/or if their import volume has increased as a result of unforeseen developments (Arts. VI, XIX GATT respectively);

---

[71] By virtue of the equivalence propositions, different instruments can achieve the same objective: chief among them the Lerner theorem establishing the equivalence between import and export duties; customs duties can be decomposed into domestic taxes (to consumers) and subsidies (to producers); through devaluation of the national currency national exports can be boosted.

[72] And, of course, as the number of signatories increases, so does the size of the carrot.

(f) With respect to domestic instruments, GATT signatories incur a non-discrimination obligation, that is, they must treat imported goods that have paid their ticket to entry (in the form of an import duty) into their national market as if they were domestic goods. Negotiators were unhappy with the manner in which they had negotiated the discipline on domestic instruments: there was dissatisfaction, for example, with the term 'like products' and a general uneasiness regarding whether this term could capture the spirit of the discipline; it was decided to keep it *faute de mieux* on a provisional basis until the ITO negotiation was completed, where this and other terms would unavoidably have been renegotiated. The end to the ITO meant, *inter alia*, the halt to renegotiation of the term 'like products'.[73] So, it was essentially left to adjudicators to ensure that the discipline on domestic instruments would function as an insurance policy to preserve the value of concessions.

Important consequences stem from the discussion above:

First, assuming a reasonable understanding of the term 'protection', the GATT allows its signatories to protect their domestic producers in their market only through tariffs. In other words, the only instrument of protection (tariffs) is negotiable. It follows that the value of tariff concessions (for which, recall, trading nations have paid a consideration by committing themselves to bound protection) will not be undone through subsequent unilateral action (e.g. through domestic instruments). Trading nations would thus continue to have an incentive to negotiate tariff reductions in the future as well:[74] binding through non-discrimination all domestic instruments is the GATT insurance policy that the value of tariff concessions will be preserved.[75]

Second, our discussion above also reveals that the GATT is a negative integration contract: its signatories are essentially free to unilaterally define their policies (which affect trade). Therefore, they are under no constraint at all, as a result of their signing the GATT, to follow a particular antitrust, environmental, labour policy, etc. All they have promised by acceding to the GATT is that, once they have decided on similar policies, they will apply them in non-discriminatory manner to both domestic and imported goods which come under their purview.

---

[73] Irwin et al. (2008).

[74] In a tariff-free world, there will be additional strain on the interpretation of the non-discrimination obligation imposed on domestic instruments in order to ensure that protectionist behaviour is punished.

[75] This feature of the GATT is exacerbated by the so-called non-violation complaints (NVCs) which appear in Art. XXIII.1b GATT. NVCs, prima facie, extend beyond non-discrimination: GATT signatories incur the obligation to compensate their trading partners if, as a result of their national policies, the value of tariff concessions has been negatively affected. This institution is akin to the obligation to perform the GATT in good faith (bona fides).

2.2 Becoming an Institution

On 6 December 1950, it was made clear that the ITO Charter would not be formally presented to US Congress for ratification.[76] There are various reasons that led to this decision and it is probably unfair to blame the US as solely responsible for the non-advent of the ITO. In the absence of published opinions by all those who participated in the negotiation (and those who were called to ratify the end product), it is difficult to measure the extent of dissatisfaction with the ITO draft. Diebold (1993) probably sums it up in a fair manner when he states:

> The efforts to go beyond traditional areas of agreement led to what I regard as a fairly promising chapter about international commodity agreements, a weak one on private business practices, and what turned out to be disastrous provisions about economic development and private investment.[77]

It is true, nevertheless, that in the US the mood was not favourable to the ITO. There was dissatisfaction in US business circles with the final outcome: an attempt to add to the brief references to investment was at the request of the US, but it also led to the inclusion of provisions that sanctioned behaviour that the US had long tried to change. The prevailing feeling was that modernized versions of treaties of friendship, commerce, and navigation (FCN), bilateral agreements that the US used to sign with a host of interested states, would better correspond to the aspirations of US business, and the question was what would be the added value were the US to sign a multilateral treaty like the ITO that would lead to an inferior

---

[76] Congress never got beyond early hearings. The Truman administration withdrew the submission to the Congress to approve the ITO Charter when it was clear that there was not going to be Congressional support for this project. Both Brown (1950) and Wilcox (1949), two prominent US negotiators, published their written version of the GATT/ITO negotiations in an effort to persuade the US public to support the multilateral endeavour. Their efforts were not, alas, crowned with success. Commentators do not agree on the reason why the US Congress failed to ratify the ITO Charter. Gardner (1956) argues that protectionist forces in the US were at least a contributing factor: many lobbies requested that President Truman draw back from asking the Senate to ratify. The wide and probably too ambitious coverage of the Havana Charter (including a full range of economic issues ranging from commodity agreements to economic development and even employment) and the threat it represented to national sovereignty was probably the other important contributing factor. On this score, see also Dam (2004). Diebold (1952, pp. 20ff) offers a different explanation: the US Council of the International Chamber of Commerce (ICC), a powerful lobby by any standard, opposed the ITO because it did not go far enough: many policies of economic nationalism were left intact. Odell and Eichengreen (1998) offer support for the thesis that the reason why the ITO project failed has to do with the failure of the Truman administration to mobilize public support on its behalf. At any rate, the ITO could not have realistically entered into force without the participation of the US, the leading trading nation at that time. Irwin (1995) takes the view that, independently of the reasons leading to it, failure was probably a blessing in light of the many arcane provisions in the ITO Charter. What is definitely true is that the early GATT experience did not do the (eventual) ratification of the ITO any favours. Leddy (1958) reports that the overarching feeling was that this was a document people could happily live with. He reports that, in the eyes of the Congress, the GATT 'was not repulsive, but neither was she fair'.

[77] Diebold (1993, p. 337).

(when compared to FCN) result.[78] The shortcomings notwithstanding, key figures in the negotiating process tried in vain to persuade the US political power to endorse the project. Clair Wilcox, one of the chief US negotiators, went as far as to state that:

> There is no hope that a multilateral trading system can be maintained in the face of widespread and protracted unemployment. Where the objectives of domestic stability and international freedom come into conflict, the former will be given priority.[79]

Their voices, however, fell on deaf ears. Besides the US business arguments, two other factors contributed to the demise of the ITO:

(a) The absence of ITO champions in the US (Truman) administration after 1949, and

(b) The realization how much could be achieved solely through the GATT.[80]

Those who would have defended the ITO had left office. We quote from Diebold (1993, p. 341):

> Clayton had gone, as had Wilcox. Nitze was doing other things. Acheson was back but he never put a high priority on trade matters except as part of larger issues. I think he regarded trade liberalization as a kind of hobby of Cordell Hull's and he did not have a lot of respect for Mr. Hull's political judgment—at least on international matters. Raymond Vernon has put forward the idea of 'policy entrepreneurs' and I wonder whether the absence of one may not have contributed to the Truman administration's dropping of the ITO.

Will Clayton, prefacing the 1949 book by Wilcox, explains that the US had embarked on a twin process aimed at leading to recovery on the European continent as well as worldwide:

> The program that is embodied in the Charter provides a necessary sequel to the program for European recovery on which the United States is now embarked. The two are interdependent; neither can be wholly successful without the other; both are parts of a common policy.[81]

European recovery would, of course, be largely achieved through the Marshall Plan. There was an increasing conviction that the second part (the Charter's programme) could be largely achieved through the GATT as it stood, that is, by one of the ITO chapters only. In this vein, some cast doubt on the value added by the ITO.

Other plausible explanations of the failure to launch the ITO have been advanced in the literature: Odell and Eichengreen (1998) invoke principal-agent

---

[78] Diebold (1952, and also later 1993) takes the view that the investment chapter was one of the key elements that led to the demise of the ITO.

[79] Wilcox (1949) at p. 131.

[80] Diebold (1952) first pointed to sequence (elaborated in Diebold 1993). Irwin et al. (2008) insist on the first point and underscore how the change in personnel affected the overall US attitude.

[81] Wilcox (1949) at pp. x–xi.

slack as the main reason for the failure of the ITO. They compare the ITO with the WTO negotiation and note that in the latter negotiation 'principals instructed their negotiating agents earlier, more often, and more precisely'.[82] As a result, the final outcome of the WTO negotiation was closer to the US Congress's preferences than was that for the ITO. The Truman administration was not, in other words, fully aware of the implications of the ITO negotiations and quite reluctant to invest substantial political capital to salvage a process that it had not fully grasped. There is arguably some truth in each of the explanations offered above and for these reasons, and probably for many more, the ITO never saw the light of the day.

The GATT, which in the meantime had entered into force on 1 January 1948, was thus left to operate in an institutional vacuum. The GATT itself contained only a few, scattered provisions of an institutional nature: reference to important institutions, like the GATT Council, was totally missing from the original text. There is nothing paradoxical about this since the GATT was supposed to be an agreement, a contractual arrangement, coming under the aegis of the ITO, the Charter of which contained all necessary institutional provisions. Eric Wyndham-White was the first Executive Secretary of the GATT, heading a small Secretariat. Eventually, in subsequent years, his post was renamed as Director-General (DG) of the GATT.

The GATT slowly evolved into an international institution in an attempt to fill the gap that had been left by the non-establishment of the ITO. The GATT integration process benefited but also suffered from the lack of an institutional foundation. On the negative side, the countries participating in the GATT could not plan far ahead; any institutional innovation was more of a practical response to an observed need, rather than a springboard which would accommodate future challenges. On the positive side, however, this functional institutionalism à la GATT gained legitimacy precisely because the edifice was built on perceived and not imaginary needs. Various bodies like the GATT Council were established, which in turn gave birth to other bodies. An appropriate illustration of the GATT functional institutionalism is offered by the advent of the Consultative Group of Eighteen (CG18), which was established by a GATT Council decision taken on 11 July 1975:

> The task of the Group is to facilitate the carrying out, by the CONTRACTING PARTIES, of their responsibilities, particularly with respect to:
>
> (a) following international trade developments with a view to the pursuit and maintenance of trade policies consistent with the objectives and principles of the General Agreement;
> (b) the forestalling, whenever possible, of sudden disturbances that could represent a threat to the multilateral trading system and to international trade relations generally; and action to deal with such disturbances if they in fact occur;

---

[82] Odell and Eichengreen (1998) at p. 183.

(c) the international adjustment process and the co-ordination, in this context, between the GATT and the IMF.

In the pursuit of its task, the Group shall take into account the special characteristics and requirements of the economies of the developing countries and their problems.

The Group shall not impinge upon the competence or authority of the CON-TRACTING PARTIES[83] or of the Council and shall not assume, or detract from, any of the decision-making responsibilities of these two bodies or of the permanent GATT Committees. Neither shall it interfere with the activities and competence of the Trade Negotiations Committee.

The Group's membership shall be balanced and broadly representative due regard being had to rotation of membership as appropriate.

Initially the composition of the Group shall be as follows:

Chairman: To be designated by members of the Group.[84]

Membership:

Argentina	India	Peru
Australia	Japan	Poland
Brazil	Malaysia	Spain
Canada	Nigeria	Switzerland
Egypt	Nordic country	United States
EU[85]	Pakistan	Zaire

The attendance of alternates shall be provided for.

In developing its procedures, the Group shall ensure that, when a matter of particular importance to any contracting party is under discussion, that contracting party shall have the opportunity fully to present its views to the Group.

The Group may invite observers to attend during the discussion of an item on the agenda of a meeting.

The Group shall meet periodically as necessary.

The Group shall report periodically to the Council. It shall submit once a year a comprehensive account of its activities.

The Group is established provisionally for a period of one year, its task, composition and terms of reference being subject to review by the Council at the end of that year.[86]

---

[83] The highest decision-making body in the GATT is the CONTRACTING PARTIES (in capital letters), which refers to the entire GATT membership adopting decisions by consensus. In many ways, the term 'CONTRACTING PARTIES' is appropriate since it was governments (and customs territories) which signed on to a *contract* liberalizing trade (the GATT), rather than adhering to become members of an institution. Evidently, the latter would have been the case had the ITO been established.

[84] DG Olivier Long was designated as Chairman.

[85] EU stands for European Union, the official name of the European integration process as of December 2009. Throughout this volume, we will refer to the previous official name, EC (European Communities), only to the extent that it is historically necessary. See WTO Docs. WT/L/779 and WT/Let/679, where it is explained that the EU assumes all the rights and obligations of the EC in respect of all agreements for which the Director General of the WTO is depositary and to which the EC is a signatory or contracting party.

[86] L/4204 of 15 July 1975, GATT Doc. BISD 22S at pp. 15ff, and GATT Doc. C/M/107.

Prior to the establishment of the CG18 there was no comparable attempt to bring senior officials from capitals to Geneva on a regular basis. Following the submission of a document by DG Olivier Long,[87] discussions on the establishment of the group were initiated. In DG Long's mind, the idea was to bring in an Executive Committee for the GATT, the membership of which was fast increasing: an organ with limited membership but quite representative of all GATT contracting parties. What he probably had in mind was a structure akin to the Committee of Twenty (C-20) of the IMF, which had been studying the reform of the international monetary system; this restricted group of high level representatives, which would not impinge upon the competence or authority of the CONTRACTING PARTIES, the Council or other permanent GATT bodies, would be able to discuss international trade matters within the political context and on the basis of the personal knowledge and authority of the group's members. Following consultations, essentially about the composition of the group, DG Long made a further submission to the Council in July 1975, where he set out the terms of reference for the group as set out above, which were approved by the Council without amendment.[88] The initial membership of the Group was as discussed above. In addition, provision was made for nine alternate members, approved each year (along with the permanent groups) by the CONTRACTING PARTIES. In the first year these were: Austria, Côte d'Ivoire, Hungary, Israel, Jamaica, Korea, New Zealand, Norway, Yugoslavia, followed by rotation within geographic regions. Alternate members could participate fully in the Group's discussions; the main formal difference between full members and alternate members was that the former were provided with two seats, one to be used by an adviser, while alternate members had only one. At the Session of CONTRACTING PARTIES in November 1985 it was decided that for 1986 the membership of the Group should be somewhat enlarged to 22 full members. The number of alternate members remained nine.

CG18 was some sort of a harbinger for global governance: representatives of the IMF attended part of the group's third meeting in June 1976. And the US choice was not accidental: it wanted to secure a 'soft' agreement in the context of CG18, an organ not entrusted with decision-making powers that could serve as a pathway to a binding decision. The US did not want to burn any bridges: it would take the time necessary to bring a critical mass of GATT players on board; almost all of them participated in CG18.

The first meeting of the Group was held in November 1975. The change of the group's name from Management Group, as originally proposed, to Consultative Group reflected the intention that this should not be a decision-making body. The group's function was essentially consultative, and on a number of occasions it

---

[87] GATT doc. L/4048. On the role of CG18 in general, see the excellent account of Blackhurst and Hartridge (2005).
[88] GATT Doc. L/4189.

made recommendations or suggestions to the GATT Council on matters of importance: thus, in July 1981 it recommended that the CONTRACTING PARTIES should envisage convening a Ministerial Meeting in 1982. This group provided the home for numerous discussions on the GATT mandate, its eventual expansion to other areas etc.

But even more telling is the institutional evolution of dispute settlement under the GATT: the two GATT provisions which explicitly refer to the settlement of disputes (Arts. XXII and XXIII) contain no specific procedures, let alone a reference to GATT Panels. Formality was added at the conclusion of the Tokyo round with the adoption of the Understanding on Notification, Consultation, Dispute Settlement and Surveillance of 28 November 1979 ('1979 Understanding'). This Understanding included an annex setting out an Agreed Description of the Customary Practice of the GATT in the Field of Dispute Settlement, which provided a description of the way in which dispute settlement procedures had evolved since the inception of the GATT:

> Panels set up their own working procedures. The practice for the panels has been to hold two or three formal meetings with the parties concerned. The panel invited the parties to present their views either in writing and/or orally in the presence of each other. The panel can question both parties on any matter which it considers relevant to the dispute. Panels have also heard the views of any contracting party having a substantial interest in the matter, which is not directly party to the dispute, but which has expressed in the Council a desire to present its views. Written memoranda submitted to the panel have been considered confidential, but are made available to the parties to the dispute. Panels often consult with and seek information from any relevant source they deem appropriate and they sometimes consult experts to obtain their technical opinion on certain aspects of the matter. Panels may seek advice or assistance from the secretariat in its capacity as guardian of the General Agreement, especially on historical or procedural aspects. The secretariat provides the secretary and technical services for panels.[89]

Three years later, acting at a Ministerial Conference,[90] the CONTRACTING PARTIES reaffirmed the 1979 Understanding and added more detail, including a requirement that:

> The contracting party to which such a recommendation [i.e. to bring a challenged measure into conformity with GATT] has been addressed, shall report within a reasonable specified period on action taken or on its reasons for not implementing the recommendation or ruling by the CONTRACTING PARTIES.[91]

---

[89] Agreed Description of the Customary Practice of the GATT in the Field of Dispute Settlement (Art. XXIII:2), GATT Doc. BISD 26S/215, 217, ¶ 6 (iv).

[90] Ministerial conferences were convened periodically throughout the GATT years to inaugurate and conclude a trade round. Sometimes they were also convened to unblock stalled negotiations. In practice ministers almost never conducted the day-to-day negotiations themselves.

[91] See GATT Doc. BISD 29S/13, 15, ¶ (viii).

Further minor steps were taken with the Decision on Dispute Settlement Procedures adopted on 30 November 1984.[92] Eventually the Montreal Rules were agreed[93] during the Uruguay round, and the Panel process began to take its current form. This illustration evidences, in quite characteristic manner, how one of the most important GATT institutions came to life following a learning-by-doing approach.

The fact that all decisions in the GATT years were taken by consensus added to the legitimacy of the whole endeavour: in the absence of explicit opposition, proposals would be voted on with tacit acquiescence sufficing for adoption of any decisions. Consensus voting signalled the adherence of all GATT signatories to whatever was being decided. There is of course a trade-off between legitimacy (through consensus) and efficiency (since any one GATT signatory could block a decision). The GATT signatories preferred to err on the latter side and sacrificed speed of the integration process in the name of consensus behind each and every step forward.[94]

Over the years, the GATT developed an institutional infrastructure that would adequately cope with its ever increasing needs. Although the participants in the GATT process continued, until the last days of the GATT, to be formally called 'contracting parties', they behaved as members of an institution, operating under a vague 'institutional' umbrella. The gradual 'institutionalization' of the GATT facilitated the two other important functions (besides settling disputes) of the GATT: reducing tariff protection, and agreeing on new trade rules. We take the two issues in turn in what immediately follows.

2.3 The GATT Rounds of Trade Liberalization

Recall that a tariff bargain was at the heart of the original GATT, and that the GATT mandate calls for progressive tariff liberalization and not for immediate tariff elimination (Art. XXVIIIbis). During the GATT years, the contracting parties conducted eight rounds of multilateral negotiations aimed at reducing tariffs (see Table 1.1).

The Doha round, which was launched in that Middle Eastern city in the autumn of 2001, is the ninth trade round since the inception of the GATT and the first since the advent of the WTO. As will be explained in more detail *infra*, these rounds managed to substantially reduce the level of tariffs over the years and gradually to focus on addressing NTBs.

---

[92] See GATT Doc. BISD 31S/9.

[93] Essentially, the right to establish a panel and the move towards compulsory third-party adjudication was introduced through these procedures, along with other modifications of less importance.

[94] A number of authors lamented the GATT pragmatic process. Dam (1970) and Hudec (1975) have been notable exceptions in this discussion.

Table 1.1 Negotiating rounds

Name of the round	Chronology	Number of participants
Geneva	1947	23
Annecy	1949	13
Torquay	1950	38
Geneva	1956	26
Dillon	1960–61	26
Kennedy	1962–67	62
Tokyo	1973–79	102
Uruguay	1986–94	123

Source: Understanding the WTO, The WTO: Geneva, p. 15.

2.4 Adding to the Legislative Framework

Up until the Kennedy round, trade negotiators were essentially preoccupied with the reduction of tariff barriers. During the Kennedy round, the focus shifted towards examining the role that NTBs play in restricting the cross-border trade in goods. Originally, negotiations on NTBs focused on barriers imposed for economic reasons (antidumping (AD), countervailing, safeguards); eventually, however (first through the negotiation of the Agreement on Technical Barriers to Trade (TBT) during the Tokyo round, and then through the renegotiation of the TBT as well as the negotiation of the Agreement on the Application of Sanitary and Phyto-sanitary Measures (SPS) during the Uruguay round), trading nations began to negotiate NTBs adopted ostensibly for public policy reasons (such as the protection of human health). In principle, these NTBs were unconnected to the competitive position of domestic industries. The agreements concluded during the Tokyo round dealing with NTBs were the following: Agreement on Implementation of Article VI of the General Agreement on Tariffs and Trade (AD); Agreement on Interpretation and Application of Articles VI, XVI and XXIII of the General Agreement on Tariffs and Trade (SCM); Agreement on Import Licensing Procedures (ILA); Agreement on Technical Barriers to Trade (TBT); Agreement on Implementation of Article VII of the General Agreement on Tariffs and Trade and Protocol to the Agreement (CV); Agreement on Government Procurement (GPA); Agreement on Trade in Civil Aircraft (CA); International Dairy Arrangement (IDA); and the International Arrangement Regarding Bovine Meat (IBM). The approach followed during the Tokyo round became known as 'GATT *à la carte*', and GATT contracting parties were given the option to decide whether or not to accede to the various codes. The list of the signatories to the various Tokyo round agreements is reproduced below (see Table 1.2):[95]

---

[95] GATT Doc. L/5517/Add. 16 of 13 May 1985.

Table 1.2 Participation in the Tokyo round agreements

COUNTRIES CONTRACTING PARTIES		Geneva 1979 Protocol	Suppl. 1979 Protocol	Tech. Barriers	Gov't Procur.	Subsid. Countervailing	Bovine Meat	Dairy	Customs Val.[96]	Import Lic.	Civil Aircraft	Anti-Dumping
Argentina	AR	A		S	O	O	A	A	S*	S	O	O
Australia	AU	A	A	O		A*	A	A[97]	A	A		A
Austria	AT	A		A	A	A	A	A	A	A	A	A
Bangladesh	BD			O	O	O	O	O	O	O	O	O
Barbados	BB											
Belgium	BE	A	A	A							A	
Belize	BZ						Prov.					
Benin	BJ											
Brazil	BR	A	A	A	O	A	A	O	A*	O	O	A
Burma	BU							O				
Burundi	BI_											
Cameroon	CM				O						O	
Canada	CA	A	A	A	A	A	A	O	A*	A	A	A
Cent. Afr. Rep.	CF											
Chad	TD											
Chile	CL		A	A	O	A		O	O	A		O
Colombia	CO			O		A	A		O	O		O
Congo	CO					O	O	O		O		
Cuba	CU			O	O	O	O	O	O	O		O
Cyprus	CY											
Czechoslovakia	CS	A		A*	O	O			A	A	O	A
Denmark	DK	A*		A*	O					A	A*	
Dominican Rep.	DO		A	A	O							
Egypt	EG	A	A	A	O	A	A	S	O	A	S	A

(Continued)

96 Including Protocol. Upon entry into force of the Agreement on 1 January 1981, the provisions of the Protocol were deemed to be an integral part of the Agreement.
97 Withdrawal to take effect on 9 June 1985.

Table 1.2 *Continued*

COUNTRIES CONTRACTING PARTIES		Geneva 1979 Protocol	Suppl. 1979 Protocol	Tech. Barriers	Gov't Procur.	Subsid. Countervailing	Bovine Meat	Dairy	Customs Val.96	Import Lic.	Civil Aircraft	Anti-Dumping
EEC	CE	A	A	A	A	A	A	A	A	A	A	A
Finland	FI	A		A	A	A	A	A	A	A		A
France	FR	A		A							A	
Gabon	GA			O	O	O	O	O		O	O	
Gambia	GM											
Germany	DE	A*			A*						A*	
Ghana	GH			O		O				O	O	O
Greece	GR			S							S	
Guyana	GY											
Haiti	HT		A		.	O	O					
Hungary	HU	A		A*	O	O	A	A	A	A		A
Iceland	IS	A				O						
India	IN	A	A	A	O	A	O		A*	A	O	A
Indonesia	ID		A	O	O	A*		O	O	O	O	O
Ireland	IE	A		A							A	
Israel	IL	S	A	O	A	O		O	O	O	O	O
Italy	IT	A		A							A	
Ivory Coast	CI	A	A	O	O	O	O	O	O	O		
Jamaica	JM	A			O	O		O		O		
Japan	JP	A*		A	A	A	A	A	A	A	A	A
Kenya	KE			A	A	A	O			A		
Korea	KR		A	A	O	A	O		A*	O		O
Kuwait	KW											
Luxembourg	LU	A		A								
Madagascar	MG						O				A	
Malawi	MW	—							A*			
Malaysia	MY			O	O	O	O		O	O		O
Maldives	MV				O	O			O	O		O
Malta	MT	A	A	O	O	O	O	O		O		O

Mauritania	MR											
Mauritius	MU									O		
Netherlands	NL	A										
New Zealand	NZ	A	A	A	A	A	A	O	O	O	O	A
Nicaragua	NI	O	O	O	O	O	O	O		O		O
Niger	NE											
Nigeria	NG	O	O	O	O	O	O	O	O	O	O	A
Norway	NO	A	A	A	A	A	A	A	A	A	A	A
Pakistan	PK	A	O	A	A	O	O	A				
Peru	PA	A		O		O		O				
Philippines	PH	A	A*	A*	A	A*	A*	A	A*		O	A
Poland	PL	A	O	A	A	O	O	O		O	O	A
Portugal	PT	O	O	A*	A	O		O	O	O	O	A
Romania	RO	A	A	A	A	A	A	A	A	A	A	A
Rwanda	RW	S	O			A						
Senegal	SN	O	O	O	O		O	O		O		O
Sierra Leone	SL											
Singapore	SG	A	A	A	O	A	A	O	O	A	O	A
South Africa	ZA	A	A*	O	O	O	O	O	O	O	O	A
Spain	ES	A	A	A	A*	A	A*	A*	A	A*	A	O
Sri Lanka	LK	O	O	A	O	O	O	O	O	O	O	A
Suriname	SR											
Sweden	SE	A	A	A	A	A	A	A	A	A	A	A
Switzerland	CH	A	A	A	A	A	A	A	A	A	A	A
Tanzania	TZ	O	O	O	O	O		O		O		O
Thailand	TH	O	O	O	O	O	O	O		O		O
Togo	TG											
Trinidad & Tobago	TT	O	O	O	A	O	O	O	O	O	O	O
Turkey	TR	O	O	O	O	O	O	O	O	O	O	O
Uganda	UG											
United Kingdom	GB	A	A*	A*	A*	A*	A*	A*	A*	A*	A*	A*
United States	US	A	A	A	A	A	A	A	A	A	A	A
Upper Volta	HV											

(Continued)

Table 1.2 *Continued*

COUNTRIES CONTRACTING PARTIES	Geneva 1979 Protocol	Suppl. 1979 Protocol	Tech. Barriers	Gov't Procur.	Subsid. Counter-vailing	Bovine Meat	Dairy	Customs Val.[96]	Import Lic.	Civil Aircraft	Anti-Dumping
Uruguay UY		A			A	A	A				O
Yugoslavia YU	A		A		S	A	O	A	A	O	A
Zaire ZR		A	O	O	O	O	O	O	O		O
Zambia ZM											
Zimbabwe ZW											
OTHER COUNTRIES											
Botswana BW								A*			
Bulgaria BG			O		O	A	A	O	O		O
Costa Rica CR						O					
Ecuador EC			O	O	O			O	O		O
Guatemala GT						A*					
Mexico MX			O		O	O	O		O		O
Panama PA						O	O				
Paraguay PY						Prov.					
Tunisia TN			A		O	A	O		O	O	
Venezuela VE					O				O	O	O

Notes:
A Accepted
B Signed (acceptance pending)
O Observer
* Reservation, condition and/or declaration
** Provisional accession to GATT

Under the single-undertaking approach that was adopted during the Uruguay round, trading nations were requested to adhere, with very few exceptions, to all agreements concluded, thus departing from prior practice (Tokyo round). The Uruguay round, however, introduced a new distinction between:

(a) Multilateral agreements, where participation was automatic upon accession to the WTO. In essence almost all Tokyo round agreements (codes) were 'multi-lateralized' and a new multilateral agreement (SPS) was added as well; and

(b) Plurilateral agreements where participation remained optional; four plurilateral agreements were concluded during the Uruguay round, namely: the Dairy Arrangement and the Arrangement Regarding Bovine Meat (which have both since expired), and the GPA and the Agreement on CA which are still in force.

2.5 The Transformations of the GATT

The original GATT underwent a series of changes over the years:

(a) In 1948, during the Havana Conference, only minor changes were made to the GATT text, the most important being the expansion of Art. XXIV GATT which as of then covers FTAs as well;

(b) In 1955, the GATT Review Session took place, which amounted to a comprehensive re-evaluation of the GATT: the provisions on balance of payments and renegotiation of duties were heavily redrafted at that time;

(c) In 1965, Part IV was added to the GATT. It was the institutional acknowledgement that MFN was not working to the benefit of developing countries, and opened the door first to the 1971 waiver, and then to the 1979 decision (Enabling Clause) which 'enabled' GATT contracting parties (developed countries) to provide, through national GSP (Generalized System of Preferences) schemes, a tariff treatment of imports originating in developing countries that was better than that of imports of the same goods originating in developed countries, without developing countries incurring the obligation to pay consideration;

(d) The ultimate transformation of the GATT came in 1995 at the end of the Uruguay round, when, as a result of its successful conclusion, the GATT reverted to its original function, an agreement coming under the institutional umbrella of a trade organization (no longer the ITO, but the WTO, the World Trade Organization).

2.6 What did the GATT Achieve?

The GATT delivered on its original promise and actually did more than that. Recall that, originally, the focus of the GATT was the dismantling of tariff protection, with commitments on domestic instruments acting as a kind of insurance policy aimed at preserving the value of tariff concessions. This is one area where the GATT has enjoyed remarkable success. There are two caveats though: first, reductions have not been symmetric across products, nor second, have they been symmetric across countries. Farm and textile products essentially lived outside the core disciplines of the GATT, the former because of Arts. XI.2 and XVI GATT (which allowed some import restrictions and subsidization respectively), and the latter because of the Multi-fibre Arrangement (MFA), which established a global quota for textile products. Developing countries, on the other hand, did not make tariff cuts comparable to those made by developed countries[98] as various tables in the WTO World Trade Report of 2007[99] clearly evidence.

Tables 1.3 and 1.4 show the tariff cuts by developed GATT contracting parties on industrial goods over the years whereas Table 1.5 reflects tariff cuts by countries acceding to the WTO after 1 January 1995.

Table 1.3 Tariff cuts by developed countries in industrial goods

Implementation Period	Round covered	Weighted tariff reduction
1948	Geneva (1947)	−26 (1939)
1950	Annecy (1949)	−3 (1947)
1952	Torquay (1950–1)	−4 (1949)
1956–8	Geneva (1955–6)	−3 (1954)
1962–4	Dillon (1961–2)	−4 (1960)
1968–72	Kennedy (1964–7)	−38 (1964)
1980–7	Tokyo (1973–9)	−33 (1977 or 1976)
1995–9	Uruguay (1986–94)	−38 (1988 or 1989)

Notes: The last column represents the year during which the MFN imports weights were based.
Source: The World Trade Report, 2007, p. 207.

Table 1.4 Tariff cuts on industrial goods during the Uruguay round

Trader	Pre-	Post-	Reduction	Imports (MFN)
	Uruguay Round		rate in %	Billion $(1988)
United States	5.4	3.5	−35	297
Japan	3.9	1.7	−56	133
EU-12	5.7	3.6	−37	197
TOTAL of above	**5.2**	**3.1**	**−39**	**627**

Source: The World Trade Report, 2007, The GATT: Geneva at p. 209.

---

[98] Thus lending some support to proponents of terms of trade theory since it would be senseless, in this view, to request concessions from countries that cannot affect the world price. In the Hullian view, they would benefit from MFN reductions.
[99] The World Trade Report, 2007, The GATT: Geneva at p. 207.

Table 1.5 Tariff cuts by countries acceding at or after the Uruguay round

	Agricultural Products		Industrial Products	
	Bound	Applied	Bound	Applied
Albania (a)	9.4	9.0	6.6	7.2
Republic of Armenia	14.7	6.6	7.5	2.3
Bulgaria	35.6	18.4	23.0	8.8
Cambodia (c)	28.1	19.5	17.7	15.9
China	15.8	16.2	9.1	9.5
Croatia (c)	9.4	9.3	5.5	4.1
Ecuador	25.5	14.7	21.1	11.5
Estonia (b)	17.5	12.2	7.3	0.1
FYR of Macedonia	11.3	12.7	6.2	8.7
Georgia	11.7	11.7	6.5	6.9
Jordan	23.7	19.6	15.2	12.1
Kyrgyz Republic (c)	12.3	7.0	6.7	4.3
Latvia (a)	34.6	11.8	9.4	2.2
Lithuania (b)	15.2	9.7	8.4	2.4
Moldova (a)	12.2	10.2	6.0	4.1
Mongolia (c)	18.9	5.1	17.3	4.9
Nepal (c)	41.4	13.5	23.7	13.7
Oman (a)	28.0	10.2	11.6	5.0
Panama (b)	27.7	14.8	22.9	7.4
Saudi Arabia (d)	22.4	7.8	10.5	4.8
Chinese Taipei (c)	15.3	16.3	4.8	5.5

Notes: 2004 is the year of applied duties by default, unless otherwise indicated: (a) refers to 2001, (b) to 2002, (c) to 2003, and (d) to 2006. The reader should not be perplexed when the bound duty is higher than the applied duty: duties have to be reduced to the bound level by the end of an agreed *staging period*, and it may be the case that the information included in this table was collected before the end of this period. For example, the Marrakesh Protocol to the GATT 1994 explains in its §2 that agreed tariff reductions should be implemented in five equal rate reductions, and provides for the time period within which all five reductions should take place.

Source: The World Trade Report, 2007, The GATT: Geneva at p. 209.

Lowering of tariffs does not exhaust the GATT success story. As noted *supra*, the lowering of tariffs revealed the importance of NTBs and the trading nations developed a series of agreements aimed at imposing multilateral disciplines on NTBs. Without bringing into question the negative integration character of the GATT,[100] these agreements provided a more fine-tuned understanding of the term 'discrimination', the cornerstone of the multilateral trade edifice, and also dealt with numerous other issues ranging from ascertaining the proper value of imported goods to constraining unilateral actions in the context of contingent protection. As tariff dismantlement has been progressing, and in light of the fact that international externalities can be imposed not only through trade but through domestic instruments as well (equivalence propositions), the law-

---

[100] Except through the addition of the Agreement on Trade Related Intellectual Property Rights (TRIPs), an agreement that requests a certain minimum level of intellectual property protection from all participants.

making function of the GATT (and now the WTO) emerges as a very important tool in the fight against protectionism.

The GATT contracting parties crystallized practice into law,[101] tried to fill the gaps in the contract through new agreements (e.g. the procedure to be followed when imposing antidumping duties), and were even bold enough to seek outside help in order to address the worries of (some) participants (e.g. the Haberler report that we discuss in Chapter 3). Renegotiation of the GATT on the other hand, was becoming an increasingly costly option as the number of participants grew, and consensus was not negotiable either.[102] The increase of participants, and the increase of agreements, unavoidably took their toll on the duration of rounds: rounds gradually took longer to complete (four years for the Kennedy round, six years for the Tokyo, eight years for the Uruguay, and we are now well into the 11th year of the Doha round). The changing subject-matter also must have had decisive influence here: it is easier to negotiate tariffs on reciprocity grounds; it is harder to do so when it comes to elaborating a legal document aiming to provide a test that will distinguish between measures that genuinely pursue say protection of public health and measures that do not do so. For these reasons and probably many more, rounds have been gradually spaced out: six rounds in the first 20 years of the GATT as opposed to three in the next 40 years, one of which (the Doha round) is yet to be completed.

Some legislative activity occurred at the Committee level at the GATT, but except for the Review Session of 1955 and the addition of Part IV, no other major change occurred throughout the GATT years: the rise in the number of participants, coupled with the religious dedication to the consensus rule when it came to adopting decisions, took their toll. The only realistic[103] way to 'complete' the contract was through adjudication. There is an important difference of course between legislation and adjudication in that the former binds all signatories, whereas the latter binds only the parties to a specific dispute. This difference nonetheless should not be exaggerated: adjudicating bodies have a strong incentive in following precedent since it is the safest way for them to acquire credibility (by applying the same law to identical transactions irrespective of the identity of the disputing parties).[104]

---

[101] See the discussion on the evolution of dispute settlement practice in Section 2.2.

[102] See the discussion on this issue in various places in Hoekman and Kostecki (2009) and especially at pp. 65–70.

[103] During round intervals, lower bodies (e.g. committees such as the Antidumping Committee) could step in and address specific issues. And indeed, as Mavroidis (2008) reports, some did and there is the emergence of secondary law, although in official GATT/WTO documents the term has so far been refuted. Most of it nonetheless occurs during the WTO years, the GATT experience in this respect being rather limited.

[104] Precedent, in turn, should be taken with a pinch of salt since, in the presence of new information, it is wise to rethink the existing paradigm. There is not binding precedent (*stare decisis*) in GATT (and now WTO) dispute adjudication, although de facto Panels almost always and with

Arts. XXII and XXIII GATT[105] established a two-phase system, whereby contracting parties would first go through a bilateral consultation phase aimed at resolving their dispute, and if this was not possible, the complainant could refer the matter to the CONTRACTING PARTIES. There was nothing like a Panel procedure explicitly established in the two aforementioned GATT provisions. The Panel procedure is thus an invention of the GATT CONTRACTING PARTIES. It all began with a complaint in the summer of 1948 by the Netherlands against Cuba, which presented the question as to whether the MFN obligation (Art. I GATT) also applied to consular taxes.[106] The matter was referred to the Chairman,[107] who ruled that Art. I GATT effectively applied to consular taxes. Rulings by the Chairman were subsequently substituted by a WP (Working Party) procedure, whereby the complaining party, the defendant, and any other contracting party that might have an interest in the dispute would participate. The GATT procedural rules were very limited, largely because it was anticipated that the ITO rules would soon come into force. The ITO Charter contained detailed dispute settlement rules that included a provision for the referral of questions to the ICJ (International Court of Justice).

The next mutation of the procedure was to eliminate the complainant and defendant from the adjudicating panel and instead assign three or five 'neutral' Panelists to prepare a report that would eventually be submitted to the CONTRACTING PARTIES for their consideration and adoption. In its early stages, dispute settlement in GATT reflected its diplomatic roots: the majority of Panelists were diplomats. No formal requirement to have legal training, let alone GATT-related legal training, was imposed. Both Hudec (1993a) and Davey (1987) have observed that the goal of the process was to end up with a mutually acceptable solution rather than to judge on the legal merits of the case—the overall tenor of the process was highly conciliatory: the accent was on removing cases from the docket.

If consultations could not lead to a satisfactory adjustment, the complainant, assuming the defendant was in agreement, could refer the matter to a Panel. The Panel would not decide the issue; it would simply submit a report which, unless adopted by the CONTRACTING PARTIES, would be of limited legal value. Assuming again that the defendant consented to the adoption of the report, the defendant would be requested to bring its measures into compliance with its GATT obligations. If implementation did not occur, the complainant could be

---

very few exceptions have followed prior rulings on the same issue; see Palmeter and Mavroidis (2004) and Mavroidis (2008).

[105] An early decision by the CONTRACTING PARTIES held that consultations under Art XXII.1 of the GATT would be considered as fulfilling the consultation requirements of Art XXIII.1 of the GATT; see GATT Doc. BISD 9S/20.

[106] This narrative about the GATT years borrows heavily from Palmeter and Mavroidis (2004).

[107] Hart (1998) mentions that 'the Havana Conference in its closing days established the Interim Commission for International Trade Organization (ICITO), composed of most members of the conference, to prepare a program for the ITO when it came into being, and to carry out related functions. Canada's Dana Wilgress was elected its first Chairman. The Commission appointed as its executive secretary, Eric Wyndham-White' (pp. 51–2).

authorized to impose countermeasures, provided that it made a request to the CONTRACTING PARTIES to this effect, and the CONTRACTING PARTIES by consensus (e.g. with the defendant's agreement) would acquiesce. Countermeasures in the GATT context amounted to an authorization to the complainant to suspend tariff concessions or other GATT obligations to the party found acting inconsistently with its obligations under the agreement. The system was transformed even more through crystallization of practice in the 1979 Understanding, described in Section 2.2 *supra*, and all additional changes that followed with the adoption of the Montreal Rules.[108]

For years, that is, before the adoption of the Montreal Rules, consensus-based decisions in dispute settlement meant that the losing party could refuse to agree to the very establishment of a Panel, thereby avoiding the embarrassment of having to face an adverse report altogether.[109] Moreover, adverse GATT Panel reports could be blocked by losing parties, irrespective of the soundness of their approach and final findings, and, consequently, winning complainants could, in theory, find themselves in an awkward situation, unable to enforce a judgment against their trading partners practising an ostensibly GATT-inconsistent measure. The literature often exacerbated the size of the problem. This is where Hudec's contribution kicks in. In Hudec's (1993a) account, there is only one case where the defendant refused to establish a Panel: the case concerned the first hormones dispute between the EU and the US, and a Panel was not ultimately established due to a disagreement between them regarding the composition of the Panel (one party privileging a scientists-only panel, whereas the other opted for a normal panel composed of trade experts and, if warranted, scientists as well).[110] Hudec's study shows that from 1947 to 1992 207 Panels were established, and the losing party eventually accepted the results of an adverse Panel report in approximately 80 per cent of cases.[111] The percentage would have been even higher (close to 90 per cent) had it not been for Panel practice in the 1980s, when blocking adoption occurred with increasing frequency, probably because trading partners moved to the adjudicating table issues that they could not agree upon while negotiating. A number of Panels during this period dealt with farm policy, a contentious issue during the Uruguay round, especially between the two transatlantic partners at that time.[112]

---

[108] Through a number of decisions, the GATT CONTRACTING PARTIES provided clarifications on auxiliary issues, such as the role of the GATT Secretariat in servicing Panels (GATT Doc. BISD 26S/215), and the duty of the party found in violation of its GATT obligations to promptly report on the implementing activities it purported to undertake (GATT Doc. BISD 29S/13).

[109] Hudec (1990) held the view that a complainant could go ahead and adopt countermeasures in case the defendant refused to even establish a Panel. This is what he termed *justified disobedience*. From a pure legal perspective, this view is questionable.

[110] Benedek (1991) described GATT practice as akin to a customary right to a Panel.

[111] See Hudec (1993a) at p. 278.

[112] The weak point in Hudec's study in this respect is probably that it does not control for the disincentive for GATT contracting parties requesting the establishment of a Panel of anticipating a possible block by the (eventual) defendant. In other words, the overall number of disputes would

Hudec's study also reveals that the only time that a GATT contracting party, facing non-compliance by the defendant, requested authorization to impose countermeasures, its wish was granted.[113]

The thrust of Hudec's argument is that the passage to negative consensus[114] through the Montreal Rules, and its subsequent extension, should not come as a surprise: the trading partners were living in a de facto world of compulsory third-party adjudication. The GATT Panel system earned its reputation through a mix of increasing legal rigour (essentially through the establishment of the GATT Legal Affairs Division back in 1982), careful intrusiveness in some sensitive areas of sovereignty (joint selection of judges; freedom as to the choice of implementing measures), and legitimacy (since the losing party would agree that it had been wrong by adhering to the consensus). By any reasonable account, the system functioned to the satisfaction of its 'clients', the trading nations, and this is probably what prompted them to move to compulsory third-party adjudication, thus giving up precious sovereignty.

We referred in Section 2.2 *supra* to the GATT successfully transforming itself into a global institution through a series of actions that, in a nutshell, provided the GATT with the necessary apparatus to take care of its (increasing) mandate.

The best proof that the GATT has been a success story is probably the fact that its membership grew steadily over time: 23 odd nations signed the original text back in the summer of 1947 in Geneva and 120 signed on the dotted line the Marrakesh Agreement that closed the GATT chapter and opened that of the WTO. There are dozens of explanatory variables for this success, and indeed many accounts to this effect. What they all have in common is the weight they accord to consensus-based decisions tailored to the problems the GATT encountered over the years: this institutional functionalism is evidence of the reigning GATT pragmatism, the idea that GATT should be there to respond to actual and not perceived needs.

---

probably be higher, if positive consensus disappeared from the face of the GATT. However, it is very difficult to measure this disincentive: under certain assumptions, the potential defendant would go ahead anyway, and under others, this would not be the case. Much of the information to properly research this area is private and not easily discernible.

[113] GATT Doc. BISD 4S/31: the CONTRACTING PARTIES authorized the Netherlands to apply a limit of 60,000 metric tons on imports of wheat flour from the United States during the calendar year 1956.

[114] This term indicates that the GATT, in its latter days, and the WTO, as of day one, have effectively moved to compulsory third-party adjudication, where there is no need for the complainant to invest in establishing a Panel: this will be the case irrespective of whether the defendant agrees, an oddity in international relations where the paradigmatic dispute adjudication is a function of the will of both parties to see their dispute adjudicated by a tribunal/arbitral body. On the issue of 'judicialization' ('proceduralization') of the WTO, see von Bogdandy (2003).

3. Regulation of Trade in Goods in the WTO Era

The establishment of the WTO marks the end of the waiting period for the advent of the ITO: the WTO[115] takes over from the GATT institution and provides the institutional coverage for a number of agreements, including the GATT. The Marrakesh Agreement Establishing the WTO (hereinafter, WTO Agreement) contains four annexes, and Annex 1 is subdivided into 1A, which covers multilateral agreements on trade in goods, 1B, on trade in services, and 1C, dealing with the TRIPs agreement. Annex 2 deals with the administration of disputes in the WTO, and the relevant source of law for this purpose is the Dispute Settlement Understanding (DSU). The Trade Policy Review Mechanism (TPRM) is included in Annex 3. We will be dealing only to the extent necessary with Annex 2,[116] whereas Annex 3 is discussed in Chapter 13. Annex 4 is of interest for this volume as well, since the plurilateral agreements covered there deal with trade in goods.

When a country (or separate customs territory possessing full autonomy in the conduct of its external commercial relations, as per Art. XII.1 of the WTO Agreement) accedes to the WTO it will accept a third (besides accession to multilateral and plurilateral agreements) layer of obligations, those assumed through its Protocol of Accession. We will discuss *infra* the nature of similar obligations, but will refrain from delving into an exhaustive discussion of this category: the reason is that similar obligations bind only the acceding country in its relations with and the WTO incumbents.

3.1 GATT 1947, GATT 1994

Art. II of the WTO Agreement refers to GATT 1994 and adds that it is a legally distinct document from the original GATT (referred to as GATT 1947). Annex 1A includes a definition of GATT 1994:

1. The General Agreement on Tariffs and Trade 1994 ('GATT 1994') shall consist of:
   (a) the provisions in the General Agreement on Tariffs and Trade, dated 30 October 1947, annexed to the Final Act Adopted at the Conclusion of the Second Session of the Preparatory Committee of the United Nations Conference on Trade and Employment (excluding the Protocol of Provisional Application), as rectified, amended or modified by the terms of legal

---

[115] The negotiation of the WTO is a totally different ball game when compared to the GATT. The number of participants increased and their interests were quite varied. OECD members still managed to leave the 'development issues' for a later round (what eventually became the Doha round) and concentrated on a serious tariff-cutting enterprise, in mutlilateralizing the Tokyo round codes, and bringing farm and textiles trade for the first time under the aegis of the WTO. We will be discussing the negotiating history of each agreement in the corresponding chapters of this volume. On negotiating tactics, especially of the US, see also Stiglitz (2003).

[116] For extensive discussion of the DSU rules, see Palmeter and Mavroidis (2004).

   instruments which have entered into force before the date of entry into
   force of the WTO Agreement;

   (b) the provisions of the legal instruments set forth below that have entered
   into force under the GATT 1947 before the date of entry into force of the
   WTO Agreement:

   (i) protocols and certifications relating to tariff concessions;

   (ii) protocols of accession (excluding the provisions (*a*) concerning
   provisional application and withdrawal of provisional application
   and (*b*) providing that Part II of GATT 1947 shall be applied
   provisionally to the fullest extent not inconsistent with legislation
   existing on the date of the Protocol);

   (iii) decisions on waivers granted under Article XXV of GATT 1947 and
   still in force on the date of entry into force of the WTO
   Agreement;[117]

   (iv) other decisions of the CONTRACTING PARTIES to GATT 1947;

   (c) the Understandings set forth below:

   (i) Understanding on the Interpretation of Article II:1(b) of the General
   Agreement on Tariffs and Trade 1994;

   (ii) Understanding on the Interpretation of Article XVII of the General
   Agreement on Tariffs and Trade 1994;

   (iii) Understanding on Balance-of-Payments Provisions of the General
   Agreement on Tariffs and Trade 1994;

   (iv) Understanding on the Interpretation of Article XXIV of the General
   Agreement on Tariffs and Trade 1994;

   (v) Understanding in Respect of Waivers of Obligations under the
   General Agreement on Tariffs and Trade 1994;

   (vi) Understanding on the Interpretation of Article XXVIII of the General Agreement on Tariffs and Trade 1994; and

   (d) the Marrakesh Protocol to GATT 1994.

There is no ambiguity regarding the legal value of Understandings, Protocols of
Accession, Protocols of Certification, and Decisions on Waivers. There is ambiguity, however, with respect to the term 'other decisions'; the reason for the
ambiguity is that, during the GATT years, there was nothing like a provision
discussing in sufficient detail the various legal acts that the CONTRACTING
PARTIES could adopt and their legal consequences. As a result, a highly varied
terminology was employed in order to achieve essentially the same outcome.

---

117 The waivers covered by this provision are listed in Doc. MTN/FA of 15 December 1993, Part
II, pp. 11–12 n. 7, and in MTN/FA/Corr.6 of 21 March 1994 (where the Ministerial Conference,
the highest WTO organ, established at its first session a revised list of waivers covered by this
provision and added those waivers that were granted under GATT 1947 after 15 December 1993
and before the date of entry into force of the WTO Agreement, and deleted the waivers which had
expired by that time).

In case law, the question has been raised whether the term 'other decisions' covers Panel reports as well. The Panel in its report on *Japan—Alcoholic Beverages II* was called upon to address, *inter alia*, this issue, since GATT Panel reports had always been submitted to the GATT CONTRACTING PARTIES for adoption: the question thus, was whether similar decisions to adopt Panel reports were in fact 'other decisions' of the CONTRACTING PARTIES to GATT 1947 within the meaning of Art. 1(b)(iv) of the GATT 1994. The Panel was of the view that adopted Panel reports enjoyed this status (§6.10). The AB (Appellate Body)[118] disagreed with the Panel and held that the 'decision' to adopt a Panel report is not a 'decision' within the meaning of Art. 1(b)(iv) of the GATT 1994, although it did acknowledge that adopted reports are 'an important part of the GATT *acquis*' (p. 15). The term 'GATT *acquis*' is a creation of the AB, and its meaning was clarified in a subsequent report: in *US—Shrimp (Art 21.5—Malaysia)* the AB held that this term covered the legitimate expectations of WTO Members to see that relevant prior case law, even in absence of *stare decisis* in the WTO legal order, will duly be taken into account in future disputes, to the extent of course that it is relevant to subsequent disputes (§§108–9). This issue arose again in the context of the dispute that led to the Panel report on *US—FSC*, where the Panel found that decisions to adopt reports should come under Art. XVI of the WTO Agreement, which provides that:

> the WTO shall be guided by the decisions, procedures and customary practices followed by the CONTRACTING PARTIES to GATT 1947.

The Panel responded in the affirmative, and the AB explicitly approved this finding (§§108–15), holding that adopted GATT reports provide guidance to future Panels dealing with the same issue. It is unclear what guidance actually entails, although it cannot amount to *stare decisis*. Guidance can be provided not only by adopted, but by un-adopted Panel reports as well: Panels in the WTO era have, on occasion, cited and followed the reasoning of un-adopted GATT reports to the extent they found it persuasive in a particular dispute. The AB, in its report on *Japan—Alcoholic Beverages II*, held that (p. 16):

> a panel could nevertheless find useful guidance in the reasoning of an un-adopted panel report that it considered to be relevant.[119]

Adopted GATT reports carry some additional legitimacy in the eyes of the WTO judge since they form part of the legitimate expectations of WTO Members (GATT *acquis*). From a strict legal perspective, though, GATT Panel reports do not form an integral part of GATT 1994.

---

[118] With the advent of the WTO, the AB was established, a second instance adjudicating body where appeals against Panel reports can be submitted.

[119] In this vein, the Panel report on *US—Lamb* looked at both adopted and un-adopted GATT reports to support one of its findings (§7.78).

3.2 The Relationship between the GATT and the other Annex 1A Agreements

Annex 1A to the WTO Agreement includes:

(a) the GATT 1994;
(b) 12 agreements (Antidumping (AD), Agriculture (AG); Textiles and Clothing (ATC); Customs Valuation (CV); Import Licensing (ILA); Pre-shipment Inspection (PSI); Rules of Origin (ROO); Subsidies and Countervailing Measures (SCM); Safeguards (SG); Sanitary and Phyto-Sanitary Measures (SPS); Technical Barriers to Trade (TBT); Trade-related Investment Measures (TRIMs));
(c) six Understandings (on Art. II.1(b) GATT; on Art. XVII GATT; on Balance of Payments (BoP); on Art. XXIV GATT; on Waivers; and on Art. XXVIII GATT); and
(d) The Marrakesh Protocol to the GATT 1994 concerning implementation of agreed tariff reductions.

The General Interpretative Note to Annex 1A establishes the legal relationship between the GATT on the one hand and the other Annex 1A Agreements in the following sense:

> In the event of conflict between a provision of the General Agreement on Tariffs and Trade 1994 and a provision of another agreement in Annex 1A to the Agreement Establishing the World Trade Organization (referred to in the agreements in Annex 1A as the 'WTO Agreement'), the provision of the other agreement shall prevail to the extent of the conflict.

The term 'conflict' emerges as key to understanding the relationship between the GATT and the other Annex 1A agreements. Earlier case law suggests that the term should be interpreted *stricto sensu*: in the absence of a true conflict (in the sense that there is a legal impossibility to respect two provisions, that is, a provision of the GATT, and a provision of another Annex 1A agreement, simultaneously), a WTO adjudicating body could start its analysis from the review of the GATT, instead of the provisions of the specialized agreements. An appropriate illustration of this case law is offered by the Panel report on *EC—Bananas III*, where the Panel decided to apply cumulatively the disciplines of GATT, ILA, and TRIMs, starting nonetheless from the provisions of the GATT itself (§§7.158–7.163). Subsequent case law construes the term 'conflict' more in line with the *lex specialis* principle: this principle is not explicitly included in the VCLT (Vienna Convention on the Law of Treaties),[120] but, to some extent, reflects the spirit of *ut regis valeat quam*

---

[120] The VCLT is not explicitly referred to in any covered agreement by the WTO. Art. 3.2 of the WTO DSU (Dispute Settlement Understanding, the agreement that administers dispute adjudication in the WTO) nevertheless requests Panels to interpret the WTO agreements in line with principles of customary international law. The AB, in its very first report (*US—Gasoline*), acknowledged that WTO adjudicating bodies are required, by virtue of Art 3.2 of the DSU, to use the VCLT rule when interpreting the covered agreements.

pereat, the principle of effective treaty interpretation, the cornerstone of the VCLT edifice, which requires from the interpreter that he/she does not interpret terms to redundancy; assuming two provisions regulate the same transaction, privileging recourse to the (relatively) more general would reduce the more specific provision to redundancy.

The relationship between TBT/SPS on the one hand, and the GATT on the other, is the area that provoked most of the discussion. Panels have never privileged recourse to Art. VI, or Art. XVI GATT ahead of recourse to the AD or SCM Agreement.[121] In §77 of its report on *EC—Asbestos*, the AB concluded that a measure which revealed the characteristics of a technical regulation which simultaneously fell under both the TBT and the GATT should have been examined under the TBT rather than under the GATT. In holding for this proposition, the AB distanced itself from the Panel's findings: the Panel had opted for a review of the measure under the GATT in the absence of a genuine conflict between the GATT and the TBT disciplines. The Panel report on *EC—Sardines* went the extra mile, so to speak, and provided the rationale for its preference to examine claims under the TBT Agreement before examining them under the GATT: it explicitly stated that, in its view, the TBT disciplines deal more specifically with the disputed transaction and for this reason provided the priority forum to entertain legal claims (§§7.14–7.16). On appeal, the Panel's approach was upheld by the AB (§195).

The relationship between two multilateral Annex 1A agreements (other than the GATT) is sometimes prescribed by legislative means (see e.g. Art 1.5 of the TBT, which clarifies the relationship between the TBT and the SPS Agreements) and, for the rest, it is left to the discretion of the WTO adjudicating bodies.[122]

Although some of the agreements mentioned in Annex 1A are officially called 'Understandings', there should be little doubt that they are treated in WTO practice as agreements and, thus, subjected to the General Interpretative Note discussed here. The AB, for example, in its report on *Turkey—Textiles* showed total deference to the Understanding on Art. XXIV of the GATT, and applied without any further discussion its clarification of the term 'general incidence of duties'. This Understanding contains additional information which is useful in interpreting the term 'general incidence of duties' (§53 of the AB report).

3.3 The Plurilateral Agreements

We mentioned above that, as a reaction to the GATT à la carte approach followed in the Tokyo round which resulted in 'messy' contractual relations with different

---

[121] What they have done is to impose cumulatively the requirements of say Art. VI GATT and the AD Agreement on antidumping disputes.

[122] The AB, in its report on *US–Upland Cotton*, requested, for example, WTO Members to simultaneously observe the disciplines of the AG and the SCM Agreements; see the relevant discussion in Chapter 7.

GATT contracting parties being parties to different contractual arrangements,[123] the advent of the WTO, which was negotiated following the single-undertaking approach, marks the end of this approach: plurilateral agreements are the only exception to this rule. Initially, there were four plurilateral agreements: the CA, the GPA, the IDA, and the IBM.

The terms for participation in the Annex 4 Agreements are spelled out in each of the four agreements (Art. XII.3 of the WTO Agreement).[124] These four Agreements are only open for accession to WTO Members, that is, to states that have accepted all the multilateral agreements (Art. II.3 of the WTO Agreement). WTO Members (Art. X.9 WTO Agreement) can, through consensus-voting, add new agreements to the existing list of plurilateral agreements. WTO Members have also the right to terminate the plurilateral agreements. This occurred in respect of the IBM and IDA Agreements, which were terminated by decisions of the General Council on 31 December 1997 and 17 December 1997 respectively.

The GPA entered into force on 1 January 1996.[125] We discuss it in detail in Chapter 12

The CA entered into force on 1 January 1980.[126] The following WTO Members have acceded to the CA so far: Albania; Canada; Chinese Taipei; Egypt; all EU Member States, and the EU itself; Georgia; Japan; Macau (China); Norway; Switzerland; and the US. On 1 January 2002, an Additional Protocol dealing with customs duties and charges applied on products coming under the purview of the CA entered into force between its signatories. Pursuant to Article 2, signatories to this agreement are required to eliminate at the latest by

---

[123] GATT Doc. L/5517/Add. 16 of 13 May 1985.

[124] A series of provisions included in the WTO Agreement make it clear that the terms of participation in plurilateral agreements are the privilege of such agreements: accession (Art. XII of the WTO Agreement); acceptance and entry into force (Art. XIV.4 of the WTO Agreement); inclusion of reservations (Art. XVI.5 of the WTO Agreement); decision-making process (Art. IX.5 of the WTO Agreement); amendments (Art. X.10 of the WTO Agreement); non-application (Art. XIII of the WTO Agreement); withdrawal (Art. XV.2 of the WTO Agreement).

[125] Some EU Member States have not ratified the GPA, and thus can be considered 'signatories' of the GPA, in the sense that they have signed that treaty. According to the WTO Status of Legal Instruments, several EU Member States have signed the GPA 1994 'subject to ratification'. Pursuant to Art. 2.1(b) of the VCLT, ' "ratification", "acceptance", "approval" and "accession" mean in each case the international act whereby a State establishes on the international plane its consent to be bound by a treaty'. Under Art. XXIV.1 GPA, consent to be bound by the GPA can be expressed on the international plane either (i) by mere signature; or (ii) by ratification following signature 'subject to ratification'. In the absence of subsequent ratification, by its very terms, signature 'subject to ratification' should not be considered as establishing consent to be bound. According to the WTO Status of Legal Instruments cited here, several EU Members have not ratified the GPA. Therefore, they have not become 'parties' to the GPA in the terms of the VCLT: Art. 2.1(g) VCLT provides that ' "party" means a State which has consented to be bound by the treaty and for which the treaty is in force'. Nevertheless, the EU is a party to the GPA, so the GPA is applicable to the EU, including with regard to the EU Member States that have not ratified it. Indeed, the EU's GPA coverage in regard to those EU Member States is included in the EU's GPA schedules (<http://www.wto.org/english/tratop_e/gproc_e/appendices_e.htm#ec>).

[126] GATT Doc. BISD 34S/22.

the date when the agreement enters into force all customs duties for products listed in the Annex to the agreement (civil aircraft, repairs on civil aircraft). It also imposes obligations with respect to technical barriers to trade, government-directed procurement, export credits, which to a large extent have been taken over by obligations assumed under the corresponding Uruguay round agreements.

The IBM entered into force on 1 January 1995. The IBM was terminated on 31 December 1997 following a decision by the IBM Council and the WTO General Council. The IDA entered into force on 1 January 1995, and was terminated on 31 December 1997.

3.4 The Protocols of Accession

Following the successful conclusion of the Uruguay round, a flurry of countries joined the WTO, and many of them had one thing in common: they were, in the eyes of the incumbents, NMEs. Now what exactly is an NME is not exact science. The Interpretative Note ad Art. VI GATT is the only legislation on this score:

> It is recognized that, in the case of imports from a country which has a complete or substantially complete monopoly of its trade and where all domestic prices are fixed by the State, special difficulties may exist in determining price comparability for the purposes of paragraph 1, and in such cases importing contracting parties may find it necessary to take into account the possibility that a strict comparison with domestic prices in such a country may not always be appropriate.

It might strike the reader as odd that the only reference to NMEs appears in the context of Art. VI GATT which deals with the conditions under which AD duties can be imposed.[127] It is true that in the context of the AD or countervailing (CVD) duties, the pricing mechanism in the exporting country is of particular relevance and non-market economies are for this reason of relevance as well. Decisions affecting trade, though, can be affected across the board and it is remarkable that recognition of NME status becomes legally relevant only in the context of contingent protection.[128] On paper, the conditions imposed for a WTO Member to be considered an NME seem quite strict: complete (or substantially complete) monopoly of trade and all domestic prices are fixed by the state. Surely, many centrally planned economies would fail the second condition, and since the two conditions must be cumulatively met, one would expect scarce practice on this score. Practice, however, evidences that non-'Western bloc' states have often been treated as NMEs by market economies in the context of AD investigations. WTO adjudicating bodies have not disturbed practice either. An appropriate illustration is offered by the recent Panel report on *EC—Fasteners*

---

[127] Czako et al. (2003, pp. 34–5).

[128] Art. XVII GATT takes care of state trading (often encountered in centrally planned economies). This provision nonetheless often finds application in disputes involving market economies as well (Canada and its marketing boards, for example, have often appeared in disputes involving application of this provision). See the discussion in Chapter 11.

(*China*) which satisfied itself with the observation that China is treated by many as NME without going any further (§§7.68ff).

NMEs have been asked to pay a price WTO incumbents have not paid upon their accession to the world trading system. The Protocols of Accession post-1995 are akin to inventories of obligations that go much further than whatever WTO incumbents must observe. For example, during the negotiations leading up to the accession of China (the People's Republic of China) to the WTO, a special safeguard mechanism was concluded which, contrary to the terms of the WTO Safeguards Agreement, allows WTO Members the possibility to impose discriminatory (i.e. country-specific) safeguards against China.[129] In similar vein, China was requested to accept a legal obligation to join the GPA, although, as we saw *supra*, accession to plurilaterals is an option for WTO Members.[130] With respect to trading rights, China accepted for all practical purposes to (partially) give up on its rights under Art. XVII GATT:

> Without prejudice to China's right to regulate trade in a manner consistent with the WTO Agreement, China shall progressively liberalize the availability and scope of the right to trade, so that, within three years after accession, *all* enterprises in China shall have the right to trade in all goods throughout the customs territory of China, except for those goods listed in Annex 2A which continue to be subject to state trading in accordance with this Protocol. Such right to trade shall be the right to import and export goods. (emphasis added)[131]

By the same token, when Saudi Arabia joined the WTO it promised, following requests by its partners, that when transforming the Gulf Cooperation Council (GCC) into a free trade area (FTA) it would respect the conditions of Art. XXIV GATT, and Art. V GATS, thus waiving the possibility to notify the preferential scheme under the Enabling Clause which, as we shall see, contains less stringent obligations;[132] notifying under the latter is a privilege that all developing countries enjoy, and the qualification of a WTO Member as developing is the exclusive privilege of the WTO Member (the lack of merits of this approach notwithstanding).

More generally, such obligations can represent either additional obligations to those assumed by the WTO membership ('WTO plus', like the obligation accepted by China), or even a lessening of the obligations assumed by incumbents ('WTO minus'):[133] for instance, Lithuania acceded to the WTO on 31 May 2001, but was given until 31 December 2005 to bring its excise taxes on beer and mead into conformity with Art III of the GATT.[134] 'WTO minus' obligations hence

---

[129] Spadi (2000).

[130] See also the accession protocol of Hungary, GATT Doc. BSID 20S/3 at §4. Several ex-centrally planned economies were requested to increase trade with the incumbents.

[131] WTO Doc. WT/L/432 of 23 November 2001 at p. 4.

[132] WTO Doc. WT/ACC/SAU/61 of 1 November 2005 at pp. 97ff.

[133] Charnovitz (2006) offers an excellent account.

[134] See the Report of the Working Party on the Accession of Lithuania to the WTO, WTO Doc. WT/ACC/LTU/52 of 7 November 2000 at §66.

have a function akin to grandfathering of obligations that some of the original GATT signatories practised. The Uruguay round marked an end to the grandfathering practice, but through protocols of accession 'WTO-minus' obligations will be tolerated, usually on a transitional basis.

During the early GATT years, before the Tokyo round Codes were negotiated, accession to the GATT was symmetric across incumbents and newly acceding countries. Art. XXVI.4 GATT read to this effect:

> Each government accepting *this Agreement* shall deposit an instrument of acceptance with . . . (emphasis added)

Arguably, nowadays, there is more leeway to negotiate conditions above and beyond the multilateral framework. Art. XII of the WTO Agreement reads:

> Any State or separate customs territory possessing full autonomy in the conduct of its external commercial relations and of the other *matters provided for in this Agreement and Multilateral Trade Agreements* may accede to this Agreement, *on terms to be agreed* between it and the WTO. (emphasis added)

This provision does implicitly impose a limit: the Protocol of Accession cannot extend beyond issues not covered by the current mandate of the WTO; in this vein, imposing obligations on a particular environmental or competition policy would go beyond the current WTO mandate.

We will not be delving any further into this issue in this volume. Suffice to say that those interested in an overview of the obligations of those WTO Members that have acceded to the organization after 1995 should be studying not only the multilateral and plurilateral agreements, but their Protocols of Accession as well.[135]

4. Organization of the Rest of the Volume

The remaining part of the volume is organized as follows: Chapters 2–5 are dedicated to the study the GATT and we will be sequentially discussing the legal disciplines on trade instruments (Chapters 2–3), on domestic instruments (Chapter 4), and the general exceptions to all obligations assumed (Chapter 5). In Chapters 6–13 we review all Annex 1A Agreements in the following manner: in Chapter 6, we discuss the agreements dealing with customs procedures (CV, ILA, PSI, ROO, as well as the Doha round negotiations on Trade Facilitation); in Chapter 7, we revert to a discussion of the three contingent protection instruments, the AD, the SCM, and the SG Agreements; in Chapter 10 we revert to a discussion of the TBT and SPS agreements which deal with specific domestic

---

[135] Even unlikely fellows had to go through turbulent times before securing accession; see Gay (2005) on the problems faced by Vanuatu.

instruments. Chapter 11 focuses on the two sectoral agreements, the AG and the ATC . The GPA is discussed in Chapter 12. Chapter 13 deals with transparency mechanisms in all agreements dealing with trade in goods. The main conclusions of this study regarding the current regulation of trade in goods by the WTO are reflected at the end of his volume.

2

DISCIPLINING TRADE INSTRUMENTS IN THE GATT

1. Quantitative Restrictions[1]

1.1 The Legal Discipline and its Rationale

WTO Members might have recourse to import and export quantitative restrictions (QRs) for a variety of reasons. One could imagine QRs imposed solely for political economy reasons in order to protect domestic producers' income; one could also imagine QRs restricting exports of raw materials in order to avoid say 'Dutch disease' or a health disease.[2] Art. XI GATT prohibits in principle import and export QRs irrespective of their rationale; we say 'in principle' because the trading nations managed to agree on a set of exceptions (like the list reflected in Art. XX GATT), recourse to which could justify use of QRs.

In their extreme form, import and export QRs totally segment markets: import and export embargoes do not allow for any trade, hence, trade liberalization will be ill-served as long as they remain a possibility. This much is clear. The question is of course how much more should be outlawed? The GATT outlaws all import and export quotas (and not only embargoes) but does not outlaw domestic (production) quotas. And yet production quotas might have effects comparable to export quotas. The reason could be that, unlike export quotas, the presumption that production quotas favour the domestic market is weaker: all in quota production could in principle be exported; the presumption is stronger in the case of export quota since, unless one wants to provide domestic market with an advantage, why impose the export quota in the first place? Only for a series of plausible public policy reasons, are export quotas permissible (Art. XX GATT).

Then there is the question of whether the GATT should have a similar attitude towards all trade instruments: for example, both QRs and tariffs are trade instruments that segment markets, yet whereas import and export QRs are prohibited outright, tariffs, as we shall see *infra* in this Chapter, are not: they can be bound and reduced through negotiations; hence, unlike import and export QRs, they are not illegal per se. Is there any reason for this differential treatment? One reason could be that many of the barriers in the post-Smoot-Hawley period have taken the form of QRs (usually exchange restrictions). This, coupled with the fact that the GATT framers wanted to introduce, as we saw in Chapter 1, MFN, probably led them to

---

[1] Trade instruments apply to imported goods only. QRs and tariffs are the most common but not the only trade instruments. Antidumping duties are tariffs as well, and so are CVDs and some safeguards. We treat them separately in Chapters 7–9 since they are not self-standing instruments but kick in only when a contingency (dumping, subsidization, increased imports respectively) occurs. Export subsidies represent a particularity: they (almost always) apply to domestic goods, and function as a negative tariff: because export subsidies are covered by the WTO SCM Agreement, we will discuss them in Chapter 8 along with domestic subsidies.

[2] The term 'Dutch disease' was in vogue when the Dutch discovered natural gas. Demand for natural gas was quite high, and thus demand for the Dutch national currency was high as well. The Dutch currency was overvalued, and Dutch exports of manufacturing products suffered as a result.

treat the two instruments in a differential manner: MFN is easily applicable in a tariffs-only context, and quite onerous in a QR setting. This is the historic explanation, and economic theory has advanced some persuasive explanations to support this argument. Krueger (1964) goes on to research the negative external effects associated with the administration of QRs: her work shows that there is a need to monitor whether a QR has been filled; whether it has been filled in a non-discriminatory manner; eventually, if (import or export) licences have been issued, whether they have been issued in a non-discriminatory manner, etc.[3] The administration of a tariff-based import system does not raise similar issues, and this is probably what explains their distinct treatment in the GATT. Negative external effects associated with QRs are thus much more important than in a tariff setting.

Bhagwati (1965) on the other hand shows that, in a perfect-competition model, tariffs have their QR equivalent. Bhagwati shows that this is not necessarily the case in imperfect competition: a monopolist in a market where a QR has been imposed will capture all residual demand (that is, demand after the QR has been exhausted). If a tariff is in place though, some competitive pressure will always be exercised on the monopolist, who might not be in position to profit as much as it would had a QR (in lieu of a tariff) been in place. This point becomes even more persuasive if one factors in the considerable time span between rounds of trade liberalization: in the in-between-rounds period, exporters facing tariffs (rather than QRs) will continue to exercise some pressure on the monopolist.

Thus, for good reasons the GATT framers decided to treat the two trade instruments in an asymmetric manner.

1.2 Coverage of the Legal Discipline

The term 'quantitative restriction' (QR)[4] is not self-interpreting; the rest of the text and the context of this provision (Art. XI GATT) provide some clarifications: first, it prohibits measures other than duties, taxes, or other charges (carve-out). This of course, is normal since otherwise the GATT would be imposing two diametrically opposed disciplines on import duties: allowed under Art. II GATT and prohibited under Art. XI GATT. The same is true with respect to the other terms appearing in this carve-out (taxes, other charges). Second, through Art. XI.2 (c) GATT, some farm quotas were excluded from the coverage of this provision. Finally, through the MFA, trade in textiles was conducted until 2005 through a

---

[3] Trading nations might have a strong incentive to do that: scarcity of the imported (or exported) good will (other things equal) push its prices up, and through auctioning of import (or export) licences, governments will be effectively dividing rents with the private operator.

[4] It is worthwhile mentioning that the term 'quantitative restriction' appears only in the heading of Art. XI GATT, while the terms 'restriction' and 'prohibition' appear in the body of the article. In light of the choice of terms, it seems reasonable to conclude (as case law has already done) that the three terms can be used interchangeably. The same is true for the term 'quota'. This is the manner in which they are being used in this volume.

quota system whereby importing nations would be importing the agreed volume from each exporting nation.[5]

For the rest, recourse to the negotiating record and the case law is necessary to better grasp the coverage of the prohibition.[6] One might legitimately ask, for example, a series of questions regarding the ambit of the term 'quantitative restriction': is it, for example, the case that only measures comprising a numerical target are envisaged by the prohibition or any measure which has a QR effect?

1.2.1 Export Taxes

Recall that Art. XI GATT exempts from its coverage 'duties, taxes, or other charges'. Does the carve-out extend to export duties (taxes) as well? For the reasons mentioned below though, we believe that export taxes are not covered by the prohibition embedded in Art. XI GATT.

Originally, a US report prepared by the Special Committee on Relaxation of Trade Barriers recommended that provision should be made, in the context of a trade agreement, to abolish all objectionable export taxes: export taxes for revenue purposes, or enforced pursuant to international agreements, or imposed under the conditions of famine or severe domestic shortage in the exporting country, or even designed to regulate the trade in military supplies under specified conditions, should not be regarded as objectionable.[7] This view did not carry the day for many good reasons and it is the same report that recognizes that there was lack of significant practice in the field of export taxes, and this is probably the single most important reason explaining why the founding fathers did not spend time and effort designing a mechanism for negotiation of export tariffs à la Art II of the GATT.[8] We read, for example, from the report:[9]

---

[5] See the discussion on MFA in Chapter 11.

[6] WTO case law consistently attaches little if any importance to the negotiating record. Numerous Panels have invoked the VCLT in order to justify their attitude in this respect. It is true that Art. 32 VCLT allows discretion to the judge when it comes to recourse to the negotiating record. Discretion, alas, has been almost always equated to no use of the negotiating record by the WTO judge. This is deplorable and legally incorrect: the judge delving into the negotiating record of the GATT and the Uruguay round agreements will typically find a wealth of information regarding the legal discipline he/she is called to interpret; he/she will of course remain free to attach a value to it and still behave in symmetry with the imperative embedded in Art. 32 VCLT. Be it as it may, and in order to ensure that references to law as completed through case law in this volume are sound, we will privilege recourse to case law and refer to the negotiating record only when warranted in our view (e.g. to show discrepancies between negotiating intent and case law interpretations).

[7] See pp. 35ff of the report of the US Special Committee on Relaxation of Trade Barriers (Report of 8 December 1943, International Trade Files, Lot File 57D-284). See also Dam (1977) discussing the US southern states' opposition to export taxes.

[8] We discuss in this section a US document where it is made clear that export taxes did occupy the minds of negotiators. Indeed, this is only normal since the economics of equivalence between export taxes and import duties were well known to negotiators. The question was whether negotiating resources should be invested in an endeavour that was not as widespread as import duties.

[9] Report of 8 December 1943, International Trade Files, Lot File 57D-284, p. 34.

Except during wartime, governmentally-imposed export duties, and prohibitions and quantitative restrictions on exports have had relatively little influence in limiting the over-all movement of commodities in world trade, although they have seriously affected the movement of specific products. Export taxes and quantitative restrictions on exports have been instituted for a variety of reasons. Some, such as export taxes on coffee in certain Latin American countries, have been imposed for revenue purposes. Some have been imposed for indirect protective reasons: for example, the United States prohibition on commercial exports of tobacco seed for the purpose of preventing the cultivation abroad of American types of tobacco. In a different category are the Mexican export taxes, which are used for revenue purposes and, in combination with an export tax-rebate system to enforce membership in export cooperatives. Some, such as the United States control of helium exports, have been imposed for security reasons. Some have been imposed pursuant to international agreements; for example, the undertaking by Cuba, in connection with the trade agreement with the United States, to prohibit the exportation of avocados to the United States except during the months of July through September...

Political economy considerations could also contribute to this outcome: exporters would not be necessarily interested in seeing their revenue divided between them and their government (that would pocket the export tax). Assuming that their lobby power matters to the government, one would expect few export taxes. The producers' interests are of course the exact opposite when it comes to import tariffs and this probably explains proliferation of import and almost total absence of export duties. Producers, if interested, could achieve the same outcome (as export taxes) through other mechanisms such as export cartels; it is at best questionable whether a domestic antitrust authority can prosecute and some jurisdictions like the US explicitly exempt them from prosecution altogether. Unlike export taxes, in an export cartel scenario they (and not the government) would be pocketing the monopoly rents.[10]

In the absence of an agreement on outright prohibition, the GATT treats import and export duties in symmetric manner: they are negotiable instruments that must anyway be applied in a non-discriminatory manner, and can be bound following an agreement to this effect. Art. XXVIIIbis GATT reads:

> The contracting parties recognize that customs duties often constitute serious obstacles to trade; thus negotiations on a reciprocal and mutually advantageous basis, directed to the substantial reduction of the general level of tariffs and other charges on imports *and exports* and in particular to the reduction of such high tariffs as discourage the importation even of minimum quantities, and conducted with due

---

[10] We elaborate on this point *infra*.

regard to the objectives of this Agreement and the varying needs of individual contracting parties, are of great importance to the expansion of international trade. The CONTRACTING PARTIES may therefore sponsor such negotiations from time to time. (emphasis added)

Nothing stops WTO Members from negotiating export concessions and in fact they often do.[11] A Note prepared by the GATT Secretariat[12] during the Uruguay round confirms the view that, absent specific commitment to this effect, WTO Members are free to impose export taxes: it states in clear language that the GATT 'permits the imposition of charges on exports' (p. 4) and explains that, if practised, export taxes must respect the MFN principle. Recently, there seems to have been proliferation of export taxes: some developing countries seem to use them more often than before in order, for example, to keep raw materials in their domestic market. This is probably what prompted WTO Members to negotiate with China a specific clause that was inserted in its Protocol of Accession whereby:

China shall eliminate all taxes and charges applied to exports unless specifically provided for in Annex 6 of this Protocol or applied in conformity with the provisions of Article VIII of the GATT 1994.[13]

Annex 6 of the Protocol of Accession contains the maximum export duties applicable on 84 products. China cannot levy an export tax on goods not included in the agreed list featured in Annex 6. In this vein, the Panel on *China— Raw Materials Exports* found that export taxes on a series of goods (bauxite, coke, etc.) were in violation of China's commitments under its Protocol of Accession and for this reason inconsistent with its obligations under the WTO (§7.105).

Minimum export prices have economic effects similar to export taxes (they should both restrict exports and create a wedge between domestic and world prices), but have been judged inconsistent with Art. XI GATT: the GATT Panel on *EEC— Minimum Import Prices* found that the requirement that importers of tomato concentrates provide additional security to guarantee that the price at the EU frontier plus the customs duty payable would equal or exceed a determined minimum import price was in violation of Art. XI GATT (§4.9).[14] In similar

---

[11] See §184 of the Working Party Report on the accession of Saudi Arabia to the WTO, WTO Doc. WT/ACC/SAU/61 of 1 November 2005.

[12] GATT Doc. MTN.GNG/NG2/W/40 of 8 August 1989.

[13] WTO Doc. WT/L/432 of 23 November 2001. See also WTO Doc. WT/ACC/SAU/61 of 1 November 2005, mentioned *supra*, Protocol of Accession of Saudi Arabia.

[14] This is a form of variable levy that the EU practised a lot before 1995: a variable component would be levied on all imports in order to equate their price to the EU price which was (almost always) higher than that of the world price for farm goods.

vein, the Panel on *China—Raw Materials* found that a system of coordinating minimum export prices imposed by China violated this provision (§7.1081). Now this might seem paradoxical and yet there is a certain logic to it, especially in the case of the Chinese dispute: the Panel essentially closed the door on the possible circumvention (by China) of its obligation under Annex 6 of its Protocol of Accession not to impose export duties.

1.2.2 Production Quotas

Film quotas are explicitly discussed in GATT: WTO Members can impose screen quotas aimed at favouring the screening of domestic films (Art. IV GATT).[15] What about other domestic (e.g. not imposed on the border) quotas? The letter of Art. XI GATT, the spirit of the GATT, as well as subsequent practice support the thesis that production quotas are not covered by the legal discipline included in Art. XI GATT.

The wording of Art. XI GATT suggests a rather restrictive understanding of its coverage in this respect: it refers to restrictions on importation/exportation, and not, for example, in connexion with importation/exportation, as is the case with Art. I GATT. If the intention of the parties was to allow for any quota to come under the purview of Art. XI GATT, they could have chosen a more appropriate (to this effect) wording. A literal interpretation of this provision would suggest that domestic quotas are GATT-consistent, since such quotas are not imposed on the exportation (or on the sale for exportation). The wording of Art. XI.2 GATT supports this reading: a limited number of exemptions have been included, and the wording chosen makes it clear that the exemptions concern import and export restrictions; Art. XI.2(c) GATT, especially, provides unambiguous support for this reading.

The argument nonetheless could still be made that production quotas de facto amount to export quotas since limited production leads, other things equal, to limited exports (the counterfactual being the absence of production quotas). Should similar arguments be upheld? The answer to this question depends on our overall understanding of the function of the GATT: does it only outlaw cases where an advantage has been granted to the domestic product which competes with a foreign competing product? Or, conversely, should we construe the GATT as outlawing cases where an advantage is provided to the domestic market, a notion that is wider than the competing good? In other words, what is the ambit of *beggar-thy-neighbour* policies covered by the GATT? The GATT, by outlawing export quotas, takes a stance against segmentation of markets and declares its intention to outlaw policies which favour domestic markets, and not only policies that favour domestic (competing) products. Production quotas, nevertheless, do not necessarily segment markets. It could be the case, for example, that all of the

---

[15] We discuss the historic rationale for this provision in Chapter 4.

limited domestic production is sold to foreign processors only. They might limit the amount of trade involved in a given commodity, but they do not necessarily segment markets. Yes, the domestic producer of a commodity might be able to extract a better price (because of the limitation imposed), but this does not seem to have been a concern for GATT negotiators.[16]

More importantly, it would be wrong, both legally and policy-wise, to construct Art. XI GATT so as to eliminate important policy choices that were supposed to observe a different legal test: production quotas being domestic instruments have to observe the non-discrimination obligation.[17] A production quota might affect both domestic and foreign goods produced in a given market depending on two factors: liberalization of investment and rules of origin. Say Home, a WTO Member, limits the production of cement: depending on how liberal investment is, it might be foreigners that are being affected; the same is true depending on what percentage of value added is necessary to confer domestic origin on cement.[18] Let us move to examine a case where the downstream market is affected as a result of the production quota. Home limits the production of steel necessary for the production of cars: one might argue that, in principle, its domestic car market (the downstream industry) would benefit as a result, at the detriment of its international competition. Now what if Home has liberal investment and the car industry is owned by Foreign? Again Home might profit since its measures help the domestic workforce (since the car industry faces less competition from abroad). But what if, according to the national definition, a car is domestic if 50 per cent of its value added is domestic and in Home's case only steel is domestic and steel represents less than 50 per cent of the added value of a car? And what if Home steel producers might find it more profitable to sell steel abroad? Limitation of production does not necessarily lead to market segmentation and does not necessarily confer an advantage on domestic production either. Art. XI GATT includes a per se prohibition with respect to import-export quotas because they necessarily segment markets: since production quotas do not necessarily do that, the GATT framers wisely did not name production quotas in the body of this provision. As to whether they violate the obligation not to discriminate, we revert to our relevant discussion in Chapter 4.

Practice supports this conclusion. The OPEC case (Organization of the Petroleum Exporting Countries) is particularly relevant since OPEC members have in place production quotas with quite meaningful trade effects. Some of the OPEC members are not WTO Members: Algeria, Iran, Iraq, and Libya belong to this category. The majority of them, however (Angola, Ecuador, Kuwait,

---

[16] Moreover, recall that the GATT was not negotiated in a vacuum. The GATT framers probably thought that the advent of the ITO, and more specifically its Chapter V dealing with Restrictive Business Practices (RBPs), would have taken care of this risk.

[17] We discuss this discipline *in extenso* in Chapter 4.

[18] We discuss rules of origin *infra* in this chapter.

Nigeria, Qatar, Saudi Arabia, United Arab Emirates, Venezuela), are WTO Members. Saudi Arabia is the most recent WTO Member and the Working Party Report on its accession reflects a rather benign discussion of this issue, where it was made clear that petroleum production quotas were not, at least in the view of the acceding country, legally challengeable before a WTO Panel.[19] There has never been a case so far where the consistency of a similar quota with the GATT rules has been litigated before a GATT/WTO Panel.

Finally, even if all arguments mentioned so far were to be judged GATT-inconsistent and thus, rejected by a Panel, production quotas can still be justified through recourse to various paragraphs of Art. XX GATT:[20]

(a) Art XX(g) allows for measures relating to the conservation of exhaustible natural resources, if such measures are made effective in conjunction with restrictions on domestic production or consumption;
(b) Art XX(i) allows for measures involving restrictions on exports of domestic materials, if such measures are part of a stabilization plan, and do not operate to increase the exports of or the protection afforded to the domestic industry;
(c) Art XX(j) allows for measures essential to the acquisition of products in general or local short supply, provided that all contracting parties are entitled to an equitable share of the international supply of that product.

1.2.3 Tariff Quotas

WTO Members often have recourse to tariff quotas. A tariff quota (TRQ) is usually an import measure whereby a lower tariff will be applied for a certain volume of imports and a higher tariff will be applied to any quota above and beyond the set quota: for example, a 5 per cent *ad valorem* duty for the first 10,000 cars, and a 50 per cent *ad valorem* duty for any additional entry. There should be no doubts as to the overall consistency of TRQs with the GATT, even though on their face they seem to function as a QR:[21] Art. XIII.5 GATT (Restrictions to Safeguard the Balance of Payments), for example, calls for application of this provision to tariff quotas. By the same token, it becomes obvious when reading §6 of the Understanding on the Interpretation of Art. XXVIII of the GATT 1994 that a TRQ can lawfully replace an unlimited tariff concession, provided that the conditions (payment of compensation) embedded in this paragraph have been met.

In practice, most TRQs concern farm products: Australia, for example, has TRQs in place, *inter alia*, for fresh cheese (HS 0406.10.00); grated or powdered cheese (HS 0406.20.00); but also for tobacco for use in manufacturing of

---

[19] WTO Doc. WT/ACC/SAU/61 of 1 November 2005 at §§179ff. Bhala (2004, pp. 799ff) agrees that OPEC participation was not a major issue during the accession of Saudi Arabia to the WTO. The author advances a different legal argument to make the same point, that is, that OPEC practices do not violate the GATT.

[20] This provision includes a list of exceptions to all GATT provisions, as we shall see *infra*.

[21] And they definitely operate as such in case the out-of-quota tariff rate is prohibitively high.

cigarettes (HS 2401.1012), and tobacco refuse (HS 2401.30.00). By the same token, Indonesia has TRQs in place for milk and cream of fat and its products (HS 0402 Ex) and rice (HS 1006 Ex). More generally, in 2006, 45 Members had in place 1,434 individual tariff quotas.[22]

1.2.4 Art. XI.2 GATT and the Agreement on Agriculture

Art. XI.2 GATT explicitly exempts practices regarding farm products from the prohibition embedded in Art. XI.1 GATT. We discuss the substantive requirements in Section 1.3 *infra*. The value of this provision has been severely reduced as a result of the conclusion of the WTO Agreement on Agriculture which we discuss in Chapter 11.

1.2.5 Trade in Textiles

Before the entry into force of the Uruguay round agreements, trade in textile products was regulated in the Multi-fibre Agreement (MFA).[23] This agreement was signed in 1974 between some developed and 31 developing countries and essentially imposed a worldwide system of bilateral quotas between exporters (usually in the southern hemisphere) and importers (in the north). The MFA is far from clear as to its relationship with the GATT: on the one hand, Art. 1.6 MFA states that this agreement will not affect the rights and obligations of contracting parties under the GATT; on the other, Art. 2 MFA makes it clear that QRs notified under the MFA will be deemed GATT-consistent if they conform to the many requirements embedded therein. There should be little doubt that Art. 1.6 MFA has cosmetic value aimed at reaffirming the commitment to the multilateral system and underscores that the MFA was but a minor deviation and nothing more: the whole idea of the MFA was to derogate from Art. XI GATT and establish a system of centrally administered bilateral quotas. Subsequent practice amply supports this conclusion.[24] The Agreement on Textiles and Clothing (ATC) was signed along with the other Uruguay round agreements, and replaced the MFA. We discuss it in more detail in Chapter 11.

1.2.6 The Relationship with Art. III GATT

The relationship between these two provisions is partly addressed in the Interpretative Note ad Art III, which relevantly reads:

> Any internal tax or other internal charge, or any law, regulation or requirement of the kind referred to in paragraph 1 which applies to an imported product and to the like domestic product and is collected or enforced in the case of the imported product at

---

[22] See WTO Doc. TN/AG/S/22 of 27 April 2006.

[23] GATT Doc. TEX.NG/1, reproduced in BISD 21S/3ff. For a concise discussion of this legal instrument, see Trebilcock and Howse (2005) at pp. 482ff.

[24] No formal challenge against the consistency of the MFA per se with the GATT rules was ever lodged.

the time or point of importation, is nevertheless to be regarded as an internal tax or other internal charge, or a law, regulation or requirement of the kind referred to in paragraph 1, and is accordingly subject to the provision of Article III.

Hence, domestic measures, even if applicable at the border, will continue to be covered by the discipline included in Art. III GATT and thus evade the purview of Art. XI GATT. There is still lack of clarity regarding which transactions should go under Art. XI and which under Art. III GATT. What if, for example, a WTO Member expresses an environmental measure as an import QR? Should it be allowed to do that?

The GATT Panel in its report on *Canada—FIRA* suggested that with the exception of truly unique circumstances, such as state trading companies which often operate as both importers and distributors, a dividing line must be drawn between measures covered by Art. III and by Art. XI GATT. In the WTO era, the Panel on *India—Autos* made the point that a priori simultaneous application of both Art. III and Art. XI GATT could not be outright discarded. This Panel did not want to distance itself from prior rulings: what it had in mind was a situation where different facets of the same measure could be regarded as border measures and some as internal measures. Since the term 'measure' is nowhere defined in the GATT, the level of disaggregation holds the key to understanding why the two reports are not inconsistent with each other. With this in mind, one can hardly envisage a scenario where a WTO Member expresses a measure in terms of an import QR rather than a domestic instrument. In the first case, the measure will be illegal outright, whereas in the second only if it is discriminatory.

1.2.7 De Jure and De Facto QRs

The question arose in case law whether one should understand the term 'QR' as referring to measures that provide a numerical target, a number (e.g.,10 tons of steel), or, conversely, whether it should extend to cover other instruments as well which, although not set as numerical targets, de facto limit imports or exports (the counterfactual being the situation where the challenged measure is absent).

The GATT Panel on *Japan—Semiconductors* was called to address a situation in which the government of Japan, as a result of an agreement it had reached with the US (the *US—Japan Semiconductor Pact*), adopted a series of measures which induced Japanese companies producing semiconductors to raise their prices when exporting to the EU market. As a result of the increase in price of Japanese semi-conductors, the EU suffered a net welfare loss as there were no domestic producers of the same product during that period in the mid to late 1980s, and consumers of semiconductors were required to pay a higher price for the same product.

The EU challenged the consistency of the Japanese measure with Art. XI GATT, arguing that exports of Japanese semiconductors to the EU market were substantially reduced as a result of the adoption of this measure: the price hike, in other words, would lead in the EU view to fewer exports to its market of semiconductors originating in Japan; Japanese producers would not have raised their export prices, so goes the argument advanced by the EU, in the absence of the incentive mechanism provided by the Japanese government. The Panel report mentions that the acknowledged purpose of the measures adopted by Japan was to avoid below cost sales in third country markets (§112): the measures consisted in the submission of detailed information of costs and export basis by concerned Japanese producers on a regular basis (§113); fines would be imposed not for failure to follow suggested prices but for failure to notify practised prices (§113). Japan, in a nutshell, using 'administrative guidance', put in place a system that aimed at eliminating dumping of semiconductors, but had not put a numerical target limiting by number its exports of semiconductors.

The Panel found that the Japanese measure was in violation of Art. XI GATT (§§109ff): in the eyes of the Panel, incentivizing producers to restrict exports was enough to establish a violation of Art. XI GATT: thus, this Panel extended the coverage of this provision to de facto QRs as well. How did the Panel on *Japan—Semiconductors* establish that in this case the QR effect was the result of incentives to act in particular manner? It did not, is the short answer. It did not even check if a QR had indeed resulted from the challenged measures, never mind whether it was explained by the provided incentives. In the name of the no-effects-cum-no-intent test that it borrowed from prior case law, it satisfied itself that Japan was in violation of its GATT obligations by the mere fact that it provided incentives that could (but did not necessarily) affect the behaviour of private parties. Indeed, it could be the case, for all we know, that private Japanese operators, when they realized that they were not facing serious competition from US producers, changed their pricing policies (or cut down their production).[25] Ideally, we would like to see some discussion of the competitive conditions in the EU market; something that would explain at the very least why the incentives were necessary in this particular case for the Japanese to behave in this particular way.

The Panel on *Argentina—Hides and Leather* attempted to do just that: in this case, the question before the Panel was whether an Argentine law that allowed for the presence of delegates of the downstream industry (leather products) at the customs clearance of hides was inconsistent with Art. XI GATT. The EU had argued that Argentine producers of hides might be unwilling to export their produce to Europe, for fear that they would be earmarked by the domestic downstream industry (§11.18). This Panel held that Art. XI GATT should not

---

[25] Smith and Venables (1991) explain why *monopoly rents* (which Japanese producers will pocket when they face less competitive foreign producers in a given market and have to observe a sales quota) might explain under certain assumptions why in the past Japan has accepted *voluntary export restraints* (VERs), which were far from voluntary since they had been requested by its trading partners, and most frequently by the US.

be construed as tantamount to an obligation to eliminate all potential for private parties to restrict trade (§11.19):

> ... we do not think that it follows either from that panel's statement or from the text or context of Article XI:1 that Members are under an obligation to exclude any possibility that governmental measures may enable private parties, directly or indirectly, to restrict trade, where those measures themselves are not trade-restrictive.

Consequently, following this approach, the Panel requested from complainants claiming that a violation of Art. XI GATT had been committed to demonstrate, at the very least, a nexus between the challenged measure and the QR effect. Now, this is quite a departure from the test established in *Japan—Semiconductors*.

To fully appreciate this report, we believe it is warranted to bring into this discussion the no-effects-cum-no-intent test on which the Panel on *Japan—Semiconductors* relied so heavily. The GATT Panel on *US—Superfund* is still considered the leading case in this respect: it stands for the proposition that Art. XI GATT (just like Art. III GATT) protects expectations that a particular behaviour will be observed by WTO Members. In this particular case, the complainants had argued that a US internal tax, which granted domestic products (petroleum products) slightly better treatment than the imported like products, was inconsistent with Art. III GATT: the tax differential (between domestic and imported goods) was close to any reasonable definition of *de minimis* and indeed this is precisely what the US submitted before the Panel. The complainants, on the other hand, maintained that there was no requirement to demonstrate trade effects since the law requested all imported goods to pay a tax higher than that imposed on the corresponding domestic goods. The US disagreed and argued that effects mattered: in this view, in light of the minimal difference in tax treatment across the two categories of goods, no trade effects could be shown, and consequently no violation of the GATT could be established. The Panel disagreed with the US argument (§5.2.2):

> The general prohibition of quantitative restrictions under Article XI, which the Panel on Japanese Measures on Imports of Leather examined, and the national treatment obligation of Article III, which Canada and the EEC invoked in the present case, have essentially the same rationale, namely to protect expectations of the contracting parties as to the competitive relationship between their products and those of the other contracting parties. Both articles are not only to protect current trade but also to create the predictability needed to plan future trade. That objective could not be attained if contracting parties could not challenge existing legislation mandating actions at variance with the General Agreement until the administrative acts implementing it had actually been applied to their trade. Just as the very existence of a regulation providing for a quota, without it restricting particular imports, has been recognized to constitute a violation of Article XI:1, the very existence of mandatory legislation providing for an internal tax, without it being applied to a particular imported product, should be regarded as falling within the scope of Article III:2, first sentence.

This report suggests that laws that have not produced any effects, but which are of a mandatory nature (in that they leave no discretion as to the behaviour that must be followed), are still violating Art. III (Art. XI) GATT. Here the Panel was dealing with a tax that had to be paid any time an import occurs. The tax as such might provide a disincentive to export to the US market (depending of course, on how the competitive relationship between the imported and the domestic good is affected by the amount of the tax differential). Art. XI (and Art. III) GATT provide an insurance policy against this risk by requesting that imported goods are not taxed in excess of like domestic goods. This was a case of de jure violation of Art. III GATT since the level of tax imposition was exclusively a function of the origin of the good: domestic goods pay low tax, imported goods pay higher taxes.

What if we are dealing with a de facto QR though? What if we are dealing with a measure which, although on its face it does not impose a numerical limit, might still result in a QR effect? The Panel on *Japan—Semiconductors* responded that the ambit of Art. XI GATT must extend to cover similar cases as well, otherwise the obligation embedded in this provision would be easily circumvented. It then rushed to apply the same standard of review in de facto cases as well, without thinking whether a more nuanced approach was appropriate here. The Panel on *Argentina—Hides and Leather* distances itself from this approach, by distinguishing between de jure and de facto QRs. With respect to the latter, the Panel was of the view that, for a successful legal challenge to be mounted, the complainant must demonstrate a causal link between the challenged measure and the (reduced) level of imports or exports, whatever the case may be. Without elaborating further on the instance of a de jure QR, the Panel articulated that the evidentiary standard should be lower in such cases (§§11.21 and 11.22):

> Finally, as to whether Resolution 2235 makes effective a restriction, it should be recalled that Article XI:1, like Articles I, II and III of the GATT 1994, protects competitive opportunities of imported products, not trade flows. In order to establish that Resolution 2235 infringes Article XI:1, the European Communities need not prove actual trade effects. However, it must be borne in mind that Resolution 2235 is alleged by the European Communities to make effective a *de facto* rather than a *de jure* restriction. In such circumstances, it is inevitable, as an evidentiary matter, that greater weight attaches to the actual trade impact of a measure.
>
> Even if it emerges from trade statistics that the level of exports is unusually low, this does not prove, in and of itself, that that level is attributable, in whole or in part, to the measure alleged to constitute an export restriction. Particularly in the context of an alleged *de facto* restriction and where, as here, there are possibly multiple restrictions, it is necessary for a complaining party to establish a causal link between the contested measure and the low level of exports. In our view, whatever else it may involve, a demonstration of causation must consist of a persuasive explanation of precisely how the measure at issue causes or contributes to the low level of exports. (italics in the original)

In a footnote to §11.22, the Panel noted:

The Appellate Body in *European Communities—Measures Affecting the Importation of Certain Poultry Products* similarly required of the complaining party in that case a demonstration of a causal relationship between the imposition of an EC licensing procedure and the alleged trade distortion. See the Appellate Body Report on *European Communities—Measures Affecting the Importation of Certain Poultry Products* (hereafter '*European Communities—Poultry*'), adopted on 23 July 1999, WT/DS69/AB/R, at paras. 126–127. While this interpretation related to a claim under the Agreement on Import Licensing Procedures, it is not apparent why the logic should be any different in the case of a claim under Article XI:1 of the GATT 1994. (emphasis in the original)

The Panel thus rejected the EU claim and found that the presence of representatives of the domestic industry was insufficient (or rather the causal link too remote) for establishing a violation of Art. XI GATT (§7.35):

We agree that it is unusual to have representatives from a downstream consuming industry involved in the Customs process of export clearance. As noted above, it seems to us that the levels of exports of raw hides from Argentina may be low. The European Communities have stated the matter to us in the form of a rhetorical question—what other purpose could these downstream industry representatives have in this government process of export clearance than restricting exports? However, it is up to the European Communities to provide evidence sufficient to convince us of that. In this instance, we do not find that the evidence is sufficient to prove that there is an export restriction made effective by the mere presence of tanners' representatives within the meaning of Article XI.

This report requests from a complainant arguing that it is facing a de facto QR, more explanation regarding the nexus between the measure challenged and the reason why it violates Art. XI GATT.

To be fair to the drafters of the report on *Japan–Semiconductors*, they might have thought that such a request would be totally unnecessary since, other things equal, a rise in price will lead to fewer transactions. Other things, however, are not always equal and while prices might have this effect, quite often this is not necessarily the case when other instruments (similar to those employed in *Argentina—Hides and Leather*) are in place.[26]

To conclude, one could schematically describe the discipline on de jure QRs as per se prohibition: WTO Members cannot set numerical targets when it comes to volumes of imports and/or exports and it suffices for the complainant to demonstrate that a similar scheme is in place for its complaint to succeed; a *rule-of-reason* approach is adopted when it comes to challenging de facto QRs, where the

---

[26] In this vein, in *India—Autos*, the Panel addressed the Indian *trade balancing condition*, that is, a threshold on the amount of exports that each manufacturer could expect to make, which in turn would determine the amount of imports that could be made. This measure, in the Panel's view, amounted to an import restriction (see §§7.254, 7.257–7.260, 7.264, 7.268, 7.270–7.272, and 7.276–7.277).

complainant needs to show that the observed trade outcome is due to the challenged measure.[27]

1.2.8 Government Involvement (Attribution)

The attribution of a practice to government is a threshold issue to the extent that Art XI. GATT becomes irrelevant if the QR is not attributed to a WTO Member. The GATT Panel on *Japan—Semiconductors* is the first dispute that dealt comprehensively with this issue. The Panel report stands for the proposition that providing incentives to private parties to act in a particular manner suffices for a measure to be attributed to government (§§109ff) and in §117 it held:

> The Panel considered that the complex of measures exhibited the rationale as well as the essential elements of a formal system of export control. The only distinction in this case was the absence of formal legally binding obligations in respect of exportation or sale for export of semi-conductors. However, the Panel concluded that this amounted to a difference in form rather than substance because the measures were operated in a manner equivalent to mandatory requirements. The Panel concluded that the complex of measures constituted a coherent system restricting the sale for export of monitored semi-conductors at prices below company-specific costs to markets other than the United States, inconsistent with Article XI:1.[28]

Subsequent GATT and WTO case law has consistently referred to this ruling when deciding whether a particular measure should be attributed to government. It is not hence only government actions that can be challenged before a Panel, but also private actions, to the extent attributable to a government. For example, in *Japan—Film*, a measure endorsed by government was attributed to it (§10.45); in *China—Raw Materials*, the Panel satisfied itself that a measure was attributable to the Chinese government because the latter had delegated authority to CCCMC (Chinese Chamber of Commerce of Metals Minerals & Chemicals Importers & Exporters), the measures of which were being challenged in that case (§7.1004–1005). Finally, in *US—Corrosion Resistant Steel Sunset Reviews*, the AB held that omissions too, to the extent attributable to a government, can be challenged before a WTO Panel (§81).

Providing incentives and delegating authority are thus two avenues for attributing behaviour to a government: while the latter seems uncontroversial (as long as there is no doubt that delegation indeed occurred), various issues can be raised with respect to the former. Did the Panel on *Japan—Semiconductors* cast the net

---

[27] How much more is still an open question, since the Panel did not adequately explain itself here. On one side of the spectrum, it could be that all the Panel would like to see is an example showing why the presence of delegates could potentially restrict exports; on the other, it could be requiring a full trade-effects analysis. The construction of Art. XI GATT as an instrument protecting competitive conditions would argue for a solution closer to the former rather than to the latter end of the spectrum, the shortcomings of this approach notwithstanding.

[28] MITI is the acronym for the Japanese Ministry of Trade and Investment, which is now known as METI (Ministry of Economy, Trade and Industry).

71

too wide? Undeniably, governments can incentivize private parties to behave in a particular way, that is, even in a GATT-inconsistent way: through a tax scheme or through subsidies, for example, it can provide traders with incentives to sell at home and not abroad. Assuming one can show that in the counterfactual, that is, absent the government scheme, the level of exports would have been different, then, in principle, a violation of Art. XI GATT could be established. The response might vary depending on the instrument used, the competitive conditions in the particular market, etc. The judge might be walking on a tightrope here. We note that so far the cases sanctioned by the WTO judge have a clear border element: in *Japan—Semiconductors*, it is exports of goods that are, theoretically at least, limited; in *Argentina—Hides and Leather*, it is again surveillance at the customs office that is being challenged, another border instrument par excellence. Opening up to de facto QRs has thus, so far, not been tantamount to violating the legislative imperative to punish only import and export QRs through Art. XI GATT.

In this vein, it is probably warranted to dedicate some lines to export cartels, as an illustration. Following the de facto acceptance of the effects doctrine, an export cartel will be prosecuted in the market that it cartelizes (and not its home market). Antitrust authorities have anyway little, if any, interest in regulating the activities of their national export cartels, since the domestic market will not be affected by similar activities (an argument could even be made that they might be affected positively, since high export prices could be used to subsidize domestic sales and lead to more intense competition in the home market). The US Webb Pomerene Act of 1918, for example, (partially) exempts export cartels from antitrust prosecution. In light of our discussion above, the question arises whether the US is violating Art. XI GATT through this law: the likelier scenario would be that an export cartel restricts output or increases prices.

Recall that, following *Japan—Semiconductors*, providing incentives is enough for behaviour to be attributed to a government. Is the US government providing incentives to its economic operators to cartelize the world market by partially exempting them from antitrust prosecution?[29] A negative response is appropriate for the following reasons: first, the ultimate decision lies with the economic operators themselves, since the US government is not imposing cartelization; second, contrary to what is the case in *Japan—Semiconductors*, the US government is not incentivizing its economic operators so that they adopt a particular behaviour; it simply promises that it will not act against them if they do; and third, economic operators know that they might, anyway, have to face a foreign antitrust authority, if they decide to cartelize foreign markets. In light of the above, and especially because of the worldwide acceptance of the effects doctrine (and the increasing sophistication of antitrust authorities around the world which can now

---

[29] Fox (1997).

rely on legal assistance treaties etc.), it seems that lack of legal pursuit in the US market is an ancillary consideration, if at all.[30]

1.3 Exceptions

The majority of the exceptions discussed below concern both import and export restrictions. Some, like the possibility to deviate from the imperative of Art. XI GATT in case a WTO Member faces critical shortages of a specific product, concern only export restrictions.

1.3.1 Critical Shortages

This is one of the three exceptions mentioned in Art. XI.2 GATT. The wording of this provision leaves much to be desired. When are we in the presence of a surplus, and what exactly is necessary 'regarding the classification of various commodities'? There are few challenges recorded in this context.[31]

With this in mind, we turn to our discussion of critical shortages: in case a WTO Member experiences critical shortage of a foodstuff or any other essential product, it can temporarily impose *export* restrictions. The key terms of this provision were discussed in the Panel report on *China—Raw Materials*. The complainants challenged a number of export restrictions on products that China considered essential. In the view of the Panel, a product is 'essential' if it is important, or necessary, or indispensable to a particular WTO Member (§7.282). The Panel added that substitutability across products could cast doubt on the essential character of one of them if other substitutable products were available (§7.344). The Panel did not go so far as to provide a numerical figure (such as e.g. the percentage of GDP that is affected by the product); it did nonetheless hold (§7.213) that it is for the WTO Member invoking the provision to make the case (the defendant, since recourse to this provision will be made only if the complainant has first shown a violation of Art. XI GATT), and also that an input to a final product could be regarded as essential and, consequently, that there was no need for a good to be final in order to be essential (§7.340). The Panel focused on the temporal character of this provision: Art. XI.2(a) deals with temporary shortages only (§7.297); in that it is distinguished from Art. XX(g) GATT which deals with conservation of exhaustible natural resources (§7.349), since addressing temporary shortages has nothing to do with long-term conservation plans.

---

[30] Caution is warranted in light of the total absence of case law dealing head on with this issue.

[31] The reason for lack of meaningful challenges has probably to do with the fact that it was primarily the EU that was profiting from lack of clarity in this respect since its CAP (common agricultural policy) was very much one of the pillars of its integration process. Few would be willing to test the ambit of unclear legal terms while running the risk of destabilizing the European integration process. There was probably a collective action problem here as well: all would profit from the dismantlement of CAP, but only the complainant would be incurring the financial cost associated with litigating similar disputes and the (probably more important) political cost of questioning one of the foundations of the EU edifice.

1.3.2 Standards for the Classification, Grading, or Marketing of Commodities

Imposing a QR in order to comply with standards and regulations for the classification, grading, or marketing of products is consistent with Art. XI.2(b) GATT. The GATT Panel on *Canada—Herring and Salmon* discussed the key terms appearing in this provision. Canada's export restrictions on pink salmon and herring had been challenged. Canada responded that it had applied quality standards to fish and it had decided to ban exports of fish not meeting these standards. In its view, allowing for high quality fish only to be exported would have a beneficial effect on all Canada's (fish) exports. Since, nevertheless, it was proven before the Panel that even exports of fish meeting the standards were prohibited, the Panel rejected the Canadian argument (§4.2). The same Panel noted that this provision was not meant to incorporate all regulations facilitating trade. It was meant to further marketing of a commodity by spreading supplies of the restricted exports over a longer (than otherwise, that is, in the absence of a QR) period (§ 4.3). It is thus within the above-mentioned narrow reading that the terms of this provisions should be understood.

1.3.3 Necessary for the Enforcement of Governmental Measures

Art. XI.2(c) GATT refers to 'restrictions' only, whereas the previous two provisions (Arts. XI.2(a) and (b)) refer to 'prohibitions and restrictions': the linguistic difference suggests that outright bans on imports on exports are not covered by this provision; the GATT Panel on *US—Canadian Tuna* has confirmed this point (§4.6).[32]

The GATT Panel report on *Canada—Ice cream and Yoghurt* laid out the requisite elements of the legal test under this provision (§62):

(a) The measure must be an import restriction;
(b) On agricultural or fisheries products;
(c) It must apply to 'like' products in any form;
(d) A governmental measure restricting the quantity of the domestic products to be marketed or produced must be in place;
(e) Public notice must be given as to the quantity that will be allowed during a future specified period;
(f) The restrictions in place should not defy the legitimate expectations regarding the proportion of domestic goods relative to imports.

The GATT Panel report on *Japan—Agricultural Products I* held that it is the trading nation imposing the restriction that carries the associated burden of proof (§5.1.3.7). The same report noted that, contrary to other provisions, no obligation to compensate for damage suffered is provided for in Art. XI.2(c) GATT; this is

---

[32] See also, the GATT Panel reports on *Japan—Agricultural Products I* (§§5.3.1.2ff), and *EEC—Dessert Apples* (§12.5).

why, in the Panel's view, this provision requires similar restrictions on domestic goods (§12.15).

During the negotiation of the GATT, the view was held that measures applying to seasonal goods at a time when like domestic goods were not available could not qualify as 'necessary' under this provision.[33] The GATT Working Party on Quantitative Restrictions in its report adopted a less stringent view, to the effect that similar measures would be GATT-consistent only if they were necessary to achieve the objectives of government measures relating to the control of domestic products.[34] The condition of a government programme is fulfilled even if the measure at hand is not a compulsory government measure, provided that it gives sufficient incentives to traders to adopt a particular behaviour.[35] The GATT Panel on *EEC—Apples (US)* echoing prior case law held that two goods that perform a similar function for the consumer are like: it is hence consumers that will decide whether two goods are like in the context of this provision (§5.7). A narrower understanding of 'likeness' has been adopted with respect to disputes concerning tariff treatment of two products, as we shall see *infra* in this chapter. The GATT Panel on *Thailand—Cigarettes* held that the reference to 'fresh' products in the Interpretative Note to this provision meant that leaf was covered but cigarettes were not (§§69–70). Following the advent of the WTO, there is relative clarity as to the coverage of this provision: the WTO Agreement on Agriculture explicitly deals with the products coming under its purview. Fisheries are not covered by the WTO Agreement on Agriculture, but there is a convention that these products come under Chapters 3 and 16 of HS 2002.[36] Before 1995, the coverage of this provision was limited to Chapters 1–24 of the Customs Cooperation Council Nomenclature.[37]

1.3.4 Balance of Payments (Arts. XII and XVIII GATT)

WTO Members can legitimately deviate from their obligations under Art. XI GATT if they encounter balance of payments problems and, to this effect, can demonstrate that they have complied with the requirements of Art. XII GATT. Developing countries facing similar concerns can invoke Art. XVIII GATT, a provision that contains less stringent requirements for compliance than Art. XII GATT.

The inclusion of these provisions was deemed necessary in light of the inflexibilities associated with the system of fixed exchange rates (fixed parities) that prevailed when the GATT/ITO was originally negotiated: under fixed parities, a country with a payments deficit could not devalue its currency easily; it would have to go through a multilateral process. The International

---

33 See §(e) of the London Conference report, cited in Irwin et al. (2008).
34 GATT Doc. L/332/Rev. 1, adopted on 5 March 1955, BISD 3S/170 at §§67ff. On its legal value, see the discussion on GATT decisions in Chapter 1.
35 *Japan—Agricultural Products I* (§5.4.1.4); see also the discussion *supra* on *Japan—Semiconductors.*
36 HS refers to Harmonized System; see the discussion *infra* in this chapter.
37 *Japan—Agricultural Products I* (§5.1.3.2).

Monetary Fund (IMF) had, by virtue of Art. XV GATT, an important role to play in this respect. Art. XV.6 GATT reads:

> Any contracting party which is not a member of the Fund shall, within a time to be determined by the CONTRACTING PARTIES after consultation with the Fund, become a member of the Fund, or, failing that, enter into a special exchange agreement with the CONTRACTING PARTIES. A contracting party which ceases to be a member of the Fund shall forthwith enter into a special exchange agreement with the CONTRACTING PARTIES. Any special exchange agreement entered into by a contracting party under this paragraph shall thereupon become part of its obligations under this Agreement.

Hence, when facing such concerns, they were allowed to take measures such as QRs in order to address, for example, an influx of imports and/or stagnation of their exports. Most countries have shifted by now to flexible exchange rates. Given that the exchange rate is a more appropriate instrument to deal with balance of payments (BoP) disequilibria—as part of a comprehensive macroeconomic adjustment programme—the GATT provisions on BoP have become largely redundant: other things being equal, WTO Members would rather devaluate and profit from the increase in export income than impose a QR and keep their exchange rate intact.[38] In other words, this provision, although still present in GATT, is largely of historical interest.

A specific committee was established to help administer the two GATT provisions, the Committee on Balance of Payments Restrictions (BoP Committee). The BoP Committee carries out consultations in order to review all restrictive import measures taken for BoP purposes. It follows the procedures for consultations on BoP restrictions which were formally approved on 28 April 1970:[39] a WTO Member willing to apply a new restriction, or to raise the general level of its existing restrictions, shall enter into consultations with the BoP Committee within four months of the adoption of such measures. The Member adopting such

---

[38] As import restrictions (in conjunction with export subsidies) are equivalent to a nominal devaluation, allowing (temporary) import barriers to deal with a balance of payments problem can make *some* sense, depending, of course, on the satisfaction of the Marshall-Lerner condition. According to the Marshall-Lerner condition, for a currency devaluation to have a positive impact on a trade balance, the sum of the price elasticities of exports and imports (in absolute value) must be greater than 1. The principle is named after economists Alfred Marshall and Abba Lerner. As a devaluation of the exchange rate means a reduction in the price of exports, demand for these will increase. At the same time, the price of imports will rise and their demand diminish. The net effect on the trade balance will depend on price elasticities. If goods exported are price-elastic, their quantity demanded will increase proportionally more than the decrease in price, and total export revenue will increase. Similarly, if goods imported are price-elastic, total import expenditure will decrease. Both will improve the trade balance. Empirically, it has been found that goods tend to be inelastic in the short term, as it takes time to change consumption patterns. Thus, the Marshall-Lerner condition is not met and devaluation is likely to worsen the trade balance initially. In the long term, consumers will adjust to the new prices and the trade balance will improve. This effect is called J-curve effect.

[39] GATT Doc. BISD 18S/45.

measures may request that consultations be held (Art. XII.4(a) and Art. XVIII.12 (a) GATT). Consultations can also be held upon invitation by the chairman of the BoP Committee. All restrictions applied for BoP purposes shall be reviewed periodically by the BoP Committee. There are notification requirements as well. Whenever recourse to BoP restrictions is made, WTO Members must notify the WTO General Council of:

(a) the introduction of, or any change in, the application of trade-restricting import measures taken for BoP purposes;
(b) any modification concerning the timing of withdrawal of such measures.

Notifications shall include information at the tariff-line level about the product coverage and trade flows affected. At the request of any Member, notifications may be reviewed by the BoP Committee. Recourse to dispute settlement procedures is also available. The role of the BoP Committee was not always pivotal: originally, BoP-related measures would be discussed in the context of Special Working Parties established to this effect; its role was strengthened during the Tokyo round, when the CONTRACTING PARTIES adopted the Declaration on Trade Measures taken for Balance-of-Payments Purposes,[40] which subjected all measures taken for BoP purposes to an examination by the BoP Committee (and not by a Special Working Party).

Art. XII GATT was designed as an exception to Art. XI GATT.[41] In practice, however, trading nations often had recourse to measures such as import surcharges in order to safeguard their BoP position. It was not clear whether such measures could be justified through a textual reading of Art. XII GATT; it was clear, on the other hand, that such measures could have had a less disruptive effect on trade than a QR. The Declaration on Trade Measures taken for Balance-of-Payments Purposes (1979) is the first legal document which acknowledged in its preamble the use of measures other than QR for BoP purposes, and in fact, encouraged their use. Through this Declaration, the GATT CONTRACTING PARTIES expressed the common preference for the use of measures which have the least disruptive effect on trade. In the same vein, during the Uruguay round, the Understanding on the BoP Provisions of the GATT 1994 was concluded, which strengthened the surveillance of restrictions (§§9–12), and contained provisions which reproduced the essence of the 1979 *Declaration*:

(a) WTO Members are encouraged to give preference to measures which have the least disruptive effect on trade (called price-based measures). Such measures include import surcharges, import deposit requirements, which can lawfully apply in excess of bound duties (§2);

---

40 GATT Doc. L/4904, adopted on 28 November 1979, GATT Doc. BISD 26S/205.
41 The opening sentence of this provision makes it clear beyond doubt that it was meant to function as exception to Art. XI GATT.

(b) WTO Members should seek to avoid applying QR, and, whenever they do so, they should explain why they did not have recourse to price-based measures (§3);

(c) WTO Members should apply restrictions across the board, except for essential products, that is products which meet basic consumption needs, or which contribute to the Members' efforts to improve their BoP situation, such as capital goods (§4).

Developed countries almost never made use of this provision.[42] Developing countries, on the other hand, made use of Art. XVIII(b) GATT, that is, the corresponding provision that developing countries can invoke when facing BoP problems (see Table 2.1). The requirements for compliance with this provision are less stringent[43] than the corresponding requirements for compliance with Art. XII GATT:

(a) the former can be used by WTO Members with inadequate monetary reserves, whereas the latter can be used by WTO Members with very low monetary reserves. Arguably, the former term leaves more discretion to the state and, consequently, would entail a more deferential standard of review, should litigation occur;

(b) whereas Art. XII GATT requires WTO Members to progressively relax the restrictions imposed, Art. XVIII(b) GATT provides that no Member shall be required to modify restrictions on the ground that a change in its development policy would render such restrictions unnecessary;[44]

(c) a simplified procedure for consultations is available: it was approved on 19 December 1972.[45] This procedure is available to all developing countries and LDCs (least developed countries); the latter, however, can have recourse to it, provided that they are pursuing trade liberalization efforts in conformity with the schedule presented to the BoP Committee in previous consultations.

Developing countries have made frequent use of Art. XVIII(b) GATT.

The GATT has in place a centralized regime to discuss BoP-based restrictions, where the BoP Committee plays an important rule. In practice, several issues arise:

---

[42] The GATT Analytical Index (6th edition, 1994) contains information about the invocations of Art. XII GATT at p. 361. Israel is the only developed country that invoked this provision in the past, but has ceased to do so.

[43] The Panel report on *India—Quantitative Restrictions* explicitly acknowledged that Art. XVII (b) GATT constitutes an expression of special and differential treatment reserved for developing countries (§5.155). On this issue, see also the Ministerial Decision adopted during the Ministerial Conference that launched the Doha round, WTO Doc. WT/MIN(01)/17 of 20 November 2001, at §1.1.

[44] Van den Bossche (2005, pp. 667–74). See also the AB report on *India—Quantitative Restrictions* at §§125ff.

[45] GATT Doc. BISD 20S/47. The WTO Understanding on BoP restrictions refers to this document as 'simplified consultation procedures'.

Table 2.1 Invocations of Art. XVIII(b) GATT

WTO Member	Period
Argentina	(1972–1978), (1986–1991)
Bangladesh	(1974–2008)[46]
Brazil	(1962–1971), (1976–1991)
Chile	(1961–1980)
Colombia	(1981–1992)
Egypt	(1963–1995)
Ghana	(1959–1989)
India	(1960–1997)
Indonesia	(1960–1997)
Korea	(1969–1989)
Nigeria	(1985–1998)
Pakistan	(1960–2002)
Philippines	(1980–1995)
Peru	(1968–1991)
Sri Lanka	(1960–1998)
Tunisia	(1967–1997)

what if, for example, the same issue is raised before a WTO Panel? Are WTO Panels obliged to follow the BoP Committee decisions? And what if the latter has not decided when a matter is referred to a Panel?[47] This issue was comprehensively discussed in the context of a dispute relating to an invocation of BoP. In *India—Quantitative Restrictions*, India attempted to justify its QRs on over 2,700 agricultural and industrial product tariff lines by invoking Art. XVIII(b) GATT. The Panel found India's measures to be inconsistent with Art. XI.1 GATT; it also went on to find that they could not be justified through recourse to Art. XVIII.11 GATT either.[48] Most importantly, the Panel found (and the AB upheld) that, in

---

[46] Bangladesh notified its intention to phase out its remaining restrictions by 1 January 2005 (WTO Doc. WT/BOP/N/54 of 15 December 2000 and WT/BOP/N/62 of 18 February 2004). Subsequent to this notification, Bangladesh imposed import restrictions under Art. XVIII(c) of the GATT, invoking *infant industry* protection; see WTO Doc. G/C/7 of 16 January 2002.

[47] Barfield (2001), Roessler (2000), and Mavroidis (2002) have expressed different views on this score. While Mavroidis espouses the thrust of the argument developed by the AB in the case we discuss here, Roessler takes the opposite view (arguing that the AB undid the institutional balance as struck by the WTO framers), whereas Barfield believes that there is overreliance in the adjudicating process.

[48] The US carried the burden of proof with respect to Art. XI GATT, and India then carried the burden of proof with respect to Art. XVIII GATT defence, an exception to the former provision. The Panel also held (and the AB upheld in §138 of its report) that the burden of proof shifted back to the US with respect to the Interpretative Note ad Art XVIII.11 of the GATT. This note concerns the conditions under which a WTO Member should progressively relax import restrictions that have been in place. It is highly unlikely that a WTO member affected by such restrictions adequately knows the facts mandating similar behaviour. The Panel probably relied on the solemnity accompanying the IMF involvement on this score. Still, it would have been on safer grounds had it imposed the burden of proof on India.

contrast to the argument advanced by India, BoP restrictions could be the subject of judicial review. On appeal, the AB noted the relevance of institutional balance within the framework of the WTO Agreement, and rejected India's argument that only the WTO BoP Committee could review the consistency of its measures with the GATT, noting that (§105):

> such a requirement would be inconsistent with Article XXIII of the GATT 1994, as elaborated and applied by the DSU, and footnote 1 to the *BOP Understanding* which, as discussed above, clearly provides for the availability of the WTO dispute settlement procedures with respect to any matters relating to balance-of-payments restrictions.

The AB upheld this finding and went on to find against India, because it had not demonstrated that it had met its burden of proof and had not explained why the removal of the QRs would lead to a change in its development policy, and ultimately to a deterioration of its overall situation (§150).

1.3.5 Exchange Restrictions

The relationship between trade and the financial system was in the mind of negotiators already during the ITO negotiations,[49] as we saw in Chapter 1, and was eloquently presented in the Declaration of Ministers at the opening of the Tokyo round:[50]

> The policy of liberalizing world trade cannot be carried out successfully in the absence of parallel efforts to set up a monetary system which shields the world economy from the shocks and imbalances which have previously occurred. The Ministers will not lose sight of the fact that the efforts which are to be made in the trade field imply continuing efforts to maintain orderly conditions and to establish a durable and equitable monetary system.
>
> The Ministers recognize equally that the new phase in the liberalization of trade which it is their intention to undertake should facilitate the orderly functioning of the monetary system.

There are two key provisions in Art. XV GATT that deal with the issue of exchange restrictions, XV.4 and XV.9, and we reproduce them in full here:

> Contracting parties shall not, by exchange action, frustrate* the intent of the provisions of this Agreement, nor, by trade action, the intent of the provisions of the Articles of Agreement of the International Monetary Fund.
>
> ...
>
> Nothing in this Agreement shall preclude:
>
> (*a*) the use by a contracting party of exchange controls or exchange restrictions in accordance with the Articles of Agreement of the International Monetary Fund

---

[49] Many have written on this score; none, in our view, as lucidly as Gardner (1956).
[50] GATT Doc. BISD 20S/19ff at §7.

or with that contracting party's special exchange agreement with the CON-
TRACTING PARTIES, or

(*b*) the use by a contracting party of restrictions or controls in imports or *exports*, the
sole effect of which, additional to the effects permitted under Articles XI, XII,
XIII and XIV, is to make effective such exchange controls or exchange
restrictions

The term 'frustrate', appearing in Art. XV.4 GATT, is further interpreted in an
interpretative note as follows:

> The word 'frustrate' is intended to indicate, for example, that infringements of the
> letter of any Article of this Agreement by exchange action shall not be regarded as a
> violation of that Article if, in practice, there is no appreciable departure from the
> intent of the Article. Thus, a contracting party which, as part of its exchange control
> operated in accordance with the Articles of Agreement of the International Monetary
> Fund, requires payment to be received for its exports in its own currency or in the
> currency of one or more members of the International Monetary Fund will not
> thereby be deemed to contravene Article XI or Article XIII. Another example would
> be that of a contracting party which specifies on an import licence the country from
> which the goods may be imported, for the purpose not of introducing any additional
> element of discrimination in its import licensing system but of enforcing permissible
> exchange controls

Consequently, WTO Members are entitled, by virtue of Art. XV.9 GATT, under
certain conditions, to impose exchange restrictions in accordance with the IMF
provisions and they will be violating these provisions only if they frustrate the
intent of the GATT provisions. The intent of the GATT provisions should be that
WTO Members do not, say through currency manipulations, confer an advantage
on their exports.[51]

There is scant practice in this context. Practice so far evidences that WTO
Panels have shown considerable deference to the IMF when dealing with exchange
restrictions. The Panel, in its report on *Dominican Republic—Import and Sale
of Cigarettes*, dealt with an exchange restriction imposed by the Dominican
Republic.[52] Essentially, the Dominican Republic had modified its original

---

[51] BoP and exchange restrictions could be related. It could be the case, for example, that a BoP
restriction is complemented by an exchange restriction, where, for example, there is increased
speculation about the exchange rate of the country imposing the restriction. It could also be that a
WTO Member imposes only an exchange restriction, and thus could be opening the door to barter
trade; if it does not want to practise barter trade, it will have to contemplate imposing a BoP
restriction as well. In general, whether a measure is an exchange restriction has to do with the
question of whether it involves a direct governmental limitation on the availability or use of foreign
currencies. §7.132 of the Panel report on *Dominican Republic—Import and Sale of Cigarettes* said as
much. Exchange restrictions do not have to be recorded in the schedules of concession, discussed in
Section 2 of this chapter, because they are a contingency which could not have been anticipated
when concessions were scheduled.
[52] The facts of the case are reflected in §§7.135–7.137 of the report.

measure, which covered all transactions, but subsequently replaced it with a measure which covered only imports. It was thus discriminating against imports. In the Panel's view, this change was evidence that it was not genuinely addressing the issue that, in name, it was purporting to address. In order, however, to cement its opinion on this issue, the Panel decided to consult with the IMF. With the passage from a system of fixed parities to a world of fluctuating parities, the IMF's mandate to ensure exchange rate stability became a more arduous task. In recent years, cooperation between the WTO and the IMF has been strengthened. An agreement was signed[53] that provides for the establishment of a steady channel of information between the two institutions, and the WTO has invited the IMF to participate as observer in meetings relating to its areas of competence, and vice versa. In the Panel's view, in case the IMF authorities held that the measures imposed by the Dominican Republic were in accordance with the IMF Articles of Agreement, these measures would *ipso facto* be deemed to be GATT-consistent as well (§7.139). This result is the only one which, in the Panel's view, is consistent with a textual reading of Art. XV.2 GATT. So, the Panel decided to request the IMF's advice on whether the restriction applied by the Dominican Republic could be regarded as an exchange restriction in the sense of Art. XV GATT that had its approval. The IMF responded that the measure at hand was not a multiple currency practice (since it was only targeting imports, and, as such, could not qualify as an exchange restriction in accordance with Art. XV GATT), and, hence, was no longer approved by the IMF. Against this background, the Panel concluded that the Dominican Republic could not justify its measures through recourse to Art. XV.9 GATT (§§ 7.143–7.145).[54] This finding was not appealed. In the same report, the Panel held that the party invoking Art. XV GATT carries the burden of proof associated with this provision (§7.131). An example of a typical notified exchange restriction is provided here:

1. Iceland maintains exchange restrictions subject to Fund jurisdiction under Article VIII, Section 2(a) arising from the capital control regime that restrict the transfer of: (i) interest on bonds (whose transfer the FX rules apportion depending on the period of the holding); and (ii) the indexed portion of amortized principal on bonds.
2. In the circumstances of Iceland, the Fund grants approval for the retention of these exchange restrictions for a period of twelve months from the date of this

---

[53] WTO Doc. WT/L/195 of 18 November 1996.

[54] See also §7.150 of the Panel report which states that 'In fact, the reply of the IMF General Counsel concludes that since the foreign exchange commission does not constitute an exchange restriction, "the issue of its consistency or inconsistency with the Funds Articles for purpose of paragraph 8 of the Co-operation Agreement does not arise". The Panel fully agrees with this statement'.

decision or the completion the next Article IV consultation with Iceland, whichever is earlier.[55]

The issue of exchange rates gained prominence recently, with voices heard, essentially in the US, that China was engaging in currency manipulation, keeping its domestic currency (*renminbi*, RMB) artificially low and thus boosting its exports. More forcefully, Mattoo and Subramanian (2009) have argued for the WTO to be given a role in addressing similar practices. A number of possible legal bases have been offered as potentially relevant to attack the Chinese practices, although none of them seems appropriate. Art. XV GATT would lead Panels to defer to the IMF, an issue we discuss *infra*. The SCM context is highly inappropriate since there is a financial contribution by the government involved here, and since, even if one extends the concept of 'financial contribution' to cover similar instances, the specificity requirement would not be met.[56] Finally, a WTO Member raising a non-violation complaint would have a mountain to climb when arguing that it legitimately expected China to act against its own interests. Staiger and Sykes (2010) visit all the literature to this effect and conclude that there is some difficulty in identifying trade effects stemming from currency practices and, because of this factor, the role of WTO dispute settlement is limited. They note that, with respect to arguments raised under Art. XV GATT, there is not much a Panel could do in light of the high burden of proof ('frustrate' the intent) associated with this provision. This point is further supported by practice and the deference that Panels show to the IMF.[57] One could add two further points: first, it would be quite awkward to entrust Panels composed of trade delegates with the authority to decide on monetary issues: deference to IMF is highly warranted in this context. Second, even the IMF itself, the body with expertise on such issues, has found it difficult to conclude whether currency manipulation has occurred, although it has been treating similar questions on hundreds of occasions.

1.3.6 *Infant Industry Protection (Art. XVIII(c) GATT)*

Art. XVIII(c) GATT allows developing countries that are WTO Members to deviate from their obligations in order to protect their infant industry. Such practices were quite popular in the 1960s and 1970s, but recently developing countries have not made use of this provision. In theory, one could make the case

---

[55] WTO Doc. WT/TF/IMF/53 of 12 November 2009. Almost identical language has been included in the document allowing Colombia to avail itself of this possibility, WTO Doc. WT/TF/IMF/49 of 26 January 2009.

[56] See the relevant discussion in Chapter 8.

[57] The authors identify a situation where acting consistently with the GATT and inconsistently with the IMF is possible, but fail to see functional consequences in their example.

in favour of protection during the early stages of development.[58] The manner in which similar measures have been practised has, nevertheless, quite often been counter-productive. The GATT does not take a stance on the welfare implications of similar invocations; it is for WTO Members to make their calculation and decide whether or not to avail themselves of this possibility. All the GATT does is to explain the substantive and procedural requirements in case recourse to this provision has been decided: in essence, the invoking state must show that the measure favouring a particular industry is meant to raise the general standard of living (a judgment that can hardly be brought into question by its trading partners), and has to respect notification requirements, as well as an obligation to enter into consultations in case the measure envisaged concerns a commodity which has to respect a tariff binding.

The Panel on *India—Quantitative Restrictions* made it clear that an invocation of Art. XVIII(c) GATT is justiciable. At the time of writing, the only such restriction in place is by Bangladesh.[59]

1.3.7 General Exceptions (Art. XX GATT)

Assuming that a violation of Art. XI GATT has been established, the violating WTO Member can seek justification by invoking one of the grounds mentioned in Art. XX GATT. We discuss this provision in Chapter 5.

1.3.8 National Security (Art. XXI GATT)

Assuming that a violation of Art. XI GATT has been established, the violating WTO Member can seek justification by invoking one of the grounds mentioned in Art. XXI GATT. We discuss this provision in Chapter 5.

1.3.9 Safeguards (Art. XIX GATT)

WTO Members can limit the amount of imports in their market (and thus legitimately have recourse to a QR), if they have complied with the various conditions included in Art. XIX GATT and the SG Agreement, which we discuss in Chapter 9.

---

[58] This provision was negotiated during the 1955 Review Session of the GATT to provide developing countries with the necessary legal space to adopt import substitution policies. We discuss this issue in more detail *infra* in Section 5. It is not necessarily the case that temporarily closing down a market is bad economics: Lucas (1988), for example, offers a skill acquisition model of endogenous growth and suggests that, by allowing countries to establish a comparative advantage in the production of high learning goods, the erection of trade barriers during the early stages of development may enhance their long-term growth. It is, of course, a totally different issue whether Lucas is followed in Art. XXVIII(c) GATT practice.

[59] WTO Doc. G/C/7 of 16 January 2002. The United States first (WTO Doc. G/C/8 of 18 February 2002) and the EU subsequently (WTO Doc. G/C/9 of 20 February 2002) requested consultations with the government of Bangladesh. No subsequent notification took place.

1.3.10 Avoiding Dumping

In *Japan—Semiconductors*, Japan was found to be in violation of its GATT obligations, because it provided its economic operators with incentives not to dump.[60] Japan argued before the Panel that, even if its actions were considered to be inconsistent with the discipline embedded in Art. XI GATT, it was still justified in acting in this way since it was aiming to dissuade Japanese economic operators from dumping, a practice condemned by Art. VI GATT. The Panel was thus led to discuss the relationship between Art. VI and Art. XI GATT. It held that Art. VI GATT did not address actions by exporting countries; it addressed only actions by importing countries, since it allowed them to impose AD duties in order to counteract dumping. It then went on to conclude that (§120):

> Article VI did not provide a justification for measures restricting the exportation or sale for export of a product inconsistently with Article XI:1.

Consequently, one cannot justify an export QR in the name of an effort to avoid dumping practices.

1.4 Legal QRs Must Respect Historic Quotas

Assuming the conditions, say, of Art. XII GATT have been respected, and a QR has been imposed as a result, Art. XIII GATT kicks in. The title of Art. XIII GATT leaves us with the impression that what is required from this provision is that otherwise lawful QRs are being administered on a non-discriminatory basis. Art. XIII.2 GATT, however, which constitutes the operational arm of this provision, does not share the impression given by the title when it states that:

> ...contracting parties shall aim at a distribution of trade...approaching as closely as possible the shares that the various contracting parties might be expected to obtain in the absence of such restrictions.

Pursuant to Art XIII.2(d) GATT, a WTO Member lawfully imposing a QR is required to allocate quotas to various suppliers in a manner that respects their pre-QR market shares. A reference period (usually the previous three to five years) will be used as benchmark for the calculation of market shares. Hence, it is not non-discriminatory administration of quotas that is privileged through Art. XIII GATT; it is respect for historic market shares—a rather discriminatory policy (since new aggressive suppliers will not be put on an equal footing with old suppliers).

Art. XIII GATT thus, by preserving historic shares, does not account for changes in supply and demand. One cannot thus exclude an 'alignment' of

---

[60] Dumping is a price differentiation scheme, whereby the export price is lower than the price practised by economic operators in their home market. Dumping is not prohibited but it is condemned. We discuss it in detail in Chapter 7.

incentives between exporters and importers: exporters fearing a maverick would support QRs as a means of preserving (at least in the short run) their market share.

Art. XIII GATT does not mention the period of time that a QR can remain in place. Ostensibly, the length of time a QR can be imposed depends on the rationale behind the QR: for instance, if a member experiences BoP problems for two years, a QR should logically be in place for the same period of time; conversely, safeguard action that takes the form of QRs can remain lawfully in place for a maximum of eight years, by virtue of Art. 7.3 SG.

The title of Art. XIII GATT is 'Non discriminatory administration of QRs'. It follows that obligations regarding the administration of QRs kick in only after the consistency of a QR with the GATT has first been established. For example, if a QR has been justified on BoP grounds, it must also, in principle, comply with Art. XIII of the GATT.[61] In the opposite scenario, that is, if a QR has been judged GATT-inconsistent, recourse to Art. XIII GATT would have been superfluous. This is not nevertheless what happened in *EC—Bananas III*, a dispute between the EU and some banana-exporting countries.[62] The EU had in place two QRs, one applicable to bananas originating in the so-called ACP countries (African, Caribbean, and Pacific)[63] and another applicable to bananas originating in the rest of world. The tariff rate for the former was much lower than that for the latter, and, as a result, non-ACP producers had suffered an important trade loss. The EU also agreed during the Uruguay round to provide preferential treatment for bananas originating in countries that had signed the so-called Framework Agreement with it (which the EU had attached in its schedule). The Panel and the AB upheld the claim advanced by the complainants to the effect that the two-quotas system ran foul of the MFN requirement (§191 of the AB report). Still, the AB went on to find that the EU regime was in violation of Art. XIII GATT. But of course such a finding is unwarranted absent a prior finding that Art. XI GATT has been violated as well. This is a one-off incident that deserves to be mentioned for the sake of completeness but which ultimately is probably not representative of the AB attitude in this respect.

1.5 Discriminatory QRs

Art. XIV GATT allows WTO Members that have invoked either Art. XII or Art. XVIII GATT to deviate from their obligations under Art. XIII GATT. The rationale for this provision is that a WTO Member invoking the BoP provisions may, by virtue of Art. VIII of the IMF Articles of Agreement (which is explicitly

---

[61] Jackson (1969) succinctly points to the sequence between Arts. XI, XII, and XIII GATT.

[62] This dispute is one of the longest standing and eventually the EU agreed to move to a single tariff applied to all its bananas imports following a transitional period; see Guth (2012).

[63] The group is composed of numerous countries that are former colonies of some members of the EU and had concluded agreements to grant them preferential access in the EU market (successively, the Arusha, Lomé, and Cotonou Agreements).

mentioned in Art. XIV.1 GATT), be authorized to deviate from its obligations not to discriminate on the origin of the goods which it will be restricting into its own market.[64] The following two conditions must be met:

(a) the quota must have been imposed to address problems relating to BoP;
(b) the discriminatory quota must affect a small part of its trade.

1.6 Import Licensing

The ILA (Import Licensing Agreement) is *lex specialis* to Art. XIII GATT and deals with the obligations imposed on WTO Members wishing to have recourse to an import licensing scheme. We discuss it in detail in Chapter 6.

2. Tariffs

2.1 The Legal Discipline and its Rationale

Tariffs (customs duties), loosely defined as a monetary burden on imports, are imposed for a variety of reasons: because, for example, governments want to protect domestic producers; because, assuming they have the necessary bargaining power to this effect, they might want to affect the terms of trade; or simply to raise income.[65] The GATT discipline on tariffs does not distinguish tariff treatment depending on their rationale: it allows tariffs (irrespective of their rationale) and WTO Members are free to enter into negotiations aiming at capping their level; irrespective of whether negotiations to this effect have been held, tariffs must be applied in non-discriminatory way.

One way to understand the discipline imposed is to think of the pre-GATT situation as the counterfactual: trading nations were free to change their level of tariffs as they deemed appropriate (tariff volatility), and also free to distinguish their tariff treatment based on the source of supply (discrimination). The advent of the GATT signalled the end of these two practices: duties would be bound, that is, following negotiations to this effect, trading nations would accept a 'ceiling' on their freedom to impose import duties in return for a 'ceiling' that their partners would impose on their imports; they would also accept to, in principle, impose the same import duty on all like imports irrespective of their origin: this is the notorious MFN (most favoured nation) clause, which we discuss *infra*. Bound duties will be reflected in schedules of concessions (commitments). By virtue of Art. II.7 GATT:

---

[64] Report of the Working Party on Quantitative Restrictions, GATT Doc. BISD 3S/170ff at §26.

[65] As we shall see *infra*, the relative absence of export duties casts some doubt on this last rationale.

> The Schedules annexed to this Agreement are hereby made an integral part of Part
> I of this Agreement.

The reason for introducing the 'ceiling' has to do with the need for some certainty
regarding transaction costs: absent this discipline, trade would suffer since exporters would find it impossible to predict what the final price of their goods would be
in export markets and this uncertainty might in and of itself dissuade them from
exporting in the first place. A tariff ceiling is preferable to a tariff floor because of
the incentive of WTO Members to occasionally cheat and shift costs to their
trading partners, as explained in Chapter 1. A ceiling is also preferable to a rigid
tariff because it allows for 'downward flexibility' to preference shocks and permits
efficiency-enhancing tariff reductions. Maggi and Rodriguez-Clare (2007) explain
that, from a political economy perspective, tariff ceilings and exact tariff commitments have very different implications: whereas when exact tariff commitments are
being negotiated, lobbying effectively ends at the time of the agreement (since the
agreement leaves no discretion for governments to choose tariffs in the future),
when tariff ceilings are being negotiated, governments retain the option of setting
tariffs below their maximum levels,[66] and thus they might be inviting lobbying
and contributions also after the agreement has been signed. Governments thus
might have a strong incentive to opt for ceilings rather than rigid commitments.

Duties that have been bound cannot be unilaterally revised upwards; the
multilateral process embedded in Art. XXVIII GATT has to be observed in this
case. In principle, compensation has to be agreed between the WTO Member
wishing to revise upwards its bound duties and a subset of WTO Members
particularly affected by the decision to revise bound duties. Reciprocity is very
much behind the procedure established in Art. XXVIII GATT, the idea being that
the balance of rights and obligations established in the original negotiation should
be preserved in subsequent negotiations, irrespective of the agreed level of duties.
This mechanism is the insurance that the value of tariff promises (bindings) will
not be altered unless both the promisor and the promisee agree that this should be
the case. Trading nations have thus an incentive to continue negotiating tariff
levels in the future as well.

Negotiations on tariff liberalization are based on reciprocal commitments. In
the words of Eric Wyndham-White, one-time DG of the GATT, when speaking
during the Torquay round:

> ...a number of European countries with a comparatively low level of tariff rates
> considered that they had entered the Torquay negotiations at a disadvantage. Having
> bound many of their rates of duty in 1947 and 1949, what could these low tariff

---

[66] Nothing legally stops WTO Members from applying a duty lower than the agreed ceiling (the
difference between the two numbers is known as 'water'), provided that they adhere to the MFN
discipline.

countries offer at Torquay in order to obtain further concessions from the countries with higher level of tariffs?[67]

Reciprocity is often referred to as a GATT legal principle. Reciprocity was, on the other hand, the negotiating principle adopted in the original negotiation for tariff concessions to be exchanged.[68] It does not, however, amount to a legal principle exonerating WTO Members from observing the contract when another WTO Member has failed to do so: if A violates the contract, B cannot, by invoking *non adimplenti contractus* (reciprocity), unilaterally stop honouring its own commitments. B can at most challenge A's practices before the WTO adjudicating bodies, and A will, if found guilty, have to implement the rulings. In the meantime, B will have to continue observing the contract. Only in the case when A refuses to implement the multilateral rulings can B request authorization to stop honouring its own commitments, on a transitional basis, until A starts respecting the contract once again.

Tariff reduction is hailed as one of the biggest successes of the multilateral trading system, even though, as Irwin (1996 and 1998a) has persuasively argued, one has probably exaggerated the size of the success. In his view, average duties across all goods calculated on dutiable imports stood at 19.34 per cent in 1947 and 13.87 per cent in 1948. However, were one to include duty-free trade, the ratio of duties collected to total imports amounted to 7.55 per cent in 1947 and 5.71 per cent in 1948. The average tariffs on dutiable imports (weighted with the 1939 trade values) in 1947 was 32.2 per cent and 25.4 per cent in 1948. As 60 per cent of US imports were duty free in 1947, the average tariff for total imports was much lower. In addition, were tariff averages to be weighted with the 1947 trade weights (and prices and not with 1939 values), then the post-Geneva average tariff on dutiable imports drops from 25.4 per cent to 15 per cent. Including duty-free imports, the pre-Annecy (GATT 1948) tariff average of all US imports was estimated by the US Tariff Commission to amount to 5.9 per cent. This number fits unusually well with the ratio of duties to total imports (free and dutiable) of 5.97 per cent in 1950.

Tariff reductions have been asymmetric in the sense that big important markets exhibit the highest number of bindings as well as the lowest level of bound tariffs.[69] During the Uruguay round, LDCs for the first time agreed to bind many of their duties; Diakantoni and Eskaith (2009) note that, with respect to

---

[67] ICITO, 1952 at p. 9.

[68] On the role of reciprocity in the original negotiation of the GATT, see E/PC/T/33, Annexure 10.

[69] Lack of interest in some developing countries' markets (and especially the LDCs) and the fact, that following the enactment of the which we discuss *infra* in this chapter, developing countries are not expected to make as many concessions as developed countries, help explain in large part why this is the case. As a result, it is almost always the case that developing countries exhibit nowadays (with few exceptions) higher tariffs than developed countries. Some researchers have cast doubt on the idea that high tariffs are universally detrimental to growth, arguing that policy prescriptions (such as low tariffs) designed to promote growth within developed economies may not be appropriate for universal adoption. See on this score, Rodriguez and Rodrik (2001), and more recently, de Jong and Ripoli (2006), who use a panel data set comprising 60 countries and spanning 1975–2000.

commitments entered by LDCs during the Uruguay round, their bound level is higher than the de facto applied level in practice.[70]

2.2 Expressing Goods in Common Language: The Harmonized System

To bind duties, WTO negotiators have first to agree on a common language to describe goods and, based on this common language, exchange concessions. The need for a common language is a consequence of the possibility that exists to express the same item in different ways, and the fact that various languages are being used by WTO Members to express the same idea: these are complicating factors that need to be set aside. The Harmonized System (HS) supplies the common language. The HS is a document elaborated in the WCO (World Customs Organization),[71] an international organization with headquarters in Brussels, Belgium. Its function is to describe goods in a multilaterally agreed manner. It comprises about 5,000 commodity groups. Goods' descriptions are expressed in two, four, and six digits: the lower the number of digits, the more generic the product category; the higher the number of digits, the more specific the product category. For example, at the two-digit level one might find the term 'vehicles', whereas, at the six-digit level, the term 'passenger cars of less than 2 tons'.

The HS Convention originates in the Geneva Nomenclature (GN), which came into being on 1 July 1937. The GN was replaced by the Brussels Convention on Nomenclature for the Classification of Goods in Customs Tariffs (BTN) in 1959, and the BTN was, in turn, replaced in 1974 by the Customs Cooperation Council Nomenclature (CCCN) in 1974, which was eventually replaced by the HS in 1988. The HS has been amended five times since 1988 (largely in order to account for changes in technology): 1992, 1996, 2002, 2007, and 2011 (the last of these will enter into force in 2012). The WTO Committee on Tariff Concessions established simplified procedures to implement these changes and any future changes in the HS relating to GATT concessions.[72] The HS is administered by the HS Committee, which is composed of representatives from each HS contracting party.

What the HS ensures is that any given good will be classified under the same tariff line (*heading*) across national jurisdictions. For example, bumpers will come

---

[70] That is, the binding of their duties did not generate any trade liberalization. It simply removed the possibility of tariff volatility above the bound level. The WTO webpage refers to the fact that all WTO Members increased their absolute number of tariff bindings. In percentage terms (out of 100 total tariff bindings), developed countries moved from 78 (pre-Uruguay round) to 99 per cent (following the successful conclusion of the Uruguay round), developing countries from 21 to 73 per cent, and economies in transition from 73 to 98 per cent. The insight in Diakantoni and Eskaith (2009) is that these numbers may simply correspond to crystallization of prior practice, and sometimes even less than that.

[71] This institution used to be known as the CCC (Customs Cooperation Council).

[72] GATT Doc. BISD 39S/300.

under the heading 8708.10, which reads 'Bumpers and Parts Thereof' in the schedules of all WTO Members alike. What might vary is the tariff treatment of bumpers: the US might impose a 2 per cent import duty, whereas Pakistan might impose a 10 per cent duty. The system is used by more than 190 countries as the basis for their customs tariffs. Not all WTO Members have formally adhered to the HS; however, either for legal reasons (formal adherence to the HS) or de facto, all WTO Members follow the HS classification up to the six-digit level.

From the six-digit level onwards, WTO Members are free to 'shape' their concessions to their liking. In this respect, Art. 3.3 HS reads:

> Nothing in this Article shall prevent a Contracting Party from establishing, in its Customs tariff or statistical nomenclatures, subdivisions classifying goods beyond the level of the Harmonized system, provided that any such subdivision is added and coded at a level beyond that of the six-digit numerical code set out in the Annex to this Convention.

Assuming a WTO Member has made a concession at the four-digit level, it can only treat subclassifications more favourably. An example from the US Tariff Schedule can help explain this point: Chapter 87 of the HS is entitled 'Vehicles other than Railway Rolling-Stock, and Parts and Accessories thereof'. 8708 is entitled 'Parts and Accessories of the Motor Vehicles of Headings 8701 to 8705' (the two categories corresponding to tractors, motor vehicles for the transport of ten or more persons, and motor cars principally designed for the transport of persons). 8708.10 reads 'Bumpers and Parts thereof'. 8708.10.60 reads 'Bumpers' (i.e. stampings).[73] The US bound its tariffs in Chapter 87 at the eight-digit level at 2.7 per cent. This means that, if it enters a new subcategory (of 8708.10.60) at the 10- or 12-digit level, it will be able to impose a maximum duty of 2.7 per cent. A similar outcome would obtain had the US committed to observe a 2.7 per cent ceiling at the four-digit level, that is, for the entry 8708. Any subclassification of this entry (i.e. 8708.01, 8708.02, but also 8708.0101) would have to observe this ceiling and goods classified under these entries could never be subjected to an import duty higher than 2.7 per cent.

Eight-digit descriptions are national classifications. They can be challenged before the WTO for not observing Art. 3.3HS.[74]

The language used in the various nomenclatures is quite generic in light of the fact that the intention was to subsume to each one of them a large number of transactions. As a result, disputes may arise as to the appropriate classification of a

---

[73] It is not the case that in the pre-HS years precise classifications and subclassifications were unknown in customs practice. Irwin (2011, p. 35) refers to the following entry in the Smoot-Hawley Tariff Act: 'bottle caps of metal, collapsible tubes, and sprinkler tops, if not decorated, colored, waxed, lacquered, enamelled, lithographed, electroplated, or embossed in color, 45 per centum ad valorem'.

[74] As we shall see *infra*, the process of certification of schedules of concessions does not at all immunize them from subsequent legal challenges. The AB *EC—Bananas III* report made this point abundantly clear.

particular transaction. Art. 10 HS reflects the dispute settlement provisions available to its signatories. Disputes will be submitted to the HS Committee, which will consider the dispute and make recommendations to the parties. The HS Committee will base its decision on the text of the HS Convention, but also on the General Interpretative Rules (GIR) that it has adopted over the years, as well as, their Explanatory Notes (HSEN). GIR 1, for example, subjects classification according to the terms of a heading, whereas GIR 3(a) stipulates that the heading which provides the most specific description shall be preferred to headings providing a more general description. There are specific GIRs for composite goods.[75]

The legal status of the HS in WTO law is not addressed in the Agreement Establishing the WTO but has been clarified in case law. The Panel report on *EC—Chicken Cuts* held that the HS provides context, in the VCLT sense of the term (Art. 31.2), for the schedules of concessions submitted by WTO Members; as a result, Panels must always take it into account when the issue of interpretation of a particular concession arises. The relevant facts are adequately described in §§7.2 and 7.3 of the report:

> The EC Schedule provides for a tariff of 102.4€/100kg/net for products covered by subheading 0207.14.10 and allows the European Communities to use special safeguard measures under Article 5 of the Agreement on Agriculture in respect of such products. The EC Schedule provides for a tariff of 15.4 per cent *ad valorem* for products covered by subheading 0210.90.20 and there is no reservation for the use of special safeguard measures under Article 5 of the Agreement on Agriculture in respect of such products.
>
> Brazil and Thailand (the complainants) submit that less favourable treatment has been accorded to frozen boneless salted chicken cuts in violation of Article II:1(a) and Article II:1(b) of the GATT 1994 because, through the relevant EC measures, the European Communities changed its customs classification so that those products, which had previously been classified under subheading 0210.90.20 and were subject to an *ad valorem* tariff of 15.4 per cent, are now classified under subheading 0207.14.10 and are subject to a tariff of 102.4€/100kg/net as well as being potentially subject to special safeguard measures pursuant to Article 5 of the Agreement on Agriculture. (italics in the original)

Brazil exported salted meat to the EU market. The EU had entered commitments on meat and salted meat, the latter being more favourable to exports but refused to treat Brazilian exports as 'salted meat'; it maintained that salted meat, if not salted for preservation purposes, could not benefit from the lower tariff since that tariff line was intended to cover meat salted for preservation purposes only. This was not the case with Brazil's exports which, in the EU view, was meat sprinkled with salt, but the quantity of salt would not suffice in order to preserve the meat exported. The Panel rejected the arguments advanced by the EU, and agreed with

---

[75] GIR 3(b).

Brazil.[76] In its view, nothing in the HS description conditioned the classification of salted meat under 02.10 (the relevant HS tariff heading) on the purpose of salting, that is, meat preservation. In doing that, however, it went through all interpretative elements of the VCLT system, paying particular attention to the HS system since it considered it to be the context of the negotiation. There is evidence in the Panel report that the Panel corresponded with the HS Committee to this effect. At the end of the day, however, it decided the issue before it itself (§§7.104ff). The AB upheld the Panel's findings in this respect (§§199ff).[77]

The LAN dispute (*EC—Computer Equipment*) between the US and the EU involved a disagreement between the two parties as to the proper classification of certain computer equipment that the US was exporting to the EU market. The particular commodity (LAN equipment) could, conceivably, come under two different HS classifications; in light of the substantial discrepancy with respect to their tariff treatment, the US had a strong trade interest in seeing it classified under the heading with the lower import duty.[78] To make matters even more complicated, there was divergent practice with respect to the classification of LAN equipment among individual EU Member States. The Panel was asked whether the legitimate expectations of the WTO Member which had negotiated the concession (the US) mattered regarding the classification of the goods. The Panel agreed with the US finding that legitimate expectations, in case of ambiguity, matter. The AB rejected the Panel's interpretation. In its view, if at all, it should be the legitimate expectations of the WTO Membership *in toto* that could be relevant (§§80–96). In its words (§84):

> The purpose of treaty interpretation under Article 31 of the *Vienna Convention* is to ascertain the *common* intention of the parties. These common intentions cannot be ascertained on the basis of the subjective and unilaterally determined 'expectations' of *one* of the parties to a treaty. Tariff concessions provided for in a member's Schedule—the interpretation of which is at issue here—are reciprocal and result from a mutually advantageous negotiation between importing and exporting members. A Schedule is made an integral part of the GATT 1994 by Article II:7 of the GATT 1994. Therefore, the concessions provided for in that Schedule are part of the terms of treaty. As such, the only rules which may be applied in interpreting the

---

[76] Remarkably, in this case, as in *EC—Computer Equipment* before it, the parties to the dispute defended before the Panel the view that their dispute did not concern a classification issue (although this is precisely what this case was all about). The Panel did not disagree with the parties.

[77] The AB took a slightly different view on the use of the interpretative elements, but did not disturb the Panel's findings on the proper classification of salted meat at all. The parties to the dispute could have submitted their dispute to the HS dispute settlement procedures explained *supra*, which they did not. On the other hand, the Panel itself could have used its powers under Art. 13 DSU to request an expert testimony from HS officials. It did not do that either. It did address questions to the HS Committee, but exercised its own discretion when evaluating the responses granted.

[78] This was the first dispute concerning products covered by the Information Technology Agreement (ITA). We discuss its content in more detail *infra*; suffice to state here that classification of products coming under the purview of the ITA was not an exact science, and considerable room for discretion was left to the importing states.

meaning of a concession are the general rules of treaty interpretation set out in the *Vienna Convention*. (italics and emphasis in the original)[79]

This passage is to some extent cryptic,[80] but it seems to provide even more support for the proposition that HS should be the context for all concessions and thus, through this acknowledgement, intense cooperation between Panels and the HS Committee should be encouraged.

2.3 What is Bound?

Art. II GATT explains the process for binding tariff protection. The key terms in this provision are 'ordinary customs duty' (OCD) and 'other duties and charges' (ODC). Neither of the two terms is detailed any further in this provision. Art. II GATT, however, suggests that a dividing line must be drawn between the two terms, since different obligations were, initially at least, assumed with respect to each one of them; the Panel on *Chile–Price Band* first, and the AB later, confirmed that a measure cannot simultaneously be both an OCD and an ODC. This Panel attempted an interpretation of the term OCD. The issue before the WTO adjudicating bodies was the notorious price band system that Chile practised, whereby Chile would not impose a fixed rate of duty on some imports but, instead, a duty which was calculated on the basis of the world price of a given commodity and the corresponding domestic price. Argentina complained that, when applying this system, Chile sometimes imposed duties beyond its bound level. The question was whether the Chilean system qualified as an OCD. The Panel defined OCDs as either *ad valorem* or specific duties that are levied without regard to exogenous factors such as current market prices. The AB disagreed, arguing that many applied duties take into account exogenous factors such as the needs of producers and consumers; it stopped short of providing a precise definition of OCDs since Chile

---

[79] Van Damme (2007) does not agree with this view. She has argued that, although schedules of commitments are undeniably treaty language (and, consequently, it is only appropriate that the starting-point of interpretation is the VCLT), some adjustments are in order in light of their special characteristics. She imports notions of public international law, paying attention to the negotiating record that will help the WTO judge to develop future case law in this field in a coherent manner. She is probably right in that adjustments (in the sense of placing some additional weight on the negotiating record) are warranted in this context. As it stands, the VCLT does not include a coefficient for each of the elements reflected in Arts. 31–2 VCLT: we know that recourse to preparatory work is optional (hence, Art. 32 VCLT plays second fiddle to the elements included in Art. 31 VCLT), and we also know that a conscious attempt was made during the negotiation of the VCLT to downplay the importance of object and treaty; see Jimenez de Arréchaga (1978). The remaining elements of Art. 31 VCLT (text, context, subsequent treaty/practice, other relevant public international law) are prima facie at par, although good arguments can be made in favour of contextual interpretations: words are not a-contextual, and context (not only the 'historic' context) is informative about the rationale for signing a particular agreement.

[80] The AB did not explain at all how one could establish the common intentions of the WTO Membership. It should be noted that the parties to the dispute, by insisting that their dispute was not a tariff classification issue (which it actually was), deprived the WTO adjudicating bodies of the opportunity to address the 'heart' of the claim.

had anyway violated its *tariffication* requirements under Art. 4.2 AG.[81] In the AB's view, all that is required, anyway, for a measure to constitute an OCD is that it is expressed in a particular form (§§264–78).

In practice, OCDs take the following forms:

(a) *ad valorem* duties;
(b) specific duties;
(c) compound duties;
(d) alternative duties (or mixed duties); and
(e) technical duties.

A duty is *ad valorem* when it is a percentage of the value of the imported product (e.g. 15 per cent of a fax machine, the import price of which is $400). A duty is specific when it is related to the weight, volume, surface, etc. of the good at hand (e.g. $20 per ton of imported wheat). A duty is compound when it comprises an *ad valorem* duty to which the customs authority adds or from which it subtracts a specific duty (e.g. 10 per cent on the import price of wheat plus $2 per imported kg of wheat). A duty is alternative or mixed when it ensures a minimum or maximum tariff protection through the choice between, in most cases, an *ad valorem* and a specific duty (e.g. 10 per cent on the import price of or $2 per imported ton of wheat, whichever is the maximum). Finally, particularly where agricultural products are concerned, a technical duty is determined by complex technical factors such as alcohol or sugar content.

The situation is different with respect to ODCs. In the absence of legislative definition the GATT Secretariat was requested to produce a document[82] which provided a road map towards the criteria that should be used in order to define ODCs. The Secretariat document made a number of very important points:

(a) ODCs should be applicable only to imports;
(b) there was nothing like an agreed definition of ODCs;
(c) the applicable date concerning the binding of an ODC;
(d) the legal effect of inscribing an ODC in a schedule of concessions.

Most of these points found their way into the Understanding on the Interpretation of Art. II.1(b) of the GATT, concluded during the Uruguay round. The *travaux préparatoires* of the Understanding reveal the willingness of negotiators to define ODCs by exclusion; it was agreed that it would have been a daunting task to attempt to draw up an exhaustive list of ODCs, a point that the Panel, in its report

---

[81] *Tariffication* refers to the process whereby all pre-existing (pre-Uruguay round) protection of farm goods had to take the form of a tariff. We discuss this concept in Chapter 11. Bagwell and Sykes (2007a) conclude that from an economic perspective it is difficult to state outright whether the Chilean system is trade restrictive or trade liberalizing, since it all depends on the final fixed rate that Chile would ultimately choose. They agree nonetheless that, from a pure legal perspective, the complainant (Argentina) had some strong arguments, which we discuss in more detail in Chapter 11.
[82] GATT Doc. MTN.GNG/NG7/W/53 of 2 October 1989.

on *Dominican Republic—Import and Sale of Cigarettes*, fully endorsed (§7.114). The Understanding provides that:

(a) ODCs have to be recorded in schedules of concessions, otherwise they are *ipso facto* GATT-inconsistent. However, since ODCs are linked to customs duties, and since only bound customs duties appear in a schedule, in practice, ODCs applicable to unbound duties do not have to be included in schedules of concessions;[83]

(b) ODCs are not by virtue of their inclusion in a schedule of concession GATT-consistent. WTO Members can, for a period of three years after the entry into force of the WTO, challenge ODCs reflected in a schedule of concessions either because an ODC did not exist at the time of the original binding of the item in question or because it exceeded its prior level (§4);

(c) Even after this period of three years, WTO Members can still challenge ODCs on grounds other than those mentioned above, that is, challenge them for being GATT-inconsistent (§5).

In practice, ODCs are usually expressed in *ad valorem* terms.[84] The lack of precise definitions for both OCDs and ODCs has not hampered the negotiating process. Nowadays ODCs are being negotiated just like OCDs. As is the case with OCDs, ODCs have to respect the negotiated ceiling through negotiations; they will be reduced, if not eliminated altogether.

2.4 Defining the Value for Customs Purposes

2.4.1 Customs Valuation

When duties are shipped from one country to another, they will form the object of customs valuation (CV). CV is a customs procedure applied to determine the customs value of imported goods upon which import duties will be imposed. CV procedures are applicable only when imported items have to face *ad valorem* duties. In similar transactions, the customs value is essential to determine the duty to be paid on an imported good. Art. VII GATT states that the value of imported merchandise for customs purposes should be based on the actual value of the imported merchandise on which the duty is assessed, and should not be based on the value of merchandise of national origin or on arbitrary or fictitious values. Art VII.2(b) GATT defines actual value in the following terms:

---

[83] The argument, however, could be made that unbound ODCs must observe the transparency requirement laid down in Art. X of the GATT. Assuming this view is upheld in case law, it does not necessarily eliminate all problems that might arise in practice. Interested traders will have to inquire into (sometimes arcane and hard to localize) national laws, instead of simply checking the national schedule of concessions notified to the WTO.

[84] ODCs feature under column 6 of the Uruguay round schedules. Only Botswana, Côte d'Ivoire, Namibia, Swaziland, and South Africa have used compound ODCs.

'Actual value' should be the price at which, at a time and place determined by the legislation of the country of importation, such or like merchandise is sold or offered for sale in the ordinary course of trade under fully competitive conditions. To the extent to which the price of such or like merchandise is governed by the quantity in a particular transaction, the price to be considered should uniformly be related to either (i) comparable quantities, or (ii) quantities not less favourable to importers than those in which the greater volume of the merchandise is sold in the trade between the countries of exportation and importation.

The 1950 Convention on the Valuation of goods for Customs Purposes, better known as the Brussels Definition of Value (BDV), contained a similar concept, the normal price, defined as follows:

The price which [the imported goods] would fetch at the time when the duty becomes payable on a sale in the open market between buyer and seller independent of each other.[85]

It was the Customs Cooperation Council, now known as the World Customs Organization, with its headquarters in Brussels, that would administer customs valuation using BDV, the widest known method at that time. During the Tokyo round, a CV Agreement was adopted which introduced new disciplines, and which has since been superseded by the Uruguay round Agreement on Customs Valuation which we discuss in Chapter 6.

2.4.2 *The Agreement on Pre-shipment Inspection*

Through pre-shipment inspection, one aims to ensure that the quantity and quality of the goods to be exported conform to the specifications reflected in a sales contract. Therefore, while the CV Agreement deals with the value of goods at the point of importation, pre-shipment inspection deals with similar issues (but with a wider range of issues as well) at the point of exportation. We discuss this agreement in more detail in Chapter 6 as well.

2.5 The Forum for Binding Duties: Multilateral Trade Negotiations (Rounds)

Concessions will be exchanged in the context of multilateral trade negotiations, the so-called trade rounds. Art. XXVIIIbis GATT does not set a specific date on which rounds must start; it is the WTO Membership that will decide when to open up multilateral talks. At the moment of writing, we are in the middle of the ninth round since the inception of the GATT, the Doha round.[86] All WTO Members participate in a trade round.

---

[85] This international treaty entered into force on 28 July 1953, and has been reproduced in 171 UNTS 307 (15 December 1950). The provision on *normal price* is included in Annex I.

[86] Rounds, with few exceptions, tend to get their name from the place where negotiations are launched (exceptions include the Kennedy and the Dillon rounds).

The TNC (Trade Negotiating Committee), where representatives of all WTO Members participate, is usually headed by the Director-General of the GATT/WTO who oversees the progress in any multilateral round.

Customs duties will be bound following the procedures laid down in Art. II GATT. There is no obligation to bind all duties and the extent of bindings varies from one WTO Member to another and is the outcome of trade negotiations. Duties will be bound following different procedures: it could be, for example, that WTO Members engage in bilateral negotiations and incur, of course, the obligation to multilateralize the outcome. In this case, things are left 'to the market', so to speak, and one would expect those with the greatest interest in negotiating the tariff treatment of a particular commodity with a specific WTO Member to do so. In other words, the WTO Member with the bargaining power to extract the maximum promise from another WTO Member would be expected to conduct a negotiation, the outcome of which will benefit the rest of the WTO Membership. Yes, in this scenario, there will be free-riding, but since different WTO Members are best placed to negotiate different tariff treatment of different commodities with different WTO Members, there is some sort of distribution of the negotiating costs across the Membership. There should be no doubt nonetheless that the outcome of the distribution is far from being equal for each WTO Member; it is expected that WTO Members enjoying the greatest bargaining power (and which usually also enjoy the largest negotiating resources) will carry most of the negotiating burden as well. As a result, it is expected that those interested in negotiating the tariff treatment of a particular commodity with a particular partner are best placed to extract the best promise.

One cannot exclude outright, however, that some might be unhappy with the outcome of the first negotiation. Assume, for example, that A and B negotiate the import duty on wheat that A will be applying. Assume further that B manages to extract from A a promise that the latter will be applying a 10 per cent duty *ad valorem*. B and A will notify the outcome of their negotiation to the WTO Secretariat. Their agreement, however, remains confidential until the end of negotiations. Nothing, in the meantime, stops C from negotiating with A. A can either repeat its promise to B or move even further if C has something to offer that B could not. In this latter case, one cannot exclude that C might extract a promise from A that the latter imposes a 7 per cent duty on imports of wheat. C will also notify the WTO Secretariat of the bilateral agreement it has reached with A. At the end of the negotiations, A will have to impose, by virtue of the MFN obligation, a 7 per cent import duty on all wheat imported into its market, irrespective of its origin. The promise of a 10 per cent duty it gave to B is not void of consequences: as we shall see *infra*, assuming A wishes, subsequent to the original negotiation and following the procedures established by Art. XXVIII GATT, to revise its duty on wheat upwards, to say 12 per cent, B will be recognized as initial negotiating right (INR) holder, and will have the right to participate in the negotiation.

During some rounds, instead of opting for bilateral negotiations the outcome of which would be multilateralized, trading partners privileged tariff cuts across the board. For example, they have agreed on reducing tariffs by a fixed percentage compared to the level of duties they had bound (or applied) during the previous round. Sometimes, as recently in the context of the Doha round, they have adopted a formula for tariff reductions that would provide some credit to those WTO Members with already low duties and request from those with relatively higher duties to make more important cuts. This is in essence what the *Swiss formula* amounts to: this formula was adopted during the Doha round for the NAMA (non-agricultural market access) negotiations, which cover tariff reductions for manufactured goods. The various modalities for negotiating tariff cuts practised so far can be described as follows:

(a) *Request–offer*: two WTO Members will negotiate tariff cuts (and the identity of the negotiating pair can change as noted above) until a mutually advantageous solution has been reached and the WTO has been notified thereof;

(b) *Linear reduction*: all bound duties are reduced by the same agreed method;

(c) *Harmonized formula*: this method leads to more substantial reduction of higher than of lower tariffs. This is the notorious *Swiss formula* briefly referred to above, which owes its name to the fact that a Swiss delegate first proposed it during the Tokyo round;[87]

(d) *Tiered cuts*: this is reminiscent of but not identical to the Swiss formula. Duties will be divided into bands (tiers) and the duties of higher bands will be cut more drastically than those of the lower band;[88]

(e) *Sectoral approach*: duties will be lowered in a particular sector (it was applied in the negotiation of the Information Technology Agreement which we discuss *infra*).

Once the WTO Membership is satisfied with the content of negotiations, the WTO Secretariat will circulate the members' schedules of concessions (or, as it is sometimes referred to, list of commitments) for verification and certification.[89] Customs duties, irrespective of whether they have been bound or are left unbound, have to be applied, in principle, that is, absent legal justification to this effect, on a

---

[87] Mathematically, linear reduction would look like this: $T^* = C \times T$ (where T^* is the new final rate, C the coefficient for agreed reductions, say 80 per cent, and T the base rate); the Swiss formula, in turn, would look like this: $T^* = C \times T/C + T$.

[88] The difference between (b) and (c), on the one hand, and (d), on the other, is that whereas the former is a formula applied on a tariff line-by-line basis, the latter is not. The latter can take different forms: *simple average reduction*, where one aims at reducing on the average the tariffs of various tariff lines; *reduction in the average*, whereby one compares the average base rates, the average final rates, and then determines the reduction of the latter vis-à-vis the former; *target average*, whereby a specific average that must be met by new bindings is agreed.

[89] We discuss this process in the following sections.

non-discriminatory basis. It has been the case so far that, in an effort to increase bargaining power, alliances have been formed during rounds across like-minded countries to push forward a particular agenda. The CAIRNS group, for example, named after the Australian city where it was first established, became notorious during the Uruguay round for pushing for lower duties in farm goods. Brazil, India, and South Africa head the NAMA 11 group, which has been very active during the NAMA negotiations of the Doha round. During the Doha round, negotiations have mainly centred around three groups:

(a) the OECD (Organisation for Economic Co-operation and Development, that is, the rich countries' club) countries;
(b) the G 20, comprising the leading developing countries, such as Argentina, Brazil, and India;
(c) the G 90, comprising the LDCs (least developed countries), as well as other developing countries.

Most of the negotiations of the Doha round concern demands that the G 20 has been formulating and are directed towards the OECD group (and some counter-demands by the latter directed to the former). The G 90 has been to a considerable extent absent from the negotiating scene, partly motivated by declarations from EU officials that they should have the round for free (that is, without making any concessions). The composition of some of the groups changes over time: the Quad, for example, used to be the all-powerful group comprising the EU, the US, Canada, and Japan. During the Doha round, a new Quad was established, with Brazil and India replacing Canada and Japan.

Notorious across rounds are the so-called Green room meetings, where chosen delegations only participate in meetings in the Director-General's office (which used to be green). The objective is to restrict access to a few key delegations in order to favour agreement. The meetings of Heads of Dels (Heads of Delegations) regroup all heads of delegations to the WTO.

WTO Members will, of course, have to faithfully implement the results of the negotiations. This is what *pacta sunt servanda* amounts to. Accepting the final package engages the international responsibility of those accepting. WTO Members cannot, following acceptance, unilaterally modify the agreed package. Yet, this is what can happen if the US does not enjoy fast-track authority, or Trade Promotion Authority (TPA) as it is officially known. This is a particularity of the US constitutional procedures which should have no bearing on the negotiations, at least from a legal perspective (since the US government is bound by the *pacta sunt servanda* principle, just like any other WTO Member). By agreeing to a fast-track procedure, the US Congress approves or disapproves the final product of negotiations, without being in a position to modify their content. The TPA is accorded for a fixed period of time and can be renewed. To avoid trouble and endless debate on the primacy of international law, the WTO negotiating community strives to conclude a round while the TPA is still in force.

At the end of the negotiating process, some schedules will reflect one (the MFN) and some two tariff rates: the MFN rate, applicable by default, and the preferential rate, applicable to a subset of the WTO Membership (the developing countries, and the countries with which the WTO Member making the tariff promise has entered into a preferential trade agreement). Over subsequent rounds, WTO Members will make new concessions, that is, they will agree to lower bound tariffs. This does not mean, however, that entries prior to the most recent entry become legally irrelevant. In fact, the opposite is true: it is necessary to look, not only at the most recently negotiated concessions, but also to the situation before for the purposes of identifying those entitled to participate in a renegotiation of duties following the procedures established in Art. XXVII GATT, which we discuss *infra* in this chapter.

It could also be the case that an amendment is introduced to a concession, or an amendment is introduced in the period between multilateral trade rounds. These amendments may be termed renegotiations or modifications resulting from action under Arts. II (schedules of concession), XVIII (governmental assistance to economic development), XXIV (PTAs, preferential trade agreements), XXVII (withholding or withdrawal of concessions), or XXVIII GATT (modification of schedules), or even rectifications to correct errors found in the schedules. The value of the amendment will be hard to ascertain absent a look at the history of the concession.

Concessions have also, on occasion, been exchanged in negotiations where only a subset of the WTO Membership participated. For instance, a few WTO Members have taken the initiative and liberalized trade in information technology goods; this is the story of the Information Technology Agreement (ITA).

The ITA was concluded at the Singapore Ministerial Conference[90] in December 1996. At that time, 29 countries (including the then 15 member states of the EU) or separate customs territories signed the declaration. However, it was still unclear at that time whether the provisions of the Declaration would come into effect, as the Declaration stipulated that participants representing approximately 90 per cent of world trade would have to notify their acceptance by 1 April 1997. The original 29 signatories did not reach the 90 per cent trade coverage criterion, since they collectively accounted for only 83 per cent of world trade in information technology (IT) products. However, in the ensuing months after the Singapore Ministerial Conference and leading up to 1 April 1997, a number of other countries expressed an interest in becoming participants in the ITA and notified

---

[90] According to Art. IV of the WTO Agreement, a Ministerial Conference is composed of representatives of all Members and meets at least once every two years. The Ministerial Conference can take decisions on all matters under any of the multilateral trade agreements. Santana (2012) mentions that sectoral initiatives were initiated as early as the Tokyo round. A negotiating group called Sectoral Approach was instituted, aimed at discussing liberalization of trade in electronics, chemicals, etc. In the Uruguay round, the US followed up with a 'zero for zero' initiative on electronics the aim of which was to reduce tariffs in selected goods to 0 per cent.

their acceptance. Thus, the 90 per cent criterion was met, and the ITA entered into force, with the first staged reduction in tariffs occurring on 1 July 1997. Following ITA I, an ITA II was successfully concluded.

All results of the ITA negotiations were subsequently 'multilateralized' and are now applied on non-discriminatory basis. The ITA now has 67 members (counting the EU as 27), 35 of which are developing countries. Together, the 67 members of the ITA represent approximately 97 per cent of world trade in IT products. Mexico and Brazil are the most important non-ITA participants, accounting for more or less 3 per cent of world ITA trade. After its peak in 2000 (16.5 per cent), the ITA now accounts for approximately 12 per cent of total world exports; the share of ITA products in world trade exceeds (in 2006) that of farm products. With the outcome of the Doha round still pending, it is probably fair to state that the ITA is the most important MFN trade liberalization initiative after the Uruguay round.[91]

The ITA has given rise to disputes regarding classification of products coming under its purview. This is probably due to the fact that it suffers from a birth defect: when concluded, its product coverage was reflected in two attachments, the first of which (Attachment A) would include HS numbers (and, hence, no or little doubt would exist as to its coverage); this Attachment was divided into two Sections: Section 1 dealt with specific products, the tariff classification of which was undisputed, whereas in Section 2 machinery necessary to produce specific products had been included and, for some of the items there, an initial agreement was reached to discuss them in the same manner as the goods featured in Attachment B. The second, the notorious 'Attachment B', included product descriptions, the tariff classification of which was in dispute among the WTO Members. We read, for example, entries such as 'network equipment', or 'flat panel displays', or 'multimedia upgrade kits'. Such entries were prone to creating a divergence of views across participants as to what precisely was covered. To make matters worse, technology moves faster than the relevant WCO Committee meets and adds new products to the existing HS list. Signatories to the ITA agreed to meet periodically in order to specify and update the coverage of the ITA, and ideally to make unanimous suggestions to the WCO Committee.[92]

The periodic meetings notwithstanding, divergences still exist between the various players[93] and often give rise to disputes. The question, for example, did arise in practice what to do between the advent of a new good and its classification.

---

[91] There have been calls to conclude an ITA III, estimating an additional $800 billion of gains to be added to the staggering $4 trillion already created through prior liberalization; see for example the estimations offered in Conconi and Howse (2012). At the time of writing, similar views have fallen on deaf ears; see New ITA Talks Would Face Challenge of Building 'Critical Mass' of Support, *Inside US Trade*, 17 June 2011. Feenstra et al. (2009) measure the remarkable productivity growth as a result of the ITA.

[92] WTO Doc. WT/MIN(96)/16 of 13 December 1996; WTO Doc. G/L/160 of 2 April 1997.

[93] For an illustration, see the discussions reflected in WTO Doc. G/IT/W/33 of 18 May 2011.

And what if the new good is 'multifunctional' and could thus be described either as an ITA or as a consumer good? In theory, various criteria are available: one could use, for example, in case of ambiguity, the preponderant commercial use when multifunctional goods are at issue. Absent agreement nonetheless, practice often evidences disagreements and the result is uncertainty with respect to classification. Uncertainty is an obstacle and ultimately investment in innovation might be negatively affected.[94]

The LAN dispute (*EC—Computer Equipment*), quoted briefly above, between the US and the EU involved a disagreement between the two parties as to the proper classification of certain computer equipment. The products concerned were computers and network equipment. Computers are defined in the ITA as automatic data processing machines capable of storing the processing program or programs and at least the data immediately necessary for the execution of the program; being freely programmed in accordance with the requirements of the user; performing arithmetical computations specified by the user; and executing, without human intervention, a processing program which requires them to modify their execution by logical decision during the processing run. The agreement covers such automatic data processing machines whether or not they are able to receive and process with the assistance of central processing unit telephony signals, television signals, or other analogue or digitally processed audio or video signals. Machines performing a specific function other than data processing, or incorporating or working in conjunction with an automatic data processing machine, and not otherwise specified under Attachment A or B, are not covered by this agreement. Network equipment is defined as Local Area Network (LAN) and Wide Area Network (WAN) apparatus, including those products dedicated for use solely or principally to permit the interconnection of automatic data processing machines and units thereof for a network that is used primarily for the sharing of resources such as central processor units, data storage devices, and input or output units—including adapters, hubs, in-line repeaters, converters, concentrators, bridges and routers, and printed circuit assemblies for physical incorporation into automatic data processing machines and units thereof. One can immediately understand that a number of products can either totally or partially come under this definition. The classification issue is with respect to the latter category. Neither the Panel nor the AB decisively addressed the main issue at dispute and the final outcome could be described as a 'pyrrhic' victory for the US, in the sense that EU practice was not decisive for the classification of the goods concerned.

A first response comes to this question in *EC—IT Products*. The Panel dealt with a challenge against the EU classification of three goods that, in the complainants' opinion, were ITA goods and hence should be benefiting from tariff-free entry, whereas in the EU view they should be classified as consumer goods and

---

[94] Arrow (1962).

accordingly burdened by a 14 per cent duty.[95] The Panel did not accept the EU view that the products, because of their additional function, were totally new, and requested the EU to take corrective action. Key to the Panel's findings (based in part on a headnote appearing across various schedules) was that it asked whether the disputed good could come under one of the product descriptions included in Attachment B: if the response was affirmative, then the good would enjoy zero tariff treatment; if the response was negative, then it would be subjected to the tariff treatment provided for in the national schedule and applicable to the relevant consumer good. The remedy that the Panel recommended was not identical across the three products, the classification of which was an issue: when the Panel felt more at ease that the additional function did not substantially alter the nature of the original product, it would recommend that the EU applied the lower tariff treatment.

2.6 Certification, Modification, and Rectification of Schedules

Until 1959 changes at the tariff level were incorporated into the GATT and its schedules through a series of protocols. There were five protocols of rectification in total, one protocol of modification, and nine protocols of rectification and modification: the term *rectification* essentially captures mundane changes (whereby the level of the tariff concession is not affected), whereas the term *modification* refers to substantive changes, such as those resulting from a renegotiation of duties conducted under Art. XXVIII GATT. Eventually, the Protocol would be registered in accordance with the provisions of Art. 102 of the UN Charter.[96]

In 1959, the CONTRACTING PARTIES agreed to adopt a procedure of certification and discontinue the practice of preparing protocols of rectifications and modifications, subject to the revised text of Art. XXX GATT being accepted. This was indeed the case; the protocol amending Art. XXX GATT was adopted, but its authority lapsed in 1967. Following this, the CONTRACTING PARTIES decided in November 1968 to establish certification procedures applicable to both modifications and rectifications as well. To this effect, they adopted a decision aimed at introducing formalism and thus establishing some sort of an institutional 'gatekeeper': the 1968 Procedures for Modification and Rectification[97] explain that all *modifications* and *rectifications* would have to take place through *certifications*; the idea is that certifications will constitute some sort of formal multilateral approval of all modifications and/or rectifications effected. Six collective

---

[95] This is also what happened in the *EC—Computer Equipment* dispute. A new product appears in the market and the various EU Member States adopt different tariff policies until the issue is resolved either through the intervention of the EU Commission or through the WTO in case of adjudication. The latter is of course a substantially longer process and political economy might push resolution in one direction or the other.

[96] Jackson (1969, pp. 211ff).

[97] GATT Doc. BISD 16S/16ff.

certifications were adopted under this decision, which was finally replaced by another, more detailed, decision adopted in 1980, the Decision on Procedures for Modification and Rectification of Schedules of Tariff Concessions.[98] Although the 1980 Decision refers to modifications resulting from actions under specified Articles, in practice these procedures have also been used to include schedules of unilateral commitments made pursuant to, for example, the ITA.

The 1980 Decision confirms that modifications imply substantive change of the concession (§1 of the 1980 Decision), whereas rectifications imply no such change (§2 of the 1980 Decision). Modifications could be the outcome of action under various provisions, and the 1980 Decision mentions to this effect Arts. II, XVIII, XXIV, XXVII, and XXVIII GATT. The 1980 Decision further confirms that multilateral review for both rectifications and modifications was necessary, probably because there is often a fine line between the two, or even because WTO Members might have an incentive to cheat and call rectification what should be understood as modification. Consequently, both modifications and rectifications will be communicated to the Director-General of the WTO. Modifications have to be communicated within three months after the action (under one of the provisions mentioned above) has been completed. Rectifications must be communicated within six months after the amendment has been introduced in national legislation or, in case of other rectifications, whenever the circumstances permit this to be the case. If no objection has been raised within three months from the communication, the notified modifications and/or rectifications become certifications (§3 of the 1980 Decision).

There should be no doubt that the 1980 Decision is part of GATT 1994 by virtue of Art. 1(b)(iv) of this agreement, since it is a formal decision adopted by the CONTRACTING PARTIES.

Certification does not confer legality: as we discuss in detail *infra* (when we examine the AB report on *EC—Bananas III*), it seems safe to conclude that consenting to a modified schedule means that the WTO Membership has conceded that the schedule at hand is accurate, but it does not necessarily also mean that it has consented to its legality. WTO Members have not, by virtue of the 1980 Decision, given up their rights to subsequently challenge the consistency of modified (or rectified) schedules with the multilateral rules. Indeed, this is exactly what happened in *EC—Bananas III*, where a host of trading nations challenged the certified EU schedule and their challenge was deemed perfectly legitimate by the WTO adjudicating bodies.

Unilateral actions that have not been certified risk being challenged before the WTO and eventually being deemed illegal. This issue arose for the first time during the proceedings that led to the GATT Panel report on *Spain—Unroasted*

---

[98] Decision of 26 March 1980, L/4962, GATT Doc. BISD 27S/25–6, hereinafter the 1980 Decision.

Coffee. Spain had originally made a tariff concession on unroasted coffee whereby it was not differentiating between the various types.[99] It then modified its negotiated concession by reserving a tariff treatment to 'unwashed Arabia' and 'Robusta' coffees that was less favourable than that reserved for 'mild' coffee (all three types of coffee being unroasted coffee): whereas it kept a 0 per cent duty on the latter, it imposed a 7 per cent duty on the former. Brazil complained since, as a result of this intervention, its coffee exports to the Spanish market were being negatively affected. The Panel outlawed the Spanish measure (§4.4):

> The Panel found that there was no obligation under the GATT to follow any particular system for classifying goods, and that a contracting party had the right to introduce in its customs tariff new positions or sub-positions as appropriate.

A footnote to this paragraph reads:

> Provided that a reclassification *subsequent* to the making of a concession under the GATT would not be a violation of the basic commitment regarding that concession (Article II:5). (emphasis added)

In this case, the Panel found that the various types of coffee were like products and that, in the absence of prior distinction across the three types, Spain was in violation of its obligations (§4.10).[100]

Usually, schedules will be annexed to the final agreement concluding a round and will be open for signature to all WTO Members.[101]

In *EC—Bananas III,* a dispute between the EU and various banana-exporting countries, the AB had the opportunity to address the obligations of WTO Members when scheduling their tariff commitments. The EU had included in its schedule of concessions a condition, according to which some WTO Members (which had concluded the so-called Framework Agreement with the EU) could profit from a preferential rate on bananas, as did the ACP countries, whereas the remaining WTO Members would not profit from similar treatment. A series of banana-exporting WTO Members complained, claiming that the measure at hand was inconsistent with the MFN rule. The EU argued in response that its regime was consistent with Art. II.1(b) GATT, that it had been notified the WTO

---

[99] GATT Doc. BISD 28S/102ff.

[100] A case similar to *Spain—Unroasted Coffee* arose recently: Panama eliminated from its schedule item 1901.10.10 (modified milk), to which it applied a 5 per cent duty. It then created two new tariff items: 1901.10.11 (infant milk formula), with an import tariff of 0 per cent, and 1901.10.19 (other), with an import tariff of 65 per cent. Mexico complained since, in its view, this unilateral modification violated, *inter alia*, Art II. of the GATT (WTO Doc. WT/DS329/1). The parties to the dispute reached a mutually agreed solution (MAS) that they notified to the WTO, whereby Panama agreed to reduce the tariff on item 1901.10.19 to 5 per cent (WTO Doc. WT/DS329/2).

[101] See, for example, GATT Doc. L/7463 of 24 May 1994, reflecting the Geneva (1994) Protocol to the GATT to which the schedules of concessions made during the Uruguay round were annexed. See also GATT Doc. PC/M/2 of 2 June 1994 at p 3. Hoda (2001) includes at pp. 227ff all protocols signed at the end of each GATT round since the inception of the GATT and until (and including) the Uruguay round.

Membership, and had also gone through the certification process without any WTO Member raising an issue as to its legality. It consequently requested the Panel to dismiss all claims.[102]

The Panel first, followed by the AB, recalling the earlier *Headnote* jurisprudence, rejected the argument of the defendant. In their view, a WTO Member can, through conditions attached to its schedule, grant other WTO Members rights, but it cannot, through this means, diminish its obligations (§§157–8):

> That said, we do not see anything in Article 4.1 to suggest that market access concessions and commitments made as a result of the Uruguay Round negotiations on agriculture can be inconsistent with the provisions of Article XIII of the GATT 1994. There is nothing in Articles 4.1 or 4.2, or in any other article of the *Agreement on Agriculture*, that deals specifically with the allocation of tariff quotas on agricultural products. If the negotiators had intended to permit Members to act inconsistently with Article XIII of the GATT 1994, they would have said so explicitly. The *Agreement on Agriculture* contains several specific provisions dealing with the relationship between articles of the *Agreement on Agriculture* and the GATT 1994. For example, Article 5 of the *Agreement on Agriculture* allows Members to impose special safeguards measures that would otherwise be inconsistent with Article XIX of the GATT 1994 and with the *Agreement on Safeguards*. In addition, Article 13 of the *Agreement on Agriculture* provides that, during the implementation period for that agreement, Members may not bring dispute settlement actions under either Article XVI of the GATT 1994 or Part III of the *Agreement on Subsidies and Countervailing Measures* for domestic support measures or export subsidy measures that conform fully with the provisions of the *Agreement on Agriculture*. With these examples in mind, we believe it is significant that Article 13 of the *Agreement on Agriculture* does not, by its terms, prevent dispute settlement actions relating to the consistency of market access concessions for agricultural products with Article XIII of the GATT 1994. As we have noted, the negotiators of the *Agreement on Agriculture* did not hesitate to specify such limitations elsewhere in that agreement; had they intended to do so with respect to Article XIII of the GATT 1994, they could, and presumably would, have done so. We note further that the *Agreement on Agriculture* makes no reference to the *Modalities* document or to any 'common understanding' among the negotiators of the Agreement *on* Agriculture that the market access commitments for agricultural products would not be subject to Article XIII of the GATT 1994.
>
> For these reasons, we agree with the Panel's conclusion that the *Agreement on Agriculture* does not permit the European Communities to act inconsistently with the requirements of Article XIII of the GATT 1994. (emphasis in the original)

The AB did not even summarily discuss the legal value of the certification process. By finding against the EU though, the AB at the very least implicitly accepted that certification does not confer legality. The outcome is not intellectually indefensible: were one to introduce a comprehensive legal review of all schedules at the end

---

102 The case concerned consistency with Art. 4.1 AG, which deals with farm goods only and is the parallel provision to Art. II GATT. There should be no doubt that, in light of the symmetric expression adopted in the two provisions and their identical function, the AB decision is relevant for all tariff concessions.

of a negotiation, the process would be disproportionately burdened; in the absence of centralized control of legality in the WTO (the Secretariat does not have any powers to this effect), it would be essentially incumbent upon WTO Members to check each other's schedule from a GATT-consistency perspective. Disagreements would have, by virtue of Art. 23.2 DSU, to be submitted to Panels, and one could potentially imagine dozens of Panels introduced at this stage. It thus seems reasonable to defend, from a policy perspective at least, the (implicit) thesis advocated by the AB: the multilateral review occurring with the exchange of schedules is limited to verification of the accuracy of commitments; the multilateral review has no bearing on their legality (GATT consistency). The conclusion should be the same from a pure legal perspective as well: an agreement like the one described here has undeniable negative external effects for non-participants; by reducing tariffs to those that signed the agreement with it, the EU would be diverting trade of bananas from historic suppliers to those who had now signed the agreement with it. Those that did not participate in the agreement would be facing adverse trade consequences although they had been promised MFN trade. The AB was, for all practical purposes, addressing these negative external effects here. Essentially, the AB, in *EC—Bananas III*, closed the door to the MFN deviations that the EU was opening up: MFN deviations cannot be the subject-matter of negotiations that lead to *inter se* agreements. Deviations from the MFN principle will have to be based on provisions of the GATT.[103]

Schedules of concessions differ across rounds. The agreed form of the Uruguay round schedules is schedules consisting of four parts.[104] Part I is divided into two sections, the first referring to agricultural tariff concessions (and is subdivided into two parts, tariffs and tariff quotas), whereas the second deals with all other products. Part II concerns preferential tariffs from the early GATT days (no entries are reported). Part III deals with non-tariff measures (only El Salvador and Indonesia have included entries); and Part IV concerns commitments with respect to domestic and export subsidies on farm goods. Part I contains occasional Headnotes (where a WTO Member might explain the implementation of its commitments),[105] and ten columns. Column 1 reflects the tariff line (e.g. HS 224646); column 2, the product description; column 3, tariff quotas (if applicable); column 4, the *base rate of duty* (the point of departure for the Uruguay round

---

[103] The AB confirmed this ruling in its report on *EC—Poultry* (§§ 98–9). Another argument in favour of the AB approach would be the following: certification does not take place within a forum, such as the Ministerial Conference, with the powers to confer legality on the outcome of negotiations.

[104] WTO doc. MTN.GNG/MA/W/25 of 25 December 1993. In 2009, the WTO issued a substantial booklet explaining the content of schedules of concessions, entitled *A Handbook on Reading WTO Goods and Services Schedules*, WTO and Cambridge University Press: Geneva.

[105] For example, we read in Canada's Uruguay round schedule the following headnote: 'Unless otherwise specified in column 5, the reductions in tariffs provided for in Section IA shall be implemented in equal annual installments beginning in the year 1995 and ending in the year 2000, with the exception of tariff items . . .'.

cuts, either bound or applied on 1 September 1986); column 5, the *final bound rate of duty* (that is, the bound level committed during the Uruguay round); column 6, the implementation period (at the end of which the WTO Member must at the very least apply its final bound rate of duty); column 7, special provision for agricultural products;[106] column 8, initial negotiating rights;[107] column 9, ODCs; and column 10, other terms and conditions (clarifications on the scope of the commitment which, the AB recognized in §7.151 of its report on *Canada–Dairy*, have legal impact).

It follows that the schedules of the Uruguay round do not contain any information regarding preferential rates applied to preferential partners (such as those belonging to the same free trade area or those benefiting by reason of their status as developing countries): tariff treatment of this sort will be reflected elsewhere.[108]

2.7 Switching between Different Types of Duties

The AB, in its report on *Argentina—Footwear*, faced the following situation: Argentina had bound its duties on footwear, during the Uruguay round, as *ad valorem*. Subsequently, it had been applying to imports of footwear either an *ad valorem* duty of 35 per cent or a specific duty which was calculated on the basis of the world price. It later decided to apply specific duties only. Since, in its view, the case did not concern a change in the bound duties, it did not notify it in accordance with the 1980 Decision. The complainant argued that such a change was not permissible (essentially because, in its view, through binding, WTO Members agreed neither to impose tariffs beyond the ceiling imposed nor to change the type of duties). The Panel upheld its claim. Overturning the Panel finding in this respect, the AB held that switching between different types of duties is perfectly legitimate as long as the overall ceiling of protection has not been violated (§§44–55). The AB did, nevertheless, find that Argentina had violated its obligations since, following the conversion, the resulting duty was higher than the negotiated ceiling.

The ruling by the AB is not totally unproblematic. When duties are bound at an *ad valorem* rate, a promise is given that a certain rate will be applied independently of price fluctuations. It is expected that, to the extent that prices decrease, a rather reasonable assumption for many goods, imported goods will be burdened less. Consequently, when duties are being negotiated and an *ad valorem* duty has been agreed, the eventual decreasing burden of the duty is something contracting partners will reasonably have in mind and, arguably, pay for when they reciprocally

---

[106] Such as the Special Agricultural Safeguard (SSG), the Special Safeguard Mechanism (SSM), Special Products (SP): we discuss these issues in Chapter 11.

[107] See *infra* in this chapter our discussion on renegotiating tariff commitments.

[108] We discuss both cases in the next chapter.

agree their own concessions. Specific duties on the other hand, are delinked from the price of the imported item. As a result, the advantage mentioned above (that is, the decreasing burden of the duty when prices fall) is lost any time duties are expressed in terms of specific duties. Allowing for conversion might thus amount to undoing the balance of rights and obligations as struck by the trading nations. On this line of thinking, even if one were to go back in time at the moment when the concession was negotiated and convert the rate of protection from an *ad valorem* to a specific duty (as the report suggests), one would still not account for the fact that a higher price (in the form of reciprocal tariff binding) has probably been paid in order to persuade (in this case) Argentina to express its commitment in *ad valorem* rather than in specific duty terms.

Argentina, as noted *supra*, did not have to follow the procedures of the 1980 Decision since the case concerned applied and not bound duties. Argentina, nonetheless, could not argue that there is a void in the WTO arsenal in this respect: a General Council Decision dating from 1997[109] requests WTO Members to notify all information regarding not only current bound, but also current applied, duties on an annual basis.[110] Argentina, alas, did not do so. The Panel and the AB report did not insist on this failure; wrongly so, in our view.[111]

2.8 Withdrawing Concessions from Members Leaving the WTO

Art. XXVII GATT allows WTO Members to withhold or withdraw concessions vis-à-vis other trading nations that never joined the institution or that left it (see Table 2.2). There has been some practice in this context. A very representative example is offered by the United Kingdom-Palestine negotiations. Upon termination of the mandate that the League of Nations provided the United Kingdom with respect to Palestine, the successor state could not be regarded as being bound by obligations under the GATT; the Declaration adopted by the CONTRACTING PARTIES on 9 May 1949 provides:

> *Whereas* the Government of the United Kingdom in the course of the negotiations leading up to the drawing up of the General Agreement on Tariffs and Trade in 1947, negotiated on behalf of the mandated territory of Palestine for concessions to be accorded to products originating in such territory and for concessions to be accorded to the products of other contracting parties entering such territory, and
>
> *Whereas* the Government of the United Kingdom ceased to be responsible for the mandated territory of Palestine on 15 May 1948,

---

[109] WTO Doc. WT/L/225 of 18 July 1997.

[110] WTO Doc. G/MA/IDB/1/Rev. 1 of 27 June 1997.

[111] Additionally, Argentina overlooked a best endeavours commitment it had undertaken by virtue of the Uruguay round Decision on Notification Procedures 'to notify, to the maximum extent possible, adoption of trade measures affecting the operation of GATT 1994'. A change in the type of duty imposed arguably falls squarely within the class of measures that should be notified.

Table 2.2 Withdrawal of concessions under Art. XXVI GATT

Concessions granted by	Initially negotiated with	Reference
Australia	China, Syria/Lebanon, Philippines	L/1266
Benelux: Section A—Metropolitan Territories	China, Syria/Lebanon, Liberia, Philippines	L/674
Benelux: Section C—Netherlands New Guinea	China	L/658 and Add.1
Canada	China, Liberia, Philippines, Korea	L/553
Ceylon	China	L/1102, L/1505
Chile	Colombia	L/3191
Czechoslovakia	Palestine	GATT/CP/23
Finland	China	L/659
France	China, Syria/Lebanon, Philippines	L/460 and L/1269
Germany, Fed. Rep.	Philippines	L/1264
India	China, Colombia, Philippines	G/77 and L/1430
Pakistan	China	L/1293
Sweden	Colombia, Philippines, China	L/950
United Kingdom	China	L/786
United States	China	GATT/CP/115 and Add.3
Uruguay	China, Colombia	L/1613

The CONTRACTING PARTIES

Declare that, since the United Kingdom ceased, as from 15 May 1948, to be a contracting party in respect of the territory formerly included in the Palestine mandate,

1. Section E shall be deemed to be no longer part of Schedule XIX; and
2. Any contracting party shall, in accordance with Article XXVII of the General Agreement, be free to withhold or withdraw, in whole or in part, any concession provided for in the appropriate schedule annexed to the GATT which such contracting party determines was initially negotiated with the United Kingdom on behalf of Palestine, provided that the contracting party taking such action shall give notice to all other contracting parties and, upon request, consult with the contracting parties which have a substantial interest in the product concerned.

There have been other cases, namely, in the late GATT years, when we came close to adding to the above list with the 'freezing' of Yugoslavia's participation in the GATT. During the late 1980s/early 1990s, the Yugoslav Federation slowly collapsed and new state entities appeared on the international scene. One of them, the Federal Republic of Yugoslavia, claimed to be the successor of the Yugoslav Federation and requested to be acknowledged as such: the consequence, had its request been accepted, would have been that the new state would have preserved the GATT contracting-party status originally obtained by the Yugoslav Federation. However, other GATT contracting parties reacted negatively to this request and, through collective action, 'froze' the participation of the Federal Republic of Yugoslavia in the GATT:[112]

> Yugoslavia
>
> - Status as a contracting party (L/7000, L/7002, L/7007, L/7008, L/7009, L/7022)
>
> The Chairman said that the break-up of the former Socialist Federal Republic of Yugoslavia had posed the question of its status as a contracting party. While the delegation speaking in the name of the Federal Republic of Yugoslavia (FRY) had laid claim to the status of successor to the former Socialist Federal Republic of Yugoslavia (L/7000), this claim had been contested by some contracting parties and some others had reserved their position on the issue. Some contracting parties had also suggested that the delegation claiming to represent the FRY as a successor to the Socialist Federal Republic of Yugoslavia (SFRY) in GATT should not participate in GATT activities until the FRY had sought fresh membership, while others held the view that its participation should be without prejudice to the FRY's claim to successor status. He had held extensive informal consultations with contracting parties and believed there was agreement that this issue would need consideration by the Council. In these circumstances, without prejudice to the question of who should succeed the former SFRY in the GATT, and until the Council considered this issue, he proposed that the representative of the FRY should refrain from participating in the business of the Council. The Council so agreed.

What exactly was meant by the phrase 'that the representative of the FRY should refrain from participating in the business of the Council' was made clear in subsequent practice: the Federal Republic of Yugoslavia did not participate in the General Council meetings. Later, with the advent of the WTO, Serbia and Montenegro first (a state entity corresponding geographically to the Federal Republic of Yugoslavia) and then other former Yugoslav republics requested accession anew to the WTO and working parties were established to this effect.[113]

In recent years, there have been no cases concerning application of Art. XXVII GATT. Although there is a specific provision in the Agreement Establishing the WTO regulating withdrawal from the WTO (Art. XV), there are no reported cases of withdrawal.

2.9 Renegotiating Tariff Protection

A WTO Member can increase its bound protection on a given tariff line provided that the multilateral process included in Art. XXVIII GATT has been followed: in

---

[112] GATT Doc. C/M/257 of 10 July 1992.

[113] Subsequently, Montenegro seceded and the two states (Serbia, Montenegro) are currently negotiating their accession to the WTO. In the meantime, they have both obtained observer status. Croatia (2000), the Former Yugoslav Republic of Macedonia (2003), Montenegro (2011), and Slovenia (1995) have all joined the WTO since the splitting up of the Yugoslav Federation.

the typical case, the Member wishing to raise its duties on a bound item will negotiate and agree compensation (that is, a lowering of protection on items other than the one where an increase of protection is being requested) with a subset of the WTO Membership that has been more severely affected by the tariff change. The agreed compensation will be applied on an MFN basis. According to Art. XXVIII.2 GATT, the WTO Members participating in the renegotiation of the concession:

> shall endeavour to maintain a general level of reciprocal and mutually advantageous concessions not less favourable to trade than that provided for in this Agreement prior to such negotiations.

Art. XXVIII GATT epitomizes the idea that the GATT is about maintaining a level of reciprocally negotiated concessions: tariff adjustments might be deemed necessary for a variety of reasons over time, and what matters is that WTO Members feel that they 'get their concession's worth' at all times. In principle, tariff flexibility can help induce more meaningful commitments in the first place: other things equal, a trading nation will be more willing to make a deep tariff cut (and benefit from the corresponding tariff cuts that its partners will make) if it knows it can always go back to another less trade-liberalizing equilibrium than if it makes only rigid tariff cuts that it can never revise upwards. The GATT does not inquire into the reasons why a WTO Member might want to avail itself of this provision. Consequently, although good theoretical arguments could support the inclusion of this provision in the GATT system, there is nothing wrong with invoking it out of mere political expediency. For example, for political economy reasons, a WTO Member might be willing to redistribute wealth among its constituencies, by over-exposing some producers to international competition (this is what the Art. XXVIII GATT compensation essentially amounts to), while sheltering others from it (this is what the increase in the level of tariff protection will lead to). It can use the procedures established in this provision to this effect.

2.9.1 The Participants in the Negotiation

The procedure starts with a request by the WTO Member interested in renegotiating its bound level of duties on a tariff line (the requesting WTO Member). In principle, all WTO Members, either actually or potentially, will be affected by the new higher duty that will be agreed at the end of the negotiation. Had they all participated in the negotiation, the negotiation itself would have been quite costly. The GATT, in an effort to speed up the negotiation process, limits participation to those WTO Members that are primarily affected by the request to renegotiate the concession, namely,[114] the INR (initial negotiating rights) holders; and the PSI

---

[114] Speeding up the process is not an innocent legislative option: the GATT thus takes a stance in favour of contract flexibility (since the counterfactual is a slower negotiation which could go on for a

(principal supplying interest) WTO Members. These two categories of WTO Members, along with the requesting WTO Member, are the *primarily concerned parties*. A third category, the WTO Members having a *substantial interest* (SI), will be consulted, but have no legal right to participate in the negotiations.

In case negotiations do not manage to produce an agreement, the requesting WTO Member will still be free to increase its tariff protection. INR holders, PSIs, and SIs will have, according to Art. XXVIII.3 GATT, the right to withdraw substantially equivalent concessions. The text of the agreement, as we shall see *infra*, leaves unanswered the question whether such withdrawal of concessions will be on a bilateral or on an *erga omnes* basis. This provision allows for efficient breach of contract without explicitly saying so, since injured parties will be removing equivalent (to the damage suffered) concessions. SIs, on the other hand, have the legal right to withdraw substantially equivalent concessions if they are not satisfied with the offer of the requesting WTO Member, even if the *primarily concerned parties* have reached an agreement between them (Art. XXVIII.3(b) GATT).

INR holders: A WTO Member is an INR holder if it has originally negotiated a specific concession with another WTO Member. The form of international negotiations, however, can prejudge the manner in which INR holders will be identified. During some trade rounds, concessions were negotiated and concluded on a bilateral basis. In such cases, the identification of the INR holder is a simple factual question: these are the so-called fixed INRs. Fixed INRs are subdivided into historic INRs and current INRs. Take the example of a concession on fax machines. Assume that during the Tokyo round India bound the duties on fax machines at 15 per cent as a result of a negotiation that it conducted with Japan. During the Uruguay round, India agrees to reduce the duty on fax machines to 10 per cent. This time, however, it negotiated the concession with Korea. Japan is the historic INR holder and Korea is the current INR holder (until, of course, in the context of a new round, India agrees to further reduce its customs duty on fax machines and then negotiates with a third country). Historic INR holders retain their legal right to participate in an Art. XXVIII GATT negotiation only if the proposed tariff increase exceeds the level of the duty at its historical level (e.g. in the example of fax machines, India requests, after the conclusion of the Uruguay round, an increase of its duty for fax machines at a level higher than 15 per cent). Otherwise, they will not be participating.

During some other trade rounds (e.g. the Kennedy round) concessions were not negotiated bilaterally. Trading nations agreed tariff cuts using a formula: for example, they all agreed to reduce tariff protection on industrial goods by 50 per cent independently of the level of protection on these goods in each individual

---

long time). The fact that at the end of the day, even in the absence of agreement, the requesting WTO Member can go ahead and modify its concession (albeit at the risk of facing countermeasures) is yet another step towards favouring contract flexibility.

country. In such cases, it is impossible to have fixed INRs. At the end of the Kennedy round, the GATT CONTRACTING PARTIES adopted the following decision to address this issue:

> In respect of the concessions specified in the Schedules annexed to the Geneva (1967) Protocol, a contracting party shall, when the question arises, be deemed for the purposes of the General Agreement to be the contracting party with which a concession was initially negotiated if it had during a representative period prior to that time a principal supplying interest in the product concerned.[115]

These are known as floating INRs. Floating INRs will be identified in practice subsequent to the Kennedy round in the same way as PSI countries.

Historic INRs have not always been incorporated into successive schedules of concessions. To reduce uncertainty in this respect, the WTO membership has undertaken a series of initiatives. For example, the Council for Trade in Goods (CTG) adopted the Decision on the Establishment of Loose-Leaf Schedules in November 1996 (WTO Doc. G/L/138):

> Each Member shall include in its schedule all INRs at the current bound rate. Other Members may request the inclusion of any INR that had been granted to them. Historical INRs different from the current bound rate not specifically identified shall remain valid where a Member modifies its concession at a rate different from the rate at which the INR was granted.

The situation has further improved with the finalization of the Consolidated Tariff Schedules (CTS) Database which provides consolidated information on the schedules of concessions of members.

One may wonder what nowadays explains the inclusion of INRs in the negotiation. Trade patterns change quite fast and the presumption that INRs continue to be big players in the market of the WTO Member requesting a renegotiation of duties should not hold. Indeed, the fact that, as we shall see in what immediately follows, the number of PSIs is limited to one or two per negotiation suggests that WTO Members with a bigger interest than INRs will not be allowed to participate in a negotiation, the outcome of which might have more of an impact on them rather than on the INR holder(s). There is a presumption that there is still an export interest in the market requesting

---

115 Recommendation adopted on 16 November 1967, GATT Doc. BISD 15S/67. Although the term 'recommendation' was privileged, there should be no doubt that this is a Decision by the GATT CONTRACTING PARTIES and part of GATT 1994. As Mavroidis (2008) explains, contracting parties used different names when adopting decisions without ever clarifying why this had been the case. What mattered is whether they would in practice conform to whatever they had decided and this is what happened in this case as well.

renegotiation; however, this presumption becomes weaker and weaker as time passes by.

PSI countries: there are two definitions of a PSI. First, the Interpretative Note ad Art. XXVIII GATT defines a PSI as a member which:

> has had, over a reasonable period of time prior to the negotiations, a *larger share in the market of the applicant contracting party* than a contracting party with which the concession was initially negotiated or would, in the judgment of the CONTRACT-ING PARTIES, have had such a share in the absence of discriminatory quantitative restrictions by the applicant contracting party. (emphasis added)

Second, the same Interpretative Note ad Art. XXVIII GATT provides a second (exceptional) definition of the term:

> the CONTRACTING PARTIES may exceptionally determine that a contracting party has a principal supplying interest if the concession in question affects trade which constitutes *a major part of the local exports of such contracting party*. (emphasis added)

During the Uruguay round negotiations, an Understanding on the Interpretation of Art. XXVIII GATT was adopted which, *inter alia*, defines PSIs in §1:

> For the purposes of modification or withdrawal of a concession, the WTO member which has *the highest ratio of exports affected by the concession* (i.e., exports of the product to the market of the Member modifying or withdrawing the concession) to its total exports shall be deemed to have a principal supplying interest *if it does not already have an initial negotiating right or a principal supplying interest as provided for in paragraph 1 of Article XXVIII*. (emphasis added)

This clause, as made explicit in the Understanding, would be reviewed within five years in order to check whether it has functioned in a satisfactory manner or whether it would have to be amended:

> ...with a view to deciding whether this criterion has worked satisfactorily in securing a redistribution of negotiating rights in favour of small and medium-sized exporting Members.

This clause was discussed, as it was supposed to be, in early 2000. In early 2000, the CTG requested the Committee on Market Access to undertake the review and the Committee in its report noted that:

> ...at this stage, there was no basis to change the criterion contained in paragraph 1 of the aforementioned Understanding.[116]

It follows from the discussions in the Committee that no use of this possibility was ever made between 1995–2000. However, developing countries were keen to keep this clause in place, in light of its potential use.[117] This item was discussed again at

---

[116] WTO Doc. G/MA/111.
[117] WTO Doc. G/MA/M/23 of 12 May 2000.

the next Committee meeting.[118] No action was taken and, as a result, the clause was neither amended nor abolished.

The rationale for including PSIs in the negotiation is explained in the Interpretative Note ad Art. XXVIII of the GATT which relevantly provides:

> The object of providing for the participation in the negotiation of any contracting party with a principal supplying interest, in addition to any contracting party with which the concession was originally negotiated, is to ensure that a contracting party with a larger share in the trade affected by the concession than a contracting party with which the concession was originally negotiated shall have an effective opportunity to protect the contractual right which it enjoys under this Agreement.

The same document adds that:

> It would ... not be appropriate for the CONTRACTING PARTIES to determine that more than one contracting party, or in those exceptional cases where there is near equality more than two contracting parties, had a principal supplying interest.

It follows that the inclusion of PSIs is justified because these are the WTO Members that will suffer most from the change in tariffs. The Interpretative Note ad Art. XXVIII of the GATT recognizes that much (§1.4):

> On the other hand, it is not intended that the scope of the negotiations should be such as to make negotiations and agreement under Article XXVIII unduly difficult nor to create complications in the application of this Article in the future to concessions which result from negotiations thereunder.

Art. XXVIII GATT aims to strike a balance between the old and the new market situation: the inclusion of INRs is justified on the grounds that, historically at least, they had a strong export interest in this particular market. PSIs take a seat around the table because the legislator wanted to account for the new market situation and ensure that those which suffer the larger damage are those who will be participating in the negotiated settlement. To what extent a balance of this sort should be maintained is open to discussion. Adoption of horizontal cuts, like the Swiss formula mentioned *supra*, suggests that we are probably moving towards an era where it is current market situation that matters most.

SI countries: This term as well is defined in the Interpretative Note ad Art. XXVIII:

> The expression 'substantial interest' is not capable of a precise definition and accordingly may present difficulties for the CONTRACTING PARTIES. It is however, intended to be construed to cover only those contracting parties which have, or in the absence of discriminatory quantitative restrictions affecting their exports could reasonably be expected to have a significant share in the market of the contracting party seeking to modify or withdraw the concession.

---

[118] WTO Doc. G/MA/M/24 of 20 July 2000.

In practice, WTO Members having 10 per cent or more of the market of the WTO Member seeking to modify the concession have been considered as having substantial interest in the concession. A report of the Committee on Tariff Concessions dating from July 1985 confirms that the 10 per cent share has been generally applied in the definition of SI countries.[119] Hence, SIs, unlike PSIs, do not have to have a market share larger than that of INRs in order to claim a right to participate in the negotiation.

MFN trade is the basis for defining PSIs and SIs: The Uruguay round Understanding on the Interpretation of Art. XXVIII GATT states in §3:

> In the determination of which Members have a principal supplying interest . . . or substantial interest, only trade in the affected product which has taken place on a MFN basis shall be taken into consideration. However, trade in the affected product which has taken place under non-contractual preferences shall also be taken into account if the trade in question has ceased to benefit from such preferential treatment, thus becoming MFN trade, at the time of the negotiation for the modification or withdrawal of the concession, or will do so by the conclusion of that negotiation.

WTO Members that have some form of preferential arrangement with the requesting WTO Member can thus never become PSIs or SIs.

New products: the question arises what to do in the case of new products where no trade statistics are available and, thus, it is impossible to measure market shares to define PSIs and SIs. In this case, recourse to other proxies such as production capacity and investment will be made. The Uruguay round Understanding on the Interpretation of Art. XXVIII GATT states in §4:

> When a tariff concession is modified or withdrawn on a new product (i.e., a product for which three years' trade statistics are not available) the Member possessing initial negotiating rights on the tariff line where the product is or was formerly classified shall be deemed to have an initial negotiating right in the concession in question. The determination of principal supplying and substantial interests and the calculation of compensation shall take into account, *inter alia*, production capacity and investment in the affected product in the exporting Member and estimates of export growth, as well as forecasts of demand for the product in the importing Member. For the purposes of this paragraph, 'new product' is understood to include a tariff item created by means of a breakout from existing tariff line. (italics in the original).

2.9.2 The Mechanics of the Negotiation

Art. XXVIII GATT distinguishes between three different forms of negotiation: in two of them, the requesting WTO Member (the 'applicant contracting party', in the terminology employed in Art. XXVIII GATT) does not need to secure the approval of the WTO Membership before it enters into negotiations; in one, it

---

[119] GATT Doc. TAR/M/16.

does. There are some common elements in all three negotiations, such as the limited number of participants: in all three types of negotiation, it is the primarily concerned parties which will negotiate. The INRs and PSIs derive, by virtue of their participation, an advantage since they can, in principle, either acting separately or collectively, identify the commodity (or list of commodities) where compensation will be paid. There should further be equivalence between the damage suffered because of the modification and the compensation offered, irrespective of the procedure followed. Art. XXVIII.2 GATT reads:

> In such negotiations and agreement, which may include provision for compensatory adjustment with respect to other products, the contracting parties concerned shall endeavour to maintain a general level of reciprocal and mutually advantageous concessions not less favourable to trade than that provided for in this Agreement prior to such negotiations.

The Interpretative Note ad Art. XXVIII of the GATT adds (§4.6):

> It is not intended that provision for participation in the negotiations of any contracting party with a principal supplying interest, and for consultation with any contracting party having a substantial interest in the concession which the applicant contracting party is seeking to modify or withdraw, should have the effect that it should have to pay compensation or suffer retaliation greater than the withdrawal or modification sought, judged in the light of the conditions of trade at the time of the proposed withdrawal or modification, making allowance for any discriminatory quantitative restrictions maintained by the applicant contracting party.

Procedures where no prior approval is required: Art. XXVIII GATT distinguishes between two procedures. The first is described in Art. XXVIII.1 GATT and the requesting WTO Member must initiate negotiations during a specified period (July to October) in any three-year period, starting on 1 January 1958. The requesting WTO Member will notify the CTG of its interest in initiating negotiations and the CTG will determine the identity of the other primarily concerned parties.[120] Assuming that, at the end of the negotiations, an agreement has been reached between the participants, the requesting WTO Member will notify the WTO of its new schedule of concessions, which will be applied on an MFN basis. If no agreement has been reached, the requesting WTO Member can go ahead and unilaterally modify its concessions. If it decides to exercise this option, the WTO Member runs the risk of facing retaliation, not only from the Members participating in the negotiation, but from the rest of the WTO Membership as well. Art. XXVIII.3(a) and (b) GATT relevantly reads in this respect:

> If agreement between the contracting parties primarily concerned cannot be reached before 1 January 1958 or before the expiration of a period envisaged in paragraph 1 of this Article, the contracting party which proposes to modify or withdraw the

---

[120] Art. XXVIII GATT states that it is the CONTRACTING PARTIES that will be entrusted with this task. However, following the advent of the WTO, this task has been entrusted to the CTG.

concession shall, nevertheless, be free to do so and if such action is taken any contracting party with which such concession was initially negotiated, any contracting party determined under paragraph 1 to have a principal supplying interest and any contracting party determined under paragraph 1 to have a substantial interest shall then be free not later than six months after such action is taken, to withdraw, upon the expiration of thirty days from the day on which written notice of such withdrawal is received by the CONTRACTING PARTIES, substantially equivalent concessions initially negotiated with the applicant contracting party.

If agreement between the contracting parties primarily concerned is reached but any other contracting party determined under paragraph 1 of this Article to have a substantial interest is not satisfied, such other contracting party shall be free, not later than six months after action under such agreement is taken, to withdraw, upon the expiration of thirty days from the day on which written notice of such withdrawal is received by the CONTRACTING PARTIES, substantially equivalent concessions initially negotiated with the applicant contracting party.

This paragraph suggests that two categories of WTO Members can react, in case the requesting WTO Member has decided to modify its concession, the absence of agreement notwithstanding: both the participants in the negotiations (PSIs and INRs), and the SIs, provided that they do so on goods initially negotiated with the requesting WTO Member. The provision is nonetheless incomplete and the following questions might legitimately arise:

(a) What if PSIs and SIs have no concessions initially negotiated with the requesting WTO Member? Should they lose their right to retaliate?
(b) Should the retaliation by PSIs and SIs be on a bilateral (e.g. only vis-à-vis the applicant WTO Member) or on *erga omnes* basis (e.g. vis-à-vis the WTO Membership)?
(c) It could be the case that WTO Members, other than INRs, PSIs, or SIs, are also affected by the unilateral modification of the concession.[121] Should they not be entitled to react?

The number of WTO Members nowadays makes it quite likely[122] that affected primarily concerned parties and/or SIs have no initially negotiated concessions with the requesting WTO Member. Practice (like the Canada/EC dispute, discussed *infra*) seems to suggest that retaliating WTO Members indicate the goods where they purport to increase tariffs in retaliation, irrespective of whether they have initially negotiated concessions on these goods with the applicant state or not.

---

[121] Some might indeed have a trade interest that supersedes that of the INR holder since, as we saw *supra*, the number of PSIs participating in a negotiation is limited to a maximum of two. It could also be the case that WTO Members with market shares less than that of the INR holder care about this product market a lot since it might represent a substantial percentage of their gross domestic product (GDP) or of their export income. Others might be deterred from investing in this commodity.

[122] It is, of course, to be expected that the smaller the number of participants, the higher the likelihood that PSIs and/or SIs are also INRs.

Although such practice runs counter to the explicit wording of Art. XXVIII GATT, no formal challenge against it by affected WTO Members has taken place as yet. Practice suggests that this condition has, de facto, been relaxed.[123]

With respect to the second question, we observe that, although Art. XXVIII GATT is not explicit in this respect, it should be the case that retaliating WTO Members should do so only on a bilateral basis, that is, they should be barred from raising their tariffs in retaliation *erga omnes*. Indeed, why should innocent states pay for the absence of agreement in a negotiation where they did not participate? However, although probably counter-intuitively so, there are at least two instances in practice where the WTO Member reacting to a unilateral modification threatened to do so on an *erga omnes* basis. First, the 1990 award by the Arbitrator on *Canada/European Communities—Article XXVIII Rights* notes, with respect to Canada's threat to withdraw concessions substantially equivalent to those modified by the EU, that:

> should Canada exercise her right to withdraw concessions, she undertakes obligations to compensate third countries having negotiating rights in respect of Canada for the products on which concessions would be withdrawn.[124]

Canada assumed that it would incur no obligations to compensate anyone, had its retaliation taken place on a bilateral basis. Implicitly, therefore, this passage suggests that Canada would be raising duties, not only vis-à-vis the EU, but also vis-à-vis the rest of its trading partners on an MFN basis. This view has been confirmed in subsequent practice. Canada and the EU ran into the same argument in the context of the EU's enlargement from 12 to 15 member states (with the accession of Austria, Finland, and Sweden). The three acceding countries had to raise their duties with respect to some products, from their prior unilateral level to the new harmonized EU level. According to Art. XXIV.6 GATT (see *infra*), in such cases, the members of the preferential trade agreement, and the outsiders, enter into Art. XXVIII GATT negotiations aiming to compensate those affected by tariff increases. When discussing the amount of compensation, 'built-in' compensation, that is, compensation already paid since the acceding countries had to lower their tariffs, with respect to certain goods, to meet the CU, will be taken into account. This is where Canada and the EU disagreed: the former believed that the 'built-in' compensation was not adequate; the latter believed that the opposite was the case. Canada threatened to retaliate:

> As a result of tariff modifications which became effective 1 January 1995, the access of Canadian exporters to the acceding countries has been impaired. Consequently, Canada wishes to notify Members that it will exercise its rights under Article XXVIII:3 to withdraw substantially equivalent tariff concessions on products of

---

[123] Assuming, however, a legal challenge against such practice, it is hard to imagine how a WTO Panel will neglect the explicit wording of Art. XXVIII GATT in this respect.

[124] GATT Analytical Index, p. 947.

interest to the European Union as outlined in the attached table. These modifications shall take effect 30 days after distribution of this notification to WTO members.

Members may wish to note that in this respect, these modifications will not affect the application of rates under the Generalized System of Preferences.

Any Member that believes it has supplier rights which are affected by this action is invited to inform the Permanent Representative of Canada to the WTO.[125]

The last quoted sentence indicates that Canada's purported retaliation was supposed to take place on an *erga omnes* basis. Although Canada targeted products originating in the EU, a negative trade impact on other WTO Members producing the same goods could not be avoided. The parties to the dispute finally agreed to a settlement and, as a result, Canada never enacted its threat.[126] This practice suggests that, for some WTO Members at least, *erga omnes* retaliation in response to unilateral modifications is very much on the cards. This is regrettable for two reasons: innocent bystanders will have to pay the price; on the other hand, since the incentive of the retaliating Member is, absent agreed compensation, to overshoot the amount of suspended concessions, in order to provide the applicant state with an incentive not to modify unilaterally the concession in the first place, and as a result, one might end up with trade wars spiralling: there is no mechanism to *ex ante* ensure that retaliation will be kept within the statutory limits.[127]

From a pure policy perspective, *erga omnes* retaliation might lead to an endless spiral of counter-retaliation by WTO Members, if, of course, compensation has not been agreed. Affected parties are between a rock and a hard place:

(a) If they choose the legal route, they will have to challenge the legality of retaliation against them (themselves being innocent bystanders watching from afar a failed attempt between primarily concerned parties to agree on the amount of compensation due) before a Panel. The Panel would have to decide if *erga omnes* retaliation is legal; and, if so, what is the appropriate amount. Based on this calculation, affected parties will have to calculate the amount of substantially equivalent concessions that they themselves might wish to suspend. They will undoubtedly suffer trade damage

---

[125] WTO Doc. G/SECRET/1 of 1 March 1995.

[126] WTO Docs. G/SECRET/1 Add. 1 of 7 March 1995 and Add. 2 of 5 February 1998.

[127] This term (*'substantially equivalent concessions'*) appears in Art 22.4 DSU as well. According to this provision, retaliation must be substantially equivalent to the damage suffered because of the commission of the illegal act. It is difficult to sustain that a unilateral modification of a concession, the absence of agreed compensation notwithstanding, amounts to an illegality: Art. XXVIII GATT *allows* WTO Members to unilaterally modify their tariff bindings even in the absence of agreement with PSIs and INRs. So one can only wonder as to the rationale behind introducing the same standard of compensation as appropriate in order to address two diametrically opposed situations. Still, in light of the identical wording across the two provisions, one would probably expect to see case law under Art. 22.4 DSU to be of relevance to the calculation of compensation under Art. XXVIII GATT.

since WTO remedies are de facto not retroactive: assuming that the process extends over say four years, they will have to 'bite the bullet' and accept a pyrrhic victory since they will be allowed to retaliate only if, after the end of a reasonable period of time within which the applicant WTO Member must implement its obligations, it has not done so;[128]

(b) If they decide to act illegally, and adopt retaliatory measures, they risk opening themselves up to counter-retaliation.[129]

From a pure legal perspective, it is at least debatable that the Canadian view described above is GATT-consistent: assume that Canada carried out its threat and suspended concessions *erga omnes*. In this scenario, innocent bystanders have to pay the price because the EU has unilaterally modified its concession and it could not agree compensation with Canada. It seems highly unlikely that Art. XXVIII GATT was intended to condone such practices.[130] Art. XXVIII GATT is silent in

---

[128] According to Art. 21 DSU, if immediate implementation is not on the cards, WTO Members will be given a reasonable period of time (RPT) to bring their measures into compliance with their obligations under the WTO. The extent of RPT will be decided either by agreement between the interested parties or through recourse to arbitration. Standard case law suggests that affected WTO Members might be authorized to retaliate against their recalcitrant partners only as of the end of the RPT and assuming no compliance has been achieved at that moment. Of course, bargaining power considerations might affect behaviour in one way or another depending on who retaliates and who is the affected party.

[129] The calculation of compensation can be very problematic. Let us stick to the Canada/EU dispute and assume that Canada includes cars in its list and that Korea produces steel and cars. Korea will see its market share in Canada's market drop if its steel gets exported to the EU. This loss cannot even in part be compensated since, if at all, trade diversion will favour Canadian cars (since the Canadian retaliatory tariff is MFN and thus hits Korean cars as well). The Arbitrator's report on *EC—Bananas III* (*Ecuador*) (*Article 22.6—EC*) refused to entertain claims on indirect benefits: the US had claimed in that case that it should be compensated for lost profits resulting from the EU bananas import regime. In its view, the EU, by blocking imports into its market of bananas originating in Mexico, was *ipso facto* blocking exports to the Mexican market of fertilizers originating in the US. In other words, in the US view, Mexico would have little need for US fertilizers in light of the reduced export opportunities of bananas to the EU market. The Arbitrators decided against the US claim in this respect. In their view, the EU could be held liable for trade in bananas lost by Mexican exporters, but not for trade in fertilizers lost by US exporters as a result of Mexico's decision to reduce imports of the said commodity. Art. 22 DSU, consequently, must be construed so as to disallow the inclusion of indirect benefits when calculating the amount of countermeasures. To what extent this case law will be followed in the context of Art. XXVIII GATT is still an open question. There are good reasons to believe that this will indeed be the case though: if indirect benefits are excluded in cases of illegal actions, *a fortiori* they will be excluded when legal actions are at stake (assuming Canada's view holds).

[130] One could make the argument that facing the prospect of MFN retaliation would provide WTO Members with an incentive not to modify unilaterally in the first place: if they did, they would be credited with spiralling countermeasures across the board. Consequently, in light of the reputation costs that they would suffer, WTO Members would rather refrain from modifying unilaterally. Such arguments are debatable: for one, the text of Art. XXVIII GATT itself states that they remain free to modify unilaterally; hence, they are in fact exercising their rights under the GATT. On the other hand, one can legitimately cast doubt on the force of reputation costs in the WTO era: the original GATT with fewer participants and more or less like-minded countries that would interact across the board of international relations was probably appropriately viewed as a relational contract. This is hardly the case as far as the WTO is concerned.

this respect and it is true that silence can be interpreted in different ways. While, however, this provision acknowledges the right of the applicant WTO Member to raise its duties even in the absence of agreements with the PSIs and INRs, it does not acknowledge the right of the latter to react on an *erga omnes* basis. A contextual reading of this provision would suggest that similar actions would violate Art. II GATT.

From a purely practical perspective, the current institutional framework is ill-equipped to deal with the scenario of MFN retaliation: assume that Canada retaliates on an MFN basis and that it then invites affected parties to negotiate their compensation with it. Under what GATT provision would such negotiations take place? Arguably, Art. XXVIII GATT is not applicable to this context since none of the three statutory procedures for renegotiation applies here and no other provision emerges as candidate to host similar negotiations.

An amendment of Art. XXVIII GATT emerges as a necessity if clarification is sought in this respect. Two elements should be introduced into the current text:

(a) In case of no agreement, retaliation shall be bilateral; and
(b) The amount of retaliation, in the case of disagreement, shall be fixed through recourse to binding arbitration (as per Art 22.6 of the DSU).[131]

What about the rights of WTO Members which do not belong to any of the two categories envisaged in Art. XXVIII.3 GATT? The current text does not explicitly acknowledge that they have a legal right to retaliate under this provision. On the other hand, they will, in all likelihood, be affected by a modification of the schedule, irrespective of whether an agreement between the primarily concerned parties has been reached or not. What can be done if such an occasion arises? The most reasonable way out would be to acknowledge the right of such WTO Members to take a non-violation complaint (NVC) against the requesting WTO Member.[132] This solution seems warranted, in light of the explicit acknowledgement in Art. XXVIII.3 GATT that the applicant WTO Member has the right to unilaterally modify its schedule of concessions *even* in the absence of agreed compensation; hence, such behaviour cannot be deemed to be illegal. The only

---

[131] Voices of this type have already been raised. During the Uruguay round negotiations, Switzerland, in a communication to the GATT (GATT Doc. MTN.GNG/NG7/W/65 of 23 December 1989) proposed 'the introduction of an interpretative note to paragraph 3 of Article XXVIII explicitly authorizing contracting parties to take retaliatory action on a bilateral basis against the contracting party which originally withdraws its concession. To avoid possible misuse, the implementation of retaliatory measures should be subject to the prior approval of the CONTRACT-ING PARTIES.' Its proposal, unfortunately, was not met with enthusiasm by its trading partners.

[132] According to case law, for an NVC to be successfully launched, the following must be cumulatively met: (a) a concession must have been negotiated; (b) a subsequent action has occurred which (c) could not have been reasonably anticipated by the affected WTO Members and which (d) reduces the value of the tariff concession. Case law (*Japan–Film*) has clarified that it is the complainant that must show (c) above if the action occurs *before* the negotiation of the concession, whereas the burden shifts to the defendant in the opposite case.

question remaining in this context is whether the right to file an NVC can be exercised irrespective of whether an agreement between the primarily concerned parties has been reached. In the absence of relevant practice, we tend to respond to this question in the affirmative: from the perspective of the affected state, it could be totally immaterial whether an agreement occurred or not, since in either scenario its rights might be negatively affected.[133]

The second category of procedures where no prior approval is required is described in Art. XXVIII.5 GATT: WTO Members can reserve their right to renegotiate, and eventually exercise this right at a later date:

> Before 1 January 1958 and before the end of any period envisaged in paragraph 1 a contracting party may elect by notifying the CONTRACTING PARTIES to reserve the right, for the duration of the next period, to modify the appropriate Schedule in accordance with the procedures of paragraph 1 to 3. If a contracting party so elects, other contracting parties shall have the right, during the same period, to modify or withdraw, in accordance with the same procedures, concessions initially negotiated with that contracting party.

Practice in this context constitutes the majority of Art. XXVIII GATT negotiations. The discussion above is *mutatis mutandis* applicable in this context.

Procedures where prior approval is required: The procedure explained *supra* has one important downside: the right can be exercised only within a particular time period. WTO Members which have not reserved their right to renegotiate or those that wish to negotiate outside the period prescribed in Art. XXVIII.1 GATT can do so only if they have first secured the authorization of the WTO Membership (following the procedure included in Art. XXVIII.4 GATT). To this effect, the WTO Member concerned will submit its request to the CTG, the competent organ to decide. A request for authorization must include the elements specified in the Interpretative Note ad Art. XXVIII GATT (§4.1):

> Any request for authorization to enter into negotiations shall be accompanied by all relevant statistical and other data. A decision on such request shall be made within thirty days of its submission.
>
> The time-period within which the negotiation must be completed should be short (60 days), but could be extended. The Interpretative Note ad Art XXVIII of the GATT relevantly provides in this respect (§ 4.3):
>
> It is expected that negotiations authorized under paragraph 4 for modification or withdrawal of a single item, or a very small group of items, could normally be brought to a conclusion in sixty days. It is recognized, however, that such a period will be inadequate for cases involving negotiations for the modification or withdrawal of a larger number of items and in such cases, therefore, it would be appropriate for the CONTRACTING PARTIES to prescribe a longer period.

---

[133] It is immaterial, if compensation, for example, is paid in commodities of no interest to the state at hand.

Assuming that negotiations have been successfully concluded, the new schedule of concessions notified by the requesting WTO Member will enter into force. It could, however, be the case that no agreement can be reached. In this case, according to Art. XXVIII.4 GATT:

> the applicant contracting party shall be free to modify or withdraw the concession, unless the CONTRACTING PARTIES determine that the applicant contracting party has unreasonably failed to offer adequate compensation.

Hence, in case of disagreement between the negotiating partners, the CTG will determine whether adequate compensation has been offered. The Interpretative Note ad Art. XXVIII GATT states that the CTG must decide within 30 days from the submission of the matter before it, unless the applicant Member agrees to a longer period (§4.4). The Interpretative Note ad Art. XXVIII GATT further provides some useful information as to the elements that the CTG should take into account, when determining whether adequate compensation had indeed been offered (§4.5):

> In determining under paragraph 4 *(d)* whether an applicant contracting party has unreasonably failed to offer adequate compensation, it is understood that the CONTRACTING PARTIES will take due account of the special position of a contracting party which has bound a high proportion of its tariffs at very low rates of duty and to this extent has less scope than other contracting parties to make compensatory adjustment.

If the CTG determines that adequate compensation has indeed been offered, the modified concession will be allowed to stand. In the opposite case, the applicant WTO Member might still go ahead and unilaterally modify the concession. In this case, INRs, PSIs, and SIs have the right to suspend substantially equivalent concessions (Art. XXVIII.4 GATT):

> If such action is taken, any contracting party with which the concession was initially negotiated, any contracting party determined under paragraph 4 *(a)* to have a principal supplying interest and any contracting party determined under paragraph 4 *(a)* to have a substantial interest, shall be free, not later than six months after such action is taken, to modify or withdraw, upon the expiration of thirty days from the day on which written notice of such withdrawal is received by the CONTRACT-ING PARTIES, substantially equivalent concessions initially negotiated with applicant contracting party.

In light of the fact that:

(a) An authorization is required before the applicant WTO Member enters into an Art. XXVIII.4 GATT negotiation;
(b) The authorization will be granted following a consensus decision to this effect; and
(c) The agreement of potential INRs, PSIs, SIs is essential, indeed the *conditio sine qua non* for a favourable decision,

it is to be expected that the negotiation on the level of compensation, in such cases, effectively takes place before the authorization has been granted. This might explain why some requests are being withdrawn (in the absence of agreement on the compensation).[134]

3. Fees and Charges for Services Rendered

WTO Members remain free to adopt additional (to OCDs and ODCs) measures related to importation of goods, to the extent that they respect the requirements of Art. VIII GATT. Art. VIII.1 GATT imposes a limit on the amount that can be charged through similar measures:

> All fees and charges of whatever character (other than import and export duties and other than taxes within the purview of Article III) imposed by contracting parties on or in connection with importation or exportation shall be limited in amount to the approximate cost of services rendered and shall not represent an indirect protection to domestic products or a taxation of imports or exports for fiscal purposes.

Measures such as statistical taxes or public health-related controls may come under the purview of this provision: Art. VIII.4 GATT provides that fees and formalities necessary to service an indicative list of measures come under its purview: consular transactions, such as consular invoices and certificates; quantitative restrictions; licensing; exchange control; statistical services; documents, documentation and certification; analysis and inspection; and quarantine, sanitation, and fumigation.

Impositions under this provision do not overlap with impositions under Art. II GATT; the Panel on *Dominican Republic—Import and Sale of Cigarettes* confirmed this point (§7.115).[135] The GATT Panel report on *US—Customs User Fee* provided a series of additional clarifications regarding the ambit of Art. VIII GATT. The facts of the case that are crucial to our study are summarized in §7 of the report:

> The term 'customs user fee' refers to a number of fees imposed by the United States for the processing by the US Customs Service of passengers, conveyances and merchandise entering the United States. Only one of these fees is at issue in this dispute. It is the 'merchandise processing fee,' an *ad valorem* charge imposed for the

---

[134] Grenada, for example, withdrew its request, arguing that it could not be present during the discussions (see WTO Doc. G/C/M/59 of 22 March 2002). Subsequently, it reintroduced its request and managed successfully to conclude the negotiations (see WTO Doc. G/SECRET/16 and Add. 1).

[135] There is, however, some dubious practice in this context: Honduras bound all its customs duties during the Uruguay round at 35 per cent *ad valorem*. It also included an additional 3 per cent ODC. In its schedule, Honduras explains that the ODC will be reduced to 1.5 per cent by 31 December 1995 and then further modified in order to comply with the requirements of Art. VIII GATT. An ODC was thus transformed into an imposition under Art. VIII GATT.

processing of commercial merchandise entering the United States. (italics in the original)

The Panel went on to explain that the services rendered, for which a charge would be imposed, did not have to be requested by the traders; they could be unilaterally decided by the importing state (§77). The Panel also explained that the service rendered must be linked to a particular transaction and not to the total cost of service (§81). Based on this analysis, the Panel went on to find that the US measure at hand was GATT-inconsistent, since, by virtue of its nature (*ad valorem*), the duty imposed was not linked to the cost of the provided service: minor value transactions would pay less than major value transactions for exactly the same service (§§84–6). As a result, fees and formalities coming under the purview of this provision cannot be expressed in *ad valorem* terms.

The analysis in *US—Customs User Fee* has not been brought into question in subsequent practice. WTO Panels that had to deal with this issue borrowed from it and explicitly referred to this case law when dealing with a legal claim under Art. VIII GATT. The Panel report on *Argentina—Footwear* reflects a quasi-identical ruling on a similar issue: Argentina had an *ad valorem* charge for services rendered in connection with the importation of goods. The Panel, applying the same logic as in *US—Customs User Fee*, found the Argentine measure to be GATT-inconsistent. It went on to address an argument by Argentina that this imposition was in line with the obligation it had assumed (by virtue of its contract with the IMF). The Panel rejected this argument as well, finding that nothing in the contractual arrangement between the WTO and the IMF could support the Argentine argument (§§6.74–80). This Panel confirmed that *ad valorem* schemes are by construction inconsistent with Art. VIII GATT, while leaving the door open to justify them under the WTO/IMF arrangement, assuming that they have been recommended by the IMF.[136]

---

[136] The Panel report on *US—Certain EC Products* is yet another illustration that the analysis in *US—Custom User Fee* is still good law (§6.69).

3

MOST FAVOURED NATION AND
EXCEPTIONS

1. Most Favoured Nation

1.1 The Legal Discipline and its Rationale

WTO Members must, by virtue of the MFN obligation, accord automatically and
unconditionally to all WTO Members any trade advantage they have accorded to
another nation, irrespective of whether the latter is a WTO Member or not.

Non-discriminatory trade liberalization is not an invention of the GATT system: Hudec (1988) explains that, as early as medieval times, the city of Mantua (Italy) obtained from the Holy Roman Emperor the promise that it would always benefit from any privilege granted by the Emperor to 'whatsoever other town'. Jackson (1997, p. 158) notes that the term 'MFN' appears for the first time at the end of the seventeenth century. During the nineteenth century, the provision appeared in a number of treaties across European states. For instance, the Cobden-Chevalier Treaty of 1860, liberalizing trade between Great Britain and France, included an MFN clause guaranteeing that a signatory would not be treated worse than any other state with which the other signatory had, or would assume, trade relations. Such schemes, however, were not tantamount to worldwide non-discriminatory trade.

It is questionable whether, except for the very general idea of non-discrimination, these first formulations of MFN can provide guidance for the understanding of the term as currently employed in GATT. The drafters of the MFN clause were inspired by the formulation of the MFN clause as developed by the League of Nations. In turn, the League of Nations based its formulation of the MFN clause on the numerous bilateral trade treaties during the 1920s and before World War I.[1] Many of those treaties were signed by the US.[2]

There is a widespread view among policy-makers, lawyers, and many economists that there are a number of strong economic rationales for non-discrimination. For instance, it seems to be rather commonly held (in particular among non-economists) that non-uniform tariff structures give rise to inefficient production and consumption patterns in a static sense. Other arguments in favour of non-discrimination hold that it eases tariff negotiations or may prevent the formation of preferential trading agreements that are formed to exploit market power in world markets. However, a general theoretical prima-facie case for non-discrimination is not as easily advanced as might be thought. Indeed, Johnson (1976, p.18) goes as far as to argue that:

> ...the principle of non-discrimination has no basis whatsoever in the theoretical argument for the benefits of a liberal international trade order in general, or in any rational economic theory of the bargaining process in particular.

Economic analyses of MFN can be broadly divided into two categories.[3] The first comprises models in which governments set tariffs unilaterally. In a typical set-up,

---

[1] E/PC/T/C/33 at p. 9. For a concise discussion of the historical underpinnings of MFN, see Horn and Mavroidis (2009).

[2] In the 1942 reciprocal trade agreement with Mexico, Art. I read: 'With respect to customs duties and charges of any kind imposed on or in connection with the importation or exportation, and with respect to the method of levying such duties and charges...any advantage, favor, privilege or immunity which has been or may hereafter be granted by the United States of America or the United Mexican States to any article in or destined for any third country shall be accorded immediately and unconditionally to the like article originating in or destined for the United Mexican States or the United States of America, respectively.' 57 Stat. 835.

[3] For a concise overview of the economics literature, see Horn and Mavroidis (2001).

firms decide on investment, the level of which is influenced by firms' perceptions about tariff treatment and, thus, on whether MFN has to be respected or not. A basic mechanism here is that MFN hinders *ex post* opportunistic taxation of economic rents and may thereby increase the *ex ante* private incentives for the creation of such rents. This mechanism lies behind several observations. For instance, by affecting the strategic interaction between firms and governments, an MFN clause may have a positive welfare impact even if the government would choose to set non-discriminatory tariffs in its absence; and a government that, absent an MFN clause would choose to discriminate, may gain from being prevented from discriminating.

A second and more recent strand of literature is concerned with the role of MFN for multilateral trade liberalization and, in particular, tariff negotiations. One fundamental role of trade agreements, as argued in Chapter 1, is to prevent negative externalities from nationally pursued trade policies. These international externalities may work through a number of different routes. For instance, they may take the form of changes in terms of trade or through domestic prices affecting import demand. Bagwell and Staiger (2002) suggest that a central role of MFN is to channel these externalities through the terms of trade. This is important, since tariff negotiations can directly address terms of trade externalities, but are less effective in addressing other forms of externalities.

The complexity of multi-country tariff negotiations is reflected in the wide variety of arguments that have been advanced in the informal academic literature and in policy discussions. MFN is said to promote tariff liberalization by making trade agreements more credible: the increased cost of giving concessions makes it less attractive for a party to undermine an agreement by subsequently offering better terms of market access to a third country (concession diversion). Here is how it works: the value to A of concessions negotiated between A and B risks being eroded through subsequent negotiations between B and C, assuming B has 'conceded' to C more than it did to A.[4] MFN is the insurance policy against similar behaviour and because of it, A and B (like any other trading nations) will continue to have an incentive to negotiate and liberalize trade.

The role of MFN to prevent concession erosion (diversion) is at focus in Ethier (2004), who takes a long-term perspective on its impact. Governments are assumed to initially form reciprocal bilateral agreements. These must include MFN to avoid concession diversion, to be meaningful. As more and more bilateral agreements are formed, the incentives to participate in further agreements gradually diminish, since each agreement has through the partner's MFN commitment to be shared by more and more other countries, and more and more market access has to be given away through a country's own MFN commitments. A process of

---

4 See, on this score, Schwarz and Sykes (1998). Close to this concept (preference erosion) is the concept of bilateral opportunism advanced by Bagwell and Staiger (2002).

liberalization through bilateral agreements will, therefore, eventually come to a halt. It will become necessary to internalize the external effects of any further agreements by making the agreements multilateral. Hence, MFN causes multilateralism, not the other way around. This study can also be seen as an illustration of the more general point that bilateral negotiations conducted under MFN generally are associated with externalities, since the outcome of such negotiations affect parties who are not present in the negotiations.

Ethier (2004) adds that the role of MFN becomes all the more important as the number of participants in trade deals increases. Assume that A and B have signed an agreement and included an MFN clause. A subsequently negotiates with C and knows that whatever benefit it will grant to C will have to be automatically extended to B as well. B, in other words, will be free-riding on A's negotiation with C. Any subsequent negotiation involves additional negotiating costs for A, and additional advantages only for B. A and B might thus be dissuaded from entering into subsequent negotiations. They would rather invite all interested parties to participate in the initial negotiation, where they all make commitments, and all profit, in a non-discriminatory manner, from the concessions entered. But what if they do not accept? One would expect in a similar scenario that trade liberalization will stall. The free-rider problem is thus real. The GATT system knows of two mechanisms (instruments) that reduce the size of the problem: the first is reciprocity, where negotiations are based on reciprocal concessions. It is true that this instrument reduces the problem only with respect to some trading nations. The second instrument reduces the size of the problem with respect to those that matter: as discussed *supra*, it is to be expected that principal suppliers will participate in tariff negotiations and, consequently, free-riders will be in most cases those that do not matter (or do not matter much) in the trade context.[5]

There are some intuitively important aspects of MFN that have not been formally scrutinized. For instance, Viner (1924) notes that the administration of discriminatory tariffs is costly because of the need to keep track of product origin; MFN significantly simplifies customs procedures. Another aspect of considerable importance is the fact that MFN reduces the cost and complexity of negotiations by reducing the number of possible bids and outcomes.

MFN also makes it attractive for outsiders to enter into an existing agreement, since they get access to a package of low tariffs. And since entrants have to grant MFN, insiders get access to many foreign markets through the incentives for entry.

On the other hand, MFN is also claimed to reduce the incentives to liberalize. It increases the costs of giving concessions, since the latter have to be given to all

---

[5] Incidentally, Hawkins (1951, pp. 81ff) reports that the unwillingness to compensate free-riders is what motivated the US government to grant MFN under the RTAA only to the countries that it considered principal suppliers of a particular commodity. Recall also from Chapter 1 that, in Hull's view, MFN was the price developed nations had to pay to developing countries as a token for re-establishing world peace.

countries with which a country has MFN agreements. MFN makes large countries unwilling to make concessions to small countries, since in return for 'peanuts' large countries have to extend their concessions to a large volume of trade; MFN reduces the benefit from a given concession since it has to be shared with other countries;[6] MFN promotes free-riding, since countries may opt to wait for agreements between other countries to spill over via MFN, rather than contribute with concessions themselves, and MFN also prevents countries from punishing free-riding; or MFN prevents subsets of countries from going further in liberalization than what is desired by the rest of the world.[7] MFN may potentially cause free-riding in at least two ways. One is that a country rejects an offer in order to let other countries reach agreements that it can benefit from without having to make concessions itself. This would be inefficient either because there would be delays in achieving an agreement or because the agreement would feature higher tariffs compared to some other (undefined) situation. This possibility has as far as we know not found any support in the literature so far. For instance, Ludema (1991), in one of the few studies that employs a non-cooperative sequential bargaining model to study the impact of MFN on multilateral bargaining, shows how negotiators may find it optimal to devise equilibrium offers such that free-riding does not occur, despite there being incentives and possibilities to free-ride. In support, note that, following tariff cuts, resources will be re-employed in other sectors—those with export potential. Those who have not made tariff cuts will be facing more competition than they had imagined.

Finally, under MFN, countries may have incentives to use narrow product classifications in order to avoid having to extend concessions granted on an MFN basis. There should thus be reasons for countries to try to manipulate customs classification schemes.

To conclude, the implications of MFN for multi-party tariff negotiations are inherently complex. Economic theory does support some of the claims concerning the beneficial effects of MFN, but provides a far too scattered picture to serve as the basis for any more general claim concerning the desirability of MFN. The proliferation of non-MFN schemes is testimony to this. A series of empirical works have demonstrated[8] that most trade is conducted nowadays on non-MFN terms. The proportion of non-MFN trade in the overall volume of trade is ever increasing. In inimitable manner, Bhagwati has described MFN as LFN, the *least favoured*

---

6 This is why Cordell Hull insisted, as we saw in Chapter 1, that MFN was the contribution to peace by the leaders of this world. Other things equal, big countries would be rather unwilling to have smaller states free-ride on the commitments they managed to extract by paying back in reciprocal terms.

7 Several of these arguments were made by Viner (1924).

8 See, *inter alia*, Sapir (1998a), Schott (1989), and compare with more recent studies such as Limão (2006c).

nation clause: MFN is the default payment to WTO Members, assuming one of the many preferential payments[9] does not occur.

1.2 Coverage of the Legal Discipline

The AB, in its report on *Canada—Autos*, held the view that both de jure as well as de facto discrimination are covered by the prohibition included in Art. I.1 GATT. Consequently, not only measures discriminatory on their face (e.g. a law whereby an advantage is granted by explicitly using origin as the criterion for conferral), but also measures which on their face are origin-neutral can be successfully challenged to the extent that they de facto discriminate in favour of particular sources of supply (§78):

> In approaching this question, we observe first that the words of Article I:1 do not restrict its scope only to cases in which the failure to accord an 'advantage' to like products of all other Members appears *on the face* of the measure, or can be demonstrated on the basis of the words of the measure. Neither the words '*de jure*' nor '*de facto*' appear in Article I:1. Nevertheless, we observe that Article I:1 does not cover only 'in law', or *de jure*, discrimination. As several GATT panel reports confirmed, Article I:1 covers also 'in fact', or de facto, discrimination. Like the Panel, we cannot accept Canada's argument that Article I:1 does not apply to measures which, on their face, are 'origin-neutral.' (italics in the original)

The problem with de facto discrimination is that it effectively amounts to opening Pandora's box. GATT/WTO case law has struggled over the years to come up with a coherent test that would distinguish wheat from chaff. Although some steps have been taken to this effect over the years, we are still miles away from establishing a watertight test to deal with de facto discrimination. At this stage, WTO adjudicating bodies apply (in name at least) the no-effects, no-intent standard of review that we briefly discussed *supra* in Chapter 2. According to this standard, a measure will be GATT-inconsistent if it modifies condition of competition to the detriment of imported goods and assuming that no explanation other than the origin of the good has been persuasively offered. Because the majority of cases that deal with this issue come under the purview of Art. III GATT, it is in Chapter 4 that we will be discussing it in detail. Since the MFN requirement covers measures coming under the purview of Art. III GATT as well, the discussion there is applicable here as well. Suffice to mention here the relevant excerpt of the Panel report on *EC—Bananas III* (§7.239):

> The requirement to match EC import licenses with BFA export certificates means that those BFA banana suppliers who are initial holders of export certificates enjoy a commercial advantage compared to banana suppliers from other third countries. We note that it is not possible to ascertain how many of the initial BFA export certificate

---

[9] We discuss them *infra*, namely, preferential trade agreements, special and differential treatment, etc.

holders are BFA banana producers or to what extent the tariff quota rent share that accrues to initial holders of BFA export certificates is passed on to the producers of BFA bananas in a way to create more favourable competitive opportunities for *bananas* of BFA origin. However, we also note that the possibility does exist to pass on tariff quota rent to BFA banana producers in such a way, whereas there is no such possibility in respect of non-BFA third-country banana producers. Thus, the EC's requirement affects the competitive relationship between *bananas* of non-BFA third-country origin and bananas of BFA origin. It is certainly true that Article I of GATT is concerned with the treatment of foreign *products* originating from different foreign sources rather than with the treatment of the suppliers of these products. In this respect, we note that the transfer of tariff quota rents which would normally accrue to initial holders of EC import licenses to initial holders of BFA export certificates does occur when *bananas* originating in Colombia, Costa Rica and Nicaragua are, at some point, traded to the EC. Therefore, in our view, the requirement to match EC import licenses with BFA export certificates and thus the commercial value of export certificates are linked to the *product* at issue as required under Article I. In practice, from the perspective of EC *importers* who are Category A or C operators, bananas of non-BFA third-country origin appear to be more profitable than bananas of BFA origin. This is confirmed by the fact that EC import licenses for non-BFA third-country bananas and Category B licenses for BFA bananas are typically oversubscribed in the first round of license allocations, while Category A and C licenses for BFA bananas are usually exhausted only in the second round of the quarterly license allocation procedure. The EC argues that the fact that licenses allowing the importation of non-BFA bananas at in-quota tariff rates are usually exhausted in the first round amounts to an advantage for bananas of Complainants' origin. While we do not endorse the EC's view, even if this were to constitute an advantage, we note 'that Article I:1 does not permit balancing more favourable treatment under some procedure against a less favourable treatment under others.' (emphasis in the original)

1.2.1 Any Advantage with Respect to . . .

Art I.1 GATT states that its coverage extends to any 'advantage', 'favour', 'privilege', and 'immunity' with respect to three categories of measures. The terms 'favour', 'privilege', and 'immunity' that follow the term 'advantage' suggest that the intention of the GATT framers was to make sure that it is the effect of and not the type of the measure that matters: what matters is whether a WTO Member is treated better than others. The three categories mentioned are:

(a) customs duties and charges of any kind imposed on or in connection with importation and exportation;
(b) rules and formalities in connection with importation and exportation;
(c) internal measures.

The ambit of this provision has been clarified through a series of GATT Panel reports. The term 'customs duties and charges of any kind' covers transactions coming not only under the purview of Art. II, but also under Art. VIII GATT: the above-cited Panel report on *US—Customs User Fee* is authority for the latter proposition. The GATT Panel on *Spain—Unroasted Coffee* clarified that the MFN clause is equally applicable to both bound and unbound customs duties (§4.3):

> Having noted that Spain had not bound under the GATT its tariff rate on unroasted coffee, the Panel pointed out that Article I:1 equally applied to bound and unbound tariff items.[10]

The AB held, in its report on *EC—Poultry* (§§96ff), that Art. I.1 GATT covers tariff quotas as well. That is, when deciding on rates within and outside the tariff quota, WTO Members must ensure that they have adhered to the non-discrimination principle. In this vein, in *EC—Bananas III*, the Panel found that conditioning the imposition on certain bananas of the in-quota (lower) tariff rate upon their origin (§§7.235ff, confirmed by the AB in its report in §207) was an advantage coming under the purview of Art. I GATT.

The drafters of the GATT, by opting for the term 'rules and formalities in connection with importation and exportation', although hardly a self-interpreting term, showed their willingness to cover the widest possible number of transactions under this heading: this is why the phrase 'in connexion with' was chosen. The GATT explicitly mentions one formality: Art. IX GATT deals with marks of origin, and imposes the obligation that marks of origin be applied on an MFN basis. Case law has identified a number of other rules and formalities that come under the purview of Art. I GATT. The leading case in this respect is *EC—Bananas III*. This Panel found that:

(a) the use of a less complicated licensing procedure (§§7.188ff);[11]
(b) the incentive given to operators to purchase bananas of a particular origin (§7.194);
(c) the issuance of a licence to import bananas of a particular origin upon the economic activity performed by the economic operator requesting the licence (§§7.220ff);
(d) the granting of licences to operators representing producers from certain countries only (§§7.251ff); and
(e) the imposition on certain bananas of the in-quota tariff rate provided that they originate in particular countries (§§7.235ff)

were all advantages with respect to rules and formalities in connection with importation and thus covered by Art. I.1 GATT. These findings were confirmed by the AB (§§206ff).[12]

---

[10] GATT practice suggests that a host of customs-related activities like consular fees come under the purview of Art. I GATT; GATT Doc. BISD II/12.

[11] Recall that, through its express wording, Art I.1 GATT states that the MFN clause does not extend only to duties and charges as such, but also to the methods of levying them. What is described here is of course an indicative list. Other practices as well might in the future be considered as conferring an advantage.

[12] On the reaction of European courts to this decision, see Snyder (2003). The bananas saga ended on 15 December 2009. The EU agreed to gradually cut its import tariff on bananas from Latin

The GATT Panel on *US—MFN Footwear* further found that the automatic backdating of the revocation of a countervailing duty order without the need to have an injury review conducted in this respect is an advantage in the sense of Art. I.1 GATT.

Art I.1 GATT makes it clear that, by virtue of the explicit reference to Art. III.2 and III.4 GATT, MFN covers internal measures as well. It was the GATT Panel on *Belgian Family Allowances* that first confirmed this by finding that internal tax exemptions for products purchased by public bodies were covered by Art. I.1 GATT.

Not only actions but also omissions, to the extent that they confer an advantage, are covered by the discipline laid down in Art. I.1 GATT: the GATT Panel on *US—Customs User Fee* held that an exemption from the imposition of a customs fee should be considered to be an advantage in the sense of Art. I.1 GATT.[13]

1.2.2 *Granted to a Product Originating in or Destined for another Country*

Art. I.1 GATT refers to

> any advantage, favour, privilege or immunity granted by any contracting party to any product originating in or destined for *any other country.* (emphasis added)

As a result, WTO Members cannot treat outsiders (non-WTO Members) better than they treat insiders (WTO Members). So MFN denotes not only the non-discrimination character of the obligation assumed under this provision, but also the fact that WTO Members enjoy the best possible (trade) treatment by their partners in the WTO. At the inception of the GATT, this provision was thought as the carrot offered to the numerous outsiders to join the club. Since only 23 had originally joined, its value was limited. Its practical importance has substantially increased as a result of the rise, in absolute numbers, of the WTO Membership from 23 (the original GATT) to 157 nowadays.

Although this provision refers to 'country', there should be no doubt that it covers customs territories as well. By virtue of Art. XII of the Agreement Establishing the WTO, a 'separate customs territory possessing full autonomy in the conduct of its external commercial relations' can join the WTO. It would be odd to allow customs territories to be WTO Members bound by the MFN and then, thanks to a narrow reading of Art. I.1 GATT, disallow them from profiting from additional advantages. This reading would run counter to the *effet utile* of this provision and as such should be dismissed. The key question here is of course:

America from €176/ton to €114/ton. The Latin American bananas exporters promised not to make any additional demands for tariff cuts on bananas during the Doha round. ACP exporters will continue to enjoy duty- and quota-free access to the EU market, while the EU will mobilize up to $200 million from the EU budget to support the main ACP exporters' adaptation to the changing conditions of competition in the EU market.

[13] §§121ff. The Panel did not formally rule on this issue since no claim had been made to this effect before it and, consequently, any ruling would be *ultra petita*. Still, in §123 of its report, it left no doubt that it considered that exemptions as well could come under the purview of Art. I GATT.

what is a good originating in a WTO Member? We discuss it in what immediately follows.

1.2.3 Originating in a WTO Member

WTO Members have to extend any advantage granted to a product originating in one country to all like goods originating in all other WTO Members. There is nothing like a horizontal definition of origin that applies across the board, that is, across all WTO Members: the WTO ROO (Agreement on Rules of Origin) does not impose a harmonized set of rules that WTO Members must observe when it comes to conferring origin: they remain free to adopt their rules of origin and apply them in a non-discriminatory manner.

One, if not the most important, objective of the ROO is, as per its Art. 9, to eventually harmonize non-preferential rules of origin.[14] This requires work on 5,000 tariff lines. Some progress has been made, but a lot still needs to be done. The work was originally due to end in July 1998, but several deadlines have been missed since that date and conclusion of the negotiation is still elusive. The negotiation is being conducted under the aegis of the WTO Committee on Rules of Origin,[15] and the Technical Committee operating under the auspices of the WCO. A Work Programme is in place, aiming, in principle, to provide for some sort of harmonized rules in this respect (Art. 9 ROO). The Committee on Rules of Origin has been actively pursuing this endeavour, known as HWP (Harmonization Work Programme), since 1995. Although meaningful discussions did take place, trading partners are still quite far from agreeing on a harmonized way of conferring origin.[16] It is reported that Members have made some progress: they have reached consensus on rules of origin for 55 per cent of the products negotiated; some core policy issues have been heavily negotiated; product-specific rules of origin are also being negotiated. Still, some hard issues remain open: the rules of origin applied to antidumping, countervailing, safeguards, SPS, TBT, and labelling figure among the thorniest issues where no consensus has been reached as yet.[17] The question has been repeatedly raised whether the Committee of Rules of Origin is the appropriate forum for the negotiation of the HWP, in view of the fact

---

[14] This is not the first multilateral initiative to this effect. The Kyoto Convention of 1977 pursues the same objective, but has had very little impact so far in WTO practice.

[15] As is the case with all WTO Committees, all WTO Members are represented in this committee.

[16] See, for example, some of the discussions as reflected in WTO Doc. WT/GC/M/109 of 24 October 2007.

[17] Discussions are ongoing on other issues as well, for example, on the so-called 'dual-rule approach', whereby, although each product must have one rule of origin, exceptionally for machinery, a WTO Member shall be allowed to choose either a value-added rule (where a fixed percentage of value confers origin) *or* a tariff-shift (where, because of value added, a product changes tariff line) rule.

that some of the issues involved are not purely technical, but also of a political nature.[18] Negotiations were ongoing at the moment of writing.[19]

Until then, nevertheless, Art. 2(d) ROO condones regulatory diversity:[20]

> Until the work programme for the harmonization of rules of origin set out in Part IV is completed, Members shall ensure that:
>
> . . .
>
> the rules of origin that they apply to imports and exports are not more stringent than the rules of origin they apply to determine whether or not a good is domestic and shall not discriminate between other Members, irrespective of the affiliation of the manufacturers of the good concerned.

WTO Members have employed a variety of methods to confer origin and sometimes a combination of distinct processes. Some employ added value, where origin is conferred if a certain threshold value has been met. Others confer origin depending on where the last substantial transformation of a given commodity has occurred. To decide whether substantial transformation occurred, countries will have recourse to criteria such as the 'percentage criterion' (where the question is whether a certain percentage of value added has been added), the change in tariff heading (as a result of the transformation),[21] or the so-called 'technical criterion', which prescribes certain production or sourcing processes that may (positive technical criterion) or may not (negative technical criterion) confer originating status. Some of the rules employed to decide whether substantial transformation has occurred leave substantial discretion to the administering authority and, as a result, disputes arise frequently.[22]

Nevertheless, because WTO rules of origin condone regulatory diversity and, essentially, hinge on non-discrimination, disputes will be submitted very infrequently to the WTO. The only reported case so far is the *US—Textiles Rules of Origin*, where the Panel in §§6.23–4 underscored the wide discretion that WTO Members enjoy when designing their rules of origin in the following terms:

> With regard to the provisions of Article 2 at issue in this case—subparagraphs (b) through (d)—we note that they set out what rules of origin should not do: rules of origin should not pursue trade objectives directly or indirectly; they should not themselves create restrictive, distorting or disruptive effects on international trade; they should not pose unduly strict requirements or require the fulfilment of a condition unrelated to manufacturing or processing; and they should not discriminate between other Members. These provisions do not prescribe what a Member must do.

---

[18] WTO Doc. WT/GC/M/126 of 22 June 2010.

[19] WTO Doc. G/RO/M/55 of 17 December 2010; see Vermulst and Imagawa (2005) for a discussion on the main themes.

[20] Vermulst (1995).

[21] It is usually substantial if the transformation leads to a change in the tariff classification say from one six-digit to another six-digit classification.

[22] Some of the most notorious disputes are reported in Vermulst and Waer (1990).

It is common ground between the parties that Art. 2 does not prevent Members from determining the criteria which confer origin, changing those criteria over time, or applying different criteria to different goods.

In practice, WTO Members often adopt different rules of origin depending on their intended function: for example, a WTO Member states that 25 per cent of domestic added value is necessary for a product to originate in a particular market for all customs purposes, but only 15 per cent for antidumping purposes. The consistency of similar practices with the WTO rules has not been contested so far. And, indeed, it seems quite hard to do so: there is no obligation to act consistently across agreements when conferring origin. By acting inconsistently across agreements (while respecting MFN), WTO Members have more discretion to accommodate domestic lobbies' demands.[23]

Besides non-discrimination, WTO Members must also ensure that their rules of origin are transparent, that they do not have restricting effects on international trade, and that they are administered in a consistent, uniform, impartial, and reasonable manner.[24] In an exclusively MFN world, where no preferences could exist, the rules of origin question would be far less dramatic than it currently is: all that would be requested is to ensure that a good is of *some* WTO origin in order to benefit from MFN treatment. Conferring *some* WTO origin is, alas, not enough in a world like ours, where preferences, as we shall see in more detail *infra*, are the dominant example and MFN the exception in international trade. In this world, it is imperative to confer the origin that is required for preferential treatment to be granted.

Questions regarding rules of origin do not arise at all if a product is wholly obtained or produced in one country. Issues arise only if more than one country is involved in its production. This is a very likely scenario in today's world. The picture of the origin of a Volvo car given in Figure 3.1 is quite telling in this respect.

Figure 3.1 is the natural outcome of the current explosion of *outsourcing*, or *offshoring*,[25] or, less colloquially, *trade in tasks*. Information technology has certainly contributed to the rise of fragmentation in the production process across firms and countries. It is definitely not wine for cloth any more, the transaction that Ricardo had in mind when constructing his theory of comparative advantage.

---

[23] Note that the US has officially cast doubt on the idea that an eventual agreement on a WTO ROO should automatically entail that the final outcome must be applied in AD investigations; WTO Doc. G/RO/W/65 of 18 May 2001.

[24] Vermulst (1992) offers a very comprehensive comparative study in this respect, with examples from state practice across various jurisdictions.

[25] The terms 'outsourcing' and 'offshoring' refer to different activities but have not been used in the same manner across the literature: a recent WTO study uses *outsourcing* to denote activities that a company outsources in general, whereas *offshoring* is used for activities outsourced in a foreign country; see *Trade Patterns and Global Value Chains in East Asia: From Trade in Goods to Trade in Tasks*, the WTO, Geneva, 2011; Helpman (2011, p. 127) uses 'outsourcing' to refer to the acquisition of goods or services from an unaffiliated party, and independently of whether the unaffiliated party is located at home or abroad, and the term 'offshoring' to refer to the sourcing of goods or services in a foreign country, either from an affiliated or from an unaffiliated party.

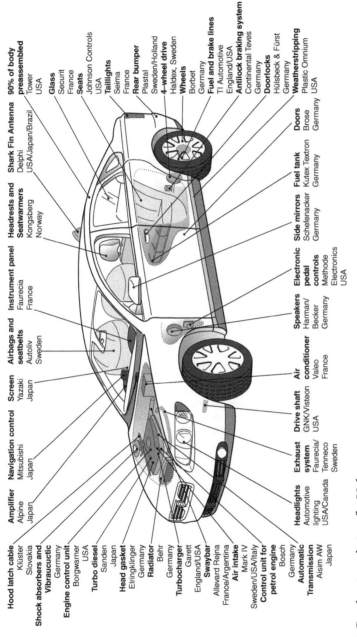

Figure 3.1 Production chain of a Volvo car

Source: Reproduced from Richard Baldwin and Philip Thornton, 'Multilateralising Regionalism', Centre for Economic Policy Research, 29 February 2008.

Hood latch cable
Klüster
Slovakia
Shock absorbers and
Vibraucuctic
Germany
Engine control unit
Borgwarner
USA
Turbo diesel
Sanden
Japan
Head gasket
Elringklinger
Germany
Radiator
Behr
Germany
Turbocharger
Garett
England/USA
Swaybar
Allevard Rejna
France/Argentina
Air intake
Mark IV
Sweden/USA/Italy
Control unit for
petrol engine
Bosch
Germany
Automatic
Transmission
Aisim AW
Japan

Amplifier
Alpine
Japan

Navigation control
Mitsubishi
Japan

Screen
Yazaki
Japan

Airbags and
seatbelts
Autoliv
Sweden

Instrument panel
Faurecia
France

Headrests and
Seatwarmers
Kongsberg
Norway

Shark Fin Antenna
Delphi
USA/Japan/Brazil

90% of body
preassembled
Tower
USA
Glass
Securit
France
Seats
Johnson Controls
USA
Taillights
Seima
France
Rear bumper
Plastal
Sweden/Holland
4-wheel drive
Haldex, Sweden
Wheels
Borbet
Germany
Fuel and brake lines
TI Automotive
England/USA
Antilock braking system
Continental Teves
Germany
Doorlocks
Hülsbeck & Fürst
Germany
Weatherstripping
Plastic Omnium
USA

Headlights
Automotive
lighting
USA/Canada

Exhaust
system
Faurecia/
Tenneco
Sweden

Drive shaft
GNK/Visteon
USA

Air
conditioner
Valeo
France

Speakers
Harman/
Becker
Germany

Electronic
pedal
controls
Methode
Electronics
USA

Side mirrors
Schefenacker
Germany

Fuel tank
Kutex Textron
Germany

Doors
Brose
Germany

Tempest (1996) shows how and why China, Indonesia, Japan, Malaysia, and Taiwan were all participating in the production process of a Barbie doll, along with the US.[26] The WTO Annual World Trade Report of 1998 explains that a typical US car includes 30 per cent Korean added value, 17.5 per cent Japanese, 7.5 per cent German, etc. The explosion of offshoring is the outcome of economically rational decisions,[27] but it does pose new problems regarding the identification of the origin of a good.[28]

The ROO deals with MFN rules of origin (Art. 1.2 ROO). There are preferential rules of origin as well: in fact, there is a menu of preferential rules of origin. Different rules are applied depending on the percentage of value added, the overall integration process pursued, etc.[29] Sometimes cumulation might be allowed and sometimes not: assume, for example, that A (developed) signs an agreement with B and C (developing); it could be that it confers origin on imported goods if a certain threshold added value has been met in either A or B or in A and B together (cumulation), or it could be that the agreement does not provide for this latter possibility. And then there are different forms of cumulation; there is bilateral cumulation, diagonal cumulation, etc. We quote from the EU webpage:[30]

> The existing Free Trade Agreements with the Western Balkans (Stabilisation and Association Agreements with Croatia and the former Yugoslav Republic of Macedonia) are based on a system of bilateral cumulation. This means Croatia and

---

[26] Ron Tempest, Barbie in the World Economy, *The Los Angeles Times*, 22 September 1996. See also Friedman (2005).

[27] Grossman and Rossi-Hansberg (2008) introduce a 'productivity-effect' and provide the theoretical framework to explain gains from trade thanks to offshoring. Before their contribution, analysts focused on the 'labour supply' and 'relative price' effects. Grossman and Rossi-Hansberg show that the 'productivity effect' can dominate the other two: put simply, improved opportunities for offshoring low-skilled jobs will raise wages for domestic workers performing similar jobs. This is so because the companies that profit from offshoring are those companies that perform similar tasks intensively. Their increased profitability will enhance their labour demand and some of it will be directed at domestic workers who perform tasks that cannot easily be moved.

[28] Of course, rules of origin is just one challenge posed by the rise in offshoring and probably not the most important. Antras and Staiger (2011) show that, whereas only trade policies get distorted in Nash equilibrium (terms of trade), both trade and domestic policies get distorted because of offshoring. They thus contemplate that the rise in offshoring may necessitate a reorientation from shallow market access to deep integration. They thus argue in favour of positive integration in the WTO. WTO officials are fully aware of the issue: they recognize the challenges posed by offshoring and have no trouble admitting that they are still in search of solutions. In a recent speech (available at <www.wti.org>), DG Lamy publicly stated:

> ... we have not yet figured out how to deal with the interdependent world economy we have created. This (GATT) system was initially designed to tackle problems specific to the mid-twentieth century. ... The basic architecture of the system reflected its origins in an Atlantic-centric world of shallow integration. The question now is what is needed to manage a globalized world of deep integration.

[29] A good illustration is offered in an ECJ judgment (C-386/08, *Brita GmbH v Hauptzollamt Hamburg-Hafen*, judgment of 25 February 2010), where the ECJ refused to accept that there is an obligation for customs authorities to accept the origin of goods as declared by the exporter.

[30] <http://ec.europa.eu/enlargement/questions_and_answers/diagonal_cumulation_en.htm>.

the former Yugoslav Republic of Macedonia can cumulate with the Community but not amongst each other. Under the system of diagonal cumulation they will also be able to cumulate amongst each other. For a system of diagonal cumulation to work, it requires that all partners have Free Trade Agreements with the same rules of origin amongst each other.

. . .

The benefits can best be illustrated by using simple example: A product receives 30% value added in Croatia and 30% value added in the former Yugoslav Republic of Macedonia. Let's assume the EU requirement for the import of a good as 'originating in Croatia' is 50% value added in that country. Under bilateral cumulation, this product will not be exportable to the EU under preferential conditions, while with diagonal cumulation these percentages can be cumulated and the product qualifies with 60% as originating in Croatia or the former Yugoslav Republic of Macedonia.

In short, there is a panoply of similar schemes, a real mess which increases transaction costs often in a highly disproportionate manner.[31] Preferential rules of origin are often more restrictive than non-preferential rules. This aspect, along with many other negative aspects of preferential rules of origin, has been highlighted in literature. Vermulst (1992, pp. 37ff) cites numerous EU court judgments in support of this claim. Brenton and Manchin (2003) investigate EU preferential schemes (such as 'Everything But Arms') and suggest that, for them to generate substantial improvements for developing countries, the EU should reconsider its current rules of origin.[32] Mattoo et al. (2003) estimate the medium-term benefits for African exporters stemming from the US AGOA (Africa Growth and Opportunity Act) and argue that the gains would be five times as much, were the US to relax the current stringent rules of origin.[33] There is ample empirical evidence that preferential rules of origin have substantially contributed

---

[31] See Inama (2003) and Krueger (1997) on this issue.

[32] The new EU GSP (Commission Regulation EU 1063/2010, in force as of 1 January 2011) includes a simplification of rules of origin, especially for LDCs (least developed countries): a uniform local content rule of 30 per cent is applied and this threshold confers LDC origin for most manufactured goods (the percentage being 50 per cent for developing countries which are not LDCs). The percentages are calculated on the basis of the ex-works price (including profits and general expenses). *Ex-works price* means the price to be paid for the product obtained to the manufacturer in whose undertaking the last working or processing is carried out. The same regulation divides LDCs into four groups (based on geographic-proximity considerations; Art. 85), and allows for *regional cumulation* if the working in the beneficiary country goes beyond minimal operations (defined in Art. 78.1 and in Annex 16 of the Regulation). Still, there are some features that continue to be debated, such as '*double jumping*', whereby a country that produces a garment from imported fabric from imported yarn can be the country of origin of the final exported good. As explained in detail *infra*, a UN list reflects all LDCs, whereas non-OECD countries are usually considered to be developing countries. LDCs have tabled their own proposal in this respect (WTO Doc. TN/MA/W/74/Rev. 1 of 10 February 2011), where they advocated even lower percentage thresholds for conferring LDC origin.

[33] Similar evidence concerning US trade with other American countries is provided in Estevadeordal and Garay (1996).

to trade diversion.[34] Cadot and de Melo (2008) explain how rules of origin oblige developing countries to buy inefficient intermediate goods from developed countries in order to qualify for favourable treatment. Cadot et al. (2005) look at the EU (the PANEURO) and US NAFTA regimes and conclude that the rules employed are tailor-made to fit protectionist requests by EU and US lobbies. The low utilization rate is explained in their view by a number of product-specific rules of origin.[35]

The current ROO, in its Annex II, includes a common declaration with regard to preferential rules of origin. In essence, this Annex imposes a transparency obligation and nothing beyond that. Does exclusion from the ROO coverage amount to exclusion from the WTO disciplines altogether? In other words, should WTO Members be allowed to deviate even from MFN when designing their preferential rules of origin? In theory, the consistency of preferential rules of origin with the WTO can be discussed in the context of the notification of a preferential trade agreement with the WTO: they could come under either the term 'other regulations of commerce' (Art. XXIV.5 GATT), or 'restrictive regulations of commerce' (Art. XXIV.8 GATT). Indeed, this issue has already been discussed (even tangentially sometimes) in this context. WTO Members did not manage to come to an agreed solution and all we have before us is a series of inconclusive debates. Following 2006 and the advent of the Transparency Mechanism discussed *infra*, there have been no more multilateral discussions on the consistency of similar schemes with the WTO rules. Still, in the absence of a definitive head-on response to this question, the correct response should be that they must observe non-discrimination: the Enabling Clause that we discuss *infra* in this chapter allows for better treatment of goods originating in developing countries provided that all developing countries are treated the same; the only permissible exception is in favour of LDCs that can be treated better than developing countries, but no discrimination across LDCs is allowed. Case law (*EC—Tariff Preferences*) allows for subdivisions beyond the division between developing countries and LDCs provided for in the body of the Enabling Clause, if similar subdivisions rely on 'objective criteria'. It follows that the multitude of preferential rules of origin is not per se inconsistent with the WTO; a WTO Member wishing to challenge the consistency of a scheme must establish that it does not rely on objective criteria. Unfortunately, the absence of any explanation by the WTO adjudicating bodies so far as to what constitutes an 'objective criterion' makes it difficult even to speculate on what could be a winning argument here. Intuitively, one would imagine that A, in case A and B are two developing countries with similar endowments and GDP per capita and face differential rules of origin (A facing more stringent conditions than B), could have a strong case before a WTO Panel.

---

[34] For a survey of the literature, not only on this score, but on all other aspects concerning rules of origin, see Inama (2009), Krishna (2005), and Puccio (2012).

[35] Compare the analysis by Inama (2009), who arrives at similar conclusions.

Finally, note that preferential schemes were supposed to provide developing countries with better, not worse, trade opportunities, and donors cannot distinguish between beneficiaries on any grounds other than their level of development or related objective criteria that we discuss in more detail *infra*. Imaginative proposals have been tabled aimed at reducing the costs in the meantime, that is, while awaiting the advent of a comprehensive legal regime.[36]

1.2.4 Immediately and Unconditionally

WTO Members must extend any advantage (as understood above) immediately and unconditionally to all other WTO Members. WTO adjudicating bodies will typically review the consistency of a measure with the two terms simultaneously: the AB report on *Canada—Autos* is a good illustration of this point (§§75–86). Most of the interpretative problems have to do with the understanding of the term 'unconditionally', since the term 'automatically' suggests the absence of time lapse between granting an advantage to one country and extending it to all WTO Members. The issue that has occupied Panels is to what extent only conditions additional to those which are necessary for the granting of an advantage in the first place should be relevant for the interpretation of the term 'unconditionally' or, conversely, whether no conditions at all should be imposed in the first instance. The following reports have outlawed imposing conditions:

(a) the GATT Panel report on *Belgian Family Allowances*: tax exemptions for products purchased by public bodies made conditional on the existence of a certain system of family allowances to be in force in the exporting country were found to be inconsistent with Art I.1 GATT;

(b) the GATT Panel report on *EEC—Imports of Beef*: conditioning a duty waiver upon certification by a particular government violates the obligation to grant MFN unconditionally;

(c) the report of the Working Party on Accession of Hungary:[37] to condition a tariff treatment upon the prior acceptance of a cooperation agreement is a violation of the requirement imposed by Art I.1 GATT;

(d) the WTO Panel on *Indonesia—Autos*: granting tax advantages to Korean companies which had entered into arrangements with Indonesian companies was inconsistent with the obligation under Art I.1 GATT;

(e) the Panel on *EC—Tariff Preferences* in §§7.59 and 7.60 adopts an interpretation of the term 'unconditionally', whereby it becomes impossible to attach any conditions, even when the advantage is granted in the first place:

In the Panel's view, moreover, the term 'unconditionally' in Article I:1 has a broader meaning than simply that of not requiring compensation. While the Panel

---

36 See, for example, Lloyd (1993), who proposes the introduction of a tariff equivalent that will be negotiable.
37 Report adopted on 30 July 1973; see GATT Doc. BISD 20S/34.

acknowledges the European Communities' argument that conditionality in the context of traditional MFN clauses in bilateral treaties may relate to conditions of trade compensation for receiving MFN treatment, the Panel does not consider this to be the full meaning of 'unconditionally' under Article I:1. Rather, the Panel sees no reason not to give that term its ordinary meaning under Article I:1, that is, 'not limited by or subject to any conditions.'

Because the tariff preferences under the Drug Arrangements are accorded only on the condition that the receiving countries are experiencing a certain gravity of drug problems, these tariff preferences are not accorded 'unconditionally' to the like products originating in all other WTO members, as required by Article I:1. The Panel therefore finds that the tariff advantages under the Drug Arrangements are not consistent with Article I:1 of GATT 1994.

There is a second batch of cases which compare two situations and essentially try to ascertain to what extent additional conditions have been imposed when extending an already granted advantage:

(a) the GATT Panel on *EEC—Minimum Import Prices*: the EU authorities required a payment deposit from all countries that could not guarantee a specified minimum import price. However, since the payment of the deposit was requested by all exporting countries falling into this category, the EC scheme was not considered to be a violation of Art. I.1 GATT;

(b) the WTO Panel on *Canada—Autos* held the view that the term 'unconditionally' does not mean that all conditions are prohibited. Rather, 'unconditionally' refers, in the Panel's view, to the notion that MFN treatment towards another WTO Member shall not be conditional on reciprocal conduct by that other WTO Member. Thus, conditions that are non-discriminatory across two transactions involving like goods originating in two different WTO members do not violate Art. I GATT (§§10.22 and 10.24):

In our view, whether an advantage within the meaning of Article I:1 is accorded 'unconditionally' cannot be determined independently of an examination of whether it involves discrimination between like products of different countries.

. . .

In this respect, it appears to us that there is an important distinction to be made between, on the one hand, the issue of whether an advantage within the meaning of Article I:1 is subject to conditions, and, on the other, whether an advantage, once it has been granted to the product of any country, is accorded 'unconditionally' to the like product of all other Members. An advantage can be granted subject to conditions without necessarily implying that it is not accorded 'unconditionally' to the like product of other Members. More specifically, the fact that conditions attached to such an advantage are not related to the imported product itself does not necessarily imply that such conditions are discriminatory with respect to the origin of imported products. We therefore do not believe that, as argued by Japan, the word 'unconditionally' in Article I:1 must be interpreted to mean that making an advantage conditional on criteria not related to the imported product itself is *per se* inconsistent with Article I:1, irrespective of whether and how such criteria relate to the origin of the imported products.

But is there really a difference between the two strings of cases? The first string of cases simply dealt with impermissible conditions, or flat violations of MFN: indeed, granting tax advantages only to those WTO Members that have entered into contractual agreements with Indonesian companies, or accepting the certification process operated by specific WTO Members without any further explanation violate MFN outright.

The Panel on *US—Non-Rubber Footwear* dealt with a US practice that could be described as rebalancing: the US claimed that it could legitimately rebalance (offset) the damage done to some imports with respect to some measures affecting them through more favourable treatment of the same imports through other measures. In its view, in other words, it is permissible under Art. I.1 GATT to discriminate negatively with respect to some measures as long as some positive discrimination is provided through other measures. What matters, in the US view, is the total treatment of imports, that is, the treatment with respect to all of the legislation applied to a particular import transaction. The Panel disagreed. In its view, no rebalancing is permissible under Art. I GATT (§§6.10ff).

1.2.5 Like Products

The reason why the obligation to accord MFN is restricted to like products only has to do with the type of beggar-thy-neighbour policies that the GATT framers wanted to outlaw. The GATT outlaws advantages granted to like products only; as a consequence, other beggar-thy-neighbour policies remain unpunished. If Home, for example, imposes a 2 per cent import duty on cars (that it produces) and a 52 per cent import duty on wheat (that it also produces), there is nothing wrong as long as all cars and all wheat imported are burdened with the same amount even if subsequently some of the money received from duties on wheat is channelled to production of cars.[38]

Art. I GATT covers behaviour with respect to both trade and domestic instruments. We will be dealing with the latter in Chapter 4, so our comments here are confined to the MFN obligation as applied to tariffs: tariff classification emerges as the dominant criterion in this context.[39] First, the 1978 Panel on *EEC—Animal Feed Proteins* employed this criterion to decide whether two goods were like: the question arose as to whether, by treating different protein products in different ways, the EU was violating its obligations. There was little doubt that the products at hand could be regarded as substitutable, that is, as belonging to the same relevant product market. The question, however, was whether such a criterion

---

[38] Similar behaviour could be caught by the SCM disciplines, but is totally safe from challenge under the MFN clause. Money is of course fungible and higher prices for good A might induce consumers to buy more of good B even if A and B do not compete in the same relevant product market. Still, a high degree of substitutability across products is a better indicator of affording an advantage to a particular good (and, thus, diverting a concession).

[39] See on this issue the comprehensive analysis of Davey and Pauwelyn (2000).

(substitutability) was still appropriate to decide likeness under Art. I GATT.[40] The Panel decided that this should not be the case, noting that (§4.20):

> ... such factors as the number of products and tariff items carrying different duty rates and tariff bindings, the varying protein contents and the different vegetable, animal and synthetic origins of the protein products before the Panel—not all of which were subject to the EEC measures. Therefore, the Panel concluded that these various protein products could not be considered as 'like products' within the meaning of Articles I and III (§ 4.2).
>
> ...
>
> The Panel noted that the general most-favoured-nation treatment provided for in Article I:1 ... did not mention directly competitive or substitutable products. In this regard the Panel did not consider animal, marine and synthetic proteins to be products like those vegetable proteins covered by the measures.

The Panel on *Japan—SPF Dimension Lumber* went even further and provided an explicit acknowledgement of the relevance of tariff classification as the dominant criterion to establish likeness (§§5.11–12):

> ... if a claim of likeness was raised by a contracting party in relation to the tariff treatment of its goods on importation by some other contracting party, such a claim should be based on the classification of the latter, i.e., the importing country's tariff.
>
> The Panel noted in this respect that 'dimension lumber', as defined by Canada, was a concept extraneous to the Japanese Tariff ... nor did it belong to any internationally accepted customs classification. The Panel concluded therefore that reliance by Canada on the concept of dimension lumber was not an appropriate basis for establishing 'likeness' of products under Article I:1 of the General Agreement.

GATT Panels have even gone so far as to dismiss the relevance of factors other than tariff classification, arguing that they are irrelevant for the purposes of defining likeness. The GATT Panel on *Spain—Unroasted Coffee*, for example, set aside the relevance of process-based distinctions in defining likeness (§§4.7–4.10):

> The Panel examined all arguments that had been advanced during the proceedings for the justification of a different tariff treatment for various groups and types of unroasted coffee. It noted that these arguments mainly related to organoleptic differences resulting from geographical factors, cultivation methods, the processing of the beans, and the genetic factor. The Panel did not consider that such differences were sufficient reason to allow for a different treatment. It pointed out that it was not unusual in the case of agricultural products that the taste and aroma of the end-product would differ because of one or several of the above-mentioned factors.
>
> The Panel furthermore found relevant to its examination of the matter that unroasted coffee was mainly, if not exclusively, sold in the form of blends, combining various types of coffee, and that coffee, in its end-use, was universally regarded as a well-defined and single product intended for drinking.

---

[40] As we shall see in Chapter 4, substitutability is a key criterion to decide likeness in the context of the discipline applied to domestic instruments.

The Panel noted that no other contracting party applied its tariff regime in respect of unroasted, non-decaffeinated coffee in such a way that different types of coffee were subject to different tariff rates.

In light of the foregoing, the Panel *concluded* that un-roasted, non-decaffeinated coffee beans listed in the Spanish Customs Tariff...should be considered as like products within the meaning of Article I:1. (emphasis in the original)

Distinctions like the ones mentioned in the Panel report on *Spain—Unroasted Coffee* could well be part of a national schedule of commitments in today's world: recall that the HS extends up to the six-digit level, but WTO Members can shape their tariff bindings using eight-digit or more classifications. Should we keep the harmonized regime (up to six-digit classifications) as benchmark for deciding on likeness? Or should we allow for likeness definitions under national classifications as well? The latter might be highly idiosyncratic and, as we saw above, probably challengeable before a WTO Panel. Case law has not provided us with a number. The six-digit level provides detailed enough classifications. A similar criterion (detailed classifications) has been privileged by the AB to decide on likeness under Art III.2 GATT in its report on *Japan—Alcoholic Beverages II*, as we will see in Chapter 4. Should we use the same criterion here?

There has been no definitive answer to this question so far. One should keep in mind that, by virtue of Art. 3.3 HS, national classifications beyond the six-digit level are not illegal as long as they specify a six-digit classification. Specification can come under various forms and colours. Assume, for example that at the six-digit level the commodity 'construction material' appears, and Home has bound import duties for this good at 10 per cent *ad valorem*. Home has also introduced in its schedule, at the eight-digit level, a distinction between asbestos-containing and asbestos-free construction material, imposing a 10 per cent import duty on the former and a 0 per cent import duty on the latter. Foreign produces asbestos-free and External, asbestos-containing material; External, because of the disadvantage it has suffered (assume pre-tariff prices of construction material across the two WTO Members are symmetric), challenges the eight-digit classification, arguing that both types of construction material are like products and should receive the same treatment. If the WTO judge sticks to the six-digit classification, External wins, but if the judge moves to discuss likeness under the eight-digit classification, External might lose depending on whether the judge finds the eight-digit classifications to be in conformity with Art. 3.3 HS (which, recall, is the legal context of GATT): the question here for the judge will be to what extent asbestos-containing and asbestos-free construction material are like products.

In the absence of case law directly addressing this issue, the only case from which one could draw useful references is the AB report on *EC—Tariff Preferences*. There the AB judged that an EU scheme conferring tariff preferences on a subset of developing countries upon satisfaction of criteria unilaterally set by the EU would be GATT-consistent to the extent that the criteria on which distinctions relied were objective. The AB left it for later to decide what an objective criterion is. In this case, the AB did not use the term 'objective criterion' as standard to draw permissible regulatory distinctions across goods, but across beneficiaries of preferences. The question was whether a country that combats drug trafficking and a country that does not should benefit from the same level of tariff preferences. The AB responded negatively to this question. It is also true that this case was decided under the Enabling Clause which, as we will see *infra*, allows for distinctions between developing countries, whereas the MFN does not. Still, one cannot exclude that WTO adjudicating bodies could use this case law in order to decide whether eight-digit classifications rely on objective criteria: one cannot exclude, for example, that worldwide concerns such as the protection against climate change could, prima facie, satisfy the criterion for objectivity and thus provide the basis for lawfully distinguishing between two products which would otherwise have been considered 'like products'.[41]

1.3 Exceptions

There are numerous exceptions to the MFN clause. Besides Arts. XX and XXI GATT, which we discuss in Chapter 5, WTO Members can treat goods originating in a subpart of the WTO Membership better than the rest of the Membership on two occasions: if the recipient of the favour is a developing country or if two WTO Members have signed a preferential trade agreement between them.[42] Grandfathering and waivers can also serve as exceptional grounds justifying deviations.

1.3.1 Grandfathering

Art. I.2 GATT contains the so-called 'grandfathering' clause: GATT contracting parties agreed to exempt from the coverage of the MFN first the imperial preferences (granted by the UK to countries and territories participating in its Commonwealth) and then, as quid pro quo, other preferences in place before 1 January 1948 across other GATT contracting parties. Annexes A–F to the GATT contain the list of the grandfathered preferences.[43]

This scheme of imperial preferences involved both higher duties on non-British Empire goods and lower duties on Dominion goods, and drew the ire of excluded countries for discriminating against their trade. Cordell Hull was an especially sharp critic of imperial preferences because of their adverse effect on US exports,

---

[41] WTO Members might prefer to use a trade (elaborate tariff classification) instead of a domestic instrument in order to advance social preferences: WTO Members might wish to commit at the border in order to avoid subsequent pressures to enact domestic laws to the contrary. Moreover, providing for policies that meet the approval of their trading partners (especially the most powerful ones) could be compensated through benefits they might receive in return.

[42] We discuss both *infra* in this chapter.

[43] See, on this score, Jackson (1969) and Irwin et al. (2008).

particularly to the UK and Canada, two of America's most important markets. Testifying before Congress in 1940, Cordell Hull called imperial preferences.

> the greatest injury, in a commercial way, that has been inflicted on this country since I have been in public life.[44]

Hull thought that the GATT was desirable also as a means to reduce the discriminatory effect against US exports. In 1938, the US and the UK signed a reciprocal trade agreement, but the negotiation was difficult and the results were limited. Despite Hull's best efforts, the agreement failed to put a dent in Britain's system of tariff preferences. Britain's entry into World War II in September 1939 and the ensuing trade controls reduced its value even further.

The negotiation of MFN was intimately linked to the issue of imperial preferences. As Brown (1950, pp. 70ff) points out, the MFN was the principle and the imperial preferences the exception: the latter could not be increased beyond the level existing on 1 July 1939, or 1 July 1946, whichever was lower. We briefly noted in Chapter 1 the widespread agreement in the literature that there was an implicit quid pro quo throughout the negotiation between the US and the UK that the extent of the MFN (the US commitment) would be a function of the reduction of the imperial preferences (the commitment by the UK).[45] During the London Conference, it was agreed that, in addition to imperial preferences, other long-standing preferences, such as those between Cuba and the US, would be permitted temporarily.[46] Eventually, others joined in: the various Annexes (A–F) to the GATT refer to colonial preferences by France, Belgium, as well as other bilateral preferences like US-Cuba. In this vein, §3 was added to Art. I GATT at the Havana Conference: this paragraph deals with preferences across certain countries of the Near East (Ottoman Empire).[47] Other annexes were added so that some preferences could qualify for exemption. The annexes concerned Portuguese territories, and the special regime between Italy, San Marino, and the Vatican.

Clayton was very much in line with Hull with respect to his attitude towards imperial preferences. The presidential decision to override Clayton's council to abandon hopes of an agreement with the UK because of the latter's refusal to reduce its imperial preferences ultimately ensured the success of the Geneva tariff negotiations and the advent of the GATT: to Clayton's disappointment, Britain's imperial preferences remained largely intact.[48] Their dismantlement had to wait almost 50 years: it was the advent of the WTO that signalled the end of grandfathering.

---

[44] Quoted in Gardner (1956) at p. 19.
[45] Irwin et al. (2008).
[46] E/PC/T/C/30 at p. 3.
[47] The GATT Analytical Index, 3rd revision, The GATT: Geneva, 1970 at pp. 3ff.
[48] See Zeiler (1999) and Toye (2003) for details on the conclusion of the negotiations.

1.3.2. Waivers

A WTO Member may, in exceptional circumstances, request that it be exempted from its obligations under the WTO. To this effect, a Member must submit a request for a waiver to the WTO Membership (Art. IX of the Agreement Establishing the WTO). We discuss waivers in Chapter 5 since they constitute an exception not only to MFN, but also to other obligations assumed under the GATT.

2. Special and Differential Treatment for Developing Countries

2.1 The Legal Discipline and its Rationale

Recall from our discussion in Chapter 1 that the original GATT membership was a rather homogeneous group of 23 countries. Following the advent of the GATT, a number of countries acceded to independence and eventually joined the GATT. A large number of them were rather poor, developing countries who were encouraged to join the GATT in light of the unambiguous desire of the GATT contracting parties to increase participation in the agreement. Developing countries were joining an agreement which was not designed as a two-tier system: the GATT provisions, with very few exceptions, were one fit for all irrespective of the level of development of participants. From the early days of their participation, developing countries aimed at changing this picture, first by introducing the possibility for preferential tariffs for developing countries' products, and eventually by encouraging that the WTO, the successor of the GATT, receives a place in the world inter-institutional dialogue on development. This is how the story unfolds.[49]

Developing countries initially felt that they could not compete for export markets on an equal basis with developed countries. In their view, the MFN tariff rate amounted to an impediment to their export trade, in that it provided for non-discriminatory access to export markets irrespective of the level of development of the exporting country. They requested the establishment of a new mechanism that would allow them to access their export markets at preferential (when compared to developed countries' exports) tariff rates. This is what Part IV of the GATT, which was introduced in 1965, and the Enabling Clause enacted in 1979 are supposed to achieve.

Already during the negotiation of the GATT, Lebanon had argued in favour of introducing tariff preferences for trade across developing countries, although it was

---

[49] There are dozens of accounts on this issue, and Hudec (1987) figures prominently among them. Graham (1978) discusses the origins of the US system.

not accepted.[50] And, as Irwin et al. (2008) note, India (before partition) had a hostile reaction when it was presented with the Suggested Charter and was requested to comment upon it: its criticism focused on MFN, arguing that this instrument was ill-equipped to deal with countries at different stages of development.[51] One could trace various other sporadic initiatives to this effect in the early years of the GATT as well. Still, the first time a comprehensive discussion on trade and development took place in the GATT was in 1958 with the circulation of the Haberler report.

Haberler, professor of economics at Harvard, was requested by the GATT to examine the validity of claims by the less developed trading partners that the existing rules on trade liberalization would not necessarily work to their advantage. He ended up concluding that similar claims were not entirely unjustified.[52] In his report, both the short- and the long-term trends in commodity prices and the factors influencing them were examined. The report concluded, *inter alia*, that existing protectionist policies in the farm sector by developed (industrialized) nations, as well as tariff escalation practices by many developed nations, were contributing factors to lack of growth in developing countries. It is worth recounting, in this respect, that the US had obtained a waiver in 1955 which allowed it to grossly subsidize its farm production over the subsequent years and essentially shield domestic producers from the challenges of international competition.[53]

The Haberler report made a series of recommendations to address the issue, and reduction of the existing protectionism was one of the measures suggested. Importantly, it sensitized the trading partners to the fact that not all gain alike

---

[50] In the words of the Lebanese delegate: 'Members recognize that the development of industry in small nations is hampered by the lack of a sufficiently large market for manufactured goods. Consequently, the Organization shall give the most favourable consideration to any proposal for preferential tariff arrangements presented to it by small Member nations belonging to one economic region, aiming at the development of that region, with a view to releasing from their obligations under Chapter V.' This proposal did not concern north-south preferences, but rather, south-south preferences aiming at developing industries within regional blocks; see E/PC/T/C.6/W/25 at p. 14.

[51] Trade, of course, is only part of a development strategy and there are inherent limits to how much development can be achieved through trade liberalization. This much should be obvious. Tupy (2005), for example, commenting on how much the Doha round can do to alleviate the problems that African states are facing (and obviously trying to bring some sense to those who saw the round as a cure-all), eloquently stated that 'trade liberalization as a cure for African poverty is often over-emphasized. The main causes of African impoverishment are internal'.

[52] GATT (1958), *Trends in International Trade*, Geneva. Gottfried Haberler, of Harvard University, was one of the best trade economists of his time.

[53] The EU barely existed in 1958 when Haberler issued his report. In subsequent years, nevertheless, the EU farm market remained hermetically closed to exports from developing countries: by adopting the notorious *variable levies*, whereby any imported product, when imported into the EU, would be burdened with a customs duty which equalled the difference between the world and the EU, exports to the lucrative European market were discouraged. As a result, the two most attractive markets were at the mercy of their domestic producers and not open to world competition. The subsequent enactment of the MFA, as we saw *supra* in this chapter, ensured that trade in textiles, yet another labour-intensive industry, would be limited in quantities. Limiting exports of farm and textile products worked to the huge disadvantage of developing countries.

from the existing regime; something needed to be done to address the concerns of those who were being left behind, essentially the producers of labour-intensive goods.

Haberler's report was not, alas, the only game in town. Hans Singer, a German professor of economics at Cambridge, and Raoul Prebisch, an Argentine economist, were advocating industrialization through import substitution policies as the safest way to development. The argument for import substitution was justified as the adequate response to what was termed '*terms of trade pessimism*', the idea that exports of developing countries were progressing at a slower pace than total exports.[54] Note that, during that time, liberal market economies were discredited in the eyes of many observers, especially in developing countries, and a strong argument in favour of government-driven economies was falling onto fertile ground. Prebisch and Singer had a head start over Haberler in some quarters.[55]

The view that development essentially equalled industrialization (supported by the influence of terms-of-trade elasticity pessimism) provided developing countries with the necessary impetus to adopt negotiating strategies aimed at achieving preferential access in developed countries' markets: in a nutshell, their request would be framed in terms of non-reciprocal preferential access to developed countries' markets. Thanks to economies of scale resulting from non-reciprocal preferential access of their products (so the argument goes), developing countries would gradually become more competitive in the production of industrial goods, which should be their objective anyway. Haberler lost then and there: developing countries started submitting their requests for a negotiation on preferential tariff rates for developing countries only.

A Working Party on Commodities was established to review trends and developments in international commodity trade; the Singer-Prebisch thesis was reflected therein, as the quoted passage from the report in 1961 evidences:

> ... in the long term, only the industrialization of the less-developed countries would enable these countries to overcome the present difficulties in their external trade; in turn, this industrialization and the economic development generally of the less-developed countries would only be achieved through an increase in their exports,

---

[54] A related idea was what became known as '*elasticity pessimism*': devaluation will improve the trade balance assuming the Marshall-Lerner condition holds, that is, the sum of import and export demand elasticities exceeds one in absolute value. If elasticities are too low, other means (possibly QR) are needed to change an adverse trade balance. There is almost no evidence that the elasticities are so low, but that was the post-war fear of many developing countries: see Lal (2000).

[55] Their position has become known as the *Singer-Prebisch thesis*: by looking at examined data over a certain period of time, they came to conclude that the terms of trade for primary commodity exporters (the commodities where developing countries had comparative advantage) had a tendency to decline. The explanation for this was that, for manufactured (industrial) goods, the income elasticity of demand is greater than it is for farm goods: as incomes rise, the demand for the former increased more rapidly than did demand for the latter. Consequently, the argument goes, it is the structure of the market that creates inequality in the world system. For a number of reasons, this thesis is not popular among economists any more.

including exports of manufactured and semi-manufactured goods. Direct investment and financial aid alone would not solve this problem.[56]

During the Kennedy round of international trade negotiations (1962–7), the
Committee on Legal and Institutional Framework of GATT in Relation to Less-
Developed Countries (one of the negotiating groups) worked on a chapter on
Trade and Development. This chapter was finalized at a Special Session of the
CONTRACTING PARTIES, held from 17 November 1964 to 8 February 1965.
It was annexed to the GATT as an amending protocol. It now appears as Part
IV. Part IV came into effect on 27 June 1966, and consists of three new legal
provisions: Principles and Objectives (Art. XXXVI GATT), Commitments (Art.
XXXVII GATT), and Joint Action (Art. XXXVIII GATT).

A look at the wording of each provision leaves the reader in no doubt that these
were meant to be 'best endeavours' clauses aiming at opening the door to
discriminatory (preferential) trade.

Following this negotiation, the feeling among developing countries was that
Part IV had fallen short of substantively contributing to the development policies
pursued, and that an additional mechanism was needed to, at the very least, make
the language included in these provisions operational. This mechanism was,
initially, a ten-year waiver allowing for preferential rates applicable to imports
originating in developing countries only; this was subsequently replaced by the
Enabling Clause. The Enabling Clause reproduces the non-reciprocity idea, first
embedded in Art. XXXVI.8 GATT, and provides for the possibility to make
commitments in this vein.[57] The Panel on *EC—Tariff Preferences* recounts the
advent of the Enabling Clause in the following terms:

> During the Second Session of UNCTAD, on 26 March 1968, a Resolution was
> adopted on 'Expansion and Diversification of Exports and Manufactures and semi-
> manufactures of Developing Countries' (Resolution 21 (II)). In this Resolution,
> UNCTAD agreed to the 'early establishment of a mutually acceptable system of
> generalized, non-reciprocal and non-discriminatory preferences which would be
> beneficial to the developing countries' and established a Special Committee on
> Preferences as a subsidiary organ of the Trade and Development Board, with a
> mandate to settle the details of the GSP arrangements. In 1970, UNCTAD's Special
> Committee on Preferences adopted Agreed Conclusions which set up the agreed
> details of the GSP arrangement. UNCTAD's Trade and Development Board took
> note of these Agreed Conclusions on 13 January 1970. In accordance with the
> Agreed Conclusions, certain developed GATT contracting parties sought a waiver
> for the GSP from the GATT Council. The GATT granted a 10-year waiver on

---

[56] GATT Doc. L/1656 of 4 December 1961, published in GATT Doc. BISD 10S/83ff, at p. 93.
During the 1955 review of the GATT, Art. XXVIII GATT was redrafted in order to help the quest
for import substitution policies which was largely reflected in Art. XXVIII(c) GATT.

[57] A GSP is a list of products for which a tariff preference is accorded in favour of goods
originating in developing countries. See, *inter alia*, Inama (2003), Keck and Low (2003),
Michalopoulos (2001), Rodrik (1999), Srinivasan (1998), Wang and Winters (2000), and
Whalley (1989).

25 June 1971. Before the expiry of this waiver, the CONTRACTING PARTIES adopted a decision on 'Differential and More Favourable Treatment, Reciprocity and Fuller Participation of Developing Countries' (the 'Enabling Clause') on 28 November 1979.

The Enabling Clause is, thus, the decision of the GATT CONTRACTING PARTIES which allowed ('enabled') deviations from the MFN rate in favour of goods originating in developing countries to become a permanent feature of the GATT—and now the WTO legal order. Through the Enabling Clause, WTO Members can now legitimately accord tariff preferences to developing countries: national GSP (Generalized System of Preferences) schemes are the vehicle to make this happen.[58] Of course, similar treatment is reserved to developing countries that are Members of the WTO and not to any developing country irrespective of whether it has joined the WTO or not.

2.2 Coverage of the Legal Discipline

2.2.1 Part IV

Art. XXXVI GATT constitutes the formal recognition that market access for products of export interest to developing countries has to be improved. It stops short, nevertheless, of prescribing measures that should be adopted to this effect. It does, on the other hand, provide the foundation for non-reciprocity to come under the aegis of the GATT (§8):

> The developed contracting parties do not expect reciprocity for commitments made by them in trade negotiations to reduce or remove tariffs and other barriers to the trade of less-developed contracting parties.

The Interpretative Note to this provision sheds some additional light:

> It is understood that the phrase 'do not expect reciprocity' means, in accordance with the objectives set forth in this Article, that the less-developed contracting parties should not be expected, in the course of trade negotiations, to make contributions which are inconsistent with their individual development, financial and trade needs, taking into consideration past trade developments.

During the Kennedy round, this provision was further interpreted as follows:

> There will, therefore, be no balancing of concessions granted on products of interest to developing countries by developed participants on the one hand and the contribution which developing participants would make to the objective of trade liberalization on the other and which it is agreed should be considered in the light of the development, financial and trade needs of developing countries themselves. It is,

---

[58] The best-known GSP schemes are the EU (discussed in Candau and Jean (2009)); the US (Dean and Wainio (2009)); the Japanese (Komuro (2009)); the Canadian (Kowalski (2009)); and the Australian (Lippoldt (2009)).

therefore, recognized that the developing countries themselves must decide what contributions they can make.[59]

Art. XXXVII GATT is a general clause recommending various actions that developed countries should undertake in order to help promote issues of interest to developing countries: chief among them, the incitation to reduce the gap between (high) barriers on processed goods, and (low) barriers on primary products: this is, of course, tariff escalation. The validity of this argument, though, is at best doubtful: in this scenario (high tariffs for processed, low tariffs for primary goods), the problem seems to be the high tariff on processed goods and not the gap in the level of tariffs between processed and primary goods. The remaining part of this provision deals with issues that were further detailed in other agreements: for example, developed countries, when imposing CVD or AD duties, or introducing safeguard measures, were to 'have special regard to the trade interests' of developing countries and 'explore all possibilities of constructive remedies before applying such measures': in the AD Agreement concluded during the Uruguay round, WTO Members agreed to transform this into a binding legal obligation. It has since been consistently interpreted as an obligation to examine the feasibility of introducing price undertakings on dumped imports originating in developing countries, before AD duties have been eventually imposed.

Art. XXXVIII GATT was meant to provide the institutional vehicle that would make the best-endeavours clauses reflected in the two aforementioned provisions operational: institutional arrangements for furthering the objectives of Part IV should be made, collaboration to this effect with the United Nations and its organs and agencies was envisaged, and some monitoring of the rate of growth of the trade of developing countries should be introduced. This is where the Enabling Clause kicks in.

2.2.2 *The Enabling Clause*

The most important features of the Enabling Clause can be recapped as follows:[60]

(a) It announces the general principle that deviations from MFN are allowed for products originating in developing countries (§1);

(b) Concessions (§2) can be expressed in tariff (§2(a)), as well as non-tariff terms (§2(b));

(c) It provides the legal basis for developing countries to form preferential trade agreements between them while respecting less onerous requirements than those established by Art. XXIV GATT (§2(c));[61]

---

[59] GATT, COM.TD/W/37, p. 9.

[60] Decision on Differential and More Favourable Treatment Reciprocity and Fuller Participation of Developing Countries of 28 November 1979 (GATT Doc. L/4903), GATT BISD 26S/203ff.

[61] We discuss Art. XXIV GATT *infra* in this chapter.

(d) It distinguishes between developing countries and least developed countries (LDCs), the latter being a subgroup of the former, allowing for additional (to those granted to developing countries) preferences for LDCs (§2(d));

(e) Measures coming under its purview must be designed to correspond to the 'development, financial and trade needs of developing countries' (§3(c));

(f) WTO Members that have recourse to measures coming under the purview of the Enabling Clause must notify the WTO Membership, and consult with them, whenever appropriate (§4);

(g) Donors should not expect reciprocity from beneficiaries (§5);

(h) LDCs should not, in general, be expected to make commitments that might jeopardize their development, financial, and trade needs (§8);

(i) Graduation is established in terms of a reflected acknowledgement that developing countries are expected to participate more fully in the multilateral trading system as long as their economic situation improves (§7).[62]

The AB, in its report on *EC—Tariff Preferences*, held that the Enabling Clause had become an integral part of the GATT, by virtue of Art. 1(b)(iv) GATT 1994.[63] In the same report, it notes that, since the Enabling Clause enables WTO Members to grant tariff preferences to a subset of the WTO Membership (namely, developing countries), it constitutes a legal exception to Art. I GATT (§99). The legal implication, in the AB's view, is that the Enabling Clause takes precedence over Art. I GATT (§102). As to the allocation of the burden of proof, the AB, reversing the Panel in this respect, held that it is insufficient for a complaining party, when challenging a measure taken pursuant to the Enabling Clause, to simply claim violation of Art. I GATT (§110). Due process considerations (§113) require that the complaining party:

> *identify* those provisions of the Enabling Clause with which the scheme is allegedly inconsistent, without bearing the burden of *establishing* the facts necessary to support such inconsistency. (§115; emphasis in the original)

Identification, of course, does not amount to an obligation to respect the standard of review associated with a claim under the Enabling Clause. The soundness of this approach can, of course, be questioned. It would,probably have made better sense for the AB to go all the way and construct the Enabling Clause, not as an exception to Art. I GATT, but as a self-standing obligation: WTO Members apply one set of tariffs to imports from developed nations, and another on imports originating in developing countries. Complainants will carry a similar burden of proof irrespective of whether they attack violations of MFN or of the Enabling Clause. More

---

[62] The terminology is a bit confusing in this respect since the Enabling Clause here refers to 'less-developed', whereas before reference was to developing and least developed countries. The fact that in §7 it refers to less-developed in the same context with developed countries should leave no doubt that the terms 'less-developed' and 'developing' are used alternatively.

[63] See the discussion in Chapter 1.

than anything else, the functionality of the AB innovation in the allocation of the burden of proof here is hard to fully grasp.

WTO Members (donors) can but do not have to provide preferences. If they decide to do so, then they must respect the Enabling Clause. The letter and the spirit of the Enabling Clause make it clear that preferences can be granted to developing countries (and not to other developed countries): the clause does not, however, lay down any specific criteria to decide which WTO Members will be classified as developing countries. Developing countries in the WTO are designated on the basis of the 'self-selection' principle (itself an expression of the principle of sovereignty).

There is no doubt as to the identity of the LDCs, a subset of the developing countries' group as per §2(d) of the Enabling Clause: WTO recognizes as LDCs those countries which have been designated as such by the UN. There are currently 48 LDCs on the UN list,[64] 33 of which are WTO Members: Angola; Bangladesh; Benin; Burkina Faso; Burundi; Cambodia; Central African Republic; Chad; Congo, Democratic Republic of the; Djibouti; Gambia; Guinea; Guinea Bissau; Haiti; Lesotho; Madagascar; Malawi; Mali; Mauritania; Mozambique; Myanmar; Nepal; Niger; Rwanda; Samoa, Senegal; Sierra Leone; Solomon Islands; Tanzania; Togo; Uganda; Vanuatu, Zambia.[65] Ten more LDCs are currently negotiating their accession to the WTO: Afghanistan, Bhutan, Comoros, Equatorial Guinea, Ethiopia, Laos, Liberia, São Tomé and Príncipe, Sudan, and Yemen. Geographically, 33/48 are located in Africa, 14 in Asia, and only one (Haiti) in the Caribbean.

Preferences for LDCs vary across donors (see Table 3.1). The EU has its own initiative in place aiming to help LDCs, the so-called EBA (Everything But Arms).

---

64 <http://www.unohrlls.org/en/ldc/related/62/>. On this webpage we find the UN criteria for including a country among the LDCs. We quote: In its latest triennial review of the list of LDCs in 2009, the UN Committee for Development Policy used the following three criteria for the identification of the LDCs: (i) A low-income criterion, based on a three-year average estimate of the gross national income (GNI) per capita (under $905 for inclusion, above $1,086 for graduation); (ii) A human capital status criterion, involving a composite Human Assets Index (HAI) based on indicators of: (a) nutrition: percentage of population undernourished; (b) health: mortality rate for children aged five years or under; (c) education: the gross secondary school enrolment ratio; and (d) adult literacy rate; and (iii) An economic vulnerability criterion, involving a composite Economic Vulnerability Index (EVI) based on indicators of: (a) population size; (b) remoteness; (c) merchandise export concentration; (d) share of agriculture, forestry, and fisheries in gross domestic product; (e) homelessness owing to natural disasters; (f) instability of agricultural production; and (g) instability of exports of goods and services. To be added to the list, a country must satisfy all three criteria. In addition, since the fundamental meaning of the LDC category, i.e. the recognition of structural handicaps, excludes large economies, the population must not exceed 75 million. To become eligible for graduation, a country must reach threshold levels for graduation for at least two of the aforementioned three criteria or its GNI per capita must exceed at least twice the threshold level, and the likelihood that the level of GNI per capita is sustainable must be deemed high.

65 Graduation applies here. The UN removed as of 1 January 2008 Cape Verde from this list where it previously featured; see UN GA Res. A/Res/59/210 of 20 December 2004. Donors followed suit: the EU, for example, removed Cape Verde from its list of LDCs beneficiaries of preferences through Regulation 1547/2007 of 21 December 2007, OJ L337/70.

Table 3.1 Preferences in favour of LDCs[a]

Preference-granting country	Description	Beneficiary(ies)	Coverage/margin of preference	References
Australia	Duty- and quota-free entry. Entry into force: 1 July 2003	LDCs	All products	WT/COMTD/N/18
Belarus	Harmonized System of preference by the Eurasian Economic Community (EAEC) Entry into force: May 2001	47 LDCs	Duty-free access for all products	WT/TPR/S/170
Brazil	Duty-free and quota-free scheme for LDCs	LDCs	Duty-free and quota-free access for products from LDCs covering 80 per cent of all tariff lines to be granted by mid-2010.	WT/COMTD/LDC/M/55
Canada	GSP—Least-developed Countries' Tariff Programme (LDCT) Entry into force: 1 January 2003, extended until 30 June 2014	LDCs	With the exception of over-quota tariff items for dairy, poultry, and egg products, Canada provides duty-free access under all tariff items for imports from LDCs	WT/COMTD/N/15/ Add.1 and Add.2 WT/ COMTD/W/159
China	Asia-Pacific Trade Agreement (APTA)[b]— amendment to the Bangkok Agreement	Bangladesh	In addition to 1,697 products (with average margin of preference of 26.7 per cent) available to all APTA members, tariff concessions granted exclusively to LDC members on 161 products with average margin of preference of 77.9 per cent	WT/COMTD/N/22
	Entry into force: 1 September 2006	Lao PDR		
		Bangladesh	On top of Asia-Pacific Trade Agreement (APTA), unilateral special preferential tariffs (zero rated) are offered on additional 87 tariff lines	Information received from the Government of China

China (cont'd)	Framework Agreement on Comprehensive Economic Co-operation between ASEAN and China Entry into force: 1 January 2006	Cambodia	Duty-free treatment on 418 tariff lines	Information received from the Government of China
	Framework Agreement on Comprehensive Economic Co-operation between ASEAN and China	Cambodia	On top of Framework Agreement on Comprehensive Economic Co-operation between ASEAN and China, unilateral special preferential tariffs (zero rated) are offered on additional 420 tariff lines	Information received from the Government of China
	Framework Agreement on Comprehensive Economic Co-operation between ASEAN and China Entry into force: 1 January 2006	Lao PDR	Duty-free treatment on 330 tariff lines	Information received from the Government of China
	Framework Agreement on Comprehensive Economic Co-operation between ASEAN and China Entry into force: 1 January 2006	Lao PDR	On top of Framework Agreement on Comprehensive Economic Co-operation between ASEAN and China, unilateral special preferential tariffs (zero rated) are offered on additional 399 tariff lines	Information received from the Government of China
	Framework Agreement on Comprehensive Economic Co-operation between ASEAN and China Entry into force: 1 January 2006	Myanmar	Duty-free treatment on 220 tariff lines	Information received from the Government of China
	Framework Agreement on Comprehensive Economic Co-operation between ASEAN and China	Myanmar	On top of Framework Agreement on Comprehensive Economic Co-operation between ASEAN and China, unilateral special preferential tariffs (zero rated) are offered on additional 226 tariff lines	Information received from the Government of China
	Forum on China-Africa Co-operation	African countries including LDCs having diplomatic relations with China	As of 1 July 2010, China grants zero-tariff to 4,762 tariff lines imported from 33 LDCs which had completed the exchange of letters for that purpose. Eight more LDCs will enjoy the same treatment once the exchange of	WT/COMTD/W/164 WT/COMTD/M/77 WT/COMTD/LDC/M/57

(Continued)

Table 3.1 *Continued*

Preference-granting country	Description	Beneficiary(ies)	Coverage/margin of preference	References
			letters is completed. The 4,762 tariff lines account for roughly 60 per cent of China's total tariff lines, and represented 98.2 per cent of all LDC exports to China in value in 2008. Zero-tariff treatment will be expanded with the aim of achieving the final objective of including 95 per cent of China's total tariff lines	
	Special preference tariff	Afghanistan, Maldives, Samoa, Vanuatu, and Yemen	Unilateral special preferential tariffs (zero rated) are offered on 286 categories of products	Information received from the Government of China
EU	GSP—Everything But Arms (EBA) initiative	LDCs	Since 1 October 2009, the EBA has been granting DFQF access for all products from all LDCs (except arms and ammunitions). The EU introduced revised rules of origin for the GSP, as of 1 January 2011, simplifying rules specially for the LDCs	WT/COMTD/N/4/Add.2 and Add.4 WT/TPR/S/ 214/Rev.1
	Entry into force: 5 March 2001 Economic Partnership Agreements (EPAs)	79 African, Caribbean and Pacific (ACP) countries, 40 of which are LDCs	EPAs include provision for duty-free and quota-free market access. As of February 2011, a full EPA was signed by the 15 countries in the Caribbean Forum of ACP states (CARIFORUM), of which Haiti is an LDC. Interim EPAs are signed by the following LDCs: (i) Southern African Development Community (SADC): Lesotho and Mozambique; (ii) Eastern and Southern	ec.europa.eu WT/TPR/S/214/Rev.1 WT7COMTD/LDC/W/ 46/Rev.1/Corr.1 <http://ec. europa.eu/trade/index_en. htm>

(Continued)

			Africa (ESA): Madagascar (signatures by Comoros and Zambia are pending). Interim EPAs are initialled with the East African Community (EAC), which includes four LDCs: Burundi, Rwanda, Tanzania and Uganda.	
Iceland	GSP—Tariff Preferences in Regard to the Importation of Products Originating in the World's Poorest Developing Countries. Entry into force: 29 January 2002	LDCs	Essentially all products with some exceptions in agricultural products (HS chapters: 04, 15, 18, 19, 21, and 22) and non-agricultural products (HS subheadings: 3502 and 3823, and all of HS 16 with the exception of subheadings 1603 to 1605)	WT/COMTD/N/17 and Corr.1 WT/TPR/S/164
India	Asia-Pacific Trade Agreement (APTA)—amendment to the Bangkok Agreement. Entry into force: 1 September 2006	Bangladesh	In addition to 570 products (with average margin of preference of 23.9 per cent) available to all APTA members, tariff concessions granted exclusively to LDC members on 48 products with average margin of preference of 39.7 per cent	WT/COMTD/N/22
	Duty-Free Tariff Preference Scheme (DFTP)	Lao PDR LDCs	DFTP Scheme announced in April 2008. Duty-free access on 85 per cent tariff lines at HS six-digit level within a five-year time frame	WT/COMTD/M/69
	South Asian Free Trade Agreement (SAFTA)ᶜ Entry into force: 1 January 2006	Bangladesh	In addition to tariff concessions on 2,940 line at the HS six-digit level to all SAFTA members, special concessions exclusively granted to LDC members. In 2006/2007, preferential rates were granted on 84.4 per cent of all tariff lines at average rate of 10.6 per cent (while 15 per cent for non-LDC members)	WT/COMTD/10 WT/TPR/S/182.Rev.1 and WT/COMTD/N/26

Table 3.1 *Continued*

Preference-granting country	Description	Beneficiary(ies)	Coverage/margin of preference	References
		Bhutan		
		Maldives		
		Nepal		
	Bilateral agreement Entry into force: 13 May 2003	Afghanistan	Tariff reductions on 38 HS six-digit lines, with margins of preferences of 50 per cent or 100 per cent of MFN tariff	WT/TPR/S/182.Rev.1
	Bilateral agreement Entry into force: extended on 29 July 2006 for 10 years	Bhutan	All products	WT/TPR/S/182.Rev.1 and WT/COMTD/N/28
	Bilateral agreement	Nepal	Tariff exemptions for all goods subject to rules of origin. Imports of certain goods (vanaspati, copper products, acrylic yarn, and zinc oxide) are subject to annual quota	WT/TPR/S/182.Rev.1
Japan	GSP—Enhanced duty- and quota-free market access Entry into force: 1 April 2007	LDCs	Duty-free access on 8,859 tariff lines (or 98 per cent of the tariff line level), covering over 99 per cent in terms of the import value from LDCs	WT/COMTD/N/2/Add.14
Kazakhstan	Harmonized System of preference by the Eurasian Economic Community (EAEC) Entry into force: May 2001	47 LDCs	Duty free for all products	WT/TPR/S/170
Korea, Rep. of	Presidential Decree on Preferential Tariff for LDCs Entry into force: 1 January 2000	LDCs	Duty-free access is granted on 87 tariff items (HS six-digit)	WT/COMTD/N/12/Rev.1 WT/TPR/S/137
	Asia-Pacific Trade Agreement (APTA)—amendment to the Bangkok Agreement	Bangladesh	In addition to 1,367 products (with average margin of preference of 35.4 per cent)	WT/COMTD/N/22

Country	Measure / Entry into force	Beneficiaries	Product coverage	Source
	Entry into force: 1 September 2006	Lao PDR	available to all APTA members, tariff concessions granted exclusively to LDC members on 306 products with average margin of preference of 64.6 per cent	WT/TPR/S/170
Kyrgyz Republic	Harmonized system of preference by the Eurasian Economic Community (EAEC) Entry into force: May 2001	47 LDCs	Duty free for all products	WT/LDC/SWG/IF/18 and G/C/6
Morocco	Preferential tariff treatment for LDCs Entry into force: 1 January 2001	33 African LDCs	Duty-free access on 61 products (at the HS four- to ten-digit level)	WT/COMTD/27
New Zealand	GSP—Tariff Treatment for LDCs Entry into force: 1 July 2001	LDCs	All products	WT/TPR/S/115
Norway	GSP—Duty- and quota-free market access Entry into force: 1 July 2002	LDCs	All products	WT/TPR/S/138
Pakistan	South Asian Free Trade Area (SAFTA) Entry into force: 1 January 2006	Bangladesh Bhutan Maldives Nepal	Special concessions available for least-developed contracting states.	WT/COMTD/N/6/Add.4 SAARC Secretariat website (www.saarc-sec.org) WT/TPR/S/193
Sri Lanka	South Asian Free Trade Area (SAFTA) Entry into force: 1 January 2006	Bangladesh Bhutan Maldives Nepal	Special concessions available for least-developed contracting states	SAARC Secretariat website (www.saarc-sec.org)

(Continued)

Table 3.1 *Continued*

Preference-granting country	Description	Beneficiary(ies)	Coverage/margin of preference	References
	Asia-Pacific Trade Agreement (APTA)—amendment to the Bangkok Agreement. Entry into force: 1 September 2006	Bangladesh	In addition to 427 products (with average margin of preference of 14 per cent) available to all APTA members, tariff concessions granted exclusively to LDC members on 72 products with average margin of preference of 12 per cent	WT/COMTD/N/22
		Lao PDR		
Switzerland	GSP—Revised Preferential Tariffs Ordinance. Entry into force: 1 April 2007	LDCs	Duty-free access for all products originating from all LDCs as of September 2009	TN/CTD/M/28 WT/COMTD/N/7/Add.2 and Add.3
Tajikistan	Harmonized System of preference by the Eurasian Economic Community (ECEA). Entry into force: May 2001	47 LDCs	Duty free for all products	WT/TPR/S/170
Turkey	GSP. Entry into force: 31 December 2005	LDCs	Duties are eliminated for LDCs on the basis of EU's Everything But Arms (EBA) Initiative	WT/TPR/S/192
Russia	Harmonized System of preference by the Eurasian Economic Community (ECEA)	47 LDCs	Duty free for all products	WT/TPR/S/170
United States	GSP for least-developed beneficiary developing countries (LDBDC). Entry into force: 1 January 1976, extended until 31 December 2010 (further extensions are currently being considered)	43 designated LDCs[d]	In addition to the standard GSP coverage of nearly 5,000 products, 1,450 articles exclusively available for LDC beneficiaries for duty-free treatment	WT/COMTD/N/1/Add.4 & Add.5
				WT/TPR/S/235

Measure	Beneficiaries	Description	Reference
African Growth and Opportunity Act (AGOA) Entry into force: May 2000, extended until 30 September 2015[e]	38 designated Sub-Saharan African Countries (including 25 LDCs[f])	1,835 products, including textiles and apparel,[g] available for duty-free treatment, in addition to duty-free treatment on products benefiting from GSP	www.ustr.gov WT/COMTD/N/1/Add.3 WT/TPR/S/235 WT/L/754
Caribbean Basin Trade Partnership Act (CBTPA)	19 designated beneficiaries (including one LDC, i.e. Haiti) in Central America and the Caribbean	Duty free for most products, including textiles and apparels. The Haitian Hemispheric Opportunity through Partnership Encouragement Act enhanced Haiti's benefits under CBERA. The Haiti Economic Lift Program Act of 2010 further expanded Haiti's benefits, including broadening duty-free access for Haitian textile and apparel exports	WT/TPR/S/235
Uzbekistan	Harmonized System of preference by the Eurasian Economic Community (ECEA)	47 LDCs	Duty free for all products	WT/L/753 www.ustr.gov WT/TPR/S/170

Notes: [a] This table, which represents a non-exhaustive list of market access initiatives undertaken in favour of LDCs, updates the information contained in the previous report by the Secretariat (WT/COMTD/LDC/W/46/Rev.1). For those measures taken in favour of exports originating from LDCs prior to 2001, please see document WT/COMTD/LDC/W/38.

[b] Members of the APTA are: Bangladesh, China, India, Lao PDR, Republic of Korea, and Sri Lanka.

[c] Members of SAFTA which superseded the South Asian Preferential Trade Agreement (SAPTA) in 2006 are: Bangladesh, Bhutan, India, Maldives, Nepal, Pakistan, and Sri Lanka.

[d] Afghanistan, Angola, Bangladesh, Benin, Bhutan, Burkina Faso, Burundi, Cambodia, Central African Republic, Chad, Comoros, Democratic Republic of Congo, Djibouti, East Timor, Equatorial Guinea, Ethiopia, The Gambia, Guinea, Guinea-Bissau, Haiti, Kiribati, Lesotho, Liberia, Madagascar, Malawi, Mali, Mauritania, Mozambique, Nepal, Niger, Rwanda, Samoa, São Tomé and Príncipe, Sierra Leone, Solomon Islands, Somalia, Tanzania, Togo, Tuvalu, Uganda, Vanuatu, Yemen, and Zambia.

[e] The Africa Investment Incentive Act of 2006 or AGOA IV extended the third-country fabric provision from September 2007 until September 2012; added an abundant supply provision; designated certain denim articles as being in abundant supply; and allows lesser developed beneficiary Sub-Saharan African countries to export certain textile articles under AGOA. Section 3 of the Andean Trade Preference Extension Act of 2008 (Public Law 110–436) removed the abundant supply provisions, and redesignated Mauritius as a lesser developed beneficiary Sub-Saharan African Country for AGOA apparel benefits. See more information on the official AGOA website at <http://www.agoa.gov>.

[f] Angola, Benin, Burkina Faso, Burundi, Chad, Comoros, Democratic Republic of Congo, Djibouti, Ethiopia, The Gambia, Guinea-Bissau, Lesotho, Liberia, Malawi, Mali, Mauritania, Mozambique, Rwanda, São Tomé and Príncipe, Senegal, Sierra Leone, Tanzania, Togo, Uganda, and Zambia.

[g] Twenty-five Sub-Saharan African countries, including 15 LDCs (Benin, Burkina Faso, Chad, Ethiopia, The Gambia, Lesotho, Malawi, Mali, Mozambique, Rwanda, Senegal, Sierra Leone, Tanzania, Uganda, Zambia), are eligible for AGOA apparel benefits.

First, in February 2001, the Council adopted Regulation (EC) 416/2001, granting duty-free access to imports of all products from LDCs, except arms and ammunitions, without any quantitative restrictions (with the exception of bananas, sugar, and rice for a limited period). EBA was later incorporated into the GSP Council Regulation (EC) No. 2501/2001. The Regulation foresees that the special arrangements for LDCs should be maintained for an unlimited period of time and not be subject to the periodic renewal of the EU GSP.[66] There is no absolute overlap between the list of LDCs and the EBA beneficiaries:

(a) The EU has removed Myanmar from the list of beneficiaries following charges that Myanmar was violating the ILO (International Labour Organization) conventions on forced labour (Council Regulation 552/97);

(b) The EU has kept Maldives among the beneficiaries, although as of 1 January 2011 Maldives does not figure among the LDCs.[67]

Unilateral declarations (to the effect that a WTO Member is a developing country) can, in principle, be challenged before a WTO Panel. No formal challenge has been launched so far in this context. Following the advent of the WTO, we have witnessed more elaborate discussions on this issue than before. While negotiating on the implementation of TRIPs, the US and the EU voiced their wish that WTO Members like Singapore, Korea, and Hong Kong, China be considered as developed nations at least for the purposes of complying with TRIPs. The discussions in the TRIPs Council evidence that, although a mutually satisfactory solution was agreed among the interested parties, the principle of self-election as such was not questioned.[68] The EU delegate, to cite another example, during the discussions before the Dispute Settlement Body (DSB) regarding the adoption of the AB report on *Korea—Various Measures on Beef*:

> . . . noted with surprise that Korea had been treated as a developing country for the purposes of the Agreement on Agriculture. Although this issue did not seem to have been in dispute, the EC was compelled to underline its disagreement with Korea's self-characterization as a developing country.[69]

In the Chinese Protocol of Accession, we read that the *de minimis* threshold for calculation of the AMS (Aggregate Measurement of Support)[70] in accordance with Art. 6.4 AG should be 8.5 per cent, when the corresponding numbers are 10 per cent for developing and 5 per cent for developed countries.

Since development is an ongoing process, one would normally expect that the group of developing countries is a dynamic and not a static one. Indeed §7 of the Enabling Clause, as mentioned *supra*, says as much ('graduation'). Several

---

[66] The current EU GSP is reflected in Regulation 732/2008 (22 July 2008) OJ L211/1.
[67] Commission Regulation (EU) 1127/2010 of 3 December 2010, OJ L318/15.
[68] WTO Doc. IP/C/M/8 of 14 August 1996, pp. 58ff.
[69] WTO Doc. WT/DSB/M/96 of 22 February 2001, p. 14.
[70] Chapter 8.

discussions have taken place within the GATT/WTO aiming to 'beef up' the language included in this provision, but, alas, none of them has been conclusive.[71] As things stand, exclusion from the group of beneficiaries of tariff preferences remains largely at the discretion of donor countries.

The discussion above points to the following conclusions: there is definitely legal certainty as to the identity of LDCs; developing countries are defined by virtue of the self-election principle; donors can challenge invocations. De facto, in the WTO world, OECD members are part of the camp of developed and non-OECD of developing countries.

In *EC—Tariff Preferences*, the Panel and the AB faced the following question: is the distinction between developing countries and LDCs the only permissible distinction across beneficiaries that could provide the basis for the level of preferences granted? Or could other distinctions be lawfully used? And, if yes, where could one look for inspiration? The narrow question before the Panel was whether the EU had legitimately excluded India from some of its preferences; the wider policy issue was whether donors can make distinctions between beneficiaries other than the distinction between developing countries and LDCs operated in §2(d) of the Enabling Clause. The facts in this dispute were as follows: India and Pakistan both benefited from the EU GSP. Pakistan, however, received extra preferences because it qualified under the so-called Drug Arrangements, a scheme aimed at compensating those WTO Members that had adopted active policies against drug production and trafficking. India complained that, by discriminating in favour of Pakistani imports, the EU was in violation of Art. I GATT, a claim upheld by the Panel (§7.60). The Panel went on to examine to what extent recourse to the Enabling Clause could be offered as justification. In the Panel's view, the Enabling Clause requires that developed countries must, by virtue of the term 'non-discriminatory' featuring in footnote 3 of the Enabling Clause, give identical tariff preferences to all developing countries.[72] The AB reversed the Panel's findings in this respect. It started its analysis (§157) by pointing to the terms used in §3(c) of the Enabling Clause, which specifies that 'differential and more favourable treatment' provided under the Enabling Clause:

> . . . shall in the case of such treatment accorded by developed contracting parties to developing countries be designed and, if necessary, modified, to respond positively to the development, financial and trade needs of developing countries.

In its view, this paragraph made it plain that development needs are not necessarily shared to the same extent by all developing countries (§162):[73] as a result, a donor

---

71 See, for example, GATT Doc. C/M/152.

72 The Panel accepted that LDCs could be benefit from additional preferences in light of the unambiguous wording of the Enabling Clause in this respect.

73 The AB suggests that the drafters could easily have inserted the term '*all*' before developing countries, if they had really wanted to drive home the point that no discrimination across developing countries is permitted. Grossman and Sykes (2005) take issue with this statement, arguing that the

wishing to do justice to this provision might have to provide tailor-made (differential) treatment to different beneficiaries; in this case, the scheme would not *ipso facto* (e.g. because of the differentiation) be judged to be discriminatory since, as the quoted passage makes it plain, differentiation might be warranted, indeed necessary, in order to respect the *effet utile* of this provision (§165). As a result, additional preferences cannot be outright excluded (§169). It went on to rule that:

> in granting such differential tariff treatment, however, preference-granting countries are required, by virtue of the term 'non-discriminatory', to ensure that identical treatment is available to all similarly-situated GSP beneficiaries, that is, to all GSP beneficiaries that have the 'development, financial and trade needs' to which the treatment in question is intended to respond. (§173)

Applying its test to the specific case, the AB found that the Drug Arrangements were not WTO-consistent, only because the EU had included in its scheme a closed list of beneficiaries (§§180 and 187). In §183, we find the core of the AB argument:

> What is more, the Drug Arrangements themselves do *not* set out any clear prerequisites—or 'objective criteria'—that, if met, would allow for other developing countries 'that are similarly affected by the drug problem' to be *included* as beneficiaries under the Drug Arrangements. Indeed, the European Commission's own Explanatory Memorandum notes that 'the benefits of the drug regime . . . are given without *any* prerequisite.' Similarly, the Regulation offers no criteria according to which a beneficiary could be *removed* specifically from the Drug Arrangements on the basis that it is no longer 'similarly affected by the drug problem'. Indeed, Article 25.3 expressly states that the evaluation of the effects of the Drug Arrangements described in Articles 25.1(b) and 25.2 'will be without prejudice to the continuation of the [Drug Arrangements] until 2004, and their possible extension thereafter.' This implies that, even if the European Commission found that the Drug Arrangements were having no effect whatsoever on a beneficiary's 'efforts in combating drug production and trafficking', or that a beneficiary was no longer suffering from the drug problem, beneficiary status would continue. Therefore, even if the Regulation allowed for the list of beneficiaries under the Drug Arrangements to be modified, the Regulation itself gives no indication as to how the beneficiaries under the Drug Arrangements were chosen or what kind of considerations would or could be used to determine the effect of the 'drug problem' on a particular country. In addition, we note that the Regulation does not, for instance, provide any indication as to how the European Communities would assess whether the Drug Arrangements provide an 'adequate and proportionate response' to the needs of developing countries suffering from the drug problem. (emphasis in the original)

AB has treated silence in a very inconsistent manner in its case law. They argue that, by the same token, the drafters could have inserted the term *'certain'* before developing countries, if they had wanted to allow for discrimination. The fact that they did not is probably equally relevant to their intent. They take the view that based not on silence, but on actual expression, the Enabling Clause makes one distinction only between developing and LDCs. This is the only relevant distinction, in their view. Howse (2003) has defended the view that neither the panel nor the AB should have entered into any discussion of the issue at all since, in his view, the Enabling Clause is not justiciable to start with.

For its scheme to be WTO-consistent, the EU would have to modify its Regulation so as to ensure that it reflects:

criteria or standards to provide a basis for distinguishing beneficiaries under the Drug Arrangements from other GSP beneficiaries. (§188)

It follows from this case law that WTO Members can distinguish between recipients of preferences between developing countries beyond the distinction between developing countries and LDCs included in the Enabling Clause, provided that their distinctions correspond to (objective) criteria. The AB, alas, did not provide any guidance as to how we should understand the term 'objective criteria and standards' that it first employed in *EC—Tariff Preferences*. All we know is that distinctions are possible, but we have no clue, not even an indicative list, as to how they should be made. We do know nonetheless that a closed list cannot meet this criterion; quite reasonably so, since countries that aspire to emulate those included in the list of beneficiaries will never be included. A closed list thus does not meet the AB standard for objectivity since countries in a similar position will be treated differently.

The EU expanded on its prior practice: it had originally included Sri Lanka in its list for GSP + preferences, although Sri Lanka is no LDC. In a press release dated 15 December 2009 by the Commission of the EU (DG Trade),[74] however, it was announced that the EU would remove with immediate effect Sri Lanka from the list of GSP + beneficiaries for failure to implement three UN Human Rights Conventions (the ICCPR (International Covenant on Civil and Political Rights); the CAT (Convention against Torture); and the CRC (Convention on Rights of the Child)).

Recall that the criteria for benefiting under the Drugs Arrangements scheme had been established unilaterally. The AB did not bring into question EU discretion to unilaterally draw up objective criteria and standards. It is at best debatable, nonetheless, whether donors have (any) incentives to adopt criteria that will promote development of the recipients and not simply their own social preferences. It might sound cynical, but was not the EU addressing (in part at least) its own domestic problems through the Drug Arrangements? Moreover, opening the door to all sorts of distinctions might undo the prioritization of development options that the recipients have decided for themselves, since the perks might be too good to turn down.[75] This is an area where some additional thinking is required before we embark on the exercise as currently designed by the WTO adjudicating bodies.

In 1999, WTO Members adopted a waiver that allows developing countries to provide preferential tariff treatment to products of least-developed countries,

---

[74] <http://trade.ec.europa.eu/doclib/press/index.cfm?id = 499>.
[75] Diverging views have been expressed on this score; see, *inter alia*, Brenton (2003), Hoekman et al. (2004), Rodrik (2002), Stevens (2002).

designated as such by the United Nations, without being required to extend the same tariff rates to like products of any other Member.[76]

This waiver allows for one-way preferential treatment for products originating in LDCs and it should not be confused with preferential trade agreements across developing countries. Recall that the Enabling Clause provides the basis for facilitating preferential trade agreements across developing countries (usually referred to as 'south-south cooperation') that do not have to follow the requirements embedded in Art. XXIV GATT. According to §2(c) of the Enabling Clause:

> Regional or global arrangements entered into amongst less-developed contracting parties for the mutual reduction or elimination of tariffs and, in accordance with criteria or conditions which may be prescribed by the CONTRACTING PARTIES, for the mutual reduction or elimination of non-tariff measures, on products imported from one another.

This provision does not explain the specifics of the test that will be applied when a PTA among developing countries is examined. Following the advent of the Transparency Mechanism that we discuss in more detail *infra*, there is a standard procedure applicable to all PTAs, irrespective whether they have been notified under Art. XXIV GATT, V GATS, or §2(c) of the Enabling Clause; the only difference is that, whereas it is the CRTA (Committee on Regional Trade Agreements) that is notified of the first two, it is the CTD (Committee on Trade and Development) that is notified of the latter. There are very few completed reports, such as the report concerning the Bangkok Agreement, and hence no meaningful conclusion can be drawn on the nature of multilateral review of south-south cooperation.[77] To date, no direct legal challenge has been raised against south-south preferences.[78] For a list of arrangements notified under §2(c) of the Enabling Clause, see Table 3.2.

Finally, as mentioned, non-tariff preferences are possible as well. To our knowledge, it is in multilateral agreements that we see evidence of similar provisions and not in GSP schemes. We turn to this discussion in what immediately follows.

2.3 WTO Provisions on Special and Differential Treatment

There are numerous provisions in the covered agreements that qualify as special and differential treatment-type provisions. This is how a document prepared by the WTO Secretariat has classified these provisions:

---

[76] WTO Doc. WT/L/304 of 17 July 1999.
[77] GATT Doc. BISD 25S/109.
[78] de Melo (2007).

Table 3.2 Preferential arrangements notified under §2(c) of the Enabling Clause

RTA Name	Coverage	Type	Date of notification	Notification	Date of entry into force
Andean Community (CAN)	Goods	CU	1 October 1990	Enabling Clause	25 May 1988
ASEAN—China	Goods & Services	PSA & EIA	21 September 2005(G) 26 June 2008(S)	Enabling Clause & GATS Art. V	1 January 2005 (G) 1 July 2007(S)
ASEAN—India	Goods	FTA	19 August 2010	Enabling Clause	1 January 2010
ASEAN—Korea, Republic of	Goods & Services	FTA & EIA			1 January 2010 (G) 1 May 2009(S)
ASEAN Free Trade Area (AFTA)	Goods	FTA	30 October 1992	Enabling Clause	28 January 1992
Asia Pacific Trade Agreement (APTA)	Goods	PSA	02 November 1976	Enabling Clause	17 June 1976
Asia Pacific Trade Agreement (APTA)—Accession of China	Goods	PSA	30 April 2004	Enabling Clause	01 January 2002
Common Market for Eastern and Southern Africa (COMESA)	Goods	FTA	04 May 1995	Enabling Clause	08 December 1994
East African Community (EAC)	Goods	CU	9 October 2000	Enabling Clause	7 July 2000
Economic and Monetary Community of Central Africa (CEMAC)	Goods	CU	21 July 1999	Enabling Clause	24 June 1999
Economic Community of West African States (ECOWAS)	Goods	CU	06 July 2005	Enabling Clause	24 July 1993
Economic Cooperation Organization (ECO)	Goods	PSA	10 July 1992	Enabling Clause	17 February 1992
Egypt—Turkey	Goods	FTA	5 October 2007	Enabling Clause	1 March 2007

(*Continued*)

Table 3.2 *Continued*

RTA Name	Coverage	Type	Date of notification	Notification	Date of entry into force
Global System of Trade Preferences among Developing Countries (GSTP)	Goods	PSA	25 September 1989	Enabling Clause	19 April 1989
Gulf Cooperation Council (GCC)	Goods	CU			01-January-2003
India—Afghanistan	Goods	PSA	08 March 2010	Enabling Clause	13 May 2003
India—Bhutan	Goods	FTA	30 June 2008	Enabling Clause	29 July 2006
India—Nepal	Goods	PSA	02 August 2010	Enabling Clause	27 October 2009
India—Sri Lanka	Goods	FTA	17 June 2002	Enabling Clause	15 December 2001
Korea, Republic of—India	Goods & Services	FTA & EIA			01 January 2010
Lao People's Democratic Republic—Thailand	Goods	PSA	26 November 1991	Enabling Clause	20 June 1991
Latin American Integration Association (LAIA)	Goods	PSA	1 July 1982	Enabling Clause	18 March 1981
Melanesian Spearhead Group (MSG)	Goods	PSA	3 August 1999	Enabling Clause	1 January 1994
MERCOSUR—India	Goods	PSA	23 February 2010	Enabling Clause	1 June 2009
Pacific Island Countries Trade Agreement (PICTA)	Goods	FTA	28 August 2008	Enabling Clause	13 April 2003
Pakistan—Malaysia	Goods & Service	FTA & EIA	19 February 2008	Enabling Clause & GATS Art. V	01 January 2008
Pakistan—SriLanka	Goods	FTA	11 June 2008	Enabling Clause	12 June 2005

(a) provisions aimed at increasing the trade opportunities of developing country Members;

(b) provisions under which WTO Members should safeguard the interests of developing country Members;

(c) flexibility of commitments, of action, and use of policy instruments;

(d) transitional time periods;

(e) technical assistance;

(f) provisions relating to least-developed country Members.[79]

The same document includes a table with all such provisions (see Table 3.3).[80]

In essence, these provisions aim to improve the position of developing countries within the WTO either by introducing 'lighter' disciplines that are applicable to developing countries only or by increasing the embedded expertise of developing countries on WTO-related issues. There is an institutional acknowledgement that participation in the WTO is a function of similar expertise and empirical evidence to support this perception.[81]

Various WTO Members participate in numerous other initiatives outside the WTO aimed at improving the position of developing countries in the WTO. The Advisory Centre for WTO Law (ACWL) is the best-known initiative of the sort and aims at providing legal expertise to developing countries at non-market (e.g. subsidized) rates.[82]

It is difficult to make a general pronouncement on the merits of all special and differential provisions since, by subject-matter, they constitute a heterogeneous group. If at all, one can side with Low's (2007) reservations regarding the well-foundedness of an approach that preaches 'one size fits all': it is quite true that developing countries present a very diverse group of countries which is becoming increasingly diverse over the years. The various provisions echo the very basic developing countries/LDCs distinction first reflected in the Enabling Clause. Rodrik (2001) has forcefully argued in favour of adding to the existing arsenal, pointing to the very limited usefulness (and even to the total uselessness) of some of the existing provisions: technical capacity, for example, as nowadays practised, has come under a lot of criticism, a point to which we return later. At the other end of the spectrum, Hoekman (2005) warns against the dangers of an over-expanded class of provisions coming under the heading 'special and differential treatment': WTO could become an irrelevant policy prescription for beneficiaries and thus all gains from trade liberalization and participation in the negotiating process could be severely undermined. It seems that too much is wrong medicine, and the

---

[79] WTO Doc. WT/COMTD/W/77/Rev.1 of 21 September 2001.

[80] On the legal status of the provisions on special and differential treatment, see Kessie (2007).

[81] Nordström (2007).

[82] Meagher (2007) discusses its mandate *in extenso*. The WTO also provides similar services, albeit in more limited manner, by making two legal experts available to developing countries on a part-time basis (Art. 27.2 DSU).

Table 3.3 Special and differential treatment provisions in multilateral agreements

Agreement	(i) Provisions aimed at increasing the trade opportunities of developing country Members	(ii) Provisions that require WTO Members to safeguard the interests of developing country Members	(iii) Flexibility of commitments, of action, and use of policy instruments	(iv) Transitional time periods	(v) Technical assistance	(vi) Provisions relating to measures to assist least-developed country Members	Total by Agreement
Agriculture	1		9	1		3	14
Decision on NFIDCs		4			1		5
Application of SPS Measures		2		2	1		5
Textiles and Clothing	1	3				2	6
Technical Barriers to Trade		6	1	1	7	1	16
Trade-Related Investment Measures			1	2		1	4
Implementation of Article VI of GATT 1994		1					1
Implementation of Art. VII of GATT 1994		1	2	4	1		8
Decision on Texts Relating to Minimum Values and Imports by Sole Agents, Sole Distributors and Sole Concessionaires		2					2
Pre-shipment inspection							0
Rules of Origin		3		1			4
Import Licensing Procedures		2	8	6			16

Agreement							Total
Subsidies and Countervailing Measures	3						
Safeguards		1		2	2	2	2
GATS		4		1	3		15
TRIPs				1			6
Understanding on Rules and Procedures Governing the Settlement of Disputes	7		2	1			11
GATT 1994 Art. XVIII	4	3					3
GATT 1994 Art. XXXVI	2	6	1				8
GATT 1994—Art. XXXVII	2	5					8
GATT 1994—Art. XXXVIII							7
Enabling Clause	1	2	2			1	4
Decision on Measures in Favour of Least-Developed Countries						7	7
Waiver preferential tariff treatment of LDCs					1	1	1
Total	14	50	33	19	14	24	155

existing measures are not good medicine either. The WTO has embarked, explicitly and implicitly, in a re-evaluation of its development tools in the context of the Doha Development Agenda (DDA), a point to which we come back in what follows.

2.4 Institutional Provisions

In 1964, the GATT undertook its first substantive initiative to provide an institutional infrastructure to its provisions regarding special and differential treatment: the GATT CONTRACTING PARTIES agreed on the establishment of the Committee on Trade and Development (CTD). Its mandate was to review the application of the provisions of Part IV. Art. IV.7 of the Agreement Establishing the WTO, which describes the current mandate of the CTD, provides:

> The Ministerial Conference shall establish a Committee on Trade and Development ... which shall carry out the functions assigned to them by this Agreement and by the multilateral trade agreements, and any additional functions assigned to them by the General Council.... As part of its function, the Committee on Trade and Development shall periodically review the special provisions in the multilateral trade agreements in favour of LDC members and report to the General Council for appropriate action.

Eventually, the CTD evolved into the forum where the discussion on Trade and Development in the widest possible connotation of the term takes place under the aegis of the WTO. It is a multi-task institution where all WTO Members participate:

(a) it is the depositary for all GSP schemes;
(b) it is the forum where the notification of and the discussion about preferential arrangements under §2(c) of the Enabling Clause take place;[83]
(c) it supervises the implementation of provisions favouring developing countries (special and differential treatment);
(d) it issues guidelines for technical cooperation. The CTD serves as a focal point for consideration and coordination of technical assistance work on development in the WTO and its relationship to development-related activities in other multilateral agencies;
(e) it adopts measures aiming to increase participation of developing countries in the trading system, paying particular attention to the position of LDCs.

At the same time (1964), the International Trade Centre (ITC) was established, with the aim of promoting trade of developing countries. The ITC later became a joint agency of the United Nations Conference on Trade and Development (UNCTAD) and GATT (and eventually the WTO). In 1998, The WTO,

---

[83] WTO Docs. WT/L/671 and 672 of 14 December 2006.

together with UNCTAD and the ITC, established the Common Trust Fund, meant to finance technical capacity in developing countries.

The mandate of the CTD and, more generally, the involvement of the WTO in development-related issues has widened over the years and extended beyond the 'classic' trade content it was originally endowed with. In the minds of the original framers of the GATT, the contribution of the world trading system towards development was uni-dimensional: non-discriminatory trade liberalization. Following the discussion in the late 1950s, as we saw above, the rules of the trading system were amended so as to make room for discriminatory (preferential) trade for goods originating in developing countries and, in the aftermath of the Uruguay round, the discussion moved to non-trade development-related issues.

It is difficult to be precise about the starting-point of this negotiation. It is clear, nevertheless, that at the Doha Ministerial Conference, in November 2001, Trade Ministers mandated the CTD to identify which special and differential treatment provisions are mandatory, and to consider the implications of making mandatory those which are currently non-binding. During this meeting, the Sub-Committee on LDCs saw the light of the day: this institution, in which all WTO Members participate, focuses on the implementation of the WTO Work Programme for the LDCs, namely:

(a) market access for LDCs;
(b) trade-related technical assistance and capacity-building initiatives for LDCs;
(c) providing, as appropriate, support to agencies assisting with the diversification of LDCs' production and export base;
(d) mainstreaming, as appropriate, into the WTO's work the trade-related elements of the LDC III Programme of Action, as relevant to the WTO's mandate;
(e) participation of LDCs in the multilateral trading system;
(f) accession of LDCs to the WTO; and follow-up to WTO Ministerial Decisions/Declarations.[84]

The WTO Work Programme for the LDCs is the platform that essentially placed the WTO in the wider inter-institutional discussion on poverty reduction and development (where notably the World Bank participates). Sure the WTO can only, by reason of its mandate, have limited impact since trade is but a component (and often a small one) of the development discourse. This initiative nonetheless gave the WTO much more visibility in wider than trade policy discussions. More on this later.

---

[84] WTO Doc. WT/COMTD/LDC/11 of 13 February 2002. This Work Programme was adopted shortly after the kick-off of the Doha round and was thought to be one of the main pillars of the ongoing negotiations, since the round aimed to address on a priority basis development-related issues; hence the denomination Doha Development Agenda (DDA). There is of course only so much that one can do through trade and its overall contribution to development should not be exaggerated.

At the Hong Kong Ministerial Conference (2005), the CTD adopted five decisions in favour of the LDCs, including a decision to grant duty-free and quota-free market access for at least 97 per cent of LDC exports. It has further been quite active in implementing a number of development-related initiatives, such as the WTO Work Programme for Small Economies. The Doha Declaration mandated the WTO General Council to examine this issue, and to make recommendations regarding measures that could improve the integration of small economies into the multilateral trading system. On 1 March 2002, the WTO General Council agreed that:

> The question of small economies would be a standing agenda item of the General Council; The Committee on Trade and Development (CTD) would hold Dedicated Sessions on this question and report regularly to the General Council.[85]

In similar vein, §55 of the Hong Kong Ministerial Declaration instructs the CTD to intensify its work on commodity issues in cooperation with other relevant international organizations and to report to the General Council with possible recommendations.

The CTD has also been active in promoting electronic commerce[86] and Aid for Trade, which we discuss *infra*. Besides the CTD, during the Doha round, ministers set up working groups on Trade, Debt and Finance, and on Trade and Technology Transfer, the former influenced by the discussion about the impact that the financial crisis in the first years of the new century would have on trade liberalization.

The WTO now cooperates with other international organizations in programmes of common interest. The two most prominent initiatives aimed at providing technical assistance to developing countries are the Integrated Framework (IF) and the Joint Integrated Technical Assistance Programme (JITAP).[87] The IF, or EIF (Enhanced Integrated Framework) as it has become (1997),[88] is an inter-agency coordination mechanism for the delivery of technical assistance, promotion of economic growth and sustainable development, and more generally for helping lift LDCs from the poverty trap. It comprises five multilateral agencies—ITC, IMF, UNCTAD, UNDP (United Nations Development Programme), World Bank, in partnership with bilateral donors and LDC beneficiaries. Note that only LDCs can take advantage of the IF facility. The WTO serves as coordinator of the IF and accommodates a Secretariat, with a view to

---

[85] The CTD issued a report to this effect; see WTO Doc. WT/COMTD/SE/5 of 29 September 2006.

[86] WTO Doc. WT/L/274 of 30 September 1998.

[87] For details concerning the operation of these programmes, see WTO Doc. WT/COMTD/W/102 of 16 July 2002.

[88] The move from IF to EIF signalled a wider portfolio for the established entity and substantial 'ownership' by the beneficiaries (LDCs), who would now have more of a say in shaping the agenda and the programmes that should be financed.

taking maximum advantage of each agency's expertise, to ensure optimal coordination. The inter-agency aspect of the coordination is primarily dealt with by the Inter-Agency Working Group (IAWG).[89] The IF aims to place trade in the context of a wider development agenda. The revamped IF is currently under extension to the following countries: Cambodia, Madagascar, Mauritania, Burundi, Djibouti, Eritrea, Ethiopia, Guinea, Lesotho, Malawi, Mali, Nepal, Senegal, and Yemen. Roughly 40–50 LDCs in total have benefited from it.

The Members of the WTO have approved the work of the IF. During the Doha Ministerial Conference, they decided to reinforce the IF, as illustrated by §43 of the Doha Ministerial Conference Decision:

> We endorse the Integrated Framework for Trade-Related Technical Assistance to Least-Developed Countries (IF) as a viable model for LDCs' trade development. We urge development partners to significantly increase contributions to the IF Trust Fund and WTO extra-budgetary trust funds in favour of LDCs. We urge the core agencies, in coordination with development partners, to explore the enhancement of the IF with a view to addressing the supply-side constraints of LDCs and the extension of the model to all LDCs, following the review of the IF and the appraisal of the ongoing Pilot Scheme in selected LDCs. We request the Director-General, following coordination with heads of the other agencies, to provide an interim report to the General Council in December 2002 and a full report to the Fifth Session of the Ministerial Conference on all issues affecting LDCs.[90]

More recently, echoing the Decision above and following active monitoring of its activities, the WTO decided to redirect the IF towards the preparation of poverty-reduction strategic papers and towards reducing the observed implementation gap (between IF prescriptions and follow-up at the national level).[91]

The JITAP, on the other hand, is a multi-country capacity-building programme implemented jointly by ITC, UNCTAD, and WTO. Following JITAP I, JITAP II was launched in February 2003, and originally covered 16 African countries,[92] which included the original eight JITAP countries plus an additional eight countries selected on the basis of criteria determined jointly by the implementing agencies and the donors to the programme. The eight original JITAP countries[93] have since 'graduated' from the programme as of 31 December 2005. The JITAP

---

89 IF coordination further rests with the Integrated Framework Steering Committee (IFSC) and National IF Steering Committees. The IFSC consists of representatives of the agencies, all donors and LDC beneficiaries, and provides *overall* policy guidance on the functioning of the IF. It meets, in principle, three times a year. The task of coordination at the country level rests with the beneficiary country itself through the establishment of a national IF Steering Committee and with the support of a lead donor.

90 WTO Doc. WT/IFSC/1 of 28 February 2002.

91 WTO Doc. WT/IFSC/W/15 of 29 June 2006.

92 Benin, Botswana, Burkina Faso, Cameroon, Côte d'Ivoire, Ghana, Kenya, Malawi, Mali, Mauritania, Mozambique, Tanzania, Tunisia, Uganda, Senegal, and Zambia.

93 Benin, Burkina Faso, Côte d'Ivoire, Ghana, Kenya, Tanzania, Tunisia, and Uganda.

aims at building capacity and strengthening the national knowledge base on the multilateral trading system. Its objective is to ensure:

(a) more effective participation in trade negotiations;
(b) better implementation of the WTO agreements;
(c) informed formulation of trade-related policies;
(d) improved supply capacity and market knowledge of exporting and export-ready enterprises to derive benefits from business opportunities resulting from better market access under the multilateral trading system.

In 2006, JITAP consolidated the implementation of the various modules in the remaining eight JITAP countries.[94] The JITAP Common Trust Fund Steering Group was to determine before the end of 2007 whether it was necessary to commission a future phase of JITAP. JITAP II ended in June 2007, with the nature and scope of its future phase not agreed between the agencies and the donors to the programme. JITAP III never saw the light of day. The donors felt that the IF and the new Aid for Trade initiative that was successfully negotiated during the Doha round would take care of the issues that JITAP was supposed to address.

2.5 Aid for Trade

The WTO webpage describes Aid for Trade as:

> part of overall development aid, but with the specific objective of helping developing countries, in particular the least developed, to play an active role in the global trading system and to use trade as an instrument for growth and poverty alleviation.

Aid for Trade concentrates on trade policy and regulation, economic infrastructure, productive capacity building, and adjustment assistance ('supply side-challenges'). It is individual donors and multilateral agencies that will assume the financing, with the WTO limiting itself to a monitoring and evaluation role. It is probably the most prominent illustration of the DDA (Doha Development Agenda) and the fact that the WTO is now part of the worldwide discussion on trade and development: various studies, including Finger and Schuler (2000), supported the view that the implementation of the Uruguay round was costly and, as Stiglitz (2000) has argued, that on top of it the final compromise was quite unbalanced. Aid for Trade was perceived as (one of the) means to redress the situation.

This initiative is, implicitly, at the very least, an admission that GSP schemes did not produce the expected results: it turns out that a series of internal barriers, such as lack of knowledge about trading opportunities, on occasion excessive red tape, inadequate financing of trading operations, as well as poor infrastructure,

---

[94] Botswana, Cameroun, Malawi, Mali, Mauritania, Mozambique, Senegal, and Zambia.

have proved a formidable obstacle for those aspiring to trade. The trading partners did not, nevertheless, proceed to abolishing GSP schemes; Aid for Trade has been thought as more of a complement to rather than a direct substitute for existing special and differential treatment.

Besides, many LDCs held the view that instruments such as the IF were better suited as mechanisms of studies rather than as a response to identified priorities. In this vein, Aid for Trade would be more of an operational arm rather than a replication of the IF.

There are four main areas where Aid for Trade is relevant:

(a) Capacity building : participation of developing countries in trade negotiations has been severely damaged by scarcity of negotiating resources and lack of expertise. While there is not much that can be done, in the short run, to address the former, a lot can be probably done with respect to the latter;

(b) Infrastructure: construction of roads, ports, airports, upgrading of existing infrastructure on telecommunications, and energy networks emerge as key issues in expanding the current participation of developing countries in world trade;

(c) Increased productivity: very often it is the case that developing countries cannot compete in product markets and some of the Aid for Trade money is meant to address this type of concern;[95]

(d) Adjustment assistance: as a result of the reduction of MFN tariffs worldwide, developing countries have suffered from preference erosion, that is, the margin of preference that they previously enjoyed has been gradually curtailed. Aid for Trade money could provide some short-term relief. Most importantly, it could go some way towards avoiding the risk that those who have suffered from preference erosion turn into enemies of trade liberalization (because of the ensuing preference erosion).[96]

The idea is that donors and beneficiaries participate in designing the various projects to be financed and it is to be expected that the latter actively participate in designing them. In that, Aid for Trade is in marked contrast to the GSP schemes

---

[95] Various contributions in Maskus et al. (2001) show the welfare implications of product standards for developing countries and especially LDCs. According to Wilson and Abiola (2003), standards rank as the most important factor blocking exports, right behind freight and transport charges. The creation of the STDF (Standards and Trade Development Facility), a joint venture between the FAO (Food and Agriculture Organization), the OIE (Organisation international des epizooties: World Organization for Animal Health), the WB, the WHO (World Health Organization), and the WTO, aims to assist developing countries to implement sanitary and phyto-sanitary standards.

[96] Hoekman and Prowse (2009). Prima facie, at least, points (b), (c), and (d) seem to endorse the approach advanced by Sachs (2005) that an original down-payment is necessary to get LDCs (the bottom billion) out of their poverty trap. There are serious counter-arguments against this thesis, notably Easterly (2001). For an overview and critical appraisal of this discussion, see Banerjee and Duflo (2011).

that were designed solely by donors, where beneficiaries could only choose (assuming a choice was an option) between complying with the various requirements and benefiting from them, and not complying and foregoing the benefits.

What is the WTO role in all this? The WTO is not a development agency and cannot provide any assistance. Conversely, the WTO can and will exercise monitoring activities. Its experience from running the TPRM (Trade Policy Review Mechanism) could be quite relevant here: it will aim to bridge the gap between the aspirations of donors and requests by beneficiaries. The WTO will be working hand in hand with other institutions in this context, as indeed it has been doing while participating in the JITAP and the IF, discussed *supra*. Monitoring will take place at three levels: global monitoring, carried out by the OECD (OECD Aid for Trade statistics come from the Creditor Reporting System, the CRS); donor monitoring, in the form of self-evaluations; and in-country monitoring, also in the form of self-assessments. These various threads will be woven together in an annual Report and an Aid for Trade debate in the WTO General Council. A WTO Aid for Trade taskforce has been established to assist this endeavour.[97] Two Declarations by the TNC (Trade Negotiating Committee) adopted at the end of the Uruguay round (15 December 1993) provide the foundation for this collaboration: the Decision on Contribution of the WTO to Achieving Greater Coherence in Global Economic Policymaking; and the Decision on the Relationship of the WTO with the International Monetary Fund.

The amount committed so far (according to OECD data) is estimated at between $25–30 billion per year, of which capacity building absorbs roughly $0.9 billion (in 2005); infrastructure roughly $9.5 billion (2005); increased productivity $12.1 billion (2005); and adjustment assistance between $3–6 billion (2005–8). According to the World Bank, Aid for Trade has increased by 21 per cent in real terms between 2002–5 (baseline) and 2007.[98]

It is probably too soon to assess the WTO impact on this discussion, and probably too soon as well to assess the effectiveness of Aid for Trade. Still, recently, studies have emerged that have questioned the efficacy of this instrument: Gamberoni and Newfarmer (2009) have constructed an index for potential demand for Aid for Trade money based on ten indicators for trade performance and trade capacity. They conclude that those who score the lowest receive most of the money. They also conclude, however, that some have received much less money in relation to their needs. Hoekman and Nicita (2010) point to the problems that might eventually be posed by the absence of a central entity or global financial coordination mechanism, since the whole enterprise builds on existing mechanisms and coordination might prove to be a formidable task. Delpeuch et al. (2011), while not denying that there is an impact (probably

---

[97] WTO Doc. WT/AFT/1 of 27 July 2006. See Hoekman and Nicita (2010).

[98] World Bank. 2009. *Unlocking Global Opportunities: The Aid for Trade Program of the World Bank Group*, The World Bank: Washington, DC.

indirect) on poverty reduction, find no evidence supporting the thesis that Aid for Trade has had a beneficial effect on trade.

In a nutshell, a number of commentators make more or less the same point: Aid for Trade is not a perfect substitute for domestic reform, and its contribution to development should be viewed and appreciated within its limits.

2.6 From Enabling Clause to Trade and Development

The discussion above evidences that what started as an exception from MFN eventually became a wide discussion on trade and development. The DDA is the culmination so far. §51 of the Doha Ministerial Declaration reads:

> The Committee on Trade and Development and the Committee on Trade and Environment shall, within their respective mandates, each act as a forum to identify and debate developmental and environmental aspects of the negotiations, in order to help achieve the objective of having sustainable development appropriately reflected.

Soon thereafter, the TNC (Trade Negotiations Committee) decided that the CTD should convene in special sessions to discuss all provisions relating to special and differential treatment, evaluating and complementing them if need be:

> As reaffirmed by Ministers at Doha, provisions for special and differential treatment are an integral part of the WTO Agreements. The negotiations and other aspects of the work programme shall take fully into account the principle of special and differential treatment for developing and least-developed countries as provided for in paragraph 50 of the Ministerial Declaration. The review of all special and differential treatment provisions with a view to strengthening them and making them more precise, effective and operational provided for in paragraph 44 of the Ministerial Declaration shall be carried out by the Committee on Trade and Development in Special Sessions.[99]

Without saying so, the feeling was that past efforts were simply not enough and more needed to be done to redress an imbalance. Jawara and Kwa (2003) capture to a T the feeling across developing countries when they note (p. 269):

> Developed countries are benefiting from the WTO, as are a handful of (mostly upper) middle income countries. The rest, including the great majority of developing countries, are not. It is as simple as that.[100]

There are of course two important caveats: first, trade is but one component of a wider development agenda. Its contribution to GDP is asymmetric across countries, but it is never a perfect substitute for development which is a function of many other policies as well. Second, the WTO is no development agency; hence, it can only do so much in the development context where it has to cooperate with other more specialized institutions (as is the case; see our discussion

---

[99] WTO Doc. TN/C/1 of 4 February 2002.
[100] Subramanian and Wei (2007) have provided empirical support for this finding.

supra). Hence, by reason of its institutional mandate and the limits inherent in its content, the WTO can contribute towards the goal of development and poverty reduction only to a limited extent.

The UN (and its specialized agencies) adopted the Brussels Programme of Action for the LDCs for the decade 2001–10 (BPOA) at the third UN Conference on LDCs (Brussels, 2001).[101] Among the various commitments, 'Commitment 5', entitled 'Enhancing the Role of Trade in Development', is what is most relevant to the WTO activities.[102] The DG of the WTO circulated a report explaining the WTO activities aimed at implementing Commitment 5:[103]

(a) In his view, the DDA agenda has embraced the spirit and objectives of the BPOA. In the negotiations, WTO Members aim to address on a priority basis the marginalization of LDCs in international trade and improve their effective participation in the multilateral trading system;

(b) Capacity building has become a fundamental activity of the WTO. The WTO Secretariat has been attaching special priority to LDCs when organizing technical assistance and training programmes. During the period 2002–9, LDCs have been associated with 40 to 45 per cent of all trade-related technical assistance (TRTA) delivered by the Secretariat. An LDC Unit was established in the WTO Secretariat in early 2003, aimed at building more informed participation by LDCs in the multilateral trading system and in their effective participation in DDA negotiations;

(c) The growth of LDC exports was higher than the world average during 2000–9. Their share in world merchandise trade was just under 1 per cent in 2009, which represents a 100 per cent increase from 1999;

(d) The Hong Kong Decision on duty-free and quota-free (DFQF) market access for LDC products was a milestone in improving the market access opportunities for LDC exports. Most of the developed Members of the WTO provide close to 100 per cent DFQF market access to LDC products. Following the decision at the Sixth Ministerial Conference on Measures in Favour of Least-Developed Countries, the CTD is mandated to annually review the steps taken to provide duty-free and quota-free market access to the LDCs. The first review was held on 28 November 2006. A number of developing countries, which are increasingly becoming key trading partners of LDCs, have either adopted or are in the process of granting a significant degree of DFQF access to LDC products;

(e) LDCs are being accorded a high degree of flexibility in all areas of negotiations, ranging from agriculture to non-agriculture, services, trade facilitation, rules,

---

etc., which is expected to help them pursue their development objectives. The LDCs are exempted from making any tariff-reduction commitments and are not expected to undertake any new commitments in the services negotiations;

(f) The LDC Group, which was formed in 2001, has become an active constituency over the years and today represents an important player in the decision-making process of the WTO;

(g) Accession of LDCs to the WTO is being encouraged: there were already 30 LDC Members of the WTO in 2001, that is, before the advent of BPOA. Since then, three LDCs (Cambodia, Cape Verde, and Nepal) have acceded to the WTO.[104] Twelve LDCs are at various stages of their accession process. The LDC Accession Guidelines were adopted in 2002, aiming to facilitate the accession of LDCs to the WTO;

(h) Aid for Trade was launched in 2005, aimed at strengthening the supply-side capacity and trade-related infrastructure in developing countries, especially in the LDCs, through a strong global partnership;

(i) The EIF has become the vehicle for the LDCs to access Aid for Trade funding and is now on the verge of covering all LDCs: 47 LDCs are at different stages of the EIF process.

The report is not only self-congratulatory. The DG acknowledges that a number of trade and development challenges remain: LDC exports continue to be characterized by concentration on a limited number of products, making them vulnerable to external shocks; supply-side constraints continue to be one of the major challenges for expansion of LDCs' trade; market access opportunities have not been fully utilized, *inter alia*, due to certain non-tariff measures such as difficulty in meeting rules-of-origin requirements; transaction costs are another area where immediate attention is warranted. Indeed, another WTO document surveying the progress of the Doha round negotiations from a developing countries' angle takes a more cautious approach:

> Two conclusions stem from this document: first, development issues suffuse all areas being negotiated, including in the market access and rule-making aspects of the negotiations. Second, a large number of proposals already on the table are aimed at addressing the development aspects of each subject. The possible gains to developing countries would largely depend on the outcome of the ongoing negotiations and manner in which the various proposals are operationalized after being adopted.[105]

There is arguably more to criticize in the broad picture: it is increasingly questionable why the various mechanisms adopted keep developing countries and LDCs (almost) totally outside the WTO disciplines. Is it that the WTO disciplines are inappropriate for LDCs? Are they inappropriate for developing countries as well? Is it that the GSP schemes need a change of focus? Is Aid for Trade the

---

[104] As of December 2007, Cape Verde has graduated and is not considered an LDC any more.
[105] WTO Doc. WT/COMTD/LDC/17 of 28 October 2010.

confirmation that GSP schemes, the traditional GATT/WTO workhorse to address development needs, have failed to deliver?

It would be highly unfair to blame the WTO for all troubles associated with LDCs: its limited mandate is a curse but also a blessing in this respect. In this vein, it is probably warranted to rethink the value of preferences, at the very least, their value within the regulatory context within which they have been operating since the 1970s, the GSP schemes. Preferential schemes have undeniably had beneficial effects for developing countries. They have also caused concern. The (academic and policy) debate has shifted from an unambiguous 'trade not aid' perspective in the 1950s to 'aid rather than (preferential) trade' nowadays. The idea is that, assuming that one can target it at the intended beneficiaries (and thus eliminate corruption, administrative costs etc.), aid could probably prove a more efficient tool to increase the income of developing nations (the ultimate goal of preferential schemes) than preferential rates. If GSP schemes were fulfilling their intended function, why bother with the whole Aid for Trade endeavour?

The margin of preferences has been affected over the years by MFN tariff liberalization: in the 1970s, MFN rates were much higher than they are now across all products. The reduction of MFN rates led to preference erosion. Because of preference erosion, developing countries have less of an incentive to liberalize trade on an MFN basis (§3 of the Enabling Clause would request them to do so).[106] Although preference erosion does not seem to be much of an issue for low income countries in high income export markets,[107] it is still an important issue for others concerned. Hoekman et al. (2001) ran the following simulation: they assumed that any tariff rate greater than 15 per cent should be treated as a tariff peak. In this vein, assuming LDCs benefited from a 0 per cent tariff rate on all tariff peaks, their exports would increase by 11 per cent. If all GSP beneficiaries benefit from a 0 per cent tariff rate on all tariff peaks, then LDC exports would increase by 5 per cent only. Finally, if the MFN rate for tariff peaks drops to 5 per cent, then LDC exports would not increase at all.

There are dozens of papers pointing in the direction that the benefits of GSP schemes should not be exaggerated. Grossman and Sykes (2005), citing abundant empirical evidence to this effect,[108] conclude that the flame is not worth the candle: there is little support for the proposition that GSP schemes have had substantial positive welfare effects on recipients. Take the EU scheme, for example, which distinguished between non-sensitive, semi-sensitive, sensitive, and very sensitive products. Grossman and Sykes (2005) calculate that, roughly speaking, developing countries receive tariff reductions of 100 per cent (for non-sensitive), 65 per cent (for semi-sensitive), 30 per cent (for sensitive), and 15 per cent (for

---

[106] Limão (2006c).
[107] van der Mensbrugghe (2009).
[108] Sapir and Lundberg (1984); Karsenty and Laird (1986); MacPhee and Oguledo (1991); Brown (1987 and 1989).

very sensitive products) compared with the usual MFN rate for goods in each category.[109] The export interest of most developing countries is of course concentrated on the very sensitive category of products, the one that receives the smallest preference margin. Dean and Wainio (2009) discuss the effects of US GSP on beneficiaries and conclude that high utilization rates should not hide the fact that preference margins for non-agricultural goods are low (preference erosion here is the direct result of low US MFN tariffs), whereas preference margins are low for agricultural goods largely because of the exclusion of products that face high tariffs from GSP schemes. Their data supports the view that the US is more generous towards its PTA partners than it is to its GSP beneficiaries. Candau and Jean (2009) conclude that the EU GSP scheme is quite important for Sub-Saharan LDCs, but not for South Asian LDCs, essentially because of the constraints imposed by rules of origin on textile and clothing exports. In similar vein, Kowalski (2009) concludes that the welfare impact of Canadian preferences is very small for developing countries. Lippoldt (2009) concludes that the Australian GSP scheme has had unambiguously beneficial effects only for those developing countries in geographic proximity to the donor.

Why is this so? GSP schemes simply do not reproduce a negotiation based on reciprocal concessions. Developing countries are not there to request the opening up of the export markets they are interested in; they are at home waiting for donors to draw up their GSP lists. Donors will do so in discussion with their domestic lobbies and the opening up of their markets corresponds to the question 'where and how much would my lobbies want me to open up to international trade?' rather than 'where would you developing countries want me to open up?' This is the simple truth. This explains the distinction between sensitive and semi-sensitive products, for example, in the EU GSP list and the other distinctions in other lists as well.[110]

Subdividing beneficiaries into various categories which are not necessarily linked to their development level might entail various negative (external) effects.[111]

---

[109] Similar conclusions in Joshi (2011).

[110] This rests on the very safe assumption that donors are democracies, and lobby power cannot be neglected. Indeed, this is true of the major donors (EU, Japan, Korea, US). Bagwell and Staiger (2011b) go a step further and provide theoretical support for the argument that, even if concessions are made on products of export interest to developing countries, the free pass they receive puts them in a disadvantaged position vis-à-vis those who paid for the concession. Their argument goes like this: the 'free pass' (in the form of unilateral tariff reductions) offered to developing countries 'to greater export volume is thwarted by the fact that, while the home country . . . offers a more open market on a non-discriminatory basis to all comers, foreign country 2 [NB: the beneficiary developing country] must compete for sales in that market with a more "high-export-performing foreign country 1" [NB the country that exchanged concessions with home country]. This is so because, following trade liberalization, productive resources in foreign country 1 (in the Bagwell-Staiger terminology) will shift from the import good (which foreign country 1 will now be importing from home country) to the export good'. See the argument in more detail in Bagwell and Staiger (2011b) at pp. 7ff.

[111] Low (2007) very sensibly argues for the opposite point: that preferences should be tailor-made for each developing country since it is a mistake to treat them as one homogeneous group. In a

We use again the EU GSP scheme (referred to above) for illustration purposes. There are three classes of beneficiaries under this scheme:

(a) All developing countries enjoy the default preference;

(b) There is a special incentive arrangement for sustainable development and good governance, the notorious GSP + scheme, which provides additional benefits for countries implementing certain international standards in human and labour rights, environmental protection, the fight against drugs, and good governance. This scheme is available to developing countries as well as to LDCs;[112]

(c) Finally, there is a special arrangement available to LDCs only, the Everything But Arms (EBA) initiative, which provides for duty- and quota-free access in the EU market for all products (but arms) originating in LDCs. The EBA was first adopted by the Council of the EU in February 2001 (Regulation (EC) 416/2001). The provisions of the EBA Regulation were incorporated into the GSP Regulation (then, Council Regulation (EC) No. 2501/2001): only imports of fresh bananas, rice, and sugar were not fully liberalized immediately. Duties on those products were gradually reduced until duty-free access was granted for bananas in January 2006, for sugar in July 2009, and for rice in September 2009. In the preceding period, duty-free tariff quotas for rice and sugar were agreed (Regulations 1381/2002 and 1401/2002). The special arrangements for LDCs will last for an unlimited period of time and are not subjected to the periodic renewal of the EU GSP.

Point (b) above is, in principle, WTO-consistent, following the AB report on *EC—Tariff Preferences*, assuming of course that the criteria used for compensating beneficiaries are objective. Legality nonetheless does not always equal rationality: the subdivision operated in the EU framework might lead to a race across developing countries in order to secure benefits, which might undo legitimate policy priorities[113] (especially if one factors in political economy)[114] and, eventually, might comport externalities of a political nature: the alliance across developing countries might be damaged because of the resulting trade diversion, if some developing countries race in to secure benefits under GSP +. Grossman and Sykes (2005) show, when discussing the *EC—Tariff Preferences* dispute, that the EU was essentially paying Pakistan (and all beneficiaries of the Drug Arrangements) with

---

way, this is what the Enabling Clause aimed to do as well, albeit in a very uninformed (e.g. not specific enough) manner by dividing the group into developing countries and LDCs. Additional subclassifications are warranted.

[112] See e.g. Commission Decision 2005/924/EC for the list of beneficiary countries.

[113] Rodrik (2011) builds his argument around this issue: in his view, the world trading system is no longer subservient to domestic policy objectives, but to some extent dictates policies to its participants. One might legitimately question the 'sweeping' character of this view, but has to agree that this conclusion is spot-on when confined to the four corners of GSP schemes.

[114] The point here is not that the EU scheme causes in and of itself the undoing of legitimate policy priorities; the point is that EU preferences might be a facilitating factor.

India's money. And it is worth repeating that donors when designing GSP +
schemes would rather include criteria that respond to their needs and not necessarily to those of beneficiaries.

The US GSP scheme excludes communist countries from its coverage, as well as
countries that withhold the supply of vital commodity resources (probably aimed
at OPEC countries), countries that injure US commerce by affording preferences
to other developed countries, countries that do not enforce arbitral awards in
favour of US citizens, countries that aid terrorism, countries that do not protect
internationally recognized workers' rights, and countries that do not address child
labour.[115] As a result, the list of beneficiaries might be a function of political
decisions rather than development needs. In that, the US scheme does not seem
to be worlds apart from the EU special incentive arrangement for sustainable
development and good governance.

Özden and Reinhardt (2003), in an empirical study, point to yet another
disturbing factor linked to GSP schemes: countries that gradually extricated
themselves from GSP schemes subsequently undertook greater liberalization
than those that chose to retain their eligibility to participate in them. It is a sort
of wicked variation on the Jevons paradox: preferences were supposed to help
beneficiaries graduate to non-beneficiary status. Instead, beneficiaries become
'hooked' to the benefit granted, use it more than before (or as much as they
can), and never graduate. The WTO becomes an irrelevance to them; they live
within the WTO world, but outside the WTO legal disciplines. The countries that
got out of this vicious circle are those that liberalized and enjoyed gains from trade.
And recall that Sachs and Warner (1995) have shown that developing countries
with more liberal trade policies have achieved higher rates of growth and development than countries that are more protectionist.[116]

A number of more recent studies point to the same result: Trefler (2004) shows
how tariff cuts can increase the industry-level productivity of the country
performing similar cuts. Tokarick (2006) examines import protection in 26
developing countries. The sample is quite disparate and hence largely representative of the situation prevailing across all developing countries: Argentina, Brazil,
Botswana, Malawi, China, India, but also Albania and Romania are being reviewed. His main objective is to quantify the extent to which import protection
acts (implicitly) as a tax on a country's export sector. He finds that this is indeed
the case and arrives at a rather substantial tax level: 12 per cent for the 26 countries
in his sample.[117] Mostashari (2010) shows that tariff cuts by countries exporting

---

115 See 19 USC §§2461 and 2462 and the discussion in Grossman and Sykes (2005).

116 In the literature, one often sees references to Korea and Chile as the two most prominent
examples of countries which, post-exclusion from GSP schemes, unilaterally liberalized trade and
boosted their growth rates.

117 The equivalence between import tariffs and export taxes was first established by the economist Abba Lerner and is known as the *Lerner symmetry theorem*. Based on the assumption of a zero
balance of trade (that is, the value of exported goods equals the value of imported goods for a given

to the US market are more important in explaining the success that these countries have enjoyed than the US import tariff cuts.

The complexities associated with the administration of preferential schemes should not be underestimated either. Most of these complexities have been linked to the preferential rules of origin, which make evidence of the origin of a product a particularly cumbersome exercise.[118] It is true that there has recently been a considerable easing of similar rules, as we pointed out in our discussion about rules of origin *supra*. There is still some way to go though.

Hudec (1987) took the view back in 1987 that GSP schemes were not all that beneficial to developing countries: they essentially blocked beneficiaries from adopting changes beneficial to them. In his view, developing countries would have been better off simply abandoning such schemes in exchange for non-discriminatory access to the agricultural and textiles markets of donors. He urged (p. 235):

> Governments of developing countries will have to be persuaded that it is in their own national economic interest to respond with a fuller commitment to GATT law.

Developing countries, alas, turned a blind eye to this and similar calls. They preferred to continue with one-way preferences and have not changed this strategy even in the presence of evidence that similar schemes do not work. Hudec's intuition that one-way preferences will have the opposite of the desired outcome has sadly been largely confirmed by subsequent practice and research.[119]

3. Preferential Trade Agreements (PTAs)[120]

3.1 The Legal Discipline and its Rationale

WTO Members that have satisfied the requirements included in Art. XXIV GATT can justifiably treat products originating in some WTO Members (those

---

country), Lerner showed that an *ad valorem* import tariff would have the same effects as an export tax. Thus, the effect on relative prices is the same, regardless of which policy—import duties or export taxes—has been privileged.

[118] Recall our discussion above about cumulation, diagonal cumulation, etc.

[119] To paraphrase Spence (2011, p. 5), it seems that the 'Inclusiveness Revolution', leading to convergence between the OECD and some fast developing countries, is taking place anyway, and the WTO is at best playing a 'catching up' game. WTO Members have been negotiating a DTQF regime for all products originating in LDCs, their token way to help the 'bottom billion', as Collier (2007) put it. The chances of success were slim and got nowhere. Helping the bottom billion out of its doldrums is not an exclusively government operation: Prahalad (2010) has made a forceful argument in favour of private sector involvement.

[120] Throughout this volume we privilege the use of the term 'PTA' over the term 'regional integration': the former captures the essence of these schemes, since participants in such arrangements will be treated better than outsiders; the latter term reflects a historical feature. Not all such schemes are regional in the sense of geographic proximity any more. One-third of FTAs currently under investigation are among countries that are not in geographic proximity: the number of cross-

with which they have formed a PTA) better than like products originating in the remaining WTO Members. Art. XXIV GATT is thus an exception to Art. I GATT. Art. XXIV GATT distinguishes between two forms of PTAs: free trade areas (FTA) and customs unions (CU). For an FTA to be GATT-consistent, its members must liberalize trade between themselves whereas, for a CU to be GATT-consistent, its members must also agree on a common trade policy vis-à-vis the rest of the WTO Membership.

There is thus a notable difference between the two forms of integration, in the sense that the CU implies substantial loss of sovereignty through the emergence of a common external tariff. FTAs and CUs do not of course exhaust the forms of market integration, as indeed the EU experience shows. Balassa (1967) provided a classification of 'stages of integration' where FTA and CU were the two 'shallow-est' forms of market integration; next would come the common market, where factors of production (and not only trade restrictions) would be eliminated; then, the economic union, where some form of harmonization of economic policies would occur, and finally a complete economic integration which would entail unification of monetary, fiscal, social policies and where a central authority entrusted with the capacity to issue binding rules would be established. Balassa did see some sequence across the various stages.[121] Sapir (2011) does not: in his view, there is no reason to believe that there is some form of automaticity in the integration process that leads from FTAs to CUs. Indeed, the numbers here tell a story since there is only a handful of CUs that have been notified to the WTO and for some of them there are legitimate doubts as to whether they have established a genuine common external tariff.[122] He bases his conclusion in part on the unwillingness of states to yield sovereignty to supranational institutions, and this is why there are so many FTAs and so few CUs.

The negotiating history of Art. XXIV GATT does not reveal a dominant explanation for its inclusion. What is clear is that the view held by many that

---

regional schemes has risen from six in 1995 to 80 in 2008. The FTAs between the EU and Mexico, Australia and Chile, Mexico and Japan underscore this point. Moreover, as Sapir (2011) points out, the origin of the term 'regional integration' is uncertain as the term does not appear in the body of Art. XXIV GATT. He notes that this term was first used in an official GATT document in February 1996 when the WTO established the Committee on Regional Trade Agreements to examine the consistency of FTAs and CUs with the WTO. Dam (1963) is credited by Sapir as the first author to use the term 'regional trade agreements', probably because in the early 1960s all preferential schemes were across regional partners.

121 He was not alone: Viner (1950, pp. 3ff) took the view that a sequence across the various forms of market integration corresponded to sound intellectual criteria; in his view, political unions should come before customs unions and that the German Zollverein, where the customs union preceded the political union, was quite idiosyncratic.

122 At the time of writing (December 2011), the WTO has been notified of only the following CUs: the Caribbean Community and Common Market (CARICOM); the Central American Common Market (CACM); the Eurasian Economic Community (EAEC); the European Union (EU); the EU CUs with Andorra, San Marino, and Turkey; the South African Customs Union (SACU).

the inclusion of a provision was meant to accommodate the European integration process is wrong: in Acheson's (1969) record, Jean Monnet revealed his plans on European integration after the Havana Conference had taken place. Two CUs participated in the negotiation of the original GATT, the Syro-Lebanese customs union (Syria, Lebanon) and Benelux (Belgium, Netherlands, Luxembourg), but neither of them requested institutional arrangements to accommodate their CU. Chase (2006), drawing on a series of archival records, explains the extension of the original provision (which was limited to CUs) to cover FTAs as well: the author demonstrates that it was the US negotiators that designed this provision in order to accommodate a trade agreement that they had secretly reached with Canada. References to FTAs were thus included in Art. 44 of the Havana Charter (the corresponding provision to Art. XXIV GATT) and appear for the first time only in 1948.[123] The US–Canada FTA, alas, was never ratified.

Economists and political scientists have advanced various explanations why one might opt to go preferential;[124] if there is one characteristic that is common to all of them it is that they are all idiosyncratic. The EU, for example, has been an early champion of preferential trade, recently copied by various eager beavers. Trade policy was for years the only genuine EU common policy and one cannot resist the temptation to ask the question whether PTAs were not part of a wider 'I sign, *ergo* I exist' strategy: with every PTA signed, the EU was affirming its international persona, becoming thus more of a figure in international relations.[125]

There are other, more generally applicable explanations for going preferential. To start with, PTAs are close to 'natural' integration schemes across geographically proximate partners. Tinbergen (1962) was the first to explain that the formation of PTAs was in some ways quite natural: he developed the gravity equation, aimed at predicting trade in the absence of distortions. Trade is an increasing function of the gross national product (GNP) of both the exporting and the importing country; trade is further negatively influenced by the distance between the countries. Gravity models have been successfully used to explain the formation of PTAs, especially between partners in geographic proximity to each other.[126] Krugman (1991) and Summers (1991) have gone one step further and have argued that PTAs among countries in geographic proximity should be encouraged, whereas PTAs among countries which are not neighbours (in a geographic sense)

---

[123] Compare Viner (1950) at pp. 113ff.

[124] Schiff and Winters (2003).

[125] This is not to say that this is the only reason why the EU signed PTAs. For a start, PTAs have been used as an antechamber for EU accession. Cremona (2010) and Mattli (1999) provide a very comprehensive and analytical account of European regionalism in its historical dimension.

[126] The term 'distance' refers not only to geographical distance (e.g. transportation costs), but also to other associated obstacles, such as the cost of information on the export market due to, for example, language differences, historical and cultural factors, etc. The term 'gravity' was chosen in reference to Newton's law describing the force of gravity as a function of the product of the masses of the two objects, and the distance between them.

should be discouraged. In their analysis, the former are more likely to avoid the adverse possibility of welfare reduction and to lead to a larger improvement in welfare.[127]

But of course, PTAs come at a cost. Viner (1950) was the first to explain why PTAs are welfare reducing in light of the resulting trade diversion (deflection):[128] when A and B form a PTA they create trade, since they dismantle pre-existing protection between them. They also divert trade, though, since intra-PTA trade might displace extra-PTA trade (trade deflection): it could be the case that the most efficient sources of a particular commodity is C and that by privileging trade from B, A will be diverting trade from the absolutely most efficient source (C) to the relatively (that is, intra-PTA) more efficient source (say B). Trade diversion comes at a cost, and this is what Viner's work alerted us to. There is cost of course not only for the consumers located inside the PTA (who now pay a higher price) but also for traders outside the PTA who now have to look for new markets.[129]

Influenced by Viner's analysis, economists initially viewed regional integration with a lot of scepticism.[130] Scholarship went one step further to provide support for scepticism: influential papers such as Grossman and Helpman (1995) and Krishna (1998) established the incentive for PTA partners to choose integration in those sectors where the possibility for preference (and thus trade deflection) is the greatest possible. True, the GATT legal test does provide some insurance policy against this possibility (through the requirement to liberalize 'substantially all trade', as we shall see *infra*), but the legal test was almost never respected in the first place. The natural consequence of this analysis is that PTA partners are missing incentives to agree, following establishment of a PTA, on MFN tariff cuts for fear of preference erosion. Bhagwati (2002), Krishna (1998), and Limão (2006a) have all contributed theoretical and empirical papers in this vein. Besides trade diversion generated through the establishment of PTAs, members of PTAs behave like enemies of non-discriminatory trade liberalization in the future as well,

---

[127] It is questionable how strong this claim is since there is empirical evidence that there are substantial border effects. Anderson and Van Wincoop (2003), for example, have estimated that national borders reduce trade between industrialized countries by moderate amounts of 20–50 per cent.

[128] It is not the case that trade diversion is a necessary evil stemming from the creation of PTAs: the Kemp-Wan theorem posits that trade diversion can be eliminated by reducing external tariffs so as to keep trade with non-members unchanged, keeping prices constant in other words. The result in the Kemp-Wan theorem applies in a set of given circumstances. The Kemp-Wan theorem, none-theless, is not a *passage obligé* in order to support a claim that PTAs can be welfare improving.

[129] And there is a lot of empirical evidence in this context: Sapir (2001), for example, examines trade deflection as a result of the deepening of the EU integration process following the single market project. He finds substantial negative welfare implications for EFTA (European Free Trade Association) exporters to the EU which he attributes to the 'quality' of market integration at the EU level. It is similar data that lends support to Baldwin (1995) who argues that EU integration had a domino effect and led EFTA members to knock on the door in Brussels and request full accession to the EU.

[130] Baldwin and Venables (1995), Panagariya (2000), and Winters (2011) have contributed an excellent survey on the economics of PTAs.

since they are unwilling to cut tariffs on an MFN basis for fear of eroding the margin of preference that they have already granted to their PTA partners. They thus become, as Bhagwati and Panagariya (1999) put it, stumbling blocks (as opposed to building blocks) in the multilateral trading system, opposing MFN trade liberalization and frustrating the achievement of the basic WTO objective. In other words, trade diversion is here to stay as a result of the incentives of PTA partners.[131] Bhagwati (2008) goes so far as to state that (p. 88):

> It is hard to contemplate the consequences of PTAs with equanimity. The most important item in our policy agenda has to be to devise an appropriate response to their spread and the damage they impose on the multilateral trading system.

Against this background, why do rational agents go preferential? As we shall see *infra*, the number of PTAs in place is staggering and their increase in the post-Uruguay round era (when tariffs were cut like never before) dramatic. As is the case with costs where we distinguish between static (trade deflection) and dynamic costs (refusal to make MFN cuts for fear of preference erosion), we can distinguish between static and dynamic gains. Baldwin (1992 and 1993) correctly suggests that it is an onerous exercise to estimate the dynamic effects of preferential agreements. Some of them, for example, might be shielded within the realm of private information that is never revealed to the rest of the world (e.g. side payments in the form of support for a permanent or temporary seat on the UN Security Council). Baldwin notes that the difficulty of calculating similar benefits is no intellectual reason to exclude them outright from any calculation. Krugman (1991, p. 10) observes that a trading bloc could be formed in order to improve the terms of trade for its participants. In this view, a similar arrangement:

> will normally have more monopoly power in world trade than any of its members alone. The standard theory of the optimal tariff tells us that the optimal tariff for a country acting unilaterally to improve its terms of trade is higher, the lower the elasticity of world demand for its exports. So for a trading bloc attempting to maximize the welfare of its residents, the optimal tariff rate will normally be higher than the optimal tariff rates of its constituent countries acting individually.[132]

Kowalczyk (1990) has shown, employing terms-of-trade and volume-of-trade analysis, that trade creation and diversion do not necessarily equate with welfare gains and losses. WTO Members might be deriving important political benefits

---

[131] Note that theory is not unanimous in this respect. Saggi and co-authors design models with endogenous cuts in order to ascertain whether MFN cuts are a counterfactual to preferential cuts: Saggi and Yildiz (2011) find that when countries have asymmetric endowments or when governments value producer interests more than tariff revenue and consumer surplus, there exist circumstances where global free trade is a stable equilibrium only if countries are free to pursue bilateral trade agreements. Saggi et al. (2010) argue that, if the players have asymmetric endowments, Art. XXIV GATT (regionalism) might, on occasion, help further the cause of multilateral liberalization.

[132] Winters and Won Chang (2000), for example, find that non-EU countries experienced terms-of-trade losses when Spain and Portugal joined the EU in 1986.

by association with their preferential partners, and this is most likely the case when associating themselves with the two main hubs, the EU and the US. This observation might also explain why those originally left out might wish to join in subsequently.[133] NAFTA was beneficial to Mexico not simply because the US lowered its tariff barriers to Mexican goods and services, but also because Mexico benefited from other dynamic benefits, such as increased investment over the years as a result of rationalization of its policies, etc.[134] In similar vein, Baltagi et al. (2008) discuss the relationship between PTAs and FDI (foreign direct investment) and conclude in an empirical paper regarding the Europe Agreements that removal of trade barriers has led to substantial flows of FDI for those participating: recourse to PTAs could thus be privileged because a country sees a PTA as a way to get investment/access to foreign technology that can increase its income, or access to low-cost production of inputs that can increase its ability to export certain products; or even that trade is a component of a wider public policy package.[135] Dynamic (indirect) benefits can be of a different nature as well. It could also be, for example, that PTAs serve as 'signalling mechanisms': Mexico, by joining NAFTA, did not only enjoy trade and investment benefits, but also signalled to the world that it was abandoning its policies of the past and was espousing a different model. Association with this particular hub (US) was a strong signal to this effect. This, in turn, might have eased the relationship of Mexico with international organizations, financial markets, etc. Becoming a preferential partner in trade might thus open the door to all sorts of political cooperation. Obtaining political perks, which might be indirect or uncertain, could on occasion be the key motivation why spokes decide to go preferential with hubs. PTAs are part and parcel of wider foreign policy and might be motivated only or mainly by concerns of a political order: China, for example, has not signed any PTA with WTO Members that have recognized Chinese Taipei.

In short, it is as impossible to respond in a horizontal manner to the question why are PTAs formed as it is to decide on their (positive or negative) welfare implications.

3.2 Coverage of the Legal Discipline

The legal test and the economics test for giving the green light to a PTA are like two ships passing in the night. Irrespective of their differences, what stems from the discussion *supra* is that economists care about the welfare implications of

---

[133] On the point that one might come close to accurate predictions as to who will join, see Baldwin (1997 and 1995).

[134] Caliendo and Parro (2009).

[135] One might legitimately ask the question whether a PTA is the necessary vehicle for this kind of perk. As things stand, we know that PTAs have proved to be the vehicle by comparing the *ex ante* with the *ex post* situation, without asking the additional question whether similar perks would have been obtained in a non-PTA scenario (a difficult, if not altogether impossible, counterfactual).

PTAs. This is the question that the legal test embedded in Art. XXIV GATT does not ask. This provision aims at avoiding PTAs à la carte and ensuring that intra-PTA trade liberalization will not be accompanied by new protection vis-à-vis the rest of the world. The result could be very substantial trade diversion (especially for early PTAs in the 1950s and the 1960s when MFN tariffs were quite high).[136] This is not a concern for the GATT legislator. Before we move to a detailed discussion of the legal discipline though, note that Art. XXIV.4 GATT leaves no doubt that there is room for PTAs under the aegis of the multilateral framework:

> The contracting parties recognize the desirability of increasing freedom of trade by the development, through voluntary agreements, of closer integration between the economies of the countries parties to such agreements. They also recognize that the purpose of a customs union or of a free-trade area should be to facilitate trade between the constituent territories and not to raise barriers to the trade of other contracting parties with such territories.

3.2.1 The Placement of Art. XXIV GATT in the WTO System

The wording and the negotiating history should leave no doubt that Art. XXIV GATT was meant to be an exception to Art. I GATT.[137] With the advent of the WTO, the question arises whether it is an exception to other provisions as well. The AB, in its report on *Turkey—Textiles*, responded in the affirmative and held that recourse to this provisions could justify deviations from Art. 2.4 ATC:

> Article XXIV may justify a measure which is inconsistent with certain other GATT provisions.

The AB explained in the same report the conditions under which this exception can be successfully invoked, and stated in unambiguous terms that the party invoking Art. XXIV GATT to justify deviations from MFN trade carries the associated burden of proof (§58):

> First, the party claiming the benefit of this defence must demonstrate that the measure at issue is introduced upon the formation of a customs union that fully meets the requirements of sub-paragraphs 8(a) and 5(a) of Article XXIV. And, second, that party must demonstrate that the formation of that customs union would be prevented if it were not allowed to introduce the measure at issue.

The Panel on *Canada—Autos* added that, for a WTO Member to successfully invoke this provision, it must show that the measure it wishes to justify is granted to all PTA partners and is not granted to non-PTA partners. Unless this is the case, an otherwise GATT-inconsistent measure cannot find shelter in Art. XXIV GATT (§§10.55–6).

---

[136] As noted by Grossman and Helpman (1995) though, the result is also that good faith WTO Members will not integrate only those sectors where the maximum trade deflection is possible.

[137] Gantz (2009) offers a comprehensive account in this respect.

3.2.2 *Notification*

WTO Members deciding to enter into a PTA have to notify the WTO of their intention to do so (Art. XXIV.7 GATT).[138] Notifications will be submitted to the CRTA (Committee on Regional Trade Agreements), where the compatibility of the notified scheme with the multilateral rules will be reviewed.[139] The CRTA[140] is the successor to Art. XXIV GATT Working Parties, the organ that would examine the consistency of notified PTAs with the multilateral rules. There is not much substantive difference between the two bodies other than the fact that the CRTA is the consolidation of prior practice into a 'permanent' organ: participation in Working Parties was open to all GATT contracting parties, and this is the case with respect to the CRTA as well.

The CRTA was established through a decision by the WTO General Council on 7 February 1996 which in part requests from the CRTA:[141]

(a) to carry out the examination of agreements in accordance with the procedures and terms of reference adopted...and thereafter present its report to the relevant body for appropriate action;

   ...

(b) to consider the systemic implications of such agreements and regional initiatives for the multilateral trading system.

The CRTA adopts its decisions by consensus as per Rule 33 of the Rules of Procedure for Meetings of the Committee on Regional Trade Agreements:[142]

> Where a decision cannot be arrived at by consensus, the matter at issue shall be referred, as appropriate, to the General Council, the Council for Trade in Goods, the Council for Trade in Services or the Committee on Trade and Development.

There is no reported case of referral to a higher body. In principle, the CRTA has wide powers. Art. XXIV.7 GATT relevantly provides that the organs examining the consistency of notified PTAs have the power:

> ...to make such reports and recommendations to contracting parties as they may deem appropriate.

---

[138] WTO Members will notify a CU, an FTA, or an interim agreement leading to a FTA or a CU. In this latter case there is a requirement to report in set periods the implementation of the PTA; WTO Doc. TN/RL/W/8/Rev. 1 of 1 August 2002.

[139] There have not been many complaints regarding absence of notification of PTAs. Still, the issue has been raised and a proposal has been tabled to eventually introduce the possibility of cross-notification of PTAs that had not been previously notified; WTO Doc. TN/RL/W/8/Rev. 1 of 1 August 2002. There is a standard notification format for PTAs irrespective of under which provision (GATT, GATS, Enabling Clause) they are notified; WTO Doc. G/L/834 of 8 November 2007.

[140] For a more detailed discussion on the inception of the CRTA, see Mavroidis (2006).

[141] WTO Doc. WT/L/127.

[142] WTO Doc. WT/REG/1 of 14 August 1996.

In principle, one cannot exclude the possibility that the CRTA concludes that a notified PTA is WTO-inconsistent. This conclusion is underscored by the explicit wording of Art. XXIV.7(b) GATT, which explains the powers of the CRTA when it reviews an interim agreement leading to the establishment of a CU or an FTA:

> If...the CONTRACTING PARTIES find that such agreement is not likely to result in the formation of a customs union or of a free-trade area...the CONTRACTING PARTIES shall make recommendations to the parties to the agreement. *The parties shall not maintain or put into force, as the case may be, such agreement if they are not prepared to modify it in accordance with these recommendations.* (emphasis added)

Never in the history of the GATT have GATT CONTRACTING PARTIES reached a decision that a notified scheme was inconsistent with the multilateral rules. For years, the final report of an Art. XXIV Working Party would look like an expression of disagreement regarding the consistency of various aspects of the notified PTA with the multilateral rules between those being reviewed (and their allies) and those reviewing. The situation has not changed in the WTO era either, as we will see in what follows. The CRTA will circulate two documents: a factual abstract (an executive summary of the discussions held in the CRTA) and a factual presentation (the final report, which will provide factual information on various aspects of the notified PTA).

Recall that it is the CTD that should be notified of arrangements across developing countries (south-south cooperation). We are consequently left with the following possible constellations for PTAs notified under Art. XXIV GATT:

(a) between developed countries all of which are WTO Members;
(b) between WTO Members some of which qualify as developed and some as developing countries;
(c) between a WTO Member which qualifies as developed country and a non-WTO Member.

There should be no doubt that the CRTA should be notified of PTAs coming under the first two categories. The last category legitimately raises issues. One would think that Art. XXIV GATT is a discipline to be observed by WTO Members only. Art. XXIV.5 reads:

> Accordingly, the provisions of this Agreement shall not prevent, *as between the territories of contracting parties*, the formation of a customs union or of a free-trade area or the adoption of an interim agreement necessary for the formation of a customs union or of a free-trade area; (emphasis added)

In this vein, to the extent a WTO Member grants an advantage to a non-WTO Member by signing a PTA to this effect, it would have to, by virtue of Art. I GATT, automatically and unconditionally extend it to all WTO Members. Yet, practice has developed in a different way. WTO Members, whether developed or developing, notify the CRTA and/or the CTD of their PTAs with non-WTO

Members as well: *EC–CARIFORUM* (Bahamas is part of the agreement, but not a WTO Member) is an example of the former, and *Ukraine–Uzbekistan* of the latter.[143] Practice has arguably developed *contra legem* in this respect since WTO Members now, when signing PTAs with non-WTO Members, do not have to automatically and unconditionally extend benefits to all other WTO Members.

Practice also evidences dual notifications simultaneously to the CRTA and the CTD. When MERCOSUR was established, it was notified under the Enabling Clause only, since all participants were developing countries. It was later agreed that the terms of reference of the Working Party should, in this particular case, also include an examination of the consistency of MERCOSUR with Art. XXIV GATT as well:

> To examine the Southern Common Market Agreement (MERCOSUR) in the light of the relevant provisions of the Enabling Clause and of the GATT 1994, including Article XXIV, and to transmit a report and recommendations to the Committee on Trade and Development for submission to the General Council, with a copy of the report transmitted as well to the Council for Trade in Goods. The examination in the Working Party will be based on a complete notification and on written questions and answers.

Eventually, MERCOSUR was discussed before the CRTA. Both the CTD and the CRTA were also notified of the CU established by the members of the GCC (Gulf Cooperation Council), the India–Korea and Korea–ASEAN FTAs. A number of developing countries raised concerns regarding the legality of this practice: in a joint communication, China, Egypt, and India pointed to the absence of a legislative framework enabling dual notifications and the ensuing uncertainty regarding both the impact of the various provisions as well as the role that the CTD and the CRTA should be acknowledged in this process.[144] At the moment of writing, this is still an open issue. A General Council decision did not manage to clarify this issue:

> Notifying Members shall specify under which provision or provisions in paragraph 1 their PTAs are notified.[145]

The use of the plural ('provisions') could be taken as an indication that dual notifications are now possible, although it could also be taken as an indication that it refers to notifications under Arts. XXIV GATT and V GATS only.

Art. XXIV.7(a) GATT addresses the timing of notification:

> Any contracting party *deciding to enter* into a customs union or free-trade area, or an interim agreement leading to the formation of such a union or area, shall *promptly* notify the CONTRACTING PARTIES and shall make available . . . such

---

[143] The WTO was also notified of the FTAs between Turkey–Syria, and EFTA–Lebanon, although neither Syria nor Lebanon is a WTO Member.

[144] WTO Doc. WT/COMTD/W/175 of 30 September 2010.

[145] WTO Doc. WT/L/806 of 16 December 2010.

information . . . as will enable them to make such reports and recommendations to contracting parties as they may deem appropriate. (emphasis added)

The language of Art. XXIV GATT suggests the CRTA should be notified of a prospective action; according to the Transparency Mechanism (that we discuss *infra*), all PTAs should be notified as early as possible and, in any case, immediately following their ratification by participants. The WTO Secretariat (the TPRM Division) will then prepare a factual presentation of the PTA that would be circulated to all WTO Members.[146] It is quite frequent, however, for PTAs to be notified with substantial delays. For example, NAFTA was signed on 17 December 1992, entered into force on 1 January 1994, and a Working Party to examine its consistency with the GATT rules was established only on 23 March 1994. The EC–Visegrad Agreements (an FTA between the EU on one hand and Hungary, Poland, and the Czech and Slovak Federal Republics on the other) entered into force on 16 December 1991, and the Working Party was established only on 30 April 1992. Consequently, Working Parties (and now the CRTA) have often been presented with a *fait accompli*. This is an important observation, especially in light of the de facto absence of retroactive remedies in the GATT/ WTO legal system: it would suggest that the CRTA does not have to provide the necessary green light for a PTA to lawfully enter into force. One WTO Panel report at least (*US—Line Pipe*) has sided with this view. A General Council decision regarding the content of notifications formally accepted that notifications can take place after the entry into force of the notified PTA:

> The required notification of a PTA shall take place as early as possible; it will occur when practicable before the application of preferential treatment by the notifying Member and, at the latest, three months after the PTA is in force.[147]

The advent of the Transparency Mechanism has provided the official confirmation of past practice in this respect: it is through a General Council decision that the Transparency Mechanism for Regional Trade Agreements was adopted on 14 December 2006.[148] Since its advent, no discussion will be reflected in the factual presentation regarding the consistency of particular aspects of the PTA with the multilateral rules.[149] The Transparency Mechanism was originally supposed to complement the existing legal arsenal dealing with PTAs (Art. XXIV GATT; Understanding on Art. XXIV GATT; Decision on the establishment of the CRTA), by clarifying the date of notification of a PTA, imposing the obligation to notify the WTO of any negotiations that might lead to a PTA, and, in general, providing information as to the kind of information that a notification was

---

[146] WTO Doc. TN/RL/18 of 13 July 2006.
[147] WTO Doc. WT/L/806 of 16 December 2010.
[148] WTO Doc. WT/L/671 of 18 December 2006.
[149] For a typical illustration, see the CRTA report on the FTA between Thailand and New Zealand; WTO Doc. WT/REG207/3 of 3 January 2007.

required to include.[150] In practice, however, the Transparency Mechanism has not complemented, but substituted, the previous arsenal: the multilateral review has de facto been narrowed down to a mere exercise in transparency.

The multilateral review is consequently definitely not the green light for the advent of PTAs any more; the CRTA is not in this respect akin to a merger authority that has to clear a merger before the latter can be lawfully consummated. With this in mind, we turn to a discussion of the substantive requirements that GATT-consistent PTAs must meet.

The content of notification has been standardized for all PTAs irrespective of whether they are notified under the Enabling Clause or Art. XXIV GATT. WTO Members have adopted a decision, on a provisional basis (pending its permanent application), regarding the content of notified PTAs.[151] The various Annexes to the decision clarify that information regarding the identity of participants, the products treated preferentially, the volume of preferential trade, etc. must be notified.

3.2.3 Substantially All Trade (Internal Requirement)

The internal requirement is common for FTAs and CUs alike: according to Art. XXIV.8 GATT, WTO Members wishing to enter into a CU or an FTA will have to eliminate duties and other restrictive regulations of commerce (ORRC) with respect to substantially all trade (SAT) in products originating in the constituents of the PTA. Grossman and Helpman (1995) have persuasively argued that the inclusion of this requirement serves a legitimate purpose: absent this requirement, WTO Members will have an incentive to conclude preferential deals on commodities where the largest possible trade diversion could result; it is thus not only PTAs à la carte that will be avoided, but among them those PTAs that might have the most nefarious welfare implications. The merits for including it notwithstanding, this provision remains even nowadays largely uninterpreted: its terms were not clarified through subsequent legislative action, not even the Uruguay round negotiations, where other terms of this provision were successfully negotiated and clarified.[152] Inevitably, hence, we have to turn to practice, that is, the various Art. XXIV Working Parties that have dealt with this issue. But even a cursory, helicopter view of practice leaves the researcher with the impression that this is an area where trading partners found it impossible to agree on a particular meaning.

Here is an inventory of some representative views heard on this score. It has been suggested that the term 'substantially all trade' has a quantitative as well as a

---

150 There was dissatisfaction with the amount of information provided by those participating in the notified PTA. There are many reasons explaining why, and dispute settlement awareness figures, according to official WTO documents, among the most important: the fear that information provided might lead to dispute settlement cases against them. As we discuss *infra*, similar fears are probably exaggerated.

151 WTO Doc. WT/L/806 of 16 December 2010.

152 Mathis (2002).

qualitative component, in the sense that it covers a certain percentage of trade and at the same time no major sector of a national economy can be excluded.[153] The opinion has also been expressed in the *EEC Working Party* that it is:

> inappropriate to fix a general figure of the percentage of trade which would be subjected to internal barriers.[154]

In the same Working Party, various EU Member States expressed the view that:

> a free-trade area should be considered as having been achieved for substantially all trade when the volume of liberalized trade reached 80 per cent of total trade.[155]

The Working Party report on EFTA, on the other hand, records the view that:

> the percentage of trade covered, even if it were established to be 90 per cent, was not considered to be the only factor to be taken into account.[156]

Other Working Party reports reflect the view that the exclusion of a whole sector, no matter what percentage of trade is involved, is contrary to the spirit of both Art. XXIV GATT and the GATT itself.[157] Nothing has changed in this respect in more recent years.[158] Discussions in the context of the CRTA are hardly illuminating. The GATT Analytical Index (vol. 2, p. 824, footnote 162) provides an exhaustive list of Working Party reports dealing with this issue; the inescapable conclusion is that trading partners did not manage to clarify this term in subsequent practice. In a series of papers that the WTO Secretariat prepared for the CRTA,[159] this conclusion was reconfirmed: 50 years of practice notwithstanding, WTO Members have failed to come up with a workable definition of the term.

Probably the most appropriate way to sum up practice in this field is offered by the Working Party report on *EC—Agreements with Portugal*,[160] where the EU delegate noted that:

> there is no exact definition of the expression referring to the term 'substantially all trade'.

After the conclusion of the Uruguay round, Australia tabled a proposal to clarify the term 'substantially all trade'.[161] Australia parted company with the

---

[153] GATT Analytical Index, pp. 824–5.

[154] Working Party report on *EEC*, GATT Doc. BISD 6S/100, §34.

[155] See GATT Doc. BISD 6S/70, §30.

[156] GATT Doc. BISD 96/83, §48.

[157] Working Party report on *EEC—Agreements with Finland*, GATT Doc. BISD 29S/79, §12.

[158] Working Party report on *Free Trade Area between Canada and the US*, GATT Doc. BISD 38S/73, §83.

[159] WTO Docs. WT/REG/W/17 of 31 October 1997; WT/REG/W/17/Add 1 of 5 November 1997; WT/REG/W/17/Corr. 1 of 15 December 1997); WT/REG/W/17/Rev. 1 of 15 February 1998.

[160] GATT Doc. BISD 20S/171, §16.

[161] WTO Doc. WT/REG/W/18 of 17 November 1997.

oft-mentioned but nebulous idea that the term reflects both a quantitative and a qualitative element. Australia proposed that, to comply with this requirement, WTO Members should be requested to liberalize 95 per cent of all the six-digit tariff lines listed in the HS. In its response to questions by other WTO Members,[162] Australia accepted that the 95 per cent figure was an arbitrary benchmark; in its view, nonetheless, coming up with a number was an appropriate device intended to move negotiations out of deadlock and provide a workable and reasonable rule of thumb. Australia was also mindful of the fact that in cases where trade is concentrated in only a few products, the 95 per cent figure could exempt sizeable trade flows. This is why it also proposed an assessment of prospective trade flows under an arrangement at various stages. Australia did not manage to persuade its partners about the well-foundedness of its proposal, which has since died a slow death. This was one of the very few proposals to interpret SAT in a meaningful manner: a document of the WTO Negotiating Group on Rules underscores that very few proposals aiming to clarify its meaning have been tabled.[163]

More recently, a General Council decision suggests, at least implicitly, that the SAT requirement does not require liberalization of all trade involved.[164] In its Annex 2, it requires notifying WTO Members to provide information regarding the list of ineligible products as well as the preferential trade volume affected in the last three years (prior to the notification).

The other term featured in this provision is 'duties and other restrictive regulations of commerce'. Art. XXIV.8 GATT does not define this term any further, but, in a notorious parenthesis, exempts from its coverage measures coming under the purview of Arts. XI, XII, XIII, XIV, XV, and XX. There should be no doubt that the term 'duties' refers to customs duties and hence interpretative issues arise only with respect to the term 'other restrictive regulations of commerce'. Two issues arise: first, whether the list of measures mentioned in the parenthesis and thus exempted is exhaustive or not; second, whether the exempted measures can help the interpreter define the full ambit of the term 'other restrictive regulations of commerce'.

Practice does not address this issue in a dispositive manner; it seems to suggest that inferences from the omission of Art. XXI GATT from the list reflected in the parenthesis can legitimately be drawn. The issue was discussed in the *Working Party on EEC*. The view of the (then) EEC member states was that:

> it would be difficult, however, to dispute the right of contracting parties to avail themselves of that provision which related, inter alia, to traffic in arms, fissionable materials, etc., and it must therefore be concluded that the list was not exhaustive.[165]

---

[162] WTO Doc. WT/REG/W/22/Add. 1 of 24 April 1998.
[163] WTO Doc. JOB/RL/3 of 25 January 2011.
[164] WTO Doc. WT/L/806 of 16 December 2010.
[165] GATT Doc. BISD 6S/70, p. 97.

Similar voices have been raised in the context of other Working Party reports.[166] The argument in favour of acknowledging the indicative character of the list has been reinforced by discussions regarding the exclusion of Art. XIX GATT. During the Uruguay round negotiations, a draft decision was tabled to clarify this issue:

> When an Article XIX action is taken by a member of a customs union or free-trade area, or by the customs union on behalf of a member, it [need not] [shall not] be applied to other members of the customs union or free-trade area. However, when taking such action it should be demonstrated that the serious injury giving rise to the invocation of Article XIX is caused by imports from non-members; any injury deriving from imports from other members of the customs union or free-trade area shall not be taken into account in justifying the Article XIX action.[167]

Had this proposal been accepted, it would have provided a much-needed clarification on this score and would have laid to rest the relationship between Art. XIX and Art. XXIV GATT. The proposal was, alas, rejected. WTO adjudicating bodies have already faced the question whether a member of a PTA (a CU in the first[168] and an FTA in the second case[169]) could impose safeguards against other members of the PTA where it belongs. They held that members of a PTA can impose safeguards against other members of a PTA, provided that they respect a parallelism: they can do so if they have counted PTA imports when assessing injury; they cannot do so, however, in the opposite case (when they have not counted PTA imports when assessing injury). Although the WTO adjudicating bodies explicitly declared that they were not influencing the relationship between the two provisions (Arts. XIX–XXIV GATT), de facto they did: had they followed a 'narrow' reading of the list in the parenthesis, it would have been impossible to open the door to safeguards between PTA members. Following these events, one can reasonably conclude that WTO practice supports the view that the list in the parenthesis of Art. XXIV.8 GATT is not exhaustive.

Including the possibility for intra-PTA safeguards *ipso facto* suggests that the list featured in parentheses is of an indicative nature. Assuming that this is the case, the next question is what else should be included. The items included (in the enlarged parentheses) should inform the interpreter about the other items that should be included. Yet, there is remarkable heterogeneity with respect to the subject-matter of the provisions included in parentheses: indeed, whereas the first five provisions mentioned deal with trade instruments, Art. XX GATT covers a wide range of domestic instruments. Should we understand the term 'other restrictive regulations of trade' as extending to cover any domestic instrument that restricts trade?

The 1970 Working Party on *EEC—Association with African and Malgasy States* dealt with this issue. There, the opinion was raised that trade had not been

---

166 The GATT Analytical Index, pp. 820ff.
167 WTO Doc. WT/REG/W/17/Rev. 1, p. 4.
168 *Argentina—Footwear (EC)*.
169 *US—Wheat Gluten*.

substantially liberalized, in view of the continued imposition by certain parties to the Convention (the Association of EEC with African and Malgasy States) of fiscal charges on imports from other members. In response, the members of the PTA argued that:

> the provisions of Article XXIV, concerning the concept of a free-trade area, concerned only protective measures. The taxes referred to were of a fiscal character, not protective.[170]

Where the line between 'protective' and 'fiscal' should be drawn was not discussed (or explained) any further. A series of PTAs now include standards on environmental protection, labour standards, human rights, etc. The question could arise whether members of a PTA could adopt, say, two sets of environmental policies, one applicable to its PTA partners and one applicable to the rest of the world.

There are good arguments to support the thesis that the term 'other restrictive regulations of commerce' should be confined to trade instruments only. The purpose of Art. XXIV GATT is to reduce protection for a subset of the WTO Membership, that is, WTO Members participating in a PTA. Since QRs are illegal, and domestic instruments are non-negotiable and have to abide by the non-discrimination obligation as we saw in Chapter 1, the only permissible (e.g. legal) protection in GATT is protection through tariff protection: consequently, the only advantage that WTO Members can give each other when forming a PTA should be a tariff advantage. For the rest, WTO Members must respect the MFN obligation. Case law has by now repeatedly acknowledged that the very purpose of the discipline on domestic instruments is to safeguard the value of tariff concessions and not to protect. The AB, in its report on *Japan—Alcoholic Beverages II*, confirmed this understanding (p. 16):

> The broad and fundamental purpose of Article III is to *avoid protectionism* in the application of internal tax and regulatory measures. More specifically, the purpose of Article III 'is to ensure that internal measures not be applied to imported or domestic products so as to afford protection to domestic production.' Toward this end, Article III obliges Members of the WTO to provide equality of competitive conditions for imported products in relation to domestic products. (emphasis added)

Domestic instruments are not meant to protect domestic production. Since they are not meant to protect domestic production, then it is impossible that a member of a PTA be allowed to give one subset of the WTO Membership an advantage that it does not extend to the remaining membership.[171]

---

[170] GATT Doc. BISD 18S/133, pp. 135–7.

[171] Compare Mathis (2006), who expressed similar thoughts on this score, as well as various other contributions in Bartels and Ortino (2006) that do not necessarily share this view. Kim (2011) reaches the same outcome based on the necessity requirement as explained by the AB in *Turkey—Textiles*: in this view, two sets of domestic instruments—one for PTA partners and one for outsiders—are not necessary.

It is probably striking that after all these years of intense practice WTO Members have not managed to agree on a more precise definition of the term 'substantially all trade'. The explanation probably lies in the missing incentives to do so: from a pure trade perspective, the less PTA partners liberalize trade between them, the better off outsiders are, since the resulting trade diversion will be less important than it would have been had PTA partners integrated their markets in a more meaningful way; moreover, specifying the SAT requirement might prove to be a Damocles' sword for outsiders since they can only profit from the current 'fuzziness' assuming they want to go preferential in the future. Consequently, for both trade as well as strategic reasons outsiders are better off with the current situation. Were one to take into account that only one current WTO Member has not signed a PTA (Mongolia), one can even better understand the strategic reasons for staying idle.

3.2.4 No New Protection (External Requirement)

Broadly speaking, by virtue of the external requirement, WTO Members should not, when entering into a PTA, raise their protection vis-à-vis the remaining WTO Membership. Contrary to what is the case with respect to the internal requirement, the conditions for meeting the external requirement are different for FTAs and CUs. With respect to FTAs, Art. XXIV.5(b) GATT reads:

> ... duties and other regulations of commerce ... shall not be higher or more restrictive than the corresponding duties and other regulations of commerce existing in the same constituent territories prior to the formation of the free-trade area ...

Art. XXIV.5(b) GATT does not explicitly state that WTO Members participating in an FTA cannot modify their external protection when joining the FTA, although wording of this sort would have been dictated by the very nature of an FTA: FTAs aim at liberalizing trade within their constituents only, without addressing external protection at all; FTA members continue to unilaterally define their foreign commercial policy, even after they have joined an FTA. Still, the wording of this provision suggests that changes are possible. Note that the obligation enshrined in this legal provision does not refer to duties and other regulations of commerce as a whole, but to individual instruments: the obligation assumed is not to come to more or less the pre-FTA situation by rebalancing various instruments; it is to ensure that each and every individual trade instrument will not become more restrictive, post-establishment of the FTA. What is the level of comparison though? Should it be the level of applied or bound duties practised in the period before the establishment of the FTA? The Understanding on the Interpretation of Article XXIV of the GATT allows WTO Members entering into an FTA to raise their level of duties from the applied level to the bound level, assuming a discrepancy between the two levels. Hence, those forming a PTA can afford each other an extra margin of preference, that captured by the difference between the level of the applied and that of the bound duty.

Note that, in contrast to Art. XXIV.8 GATT, this provision refers to other regulations of commerce, and not to other restrictive regulations of commerce, the latter, prima facie at least, being a subset of the former. Art. XXIV.5(b) GATT contains neither an indicative nor an exhaustive list of regulations of commerce (other than duties). It should not be in doubt though, that, in light of our analysis in Chapter 2, ODCs should be covered by this provision. The question, is of course, what else? The other instrument most likely to change as a result of the establishment of a PTA is the rules of origin. Rules of origin are of particular interest in the FTA context: unless goods are accompanied by a certificate of origin, exporters will have an incentive to ship to the cheapest port of entry in an FTA (since external protection remains a matter for national sovereignty and it could very well be the case that there are asymmetries as to the level of customs duties across FTA members). Rules of origin have on occasion been discussed in the context of Art. XXIV.5 GATT.[172] Since PTAs are meant to allow the conferral of WTO-consistent preferences, the rules of origin contracted in the context of a PTA should be more favourable (or, at the very least, not more burdensome) than those applied on an MFN basis. And yet, as our discussion *supra* shows, it is difficult to state whether this has indeed been the case across PTAs. Preferential rules of origin have been excluded from the mandate of the HWP; they are also quite asymmetric and quite often difficult to use. This is definitely one area where improvements and simplifications of procedures are necessary.[173]

Discussions in this context also evidence the opinion that (unilateral or mutual) recognition under SPS or TBT should come under Art. XXIV.5 GATT, and there was even a formal proposal that all measures relating to recognition must be notified to the CRTA, or the CTD, depending on whether the PTA was coming under the purview of Art. XXIV GATT or the Enabling Clause.[174]

With respect to CUs, Art. XXIV.5(a) GATT reads:

> ... duties and other regulations of commerce ... shall not *on the whole* be higher or more restrictive than *the general incidence* of the duties and regulations of commerce applicable in the constituent territories prior to the formation of such union ... (emphasis added)

The words in italics mark the difference between the text of Art. XXIV.5(b) GATT, and that of Art. XXIV.5(a) GATT: 'on the whole' and 'general incidence' invite a comparison of the general (and not item by item) situation before and after the formation of the CU. This was the intention of the drafters:

---

[172] WTO Doc. TN/RL/W/8/Rev. 1 of 1 August 2002. The General Council decision mentioned *supra* (WTO Doc. WT/L/806 of 16 December 2010) explicitly refers to the obligation to notify rules of origin when notifying a PTA.

[173] Serra et al. (1997) show that rules of origin are one of the most important causes of trade diversion. We have provided *supra* studies on their economic impact.

[174] WTO Doc. JOB/RL/3 of 25 January 2011.

The phrase 'on the whole'...did not mean that an average tariff should be laid down in respect of each individual product, but merely that the whole level of tariffs of a customs union should not be higher than the average overall level of the former constituent territories.[175]

The Sub-Committee recommended that the words 'average level of duties' be replaced by 'general incidence of duties' in paragraph 2(a) of the new Article. It was the intention of the Sub-Committee that this phrase should not require a mathematical average of customs duties but should permit greater flexibility so that the volume of trade may be taken into account.[176]

Subsequent practice sides with the view that an item-by-item approach is unwarranted in the context of Art. XXIV.5(a) GATT; there is, nonetheless, disagreement as to the precise level on which comparisons will take place. The report of the 1983 Working Party on Accession of Greece to the European Communities reflects the view expressed by the EU, that:

Article XXIV.5 required only a generalized, overall judgment on this point.[177]

By the same token, the report of the 1988 Working Party on Accession of Portugal and Spain to the European Communities includes the view of the EU that:

Article XXIV.5 only required an examination on the broadest possible basis.[178]

This view, however, failed to convince other members of the Working Party. One member:

could not accept the Communities' contention that the extension of the tariff of the EC/10 to the EC/12 was compatible with their obligations under Article XXIV.5(a) regardless of the effect on the tariffs of Spain and Portugal. Article XXIV.5(a) required a comparison with the pre-accession tariffs of the constituent territories and the relative size of those territories was not a relevant factor.[179]

Disagreements appeared often among members of the Working Party as to whether bound or applied rates should be used in the context of Art. XXIV.5(a) GATT.[180] This issue has been clarified with the entry into force of the WTO Understanding on the Interpretation of Article XXIV of the GATT:

---

[175] GATT Doc. EPCT/C.II/38 at p. 9, reproduced in the GATT Analytical Index: Guide to GATT Law and Practice, updated 6th edition (1995) at p. 803.

[176] Havana Reports reproduced in the GATT Analytical Index at p. 803.

[177] See GATT Doc. BISD 30S/168, p. 184.

[178] See GATT Doc. BISD 35S/293, pp. 295–6.

[179] Idem, p. 311.

[180] See, for example, the discussions of the Working Party examining the compatibility of the EEC with Art XXIV, GATT Doc SR.18/4, pp. 46–54 and also in C/M/8, SR.19/6–7; see the Working Party report on *Accession of Greece to the European Communities, op cit*, p. 175; see also the 1991 Working Party report on *Free Trade Agreement between Canada and the United States*, BISD 38S/47, p. 66.

The evaluation under paragraph 5(a) of Article XXIV of the general incidence of the duties and other regulations of commerce applicable before and after the formation of a customs union shall in respect of duties and charges be based upon an overall assessment of weighted average tariff rates and of customs duties collected. This assessment shall be based on import statistics for a previous representative period to be supplied by the customs union, on a tariff-line basis and in values and quantities, broken down by WTO country of origin. The Secretariat shall compute the weighted average tariff rates and customs duties collected in accordance with the methodology used in the assessment of tariff offers in the Uruguay Round of Multilateral Trade negotiations. For this purpose, the duties and charges to be taken into consideration shall be the *applied rates* of duty. It is recognized that for the purpose of the overall assessment of the incidence of other regulations of commerce for which quantification and aggregation are difficult, the examination of individual measures, regulations, products covered and trade flows affected may be required. (emphasis added)[181]

It follows that it is applied rates that matter when a CU is established. There is an additional provision for CUs embedded in Art. XXIV.6 GATT:

If, in fulfilling the requirements of subparagraph 5(a), a contracting party proposes to increase any rate of duty inconsistently with the provision of Article II, the procedure set forth in Article XXVIII shall apply. In providing for compensatory adjustment, due account shall be taken of the compensation already afforded by the reduction brought about in the corresponding duty of the other constituents of the union.

Art. XXIV.6 GATT deals only with customs duties and not other regulations of commerce. An example can help illustrate the function of Art. XXIV.6 GATT. Assume that A, B, and C decide to enter into a CU. Assume that before the formation of the CU the tariff protection (to avoid any unnecessary complications, assume equivalence between bound and applied rates) of the automotive sector in the three countries was the following:

A 20 per cent
B 30 per cent
C 40 per cent

A, B, and C bind customs duties on cars at 30 per cent at the CU level. Arguably, they have met their obligations under Art. XXIV.5(a) GATT. They have not, however, necessarily met their obligations under Art. XXIV.6 GATT as well: when Art. XXIV.5(a) GATT is violated, Art. XXIV.6 GATT will be *ipso facto* violated as well. Compliance with Art. XXIV.5(a) GATT, on the other hand, does not

---

181 It is interesting that the Understanding focuses on *applied* as opposed to *bound* duties. By adopting this focus, it is going further than simply stating that WTO Members cannot use a CU to undo tariff obligations that were previously bound; it is also stating that WTO Members cannot use a CU to jointly raise applied tariffs. This is interesting because one prediction of the theory would be that a CU would have the incentive to set higher external tariffs than the Members would acting individually (i.e. before the CU) and that this would be one bad thing about the CU in terms of its multilateral effects. So, from the multilateral perspective, this rule makes sense.

automatically lead to compliance with Art. XXIV.6 GATT. Compliance with Art. XXIV.5(a) GATT is, in other words, a necessary but not sufficient condition for compliance with Art. XXIV.6 GATT. Art. XXIV.6 GATT comes into play any time a member of a CU (in our illustration, A) has to raise its pre-CU duty to meet the duty at the CU level. In such cases, Art. XXVIII GATT negotiations will kick in. This means that WTO Members which qualify as INRs or PSIs will participate in the negotiations with the members of the CU; such negotiations aim to compensate those WTO Members which will have more difficult access to A's market as a result of the formation of the CU. Art. XXIV.6 GATT, second sentence makes it clear that built-in compensation will be taken into account. An obligation to compensate will exist only if the built-in compensation does not suffice to take care of the injury suffered as a result of A's new, higher duties. Let us go through two factually different scenarios to illustrate this point.

First scenario: A is a low per capita income, small country, whereas C is a high per capita income, large country. Neither A nor C produces cars. The fact that C lowers its duties from 40 per cent to 30 per cent will, in all likelihood, overcompensate for the fact that A raised its own duties from 20 per cent to 30 per cent. This is the notion of built-in compensation. C will import so many more cars than before that exporters will be compensated for their losses resulting from fewer exports to A.

Second scenario: A is a high per capita income, large country, whereas C is a low per capita income, small country. In this case, the amount of trade lost because A had to raise its duties is, most likely, not compensated by the fact that C lowered its own duties. In such cases, there is nothing like sufficient built-in compensation. Hence, something needs to be done. Art. XXIV.6 GATT calls for compensation to be offered to the WTO Members following an Art. XXVIII GATT negotiation.[182]

3.3 Litigating PTAs

When judged against its original mandate (to review consistency of notified PTAs with the relevant multilateral rules), the multilateral review has been a failure by any reasonable benchmark: 462 PTAs in total had been notified to the WTO at the time of writing, of which 345 were under Art. XXIV GATT, almost two-thirds of which are now in force,[183] and only on a handful of occasions have the WTO organs managed to unanimously decide on the consistency of the notified scheme. Schott (1989) identifies four cases where PTAs were judged broadly consistent with the GATT. Since his study, the CU between the Czech and the Slovak Republics has been judged GATT-consistent; this is a highly idiosyncratic case, though, since the establishment of the CU was the interregnum between the dissolution of a unitary state (Czechoslovakia) and the accession of its two

---

[182] Hoda (2001) discusses practice in this context.

[183] According to the WTO 2011 World Trade Report dedicated to PTAs ('The WTO and Preferential Trade Agreements: From Coexistence to Coherence'), 300 PTAs were in force in 2010, whereas there were only 70 in 1990.

constituent parts to the EU. We are simply in the dark as to the GATT-consistency of all other remaining PTAs. And there are many. The overwhelming majority of Art. XXIV Working Party reports reflect disagreement among its members.

Hudec (1972, p. 1362) noted:

The seeming collapse of the MFN rules is probably the single most important cause of the present day pessimism about the GATT substantive rules.

Hudec, 20 years later (1993a, p. 154), remarks:

the GATT's somewhat benign attitude toward RAs is merely one part of this larger tolerance toward departures from MFN in general.

Roessler (1993, p. 321) is in agreement:

The record under the current procedures is not encouraging. During the past three decades about 50 working parties have been established to examine RIAs. None of them was able to reach a unanimous conclusion on the GATT-consistency of the agreement examined.

The advent of the Transparency Mechanism, as we saw *supra*, signalled the end of reports aimed at deciding on the consistency of PTAs. Before, as well as after its advent, WTO Members could always challenge the consistency of PTAs before WTO adjudicating bodies. Case law is quite clear on this. Voices have been heard in the literature, though, arguing that, according to Panels the power to adjudicate on the overall consistency of PTAs with the multilateral rules would undo the institutional balance across WTO organs as struck by the WTO framers. The AB has put to rest similar arguments which are, nonetheless, worth recounting in light of their (potential) repercussions for other issues as well.

Roessler (2000) has argued that, for reasons having to do with the institutional balance of the WTO, a limited judicial review by WTO adjudicating bodies is the most appropriate outcome. A similar argument was raised by India in *India—Quantitative Restrictions*: India argued that the question of whether a restriction could be justified on balance-of-payments grounds was inherently political. Borrowing from the political question doctrine, familiar to some legal orders, India argued that a comprehensive review of such issues should be entrusted to WTO Committees and not to Panels. In other words, the overall consistency of a PTA with the WTO should be the exclusive *domaine reservé* of the CRTA. The AB rejected India's argument, essentially on textual grounds.[184] The wording of the Understanding on Art XXIV of the GATT supports this view (§12):

The provisions of Articles XXII and XXIII of GATT 1994 as elaborated and applied by the Dispute Settlement Understanding may be invoked with respect to any matters arising from the application of those provisions of Article XXIV relating to

---

[184] See *India—Quantitative Restrictions* at §§98ff.

customs unions, free-trade areas or interim agreements leading to the formation of a customs union or a free-trade area.[185]

Hence, in theory, the consistency of a PTA could be simultaneously before a Panel and the CRTA, and the two could reach divergent conclusions on the same issue unless some sort of coordination mechanism is introduced. Of course, this is a non-issue for all PTAs notified after the advent of the Transparent Mechanism: CRTA will not discuss the consistency of PTAs any more. It is nonetheless an issue for past PTAs for which reports have been issued. Can a challenge against PTAs examined before 2006 be brought nowadays before a Panel? The Panel on *EEC— Imports from Hong Kong* held that:

> It would be erroneous to interpret the fact that a measure had not been subject to Article XXIII over a number of years, as tantamount to its tacit acceptance by contracting parties.

In the absence of statutory prescription and in light of this ruling, it is worth examining this issue a bit further. There is no obligation to suspend Panel proceedings while an issue is being discussed before the CRTA (*lis pendens*).[186] The Panel on *US—Line Pipe* did not stop its review only because the CRTA had not issued its report at the time the dispute was submitted to it (§7.144):

> Concerning Article XXVIII:8(b), we do not consider the fact that the CRTA has not yet issued a final decision that NAFTA is in compliance with Article XXIV:8 is sufficient to rebut the prima facie case established by the United States. Korea's argument is based on the premise that a regional trade arrangement is presumed inconsistent with Article XXIV until the CRTA makes a determination to the contrary. We see no basis for such a premise in the relevant provisions of the Agreements Establishing the WTO.

If the CRTA concludes by consensus (irrespective of whether it concluded on the consistency or the inconsistency of the notified PTA with the multilateral rules), there are good reasons to believe that the Panel subsequently dealing with the issue will follow the opinion reflected in the CRTA. The Panel on *India—Quantitative Restrictions*, which dealt with a similar issue,[187] held in §5.94:

> we see no reason to assume that the panel would not appropriately take those conclusions into account. If the nature of the conclusions were binding . . . a panel should respect them.

---

[185] Roessler (2000) argues that the terms of the Understanding lean towards a restrictive understanding of its scope: the reference made is to the application of Art. XXIV and not to Art. XXIV GATT as such. It is nonetheless quite difficult to distinguish between the two.

[186] Art. 12.12 DSU allows the complaining party to request suspension of panel proceedings. This is a right bestowed upon the complainant and not an obligation to behave in this way assuming certain contingencies (e.g. discussions of the issue before a WTO committee) have been met.

[187] The issue before this Panel was to what extent a Panel dealing with an issue which had already been decided by the WTO Balance of Payments Committee should follow the decision reached in this Committee.

There is, however, no legal compulsion for the Panel to follow a CRTA decision. Should Panels stop short of deciding whether a PTA is WTO-consistent, if the CRTA has not yet pronounced on its consistency? This is a non-issue nowadays since, as stated *supra*, the CRTA does not pronounce on the consistency of notified PTAs any more. On the other hand, should the CRTA be bound by a Panel's (and/or AB's) decision on the consistency of a PTA with the relevant WTO rules? This seems to be a likelier scenario in light of the time constraints that Panels have to adhere to and the absence of such constraints when the CRTA reviews a scheme. The formal answer has to be, once again, no. The legal effect of the judiciary's decision is not such that it acknowledges the force of *res judicata* (binding any discretion of the CRTA to subsequently deviate from its reasoning/outcome). But, once again, this is a non-issue in light of the current mandate of the CRTA following the advent of the Transparency Mechanism.

3.3.1 Litigation in the GATT Era

The view that the consistency of PTAs with the multilateral rules can be the subject of judicial review was endorsed by GATT contracting parties long before the AB explicitly accepted that to be the case. A representative view is offered by the EU delegate and is reflected in the report issued by the 1978 Working Party on the Agreement between the EEC and Egypt:

> ... as regards the possibility of consultations with the contracting parties concerning the incidence of the Agreement on their trade interests... nothing prevented these countries from invoking the relevant provisions of the General Agreement, such as Articles XXII and XXIII.[188]

During the GATT years (1948–94), three Panels were established to examine claims relating to the consistency of a PTA with the multilateral rules.[189] Two reports were issued and they both remain un-adopted. The first of these, the *EC—Citrus* Panel report, argues in favour of an examination (by Panels) of individual measures only and, based on this position, refused to pronounce on the overall consistency of the PTA with the multilateral rules. The Panel did not see its role as a surrogate to the (then) Art. XXIV Working Parties:

> The Panel noted that at the time of the examination of the agreements entered into by the European Community with certain Mediterranean countries, there was no consensus among contracting parties as to the conformity of the agreement with Article XXIV.5
>
> ...

---

[188] GATT Analytical Index, p. 781.

[189] The first, after a request by Canada in 1974 in connection with the accession to the European Community of Denmark, Ireland, and the United Kingdom (GATT Doc. C/W/250) was not activated because the parties to the dispute reached an agreement (GATT Doc. C/W/259). The second led to an un-adopted Panel report in *EC—Citrus*, GATT Doc. L/5776. The third report is on *EEC—Bananas II*, GATT Doc. DS38/R of 11 February 1994, which also remains un-adopted.

The agreements had not been disapproved, nor had they been approved. The Panel found therefore that the question of conformity of the agreements with the requirements of Article XXIV and their legal status remained open.[190]

This report remains un-adopted and, hence, of limited legal relevance.

EEC—Bananas II is the second report in this vein. This report made one important interpretative contribution by holding that one-way preferential arrangements are per se inconsistent with Art. XXIV GATT; obligations to liberalize must be assumed by all participants (§159):

> This lack of *any* obligation of the sixty-nine ACP countries to dismantle their trade barriers, and the acceptance of an obligation to remove trade barriers only on imports into the customs territory of the EEC, made the trade arrangements set out in the Convention substantially different from those of a free trade area, as defined in Article XXIV:8(b).

Unsurprisingly, the same Panel went on to conclude (§164) that the *Lomé Convention* (the agreement between the EU and a series of African, Caribbean, and Pacific states) did not meet the requirements of Art. XXIV GATT. This report remains un-adopted as well and, although the view expressed in the cited passage is sound, the legal value of the report is minimal.[191]

3.3.2 Litigation in the WTO Era

During the WTO era, practice in this area continues to be scarce. The Panel on *Turkey—Textiles* records the most comprehensive discussion yet concerning the ambit of judicial review of a PTA by Panels. India had argued before the Panel that it had suffered damage as a result of Turkey's decision to erect new barriers to its textiles exports, following the signature and the entry into force of the CU between the EU and Turkey. India argued that its MFN rights had been impaired as a result. Turkey did not deny that this had indeed been the case (that is, that it had erected new barriers), but invoked Art. XXIV GATT to justify its deviation from MFN. The Panel first addressed the question whether it was competent to discuss the overall consistency of a PTA with the GATT. Responding to an argument by the complainant, it held that WTO adjudicating bodies are competent to examine PTA-related issues, but should stop short of providing an overall assessment regarding the consistency of a PTA with the WTO. This Panel followed the findings in the Panel report on *EC—Citrus* (§§9.52–3):

> As to the second question of how far-reaching a panel's examination should be of the regional trade agreement underlying the challenged measure, we note that the Committee on Regional Trade Agreements (CRTA) has been established, *inter alia*, to assess the GATT/WTO compatibility of regional trade agreements entered into by Members, a very complex undertaking which involves consideration by the

---

190 GATT Doc. L/5776, dated 7 February 1985, at §4.6 and at §4.10.
191 In the WTO era, the AB report on *EC—Bananas III* reproduced this view almost verbatim.

CRTA, from the economic, legal and political perspectives of different Members, of the numerous facets of a regional trade agreement in relation to the provisions of the WTO. It appears to us that the issue regarding the GATT/WTO compatibility of a customs union, as such, is generally a matter for the CRTA since, as noted above, it involves a broad multilateral assessment of any such custom union, i.e. a matter which concerns the WTO membership as a whole.

. . .

As to whether panels also have the jurisdiction to assess the overall WTO compatibility of a customs union, we recall that the Appellate Body stated that the terms of reference of panels must refer explicitly to the 'measures' to be examined by panels. We consider that regional trade agreements may contain numerous measures, all of which could potentially be examined by panels, before, during or after the CRTA examination, if the requirements laid down in the DSU are met. However, it is arguable that a customs union (or a free-trade area) as a whole would logically not be a 'measure' as such, subject to challenge under the DSU. (italics in the original)

On appeal, the AB held a different view, arguing that those availing themselves of justifying their measures through recourse to Art. XXIV GATT must explain why their PTA is GATT-consistent. Consequently, Panels should always have the power to discuss the overall consistency of PTAs with the multilateral rules (§§58–9):

First, the party claiming the benefit of this defense must demonstrate that the measure at issue is introduced upon the formation of a customs union that *fully meets the requirements of sub-paragraph 8(a) and 5(a) of Article XXIV*. And second, that party must demonstrate that the formation of that customs union would be prevented if it were not allowed to introduce the measure at issue.

. . .

We would expect a panel, when examining such a measure, to require a party to establish that both of these conditions have been fulfilled. It may not always be possible to determine whether the second of the two conditions has been fulfilled without initially determining whether the first condition has been fulfilled. (emphasis added)

More recently, the Panel on *US—Line Pipe* faced an argument by the US that, as a member of NAFTA, it was entitled to treat imports from NAFTA differently than imports from non-NAFTA sources when imposing a tariff quota. The Panel repeated that the US had the burden of proof to show consistency of NAFTA with Art. XXIV GATT (§7.142); it then addressed the issue of the quantum of proof (burden of persuasion) that the party carrying the burden of proof has to provide in order to establish a prima-facie case for the consistency of a PTA with the multilateral rules (§ 7.144):

In our view, the information provided by the United States in these proceedings, the information submitted by the NAFTA parties to the Committee on Regional Trade Agreements ('CRTA') (which the United States has incorporated into its submissions to the Panel by reference), and the absence of effective refutation by Korea, establishes a prima facie case that NAFTA is in conformity with Article XXIV:5(b) and (c), and with Article XXIV:8(b).

The information provided by the US in the proceedings is confined to a statement (§7.142) that duties on 97 per cent of the NAFTA parties' tariff lines would be eliminated within 10 years from the inception of NAFTA, whereas, with respect to other regulations of commerce, a reference to the principles of national treatment, transparency, and a variety of other market access rules is made. In the Panel's view, the submitted information was enough to make a prima-facie case of consistency of NAFTA with Art. XXIV GATT. In subsequent cases as well (*Argentina—Poultry Antidumping Duties, Mexico—Taxes on Soft Drinks*), Panels have confirmed the view that they have the power to decide on the overall consistency of notified PTAs with the multilateral rules.

3.3.3 Why so Little Litigation?

Only a handful of Panels have so far been established in order to discuss the consistency of PTAs with the multilateral rules, and this is certainly not much when one takes into account the sheer number of PTAs and the absence of meaningful review by the CRTA over the years. Moreover, serious procedural hurdles were removed with the advent of the WTO and the recent case law. Panels are now established at the sole request of the complainant, and the original burden of proof is easy to meet (the complainant would be required to demonstrate deviation from MFN and, upon such demonstration, the burden of proof would shift to the defendant); it is the defendant that will have to demonstrate the overall consistency of the PTA with the GATT rules.

So why have WTO Members stayed idle?[192] Historically, the first integration was that of Europe and there should be no doubt that the ECSC (European Coal and Steel Community) was a blatant violation of GATT rules since it integrated markets only with respect to two goods. No one wanted to question the wider European integration process, though, by bringing into question the GATT-consistency of ECSC. Contracting parties, having committed the original sin (by demonstrating a benign attitude towards the European integration), refrained from changing attitude subsequently for fear of being inconsistent. Finger (1993) has defended this line of argument.

A risk-averse WTO Member would rationally choose not to challenge a PTA since:

(a) there is a collective action problem;
(b) strategic reasons might argue against a challenge;
(c) the agency design for WTO adjudicating bodies probably does not inspire challenges of this sort.

Let us discuss the collective action problem first, that is, the point that the complainant will not benefit from the full cost of its investment. The cost of

---

[192] This part is largely based on Mavroidis (2006). See also Limão (2006b) on this score, as well as Levy and Srinivasan (1996).

WTO litigation should not be underestimated. Bown and Hoekman (2005) provide some numbers in this regard and point to the fact that the numbers they cite in and of themselves might dissuade (some) potential complainants from launching complaints. Nordström et al. (2007) concludes along the same lines and his empirical study cautions against those who tend to underestimate the cost of WTO litigation. Of course, a potential complainant will measure the cost of litigation against the probability of prevailing and the expected profits if it does prevail. The potential complainant will actually be subsidizing all other WTO Members that will be profiting (one way or the other) without having invested at all in the process. The cost is not only monetary: it can extend beyond that since litigation could be perceived as 'unfriendly' behaviour. It is not therefore irrational to think in terms of 'if I don't do it, somebody else will'.

For strategic reasons as well, a WTO Member might rationally decide to abstain from challenging the consistency of a PTA with the WTO rules: it might not only provoke negative reactions from those participating in the PTA it attacks, but it might also prejudge its own future options. We explain. A WTO Member might be foregoing the possibility to obtain perks of various sorts from signing a PTA itself with one (or more) of the members of the PTA it now challenges, as well as to obtain all sorts of political benefits in the future: especially nowadays where PTAs go beyond the classic trade issues, challenging a PTA could be perceived as a challenge against the wider concerns of its constituent parts. Although the term 'diplomatic war' might be an exaggeration here, it would not be too far off the mark to argue that tension could be the result of similar challenges. One cannot exclude, either, that a legal challenge might provoke another legal challenge against the complainant under a different legal provision. Indeed, there is increasing empirical evidence that action by A against B in antidumping increases the likelihood that B might attack A in the same field. Martin and Vergote (2008) find that AD is increasingly being used in a strategic, retaliatory fashion. In the Martin-Vergote setting, retaliation actually occurs in equilibrium as part of a cooperative relationship among privately informed governments.[193] Today's outsiders might be tomorrow's incumbents. Successfully arguing a PTA-related case might come at a cost, since, in the event that today's successful complainant might decide to go preferential tomorrow, it might face the music it helped compose: specifying the requirements of Art. XXIV GATT might make the test more difficult to meet. Any interpretation, in other words, could become the benchmark in any (fresh) discussion of the consistency of a member's PTA with the multilateral rules. Finally, the less PTA partners integrate their markets, the less trade diversion will result. The less, for example, members of a PTA liberalize their trade in cars, the better export opportunities outsiders will have to export cars to the PTA. This should be the case always, except for cases where outsiders are interested

---

[193] But check Zanardi (2004).

in exporting to the PTA complementary products. The more members of a PTA liberalize trade in cars, the likelier it would be for WTO Members to sell wheels in the PTA market. Challenging a PTA is not necessarily the best way to receive compensation for trade diversion, since it might exacerbate the original trade diversion, if, for example, PTA partners decide to go the full nine yards and fully integrate their markets as a response. Staying idle might work just as well.

The agency design does not 'invite' similar challenges either: a Panel is usually composed of trade delegates, who are career diplomats serving in Geneva.[194] When facing a question relating to the consistency of a PTA with the WTO, they know that they are not prejudging just one transaction (as is the case, for example, when they face a challenge against an allegedly illegal imposition of AD duties); through their response, they will be bringing into question all subsequent trade-related behaviour of the PTA hopefuls. They also know that:

(a) no WTO adjudicating body before them ever moved to pronounce on the inconsistency of a PTA with the WTO, except in very obvious cases (such as the EC/ACP arrangement quoted above);
(b) that they have little legislative guidance to draw on, since the terms of Art. XXIV GATT, with the few notable exceptions mentioned *supra*, have not been further elaborated/interpreted either through legislative activity or through subsequent (CRTA) practice; and
(c) that there is probably a relationship between (a) and (b), that is, wisely, previous Panels chose to abstain from far-reaching pronouncements in the absence of a clear legislative document.

They are also aware that PTAs are being tolerated in the WTO. As Schott (1989, p. 25) observes:

> Besides the ambiguity of its provisions, political considerations have often outweighed other factors in decisions to accede to the terms of the agreements. In addition, affected third countries have been reticent to criticize preferential deals because the majority of GATT members participate in such agreements.

To a large extent, WTO Members have learned to live in a world where PTAs will not be challenged and, by now, they might rationally be expecting to receive a 'no challenge' status when they enter into PTAs. Finally, there is a question of expertise: the terms in Art. XXIV GATT are characterized by their indeterminacy; what kind of expertise by Panellists can help them overcome this hurdle? Unless the PTA is on very shaky grounds, Panels might rationally choose to abstain from making a definitive pronouncement on the question asked; they do not have to hide behind *non liquet* to do that, since they can always communicate the message that, for example, the burden of proof has not been met, or evidence provided has not been effectively refuted, and ask for additional homework from the complainant.

---

[194] Nordström (2005).

It is thus not irrational that WTO Members have chosen to abstain from challenging PTAs *en masse* so far. No multilateral review and no challenges before Panels inevitably have led to a tolerance policy towards PTAs. Is this a serious problem? We turn to this question in what immediately follows.

3.4 They Multiply, but What is the Risk?

The numbers are there and the numbers tell one story: there is a proliferation of PTAs, the consistency of which with the multilateral rules remains unchecked.[195] To decide on their legal consistency with the multilateral rules one needs to do the exercise that the Transparency Mechanism is not currently doing: inquire whether each and every PTA notified respects the external and internal requirements. But, more fundamentally, to decide whether PTAs have been a threat to multilateralism, to decide that is, whether they are stumbling or building blocks (as Bhagwati and Panagariya (1999) put it), one needs to undertake a more serious analysis and examine, beyond a case-by-case approach, strategic interactions across PTA partners and outsiders, the incentive for outsiders to go preferential themselves, the interaction between the preferential and the multilateral agenda, etc. This is a very difficult exercise and often suffers from the difficulty in establishing the counterfactual.

There are reasons to believe though, from a pure trade perspective, that they are less of a threat than they used to be.[196] Scholarship, as mentioned above, points to the (missing) incentives to agree on MFN tariff cuts following establishment of a PTA; Bhagwati (2002), Krishna (1998), and Limão (2006a) have all contributed to making the point that, besides trade diversion generated through the establishment of PTAs, members of PTAs behave as enemies of non-discriminatory trade liberalization, since they are unwilling to cut tariffs on MFN basis for fear of eroding the margin of preference that they have granted to their PTA partners: they behave like stumbling blocks, that is, they would cut tariffs less in areas where they had preferential tariffs. The ongoing tariff liberalization of tariffs at MFN level would strongly argue in favour of the thesis that the problem is not of the magnitude that it used to be. Recent empirical studies provide us with mixed evidence regarding the extent of trade diversion resulting from the formation of PTAs. On the one hand, studies like Karacaovali and Limão (2008), looking at the EU, and Limão (2006a), looking at the US, have provided empirical evidence that PTAs have behaved like stumbling blocks. More generally, Flam and Nordstrøm (2011) show how much MFN trade is affected by even the shallowest of preferences. Other studies, however, find the opposite: Estevadeordal et al. (2008) and Freund (2011) examine the Latin experience with PTAs and find that Latin nations cut their MFN rates most in products where they had preferences in place. Baldwin and Seghezza (2010) use tariff data for 23 large trading nations and

---

195 The WTO webpage has a very informative dataset on PTAs: <http://rtais.wto.org>.
196 The following builds on Mavroidis (2011).

find that MFN cuts and preferences are complements not substitutes: margins of preferences in the real world tend to be zero or close to zero where nations have high MFN tariffs. Intuitively, one would associate the stumbling-block thesis with large preferences in cases of high MFN tariffs, but the authors show that this is not the case in practice. The authors thus discard the stumbling-block without supporting the building-bloc thesis. Acharya et al. (2011), in similar vein, find that the impact of plurilateral PTAs on extra-PTA imports and exports is large and positive. Thus recent empirical evidence lends little or no support to the conclusion that PTAs are stumbling blocks per se. Of course trade diversion can result from instruments other than tariffs. Trade diversion can be due to other factors as well, for example regional technical standards, as the work of Chen and Mattoo (2008) shows. It can result from, say, convergent environmental or public health policies across PTA partners. Trade diversion can also result from, say, increased use of antidumping (AD) proceedings against non-PTA partners, as the work of Prusa and Teh (2011) shows.[197] But there is nothing that can be done against that: domestic standards have to be applied on an MFN basis as we saw *supra*, whereas the only MFN obligation with respect to AD, as we shall see in Chapter 7 is to collect duties on an MFN basis, but not to start investigations on an MFN basis.

There is the additional argument whether we want to enforce an ill-informed test. Recall that the legal test does not inquire into the welfare implications of the PTA. True, as Grossman and Helpman (1995) have shown, absent the SAT requirement, countries would have an incentive to offer cuts where trade diversion is likely. This could severely undermine MFN, the cornerstone of the GATT edifice. But one cannot escape the conclusion that GATT framers who could not live with a GATT à la carte could live with GATT-consistent PTAs which resulted in trade diversion. Indeed, especially in the 1950s and the 1960s when MFN rates were high (and thus the potential margin of preference large), PTAs that would take the intra-PTA tariff rates to 0 per cent could create substantial trade diversion if the PTA partners were relatively inefficient (uncompetitive): the GATT would applaud, while Viner's worst fears would have been confirmed. One could go deeper into this issue and ask what exactly we are called to enforce. As we saw above, there is an indeterminacy inherent in Art. XXIV GATT and subsequent practice has not managed to 'complete' an 'incomplete' contract: the Australian proposal we discussed *supra* met with the approval of the proposing state only. And even if we come up with something akin to the Australian proposal, the question will arise what to do with the existing PTAs. 'Bygones are bygones' seems not to be an option in light of the sheer number of existing PTAs (see Table 3.4). To say that we care only about the future and forget past sins would amount to creating two classes of PTAs and yet another layer of discrimination in the name of rigorous enforcement of the GATT contract.

---

[197] See Gantz (2011).

Table 3.4 Preferential Trade Agreements notified under Art. XXIV GATT

RTA Name	Coverage	Type	Date of notification	Notification	Date of entry into force
Armenia—Kazakhstan	Goods	FTA	17 June 2004	GATT Art. XXIV	25 December 2001
Armenia—Moldova	Goods	FTA	17 June 2004	GATT Art. XXIV	21 December 1995
Armenia—Russian Federation	Goods	FTA	17 June 2004	GATT Art. XXIV	25 March 1993
Armenia—Turkmenistan	Goods	FTA	17 June 2004	GATT Art. XXIV	7 July 1996
Armenia—Ukraine	Goods	FTA	17 June 2004	GATT Art. XXIV	18 December 1996
ASEAN—Australia—New Zealand	Goods & Services	FTA & EIA	8 April 2010	GATT Art. XXIV & GATS V	1 January 2010
ASEAN—China	Goods & Services	PSA & EIA	21 September 2005(G) 26 June 2008(S)	Enabling Clause & GATS Art. V	1 January 2005(G) 1 July 2007(S)
ASEAN—Japan	Goods	FTA		GATT Art. XXIV	1 December 2008
ASEAN—Korea, Republic of	Goods & Services	FTA & EIA	23 November 2009	GATT Art. XXIV	1 January 2010(G) 1 May 2009(S)
Australia—Chile	Goods & Services	FTA & EIA	3 March 2009	GATT Art. XXIV & GATS V	6 March 2009
Australia—New Zealand (ANZCERTA)	Goods & Service	FTA & EIA	14 April 1983(G) 22 November 1995(S)	GATT Art. XXIV & GATS V	1January 1983(G) 1 January 1989(S)
Australia—Papua New Guinea (PATCRA)	Goods	FTA	20 December 1976	GATT Art. XXIV	1 February 1977
Brunei Darussalam—Japan	Goods & Services	FTA & EIA	31 July 2008	GATT Art. XXIV & GATS V	31 July 2008
Canada—Chile	Goods & Services	FTA & EIA	30 July 1997	GATT Art. XXIV & GATS V	5 July 1997
Canada—Costa Rica	Goods	FTA	13 January 2003	GATT Art. XXIV	1 November 2002
Canada—Israel	Goods	FTA	15 January 1997	GATT Art. XXIV	1 January 1997
Canada—Peru	Goods & Services	FTA & EIA	31 July 2009	GATT Art. XXIV & GATS V	1 August 2009
Caribbean Community and Common Market (CARICOM)	Goods & Services	CU & EIA	14 October 1974(G) 19 February 2003(S)	GATT Art. XXIV & GATS V	1 August 1973 (G) 1 July 1997(S)

(Continued)

Table 3.4 *Continued*

RTA Name	Coverage	Type	Date of notification	Notification	Date of entry into force
Central American Common Market (CACM)	Goods	CU	24 February 1961	GATT Art. XXIV	4 June 1961
Central European Free Trade Agreement (CEFTA) 2006	Goods	FTA	26 July 2007	GATT Art. XXIV	1 May 2007
Chile—China	Goods & Services	FTA & EIA	20 June 2007(G) 18 November 2010(S)	GATT Art. XXIV & GATS V	1 October 2006(G) 1 August 2010(S)
Chile—Colombia	Goods & Services	FTA & EIA	14 August 2009	GATT Art. XXIV & GATS V	8 May 2009
Chile—Costa Rica (Chile—Central America)	Goods & Services	FTA & EIA	16 April 2002	GATT Art. XXIV & GATS V	15 February 2002
Chile—El Salvador (Chile—Central America)	Goods & Services	FTA & EIA	29 January 2004(G) 5 February 2004(S)	GATT Art. XXIV & GATS V	1 June 2002
Chile—Japan	Goods & Services	FTA & EIA	24 August 2007	GATT Art. XXIV & GATS V	3 September 2007
Chile—Mexico	Goods & Services	FTA & EIA	27 February 2001	GATT Art. XXIV & GATS V	1 August 1999
China—Hong Kong, China	Goods & Services	FTA & EIA	27 December 2003	GATT Art. XXIV & GATS V	1 January 2004
China—Macao, China	Goods & Services	FTA & EIA	27 December 2003	GATT Art. XXIV & GATS V	1 January 2004
China—New Zealand	Goods & Services	FTA & EIA	21 April 2009	GATT Art. XXIV & GATS V	1 October 2008
China—Singapore	Goods & Services	FTA & EIA	2 March 2009	GATT Art. XXIV & GATS V	1 January 2009
Colombia—Mexico	Goods & Services	FTA & EIA	13 September 2010	GATT Art. XXIV & GATS V	1 January 1995
Common Economic Zone (CEZ)	Goods	FTA	18 August 2008	GATT Art. XXIV	20 May 2004
Commonwealth of Independent States (CIS)	Goods	FTA	29 June 1999	GATT Art. XXIV	30 December 1994
Costa Rica—Mexico	Goods & Services	FTA & EIA	17 July 2006	GATT Art. XXIV & GATS V	1 January 1995

Agreement	Coverage	Type		Legal basis	
Dominican Republic—Central America—United States Free Trade Agreement (CAFTA-DR)	Goods & Services	FTA & EIA	17 March 2006	GATT Art. XXIV & GATS V	1 March 2006
East African Community (EAC)	Goods	CU	9 October 2000	Enabling Clause	7 July 2000
EC—Albania	Goods & Services	FTA & EIA	7 March 2007(G); 7 October 2009(S)	GATT Art. XXIV & GATSV	1 December 2006 (G); 1 April 2009(S)
EC—Algeria	Goods	FTA	24 July 2006	GATT Art. XXIV	1 September 2005
EC—Andorra	Goods	CU	23 February 1998	GATT Art. XXIV	1 July 1991
EC—Bosnia and Herzegovina	Goods	FTA	11 July 2008	GATT Art. XXIV	1 July 2008
EC—Cameroon	Goods	FTA	24 September 2009	GATT Art. XXIV	1 October 2009
EC—CARIFORUM States EPA	Goods & Services	FTA & EIA	16 October 2008	GATT Art. XXIV & GATS V	1 November 2008
EC—Chile	Goods & Services	FTA & EIA	3 February 2004(G); 28 October 2005(S)	GATT Art. XXIV & GATS V	1 February 2003(G); 1 March 2005(S)
EC—Cote d'Ivoire	Goods	FTA	11 December 2008	GATT Art. XXIV	1 January 2009
EC—Croatia	Goods & Services	FTA & EIA	17 December 2002(G); 12 October 2009(S)	GATT Art. XXIV & GATS V	1 March 2002(G); 1 February 2005(S)
EC—Egypt	Goods	FTA	3 September 2004	GATT Art. XXIV	1 June 2004
EC—Faroe Islands	Goods	FTA	17 February 1997	GATT Art. XXIV	1 January 1997
EC—Former Yugoslav Republic of Macedonia	Goods & Services	FTA & EIA	23 October 2001(G); 2 October 2009(S)	GATT Art. XXIV & GATS V	1 June 2001(G); 1 April 2004(S)
EC—Iceland	Goods	FTA	24 November 1972	GATT Art. XXIV	1 April 1973
EC—Israel	Goods	FTA	20 September 2000	GATT Art. XXIV	1 June 2000
EC—Jordan	Goods	FTA	17 December 2002	GATT Art. XXIV	1 May 2002
EC—Lebanon	Goods	FTA	26 May 2003	GATT Art. XXIV	1 March 2003
EC—Mexico	Goods & Services	FTA & EIA	25 July 2000(G); 21 June 2002(S)	GATT Art. XXIV & GATS V	1 July 2000(G); 1 October 2000(S)
EC—Montenegro	Goods & Services	FTA & EIA	16 January 2007; 22 February 2008(G); 18 June 2010(S)	GATT Art. XXIV & GATS V	1 January 2008(G); 1 May 2010(S)
EC—Morocco	Goods	FTA	13 October 2000	GATT Art. XXIV	1 March 2000
EC—Norway	Goods	FTA	13 July 1973	GATT Art. XXIV	1 July 1973
	Goods	FTA	14 December 1970	GATT Art. XXIV	1 January 1971

(Continued)

Table 3.4 *Continued*

RTA Name	Coverage	Type	Date of notification	Notification	Date of entry into force
EC—Overseas Countries and Territories (OCTOBER)					
EC—Palestinian Authority	Goods	FTA	29 May 1997	GATT Art. XXIV	1 July 1997
EC—South Africa	Goods	FTA	2 November 2000	GATT Art. XXIV	1 January 2000
EC—Switzerland—Liechtenstein	Goods	FTA	27 October 1972	GATT Art. XXIV	1 January 1973
EC—Syria	Goods	FTA	15 July 1977	GATT Art. XXIV	1 July 1977
EC—Tunisia	Goods	FTA	15 January 1999	GATT Art. XXIV	1 March 1998
EC—Turkey	Goods	CU	22 December 1995	GATT Art. XXIV	1 January 1996
EC (10) Enlargement	Goods	CU	24 October 1979	GATT Art. XXIV	1 January 1981
EC (12) Enlargement	Goods	CU	11 December 1985	GATT Art. XXIV	1 January 1986
EC (15) Enlargement	Goods & Services	CU & EIA	22 December 1994(S)	GATT Art. XXIV & GATS V	1 January 1995
EC (25) Enlargement	Goods & Services	CU & EIA	26 April 2004	GATT Art. XXIV & GATS V	1 May 2004
EC (27) Enlargement	Goods & Services	CU & EIA	27 September 2006(G) 26 June 2007(S)	GATT Art. XXIV & GATS V	1 January 2007
EC (9) Enlargement	Goods	CU	7 March 1972	GATT Art. XXIV	1 January 1973
EC Treaty	Goods & Services	CU & EIA	24 April 1957(G) 10 November 1995(S)	GATT Art. XXIV & GATS V	1 January 1958
EFTA—Albania	Goods	FTA	7 February 2011	GATT Art. XXIV	1 November 2010
EFTA—Canada	Goods	FTA	4 August 2009	GATT Art. XXIV	1 July 2009
EFTA—Chile	Goods & Services	FTA & EIA	3 December 2004	GATT Art. XXIV & GATS V	1 December 2004
EFTA—Croatia	Goods	FTA	14 January 2002	GATT Art. XXIV	01 January 2002
EFTA—Egypt	Goods	FTA	17 July 2007	GATT Art. XXIV	01 August 2007
EFTA—Former Yugoslav Republic of Macedonia	Goods	FTA	11 December 2000	GATT Art. XXIV	1 January 2001
EFTA—Israel	Goods	FTA	30 November 1992	GATT Art. XXIV	1 January 1993
EFTA—Jordan	Goods	FTA	17 January 2002	GATT Art. XXIV	1 September 2006
EFTA—Korea, Republic of	Goods & Services	FTA & EIA	23 August 2006	GATT Art. XXIV	1 September 2006

	Coverage	Type		Legal Basis	
EFTA—Lebanon	Goods	FTA	22 December 2006	GATT Art. XXIV & GATS V	1 January 2007
EFTA—Mexico	Goods & Services	FTA & EIA	25 July 2001	GATT Art. XXIV & GATS V	1 July 2001
EFTA—Morocco	Goods	FTA	20 January 2000	GATT Art. XXIV	1 December 1999
EFTA—Palestinian Authority	Goods	FTA	23 July 1999	GATT Art. XXIV	1 July 1999
EFTA—SACU	Goods	FTA	29 October 2008	GATT Art. XXIV	1 May 2008
EFTA—Serbia	Goods	FTA	24 November 2010	GATT Art. XXIV	1 October 2010
EFTA—Singapore	Goods & Services	FTA & EIA	14 January 2003	GATT Art. XXIV & GATS V	1 January 2003
EFTA—Tunisia	Goods	FTA	3 June 2005	GATT Art. XXIV	1 June 2005
EFTA—Turkey	Goods	FTA	6 March 1992	GATT Art. XXIV	1 April 1992
EFTA accession of Iceland	Goods	FTA	30 January 1970	GATT Art. XXIV	1 March 1970
EU—San Marino	Goods	CU	24 February 2010	GATT Art. XXIV	1 April 2002
EU—Serbia	Goods	FTA	31 May 2010	GATT Art. XXIV	1 February 2010
Eurasian Economic Community (EAEC)	Goods	CU	21 April 1999	GATT Art. XXIV	8 October 1997
European Economic Area (EEA)	Services	EIA	13 September 1996	GATS Art. V	1 January 1994
European Free Trade Association (EFTA)	Goods & Services	FTA & EIA	14 November 1959(G) 15 July 2002(S)	GATT Art. XXIV & GATS V	3 May 1960(G) 1 June 2002(S)
Faroe Islands—Norway	Goods	FTA	12 February 1996	GATT Art. XXIV	1 July 1993
Faroe Islands—Switzerland	Goods	FTA	12 February 1996	GATT Art. XXIV	1 March 1995
Georgia—Armenia	Goods	FTA	8 February 2001	GATT Art. XXIV	11 November 1998
Georgia—Azerbaijan	Goods	FTA	8 February 2001	GATT Art. XXIV	10 July 1996
Georgia—Kazakhstan	Goods	FTA	8 February 2001	GATT Art. XXIV	16 July 1999
Georgia—Russian Federation	Goods	FTA	8 February 2001	GATT Art. XXIV	10 May 1994
Georgia—Turkmenistan	Goods	FTA	8 February 2001	GATT Art. XXIV	1 January 2000
Georgia—Ukraine	Goods	FTA	8 February 2001	GATT Art. XXIV	4 June 1996
Gulf Cooperation Council (GCC)	Goods	CU			1 January 2003
Honduras—El Salvador and the Separate Customs Territory of Taiwan, Penghu, Kinmen and Matsu	Goods & Services	FTA & EIA	6 April 2010	GATT Art. XXIV & GATS V	1 March 2008
Hong Kong, China—New Zealand	Goods & Services	FTA & EIA	3 January 2011	GATT Art. XXIV & GATS V	1 January 2011

(Continued)

Table 3.4 *Continued*

RTA Name	Coverage	Type	Date of notification	Notification	Date of entry into force
Iceland—Faroe Islands	Goods & Services	FTA & EIA	10 July 2008	GATT Art. XXIV & GATS V	1 November 2006
India—Singapore	Goods & Services	FTA & EIA	3 May 2007	GATT Art. XXIV & GATS V	1 August 2005
Israel—Mexico	Goods	FTA	22 February 2001	GATT Art. XXIV	1 July 2000
Japan—Indonesia	Goods & Services	FTA & EIA	27 June 2008	GATT Art. XXIV & GATS V	1 July 2008
Japan—Malaysia	Goods & Services	FTA & EIA	12 July 2006	GATT Art. XXIV & GATS V	13 July 2006
Japan—Mexico	Goods & Services	FTA & EIA	31 March 2005	GATT Art. XXIV & GATS V	1 April 2005
Japan—Philippines	Goods & Services	FTA & EIA	11 December 2008	GATT Art. XXIV & GATS V	11 December 2008
Japan—Singapore	Goods & Services	FTA & EIA	8 November 2002	GATT Art. XXIV & GATS V	30 November 2002
Japan—Switzerland	Goods & Services	FTA & EIA	1 September 2009	GATT Art. XXIV & GATS V	1 September 2009
Japan—Thailand	Goods & Services	FTA & EIA	25 October 2007	GATT Art. XXIV & GATS V	1 November 2007
Japan—Viet Nam	Goods & Services	FTA & EIA	1 October 2009	GATT Art. XXIV & GATS V	1 October 2009
Jordan—Singapore	Goods & Services	FTA & EIA	7 July 2006	GATT Art. XXIV & GATS V	22 August 2005
Korea, Republic of—Chile	Goods & Services	FTA & EIA	8 April 2004	GATT Art. XXIV & GATS V	1 April 2004
Korea, Republic of—India	Goods & Services	FTA & EIA	21 February 2006	GATT Art. XXIV & GATS V	1 January 2010
Korea, Republic of—Singapore	Goods & Services	FTA & EIA			2 March 2006
Kyrgyz Republic—Armenia	Goods	FTA	12 December 2000	GATT Art. XXIV	27 October 1995

Agreement	Coverage	Type	Notification date	Legal basis	Entry into force
Kyrgyz Republic—Kazakhstan	Goods	FTA	29 June 1999	GATT Art. XXIV	11 November 1995
Kyrgyz Republic—Moldova	Goods	FTA	15 June 1999	GATT Art. XXIV	21 November 1996
Kyrgyz Republic—Russian Federation	Goods	FTA	15 June 1999	GATT Art. XXIV	24 April 1993
Kyrgyz Republic—Ukraine	Goods	FTA	15 June 1999	GATT Art. XXIV	19 January 1998
Kyrgyz Republic—Uzbekistan	Goods	FTA	15 June 1999	GATT Art. XXIV	20 March 1998
Mexico—El Salvador (Mexico—Northern Triangle)	Goods & Services	FTA & EIA	23 May 2006	GATT Art. XXIV & GATS V	15 March 2001
Mexico—Guatemala (Mexico—Northern Triangle)	Goods & Services	FTA & EIA	3 July 2006	GATT Art. XXIV & GATS V	15 March 2001
Mexico—Honduras (Mexico—Northern Triangle)	Goods & Services	FTA & EIA	10 July 2006(G) 20 June 2006(S)	GATT Art. XXIV & GATS V	1 June 2001
Mexico—Nicaragua	Goods & Services	FTA & EIA	17 October 2005	GATT Art. XXIV & GATS V	1 July 1998
New Zealand—Singapore	Goods & Services	FTA & EIA	4 September 2001	GATT Art. XXIV & GATS V	1 January 2001
Nicaragua and the Separate Customs Territory of Taiwan, Penghu, Kinmen and Matsu	Goods & Services	FTA & EIA	9 July 2009	GATT Art. XXIV & GATS V	1 January 2008
North American Free Trade Agreement (NAFTA)	Goods & Services	FTA & EIA	29 January 1993(G) 1 March 1995(S)	GATT Art. XXIV & GATS V	1 January 1994
Pakistan—China	Goods & Services	FTA & EIA	18 January 2008(G) 20 May 2010(S)	GATT Art. XXIV & GATS V	1 July 2007(G) 10 October 2009(S)
Pakistan—Malaysia	Goods & Services	FTA & EIA	19 February 2008	Enabling Clause & GATS Art. V	1 January 2008
Pakistan—Sri Lanka	Goods	FTA	11 June 2008	Enabling Clause	12 June 2005
Panama—Chile	Goods & Services	FTA & EIA	17 April 2008	GATT Art. XXIV & GATS V	7 March 2008
Panama—Costa Rica (Panama—Central America)	Goods & Services	FTA & EIA	7 April 2009	GATT Art. XXIV & GATS V	23 November 2008
Panama—El Salvador (Panama—Central America)	Goods & Services	FTA & EIA	24 February 2005	GATT Art. XXIV & GATS V	11 April 2003

There is one final issue with respect to the current legal test: Horn et al. (2010) examine the subject-matter of PTAs concluded by two hubs (EU, US) with various spokes between 1992–2008 and divide it into WTO + ('WTO plus', say tariff cuts beyond the MFN level), and WTOx ('WTO extra', issues that do not come under the mandate of the WTO, say positive integration in fields such as environmental policy, fight against corruption, etc.). The WTOx part of the PTAs is quite substantial. Horn et al. (2010) thus suggest that the rationale for going preferential should also be sought in WTOx-type obligations. The problem, however, is that we lack a test (other than MFN) to measure the consistency of WTOx provisions with the WTO.[198]

PTAs are formed for many, often idiosyncratic, reasons. We cited some of the reasons *supra* and there are many more: Winters and Schiff (1998) discuss the political benefits stemming from the formation of PTAs. Baldwin (1997), for example, tries to explore the validity of some of the rationales and, more recently, Whalley (2008) attempts a similar endeavour. Baldwin (2008) even develops a theory aimed at predicting who goes preferential depending on the identity of the spoke and the hub that have already gone preferential. But we lack a dominant explanation that can serve as a rationale across PTAs. Under the circumstances, it is difficult to come up with one 'medicine' for all. The counter-argument here is that the WTO being a trade contract should be limited to a discussion of the trade agenda and discard all the rest. But even then, we have to change the current legal test, which does not enquire at all into welfare implications. Critically, we have to rethink it in light of the overall mandate of the WTO: it seems that the preferential agenda, with its WTOx elements, is moving in directions where no WTO mandate currently exists. Under the circumstances, the Transparency Mechanism is probably a blessing in disguise that will provide trading nations with the necessary time to rethink their attitude towards PTAs.[199]

The one issue that requires additional reflection is the observed discrepancy between the content of the WTO rules and those of PTAs. WTOx could give food for thought to WTO negotiators who, unless they ponder seriously on this issue, might see PTAs run away with the trade agenda and thus contribute to the relative irrelevance of the WTO.[200]

---

[198] Compare Limão (2011), Trachtman (2011), and Kenner (2011) on this score. Bartels (2005) discusses human rights clauses in PTAs signed by the EU and more specifically the enforceability of similar clauses.

[199] Davey (2011), Mathis (2011), and Srinivasan (2011) have all expressed sceptical views regarding the realism of the proposals to redesign Art. XXIV GATT.

[200] PTAs on occasion might be a more effective tool to advance social preferences: Hafner-Burton (2005) examines the human rights record of 177 countries between 1972–2002 and concludes that human rights enforcement has been seriously aided by including clauses to this effect in PTAs.

4

DOMESTIC INSTRUMENTS

1. The Legal Discipline and its Rationale

Art. III GATT reflects the obligation to observe national treatment (NT) whenever WTO Members have recourse to domestic instruments: this obligation requests from WTO Members to ensure that, once imported goods have paid their ticket to enter a market (e.g. tariff), they cannot be subjected to a burden of whatever nature higher than that imposed on domestic products with which they are competing. Art. III.1 GATT reflects this principle in best-endeavours terms and requests from WTO Members, when applying their domestic instruments (policies), not to afford protection to domestic production:

> The contracting parties recognize that internal taxes and other internal charges, and laws, regulations and requirements affecting the internal sale, offering for sale, purchase, transportation, distribution or use of products, and internal quantitative regulations requiring the mixture, processing or use of products in specified amounts or proportions, should not be applied to imported or domestic products so as to afford protection to domestic production.

§§2, 4, and 5 constitute the operational arm of Art. III.1 GATT. Art. III GATT does contain some clarifications: in §8 it exempts two instruments (government procurement and subsidies) from its coverage and, by virtue of §5, WTO Members are requested to abstain from using a particular instrument, namely 'local content' requirements; implicitly, the use of local content requirements is equated with protection and the judge could use this information to see, by analogy, which other measures coming under the purview of §§2 and 4 should be considered protectionist.[1] During the negotiations, it was made clear that there was no room for preferential internal taxes, such as those previously practised in some parts of the world (New Zealand, US).[2] China wanted to limit the NT obligation to taxes (fiscal measures) only, but this attempt was thwarted by others.[3] For the rest, §§2 and 4 do not refer to any specific measure, but impose an obligation not to discriminate between domestic and imported goods which are competing with each other on all domestic instruments whether of a fiscal or non-fiscal nature. Consequently, with respect to domestic instruments, the GATT is an incomplete

---

[1] In a way §5 serves as an indicative list, albeit a very short one, of measures coming under the purview of Art. III GATT. Indicative lists help the judge avoid a type II error (false negative): every time a challenged measure is judged to be a local content requirement, it must be outlawed. Bagwell and Sykes (2007b) note that the prohibition of local content requirements makes sense only when markets are not competitive (say because we are in the presence of market power): when markets are competitive and the domestic country imposing the requirement is small, local content requirements may cause a redistribution of surplus from domestic consumers to the domestic input industry with no associated international (negative) externality.

[2] UN Doc. E/PS/T/W/179 at p. 3.

[3] UN Doc. E/PC/T/W/181 at p. 3. In China's view, hence, there should be no NT obligation with respect to regulatory (non-fiscal) domestic instruments.

contract in that it provides neither an exhaustive nor even an indicative list of the measures covered. The originally 'incomplete' contract could, of course, have been completed in this respect through subsequent renegotiation. And, indeed, as we discuss *infra*, an attempt to this effect was made but failed (Working Party on Border Tax Adjustments). For the reasons explained in more detail *infra*, this failure should not come as a surprise; completing the contract in this respect is bordering on the impossible. Suffice to say for the time being that, because preferences change over time across the various trading nations, and because everything at least indirectly affects trade, and because it is quite difficult to establish reciprocity across regulatory measures, WTO Members would have to find themselves in a state of permanent negotiation if they were to (attempt to) write a complete contract in this respect. Wisely, they chose not to do so.

The legal discipline imposed is an obligation of result and not an obligation of specific conduct: this provision does not prejudge the specific measures that must be adopted by WTO Members in order to achieve the stated objective; it allows WTO Members to unilaterally choose their domestic policies but requests from them that all policies covered by this provision must be applied in an even-handed manner to domestic and imported goods alike, no matter what their final choice is. The GATT is thus, with respect to domestic instruments, a negative integration contract: WTO Members do not have to follow, say, a particular tax policy, they can define their own; their only obligation under the GATT is to impose their tax regime in a non-discriminatory manner on domestic and foreign goods.[4] Put differently, Art. III GATT is meant to equate conditions of competition *within* markets, not *across* markets.[5]

Why was the NT discipline necessary in the GATT edifice? There is a 'substitution effect' between trade and domestic policy instruments which implies that, if

---

[4] For many commentators, this is the only feasible form of integration in light of the 'heterogeneity' across the various WTO players which is, in and of itself, an impediment, so the argument goes, to a deeper form of integration. Yet even an NT agreement should not be taken for granted: in a two country model, Saggi and Sara (2008) ask whether and how each country's incentive to enter into an NT agreement with the other depends upon the relative quality of their production as well as on the relative size of their markets. They show that if market size is identical across countries, while the high quality country benefits from an NT agreement, the low quality country does not and an NT agreement fails to arise in equilibrium even when it yields higher aggregate global welfare. However, when market size also differs across countries, a welfare-improving NT agreement can arise in equilibrium. Intuitively, asymmetry in market size helps counterbalance the asymmetry in production quality. Even so, they find that an NT agreement occurs only when the quality gap between goods is itself not too large, i.e. goods are sufficiently 'like'. At the other end of the spectrum, Petersmann (2002) questions the continued legitimacy of NT (as an instrument accepting, if not altogether promoting, negative integration) in today's world. In his view, NT should be understood as a 'constitutional' provision (using this term to denote hierarchy across the various GATT provisions) and should be anchored in human rights, that is, it should be interpreted in light of jurisprudence in the field of protection of human rights.

[5] Palmeter (1993, 1999) argues that WTO Members do not, by signing the WTO agreement, usurp each other's sovereignty; they agree only to limit the exercise of their own sovereignty when they believe that such limitation is to their advantage.

no regulation of the latter exists, governments can use say a domestic tax to take back part of the market access that they promised in a tariff negotiation. They can thus through 'policy substitution' afford 'protection' to their domestic goods. Recall our discussion on equivalence propositions: a tariff can be distinguished in a domestic tax for consumers and a subsidy for producers; if tariffs are disciplined, but subsidies and (domestic) taxes are not, then WTO Members could easily circumvent their obligations not to impose tariffs beyond the agreed ceiling by taxing consumers (who would pay a tax any time they purchased foreign goods) and subsidizing producers through the tax proceeds.

The negotiating record reveals[6] that trading nations wanted to ensure that no protection will be afforded through domestic instruments in order to safeguard the value of tariff concessions. Irwin et al. (2008) reflect on all draft versions of what became Art. III GATT from the London to the Havana Conference: the term 'so as to afford protection' replaced the originally used term 'for the purpose of affording protection'. NT was incorporated in Art. 9 of the London Conference; it became Art. 15 in Lake Success (New York); and, eventually, it became, in the Havana Conference, Art. 18. This last transformation is the current Art. III GATT. The key message throughout the negotiating history has been that no protection additional to that imposed through tariffs should occur in favour of domestic products as a result of unilateral regulatory activity by the trading nations. Protection should be negotiable and not left to the discretion of those with the incentive to protect.

A note by the GATT Secretariat summarizing the meetings of the Working Party on Border Tax Adjustments on 18–20 June 1968 captures this point in the following terms:

> In the case of Article III, the rules were designed to safeguard tariff concessions and to prevent hidden discrimination.[7]

More recently, the AB, in its report on *Japan—Alcoholic Beverages II*, confirmed this understanding of NT (p. 16):

> The broad and fundamental purpose of Article III is to avoid protectionism in the application of internal tax and regulatory measures. More specifically, the purpose of Article III 'is to ensure that internal measures not be applied to imported or domestic products so as to afford protection to domestic production.' Toward this end, Article III obliges Members of the WTO to provide equality of competitive conditions for imported products in relation to domestic products.

NT is thus an insurance policy that the value of a negotiated tariff concession (for which consideration has been paid) will not be undone through subsequent unilateral action; agreeing on this insurance policy is necessary for trading nations to continue to have an incentive to negotiate tariff reduction and trade

---

[6] See Irwin et al. (2008) and Jackson (1969).
[7] GATT Doc. L/3039 of 11 July 1968.

liberalization. What is the incentive for A to negotiate tariffs on widgets with B (and pay through reciprocal commitments), if B can subsequently decide to set say the level of VAT (value added tax) on domestic widgets at 10 per cent, and that on imported widgets at 25 per cent? If knowledge about the VAT levels was *ex ante* known, A might have had the incentive to negotiate with B even if B imposed two VAT levels depending on the origin of the good. It is the uncertainty that B might impose duties at *ex ante* unknown levels that A is seeking protection from. It is thus the freedom of B to unilaterally decide on the level of differential treatment that A wants to eliminate: respect for NT guarantees that B can set its levels of VAT at any level it wishes but without treating domestic and imported goods unevenly. As a result, the only disadvantage that goods originating in A will suffer from when exported to B would be tariffs, and the level of this instrument is not unilaterally decided, as we saw in Chapter 2.

Safeguarding the value of tariff concessions, though, should not be an objective that must be reached at all costs: Art. III GATT is a negative integration contract as discussed above and Art. XX GATT clearly states that social preferences 'trump' trade commitments. It is not therefore that WTO Members must streamline their domestic policies in order to serve the value of tariff concessions; the GATT is more about providing them with the breathing space to shape their domestic policies provided that they do not apply them in a discriminatory manner across domestic and imported goods. A negative trade impact will thus be tolerated to the extent that it is not designed to disfavour imports. This much should be critical in designing the appropriate standard of review that is applicable in similar litigation.

In this vein, absence of protection through domestic instruments should not be equated with an obligation to deregulate: trading nations are free to regulate as much as they wish provided that they have not discriminated against foreign goods when doing so. Non-discrimination (NT) is legalese for absence of protectionism. 'Protection' is not defined any further, and indeed, it is a difficult term to define.[8] Yet, unless we have an idea about it, the interpretation of the terms appearing in §§ 2, 4, and 5 will suffer and it will be questionable whether they can effectively serve the objective they are called to serve. This problem could, of course, have been avoided were the WTO Members to write a 'complete' contract where they would enumerate each and every domestic instrument by each and every WTO Member and decide on their fate (legal/illegal). As things stand, it is largely left to the WTO judge to decide on the measures that come under the purview of this provision[9]

---

[8] Bagwell and Staiger (2002) have developed an intellectually appealing definition (politically optimum) which nevertheless, is difficult to translate into specific obligation and thus transform it to a workable tool in the hands of the WTO judge.

[9] As we have argued in Horn and Mavroidis (2008), although not explicitly mentioned, the public international law rules regarding allocation of jurisdiction must be read into the GATT and on occasion provide a jurisdictional halt. Indeed, the Working Party on Border Tax Adjustments was established in order to address the question: for which class of measures can a GATT contracting party adjust its taxes? This is an eminently jurisdictional issue, and the establishment of the Working

and, once this has been decided, which of them violate it: finding protection becomes by necessity the outcome of an intellectual exercise that the judge is called to apply.

Non-discrimination as discussed so far entails a requirement of even-handedness across a specific class of products: loosely speaking, those competing in the same relevant product market against each other.[10] NT should not be equated with a blanket prohibition to have recourse to beggar-thy-neighbour policies. NT addresses only some of them, those affording protection to domestic goods competing with imports.

There are other limits inherent in the non-discrimination obligation as embedded in the GATT of which we should be mindful: on its face, non-discrimination does not request from WTO Members the obligation to adopt efficient regulations. Assume, for example, that it is proven that a 5 per cent tax can take care of an environmental hazard which has been provoked by good A, produced in equal parts in Home and Foreign, two WTO Members. Assume further that Home imposes a 25 per cent taxation on good A irrespective of its origin. Nothing that we discussed so far (or that we will be discussing in what follows) can help an aspiring complainant make a persuasive case against this measure before the WTO. WTO Members can use the second- or third-best instrument to address a distortion and still be found to be WTO-consistent if the (so far loosely defined) requirement of even-handedness has been observed. The point here is that non-discrimination is no surrogate for efficiency.[11] And yet efficient interventions (using the first-best instrument) should create a strong presumption that the intervening party is genuine in what it pursues.[12] The 25 per cent taxation is a *beggar-thy-neighbour* policy, since Foreign will be requested to pay money that is

---

Party was probably decided because of the contractual certainty that a bargaining solution entails. The AB, in *US—Shrimp*, explicitly referred to the jurisdictional nexus that must be present whenever a WTO Member exercises jurisdiction, as we will see *infra*. There are many accounts of how public international law addresses jurisdiction and the contributions in Meessen (1996) must rank among the most complete. On the limits of jurisdiction, see the divergent views of Kramer (1995), Lowenfeld (1995), Raustiala (2006), and Vagts (2003).

[10] We shall see *infra* in sufficient detail how this feature of NT has been understood in case law and whether, in our view, this understanding is reasonable.

[11] Staiger and Sykes (2010) deal with the limits of the current draft of Art. III GATT. They observe that WTO rules and disputes centre on complaints about excessively stringent regulations. Employing the international externalities (terms-of-trade) framework for the modelling of trade agreements, they show how large nations may have an incentive to impose discriminatory product standards against imported goods once border instruments are constrained, and how inefficiently stringent standards may emerge under certain circumstances even if regulatory discrimination is prohibited. They then assess the WTO legal framework in light of their results, arguing that it does a reasonably thorough job of policing regulatory discrimination, but that it does relatively little to address excessive non-discriminatory regulations.

[12] For a theoretical understanding of the *targeting literature* (addressing distortions through the appropriate instrument), see Bhagwati and Ramaswami (1963); for an application in WTO case law, see Mattoo and Mavroidis (1997).

not necessary to address the observed distortion; yet this type of beggar-thy-neighbour policy remains unpunished by WTO law as it currently stands.

Art. III GATT does not contain a consistency requirement either. Yet, a similar requirement makes eminent sense as means to fight 'protectionism' and is indeed used in the SPS Agreement as we shall see in Chapter 10. Think of it this way: A and B are two environment polluting goods; assume that A is responsible for tenfold more environmental pollution than B is, and also that A and B do not compete in the same market. Home and Foreign produce both A and B in a symmetric manner. Now Home decides, for whatever implausible reasons, to tax B but not A. Assume further that Foreign has taken active measures to address pollution by A and its investment is paying off; it does not address B pollution since it is negligible. Foreign, when called to pay tax on its B exports, cannot request from A to tax A pollution as well or to rebalance its tax imposition because it has already invested in addressing pollution by A. It will have to pay the unilaterally set tax and Home, if challenged, will prevail in WTO litigation as long as domestic and imported B are treated in an even-handed manner. Home, of course, might use some of the proceedings to address pollution by A in its market. In that it will be engaging in beggar-thy-neighbour practice yet again. And, yet again, its measure will carry the day in WTO litigation.[13] Or, think of the importation of natural resources such as oil. In these sectors, import tariffs are typically close to zero, but consumption taxes are extremely high.

How does all this tie with terms of trade? It is clear from the theory that terms of trade can be affected not only through trade, but also through domestic, instruments. Indeed, a WTO Member with substantial bargaining power on widgets could in theory affect terms of trade either by imposing a customs duty or a consumption tax. If terms of trade was the basic rationale for concluding the GATT (the 'GATT-think'), why then did not trading nations move on and negotiate on domestic instruments as well? Why did not trading nations exchange concessions on domestic instruments in the same way as they did with respect to customs duties? Recall our discussion above about contract 'incompleteness': trading nations would have found it almost impossible to contract in all domestic instruments affecting trade. Rationally then, the trading nations opted for a second-best regulation of domestic instruments where non-discrimination becomes the dominant legal discipline (and not exchanges of concessions having measured the impact of domestic instruments on terms of trade), and effectively must have accepted to live with some terms-of-trade manipulation in light of the sheer difficulty in contracting the full nine yards: those with the more demanding regulatory regime happen to be those with the bargaining power to affect terms of

---

[13] As we shall see in Chapter 10, a consistency requirement has been included in the WTO SPS Agreement.

trade.[14] There is some insurance policy against this danger since, unlike tariffs, domestic instruments bind domestic goods as well, and the resulting effect on terms of trade will thus be mitigated.[15]

There is an additional reason why opting for non-discrimination (instead of policy-by-policy negotiation) is the sensible way to achieve contracting with respect to domestic instruments. Domestic instruments are of both a fiscal and a non-fiscal nature. The former look very much like tariffs; in fact they are tariffs. The latter are different: governments have different utility scales and comparisons might be difficult if not altogether impossible. Say Home has a requirement that no TV advertising is allowed during evening hours and Foreign bans hormone-treated chicken from its market. How can reciprocity work in a similar scenario?

2. The Coverage of the Legal Discipline

The drafters of Art. III GATT followed a hybrid approach with respect to its coverage: recall that one instrument (local content requirements) was specifically mentioned in the body of this provision and, two instruments (subsidies, government procurement) have been explicitly excluded from its coverage; moreover, a contextual reading of Art. III GATT leads to the conclusion that film quotas are also excluded from its coverage, as are probably goods in transit. For the rest, the wording and the negotiating record of this provision leave us with no doubt that it was meant to cover dozens of other instruments but that for reasons explained *infra* its framers thought it wiser to avoid enumerating them one by one. An attempt to add some information regarding its coverage to this provision was undertaken through the establishment of the Working Party on Border Tax Adjustments. Although the final outcome was not as successful as originally hoped, this report still left us with some additional information as to what the GATT framers had in mind with respect to the coverage of Art. III GATT. We know, for example, that direct taxation escapes the coverage of this provision. As things stand now, national treatment applies, with very few exceptions, to each and every domestic policy affecting trade irrespective of whether tariffs on the goods concerned have been bound or left unbound.

2.1 Explicitly Covered: Local Content Requirements

Art. III.5 GATT explicitly outlaws local content requirements: under this provision, all measures whereby a government privileges goods containing a set amount

---

[14] There are of course exceptions such as Switzerland or Norway.

[15] Although, as argued above, the risk of manipulation still exists since, for example, ineffective yet non-discriminatory domestic regulations are perfectly legitimate under the current GATT legal discipline; compare Horn (2006). The agreements on TBT and SPS are discussed in Chapter 10.

of domestic added value are outlawed. Local content requirements are not only trade- but also investment-related measures. Actually, this is not the only invest-ment measure regulated by the GATT: export performance requirements are outlawed by Art. XI GATT. The question might, thus, naturally arise: how much does the GATT regulate investment protection? The answer is that the GATT does not contain comprehensive disciplines on investment protection: it does not regulate anything beyond the two measures mentioned. This point was made clear by the GATT Panel on *Canada—FIRA*. In this case, the US had challenged the consistency of the Canadian Foreign Investment Review Act (FIRA) with various GATT provisions, including Art. III.4 GATT. The Canadian Act subjected approval of foreign investment into Canada only if it could be demonstrated that the investment would have 'significant benefit to Canada'.[16] In this vein, foreign investors would be required to make specific undertakings, whereby they would be promising, *inter alia*, to purchase Canadian goods (roughly, to ensure a certain level of Canadian added value in their production process). The Panel explained in three different places the limits of the coverage of investment protection under the GATT (§§5.1, 5.9, 6.5):

> In view of the fact that the General Agreement does not prevent Canada from exercising its sovereign right to regulate foreign direct investments, the Panel examined the purchase and export undertakings by investors subject to the Foreign Investment Review Act of Canada solely in the light of Canada's trade obligations under the General Agreement.
> . . .
> The purpose of Article III:4 is not to protect the interests of the foreign investor but to ensure that goods originating in any other contracting party benefit from treatment no less favourable than domestic goods . . .
> . . .
> . . . the national treatment obligations of Article III of the General Agreement do not apply to foreign persons or firms but to imported products.

Local content requirements are now regulated both at the GATT and at the TRIMs level (Agreement on Trade Related Investment Measures), following the advent of the latter as a result of the successful conclusion of the Uruguay round. Their regulation, nonetheless, is not identical, since TRIMs contains additional obligations to those imposed by Art. III GATT. We will discuss them *infra* in this chapter.

2.2 Explicitly Excluded from Coverage

2.2.1 Subsidies

By virtue of Art. III.8 GATT, subsidies are excluded from the coverage of Art. III GATT. We discuss their treatment in WTO law in Chapter 8.

---

[16] §2.2 of the report.

2.2.2 *Government Procurement*

By virtue of Art. III.8 GATT, government procurement is excluded from the coverage of Art. III GATT. A plurilateral agreement (that is, an agreement where participation is optional for WTO Members) nonetheless has been agreed: the WTO agreement on government procurement (GPA) was successfully negotiated during the Uruguay round, and we discuss it in detail in Chapter 12.

2.2.3 *Film Quotas*

Art. IV GATT allows for screen quotas for cinematographic films of national origin (or originating in another specific contracting party)[17] if they are not allocated to a specific source of supply. The quota as such is not a proper import or export quota. If this were the case, then it would have been outlawed by virtue of Art. XI GATT. It is not a production quota either. The placement of this provision immediately after Art. III GATT evidences the mindset of the negotiators, who considered screen quotas in favour of national films as an exception to the NT obligation. As Ehring (2011, p. 114) nevertheless correctly points out, this provision should be considered as *lex specialis* and not as an exception to Art. III GATT. This understanding of the provision is not void of legal consequences since in the former case (*lex specialis*) it is still the complainant that carries the burden of proof, whereas in the latter it is the defendant, that is, the WTO Member, imposing the film quota.

It must be that cinematographic films were considered as goods and not as services, since otherwise why bother to regulate this issue under the GATT in the first place? This classification is not totally unproblematic as we will explain in what follows. It is probably warranted, though, to first take a look at the negotiating record. It was the UK delegation that initially proposed (in what later became Art. IV GATT) the exclusion of films from the coverage of Art. 15 of the London Draft. In the words of the UK delegate (Mr Rhydderch):

> he would prefer a note to the Article to say it did not apply to films. There were cultural, as well as commercial, considerations to be taken into account in the case of films.[18]

And the same UK delegate:

> In the case of films it is not merely an economic and not even material question; it brings in a very important cultural consideration such as does not come in the case of other commodities. We think it is quite clear that countries will not allow their own film production which affects their own culture and ideas, to be swamped by imported films simply because the latter happen to be better organised commercially.

---

[17] The rationale for this extension could be that two countries share common cultural factors such as language and in this vein it would be appropriate say for Canada to keep screen quotas for French-speaking films originating in France.

[18] E/PC/T/C.II/E.14 of 4 November 1946 at p. 5.

Some perfectly reliable method of safeguarding domestic film production is needed and will in fact be insisted on by a great many countries. The method of the screen quota is much the most effective, perhaps the only effective method of attaining this desired object. We must therefore preserve our right to use this method.[19]

This is probably one of the first expressions in favour of a cultural exception in the world trading system. The UK delegation thought of films not only as economic, but as cultural goods as well. The support of Chile, Czechoslovakia, New Zealand,[20] and eventually Norway and South Africa, left only the US delegation opposing the UK view. The US saw no reason to treat films differently from other goods; in the view of its delegates, the preference of the audience should determine the amount of trade in films.[21] It was clear, nonetheless, that the US delegation was fighting a losing battle on this issue. Eventually, a separate provision applicable only to films and justifying an exception to national treatment would be agreed to in subsequent negotiations (the current Art. IV GATT). We quote from Wilcox (1949, pp. 44–5):

> Almost without exception, the changes that had been suggested in the United States were accepted and the draft was amended accordingly. Of particular importance was the inclusion of two new articles, one limiting the freedom of nations to discriminate against foreign motion-picture films and the other dealing with the treatment of foreign investment. The latter article, while unacceptable in substance, did serve to bring the subject of foreign investment within the scope of the Charter.

An unlikely, by today's standards, nation was thus at the origin of Art. IV GATT.[22] We stated before that the assumption underlying this provision must be that cinematographic films are a good. And had the WTO never seen the light of the day, there would have been no interest in pursuing this discussion any further. The advent of the WTO, however, signalled the advent of GATS as well and the issue of classification of cinematographic films gained new interest. Services grew as part of domestic GDP in developed countries after the advent of the GATT. Interest in liberalizing the market for films grew in this context. The US first tabled a proposal to the effect that barriers to trade in television programming were technically a violation of GATT rules, accepting nonetheless that some of the principles of Art. IV GATT might well apply to them. In 1961, the US raised the question of introducing new language into GATT that would address restrictions by a number of countries on trade in television programming. There

---

[19] E/PC/T/A/SR/10.

[20] New Zealand insisted on an arrangement that would take care of its 'film hire tax'; see E/PC/T/C.6/8 of 23 January 1947. The film hire tax was a delayed customs duty levied at the point where the real value of the film had become apparent. The New Zealand delegate eventually conceded that this imposition could form the subject-matter of tariff negotiations under Art. 24 of the London Draft. New Zealand was not, at the time, producing films, other than educational and newsreels; see E/PC/T/C.6/55/Rev. 1 at pp. 7–8.

[21] E/PC/T/W/181 at pp. 7–8.

[22] Originally it was Art. 19 of the Havana Charter; see Wilcox (1949) at pp. 76ff.

was no unanimity across GATT contracting parties on this score, and they decided to set up a Working Party to examine the issue, but reached no final conclusion.[23] The uncertainty thus persisted.

In some legal orders, the question was addressed through case law. In the EU legal order, for example, the *Saachi* jurisprudence made it clear that trade in television transmission involved trade in services, whereas in *Cinethèque* the ECJ held that trade in videocassettes involved goods and not services.[24] The EU, in a proposal it tabled during the negotiation of the Uruguay round on audiovisual services, was not keen to extend right away MFN and NT to foreign services suppliers. This is evidence that in its view audiovisual services had to respect neither MFN nor NT by virtue of obligations assumed under the GATT. We quote:

> Article 3: Most favoured nation treatment
> As far as the origin of a work determines its cultural content, the Agreement shall not affect the right of a party not to accord a treatment as favourable as that accorded in like circumstances to services or providers of services of any other party.
> Article 4: National treatment
> Parties may apply or introduce measures providing for some requirements of origin applicable to audiovisual works for cultural reasons. The Agreement shall not affect the right of a party not to accord, on the basis of measures referred to in paragraph 1, a treatment as favourable as that accorded in like circumstances to its own services or providers of services.[25]

The question of overlap between GATT and GATS in the audiovisual sector occupied the minds of the negotiators during the Uruguay round and was vividly discussed on more than one occasion.[26] There is certainly an overlap. In theory, though, the GATS regime may be less liberalizing than the GATT: WTO Members can, under GATS, take MFN exemption and avoid commitments, thus keeping not only their markets closed but also the possibility of discriminating among different sources. So the question, with the advent of GATS, is whether Art. IV GATT still means something. De jure it does, since it has not been abolished. De facto, nonetheless, it has gone with the wind. We explain. One caveat first: Art. IV GATT covers quotas for imported films and not cross-border transmission of audiovisual works through satellites.

The issue of the boundary between a good and a service, that is, the relationship between GATT and GATS, is far from obvious and has been addressed by WTO adjudicating bodies: the two agreements were not negotiated simultaneously

---

[23] Report of the Working Party, Application of GATT to International Trade in Television Programmes, in GATT Doc. L/1741 of 13 March 1962. See also Jackson (1969) at p. 294.
[24] Cases 155/73 (1974), and 60-61/84 (1986) respectively. See Acheson and Maule (2001) at pp. 58ff.
[25] MTN.GNS/AUD/W/2 of 4 October 1990.
[26] See, for example, MTN.GNS/AUD/1 of 27 September 1990; MTN.GNS/AUD/2 of 20 December 2010; MTN.GNS/W/1 of 4 October 1990.

and, unfortunately, negotiators did not pay particular attention to the potential overlap between them.[27] In *Canada—Periodicals*, the issue arose whether the Canadian *Excise Tax Act* should come under the purview of GATT or GATS since, as Canada had argued, the tax (equal to 80 per cent of the value of all the advertisements contained in the so-called split-run magazines) was imposed on a service (advertising) and was therefore only subject to the disciplines of the GATS. Canada further argued that the measure at hand could only be reviewed under the national treatment obligation of the GATS (Art. XVII), in respect of which no specific commitments on advertising had been taken. Both the Panel and the AB disagreed with the Canadian argument, stating that the measure at hand (a tax) was also a measure affecting trade in goods. On the wider issue regarding the frontier between GATT and GATS, the AB provided a rather non-committal statement along the following lines (p. 19):

> The entry into force of the GATS, as Annex 1B of the *WTO Agreement*, does not diminish the scope of application of the GATT 1994. Indeed, Canada concedes that its position 'with respect to the inapplicability of the GATT would have been exactly the same under the GATT 1947, before the GATS had ever been conceived'.

We agree with the Panel's statement:

> The ordinary meaning of the texts of GATT 1994 and GATS as well as Art. II:2 of the WTO Agreement, taken together, indicates that obligations under GATT 1994 and GATS can co-exist and that one does not override the other.
>
> We do not find it necessary to pronounce on the issue of whether there can be potential overlaps between the GATT 1994 and the GATS, as both participants agreed that it is not relevant in this appeal. (italics in the original)

The AB then held that the Canadian measure at issue applied to trade in goods and subsequently examined the measure under Art. III:2 GATT. In short, in *Canada—Periodicals*, the AB held that the obligations of both agreements can co-exist, rather than the obligation of one being overridden by those of the other, but did not find it necessary to pronounce on the overlap issue. This finding amounted to a non-finding when it comes to clarifying the relationship between GATT and GATS. It was no surprise therefore that it was not long before this issue was brought before WTO adjudication again: in *EC—Bananas III*. There, the EU defended the view that GATT and GATS cannot overlap, as a matter of principle. The Panel disagreed essentially because, in its view, in the absence of overlap, WTO

---

[27] Unlike the Treaty Establishing the European Community (ECT), the predecessor to the Treaty on the Functioning of the European Union (TFEU), which abolishes any overlap between measures affecting trade in goods and measures affecting trade in services, there is no provision in the WTO Agreement regulating the relationship between the GATT and the GATS. Art. 50 (ex Art. 60) ECT reads: 'Services shall be considered to be "services" within the meaning of this Treaty where they are normally provided for remuneration, insofar as they are not governed by the provisions relating to freedom of movement of goods, capital and persons'.

Members would easily be in a position to circumvent their WTO obligations. The Panel offered the following example to highlight its view at §7.283:

> For example, a measure in the transport sector regulating the transportation of merchandise in the territory of a Member could subject imported products to less favourable transportation conditions compared to those applicable to like domestic products. Such a measure would adversely affect the competitive position of imported products in a manner which would not be consistent with that Member's obligation to provide national treatment to such products. If the scope of GATT and GATS were interpreted to be mutually exclusive, that Member could escape its national treatment obligation and the Members whose products have been discriminated against would have no possibility of legal recourse on account that the measure regulates 'services' and not goods.

In §7.285, the Panel defined the scope of application of the GATS in the following terms:

> [N]o measures are excluded a priori from the scope of the GATS as defined by its provisions. The scope of the GATS encompasses any measure of a Member to the extent it affects the supply of a service regardless of whether such measure directly governs the supply of a service or whether it regulates other matters but nevertheless affects trade in services.

Based on this interpretation of the scope of the GATS, the Panel on *EC—Bananas III* concluded that there was (§7.286):

> no legal basis for an a priori exclusion of measures within the EC banana import licensing regime from the scope of the GATS.

The AB upheld this finding (p. 220). Further to its determination in *Canada—Periodicals*, the AB, in *EC—Bananas III*, reaffirmed that in certain circumstances GATT and GATS may overlap (p. 221):

> there is yet a third category of measures that could be found to fall within the scope of both the GATT 1994 and the GATS. These are measures that involve a service relating to a particular good or service supplied in conjunction with a particular good. In all such cases in this third category, the measure in question could be scrutinized under both the GATT 1994 and the GATS. However, while the same measure could be scrutinized under both agreements, the specific aspects of that measure examined under each agreement could be different. Under the GATT 1994, the focus is on how the measure affects the goods involved. Under the GATS, the focus is on how the measure affects the supply of the service or the service suppliers involved. Whether a certain measure affecting the supply of a service related to a particular good is scrutinized under the GATT 1994 or the GATS, or both, is a matter that can only be determined on a case-by-case basis.

Although the quoted passage is not very illuminating, at the end of the day, the AB seems to suggest that it could offer no clear definition of what a measure is: is it the same transaction that falls simultaneously under GATT and GATS, or different features of it? Probably the latter, but we will have to await clarifications in this respect in the future. Until then, what matters are commitments made under GATS. See Tables 4.1 and 4.2 for the commitments entered into by WTO Members in the audiovisual sector.[28]

In the same WTO document where the tables appear we read (§69):

> Many Members (48) have scheduled one or more MFN exemptions pertaining to audiovisual services. Most of these Members have no specific commitments in the sector. Overall, 114 MFN exemptions have been listed for audiovisual services, making it the sector with most exemptions. These often relate to the conferring of national treatment to works covered by co-production agreements, support programmes, or, in the case of European countries, the Council of Europe Convention on Transfrontier Television. Some MFN exemptions also reserve the right to retaliate against adverse, unfair or unreasonable trading conditions abroad. MFN exemptions in the sector are often justified by the relevant Members on the basis of cultural policy purposes.

No challenge has been raised so far against the MFN exemptions appearing in the schedules. As stated above, though, these exemptions constitute an undeniable backtracking from the GATT regime established in Art. IV. Hence, our conclusion that, de facto, Art. IV GATT does not mean much any more. The relevant tables are featured on p. 246.

2.3 Goods in Transit

Art. V GATT condones the freedom of transit. According to Art. V.1 GATT, a good is in transit if the passage through a territory is only a portion of the complete journey. It is clear that transiting goods are not destined to be sold in the market of a transiting state. Hence, the WTO Member through which goods are transiting cannot invoke the Interpretative Note ad Art. III GATT and subject similar goods to taxes applied to goods consumed in its market:

> Any internal tax or other internal charge, or any law, regulation or requirement of the kind referred to in paragraph 1 which applies to an imported product and to the like domestic product and is collected or enforced in the case of the imported product at the time or point of importation, is nevertheless to be regarded as an internal tax or other internal charge, or a law, regulation or requirement of the kind referred to in paragraph 1, and is accordingly subject to the provisions of Article III.

The wording and the negotiating record of this provision[29] make it clear that, as a matter of WTO law, WTO Members incur three obligations with respect to transit:[30]

---

[28] WTO Doc. S/C/W/310 of 12 January 2010.

[29] Irwin et al. (2008). Art. V.1, as well as the second sentence of Art. V.2 GATT, is based on the corresponding provisions (Arts. 1 and 2) of the Convention and Statute on Freedom of Transit, signed in Barcelona, on 29 April 1921; see UN Doc. E/PC/T/C.II/54/Rev.1.

[30] Actually, Art. V.6 GATT applies to WTO Members whose territory is the final destination for goods in international transit and not to WTO Members through which goods are transiting. The Panel on *Colombia—Ports of Entry* concluded that much (§7.475). The rest of the provision concerns transiting goods.

Table 4.1 Specific commitments in audiovisual services

Members	02.D.a.	02.D.b.	02.D.c.	02.D.d.	02.D.e.	02.D.f.	Total
Armenia	X	X	X		X		4
Cape Verde	X		X		X		3
Central African Rep.	X	X	X	X	X	X	6
China	X	X			X		3
Dominican Republic				X		X	2
El Salvador				X		X	2
Gambia	X	X	X	X			4
Georgia	X	X	X		X		4
Hong Kong, China	X				X	X	3
India	X						1
Israel	X						1
Japan	X	X			X		3
Jordan	X	X			X		3
Kenya	X	X					2
Korea RP	X				X		2
Kyrgyz Republic	X	X	X	X	X		5
Lesotho	X	X	X	X			4
Malaysia	X			X			2
Mexico	X	X					2
New Zealand	X	X	X	X		X	5
Nicaragua	X	X					2
Oman	X	X					2
Panama	X	X	X		X		4
Saudi Arabia	X		X				2
Singapore	X				X		2
Chinese Taipei	X	X	X		X		4
Thailand	X		X				2
Tonga	X	X	X		X		4
United States	X	X	X	X	X	X	6
Viet Nam	X	X			X		3
Total	28	19	14	9	16	6	92

Note: D.a. corresponds to motion picture video tape production and distribution services; D.b. to motion picture projections; D.c. to radio and television services; D.d. to radio and television transmission services; D.e. to sound recordings; and D.f. to other audiovisual services.

Table 4.2 Level of commitments

Percentage of entries per level of commitment (market access and national treatment columns)	Mode 1	Mode 2	Mode 3
Full commitments	66.7%	87.3%	66.8%
Partial commitments	11.1%	3.7%	22.6%
Unbound	22.2%	8.9%	10.5%

(a) All costs and charges must be reasonable (Art.V.3 and V.4 GATT);

(b) To allow transiting goods to use 'the routes most convenient for international transit' (Art. V.2 GATT);[31]

---

[31] In *Colombia—Ports of Entry*, the Panel concluded that Art. V.2 GATT required the extension of unrestricted access via the most convenient routes for the passage of goods in international transit

(c) They cannot discriminate across different foreign sources of supply (Art. V.5 GATT, MFN).

The question has recently arisen whether transiting goods should be subjected to other laws and regulations as well, which are not intimately linked to customs procedures. Could, for example, counterfeit goods be subjected to domestic laws regarding protection of intellectual property rights, even if they are simply transiting through a WTO Member? If yes, then the NT obligation would have to apply. The issue of goods in transit has been discussed in the TRIPs Council since May 2009, without, however, WTO Members being in a position to arrive at a common solution and eventually at an agreed interpretation/amendment of the current agreement.[32] Under the DSU, two requests for consultations have been submitted, one by India (11 May 2010; DS/408/1), and one by Brazil (12 May 2010; DS/409/1), and the two cases are almost identical: they concern repeated seizures on patent infringement grounds of generic drugs originating in India, but transiting through ports and airports in the Netherlands to third-country destinations, including Brazil. Brazil and India have alleged that the measures at issue (seizures) were, *inter alia*, inconsistent with the obligations of the EU under Art. V GATT. At the moment of writing, negotiations were still pending and no one had requested the establishment of a Panel. It has been unofficially reported that the EU has started the regular review of the relevant Regulation 1383/2003 (customs action against suspected infringing goods).

Irrespective of the eventual resolution of the two disputes, they have presented us with an interesting issue: can a WTO Member impose its public order on transiting goods or does this provision impose a jurisdictional halt with respect to some transactions? It would be quite odd to accept that there are no exceptions to freedom of transit: a similar construction of the GATT would be elevating trade liberalization to a higher hierarchical value than public order, a thesis that Art. XX GATT (as we shall see in more detail in Chapter 5) blatantly refutes: Art. XX GATT is a general exception to all obligations assumed under the GATT; recourse to this provision would thus suggest that WTO Members can deny freedom of transit if they can successfully invoke one of the grounds mentioned therein. In similar vein, Art. XXI GATT would allow WTO Members to invoke national security and deny freedom of transit.

---

whether or not the goods have been trans-shipped, warehoused, break-bulked, or have changed modes of transport. Accordingly, goods in international transit from any WTO Member must be allowed entry whenever destined for the territory of a third country. In the Panel's view, a WTO Member is not required, by virtue of this provision, to guarantee transport on necessarily any or all routes in its territory, but only on the ones 'most convenient' for transport through its territory (§7.401).

[32] There is a record of these discussions in the respective TRIPs Council minutes—originally under 'Public Health Dimension of the TRIPs Agreement' and later under 'Enforcement Trends'.

2.4 Social Security and Payroll Taxes

The coverage of Art. III GATT was further specified in 1971 as a result of the partial agreement obtained at the Working Party on Border Tax Adjustments. It is worth providing a short narrative of the work of this group. The group was established following a request by the US: in the 1960s and 1970s, there was a lot of concern in the US about the impact of European indirect taxes, such as value added taxes (VAT) on international trade. European economies were becoming more competitive in this period. Actually, though, the relevant story starts earlier: Art. XVI GATT underwent a substantial revision during the GATT Review Session of 1955, when it was agreed that:

> The exemption of an exported product from duties or taxes borne by the like product when destined for domestic consumption, or the remission of such duties or taxes in amounts not in excess of those which have accrued shall not be deemed to be a subsidy.

Now, few would disagree with the statement that this provision is far from being a paragon of clarity. It was felt that it was an attempt to formally endorse the destination principle to indirect taxes: according to this principle, internationally traded commodities should be subjected to taxes of the imported country and exempted from similar taxes of the exporting country in order to avoid double taxation. The principle contrasts with the origin principle as applied to other forms of taxation on transactions, income taxes levied according to source of income, or domicile or residence of the taxpayer, and property taxes imposed according to the *situs* of the taxable product. In 1960, the Working Party on Subsidies was established.[33] This Working Party was meant to reinforce the disciplines on subsidies, and adopted a number of practices construed to be subsidies. Point 5 of this report referred, *inter alia*, to:

> . . .
> (c) The remission, calculated in relation to exports, or direct taxes, or social welfare charges on industrial or commercial enterprises;
> (d) the exemption, in respect of exported goods, of charges or taxes, other than charges in connexion with importation or indirect taxes levied at one or several stages on the same goods if sold for internal consumption; or the payment, in respect of exported goods, of amounts exceeding those effectively levied at one or several stages on these goods in the form of indirect taxes or of the charges in connexion with importation or in both forms;

The Working Party report was adopted along with a Declaration giving effect to Art. XVI.4 GATT:

---

[33] GATT Doc. L/1381, adopted on 19 November 1960, GATT Doc. BISD 9S/185.

The Working Party agreed that this list should not be considered exhaustive or to limit in any way the generality of the provisions of paragraph 4 of Article XVI. It noted that the governments prepared to accept the declaration contained in Annex A agreed that, for the purpose of that declaration, these practices generally are to be considered as subsidies in the sense of Article XVI:4 or are covered by the Articles of Agreement of the International Monetary Fund. The representatives of governments which were not prepared to accept that declaration were not able to subscribe at this juncture to a precise interpretation of the term 'subsidies', but had no objection to the above interpretation being accepted by the future parties to that declaration for the purposes of its application.[34]

This report thus condoned the origin principle for direct taxes and the destination principle for indirect taxes. Recall that the GATT does not impose specific tax policies that have to be observed by its adherents: GATT contracting parties are left free to choose whether they opt for direct taxes, indirect taxes, or a combination of the two. The US tax system is based on direct taxation, whereas most European economies opted for indirect taxation. Voices were being raised in the US regarding the GATT's benign attitude towards indirect taxes, as opposed to its hostile stance towards direct taxes.[35] The argument was that it was the US that suffered as a result, and the European economies that profited. The fast growth of the European economies in the 1960s did not help pacify those arguing for some form of action at the GATT level.

The WP on Border Tax Adjustments was thus established in order to address a perceived imbalance regarding the GATT stance towards direct and indirect taxation: the GATT was supposed to be neutral vis-à-vis this choice in light of its negative integration character. The WP was requested to pronounce on the GATT consistency of practices by the GATT contracting parties referred to as 'border tax adjustments', that is, cases where the customs tariff was adjusted by the amount of an internal tax already imposed on domestic production. In the words of the drafters of the WP final report, the mandate was (§1):

> Acting under paragraph 1 of Article XXV and with a view to furthering the objectives of the General Agreement, and taking into account the discussions in the Council:
> 1. To examine:
>   (*a*) The provisions of the General Agreement relevant to border tax adjustments;
>   (*b*) The practices of contracting parties in relation to such adjustments;
>   (*c*) The possible effects of such adjustments on international trade.

---

[34] Seventeen governments adhered; GATT Doc. MTN.GNG/NG10/W/4 of 28 September 1987.

[35] The distinction between direct and indirect taxes was probably acceptable in economics three generations ago, but has since been widely questioned. In practice, indirect taxes are not fully shifted into product prices, and certain direct taxes (in particular corporate profits taxes) may be shifted into product prices, although the degree of shifting may vary from country to country. Classification of some taxes is questionable as well: value added taxes are classified as indirect taxes, but they fall on both costs and profits of the producer (value being defined as the difference between the value of a firm's purchases and sales), and to the extent that they fall on profits, how can they be distinguished from a profit tax in effect?

2. In the light of this examination, to consider any proposals and suggestions that may be put forward; and

3. To report its findings and conclusions on these matters to the Council or to the CONTRACTING PARTIES.

The term 'border tax adjustment' is explained in §4 of the final report:[36]

> ... as any fiscal measures which put into effect, in whole or in part, the destination principle (i.e. which enable exported products to be relieved of some or all of the tax charged in the exporting country in respect of similar domestic products sold to consumers on the home market and which enable imported products sold to consumers to be charged with some or all of the tax charged in the importing country in respect of similar domestic products).[37]

§5 of the final report makes it clear that, for a measure to be considered a BTA, the adjustment does not have to take place at the border, that is, at the moment a good goes through customs; it can take place at a later stage, that is, after the importation-related procedures have been completed, assuming, of course, that the rationale for its imposition is the crossing of the border: undeniably, the work of the WP concerned instruments which normally come under the purview of Art. III.2 GATT.

Some discussion regarding precisely which taxes should come under the purview of Art. III GATT had already occurred even during the negotiation stage. At the Havana Conference, for example, the following view was reflected:

> neither income taxes nor import duties fall within the scope of Art 18 (of the Havana Charter—Art III of the GATT) which is concerned solely with internal taxes on goods.[38]

No agreement was reached, but this view is typical of trading nations that were becoming increasingly anxious about the open-ended expression of the NT

---

[36] GATT Doc. BISD 18S/97ff.

[37] The destination principle was taken over from bilateral agreements negotiated in the 1930s, such as the agreement of 6 May 1936 between the US and France; see §10 of the Annex to the Working Party report on Border Tax Adjustments, op. cit. See also Irwin et al. (2008). Economists have used more or less the same definition for the term BTA. This is, for example, how Johnson and Krauss (1970) describe border tax adjustments (pp. 596–7): 'A border tax, properly interpreted, is a tax imposed when goods cross an international border, and as such must be inimical to international trade and therefore to the achievement of the economic benefits of international specialization and division of labour. A border tax adjustment, on the other hand, is an adjustment of the taxes imposed on a producer when the goods he produces cross an international border....Under the origin principle, a tax is imposed on the domestic production of goods, whether exported or not, and under the destination principle, the same tax is imposed on imported goods as on domestically-produced goods destined for consumption by domestic consumers, while domestically-produced goods destined for consumption by foreigners enjoy a rebate of the tax. The origin principle involves no tax adjustment, but the destination principle involves a border tax adjustment to the full extent of the tax.' Compare Meade (1974).

[38] §12 of the annex to the working party report on Border Tax Adjustments, op cit. These were the words of the UK delegate, one of the key delegations in the drafting of Art. III GATT; see Irwin et al. (2008) and the corresponding discussion on 'property rights on the GATT'.

provision. The WP was probably established because of the perceived 'asymmetric' attitude that GATT exhibited towards national fiscal regimes. The attempts to narrow down the scope of NT had started much earlier.

Art. III.2 GATT is not the only GATT legal provision that is relevant when it comes to operating border tax adjustments. The members of the WP agreed that five other GATT legal provisions were relevant in the examination of the GATT consistency of BTAs: Arts. I, II, VI, VIII, XVI GATT.[39]

Art. II.2(a) GATT provides that:

> Nothing in this Article shall prevent any contracting party from imposing at any time on the importation of any product:
> (a) a charge equivalent to an internal tax imposed consistently with the provisions of paragraph 2 of Article III in respect of the like domestic product or in respect of an article from which the imported product has been manufactured or produced in whole or in part.

Thus, this provision makes it clear that the trading partners can impose (domestic) taxes beyond customs duties to the extent that their taxes observe the discipline embedded in Art. III GATT.[40] Recently, the AB, in its report on *India— Additional Import Duties*, confirmed this understanding of the ambit of Art. II.2 (a) (§153).[41]

The negotiators agreed that the destination principle circumscribed the taxes that could be lawfully adjusted. §4 of the final report of the WP explains the destination principle in the following terms:

---

[39] Art. I GATT also comes into play because, unless respected, trading partners could afford a trade advantage by, for example, adjusting taxes for goods of a certain origin and not for others. Art. XVI GATT allows trading partners to exempt from taxation goods destined for consumption abroad without qualifying similar practices as subsidy. Art. VI GATT comes into play, because, unless otherwise specified, the lower price of a good that is being exported (resulting from non-taxation) *could* qualify as dumping. Finally, Art. VIII GATT was also relevant since a BTA should not be equated to a customs fee or formality for service rendered: no service is rendered in the first place when BTAs are imposed.

[40] Pauwelyn (2007) argues that a textual reading of Art. II.2(a) GATT suggests that regulatory distinctions based on non-incorporated PPMs (production process methods) are illegal. Roessler (1996 and 2003) has expressed similar views. Were this view to be upheld, a lot of policies aimed at addressing climate change would be *ipso facto* inconsistent with the GATT. In Horn and Mavroidis (2010), we have explained why similar views should be dismissed. Briefly, Art. II GATT deals with bound tariffs. Since the overwhelming majority of tariff classifications included in the HS do not include distinctions based on non-incorporated PPMs (some classifications deal with inputs), it is only to be expected that Art. II.2(a) GATT refers to inputs and final products only. Art. II GATT was not intended to circumscribe the ambit of Art. III GATT; it serves as the mechanism to exchange tariff concessions. Art. III GATT outlaws only the use of local content requirements, and as we will see *infra*, the WP on BTAs did not outlaw the use of environmental or public health measures, including regulatory distinctions on PPMs. As a result, Art. II GATT should not be read as Pauwelyn (2007) suggests. Howse and Eliason (2009) follow a different route but end up with similar results. See also Hufbauer et al. (2009).

[41] Conconi and Wouters (2010).

... enable exported products to be relieved of some or all of the tax charged in the exporting country in respect of similar domestic products sold to consumers on the home market and which enable imported products sold to consumers to be charged with some or all of the tax charged in the importing country in respect of similar domestic products.

Taxation could thus, in principle, be adjusted by both the importing and the exporting states, and the question was who should, or rather who should not, perform the adjustment? The GATT contracting parties reached agreement on some measures, and did not on many others. The extent of their agreement is reflected in the following paragraph:

> ... the Working Party concluded that there was convergence of views to the effect that taxes directly levied on products were eligible for tax adjustment. Examples of such taxes comprised specific excise duties, sales taxes and cascade taxes and the tax on value added. It was agreed that the TVA, regardless of its technical construction (fractioned collection), was equivalent in this respect to a tax levied directly—a retail or sales tax. Furthermore, the Working Party concluded that there was convergence of views to the effect that certain taxes that were not directly levied on products were not eligible for tax adjustment. Examples of such taxes comprised social security charges whether on employers or employees and payroll taxes.[42]

There was divergence of views regarding the eligibility for adjustment of *taxes occultes* and some other taxes such as property taxes. The scarcity of complaints with respect to either of these two taxes, however, persuaded negotiators to stop negotiating on them (§15 of the final report):

> The Working Party noted that there was a divergence of views with regard to the eligibility for adjustment of certain categories of tax and that these could be sub-divided into
>
> (*a*) 'Taxes occultes' which the OECD defined as consumption taxes on capital equipment, auxiliary materials and services used in the transportation and production of other taxable goods. Taxes on advertising, energy, machinery and transport were among the more important taxes which might be involved. It appeared that adjustment was not normally made for taxes occultes except in countries having a cascade tax;
>
> (*b*) Certain other taxes, such as property taxes, stamp duties and registration duties ... which are not generally considered eligible for tax adjustment. Most countries do not make adjustments for such taxes, but a few do as a few do for the payroll taxes and employers' social security charges referred to in the last sentence of paragraph 14.
>
> It was generally felt that while this area of taxation was unclear, its importance—as indicated by the scarcity of complaints reported in connexion with adjustment of taxes occultes—was not such as to justify further examination.[43]

---

[42] §14 of the final report.
[43] On the extent of disagreement, see also Genasci (2008).

Finally, there was agreement between negotiators that some taxes, such as *cascade taxes*,[44] were eligible for adjustment, though the modalities for adjusting them were not clear (§16 of the final report):

> The Working Party noted that there were some taxes which, while generally considered eligible for adjustment, presented a problem because of the difficulty in some cases of calculating exactly the amount of compensation. Examples of such difficulties were encountered in cascade taxes. For adjustment, countries operating cascade systems usually resorted to calculating average rates of rebate for categories of products rather than calculating the actual tax levied on a particular product. It was noted, however, that most cascade tax systems were to be replaced by TVA systems, and that therefore the area in which such problems occurred was diminishing. Other examples included composite goods which, on export, contained ingredients for which the Working Party agreed in principle it was administratively sensible and sufficiently accurate to rebate by average rates for a given class of goods.

The preceding analysis unambiguously supports the conclusion that the WP on BTAs did not manage to resolve all ambiguities and disagreements regarding tax adjustability. Disagreements between trading partners regarding similar issues continued to persist and some of them found their way into GATT/WTO adjudication. Notoriously, the US subsequently enacted the DISC and FSC legislations,[45] both of which were condemned, the first by a GATT Panel, the second by a WTO Panel and the AB.[46] Nevertheless, there was agreement in the WP concerning at least some of the taxes. Of interest to the coverage of Art. III GATT, which is the issue we debate here, is the following:

(a) it is clear that social security taxes are not adjustable, hence WTO Members cannot impose them on imported goods. Yes, §15 notes that some trading nations imposed them, but in §14 a convergence not to do so is reflected. No dispute on this issue has taken place since;

(b) there is uncertainty with respect to *taxes occultes*. Since no subsequent negotiation ever took place, by virtue of the *in dubio mitius* principle, one should conclude that similar taxes, in the absence of outright prohibition to do so, can lawfully be imposed and have to respect NT.

The report of the WP on BTAs was adopted by the GATT CONTRACTING PARTIES, that is, the highest organ of the GATT and the sole organ that was

---

[44] A cascade tax is a turnover tax which is applied at every stage of the production process.

[45] The FSC dispute is discussed in Chapter 6. *US—DISC*, its GATT predecessor, was adjudicated during the GATT years. At stake was US tax legislation on Domestic International Sales Corporations. In brief, a US company that qualified as a DISC company would not be subjected to US federal income tax on its current or retained export earnings. Following a complaint, the Panel found that the US tax legislation constituted an export subsidy and was thus inconsistent with Art. XVI GATT. See GATT Doc. BISD 23S/98, and 28S/114. See also the very thorough analysis of the case by Jackson (1978).

[46] On the overall stance of adjudicating bodies with respect to BTAs, see Bhagwati and Mavroidis (2004) and Démaret and Stewardson (1994).

competent to adopt similar acts. It is unclear whether it is a decision by the CONTRACTING PARTIES, and thus comes under the purview of Art. 1(b)(iv) GATT 1994, or whether it is part of the GATT *acquis*, and thus comes under the purview of Art. XVI of the Agreement Establishing the WTO.[47] No matter how it is classified, the WP report will have legal significance: if it comes under the former it should be regarded as binding on all WTO Members, whereas if it comes under the latter it should be regarded as creating legitimate expectations that WTO practice will be guided by it.[48] It seems that the better arguments lie with the view that the WP report should come under Art. 1(b)(iv) GATT 1994. After all, the WP was not convened to adjudicate a dispute between two GATT contracting parties; it was requested to discuss the treatment of tax adjustments at the GATT-wide level. In subsequent practice, a number of WTO Panel and AB reports have referred to this report, without however classifying it either as part and parcel of Art. 1(b)(iv) GATT 1994 or under Art. XVI WTO Agreement.[49] But even if one takes the view that it should be considered to be part of the GATT *acquis*, rather than be accepted as a decision, it would still retain legal value as explained above. The fact that it has been often cited in WTO case law leaves little room for doubt that recourse to it will be made again if, for example, the question of whether payroll taxes can be adjusted comes up.[50]

2.5 And for the Rest? Incomplete Contracting

We argued above that the inclusion of domestic instruments in the GATT was necessary otherwise the GATT objectives risked remaining unattained, and yet the inclusion of domestic instruments presented negotiators with more than they could have handled. First, there are an extremely large number of different domestic policy instruments with trade impact;[51] second, domestic policies are responsive to changes in the underlying economic/political environment, and as a result keep changing themselves. One possibility would have been for the

---

[47] For a detailed discussion of this issue, see Mavroidis (2008).

[48] See the relevant discussion in Chapter 1.

[49] See, for example, the Panel and AB report on *Japan—Alcoholic Beverages II*.

[50] There was some more general debate among economists as to what extent the US view that the GATT was biased against direct taxes was sensible at all. The prevailing view was that this was not the case. Grossman (1980) examined to what extent indirect taxes, like the VAT, were origin neutral. He challenged the then conventional wisdom asserting the trade neutrality of uniform indirect taxes under both the origin and destination principles and re-examined its validity in the context of a world with trade in intermediate goods. He showed that a uniform general sales tax is trade-neutral under the destination principle, but trade-distorting under the origin principle; a 'stage of processing' value added tax is non-distorting under either border tax adjustment principle.

[51] There have been some attempts to classify them. An official US document, for example (Committee on Finance, *United States Finance, Summary and Analysis of H.R 10710—The Trade Reform Act of 1973*, 26 February 1974, US Government Printing Office, Washington, DC, 1974), classifies NTBs under five broad areas (p. 2): government participation in trade; customs and administrative entry procedures; standards; specific limitations to trade; and charges on imports. Similar classifications never became policy relevant, however.

agreement to specify for each Member the policies to be pursued in each and every situation that the Member might find itself in; that is, the agreement is 'state-contingent' in economic jargon. But, of course, with the agreement intended to be in place for an extended period of time, there would be a huge number of such different economic/political situations that would call for different policy responses. As a result, WTO Members would have to be in long negotiations: the costs of negotiating and drawing up such a grand contract would be huge, and would most likely dominate the gains it would bring. Indeed, it would amount to central planning on a global scale. As well as long, negotiations would have to be consistently ongoing: societal preferences change over time as a result of knowledge, culture, religion, fashion, etc.; the larger the number of participants, the greater the likelihood that change might occur somewhere and, hence, the stronger the case for ongoing negotiations. This is one reason why trade agreements are 'incomplete', in the sense that they do not contain all the information necessary for their operation at the moment of their inception.[52] Besides, contracting social policies might be deemed politically undesirable in some quarters. Moreover, negotiators might have found it difficult to *ex ante* decide on the legality of each and every measure reflected in the agreement. Finally, for some trading nations it was unthinkable to transfer sovereignty regarding behind the border measures. Hudec (1990) reflects the following discussion (p. 24):

> Governments would have never agreed to circumscribe their freedom in all these other areas for the sake of a mere trade agreement.

Contractual incompleteness can, of course, take many forms:[53] undertakings may not be conditioned on changes in the environment; they can be 'rigid'. Undertakings can also leave 'discretion' to individual governments to determine their policies unilaterally. The problem, of course, is that in this scenario, when discretion is permitted, there are good reasons to believe that governments have incentives to use such discretion for protectionist purposes, as a substitute for the border instruments that have been bound: this is essentially where the political economy literature kicks in. Contractual incompleteness by itself is not necessarily a problem; governance problems are posed when incomplete contracts are combined with opportunism (Williamson 2005). The GATT does not eliminate the potential for such behaviour: WTO Members will usually have private information when regulating which they only in part have to reveal (by virtue of the transparency obligation)[54] and a strong incentive to cheat (by pretending, for example, to be internalizing environmental externalities when acting solely, or predominantly, in the interest of their domestic producer, and thus imposing costs

---

[52] Grossman et al. (2012).
[53] Horn et al. (2010).
[54] See the discussion on transparency in Chapter 13.

on their trading partners through beggar-thy-neighbour policies).[55] *Ex post* detection is not guaranteed, and suspicion of cheating might lead trading nations to uncooperative behaviour (e.g. fewer commitments than otherwise to liberalize trade).

Economic theory and the negotiating record see eye to eye on this score: the Chairman of the Technical Sub-Committee in charge of preparing the draft provision on NT during the London Conference (1946) noted to this effect:[56]

> Whatever we do here, we shall never be able to cover every contingency and possibility in a draft. Economic life is too varied for that, and there are all kinds of questions which are bound to arise later on. The important thing is that once we have this agreement laid down we have to act in the spirit of it. There is no doubt there will be certain difficulties, but if we are able to cover 75 or 80 or 85 per cent of them I think it will be sufficient.

They thus knowingly left the provision 'incomplete', to be gradually 'completed' through subsequent adjudication (and, eventually, renegotiation). The GATT could, of course, have been completed through renegotiation. Some renegotiation did indeed take place: the WP on BTAs nevertheless did not manage to resolve many issues. The negotiating costs of renegotiation of the GATT are anyway quite high since de facto all of the WTO Membership has to be on board. Kennedy (2010) discusses the implementation of an agreed TRIPs amendment to provide empirical evidence of the very sizeable costs associated with this procedure.

In the absence of a (re-)negotiated solution, it will be left to the WTO judge to decide whether particular interventions contravene the spirit of the 'incomplete' contract or not. The GATT/WTO judge has indeed been called to do that through case law.[57] Pushing the decision to the adjudicating bodies is not risk free, as we will see *infra*. The allocation of the burden of proof, as well as the quantum of proof required, will hold the key in developing a clear judicial strategy towards distinguishing the wheat from the chaff, so to speak. The WTO judge does not start with a clean slate and his/her hands are not free. The judge is an agent bound by the agency contract signed with the principals, the WTO Members. The contract reads:

> The dispute settlement system of the WTO is a central element in providing security and predictability to the multilateral trading system. The Members recognize that it serves to preserve the rights and obligations of Members under the covered agreements, and to clarify the existing provisions of those agreements in accordance with

---

[55] Maskin and Tirole (1999) have persuasively argued that the manner in which we think about incomplete contracts is not optimal. They point out that, instead of discussing contingencies, contractual parties could be discussing payoffs. There are doubts, however, as to whether their model can fit the GATT. With respect to some of the policies (potentially) covered by NT, it is at least doubtful that governments would be willing to negotiate specific disciplines and (eventually) payoffs.

[56] UN Doc. E/PC/T/C.II/PRO/PV/7.

[57] Maggi and Staiger (2011). Similar thoughts have been expressed in Saggi and Trachtman (2011).

customary rules of interpretation of public international law. Recommendations and rulings of the DSB cannot add to or diminish the rights and obligations provided in the covered agreements.

It follows that WTO judges cannot undo the balance of rights and obligations as struck by the WTO Members: they must respect the policy space entrusted to the WTO by all trading nations and cannot transfer sovereignty to the international plane if principals did not agree themselves to such a transfer.[58] Their job of course would have been easier if the contract had been more clear, more 'complete'. Alas, it is not. Their discretion to clarify is not open-ended either: WTO judges, from the first case they were called to address (*US—Gasoline*), have understood the reference to 'customary rules of interpretation of public international law' included in Art. 3.2 DSU as tantamount to a reference to the VCLT. The VCLT contains many interpretative elements but does not decide how much weight should be given to each one of them.[59] Consequently, the WTO judge is in a non-enviable position: called upon to interpret one incomplete contract (the GATT) through another (the VCLT). From a pure methodological perspective, contract incompleteness demands from the judge to:

(a) decide on the coverage of this provision;
(b) decide on the understanding of its key terms.

There is some indication regarding coverage already in the body of the provision. Art. III.5 GATT refers to mixing requirements (local content), while Arts. III.2 and III.4 GATT refer to unidentified instruments of a fiscal and non-fiscal nature. Reference to mixing requirements has a twofold function: on the one hand, the judge cannot commit a false negative and overlook challenges against similar measures since they are explicitly mentioned in the body of the provisions and hence unambiguously covered by it; on the other hand, similar to mixing requirements, measures should be covered as well since one can reasonably assume that the legislator included the most representative of a class of measures in its indicative list.

Art III.2 GATT refers to taxes and charges and requests from WTO Members to ensure that imported products will not be subjected *directly or indirectly* to taxes

---

[58] Recall our discussion in Chapter 1, that there is no *stare decisis* in WTO. Still, the legitimacy of WTO courts depends largely on the manner in which they treat their own case law. They are expected to apply the same law to the same transactions irrespective of the identity of the parties involved in a particular dispute. There is definitely something in the colloquial saying 'justice must be blind'. In doing that, judges and courts will be preparing their own demise: they will make law so predictable that in good faith there will be little to argue about. Of course, new laws, and new knowledge regarding the manner in which specific issues should be treated, cast some doubt on this statement. The basic mould should hold though.

[59] When following contextual—as opposed to teleological interpretations—respecting the *in dubio mitius* maxim, the WTO judge runs a substantially lower risk of undoing the balance of rights and obligations as struck by the principals.

in excess of those applied to domestic like products.[60] Art. III.4 GATT, on the other hand, covers all internal laws, regulations, and requirements 'affecting' the life of imported products in a given market. The term 'affecting' denotes the legislative will to cast the net, if in doubt, wide rather than narrow. To our knowledge, there is no negotiating record indicating that specific transactions were intended to be excluded.[61] The wording of this provision, as well as its negotiating record, thus give support to the view that it was intended to be an all-encompassing provision.

The term 'affecting' nevertheless should not be taken as carte blanche to bring under the NT discipline anything that affects trade. Trade of course, directly or indirectly, actually or potentially, is affected by every field of regulatory activity. This does not mean that every field of regulatory activity has to observe NT across the board. The GATT is about trade in goods, and its discipline cannot extend, for example, to services. The very signing of a separate agreement, the GATS, is proof of this point. Moreover, it cannot extend to investment protection. This point was made clear in the GATT Panel report on *Canada—FIRA*, as we saw *supra*.[62]

GATT Panels and WTO adjudicating bodies have consistently held that not only de jure, but also de facto discrimination is punished by Art. III GATT. Discussing MFN in the services context, the AB in its report on *EC—Bananas III* explained why the extension to de facto discrimination was necessary (§233):

> [I]f Article II was not applicable to *de facto* discrimination, it would not be difficult—and, indeed, it would be a good deal easier in the case of trade in services, than in the case of trade in goods—to devise discriminatory measures aimed at circumventing the basic purpose of that Article. (italics in the original)

Art. III GATT deals with non-discrimination as well, and for this reason the same logic should find application in its context as well. While de jure discrimination is easy to define (since by law a measure confers an advantage on a class of goods because of their origin), it is not easy to define de facto discrimination. Indeed, rare are definitions of this term in case law. The passage quoted *infra* from the Panel report on *Canada—Pharmaceutical Patents* is a rarity (§7.101):

> [d]e facto discrimination is a general term describing the legal conclusion that an ostensibly neutral measure transgresses a non-discrimination norm because its actual

---

[60] §13 of the annex to the Working Party report on Border Tax Adjustments, GATT Doc. L/3464, adopted on 2 December 1970, GATT Doc. BISD 18S/97ff.

[61] Irwin et al. (2008). This is not to suggest that NT can *equally* meaningfully apply to *all* domestic policies/measures. Its application to substantive (as opposed to procedural) antitrust laws is, for example, problematic: a WTO Member which accepts a merger between two domestic companies and, subsequently, rejects a merger between a foreign and a domestic company when all four operate in the same relevant product market has not necessarily violated NT; moving from say six to five or from five to four companies in a market involves different considerations (*inter alia*, because the degree of concentration as measured in Herfindal-Hirschman Index terms will be different).

[62] §2.2 of the report.

effect is to impose differentially disadvantageous consequences on certain parties, and because those differential effects are found to be wrong or unjustifiable. (italics in the original)

Moreover, they have further held that NT covers all goods irrespective of whether their import duties had been bound or left unbound. The AB left no doubt of its interpretation in this respect (*Japan—Alcoholic Beverages II*, p. 17):

> The Article III national treatment obligation is a general prohibition on the use of internal taxes and other internal regulatory measures so as to afford protection to domestic production. This obligation clearly extends also to products not bound under Article II.

Finally, we should note that the *locus* where the measure will be enforced does not necessarily prejudge the coverage of Art. III GATT: domestic measures enforced at the border come, according to the Interpretative Note ad Art. III of the GATT, under the purview of Art. III GATT. Thus, a sales ban which is enforced at the border (and could be mistaken for a trade embargo) will still be considered to be a sales ban (and, consequently, come under the purview of Art. III GATT).

The judge can rely on a very rich negotiating record when it comes to the interpretation of the key terms ('like products' etc.). Although recourse to the *travaux préparatoires* is at the discretion of the judge in the VCLT system, the judge would be well-advised to check there in order to form an idea regarding the rationale for this provision. In completing a contract, the national judge is in a privileged position compared to the international judge. Assume, for example, that an heir kills a relative in order to accelerate his becoming wealthy; even if the will says nothing about this contingency, the judge can always rely on domestic penal/criminal law and punish the heir: in doing that, the judge will be completing the will through recourse to domestic public order. What is the equivalent to domestic public order in international law? For some, it is the *jus cogens*, the law linking the whole international community, and WTO adjudicators should strive to interpret the WTO in this context.[63] Although, so far, there has been no case where the WTO judge has had to ask this question, one might legitimately ask the question whether *jus cogens* exhausts the non-WTO law that the WTO judge can legitimately use in interpreting the WTO contract. The response, as we have seen, is negative: WTO Panels and the AB have already accepted the HS Convention as the legal context for the GATT.[64] There are other rules of customary international law which, if neglected, could render WTO legal institutions, if not obsolete, highly unmanageable: how could, for example, Art. III GATT function unless one

---

[63] Benedek (1991) was the first to provide a comprehensive discussion of this issue followed by Pauwelyn (2003). Whereas the former takes an outside-in look and attempts to review the GATT from a public international law perspective, the latter takes an inside-out look, asking the question how much of public international law is relevant when interpreting the GATT.

[64] For a comprehensive discussion regarding the attitude of the WTO adjudicating bodies in this respect, see Mavroidis (2008).

sees around it a well-defined jurisdictional scope?[65] The WTO judge has not made direct reference to jurisdictional rules in public international law, although the AB in *US—Shrimp* did mention the need for a nexus between the regulating state and the regulated transaction. The WTO judge has been, for good reasons, cautious when it comes to completing the contract through non-WTO law: silence in the WTO contract could be interpreted either as tacit acceptance of an unidentified legal context or as an expression of outright irrelevance. Conscious of the limits imposed by Art. 3.2 DSU, the WTO judge should always pick the latter option where silence speaks volumes.[66]

Non-WTO law, though, is only marginally interesting for our discussion here. After all, what matters when say an environmental measure is being challenged before a WTO Panel is not whether it has been agreed within the context of an MEA (multilateral environmental agreement), but whether it meets the various requirements of Art. III GATT.

With this in mind, we can proceed to our discussion of the substantive requirements of NT. Art. III GATT divides the measures coming within its ambit into fiscal and non-fiscal measures, and we will follow the statutory taxonomy.

2.6 Fiscal Measures

Art. III.2 GATT reflects the discipline with respect to fiscal measures. 'Fiscal measures' is a generic term that should be understood as covering domestic taxes and other charges of pecuniary nature, e.g. value added taxes (VAT), consumption taxes etc. The only indication we have as to what criterion Panels should employ in order to decide whether a measure is a fiscal measure coming under the purview of this provision comes from the report on *China—Auto Parts*, where the AB held in §§163–5:

> ...a key indicator of whether a charge constitutes an 'internal charge' within the meaning of Article III:2 of the GATT 1994 is 'whether the obligation to pay such charge accrues because of an *internal* factor (e.g., because the product was *re-sold* internally or because the product was *used* internally), in the sense that such 'internal factor' occurs *after the importation* of the product of one Member into the territory of another Member.' We also observe that the Harmonized System does not serve as relevant context for the interpretation of the term 'internal charges' in Article III:2. In sum, we see the Harmonized System as context that is most relevant to issues of classification of products. The Harmonized System complements Members' Schedules and confirms the general principle that it is 'the 'objective characteristics' of the product in question when presented for classification at the border' that determine their classification and, consequently, the applicable customs duty. The Harmonized System, and the product categories that it contains, cannot trump the criteria

---

[65] Horn and Mavroidis (2008).
[66] Ibid.

contained in Article II:1(b) and Article III:2, which distinguish a border measure from an internal charge under the GATT 1994. Among WTO Members, it is these GATT provisions that prevail, and that define the relevant characteristics of ordinary customs duties for WTO purposes. Thus, even if the Harmonized System and GIR 2(a) would allow auto parts imported in multiple shipments to be classified as complete vehicles based on subsequent common assembly, as China suggests, this would not *per se* affect the criteria that define an ordinary customs duty under Article II:1(b). In any case, the Panel did not accept the broad interpretation of GIR 2(a) suggested by China. Rather, the Panel remarked that its findings on the meaning of 'as presented' in GIR 2(a) did not appear to contradict its finding as to the meaning of 'on their importation' in Article II:1(b).

In our view, accepting that a charge imposed on auto parts following, and as a consequence of, their assembly into a complete motor vehicle can constitute an ordinary customs duty would significantly limit the scope of 'internal charges' that fall within the scope of Article III:2 of the GATT 1994. We also share the concerns expressed by the Panel to the effect that the security and predictability of tariff concessions would be undermined if ordinary customs duties could be applied based on factors and events that occur internally, rather than at the moment and by virtue of importation, and that this, in turn, would upset the carefully negotiated and balanced structure of key GATT rights and obligations, including the different disciplines imposed on ordinary customs duties and internal charges.[67]

Art. III.2 GATT distinguishes between two classes of goods, directly competitive or substitutable (DCS) and like goods. Case law has established that like goods are a subset of DCS goods (in the sense that sharing a DCS relationship is a necessary but not sufficient condition for likeness), The AB in its report on *Korea—Alcoholic Beverages* held as much (§118):

> 'Like' products are a subset of directly competitive or substitutable products: all like products are, by definition, directly competitive or substitutable products, whereas not all 'directly competitive or substitutable' products are 'like'.

It follows that case law regarding the definition of DCS is *ipso facto* relevant for the interpretation of the term 'like products'. For this reason, we will start our discussion with an explanation of the discipline on DCS goods.

2.6.1 DCS Products

A WTO Member cannot tax an imported good so as to afford protection to the domestic DCS good. What is the rationale for including a discipline on DCS goods? Recall from our discussion earlier on in this chapter that the overall purpose of NT is to introduce in the GATT an insurance policy against the risk that the value of tariff concessions be eviscerated through subsequent (to the conclusion of a concession) unilateral action. What was needed then was a guarantee that if say

---

[67] Following this reasoning the Panel and the AB found that a 25 per cent duty imposed by China on auto parts was an internal charge in violation of Art. III.2 GATT; see the discussion in Wauters and Vandenbussche (2010).

Home agreed to bind its tariffs on butter at say 5 per cent, this 5 per cent *ad valorem* imposition would be the only imposition that would fall exclusively on imported butter. If butter originating in Foreign would then be subjected to a VAT scheme applied by Home, this scheme should fall in an even-handed manner on domestic and imported butter. Should it also fall in an even-handed manner on domestic butter and foreign margarine? Yes, is the response suggested by the inclusion of DCS products in the NT discipline. The records of the Havana Conference support this response: they reveal some interesting discussions whereby negotiators advance specific examples to demonstrate their understanding of the inclusion of DCS products in the NT provision. It was stated, for example, that an internal law that might help a domestic product (say, butter), but which hit equally imported and domestic oleomargarine (a DCS product), would not violate NT, if domestic production of oleomargarine were substantial.[68] Moreover, existing internal taxes which afforded protection to DCS products in cases in which there was no substantial production of the like product could be maintained, subject to negotiation for their elimination or reduction.[69] Following a US proposal to this effect, the obligation to accord NT was extended to cover not only like, but also DCS products,[70] the intent being to ensure that, in the absence of domestic production of like products, taxes could not be used to favour domestic DCS products.[71]

Eventually, negotiators agreed to drop references to 'substantial production' and provide for a blanket prohibition to use fiscal measures so as to afford protection to all domestic DCS goods. In this vein, §17 of the report of the Working Party on Border Tax Adjustments, quoting from the preparatory work of the GATT, reflects the following passage:

> During the drafting of the Havana Charter, and thus the GATT, it was felt that this might occur where there was no, or negligible, domestic production of the imported product. Various examples were quoted; it was for instance suggested that a country which did not produce coffee could not impose tax on coffee, unless it placed a similar tax on chicory, a competitive product.

It seems thus that the reason for including the DCS category was that, since tariff concessions would not cover all products, the value of tariff concessions could be negatively affected if the coverage of the NT discipline did not extend beyond identical (like) to competing products as well. Assume that Home produces chicory but no coffee, and Foreign produces coffee but no chicory. Home has no interest at all in securing a promise from Foreign that it will apply a certain tariff

---

[68] Havana Reports at pp. 61–7. The Havana Conference signals the end of the negotiation on NT: Art. III GATT has remained unchanged since the last negotiations in the early months of 1948 in Havana.

[69] UN Doc. E/PC/T/186.

[70] UN Doc. E/PC/T/W7150 at p. 5.

[71] UN Doc. E/PC/T/174 at p. 6.

binding on coffee and it will not request one; the same is true of Foreign and chicory. Yet, when Home exports chicory to Foreign, its exports will compete with coffee in the market of Foreign. Home has secured a tariff promise on chicory from Foreign; it needs insurance that this tariff promise will be safeguarded in the product market where its chicory will compete, otherwise the tariff binding it secured is of no use. What is the use of a 10 per cent tariff promise to Home by Foreign on chicory, if subsequently Foreign can unilaterally impose a 0 per cent non-discriminatory consumption tax on coffee, and a 100 per cent non-discriminatory consumption tax on chicory? Most likely, Foreign consumers will vote with their feet and turn to coffee, walking away from chicory. To safeguard the value of the tariff concession hence, NT must cover DCS goods as well. The inclusion of DCS de facto amounts to an obligation assumed by trading nations to behave consistently within this category.[72]

In a nutshell:

(a) because concessions are exchanged by looking at tariff lines, but their value depends on competition with other products—that is, products with which they might be substitutable although they do not share the same tariff classification—in specific markets; and

(b) because the purpose of NT is to safeguard the value of concessions;

(c) it is imperative to include the DCS category in the NT provision.

Point (a) deserves an additional explanation: tariff classifications are not and cannot be a perfect reproduction of what would be termed in antitrust a relevant product market. This is so because for geographic, cultural, and other reasons markets differ. Recall that the objective of NT is to harmonize conditions of competition *within* and not *across* markets.[73] Tariff classifications are an approximation but no reproduction of relevant product markets. Yet, it is the latter that matters in our discussion since, when entering a foreign market, goods will be competing with substitutable goods irrespective of their tariff classification. It is consumers and not WCO bureaucrats that will decide on their fate. If tariff classifications were in a one-to-one correspondence with relevant product markets across the world, there would be no need for the DCS category. Introducing thus, the DCS category was some sort of an anti-circumvention device aimed at ensuring that the overarching purpose of Art. III GATT (not to undo the value of tariff concessions through subsequent unilateral action) would be honoured.

---

[72] Consistency is a proxy for the absence of protectionist intent, and we will discuss it in detail in Chapter 7, since it is a legal requirement that adopted SPS measures must observe.

[73] Through non-violation complaints (NVCs), WTO Members can further protect the value of their concessions. To this effect, they would have to show that an unanticipated change in the policy of their trading partners has had a negative impact on the trade of their goods; see Bagwell et al. (2002) for a more detailed explanation of its rationale, and Palmeter and Mavroidis (2004) for a discussion of the legal requirements.

The AB in its report on *Japan—Alcoholic Beverages II* provided its understanding of the term 'DCS' products. This dispute arose because of a Japanese taxation scheme which, while on its face neutral, subjected predominantly Western products to a heavier taxation than predominantly Japanese products: as a result, '*sochu*' (an alcoholic beverage predominantly produced in Japan) was subjected to less burdensome taxation than, *inter alia*, whisky (an alcoholic beverage predominantly produced in Europe and the US). Europe and the US protested, arguing that the products at hand were at least DCS if not like products. The Panel had already accepted that all of the products concerned (with the exception of vodka, which was deemed to be a like product to *sochu*) were DCS products. The AB upheld the Panel's findings in this regard. In its view:

(a) physical properties and characteristics;
(b) consumer preferences;
(c) end-uses; and
(d) tariff classification

are appropriate elements to take into account when defining whether two products are DCS. Importantly, upholding the Panel's findings in this regard, the AB made it clear that the test to define whether two products are DCS is in the marketplace, in the sense that it is consumers who will ultimately decide whether two products are indeed in competition with each other. To this effect, econometric indicators (for instance, cross-price elasticity)[74] are relevant when defining whether two products are indeed in competition with each other. The EU had submitted some consumer surveys to this effect, suggesting that Japanese consumers in the absence of discriminatory taxation would be prepared to substitute a host of Western drinks for *sochu* (p. 25):

> In this case, the Panel emphasized the need to look not only at such matters as physical characteristics, common end-uses, and tariff classifications, but also at the 'market place.' This seems appropriate. The GATT 1994 is a commercial agreement, and the WTO is concerned, after all, with markets. It does not seem inappropriate to look at competition in the relevant markets as one among a number of means of identifying the broader category of products that might be described as 'directly competitive or substitutable'.
>
> Nor does it seem inappropriate to examine elasticity of substitution as one means of examining those relevant markets. The Panel did not say that cross-price elasticity of demand is '*the* decisive criterion' (footnote omitted) for determining whether products are directly competitive or substitutable. The Panel stated the following:

---

[74] Cross-price elasticity of demand provides information about the demand relationship between two products, by capturing how a price increase for one product increases the demand for another product. (Formally, it is defined as the percentage change in quantity demanded of some good X divided by the percentage change in price for good Y.) Adjudicating bodies have not so far provided any guidance on what values of cross-price elasticity (e.g. 1, more than 1?) would normally be necessary for two products to be considered DCS.

In the Panel's view, the decisive criterion in order to determine whether two products are directly competitive or substitutable is whether they have common end-uses, *inter alia*, as shown by elasticity of substitution.

We agree. And, we find the Panel's legal analysis of whether the products are 'directly competitive or substitutable products' in paragraphs 6. 28–6.32 of the Panel Report to be correct. (italics and emphasis in the original)

What followed after this case is a consistent dilution of this test: in *Korea— Alcoholic Beverages*, the AB held that a decision that two goods are DCS can be based on either econometric or non-econometric indicators, the two methods used to define whether two goods are DCS being of equal value in the eyes of the AB. In this case, the facts were similar to those in *Japan—Alcoholic Beverages II*: beverages predominantly produced in Korea (*soju* and diluted *soju*) were hit by a substantially lower tax burden than their counterparts which were predominantly produced in the EU, Canada, and the US (vodka, whisky, etc.). The EU, Canada, and the US complained, arguing that the Korean regime was GATT-inconsistent. Korea argued that the products concerned were not DCS in the first place: the price of (diluted) *soju* was only a small fraction of the price of the Western drinks at hand, and consequently changes in the price of *soju* would not lead its consumers to consumption of Western drinks. Following the analysis in *Japan—Alcoholic Beverages II* and the relevance of econometric indicators in deciding whether two products are DCS, Korea argued that with respect to (diluted) *soju* at least, no claim under Art. III.2 GATT could be sustained.

Complaining parties claimed that the fact that the Western drinks hit by higher taxation were in a DCS relationship with a similar drink (*sochu*) in a similar market (Japan) provided enough evidence that *soju* was also a DCS product to the same drinks. The Panel essentially upheld the complaining parties' view, holding that the products were indeed in a DCS relationship. Only a reading of the AB report on *Japan–Alcoholic Beverages II*, whereby cross-price elasticity would be elevated to *the* decisive criterion conferring DCS status, would lead the Panel to rule otherwise. Such a reading of Art. III.2 GATT, however, was in the Panel's eyes unwarranted. The AB upheld the Panel's findings and explained which non-econometric indicators can help establish a DCS relationship across two goods (§§114ff and especially 133–4, 135–8):

1. Potential Competition
   . . . In our view, the word 'substitutable' indicates that the requisite relationship *may* exist between products that are not, at a given moment, considered by consumers to be substitutes but which are, nonetheless, *capable* of being substituted for one another . . . .
2. Expectations
   As we have said, the object and purpose of Article III is the maintenance of equality of competitive conditions for imported and domestic products.
3. 'Trade Effects' Test
   . . . the Panel stated that if a particular degree of competition had to be shown in quantitative terms, that would be similar to requiring proof that a tax measure has

a particular impact on trade. It considered such an approach akin to a 'type of trade effects' test.

We do not consider the Panel's reasoning on this point to be flawed.

4. Nature of Competition

The Panel considered that in analyzing whether products are 'directly competitive or substitutable,' the focus should be on the *nature* of competition and not on its *quantity*... For the reasons set above, we share the Panel's reluctance to rely unduly on quantitative analyses of the competitive relationship. In our view, an approach that focused solely on the quantitative overlap of competition would, in essence, make cross-price elasticity *the* decisive criterion in determining whether products are 'directly competitive or substitutable.' We do not, therefore, consider that the Panel's use of the term 'nature of competition' is questionable.

5. Evidence from the Japanese Market

...It seems to us that evidence from other markets may be pertinent to the examination of the market at issue, particularly when demand on that market has been influenced by regulatory barriers to trade or to competition. Clearly, not every other market will be relevant to the market at issue. But if another market displays characteristics similar to the market at issue, then evidence of consumer demand in that other market may have some relevance to the market at issue. This, however, can only be determined on a case-by-case basis, taking account of all relevant facts. (emphasis in the original)[75]

The AB, in a subsequent case that we discuss *infra* (*EC—Asbestos*), went one step further and held that on occasion there is no need to look at the market at all, applying either econometric or non-econometric indicators, since the opinion of the 'reasonable consumer' could be decisive.

In *Korea—Taxes on Alcoholic Beverages,* the AB repeated that the criteria already mentioned in the WP on BTAs were appropriate in deciding whether two goods are DCS: physical characteristics, properties of the product, end-uses, consumer preferences, and even tariff classification can be used to this effect. It did not establish any hierarchy across the various criteria, nor did it clarify whether they must be cumulatively met for two goods to be DCS. It kept its cards close to its chest in this and subsequent cases, leaving the impression that some sort of 'qualitative' judgment was appropriate in similar cases. The precise parameters of this intellectual process remain unknown.

One can take issue with the decision of the AB not to insist on and strengthen its decision in *Japan—Alcoholic Beverages II.* True, it did not hold there that econometric indicators are the only way to define whether two goods are DCS. And indeed this cannot be the case always. But it is problematic that the

---

[75] In the case at hand, the argument was made that demand in Korea was *latent* because of the regulatory barriers that impeded access for Western drinks. It did not, however, beyond the generic references in the passage included above, refer specifically to these barriers. Hence, evidence from third-country markets was necessary to establish whether *soju* and a series of Western beverages were indeed *DCS* products. Korea pointed out that the price of *shochu* was higher than that of *soju*, and closer to that of the Western drinks. Note also that there have not been any *serious* challenges regarding likeness in subsequent case law.

relative price of the goods that are compared does not feature among the criteria that it uses to define whether two goods are DCS. There are of course some goods with inelastic demand, as there are a few consumers with unlimited purchasing power. But the overwhelming majority of consumers base their purchasing decisions for the overwhelming majority of the goods they buy in the market on scarcity of financial resources: every purchase has an opportunity cost, and price decisively affects purchasing behaviour. The AB decided to close its eyes to this simple reality of life by pronouncing in favour of the, under all circumstances, equal validity of decisions to show DCS relationship through use of econometric and non-econometric indicators.[76]

Demonstrating DCS relationship is only the first step towards establishing violation of Art. III.2 GATT; the second step is to show that the challenged fiscal measure is applied so as to afford protection to domestic production (ASATAP). To be precise, Art. III.2 GATT makes it clear that taxation of two DCS products is GATT-inconsistent, if it operates in a manner that is not consistent with Art. III.1 GATT. This is where the ASATAP requirement is featured. The Interpretative Note ad Art III of the GATT (to which Art. III.2 GATT refers) further explains that a taxation scheme operates ASATAP if a pair of products is not 'similarly' taxed: it does, in other terms, offer (at least) one instance where taxation across DCS products operates ASATAP, that is, the case of dissimilar taxation. Two interrelated interpretative questions arise in this context:

(a) How should we understand the terms 'not similarly taxed' appearing in the Interpretative Note ad Art III of the GATT?
(b) Does *any* dissimilar taxation suffice for a tax scheme to operate ASATAP?

In *Japan—Alcoholic Beverages II*, the AB provided its first comprehensive response to these questions when it held (p. 27):

> Unlike that of Article III:2, first sentence, the language of Article III:2, second sentence, specifically invokes Article III:1. The significance of this distinction lies in the fact that whereas Article III:1 acts implicitly in addressing the two issues that

---

[76] Horn and Mavroidis (2004) do not agree with the methodology the AB used in its report on *Korea—Alcoholic Beverages* to define whether the products concerned were like/DCS. In particular, in their view, the AB does not seem to recognize that the characteristics it considers to assess the extent of consumer likeness (end-uses, physical characteristics, etc.) are reflected in a cross-price elasticity estimation. In the author's view, statistical analysis should be the primary method of establishing consumer preferences for the products at stake. These other indicators are imperfect substitutes to employ in cases where there is not enough data, or its quality is too poor, to undertake statistical analysis. In contrast, the AB seemed to view neither of the two approaches as being conceptually superior. In a subsequent case, *EC—Asbestos*, which we discuss in detail *infra*, the AB diluted its test even further: it held that likeness (and DCS relationship) can be defined by asking whether a 'reasonable' consumer would have treated two goods as competing with each other. In name, the test is still in the marketplace. In name only, though, is this the case: not only is there no need to use econometric indicators, there is probably (in some cases at least) no need to conduct consumer surveys since it is the opinion of 'reasonable' consumers that matters.

must be considered in applying the first sentence, it acts explicitly as an entirely separate issue that must be addressed along with two other issues that are raised in applying the second sentence. Giving full meaning to the text and to its context, three separate issues must be addressed to determine whether an internal tax measure is inconsistent with Article III:2, second sentence. These three issues are whether:

(1) the imported products and the domestic products are '*directly competitive or substitutable product*' *which are in competition with each other*;

(2) the directly competitive or substitutable imported and domestic products are '*not similarly taxed*' (attr); and

(3) the dissimilar taxation of the directly competitive or substitutable imported domestic products is '*applied . . . so as to afford protection to domestic production.*' (emphasis in the original)

Hence, in the AB's view, Art III.1 GATT is relevant for the whole of Art. III.2 GATT, but its impact on the interpretation of the first sentence (dealing with like products) is not symmetric with its impact on the second sentence (dealing with DCS products):

(a) with respect to like products, taxation in excess of the imported like product *ipso facto* amounts to a violation of the ASATAP requirement;

(b) whereas with respect to *DCS* products, establishment of taxation in excess of the imported product is a necessary but not sufficient condition for finding that a measure operates so as to afford protection.

The AB effectively reduced the value of the Interpretative Note ad Art. III GATT: dissimilar taxation across *sochu* and whisky was not in its eyes in and of itself enough to condemn Japan. It was in the Panel's eyes; the AB wanted something more. What exactly? It provided the response to the question at pp. 29–32 of its report, the relevant passages of which we quote:

> The Panel was of the view that also small tax differences could influence the competitive relationship between directly competing distilled liquors, but the existence of protective taxation could be established only in the light of the particular circumstances of each case and there could be a *de minimis* level below which a tax difference ceased to have the protective effect prohibited by Article III:2, second sentence.
>
> . . .
>
> To detect whether the taxation was protective, the panel in the 1987 case examined a number of factors that it concluded were 'sufficient evidence of fiscal distortions of the competitive relationship between imported distilled liquors and domestic shochu affording protection to the domestic production of shochu.'
>
> . . .
>
> These factors included the considerably lower specific tax rates on shochu than on imported directly competitive or substitutable products; the imposition of high *ad valorem* taxes on imported alcoholic beverages and the absence of *ad valorem* taxes on shochu; the fact that shochu was almost exclusively produced in Japan and that the lower taxation of shochu did 'afford protection to domestic production'; and the mutual substitutability of these distilled liquors.
>
> . . .

Although it is true that the aim of a measure may not be easily ascertained, nevertheless its protective application can most often be discerned from the design, the architecture, and the revealing structure of a measure. The very magnitude of the dissimilar taxation in a particular case may be evidence of such a protective application, as the Panel rightly concluded in this case. Most often, there will be other factors to be considered as well. In conducting this inquiry, panels should give full consideration to all the relevant facts and all the relevant circumstances in any given case.

Thus, having stated the correct legal approach to apply with respect to Article III:2, second sentence, the Panel then equated dissimilar taxation above a *de minimis* level with the separate and distinct requirement of demonstrating that the tax measure 'affords protection to domestic production.' As previously stated, a finding that 'directly competitive or substitutable products' are 'not similarly taxed' is necessary to find a violation of Article III:2, second sentence. Yet this is not enough. The dissimilar taxation must be more than *de minimis*. It may be so much more that it will be clear from that very differential that the dissimilar taxation was applied 'so as to afford protection.' In some cases, that may be enough to show a violation. In this case, the Panel concluded that it was enough. Yet in other cases, there may be other factors that will be just as relevant or more relevant to demonstrating that the dissimilar taxation at issue was applied 'so as to afford protection.' In any case, the three issues that must be addressed in determining whether there is such a violation must be addressed clearly and separately in each case and on a case-by-case basis.

. . .

Thus, through a combination of high import duties and differentiated internal taxes, Japan manages to 'isolate' domestically produced shochu from foreign competition, be it foreign produced shochu or any other of the mentioned white and brown spirits. (italics in the original)

Were we to attempt to distil the methodology that will help us establish whether the ASATAP requirement has been met in future cases, then the following seems pertinent as far as the AB attitude is concerned:

(a) there is an undefined *de minimis* level below which no ASATAP requirement can be established. The AB did not come up with a number here but the context supports the idea that the tax differential must affect the competitive relationship across two goods (domestic, imported), and if not, then Art. III.2 GATT is not violated;

(b) the tax differential (above *de minimis* anyway) does not necessarily equate to the ASATAP requirement;

   a. sometimes the tax differential because of its magnitude might in and of itself prove that a measure is ASATAP to domestic production;[77]

   b. some other times, when the tax differential is more than *de minimis* but not substantial enough, recourse to other relevant factors and relevant circumstances might be necessary;

---

[77] For a case falling into this category, see the Panel report on *Philippines—Distilled Spirits* at §§ 7.180ff.

(c) relevant other factors could be the design, the architecture, and the revealing structure of the measure;

(d) relevant circumstances could be the import regime for the particular goods.

In *Chile—Alcoholic Beverages*, the AB was asked to pronounce on the consistency of the Chilean tax system for alcoholic beverages with the GATT: the scheme distinguished between two categories of alcoholic beverages, using alcoholic content as the distinguishing criterion: below 35° and above 39°. The complaining party (EU) had argued that many Western products of slightly more than 39° were DCS products to Chilean products of less than 35° and that the tax differential operated ASATAP. In the view of exporters of 'Western' alcoholic drinks, the Chilean tax regime favoured predominantly locally produced alcoholic beverages (some categories of *pisco*). Chile responded that its scheme did not condition the payment of the higher tax on the origin of the product, and, moreover, that in the 39° and above tax category the majority of the products hit by high taxation were domestic. As a result, in Chile's view, no protection could result from such a taxation scheme (§58).

The AB upheld the Panel's finding, and condemned the Chilean fiscal scheme. It first held that the tax differential (27 per cent and 47 per cent) across the two categories of lower and higher alcoholic content drinks was more than *de minimis* (§§44ff). It then asked the question whether the dissimilar taxation supported the conclusion that it was ASATAP to the domestic product (§§64–6):

> We note, furthermore, that, according to the Panel, approximately 75 per cent of all domestic production has an alcohol content of 35° or less and is, therefore, taxed at the lowest rate of 27 per cent *ad valorem*. Moreover, according to figures supplied to the Panel by Chile, approximately *half* of all domestic production has an alcohol content of 35° and is, therefore, located on the line of the progression of the tax at the point *immediately before* the steep increase in tax rates from 27 per cent *ad valorem*. The start of the highest tax bracket, with a rate of 47 per cent *ad valorem*, coincides with the point at which most imported beverages are found. Indeed, according to the Panel, that tax bracket contains approximately 95 per cent of all directly competitive or substitutable imports.
>
> Although the tax rates increase steeply for beverages with an alcohol content of more than 35° and up to 39°, there are, in fact, very few beverages on the Chilean market, either domestic or imported, with an alcohol content of between 35° and 39°. The graduation of the rates for beverages with an alcohol content of between 35° and 39° does not, therefore, serve to tax distilled alcoholic beverages on a progressive basis. Indeed, the steeply graduated progression of the tax rates between 35° and 39° alcohol content seems anomalous and at odds with the otherwise linear nature of the tax system. With the exception of the progression of rates between 35° and 39° alcohol content, this system simply applies one of two fixed rates of taxation, either 27 per cent *ad valorem* or 47 per cent *ad valorem*, each of which applies to distilled alcoholic beverages with a broad range of alcohol content, that is, 27 per cent for beverages with an alcoholic content of *up to 35°* and 47 per cent for beverages with an alcohol content of *more than 39°*.

> In practice, therefore, the New Chilean System will operate largely as if there were only two tax brackets: the first applying a rate of 27 per cent *ad valorem* which ends at the point at which most domestic beverages, by volume, are found, and the second applying a rate of 47 per cent *ad valorem* which begins at the point at which most imports, by volume, are found. The magnitude of the difference between these two rates is also considerable. The absolute difference of 20 percentage points between the two rates represents a 74 per cent increase in the lowest rate of 27 per cent *ad valorem*. Accordingly, examination of the design, architecture and structure of the New Chilean System tends to reveal that the application of dissimilar taxation of directly competitive or substitutable products will 'afford protection to domestic production.' (italics and emphasis in the original)

Note that the AB agreed that, as a matter of fact, most of the alcoholic drinks hit by the higher taxation were of Chilean origin. It dismissed the relevance of this observation for the interpretation of the ASATAP requirement in the following terms (§67):

> It is true, as Chile points out, that domestic products are not only subject to the highest tax rate but also comprise the major part of the volume of sales in that bracket. This fact does not, however, by itself outweigh the other relevant factors, which tend to reveal the protective application of the New Chilean System. The relative proportion of domestic versus imported products within a particular fiscal category is not, in and of itself, decisive of the appropriate characterization of the total impact of the New Chilean system under Article III:2, second sentence, of the GATT 1994. This provision, as noted earlier, provides for equality of competitive conditions of *all* directly competitive or substitutable imported products, in relation to domestic products, and not simply, as Chile argues, those imported products within a particular fiscal category. The cumulative consequence of the New Chilean System is, as the Panel found, that approximately 75 per cent of all domestic production of the distilled alcoholic beverages at issue will be located in the fiscal category with the lowest tax rate, whereas approximately 95 per cent of the directly competitive or substitutable imported products will be found in the fiscal category subject to the highest tax rate. (emphasis in the original)

It seems that, for the AB, the sharp increase in the tax rate is what triggered its decision to find against Chile. In its view, the sharp increase was the quintessential element in the design, structure, and architecture of the challenged measure that made a prima-facie case of violation of the GATT, which Chile did not rebut (§71):

> In the present appeal, Chile's explanations concerning the structure of the New Chilean System—including, in particular, the truncated nature of the line of progression of tax rates, which effectively consists of two levels (27 per cent *ad valorem* and 47 per cent *ad valorem*) separated by only 4 degrees of alcohol content—might have been helpful in understanding what *prima facie* appear to be anomalies in the progression of tax rates. The conclusion of protective application reached by the Panel becomes very difficult to resist, in the absence of countervailing explanations by Chile. The mere statement of the four objectives

pursued by Chile does not constitute effective rebuttal on the part of Chile. (italics in the original)[78]

This passage makes us think that the same law would be GATT-consistent if for example the rate of tax progression was the same for alcoholic drinks below and above the two categories. Alternatively, the measure would have been found to be GATT-consistent if the tax progression was not as steep. Finally, Chile could have saved its measure had it effectively explained the steep graduation in the tax rate. It follows that it is not the steep graduation per se that tilted the AB towards its decision, but rather the lack of explanation for it. The steep graduation was thus a 'warning signal', the effects of which were not mitigated by the fact that the bulk of the taxation in the higher alcoholic category fell on Chilean shoulders. Recall the cited passage above (§67):

> This provision, as noted earlier, provides for equality of competitive conditions of *all* directly competitive or substitutable imported products, in relation to domestic products, and not simply, as Chile argues, those imported products within a particular fiscal category. (emphasis in the original)

The quoted passage raises a number of questions:

(a) Why is the fact that Chileans shoulder the majority of the taxation not a countervailing factor to the prima-facie case? What is the significance of the comparison of the volume represented by the 25 per cent of Chilean goods in the highest alcoholic category and by the 95 per cent of the Western drinks?

(b) Would Chile, in case its objective was to confer an advantage on domestic production, impose such a heavy burden on its domestic producers?[79]

(c) Why is it so clear that the design, structure, and architecture of the measure support the AB finding in this respect?

The problem does not lie in this report. In all reports discussed, the AB did not provide any methodology regarding its findings on the ASATAP requirement. Yes, we look at the design, structure, and architecture of the challenged measure, but what are we looking for exactly? The AB keeps its cards close to its chest and simply repeats that subjective intentions are immaterial, and what matters is the objective intent as revealed through the design etc. But similar statements raise more questions than they purport to answer. What is objective intent? And how is it revealed? What if the 95 per cent mentioned in the decision, for example, was 1 per cent of the 25 per cent of the Chilean production burdened by the highest tax? What if it was 1‰ of the Chilean production?[80]

---

[78] Chile invoked four grounds to explain its measure including revenue collection but did not elaborate on any of them (§69). In §72 of its report, the AB held that there was a necessity requirement in Art. III.2 GATT: Chile did not have to demonstrate that its measures were necessary (e.g. least restrictive) in order to be consistent with Art. III GATT.

[79] Similar thoughts have been expressed by Ehring (2002).

[80] This is in essence what Ehring (2002) complains about.

The AB report did not respond to these questions. It reaffirmed that an inquiry into the objective intent of a measure is necessary in order to respond to the question whether the challenged measure is ASATAP, but did not explicitly state the methodological steps that need to be taken in this perspective. We are in the dark as to what exactly we are looking for through this inquiry. Is intent the decisive element? Are trade effects a proxy to denote intent? Case law, thus, leaves many questions unanswered.

2.6.2 Like Products

For a complainant to demonstrate that a violation of Art. III.2 GATT, first sentence, has occurred, it will have to demonstrate that:

(a) the domestic and the foreign products are like; and
(b) the latter is taxed in excess of the former.

The term 'like product' appears in various provisions of the GATT. Case law has not advanced one consistent interpretation of the term, irrespective of the function that it is supposed to serve: to the contrary, as we shall see in this and the following chapters, the term has been understood in different ways across the various agreements (and/or even provisions within the same agreement) where it appears. It is the tariff classification that defines 'like products' when it comes to establishing whether the non-discrimination principle has been adhered to with respect to tariff treatment;[81] it is the marketplace that will define likeness with respect to two products subjected to a domestic instrument as we shall see in this chapter; and it is the petitioner's request that will largely define likeness for the purposes of an antidumping investigation as we will see in Chapter 7. Even within the same provision, the term does not have a symmetric meaning: 'like' in Art. III.2 GATT has a substantially narrower content than 'like' in Art. III.4 GATT. This is one of the case law contributions that we will be discussing *infra* in this chapter.[82]

Why then, since negotiators agreed that these provisions were intended to serve different purposes, was the same term used? After all, such a choice could only lend to confusion. *Faute de mieux*, is the short answer. Irwin et al. (2008) reveal a discussion in which Brazil mentioned the existence of a national committee (Comisáo de Similares) that it had established to deal with determinations of like products precisely because the term was hard to define. It was felt that some similar action should be undertaken at the multilateral level as well. It was decided, however, not to overburden the GATT negotiations with a similar task. Since the GATT would eventually come under the aegis of the ITO, and the ITO would possess sufficient institutional structure to deal adequately with similar concerns, it was decided to leave it to the ITO

---

81 Recall our discussion to this effect in Chapter 2.
82 On the various meanings of the term, see Hudec (2000), and also Davey and Pauwelyn (2000) and Mavroidis (2000a).

... later on to establish a jurisprudence on the meaning of this term.[83]

The non-advent of the ITO and the subsequent lack of any negotiating initiative to this effect left GATT Panels first, and WTO adjudicating bodies subsequently, with yet another 'hot potato': come to grips with this term.[84] The term 'like product' has been interpreted in many GATT/WTO Panels. GATT case law evidences two trends:

(a) there are a number of cases that follow a marketplace test: likeness is defined by reference to consumers' reactions;[85]
(b) there are two cases which reveal a willingness to take into account regulatory intent when establishing likeness among domestic and foreign products.

Let us start with the former. The WP on BTAs established four criteria to define likeness (§18):

(a) the properties, nature, and quality of the products;
(b) the end-uses of the products;
(c) consumers' tastes and habits—more comprehensively termed consumers' perceptions and behaviour—in respect of the products; and
(d) the tariff classification of the products.

It did not assign a particular weight to each one of the four criteria it employed. It did not even explain whether all four criteria must be cumulatively met. Relying on these four criteria, the Panel report on *Japan—Alcoholic Beverages I* held that alcoholic beverages (§5.6):

> should be considered as 'like products' in terms of Article III:2 in view of their similar properties, end-uses and usually uniform classification in tariff nomenclatures.

The AB endorsed this approach and explicitly stated that it is the sum of the criteria mentioned in the report on Border Tax Adjustments that will decide on likeness. In a famous and oft-quoted passage, it used an accordion metaphor to explain its views on how likeness should be determined (p. 21):

> No one approach to exercising judgment will be appropriate for all cases. The criteria in *Border Tax Adjustments* should be examined, but there can be no one precise and absolute definition of what is 'like'. The concept of 'likeness' is a relative one that evokes the image of an accordion. The accordion of 'likeness' stretches and squeezes

---

[83] UN Doc. E/PC/T/A/PV/40(1) at p. 14.

[84] Hudec (1990) mentions that non-discrimination as such was considered a non-satisfactory discipline to apply to domestic instruments. He refers to pre-GATT/ITO discussions across trading nations which reveal that non-violation complaints (NVCs) were thought to be the necessary complement to the contracted obligation not to discriminate. NVCs go beyond non-discrimination, as discussed in Chapter 1.

[85] So far, there has not been a single case where supply-substitutability has been accounted for when defining likeness or DCS relationship.

in different places as different provisions of the WTO Agreements are applied. The width of the accordion in any one of those places must be determined by the particular provision in which the term 'like' is encountered as well as by the context and the circumstances that prevail in any given case to which that provision may apply. (italics in the original)

In *EC—Asbestos* (§109), the AB underscored this point when it ruled that Panels which are called to pronounce on likeness must examine 'the evidence relating to each of those four criteria and, then, weigh all of that evidence, along with any other relevant evidence, in making an overall determination of whether the products at issue could be characterized as "like"'.

Then there are two cases that dismissed marketplace as the relevant criterion to decide on likeness: the Panel reports on *US—Malt Beverages* and on *US—Taxes on Automobiles* ('*Gas Guzzler*', as it is widely known).[86] In *US—Malt Beverages*, the Panel defines likeness in §5.25 in the following manner:

Consequently, in determining whether two products subject to different treatment are like products, it is necessary to consider whether such product differentiation is being made 'so as to afford protection to domestic production'. While the analysis of 'like products' in terms of Article III:2 must take into consideration this objective of Article III, the Panel wished to emphasize that such an analysis would be without prejudice to the 'like product' concepts in other provisions of the General Agreement, which might have different objectives and which might therefore also require different interpretations.

In *US—Taxes on Automobiles*,[87] the Panel had the opportunity to elaborate further on this proposition by introducing the so-called 'aims and effects' test (§§5.7 and 5.10):

In order to determine this issue, the Panel examined the object and purpose of paragraphs 2 and 4 of Article III in the context of the article as a whole and the General Agreement.

. . .

The Panel then proceeded to examine more closely the meaning of the phrase 'so as to afford protection.' The Panel noted that the term 'so as to' suggested both aim and effect. Thus the phrase 'so as to afford protection' called for an analysis of elements including the aim of the measure and the resulting effects. A measure could be said to have the *aim* of affording protection if an analysis of the circumstances in which it was adopted, in particular an analysis of the instruments available to the contracting

---

86 This report remains un-adopted and is, hence, of limited legal value. In fact, as we shall see *infra*, it was totally rejected by a subsequent WTO Panel dealing with the same issue.

87 In this case, the EU had challenged the consistency of a US tax scheme applicable to cars, according to which the total fleet of passenger vehicles produced by an individual producer would be taken into account in order to decide on the tax that would be imposed on specific items. Producers with a fleet that consisted of large, more powerful cars (gas guzzlers) would suffer most, as a result. Many European producers belonged to this category. Note that the US regime was enacted at a time when those suffering most were US producers: it was a legislative effort to dissuade consumers eager to buy gas guzzlers. See Mattoo and Subramanian (1998).

party to achieve the declared domestic policy goal, demonstrated that a change in competitive opportunities in favour of domestic products was a desired outcome and not merely an incidental consequence of the pursuit of a legitimate policy goal. A measure could be said to have the *effect* of affording protection to domestic production if it accorded greater competitive opportunities to domestic products than to imported products. The effect of a measure in terms of trade flows was not relevant for the purposes of Article III, since a change in the volume or proportion of imports could be due to many factors other than government measures. (emphasis in the original)

According to this view, consequently, likeness will not be defined by reference to prevailing perceptions in the marketplace about the products concerned, but instead by reference to the regulatory aims pursued by the intervening government.

What prompted the drafters of these two reports? Arguably, the automaticity in the sanction embedded in Art. III.2 GATT, first sentence: *any* tax differential across two like goods would lead *ipso facto* to a violation of Art. III GATT. If likeness was left totally to consumers to define, so the argument goes, then governments would have to justify their measures through recourse to Art. XX GATT; but the list of Art. XX GATT is a narrow, exhaustive list, and moving the discussion to this provision would be tantamount to understanding GATT as an instrument of deregulation and not as an instrument punishing only discrimination any time a regulatory intervention occurred for reasons other than those mentioned in the body of Art. XX GATT.[88] This was not the intention of the GATT framers who, as we saw in Chapter 1, would rather see trading nations unilaterally pursue any goal they deem legitimate, provided that when doing so they do not discriminate across domestic and imported (like) goods: 'aims and effects' is the necessary method that must be used in interpreting likeness if we are to understand the GATT as originally designed.[89] Consequently, what 'aims and effects' actually did was to interpret likeness in light of the overarching purpose of Art. III GATT, as it has been expressed in the opening paragraph of this provision.

The report on *US—Taxes on Automobiles* was the last one to discuss a claim under Art. III GATT in the GATT era. The first report in the WTO era was that on *Japan—Alcoholic Beverages II*, the facts of which almost verbatim reproduced that of *Japan—Alcoholic Beverages I*. The Panel explicitly rejected for various reasons the relevance of the 'aims and effects' test when deciding on likeness (§§ 6.15–19). The AB endorsed the Panel's approach (pp. 16ff) The AB (pp. 19 ff) ruled that the term 'like products' should be defined by reference to the marketplace. It explicitly stated that the term 'like products' invites a narrow reading, that is, a reading narrower than DCS, and that customs classification is relevant to establish likeness.

---

[88] *Infra* in this chapter, we advance similar grounds.
[89] Hudec (1988 and 1998) and Roessler (1996) should be credited with the original formulation of this approach. Howse and Regan (2000), Petersmann (2000), Regan (2002, 2003), and Marceau and Trachtman (2002) have elaborated it further.

A necessary condition is that the classification be precise (pp. 23–4):

> If sufficiently detailed, tariff classification can be a helpful sign of product similarity.
>
> . . .
>
> It is true that there are numerous tariff bindings which are in fact extremely precise with regard to product description and which, therefore, can provide significant guidance as to the identification of 'like products.'

This would usually be the case with respect to six-digit classifications. Four-digit classifications are in the overwhelming majority of cases uninformative, and eight-digit classifications are a matter of national definition, and not of worldwide acceptance.[90]

In a subsequent case (*Philippines—Distilled Spirits*), the AB faced the following facts (§98): distilled spirits produced from one of the following materials, sap of the nipa, coconut, cassava, camote etc. (predominantly produced in Philippines), were subjected to a flat-rate tax, whereas distilled spirits produced from other materials (predominantly imported) were subjected to a higher excise tax. The AB suggested that DCS products are those with low substitutability between them, whereas like products have high, almost perfect substitutability (§§120–2, 148).[91] In sharp contrast with its prior case law (*Japan—Alcoholic Beverages II*), the AB did not condition a finding on likeness on common tariff classification across two products: it first held that a four-digit tariff classification was uninformative, since not sufficiently detailed, and no conclusions on likeness could be drawn (§182). It then noted that two of the goods did not share the same six-digit tariff classification. It still found that they were like, thus overlooking the significance of tariff classification, satisfying itself that the goods were like since they were in an intense competitive relationship (§164).

When it comes to 'taxation in excess', the AB has held that even a minimal tax differential will suffice to satisfy this criterion. We quote from *Japan—Alcoholic Beverages II* (p. 23):

> Even the smallest amount of 'excess' is too much. The prohibition of discriminatory taxes in Article III:2, first sentence, is not conditional on a 'trade effects test' nor is it qualified by a *de minimis* standard. (italics in the original)

---

90 Charnovitz (1996) takes issue with the rejection of the aim and effect test. Noting first how two GATT panels had interpreted Art. III.2 GATT, first sentence, 'narrowly in order to reduce interference with national tax sovereignty', Charnovitz warned that the decision 'has important implications for the autonomy of national governments' and explained that with the door to Art. III GATT closed, environmental regulations will be reviewed under the restrictive rules of Art. XX GATT. We will come back to this issue in Section 3 *infra*.

91 It upheld a finding that cross-price elasticity measured between -0.01 and 0.07 (considered low by those who prepared the study) was not in and of itself a factor that prohibited a finding of likeness, especially since in a tax-neutral environment imports were expected to rise since high tax differentials often 'freeze' consumers' preferences (§§235ff).

In the same report, the AB held that, with respect to like products, taxation in excess should be understood as an instance of a measure meeting the ASATAP requirement. Consequently, a complainant who has established that taxation on imported products is in excess of that on domestic like products does not also have to establish that the measure at hand meets the ASATAP requirement (pp. 18–19):

> Article III:1 informs Article III:2, first sentence, by establishing that if imported products are taxed in excess of like domestic products, then that tax measure is inconsistent with Article III. Article III:2, first sentence does not refer specifically to Article III:1. There is no specific invocation in this first sentence of the general principle in Article III:1 that admonishes Members of the WTO not to apply measures so as to afford protection. This omission must have some meaning. We believe the meaning is simply that the presence of a protective application need not be established separately from the specific requirements that are included in the first sentence in order to show that a tax measure is inconsistent with the general principle set out in the first sentence. However, this does not mean that the general principle of Article III:1 does not apply to this sentence. To the contrary, we believe the first sentence of Article III:2 is, in effect, an application of this general principle. The ordinary meaning of the words of Article III:2, first sentence leads inevitably to this conclusion. Read in their context and in the light of the overall object and purpose of the *WTO Agreement*, the words of the first sentence require an examination of the conformity of an internal tax measure with Article III by determining, first, whether the taxed imported and domestic products are 'like' and, second, whether the taxes applied to the imported products are 'in excess of' those applied to the like domestic products. If the imported and domestic products are 'like products,' and if the taxes applied to the imported products are 'in excess of' those applied to the like domestic products, then the measure is inconsistent with Article III:2, first sentence. (italics in the original)

2.7 Non-fiscal Measures

Art. III.4 GATT deals with domestic instruments of a non-fiscal nature. The list is endless here as per our discussion *supra* on incomplete contracting: public health, environmental, human rights, antitrust, consumer protection laws, etc. come under the aegis of this provision. Irrespective of the precise subject-matter, a complainant aiming to establish that this provision has been violated will have to demonstrate that:

(a) with respect to laws, regulations, or requirements;
(b) affecting internal sale, offer for sale, purchase, transportation, distribution, or use;
(c) a foreign good is afforded in comparison to a domestic like good;
(d) less favourable treatment (LFT).

2.7.1 Laws, Regulations, or Requirements

GATT/WTO case law has understood the term 'laws, regulations and requirements' featured in Art. III.4 GATT as equivalent to the term 'measure' featured in

Art. XXIII.1(b) GATT and Art. XI GATT: case law under these provisions has consistently refused to understand the term 'measure' in a narrow manner.[92] The same should consequently hold true in the context of Art. III.4 GATT as well: indeed, so far we have witnessed no case where a WTO adjudicating body has rejected a claim because the complainant failed to show that a 'law, regulation or requirement' was being challenged. The inclusion of the term 'requirements' supports this construction: it was meant to extend the coverage of this provision and ensure that it is not restricted to formal laws only.

The GATT does not regulate private behaviour, so the next question is to what extent a measure is attributed to a government. Or, what is the degree of government intervention for a particular measure to be attributed to a government? WTO case law addressed the issue of attribution in the context of Art. III.4 GATT, in parallel with the approach followed in the context of Art. XI GATT. What matters is that a government has provided private parties with enough incentives to act in a particular way.[93,94] We read in the Panel report on *US—FSC* (§10.376):

> A literal reading of the words *all laws, regulations and requirements* in Article III:4 could suggest that they may have a narrower scope than the word *measure* in Article XXIII:1(b). However, whether or not these words should be given as broad a construction as the word *measure*, in view of the broad interpretation assigned to them in the cases cited above, we shall assume for the purposes of our present analysis that they should be interpreted as encompassing a similarly broad range of government action and action by private parties that may be assimilated to government action. In this connection, we consider that our previous discussion of GATT cases on administrative guidance in relation to what may constitute a 'measure' under Article XXIII:1(b), specifically the panel reports on *Japan—Semi-conductors* and *Japan—Agricultural Products*, is equally applicable to the definitional scope of 'all laws, regulations and requirements' in Article III:4. (italics and emphasis in the original)

2.7.2 *Affecting Sale, Offering for Sale*

Under this term, measures that not only actually, but also potentially and/or indirectly, affect trade have been subjected to judicial review. The AB, in its report on *US—FSC*, had the opportunity to confirm the wide interpretation of the term 'affecting' (§§208–10):

---

[92] See, for example, the Panel report on *Japan—Trade in Semiconductors*, discussed in Chapter 2, which has been cited in every single case dealing with Art. XI GATT ever since. See also the Panel report on *Japan—Film (Kodak/Fuji)* on this score.

[93] Although this point has not been discussed thoroughly in case law, our discussion here is most likely interesting only as far as the term 'requirements' is concerned, a term which leaves some doubt as to its origin. The terms 'laws' and 'regulations' are exhaustively government actions.

[94] Note that the issue of attribution is a non-issue in the context of Art. III.2 GATT: fiscal impositions can only be imposed by governments, or by non-governmental organs, following delegation of authority by governments.

...the word 'affecting' assists in defining the types of measure that must conform to the obligation not to accord 'less favourable treatment' to like imported products, which is set out in Article III:4.

The word 'affecting' serves a similar function in Article I:1 of the *General Agreement on Trade in Services* (the 'GATS'), where it also defines the types of measure that are subject to the disciplines set forth elsewhere in the GATS but does not, in itself, impose any obligation....

In view of the similar function of the identical word, 'affecting', in Article III:4 of the GATT 1994, we also interpret this word, in this provision, as having a 'broad scope of application.' (italics in the original)

There is not one single reported case where a challenged measure failed to meet the 'affecting' requirement.

2.7.3 Like Products in Art. III.4 GATT

Art. III.4 GATT does not, in contrast to Art. III.2 GATT, distinguish between like and DCS products. The question, hence, arises whether the term 'like product' should have the same meaning across the two paragraphs. The AB decided that this should not be the case. In its report on *EC—Asbestos*, the AB had to deal with a French decree which banned the sales of asbestos containing construction material: asbestos-containing construction material was banned, irrespective of its origin. The question before the Panel (and the AB) was whether all construction material, irrespective of whether asbestos-containing or asbestos free-, were like products. In order to respond to this question, the AB had first to define the scope of like products. It held that the term 'like products' in Art. III.4 GATT should be interpreted in light of the overarching purpose of Art. III GATT to punish protectionism with respect to both fiscal and non-fiscal measures: absent some parallelism in the coverage across the two paragraphs (III.2 and III.4 GATT), WTO Members would be incurring obligations of different scope with respect to fiscal and non-fiscal instruments. This view was, in the eyes of the AB, supported neither by the negotiating record nor by the function that this provision is called to perform in the GATT context. The AB, consequently, held that the term 'like products' in Art. III.4 of the GATT should be understood as covering products that are in a competitive relationship with one another. It explicitly accepted that it was acknowledging a wide coverage to the term, but not wider than the scope of products coming under the purview of Art. III.2 GATT, that is, the combined coverage of like and DCS products (§§98–100).

Next, the AB turned to the comparator (the *tertium comparationis*) for likeness in Art. III.4 GATT: should it be the marketplace or should it be something else?[95] France's prohibition (administrative decree) of sales of asbestos-containing construction material was based on scientific evidence: asbestos-containing

---

[95] See the excellent discussion of the AB report in Horn and Weiler (2007) which forms the basis for the analysis here.

construction material contributed to mesothelioma, a form of cancer. The asbestos-containing construction material was chrysotile fibres (an input to the final product) heavily produced in the province of Québec in Canada. Canada had argued that there was no difference between construction material containing chrysotile fibres, on the one hand, and construction material containing PCG fibres (which is an asbestos-free input to the final product), on the other. Construction material containing PCG fibres was being legally sold in France. Canada argued that the French ban on construction material containing chrysotile fibres, while allowing for sales of construction material containing PCG fibres, amounted to according to the Canadian good a less favourable treatment than that accorded to the French like good.

The Panel had at first instance decided that the two products were indeed like and, consequently, held that Art. III.4 GATT had been violated. The Panel paid particular attention to the end-uses of the two products: since they were the same (construction material), the Panel held that the two products were like. The Panel then held that, by allowing sales of domestic asbestos-free and banning sales of imported asbestos-containing construction material, France was according imported products less favourable treatment than that accorded to domestic like products. Since Art. III.4 GATT had, in the eyes of the Panel, been violated, the Panel moved to examine the French (EU) defence under Art. XX GATT.

On appeal, the AB reversed the Panel's findings with respect to likeness. In its view, the Panel should have examined all four criteria mentioned in the WP on BTAs, and not just one of them (end-uses): it should have also discussed the other criteria conferring likeness, such as physical characteristics. Had it done so, the Panel would, in the AB's view, have observed the differences in physical characteristics between the two products. In the AB's view, the composition of a product is very much part of the analysis concerning physical characteristics. Chrysotile fibres and PCG fibres are not the same: the first are carcinogenic, whereas the latter are not. This, in the AB's view, most likely would have led reasonable consumers to stop purchasing material containing chrysotile fibres. The likelihood that the different composition, because of the danger to human health that it represents, might affect consumers' choices in this regard was sufficient reason to raise a presumption that the two products were unlike (§§101–54). What's more, these buyers of the imported material would often not be exposed themselves to the health risk, but would be indirectly affected, since their customers could be affected. The finding of non-likeness was hence based on the AB's assessment of the construction companies' assessment of how the latter would be affected, through the market mechanism, by their customers' assessment of differences in risk.

The burden of proof for Canada, in light of the difference in physical characteristics, would be now, in the words of the AB, much higher. The AB effectively held that the presence of health risk in asbestos-containing construction material raised a presumption that the two products were unlike. Canada was called to rebut this presumption (which, *in casu*, Canada did not and, consequently, its original legal challenge against the French decree was rejected).[96]

The *EC—Asbestos* dispute hence contains a novelty from a burden-of-proof point of view; when making its likeness determination, the AB did not rely on studies or information concerning actual buyer behaviour. The AB uses its own interpretation of what reasonable buyers would do, if facing a choice between the two products (§122):

> In this case especially, we are also persuaded that evidence relating to consumers' tastes and habits would establish that the health risks associated with chrysotile asbestos fibres influence consumers' behaviour with respect to the different fibres at issue. We observe that, as regards *chrysotile asbestos and PCG fibres*, the consumer of the fibres is a *manufacturer* who incorporates the fibres into another product, such as cement-based products or brake linings. We do not wish to speculate on what the evidence regarding these consumers would have indicated; rather, we wish to highlight that consumers' tastes and habits regarding *fibres*, even in the case of commercial parties, such as manufacturers, are very likely to be shaped by the health risks associated with a product which is known to be highly carcinogenic. A manufacturer cannot, for instance, ignore the preferences of the ultimate consumer of its products. If the risks posed by a particular product are sufficiently great, the ultimate consumer may simply cease to buy that product. This would, undoubtedly, affect a manufacturer's decisions in the marketplace. Moreover, in the case of products posing risks to human health, we think it likely that manufacturers' decisions will be influenced by other factors, such as the potential civil liability that might flow from marketing products posing a health risk to the ultimate consumer, or the additional costs associated with safety procedures required to use such products in the manufacturing process. (§122, italics in the original; underlining added)

In the preceding recital to the above quoted passage, the AB had, however, noted:

> Furthermore, in a case such as this, where the fibres are physically very different, a panel *cannot* conclude that they are 'like products' if it *does not examine* evidence relating to consumers' tastes and habits… (italics in original)

Still, the AB did not think it was necessary to look for market evidence when deciding on the likeness of the products concerned. So the test for likeness stays in the market in name only, since it is the reactions of a reasonable and not an actual consumer that will define, according to this test, whether two products are like.[97]

---

[96] The AB held that the presence of health risk in asbestos-containing construction material raised a presumption that the two products were unlike. Canada was called to rebut this presumption (which, *in casu*, Canada did not). In a separate but concurring opinion, an unnamed member of the AB held the view that the scientific proof cited in this case was *sufficient* to conclude that the two products were *unlike*. One way to understand the need for a separate opinion is probably that, in this member's eyes, the difference in physical characteristics, and the ensuing consumers' reaction, does not merely raise a presumption, but amounts to a home run: Canada could never rebut such evidence.

[97] The AB found additional support for its overall finding in the fact that chrysotile fibres and PCG fibres do not share the same tariff classification, and, also, in the fact that scientific evidence was cited in support of the carcinogenic nature of chrysotile fibres.

In other words, what the AB did here was to reduce the probative value of evidence like market surveys, irrespective of whether econometric indicators had been used. This finding in the report raises a number of issues:

(a) if reasonable consumers, as the AB asserts, would never treat the two products as like, then what was the need for France to impose the sales ban in the first place? Arguably, France would have to act this way precisely because consumers did treat the two goods as substitutes. Indeed, depending on their risk aversion and taking into account the price difference, some consumers might opt for asbestos-containing goods. There is nothing unreasonable about that. The axiomatic distinction that the AB drew is probably not supported by facts;[98]

(b) this is not to say that France should have lost this case. Indeed, what more persuasive than the scientific studies that France produced linking exposure to asbestos-containing construction material and increased likelihood to contract mesothelioma? France should have prevailed since by treating the two like goods differently, it did not afford less favourable treatment to the imported goods since its objective was not to confer an advantage on domestic goods. It was French producers after all who had to adjust their production of construction material by abandoning the relatively cheaper chrysotile for the more expensive PCG fibres.[99] But more on this *infra* in Section 3.

2.7.4 Less Favourable Treatment

The question whether the requirement not to afford imported goods less favourable treatment (LFT) than that afforded to domestic like goods should be understood in a similar manner to the ASATAP requirement has naturally arisen before the WTO adjudicating bodies. In *EC—Bananas III*, the AB clarified this issue when holding that:

> Article III:4 does *not* specifically refer to Article III:1. Therefore, a determination of whether there has been a violation of Article III:4 does *not* require a separate

---

[98] Lydgate (2011) reaches similar conclusions. Palmeter (2006), citing Hudec, argues that tribunals frequently decide the case as best they can by making a 'seat-of-the-pants' judgment about whether the defendant government is behaving correctly or incorrectly—a process of judgment known in some circles as the 'smell test'. The decisions of panels and the AB in disputes involving health and safety measures suggest, in the author's view, that the 'smell test' is alive and well in the WTO.

[99] The report has received mixed reactions. At one end of the spectrum, Yavitz (2002) criticizes this case law for not interpreting the key terms in this provision in a manner that would honour its agreed function, that is, to avoid WTO Members using non-fiscal instruments so as to afford advantages to their domestic production. In contrast, Howse and Türk (2001) agree with the basis of the reasoning of the AB report and disagree vehemently with the Panel approach. The authors defend a comprehensive discrimination test that should take place within the four corners of Art. III GATT (instead of moving the discussion to Art. XX GATT). They thus see the AB report as a positive step in this direction. These and other views are not necessarily mutually inconsistent, since they focus on different parts of the report.

consideration of whether a measure afford[s] protection to domestic production. (emphasis in the original)

In its report on *EC—Asbestos*, the AB repeated in even clearer terms that the LFT requirement echoes the principle set forth in Art. III.1 GATT (§100):

> The term 'less favourable treatment' expresses the general principle, in Article III:1, that internal regulations 'should not be applied...so as to afford protection to domestic production.' If there is 'less favourable treatment' of the group of 'like' imported products, there is, conversely, 'protection' of the group of 'like' domestic products. However, a Member may draw distinctions between products which have been found to be 'like,' without, for this reason alone, according to the group of 'like' *imported* products 'less favourable treatment' than that accorded to the group of 'like' *domestic* products. (emphasis in the original)

What needs to be shown besides differential treatment and who should carry the burden of proof?[100] This is an area where case law has not progressed smoothly and coherently. Let us unravel the narrative. The AB report on *Korea—Various Measures on Beef* discussed in detail the nuts and bolts of the LFT test. This dispute between Korea, on the one hand, and a host of beef exporters, on the other, concerned the distribution of beef in the Korean market. Korea had enacted a law, whereby traders at the retail level could sell either domestic or imported beef: this was the notorious Korean *dual retail system*. The complainants had argued that, as a result of the dual retail system, there were only 5,000 points of sale for imported beef, whereas there were over 45,000 points of sale for domestic beef. In this vein, they claimed that the dual retail system amounted to a violation of Art. III.4 GATT. Korea defended itself by arguing that the background to this dispute mattered and that, absent thorough examination of the background, the Panel would risk committing a type I error, outlawing a scheme that neither intended to be protectionist nor had a similar effect. It pointed to the fact that it had in place an import quota for beef, the legality of which was not put into question during the proceedings. Indeed, Korea had invoked the balance-of-payments provisions of the GATT to impose a quota on the import of beef and complainants did not question the legitimacy of this action. Korea added that the quota had been absorbed in all years when the system was in place, with one exception only: following the financial crisis in 1997, when overall consumption (of both domestic and foreign beef) fell dramatically. Hence, in Korea's view, complainants suffered trade damage in only one year since the dual retail system had been in place for a reason that had nothing to do with the existence of the distribution system. Korea also argued before the Panel that the dual retail system was not discriminatory, in

---

[100] Sometimes, the issue is quite straightforward: for example, as discussed in Howse and Neven (2007f), in *US—Section 211 Appropriations Act*, the US law imposed one additional administrative hurdle on foreigners when requesting registration of a trademark and it is this additional step that made the law inconsistent with Art. III GATT. The facts in the majority of cases brought to WTO dispute settlement are more nuanced.

light of the fact that traders were free to choose whether they would sell domestic or foreign beef, and that there was no legal compulsion obliging them to choose one category of beef over the other; they could further subsequently switch at no cost, and sell say imported beef when they had previously been selling domestic beef. Pointing to standing case law, Korea argued that the dual retail system established equality of competitive conditions for domestic and imported like goods.[101]

Korea requested the Panel to reject the complaint for all the reasons mentioned above, as well as because there was incoherence in the formulation of the basic claim: the number of outlets should be immaterial, since, as they had argued, there was no need to show trade effects for a claim under Art. III GATT to be successful. Korea claimed that a legislation which establishes equality of competitive conditions passes the test of consistency with Art. III GATT even if some trade effects might look harmful to exporters. Korea was effectively arguing that the complainants could not, on the one hand, claim that trade effects are immaterial and, on the other, base their complaint on trade effects.[102] The Panel rejected all of Korea's claims and found in favour of the complainants.

On appeal, the AB held that this system, although formally non-discriminatory, still modified the conditions of competition to the detriment of the imported product and found Korea's practices to be inconsistent with Art. III.4 GATT since it afforded LFT to imported like products. The modification of conditions of competition was evident, in the AB's view, in the fact that fewer retailers decided to sell imported beef (§§143–51). The AB accepted that the choice to distribute domestic or imported beef was in the hands of private retailers. In a rather cryptic passage, it held that LFT resulted from Korea's decision not to stick to the prior regime (§146):

> We are aware that the dramatic reduction in number of retail outlets for imported beef followed from the decisions of individual retailers who could choose freely to sell the domestic product or the imported product. The legal necessity of making a choice was, however, imposed by the measure itself. The restricted nature of that choice should be noted. The choice given to the meat retailers was *not* an option between remaining with the pre-existing unified distribution set-up or going to a dual retail system. The choice was limited to selling domestic beef only or imported beef only. Thus, the reduction of access to normal retail channels is, in legal contemplation, the effect of that measure. In these circumstances, the intervention of some element of private choice does not relieve Korea of responsibility under the GATT 1994 for the resulting establishment of competitive conditions less

---

[101] Korea did not contest before the Panel the assertion of complainants that domestic and imported beef were like goods.

[102] Korea also made claims under Art. XX GATT, arguing that the system was in place in order to combat tax fraud: traders had the incentive to sell imported beef as domestic beef, in light of the very substantial price differential between imported and domestic beef (the latter being substantially more expensive than the former).

favourable for the imported product than for the domestic product. (emphasis in the original)

The AB was quick to highlight what it had not been prejudging through its decision (§149):

It may finally be useful to indicate, however broadly, what we are *not* saying in reaching our above conclusion. We are *not* holding that a dual or parallel distribution system that is *not* imposed directly or indirectly by law or governmental regulation, but is rather solely the result of private entrepreneurs acting on their own calculations of comparative costs and benefits of differentiated distribution systems, is unlawful under Article III:4 of the GATT 1994. What is addressed by Article III:4 is merely the *governmental* intervention that affects the conditions under which like goods, domestic and imported, compete in the market within a Member's territory. (emphasis in the original)[103]

This case raised many questions, casting serious doubt on the intellectual legitimacy of the approach adopted:

(a) what exactly does the LFT test consist of in this case? Is it the fact that imported beef was previously being sold through the same channel as domestic beef, or is it the fact that only 5,000 outlets sell imported beef, whereas 45,000 outlets sell domestic beef? It cannot be the former, since the same requirement was imposed on domestic beef (it cannot be sold through the same channels as imported beef); hence no LFT results from this modification of conditions of competition. It cannot be the latter either since trade effects, so says consistent case law, are immaterial. Or are they?

(b) If trade effects do matter, how can we judge whether availability of imported beef in 5,000 as opposed to 45,000 outlets operates to the detriment of imported beef unless we have information about the size of outlets, their location etc.?

(c) What exactly did the AB mean when stating that the measure operates to the detriment of imported beef when the quota was absorbed in all the years that it was in place except for one, when indeed extraordinary circumstances (by any reasonable account) occurred? Was the AB effectively judging the post-quota period? We should add here that it cannot be that the modification of conditions per se that constitutes a GATT violation: the GATT is a negative integration contract and trading partners retain the right to modify their laws

---

[103] So, the AB did not go so far as to outlaw exclusivity contracts signed between suppliers and retailers. Did it outlaw similar contracts if they benefit from government authorization? Arguably, exclusivity contracts, assuming market power in the upstream (or even, in some legal orders, in the downstream) market, will be judged illegal under many national antitrust statutes and, unless they have benefited from antitrust exemption, cannot lawfully take place. Is this degree of government intervention sufficient for the AB to outlaw similar practices? Probably yes, if exclusivity contracts concern domestic goods and are denied when imported like goods place similar requests, although the comparability across transactions might be too high a hurdle for the complainant to overcome. This is nonetheless a side issue.

whenever appropriate as long as they observe the basic non-discrimination obligation. Hence, it is the notion that the modification of conditions of competition was to the detriment of imported goods that must form the basis of the AB judgment;

(d) Since LFT equals ASATAP, should not the AB inquire into the design, structure, and architecture of the law? Well, it did so in the context of Art. XX GATT and did not cast doubt on the Korean justification that it was done for consumer protection purposes: there was (and is) a very substantial price differential between imported and domestic beef in Korea in the sense that the latter's price is much higher than the former's. Korea had argued that the dual retail system (along with other repressive measures) were meant to guarantee that traders, through fraudulent practices, would not sell imported beef for Korean beef and pocket the price mark-up. If this is acceptable, how does the design, structure, and architecture of the measure support a finding of LFT?[104]

It seems that the Panel and the AB were quick to find against Korea because the measure was origin-based: imported beef would be distributed through one channel, domestic through another. They thus equated de jure discrimination with a per se violation. This is not necessarily correct though: in a case like this, the distinction is origin-based simply because the imported good is less expensive and that domestic traders might have an incentive to pocket the price difference by selling imported as Korean beef. Arguably, Korea would have done the same thing if the price of Korean beef had exceeded that of imported beef.[105]

In a subsequent case, the AB, in order to define whether LFT had indeed resulted from a particular measure, asked the question whether the resulting detriment for imported goods was due to their origin; if yes, then less favourable treatment had been accorded, but if no, then the NT provision had not been violated. In its report on *Dominican Republic—Import and Sale of Cigarettes*, the AB upheld the Panel's rejection of Honduras's claim under Art. III.4 GATT. It agreed

---

[104] In §§172ff of its report, the AB held that Korea had violated its obligations under Art. XX(d) GATT not because the measure was not authentically pursuing consumer protection, but because it was unnecessary, in the sense of being more trade-restrictive than necessary. We discuss this aspect of the report in Chapter 5. Suffice, nonetheless, to mention here that there is no necessity requirement in Art. III GATT: if the measure did indeed modify conditions of competition to the detriment of imported goods (a highly doubtful proposition for the reasons mentioned above), *and* was not origin-based (as the Panel and the AB accepted), then it should have passed the test of consistency under Art. III GATT as the AB report on *Dominican Republic—Import and Sale of Cigarettes* that we discuss *infra* has held.

[105] Interestingly, antitrust, where the distinction between per se (a practice is illegal because of its inherent characteristics) and rule of reason (the antitrust authority will weigh the pros and cons of a challenged scheme) comes from, is moving undeniably towards a restriction of the former—and an expansion of the latter standard. The US Supreme Court, probably the most influential court in this context, has accepted that even a naked restriction of trade across competitors might on occasion be more appropriately dealt with under a 'truncated rule of reason' standard of review; see *California Dental Association v Federal Trade Commission* (976–1625) 576 US 759 (1999), 128 F.3d 720.

with the Panel that a detrimental effect of a measure (the measure here was the bond requirement, under which cigarette importers had to post a bond to ensure payment of taxes) on a given imported product does not necessarily imply that the measure accords less favourable treatment to imports if the effect is explained by factors unrelated to the foreign origin of the product. In this case, the factor explaining the treatment was the market share of the importer, in the sense that the level of the bond requirement depended on the market share that the importer (or the domestic producer) attained in the Dominican Republic market (§96):

> The Appellate Body indicated in *Korea—Various Measures on Beef* that imported products are treated less favourably than like products if a measure modifies the conditions of competition in the relevant market *to the detriment of imported products*. However, the existence of a detrimental effect on a given imported product resulting from a measure does not necessarily imply that this measure accords less favourable treatment to imports if the detrimental effect is explained by factors or circumstances unrelated to the foreign origin of the product, such as the market share of the importer in this case. In this specific case, the mere demonstration that the per-unit cost of the bond requirement for imported cigarettes was higher than for some domestic cigarettes during a particular period is not, in our view, *sufficient* to establish 'less favourable treatment' under Article III:4 of the GATT 1994. Indeed, the difference between the per-unit costs of the bond requirement alleged by Honduras is explained by the fact that the importer of Honduran cigarettes has a smaller market share than two domestic producers (the per-unit cost of the bond requirement being the result of dividing the cost of the bond by the number of cigarettes sold on the Dominican Republic market). In this case, the difference between the per-unit costs of the bond requirement alleged by Honduras does not depend on the foreign origin of the imported cigarettes. Therefore, in our view, the Panel was correct in dismissing the argument that the bond requirement accords less favourable treatment to imported cigarettes because the per-unit cost of the bond was higher for the importer of Honduran cigarettes than for two domestic producers. (italics and emphasis in the original)

The AB did not explain the exact nature of the test that determines whether the detriment is due to the origin of good (or not). In this case, it found in favour of the defendant because on its face the law did not link the level of bond requirements to anything other than market share. There is thus a marked difference between the two reports: a measure that operates to the detriment of imported goods is in violation of Art. III.4 GATT in the world of *Korea—Various Measures of Beef.* This is not necessarily the case in the world of *Dominican Republic—Import and Sale of Cigarettes*: if the measure is justified for reasons other than the origin of the goods then, even in the presence of detrimental effects for imported goods, it will pass muster under Art. III.4 GATT.[106]

---

[106] The word 'however' in the fourth line of the quoted passage should leave little room for doubt that the AB was reversing its previous report on *Korea—Various Measures on Beef.*

The AB held, in similar vein, in its report on *US—FSC (Article 21.5—EC)* that a careful analysis of the implications of a measure in the marketplace must be performed in order to decide on whether the LFT requirement has been met (§215):

> The examination of whether a measure involves 'less favourable treatment' of imported products within the meaning of Article III:4 of the GATT 1994 must be grounded in close scrutiny of the 'fundamental thrust and effect of the measure itself'. This examination cannot rest on simple assertion, but must be founded on a careful analysis of the contested measure and of its implications in the marketplace. At the same time, however, the examination need not be based on the *actual effects* of the contested measure in the marketplace. (emphasis in the original)

Yet, in a more recent case, we see no mention of the AB report on *Dominican Republic—Import and Sale of Cigarettes*. In *Thailand—Cigarettes*, the AB was asked to pronounce on the consistency of a Thai tax measure with Art. III.4 GATT. Thailand had argued before the Panel and the AB that its measures were not origin-related and hence not in violation of Art. III.4 GATT. In §126 of its report, the AB discusses LFT, referring time and again to *Korea—Various Measures on Beef* and avoiding any reference to *Dominican Republic—Import and Sale of Cigarettes*. To make things even more confusing on this front, in *US—Clove Cigarettes*, a Panel report released in September 2011, the Panel discusses (§§ 7.268ff) the LFT requirement exclusively in light of the findings of the AB report on *Dominican Republic—Import and Sale of Cigarettes*. This Panel report was issued months after the AB report on *Thailand—Cigarettes*, and it is quite legitimate to suspect that its authors were fully aware of its content. The only fitting conclusion here is that WTO adjudicating bodies are still struggling with the test that should be applied in order to decide whether the LFT requirement has been established or not.[107]

So far, there has been no case in the WTO where an omission was found to be a measure inconsistent with Art. III GATT. In the EU context, the court has found that France was in breach of its obligations under the ECT (Art. 28) by not taking measures sufficient to deter French farmers from emptying trucks and destroying Spanish farm products that had been cleared through customs.[108]

Finally, there are some measures that de facto are probably often discriminatory. A natural candidate for this category is advertising: the question has arisen in the GATT whether an outright ban on advertising would be considered GATT-consistent or not. The GATT Panel on *Thailand—Cigarettes* explained why, in its view, a ban on advertising applied on both domestic and foreign cigarettes will always operate in favour of the domestic product (§78):

---

[107] The Panel reports on *US—COOL* and *US—Tuna II (Mexico)*, both issued in the fall 2011, reflect the test for the LFT requirement developed in *Dominican Republic—Import and Sale of Cigarettes*.

[108] C-265/95, *Commission of the European Communities v French Republic* [1997] ECR I-6959.

> A ban on the advertisement of cigarettes of both domestic and foreign origin would normally meet the requirements of Article III:4. It might be argued that such a general ban on all cigarette advertising would create unequal competitive opportunities between the existing Thai supplier of cigarettes and new, foreign suppliers and was therefore contrary to Article III:4. Even if this argument were accepted, such an inconsistency would have to be regarded as unavoidable and therefore necessary within the meaning of Article XX(b) because additional advertising rights would risk stimulating demand for cigarettes.

The rationale for this finding has to do with the idea that consumers are better acquainted with local goods and a ban on advertising would always fall more heavily on imported goods. The validity of this proposition critically rests on the assumption that the market at hand is segmented and only trades with the rest of the world. Liberalizing investment will, of course, cast substantial doubt on this view.[109]

3. NT Revisited

We started with the observation that Art. III GATT is incomplete, although the 'spirit' of the provision is more or less defined: avoid protection through use of domestic instruments. As stated above, we still lack an operational definition of the term 'protection'. The contract has not been completed through subsequent renegotiation, and the WTO judge, as the preceding analysis shows, did not manage to come up with a watertight methodology that will distinguish protectionist from non-protectionist measures and thus honour the spirit of NT.[110] One can, of course, only sympathize with the WTO judge and the enormity of the task it faces when adjudicating disputes under Art. III GATT:

(a) it is called to decide at the end of the day what protection is, an intellectually very demanding exercise, since there is nothing like a dictionary definition of the term;

(b) it will typically be dealing with a scenario where there is private information (the regulator knows the rationale for the challenged measure);

---

[109] Compare the view expressed here with that of the Advocate General, and the European Court of Justice (ECJ) in their judgment of 9 February 1995, on *Leclerc-Siplec/TF1 et M6*, C-412/93, ECJ Reports 1995, p. I-179.

[110] When referring to contract incompleteness, we pointed to the agency contract that links the WTO judge to the WTO principals, and raised two issues: the WTO judge must respect its institutional mandate (and remain an agent within the limits defined in Art. 3.2 DSU); the WTO judge must interpret the terms of the provision with the limited set of tools at its disposal. The discussion here concerns the second point. Suffice to say that the WTO judge, in general, has not provoked much acrimony regarding the first point. Ironically, it was in an Art. III GATT case that many (the overwhelming majority of) WTO Members thought it had trespassed its mandate when accepting *amicus curiae* briefs in *EC—Asbestos*. This was nonetheless a procedural issue totally de-linked from our discussion of key terms in what follows; see Mavroidis (2004a).

(c) the party possessing private information has a strong incentive to act opportunistically:

  a. if the regulator did intend to violate the ASATAP requirement when enacting the challenged measure and reveals the truth, it will be violating the GATT and will have to pay the consequences;

  b. if, in the same constellation of facts, it pretends that its measure was enacted for a different purpose, then it might get away with it;

(d) the WTO judge, recall, will have to interpret one incomplete contract (the GATT) through another (the VCLT).

What are the tools that the WTO judge can use to honour its task under the circumstances? Essentially, it can make use of the burden of proof as a tool to reach its conclusions. The burden of proof is made up of:

(a) the burden of production of proof, where the question asked is who is supposed to bring forward the required evidence;

(b) the burden of persuasion, where the question asked is how much evidence is required for the burden (of production of proof) to shift to the other party. This second aspect is intimately linked to the standard of review that WTO adjudicating bodies will apply across disputes.

In what follows, we first ask the question whether the outcome is reasonable and, if not, whether the source of 'dissatisfaction' rests within the case law or the law itself. The bulk of the criticism advanced here has to do with the manner in which the original contract has been interpreted.

3.1 Burden of Production of Proof[111]

The GATT does not explicitly regulate the burden of proof. The current practice has instead been developed in case law. Case law has endorsed the *in dubio mitius* principle, according to which WTO Members' actions should be presumed legitimate, unless challenged and proven inconsistent before a WTO panel (and/ or the AB, as the case may be). This principle hence imposes the original burden of production of proof on the complainant (*actori incumbit probatio*). If the law distinguishes between a rule and an exception, then legal orders follow the maxim *quicunque exceptio invokat ejusdem probare debet*: the party invoking the exception carries the burden of proof to demonstrate compliance with the conditions reflected in the exception. In this case, there is a presumption of illegality since, the party invoking an exception has by definition broken the rule, that is the legal canon for which the presumption of legality has been agreed.[112] Assuming the

---

111 This section relies heavily on Grossman et al. (2012).

112 This principle is of no use here but will be of use in Chapter 5 when we discuss General Exceptions to the basic obligations assumed under GATT.

complainant produces sufficient evidence to raise a presumption (an undefined notion in case law), the burden shifts to the other party.

It follows from the above that, in the context of NT, it is the complainant that must demonstrate that either two goods are DCS (like) and the fiscal (or non-fiscal) measure meets the ASATAP (LFT) requirement, as the case may be. Reading the actual case law, it is difficult to form an opinion as to what actually happened in terms of who provided what proof. One thing is for sure: WTO adjudicating bodies are not umpiring a tennis game where, unless the ball goes over the net, the burden of production of proof does not shift to the other party. They rather invite both parties to submit evidence and they will make up their mind and reach a decision based on all evidence submitted. In this vein, we note that the Panel, in its report on *Turkey—Rice* summing up prior case law, held that it would not request the defendant to respond only after the complainant had successfully made a prima-facie case; rather, it would decide whether a prima-facie case had been made on the basis of the totality of evidence brought by the parties to the dispute.[113] There is not one single case so far that does not evidence this approach.

This does not mean that say the defendant cannot object to a request to submit evidence if in its view it should be incumbent on the other party to provide the requested evidence. Similar incidents are rare though: since Panels have the possibility to draw inferences[114] from non-cooperative behaviour, parties to a dispute have an incentive to acquiesce to similar requests, within the bounds of reasonableness of course.

There are in theory three possible outcomes:

(a) The complainant makes a prima-facie case that has not been refuted;
(b) There is effective refutation of the prima-facie case;
(c) Evidence and counter-evidence are evenly balanced.

The prima-facie requirement was first introduced by the AB in its report on *US—Wool Shirts and Blouses*. It has been cited in practically all disputes ever since when a burden of proof issue arose (§14):

(a) It is a generally accepted canon of evidence in civil law, common law, and, in fact, most jurisdictions that the burden of proof rests upon the party, whether complaining or defending, who asserts the affirmative of a particular claim or defence. If that party adduces sufficient evidence to raise a presumption that what is claimed is true, the burden then shifts to the other party, who will fail unless it adduces sufficient evidence to rebut the presumption.

---

[113] Gantz and Schropp (2009) offer an excellent account of the discussion on burden of proof in this dispute from a law and economics perspective.

[114] In *Canada—Aircraft*, the AB noted (§203): 'Clearly, in our view, the Panel had the legal authority and the discretion to draw inferences from the facts before it—including the fact that Canada had refused to provide information sought by the Panel.'

(b) This passage provides only an indication as to the burden of persuasion; making a prima-facie case is shorthand for observing the burden of persuasion. In subsequent cases, panels have used the term 'to make a *prima facie* case' as equivalent to the obligation to 'raise a presumption' that what is claimed is true (*US—Stainless Steel* at §6.2). Raising a presumption is not a self-interpreting term either and, as a result, the question of the quantum of proof needed to discharge the obligation of burden of persuasion can only be evaluated on a case-by-case basis in WTO jurisprudence.

(c) The Panel on *Mexico—Taxes on Soft Drinks* ruled that the duty of the complainant to make a prima-facie case is not affected by the defendant's decision not to challenge the claims and arguments made. In the case at hand, Mexico had chosen not to raise any defence in some of the claims advanced by the US. In the Panel's view, Mexico's inaction did not amount to an admission that the US had made a prima-facie case (§§8.16ff).

(d) The AB noted in its report on *Korea—Dairy* that there is (§145):

> ... no provision in the DSU ... that requires a panel to make an explicit ruling on whether the complainant has established a *prima facie* case of violation before a panel may proceed to examine the respondent's defence and evidence. (italics in the original)

Consequently, the issue whether a party has indeed established a prima-facie case, and/or the adjunct issue whether the prima-facie case was effectively refuted, will form an integral part of the general evaluation by the panel. In this vein, Panels can at the end of the process, that is, after they have invited evidence from both parties, decide that the complainant did not make a prima-facie case (*India—Autos* §§ 7.231–3).

The Panel, in its report on *US—1916 Act* (*EC*) concluded that evidence submitted by the complainant and the defendant was in equipoise. It then asked itself what the legal consequence of this finding should be. It held that, in such cases, the advantage rests with the party responding to the claim (§6.58):

> If, after having applied the above methodology, we could not reach certainty as to the most appropriate court interpretation, i.e. if the evidence remains in equipoise, we shall follow the interpretation that favours the party against which the claim has been made, considering that the claimant did not convincingly support its claim.

So equipoise works in favour of the regulator (defendant in NT cases). This would mean that, assuming prima facie comes close to preponderance of evidence,[115] the complainant will have to be, relatively speaking, more persuasive than the defendant for its claim to be accepted.

---

[115] Grando (2009) checks the vast majority of reports since the inception of the WTO and concludes that this has indeed been the case.

Where does all this lead us? It is clear that it is the complainant that must bring in evidence first. It is also clear that, even in the absence of rebuttal, the evidence will be freely evaluated by the Panel. From then onwards, the WTO judge is an umpire who will evaluate all evidence submitted to it by both parties. The WTO judge might provoke the quantum of the evidence through questions it can pose to both parties (Art. 13 DSU).

The economic literature suggests a number of additional considerations that may affect the optimal allocation of the burden of proof. A basic notion in this literature is that it may be desirable to allocate the burden to the party that is better informed concerning a contested issue. Since the importing country government is likely to be much better informed concerning the reasons for the contested measure, this would suggest that the regulator should be asked to explain the rationale for its policies. This would also be natural given the fact that a fundamental obstacle to the implementation of NT is lack of information concerning the government preferences that have led to the regulation.

Now there are some important countervailing arguments here: assigning the bulk of burden of proof to the regulator might provoke a flurry of complaints. There is an obvious cost: administrative resources will have to be committed to discussing those disputes. Moreover, more cases will increase, other things equal, the probability to commit an error. The economics literature also addresses to what extent the likelihood and cost of judicial errors should affect the allocation of the burden of production of proof. The allocation of the burden of proof should preferably weigh the costs of false positive findings of violations against the costs of erroneous acquittals, while, at the same time, taking into consideration the benefits of making tariff liberalization commitments meaningful. The costs of judicial errors of type I and type II partly depend on the context. For the complainant, the costs of losing a dispute in which it should prevail typically stem from reduced market access in its export market. For the respondent, the costs of having to treat a domestic and imported product identically, when it should not need to do so, may partly take the form of reduced sales for its import-competing industry. But the importing country may also suffer a cost if the prohibition of its measure induces a lower level of ambition with regard to the policy objective it was pursing. Assigning the burden to the better informed party (defendant) might also lead to under-regulation ('regulatory chill').[116] Another consideration is the desire to minimize legal costs. It is often suggested that this aspect has a special importance in the context of WTO dispute settlement, where it is argued that poorer

---

[116] Already in 1933, Neyman and Pearson (p. 296) wrote of type I and type II errors: 'Is it more serious to convict an innocent man or to acquit a guilty? That will depend on the consequences of the error; is the punishment death or fine? What is the danger to the community of released criminals? What are the current ethical views on punishment? From the point of view of mathematical theory all that we can do is show how the risk of errors may be controlled or minimized. The use of these statistical tools in any given case, in determining just how the balance should be struck, must be left to the investigator'. Compare Stein (2005) at pp. 214ff.

Members cannot afford to defend their rights due to the substantial legal costs involved. Finally, the allocation of the burden of proof concerns the willingness of Members to pursue disputes. If the chances of winning even justified disputes are small, Members may refrain from bringing complaints because of the costs involved. This may adversely affect not only the Member that refrains from bringing a justified complaint, but also the rest of the membership, in that there are certain positive externalities from such complaints which contribute to maintaining the integrity of the self-enforcing agreement. The allocation of the burden of proof will also have implications for the incentives for countries to pursue illegal or legally questionable measures.

In short, in the absence of solid arguments in favour of viewing the allocation of burden of proof as a tennis match, there is no reason to discard the current system: inviting parties to produce evidence and judging whether the burden has been met against this background.

3.2 Burden of Persuasion (Standard of Review)

The leading case regarding the standard of review is the GATT Panel report on *US—Superfund*. We briefly referred to it in Chapter 2, but here are the facts in some more detail: the US had been taxing imported petroleum (and petroleum substances) slightly higher than their domestic counterparts. When the measure was challenged before the GATT dispute settlement process, the US response was that the difference was so minimal that it could not reasonably have an impact on the prices in the US market. The products affected by the US taxation scheme were like products, a point conceded by the US attorneys before the GATT Panel: they did not advance any defence other than the absence of impact on prices.

The GATT Panel dismissed the US argument. In its view, the fact that the effects on the market were negligible was a non-issue: Art. III GATT should be construed as a mechanism protecting legitimate expectations as to the quality of competitive conditions (§5.1.9):

> ...Article III:2, first sentence, cannot be interpreted to protect expectations on export volumes; it protects expectations on the competitive relationship between imported and domestic products. A change in the competitive relationship contrary to that provision must consequently be regarded ipso facto as a nullification or impairment of benefits accruing under the General Agreement. A demonstration that a measure inconsistent with Article III:2, first sentence, has no or insignificant effects would therefore in the view of the Panel not be a sufficient demonstration that the benefits accruing under that provision had not been nullified or impaired even if such a rebuttal were in principle permitted. (underlining in the original)

The AB in its report on *Japan—Alcoholic Beverages II* referred to this statement when deciding on the applicable standard of review (p. 16):

> ... it is irrelevant that 'the trade effects' of the tax differential between imported and domestic products, as reflected in the volumes of imports, are insignificant or even

295

non-existent; Article III protects expectations not of any particular trade volume but rather of the equal competitive relationship between imported and domestic products.[117]

In this report the AB extended the irrelevance of a trade effects test to cases where DCS products are involved and where de facto as opposed to de jure discrimination was at issue: in *US—Superfund* imported goods were being taxed higher than US goods because of their origin; in *Japan—Alcoholic Beverages II*, it was whisky that was being taxed higher than *sochu* irrespective of its origin.[118] The damage was done there and then:[119] it is one thing to extend the coverage of the NT provision to cases of de facto discrimination: indeed good arguments could be made in support of the case law subjecting cases of de facto discrimination to the coverage of NT since, absent this extension, the intended coverage of this provision would, inevitably, be severely curtailed.[120] One would expect, nevertheless, a more demanding standard when the claim is that the challenged measure leads to de facto discrimination. Yet applying the same standard to cases of both de jure and de facto discrimination seems prima facie an untenable proposition:[121] if at all, in the latter case it is not clear *ab initio* that the regulatory distinction is origin-based. Sykes (1999) correctly observes that regulatory measures that raise the costs of foreign firms relative to domestic firms are exceptionally wasteful protectionist devices, but with deadweight costs that can greatly exceed those of traditional protectionist instruments such as tariffs and quotas. The presumption hence would be that WTO Members wishing to protect their own market would rather use a trade than a domestic instrument.[122] The point here is that, since NT punishes protectionism, one would inevitably need more information (than in a de jure case) to establish that what was really meant through the challenged measure was to confer an advantage on domestic production.[123]

Logically, applying such a low threshold to adjudicating cases of de facto discrimination should have led to type I errors (false positives): WTO adjudicating bodies would be outlawing measures that should have been found GATT-consistent. And probably some false positives have been committed: it is difficult to

---

[117] Compare Oesch (2003).

[118] In similar vein, in *US—FSC*, the AB calls for a review of the impact of the challenged measure in the marketplace, while explicitly holding that there is no need to check actual effects (§215).

[119] To be fair, even the Panels on *US—Taxes on Automobiles*, which introduced the 'aims and effects' test, refused to inquire into trade effects invoking the prior ruling of *US—Superfund*.

[120] Jackson (1989, 1998, 2006) and Jackson and Aldonas (2003).

[121] Compare the corresponding analysis in Chapter 2 where we advocated a similar pattern.

[122] Renegotiation of duties comes at a cost as we saw in Chapter 2. But it can provide a stable environment post-payment of compensation. On the other hand, there is no guarantee that a protectionist measure will survive a challenge before a WTO Panel. WTO Members will thus have to weigh their options. The point here is that at least risk-averse WTO Members will not use a domestic instrument to afford protection to domestic production. Other considerations, of course, will also weigh in: for example, in light of its bargaining power, can the regulating WTO Member afford not to comply and see its trading partners suspend concessions (Art. 22 DSU)?

[123] Compare Di Mascio and Pauwelyn (2008).

understand how Korea lost the beef dispute discussed above in the absence of any (market) evidence that exporters of beef had suffered (or would in the future suffer) damage. In the same vein, for the reasons already mentioned, one might raise doubts on the soundness of the approach followed in *Chile—Alcoholic Beverages*.

More recently, WTO adjudicating bodies have seemed quite worried that they might commit a type I error and over time have adopted a cautious approach when the dispute brought before them concerns a domestic instrument. Error costs are important. Type II errors (false negatives) would amount to not striking down otherwise GATT-inconsistent legislation. The ensuing cost would be loss of trade income for the exporting country.[124] In case of type I error though, the cost is difficult to measure and for this reason probably more fearsome: striking down a GATT-consistent public health legislation comports, beyond the obvious casualties, a negative external effect that will haunt the institution. The GATT paid a heavy price with *US—Tuna*, when it outlawed a non-discriminatory US measure that banned sales of tuna that had been caught in a manner that accidentally took the life of dolphin simply because the measure was unilateral (as indeed would always be the case since there are no common policies in the GATT). At stake in that case was dolphin life. WTO turned a corner with *US—Shrimp* which marks the beginning of a change in case law, a sea change to be more precise: here the AB accepted that measures aiming to protect the environment should not be declared illegal simply because they are unilateral.[125]

Sykes (2003a) astutely observes that case law is more deferential to the proffered justifications of regulators in cases where human life is at stake (*EC—Asbestos*), for example, than in cases involving small stakes consumer fraud (*Korea—Various Measures on Beef*). In §172 of the AB report on *EC—Asbestos*, we read:

> We indicated in *Korea—Beef* that one aspect of the 'weighing and balancing process ... comprehended in the determination of whether a WTO-consistent alternative measure' is reasonably available is the extent to which the alternative measure 'contributes to the realization of the end pursued'. In addition, we observed, in that case, that '[t]he more vital or important [the] common interests or values' pursued, the easier it would be to accept as 'necessary' measures designed to achieve those ends. In this case, the objective pursued by the measure is the preservation of human life and health through the elimination, or reduction, of the well-known, and life-threatening, health risks posed by asbestos fibres. The value pursued is both vital and important in the highest degree. The remaining question, then, is whether there is an alternative measure that would achieve the same end and that is less restrictive of trade than a prohibition. (italics in the original, underlining added)

---

[124] In theory, the cost could be higher: what if, in the name of de facto precedent (*stare decisis*), subsequent Panels follow previous reports dealing with the same issue? This is quite probable, but there is an important mitigating factor: there is no binding precedent in the WTO, and there is always hope that subsequent Panels will not follow prior reports in case they can justify their deviation.

[125] See the discussion in Chapter 5.

One might take issue with this approach, since nowhere does the GATT state that a more deferential standard is warranted whenever human health is at stake. Moreover, the negative integration of the GATT would necessarily entail different social preferences and only by coincidence would there be unanimity across the various WTO Members as to what is vital or important.[126] But more generally, we observe a tendency to escape the automaticity of punishing any differential treatment distinguishing between two products competing in the same market:

(a) The introduction of the objective-intent test, which opens up an in-depth inquiry into the challenged measure;
(b) The consistent dilution of the econometrics test applied in the Japanese case involving alcoholic drinks all the way to *EC—Asbestos*: allowing for a 'reasonable consumer' test, coupled with the observed tendency to show additional deference when public health is at stake;
(c) The holdings first in *EC—Asbestos*, and then in *Dominican Republic—Import and Sale of Cigarettes*, where the AB took the view that regulatory distinctions that are unrelated to origin of goods are consistent with NT even if the trade impact falls disproportionately on imported goods.

This last point, as discussed, needs to be taken with a pinch of salt: following *Thailand—Cigarettes*, we are in the dark as to whether the holding applies only to cases where public health is at stake (*EC—Asbestos*) or to all other cases coming under the purview of Art. III GATT (*Dominican Republic—Import and Sale of Cigarettes*).

WTO adjudicating bodies and more particularly the AB seem to be moving in the intended direction of the GATT framers. Yet, they seem to be painting the broader picture for now, while leaving details for later. Case law has not managed to pin the key terms down in one measurable dimension and, as a result, there is still considerable uncertainty regarding the understanding of 'like products', 'ASATAP', 'LFT'. We are clearer as to what case law has rejected than as to what it has accepted: Ortino (2003) put his finger on the real issue when he argued that, while it is clear that WTO adjudicating bodies have rejected the aims-and-effects test,[127] it still remains unclear what they have replaced it with.

In light of the rather disappointing status of case law,[128] some voices have been heard arguing that it would be best to opt for legislative rather than judicial

---

126 On this issue, see Petersmann (2000).

127 Still, Porges and Trachtman (2003) use a legal-realist methodology and hypothesize that tribunals will, when examining domestic regulation under Art. III GATT, always look at aim and effects (no matter what they say). The authors then review the post *Japan—Alcoholic Beverages II* case law to make the point that tribunals have indeed looked at aim and effects.

128 The criticism against the AB decisions comes from academics from all walks of life: Choi (2003) discusses exhaustively all of the case law until 2003. Her main conclusion is that the key term in the NT provision, 'like products', has been interpreted inconsistently. She pleads for an interpretation in line with the overall WTO aims, that is, trade liberalization that takes sufficient account of

solutions in this respect. Bronckers and McNelis (2000) are of the view that, in light of the experience so far, it is probably too risky to leave it to adjudicating bodies to continue interpreting terms such as 'like products'. They argue that it would be wiser to legislate further (in an effort to attempt to complete the contract to the extent possible) and pre-empt judicial action by clarifying this concept. Verhoosel (2002) and Bartels (2009) have advanced more or less the same argument: they call for the application of an 'integrated necessity test' (the term first coined by Verhoosel) whereby the WTO adjudicator will decide whether de facto discrimination has occurred by engaging in a two-prong test: first, ask whether a measure specifically affects imported products, and if the response to this question is affirmative, then check whether the measure is necessary to achieve a legitimate policy goal. This approach too would require some change in the current text. Both are meritorious opinions in that, assuming a legislative change can be obtained through negotiations, the road will be clear. The problem is what change? Verhoosel proposes something concrete. Yet, his approach raises new questions: how should burden of proof be allocated? In light of how costly the supply of information is? Or, in light of other concerns, e.g. how many cases risk being brought to the WTO as a result of the allocation of burden of proof (and the ensuing administrative and opportunity costs)? Is necessity enough or should we be looking into other proxies for non-protectionism as well? Who will decide on a list of legitimate goals and how? More importantly, what is wrong with the (beginning of an) approach, as reflected in the AB report on *Dominican Republic—Import and Sale of Cigarettes*, whereby regulatory distinctions based on the origin of the good are the only ones that need to be punished under Art. III GATT?

There are limits on how much we can achieve through legislation. It is probably more appropriate to provide the judge with some workable rules of thumb. We

---

the negative-integration model established by the GATT. Trebilcock and Fishbein (2007) and Giri and Trebilcock (2005) believe that WTO adjudicating bodies have not managed to successfully distinguish cases of the legitimate exercise of regulatory autonomy from cases of regulatory protectionism, precisely because of their incapacity to design the proper standard of review to be applied in similar cases. Dunoff (2009) discusses how WTO Members can through domestic instruments advance social goals, paying particular attention to cases where the regulating government acts as purchaser. He points to the difficulties that might arise in this context as a result of the manner in which WTO adjudicating bodies have understood the key terms that appear in the body of Art. III GATT. Melloni (2005) agrees with the view espoused by adjudicating bodies that the NT provision is there to guarantee that no recourse will be made to regulatory protectionism. In his view, however, this test has been misapplied largely because the WTO adjudicating bodies (and more especially the AB) have refused to entertain any analysis grounded in economics. Eeckhout (2010), based on this case law, takes the view that WTO law has yet to mature on this issue. Charnovitz (2002) expresses disagreement with the manner in which WTO adjudicating bodies have, by applying an erroneous standard of review that does not inquire into the intent of the challenged measure, de facto subjected the pursuit of social preferences (often pursued in non-discriminatory terms) to trade concerns. This goes against the negotiating intent (that Charnovitz has explored in this and other work) and undoes the balance of rights and obligations as struck by the WTO Members during negotiations.

will turn to them in what follows. But first, we need to discuss the allocation of production of burden of proof.

3.3 Constructing NT as an Instrument to Punish Protectionism[129]

With all the analysis above in mind, we can now turn to a normative discussion and ask how WTO Panels should approach claims coming under the aegis of Art. III GATT. The term 'normative' needs some additional explanation since it might lead to confusion: the idea advanced here is that, without changing an iota in the current legal text, WTO adjudicating bodies could interpret the terms appearing in the NT provision in a manner that will honour its intended function. The suggested approach is guided by realism. Realism is in turn aided by the fact that what is left out as a result of our privileged approach is something that, although desirable to address, would be too costly to address in a meaningful manner. We noted *supra* that Art. III GATT aims at eliminating protectionism (an objective that we approve), but does not oblige WTO Members to adopt efficient regulations, and that inefficient regulations, to the extent that they are non-discriminatory, will pass the test for consistency with Art. III GATT. This is not satisfactory. Yet, if we were to introduce a similar requirement, we would have to push for legislative amendment of the GATT, a costly operation as noted *supra*. Moreover, the domestic democratic dialogue can anyway push in this direction, so why make it an international issue?

3.3.1 The Important Parameters of the Proposed Test for Consistency with Art. III GATT

Art. 3.2 DSU clearly states that it is not for the interpreter to undo the balance of rights and obligations as struck by the framers of the WTO. So, even if desirable to do so, the interpreter should stop short of imposing its own rationality, thus relegating negotiating intent to a second-order consideration. This provision is very important in light of the decision to advance an 'interpretative' rather than a 'legislative' proposal.

The basic idea of the NT provision is deceptively simple: since inefficiencies in the use of domestic instruments stem from less favourable treatment of imported products, countries should not be allowed to treat domestic products better than foreign products solely by virtue of their different origin. While persuasive at a general level, the practical implementation of this simple idea has proved to be far from trivial. The basic thrust of the GATT is to leave Members discretion over domestic instruments, while punishing only 'protectionist' policies.

'Protection' is nowhere defined in the GATT. It can be interpreted to mean 'to shield from competition', without any value judgment attached as to whether this is desirable or not. Alternatively, it could be interpreted to refer to measures giving

---

[129] This section draws on Grossman et al. (2012).

rise to negative international externalities. Moreover, it is simply not the case that all protection is undesirable in the GATT: for instance, when using the phrase 'so as to afford protection', Art. II.4 GATT states, with respect to government mandated or operated monopolies, that:

> ... such a monopoly should not ... operate so as to afford protection on the average in excess of the amount of protection provided for in that Schedule.

Hence, a certain degree of 'protection' is legitimate–the protection provided for in the national schedule of concessions—while any additional protection is illegal.[130] It is clear that, when Art. III.1 GATT sets its sights on domestic policy measures that are 'applied so as to afford protection', it refers to an undesirable form of 'protection': there is no corresponding legitimate protection mentioned for domestic instruments. It is also clear that many policy measures that WTO Members would consider to be legitimate (and thus not protectionist), at the same time protect import-competing industries in the sense of shielding them from competition. Those affected by such measures might disagree on their legitimacy. All this is the natural consequence of the incompleteness of Art. III GATT.

At the core of the rationale for NT is an informational problem: the need for the provision stems from the fact that government preferences are not easily observable. But very little work has been done to date on informational aspects of NT. Consider the following illustrative example. An importing country government can have two different motives to impose a higher tax on imports than on domestic competing products: all governments probably have the standard protectionist motive, and some governments face local environmental problems stemming from the transportation or consumption of the imported product. Outside observers cannot tell whether a higher tax on an imported product is motivated by one or both of these motives. We can thus, in theory, think of governments:

(a) with only protectionist motives for differential taxation;
(b) with only environmental motives; or
(c) with both protectionist and environmental motives.

For the sake of simplification, assume category (b) does not exist. Now note two features: first, since a government coming under (c) faces the same protectionist motives as the other type of government, that is, government (a), its unilaterally optimal tax differential will be larger than if only protectionism motivated the tax setting, since the environmental problem adds a reason for taxing the imported products higher; second, if the negotiated tariff is sufficiently high, there is no need to use domestic taxes to achieve any of these objectives. The importing country can set the same tax rate (perhaps equal to zero), and can achieve both its protectionist

---

[130] Economic theory would suggest that the legitimacy of the protection provided by the measures that are bound in the Schedule stems from the fact that it has been negotiated.

	Market like	Not market like
Policy like	Like: no tax differential is allowed	Art. III not applicable; any tax differential is allowed
Not policy like	DCS: some tax differential is allowed	Art. III not applicable; any tax differential is allowed

and a possible environmental target in a NT-compatible fashion through the tariff. As the tariff is gradually lowered from this level, however, it becomes increasingly likely that there is not enough of a difference in total taxation between the imported and the domestic product. The government to first experience this problem is the government that faces environmental problems from imports, since it has stronger incentives to maintain a large tax differential than the government that is solely motivated by protectionism. The environmentally conscious government will hence be the first to switch to lower taxation of the domestic product, and thus come under NT. In this sense, as trade is liberalized, NT first affects those governments that desire high total taxation of the imported product not only for protectionist reasons, but also for environmental reasons. NT in this sense starts to bind from the wrong side of the spectrum of government types.

Of course, this feature of NT may be immaterial if the adjudication process flawlessly determines whether countries have been exposed to environmental hazards of a sufficiently severe nature for it to be in the global interest to let these countries continue with their differential taxation. But if there are e.g. litigation costs, or if adjudicating bodies occasionally commit judicial mistakes, this aspect may take on significance. As we have argued above, judicial errors are not only probable (or possible), but in our view they have already occurred. And the possibility that a judicial error might be committed is taken on board in our proposal.

All these considerations have guided us when formulating the test for consistency with Art. III GATT that we would like to see WTO adjudicating bodies applying in future cases.

3.3.2 A Test for Consistency with Art. III GATT

Our preferred test could be summarized as follows:

Two goods are like if they are both market and policy like. Because of their shared properties, there will be absolutely no reason to differentiate their treatment. One might of course legitimately ask why, in light of policy likeness, there is any need for market likeness as well? The main reason for including the market likeness criterion is to prevent the provision binding importers in instances where by coincidence the products would be treated equally despite not being in competition. For instance, there are many reasons why a country may apply a lower tax on domestically produced coffee cups (which are not imported) than on diesel trucks (which are only imported). It could by chance be the case that the joint welfare of the exporting and importing country governments would increase if the importing country government were requested to tax the two products identically—the products thus being policy like by chance. But it is obviously highly unlikely that the differential taxation would reflect protectionism.

The next question[131] would be: what should be the test when DCS goods[132] are at stake? How should we understand DCS, and how should we understand ASATP/LTF?

Let us start with DCS goods. Recall that case law has consistently held that the test for DCS goods is in the marketplace. Yet, case law, although in name it has been following the same test, has not been internally consistent: indeed, as we pointed out *supra*, it is scarcity of monetary resources (and the ensuing opportunity cost) that dictate consumption for the majority of consumers; hence, price is the key element in deciding whether two goods are DCS, and price is the relevant criterion in *Japan—Alcoholic Beverages II*, but not in *Korea—Alcoholic Beverages*. More generally, although the test is in the marketplace, the quantity of market information is not symmetric across the discussed cases: a consumer survey was submitted in re: *Japan—Alcoholic Beverages II*; a 'reasonable-consumer test' was adopted in *EC—Asbestos*, where it was judged unnecessary to ask consumers whether the asbestos-containing and asbestos-free construction materials are DCS goods. Table 4.3 aims to capture the quantity of market information associated with each of the three leading cases in this respect. Over time, WTO adjudicating bodies have moved to a market uninformed test, although probably this was done because of the subject-matter of *EC—Asbestos*.[133]

---

[131] This understanding of the key terms does not require redrafting either of §2 or of §4 of Art. III GATT: recall that following *EC—Asbestos*, 'like' in Art. III.4 covers both like and DCS goods as the two terms are understood in Art. III.2 GATT. One can thus distinguish between cases where like or DCS goods are being discussed in litigation under Art. III.4 GATT.

[132] The evaluation of the competitive relationship between the products should preferably be based on data collected from the actual market at hand. But lacking such data, as when the differential policy treatment is sufficiently pronounced to deny market access to the exportable, one must resort to more indirect sources of information. This could for instance be evidence on the relationship between the products in other countries or between similar products in the importing country. One could also use the indicators suggested in the WP on BTAs (such as end-uses, physical characteristics, etc.). Another source of information is tariff classification. For the most part, if two products are in the same six-digit Harmonized System category, they are likely to be in close competition, even though such tariff classifications are not always informative about the properties of the products. With finer HS classification, it is of course even more likely that the products are highly competitive. The data should as far as possible be examined through econometric analysis. Indeed, such analysis is commonplace in the antitrust context where the relevant product market within which market power will be estimated is routinely defined in this way. But since the quality of both data and econometric analyses are likely to vary, such analysis should be complemented with other forms of market analysis. The basic purpose of such exercises is to assess the extent to which the contested measure enhances the competitive position of the domestic product relative to the importable.

[133] Korea did not offer any policy rationale for tax differentials other than that the two goods were not in DCS relationship because of their price differential. Japan did offer some justification (e.g. protecting artisanal production), but it was considered *ex post facto* justification by the Panel since it was nowhere reflected in the Order imposing the tax differential.

Table 4.3 Market information in deciding DCS relationship

Quantity of Market Information	High	Japan—Alcoholic Beverages II	Korea—Alcoholic Beverages	EC— Asbestos
	Low	1996	1998	2003

Recourse to econometric indicators should be the starting-point of analysis inquiring into the DCS relationship between two goods: it is by far the most reliable tool we possess at this stage to discuss this relationship. On occasion, recourse to econometric indicators might be impossible: for example, in case one of the goods concerned is not physically present in the market under examination. In similar cases, recourse to non-econometric indicators will be warranted and it is there that the various criteria first established in the Working Party report on BTAs could find application.[134]

Finally, the mere presence of regulation should alert the WTO judge to the possibility that the goods concerned are market-like (DCS). The natural question to ask here would be why regulate if goods are anyway (in the eyes of consumers) market-unlike? We say presumption because even if consumers through their behaviour have 'internalized' the externality, there might still be reason to regulate: it could be, for example, that some consumers continue to behave in the opposite way to the majority of consumers and their behaviour might comport negative external effects for the society; it could also be that the regulator wants to buy an insurance policy against uncertainty since future behaviour of consumers is not given; or, even, for political economy reasons, a government might want to be perceived as doing the right thing, even though the right thing is practised anyway.

Turning to the question regarding the understanding of the ASATAP/LFT requirement, recall from our discussion above that a fundamental problem facing the adjudicator is to determine the true preferences of the importing country. Since preferences are not directly observable, and since the regulating state has a strong incentive to behave opportunistically, the judge must rely on indirect evidence of their nature. Information (or indications) concerning intent could be relevant here.[135] Examples of such indicators are the following:

---

[134] The Panel report on *Philippines—Distilled Spirits* is an excellent illustration of the limits of using econometric indicators not based on historical quantity and price data so that the emerging picture should correspond to actual and not imaginary consumption of particular goods and their relationship to other DCS goods; see §§7.110ff of the Panel report.

[135] Zhou (2012) supports the view that the negotiating history of Art. III GATT suggests that the intent of the regulator was considered relevant in an evaluation of the consistency of a policy with Art. III GATT.

(a) As a threshold issue, the measure should be origin-neutral. Even if today say only domestic cars conform to the desired environmental standard, there is no good reason to ban foreign cars from the market only because they are foreign. After all, it is the environmental friendliness of the goods that will provide them with the regulatory 'passport' to this market and no one can exclude that in the future foreign cars will conform to this standard;

(b) The question whether the regulating state has had recourse to the first-best instrument to address the perceived distortion;

(c) Scientific evidence: Measures based on scientific evidence are in general more likely to respond to a genuine need to intervene, at least in light of the best current knowledge about a particular issue. Of course, this does not mean that measures based on the precautionary principle are necessarily protectionist: for such measures, recourse to some or all of the criteria mentioned above might be warranted;

(d) The consistency by which the alleged objective is pursued across products: if the same objective is disregarded in other industries, the differential treatment of the product at hand might indicate that the protection is intentional; indeed, Art. 5.5 SPS reflects a very similar idea;

(e) The use of international standards: assume for example that an international standard exists that can appropriately take care of the legislative objective sought. Deviations from the standard, while not necessarily unwarranted, should then be viewed with suspicion: it should be normal in similar cases to request from the deviating state to explain itself on its choice to deviate, rather than allocate the burden of production of proof à la *EC—Sardines* (AB report);[136]

(f) The magnitude of trade effects: The larger are the trade effects, the more likely it is that they are intended. The choice of less trade-restrictive should be understood as a proxy (albeit an imperfect one) that the measure has been enacted for motives other than protectionism;[137]

(g) In similar vein, the question whether domestic producers have had to incur adjustment costs in order to conform to the new regulatory standard.

This list is by no means exhaustive, but only intended to illustrate the type of criteria that could be used to evaluate whether a measure is protectionist. Two

---

[136] See the discussion in Chapter 10.

[137] Doing away with a trade-effects test not only deprived WTO adjudicating bodies of useful evidence with which to evaluate protectionism, but had another side-effect: in order to satisfy standing requirements (*locus standi*) all that complainants need to satisfy before a WTO adjudicating body is legal interest to observe the WTO contract; there is no need to demonstrate trade damage resulting from the challenged measure. But legal interest exists for all since all WTO Members are interested in seeing that the WTO contract is respected. Hence, in principle, all WTO Members can challenge the consistency of any measure with the WTO rules irrespective of whether they have actually suffered from it. This could of course lead to a flurry of litigation. Indeed, the AB ruled as much in its *EC—Bananas III* report.

points are in order here: first, the above are proxies, not legal obligations. That is, the judge cannot, for example, request WTO Members to always perform a scientific risk assessment or punish them for not doing so. It can, however, if presented with similar evidence, reach a more informed judgment on the consistency of the challenged measure. Second, it is difficult to establish a hierarchy across the various criteria established above. It seems however that, besides the threshold issue, criteria (b)–(d) are the least controversial and for that reason should be the priority-criteria, so to speak. Adjudicators should think twice before striking down measures that are science-based and are adopted by WTO Members with consistent (in the sense of Art. 5.5 SPS)[138] policies, for the risk of committing a false positive in this constellation is quite high.[139]

In sum, both effect and intent are relevant to the definition of the substantive obligation. Effect matters since the purpose is to regulate measures that cause international externalities, and intent matters since it is closely related to the question whether international externalities are present. Effects, moreover, can be a proxy for regulatory intent. Intent and effect are also relevant from an evidentiary perspective, since both perceived intent as well as observed effects in the market could serve as evidence concerning the extent to which the substantive requirements for a violation are at hand.

In what respect does the approach suggested above differ from the aims-and-effects test? First, likeness is not only policy likeness, but also market likeness in our approach. Second, the realized effects of the contested measure matter, but are explicitly irrelevant in the aims-and-effects test.

One might legitimately ask the question where does this approach lead and what does it mean for Art. XX GATT? Is not this provision supposed to be an exception to all GATT provisions, including Art. III GATT? It is true that what we describe above comes close to constructing Art. III GATT as a one-stop shop where claims that NT has been violated will be discussed exclusively within its four corners. That much is probably true. We should note nonetheless that, through this construction, we have not committed the cardinal mistake of the interpreter of reading Art. XX GATT into redundancy. Art. XX GATT will continue to have a role as exception to trade instruments, such as tariffs and QRs. Moreover, it can continue to have a limited role with respect to domestic instruments:[140] assume for example that Home taxes (VAT) domestic cars at 5 per cent and imported cars at 25 per cent, although both sets of cars are equally polluting or equally environmentally friendly. Home will then be violating Art. III GATT. It could then seek

---

[138] See the discussion in Chapter 10.

[139] One might have a similar reaction with respect to measures based on international standards. The discussion in Büthe and Mattli (2011), however, reveals that it is not unwarranted to view (many) international standards with some scepticism. We discuss this issue in more detail in Chapter 7.

[140] This view has not been accepted in case law, which continues to construct Art. XX GATT as an exception to Art. III GATT.

justification in Art. XX GATT, and argue that this measure relates to the protection of clean air that Foreign pollutes when producing steel. If Foreign does not export steel, Home will have no other way to punish Foreign for its behavior which it is assumed affects Home as well. In this vein, Home will have to demonstrate that it applies similar measures to domestic production of steel in order to justify the conditions of the *chapeau* of Art. XX GATT.[141]

There are two reasons for limiting the role of Art. XX GATT in this respect: first, the two provisions (Art. III, Art. XX GATT) share a non-discrimination clause. How can a measure that has been found to be discriminatory under Art. III GATT also be found to be non-discriminatory under Art. XX GATT?[142] Second, the GATT framers did not conceive the GATT as an instrument for deregulation or for efficient domestic regulation, but rather for non-discrimination, where the disciplining of domestic instruments served one purpose only: to ensure that the value of tariff concessions would not be impaired through their discriminatory use. Moving the discussion to Art. XX GATT inherently entails the risk of constructing the GATT as an instrument of deregulation.[143] This is why: Art. XX GATT contains an exhaustive list of policy objectives that serve as a blanket basis for exceptions from undertakings in the rest of the GATT, provided they are not disguised protection. For example, a WTO Member distinguishing between 'ordinary' and 'luxury' items in such a manner as to indirectly tax an imported product higher than a competing domestic product will have a hard time finding justification under Art. XX GATT. Another example would be domestic taxation that treats products originating from small and medium enterprises more favourably than products of bigger players. According to current case law (*Chile—Alcoholic Beverages*), it suffices that in both instances one imported product is taxed more heavily than its domestic counterpart, the overall tax effect being a non-issue. The defendant would then have a hard time justifying its measures under Art. XX GATT. Yet another policy would be the promotion of culture.

It might sound cavalier, even aloof, but discrimination does not have an inherent value; it is an empty shell. It means nothing beyond being a point on a

---

141 See the relevant discussion in Chapter 5.

142 WTO case law tried to respond to this question, quite unsuccessfully in our view, as we will see *infra*.

143 In EU law, the Court (European Court of Justice, ECJ) has adopted a more expansive understanding of the exceptions to free movement of goods (the provisions in the EU legal order corresponding to Arts. III/XX GATT): in C-112/00, *Schmidberger*, the Court found nothing wrong with the fact that Austrian citizens had blocked a highway and thus made free movement of goods more onerous, since it found that this action was an exercise of freedom of speech and thus a legitimate restriction on trade; in C-265/95, *Commission v France*, though, it found that France was in violation of its obligations because it did not take adequate measures to stop rioters from destroying strawberries imported from Spain. In this latter case, no defence other than the desire to protect domestic production was at stake. Freedom of speech is not explicitly mentioned in the body of EU law as a legitimate defence against free movement of goods; the Court was interpreting the term 'public order'.

continuum which serves as a distinctive factor between policies that a society (local or international) has accepted as lawful and policies that it wants to condemn. Think of it this way: assume two identical twins take the Bar exam and score identical scores. They are ranked 100th and 101st. Now the Bar accepts only 100 new attorneys for reasons having to do with the distribution of income across incumbents. One of the two must fail, yet there is no distinctive feature between them. Still, one will fail in the name of the policy objective pursued by the Bar. In the GATT world, the policy objective pursued is the fight against protectionism, and discrimination is legalese for protectionism.

4. TRIMs (Trade Related Investment Measures)

4.1 The Legal Discipline and its Rationale

WTO Members must, by virtue of the various obligations included in the WTO TRIMs Agreement, notify the WTO of all measures coming under its aegis, respect a standstill-obligation during a transition period, at the end of which they must have eliminated all measures judged inconsistent with the TRIMs disciplines. The TRIMs Agreement is *lex specialis* to Arts. III and XI GATT since it specifically outlaws two instruments covered by these provisions, export performance and local content requirements. It was considered necessary to add this agreement for essentially two reasons: on the one hand, it would provide some clarity judged necessary with respect to the two instruments mentioned *supra*; on the other, the advent of this Agreement was considered a precursor to a more 'comprehensive' agreement on trade and investment. Investment and trade could be complements[144] and/or substitutes,[145] and one might affect the other. A comprehensive agreement nevertheless could not see the light of the day, the various initiatives inside and outside the WTO notwithstanding. We turn to this discussion in what immediately follows.

4.2 Trade and Investment: From ITO to the GATT

Investment was not regulated in a comprehensive manner in the Havana Charter. Two provisions (Arts. 11 and 12) in Chapter III entitled 'Economic Development and Reconstruction' deal with this issue, and the placement of investment-related provisions in this Chapter probably denotes the overarching objective that investment

---

[144] There is ample literature on this score. Recently, Baltagi et al. (2008) discuss the relationship between PTAs (preferential trade agreements) and FDI (foreign direct investment) and conclude in an empirical paper discussing the Europe Agreements that removal of trade barriers can lead to substantial flows of FDI for those participating.

[145] The foundational paper for viewing investment and trade as substitutes is that by Bhagwati et al. (1987), who have argued that foreign export-oriented firms may establish import-competing subsidiaries in an effort to jump an existing tariff or to defuse a protectionist threat (*tariff jumping*).

regulation should serve. The regime was thus not geared towards protecting property rights, although this would have been the natural outcome; it was thought of rather as a tool to promote economic development faithful to the '*dirigiste*' spirit of the ITO.

The provisions are all couched in hortatory language, leaving ample discretion to interested parties to adopt specific measures, the content of which is not specified *ex ante*:

(a) ITO Members could reflect on the appropriateness of signing bilateral or even multilateral agreements protecting international investment, the possibility of one multilateral agreement being retained;

(b) In the meantime, they should strive to provide foreign investors with equitable treatment, the parameters of the treatment remaining unspecified.

Two more specific provisions were included in the ITO Charter:

(a) ITO Members should reflect on avoiding double taxation as a means to promote international investment;

(b) They should further reflect on the appropriateness of avoiding discrimination against foreign investors (the benchmark of comparison being domestic investors).

Again the language was hortatory. Anyway, the non-advent of the ITO[146] meant the de facto irrelevance of these provisions: we say de facto and not de jure because, by virtue of Art. XXIX GATT, GATT contracting parties undertook to observe, pending the entry into force of the ITO, to the fullest extent possible the general principles of Chapters I–VI of the Havana Charter.[147]

The GATT does not deal with investment in an explicit manner. Proponents of a wide GATT mandate might point to the term 'affecting' appearing in Art. III.4 GATT, and argue that the non-discrimination obligation extends to any measure affecting trade. Similar arguments were put to rest by a GATT Panel, the Panel on *Canada—FIRA*, as explained above. Subsequent practice amply confirms this point: WTO Members do not treat investors from other states in a non-discriminatory manner and no legal challenge against similar practices has ever been raised. The GATT requires WTO Members to abolish two types of investment measures:

(a) local content and

(b) export performance requirements (Arts. III.5 and XI GATT respectively).

---

[146] Irwin et al. (2008); Jackson (1969); Wilcox (1949).
[147] See Chapter 1 on this score.

The historic record indicates that, in the 1940s, there was very frequent use of the two types of investment measures, and negotiators felt that these types of measures would undermine the very basis of the GATT.[148]

4.3 The Coverage of the Legal Discipline

4.3.1 Measures Coming under the Purview of TRIMs

Art. 2.1 TRIMs prohibits WTO Members from applying any investment measure that is inconsistent with Art. III, or Art. XI GATT. An illustrative list annexed to TRIMs provides the following examples of measures that are inconsistent with Art. III or Art. XI GATT:

(a) Local content requirements;
(b) Export performance requirements;
(c) Trade balancing requirements;
(d) Foreign exchange balancing restrictions; and
(e) Restrictions on an enterprise's export or sale for export of products.

WTO Members must phase out similar measures during a transitional period, assuming that they have notified the WTO of these measures. A longer transition period is available to developing countries. The content of the illustrative list is inspired by the plain text of GATT provisions, and by the relevant case law as well. So one might legitimately ask whether there is any value added in concluding the TRIMs? Besides keeping the wider trade and investment discussion alive, a point to which we will come back later, the TRIMs adds to the GATT provision in different ways. First, the TRIMs facilitates the work of WTO adjudicating bodies, since it identifies specific types of trade-related investment measures (other than local content that is explicitly included in the body of Art. III GATT) that are considered to be inconsistent with GATT Art. III or XI. The Panel on *India—Autos* held that (§7.157), the illustrative list:[149]

> provides additional guidance as to the identification of certain measures considered to be inconsistent with Articles III:4 and XI:1 of the GATT 1994.

Assuming a measure challenged falls under the illustrative list, it will be *ipso facto* judged WTO-inconsistent; the judge will not have to see to what extent it violates a specific provision. The *Indonesia—Autos* Panel ruled to this effect (§14.83):

> An examination of whether the measures [in question] are covered by Item (1) of the Illustrative List . . . will not only indicate whether they are trade-related but also whether they are inconsistent with Article III:4 and thus in violation of Article 2.1 of the TRIMs Agreement.

---

[148] See, on this score, Irwin et al. (2008) and Trebilcock and Howse (2005).
[149] See Bagwell and Sykes (2007b).

The TRIMs agreement also provides extra transparency. Under GATT, WTO Members have to notify the WTO of only measures of general application (Art. X GATT). Arguably, many measures covered by TRIMs are of general application. Art. X GATT, however, leaves substantial discretion to WTO Members (although their exercise of discretion is justiciable). The TRIMs reduces the scope for discretion by obliging them to notify all TRIMs.

Finally, the TRIMs Agreement includes a transitional period during which WTO Members agreed to phase out WTO-inconsistent measures that had been notified to the WTO.

This raises the more general question regarding the relationship between GATT and TRIMs: there is now an agreed transition period for measures which violate Arts. III and/or XI GATT which did not exist before the advent of the WTO. Several WTO Panels have dealt with measures challenged under both GATT and Art. 2.1 TRIMs. In analysing the legal relationship between GATT and TRIMs, a preliminary issue is whether there is a conflict between the two agreements. Recall that, according to the General Interpretive Note to Annex 1A of the WTO Agreement, when a conflict exists between a provision of the GATT and a provision of another agreement in Annex 1A (like TRIMs), the provision of the other agreement 'shall prevail to the extent of the conflict'. In the event of a conflict between the provisions of GATT and TRIMs, the provisions of the TRIMs would, therefore, prevail. The term 'conflict' is not defined any further. As we saw, the originally narrow understanding of the term conflict quickly gave way to the concept of *lex specialis*: according to this interpretative principle, even if no genuine conflict exists between two provisions in two different agreements, a transaction which potentially could be submitted under two different agreements should always be submitted to the one that regulates in more detail the transaction at hand. There have been disagreements, nevertheless, in earlier case law as to which of the two (GATT, TRIMs) is the more specific agreement. For example, in *Indonesia—Autos*, the Panel reflects the view that TRIMs is the more specific agreement (§14.63):

> first examine[d] the claims under the TRIMs Agreement since the TRIMs Agreement is more specific than Article III:4 [of the GATT] as far as the claims under consideration are concerned.

However, in *Canada—Autos*, while the Panel accepted (§10.63)

> that a claim should be examined first under the agreement which is the most specific with respect to that claim . . .

it concluded that TRIMs could not be (§10.63)

> properly characterized as being more specific than Article III:4 in respect of the claims raised by the complainants in the present case.

In the same vein, in *India—Autos*, the Panel stated that, as a general matter, it might be difficult to characterize the TRIMs Agreement as necessarily more specific than the relevant GATT provisions (§7.157). The Panel analysed the measures in question under the GATT first, partly because India, the responding party, encouraged the Panel to refrain from evaluating the consistency of the challenged measures with the relevant provisions of the TRIMs Agreement (§7.158). The order of analysis of the various claims presented should not, in principle, affect the outcome, assuming that an examination under the TRIMs will follow that under the GATT. Nevertheless, as the Panel itself implicitly recognized, the situation could be different in case judicial economy has been exercised: in this case, the outcome of the dispute might be different had a Panel examined the challenged measure under the more detailed agreement (TRIMs) as well (§§7.158–61).[150]

There has been a drastic change in the attitude of the WTO adjudicating bodies since the report on *EC—Sardines*. There, the AB made it abundantly clear that WTO adjudicating bodies should always start from the agreement regulating a matter in a more specific manner; by privileging the TBT over the GATT (§204), and, hinting that the GATT is the default agreement, one should expect that Panels now confronted with this issue will start their analysis from the claims under TRIMs.

The measures appearing in the illustrative list discussed above cover measures that come under the purview of both Art. III as well as Art. XI GATT (if, of course, no TRIMs Agreement existed). The following come under the purview of the former:

(a) Required purchase or use by an enterprise of products of domestic origin or from any domestic source; or
(b) Requirements to the effect that an enterprise's purchases or use of imported products be limited to an amount related to the volume or value of local products that it exports.

In *Indonesia—Autos*, the Panel ruled on the legality of an Indonesian car programme, linking tax benefits for cars manufactured in Indonesia to local content requirements, and linking customs duty benefits for imported components of cars manufactured in Indonesia to similar local content requirements. The Panel found that these were indeed local content requirements which had a significant impact on investment in the automotive sector (§14.80), and that they were trade-related, because they affected trade (§14.82). The Panel also found that compliance with the requirements for the purchase and use of products of domestic origin was necessary to obtain the tax and customs duty benefits and that such benefits were advantages within the meaning of the illustrative list

---

[150] For examples of judicial economy, see the Panel reports on *Indonesia—Autos* (§14.93); *India—Autos* (§7.324); *EC—Bananas III* (§7.185); and *Canada—Autos* (§10.91).

(§§14.89–91). As a result, the Panel ruled that the local content requirements imposed by Indonesia violated the TRIMs Agreement (§14.91).

Three categories of measures come under the purview of Art. XI.1 GATT:

(a) The importation by an enterprise of products used in or related to its local production, generally in an amount related to the volume or value of local production that it exports;

(b) The importation by an enterprise of products used in or related to its local production by restricting its access to foreign exchange to an amount related to the foreign exchange inflows attributable to the enterprise; or

(c) The exportation or sale for export by an enterprise of products.

All these measures are (in varying degree) export-related performance requirements. The *India—Autos* litigation[151] involved the review of an Indian trade-balancing measure: the import (by domestic car manufacturers) of parts and components necessary for the production of cars was conditioned on a certain FOB (free on board) value of exports of cars and components over the same period; if the statutory thresholds had not been met, no imports would occur. The legislation thus gave an incentive to Indian car manufacturers to export (so that they could profit from cheap inputs). The Panel addressed this measure in the following manner (§§7.277–8):

> [As of the date of the establishment of the trade balancing condition,] there would necessarily have been a practical threshold to the amount of exports that each manufacturer could expect to make, which in turn would determine the amount of imports that could be made. This amounts to an import restriction. The degree of effective restriction which would result from this condition may vary from signatory [of a memorandum of understanding with the Indian government] to signatory depending on its own projections, its output, or specific market conditions, but a manufacturer is in no instance free to import, without commercial constraint, as many kits and components as it wishes without regard to its export opportunities and obligations. The Panel therefore finds that the trade balancing condition [,] ... by limiting the amount of imports through linking them to an export commitment, acts as a restriction on importation, contrary to the terms of Article XI:1.

Having found that the trade balancing requirements violated Art. XI.1 GATT, the *India—Autos* Panel invoked the principle of judicial economy and concluded that it was not necessary to analyse the measures under the TRIMs Agreement as well (§§7.323–4).

4.3.2 Obligations during and after the Transitional Phase

Art. 5.2 TRIMs provides for three different transition periods during which WTO Members, according to their level of development, must phase out WTO-inconsistent measures that the Council on Trade in Goods (CTG) has been notified of:

---

151 Bagwell and Sykes (2007b) discuss this case.

(a) Developed country Members were required to eliminate their WTO-inconsistent measures by 1 January 1997;

(b) Developing country Members were required to eliminate their WTO-inconsistent measures by 1 January 2000;

(c) LDCs were required to eliminate their WTO-inconsistent measures by 1 January 2002.[152]

Art. 5.1 TRIMs subjects to prior notification all measures that can benefit from the transitional period established: new measures introduced within 180 days before the entry into force of the Agreement shall not profit from the transitional period (Art. 5.4 TRIMs). During the transitional period, a WTO Member could not modify the terms of any WTO-inconsistent measure (Art. 5.4 TRIMs): this is the standstill-obligation imposed on WTO Members with respect to all notified TRIMs.

The notification record probably leads to suspicion that not all WTO Members took this obligation seriously: for example, among least developed countries, only Uganda notified its local content-type trade-related investment measures.[153] Some developing countries were unable to eliminate WTO-inconsistent measures during the transitional period and made use of the possibility provided in the TRIMs Agreement (Art. 5.3) to request extension of the deadline for compliance from the CTG.[154]

4.3.3 Procedural Obligations

WTO Members must (Art. 6.2 TRIMs):

> notify the Secretariat of the publications in which TRIMs can be found, including those applied by regional and local governments and authorities within their territories.

The purpose of this obligation is to ensure transparency. This transparency obligation covers both WTO-consistent and WTO-inconsistent measures.

The CTG was required to review the TRIMs by 1 January 2000 (Art. 9 TRIMs) to:

> consider whether the Agreement should be complemented with provisions on investment policy and competition policy.

The review process began in 1999 and is still ongoing. There is no consensus on the need to amend the Agreement: while developing countries are seeking

---

[152] The transition period for LDCs was extended until 2012 by virtue of Annex F of the Hong Kong Ministerial Declaration; see *infra* for more detail.

[153] WTO Doc. G/TRIMS/N/1/UGA/1 of 7 July 1997.

[154] Extensions were granted to Argentina, Colombia, Malaysia, Mexico, Pakistan, Thailand (until 31 December 2003), Philippines (30 June 2003), and Romania (31 May 2003).

greater flexibility to apply TRIMs for development purposes, developed countries generally would like to see the current balance of rights and obligations maintained.

4.3.4 The Relationship with Other Annex 1A Agreements

The legal relationship between TRIMs and other Annex 1A agreements was discussed in a case involving a measure challenged under TRIMs- and the SCM Agreements. In *Indonesia—Autos*, the Panel concluded that measures challenged under both TRIMs and the SCM must be reviewed under both agreements. The Panel examined whether there was conflict between the two agreements. In its view, the General Interpretive Note did not apply to the relationship between TRIMs and SCM (§14.49). It used a narrow definition of the term 'conflict' to arrive at its final judgment. It held that (§14.55):

> there is no general conflict between the SCM Agreement and the TRIMs Agreement.

It thus moved on and applied the two agreements cumulatively to the transaction before it.

4.3.5 Special and Differential Treatment

The TRIMs Agreement provides for special and differential treatment by making available longer transitional periods in order to eliminate notified TRIMs to developing countries and LDCs. Following negotiations, it was agreed during the Hong Kong Ministerial Conference (2005) that additional measures were required. Annex F of the Hong Kong Ministerial Decision[155] reflects these new measures:

(a) LDCs were allowed to maintain existing TRIMs until the end of a new transition period lasting for seven years:
   (i) The transitional period may be extended by decision of the CTG, in light of the individual financial, trade, and development needs of the Member in question;
   (ii) LDCs would have to notify the CTG within two years of their TRIMs, their notification duty starting on 17 January 2006;
(b) LDCs were further allowed to introduce new TRIMs:
   (i) The duration of the new TRIMs shall not exceed five years, and they could be renewed subject to review and decision by the CTG;

---

[155] Decision adopted on 18 December 2005, see WTO Doc. WT/MIN(05)/DEC of 22 December 2005.

(ii) To this effect, LDC will have to notify the CTG of their new TRIMs within six months of their adoption;

(iii) The CTG is encouraged to give positive consideration to such notifications.

4.3.6 Institutional Issues

A Committee on Trade-Related Investment Measures (TRIMs Committee) is established by virtue of Art. 7 TRIMs. The main task of the TRIMs Committee is to monitor the operation and implementation of the TRIMs Agreement. It further provides a forum for consultations among WTO Members on trade and investment issues. The TRIMs Committee reports annually to the CTG.

4.4 Trade and Investment Revisited

The inevitable conclusion from the discussion above is that the WTO, as it now stands, does not deal with investment in a comprehensive manner. This is not for lack of trying: a Working Group was established soon after the advent of the WTO to discuss this issue. It was short-lived, and did not manage to bring its mandate to conclusion. Attempts to multilateralize investment protection have also taken place outside the WTO, most notably within the OECD where the Multilateral Agreement on Investment (MAI) was launched. This initiative too has not led to a fruitful conclusion. As a result, investment protection nowadays takes place within bilateral investment treaties (BITs), regional schemes, and PTAs. We will take each issue in turn in what follows.

4.4.1 The Working Group on Trade and Investment

Following an initial discussion in the Singapore Ministerial Conference (1996), WTO Members agreed at the Doha Ministerial Conference (November 2001), to undertake negotiations on trade and investment beginning in 2003.[156] The scope of these negotiations was not initially defined. The negotiators nonetheless recognized the interrelationship between trade and investment and decided to start the negotiating process with a clean slate.[157]

The life of this group was short and left little to cheer about for those aspiring to see a multilateral agreement on investment in the WTO. During the Cancun Mid-Term Review meeting (September 2003), which was supposed to signal that trading partners were half way towards the successful conclusion of the Doha round, the WTO Membership took the dramatic decision to stop the negotiation

---

[156] See WTO Doc. WT/MIN(01)/DEC/1 of 20 November 2001 at §20.

[157] See WTO Working Group on the Relationship between Trade and Investment, WTO Doc. WT/WGTI/W/7 of 18 September 1997. See the excellent analysis by Koulen (2001).

on trade and investment.[158] As a result, the WTO Membership abandoned the negotiating group on trade and investment.[159] We quote from a decision adopted by the WTO General Council on 1 August 2004:

> Relationship between trade and investment, interaction between trade and competition policy and transparency in government procurement: the Council agrees that these issues, mentioned in the Doha Ministerial Declaration in paragraphs 20–22, 23–25 and 26 respectively, will not form part of the Work Programme set out in that Declaration and therefore no work towards negotiations on any of these issues will take place within the WTO during the Doha Round.[160]

Many are the reasons that contributed to this outcome. Without any intent to provide a hierarchy, we start from the reason most frequently heard in the literature: developing countries (especially Asian) were quite hostile to the idea of a multilateral agreement on investment. They voiced their concerns to this effect, citing the negative impact that a similar agreement would have had on their sovereignty and related issues. The ideological opposition was aided by the fact that for many developing countries the attitude of the OECD countries on the investment front had been unacceptable: few would forget that they had previously been essentially presented with a 'take it or leave it' deal in the form of the MAI. At the same time, they frequently expressed the view that bilateral and regional approaches to investment liberalization allowed them more opportunity to take into account national policy priorities than multilateral rules. In their view, similar contractual arrangements could better adapt to their national specificities and idiosyncratic elements.[161] It is important to note that these views were not universally shared by developing countries. Some developing countries (Chile, Korea, Costa Rica) were advocates of investment rules in the WTO which they saw as preferable to bilateral and regional investment agreements. On the other hand, certain Asian countries (India, Indonesia, Malaysia) were very strongly opposed to any negotiations on investment for the reasons that I described above. Another group of countries (Brazil, Argentina) would have been willing to go along with investment negotiations in the WTO if this would have helped them elsewhere in the Doha round (especially agriculture vis-à-vis the EU and Japan). The likelihood that this would happen, that investment could be used as a quid pro quo to extract concessions on other fronts and primarily agriculture, was questionable though and indeed eventually questioned by developing countries:

---

[158] Along with the negotiation on trade and competition.

[159] See Trachtman (1998) on the issue of linkage between trade and investment, and Sauvé and Wilkie (2000) on the negotiation in the WTO.

[160] See WTO, Doha Work Programme, Decision Adopted by the General Council on 1 August 2004 (2004). WTO Doc. WT/L/579 at §3.

[161] The quintessential elements of discussions that took place have been reproduced in the annual reviews of the negotiation published in WTO Docs. WT/WGTI/2, 3, 4, 5, 5 Add. 1, 6, and 7 of 8 December 1998, 22 October 1999, 27 November 2000, 8 October 2001, 22 October 2001, 9 December 2002, 11 July 2003 respectively.

part of the reason officials in Delhi were so sceptical about investment was that they did not believe that a deal on investment would make it significantly easier for Japan and the EU to make concessions in areas of interest. In fact, there was sometimes a suspicion that the EU, Japan, and Korea, with an important defensive interest in agriculture, were interested in investment not to create positive linkages but to create negative linkages, i.e. that they would drop investment as the price for lowering ambitions in agriculture.

Then there was also scepticism that investment rules actually had a real impact on the pattern of international investment flows. Many wondered whether a multilateral agreement would be the necessary price to pay to attract investment. For them the flame could light up anyway for reasons other than the conclusion of an agreement, so why pay the price of the candle?

On the other hand, it would probably be a mistake to focus exclusively on the position of developing countries as the principal factor explaining the lack of agreement on investment negotiations in the WTO. Developed countries did not manage to present a unified position throughout the negotiation process. In fact, from the outset, i.e. 1996 (Singapore Ministerial Conference) there was tension between the EU Commission (the EU spokesman), Japan, and Canada, on the one hand, and the US and certain EU Member States,[162] on the other, in that the former preferred to negotiate on investment in the WTO, whereas the latter considered that priority should be given to concluding a high standard multilateral investment agreement in the OECD. This tension dissipated in 1998–9 after the collapse of the MAI negotiations, but the US did not change its attitude and never became an enthusiastic supporter of investment negotiations in the WTO. It should be noted here that the US had historic reasons to believe that this would be the case: they had advocated a top-down investment model in the GATS and ended up with a positive-list approach as the only tangible result.[163] They did not want to see history repeat itself in this context.

Finally, one should bear in mind that the NGO community was extremely hostile to the notion of investment negotiations in the WTO; this probably explains why Canada, which was a staunch supporter of investment negotiations in the WTO in the period 1996–9, was clearly less enthusiastic at the time of the Doha and Cancun conferences. For all these reasons and probably more, the WTO group came away empty-handed.

4.4.2 Attempts to Multilateralize outside the WTO

The only attempt to multilateralize investment protection conducted under the aegis of the WTO was a failure: negotiated at the OECD, the MAI was intended

---

[162] The EU, when the negotiation started, did not have exclusive competence to negotiate on international investment. It had to share it with its Member States.

[163] On the reasons why this was the case, see Marchetti and Mavroidis (2011).

to be eventually 'exported' to the WTO. The MAI would have removed barriers to investment, provided protection against expropriation and measures diminishing its value, and instituted a dispute settlement system.

The MAI deserves a short narrative: in 1992, the OECD Investment Committee started its preparatory work.[164] The mandate for the negotiations was to achieve a multilateral framework for investment, with high standards of investment liberalization and protection. Negotiators further aimed at providing an effective dispute settlement system that would be accessible to OECD and non-OECD Members. The negotiations formally began in September 1995, continued until April 1998, and extended into the fall of 1998. The 29 OECD Members as well as the Commission of the EU participated in the negotiations. Participation was not confined to OECD Members only:

(a) Eight non-OECD Members participated as observers: Argentina; Brazil; Chile; Estonia; Hong Kong, China; Latvia; Lithuania; and the Slovak Republic;

(b) Other (than the eight who acquired observer status) non-OECD Members were informed on a regular basis about the status and substance of the negotiations.

The negotiators felt the time was ripe for a global framework for investment, mainly because foreign direct investment (FDI) grew 14 times between 1973 and 1996 (from $25 to $350 billion), significantly faster than growth in international trade.[165] The MAI was a very ambitious project. Unlike the regime envisaged by most bilateral investment treaties, the MAI purported to cover the pre-establishment phase as well.[166] Hence, the MAI included provisions on privatization, behaviour of monopolies, and the temporary entry and stay of key personnel, such as investors, managers, and experts. It had three pillars:

(a) Investment liberalization;

(b) Investment protection; and

(c) Dispute settlement.

With respect to the first and the second pillars, the MAI enshrined the principle of non-discrimination:[167]

(a) First, the MAI signatories committed to treat foreign investors and their investments no less favourably than they treat their own (NT);

---

[164] See Karl (1998) and Daly (1998) for an insider's narrative on the MAI. See also Trebilcock and Howse (2005) who provide a slightly different account.

[165] See, on this score, Trebilcock and Howse (2005).

[166] On this issue, see the comprehensive analysis in Sacerdotti (1997), and also in Sauvé and Wilkie (2000).

[167] For an excellent exposé of this principle, see Ortino (2009).

(b) Second, the MAI signatories agreed not to distinguish between investors and investments of other MAI parties (MFN).

With respect to the third pillar, the MAI contained provisions on cross-border transfer of funds, fair and equitable treatment, and the standard of compensation in case of expropriation. The coverage of the MAI was quite broad: FDI, portfolio investment, and rights under contract formed part of its subject-matter. The MAI negotiations provoked a series of negative reactions and the project was abandoned in late 1998. The defeat was attributable in large part to two main factors: developing country Members of the WTO were not willing[168] to sign up to an instrument in the negotiation of which they had not participated. It is noteworthy that history does not seem to touch trading partners much. A similar OECD initiative that was supposed to be exported to the WTO had previously known similar failure: a 1987 study prepared by the OECD, entitled 'Elements of a Conceptual Framework for Trade in Services', was submitted for consideration to the GATT. In this study, OECD members were making the case for expanding the (then) GATT mandate so as to cover trade in services as well. It was thwarted immediately by developing countries, only because it had been prepared by the OECD and, consequently, they had had no opportunity to debate it and negotiate it. Negotiations should start from a clean slate, not from an OECD dictum, in their view. It is also questionable whether levelling the field is an incentive-compatible structure for developing countries: these are capital-importing countries and, through regulatory concessions, they might better position themselves to attract foreign capital at the expense of other developing countries.

On the other hand, civil society demonstrated an unambiguous opposition to the MAI: an unprecedented coalition of anti-globalization groups[169] comprising over 600 non-governmental organizations (NGO) from 70 countries were reportedly involved in opposing the MAI, fearing the (negative) impact of the MAI on a variety of issues, ranging from effects on unemployment to protection of the environment.[170] The debate in civil society focused on several issues:

---

[168] See Vadcar (1998) on this score. Sornarajah (2004), writing before the Cancun failure, predicted that the negotiating lines dividing developed from developing countries were hard to cross, and absent drastic change in the approach of developed countries, there was not much hope of securing a multilateral framework. Subsequent events justified his views.

[169] Graham (2000) provides an excellent account on this issue. His work, however, is very informative on all other aspects surrounding the negotiation of the multilateral investment framework.

[170] See Dam (2001). Huner (1998), who acted as secretary to the Chair of the OECD Committee negotiating the MAI, believes that the project failed miserably because negotiators were not prepared politically to 'sell' the whole project when the time had come to do so.

(a) First, although investment creates jobs, foreign firms can, it was argued, exercise too much influence on, or dominate, economic sectors, especially in developing countries, unless they are subject to some controls;

(b) Second, there were fears that investment liberalization could lead to economic crisis when, in times of trouble, foreign investors pull their money out. Note, however, that empirical research has shown that the withdrawal of foreign investment is a problem only with portfolio investment, bank deposits, and loans, not with FDI. For example, during both the Mexican peso devaluation of 1994–5, and the Asian economic crisis of 1997–8, FDI was largely stable; there was little capital flight;[171]

(c) Third, investment liberalization was opposed, because, NGOs argued, multilateral companies would use FDI to exploit workers in low-wage countries with inadequate labour standards;[172]

(d) Fourth, NGOs argued that companies would invest in countries with low environmental standards, and use their influence to attack efforts in these countries to improve environmental standards.[173] As evidence, they cited the impact of NAFTA Chapter 11, which had been used by companies to recover damages when new, higher environmental standards had frustrated investment expectations.[174]

Voices were heard arguing for a trimmed down version of the ambitious MAI as a last hope for a multilateral agreement. Among them, Hoekman and Kostecki stand out as probably the most persuasive voice on this issue.[175]

At the moment of writing, there is no comprehensive multilateral agreement on investment protection: there is only a sector-specific agreement, the Energy Charter Treaty,[176] which liberalizes investment in the energy sector.[177] There are also some multilateral initiatives dealing with particular aspects of investment protection, such as the World Bank Multilateral Investment Guarantee Agency (MIGA).

This, however, does not mean that developing countries (or any countries for that matter) are not interested in providing an attractive environment for foreign investors. Empirical research suggests FDI policies are being liberalized quite rapidly. According to a report published by the United Nations Conference on

---

171 See Razin (2001) on this score.

172 Trebilcock and Howse (2005).

173 Environmentalists' Letter on MAI, 13 February 1997, reprinted in *Inside US Trade*, 21 February 1997, pp. 12–13.

174 The NAFTA decision on *Metalclad Corp. v Mexico*, 40 *International Legal Materials* 36 (2001), awarding damages when the company's investment in hazardous waste treatment facility approved by federal government of Mexico was blocked by local Mexican authorities.

175 Hoekman and Kostecki (2009) at pp. 418ff.

176 34 *International Legal Materials* 360 (1995).

177 Wälde (1996).

Trade and Development (UNCTAD),[178] over 90 per cent of changes in national regimes regulating FDI were of a liberalizing nature. Sauvé and Subramanian (2001) estimate that cross-border FDI activity increased in the nineties by almost 60 per cent. Investment, thus, is being liberalized at a fast pace even in the absence of a multilateral umbrella.[179] And although it is still difficult to provide a comprehensive assessment of the effects of a liberalization policy on productivity, empirical research tends to support the view that FDI liberalization contributes to productivity growth.

4.4.3 Investment Protection in BITs and PTAs

The absence of success in the MAI and the WTO Trade and Investment negotiations, as well as the current limited ambit of TRIMs, amount to absence of multilateral protection of investors who are currently protected through BITs,[180] or through investment provisions in PTAs, such as NAFTA Chapter 11[181] or the EU.[182] Inclusion of investment in PTAs deserves particular mention: a recent study by Horn et al. (2010) shows that investment protection figures prominently among many PTAs signed by the two main hubs (EU, US) and a series of spokes. It is remarkable that many developing countries are eager to sign investment protection provisions with capital-exporting countries in the context of PTAs: Horn et al. (2010) show that 12 out of 14 PTAs signed between 1992 and 2008 by the EU with a host of developing nations contain provisions relating to investment protection. Moreover, in eight of these schemes the language chosen was clearly binding, thus ensuring enforcement of property rights. The numbers for US arrangements during the same period are 11/14 and 11/11. In another recent study, Kotschwar (2010) analyses investment provisions in 52 PTAs and concludes that it is flexibility that drives the inclusion of investment provision in PTAs. If correct, then the possibility for concluding an international agreement would be severely hampered. It is probably high time that the WTO reflected seriously on why this has been the case. This is of course

---

[178] UNCTAD, *World Investment Report 2000: Cross-border Mergers and Acquisitions and Development* (New York and Geneva: United Nations Publications, 2000). Moreover, attracting investment is not just a developing countries issue. Indeed developed countries also have had recourse to measures aimed at subsidizing FDI. Discussing the Irish experience in this respect, Razin concludes that 'the heavy subsidization of FDI inflows in Ireland in the past two decades resulted in impressive GDP growth rates but with less pronounced effect on the well-being of Irish residents'. See Razin (2004).

[179] Hoekman and Kostecki, (2009) at 418ff.

[180] There is abundant literature on this issue. Very representative views on this issue can be found in Weston et al. (1999), Sornarajah (2004), and Sacerdotti (1997).

[181] 32 *International Legal Materials* 289 (1993).

[182] Free movement of capital is one of the four fundamental freedoms agreed by the EU Member States in the context of the Treaty establishing the European Community (ECT). The EU integration process aims, eventually, at complete liberalization of investment (free movement of capital). See Bermann et al. (2002).

part of a wider discussion concerning the discrepancy between the multilateral and the preferential agenda that the Doha round should have entertained but did not.

5. Exceptions

Art. XX and Art. XXI GATT have been construed in case law as exceptions to Art. III GATT. They are also exceptions to the TRIMs Agreement, by virtue of Art. 3 TRIMs. We will turn to this discussion in the next chapter.

5

DEVIATING FROM WTO OBLIGATIONS

1. Introductory Remarks

In this chapter, we discuss the legal means available to those WTO Members willing to deviate from the GATT obligations discussed in the previous two chapters. Our focus is on four instruments, the content of which is heterogeneous and thus an explanation is warranted:

(a) General exceptions (Art. XX GATT);
(b) National security (Art. XXI GATT);
(c) Non-application (Art. XXXV GATT and Art. XIII of the Agreement Establishing the WTO);
(d) Waivers (Art. XXXV GATT and Art. IX of the Agreement Establishing the WTO).

Arts. XX and XXI GATT qualify in legalese as legal exceptions to assumed obligations, in the sense that the party invoking them bears the associated onus to demonstrate that it is in compliance with the substantive (and, where appropriate, procedural) requirements embedded in these provisions; upon successful demonstration, it will be lawfully exempted from observing the obligation from which it purports to deviate.

There are of course other exceptions in the GATT: to provide but an illustration, Art. XIV GATT, as we saw in Chapter 2, exceptionally allows for discriminatory QRs if the conditions reflected in that provision have been met. The difference between Arts. XX and XXI GATT, on the one hand, and any other exception mentioned in the various agreements regulating trade in goods, on the other, is that the former offer an escape route with respect to any (as opposed to a specific) obligation assumed. While we discuss exceptions to specific provisions in the corresponding chapters of this book, in this chapter we focus on exceptions of a 'general' character so to speak.

The 'non-application' clause of the GATT is not an exception to assumed obligations. Furthermore, the country invoking it does not have to meet any specific substantive requirements in order to successfully invoke this provision. It does exhibit, nevertheless, a similar function to an exception: upon accession of a country to the WTO, an incumbent can, by invoking this provision, deviate from its obligation to observe the WTO contract vis-à-vis the acceding country. It was felt necessary to include a similar provision in the GATT since, after WWII, it was not politically feasible to immediately turn the page and for old enemies to start behaving like good friends.

Waivers are a halfway house between the two: a WTO Member must explain the reasons for requesting a waiver, but the reasons are highly idiosyncratic and specific to the requesting WTO Member: for different reasons, WTO Members might be granted a waiver, that is, permission to deviate from their WTO obligations (or some of them) on a temporary basis. A request for a waiver is a necessary but not sufficient condition for its granting: ultimately, it is WTO Members that will decide by statutory majorities whether or not to respond affirmatively to similar requests.

2. General Exceptions

2.1 The Legal Discipline and its Rationale

WTO Members can justify violations of their obligations assumed under the GATT through recourse to one of the grounds mentioned in Art. XX GATT. This list covers a variety of exceptions, ranging from the protection of public health to conservation of natural resources. The opening sentence of Art. XX GATT ('nothing in this agreement') leaves no doubt that the legislator's intent was that all grounds mentioned in this provision 'trump' trade-liberalizing obliga-tions reflected in the rest of the GATT. This provision has been modelled after the corresponding provision included in the 1927 International Convention for the Abolition of Import and Export Prohibitions and Restrictions (World Economic Conference of 1927), the first attempt to multilateralize international trade.[1]

Art. XX GATT is a flexibility clause which, at the same time, provides a hierarchy between trade commitments and (national) social preferences: public morals, protection of human health, and all the other grounds mentioned in the body of this provision 'trump' trade commitments. In other words, trading partners will not have to 'bite the bullet' and set aside important social concerns in the name of honouring their trade deals. Thus, trade is not elevated to the supreme common value that all WTO Members must observe at any cost. This understanding of GATT commitments is, of course, perfectly consistent with the negative-integration character of the GATT.[2]

At the same time, it does not suffice that a WTO Member simply invokes a ground mentioned in the body of this provision in order to lawfully de-respect its trade commitments; if this were the case, then what would be the value of committing in the first place? If this were the case, the enforcement of the contract would be relying solely on the reputation costs that the various partners would incur in case of abusive invocations. Some mechanism to distinguish good from bad invocations was deemed necessary: the 'non-discrimination', 'necessity', and other clauses included in this provision help distinguish the wheat from the chaff in this context.

2.2 The Coverage of the Legal Discipline

Art. XX GATT covers a series of grounds that, if successfully invoked, will provide WTO Members with a lawful escape route from their GATT obligations. The substantive requirements imposed are not symmetric across all grounds reflected in the provision: some are; some are not. In what immediately follows, we will review the status of all 'common' elements, that is, the requirements that a WTO Member must fulfil irrespective of the specific grounds in Art. XX GATT that it has invoked. We will then move to discussion of each of the specific grounds.

2.2.1 Elements Common to all Grounds

The list of common elements as discussed above is as follows:

(a) The GATT provisions to which Art. XX GATT is an exception;
(b) The test for compliance with the *chapeau* of Art. XX GATT;
(c) The list of grounds reflected in Art. XX GATT is exhaustive;

---

[1] On the content of the negotiations, and the reasons for the non-ratification of the final text, see Charnovitz (1991), and Irwin et al. (2008).

[2] See the corresponding discussion in Chapter 3.

(d) Art. XX GATT condones and does not suppress regulatory diversity;

(e) The allocation of the burden of proof when Art. XX GATT is invoked and the ensuing standard of review.

It seems that what the UK negotiator (one of the architects of this provision) had in mind was to include a provision which would operate as an exception to import and export restrictions only, and not to internal measures:

> The undertakings in Chapter IV of this Charter relating to import and export restrictions shall not be construed to prevent the adoption or enforcement by any member of measures for the following purposes, provided that they are not applied in such a manner as to constitute a means of arbitrary discrimination between countries where the same conditions prevail, or a disguised restriction of international trade.[3]

It is unclear whether this view, its intellectual appeal notwithstanding, was shared by all negotiators and it is anyway water under the bridge by now: GATT/WTO case law has by now accepted that recourse to Art. XX GATT can be made in order to justify violations assumed with respect to both trade and domestic instruments.

An example of the former is offered by the GATT Panel on *Thailand— Cigarettes*: in this case, the United States challenged the consistency of the Thai Tobacco Act of 1966 with Art. XI GATT. According to this law:

> the importation...of tobacco is prohibited except by licence of the Director-General (§63).

The Thai Tobacco Act of 1966 defined tobacco to include cigarettes. There was no dispute between the parties that the measure at hand constituted a quota in the sense of Art. XI GATT (§§21, 65); Thailand attempted to justify the quota in place by invoking, *inter alia,* Art. XX(b) GATT (§§72ff).

An example of the latter is offered in the report on *EC—Asbestos*, where the AB held that Art. XX GATT could serve as a legal basis to justify measures that had been previously found to be inconsistent with Art. III GATT (§115).[4]

The Panel on *China—Raw Materials* confirmed prior case law to the effect that Art. XX GATT could also serve as an exception to obligations assumed under a Protocol of Accession. Nevertheless, this would be the case only if there is explicit or even implicit reference to this provision in the relevant protocol (§§7.158–60).

The AB has constructed Art. XX GATT akin to a two-tier test. For example, assuming a WTO Member invokes Art. XX(b) GATT in order to justify an import embargo on toxic waste (which is considered to be harmful to human health), the WTO adjudicating body will first examine whether such a measure is necessary to achieve the stated objective (protection of human health), that is, whether the measure at hand conforms with the requirement included in Art. XX

---

[3] E/PC/T/C.II/50, pp. 7ff; E/PC/T/C.II/54, pp. 32ff.
[4] For confirmation, see the AB report on *Korea—Various Measures on Beef* at §§152ff.

(b) GATT, before it examines whether the provisionally justified measure under Art. XX(b) GATT has also been applied in a manner consistent with the *chapeau* of the GATT. The two obligations must be met cumulatively for a measure to be judged GATT-consistent. The AB stated as much in its report on *US—Gasoline* (p. 22):

> In order that the justifying protection of Article XX may be extended to it, the measure at issue must not only come under one or another of the particular exceptions—paragraphs (a) to (j)—listed under Article XX; it must also satisfy the requirements imposed by the opening clauses of Article XX. The analysis is, in other words, two-tiered: first, provisional justification by reason of characterization of the measure under XX(g); second, further appraisal of the same measure under the introductory clauses of Article XX.

In its report on *US—Shrimp*, the AB provided the rationale for the two-tier approach in the following manner (§§119–120):[5]

> The sequence of steps indicated above in the analysis of a claim of justification under Article XX reflects, not inadvertence or random choice, but rather the fundamental structure and logic of Article XX.
>
> . . .
>
> The task of interpreting the chapeau so as to prevent the abuse or misuse of the specific exemptions provided for in Article XX is rendered very difficult, if indeed it remains possible at all, where the interpreter (like the Panel in this case) has not first identified and examined the specific exception threatened with abuse.

The AB, in its report on *US—Gasoline*, held that the choice of words should imply that the legal test chosen should not be identical across the various subparagraphs of this provision, whereas the same test always applies when discussing the conformity of a measure with the *chapeau* (pp. 17–18):

> In enumerating the various categories of governmental acts, laws or regulations which WTO Members may carry out or promulgate in pursuit of differing legitimate state policies or interests outside the realm of trade liberalization, Article XX uses different terms in respect of different categories:
>
> 'necessary'—in paragraphs (a), (b) and (d); 'essential'—in paragraph (j); 'relating to'—in paragraphs (c), (e) and (g); 'for the protection of'—in paragraph (f); 'in pursuance of'—in paragraph (h); and 'involving'—in paragraph (i).
>
> It does not seem reasonable to suppose that the WTO Members intended to require, in respect of each and every category, the same kind or degree of connection or relationship between the measure under appraisal and the state interest or policy sought to be promoted or realized.

---

[5] In this case, the AB faced a US measure banning sales of shrimps that had been caught in a way that led to accidental taking of the life of sea turtles, an endangered species that featured in the list of CITES (Convention on International Trade of Endangered Species), a multilateral convention banning trade in similar commodities; see Howse and Neven (2007a).

The Panel on *China—Raw Materials* added that the legal consequence of the two-tier test is that, unless compliance with a subparagraph has been shown, there is no need to examine the consistency of the challenged measure with the *chapeau* of Art. XX GATT (§7.469).

The AB in its report on *US—Shrimp* expressed the view that it is the language of the *chapeau* that makes it clear that all exceptions appearing in Art. XX GATT are limited and conditional (§157):

> In our view, the language of the chapeau makes clear that each of the exceptions in paragraphs (a) to (j) of Article XX is a *limited and conditional* exception from the substantive obligations contained in the other provisions of the GATT 1994, that is to say, the ultimate availability of the exception is subject to the compliance by the invoking Member with the requirements of the chapeau. (emphasis in the original)

The word 'limited' in the above quoted passage makes it clear that the list of exceptions mentioned in Art. XX GATT is exhaustive. The AB, in its report on *Brazil—Retreaded Tyres*, eliminated any doubts on this score, by holding the following (§139):

> First, a panel must examine whether the measure falls under at least one of the ten exceptions listed under Article XX.

Recall our discussion in the previous chapter, where we held the view that the negotiating intent of the GATT framers was to establish a trading regime based on negative integration with respect to domestic instruments, such as those mentioned in Art. XX GATT. During the GATT years, two Panels outlawed legislation aimed at protecting dolphins caught in the nets of tuna fishermen, simply because the measure had been unilaterally decided: these reports thus construed the GATT contrary to its negotiating intent. The US had enacted legislation (the US Marine Mammal Protection Act) which required all fishermen wishing to sell tuna in the US market (domestic and foreigners alike) to observe a regulation that obliged them to fish for tuna using purse seine nets: this fishing technique greatly reduced the risk that dolphins would accidentally be caught and killed. This risk was particularly high in areas where tuna and dolphin swam together. Mexico was one of these areas. Mexican fishermen did not want to adapt to the new recommended fishing techniques and, as a result, were left out of the lucrative US tuna market.

The government of Mexico protested that the measure at hand amounted to a violation of Art. XI GATT. The GATT Panel that was asked to decide on Mexico's challenge first established a violation of Art. XI GATT, and then rejected the argument advanced by the US that the measure was consistent with Art. XX GATT: in its view, this could never be the case when measures are enacted unilaterally. The Panel on *US—Tuna (Mexico)* outlawed the US measure because of its unilateral character (§5.27):

The Panel considered that if the broad interpretation of Article XX(b) suggested by the United States were accepted, each contracting party could unilaterally determine the life or health protection policies from which other contracting parties could not deviate without jeopardizing their rights under the General Agreement. The General Agreement would then no longer constitute a multilateral framework for trade among all contracting parties but would provide legal security only in respect of trade between a limited number of contracting parties with identical internal regulations.[6]

This case law was overturned by the AB in its landmark *US—Shrimp* jurisprudence. A sea change indeed occurred. On this occasion, the US government enacted legislation to prevent the accidental death of sea turtles, an acknowledged endangered species by CITES (Convention on the International Trade of Endangered Species), a multilateral international convention.[7] CITES prohibits trade in endangered species that come under its purview. The US went one step further than that: it prohibited the sale of shrimp that had not been fished with TEDs (turtle-excluding devices), a US technology that allowed sea turtles to swim out of the net where shrimp had been caught; the US. thus, was not regulating directly trade in endangered species, it was regulating trade in shrimps which had an effect on the life of one endangered species, namely, sea turtles. TEDs were considered an effective means to protect the life of sea turtles, since sea turtles and shrimp often swim together: the US submitted ample empirical proof to the Panel to back up its allegations in this respect.[8] Some producers/exporters of shrimp (Malaysia and Thailand leading the way) complained. In their view, the US measure was effectively denying them access in the US market since they would have to change their production methods and incur substantial adjustment costs in order to comply with the US standard. Referring to prior GATT case law, the complainants challenged the consistency of the US measure with the GATT, arguing that it was inconsistent since it had been unilaterally defined.

The Panel that dealt with this dispute followed the ruling on *US—Tuna (Mexico)*, and condemned the US measure because of its unilateral character. The AB overturned the Panel, holding that WTO Members remained free to unilaterally regulate their market, provided that they respected the relevant GATT disciplines; in other words, a measure would not be judged to be GATT-inconsistent, simply because it had been unilaterally defined. In §121 of its report, the AB makes the sea change:

---

[6] This ruling sparked a discussion as to whether the GATT allows for PPM-based distinctions, that is, regulatory distinctions based on process and production methods. The literature discussed in the previous chapter largely addresses this issue as well, since regulatory distinctions will typically be made through domestic instruments.

[7] Actually, for the sake of accuracy, a number of categories of sea turtles have been acknowledged as endangered species.

[8] See the discussion in Howse and Neven (2007a), and Mavroidis (2000b).

...conditioning access to a Member's domestic market on whether exporting Members comply with, or adopt, a policy or policies unilaterally prescribed by the importing Member may, to some degree, be a common aspect of measures falling within the scope of one or another of the exceptions (a) to (j) of Article XX. Paragraphs (a) to (j) comprise measures that are recognized as *exceptions to substantive obligations* established in the GATT 1994, because the domestic policies embodied in such measures have been recognized as important and legitimate in character. It is not necessary to assume that requiring from exporting countries compliance with, or adoption of, certain policies (although covered in principle by one or another of the exceptions) prescribed by the importing country, renders a measure *a priori* incapable of justification under Article XX. Such an interpretation renders most, if not all, of the specific exceptions of Article XX inutile, a result abhorrent to the principles of interpretation we are bound to apply. (italics and emphasis in the original)

This case law has been consistently reproduced and emphasized in subsequent case law.[9] As a result, it is now uncontested that Art. XX GATT condones and does not suppress regulatory diversity.[10]

Case law has consistently held, by virtue of the maxim that the party invoking an exception carries the associated burden of proof (*quicunque exceptio invocat ejusdem probare debet*), that the party invoking Art. XX GATT carries the burden of proof to demonstrate that it has met its requirements. The AB, citing prior case law to this effect (*US—Gasoline*, pp. 22–3; *US—Wool Shirts and Blouses*, pp. 15–16; *US—FSC (Article 21.5—EC)*, §133) has confirmed this view in its report on *US—Gambling* (§309):

> It is well-established that a responding party invoking an affirmative defence bears the burden of demonstrating that its measure, found to be WTO-inconsistent, satisfies the requirements of the invoked defence.

The AB, in its report on *Korea—Various Measures on Beef*, clarified that its judicial review has to be confined to the means used to achieve a particular objective, and cannot extend to an examination of the legitimacy of the ends themselves (§176):

> It is not open to doubt that Members of the WTO have the right to determine for themselves the level of enforcement of their WTO-consistent laws and regulations. We note that this has also been recognized by the panel in *United States—Section 337*, where it said: 'The Panel wished to make it clear that this [the obligation to choose a reasonably available GATT-consistent or less inconsistent measure] does not mean that a contracting party could be asked to change its substantive patent law or its desired *level of enforcement* of that law.....' (italics and emphasis in the original)

Over the years, however, the AB has made it clear that it would be more deferential when human (life and) health was at stake, and less so when WTO Members were

---

9 See, for example, the AB report on *US—Shrimp (Article 21.5—Malaysia)* at §§137–8.
10 See, on this score, Howse and Türk (2001), and Mavroidis (2000a).

pursuing other regulatory objectives mentioned in the body of Art. XX GATT. The AB first announced in its report on *Korea—Various Measures on Beef*, that it would take into account the importance of the objective sought when measuring the necessity of the means employed to attain it. In its report on *EC—Asbestos*, the AB confirmed that this was indeed the case (§172):

> We indicated in *Korea—Beef* that one aspect of the 'weighing and balancing process. . .comprehended in the determination of whether a WTO-consistent alternative measure' is reasonably available is the extent to which the alternative measure 'contributes to the realization of the end pursued'. In addition, we observed, in that case, that '[t]he more vital or important [the] common interests or values' pursued, the easier it would be to accept as 'necessary' measures designed to achieve those ends. In this case, the objective pursued by the measure is the preservation of human life and health through the elimination, or reduction, of the well-known, and life-threatening, health risks posed by asbestos fibres. The value pursued is both vital and important in the highest degree. (italics in the original)

2.2.2 Public Morals

WTO Members can adopt measures necessary to protect their 'public morals': this term is not defined any further in Art. XX(a) GATT. In §296 of its report on *US—Gambling*, the AB provided the Panel's understanding of the term 'public morals' as follows:

> In its analysis under Article XIV(a), the Panel found that 'the term "public morals" denotes standards of right and wrong conduct maintained by or on behalf of a community or nation.'

In §298 it approved this definition. This case dealt with claims under Art. XIV GATS and not Art. XX GATT. Nevertheless, since the same term appears in the two provisions, and since the two provisions pursue the same objective, there are good reasons to believe that GATT case law would be inspired by this interpretation.

The term 'standards of right and wrong' nevertheless falls short of setting interpretative issues aside once and for all. Disagreements might legitimately continue to persist against this background. Feddersen (1998) points to the preparatory work of the GATT, where, in his view, it is made clear that the negotiating partners had in mind a narrow construction of the term (as opposed to some form of generic public order type of exception). He consequently held that the term was meant to cover 'public morality', that is, trade restrictions against pornography etc., and was not intended to cover public order in its widest possible connotation. Charnovitz (1998) alludes to a wider understanding of the term public morals and constructs examples where, through recourse to Art. XX(a) GATT, WTO Members can promote public order in general. As a matter of negotiating record, Feddersen is probably closer to the truth: the various examples cited by the negotiators during the process point to a public-morality type of exception.[11] There is a problem, however, with this construction of the term 'public morals' and this is what Charnovitz aimed to address: assuming an a-contextual understanding of terms 'applied so as to afford protection' and 'less favourable treatment', appearing in Art. III GATT, regulating states could find themselves forced to defend their measures by invoking Art. XX GATT even if their measures distinguish between various classes of goods without being enacted so as to afford protection to domestic production. We pointed to this danger in the previous chapter. Moving to Art. XX GATT is not free of consequences: recall this is an exhaustive list and, if the regulating state pursues an objective other than those mentioned in its list (e.g. protection of small and medium enterprises), it can find itself unable to defend its measures. This, as we have mentioned on numerous occasions in this volume, was not the intent of the GATT framers. And Charnovitz's construction effectively amounts to an insurance policy against this type of error.

Note that the GATS, an agreement signed subsequent to the GATT, used in the corresponding provision (Art. XIV) the term 'public order' in lieu of 'public morals'. Arguably, the term 'public order' is an all-encompassing term and its use would render mention of other grounds (such as human life or health) redundant. Similar views should be rejected: 'public order' is a catch-all term that should be used whenever more specific terms (such as human life or health) are ill suited to addressing a social concern. The inclusion of this term, in other words, does not automatically signal the exclusion of all other social preferences: it is meant to cover whatever has not been covered by more specific provisions. Consequently, the use of this term in GATS takes care of Charnovitz's worry about constructing the GATT as an instrument that on occasion mandates deregulation. Wu (2008) sees the potential for the GATT to be inspired by the GATS clause, especially because of the manner in which this clause has been interpreted in *US—Gambling*, where the US affirmed its rights to regulate internet gambling and imposed restrictions invoking that it was doing so to protect public morals. This is an attractive proposition that would take care of a lot of misgivings originating in the exhaustive character of the list included in Art. XX GATT. As yet, though, WTO adjudicating bodies have still to make this interpretative leap forward and construe Art. XX(a) GATT in this way.[12]

Only measures that are necessary to protect public morals will be deemed to be GATT-consistent. We discuss the necessity requirement *infra* in the immediately following subsections, as it has not been discussed in litigation concerning public morals. Note, however, that it is not necessarily the case that this term will be interpreted in exactly the same way across all subparagraphs of Art. XX GATT. For

---

11 See also Irwin et al. (2008).

12 The WTO Secretariat will reflect in its periodically conducted trade policy reviews (TPRM) national measures that have been imposed, allegedly on public morals grounds. A look at this list would support the argument advanced by Wu (2008) who points to all similar measures that the WTO has been notified of prior to 2008.

one, recall §172 of the AB report on *EC—Asbestos*: the WTO adjudicating bodies will not impose an equally stringent standard of review irrespective of the grounds invoked; as a result, one should expect a more deferential standard when public health is at stake than when public morality is invoked, even though both provisions include the same necessity requirement.

In the EU legal order, the question has arisen as to what extent public morals can provide an exception not only to import- but also to export-related measures: the United Kingdom refused to grant export licences to producers interested in exporting livestock to Spain since, in its view, Spain had not eliminated the potential for cruel treatment of animals in its slaughterhouses.[13] The dispute was resolved on technical grounds, but the interesting question remains.

2.2.3 Human, Animal, Plant Life, and/or Health

WTO Members can adopt measures necessary to protect human, animal, plant life, or health. In practice, Art. XX(b) GATT has been used in order to justify measures that aim to protect public health and/or the protection of the environment, although the latter is not explicitly mentioned in the body of Art. XX(b) GATT. Nevertheless, most of the environmental concerns are now being discussed under Art. XX(g) GATT, where, following case law interventions, the standard of review employed by WTO adjudicating bodies is more lenient towards the regulator: since it is the regulator that will invoke Art. XX GATT, it will naturally privilege invocation of subparagraph (g) over (b).

For a measure to be consistent with Art. XX(b) GATT, it must be necessary to achieve the ends pursued. The necessity requirement has been interpreted by various GATT/WTO Panels to mean that WTO Members must use the least restrictive (on international trade) measure, and the emerging case law could be described as follows:[14]

(a) The right of WTO Members to choose the level of enforcement cannot be put into question by a Panel. In other words, WTO Members cannot be requested to employ a less restrictive measure if such measure is also say less efficient in addressing the (perceived) distortion. This is a direct consequence of the acknowledgement that the WTO judge can judge the consistency of the employed means to reach a stated end, but not the appropriateness of ends themselves. Note, however, that the importance of the objective sought will

---

[13] Case C–5/94, *The Queen v Ministry of Agriculture, Fisheries and food ex p Hedley Lomas (Ireland) Ltd*, ECJ, 23 May 1996.

[14] The necessity-requirement is also included in other subparagraphs of Art. XX GATT such as Art. XX(d) GATT. We reproduce here all of the case law regarding this requirement, irrespective of the subparagraph invoked. Although there is no guarantee that case law under Art. XX(d) GATT will be reproduced 'lock, stock, and barrel' in case law regarding Art. XX(b) GATT, case law so far suggests that adjustments might be warranted only in light of the relative importance of the objective sought. With this caveat, case law under Art. XX(d) GATT regarding the necessity-requirement is legally relevant for the understanding of the same requirement in Art. XX(b) GATT.

weigh in the standard of review employed by WTO adjudicating bodies. The sum of these two sentences should lead us to the conclusion that, while WTO adjudicating bodies cannot put into question the ends sought, they still have a hierarchy of the various ends sought (appearing in the body of Art. XX GATT) and apply a more or less deferential standard of review depending on what exactly has been invoked as justification to deviate from an obligation assumed under the GATT;[15]

(b) When the choice is between using a GATT-consistent, and a GATT-inconsistent measure, assuming the two are equally efficient, the WTO Member concerned must use the GATT-consistent option;

(c) The AB held that 'necessary' should not be equated with 'indispensable', since, in its view, the term 'necessary' in Art. XX(d) GATT refers to a range of necessary options. The AB explained that it understands 'making a contribution to' to be at one end of a logical continuum, and indispensability at the other: necessary measures are closer to the latter than the former, but how much closer will depend on factors such as their contribution to realizing the objective sought, their relative impact on international trade, etc.;

(d) The necessity requirement should not be interpreted as requiring WTO Members to employ the absolutely least restrictive measure in order to attain their objectives. What is required is to employ the least restrictive option among those reasonably available to the WTO Member availing itself of this possibility. It was felt that, otherwise, WTO Members might find it impossible to pursue their social preferences since the necessity requirement would have made it very hard, if not altogether impossible, to do so;

(e) The allocation of the burden of proof has been addressed as well: assuming the regulating WTO Member has made a prima-facie case[16] that its measures are necessary, the burden will shift to the original complainant to demonstrate the existence of another (equally efficient) alternative measure that should have been used. If the original complainant is successful in this endeavour, then the burden will shift back to the WTO Member invoking Art. XX GATT to show that the alternative invoked is not reasonably available to it;

---

[15] In constitutional writings, 'necessity' constitutes the second of a three-level analysis, whereby first the question is raised whether a measure can appropriately serve the stated objective; if no, the measure would be considered inappropriate and dismissed altogether, but if yes, the next question would be whether it constitutes the least restrictive option in the hands of the regulating entity; following the same binary analysis, if yes, the last question would be whether achieving the requested value would put into question the achievement of other values equally or more important (in the eyes of the judge) to the society at large. The Swiss constitutional judge could, thus, in the name of proportionality, request from a specific canton to abandon its pursuance of specific necessary policies for endangering policies that affect the whole of the Swiss confederation. The WTO judge is no Swiss constitutional judge and cannot perform this last leg of the test.

[16] As already discussed, but worth recalling, in GATT/WTO case law this term should be understood as equivalent to a 'preponderance of evidence' standard, and not a standard akin to proving something beyond reasonable doubt.

Point (a) has been made by the AB in its reports on *EC—Asbestos* and *Brazil—Retreaded Tyres*. We start with the former, the facts of which are by now known (§174):

> In our view, France could not reasonably be expected to employ *any* alternative measure if that measure would involve a continuation of the very risk that the Decree seeks to 'halt'. Such an alternative measure would, in effect, prevent France from achieving its chosen level of health protection. On the basis of the scientific evidence before it, the Panel found that, in general, the efficacy of 'controlled use' remains to be demonstrated. Moreover, even in cases where 'controlled use' practices are applied 'with greater certainty', the scientific evidence suggests that the level of exposure can, in some circumstances, still be high enough for there to be a 'significant residual risk of developing asbestos-related diseases.' The Panel found too that the efficacy of 'controlled use' is particularly doubtful for the building industry and for DIY enthusiasts, which are the most important users of cement-based products containing chrysotile asbestos. Given these factual findings by the Panel, we believe that 'controlled use' would not allow France to achieve its chosen level of health protection by halting the spread of asbestos-related health risks. 'Controlled use' would, thus, not be an alternative measure that would achieve the end sought by France.

The facts of *Brazil—Retreaded Tyres* are reproduced in §118 of the report:

> Tyres are an integral component in passenger cars, lorries, and airplanes and, as such, their use is widespread in modern society. New passenger cars are typically sold with new tyres. When tyres need to be replaced, consumers in some countries may have a choice between new tyres or 'retreaded' tyres. This dispute concerns the latter category of tyres. Retreaded tyres are used tyres that have been reconditioned for further use by stripping the worn tread from the skeleton (casing) and replacing it with new material in the form of a new tread, and sometimes with new material also covering parts or all of the sidewalls. Retreaded tyres can be produced through different methods, one of which is called 'remoulding'.[17]

In this report, the AB held that there is no need to quantify the contribution of means to ends, for a measure to pass the consistency test with Art. XX(b) GATT: a qualitative analysis, by and large, suffices (§146). However, there is a presumption that recourse to an import embargo should be allowed only in exceptional circumstances. The AB held that, in principle, such measures would be accepted only if it was proven that they have made material contribution to the attainment of the stated objective (§150):

> As the Panel recognized, an import ban is 'by design as trade-restrictive as can be'. We agree with the Panel that there may be circumstances where such a measure can nevertheless be necessary, within the meaning of Article XX(b). We also recall that, in *Korea—Various Measures on Beef*, the Appellate Body indicated that 'the word "necessary" is not limited to that which is "indispensable"'. Having said that, when a measure produces restrictive effects on international trade as severe as those resulting

---

17 Bown and Trachtman (2009) discuss this case in detail.

from an import ban, it appears to us that it would be difficult for a panel to find that measure necessary unless it is satisfied that the measure is apt to make a material contribution to the achievement of its objective. Thus, we disagree with Brazil's suggestion that, because it aims to reduce risk exposure to the maximum extent possible, an import ban that brings a marginal or insignificant contribution can nevertheless be considered necessary.

In the same report, the AB explained itself on the relative importance of the social preference pursued and how it affects its standard of review (§143):

> In *US—Gambling*, the Appellate Body addressed the 'necessity' test in the context of Article XIV of the GATS. The Appellate Body stated that the weighing and balancing process inherent in the necessity analysis 'begins with an assessment of the "relative importance" of the interests or values furthered by the challenged measure', and also involves an assessment of other factors, which will usually include 'the contribution of the measure to the realization of the ends pursued by it' and 'the restrictive impact of the measure on international commerce'. (italics in the original)[18]

Point (b) was discussed in the GATT Panel on *Thailand—Cigarettes*. Thailand had argued that its trade embargo on the importation of cigarettes, while restricting the overall quantity sold in its market, was justified by the fact that it aimed to ensure the quality of cigarettes imported. The Panel felt that Thailand could have ensured both objectives through the use of non-discriminatory, and hence GATT-consistent, measures (ban on advertising, non-discriminatory labelling etc.) (§75):

> The Panel concluded from the above that the import restrictions imposed by Thailand could be considered to be 'necessary' in terms of article XX(b) only if there were no alternative measure consistent with the General Agreement, or less inconsistent with it, which Thailand could reasonably be expected to employ to achieve its health policy objectives.

When the Panel satisfied itself that Thailand could indeed have reached its objectives by employing GATT-consistent measures, it also found that Thailand had violated its obligations under Art. XX(b) GATT (§81). In similar vein, the GATT Panel on *US—Section 337* held (§5.26):

> It was clear to the Panel that a contracting party cannot justify a measure inconsistent with another GATT provision as 'necessary' in terms of Article XX(d) if an alternative measure which it could reasonably be expected to employ and which is not inconsistent with other GATT provisions is available to it. By the same token, in cases where a measure consistent with other GATT provisions is not reasonably available, a contracting party is bound to use, among the measures reasonably available to it, that which entails the least degree of inconsistency with other GATT provisions.

Point (c) was decided in the AB report on *Korea—Various Measures on Beef* in the following terms (§§161, 163, 164):

---

[18] Recall the discussion regarding §172 of the AB report on *EC—Asbestos* in the previous chapter.

We believe that, as used in the context of Article XX(d), the reach of the word 'necessary' is not limited to that which is 'indispensable' or 'of absolute necessity' or 'inevitable'. Measures which are indispensable or of absolute necessity or inevitable to secure compliance certainly fulfill the requirements of Article XX(d). But other measures, too, may fall within the ambit of this exception. As used in Article XX(d), the term 'necessary' refers, in our view, to a range of degrees of necessity. At one end of this continuum lies 'necessary' understood as 'indispensable'; at the other end, is 'necessary' taken to mean as 'making a contribution to.' We consider that a 'necessary' measure is, in this continuum, located significantly closer to the pole of 'indispensable' than to the opposite pole of simply 'making a contribution to'.
. . .

There are other aspects of the enforcement measure to be considered in evaluating that measure as 'necessary'. One is the extent to which the measure contributes to the realization of the end pursued, the securing of compliance with the law or regulation at issue. The greater the contribution, the more easily a measure might be considered to be 'necessary'. Another aspect is the extent to which the compliance measure produces restrictive effects on international commerce, that is, in respect of a measure inconsistent with Article III:4, restrictive effects *on imported goods*. A measure with a relatively slight impact upon imported products might more easily be considered as 'necessary' than a measure with intense or broader restrictive effects.

In sum, determination of whether a measure, which is not 'indispensable', may nevertheless be 'necessary' within the contemplation of Article XX(d), involves in every case a process of weighing and balancing a series of factors which prominently include the contribution made by the compliance measure to the enforcement of the law or regulation at issue, the importance of the common interests or values protected by that law or regulation, and the accompanying impact of the law or regulation on imports or exports. (emphasis in the original)

It follows that measures which are not, strictly speaking, indispensable to reach the objective pursued might still qualify as necessary, depending on the circumstances. In its report on *Brazil—Retreaded Tyres*, the AB added that the contribution of the measure to the overall objective could be critical in cases where a very restrictive measure, like a trade embargo, is being used (§210):

In this respect, the fundamental principle is the right that WTO Members have to determine the level of protection that they consider appropriate in a given context. Another key element of the analysis of the necessity of a measure under Article XX(b) is the contribution it brings to the achievement of its objective. A contribution exists when there is a genuine relationship of ends and means between the objective pursued and the measure at issue. To be characterized as necessary, a measure does not have to be indispensable. However, its contribution to the achievement of the objective must be material, not merely marginal or insignificant, especially if the measure at issue is as trade restrictive as an import ban. Thus, the contribution of the measure has to be weighed against its trade restrictiveness, taking into account the importance of the interests or the values underlying the objective pursued by it.

It seems that the message that the AB wanted to convey here is that it will not lightly accept the most egregious cases of market segmentation, but will do so when their contribution to the objective sought is meaningful.

Point (d) was decided in the AB report on *Korea—Various Measures on Beef* (§166):

> In our view, the weighing and balancing process we have outlined is comprehended in the determination of whether a WTO-consistent alternative measure which the Member concerned could 'reasonably be expected to employ' is available, or whether a less WTO-inconsistent measure is 'reasonably available'.

It follows that the WTO Member will respect the necessity requirement when employing the relatively necessary means, that is, the least restrictive option which is reasonably available to it. What is reasonably available depends on endowments proper to the regulating state; it is, in other words, an endogenous requirement. In *China—Audiovisual Services*, the AB stated that a hardship test might be appropriate to decide on the reasonable availability of a specific option: in its view, a measure would be reasonably available if it did not impose an undue burden on the regulating state (§327). This test would imply that adjudicating bodies retain some leeway to impose a 'costlier' option than that chosen if the gains for trade would be substantial. Where exactly they will draw the line and what kind of methodology they will choose in deciding similar cases is an issue that only future practice can respond to.

Point (e) was advanced by the AB in its report on *US—Gambling*, a GATS case: the US had adopted federal legislation banning the remote supply of gambling services. Some US states adopted similar statutes. Antigua and Barbuda complained to the WTO that such legislation was GATS-inconsistent since it amounted to a total prohibition on remote gambling when the US had committed to liberalize trade in that context. Both the Panel and the AB agreed with the complainant that the US should have indicated in its schedule of concessions that it was banning remote gambling and that, in absence of such indication, it was in violation of Art. XVI GATS. The US attempted to justify their measures under Art. XIV GATS (the GATS provision corresponding to Art. XX GATT). The AB, overturning the Panel's findings in this respect, held that, with respect to the allocation of the burden of proof (§§309–11):

> It is well-established that a responding party invoking an affirmative defence bears the burden of demonstrating that its measure, found to be WTO-inconsistent, satisfies the requirements of the invoked defence. In the context of Article XIV(a), this means that the responding party must show that its measure is 'necessary' to achieve objectives relating to public morals or public order. In our view, however, it is not the responding party's burden to show, in the first instance, that there are no reasonably available alternatives to achieve its objectives. In particular, a responding party need not identify the universe of less trade-restrictive alternative measures and then show that none of those measures achieves the desired objective. The WTO agreements do not contemplate such an impracticable and, indeed, often impossible burden.
>
> Rather, it is for a responding party to make a prima facie case that its measure is 'necessary' by putting forward evidence and arguments that enable a panel to assess the challenged measure in the light of the relevant factors to be 'weighed and

balanced' in a given case. The responding party may, in so doing, point out why alternative measures would not achieve the same objectives as the challenged measure, but it is under no obligation to do so in order to establish, in the first instance, that its measure is 'necessary'. If the panel concludes that the respondent has made a prima facie case that the challenged measure is 'necessary'—that is, 'significantly closer to the pole of "indispensable" than to the opposite pole of simply "making a contribution to"'—then a panel should find that challenged measure 'necessary' within the terms of Article XIV(a) of the GATS.

If, however, the complaining party raises a WTO-consistent alternative measure that, in its view, the responding party should have taken, the responding party will be required to demonstrate why its challenged measure nevertheless remains 'necessary' in the light of that alternative or, in other words, why the proposed alternative is not, in fact, 'reasonably available'. If a responding party demonstrates that the alternative is not 'reasonably available', in the light of the interests or values being pursued and the party's desired level of protection, it follows that the challenged measure must be 'necessary' within the terms of Article XIV(a) of the GATS.

To evaluate the reasonable availability of a measure:

> factors such as the trade impact of the measure, the importance of the interests protected by the measure, or the contribution of the measure to the realization of the end pursued, should be taken into account in the analysis

can be taken into account.[19] This is what the AB held in *Dominican Republic—Import and Sale of Cigarettes* (§70). Initially, case law concerning the issue as to whether it is for the Panel to come up with a reasonably available alternative or up to the party challenging the measure was not unanimous: the Panel on *Canada—Wheat Exports and Grain Imports* is an example of the former approach, and the AB report on *Japan—Agricultural Products II* (§§123–30) of the latter. This issue was resolved in the AB report on *US—Gambling*, where, as discussed above, assuming that a prima-facie case has been made (that the necessity requirement has been met), the burden of proof shifts to the other party (the original complainant) who will have to demonstrate that another, less restrictive (but equally effective) measure should have been privileged.

During the Uruguay round negotiations, the US had tabled a proposal according to which, whenever recourse to Art. XX(b) GATT was being made in order to protect human health, the ensuing measures would have to be based on scientific evidence.[20] This proposal did not manage to get the approval of the other trading nations. Later, the AB held in §178 of its report on *EC—Asbestos* that WTO Members can, but do not have to, have recourse to scientific expertise in order to justify a regulatory intervention through recourse to Art. XX(b) GATT.

---

[19] See Conrad (2011) at pp. 330ff who discusses in detail 'absolute' and 'relative' necessity.
[20] GATT Doc. MTN.GNG/NG5/W/118 of 25 October 1989 at p. 11.

2.2.4 Imports and Exports of Gold and Silver

WTO Members can justify their deviations from obligations assumed under the GATT if they 'relate to' the importation or exportation of gold or silver. The coverage of this provision is clear: only measures relating to the importation and exportation of two commodities, gold and silver, are covered. The GATT Panel on *Canada—Gold Coins* emerges as the only case in this context so far: Canada (the province of Ontario) had in place a retail tax on gold coins which was applicable on *Krugerrand* (South African gold coin), but exempted from this tax Maple Leaf gold coins struck by the Canadian Mint. The Panel found that gold coins were not only means of payment but also goods and thus covered by Art. III GATT (and, consequently, by Art. XX GATT as well). The report remains un-adopted.[21]

The question is how one should understand the term 'relate to' appearing in the body of Art. XX(c) GATT. There is no case law to draw on, but the same term appears in Art. XX(g) GATT. Our discussion of the term there provides useful inspiration for the understanding of the term here.

2.2.5 Compliance with Laws not Inconsistent with the GATT

WTO Members can justify their deviations from obligations assumed under the GATT, if they are necessary to secure compliance with laws or regulations which are not inconsistent with the GATT. Art. XX(d) GATT does not contain an exhaustive list of the laws, regulations that come under its purview. There is, nonetheless, an indicative list of the type of measures envisaged: customs enforcement, enforcement of monopolies (state trading enterprises), protection of patents, trademarks and copyrights, the prevention of deceptive practices.

The Panel and the AB faced in the context of *Mexico—Taxes on Soft Drinks* a question regarding the coverage of this provision. The situation they faced is clearly described in §68 of the AB report:

> the central issue raised in this appeal is whether the terms 'to secure compliance with laws or regulations' in Article XX(d) of the GATT 1994 encompass WTO-inconsistent measures applied by a WTO Member to secure compliance with another WTO Member's obligations under an international agreement.

Mexico had raised its domestic taxes on some products (soft drinks) and was found to be violating Art. III.2 GATT (since it was treating imported goods in a manner that was affording protection to domestic DCS products): Mexico was in fact taxing the process (inputs) of soft drinks in a manner that led soft drinks originating in the US to pay a higher tax burden than Mexican soft drinks, which contained different inputs. Mexico claimed before the Panel that its measures were necessary to enforce domestic laws covered by Art. XX(d) GATT. In Mexico's view, the differential taxation was necessary to enforce its

---

[21] GATT Doc. L/5863 of 17 September 1985; see especially §§50ff.

rights under the NAFTA Agreement: Mexico felt that the US had not complied with their obligations under NAFTA, and it was now retaliating, as, in its view, it had the right to do under the relevant NAFTA provisions. The Panel dismissed Mexico's defence. It held that the indicative list in Art. XX(d) GATT, as well as its preparatory work, were pointing to an understanding of this provision as covering only domestic and not international measures (§§8.162ff). On appeal, the AB upheld the Panel's findings, arguing, however, that its reason for doing so was that Art. XX(d) GATT was not designed to cover obligations of other (than the enforcing) WTO Member. Since at stake here was US compliance with NAFTA, the measures at hand were found to lie outside the four corners of Art. XX(d) GATT. This is an odd statement since it can be so easily circumvented: what if Mexico was invoking the Mexican law incorporating its rights and obligations under NAFTA? Would the Panel and AB still hold the same opinion? This case is illustrative of the attitude of WTO adjudicating bodies towards non-WTO law: we are still miles away from a consistent approach in this respect, and have been witnessing so far only knee-jerk reactions. Be it as it may, it is highly implausible that this is the last word of the AB on this score.

Panels have from early on insisted on a narrow understanding of this provision which should not be equated to a carte blanche to violate the GATT: its coverage is limited only to laws etc. which are GATT-consistent anyway. In this vein, the GATT Panel on *Japan—Agricultural Products I* dismissed an argument by Japan to the effect that a GATT-inconsistent monopoly for the import of farm goods could be justified through recourse to Art. XX(d) GATT (§5.2.2.3).

WTO adjudicating bodies have understood the necessity requirement featured in Art. XX(d) GATT in the same way as in Art. XX(b) GATT, with the proviso mentioned that the relative importance of the value protected through the challenged measure might lead the WTO judge to a more (or less, depending on the circumstances) deferential standard of review. This question arose in *Korea—Various Measures on Beef*. Korea, recall, had adopted a dual retail system, whereby retailers could sell either domestic or foreign beef but, in principle, not both. In Korea's view, this practice was necessary to secure compliance with the Korean Unfair Competition Act, a law which was not inconsistent with the GATT and, consequently, came under the purview of Art. XX(d) GATT. The Panel and the AB recognized that the dual retail system was:

> ...established at a time when acts of misrepresentation of origin were widespread in the beef sector. (§158, AB report).

The question before the AB was to what extent the dual retail system was necessary (§176):

> It is not open to doubt that Members of the WTO have the right to determine for themselves the level of enforcement of their WTO-consistent laws and regulations. We note that this has also been recognized by the panel in *United States— Section 337*, where it said: 'The Panel wished to make it clear that this [the obligation

to choose a reasonably available GATT-consistent or less inconsistent measure] does not mean that a contracting party could be asked to change its substantive patent law or its desired *level of enforcement* of that law . . . (emphasis in the original)

The importance of the ends sought mattered in the appraisal of the necessity requirement (§162):

> It seems to us that a treaty interpreter assessing a measure claimed to be necessary to secure compliance of a WTO-consistent law or regulation may, in appropriate cases, take into account the relative importance of the common interests or values that the law or regulation to be enforced is intended to protect. The more vital or important those common interests or values are, the easier it would be to accept as 'necessary' a measure designed as an enforcement instrument.

That much seems to be uncontested in subsequent WTO case law as well. In §§ 180–2, the AB invoked two grounds to dismiss the Korean defence: first, it pointed to a means for Korea to reach its objective ('selective, well-targeted, controls') which the complainants had not invoked. This flies directly against the AB holding in the subsequent *US—Gambling* report, where it held that it is for the complainant (as opposed to the Panel or the AB itself) to point to other less restrictive means; it then finds against Korea because it had not discharged its burden of proof to show that other less restrictive means were reasonably available to it. But should not the burden shift to Korea to show that another less restrictive means is not reasonably available to it only after the complainant has produced such an alternative? Is not that what *US—Gambling* is all about? We quote the paragraphs referred to:

> We are not persuaded that Korea could not achieve its desired level of enforcement of the *Unfair Competition Act* with respect to the origin of beef sold by retailers by using conventional WTO-consistent enforcement measures, if Korea would devote more resources to its enforcement efforts on the beef sector. It might also be added that Korea's argument about the lack of resources to police thousands of shops on a round-the-clock basis is, in the end, not sufficiently persuasive. Violations of laws and regulations like the Korean *Unfair Competition Act* can be expected to be routinely investigated and detected through selective, but well-targeted, controls of potential wrongdoers. The control of records will assist in selecting the shops to which the police could pay particular attention.
> There is still another aspect that should be noted relating to both the method actually chosen by Korea—its dual retail system for beef—and alternative traditional enforcement measures. Securing through conventional, WTO-consistent measures a higher level of enforcement of the *Unfair Competition Act* with respect to the retail sale of beef, could well entail higher enforcement costs for the national budget. It is pertinent to observe that, through its dual retail system, Korea has in effect shifted all, or the great bulk, of these potential costs of enforcement (translated into a drastic reduction of competitive access to consumers) to imported goods and retailers of imported goods, instead of evenly distributing such costs between the domestic and imported products. In contrast, the more conventional, WTO-consistent measures of enforcement do not involve such onerous shifting of enforcement costs which ordinarily are borne by the Member's public purse.

For these reasons, we uphold the conclusion of the Panel that Korea has not discharged its burden of demonstrating under Article XX(d) that alternative WTO-consistent measures were not 'reasonably available' in order to detect and suppress deceptive practices in the beef retail sector, and that the dual retail system is therefore not justified by Article XX(d).

In *US—Gambling*, a subsequent report, the AB has adopted a different approach regarding the allocation of burden of proof (discussed *supra*) which should be regarded as the prevailing approach nowadays.

Finally, the AB report on *Korea—Various Measures on Beef* is troublesome for one more reason: in §172, the AB sees a consistency requirement in Art. XX(d) GATT which is simply missing in the text of this provision:

> The application by a Member of WTO-*compatible* enforcement measures to the same kind of illegal behaviour—the passing off of one product for another—for like or at least similar products, provides a suggestive indication that an alternative measure which could 'reasonably be expected' to be employed may well be available. The application of such measures for the control of the same illegal behaviour for like, or at least similar, products raises doubts with respect to the objective *necessity* of a different, much stricter, and WTO-inconsistent enforcement measure. The Panel was, in our opinion, entitled to consider that the examples taken from outside as well as within the beef sector indicate that misrepresentation of origin can indeed be dealt with on the basis of basic methods, consistent with the *WTO Agreement*, and thus less trade restrictive and less market intrusive, such as normal policing under the Korean *Unfair Competition Act*. (emphasis in the original)

It is clear from the passage that the AB used the lack of consistency by Korea as a tool to cast doubt on the necessity of the measure employed by the government. This is a very far-fetched conclusion though: similarity across products does not guarantee symmetry across different product markets. This is precisely why the SPS Agreement treats the consistency requirement separately from the necessity requirement. We will revert to this discussion in Chapter 10.

2.2.6 Prison Labour

WTO Members can justify their deviations from obligations assumed under the GATT, if they relate to products of prison labour. The term 'prison labour' can be understood either in a narrow (products wholly originating in prisons) or in a wide sense (products with inputs produced in prisons and other detention establishments). Then of course, the term 'prison' could be understood as encompassing all sorts of state offices depriving humans of their freedom etc. There is total absence of practice in this area so these questions remain unanswered. On the other hand, the rationale for this provision is clear: as prisoners receive no salary for their work, exports of similar goods would be benefiting from lower prices and the ensuing competitive advantage. There is probably, on occasion, a social preference as well not to transact with goods made in prison.

The term 'relate to' appearing in the body of Art. XX(e) GATT describes the legal relationship between the challenged measure and the protection against imports of goods originating in prisons. Since this term appears also in Art. XX (g) GATT where it has been interpreted on a number of occasions, we will discuss it there, with the caveat we mentioned about the necessity requirement (appearing in two sub-paragraphs) being applicable here as well.

2.2.7 National Treasures

WTO Members can justify their deviations from obligations assumed under the GATT, if their measures have been imposed for the protection of national treasures. The qualification of an item as a 'national treasure' depends on the satisfaction of one of the three criteria included in Art. XX(f) GATT: artistic, historic, or archaeological value. This should not be a difficult test to meet since historic value has a much wider coverage than archaeological value. There is an absence of dispute settlement practice in this context.

Note that the provision exonerates measures imposed for the protection of national treasures, not measures relating to or necessary for the protection. This would suggest that the satisfaction of this condition is something close to a self-fulfilling prophecy: any measure that is imposed (is in place) for the purpose of protecting national treasures comes under its ambit. So the only remaining question is what qualifies as 'national treasure', an easy to meet standard for the reasons mentioned *supra*. Assuming willingness to protect national treasures, this provision in practice should be of help to those imposing export bans on similar transactions.

2.2.8 Conservation of Exhaustible Natural Resources

Measures that relate to the conservation of exhaustible natural resources and are made effective in conjunction with restrictions on domestic production or consumption can justifiably run counter to any obligation assumed under the GATT. The interpretation of the term 'exhaustible natural resources' by WTO adjudicating bodies has provoked a lot of discussion in the literature. By adopting a very wide understanding of the term, the AB has de facto established a (partial) overlap, subject-matter-wise, between Arts. XX(b) and XX(g) GATT; since the latter reflects a more deferential standard of review ('relating to' as opposed to 'necessary'), many environmental concerns are now being adjudicated under Art. XX(g) GATT. We explain.

A look into the *travaux préparatoires* of the GATT leaves us with the impression that the framers had in mind commodities such as petrol and minerals (i.e. non-living resources) when they drafted Art. XX(g) of the GATT.[22] Charnovitz (1991), though, correctly observes that this is not a watertight observation since some

---

[22] E/PC/T/C.II/50 at pp. 5ff.

references might argue for a wider understanding of the term. Still, the examples used during the negotiation point in the direction of constructing this term as referring to non-living organisms.[23]

Then came case law. First, in the GATT years, the Panel on *Canada—Herring and Salmon* agreed with the parties that salmon and herring stocks are exhaustible natural resources (§4.4). In the WTO years, in *US—Gasoline*, the Panel held that clean air was an exhaustible natural resource (§6.37). The dispute related to the implementation by the US of its domestic legislation known as the US Clean Air Act of 1990 (CAA) and, more specifically, to the regulation enacted by the US Environmental Protection Agency (EPA) pursuant to that Act to control toxic and other pollution caused by the combustion of gasoline manufactured in or imported into the United States. The CAA had established two gasoline programmes to ensure that pollution from gasoline combustion did not exceed 1990 levels and that pollutants in major population centres were reduced. A preliminary question was raised by the US at the oral hearing concerning arguments made by Venezuela and Brazil in their respective appellees' submissions on the issues of whether clean air was an exhaustible natural resource within the meaning of Art. XX(g) GATT. The AB agreed with the US that the issue was not properly before it (pp. 10ff). As a result, the AB did not rule on this issue and the Panel's ruling stands.

In its report on *US—Shrimp*, the AB held that the term 'exhaustible natural resources' should not be confined to non-living resources. At dispute was a US measure which banned the import of shrimp fished in a manner that led to the accidental taking of the life of sea turtles. The US had argued that the measure at hand was in full conformity with the requirements of Art. XX(g) GATT, and if not, with the requirements of Art. XX(b) GATT. The complainants (India, Malaysia, Pakistan, and Thailand) argued that the negotiating history of the term 'exhaustible natural resources' pointed to the conclusion that this term was meant to cover non-living resources only, such as minerals (§127, AB report). The question, thus, arose whether the US measure should come under the purview of Art. XX(b) or Art. XX(g) GATT. In the view of the AB, the term had to be given a meaning in accordance with today's perceptions (§130):

> ... the generic term 'natural resources' in Article XX(g) is not 'static' in its content or reference, but is rather 'by definition, evolutionary'.

The AB went on to state that sea turtles, a living organism, could very well be regarded as an exhaustible natural resource. International conventions (CITES) recognized sea turtles as an endangered species, and others which used the term 'natural resources' to cover both living and non-living organisms (UNCLOS, United Nations Convention on the Law of the Sea) were cited (§§130ff, AB

---

[23] See also Matsushita et al. (2006).

report) in support.[24] The defining criterion (which distinguishes exhaustible from non-exhaustible natural resources) was, in the AB's view, whether the item at hand was being depleted faster than it is being reproduced (§§128, 130, and 153):

> Textually, Article XX(g) is *not* limited to the conservation of 'mineral' or 'non-living' natural resources. The complainants' principal argument is rooted in the notion that 'living' natural resources are 'renewable' and therefore cannot be 'exhaustible' natural resources. We do not believe that 'exhaustible' natural resources and 'renewable' natural resources are mutually exclusive. One lesson that modern biological sciences teach us is that living species, though in principle, capable of reproduction and, in that sense, 'renewable', are in certain circumstances indeed susceptible of depletion, exhaustion and extinction, frequently because of human activities. Living resources are just as 'finite' as petroleum, iron ore and other non-living resources.
>
> . . .
>
> From the perspective embodied in the preamble of the *WTO Agreement*, we note that the generic term 'natural resources' in Article XX(g) is not 'static' in its content or reference but is rather 'by definition, evolutionary'. It is, therefore, pertinent to note that modern international conventions and declarations make frequent references to natural resources as embracing both living and non-living resources.
>
> . . .
>
> The language [of the preamble of the *WTO Agreement*] demonstrates a recognition by WTO negotiators that optimal use of the world's resources should be made in accordance with the objective of sustainable development. As this preambular language reflects the intentions of negotiators of the *WTO Agreement*, we believe it must add colour, texture and shading to our interpretation of the agreements annexed to the *WTO Agreement*, in this case, the GATT 1994. We have already observed that Article XX(g) of the GATT 1994 is appropriately read with the perspective embodied in the above preamble. (emphasis in the original)

The 'evolutionary approach' that the AB explicitly invoked when providing its understanding of the term 'exhaustible natural resources' certainly has strong underpinnings in Art. 31 VCLT, which refers to subsequent practice and subsequent agreements. The subject of both these elements, nevertheless, is the principal not the agent, the state not the adjudicator. If, in other words, WTO Members post-1947 had signed a new agreement or adopted an interpretation/amendment of the GATT whereby the term 'exhaustible natural resources' should be understood as covering both living as well as non-living organisms, then the WTO judge should respect it and apply it in subsequent litigation. By the same token, the judge should do the same if it witnesses practice conforming to this interpretation. The question to ask under the circumstances should be practice by whom: by all or only by those litigating? The AB did not respond to this question, but did underline the fact that all parties to the dispute were parties to

---

[24] Although the AB did not prescribe in definitive manner the precise legal relevance of similar instruments in the WTO legal order, it used them in support of an opinion it had already reached; hence, extra-WTO international treaties were used in this case as supplementary means of interpretation. For a more extensive analysis of this point, see Mavroidis (2008).

CITES. CITES, however, is of not much help since there is not necessarily a one-to-one relationship between endangered species and exhaustible natural resources. Moreover, what about the WTO Members that did not sign CITES? Why should they be bound by similar jurisprudence? It is highly unlikely that the AB's intention was to create a two-tier jurisprudence, whereby some WTO Members will, while others will not, be bound by case law depending on the circumstances. The judge applied evolutionary interpretation here in light-hearted manner without giving it much thought: it is definitely the case that the judge by virtue of its agency contract (Art. 3.2 DSU) cannot undo the balance of rights and obligations struck by the principals: evolutionary interpretation, in other words, does not trump the agency contract.

The shortcomings of the approach notwithstanding,[25] this is by now water under the bridge: living organisms could be considered to be exhaustible natural resources and this recognition has opened the door to discussing a flurry of environmental cases under Art. XX(g) GATT.

Two requirements must be cumulatively met for a measure protecting exhaustible natural resources to be judged GATT-consistent:

(a) It must relate to the conservation of exhaustible natural resources; and
(b) It must be made effective in conjunction with restrictions on domestic production or consumption.

We take each point in turn. The Panel, in its report on *US—Gasoline*, went on to apply the GATT Panel's reasoning and conclusion in *Canada—Herring and Salmon* as to the interpretation of the term 'relating to': in this Panel's view, this term was tantamount to the term 'primarily aimed at', that is, a measure is relating to protection of exhaustible natural resources if its primary aim and not an ancillary or even accidental effect is to protect similar resources. The AB disagreed. It noted in *US—Gasoline* that, although past case law had construed the term in this way, the AB was not at ease with this understanding, even though the parties to the dispute seemed to endorse it (pp. 18–19):

> All the participants and the third participants in this appeal accept that a measure must be 'primarily aimed at' the conservation of exhaustible natural resources in order to fall within the scope of Article XX(g). Accordingly, we see no need to examine this point further, save, perhaps, to note that the phrase 'primarily aimed at' *is not itself treaty language and was not designed as a simple litmus test for inclusion or exclusion from Article XX(g)*..... (emphasis added)

---

[25] Another unintended consequence of this case law is that, as a result of the AB report on *US—Shrimp*, the standard of review when a claim regarding public health is discussed under Art. XX GATT is more stringent than when a claim regarding animal health is discussed, since the former arguably continues to come under the purview of Art. XX(b) GATT and the ensuing necessity requirement.

In its report on *US—Shrimp*, the AB distanced itself from prior practice and held that 'relating to' implied a rational connection between a measure and the conservation of exhaustible natural resources and nothing beyond that (§141):

> In its general design and structure, therefore, Section 609 is not a simple, blanket prohibition of the importation of shrimp imposed without regard to the consequences (or lack thereof) of the mode of harvesting employed upon the incidental capture and mortality of sea turtles. Focusing on the design of the measure here at stake, it appears to us that Section 609, *cum* implementing guidelines, is not disproportionately wide in its scope and reach in relation to the policy objective of protection and conservation of sea turtle species. The means are, in principle, reasonably related to the ends. The means and ends relationship between Section 609 and the legitimate policy of conserving an exhaustible, and, in fact, endangered species, is observably a close and real one. (emphasis in the original)

Arguably, the rational-connection standard endorsed by the AB is more deferential towards the regulating WTO Member than the previously employed primarily aimed standard, since even measures which do not primarily aim at the conservation of exhaustible natural resources can be justified through recourse to Art. XX (g) GATT, if they are not inappropriately used for a particular purpose. At the same time, it is quite clear that measures that pass the rational-connection standard do not *ipso facto* meet the necessity requirement as well. The latter requires that the measure is the (reasonably available) least-restrictive (on international trade) option, the former does not care about the magnitude of restrictive effects.

Art. XX(g) GATT further requires that, when imposing trade restrictions to protect exhaustible natural resources, WTO Members also adopt measures aimed at restricting domestic consumption or production (as the case may be). The GATT Panel on *US—Canadian Tuna* outlawed US measures restricting imports of some tuna because similar measures had not been adopted with respect to domestic tuna of the same kind (§§4.5ff). The AB, in its report on *US—Gasoline*, explained that the requirement to demonstrate that import-restricting measures are taken in conjunction with domestic measures aimed at the conservation of exhaustible natural resources was an even-handedness requirement. It went on to stress that there was no need for an effects test in order to comply with Art. XX(g) GATT in this respect (pp. 20–1):

> ... the clause 'if such measures are made effective in conjunction with restrictions on domestic product or consumption' is appropriately read as a requirement that the measures concerned impose restrictions, not just in respect of imported gasoline but also with respect to domestic gasoline. The clause is a requirement of *even-handedness* in the imposition of restrictions, in the name of conservation, upon the production or consumption of exhaustible natural resources.
> ... if *no* restrictions on domestically-produced like products are imposed at all, and all limitations are placed upon imported products *alone*, the measure cannot be accepted as primarily or even substantially designed for implementing conservationist goals. The measure would simply be naked discrimination for protecting locally-produced goods.

> We do not believe... that the clause 'if made effective in conjunction with restrictions on domestic production or consumption' was intended to establish an empirical 'effects test' for the availability of the Article XX(g) exception. (emphasis in the original)

In *China—Raw Materials*, the AB held (§§360–1) that Art. XX(g) GATT requests from WTO Members to take measures restricting imports in conjunction with measures restricting domestic production; it does not also request that the measures adopted be of such nature that they render effective measures aimed at restricting domestic production.

Environmental harms are normally trans-boundary and the question of jurisdiction will inevitably arise. In fact, it did arise: the AB, in its report on *US—Shrimp* faced, *inter alia*, the question whether Art. XX(g) GATT included a jurisdictional limit, in the sense that WTO Members could intervene to protect exhaustible natural resources only within their jurisdiction, as the latter is defined by public international law.[26] In §133, the AB, while avoiding a direct response to the question whether the US measure respected the territoriality principle, did point to the nexus between the subject-matter and the US interest in prescribing legislation:

> We do not pass upon the question of whether there is an implied jurisdictional limitation in Article XX(g), and if so, the nature or extent of that limitation. We note only that in the specific circumstances of the case before us, there is a sufficient nexus between the migratory and endangered marine populations involved and the United States for purposes of Article XX(g).

WTO case law is taking its first steps in this direction and it is way too early to have a meaningful discussion of the issue.

Finally, environmental disputes point to a developed–developing countries divide within the WTO. Environmental pollution appears first to worsen and later to improve as countries' incomes grow: because of its resemblance to the

---

[26] Nationality and territoriality are the two most common bases, in public international law, for exercising jurisdiction: under the former, a state can regulate the behaviour of its nationals; under the latter, a state can regulate transactions taking place in its territory. Public international law practice gives the edge to the latter, when a conflict between the two arises. On the other hand, one can further distinguish between *objective* and *subjective* territoriality: the former captures activities occurring within national frontiers; the latter captures activities which occur in state A, but which affect state B. B could legitimately, by virtue of subjective territoriality (effects doctrine), punish, for example, A's export cartels, which cartelize its own (B's) market. Indeed, except for some extreme cases, state A would have little incentive to regulate the behaviour of an export cartel operating from its market but affecting the rest of the world. Antitrust advocacy usually attributes such inactivity to the fact that domestic antitrust laws are there to protect domestic (as opposed to foreign) consumers' welfare. On this issue, see the various contributions in Meessen (1996) regarding the status of these principles in public international law; Mavroidis and Neven (1999) for a discussion on antitrust; and Bagwell et al. (2002), Bartels (2002), Charnovitz (1998 and 2002), and Horn and Mavroidis (2008) for a discussion regarding the status of these principles in WTO law.

pattern of inequality and income described by Kuznets, this pattern of pollution and income has been labelled an 'Environmental Kuznets Curve'. It is true that many pollutants exhibit this pattern; peak pollution levels, nonetheless, occur at different income levels for different pollutants, countries, and time periods. Social preferences, and the ensuing establishment of environmental institutions, explain why environmental protection rises as incomes rise. This issue was briefly discussed in the Panel report on *China—Raw Materials* (§§7.551ff) when China tried to justify its measures by arguing that its environmental awareness had risen as a result of its recent high growth rates. The Panel dismissed the arguments by China. As a matter of descriptive statistics nonetheless, it is very much the case in the WTO that the environmental regulator is an OECD country asked to defend its measures before a Panel.

2.2.9 Intergovernmental Commodity Agreements

WTO Members can justify their deviations from obligations assumed under the GATT, if their measures have been undertaken under one of the international commodity agreements (ICA) submitted to the WTO Members and not disapproved by them. The story behind the conclusion of ICAs deserves a few words. ICAs were signed by governments in order to promote cooperation between producers and consumers of particular commodities.

The following ICAs are currently in place: International Cocoa Organization (ICCO); International Coffee Organization (ICO); International Cotton Advisory Committee (ICAC); International Grains Council (IGC); International Olive Oil Council (IOOC); International Sugar Organization (ISO); International Tropical Timber Organization (ITTO).

Initially, ICAs aimed at stabilizing international prices for commodities. Over time, only three of them were successful in doing so: the ICAs on coffee and cocoa through retention schemes, and the ICA on natural rubber through a buffer stock. At present, none of the existing ICAs attempts to regulate markets by supply or price management. All ICAs now exhibit a pure administrative nature and serve as fora for producer-consumer cooperation and consultations, market transparency, development projects, and sources of statistical information. In practice, ICAs have now a function very comparable to that of ISGs (International Study Groups), the other forum for cooperation between producers and consumers.

The following ISGs are currently in place: International Rubber Study Group (IRSG); International Lead and Zinc Study Group (ILZSG); International Nickel Study Group (INSG); International Copper Study Group (ICSG); International Jute Study Group (IJSG). Both ICAs and ISGs were established in order to promote the cooperation of consumers and producers of specific commodities, although the function of the latter, as will be explained *infra*, was not to intervene in world prices. ICAs, ISGs, as well as the FAO intergovernmental groups and subgroups of individual agricultural commodities have been designated by the

Common Fund for Commodities (CFC) as International Commodity Bodies (ICB) eligible for CFC projects.[27]

There have been some initiatives to reintroduce price stabilization schemes (coffee, natural rubber), but there is general unwillingness to proceed in this way. Participation in the various ICAs and ISGs varies, but, in general, both developed and developing countries participate.[28]

The Interpretative Note ad Art. XX(h) GATT makes it clear that this exception extends to any ICA which conforms to the principles approved by the UN Economic and Social Council (ECOSOC) in its resolution 30(IV) of 28 March 1947. This resolution reads as follows:

The Economic and Social Council,

Noting that inter-governmental consultations are going forward actively with respect to certain internationally trade commodities, and

Considering the significant measure of agreement regarding commodity problems and the co-ordination of commodity consultations already reached both in the First Session of the Preparatory Committee of the United Nationals Conference on Trade and Employment, and in the Preparatory Commission on World Food Proposals of the Food and Agriculture Organization of the United Nations.

Recommends that, pending the establishment of the International Trade Organisation, Members of the United Nations adopt as a general guide in inter-governmental consultation or action with respect to commodity problems the principles laid down in Chapter VII as a whole—i.e., the chapter on inter-governmental commodity arrangements of the draft Charter appended to the Report of the First Session of the Preparatory Committee of the United Nations Conference on Trade and Employment—although recognizing that discussion in future sessions of the Preparatory Committee of the United Nations Conference, as well as in the Conference itself, may result in modifications of the provisions relating to commodity arrangements, and

Requests the Secretary-General to appoint an interim co-ordinating committee for international commodity arrangements to keep informed of and to facilitate by appropriate means such inter-governmental consultation or action with respect to commodity problems, the committee to consist of a chairman to represent the Preparatory Committee of the United Nations Conference on Trade and Employment, a person nominated by the Food and Agriculture Organization of the United

---

[27] The CFC provides assistance to commodity producers to enable them to strengthen the quality of their production systems and to develop new products which will enable them to effectively compete with these synthetic products. For example, a recent CFC project concerns the promotion of exports of organic bananas from Ethiopia and Sudan. The CFC has a membership of 105 Member States as well as institutional members, such as the EU, the African Union/African Economic Community (AU/AEC), the Common Market for Eastern and Southern Africa (COMESA), and most recently, the Caribbean Community (CARICOM). The Agreement Establishing the CFC was adopted on 27 June 1980 in Geneva by the United Nations Negotiating Conference on a Common Fund under the Integrated Programme for Commodities. The Agreement entered into force on 19 June 1989.

[28] UNCTAD/ITCD/COM/11.

Nations to be concerned in particular with agricultural primary commodities, and a person to be concerned in particular with non-agricultural primary commodities.[29]

ICAs were included in Chapter VI of the Havana Charter, which, as we saw in Chapter 1, never entered into force. WTO Members have, nevertheless, incurred an obligation, by virtue of Art. XXIX GATT, to

> observe to the fullest extent of their executive authority the general principles of Chapters I to VI inclusive and of Chapter IX of the Havana Charter.

For the reasons developed in Chapter 1, this provision is of limited, if any, value. Conformity with the principles approved by the UN Economic and Social Council in its resolution 30(IV) of 28 March 1947 is one of the three ways in which an ICA can be legally relevant in the GATT (and, consequently, a WTO Member can invoke it by virtue of Art. XX(h) GATT). The other two ways mentioned in Art. XX(h) GATT are:

(a) either the ICA conforms to criteria which have been submitted to the CON-TRACTING PARTIES and not disapproved by them; or
(b) the agreement itself is submitted to and not disapproved by the CON-TRACTING PARTIES.

The GATT Panel on *EEC (Member States)—Bananas I* faced, *inter alia*, an argument to the effect that the Lomé Convention, an agreement between the EU and a series of developing countries, should be regarded as an ICA. The Panel report, which remains un-adopted and, hence, of limited legal value, did provide some clarifications as to the understanding of the obligation embedded in Art. XX (h) GATT: for example, the Panel stated that no ICA was ever submitted for approval to the CONTRACTING PARTIES, and no criteria to review conformity of ICAs were submitted. Hence, the only way an ICA can be successfully invoked under Art. XX(h) GATT is if it conforms to the principles approved by the UN Economic and Social Council in its resolution 30(IV) of 28 March 1947. These principles required that participation in ICAs were open to trading nations and not limited to a select group of countries, and for this reason the Panel found that the Lomé Convention could not qualify as an ICA in the sense of Art. XX(h) GATT. We quote from §166:

> Turning to the principles in the ECOSOC Resolution 30(IV), the Panel noted that this Resolution required, *inter alia*, that the negotiation of, and participation in, an international commodity agreement must be open to all interested countries and must avoid, as also stipulated in the requirements set out at the beginning of Article XX of the General Agreement, unjustifiable discrimination between countries. The Panel, noting the limited membership of the Lomé Convention and noting further that the EEC had never claimed the Lomé Convention to be a non-discriminatory

---

[29] The text has been reproduced on p. 588 of the GATT Analytical Index, The GATT: Geneva, 1995.

commodity agreement open to all banana producer and consumer countries, found that the criteria of the ECOSOC Resolution 30(IV) had not been met. The Panel therefore concluded that Article XX(h) could not justify the inconsistency with Article I:1 of the EEC's banana preferences. (italics in the original)

This passage of the Panel report should be good law, the absence of adoption of the report notwithstanding: the Resolution is quite clear in requesting that an ICA be open to all interested nations, and this was definitely not the case with the challenged scheme.

2.2.10 Government Stabilization Plans

WTO Members can justify their deviations from obligations assumed under the GATT, if their measures are part of a government stabilization plan (of prices). Through this exemption, WTO Members can legitimately impose, for example, export quotas, and provide the domestic processing industry with essential quantities of material at prices held below the world price which otherwise would have been exported to the world market where prices were higher.

Only measures which are parts of government stabilization plans, as discussed *supra*, can profit from this exception. New Zealand, one of the initiators of this provision, explained that, unless an exemption was provided, those with government stabilization plans (of prices) in place would be forced to dismantle either their domestic processing industry or their stabilization plan altogether: if, for example, the price of leather were below the world price, then New Zealand producers would be selling all production abroad and any attempt by the government to stop them would fall foul of Art. XI GATT: this is where this exception kicks in.[30] For such a scheme to be judged GATT-consistent, the WTO Member concerned must not use it in order to increase its exports, and it must respect non-discrimination.[31] This is of course a hard condition to fulfil in practice: if leather is used as input for other goods, then the New Zealand (or elsewhere) producers of the downstream industry would profit from cheaper inputs. It should be stated nonetheless that government stabilization plans were in vogue when the GATT was being negotiated, but are far from being popular nowadays: regulators are well aware of the (negative) externalities that price caps and price floors give rise to and generally avoid them; for political economy reasons as well, governments might have little incentive to pursue similar policies.

2.2.11 Products in General or Local Short Supply

WTO Members can justify their deviations from obligations assumed under the GATT, if their measures are essential to the acquisition or distribution of products in general or in local short supply.

---

[30] EPCT/A/PV/36 at pp. 22ff, and Irwin et al. (2008).
[31] GATT Doc. GATT/CP.4/33.

The term 'in short supply' appearing in the body of this provision (Art. XX(j) GATT) has not been meaningfully interpreted in case law, except once when the AB, in its report on *China—Raw Materials*, noted (§325) that the term 'shortages' referred to in Art. XI.2(a) GATT must be 'critical' and consequently, the coverage of this term is narrower than that of shortages referred to in Art. XX(j) GATT.

Only measures which are essential, that is, indispensable, for the acquisition or distribution of goods in general or in local short supply, a rather stringent requirement indeed, will be exempted. This provision was meant to address the post-WWII observed short supply of goods, and it was intended to be eliminated at the latest by 1 January 1951.[32] Following a series of meetings where trading nations found it impossible to decide this issue in definitive manner, it was decided, within the context of the Working Group on Other Barriers to Trade convened during the Review Session of 1954–5, to maintain this provision. The rationale for retaining it had to do with the awareness that this provision was considered relevant not only for the post-war period of short supply of various goods, but also for cases of natural disaster which could occur at any time.[33]

The WTO Member invoking this provision must ensure that all WTO Members will be entitled to an equitable share of the international supply of products the sale of which is being restricted, and that any measure which is GATT-inconsistent will cease to exist as soon as the conditions giving rise to it have ceased to exist.

2.2.12 Complying with the Chapeau

Recall that, for WTO Members to justify their deviations from obligations assumed under the GATT, they must not only ensure their consistency with one of the substantive provisions discussed so far; they must also apply their measures in a non-discriminatory manner, in accordance with the requirements of the *chapeau*. The AB held in its report on *US—Gasoline* that a WTO adjudicating body cannot review the substantive consistency of a national measure with Art. XX GATT under the *chapeau* of Art. XX GATT. When moving to the *chapeau*, the only remaining question is to what extent the measure at hand is applied in a GATT-consistent manner (p. 22):

> The chapeau by its express terms addresses, not so much the questioned measure or its specific contents as such, but rather the manner in which that measure is applied. It is, accordingly, important to underscore that the purpose and object of the introductory clauses of Article XX is generally the prevention of 'abuse of the exceptions'.

The *chapeau* must be always complied with, irrespective of the subparagraph of Art. XX GATT that has been invoked in a particular case. The AB, in its report on *US—Shrimp (Art 21.5—Malaysia)*, explained the three conditions that must be cumulatively met for a measure to be *chapeau*-consistent (§118):

---

[32] EPCT/A/PV/30 at p. 20.
[33] GATT Doc. BISD 3S/249 at §42.

The chapeau of Article XX establishes three standards regarding the *application* of measures for which justification under Article XX may be sought: first, there must be no 'arbitrary' discrimination between countries where the same conditions prevail; second, there must be no 'unjustifiable' discrimination between countries where the same conditions prevail; and, third, there must be no 'disguised restriction on international trade'. The Panel's findings appealed by Malaysia concern the first and second of these three standards. (emphasis in the original)

The AB, in its report on *US—Gasoline*, discusses the issue whether the term 'between countries where the same conditions prevail' should be understood as referring only to exporting countries or, conversely, whether it should encompass the importing country as well. Although the AB did not formally rule on this issue on this occasion, it saw no reason to deviate from the prevailing practice which privileged the latter interpretation (pp. 23–4):

> It was asked whether the words incorporated into the first two standards 'between countries where the same conditions prevail' refer to conditions in importing and exporting countries, or only to conditions in exporting countries. The reply of the United States was to the effect that it interpreted that phrase as referring to both the exporting countries and importing countries and as between exporting countries . . . . At no point in the appeal was that assumption challenged by Venezuela or Brazil.
> . . . we see no need to decide the matter of the field of application of the standards set forth in the chapeau nor to make a ruling at variance with the common understanding of the participants.

As a result of this interpretation, a regulating state, for the purposes of compliance with the *chapeau*, must subject its own products to the regime that it applies to all imported goods as well. The *chapeau* thus contains some sort of a 'non-discrimination' clause, a point to which we will come back *infra*. Discriminatory treatment has been punished in the past. The GATT Panel on *US—Canadian Tuna*, for example, found that the US was violating its obligations under the *chapeau* by subjecting Canada to import restrictions while exempting Costa Rica (§4.8). In its report on *Brazil—Retreaded Tyres*, the AB went one step further and clarified that there is no effects test in the *chapeau* and that, consequently, all WTO Members must, in principle, be subjected to the same regulatory requirements, even if their respective volumes of trade are highly asymmetric. The question before the AB was whether, by allowing imports of retreaded tyres from its MERCOSUR partners while banning similar imports from all other sources, Brazil was violating Art. XX GATT. Brazil's response was that MERCOSUR countries exported a very small volume of retreaded tyres to Brazil (§§228–9):

> In this case, the discrimination between MERCOSUR countries and other WTO Members in the application of the Import Ban was introduced as a consequence of a ruling by a MERCOSUR tribunal. The tribunal found against Brazil because the restriction on imports of remoulded tyres was inconsistent with the prohibition of new trade restrictions under MERCOSUR law. In our view, the ruling issued by the MERCOSUR arbitral tribunal is not an acceptable rationale for the discrimination, because it bears no relationship to the legitimate objective pursued by the Import

356

Ban that falls within the purview of Article XX(b), and even goes against this objective, to however small a degree. Accordingly, we are of the view that the MERCOSUR exemption has resulted in the Import Ban being applied in a manner that constitutes arbitrary or unjustifiable discrimination.

The Panel considered that the MERCOSUR exemption resulted in discrimination between MERCOSUR countries and other WTO Members, but that this discrimination would be 'unjustifiable' only if imports of retreaded tyres entering into Brazil 'were to take place in such amounts that the achievement of the objective of the measure at issue would be significantly undermined'. The Panel's interpretation implies that the determination of whether discrimination is unjustifiable depends on the quantitative impact of this discrimination on the achievement of the objective of the measure at issue. As we indicated above, analyzing whether discrimination is 'unjustifiable' will usually involve an analysis that relates primarily to the cause or the rationale of the discrimination. By contrast, the Panel's interpretation of the term 'unjustifiable' does not depend on the cause or rationale of the discrimination but, rather, is focused exclusively on the assessment of the *effects* of the discrimination. The Panel's approach has no support in the text of Article XX and appears to us inconsistent with the manner the Appellate Body has interpreted and applied the concept of 'arbitrary or unjustifiable discrimination' in previous cases.

In the same report, the AB held that, although Brazil's import ban of some (all but MERCOSUR) retreaded tyres was the direct outcome of orders by Brazilian courts to allow imports from MERCOSUR countries, this fact in and of itself did not exonerate Brazil from responsibility; it concluded that Brazil was in violation of the requirements of the *chapeau* of Art. XX GATT (§§232–3, 246).

GATT/WTO case law has often examined the 'arbitrary or unjustifiable discrimination' requirement in tandem, without distinguishing between its two elements (AB report on *US—Shrimp*, §150). It has, on occasion though, proceeded the other way and examined the two elements separately. In *US—Shrimp*, the AB held that measures must result in discrimination and that the resulting discrimination must be unjustifiable or arbitrary (§150). This sounds like tautology. But it went further and held that actively accounting for differences among various WTO Members is a necessary component of the obligation imposed on WTO Members not to discriminate in an unjustifiable or arbitrary manner. Flexibility becomes thus a necessary component for compliance to be achieved under the *chapeau* (§§164–5 and 177):

It may be quite acceptable for a government, in adopting and implementing a domestic policy, to adopt a single standard applicable to all its citizens throughout that country. However, it is not acceptable, in international trade relations, for one WTO Member to use an economic embargo to *require* other Members to adopt essentially the same comprehensive regulatory program, to achieve a certain policy goal, as that in force within that Member's territory, *without* taking into consideration different conditions which may occur in the territories of those other Members.

We believe that discrimination results not only when countries in which the same conditions prevail are differently treated, but also when the application of the measure at issue does not allow for any inquiry into the appropriateness of the regulatory program for the conditions prevailing in those exporting countries.

. . .

Section 609, in its application, imposes a single, rigid and unbending requirement that countries applying for certification . . . adopt a comprehensive regulatory program that is essentially the same as the United States' program, without inquiring into the appropriateness of that program for the conditions prevailing in the exporting countries. Furthermore, there is little or no flexibility in how officials make the determination for certification pursuant to these provisions. In our view, this rigidity and inflexibility also constitute 'arbitrary discrimination' within the meaning of the chapeau. (emphasis in the original)

The AB had the opportunity to further explain itself on this score during the compliance stage of this litigation. The original US measure conditioning market access for shrimp upon a particular fishing method (the use of TEDs) had been found to be in substantive compliance with Art. XX(g) GATT; it was judged, however, inconsistent with the requirements of the *chapeau*. In the AB's view, the US measure should be modified to allow exports of shrimp fished through other (than TEDs) fishing methods, of comparable, to the TED, effectiveness. Subsequent to the original condemnation of its measure, the US modified its statute so as to allow for certification of other fishing methods. The AB held that this amendment brought the US measure into compliance with its obligations in this respect (§§144 and 149–50). The US was also found to be inconsistent with the requirements of the *chapeau*, because it had offered international negotiations to resolve the problems encountered by the enactment of *US Section 609* to some (Caribbean countries), but not to all WTO Members. This behaviour was judged inconsistent with the requirements of the *chapeau*, because of its inherent discriminatory content: the US did not justify why some were, and some were not, offered the chance to negotiate an agreement with it. Subsequently, the US offered the same opportunity to all other shrimp exporters affected by the US measure (including Malaysia, the complainant in this case). The AB found that, in so doing, the US had effectively complied with its obligations in this respect. Wisely, the AB added that, in its view, the US could not have been asked to achieve through international negotiations with Malaysia an outcome comparable to that achieved with other WTO Members (as Malaysia indeed had argued): some were prepared to accept fishing using a particular technique which minimizes the incidental taking of sea turtles, others were not (§§122, 123, and 130).

The GATT Panel report on *US—Canadian Tuna* held that measures publicly announced could not, for this reason alone, be judged a 'disguised restriction of trade' (§4.8).[34] On p. 25 of its report on *US—Gasoline*, the AB rejected the interpretation that the term 'disguised restriction' (of trade) is not limited to

---

[34] The Canadian delegate expressed his disappointment with this interpretation during the discussion regarding the adoption of the report; see GATT Doc. C/M/155.

concealed or unannounced restrictions only. In other words, the obligation to avoid disguised restrictions of trade is not a mere exercise in transparency:

> 'Arbitrary discrimination', 'unjustifiable discrimination' and 'disguised restriction' on international trade may, accordingly, be read side-by-side; they impart meaning to one another. It is clear to us that 'disguised restriction' includes disguised *discrimination* in international trade. It is equally clear that *concealed* or *unannounced* restriction or discrimination in international trade does *not* exhaust the meaning of 'disguised restriction'. (emphasis in the original)

That much should be obvious. On p. 25 of the same report, the AB went on and provided the framework for analysis of the term. In its view, through this term, the framers of GATT wanted to outlaw abusive invocations of Art. XX GATT:

> It is equally clear that *concealed* or *unannounced* restriction or discrimination in international trade does *not* exhaust the meaning of 'disguised restriction.' We consider that 'disguised restriction', whatever else it covers, may properly be read as embracing restrictions amounting to arbitrary or unjustifiable discrimination in international trade taken under the guise of a measure formally within the terms of an exception listed in Article XX. Put in a somewhat different manner, the kinds of considerations pertinent in deciding whether the application of a particular measure amounts to 'arbitrary or unjustifiable discrimination', may also be taken into account in determining the presence of a 'disguised restriction' on international trade. The fundamental theme is to be found in the purpose and object of avoiding abuse or illegitimate use of the exceptions to substantive rules available in Article XX. (emphasis in the original)

This view is reminiscent of the French doctrine of *abus de droit*. It has been reproduced as such in subsequent case law. The Panel in its report on *EC—Asbestos*, for example, held that the term 'disguised restriction' should be understood as outlawing interventions, which, under the guise of protection of one of the grounds mentioned in the subparagraphs of Art. XX of the GATT, aim at promoting other interests (§8.236):

> Referring also to the remark made by the Appellate Body in the same case according to which 'the provisions of the chapeau [of Article XX] cannot logically refer to the same standard(s) by which a violation of the substantive rule has been determined to have occurred', we consider that the key to understanding what is covered by 'disguised restriction on international trade' is not so much the word 'restriction', inasmuch as, in essence, any measure falling within Article XX is a restriction on international trade, but the word 'disguised'. In accordance with the approach defined in Article 31 of the Vienna Convention, we note that, as ordinarily understood, the verb 'to disguise' implies an *intention*. Thus, 'to disguise' (*déguiser*) means, in particular, 'conceal beneath deceptive appearances, counterfeit', 'alter so as to deceive', 'misrepresent', 'dissimulate'. Accordingly, a restriction which formally meets the requirements of Article XX(b) will constitute an abuse if such compliance is in fact only a disguise to conceal the pursuit of trade-restrictive objectives. However, as the Appellate Body acknowledged in *Japan—Alcoholic Beverages*, the aim of a measure may not be easily ascertained. Nevertheless, we note that, in the same case, the Appellate Body suggested that the protective application of a measure

can most often be discerned from its design, architecture and revealing structure. (emphasis in the original)

2.3 The Relationship between Art. III and Art. XX GATT Revisited

In Chapter 4, we discussed one aspect of the relationship between Art. III and Art. XX GATT, pointing to the dangers when moving the discussion to the latter provision too fast. We can now enlarge the discussion and ask the question whether Art. XX GATT should be construed as an exception to Art. III GATT at all. Our response is yes, but for a very limited class of cases. Before we explain the reasons for this approach, let us first visit the case law on this score.

The AB addressed this question (should Art. XX be construed as an exception to Art. III GATT?) head on in its report on *US—Gasoline.* It provided an affirmative response. The next question is how should we understand the term 'arbitrary or unjustifiable discrimination' appearing in the *chapeau?* Were this term to be understood as equivalent to 'less favourable treatment', then, naturally, one would legitimately doubt whether Art. XX GATT could ever be construed as an exception to Art. III GATT. The AB responded in the negative to this question, arguing that the legal tests for consistency with the two provisions (Art. III, Art. XX GATT) are not identical (p. 21):

> The enterprise of applying Article XX would clearly be an unprofitable one if it involved no more than applying the standard used in finding that the baseline establishment rules were inconsistent with Article III:4. That would also be true if the finding were one of inconsistency with some other substantive rule of the *General Agreement.* The provisions of the chapeau cannot logically refer to the same standard(s) by which a violation of a substantive rule has been determined to have occurred. To proceed down that path would be both to empty the chapeau of its contents and to deprive the exceptions in paragraphs (a) to (j) of meaning. Such recourse would also confuse the question of whether inconsistency with a substantive rule existed, with the further and separate question arising under the chapeau of Article XX as to whether that inconsistency was nevertheless justified. One of the corollaries of the 'general rule of interpretation' in the *Vienna Convention* is that interpretation must give meaning and effect to all the terms of a treaty. An interpreter is not free to adopt a reading that would result in reducing whole clauses or paragraphs of a treaty to redundancy or inutility. (italics in the original)

So far, so good. In what exactly lies the difference between the two tests? This is the response by the AB from the same report (p. 26):

> We have above located two omissions on the part of the United States: to explore adequately means, including in particular cooperation with the governments of Venezuela and Brazil, of mitigating the administrative problems relied on as justification by the United States for rejecting individual baselines for foreign refiners; and to count the costs for foreign refiners that would result from the imposition of statutory baselines. In our view, these two omissions go well beyond what was necessary for the Panel to determine that a violation of Article III:4 had occurred in the first place.

A closer look at this paragraph nevertheless raises more questions than it provides answers: why would the first grounds invoked necessarily lie beyond Art. III GATT? Assume this claim had been discussed in the context of Art. III.4 GATT, would the outcome have been any different? Assume, that is, that in Venezuela some producers meet and some do not meet the US standard: would the US in this case be justified under Art. III.4 GATT in adopting a country-wide baseline? This would hardly be the case in light of the case law as discussed in the previous chapter. More generally, what is the theory behind this statement? Is it a question of degree? In this vein, some discrimination would be allowed under Art. XX GATT, namely, discrimination that is justified or is not arbitrary, whereas none would be tolerated under Art. III GATT. This cannot be the case, for it is the same AB that in *Brazil—Retreaded Tyres* held that there is no effects test in the *chapeau*.

Take the cases that have been discussed under Art. XX GATT: *US—Shrimp* could have been discussed as a ban on sales of tuna fished in a turtle-unfriendly manner. In fact, it is under Art. III.4 GATT that this case should have been discussed and it is only for reasons known to the US legal team that the case was not discussed in this context. The US imposes the same regulatory requirement on producers of domestic and foreign goods, so where is the discrimination in the first place? The AB would have adopted exactly the same reasoning that it actually did in its report, had it reviewed the dispute within the four corners of Art. III GATT. In fact, as far as we know, there is not one single case so far where a measure was found to be inconsistent with Art. III GATT, but consistent with Art. XX GATT. The Panel report on *EC—Asbestos* came the closest, but then the AB adjudicated the dispute under Art. III GATT solely.

Does this mean that there can never be a case where a violation of Art. III GATT can be justified under Art. XX GATT? No, is the short answer. It is only for a very limited class of cases though that Art. XX could serve as an exception to Art. III GATT. This could be the case when like/DCS goods are treated asymmetrically because the importing state wants to punish goods not exported to its market. An illustration is warranted in this context: assume Home imports watches from Foreign that are like products to its domestic watches. Foreign produces steel in an environmentally unfriendly manner, but does not export steel products to Home. Home respects high environmental norms when producing steel. Now Home suffers from the environmental pollution in Foreign. It decides to impose a 150 per cent VAT on Foreign's watches when its own watches (as well as watches originating in countries that produce steel in a similarly environmentally friendly manner) pay only 15 per cent. Home will undeniably be violating Art. III GATT. It will seek refuge for its measure in Art. XX GATT. In light of our discussion *supra*, it will easily pass the test of substantive consistency of its measure with Art. XX(g) GATT and will then have to show compliance with the *chapeau*. Per construction of our example, Home treats in a symmetric manner products originating in countries where similar conditions prevail: it treats Foreign differently, but the conditions prevailing there are different from the conditions prevailing in Home.

In other words, there is room to construct Art. XX GATT as an exception justifying violations of Art. III GATT when the basis for discriminatory treatment is not the imported, but an unimported good.

2.4 Art. XX GATT and Protocols of Accession

In *China—Audiovisual Services*, the AB established that China could rely on Art. XX(a) GATT in order to justify an exception from obligations assumed under its Protocol of Accession (§§223ff and especially §233).[35] It stopped short nevertheless of making a sweeping statement to the effect that Art. XX GATT can be relied upon by any WTO Member that wishes to deviate from obligations assumed under its Protocol of Accession, although it did not refute this possibility either. The AB seems to have paid particular attention to the wording included in §5.1 of the Protocol of Accession which reads:

> Without prejudice to China's right to regulate trade in a manner consistent with the WTO Agreement . . .

The AB went on to find in favour of China (§233):

> we consider that the provisions that China seeks to justify have a clearly discernible, objective link to China's regulation of trade in the relevant products. In the light of this relationship between provisions of China's measures that are inconsistent with China's trading rights commitments, and China's regulation of trade in the relevant products, we find that China may rely upon the introductory clause of paragraph 5.1 of its Accession Protocol and seek to justify these provisions as necessary to protect public morals in China, within the meaning of Article XX(a) of the GATT 1994.

It is thus because of the obligations assumed under its Protocol that China had the right to invoke Art. XX GATT in this case and not because of its general availability. One would expect that the AB would apply a similar test in future cases dealing with this issue as well.

Note, however, that in a subsequent report (*China—Raw Materials*), the AB held (§§325ff) that Art. XX GATT can be an exception to obligations assumed under a Protocol of Accession if it is *clearly* the case that it was meant to serve as exception: for example, if a specific reference to this provision is made or if action is mandated 'without prejudice to the right to regulate', since the right to regulate encompasses the grounds reflected in Art. XX GATT. In contrast, reference to a GATT provision (in this case, Art. VIII GATT) does not in and of itself suffice to render Art. XX GATT applicable to obligations assumed under the Protocol of Accession.

---

[35] See the discussion in Conconi and Pauwelyn (2011).

2.5 Art. XX GATT and Annex 1A Agreements

The relationship between Art. XX GATT and Annex 1A Agreements is not explicitly discussed or addressed in the Agreement Establishing the WTO. It is not addressed in the General Interpretative Note regarding the relationship between the GATT and Annex 1A Agreements either: recall that this Note came to be interpreted as an acknowledgment that Annex 1A Agreements are *lex specialis* to the GATT. The construction of Annex 1A Agreements as *lex specialis* to the GATT does not provide an answer to the question whether Art. XX GATT can serve as an exception to justify deviations from them; it merely provides an order of analysis, assuming claims have been submitted under both the GATT and an Annex 1A Agreement.

In the absence of a 'horizontal' solution, the response should be the outcome of an inquiry into the relationship between the GATT and each individual Annex1A Agreement.

There should be no doubt that Art. XX GATT can serve as an exception to violations of TRIMs. Art. 3 TRIMS explicitly states:

All exceptions under GATT 1994 shall apply, as appropriate, to the provisions of this agreement.

It is also settled that Art. XX GATT cannot serve as a lawful exception to violations of the SPS Agreement, First, Art. 2.4 SPS reads:

Sanitary or phytosanitary measures which conform to the relevant provisions of this Agreement shall be presumed to be in accordance with the obligations of the Members under the provisions of GATT 1994 which relate to the use of sanitary or phytosanitary measures, in particular the provisions of Article XX(b).

Second, Art. 3.2 SPS includes a presumption to the effect that SPS measures that conform to international standards are deemed necessary and presumed consistent with the relevant provisions of the SPS Agreement and the GATT 1994. And, finally, two Panels have so far stated in unambiguous terms that violations of the SPS Agreement can be healed through recourse to Art. XX GATT. The Panel report on *US—Poultry (China)* includes the following passage at §7.482:

... where such an SPS measure has been found inconsistent with provisions of the *SPS Agreement* such as Articles 2 and 5, the disciplines of Article XX(b) cannot be applied so as to justify such a measure.[36]

For the remaining Annex 1A Agreements, in the absence of a response in law or case law, one needs to ask the question whether Art. XX GATT could be construed as an exception to them.

---

[36] See also the Panel report on *EC—Hormones* at §§8.31–2.

Agriculture: Art. 21 AG makes explicit reference to the application in principle of GATT 1994. For this reason, Art. XX GATT could in principle be construed as an exception to obligations assumed under this agreement.

Agreement on Textiles and Clothing (ATC): As we will see in detail in Chapter 11, the whole purpose of ATC was to bring the field of textiles and clothing under the usual GATT disciplines following an agreed transitional period. As a result, the ATC has now ceased to exist and the question of the applicability of Art. XX GATT does not arise.

Technical Barriers to Trade (TBT): Nothing in this agreement explicitly discusses its relationship with Art. XX GATT. The preamble explicitly mentions all Art. XX grounds that could be relevant to the TBT Agreement; if at all, this explicit mention denotes that the framers of the TBT had in mind a construction of the TBT Agreement where no recourse to Art. XX GATT would be possible. Moreover, Art. 2.2 TBT includes the necessity test, which appears in certain subparagraphs of Art. XX GATT. In *US—Clove Cigarettes*, the Panel came close to discussing this issue, but in the end it did not have to since the US had invoked Art. XX GATT as an exception to Art. III GATT only and not as an exception to the TBT (§§7.305ff). Perhaps the US attitude here is telling in and of itself. In *US—COOL*, the Panel held that the interpretation of the 'necessity-requirement' should be symmetric to the interpretation of the same term under Art. XX GATT (§§7.667ff). Hence, under the circumstances, it will be far-fetched to construct the GATT as an exception to the TBT since as a matter of logic it cannot be that the same measure fails and passes the same legal test (since the necessity test appears in various paragraphs of Art. XX GATT as well). It is still an open question in case law, though, whether justifications of the TBT Agreement could successfully find justification through recourse to those subparagraphs of Art. XX GATT where a less demanding test than the necessity test has been introduced. It seems that, in light of the content of the preamble, a construction of the TBT Agreement in line with the negotiating intent would suggest a negative response to this question.

Antidumping (AD): The title of this agreement might support the opinion that Art. XX GATT is a possible exception to obligations assumed: after all, the Agreement elaborates on Art. VI GATT, and Art. XX GATT includes a list of exceptions to all GATT provisions. Art. 18.1 AD nevertheless should suffice to tilt the balance in the opposite direction: AD duties can be imposed only in accordance with GATT 1994 'as interpreted' by the AD Agreement. The AD Agreement contains no reference to Art. XX GATT and, hence, the latter cannot serve as an exception to the former.[37]

---

[37] See also the discussion on safeguards which is applicable here as well and justifies a negative response to the question asked, albeit for a different reason.

Customs Valuation (CV): This Agreement is an elaboration of Art. VII GATT. As such, Art. XX GATT should, in principle, be applicable. Indeed, one could very well examine cases where Art. XX(c) or (d) GATT could be potentially applicable.

Pre-shipment Inspection (PSI): A similar response is warranted here, especially since the preamble explicitly states that the principles and obligations of GATT 1994 apply here as well. Art. XX GATT is not an obligation, but is a principle of GATT 1994.

Rules of Origin (ROO): As we saw in Chapter 3, there is no actual agreement on Rules of Origin; WTO Members are free to decide on the origin of goods sold in their market and have to observe an obligation not to discriminate. As a result, we are squarely into the realm of the GATT here and, consequently, Art. XX GATT should be applicable.

Import Licensing Agreement (ILA): The Agreement explicitly provides in its preamble that the provisions of GATT 1994 apply, in principle, to the ILA. In principle, one cannot exclude the applicability of various paragraphs of Art. XX GATT (like (d), for example) in the context of import licensing.

Subsidies and Countervailing Measures (SCM): This is one of the most complicated cases. Unlike, the AD Agreement, the title of the Agreement does not denote an elaboration of a specific GATT provision (unlike the situation during the Tokyo round). Art. 31.2 SCM echoes Art. 18.1 AD and consequently the same response is warranted here when it comes to responses against subsidies. The SCM nevertheless regulates subsidization as well, and not CVDs only: subsidization is a state act, and the WTO is a contract regulating government behaviour; dumping is a private act and thus escapes the ambit of the WTO obligations.[38] Two forms of subsidies are, as we shall see in more detail in Chapter 8 explicitly declared illegal per se, that is, irrespective of their effects. Thus, the question might naturally arise whether Art. XX GATT could serve as an exception to this ban: in other words, could a local content subsidy be exceptionally allowed for reasons of environmental protection? There are two problems with this construction: first, it would put into question the whole idea of establishing a 'trichotomy' between prohibited, actionable, and non-actionable subsidies embedded in the SCM Agreement. If the idea was to keep Art. XX GATT as an exception to the SCM Agreement, this idea would have been reflected somewhere in the SCM Agreement; it was not. There is, of course, partial overlap between the list of Art. XX GATT and the list in Art. 8 SCM: 'green' subsidies could come under Art. XX(b) and XX(g) GATT

---

[38] Indeed, as we will see in more detail in Chapter 7, dumping is perfectly legal. It is characterized as 'unfair' trade practice in Art. VI GATT, but nowhere is its illegality pronounced.

anyway.[39] The negotiating record strongly indicates that the idea was to examine 'green' subsidies in a self-contained manner in the SCM context: documents by the Secretariat,[40] the Chairman of the Negotiating Group on Trade Environment,[41] as well as by various WTO Members belonging to different alliances, such as New Zealand,[42] India,[43] and Austria on behalf of EFTA (European Free Trade Association),[44] strongly support the conclusion that Art. 8 SCM was not thought of as an add-on to Art. XX GATT, but rather as the only provision dealing with subsidies not bound by the disciplines embedded in the SCM Agreement. Second, the problem with an affirmative response to this question is that almost axiomatically similar schemes would fail the test of consistency with the *chapeau* of Art. XX GATT which, as we saw *supra*, calls for absence of discrimination across countries where similar situations prevail: it cannot have been the intent of WTO Members to exclude payment of subsidies to foreigners through Art. III.8 GATT, only to reintroduce them through the back door (Art. XX GATT). In light of this argument, it is probably wiser to exclude the applicability of Art. XX GATT in the SCM context. This reading might look rigid and it is not inconsequential: the argument for example could be made that since subsidies might on occasion be the least restrictive (in terms of burden to international trade) option to address a distortion, by not sheltering them from challenge one risks seeing WTO Members employ restrictive measures when deviating from their GATT obligations. This risk should not be exaggerated though. As we will see nevertheless, in Chapter 8, generally available financial contributions by the government are not considered subsidies in the SCM sense of the term; one would expect to see similar behaviour (e.g. granting generally available subsidies) when promoting one of the objectives embedded in Art. XX GATT.[45]

Safeguards: A negative response is equally appropriate here: were Art. XX GATT to be construed so as to allow, for example, for higher duties or disproportionately large import quotas (in contravention of Art. 5 SG), then the limited ambit of the right itself to impose safeguards would have been altered.

---

[39] There is no case law though.
[40] GATT Doc. L/6896 of 18 September 1991.
[41] GATT Doc. Spec (91)21 of 29 April 1991.
[42] GATT Doc. Spec (91)36 of 8 July 1991.
[43] GATT Doc. Spec (91)40 of 9 July 1991.
[44] GATT Doc. Spec (91)27 of 12 June 1991.
[45] Howse (2010) and Rubini (2010) have both advanced arguments in favour of constructing Art. XX GATT as an exception to the disciplines imposed by the SCM Agreement. Compare Lester (2011) who also advances arguments in favour of constructing the SCM Agreement as a means of fighting against 'protectionist' subsidies only, that is, subsidies void of a public policy rationale other than to increase the income of producers.

3. National Security

Trade policy can be used either aggressively (export embargo) or defensively (import embargo) in order to promote national security concerns, its effectiveness depending on the identity of the players and the circumstances of particular cases. Overall, boycotts and economic sanctions do not seem to have functioned well, their extensive use especially in the early post-WWII era notwithstanding.[46] On the other hand, trade policy broadly defined is, as Schelling (1971, p. 737) observes, in a way national security policy, since it allows trading nations to have access to markets of goods which could be critical to advance national security concerns.

The title of Art. XXI GATT (Security Exception)[47] leaves no room for doubt that it is intended to function as an exception to the obligations assumed under the GATT: a WTO Member can invoke the security exception either because it has unilaterally decided that its security is threatened, or in order to comply with its obligations under the United Nations Charter for the maintenance of international peace and security.

The *travaux préparatoires* reveal no objection regarding the inclusion of this clause in the GATT: indeed, participants found it unreasonable to request contracting parties to continue to do business with firms that transferred all or part of their profits from their sales to the enemy. The discussions focused rather on the delineation of the exception:

> We recognized that there was a great danger of having too wide an exception and we could not put it in the Charter simply by saying: 'by any Member of measures relating to a Member's security interests,' because that would permit anything under the sun. Therefore we thought it well to draft provisions which would take care of real security interests and, at the same time, so far as we could, to limit the exception so as to prevent the adoption of protection for maintaining industries under every conceivable circumstance. . . . It is really a question of balance. We have got to have some exceptions. We cannot make it too tight, because we cannot prohibit measures which are needed purely for security reasons. On the other hand, we cannot make it so broad that, under the guise of security, countries will put on measures which really have a commercial purpose.[48]

Most of the discussion on Art. XXI GATT concerns the appropriate standard of review of actions taken under the auspices of this provision. As we saw *supra*, there was originally scepticism regarding the potential that this provision might be abused in practice. This reaction was not without foundation: the world was coming out of WWII and the alliances built during that time were quite recent,

---

[46] Schelling (1971).
[47] The term exception is used in the title of two provisions only: Art. XX and Art. XXI GATT.
[48] EPCT/A/PV/33 at pp. 20–1, and also EPCT/A/SR/33 at p. 3.

as was the diffidence when approaching nations from 'the other side'. The rise of communism provided these feelings with additional ammunition. Some communist regimes joined either as original members of the GATT or later. Western states had put in place COCOM, an acronym for Coordinating Committee for Multilateral Export Controls. COCOM was established in 1947, during the Cold War, to put an embargo on Western exports to East Bloc countries, and numbered 17 Member States, namely, Australia, Belgium, Canada, Denmark, France, Germany, Greece, Japan, Luxembourg, Netherlands, Norway, Portugal, Spain, Turkey, the United Kingdom, and the US. In addition, there were a number of cooperating countries, such as Austria, Finland, Ireland, New Zealand, Sweden, and Switzerland. COCOM ceased to function on 31 March 1994, and the then-current control list of embargoed goods was retained by the member nations until the successor, the Wassenaar Agreement, was established. The Wassenaar Arrangement (Wassenaar Arrangement on Export Controls for Conventional Arms and Dual-Use Goods and Technologies) is an arms control convention with 40 participating states. It was established on 12 May 1996, in Wassenaar (the Netherlands). A Secretariat for administrating the agreement is located in Vienna, Austria. As of December 2006, the 40 participating states are: Argentina, Australia, Austria, Belgium, Bulgaria, Canada, Croatia, Czech Republic, Denmark, Estonia, Finland, France, Germany, Greece, Hungary, Ireland, Italy, Japan, Latvia, Lithuania, Luxembourg, Malta, the Netherlands, New Zealand, Norway, Poland, Portugal, Republic of Korea, Romania, Russia, Slovakia, Slovenia, South Africa, Spain, Sweden, Switzerland, Turkey, Ukraine, the United Kingdom, and the United States. These arrangements were limited to exports of arms on which no tariff concessions occur; arms, nonetheless, are often produced through a variety of inputs of a purely commercial character, and the legal vehicle permitting COCOM and later the Wassenaar Arrangement countries to lawfully impose export restrictions on similar goods is Art. XXI GATT.

Yet, on the other side, absent inclusion of the security exception, few if any would have agreed to join the GATT. The inclusion of the national security provision in GATT was a necessity. For a variety of reasons, there have been very few invocations of this provision in practice, and most of them would qualify as 'legitimate' cases. Very rarely has a Panel been established in order to address a national security claim.

There have, however, been a few instances where, although no Panel was in the end established, national security claims have been raised as a defence for trade-restricting measures. In 1949, Czechoslovakia complained that the US administration of its export licensing controls discriminated between destination countries, contrary to Arts. I and XIII GATT. The US delegate responded, *inter alia*, that the challenged measures were restrictions imposed for security reasons.[49]

---

[49] GATT CP.3/SR.22 at pp. 4ff.

The complaint was rejected by a roll-call vote of 17 to 1 with 3 abstentions.[50] In 1961, when Portugal acceded to the GATT, Ghana imposed an import embargo on Portuguese goods, arguing that it was justified by the situation in Angola which posed (in the eyes of the government in Ghana) if not an actual, at least a potential, threat to its own national security. In Ghana's view:

> . . . under this Article each contracting party was the sole judge of what was necessary in its essentially security interest.[51]

In 1970, the United Arab Republic (UAR) (Egypt) defended its boycott against Israel (both its primary boycott against Israel and its secondary boycott against firms having relations with Israel) before the members of the Working Group on the Accession of the United Arab Republic, arguing that it was necessary to defend its national security since otherwise it would be contributing to the financing of Israel. Several members of the Working Group expressed sympathy for the view that the boycott was of a political and not of a commercial nature.[52] In November 1975, Sweden introduced an import quota for some footwear products. It sought to justify its measure through recourse to Art. XXI GATT, arguing that the country's security policy necessitated the maintenance of minimum production capacity in vital industries. During the discussions that followed at the GATT General Council,[53] many delegations expressed doubts as to the applicability of Art. XXI GATT in this context, and Sweden eventually notified the termination of its measures.[54] In April 1982, the Member States of the EU (then the EEC, European Economic Community), Australia, and Canada suspended imports of products originating in Argentina into their territories. They all claimed that their measures were justified by Art. XXI GATT and that they had been taken in light of the situation addressed in the UN Security Council Resolution 502, namely the Falklands/Malvinas war.[55] Argentina complained that the measures violated a series of GATT provisions, namely, Arts. I, II, XI, XIII, and Part IV.[56] During the discussions before the GATT General Council, the representative of the EU argued that it was the sole judge of the exercise of its rights under Art. XXI GATT; he added that the measures coming under the purview of this provision did not require notification, justification, or approval. The Australian delegate held similar views, adding that the CONTRACTING PARTIES, the highest GATT organ,

---

[50] See the decision of 8 June 1949 published in GATT Doc. II/28. The *roll-call vote* was a system of voting whereby the secretary to a meeting would call those present in a meeting individually to cast their vote. Like voting in general, it has been discontinued in the GATT/WTO context, since the early 1950s.

[51] SR.19/12 at p. 196.

[52] GATT Doc. BISD 17S/40 at pp. 22f.

[53] GATT Doc. C/M/109.

[54] GATT Doc. L/4250/Add. 1.

[55] GATT Doc. L/5319/Rev. 1.

[56] See the discussions before the GATT General Council reflected in GATT Docs. C/M/157 and C/M/159.

had no powers to question that judgment. In the same vein, the Canadian delegate took the view that the GATT had neither the competence nor the responsibility to deal with the political issue that had been raised.[57] Argentina requested an interpretation of Art. XXI GATT, which was decided in November 1982, five months after the challenged measures had been removed. On 30 November 1982, the CONTRACTING PARTIES adopted a Decision Concerning Article XXI of the General Agreement, which reads as follows:

1. Subject to the exception in Article XXI:a, contracting parties should be informed to the fullest extent possible of trade measures taken under Article XXI.
2. When action is taken under Article XXI, all contracting parties affected by such action retain their full rights under the General Agreement.
3. The Council may be requested to give further consideration to this matter in due course.[58]

The dispute between the US and Nicaragua concerning the US import and export embargo against Nicaragua is the first time that a dispute where national security was an issue was submitted to a Panel.[59] The US measure came as a response to the establishment of the Sandinistas in Nicaragua and their overall attitude, which, in the eyes of the US government, was hostile to the US. Nicaragua was facing a two-way embargo from the US, which practically ended any trade relations between the two countries. Nicaragua complained that the measure at hand was in violation of Art. XI GATT. Even before the Panel had been established, the US had argued that the measure was necessary to protect its national security interests. The US also claimed that an invocation of Art. XXI GATT was not justiciable. Before the Panel, the US repeated the same arguments. The Panel report on *US—Nicaraguan Trade*, which dealt with the complaint by Nicaragua, was never adopted and, hence, remains of limited legal value. It reveals, however, the *opinio juris* of an influential WTO Member, with respect to Art. XXI GATT. The motivation for the trade embargo is reflected in §3.1 of the report, and in §3.3 the impact that the US embargo had on trade between the two countries is discussed:

> 3.1 On 1 May 1985 the President of the United States issued an Executive Order which reads:
> ... I, RONALD REAGAN, President of the United States of America, find that the policies and actions of the Government of Nicaragua constitute an unusual and extraordinary threat to the national security and foreign policy of the United States and hereby declare a national emergency to deal with that threat.

---

[57] Idem.
[58] GATT Doc. BISD 29S/23.
[59] On this issue, see the excellent analysis offered in Hahn (1991) who discusses the case law and pays particular attention to the standard of review employed in national security cases. The author further advances his own framework for analysis of such issues.

I hereby prohibit all imports into the United States of goods and services of Nicaraguan origin; all exports from the United States of goods to or destined for Nicaragua, except those destined for the organized democratic resistance, and transactions relating thereto.

I hereby prohibit Nicaraguan air carriers from engaging in air transportation to or from points in the United States, and transactions relating thereto.

In addition, I hereby prohibit vessels of Nicaraguan registry from entering into United States ports, and transactions relating thereto.

The Secretary of the Treasury is delegated and authorized to employ all powers granted to me by the International Emergency Economic Powers Act to carry out the purposes of this Order.

The prohibition set forth in this Order shall be effective as of 12:01 a.m., Eastern Daylight Time, 7 May 1985 and shall be transmitted to the Congress and published in the Federal Register.

. . .

3.3 According to calculations made by the GATT Secretariat almost all imports (more than 99 per cent) from Nicaragua into the United States are items for which the duties are bound under the General Agreement.

The parties agreed on special terms of reference for this Panel, reproduced in §§ 1.4–1.5:

1.4 At the meeting of the Council on 12 March 1986, the Chairman announced that the following terms of reference of the Panel had been agreed:

To examine, in the light of the relevant GATT provisions, of the understanding reached at the Council on 10 October 1985 that the Panel cannot examine or judge the validity of or motivation for the invocation of Article XXI:(b)(iii) by the United States, of the relevant provisions of the Understanding Regarding Notification, Consultation, Dispute Settlement and Surveillance (BISD 26S/211–218), and of the agreed Dispute Settlement Procedures contained in the 1982 Ministerial Declaration (BISD 29S/13–16), the measures taken by the United States on 7 May 1985 and their trade effects in order to establish to what extent benefits accruing to Nicaragua under the General Agreement have been nullified or impaired, and to make such findings as will assist the CONTRACTING PARTIES in further action in this matter (C/M/196, page 7).

1.5 Following this announcement, the representative of the United States said the terms of reference had been drafted specifically for this case and would govern the Panel in this particular dispute. However, this should not imply that panels in other cases would not have to determine whether nullification or impairment existed. Only in this case did the United States not dispute the effects of a two-way trade embargo. Furthermore, the above terms of reference should not be interpreted to mean that any further action by the CONTRACTING PARTIES in this matter was necessary or appropriate. The representative of Nicaragua replied that, in his view, this Panel was not an exception; its functions would be those described in the 1979 Understanding (BISD 26S/211–218). Consequently, the CONTRACTING PARTIES would have to take appropriate action on the Panel's report (C/M/196, page 8).

This Panel was, consequently, lame from birth. The main arguments of the parties focused on the standard of review to be applied by the Panel. The parties presented radically opposing views—Nicaragua argued for a substantive review of the case, whereas the US argued for the opposite:

4.5 <u>Nicaragua</u> stated that the United States could not properly rely on Article XXI: (b)(iii) in this case. This provision could be invoked only if two conditions were met: first, the measure adopted had to be necessary for the protection of essential security interest and, second, the measure had to be taken in time of war or other emergency in international relations. Neither of these conditions were fulfilled in this present case. Obviously, a small developing country such as Nicaragua could not constitute a threat to the security of the United States. The embargo was therefore not necessary to protect any essential security interest of that country. Nor was there any 'emergency' in the sense of Article XXI. Nicaragua and the United States were not at war and maintained full diplomatic relations. If there was tension between the two countries, it was due entirely to actions by the United States in violation of international law. A country could not be allowed to base itself on the existence of an 'emergency' which it had itself created. In that respect, Article XXI was analogous to the right of self-defence in international law. This provision could be invoked only by a party subjected to direct aggression or armed attack and not by the aggressor or by parties indirectly at risk. Nicaragua added that it must be borne in mind that GATT did not exist in a vacuum but was an integral part of the wider structure of international law, and that the General Agreement must not be interpreted in a way inconsistent with international law. The International Court of Justice had found that the embargo was one element of a whole series of economic and military actions taken against Nicaragua in violation of international law and that it was not necessary for the protection of any essential security interest of the United States, and it had declared that the United States must make reparation for the damage caused. The Security Council (Resolution 562) and the General Assembly (Resolution 40/188) of the United Nations had also condemned the embargo for infringing the principles of free trade and had explicitly demanded its rescinding. Consequently, Nicaragua held that the United States could not base itself on Article XXI in the particular case, and that the trade measures under consideration constituted coercive measures applied for political reasons in contravention of paragraph 7(iii) of the Ministerial Declaration of November 1982, which obliged contracting parties to abstain from taking restrictive trade measures, for reasons of a non-economic character, not consistent with the General Agreement.

4.6 The <u>United States</u> said that Article XXI applied to any action which the contracting party taking it considered necessary for the protection of its essential security interest. This provision, by its clear terms, left the validity of the security justification to the exclusive judgement of the contracting party taking the action. The United States could therefore not be found to act in violation of Article XXI. In any case, the Panel's terms of reference made it clear that it could examine neither the validity of, nor the motivation for, the United States' invocation of Article XXI:(b) (iii). The United States' compliance with its obligations under the General Agreement was therefore not an issue before the Panel. The United States added that it disagreed with Nicaragua's assessment of the security situation but it did not wish to be drawn into a debate on a matter that fell outside the competence of the GATT in general and the Panel in particular.

4.7 <u>Nicaragua</u>, while recognizing that it was not within the competence of the Panel to examine or judge the validity of or motivation for the invocation of Article XXI:(b)(iii), nevertheless felt that the Panel had sufficient legal material and other

information before it to arrive at a conclusion on the consistency of the embargo
with the provisions of the General Agreement. (emphasis in the original)

The Panel was prevented, by its terms of reference, from addressing the justification for the embargo. Moreover, the Panel realized that a recommendation to the
effect that the US withdraw the embargo would have little effect in practice, given
the clear indication of the US (repeated a number of times before and during the
Panel proceedings) that it would not comply with such a recommendation.
Finally, even if the Panel had opted for a recommendation in favour of Nicaragua
and the latter requested authorization to impose countermeasures this would have
achieved little, given the two-way embargo by the US which essentially insulated
one country from the other; the presence or absence of countermeasures by
Nicaragua would have had no effect under the circumstances. The Panel report
is of particular interest when discussing the standard of review that Panels should
employ in similar cases: should they adopt a totally deferential standard or could
Panels legitimately sanction invocations of this provision that are abusive in their
view? We quote the relevant passage:

> 5.16 ... The Panel recognized that the General Agreement protected each contract-
> ing party's essential security interests through Article XXI and that the General
> Agreement's purpose was therefore not to make contracting parties forego their
> essential security interests for the sake of these aims. However, the Panel considered
> that the GATT could not achieve its basic aims unless each contracting party,
> whenever it made use of its rights under Article XXI, carefully weighed its security
> needs against the need to maintain stable trade relations.
>
> 5.17 The above considerations and the conclusions to which the Panel had to
> arrive, given its limited terms of reference and taking into account the existing rules
> and procedures of the GATT, raise in the view of the Panel the following more
> general questions: If it were accepted that the interpretation of Article XXI was
> reserved entirely to the contracting party invoking it, how could the CONTRACT-
> ING PARTIES ensure that this general exception to all obligations under the
> General Agreement is not invoked excessively or for purposes other than those set
> out in this provision? If the CONTRACTING PARTIES give a panel the task of
> examining a case involving an Article XXI invocation without authorizing it to
> examine the justification of that invocation, do they limit the adversely affected
> contracting party's right to have its complaint investigated in accordance with Article
> XXIII:2? Are the powers of the CONTRACTING PARTIES under Article XXIII:2
> sufficient to provide redress to contracting parties subjected to a two-way embargo?
>
> 5.18 The Panel noted that in 1982 the CONTRACTING PARTIES took a
> 'Decision Concerning Article XXI of the General Agreement' which refers to the
> possibility of a formal interpretation of Article XXI and to a further consideration by
> the Council of this matter (BISD 29S/23–24). The Panel recommends that the
> CONTRACTING PARTIES, in any further consideration of this matter in accor-
> dance with that Decision, take into account the questions raised by the Panel above.

The essence of the Panel's approach is captured in §5.17: although not explicitly
stating it, the Panel seemed opposed to the view that the invocation of Art. XXI of
the GATT was not justiciable. However, in light of its limited mandate (special

terms of reference), the Panel did not have the opportunity to explore the appropriate standard of review any further.

In 1991, first the EU and then a host of countries withdrew preferential benefits from Yugoslavia, in light of the prevailing situation there (civil war), invoking Art. XXI GATT to justify these measures.[60] Yugoslavia reacted by arguing that the measures could not be justified under Art. XXI GATT. A Panel was established to discuss the dispute.[61] In light of the decision to freeze Yugoslavia's membership of the WTO, the Panel was discontinued.[62]

The notorious US Helms/Burton Act (Cuban Liberty and Democratic Solidarity Act)[63] emerges so far as the only dispute in the WTO era where Art. XXI GATT has been invoked. Through this Act, the US imposed trade sanctions on products of Cuban origin, but also on products of other (than Cuban) origin, a percentage of the value added of which was Cuban (primary embargo). Eventually, the US, through a secondary embargo, stopped trading with nations trading with Cuba. The EU complained that the US measure violated a series of GATT provisions. The official description of the EU complaint is reproduced here:

> The European Community and its Member States wish to convey to you a request for consultations with the United States of America pursuant to Article 4 of the Understanding on Rules and Procedures Governing the Settlement of Disputes (DSU), Article XXIII:1 of the General Agreement on Tariffs and Trade 1994 (GATT 1994) and Article XXIII:1 of the General Agreement on Trade in Services (GATS) concerning the Cuban Liberty and Democratic Solidarity (LIBERTAD) Act of 1996, other legislative provisions consolidated therein, and any implementing measures taken thereunder.
>
> The European Community and its Member States wish to express their profound concern about the apparent lack of conformity of certain aspects of this Act, including other legislative provisions consolidated therein and any implementing measures taken thereunder, to the international obligations of the United States under GATT 1994 and GATS. This concern relates in particular, but not necessarily exclusively, to the following aspects:
>
> The Cuban Democracy Act and its companion the Cuban Liberty and Democratic Solidarity Act contain a number of provisions which have the intent and effect to restrain the liberty of the EC to export to Cuba or to trade in Cuban origin goods, as well as to restrict the freedom of EC registered vessels and their cargo to transit through US ports.
>
> In addition, there are provisions which require the provisions of certificates in respect of trade in Cuban sugar. If such certificates are not provided, access to the US sugar quota is denied.
>
> Finally, there are measures which may lead to the refusal of visas and the exclusion of non-US nationals from US territory in a way which may contravene US commitments under GATS.

---

60 GATT Doc. L/6948.
61 GATT Doc. C/M/255 at p. 18.
62 GATT Doc. C/M/264 at p. 3.
63 Sometimes referred to as LIBERTAD.

The European Community and its Member States are of the view that these and comparable measures taken under the two laws mentioned above may not be in conformity with at least the following provisions: Articles I, III, V, XI and XIII of GATT 1994 and Articles I, III, VI, XVI and XVII of GATS and in particular in relation to the Annex on Movement of Natural Persons Supplying Services under the Agreement.[64]

Following inconclusive consultations, a Panel was established to adjudicate the EU complaint. Subsequent to the establishment of the Panel, the EU requested, in accordance with Art. 12.12 DSU, the suspension of the Panel's work, in order to allow it to reach a mutually acceptable solution with the US.[65] The Panel suspended its work on 21 April 1997, and since no request was tabled to reconvene within one year, the authority of the Panel, as per Art. 12.12 of the DSU, lapsed on 22 April 1998.[66] The WTO was never notified of any mutually acceptable solution. Nor has the EU resurrected the original Panel.[67]

The key question remains what is the standard of review that Panels will employ in similar cases? Recently, the Panel on *China—Raw Materials* suggested that a very deferential standard is appropriate in national security cases (§7.276). This seems to be in line with the AB line of thinking of adopting a more deferential standard the higher the value that is being pursued: arguably, nothing is more sacrosanct than national security in state-to-state international relations.

4. Waivers

A WTO Member may, in exceptional circumstances, request that it be exempted from its obligations under the WTO. To this effect, a Member must submit a request for a *waiver* to the WTO Membership. Art. IX WTO Agreement set out the procedure:

> 3. In exceptional circumstances, the Ministerial Conference may decide to waive an obligation imposed on a Member by this Agreement or any of the Multilateral Trade Agreements, provided that any such decision shall be taken by three fourths of the Members unless otherwise provided for in this paragraph.
>
> (a) A request for a waiver concerning this Agreement shall be submitted to the Ministerial Conference for consideration pursuant to the practice of decision-making by consensus. The Ministerial Conference shall establish a time-period, which shall not exceed 90 days, to consider the request. If consensus is not reached during the time-period, any decision to grant a waiver shall be taken by three fourths of the Members.

---

[64] See WTO Doc. WT/DS38/1 of 13 May 1996.
[65] WTO Doc. WT/DS38/5 of 25 April 1997.
[66] WTO Doc. WT/DS38/6 of 24 April 1998.
[67] See the chapter dedicated to this issue in Matsushita et al. (2006).

(b) A request for a waiver concerning the Multilateral Trade Agreements in Annexes 1A or 1B or 1C and their annexes shall be submitted initially to the Council for Trade in Goods, the Council for Trade in Services or the Council for TRIPS, respectively, for consideration during a time-period which shall not exceed 90 days. At the end of the time-period, the relevant Council shall submit a report to the Ministerial Conference.

4. A decision by the Ministerial Conference granting a waiver shall state the exceptional circumstances justifying the decision, the terms and conditions governing the application of the waiver, and the date on which the waiver shall terminate. Any waiver granted for a period of more than one year shall be reviewed by the Ministerial Conference not later than one year after it is granted, and thereafter annually until the waiver terminates. In each review, the Ministerial Conference shall examine whether the exceptional circumstances justifying the waiver still exist and whether the terms and conditions attached to the waiver have been met. The Ministerial Conference, on the basis of the annual review, may extend, modify or terminate the waiver.

5. Decisions under a Plurilateral Trade Agreement, including any decisions on interpretations and waivers, shall be governed by the provisions of that Agreement.

A footnote to §3 reads:

> A decision to grant a waiver in respect of any obligation subject to a transition period or a period for staged implementation that the requesting Member has not performed by the end of the relevant period shall be taken only by consensus.

It follows that a waiver is a transitional multilateral authorization to deviate from agreed obligations. The transitional character is underlined by the fact that all waivers will be reviewed annually, irrespective of whether they have been granted for a multi-year period: WTO Members must satisfy themselves during the review that the rationale for granting the waiver is very much alive. As briefly alluded to above, waivers can be granted for whatever reason the requesting state might find appropriate. For example, the EU requested a waiver that would allow it to provide humanitarian assistance to products originating in Pakistan. The EU's declared motive was humanitarian assistance; Pakistan had suffered floods and the EU was willing to accord Pakistan trade preferences as means to help alleviate the crisis. Many developing countries initially opposed it because of the consequential preference erosion for their goods, but eventually conceded to its adoption.[68]

Practice has led to conflicts across WTO Members as to the overall *justiciability* of waivers' decisions, as well as the terms under which waivers have been granted. Case law has provided some answers in both respects.

---

[68] See WTO Doc. WT/L/851 of 22 February 2012. A number of sensitive import-competing products were, nevertheless, largely excluded and as a result the efficacy of this measure was judged highly questionable by Khorana et al. (2012), who also cast doubt on the effectiveness of trade measures as a response to humanitarian crises.

The Panel on *EC—Bananas III* was called upon to address the EU argument that waivers[69] cannot form the subject-matter of a dispute before WTO adjudicating bodies. In rejecting this argument, the Panel held that it had the requisite jurisdiction to interpret the contents of a waiver granted by the WTO Members (§ 7.97). On appeal, the AB upheld this finding in the following terms (§167):

> The European Communities asserts that the Panel should not have conducted an objective examination of the requirements of the Lomé Convention, but instead should have deferred to the 'common' EC and ACP views on the appropriate interpretation of the Lomé Convention. This assertion is without merit. The Panel was correct in stating:
>
>> We note that since the GATT CONTRACTING PARTIES incorporated a reference to the Lomé Convention into the Lomé waiver, the meaning of the Lomé Convention became a GATT/WTO issue, at least to that extent. Thus, we have no alternative but to examine the provisions of the Lomé Convention ourselves in so far as it is necessary to interpret the Lomé waiver.
>
> We, too, have no alternative.

Having clarified that waivers are justiciable, the same Panel went on to provide its understanding on the manner in which the terms of a waiver should be interpreted. This Panel was requested, *inter alia*, to review whether the EU had respected the terms of the waiver that it had requested (and obtained) in order to treat imports of bananas from some WTO Members (the ACP countries, a group of countries from Africa, the Caribbean, and the Pacific with which it had signed a treaty, the Lomé Convention) better than imports from the rest of the world, in contravention of Art. I GATT. The precise question before the Panel was whether Art. XIII GATT, a provision that had not been explicitly included in the waiver granted to the EU, was covered by the terms of the waiver or not. Although the Panel was of the view that a waiver should be construed narrowly, it went on to hold that despite the fact Art. XIII GATT was not explicitly mentioned in the waiver granted to the EU, that provision should, nevertheless, be covered by the terms of the waiver in light of the *effet utile* of the waiver (§§7.105–8). On appeal, the AB reversed the Panel's findings and held that only what is *explicitly* reflected to in a waiver should be understood to be covered by the terms of the waiver (§§182–8). As a result, it is now the case that, unless a provision has been explicitly included in the waiver itself, it is not covered by it.

Table 5.1 provides a list of the waivers that have been granted since the advent of the WTO and those waivers that are presently in force (December 2011).[70]

---

[69] The facts of this case, which are reproduced in other parts of this volume, are immaterial here and hence are omitted: the EU claimed that waivers, as a general matter, irrespective of the reasons underlying the granting of the request, are not justiciable.

[70] WTO Doc. WT/GC/W/629 of 8 February 2011.

Table 5.1 List of Waivers

Waiver	Decision	Date of adoption of Decision	Granted until	Report in 2010[i]
Granted in 2010				
Introduction of Harmonized System 2007 changes into WTO Schedules of Tariff Concessions[ii]	WT/L/809	14 December 2010	31 December 2011	—
Introduction of Harmonized System 2002 changes into WTO Schedules of Tariff Concessions[iii]	WT/L/808	14 December 2010	31 December 2011	—
Argentina—Introduction of Harmonized System 1996 changes into WTO Schedules of Tariff Concessions	WT/L/801	29 July 2010	30 April 2011	—
Previously granted—in force in 2010				
Introduction of Harmonized System 2007 changes into WTO Schedules of Tariff Concessions[iii]	WT/L/787 and Add.1	17 December 2009	31 December 2010	—
Introduction of Harmonized System 2002 changes into WTO Schedules of Tariff Concessions[iv]	WT/L/786	17 December 2009	31 December 2010	—
Preferential Tariff Treatment for Least-Developed Countries—Decision on extension of waiver	WT/L/759	27 May 2009	30 June 2019	—
Panama—Introduction of Harmonized System 1996 changes into WTO Schedules of Tariff Concessions	WT/L/758	27 May 2009	30 April 2010	—
Argentina—Introduction of Harmonized System 1996 changes into WTO Schedules of Tariff Concessions	WT/L/757	27 May 2009	30 April 2010	—
United States—Andean Trade Preference Act—Renewal of waiver	WT/L/755	27 May 2009	31 December 2014	WT/L/796
United States—African Growth and Opportunity Act	WT/L/754	27 May 2009	30 September 2015	WT/L/795
United States—Caribbean Basin Economic Recovery Act—Renewal of waiver	WT/L/753	27 May 2009	31 December 2014	WT/L/794
European Communities—Application of Autonomous Preferential Treatment to Moldova	WT/L/722	7 May 2008	31 December 2013	WT/L/800 and Corr.1
Duties on raw cashmere Mongolia—Export	WT/L/695	27 July 2007	29 January 2012	—
United States—Former Trust Territory of the Pacific Islands	WT/L/694	27 July 2007	31 December 2016	WT/L/798
Cuba—Article XV:6 of GATT 1994	WT/L/678	15 December 2006	31 December 2011	WT/L/803

CARIBCAN	WT/L/677	15 December 2006	31 December 2011	WT/L/804
Kimberley Process Certification Scheme for rough diamonds[iv]	WT/L/676	15 December 2006	31 December 2012	—
European Communities' preferences for Albania, Bosnia and Herzegovina, Croatia, Serbia and Montenegro, and the Former Yugoslav Republic of Macedonia	WT/L/654	28 July 2006	31 December 2011	WT/L/799 and Corr.1
Least-Developed Country Members—Obligations under Article 70.9 of the TRIPS Agreement with respect to Pharmaceutical Products	WT/L/478	8 July 2002	1 January 2016	—

Notes:

[i] Applicable if so stipulated in the corresponding waiver Decision.

[ii] The Members which have requested to be covered under this waiver are: Argentina; Australia; Brazil; Canada; China; Costa Rica; Croatia; El Salvador; European Union; Guatemala; Honduras; Hong Kong, China; India; Israel; Korea; Macao, China; Malaysia; Mexico; New Zealand; Nicaragua; Norway; Pakistan; Singapore; Switzerland; Thailand; United States; and Uruguay.

[iii] The Members which have requested to be covered under this waiver are: Argentina; Australia; Brazil; China; Costa Rica; Croatia; El Salvador; European Union; Iceland; India; Republic of Korea; Mexico; New Zealand; Norway; Thailand; United States; and Uruguay.

[iv] Annex: Australia; Botswana; Brazil; Canada; Croatia; India; Israel; Japan; Korea; Mauritius; Mexico; Norway; Philippines; Sierra Leone; Chinese Taipei; Thailand; United Arab Emirates; United States; and Venezuela.

5. Non-application

In order to facilitate accession to the GATT, Art. XXXV GATT provided flexibility in that it allowed acceding countries *not* to enter into contractual arrangements *at all* with some incumbent GATT CONTRACTING PARTIES (Art. XXXV GATT). Two countries could thus both acquire the status of a GATT contracting party without being bound by the GATT at all in their *inter se* relations.

Historically, the rationale for its original inclusion in the GATT has to do with the fact that the world was emerging from the Second World War and, except for the neutral countries, many potential candidates to accede to the GATT had not healed the wounds: it would have been politically unacceptable for them to do 'business as usual' with yesterday's enemies. For example, a number of GATT contracting parties invoked Art. XXXV GATT against Japan: Australia in 1964, Austria (1976), Barbados (1967), Belgium (1964), Benin (1972), Brazil (1957), Burundi (1972), Cameroon (1974), Central African Republic (1974), Chad (1971), Congo (1973), Cuba (1961), Cyprus (1962), France (1964), Gabon (1973), Gambia (1971), Ghana (1962), Guyana (1966), Haiti (1958), India (1958), Ireland (1975), Ivory Coast (1970), Jamaica (1972), Kenya (1977), Kuwait (1970), Luxembourg (1964), Madagascar (1969), Malaysia (1963), Maldives (1988), Mali (1993), Malta (1968), Mauritania (1968), Netherlands (1964), New Zealand (1962), Niger (1970), Nigeria (1975), Portugal (1972), Rhodesia and Nyasaland (1963), Rwanda (1970), Senegal (1975), Sierra Leone (1975), South Africa (1985), Spain (1971), Trinidad and Tobago (1966), Uganda (1970), United Kingdom (1963), and Upper Volta (1970).[71]

During the Uruguay round negotiations, it was judged that the rationale for the continued inclusion of the non-application clause was still present and, consequently, it was decided that Art. XIII be included in the Agreement Establishing the WTO:

1. This Agreement and the Multilateral Trade Agreements in Annexes 1 and 2 shall not apply as between any Member and any other Member if either of the Members, at the time either becomes a Member, does not consent to such application.
2. Paragraph 1 may be invoked between original Members of the WTO which were contracting parties to GATT 1947 only where Article XXXV of that Agreement had been invoked earlier and was effective as between those contracting parties at the time of entry into force for them of this Agreement.
3. Paragraph 1 shall apply between a Member and another Member which has acceded under Article XII only if the Member not consenting to the application has so notified the Ministerial Conference before the approval of the agreement on the terms of accession by the Ministerial Conference.

---

[71] See the GATT Analytical Index, at pp. 1034ff. Japan was the most frequent target of invocations of the non-application clause. Eventually, the GATT contracting parties starting disinvoking Art. XXXV GATT against Japan. However, it took some time and often persuasion: Japan, for example, had to threaten developing countries that it would not be providing them with tariff preferences since they had invoked Art. XXXV GATT against it (GATT Doc. 2ss/SR.2 at p. 7).

4. The Ministerial Conference may review the operation of this Article in particular cases at the request of any Member and make appropriate recommendations.
5. Non-application of a Plurilateral Trade Agreement between parties to that Agreement shall be governed by the provisions of that Agreement.

The non-application clause goes far beyond a classic reservation to a treaty: reservations, in the VCLT sense of the term, are meant to vary the bindingness of particular provisions for those introducing them (the WTO Agreement does not allow reservations to be entered at all).

Table 5.2 lists the Members that have invoked the non-application clause under Art. XIII of the WTO Agreement as of the entry into force of the WTO.

Table 5.2: Instances of application of Article XIII of the WTO Agreement

Invoked by	In respect of	Date of General Council decision on accession	Date of invocation	Withdrawal
United States	Romania	N/A	WTO document dated 27 January 1995 indicates that the United States informed the Director-General on 30 December 1994 WT/L/11	WT/L/203
United States	Mongolia	18 July 1996 WT/ACC/MNG/10	Communication dated 11 July 1996 WT/L/159	WT/L/306
United States	Kyrgyz Republic	14 October 1998 WT/ACC/KCZ/28	Communication dated 9 October 1998 WT/L/275	WT/L/363
United States	Georgia	6 October 1999 WT/ACC/GEO/32/	Communication dated 30 September 1999 WT/L/318	WT/L/385
United States	Moldova	8 May 2001 WT/ACC/MOL/39	Communication dated 2 May 2001 WT/L/395	Still in force
El Salvador	China	10 November 2001 WT/ACC/CHN/49 and Corr.1	Communication dated 5 November 2001 WT/L/429	Still in force
Turkey	Armenia	10 December 2002 WT/L/ARM/23	Communication dated 29 November 2002 WT/L/501	Still in force
United States	Armenia	10 December 2002 WT/L/ARM/23	Communication dated 3 December 2002 WT/L/505	WT/L/601
United States	Viet Nam	7 November 2006 WT/L/662	Communication dated 3 November 2006 WT/L/661	WT/L/679

6

AGREEMENTS DEALING WITH CUSTOMS PROCEDURES

1. Introductory Remarks

In this and the following five chapters, we will be discussing the so-called Annex 1A Agreements, that is, the agreements besides the GATT that regulate trade in goods. In this chapter, we discuss three agreements that deal with simplification of customs procedures and, thus, reduction of 'deadweight losses': the ILA, the CV, and the PSI Agreements. We then revert to the ongoing discussions on trade facilitation, which have not so far but could soon result in a new WTO agreement: this could be the first agreement since the advent of the WTO. From a subject-matter perspective, trade facilitation deals with similar issues (e.g. simplification of customs procedures), but extends its coverage to 'behind the border' measures.

2. The ILA (Import Licensing Agreement)

2.1 The Legal Discipline and its Rationale

The ILA aims at simplifying, and bringing transparency to, import licensing procedures in an effort to ensure their fair and equitable application and administration, and to prevent the procedures applied when granting import licences having a restrictive or distortive effect on imports.

The core subject-matter of the ILA was already covered by the GATT: WTO Members are anyway subject to transparency obligations as to the administration of import licences under Art XIII.3(a) GATT. The ILA was added because transparency in and of itself is not a guarantee that no additional distortions will result from the introduction of import licensing schemes.

During the Tokyo round, the first such agreement was concluded and has since been superseded by the Uruguay round ILA. The current agreement contains stronger disciplines on transparency and notifications.

This Agreement must be observed whenever recourse to import licensing is being made.

Art. 1 ILA defines import licensing:

> For the purpose of this Agreement, import licensing is defined as administrative procedures used for the operation of import licensing regimes requiring the submission of an application or other documentation (other than that required for customs purposes) to the relevant administrative body as a prior condition for importation into the customs territory of the importing Member.

Import licensing procedures are in place irrespective of whether another restriction has also been introduced: a licence might be warranted if no QR is in place (say for statistical reasons) or if a legal QR (say on balance of payments grounds) has been introduced. The key to understanding the legal discipline is that the licensing scheme does not in and of itself add a new restriction.[1]

---

[1] In practice, import licences are imposed for a variety of reasons and usually when a QR is in place. Licences are imposed for rent-seeking reasons, for political-economy reasons or even because of a belief in a particular economic model: Douglas (1987, pp. 164ff) in his formidable book describes how the belief that balance of payments problems were the main constraint for economic growth led successive New Zealand governments to impose dozens of licence schemes and eventually to become known as 'Fortress New Zealand'.

2.2 The Coverage of the Legal Discipline

2.2.1 Two Forms of Import Licensing

There are two forms of licensing provided for in the ILA: *automatic licensing* (Art. 2 ILA), which occurs in the absence of a restriction in place; and *non-automatic licensing* (Art. 3 ILA), which takes place when a lawful restriction is in place.

Automatic import licensing, it is acknowledged, may be necessary when other appropriate procedures for reaching the regulatory objective sought are not available. Art. 2 ILA makes it clear that automatic import licensing may be maintained as long as the circumstances which gave rise to its introduction prevail and as long as its underlying administrative purposes cannot be achieved in a more appropriate way. A WTO Member will usually have recourse to automatic licensing in order to monitor imports, that is, get statistical information.

WTO Members, when having recourse to automatic import licensing, have to ensure that they will not be introducing any restrictive effects on imports. There is a presumption that automatic import licensing has restrictive effects. This is not, however, the case if the three conditions mentioned in Art. 2.2(a) ILA have been met. We quote:

(a) Any person, firm or institution which fulfils the legal requirements of the importing Member for engaging in import operations involving products subject to automatic licensing is equally eligible to apply for and to obtain import licences;

(b) Applications for licences may be submitted on any working day prior to the customs clearance of the goods;

(c) Applications for licences when submitted in appropriate and complete form are approved immediately on receipt, to the extent administratively feasible, but within a maximum of 10 working days.

The Agreement is not explicit in this respect, but it should be the case that the three conditions must be met cumulatively. Indeed, what is the use of fulfilling (a), if licences are granted five years, that is, abusively later, than the date of the request? What the ILA does make clear is that the list quoted above is of an indicative character. So what other activities could be deemed to have restrictive effects in accordance with this provision? Governments imposing QRs might, for example, have the incentive to auction off import licences to interested importers. Indeed, this would be the case any time there is substantial discrepancy between the world and the home price. In this case, the price of acquiring an import licence (auction price) will depend on the difference between the price of the domestic good and that of the imported good. Should auctioning of import licences be accepted as a restrictive effect and, thus, outright banned whenever recourse to automatic licensing is being made? An affirmative response seems appropriate in light of the definition of automatic licensing in Art. 2.1 ILA:

> Automatic import licensing is defined as import licensing where approval of the application is granted in all cases, and which is in accordance with the requirements of paragraph 2(a).

In case of auctioning, there is no approval of applications in all cases, since only the winner of the auction will be allowed to import. There is approval of the request to participate in the auction. This is not, nonetheless, what the framers of ILA had in mind as the wording of the cited provision makes it clear. If at all, auctioning could come under non-automatic licensing.

Non-automatic import licensing can occur any time a restriction (usually a quota) is in place. It can occur, nonetheless, even if another (other than quota) restriction is in place; what matters is that the restriction is lawful. The AB in its report on *EC—Bananas III* accepted the legality of imposing a licensing scheme when a tariff quota, and not a QR, was in place (§§193–5). In doing so, it understood the term 'restriction' appearing in Art. 3.2 ILA to cover at least quotas and tariff quotas.

The ILA assumes, of course, that the restriction is legitimately in place (that is, there is a justifiable exception to Art. XI GATT). Non-automatic import licensing is defined in Art. 3.1 ILA as follows:

> Non-automatic import licensing procedures are defined as import licensing not falling within the definition contained in paragraph 1 of Article 2.

Non-automatic licensing is, in practice, the more frequently used type of licensing.

Art. 3.2 ILA requests from WTO Members to ensure that no additional (to the QR in place) trade-restrictive effect will result from the adoption of the import licensing scheme. The quintessential obligation enshrined in Art. 3.2 ILA has to do with the interpretation of the terms 'trade-restrictive or -distortive effects on imports'. The second sentence of the same provision seems to suggest that the legislator had in mind instances such as the extension of the duration of the QR. Interpreting this provision, the AB, in its report on *EC—Poultry*, held that WTO Members have to ensure that, when applying import licensing schemes, no distortive effects will be caused either for the trade covered by the scheme at hand or for the trade not covered by the scheme. The onus is, however, on the complainant to show that distortive effects have resulted from the introduction of a licensing scheme. In *EC—Poultry*, the AB held that the complainant must demonstrate a causal relationship between the existence of the licensing procedure and the claimed distortion (§67):

> These arguments, however, do not address the problem of establishing a causal relationship between imposition of the EC licensing procedure and the claimed trade distortion. Even if conceded *arguendo*, these arguments do not provide proof of the essential element of causation. (italics in the original)

Additional obligations regarding non-automatic import licensing are reflected in Art. 3.5 ILA.

(a) The period of application should not be excessively long;

(b) The period of validity of the licence should not be unreasonably limited in time;

(c) WTO Members should not discourage full utilization of quotas;

(d) The desirability for issuing licences for products in economic quantities must be taken into account by the WTO Member issuing an import licence;

(e) When allocating import licences, the previous import performance of the petitioner must be taken into account;

(f) In the case where a quota is administered through a licence which is not country of origin-specific, importers shall be free to choose the source of imports;

(g) In case of variations between the amount designated in the licence and the amount actually imported (which can occur, as Art. 1.4 ILA itself acknowledges), Art. 3.5(l) ILA calls for compensatory adjustments to ensure that trade flows continue unimpeded; and finally,

(h) WTO Members undertake, in accordance with Art. 1.9 ILA, the obligation to make foreign exchange available to petitioners for an import licence under the same terms as importers of goods for which no import licensing scheme is in place.

In *Turkey—Rice*, the Panel had to entertain a claim by the US to the effect that Turkey was running foul of its obligations under Art. 3.5 ILA by restricting access to in-quota rice to traders who had previously purchased a larger quantity of domestic rice.[2] This was, in the view of the complainant, an impermissible distortive effect. The Panel for reasons of judicial economy did not formally rule on this issue, yet the overall context and discussion in the Panel report lend strong support to the view that similar practices are inconsistent with the obligations assumed under the ILA (§§7.294ff).

Should auctioning of import licences be accepted whenever recourse to non-automatic licensing is being made? Here the response should, in principle, be affirmative. The ILA does not ban auctioning. It could of course be the case that the winner of the auction might be prepared to pay in order to exclude the imported goods from the market: some importers might for strategic reasons purchase licences and contribute towards eliminating imports from their domestic market in case, for example, they are producers of a substitutable (to the imported) product. On occasion, depending on the cost of the auction, this might be a profitable enterprise. Is there any insurance policy against similar behaviour? Indirectly, yes. Recall that under Art. 3.5 ILA past performance must be taken into account. In this context, they must take into account cases where the winner of an auction has not utilized the quota in full and has not provided an adequate explanation as to why this happened. There is no obligation to exclude similar

---

[2] A tariff quota was in place and its legality was not an issue.

importers from future auctions, but there is an obligation to demonstrate that authorities are well aware of similar behaviour and have addressed it.

2.2.2 Obligations Relevant to both Forms of Import Licensing

Art. 1.4 ILA imposes a general obligation of transparency on all WTO Members availing themselves of the possibility to have recourse to import licensing schemes, whereby the conditions for obtaining a licence become public and a notification is transmitted to the WTO at the very least 21 days before the effective date of the imposition of the requirement. WTO Members are further obliged to complete on an annual basis the *Questionnaire on Import Licensing Procedures* by 30 September each year:[3] they might be requested to provide additional, detailed information about both their legislation and practice regarding import licensing, and this document serves precisely this purpose. WTO Members are, further, under the duty to notify the WTO of all laws, regulations, and the like that regulate import licensing as well as initiations of licensing procedures. Art. 5.5 ILA allows for the possibility of cross-notifications of licensing procedures instituted by other WTO Members.

Art. 1.3 ILA imposes a general obligation on WTO Members to the effect that:

> The rules for import licensing procedures shall be neutral in application and administered in a fair and equitable manner.

The AB in its report on *EC—Bananas III* clarified that this legal provision should be understood as imposing on WTO Members the obligation to apply the same procedures for import licensing to all WTO Members (§§196–8).

Art. 1.5 ILA further requests that WTO Members guarantee that application and renewal forms are 'as simple as possible'; the same obligation is imposed by virtue of Art. 1.6 ILA with respect to application and renewal procedures. Finally, Art. 1.7 ILA makes it clear that applications will not be rejected for minor documentation errors.

The treatment of confidential information is regulated in Art. 1.11 ILA:

> The provisions of this Agreement shall not require any Member to disclose confidential information which would impede law enforcement or otherwise be contrary to the public interest or would prejudice the legitimate commercial interests of particular enterprises, public or private.

Reservations to the ILA are possible, assuming the other WTO Members have provided their consent to this effect (Art. 8 ILA).

2.3 Export Licensing

The ILA deals with import and not with export licences. In fact, there is no agreement on export licences, since WTO Members have refused to enter into

---

[3] Art. 7.3 ILA and WTO Doc. G/LIC/3.

similar negotiation. During the Tokyo round, there was an attempt to negotiate on export restrictions. Winham (1986, pp. 277ff) reflects the consensus view at the time that similar measures were occasionally adopted in order to confer an advantage to domestic industries. Following a proposal in 1976 by the then Brazilian Ambassador, George A. Maciel, a negotiating group was established: the Framework Group. This group was, *inter alia*, requested to negotiate an agreement on export licensing. It is clear from the record that a negotiation on export restrictions was not a priority issue.[4] Yet, trading nations were, in principle, unwilling to commit on this score, fearing the repercussions for a similar commitment on their sovereignty over natural resources.[5] The end product of the negotiation was that an Understanding Regarding Export Restrictions and Charges was issued that dealt head on with this issue,[6] but which essentially called for treating export restrictions as a priority issue for the negotiators in the post-Tokyo round era.[7]

The discussion continued for some time immediately after the conclusion of the Tokyo round, and the Consultative Group of Eighteen (CG18) was asked to advise the GATT Council on the forum and modalities of the negotiation. This body issued a document explaining the impact of export restrictions on international trade and added an Annex reflecting illustrative examples.[8] This provided the impetus for further work in this area. During the preparations leading to the meeting at ministerial level of the CONTRACTING PARTIES in 1982, one delegation suggested the inclusion in the agenda of export restrictions with a view to pointing to the trade-distorting effects of similar practices. The matter was not included in the Declaration adopted at the end of the meeting.[9]

Trading nations nevertheless spent little time negotiating this issue in the context of the Uruguay round which was initiated in 1986. The GATT Secretariat issued a very elaborate document[10] where it discussed the rationale for imposing export restrictions as well as some illustrative examples: improving terms of trade, protection of processing industries, raising revenue, domestic price stabilization, and conservation of exhaustible natural resources were the reasons mentioned for restricting exports. Sovereignty concerns linked to, for example, national minerals might provide WTO Members with an incentive to place restrictions on the export side. In the same spirit, a country with monopoly power in the global market with respect to its (rare) minerals might seek to place restrictions on exports

---

[4] GATT Activities in 1978, May 1979, The GATT: Geneva.

[5] The Tokyo Round of Multilateral Trade Negotiations, Report by the Director-General of the GATT, April 1979, The GATT: Geneva at pp. 98ff.

[6] GATT Doc. MTN/FR/W/20/Rev. 2 of 30 March 1979.

[7] See also GATT Doc. L/4885 of 23 November 1979 at pp. 21ff, which contains a detailed discussion of the various GATT provisions dealing with export restrictions.

[8] GATT Doc. CG.18/W/43 of 10 October 1980.

[9] GATT Doc. BISD 29S/9.

[10] GATT Doc. MTN.GNG/NG2/W/40 of 8 August 1989.

in order to facilitate price discrimination across different foreign buyers. Nevertheless because of MFN, it cannot do that and hence some of the incentive to impose restrictions (such as export licences) on the export side evaporates. Following the discussion mentioned above, nothing much happened and the Uruguay round did not include an agreement on export licences.

Export licences do on occasion occur. So the question arises how should export licences be treated in WTO law? In 1949, a complaint was brought and the claim was that export licences adopted by one contracting party were discriminatory. The dispute was submitted, as was the case at the time, to the CONTRACTING PARTIES, which decided that no discrimination resulted from the application of the export licence and consequently exonerated the imposing trading nation from any responsibility.[11] Much later, the Panel on *China—Raw Materials* dealt once again with the same issue. It held that export licences must be assessed in the context of Art. XI GATT: they do not necessarily violate this provision, unless they have restrictive effects of their own; for example, an authority that requests from (potential) exporters a document attesting the right to export is not violating Art. XI GATT (§§7.881, 7.917–18), but an authority that retains discretion to request a number of unidentified documents as a precondition for issuing a licence is acting inconsistently with this provision (§§7.957–8).[12]

2.4 Institutional Issues

WTO Members are required to notify the Committee on Import Licensing of their laws and regulations by virtue of Art. 1.4(a) and 8.2(b) ILA, and by virtue of Art. 5.1–4 ILA, of their new or modified licensing procedures. Cross-notifications are permissible under Art. 5.5 ILA.

The Committee on Import Licensing has adopted procedures for notification: a questionnaire must be completed by WTO Members every year, whereby the purpose and coverage of licensing, the applied procedures, the criteria for eligibility to apply for a licence, and its period of validity are, *inter alia*, reported.[13]

The record of notifications is quite good by any reasonable standard.[14] This might be explained by the fact that there are various overlapping disciplines regarding notifications which increase transaction costs; moreover, the agreement does not establish a one-stop shop that will be notified of all issues relating to

---

[11] GATT Doc. CP.3/SR.22.

[12] During the Doha round negotiations, Japan tabled a proposal entitled Protocol on Transparency in Export Licensing to the GATT 1994 (TN/MA/W/15/Add.4/Rev.7) and the EU a proposal to discipline export restrictions (TN/MA/W/101). At the time of writing, the Doha negotiations were in stalemate.

[13] WTO Doc. G/LIC/3 of 7 November 1995.

[14] 100 Members had by October 2011 notified their laws and procedures; see WTO Doc. G/L/968 of 26 October 2011.

import licences.[15] Finally, WTO Members might on occasion be lacking the incentive to notify. The Committee has since 2009 been focusing on Members' compliance with the transparency obligations in the Agreement. As noted in the 2011 report of the Committee (G/L/968), improvements have been seen at the level of compliance with the mandatory notification obligations, particularly under Arts. 1.4(a), 8.2(b), and 7.3 ILA.

Recently, the WTO Secretariat proposed a simplified formulary that could be used for notification purposes:[16] information regarding the publication of the import licensing scheme, a translation into one of the three WTO official languages (English, French, or Spanish) if necessary, as well as the domestic institution in charge is provided. The new format will be used on a voluntary basis by WTO Members.[17]

A soft conciliation procedure is established where Members bring forward their complaints.[18] If submitted complaints do not get resolved at this stage, then the complaining party can always submit its concern to a WTO Panel.

There is no special and differential section in this Agreement. The only provision which references some special treatment for developing country Members is Art. 3.5(j), which states that:

> Consideration shall also be given to ensuring a reasonable distribution of licences to new importers, taking into account the desirability of issuing licences for products in economic quantities. In this regard, special consideration should be given to those importers importing products originating in developing country Members and, in particular, the least developed country Members.

3. The Customs Valuation Agreement

3.1 The Legal Discipline and its Rationale

Customs valuation is discussed in the original GATT (Art. VII GATT), but this provision does not contain a comprehensive definition of the term 'customs valuation'. First, during the Tokyo round, an agreement on customs valuation (CV) was adopted which aimed to complement Art. VII GATT, introducing new disciplines to this effect. This agreement has since been superseded by the Uruguay round Agreement on Customs Valuation.[19] The CV Agreement aims at

---

[15] Unlike, in this respect, the TBT and SPS Agreements which contain similar provisions; see the relevant discussion in Chapter 10.

[16] WTO Doc. G/LIC/22 of 2 August 2011.

[17] See the Chinese notification along these lines; WTO Doc. G/LIC/23 of 21 October 2011. We discuss this document in more detail in Chapter 10.

[18] The WTO Docs. G/LIC/Q and G/LIC/M series are a precious source of information on issues relating to import licensing.

[19] Rosenow and O'Shea (2010) provide a complete account of this Agreement, its function and its history.

streamlining the conditions under which specific methods for customs valuation will be legitimately used, while, at the same time, taking an active step towards transparency: traders have the right to request and receive explanations (Art. 16 CV), whereas all customs laws etc. must be published (Art. 12 CV).

In *Colombia—Ports of Entry*, the Panel provided the following definition of customs valuation (§7.83):

> Essentially, customs valuation involves the process of determining the monetary worth or price of imported goods for the purpose of levying customs duties.

The CV Agreement does not contain obligations concerning valuation for purposes of determining export duties or quota administration based on the value of goods, nor does it lay down conditions for the valuation of goods for internal taxation or foreign exchange control: its sole preoccupation is valuation of imported goods.

3.2 The Coverage of the Legal Discipline

3.2.1 The Primacy of Transaction Value

The new CV Agreement, following the approach already adopted in Art. VII GATT, confirms that CV shall, with the exception of circumstances mentioned in the agreement, be based on the actual price paid or payable for the goods to be valued, which generally appears on the invoice. This price, adjusted for certain elements featured in Art. 8 CV, constitutes the 'transaction value'. The transaction value is the most important method of valuation referred to in the agreement.

Transaction value is understood as the value of imported goods upon which the buyer and the seller have agreed for the purposes of a particular transaction. The price should be the invoice price and, consequently, activities that the buyer might undertake on behalf of the seller which relate to the sold goods (such as advertising) will not be taken into account for customs valuation purposes.[20] By the same token, internal taxes etc. cannot be added to the invoice price.

Art. 8 CV leaves it to the discretion of WTO Members to privilege a FOB (free on board) or a CIF (cost, insurance, freight) price as the basis for valuing imported goods: in §2, it provides:

> In framing its legislation, each Member shall provide for the inclusion in or the exclusion from the customs value, in whole or in part, of the following:
>
> (a) the cost of transport of the imported goods to the port or place of importation;
>
> (b) loading, unloading and handling charges associated with the transport of the imported goods to the port or place of importation; and
>
> (c) the cost of insurance.

---

[20] Interpretative Note ad Art. 1 CV.

3.2.2 Deviating from the Transaction Value

The buyer and the seller might have on occasion a strong incentive to cheat: under-invoicing can lead to less imposition in terms of customs duties, whereas over-invoicing can lead to (illegal) exodus of capital. Customs authorities might not care that much about the latter,[21] but they certainly care about the former. Double invoicing, whereby the buyer would issue one invoice for customs purposes and one that should be used for payment purposes, has happened (and probably continues to do so) quite frequently. Customs authorities thus might have legitimate reasons to doubt the accuracy of the invoice price. The CV Agreement wants to impose some limits in their exercise of discretion when they reject the invoice price. It thus provides for five methods that can be used for the purposes of customs valuation:

(a) transaction value of identical goods (Art. 2 CV);
(b) transaction value of similar goods (Art. 3 CV);
(c) deductive method (Art. 5 CV);
(d) computed method (Art. 6 CV); and, finally,
(e) fall-back method (Art. 7 CV).

These methods are to be applied in the prescribed hierarchical order[22] in cases where there is no transaction value or where the transaction value is not acceptable because the price has been distorted as a result of certain conditions.

Customs authorities cannot use other than the above-mentioned methods: in *Colombia—Ports of Entry*, the Panel found that Colombia, by basing its customs valuation of imported goods on indicative prices, was in violation of Arts. 1, 3, 5. and 7 CV (§§7.152ff)

Adjustments are possible when specifying the transaction value: Art. 8 CV contains a list of items that can be lawfully adjusted depending on who incurred the mentioned costs. Customs authorities have the right to verify the truth and accuracy of information received (Art. 17 CV).

Moreover, the Uruguay round 'Decision Regarding Cases where Customs Administrations have Reasons to Doubt the Truth or Accuracy of the Declared Value' makes it clear that customs authorities are entitled to ask questions in order to verify whether the declared value corresponds to the amount actually paid and whether adjustments took place in accordance with Art. 8 CV.

In case the transaction value has been rejected, the authorities' hands are not totally free; the CV Agreement restricts the freedom of WTO Members to act unconstrained in two ways: first, as mentioned above, in case they decide to deviate from the transaction value, they are not free to choose any valuation

---

[21] Unless of course they have exchange restrictions in place: in that case, through over-invoicing, capital flows away from their domestic market.
[22] That is, (a) before (b) before (c) before (d) before (e), as we explain in more detail *infra*.

method, as the CV Agreement establishes five methods that they must have recourse to in sequential form; second, it imposes an obligation to follow a particular procedure when they have reasons to doubt presented documentation. The Panel on *Thailand—Cigarettes (Philippines)* entertained a claim to the effect that Thailand was violating its obligations under Arts. 1 and 2(a) CV by enacting a general rule rejecting the transaction value and requiring the application of the deductive value. It first established what was in its view the appropriate standard of review to entertain this claim (§7.105), upholding:

> the Appellate Body's reasoning that panels need not necessarily confine their review of a domestic authority's determination to an examination of that determination in terms of the factual and legal arguments put forward by the interested parties during the domestic investigation. The Appellate Body in *US—Countervailing Duty Investigation on DRAMS* also stated, 'this is not to say that a panel is prohibited from examining whether the agency has given a reasoned and adequate explanation for its determination, in particular, by considering other inferences that could reasonably be drawn from—and explanations that could reasonably be given to—the evidence on record. Indeed, a panel must undertake such an inquiry.'

The Panel went on to observe that the transaction value can be discarded if the buyer and seller are related (Art. 1.1(d) CV) and if the relationship has affected the price. So, there is no automaticity resulting from the relationship between buyer and seller that would lead to the rejection of the transaction value. It must be demonstrated that the relationship did not influence the price for the transaction value to be maintained. The duties of the customs authority and the importer in making this demonstration have been clarified in the Panel report on *Thailand—Cigarettes (Philippines)* (§§7.169–71):

> The particular nature of the examination to be conducted by the customs authorities can further be inferred from Case Study 10.1 on the application of Article 1.2 of the Customs Valuation Agreement by the WTO Technical Committee on Customs Valuation:
> 'Under Article 1.2 of the Agreement the responsibility for demonstrating that relationship [between buyer and seller] has not influenced price [sic] lies with the importer. While the Agreement requires Customs to provide reasonable opportunity to the importer to provide information that would indicate that prices are not influenced by the relationship, it does not require the Customs administration to conduct an exhaustive enquiry for the purpose of justifying the price difference. Thus, any decision in this regard must, to a significant degree, be based on the information provided by the importer.'
> The WTO Technical Committee's comment supports the understanding that while customs authorities are responsible for providing a 'reasonable opportunity' to the importer to provide information, once given this opportunity, importers are in principle liable for supplying the customs authorities with information that would indicate that the relationship did not influence the price.
> In sum, we consider that the customs authorities and importers have respective responsibilities under Article 1.2(a). The customs authorities must ensure that importers be given a reasonable opportunity to provide information that would

indicate that the relationship did not influence the price. Importers are responsible for providing information that would enable the customs authority to examine and assess the circumstances of sale so as to determine the acceptability of the transaction value. Provided with such information, the customs authorities must conduct an 'examination' of the circumstance of sale, which would require an active, critical review and consideration of the information before them.

The grounds for rejecting the transaction value must be communicated to the importer by virtue of Art. 1.2(a) CV.[23] The Panel on *Thailand—Cigarettes (Philippines)* explained that this obligation is distinct from the obligation to provide an explanation for how the customs authority had proceeded with customs valuation under Art. 16 CV; in its view, communicating the grounds would entail communicating (§7.218):

> the customs authorities' *reasons for considering*, in the light of information provided by the importer or otherwise, that the relationship influenced the price. (emphasis in the original)

By contrast, a customs authority would be required under Art. 16 CV to provide:

(a) The reason for rejecting transaction value: and
(b) The basis for the alternative valuation determination.

The Panel on *Thailand—Cigarettes (Philippines)* endorsed this standard (§7.237). WTO Members must provide affected parties with a forum to launch an appeal against this type as well as any other decision customs authorities adopt in the context of customs valuation (Art. 11 CV).

If the transaction value has been rejected, customs authorities must first make an attempt to locate prior transactions of 'identical' goods (Art. 2 CV).

If this has proven impossible, then they can legitimately use previous transactions of 'similar' (a wider category than 'identical') goods (Art. 3 CV). The five methods will be applied to a different class of goods depending on whether we are in an Art. 2 CV or an Art. 3 CV scenario.

The term 'identical' is defined in Art. 15 CV as referring to goods which:

> are the same in all respects, including physical characteristics, quality and reputation. Minor differences in appearance would not preclude goods otherwise conforming to the definition from being regarded as identical.

The same provision identifies 'similar' goods as:

> goods which, although not alike in all respects, have like characteristics and like component materials which enable them to perform the same functions and to be commercially interchangeable. The quality of the goods, their reputation and the existence of a trademark are among the factors to be considered in determining whether goods are similar.

---

[23] In case they do reject the presented value, they should provide parties with a right to appeal the decision to reject the presented value (Art. 11 CV).

If none of the above is feasible, customs authorities can legitimately have recourse to the deductive value loosely defined as the price at which the importer (and not the seller) sells the imported good to an unrelated buyer (arm's length transaction). Customs authorities can deduct from this price a percentage reflecting the profit of the importer as well as expenses relating to the sale of the good to the buyer.

If recourse to the deductive value is not feasible, then customs authorities must rely on the computed value. This reflects a calculation by the customs authorities which must ascertain the production cost of the seller to which they can add general expenses, profit, and transport costs to the port of entry. One can right away understand that, absent cooperation with the foreign producer (seller), recourse to the computed value will be difficult, if not infeasible altogether.[24]

Finally, and assuming all prior methods cannot be used, customs authorities can use the fall-back method. This method would allow customs authorities to devise their own procedure as long, however, as it is reasonable and consistent with the principles of Art. VII GATT and the CV Agreement. Rosenow and O'Shea (2010, pp. 122ff) mention that this method is used when importations concern repaired (abroad) items, damaged goods etc. In this context, customs authorities might, for example, use one of the methods mentioned above in adjusted form: for example, they could look at the transaction value of similar goods by enlarging the ambit of this concept and review the price of goods with lower (than usual) substitutability. The standard of review that a WTO Panel would employ when facing a challenge against the fall-back method would, by construction, be more deferential (than when facing a challenge against the use of one of the five previous methods); a 'reasonableness' standard seems suitable here. This does not mean, however, that anything goes: in its report on *Thailand—Cigarettes (Philippines)*, the Panel concluded that the Thai Customs' failure to properly consult the importer on the information necessary for the requested deductions rendered its decision not to deduct sales allowances, provincial taxes, and transportation costs in the determination of the customs value of the entries at issue inconsistent with Article 7.1 CV (§7.332).

3.2.3 Methods that Cannot be Used

Art. 7 CV contains a list of methods that cannot be used as a basis for deciding on the customs value under any circumstances. The best known in practice was minimum customs value, whereby the customs value would not fall below a certain threshold under any circumstances. Developing countries, nevertheless, can have recourse to them, if they have made a reservation to this effect and have shown good cause: the Decision on Texts Relating to Minimum Values and

---

[24] The Interpretative Note to the CV Agreement requests from customs authorities that they use information prepared in a manner consistent with the Generally Accepted Accounting Principles (GAAP.) *The GAAP* has been defined in paragraph 1 of the Note.

Imports by Sole Agents, Sole Distributors and Sole Concessionaires, adopted during the Uruguay round, says as much.[25]

Customs authorities must, by virtue of Art. 7 CV, further refrain from using:

(a) Arbitrary or fictitious values: this term appears in Art. VII.2(g) GATT as the opposite to actual value;

(b) Price of goods in other export markets: some markets might affect terms of trade of a particular commodity and exporters will take this into account when setting their prices, whereas others do not. Opening up for this possibility would thus allow customs authority to compare incomparable situations;

(c) Price of goods in the exporting market: the competitive conditions in the two markets might not be the same,

(d) Cost of production calculated without recourse to the computed value: opening up for this possibility would allow customs authorities to end up with a totally arbitrary or fictitious value (which is anyway prohibited);

(e) Allowing the use of the highest of two alternative values: the rationale for this prohibition has to do with the relative uncertainty for traders who would not *ex ante* know which method would be applied to their exports;

(f) Selling price of goods in the importing market: Rosenow and O'Shea (2010, p. 126) mention that the rationale for this prohibition has to do with the decision to eliminate a practice, the so-called American Selling Price (ASP), which functioned almost like a variable import levy that would equate the world to the domestic price.

3.2.4 Confidentiality

It is often the case that confidential information has to be disclosed to customs authorities for customs valuation purposes. Protection of similar disclosures is guaranteed by Art. 10 CV. The rationale for this provision is that, otherwise, competitors of the disclosing company could gain an advantage through knowledge about pricing, volumes of trade, etc. In *Thailand—Cigarettes (Philippines)*, the Panel held that disclosure by the customs authorities of information regarding the pricing of a company and its overall volume of imports that had been submitted and classified as confidential constitutes a violation of this provision (§§7.405ff).

3.2.5 Special and Differential Treatment

The CV Agreement also provides for special and differential treatment for developing Members in its Art. 20 and Annex III. Art. 20 CV, for example, allows a developing country Member to delay the application of the CV Agreement for a period of five years from the date of entry of the WTO Agreement for such a Member. This right could not be availed of by those WTO Members who had

---

[25] See also Annex III to the CV Agreement at §2.

been signatories to the Tokyo round CV Code. Several WTO Members, including Bahrain, Bolivia, Jamaica, Kuwait, Senegal, Tunisia, and Sri Lanka, have had recourse to this provision. Paragraph 2 of Annex III also permits developing Members to retain minimum values (prohibited by Art 7.2(f) CV) on a limited and transitional basis under terms and conditions to be agreed to by WTO Members. WTO Members granted this reservation include Colombia, Gabon, Honduras, Morocco, and Nicaragua (see WTO Doc. G/VAL/2 and its revisions).[26] Clearly, there was recognition that developing country Members of the WTO might encounter difficulties in applying the CV Agreement without a transition phase which gave room for technical assistance: technical assistance is envisaged in paragraph 3 of Art. 20 CV. In light of the increased number of developing countries required to implement the CV Agreement, the Committee on Customs Valuation agreed that it was necessary to reinvigorate technical assistance. In July 2001, the Committee on Customs Valuation agreed to a work programme to give shape to this reinvigoration.[27]

3.2.6 Cooperation across WTO Members

The CV Agreement incites WTO Members to cooperate when appropriate: when, for example, recourse to the computed value is being made, customs authorities could be in need of information they could obtain only through cooperation and/ or the authorities in its country of origin if, for example, they suspect fraud. The WCO has agreed on a template 'Model Bilateral Agreement on Mutual Administrative Assistance in Customs Matters', the use of which it encourages for this purpose. The WTO membership has further adopted a Decision during the Doha Ministerial Conference which allows customs authorities to inquire about the accuracy of the importer's declaration in case of reasonable doubt; the inquired authority can legitimately refuse to respond if the request is not consistent with its domestic public order.[28]

In the WTO, a Committee on Customs Valuation is established where all WTO Members participate and which is entrusted with the administration of the CV Agreement (Art. 18 CV). The same provision gave birth to the Technical

---

[26] India, which was a signatory to the Tokyo round Customs Valuation Code, views itself as still being covered by this reservation. This view is not shared by others. This situation explains why the Annual Review documents from 1998 to 2009 prepared by the Secretariat for the purpose of assisting the Committee carry out the review under Art. 23 CV remain un-adopted; they do not list India as being covered by this reservation.

[27] WTO Docs. G/VAL/M/21 and G/VAL/W/82/Rev.1.

[28] Decision of 14 November 2001, WTO Doc. WT/MIN(01)/17 of 20 November 2001 at § 8.3. This matter has been discussed in the Committee since early 2000. However, to date discussions have not concluded, partly because the same subject was introduced in the Trade Facilitation negotiation which in the view of some Members was the more appropriate forum for addressing this issue. In this connection, see also WTO Doc. G/VAL/49 which provides a report of the Committee to the Trade Negotiations Committee on the outstanding implementation issues.

Committee, also composed of representatives of all WTO Members (usually customs experts) and which meets twice a year in Brussels in the headquarters of the WCO. The Technical Committee reports to the Committee on Customs Valuation and prepares technical documents aimed at helping WTO Members when dealing with customs valuation issues.[29] Its output comes under different denominations (explanatory notes, advisory opinions) and is included in a publication issued by the WCO, the WCO Compendium.[30]

4. The Agreement on Pre-shipment Inspection (PSI)

4.1 The Legal Discipline and its Rationale

This is one of the agreements introduced with the advent of the WTO as a result of the successful conclusion of the Uruguay round. Through pre-shipment inspection, traders aim at ensuring that the value of exported goods conforms to the specifications reflected in a sales contract, as well as other relevant information such as the quality and quantity of goods shipped. Therefore, while the CV Agreement deals with the value of goods at the point of importation, pre-shipment inspection deals with similar issues at the point of exportation.[31] In fact, footnote 4 of the PSI Agreement reads as follows:

> The obligations of user Members with respect to the services of pre-shipment inspection entities in connection with customs valuation shall be the obligations which they have accepted in GATT 1994 and other Multilateral Trade Agreements included in Annex 1A of the WTO Agreement.

So, in a way, the PSI Agreement allows WTO Members to outsource their customs operations without however incurring any financial cost since customs duties will be paid when cleared in the import state. It is traders that, in order to reduce uncertainty regarding customs valuation, will be prepared to incur the additional cost of pre-shipment inspection by pre-shipment entities.

---

[29] See, for example, the response (VAL/W/54) of the Technical Committee to the terms of reference sent by the Committee on Customs Valuation in connection with its work on paragraph 8.3 of the Ministerial Declaration (WT/MIN(01)/17).

[30] Its tasks are laid out in detail in Annex II of the CV Agreement.

[31] The two agreements have thus a complementary function. Low (1995) explains the rationale behind its enactment as well its basic institutions. In essence, through this agreement, exporters obtain the necessary certainty regarding the overall duty that will be imposed at the destination market, which they would not necessarily have if inspection took place in the importing market following the CV procedures. In this latter case, customs officers might put into question the invoice price. They will not, or rarely do so, if the invoice price has been certified by a pre-shipment inspection entity.

4.2 The Coverage of the Legal Discipline

4.2.1 Pre-shipment Entity

Although inspections are government-contracted, they are performed by private companies: the government of an importing WTO Member will, thus, contract a private company and ask it to perform an evaluation. The private company is the pre-shipment inspection entity.[32] The inspecting companies will perform essentially two functions:

(a) Ensure conformity of goods with the terms of the sales contract; and
(b) Verify the invoice price.

Government contracts with pre-shipment inspection companies have been either foreign exchange contracts (FOREX), where the basic objective of the government is to prevent the exodus of capital through over-invoicing, and/or customs contracts, where the main aim is to ensure that there is no loss in customs revenue as a result of under-valuation or mis-classification of the good. A pre-shipment inspection company might also provide a number of subsidiary services which include, *inter alia*, the verification of origin of the product, maintenance of data for statistical purposes, technical assistance, and training. Expertise by companies is not binding on customs authorities. They might decide to neglect it and perform their own evaluation.

There are of course other means that one can use in order to achieve these objectives. In an influential study, Low (1995) examines many of the alternative proposals, namely, the so-called 'Norwegian proposal', 'destination inspections', the application of minimum import prices, and the use of price databases. The Norwegian proposal, which requires cooperation across national jurisdictions in an effort to replicate the Agreement, is for good reasons discarded, since it is not incentive-compatible as far as the exporting trading nation is concerned. Destination inspection largely reproduces the existing customs valuation regime and thus suffers from the same weaknesses. Minimum import prices are refuted in light of the many other distortions they generate. Valuation data sets could be useful as a transparency-mechanism, but not as a substitute for pre-shipment inspection. Low concludes that a clear role exists for pre-shipment, especially in countries with weak administration.

4.2.2 The Independent Entity

Disputes might arise between the pre-shipment entities and exporters concerning the evaluation by the former. Note that such disputes are between private parties and not between state entities. In such cases, the complaining party can refer the dispute to the so-called Independent Entity (Art. 4 PSI).[33] The Independent Entity is a three-person body, including a member nominated by the pre-shipment

---

[32] SGS (Société Générale de Surveillance) is the company most frequently used.
[33] The Independent Entity was established by a decision of the WTO General Council adopted on 13 December 1995; see WTO Doc. WT/L/125 Rev. 1 of 9 February 1996.

Table 6.1 PSI Programmes for Customs Purposes

PSI Programmes for Customs Purposes (Revenue Protection)

Country	Mandated Member(s) of IFIAPSI Committee	Basis of Member Choice
Angola	BIVAC, Cotecna, SGS	Importer
Bangladesh	BIVAC, Intertek, SGS, OMIC	Geographical
Central African Rep.	BIVAC	—
Chad	BIVAC	—
Dem. Rep. of Congo	BIVAC	—
Iran[1]	BIVAC, Cotecna, OMIC, SGS	Importer
Mauritania	SGS	—
Uzbekistan[2]	BIVAC, CUI, Intertek, OMIC, SGS	Importer/Exporter

Customs Support Services (including Destination inspection and/or Selective PSI)

Country	Mandated Member(s) of IFIAPSI Committee	Basis of Member Choice
Burkina Faso[1][2]	Cotecna	—
Burundi[1]	SGS	—
Cameroon[1][2]	SGS	—
Chad [1]	Cotecna	—
Congo[1][2]	Cotecna	—
Côte d'Ivoire[1] [2]	BIVAC	—
Equatorial Guinea	Cotecna	—
Ghana[2]	BIVAC, Cotecna	Air & land/sea-freight
Guinea (Conakry) [1][2]	BIVAC	
Haiti[1]	SGS	—
Liberia[1][2]	BIVAC	
Mali[1][2]	BIVAC	
Mozambique[1] [2]	Intertek	—
Niger[1]	Cotecna	
Nigeria[2]	Cotecna, SGS	Port of Arrival
Senegal[1][2]	Cotecna	—
Togo[2]	Cotecna	—

[1] Physical inspection (quantity/quality only) for foreign exchange purposes.
[2] Including reporting for foreign exchange purposes. No programmes now include intervention on invoiced price.
[1] 'Selective': only certain shipments subject to physical PSI based on risk assessment.
[2] Cargo destination inspection which may include price verification and classification on a pre-shipment or post-shipment basis.
Source: Taken from WTO Doc. G/VAL/W/63/Rev. 14, dated 8 November 2011, which lists countries using PSI regimes. It reproduces information compiled by the IFIA (International Federation of Inspection Agencies) Preshipment Inspection Committee. According to the IFIA, the recent trend for PSI programmes shows a reduction in traditional programmes (e.g. PSI programmes for customs purposes), with considerable growth in more modern programmes (e.g. Customs support services) that are less intrusive for exporters.

entities, a member nominated by the exporters' organization, and an independent trade expert.[34] Its decisions, as per Art. 4(h) PSI, are binding on their addressees and cannot be appealed.[35]

---

[34] One expert is nominated from the list provided by the International Federation of Inspection Agencies (IFIA) (WTO Doc. G/PSI/IE/1/Rev. 1), one from the list provided by the International Chamber of Commerce (ICC), and one by the administrator of the Independent Entity, that is, the WTO Secretariat.

[35] At the time of writing, two such decisions had been issued, WTO Docs. G/PSI/IE/R/1 and 2.

One could speculate as to why in 15 years of existence the Independent Entity was only resorted to twice. One reason could be the cost of using the Independent Entity; the fact that the Independent Entity is unfamiliar territory; or that the existing dispute mechanisms work. A view expressed by the International Chamber of Commerce, as reflected in the 1999 Working Party on Pre-shipment Inspection report, noted that the 'non-use of the Independent Entity might be because the provisions of the Agreement have removed some of the principal sources of disputes between inspection agencies and exporters, or because of exporters' concern that identifying themselves to the PSI companies could result in aggravating rather than alleviating the situation, or because of the costs associated with its use'. The view of the International Federation of Inspection Agencies, also contained in the same report, was that 'in many cases problems had been settled between the PSI companies and the exporters concerned'.[36]

4.2.3 Institutional Issues

Unlike other multilateral agreements in Annex 1A of the WTO Agreement, the PSI Agreement does not establish a Committee to monitor the implementation of the Agreement. Monitoring of the Agreement takes place in the Committee on Customs Valuation where pre-shipment inspection is a standing agenda item. This was one of the recommendations by the Working Party on Pre-shipment Inspection established by the General Council in November 1996 for the purposes of conducting the review provided for in Art. 6 PSI, which states that:

> At the end of the second year from the entry into force of the WTO Agreement and every three years thereafter, the Ministerial Conference shall review the provisions, implementation and operation of the Agreement...

The Working Party submitted a first report in December 1997 (WTO Doc. G/L/214), but its life was extended by a year on two occasions. At the end of each of those extensions, a report was submitted to the General Council (WTO Docs. G/L/273, in 1998; G/L/300, in 1999). In the last report, a recommendation that future monitoring of the Agreement should be undertaken initially by the Customs Valuation Committee and that PSI should be a standing agenda item was adopted by the General Council. Another brief review of the PSI Agreement took place in 2006 in the Committee on Customs Valuation and the report of the review was issued in WTO Doc. G/L/809.

The reason for choosing the Committee on Customs Valuation to monitor the implementation of the PSI Agreement would seem to be logical given the linkages between customs valuation and pre-shipment inspection. However, one wonders why participants in the Uruguay round negotiating the PSI Agreement did not think that a Committee on PSI was warranted. One reason might be that PSI

---

[36] WTO Doc. G/L/300 at §9.

activities were considered to be of a transitional nature. The third preambular paragraph of the PSI Agreement alludes to the transitional nature of pre-shipment activities by recognizing the need for developing countries to have recourse to pre-shipment inspection:

> for as long and in so far as it is necessary to verify the quality, quantity or price of imported goods.

The Working Party report contained in G/L/300 also states that:

> All Members have accepted that recourse to PSI is a transitional measure to be used only until their national customs authorities are in the position to carry out these tasks on their own.

Concerning transparency, Members, be they Exporter Members or User Members[37] are obliged to ensure transparency and non-discriminatory application of all their laws relating to pre-shipment inspection (Arts. 2 and 3 PSI). They are further obliged to submit to the WTO Secretariat copies of the laws and regulations by which they have implemented the PSI Agreement, any other laws and regulations relating to pre-shipment inspection, as well as changes in the laws and regulations relating to pre-shipment inspection which must be notified immediately after their publication (Art. 5 PSI).[38]

The PSI Agreement does not contain provisions on special and differential treatment. A paragraph on technical assistance which falls under Art. 3 PSI, entitled 'Obligations of Exporter Members', notes that:

> Exporter Members shall offer to provide User Members, if requested, technical assistance directed toward the achievement of the objectives of this Agreement on mutually agreed terms.

A footnote to this paragraph further specifies that technical assistance could be bilateral, plurilateral, or multilateral. So technical assistance can be provided by even developing country Members to other developing country Members, unlike the CV Agreement which, as noted earlier, in its Art. 20.3 provides that developed country Members are to furnish technical assistance to developing country Members that so request.

Recently, criticism on the activities of PSI companies has been mounting, the culmination being the introduction of a paragraph in the current text of trade facilitation which will put a halt to compulsory pre- and post-shipment inspection.[39] At this stage, it is difficult to take a definitive stance on whether criticism is

---

[37] The obligations of User Members are stipulated in 22 paragraphs under Art. 2 PSI. They are expected to ensure that PSI activities abide by obligations covering matters such as the site of inspection, protection of confidential business information, delays and appeals procedures. Obligations of Exporter Members are covered in three paragraphs under Art. 3 PSI.

[38] For example, see WTO Doc. G/PSI/N/1 Add. 15 of 27 June 2011.

[39] See the relevant discussion *infra* in this chapter.

targeted more towards the agencies or the function as such. At the moment of writing and because the agreement on trade facilitation has not seen the light of the day, pre-shipment activities continue as before.

5. Trade Facilitation

5.1 Historical Background

The scope of trade facilitation is hard to define in the abstract, and this is a point to which we will come back *infra*. The WTO webpage defines it as follows:

> Once formal trade barriers come down, other issues become more important. For example, companies need to be able to acquire information on other countries' importing and exporting regulations and how customs procedures are handled. Cutting red-tape at the point where goods enter a country and providing easier access to this kind of information are two ways of 'facilitating' trade.

It all started in 1996. The Singapore Ministerial Declaration reflected this in §22, entitled 'Trade Facilitation', where the following was noted:[40]

> In the organization of the work referred to in paragraphs 20 and 21, careful attention will be given to minimizing the burdens on delegations, especially those with more limited resources, and to coordinating meetings with those of relevant UNCTAD bodies. The technical cooperation programme of the Secretariat will be available to developing and, in particular, least-developed country Members to facilitate their participation in this work.

Trade facilitation was thus originally conceived as an integral part of measures in favour of developing countries. The WTO webpage nowadays quotes a phrase that defines the scope of trade facilitation as 'simplification of trade procedures'. This phrase, nevertheless, is a direct quotation from §21 of the Singapore Ministerial Declaration entitled 'government procurement'. The confusion about the scope of the endeavour notwithstanding, the Singapore Ministerial Declaration provided the necessary impetus in order to start negotiating this issue. The WTO is not the first forum that dealt with this subject-matter. Many institutions have approached this issue in the past, IMF, UNCTAD, and the WCO being among those that produced work that was usefully utilized in the WTO negotiation.[41]

5.2 Defining Trade Facilitation

The negotiation on trade facilitation has been taking place in the context of the Doha round. Defining the scope of the negotiation represented a challenging feature of the endeavour in and of itself: at one end of the continuum, one could

---

[40] WTO Doc. WT/MIN(96)DEC of 18 December 1996.
[41] WTO Doc. G/C/W/80 Rev. 1 of 22 September 2000.

conceive the term to cover a very broad discussion of the (customs and regulatory) environment within which transactions take place, some sort of trade facilitation efforts 'inside the border'; at the other end of the continuum, a narrow definition would call for addressing issues related directly to moving goods through ports. One could even go as far as Staples (1998) and argue that Vasco da Gama by circumventing the Cape of Good Hope facilitated trade, or agree with Sengupta (2007) that GATT and now the WTO quintessentially facilitate trade. Similar wide definitions, their intellectual merit notwithstanding, risk rendering the ensuing negotiation on instruments to facilitate trade non-operational.

Over the years, the subject-matter of the negotiation has evolved: originally, it was conceived as an attempt to elaborate disciplines to smooth procedures behind the border, that is, ease customs procedures, provide more transparency regarding all sorts of regulations affecting imports etc.[42] The agreement, as it now stands,[43] is essentially a clarification of Arts. V, VIII, and XX GATT and an elaboration of some additional but related provisions. The focus on developing countries has not dwindled over the years: capacity building, technical assistance, and more generally special and differential treatment figure prominently on the agenda.[44]

National experience has been discussed extensively and it is largely based on this type of input that negotiators have managed to concretize the negotiation content, while becoming better aware of the gains from cooperation in this field.

5.3 Gains from Cooperation

The measurement of gains from cooperation in the field of trade facilitation depends on the assumptions made. There are many papers estimating similar gains and we will be referring to some of them in what immediately follows. Similar work certainly influenced from one point onwards the WTO negotiation, since there was awareness of what could be achieved through cooperation. It is doubtful however that it provided the original impetus for the negotiation which was initially conceived as a means to provide technical capacity to developing countries only.

Studies have focused on the cost side of existing regimes and the benefits in case some of the deadweight losses are dismantled. Sengupta (2007), for example, employs the WBES (World Business Economic Survey) and interviews managerial staff in 10,000 enterprises spread over 80 countries to conclude that a considerable amount of their time is spent on non-productive activities such as dealing with bureaucracy.[45] Hummels (2001) links trade facilitation measures to tariffs to find that each day saved in shipping time (thanks to faster customs clearance) is worth a

---

[42] Sengupta (2007) at pp. 126ff.
[43] WTO Doc. TN/TF/W/165/Rev. 10 of 25 July 2011.
[44] WTO Docs. TN/TF/1 of 16 November 2004; TN/TF/2 of 15 July 2005.
[45] Earlier empirical literature is detailed in Maskus et al. (2001).

0.5 percentage point reduction of *ad valorem* tariffs. Wilson et al. (2003) construct four measures of trade facilitation (port efficiency, customs environment, regulatory environment, e-business usage), using country-specific survey and hard data. They estimate independent effects for each of the four measures and find that trade flows are most closely associated with port efficiency. In a companion paper, Wilson et al. (2005) keep the four measures of trade facilitation and investigate their relationship to trade for a sample of 75 countries. They find that improvement in all forms of trade facilitation would yield an increase in global trade of $377 billion, which they decompose to shed some light on the GATT provisions under discussion in the WTO negotiation on trade facilitation (Arts. V, VIII, and XX GATT).[46] Finally, Dennis and Shepherd (2011) show that improved trade facilitation (essentially reforms to customs procedures) represents a set of policy options that would appear to have significant scope to promote export diversification.

In short, there is by now persuasive empirical evidence regarding the gains from improved trade facilitation which is a function of the term 'trade facilitation'.

5.4 The 'Agreement' as it Now Stands

As stated briefly above, the agreement as it now stands contains provisions that reinforce the existing disciplines on transit (Art. V GATT), customs fees (Art. VIII GATT), and transparency (Art. X GATT).

The transparency obligation is specified and reinforced: for example, Art. 1[47] contains a list of items such as customs fees, procedures of classification of goods etc. that must be published, while Art. 3 obliges WTO Members to provide enquiry points that will inform traders about the content of items coming under the purview of Art. 1. Art. 2 requires an interval between publication and entry into force of similar measures which could allow traders to express their opinions on the upcoming measures.

With respect to customs fees, the agreement crystalizes case law into law: Art. 6 makes it clear that WTO Members cannot impose *ad valorem* duties for services rendered during customs clearance procedures, a point made by the GATT Panel on *US—Customs User Fee*, as we saw in Chapter 2. In the same context, consular transactions (including related fees) are prohibited (Art. 8), that is, WTO Members cannot impose a procedure whereby a consular visa is obtained from the consul of the importing state prior to the transaction.

With respect to transit, a necessity requirement is introduced, whereby charges, regulations, etc. relating to transit cannot be more restrictive than necessary to fulfil a legitimate objective (Art. 11).

---

[46] In similar vein, Fink et al. (2002a and 2002b) have shown the impact of anti-competitive practices on port and transport services, and telecommunications services.
[47] WTO Doc.TN/TF/W/165/Rev. 10 of 25 July 2011.

And then there are some innovations. Pre-arrival processing is introduced in Art. 7: traders are invited to submit information regarding the upcoming transaction prior to its realization in an effort to expedite the release of goods. Members are encouraged[48] to use international standards regarding formalities and documentation requirements. Three of them are mentioned in Art. 10.2: the UN Layout Key (UNLK), which provides a simplification and standardization of documents used in export trade;[49] the UN Trade Data Elements Directory, which has a very comparable function to the UNLK; and, finally, the WCO Data Model which, besides customs-related documentation, contains information on regulatory agencies, health, and agricultural policies etc. Adoption of international standards in this context will undoubtedly reduce current transaction costs, since traders are required to compile different documentation depending on the port of exportation. WTO Members will also be required to establish a single window, that is, a single entry point where documentation relevant to the importation will be submitted (Art. 10.4). This is yet another attempt to reduce transaction costs.

At the moment of writing it is far from clear how much of this will see the light of the day.

6. From Customs Valuation to Trade Facilitation

Private behaviour is not a concern for the multilateral trading system. It is simply irrelevant whether traders might, on occasion, have the incentive to cheat through under-invoicing etc. Similar behaviour does affect trade patterns of course, but there are other statutes, typically domestic law statutes, that will take care of this. WTO cares about constraining state behaviour when facing similar issues. The rationale behind regulating the behaviour of customs authorities rests on the premise that we need to ensure that there will be no additional protection to whatever level of protection has been negotiated among trading partners and has been expressed in OCDs and ODCs. This is what drove the CV and the ILA Agreements, the two pillars of this system, which have subsequently been complemented by the PSI Agreement and eventually will be further strengthened through the adoption of the Agreement on Trade Facilitation.

The agreements discussed above provide clarity as to what is expected from customs authorities, and there are few disputes, which is always a good sign when extensive use of the covered instruments is being made. Inevitably, under the circumstances, attention shifted to other 'neighbouring' areas: practice and academic research have pointed to deadweight losses stemming from lack of expertise

---

[48] The current text contains in brackets both the terms 'are encouraged' and 'shall'. At the moment of writing, no final decision has been taken on this score.

[49] UN Layout Key, Guidelines for Application, United Nations: Geneva and New York, 2002.

regarding customs clearance, lack of information regarding customs procedures, and many other related areas. This is where first the PSI Agreement and now the ongoing negotiation on Trade Facilitation kick in. Note, though, that Art. 10.5 of the draft Facilitation Agreement (WTO Doc. TN/TF/W/165/Rev.11) provides for the elimination of mandatory pre-shipment and post-shipment inspections, all in bracketed language which indicates lack of definitive agreement. This would suggest, prima facie at least, that PSI companies' functions in the customs areas are not viewed as a success. Irrespective of the final outcome in the negotiations on trade facilitation, it is highly likely that the activities of PSI companies will be discussed again at the WTO.

Trade facilitation started, as described above, on a rather narrow basis focusing on three GATT provisions. Its aim is to streamline customs procedures through various instruments, such as standardizing the provision of information with respect to both the content as well as the 'single window' provisions, and to provide much-needed transparency regarding on and behind the border procedures. Research points to substantial gains from adopting similar mechanisms, which vary in function according to the content of trade facilitation. Wisely probably, in light of the existing problems of managing the Doha round agenda, negotiators chose to start with a rather narrow definition of the term 'trade facilitation', which in turn constrained the ambit of the agenda. It is too soon to make any predictions, but probably this is only the beginning of the negotiation. As noted above, gains from facilitating trade are all the more substantial as the ambit of the term widens. This is probably the area where issues such as export licensing will eventually be negotiated.

7

ANTIDUMPING

1. Contingent Protection

The term 'contingent protection' refers to instruments which, assuming a contingency has occurred, will allow WTO Members to introduce protection (in the form of either tariffs or quotas, or a combination thereof) in favour of their domestic producers beyond the existing consolidated tariff protection. They do not constitute a renegotiation of duties since no negotiation at all takes place; the WTO Members that want to avail themselves of this possibility will have to comply with the various obligations reflected in the law.

There are three contingent protection instruments:

(a) Antidumping (AD) duties;
(b) Countervailing duties (CVDs);
(c) Safeguards which can take the form of duties, quotas, or even tariff quotas.

They refer to different situations: AD duties can be imposed when dumping, a private activity[1] (when export price is lower than price charged for the like good in the domestic market), occurs and it causes injury to the domestic industry producing the like product; CVDs, in case subsidization—government behaviour—has taken place, and safeguards only when imports have, loosely speaking, increased in unforeseen, disproportionate amounts. Yet in the real world, they are often used interchangeably, the discretion that the statutes leave to the investigating authorities (IAs) being one major reason why. Worse, there are reasons to believe that what Bhagwati, when referring to AD duties taking the place of tariffs, called the 'law of constant protection' is indeed the case. Using data put together by Laird and Yeats (1990), Mansfield and Busch (1995) reach the conclusion that AD duties and tariffs are substitutes; it would of course be worse from a trade-liberalization perspective, if they were complements and not substitutes. And yet, there are papers like Ray (1981) that point in this direction. In short, the contingencies (especially dumping) seem to occur a bit too often and there is now widespread use of these instruments (see Tables 7.1 and 7.2).

There are dozens of papers explaining how political economy explains adoption of similar measures, and we will be referring to many of them in what follows. What is often overlooked in this literature is the agency design of IAs: there is nothing like say a World Antidumping Authority composed of international officials to impose AD duties on behalf of requesting WTO Members. Instead, IAs are national, a part of the political economy constraints that lead to the imposition of duties. Sure there are obligations of independence and evenhandedness imposed by the WTO agreements. And a reasonable reading of the successive AD agreements over the years leaves us with the impression that negotiation amounts to a continuous 'tightening' of the screws. These contracts, nevertheless, are incomplete in so many respects, leaving decisive discretion to the IAs implementing them. In turn, IAs are part and parcel of a national institutional dialogue, with everything that goes with it. This is something we should not forget when we start to study the various contingent protection instruments.

---

[1] State (e.g. Chinese) enterprises are also targets nowadays.

Table 7.1 Initiations of Antidumping investigations, 1 January 1995–30 June 2010

Reporting member	1995	1996	1997	1998	1999	2000	2001	2002	2003	2004	2005	2006	2007	2008	2009	2010	Total
Argentina	27	22	14	8	23	43	28	14	1	12	12	11	8	19	28	7	277
Australia	5	17	44	13	24	15	23	16	8	9	7	10	2	6	9	4	212
Brazil	5	18	11	18	16	11	17	8	4	8	6	12	13	23	9	5	184
Bulgaria								1									1
Canada	11	5	14	8	18	21	25	5	15	11	1	7	1	3	6	1	152
Chile	4	3		2		5						1	1	1	1	1	19
China					2	11	14	30	22	27	24	10	4	14	17	4	182
Colombia	4	1	1	6	2	3	6			2	2	9	1	6	5	2	50
Costa Rica		4		2							1	1			2		10
Czech Republic				2	1												3
Ecuador				1													1
Egypt			7	14	7	3	7	3	1		12	9	2		2		67
European Union	33	25	41	22	65	32	28	20	7	30	25	35	9	19	15	8	414
Guatemala		1															1
India	6	21	13	28	64	41	79	81	46	21	28	35	47	55	31	17	613
Indonesia		11	5	8	8	3	4	4	12	5		5	1	7	7	3	83
Israel	5	6	3	7		1	4			1	4			1	6	5	43
Jamaica						1	1	1	1						1	1	6
Japan							2						4				6
Jordan												1					1
Korea, Republic of	4	13	15	3	6	2	4	9	18	3	4	7	15	5		3	111
Latvia							1	6									7
Lithuania					1	6											7

																	Total
Malaysia	3	2	8	1	2	6	1	5	6	3	4				2		43
Mexico	4	4	6	12	11	6	6	10	14	6	6	6	6			1	98
New Zealand	10	4	5	1	4	9	1	2	5	5	6	1					53
Nicaragua				2													2
Pakistan								1	3	3	13	4		3	26		53
Panama			2												4		6
Paraguay					1					1							2
Peru	2	8	2	3	8	1	8	13	4	7	4	3	2		4		69
Philippines	1	1	2	3	6	2		1	1						1		18
Poland			1		7			3	1								12
Slovenia					1												1
South Africa	16	34	23	41	16	21	6	4	8	6	23	3	5	3	3		212
Taipei, Chinese			1	6		4	3		2			5			1	1	23
Thailand		1	3		1		3	21	3	3		3	2		1	2	43
Trinidad and Tobago		1		4	3		1		2					1			12
Turkey			4	1	8	7	15	18	11	25	12	8	6	23	6	1	145
Ukraine							2	3	2	6	2	1	5	7	2	1	31
United States	14	22	15	36	47	47	77	35	37	26	12	8	28	16	20	2	442
Uruguay					1	1	4										6
Venezuela, Bolivarian Republic of	3	2	6	10	7	1	1	1									31
Total	157	226	246	266	358	298	371	315	234	220	202	203	165	213	209	69	3752

Source: <http://www.wto.org>.

Table 7.2 Antidumping measures, 1 January 1995–30 June 2010[1]

Reporting member	1995	1996	1997	1998	1999	2000	2001	2002	2003	2004	2005	2006	2007	2008	2009	2010	Total
Argentina	13	20	11	12	9	15	16	22	20	1	8	5	10	6	15	7	190
Australia	1	1	1	20	6	5	10	9	10	4	3	4	1	3	2	1	81
Brazil	2	6	2	14	5	9	13	5	2	5	3		9	11	16	3	105
Canada	7		7	10	10	14	19		5	8	4		3	3	2	2	94
Chile	2		2	2									1		1		8
China				3	2	5		5	33	14	16	24	12	4	12	7	137
Colombia	1	1	1		6	2				1	1	1	7		3		24
Costa Rica									1				2				3
Czech Republic						1											1
Egypt				5	14	1	2	7	4	1		12	2	3		1	52
European Union	15	23	23	28	18	41	13	25	2	10	21	12	12	15	9	2	269
Guatemala			1														1
India	7	2	8	22	23	55	38	64	52	29	17	16	25	31	30	17	436
Indonesia			4	2	7		1		1	8	4	2		5	1		35
Israel	1			6	4		1	2		1		3	1			2	21
Jamaica								2									4
Japan	1							2						4			7
Korea, Republic of		5	10	8		5		1	4	10	3	8		12	4		70
Latvia								1	1								2
Lithuania							7										7
Malaysia		2	2	4	1	1		1	7	7	7						25
Mexico	16	4	7	7	7	6	3	4	7	2	8	5	3		1	1	83
New Zealand	3	4		1		2	2	1			4	2	3				22

																	Total
Nicaragua				1													1
Pakistan								2	1		1	4	6	6			24
Paraguay			1											1			2
Peru	2	2	3			4	1	7	7	8	3	4	1	6	2	1	48
Philippines		2	1	4	4	1											11
Poland			1	6				2									9
Singapore	2																2
South Africa		8	18	36	13	5	15	1	4		7	1		3	3	1	128
Taipei, Chinese			1	1	1		2				1	1	1				12
Thailand		1	1				1	20	1					3			31
Trinidad and Tobago			2			1		1	1		2	1					7
Turkey	11			1	8	2	11	28	16	9	21	6	11	9	9		142
Ukraine					1		2	2	2	6	2	1	5	3			24
United States	33	12	20	24	31	33	27	12	14	18	5	5	23	15	5		289
Uruguay		1				1											1
Venezuela, Bolivarian Republic of	2	4	8	9	1			1									25
Total	119	92	127	181	190	237	170	218	224	154	138	140	108	139	137	59	2433

Note: [1] There have been huge efforts to provide databases on antidumping cases initiated and enforced by WTO Members. Such databases are not simple matters since the antidumping procedures are so complicated (especially if one takes the reviews into account). The most complete source is provided by Bown, and it is posted on the following website: <http://econ. worldbank.org/rtbd>. See also Czako et al. (2003), as well as Prusa (2001, 2005) who tries to explain the proliferation of AD duties. Finger and Nogues (2006) have studied the practice of MERCOSUR countries, and conclude that AD has been used as a carrot to pursue economic liberalization.

Source: <http://www.wto.org>.

2. Antidumping

2.1 The Legal Discipline and its Rationale

Art. VI GATT and the WTO Agreement on Antidumping (AD)[2] do not regulate dumping, but deal with the conditions that must be met for AD duties to be imposed lawfully: briefly, a WTO Member must show that dumping (defined as the differential between two prices, the price in the home market and the price in the export market—what is known as the dumping margin) has caused injury to the domestic industry producing the like product. If these requirements have been cumulatively met, a WTO Member can impose AD duties, that is, it can add the dumping margin to its duties.[3] To do that, it will have to initiate an AD investigation and ensure that specific due process obligations have been respected throughout the process.

To understand the rationale for AD duties, we must first understand why WTO Members are allowed to constrain dumping. After all, dumping is private behaviour and the GATT was supposed to address state impediments to trade liberalization, not private behaviour. Art. VI GATT states, *inter alia*:

> The contracting parties recognize that dumping, by which products of one country are introduced into the commerce of another country at less than the normal value of the products, *is to be condemned* if it causes or threatens material injury to an established industry in the territory of a contracting party or materially retards the establishment of a domestic industry. (emphasis added)[4]

---

[2] Consistently, WTO adjudicating bodies have held that antidumping is governed not only by the WTO AD Agreement, but also by Art. VI GATT (see, for example, the AB report on *US—1916 Act*). It is difficult to confirm that such has been the negotiating intent as well. Some might have legitimately thought that the WTO AD Agreement, being later in time, had superseded Art. VI GATT. Be it as it may, the consequence of the current construction of the regulatory framework applicable to antidumping is twofold: first, dumping is recognized as 'unfair' practice, a practice to be condemned when it causes injury (there is no statement regarding its unfairness in the context of the WTO AD Agreement); second, the obligations of IAs when examining dumping practices originating in NMEs (non-market economies), an issue we will be discussing *infra*, are mentioned in Art. VI GATT but not in the WTO AD Agreement. Czako et al. (2003), Mavroidis et al. (2008), Palmeter (1995), Stewart and Dwyer (2010) provide extensive discussions of the WTO AD Agreement, its negotiating record, and objectives. The analysis in this chapter relies in part on Mavroidis et al. (2008).

[3] Arguably, importing states will have little incentive to incur administrative costs and initiate an AD procedure on goods the duties of which have not been bound. It could, however, be the case that a law needs to be formally amended for a tariff change to occur, even in cases where the practised tariff is not bound. In such a case, an AD procedure could be less costly. For what it is worth as proxy, note that, as Bown (2010) shows, a number of WTO Members imposed AD duties on imports from China before 2001, that is, before the Chinese accession to the WTO, at a time when they could simply have raised their import duties. More generally, raising unbound duties faces the additional limitation that the tariff increase would have to apply on an MFN basis when the importer would rather punish one source of production. It might legitimately want to avoid alienating a number of its trading partners, and therefore decide to have recourse to AD duties, even though it has not bound the duties of the (allegedly) dumped import.

[4] Irwin et al. (2008) mention that this sentence was added at a late stage of the negotiation of the GATT, following a proposal by the Cuban delegation to this effect.

It is by virtue of this provision that antidumping duties can be imposed because dumping, although not illegal per se, is an unfair trade practice and can be counteracted. Case law has recognized as much (§87 of the AB report on *Argentina—Footwear (EC)*; and §81 of the AB report on *US—Line Pipe*). The next logical question is how can an unfair trade practice be counteracted?[5] Art. 18.1 AD provides the response to this question:

> No specific action against dumping of exports from another Member can be taken except in accordance with the provisions of GATT 1994, as interpreted by this Agreement.

A footnote to this Article (footnote 24) pertinently adds:

> This is not intended to preclude action under other relevant provisions of GATT 1994, as appropriate.

The Panel on *US—Offset Act (Byrd Amendment)* was called to interpret this provision. It found that AD duties constitute the only permissible response against dumping. In doing that, it found that the Byrd Amendment payments, a US law whereby only the economic operators that had supported a petition to impose AD duties would receive monetary compensation resulting from the collection of AD duties, if, as a result of the petition, duties were eventually imposed, was a specific action against dumping other than AD duties and, hence, illegal (§7.18). On appeal, the AB confirmed the Panel's findings. Recalling its prior pronouncements on this issue (*US—1916 Act*), the AB held that the Byrd Amendment[6] was inconsistent with Art. 18.1 AD (§§255–6 and 265).[7]

In *US—Antidumping and Countervailing Duties (China)*, the AB added an extra dimension to this discussion: it held that a WTO Member cannot impose both AD and CVD duties to address the same situation of subsidization: it prohibited in other words 'double dipping' (§§550ff and especially 583 and 591).

Dumping is, of course, a price discrimination scheme. Characterizing a similar scheme as unfair seems odd since similar schemes are quite acceptable in business and also under domestic laws. Why then is most of domestic price differentiation accepted, while the moment an international element is introduced it becomes unfair?

---

[5] On the origins of unfairness in international trade, and the evolution of its coverage, see the excellent work by Beviglia-Zampetti (2006).

[6] Its official acronym is CDSOA (Continued Dumping and Subsidy Offset Act).

[7] The heart of the issue here was whether Byrd Amendment payments to the injured US industry would disincentivize exporters to the US market who would stop dumping as a result. Horn and Mavroidis (2005a) have voiced their criticism of the manner in which the AB has handled the interpretation of Art. 18.1 AD, and point out that it is equally plausible that, as a result of Byrd Amendment payments, exporters continue to dump and possibly more aggressively so. Consequently, the AB seems to have punished a statute that might (or might not) disincentivize exporters to continue dumping. This decision, consequently, expands considerably the coverage of Art. 18.1 AD. Where one draws the line is a question of future (jurisprudential) experience. Bhagwati and Mavroidis (2004) add their voices to this criticism, arguing that the problem with the US law is double dipping (and AD duties are in place, and a subsidy is being paid), and that this is where the AB should concentrate its analysis.

Indeed, one way to look at Art. VI GATT is as an exception to Art. III GATT: WTO Members apply one statute (domestic antitrust) to domestic price differentiation, while applying a different statute (AD Agreement) when the operator practising the scheme is of foreign origin.[8] This issue is even more pertinent nowadays in light of the rise of offshoring and outsourcing. Increasingly, it is the case that, say, EU companies request imposition of AD duties against inputs of EU goods (since many EU companies, established in the EU, outsource/offshore part of their production abroad). In October 2006, for example, the EU imposed AD duties of 16.5 per cent and 10 per cent on certain leather shoes imported into the EU market. Although many EU companies produce leather footwear inside the EU, a significant number of EU companies had outsourced the production of footwear to third countries, while keeping other parts of their operations in the EU. Some EU companies that produce leather shoes in the third countries were subjected to AD duties. Such incidents have caused concern in Brussels, to the point that the then Trade Commissioner issued a Green Paper asking, *inter alia*, whether the EU IA should somehow take into account the interests of companies which have retained significant operations and employment in Europe, even though they have moved some part of their production outside the EU market.[9]

It is probably warranted to start with a brief discussion of representative antitrust statutes to see how they deal with price discrimination.[10] In antitrust practice, which is not necessarily by definition the best reflection of cutting-edge economics[11] but has been substantially more open than trade law to economic analysis, a price differential is not necessarily viewed with scepticism. Of course, there is nothing like a world antitrust statute and, hence, we are forced to look at domestic statutes: the EU and US statutes are probably the most sophisticated instruments in this respect.

In the EU system, price differentiation will be treated as an abuse of (single or collective) dominance. As a result, for price differentiation to enter the picture of antitrust enforcement, a prior finding of dominance is required. The ECJ had the opportunity to pronounce on this issue in its *Akzo* and *Tetrapak* case law.[12] We quote

---

[8] Technically, however, since AD is a border instrument and NT covers only domestic instruments, it would be difficult to sustain such an argument before a WTO adjudicating body. Still, trade liberalization is meant to be an extension of the relevant geographic market (in the antitrust sense of the term): by removing tariff barriers and NTBs (non-tariff barriers), conditions of competition become (more) homogeneous across national jurisdictions.

[9] See pp. 6 and 7 in Commission of the European Communities, Global Europe, Europe's Trade Defense Instruments in a Changing Global Economy, A Green Paper for Public Consultation, Brussels, 6 December 2006, COM (2006).

[10] See Kovacic (2010) for an excellent discussion of the manner in which price discrimination is treated in antitrust and trade statutes.

[11] See Hovenkamp (2011, pp. 2ff).

[12] C-62/86, *Akzo Chemie BV v Commission* [1991] ECR I-3359 (3 July 1991); Case T-83/91, *Tetrapak International SA v Commission* [1995] ECR II-762 (CFI) and Case C-333/94P, [1996] ECR I-5951.

from the *Tetrapak* decision (§41), which is the most recent case and can be considered the authentic expression of the test for predatory pricing established by the ECJ:

> In AKZO this Court did indeed sanction the existence of two different methods of analysis for determining whether an undertaking has practised predatory pricing. First, prices below average variable costs must always be considered abusive. In such a case, there is no conceivable economic purpose other than the elimination of a competitor, since each item produced and sold entails a loss for the undertaking. Secondly, prices below average total costs but above average variable costs are only to be considered abusive if an intention to eliminate can be shown.

With respect to some of the sales at hand, the ECJ found that the prices charged were between average variable cost and average total cost. According to its own test, therefore, it would have to show intent to eliminate the competition. The ECJ in §44 ruled as follows on this point:

> ...it would not be appropriate, in the circumstances of the present case, to require in addition proof that Tetra Pak had a realistic chance of recouping its losses. It must be possible to penalize predatory pricing whenever there is a risk that competitors will be eliminated.... The aim pursued, which is to maintain undistorted competition, rules out waiting until such a strategy leads to the actual elimination of competitors.

A dominant company that prices below a certain threshold is thus found to be practising predatory prices, in EU practice. There is no need to further show that the company at hand would realistically recoup its original investment. In the eyes of the court, a company behaving in this manner can only intend to monopolize the market, and it is predatory intent that is ultimately being punished.[13]

The US Supreme Court also had the opportunity to pronounce on this issue. In the US statute, monopolization plays a comparable role to abuse of dominance in the EU regime, and it is under its aegis that the Supreme Court discussed this issue. The leading case is *Brooke Group*:[14]

> A plaintiff must prove (1) that the prices complained of are below an appropriate measure of its rival's costs and (2) that the competitor had a reasonable prospect of

---

13 In 2009, the EU Commission issued a Communication regarding exclusionary conduct by dominant undertakings (2009/C/45/02 OJ C45/7 of 24 February 2009). There, in §§63ff, it adopted a different standard on predation. First, it adopted a slightly different standard, since it now uses AAC (average avoidable cost) and not AVC (average variable cost) as the benchmark to evaluate if predation has occurred. AAC refers to the average of avoidable costs. In most cases, AAC and AVC will be the same, since it is variable costs that can typically be avoided. So, there is not much of a change so far. Most importantly, nonetheless, the Commission, beyond pricing below AAC, will examine whether 'the allegedly predatory conduct led in the short term to revenues lower than could have been expected from a reasonable alternative conduct, that is to say, whether the dominant undertaking incurred a loss that it could have avoided' (§65). In that, the new test is different from that applied in *Akzo*. It is still unclear whether the Communication will exert a major influence in the shaping of EU case law. Only future practice will respond to this question.

14 *Brooke Group Ltd v Brown & Williamson Tobacco Corp*, 509 US 209 (1993). See the analysis of the case in Hovenkamp (2011) at pp. 370ff.

recouping its investment in below cost prices.... The plaintiff must demonstrate that there is a likelihood that the scheme alleged would cause a rise in prices above the competitive level sufficient to compensate for the amounts expended on the predation, including the time value of the money invested in it. Evidence of below cost pricing is not alone sufficient to permit an inference of probable recoupment and injury to competition. The determination requires an estimate of the alleged predation's cost and a close analysis of both the scheme alleged and the relevant market's structure and conditions. Although not easy to establish, these prerequisites are essential components of real market injury.... Predatory pricing schemes, in general, are implausible... and even more improbable when they require coordinated action among several firms... They are least likely to occur where... the cooperation among firms is tacit, since effective tacit coordination is difficult to achieve; since there is a high likelihood that any attempt by one oligopolist to discipline a rival by cutting prices will produce an outbreak of competition; and since a predator's present losses fall on it alone, while the latter supracompetitive profits must be shared with every other oligopolist in proportion to its market share, including the intended victim.

As can be seen, the evidentiary standard in US law is higher and makes the possibility of successful challenges against predatory schemes quite unlikely. The overlap between the two regimes is that they both punish only a subset of price discrimination: predatory pricing; assuming that a similar scheme has been successfully implemented, the predator will be in a position to recoup the original investment, having driven the competitors out of the market and having ensured that there is no risk, at least for some time, that they re-enter the market once the predator raises its prices. In other words, what antitrust statutes punish is behaviour which causes injury to competition, as opposed to injury to competitors.[15] As we will see in some detail *infra* when we discuss the injury test in the AD Agreement, this is one of the key differences between the antitrust and the trade approach to price differentiation: while antitrust statutes look into the welfare implications of price differentiation for the whole of the society, the AD statute looks simply into the implications for a subset of the society, the injured producers. It is not overstating the case, if we were to state that the regulation of AD has emerged as probably the most contentious issue among policy-makers and trade economists.

Policy-makers, nevertheless, advance four categories of arguments to justify continuing recourse to AD:[16]

(a) discriminatory pricing is wrong;
(b) AD addresses predatory prices;

---

[15] The US test is more reasonable since it avoids punishing unsuccessful predatory pricing: in such cases, consumers will profit from lower prices, as the predator will not be in a position to recoup the original investment.

[16] This section borrows from Mavroidis et al. (2008). The welfare implications of AD are well documented in economics literature and there is no need to reinvent the wheel here. The reader could, *inter alia*, check Boltuck and Litan (1991), Finger (1993), Messerlin (2001), and Prusa (2001 and 2005).

(c) strategic dumping can reduce the incentives for participating in the WTO;

(d) AD is a necessary safeguard.

Antidumping demonizes price discrimination when it causes injury; it does not address the reasons that give rise to it: the importing state will raise duties and the reasons giving rise to it will remain in place. Price discrimination will occur when price arbitrage is impossible. This could be for various reasons: the absence of arbitrage may flow from intrinsic factors outside the control of the exporting firm (such as different technologies in the two markets; designs segmenting markets for more economically sound reasons—the home country consumers could be much more sensitive to the latest technologies than the foreign country consumers; or other technical barriers to trade), or it might be generated from the firm itself in its effort to protect the home market. Whatever the reason, the fact remains that dumping occurs because there is no price arbitrage. If discriminatory pricing is the true concern of the proponents of AD duties, why not address discriminatory pricing as such? Why have recourse to a second-best instrument such as AD (which leads to increasing prices to the level of the higher price) and not try to move prices to the level of the lower price? Do we really need to burn the village to save it? More practically, the first question to ask would be why importers do not simply re-export the dumped products to the exporting country charging the higher price? Arguably, this would have been quite profitable. Is it because of (state) trade barriers, product differentiation, or any other reason? The former could be decomposed into tariffs, QRs, export subsidies, and domestic instruments: QRs and export subsidies are illegal per se, and domestic instruments have to be applied in a non-discriminatory manner. Hence, the only remaining issue would be whether the reason for price arbitrage relates to import tariffs. Assuming this is indeed the case, it would be more sensible to try to reduce the level of tariffs in the context of multilateral rounds rather than increase prices by adding the dumping margin to the bound tariff. Cases of product differentiation can also be discarded, since, assuming this is indeed the case, AD duties cannot be imposed: the investigating authority will not be in a position to overcome the like product requirement.[17] Price arbitrage can also occur because of legitimate prohibition of parallel imports, since the TRIPs Agreement does not include an outright prohibition of similar instruments.[18] Inquiring into the reasons for lack of arbitrage will allow trading partners to use the first-best instruments to address distortions.[19] It will, in all likelihood, also lead to fewer AD investigations. This is not to say, of

---

[17] Admittedly, things can be much more complicated. But developing this line of thought for argument's sake will allow us to understand how much of a concern price discrimination really is. Like product definitions are, in the overwhelming majority of cases, quite narrow in AD proceedings. More on this last issue, *infra*.

[18] Li and Maskus (2006) discuss the cost of such policies.

[19] A similar pattern is described by Goldberg and Verboven (2005) who discuss the cars' price differentiation across EU Member States and the manner in which the EU Commission addressed it.

course, that one needs to address any price discrimination. This is simply to suggest that we do not know whether price discrimination is a genuine concern for those proposing the regulation of AD. It most likely is not. It can, of course, have positive welfare implications for consumers abroad, and indeed it does, in the overwhelming majority of tested cases.[20] AD, however, proceeds without inquiring at all into the overall welfare implications of dumping; injury to domestic producers competing with dumped imports suffices for duties to be lawfully imposed. This is what the injury to competitors test amounts to.[21]

Complaining firms in AD cases often suggest that dumping is driven by the will of foreign firms to eliminate domestic competitors in their own market in order to increase prices when they will ultimately be in a monopoly position in the import-competing market. Does this argument make sense? No, is the short answer. First, if this was indeed true, one could simply reduce AD actions to cases of predatory pricing. Actually, for some jurisdictions at least, this would mean that there would be no need to rely on the AD Agreement, since their own competition laws would lead to a comparable outcome.[22] Second, as we saw, US antitrust practice has adjusted to the idea that predation is unlikely and, consequently, not much time and effort should be invested in thinking about ways to address it. This is so because a predator's pricing is a strategy in two phases: eliminating competitors necessarily generates costs for predator and recouping these costs during the second phase, which almost necessarily creates incentives for old competitors to come back or new competitors to enter a market that they ignored before the price war. A predator should follow a predatory pricing strategy only if the second phase

---

[20] Finger (1993); Messerlin (2001).

[21] Bown *et al.* (2004); Prusa (2005 and 2001); Petersmann (1993); Hoekman and Mavroidis (1996a).

[22] Messerlin (2001) asked the question what would have been the outcome of AD investigations, had the investigating authorities employed an antitrust-type standard. His analysis is specific to the EU. The period of his investigation runs from 1980 to 1997 during which he examines 461 cases of initiation of investigation for which adequate information exists. To answer this question he proposes a five-screen test. The five screens include: first, a screen to assess the capacity of the foreign firms involved in AD cases to behave as predators. He proposes a screen which eliminates from investigation all foreign companies with forecasted aggregate market share of 40 per cent or less. He thus screens out 311 out of 461 cases. The second screen screens out 14 additional cases for which a negative outcome (no injury) resulted from the investigation. The third screen requests elimination of all cases where four or more countries were involved. The rationale for this screen as explained by the author (p. 358) is that 'if four or more countries are involved in simultaneous antidumping actions on the same product, the possibility of joint predatory behaviour seems rather low'. Seventy-five more cases are thus screened out. The fourth screen eliminates all cases where eight or more economic operators are involved (for the same reason as per screen three, the possibility for predatory behaviour where eight or more companies are involved is quite low). Seventeen more cases are screened out. The remaining 44 cases (i.e. less than 10 per cent of the original total) are subjected to a test whereby the author examines the market share of the economic operators involved and/or the Herfindahl-Hirschman Index (HHI) and concludes (having eliminated cases where either companies have small market share or in application of the HHI no reasonable competition authority would have intervened) that only 12 cases were worth investigating, that is, less than 2 per cent of the original total.

brings higher profits than the losses generated by the first phase. If phase one is long, the likelihood of recouping in phase two thereby becomes slimmer. At the end of the day, only an evaluation of the barriers to entry in the market where the predator operates can provide responses as to the likelihood of recouping the original investment. The unlikelihood of this occurrence is supported by an additional argument. If the goal of predation is monopolization of a market, there is a better, less costly manner to do it: merger. A predator can buy the other companies in the relevant market where it operates, at a price which would reflect their stock value in the expected monopolistic (not in a competitive) market.[23]

Strategic dumping crucially relies on cost conditions: an exporting firm will benefit from a closed home market (a safe harbour), where it can charge the home consumers the full (fixed and variable) costs of production, allowing the sale of the product in the export market at a price only inclusive of the variable cost (its competitors in the export market are assumed not to operate in a safe harbour). The competitors of the strategic dumper cannot emulate its behaviour: they thus must be disadvantaged enough, in terms of the relative size of accessible markets and scale economies, with respect to the strategic dumper. It follows that, when the safe harbour is small relative to the export market, it is highly unlikely that strategic dumping will occur. In this vein, a high percentage of AD investigations (of goods originating in say Singapore, or Hong Kong, China) cannot be justified on strategic dumping grounds.[24]

---

[23] A predator's strategy can be further complicated, depending on the facts of the case: if, for example, the other companies are small compared to the predator, they can try to convince the demand side of the market (the consumers) to help them survive to the first phase of the predator's dumping. They have a good argument: it is that if the predator wins, consumers will pay the eventual monopoly price.

[24] Independently from AD measures, there is evidence that AD measures have a pro-cartel effect at the two stages of the complaint and of the decision. Messerlin (2001) persuasively argues that exchanging information for lodging a complaint requires a minimum exchange of information from the complainant; even if handled through lawyers, plaintiffs could draw common conclusions from the complaint. On the other hand, nascent collusion between plaintiffs can be made sustainable by AD measures. It is not by accident that, at least, on his count, one-quarter of EU AD cases of the 1980s were 'twin' AD and competition cases dealing with similar products and EU firms. A more systematic indication of this pro-cartel dimension flows from the fact that the combined market shares of the plaintiffs and defendants are often extremely high—on average, around 80 per cent–85 per cent in the United States and the European Union. Defendants and complainants have a combined market share of less than 90 per cent in only 55 per cent of the US and EC AD cases examined in the 1980s and mid-1990s. Foreign cartels (that is, outside the country enforcing AD measures), as well, have been created by AD cases, as best illustrated by the quasi-official Canadian potash cartel triggered by US AD. Another interesting observation that Messerlin (2001) reports is *echoing* in AD investigations: it has been shown that EU and US AD actions against China targeted the same Chinese exports in 75 per cent of AD cases initiated against Chinese exports by the United States and in 68 per cent of the cases initiated by the European Union. Most of these cases echoed each other within a year or less, and all but three of these cases (cycles, hammers, and pocket lighters) resulted in AD measures of some kind. Such a large proportion of echoing cases and the similarity of their outcomes are signs that AD is a protectionist instrument that petitioners are using in a strategic way to segment the two largest world markets. World cartels are likely to be fostered by a series of AD cases echoing each other all over the world. Large firms almost simultaneously lodge AD complaints

In defence of antidumping, the argument has also been made that AD intro-duces a flexibility element into the WTO contract: trading partners will be induced to make more commitments than otherwise, because they know that they can always subsequently increase their protection by the dumping margin; AD thus has functions similar to that of a safeguard. It is probably true that, in practice, AD has been used as a surrogate for safeguard measures. This was not, however, its intended use: indeed the AB has time and again insisted on the distinction between fair and unfair trade, upon which, in its view, the differen-tiated legal requirements in the two agreements are predicated. Consequently, it is not that it is irrational to use AD as a safeguard; it is *contra legem*. But more to the point: recently, Finger and Nogues (2006) provided some empirical support for the argument that AD can be put to good use as a safeguard mechanism, by researching the MERCOSUR experience. In their account, national administra-tions in the MERCOSUR countries used the potential for AD as a carrot to persuade domestic lobbies to support trade-liberalizing commitments. This argu-ment rests on the premise that the current safeguard clause does not operate to the satisfaction of the trading partners. This is probably true, as we will see *infra* in this chapter. But the natural question to ask is: why do negotiating efforts not concentrate on fixing the current safeguard clause instead of adding a new one that comports numerous negative external effects?

The discussion above points to the inability to mount a serious intellectual defence of AD, and its advent in the WTO world is better explained on political economy grounds.[25] Antidumping is a means to protect producer welfare from nefarious effects caused by the pricing strategies of foreign competitors. Various provisions in the AD Agreement and especially Art. 3 (which describes injury as the effect of dumped imports on domestic producers) and Art. 6.12 (which does not place consumer organizations—arguably entities with contrary interests to domestic producers—on an equal footing with producers) support this under-standing of the AD Agreement. Its various provisions hence should be understood in light of this overarching objective, even though, for the reasons mentioned above, this objective is not persuasive.

2.2 The Coverage of the Legal Discipline

2.2.1 Negotiating History

Antidumping precedes Art. VI GATT time-wise. Canada's father of the AD legislation was the Finance Minister William S. Fielding, who is quoted as saying back in 1904:

---

in Brussels, Washington, and elsewhere in order to segment the world market as they wish (AD duties and measures increase the transaction costs, hence the firms' ability to charge different prices (discriminate) in different locations).

[25] Horlick (1993); Messerlin (2001); Moore (2002 and 2004).

It was unscientific to meet special and temporary cases of dumping by a general and permanent raising of the tariff wall and that the proper method was to impose special duties upon dumped goods.[26]

So, AD was thought to be the means to avoid punishing innocent bystanders. But punish what? The relevant Australian statute is the 1906 Industries Preservation Act and it protects against international predation, as is made clear in §19.[27] Protecting against international predation, and not simply price discrimination, seems to have been the thrust of the US laws to this effect. Stewart et al. (1993, p. 1401) reflect the following opinion by US Congressman Fodney, expressed in 1921:

> We have no law and we have no means of preventing concerns in a foreign country combining to sell their goods at a sacrifice in this country until competition here has been destroyed and thus control our markets at such prices as they wish to charge.

Indeed, in *American Banana Co v United Fruits Co*,[28] judge Oliver Wendell Holmes, writing for the US Supreme Court, held that one could not use domestic laws to attack foreign price discrimination. Citing prior case law to the effect that all legislation is prima-facie territorial,[29] he went on to write (p. 357):

> Words having universal scope, such as 'every contract in restraint of trade,' 'every person who shall monopolize,' etc., will be taken as a matter of course to mean only everyone subject to such legislation, not all that the legislator subsequently may be able to catch. In the case of the present statute, the improbability of the United States' attempting to make acts done in Panama or Costa Rica criminal is obvious, yet the law begins by making criminal the acts for which it gives a right to sue. We think it entirely plain that what the defendant did in Panama or Costa Rica is not within the scope of the statute so far as the present suit is concerned. Other objections of a serious nature are urged, but need not be discussed.

Antidumping was thus conceived as the instrument to punish foreign price discrimination (but in the form of predation). Over the years, antidumping evolved into an instrument that punishes price discrimination instead of focusing only on predation.[30] Antidumping statutes nevertheless took time to proliferate. A 1956 GATT study reveals that only 24 countries had AD laws in place, and only eight of them had used them by that time.[31] Institutions were established at the national level to deal with the procedural aspects of antidumping investigation.[32]

---

[26] Viner (1922) at p. 193.

[27] INDUSTRIES PRESERVATION, V Austl. C. Acts 19 (1906).

[28] 213 US 347 (1909).

[29] *Ex parte Blain*, LR 12 Ch. Div 522 at 528.

[30] Hoekman and Mavroidis (1996a).

[31] GATT Doc. TN.64/NTB/W/20 of 5 May 1967.

[32] In 1954, injury analysis in the US was entrusted to the then Tariff Commission (later named ITC, the International Trade Commission), whereas the US Treasury focused on the dumping investigation, US Public Law 90-63. Similar arrangements were made in the context of the EU. Institutional arrangements influence the outcome of investigations in the sense that if injury has been established first, the political pressure to attribute it to dumping might become irresistible.

The preparatory work of all AD Agreements signed since the Kennedy round leaves us with no doubt that it is price discrimination that is being sanctioned through AD duties.

The negotiation of the Uruguay round AD Agreement has been discussed in several publications.[33] They were characterized by a division between the then main users (EU, US) and the exporters. The former were fighting a rearguard fight in an attempt to keep as much discretion as possible in the hands of IAs and introduce stringent anti-circumvention mechanisms, such as third country circumvention and country-hopping.[34] A series of drafts prepared by the then New Zealand delegate Hugh McPhail (McPhail I, II, and III) were rejected and only the Cartland draft at the end of the round (named after the Hong Kong Ambassador, Michael Cartland) managed to gather the necessary crowd behind it. The main users failed in introducing anti-circumvention but, at the insistence of the US, managed to introduce a standard of review that, prima facie, looks quite deferential towards IAs. Exporters can claim victory in introducing new disciplines regarding recourse to constructed prices, best information available etc., and then there are some issues like zeroing[35] where no agreement proved possible and the matter was left for discussion at a later date and eventually to adjudication.

For AD duties to be imposed, price discrimination is a necessary but not sufficient condition: WTO Members wishing to avail themselves of this possibility must further show that dumping (price discrimination) has caused injury to the domestic industry producing the like product. The demonstration of injurious dumping must take place within an investigation that must be conducted in conformity with the various due process requirements established in the WTO AD Agreement. In what follows, we will detail these aspects one by one.

2.2.2 Establishing Dumping

According to Art. 2.1 AD, dumping exists when the home price (called normal value (NV); Art. 2.2 AD) exceeds the export price (EP), discussed in Art. 2.3 AD. The difference between the two prices constitutes the dumping margin. An IA must demonstrate that dumping margins exceed an agreed level since margins below the statutory *de minimis* level (2 per cent) cannot justify the eventual imposition of AD duties (Art. 5.8 AD). IAs are not totally free when it comes to

---

[33] See, *inter alia*, Croome (1995), Liang (2011), Paemen and Bentsch (1995), Pregg (1995), Stewart et al. (1993).

[34] There are differences between these schemes but essentially they cover cases where an exporter makes changes in its supply chain in order to avoid payment of AD duties; for a more extensive discussion, see Liang (2011).

[35] This term refers to the practice of discarding positive dumping margins during an AD investigation. As a result, the dumping margin is inflated. It gave rise to dozens of disputes in the WTO era and has by now been totally outlawed by WTO adjudicating bodies. There are of course other issues as well which are not antidumping-specific, but which have remained unresolved and have a significant impact on antidumping investigations, such as non-preferential rules of origin; see Inama and Vermulst (2010).

choosing methodologies for establishing a dumping margin: they must observe the requirements established in Art. 2.4.2 AD.

Normal Value: The NV should normally be the actual price of the allegedly dumped good in the exporting market. The AD Agreement allows an IA to disregard the actual price if one of the following situations occurs (Art. 2.2 AD):

(a) There are no sales of the like product in the ordinary course of trade;[36] or
(b) A proper comparison between the normal value and the export price cannot be made, because of
   (i) the particular market situation, or
   (ii) the low volume of sales in the home market.

The AD Agreement does not define the term 'ordinary course of trade'. Art. 2.2.1 AD provides that sales made below per unit (fixed and variable) cost of production plus selling, general, and administrative expenses (SG&A) may, under certain circumstances, be considered as not having been made in the ordinary course of trade. This is so only if sales were made within an extended period of time (normally one year but in no case less than six months), in substantial quantities (if the weighted average selling price of the transactions under consideration is below the weighted average per unit costs, or if the volume of sales at a loss represents at least 20 per cent of the volume of transactions), and at prices which do not allow for the recovery of all costs within a reasonable period of time. Sales made at prices which are below per unit costs at the time of sale, but above weighted average per unit costs for the period of investigation, shall be considered to provide for the recovery of costs within a reasonable period of time.[37]

    Case law has provided additional examples of sales outside the ordinary course of trade. In *US—Hot-Rolled Steel*, sales between parties with common ownership were identified by the AB as a case of sales outside the ordinary course of trade, but the AB was quick to point out that, even where the parties to a sales transaction are entirely independent, a transaction might not be in the ordinary course of trade (§143): a liquidation sale by an enterprise to an independent buyer, which may not reflect normal commercial principles (§148). What also matters is that the test is

---

36 The AB, in its report on *US—Hot-Rolled Steel*, clearly stated that sales outside the ordinary course of trade must be excluded by the IA from the calculation of NV (§139).

37 See footnotes 4 and 5 to Art. 2.2.1 AD. In the course of the ongoing negotiations of the Doha round, it has been argued that the test as currently set forth in Art. 2.2.1 AD has some important negative implications for those industries whose product pricing is especially sensitive to shifts in supply and demand and for agricultural and other commodity sectors whose producers are typically 'price takers'. Owing to the price volatility, the result of the current test would be higher normal values reflecting higher price levels that would not normally be sustainable in the market, thus not reflecting market realities. It has been proposed to allow for the exclusion of only those sales as being outside the ordinary course of trade, of which the weighted-average selling price is below the weighted-average total cost, regardless of the quantities of transactions that may have been made individually at prices below cost; WTO Docs. TN/RL/GEN/95 and TN/RL/GEN/9, which call for a repeal of the current 20 per cent test.

applied in an even-handed manner: the AB thus considered inconsistent the test used by the US which excluded sales transactions between related parties[38] which were marginally low-priced, while including all high-priced sales, except those proved, upon request, to be aberrantly high-priced (§154).

Footnote 2 to the AD Agreement indicates that, when it comes to 'low volume of sales', sales shall be considered sufficient in volume, if they represent at least 5 per cent of the sales of the product in the importing/investigating country; it is, nevertheless, clear from the text of this footnote that the 5 per cent benchmark is not an absolute criterion: assuming evidence that sales at a lower ratio are still of sufficient magnitude to provide for a proper comparison, a lower number of sales should be acceptable for the purposes of the NV determination.[39]

The term 'particular market situation' remains largely un-interpreted: a GATT Panel (*EEC—Cotton Yarn*) found that hyper-inflation combined with a fixed exchange rate did not necessarily constitute a particular market situation. The Panel considered that the complainant had failed to demonstrate that prices used as the basis of the NV were themselves so affected by the combination of high domestic inflation and a fixed exchange rate such that those sales did not permit a proper comparison (§§478–9).

Assuming that we are in the presence of either sales not in the ordinary course of trade, or low volume sales, or a particular market situation, the IA can set aside the price in the exporter's home market and pick one of the two alternative bases for the calculation of the NV (Art. 2.2 AD):

(a) Third-country sales, that is, the IA will use data from sales of the like product in an appropriate third country, provided the price is representative; or

(b) Constructed price, that is, the IA can calculate *de novo* the NV, which will be the arithmetic addition of the following elements: the cost of production in the country of origin, a reasonable amount for SG&A expenses, and a reasonable amount for profits.

Moving to constructed price is of course bogus for the exporter who is now left at the discretion of the IA. Over the years, negotiators of the successive AD agreements have tried to come up with language that would limit the discretion of IAs in this respect to an acceptable, reasonable exercise. Their efforts have concentrated on two fronts: first, on the definition of what should come under the key

---

[38] Prusa and Vermulst (2010) discuss this concept as it has been interpreted across cases in WTO case law.

[39] The AD Agreement does not specify whether the sufficient volume test relates to all domestic sales by an investigated exporter, or only to those sales by the exporter which are made in the ordinary course of trade. It has been argued that the purpose of the test is to determine whether the domestic market is sufficiently large to enable domestic sales to serve as a legitimate measure of NV, and all sales, even those outside the ordinary course of trade, should be taken into account in making this benchmark determination; see WTO Doc. TN/RL/GEN/9 where the FANs (*Friends of Antidumping Negotiations*) have attempted a clarification on this score.

terms ('NV', 'SG&A', 'profits'), and under what circumstances; second, what methodology IAs should be allowed to use when having recourse to constructed price. We take each issue in turn.

In principle, the cost data to be used as a basis for constructing the NV are those of the exporter or producer in question. The IA has limited discretion in constructing the NV since it must perform a calculation on the basis of (Art. 2.2.1.1 AD):[40]

(a) Actual cost data of the examined producer or exporter, provided that
   a. such records are in accordance with the generally accepted accounting principles (GAAP) of the exporting country; and
   b. they reasonably reflect the costs associated with the production and sale of the product under consideration;
(b) All available evidence on the proper allocation of costs, provided that such allocations have been historically utilized by the exporter or producer. Reversing the Panel's findings in this respect, the AB, in its report on *US—Softwood Lumber V*, held that, occasionally at least, this sentence would oblige an IA to compare alternative methodologies on cost allocation and privilege the one that better suits the facts of the case (§§138–9);
(c) Appropriate adjustment of costs for non-recurring items which benefit future and/or current production or for circumstances in which costs during the period of investigation are affected by start-up operations.

The Panel on *US—Softwood Lumber V* noted that Art. 2.2.2 AD does not define the term 'SG&A'. In its view, all costs affecting all or nearly all products manufactured by a company should be considered 'general' costs, while 'administrative' costs were defined as costs concerning or relating to the management of the company's affairs (§7.263). When constructing SG&A and profits, an IA must, in accordance with Art. 2.2.2 AD, base its calculations on the investigated exporter's actual data pertaining to the production and sales in the ordinary course of trade of the like product. In *EC—Tube or Pipe Fittings*,[41] the question arose whether data relating to sales that had been discarded by an IA under Art. 2.2 AD could still be used for the purposes of constructing SG&A and profits in the context of Art. 2.2.2 AD. Specifically, Brazil complained that the European IA used in its calculations under Art. 2.2.2 AD data relating to sales previously discarded under Art. 2.2 AD (low volume sales). The AB, upholding the Panel

---

[40] The term 'on the basis of', which is reflected in this provision, arguably leaves some room for discretion. The Panel in its report on *Egypt—Steel Rebar* emphasized that only those costs recorded in the books in accordance with GAAP and which reasonably reflect the costs associated with the production and sale of the product under consideration are to be included in the cost calculation (§7.393). In the same vein, the Panel in its report on *US—Softwood Lumber V* underscored the fact that these provisions are not absolute and apply only to the extent that the statutory conditions for their application have been met (§7.237).

[41] Horn and Mavroidis (2005b) discuss this report.

finding in this respect, made it clear that an IA which has discarded the market price for one of the reasons reflected in Art. 2.2 AD, other than for the reason that such sales were made outside the ordinary course of trade, can still use market data for the calculation of SG&A when constructing the NV (§101). The Panel, in its report on *EC—Salmon (Norway)*, added that actual domestic profit data and actual SG&A data should not be excluded because of the low volume or the low level of profitability of the sales to which they pertain (§§7.309, 7.318).

IAs are not free to decide on the methodology that they can use: paragraphs (i)–(iii) of Art. 2.2.2 AD provide for three alternative methods for calculating the SG&A and profit amount (when actual data regarding the production and sales in the ordinary course of trade cannot be used), which, in the words of the Panel in *EC—Bed Linen* (§6.60):

> are intended to constitute close approximations of the general rule set out in the chapeau of Article 2.2.2. These approximations differ from the chapeau rule in that they relax, respectively, the reference to the like product, the reference to the exporter concerned, or both references, spelled out in that rule.

In this Panel's view (§6.96), if one of these methods is properly applied, the results are by definition reasonable, as required by Art. 2.2 AD. The same Panel held that the three methods are on an equal footing (§6.66).

The first alternative methodology is reflected in paragraph (i) which provides that the amounts can be based on the actual amounts incurred and realized by the investigated exporter for the same general category of products (which may include the like product). How broad the general category of products may be is not defined in the Agreement. The Panel, in *Thailand—H-Beams*, found that the text of Art. 2.2.2 AD does not provide (§7.111):

> precise guidance as to the required breadth or narrowness of the product category.

It did note, however, that sticking to a narrower definition makes the methodology used fully consistent with the objectives of the Agreement (§7.113).

Paragraph (ii) states that SG&A and profit may be based on the weighted average (WA)[42] of actual amounts incurred and realized by other investigated exporters or producers, rather than by the specific investigated exporter or producer, but for the same like product. The AB (*EC—Bed Linen*, §80) clarified that all sales of other exporters or producers of the like product are to be included for determining SG&A and profit data, whether made in the ordinary course of trade or not.

Finally, as a third alternative methodology, paragraph (iii) provides that SG&A and profits may be based on any other reasonable method, with the proviso that

---

[42] The Panel in its report on *EC—Bed Linen (Article 21.5—India)* held that the weighting can be performed on a volume or value basis (§6.81). The use of data from one exporter only is not permitted; see AB report on *EC—Bed Linen* at §76. See, on this score, Grossman and Sykes (2007a).

the amounts shall not exceed the amounts incurred and realized by other investigated exporters for the same general category of products. The reference to any other reasonable method in paragraph (iii) led the Panel in *EC—Bed Linen* to the conclusion that (§6.98):

> in case a Member bases its calculations on either the chapeau or paragraphs (i) or (ii), there is no need to separately consider the reasonability of the profit rate against some benchmark.

SG&A costs have to be based on actual data pertaining to production and sales of the like product. The Panel on *US—Softwood Lumber V* was of the view that, since SG&A costs benefit the production and sale of all goods that a company may produce, they must certainly relate or pertain to those goods, including to the product under investigation (§7.265). It, thus, concluded that (§7.267):

> unless a producer/exporter can demonstrate that the product under investigation did not benefit from a particular G&A cost item, an investigating authority is not precluded from attributing at least a portion of that cost to the product under investigation.

The Panel went on to conclude that it was not unreasonable for the US IA to allocate part of a large settlement amount relating to claims concerning hardwood to the production and sale of softwood lumber, as this settlement was a cost borne by the company as a whole.

Does the above guarantee that discretion will always be exercised in a reasonable way? The *Korea—Certain Paper* case forms a good, albeit unfortunate, example of the slippery slope an exporter might find itself on, once the authorities have decided to construct the NV. In this case, the authority decided to construct NV because an important number of sales by two of the investigated exporters were made through a related trading company. As this company did not provide the information required to permit the authority to verify whether these sales to that company were made in the ordinary course of trade, it assumed this not to be the case. The authority thus constructed the exporters' NV, on the basis of the cost of production of the exporter, plus the exporters' SG&A and interest expenses, plus the SG&A and interest expenses of the trading company, and finally adding profits (§7.99). Since the trading company, which was not an interested party, did not provide the necessary data, the authority resorted to facts available to calculate the SG&A and interest expenses of this trading company, in spite of repeated claims by Indonesia that this trading company did not incur any financial expenses (§§7.101–2). The authority then decided not to deduct the expenses of the related trading company from the data provided by the investigated exporters in question, but rather relied on SG&A data from two other companies, A and B. The Panel agreed with Indonesia that the authority could have relied on the two investigated exporters' information in deriving the appropriate financial and SG&A expenses for the trading company. However, it did not consider that this was the only way for the authority to proceed in this regard, as the authority also had verified information relating to another investigated company which it used to determine the related trading company's costs. Therefore, and given the important discretion of the IA in this respect, the Panel did not find this course of action to be inconsistent with the AD Agreement (§7.105).

In the case of imports from a country which is a non-market economy (NME), an IA may deviate from the rules governing the establishment of normal value. NMEs are defined in the Interpretative Note ad Art. VI GATT as:

> a country which has a complete or substantially complete monopoly of its trade and where all domestic prices are fixed by the state.

The Note allows WTO Members to deviate from the obligations imposed in Art. VI GATT (as further explicated in the AD Agreement), but does not explain what methodology exactly they should be following in similar cases:

> It is recognized that, in the case of imports from a country which has a complete or substantially complete monopoly of its trade and where all domestic prices are fixed by the State, special difficulties may exist in determining price comparability for the purposes of paragraph 1, and in such cases importing contracting parties may find it necessary to take into account the possibility that a strict comparison with domestic prices in such a country may not always be appropriate.

Normally, an IA, in the absence of legislative guidance as to what to do in such cases, will either use data from third-country producers, or construct the NV. In *EU—Footwear (China)*, the Panel faced a claim by China that, by choosing Brazil as a surrogate country for China, the EU had violated its obligations under the AD Agreement. The Panel discarded the claim, underlining the wide discretion IAs have when choosing surrogate countries for NMEs (§§7.253ff).

Not surprisingly, the NME status of China was an important issue in the Chinese accession process (Accession Protocol), which starts from the principle that WTO Members have a choice either to use Chinese prices or costs for the industry (that is, to treat China as any other market economy country) or to use a methodology based on the general rule that it is up to the producers under investigation to:

> clearly show that market economy conditions prevail in the industry producing the like product with regard to the manufacture, production and sale of that product.[43]

If this has been the case, the importing WTO Member is obliged to use Chinese prices. In the opposite case, a methodology that is not based on a strict comparison with domestic prices or costs in China may be used. If this methodology is applied, it has to be notified to the WTO Antidumping Committee. At the same time, China's Accession Protocol provides that, as soon as China is able to establish that

---

[43] WTO Doc. WT/L/432 at §15.

it is (either as a whole or with regard to a particular industry) a market economy according to the criteria set forth in the importing WTO Member's national law, China (e.g. the Chinese industry in question) must be treated as a normal market economy/industry. In order to benefit from market economy status, the criteria conferring it must have existed in the importing WTO Member's law at the time of China's accession in 2001. It is not entirely clear what happens if similar criteria were not in place at the time of China's accession, and it is an open question whether WTO Members finding themselves in this situation are precluded from treating China as an NME. This will be, if at most, a short-lived situation, since the NME status of China will expire at the latest 15 years after accession, that is, by 2016. China's Accession Protocol does not set forth which methodology is to be used in cases where the importing WTO Member does not use Chinese prices and costs. The final report of the Working Party on China's Accession[44] provides some clarification in this respect: the authority shall normally utilize, to the extent possible, and where cooperation exists, the prices or costs in one or more market economy countries that are significant producers of comparable merchandise, and that are, either at a level of economic development comparable to that of China, or are otherwise an appropriate source for prices or costs to be utilized in light of the nature of the industry under investigation. Those WTO Members that do not have an established practice in this respect should make best efforts to ensure that their methodology for determining price comparability is along similar lines. In addition, it provides that due process rights of Chinese exporters be respected.

Export Price: Determining the NV is the first part of the endeavour to establish a dumping margin. The second is the establishment of export price (EP). According to Art. 2.3 AD, the IA will use the market price unless the exporter and importer are 'related'. In this case, a constructed export price can legitimately be used. The Panel, in its report on *US—Stainless Steel (Mexico)*, summed up as follows the rationale for constructed EP (§6.99):

> . . . an export price is constructed, and the appropriate allowances made, because it appears to the investigating authorities that the export price is unreliable because of association or a compensatory arrangement between the exporter and the importer or third party. By working backwards from the price at which the imported products are first resold to an independent buyer, it is possible to remove the unreliability. Thus, we agree with the United States that the purpose of these allowances is to construct a reliable export price to use in lieu of the actual export price or, as expressed by the EC as third party, to arrive at the price that would have been paid by the related importer had the sale been made on a commercial basis.

This passage seems to suggest that the relation of parties does create a presumption that observed prices are unreliable. Nevertheless, there is nothing axiomatic about it since it could be the case that exporters sell at the same price at both related and

---

44 WTO Doc. WT/ACC/CHN/49 at §151.

unrelated importers in a foreign market. In other words, it seems that an IA should test the reliability of prices between related parties by comparing them with those charged in transactions with non-related parties. It is common practice to consider that, in case of a significant difference in the average price charged to related importers compared with the price charged to other importers, the former price is not reliable and the export price will be constructed for sales to related importers. The Panel on *US—Stainless Steel* (*Mexico*) held that, as the constructed export price should be a reliable export price, costs incurred between importation and resale can only be deducted if they were foreseen: only foreseen costs can be considered to be reflected in the price (§6.100). Interestingly, the same Panel highlighted that there does not exist an obligation to make such adjustments (§6.93):

> because the failure to make allowance for costs and profits could only result in a higher export price—and thus a lower dumping margin.

In other words, not making such allowances would not constitute a disadvantage to the exporter, as it implies a higher export price and thus a lower dumping margin.

The AD Agreement does not explain when parties may be considered to be related, neither does it set forth any guidelines on how to test for and determine the lack of reliability of such sales. The absence of an agreed definition of what constitutes a related party (or affiliated party) is an important problem.[45] The Agreement does offer, though, an alternative in case the transacting parties are related: the price of the product when sold for the first time to an independent buyer may form the basis for the constructed export price.[46] In the case where the product is not resold or not resold in the condition as imported, the export price may be determined on another reasonable basis. What is reasonable will of course be ultimately determined by WTO Panels: the report on *US—Hot-Rolled Steel*, for

---

[45] In the Doha round of negotiations currently under way, the question of how to deal with affiliated parties in determining normal value and export price has been the subject of some interesting proposals. The Friends of Antidumping Negotiations (the FANs) have, as a group, as well as individually, in the case of Brazil and Chinese Taipei, submitted proposals intended to clarify and restrict the meaning of the term 'related or affiliated party' based on the control criterion. Practically, the FANs' proposal defines affiliated parties to be similar to those that are consolidated into a consolidated financial statement, into which a responding party would also be consolidated, in accordance with the accounting standards in many countries. In their view, this would avoid many of the problems relating to the provision of information we pointed to earlier. The proposals also suggest changes to the text of the AD Agreement, *inter alia* introducing an objective test for determining whether the sales, even when made to related parties, are actually unreliable, and eliminating the possibility of replacing unreliable sales to related parties with downstream sales; see WTO Docs. TN/RL/GEN/19, 67, 82.

[46] In *US—Hot-Rolled Steel*, the AB, reversing the Panel in this respect, agreed with the US that, in an NV determination, similar use of such downstream sales may be made for constructing the NV (§§ 154ff). This finding is of course at odds with the text of the AD Agreement (*contra legem*) which unambiguously provides for other alternatives, and not for this one. Still, following this report, NV can now also be constructed by using sales to the first unaffiliated party.

example, reflects a US practice (which it does not find to be inconsistent with the AD Agreement) to the effect that an investigated exporter or foreign producer may own as little as 5 per cent of another company for the sale to be considered as taking place between affiliated parties (footnote 73 to the Panel report). It is thus not unusual for importers to be 'related' to the exporters, and hence recourse to constructed EP occurs frequently.[47]

Fair Comparison: Assuming that an NV and an EP have been determined, irrespective of whether they are actual or constructed prices, the IA will then proceed to establish whether a dumping margin exists by comparing the former to the latter. To this effect, it must proceed and perform a fair comparison between the two sides of the dumping margin equation and it will be comparing two prices. In this vein, it must ensure that (Art. 2.4 AD):

(a) The two prices must be at the same level of trade; and
(b) Due allowances for any differences affecting price comparability must be made in accordance with the AD Agreement.

The purpose of this provision is, in the words of the Panel on *US—Stainless Steel (Mexico)* (§6.77):

> to neutralise differences in a transaction that an exporter could be expected to have reflected in his pricing.

The Panel on *US—Softwood Lumber V* explained what precisely the obligation under Art. 2.4 AD entails in the following manner (§§7.357–8):

> Comparability is a term which, in our view, cannot be defined in the abstract. Rather, an investigating authority must, based on the facts before it, on a case-by-case basis decide whether a certain factor is demonstrated to affect price *comparability*. We can imagine of situations where although differences exist, they do not affect price *comparability*. For instance, this could occur where in the exporting country all cars sold are painted in red, while cars exported are all black. The difference is obvious; in fact, it is one of those differences listed in Article 2.4 itself—a difference in physical characteristics. However, there might be no variable cost difference among the two cars because the cost of the paint—whether red or black—might be the same. If instead of differences in cost, we were looking at market value differences, we might reach the same conclusion if, either the seller or the purchaser, would be willing to sell or purchase at the same price, regardless whether the car is red or black.
>
> It is also important to note that there are no differences 'affect[ing] price comparability' which are precluded, as such, from being the object of an *allowance*. In addition, we consider that the obligation on an investigating authority is to examine the merits of each claimed adjustment and to determine whether the difference affects price comparability between the allegedly dumped product and the like product sold on the domestic market of the exporting country. (emphasis in the original)

---

[47] This practice would of course run foul of the FANs' proposal discussed *supra*.

In other words, Art. 2.4 AD does not require that an adjustment be made automatically in all cases where a difference is found to exist, but only where (based on the merits of the case) that difference is demonstrated to affect price comparability. For example, the fact that a trading company handles domestic or exports sales of an investigated product does not in and of itself mean that there is a difference that affects price comparability and that an adjustment has to be made; the Panel, in its report on *Korea—Certain Paper*, decided as much (§7.147): it rejected the need for an adjustment, as it was not convinced that there were sales-related services rendered by the trading company with respect to domestic sales of the exporters' products in the domestic market which were not rendered in the exporters' export sales to the importing country.

It is thus difficult to draw up an exhaustive list of factors that affect price comparability. Think of the following: Hansen and Prusa (1996) have shown that, assuming constant market share, the probability of a positive dumping finding is higher the larger the number of exporters. Hence, investigating authorities might have an incentive to cumulate. This is what they termed 'super-additivity'. Gupta and Panagariya (2006) provided a theoretical explanation for super-additivity: the larger the number of exporters involved, the higher the risk of free-riding (producers will free-ride on other producers' recourse to legal experts, etc.). It is doubtful if, as a matter of principle, Art. 2.4 AD should make room for this type of consideration as well, and a negative answer is probably warranted here, the influence of super-additivity on dumping margins notwithstanding. So where should we draw the line?

Art. 2.4 AD draws two lines: it obliges first of all that comparisons should be made at the same level of trade (and as a result some items become, *ipso facto*, non-adjustable); second, it provides for an indicative list of due allowances. The normal way to perform a fair comparison at the same level of trade is by comparing prices at the ex-factory level.[48] This does not mean, nonetheless, that an IA cannot for example compare NV and EP at the wholesale or the retail level. What matters is that both prices are at the same level of trade so the comparison is fair. Art. 2.4 AD also provides an indicative list of due allowances that can legitimately be made once prices have been brought to the same level of trade:

> Due allowance shall be made in each case, on its merits, for differences which affect price comparability, including differences in conditions and terms of sale, taxation, levels of trade, quantities, physical characteristics, and any other differences which are also demonstrated to affect price comparability. In the cases referred to in paragraph 3, allowances for costs, including duties and taxes, incurred between importation and resale, and for profits accruing, should also be made. If in these cases price comparability has been affected, the authorities shall establish the normal value at a level of trade equivalent to the level of trade of the constructed export price,

---

[48] This is also known as 'netting back' and establishing an ex factory export price and an ex factory normal value.

or shall make due allowance as warranted under this paragraph. The authorities shall indicate to the parties in question what information is necessary to ensure a fair comparison and shall not impose an unreasonable burden of proof on those parties.

It follows that both factors exogenous to the allegedly dumping company (e.g. taxation), but also factors controlled by it, such as quantity discounts or differences between the quality of the exported product and that of the product sold domestically, can affect price comparability and appropriately form the subject-matter of due allowances. Art. 2.4 AD also requires that due allowance shall be made for any other difference which affects price comparability. In *EC—Fasteners (China)*, the AB found that a failure to indicate clearly what was necessary to perform fair comparison was inconsistent with Art. 2.4 AD (§527).

The Panel on *EC—Tube or Pipe Fittings* accepted that due allowance could be made for packaging expenses, an item not explicitly mentioned in Art. 2.4 AD (§7.184). The Panel on *US—Stainless Steel (Mexico)* clarified that only differences that the exporter could reasonably have anticipated and could have taken into account in his price determination may be the subject of adjustments (§6.77).

The method to use when making due allowances is not prejudged in the AD Agreement. The Panel on *EC—Tube or Pipe Fittings* dealt, *inter alia*, with a claim by Brazil that the EU had denied a request to make due allowances for differences in indirect taxation because of the methodology it had privileged to address this issue. The Panel rejected Brazil's argument. In its view, the AD Agreement did not specify a particular manner in which differences in indirect taxation should be accounted for. As a result, any methodology used, to the extent reasonable, should be considered WTO-consistent (§7.178).

It is now well settled in case law that Art. 2.4 AD places an obligation on the investigating authority to ensure a fair comparison.[49] This implies that for those differences which have been identified as requiring an adjustment, it is incumbent upon the IA to evaluate them and decide whether an adjustment is required to maintain price comparability.[50] In *EC—Tube or Pipe Fittings*, the parties did not agree on the nature of the evidence that should be submitted in support of a claim for an adjustment nor as to whether it is the IA or the exporter that bears the burden of identifying and substantiating the claimed adjustment. According to the Panel, it is for the IA to make due allowances and abide by the disciplines of Art. 2.4 AD; the IA retains discretion as to items to be included as well as the manner in which they will be evaluated. To this effect, it could very well be the case that an IA does not accept each and every claim presented under Art. 2.4 AD. It might request clarity from the party making the argument and, if this is the case, the party concerned has a duty to cooperate (§7.158). The Panel on *Argentina—*

---

[49] *US—Hot-Rolled Steel* at §178, AB report. For a concise history of the zeroing case law, see the Panel report on *US—Orange Juice*, §§7.89–136.
[50] *Argentina—Ceramic Tiles* at §6.113, Panel report.

Poultry Antidumping Duties held in the same vein that an IA must indicate to the parties concerned the type of information that is necessary to ensure a fair comparison, and it must not impose an unreasonable burden of proof on the interested party; if it does that, it is not violating the Agreement even if it refuses to make an adjustment for certain differences for which no such sufficient evidence has been presented by the party concerned (§7.239). With respect to a request to make adjustments for differences in packaging costs of the product when sold domestically compared to when exported, the Panel, in its report on *EC—Tube or Pipe Fittings* considered that no documentary evidence had been supplied by the Brazilian producer in spite of a clear request by the IA to provide such evidence. In such circumstances, the Panel was of the view that there was no obligation on the IA to establish the need for an adjustment through on-site verification, as argued by Brazil (§7.192). The Panel on *Egypt—Steel Rebar* held that the process of determining what types of adjustments need to be made is something of a dialogue between interested parties and the IA. This Panel also seemed to accept that an IA may be required to make adjustments even when not explicitly requested or identified by the interested parties, in case it is demonstrated 'by the data itself' that a given difference affects price comparability (§7.352). This seems a correct approach in light of the overall obligation imposed on IAs to conduct their investigation in a fair and unbiased manner. It would not be consistent with this overall obligation to allow an authority to defer its obligation of making a fair comparison to the interested parties. It thus appears that, even in the absence of a request for adjustments by an interested party, the IA has an independent obligation to make all reasonable adjustments as are necessary to ensure a fair comparison between normal value and export price. It will do so on evidence provided, in principle, by the parties involved. At the end of this process, the IA will have in front of it two prices, or two sets of prices, an adjusted export price and an adjusted normal value. If the adjusted NV is higher than the adjusted EP by at least the statutory *de minimis* level of 2 per cent, then the IA has established a dumping margin that allows it in principle to impose AD duties. To do that nonetheless, besides respecting the various procedural requirements discussed *infra*, it will have to also show that dumping has caused injury to the domestic industry producing the like product. We turn to these issues in what immediately follows.

Calculating the Margin of Dumping: The AD Agreement includes three methods that could, theoretically, be used by an IA when establishing a dumping margin. Art. 2.4.2 AD reads:

> ... the existence of margins of dumping ... shall *normally* be established on the basis of a comparison of a weighted average normal value with a weighted average of prices of all comparable export transactions or by a comparison of normal value and export prices on a transaction-to-transaction basis. (emphasis added)

Hence the two normal methods to calculate the dumping margin at the disposal of an IA are:

(a) weighted average to weighted average (WA-WA);

(b) transaction to transaction (T-T).

The AB, in its report on *EC—Tube or Pipe Fittings*, made it clear that two methods (WA-WA, T-T) are offered as alternatives, and WTO Members are free to choose one or the other. The issue arose when Brazil argued that, to account for the influences that devaluation might have had when calculating the dumping margin, a particular method had to be privileged by the European IA. The AB rejected all arguments to this effect, arguing that nothing in the AD Agreement privileges one methodology over the other when a particular set of facts is present (§76). Note that the AD Agreement (Art. 2.4.2) states that, when using the WA-WA methodology, the weighted average NV should be compared to a weighted average of prices of all comparable export transactions, and not of all sales. This implies that the use of multiple averages based on, for example, different periods of sale is allowed by the AD Agreement, if it is necessary to avoid a weighted-average NV being compared to a weighted-average EP that includes non-comparable export transactions. In other words, there is no requirement to always compare a single WA NV to a single WA EP. The Panel on *US—Stainless Steel* (*Mexico*) held that differences in timing may be considered to give rise to a comparability problem, only in case two elements exist:

(a) a change in prices; and

(b) differences in the relative weights by volume within the POI (period of investigation) of sales in the home market as compared to the export market (§6.123).

The T-T methodology does not involve an evaluation of all sales: there could be a discrepancy in the number of sales in the home and the export market. As a result, in such cases, in practice, an IA will look for the domestic sale as close in time as possible to each of the export transactions. In other words, it will compare the two transactions which are as close time-wise to each other as possible, and will neglect the remaining transactions. It is clear that the choice of methodology for calculating the dumping margin may have an important impact on whether dumping is found to exist or not. Assume four domestic transactions taking place on 1 January for $80, 1 March for $100, 1 June for $120, and 1 November for $100. The volume is similar each time. The WA NV is $100. Assume three export transactions on 2 January, 2 June, and 2 July. All are made for $100, at the same weight. So on a WA-WA basis, there is no dumping. Using a T-T methodology, an export transaction on 2 January for $100 will be compared with a domestic transaction on 1 January for $80. There is no dumping margin, since the NV is higher than the NV. The export transaction on 2 June will be compared with the 1 June domestic transaction for $120: a dumping margin of 20 results. And the export transaction on 2 July will also be compared with a domestic transaction on 1 June since this is the closest in time, again finding a margin of dumping of 20. On average, using this methodology, a positive margin of dumping of $20 will have been established. The reverse could, of course, also be the case.

A third, exceptional, methodology is provided for in Art. 2.4.2 AD, which allows, in specific circumstances, a comparison between a WA NV and prices of specific export transactions. We quote:

> A normal value established on a weighted average basis may be compared to prices of individual export transactions if the authorities find a pattern of export prices which will differ significantly among different purchasers, regions or time periods, and if an explanation is provided as to why such differences cannot be taken into account appropriately by the use of a weighted average-to-weighted average or transaction-to-transaction comparison.

This provision aims to counteract targeted dumping. If, for example, during the POI, an exporter dumps substantial volumes of exports during, say, one month only, then, an IA can, for the calculation of dumping margins, legitimately take into account export prices as reflected in the transactions during this month. The AB, in its report on *EC—Bed Linen*, recognized as much (§62).[51] The Panel on *Argentina—Poultry Antidumping Duties* faced the following issue: two Brazilian companies had reported to the Argentine authorities all relevant documents concerning their domestic sales. The Argentine authorities compared the weighted average of a sample of these transactions with the weighted average of all export prices. The Panel held that this was inconsistent with Art. 2.4.2 AD since 'a weighted average normal value' is a weighted average of all domestic sales other than those which may be disregarded pursuant to Art. 2.2.1 AD (§§7.272ff). According to the Panel, the weighted average must be established by using all transactions as a benchmark.

IAs have, in the past, often had recourse to calculation practices the consistency of which with the AD Agreement has been contested: chief among them, the practice of zeroing. It appears in various forms and guises and consists in disallowing negative dumping margins (that is, cases where the NV is lower than the EP) to offset positive dumping margins (that is, cases where the NV is higher than the EP), when calculating an overall margin of dumping for the product alleged to have been dumped into the importing country's market. In other words, where the export price exceeds the normal value for the product (negative dumping margin), the transaction will either be completely disregarded or will be considered to have taken place at a non-dumped price and a fictitious margin of dumping of zero will be attributed to this transaction. As a result, the dumping margin is inflated, since negative dumping margins are not able to moderate the calculation of the overall dumping margin.

The US was the last entity to abandon zeroing. The EU, a prior heavy user, abandoned its use earlier. It has been used whenever recourse to calculation of

---

[51] See, on this score, Janow and Staiger (2007) and Grossman and Sykes (2007a).

dumping margin is being made at different stages of the original and subsequent investigations:

(a) Original investigations (Art. 5.3 AD);
(b) Administrative reviews (Art. 9.3.1 AD);
(c) Sunset reviews (Art. 11.3 AD);
(d) Interim or changed circumstances reviews (Art. 11.2 AD);
(e) New shipper reviews (Art. 9.5 AD).

There have been dozen of disputes on zeroing and the ensuing case law is made up of diverging Panel reports, dissenting opinions,[52] a Panel in a way overturning itself,[53] and the AB changing its reasoning to deal with the issue on several occasions. It even includes two Panel reports which openly disagreed with the AB and refused to follow its reasoning.[54] This is a very rare occurrence in WTO practice, where Panels almost always follow the AB reasoning. The search for the correct legal basis on which to analyse the practice of zeroing is what characterizes the zeroing case law. It is clear that the AD Agreement does not contain an express prohibition or permission of zeroing. In fact, the term 'zeroing' is not even mentioned in the AD Agreement. This does not necessarily mean that zeroing is permitted under the Agreement, as became clear from the case law. Still, the problem Panels and the AB obviously have struggled to find the right textual hook on which to hang the analysis. The legal basis for much of the Panels' and the AB's analysis has been threefold:

(a) Art. 2.1 AD, which defines dumping margins;
(b) Art. 2.4.2 AD, which deals with the methods for comparing normal value and export price in order to establish a margin of dumping; and
(c) the general requirement of Art. 2.4 AD to conduct a fair comparison between normal value and export price.

It is questionable if (a) is appropriately used. The AB did hold time and again that this is where the negotiating partners in the Uruguay round agreed to anchor the prohibition of zeroing. Yes, this provision echoes verbatim the corresponding provision in the Tokyo round AD Agreement when zeroing was practised by many IAs. The second ground is closely linked to the third and it is here that the AB should always base its ban on zeroing. Prusa and Vermulst (2009) have explained adequately how by zeroing there is an artificial increase in dumping margins and, consequently, that no fair comparison can be made. It seems though

---

[52] *US—Zeroing (EC)*, and *US—Softwood Lumber V*. See Bown and Sykes (2008); Prusa and Vermulst (2009, 2011); Crowley and Howse (2010); Crowley and Palmeter (2009); Hoekman and Wauters (2011).

[53] The reasoning in *US—Softwood Lumber V*, and *US—Softwood Lumber V (Article 21.5— Canada)* is not the same, although the former deals with a WA-WA and the latter with a T-T method.

[54] *US—Zeroing (Japan)*; *US—Stainless Steel (Mexico)*.

that this discussion is water under the bridge by now since the AB has hermetically shut the door to zeroing practices under any circumstances.[55]

2.2.3 *Establishing Dumping in a Sampling Scenario*

The practice of 'sampling' is explicitly allowed by Article 6.10 AD: assuming a large number of exporters, an IA may legitimately restrict its investigation to a few companies only (a sample) that it can reasonably investigate; it will then determine an individual dumping margin for each of the sampled companies. Non-sampled exporters will be burdened, by virtue of Art. 9.4 AD, by a duty corresponding to the WA of the dumping margins of the sampled exporters; the WA will be calculated excluding zero and *de minimis* margins, as well as margins established on the basis of the facts available.

Whenever recourse is made to sampling, the IA can either limit the examination to a reasonable number or investigate a statistically valid sample. The two alternatives are, from a purely legal perspective, substitutes. Recourse to econometrics, however, seems warranted in order to define what is a statistically valid sample. A statistically valid sample means that the properties of the sample are the same as those of the whole; in other words, one can safely argue that the dumping margins established will more or less reflect those of the non-sampled exporters. There is no similar guarantee when recourse is made to an administratively reasonable number since an IA might be tempted to pick outliers, non-representative cases: this method seems to leave more discretion to an IA, in particular, since it does not exclude the possibility that a statistically non-valid sample has been chosen. There is only a limited insurance policy against this risk in the sense that non-sampled exporters can request individual investigations (within the confines of feasibility of course). In principle, thus, the choice between the two sampling methods could lead to divergent results.

The Panel on *EC—Salmon (Norway)* cast some doubt on the understanding of the term 'statistically valid sample' as discussed so far: it held that the term refers only to a sample of known exporters. We quote from §7.162:

> Thus, the 'statistically valid' sample referred to in the second sentence of Article 6.10 is a 'statistically valid' sample of all of the 'known exporter[s] or producer[s] concerned' for whom it is 'impracticable' to calculate an individual margin of dumping. Likewise, the 'largest percentage of the volume of the exports... which can be reasonably investigated' is the 'largest percentage of the volume of the exports... which can be reasonably investigated' in respect of all of the 'known exporter[s] or producer[s] concerned' for whom it is 'impracticable' to calculate an individual margin of dumping.

---

[55] The US did initiate a procedure to repeal zeroing; see Federal Register, vol. 75 no. 248, at pp. 81533ff, Tuesday 28 December 2010; see also <http://www.ustr.gov/about-us/press-office/press-releases/2012/united-states-trade-representative-ron-kirk-announces-solu>.

Consequently, in theory it could be the case that because say important exporters are not known to the IA, the sample chosen is not statistically valid; its statistical validity will be relative, that is, restricted to the narrower circle of known exporters.

The term 'known exporter' has been interpreted by the AB as referring to all exporters that have been identified in the petition, as well as those who have voluntarily appeared before the IA (*Mexico—Antidumping Measures on Rice*). In *EU—Footwear (China)*, the Panel held that the EU criteria for sampling (largest volume of sales in both the domestic as well as the export markets) were consistent with Art. 6.10 AD (§§7.221ff).

In *EC—Fasteners (China)*, the Panel held that sampling is the only permissible exception to the obligation to calculate individual dumping margins for exporters (§7.90). The AB added that there are other cases where departures are permitted but they are all reflected in the covered agreements (§§328–9). In doing that, the AB outlawed a provision in the EU Basic AD Regulation whereby a third-country-wide rate would be applied to all exporters originating in NMEs if they had not managed to reverse the presumption that the EU law imposed. NME exporters interested in avoiding a constructed price (or application of a third-country price) would have to meet the 'MET' (market economy test) established by the EU Basic AD Regulation. Failure to do so would lead the EU authorities to impose a third-country-wide margin on all of them except for those who applied for individual treatment (IT) in accordance with the conditions included in the IT test (which was an integral part of the EU Basic AD Regulation). The AB held that the EU law was inconsistent with the AD Agreement in this respect (§364) and that, unless the EU used sampling or any other statutory exception, it could not deviate from the rule established in Art. 6.10 AD to calculate individual dumping margins for each exporter.[56] Violation of this rule would lead to violation of Art. 9.2 AD as well, that is, of the obligation to collect the appropriate amount of duty (§339).

2.2.4 Injury Analysis

An IA has to demonstrate, by looking at the volume of dumped imports, their price effects, and the injury indicators specifically reflected in the AD Agreement, that the domestic industry producing the like product has been injured (Arts. 3.2 and 3.4 AD) as a result of the dumped imports (Art. 3.5 AD). The AD Agreement does not thus request from an IA to evaluate the society-wide welfare implications of dumping: the standard embedded is an injury-to-competitors standard. So even if (as is likely to be the case) the positive welfare implications for consumers outweigh the negative ones for producers, an IA can lawfully impose duties, assuming it can also show that injury is due to dumping.[57] It is also irrelevant if

---

[56] In the same vein, the Panel report on *EU—Footwear (China)* at §§7.88ff.

[57] The AD Agreement acknowledges that WTO Members retain discretion to evaluate the implications of dumping for consumer welfare; there is no obligation to do that. We discuss this issue more at the end of this section.

the domestic industry suffering from dumping is a monopolist that might be 'tamed' through market opening measures; it suffices that it suffered injury. Finally, the AD Agreement does not condition the initiation of injury analysis on a prior finding of dumping. In practice, the two legs of the analysis, that is, the investigation of dumping margins and of injury, often take place in parallel. In fact, it is not unheard of that dumping analysis follows injury analysis. Depending on what takes place first, the signalling to the market regarding the probability that AD duties will be imposed could be different. Knetter and Prusa (2003) note, for example, that of 800 cases investigated in the period 1980–98, the DOC (US Department of Commerce), in charge of establishing dumping margin, issued a negative dumping decision only in 28 cases (3.5 per cent of the total); on the other hand, the ITC (US International Trade Commission), in charge of establishing injury, made negative injury decisions in 37.5 per cent of all cases submitted to it during the same period. If DOC kicks off the process and the ITC is not implicated until dumping margins have been established, it is relatively unclear whether duties will be imposed at the end of process; the opposite is true when ITC has moved first.

The term 'injury' is used in the AD Agreement to refer to a situation of current material injury, threat of injury, and/or the material retardation in the establishment of an industry. The latter concept should not be confused with that of infant industry: what the Agreement is referring to is a situation where an industry was about to be established, but its establishment was materially retarded because of the dumped imports. Once the industry is established, the domestic producers forming part of this new industry cannot rely on this argument any more.[58] To show injury, an IA must undertake an 'objective examination' regarding the effects of dumped imports on prices and producers of the like product and must provide 'positive evidence' that injury has indeed occurred as a result of dumping (Art. 3.1 AD).[59] The AB on *US—Hot-Rolled Steel* explained that the term 'objective examination' relates to the way in which evidence is gathered and requires an IA to conduct the process without favouring the interests of any interested party in the investigation (§193). The AB, in its report on *US—Hot-Rolled Steel*, considered that the requirement of positive evidence implied that the evidence must be objective and verifiable (§192). The positive-evidence standard does not eliminate the possibility for an IA to resort to assumptions. But, as the AB pointed out in *Mexico—Antidumping Measures on Rice* (§204):

---

[58] A proposal has been tabled to clarify the term 'material retardation' along the lines suggested here, see WTO Doc. TN/RL/GEN/122.

[59] In *Thailand—H-Beams*, the AB stated that it considered Art. 3.1 AD as an overarching provision that informed the more detailed obligations in the succeeding paragraphs of Art. 3 AD (§106).

these assumptions should be derived as reasonable inferences from a credible basis of facts, and should be sufficiently explained so that their objectivity and credibility can be verified.[60]

Volume of Dumped Imports: Art. 3.2 AD requires that an IA *consider* whether there has been a significant increase in dumped imports, either in absolute terms or relative to production or consumption in the importing Member, and also to examine its price effects. An initial question seems to be whether an IA should be requested to *prove* a (relative or absolute) increase in dumped imports as well. The Panel on *Thailand—H-Beams* was of the view that Art. 3.2 AD required an IA to consider whether there had been a significant increase, rather than requiring it to make an explicit finding or determination as to whether the increase was significant (§7.161). Eventually, the AB in its report on *EC—Tube or Pipe Fittings* accepted this approach in an explicit manner (footnote 114):

> Brazil's thesis is further predicated on the assumption that if no significant increase in dumped imports (either in absolute terms or relative to production and consumption in the importing Member) were found originating from a specific country under Article 3.2, then those imports would have to be excluded from cumulative assessment under Article 3.3. (Brazil's response to questioning at the oral hearing.) However, we find no support for this argument in the text of Article 3.2 itself: significant increases in imports have to be 'consider[ed]' by investigating authorities under Article 3.2, but the text does not indicate that in the absence of such a significant increase, these imports could not be found to be causing injury.

One would expect, however, that, although in principle possible, a lawful imposition of AD duties in the case of no absolute or relative increase in dumped imports would be more difficult, precisely because of this absence. Indeed, it seems that an increase in imports will be one of the first and most obvious consequences of the dumping practice which makes the imported products more appealing to consumers in the importing country. If dumping has not even had the effect of increasing imports, it will be highly unlikely that any other significant effect of dumping will be found. Although demonstrating increased dumped imports is not a necessary condition for demonstrating injury, the volume of dumped imports must anyway be above a statutory *de minimis* level, otherwise the injury analysis is flawed: if imports originate in one country, they must represent at least 3 per cent of total imports, and if in more than one market, they must cumulatively represent at least 7 per cent (Art. 5.8 AD).

An IA cannot cherry-pick among imports from a source that sometimes dumps and sometimes not. It must take into account the whole volume, as the AB clearly stated in its report on *EC—Bed Linen (Article 21.5—India)* as follows (§115):

---

[60] In the same report, the AB, upholding the Panel's findings, held in §205: An investigating authority that uses a methodology premised on unsubstantiated assumptions does not conduct an examination based on positive evidence. An assumption is not properly substantiated when the investigating authority does not explain why it would be appropriate to use it in the analysis.

if a producer or exporter is found to be dumping, all imports from that producer or exporter may be included in the volume of dumped imports, but, if a producer or exporter is found not to be dumping, all imports from that producer or exporter must be excluded from the volume of dumped imports.

In *EC—Bed Linen* (*Article 21.5—India*), the AB dealt with injury analysis in a sampling scenario. The EU had sampled Indian exporters, and of the five sampled exporters, three were found to be dumping. The EU did not impose duties on the two exporters found not be dumping, but it did impose the WA (of the duties imposed on the three 'dumpers') on the non-sampled Indian exporters. India protested, noting that, during the investigation of Indian exporters of bed linen, 53 per cent of imports in the EU market (the volume represented by the two non-dumping Indian exporters) were found not to be dumped. India did not bring into question the methodology used by the EU for sampling. In India's view, it was the injury analysis of the EU that was questionable: since Art. 3.2 AD required investigating authorities to focus on the effects of dumped imports only, the EU should have kept as a working hypothesis that 53 per cent of total Indian imports were not dumped and, hence, could not be taken into account for the purpose of the injury analysis. The EU disagreed. In its view, the working hypothesis of the AD Agreement was that there was no need to make a separate injury analysis for non-sampled known exporters: the very fact that Art. 6.10 AD allowed sampling and Art. 9.4 AD allowed the imposition of the WA on non-sampled known exporters amounted, in the EU's view, to a presumption that injury had been caused by such exporters. The AB rejected all EU arguments (§§132–3). In the view of the AB, Art. 9.4 AD does not provide justification for considering all imports from non-examined producers as dumped for purposes of Art. 3 AD (§ 127). The AB did not explicitly state how to determine the volume of dumped imports in the case of a sample, but it did indicate that it was difficult to perceive of any other way than to do this on the basis of some extrapolation of the evidence relating to the investigated producers/exporters (§137).[61]

---

[61] Initially, the injury test in antidumping has been exclusively based on a 'trend' approach; that is, on descriptive explanations of the evolutions of the key variables in the antidumping case, namely the transaction prices for sales of the relevant imports and domestic products and the time series on imports, with a review of the individual transactions in case of alleged lost sales (Morkre and Kruth 1989; Prusa and Sharp 2001). Such trend analyses are necessary and useful, but they have a serious weakness: they are highly sensitive to subjective interpretations. One way to improve injury determination relies on modelling the market of a product (Boltuck 1991; Francois and Hall 1993). Such user-friendly models are based on pre-specified forms of domestic supply, foreign (import) supply, and domestic demand. They take the form of spreadsheets requiring analysts to fill up a few cells defining the initial situation (domestic and foreign sales, appropriate (constant) price elasticities, and so on) before letting the model run. The main limits of this approach are being confined to the market of the product in question (it is a partial equilibrium model even if there are more sophisticated versions) and being heavily dependent on initial data (price elasticities in particular). An alternative method consists of developing an econometric model of simultaneous relations (equations) of supply and demand. From the demand side, the price of the product under investigation may be stated as a function of several exogenous variables: for instance, the domestically

Price Effects: The above concludes our discussion regarding the evaluation of dumped imports. Recall that Art. 3.2 AD requires from an IA to consider the price effects of the increase in volume of dumped imports. In particular, an IA must inquire whether, as a result of increased dumped imports:

(a) price undercutting; or
(b) price suppression; or
(c) price depression has occurred.

The term 'price undercutting' refers to a situation where imported products are priced below domestic products. A 20 per cent differential was judged substantial in *EC—Tube or Pipe Fittings* (§7.268ff). The terms 'price suppression' and 'price depression' were the subject of interpretation by the AB in its report on *US—Upland Cotton*.[62] Although this case dealt with the interpretation of the two terms as they appear in the SCM Agreement, Panels dealing with the interpretation of the same terms in the context of the AD Agreement will in all likelihood defer to this report: the terms are identical in the two agreements and serve the same function as well. We quote from §§423–4 of the AB report on *US—Upland Cotton*:

> In explaining this term, the Panel stated, in paragraph 7.1277 of the Panel Report: Thus, *'price suppression'* refers to the situation where 'prices'—in terms of the 'amount of money set for sale of upland cotton' or the 'value or worth' of upland cotton—either are prevented or inhibited from rising (i.e. they do not increase when they otherwise would have) or they do actually increase, but the increase is less than it otherwise would have been. *Price depression* refers to the situation where 'prices' are pressed down, or reduced.
>
> Although the Panel first identified 'price suppression' and 'price depression' as two separate concepts in paragraph 7.1277, footnote 1388 of the Panel Report suggests

produced quantity, the price of the imported product from countries under investigation as well as for countries not included in the investigation, the quantities produced of goods derived from the product under investigation (for instance, of autos built from the investigated cold-rolled steel), and so on. From the supply side, the price of the product under investigation may be stated as a function of several exogenous variables: for instance, the domestically produced quantity (again), the available production capacity, the prices of the various materials important for producing the product under investigation, and so on. Well-oiled econometric techniques allow estimating the coefficients of each of the chosen exogenous variables, and checking whether the corresponding calculated (predicted) price fits well the observed evolution of the price. If this is the case, the coefficients of each of the exogenous variables give a sense of their relative impact on the price of the product investigated. In particular, the coefficient of the exogenous variable 'imports' gives a sense of whether imports have played a key role in the observed decline of the product price or not, that is, in the observed injury. The econometric approach offers a more encompassing analysis than the model approach to the extent that it is based on a wider range of information (it is not just limited to the market if the product is under investigation, but can include a wide range of variables, adapted to each case, from markets of related products). The negative aspects of the econometric approach are that the model may be mis-specified (for instance, a critical exogenous variable is not taken into consideration or not in an appropriate manner) and that it may require a lot of data. Because all the methods have strengths and weaknesses, the best approach is to see these frameworks as complementary, rather than substitutable, and to use the most appropriate one(s) for each case.

[62] See the discussion in Davey and Sapir (2010); see also Grossman and Sykes (2011).

that, for its analysis, the Panel used the term 'price suppression' to refer to both price suppression and price depression. We recognize that 'the situation where "prices"... are prevented or inhibited from rising' and 'the situation where "prices" are pressed down, or reduced' may overlap. Nevertheless, it would have been preferable, in our view, for the Panel to avoid using the term 'price suppression' as short-hand for both price suppression and price depression, given that Article 6.3(c) of the SCM Agreement refers to 'price suppression' and 'price depression' as distinct concepts. We agree, however, that the Panel's description of 'price suppression' in paragraph 7.1277 of the Panel Report reflects the ordinary meaning of that term, particularly when read in conjunction with the French and Spanish versions of Article 6.3(c), as required by Article 33(3) of the *Vienna Convention on the Law of Treaties* (the '*Vienna Convention*'). (italics in the original)[63]

Domestic Industry: Recall that Art. 3.2 AD also requires an IA to consider the effects of the increase in volume of dumped imports to the domestic industry producing the like product: this is what we qualified as an injury-to-competitors standard. The term 'like product' appears in various parts of the WTO Agreement and it does not necessarily have the same meaning across provisions and across covered agreements. Art. 4.1 AD defines the 'industry producing the like product' as follows:

> For the purposes of this Agreement, the term 'domestic industry' shall be interpreted as referring to the domestic producers as a whole of the like products or to those of them whose collective output of the products constitutes a major proportion of the total domestic production of those products.[64]

The term 'like product' is in turn defined in Art. 2.6 AD as follows:

> Throughout this Agreement the term 'like product' ('produit similaire') shall be interpreted to mean a product which is identical, i.e. alike in all respects to the product under consideration, or in the absence of such a product, another product which, although not alike in all respects, has characteristics closely resembling those of the product under consideration.[65]

An investigating authority would normally have some discretion (depending on the formulation of the category in the petition requesting initiation of the investigation) in defining what the like product is, since it is highly unlikely that two

---

[63] Price suppression and/or depression must be significant. The same report a few lines after the quoted paragraph makes it clear that, as in the case of price undercutting, price suppression/depression is significant if it is notable or important. In the absence of quantitative criteria, it is difficult to be precise here, but the idea most likely is that the counterfactual prices or the depressed prices are certainly above a *de minimis* threshold.

[64] Art. 4.1 AD adds: 'except that: (i) when producers are related to the exporters or importers or are themselves importers of the allegedly dumped product, the term "domestic industry" may be interpreted as referring to the rest of the producers.'

[65] The AD Agreement does not know of the category of DCS products that we have encountered in Chapter 4. Prima facie, this would mean that injury analysis will be facilitated for the IA since the impact of dumped imports will, other things equal, be greater the narrower the class of products that comes into the equation.

products will be identical, that is, alike in all respects. The choice, nevertheless, of whether to go for a narrower or broader definition is far from obvious. It might have the incentive to define like product in a narrow sense since, otherwise, subject country (-ies) could perform slight changes in the product specifications and avoid the AD order in place. However, the caveat would be that it would not want to expand the product definition too wide if doing so meant that there was no longer an increase in import volume: if, over the period of investigation, product x increased by 1 million tons and product y decreased by 1 million tons, then a broad scope would produce a flat import trend. That would hurt the injury case. Similarly, if product scope is broadened to avoid easy product shifting but some of the widened scope is not produced domestically, that also might hurt the domestic injury case.

One thing is clear though: the understanding of this term in the AD context is totally different from the case law interpretation of the term in Art. III GATT. It could, for example, be the case that the like product is defined as 'two-door motor vehicles'. Nothing in the AD Agreement obliges WTO Members to ask the question whether this definition is abusive and, consequently, whether consumers should be asked if they treat two- and four-door cars as like products. So, in theory, one could imagine an IA treating a Fiat Cinquecento (a rather low-priced car) and a Ferrari (a high-priced car) as falling under the same category; or it could be that domestic industry produces two goods A and B, as does the exporter, and that both A and B are DCS (in the GATT-sense of the term) goods and still the petition requests that an AD investigation is initiated in order to eventually impose duties against A (even if we assume that the domestic industry is profitable in the B market). Indeed, two Panels had to deal with this question and, although on both occasions Panelists showed some sympathy for the claim that the products under investigation had been defined in an unduly restrictive manner, none of them questioned the IA's discretion on this score.[66] The only way in which the IA's discretion could be brought into question is through the requirement to make due allowances for factors affecting price comparability under Art. 2.4 AD: in the Cinquecento/Ferrari example, one could construct this requirement so as to impose on an IA to control for differences in the size of the motor etc.

Recently, however, in a case involving claims that certain practices constituted illegal subsidies, the AB followed a different attitude when discussing like products. In *EC and Certain Member States—Large Civil Aircraft*, the AB was facing a claim by the US that EU subsidies had displaced US aircraft from world markets. Displacement is one of the grounds for establishing 'serious prejudice' as we will see in the section on subsidies in this chapter. According to the SCM Agreement, like products might be displaced as a result of subsidization. The Panel had defined

---

[66] See the Panel reports on *EC—Salmon (Norway)* at §§7.13–76; *US—Softwood Lumber V* at §§7.139–58.

the market as comprising all aircraft produced by Boeing and Airbus, the duopoly in large aircraft. The EU objected to this market definition and appealed against the Panel's findings in this respect, arguing that finer distinctions across the various aircraft types should be made since they do not all compete in the same relevant product market (§1113).[67] The AB first noted the 'like product' definition in the SCM Agreement which is identical to that in the AD Agreement (§1118). It then went on to agree with the EU argument finding in §§1119–20:

> We construe the concept of displacement as relating to, and arising out of, competitive engagement between products in a market. Aggressive pricing of certain products may, for example, lead to displacement of exports or imports in a particular market. This, however, can only be the case if those products compete in the same market. An examination of the competitive relationship between products is therefore required so as to determine whether such products form part of the same market. We conclude therefore that a 'market', within the meaning of Articles 6.3 (a) and 6.3(b) of the *SCM Agreement*, is a set of products in a particular geographical area that are in actual or potential competition with each other. An assessment of the competitive relationship between products in the market is required in order to determine whether and to what extent one product may displace another. Thus, while a complaining Member may identify a subsidized product and the like product by reference to footnote 46, the products thereby identified must be analyzed under the discipline of the product market so as to be able to determine whether displacement is occurring. Ordinarily, the subsidized product and the like product will form part of a larger product market. But it may be the case that a complainant chooses to define the subsidized and like products so broadly that it is necessary to analyze these products in different product markets. This will be necessary so as to analyze further the real competitive interactions that are taking place, and thereby determine whether displacement is occurring
>
> ... Indeed, whether two products compete in the same market is not determined simply by assessing whether they share particular physical characteristics or have the same general uses; it may also be relevant to consider whether customers demand a range of products or whether they are interested in only a particular product type. In the former case, when customers procure a range of products to satisfy their needs, this may give an indication that all such products could be competing in the same market.

The AB went on to state that both demand as well as supply substitutability is relevant in establishing whether two goods are like (§1121). In light of this case law, and because of the fact that the 'like product' definition is identical in the AD and the SCM context, one cannot exclude that this line of thinking might find application in future practice in the AD context as well.

The term 'major proportion' has not been interpreted in any meaningful way so far.[68] The Panel, in its report on *Argentina—Poultry Antidumping Duties*, rejected

---

[67] In antitrust analysis, one usually distinguishes between short, medium, and long haul.

[68] This provision has some relevance in this context: Art. 5.4 AD, as we will see *infra*, requires that at least 25 per cent of the domestic industry support a petition to initiate an AD investigation.

the argument that the term 'major proportion' implies that such producers must account for at least 50 per cent of total domestic production; it sufficed that the domestic producers that constitute the domestic industry for purposes of the AD investigation represent (§7.341):

> an important, serious or significant proportion of total domestic production.[69]

The Agreement further does not allow an IA to investigate the part of the industry that better suits its case. In *US—Hot Rolled Steel*, the AB held as much (§204):

> Different parts of an industry may exhibit quite different economic performance during any given period. Some parts may be performing well, while others are performing poorly. To examine only the poorly performing parts of an industry, even if coupled with an examination of the whole industry, may give a misleading impression of the data relating to the industry as a whole, and may overlook positive developments in other parts of the industry. Such an examination may result in highlighting the negative data in the poorly performing part, without drawing attention to the positive data in other parts of the industry. We note that the reverse may also be true—to examine only the parts of an industry which are performing well may lead to overlooking the significance of deteriorating performance in other parts of the industry.[70]

In *EC—Fasteners (China)*, the AB outlawed an EU decision to examine only 27 per cent of the Chinese fasteners' industry, finding that this percentage does not constitute a major proportion (§430). The AB objected to the EU practice of restricting its review to sampled producers only even though Chinese producers, other than those sampled, had provided the EU authority with information about the case. As a result, the AB found the EU decision to be contrary to Art. 4.1 AD. In doing that, it provided its understanding, albeit not in crystal-clear terms, of what 'major proportion' is (§419):

> In sum, a proper interpretation of the term 'a major proportion' under Article 4.1 requires that the domestic industry defined on this basis encompass producers whose collective output represents a relatively high proportion that substantially reflects the total domestic production. This ensures that the injury determination is based on wide-ranging information regarding domestic producers and is not distorted or skewed. In the special case of a fragmented industry with numerous producers, the practical constraints on an authority's ability to obtain information may mean that what constitutes 'a major proportion' may be lower than what is ordinarily permissible in a less fragmented industry. However, even in such cases, the authority bears the same obligation to ensure that the process of defining the domestic industry does not give rise to a material risk of distortion.

Note, however, that the panel in *Argentina—Poultry Antidumping Duties* rejected the parallel with the *standing* requirement of Art. 5.4 AD; see § 7.341 and footnote 221.

[69] It has been proposed in the course of the Doha round negotiations to change this language and require that the domestic producers in question represent more than 50 per cent of total domestic output; WTO Docs. TN/RL/GEN/27; TN/RL/GEN/62.

[70] See also the AB report on *US—Cotton Yarn* at §§100–1.

The Panel, in its report on *Mexico—Steel Pipes and Tubes*, found that Mexico had failed to comply with this requirement as it had analysed a number of economic injury factors with respect to three firms representing 88 per cent of the national production, while its analysis of financial injury factors was based on only one firm constituting 53 per cent of national production only (§7.322). In other words, once a determination has been made as to which producers constitute the domestic industry for purposes of the investigation, and assuming of course that they represent a major proportion of the industry, it is the data from all of these producers that must be used to assess the impact of the dumped imports on the domestic industry.

The AD Agreement provides that it is possible to exclude from the definition of the domestic industry those producers who are related to the exporters or importers, or are themselves importers of the allegedly dumped product. The rationale for this provision is that these producers may not be representative, as they may be benefiting from the success of the dumped imports themselves. The term 'related' is defined in the Agreement (footnote 11) in terms of control: a company shall be deemed to control another, when the former is legally or operationally in a position to exercise restraint or direction over the latter. The fact that a producer is controlled by, or itself controls, an exporter or an importer does not suffice: there must also be grounds for believing or suspecting that the effect of the relationship is such as to cause the producer to behave differently from non-related producers. The AD Agreement does not provide for a certain minimum amount of imports that needs to be made by a domestic producer so as to allow the IA to exclude this producer from the investigation.[71]

Art. 3.4 contains an indicative list of factors that an IA must go through in order to satisfy the injury requirement of the AD Agreement. The list of factors included in Art. 3.4 AD seems to combine both indicators of the state of the domestic industry (such as sales, profits, output, market share, productivity, return on investments, and capacity utilization), and factors which may be relevant in resolving the causation question (such as factors affecting domestic prices or the magnitude of the margin of dumping). The Panel, in its report on *Egypt—Steel Rebar*, held that Art. 3.4 AD does not require a full causation analysis, and stated that (§7.62):

as a whole, these factors are more in the nature of effects than causes.[72]

---

[71] A proposal has been put forward to limit the discretion of the IA to exclude domestic producers from the injury determination where the total import value made by the producer is relatively low compared to its sales, or where the imports in question relate to a few models of the like product and were made to fill the gaps in its range of products; WTO Doc. TN/RL/GEN/62.

[72] In similar vein, the Panel on *EC—Tube or Pipe Fittings* rejected a number of Brazilian arguments which, in its view, blurred the boundaries between Art. 3.4 AD, and Art. 3.5 AD, the forum for causation analysis (§7.335).

A number of Panel[73] and AB reports[74] have held that all factors included in Art. 3.4 AD must be addressed in an investigation, although the provision explicitly states that none of them by itself or in combination with other factors mentioned therein is necessarily decisive for the outcome of the analysis.[75]

The AB, in its report on *EC—Tube or Pipe Fittings*, held that, even though in its decision to impose duties the EU had not explicitly referred to one of the factors mentioned in Art. 3.4 AD, it sufficed for the purposes of consistency with Art. 3.4 AD that it had implicitly examined it. In the case at hand, the EU had not reflected in its order a separate examination of growth, a factor listed in Art. 3.4 AD. It was clear from the record, however, that the IA had taken into account this factor (§§ 161–2). It is the overall record of the investigation that matters and not simply the final decision when it comes to deciding whether an IA has examined all factors reflected in Art. 3.4 AD.[76] Mere reference to each one of them, on the other hand, does not suffice for a WTO Member to absolve its obligations under Art. 3.4 AD. The Panel on *EC—Tube or Pipe Fittings* made it clear that such behaviour was WTO-inconsistent (§ 7.310). In the eyes of this Panel, an evaluation of the data is required (§7.314). In the same vein, the AB, in its report on *US—Lamb*,[77] indicated that an explanation of why factors which would seem to lead in the opposite direction (that is, no material injury) do not, overall, undermine the conclusion of material injury is necessary for an IA to be deemed in compliance with its obligations (§106):

> Panels must, therefore, review whether the competent authorities' explanation fully addresses the nature, and, especially, the complexities, of the data, and responds to

---

[73] See e.g. *Egypt—Steel Rebar* at §7.36; *EC—Bed Linen* at §6.159; *Mexico—Corn Syrup* at §7.128; *EC—Tube or Pipe Fittings* at §7.304.

[74] See the AB report on *Thailand—H-Beams* at §125.

[75] In other words, not each and every injury factor must be indicative of injury and it is thus not necessary that all factors show negative trends (Art. 3.4 AD, last sentence); see the Panel report on *EC—Bed Linen* (*Article 21.5—India*) at §6.213.

[76] Note, however, that in previous cases Panels had expressed the view that the consideration of the factors in Art. 3.4 AD must be apparent in the determination, so as to enable the Panel to assess whether the IA acted in accordance with Art. 3.4 AD at the time of the investigation; see the Panel reports on *Guatemala—Cement II* (§8.283); *EC—Bed Linen*, (§6.162). It is in *Egypt—Steel Rebar* where the Panel first emphasized the importance of the written record even outside the final determination(§7.49):If there is no such written record—whether in the disclosure documents, in the published determination, or in other internal documents—of how certain factors have been interpreted or appreciated by an investigating authority during the course of the investigation, there is no basis on which a Member can rebut a prima facie case that its 'evaluation' under Article 3.4 was inadequate or did not take place at all. In particular, without a written record of the analytical process undertaken by the investigating authority, a panel would be forced to embark on a post hoc speculation about the thought process by which an investigating authority arrived at its ultimate conclusions as to the impact of the dumped imports on the domestic industry. A speculative exercise by a panel is something that the special standard of review in Article 17.6 is intended to prevent.

[77] Although the AB, in this report, dealt with claims under the SG Agreement, its findings are relevant for claims made under the AD Agreement, in light of the similarity of the subject-matter.

other plausible interpretations of that data. A panel must find, in particular, that an explanation is not reasoned, or is not adequate, if some alternative explanation of the facts is plausible, and if the competent authorities' explanation does not seem adequate in the light of that alternative explanation. Thus, in making an 'objective assessment' of a claim under Article 4.2(a), panels must be open to the possibility that the explanation given by the competent authorities is not reasoned or adequate.

Note, finally, that an IA must examine all relevant economic factors, and not only those mentioned in Art. 3.4 AD. In the words of the AB (*US—Hot-Rolled Steel*, §194):

> Article 3.4 lists certain factors which are deemed to be relevant in every investigation and which must always be evaluated by the investigating authorities. However, the obligation of evaluation imposed on investigating authorities, by Article 3.4, is not confined to the listed factors, but extends to 'all relevant economic factors'.[78]

Injury analysis will normally take place with respect to dumped imports originating in a particular WTO Member. It could be the case, though, that injury is caused by dumped imports originating in various WTO Members, and in this case an IA might want to perform cumulative injury analysis: in this case, Art. 3.3 AD imposes certain disciplines on an IA that conducts similar analysis. It provides that an IA may only cumulate the effects of imports simultaneously subject to an AD investigation if it determines that:

(a) The margin of dumping established in relation to the imports from each country is more than *de minimis* (>2 per cent) and the volume of imports from each country is not negligible (>3 per cent); and
(b) Such a cumulative assessment of the effects of the imports is appropriate in light of the conditions of competition between the imported products from the various countries examined and the conditions of competition between the imported products and the like domestic product.

The AB, in its report on *EC—Tube or Pipe Fittings*, upheld the Panel's finding that cumulation is only possible after a prior country-specific analysis of volume and price effects of dumped imports, that is, after checking the conditions of competition in the marketplace. In other words, the determination of a significant increase in dumped imports and significant price effects may be based on an examination of the volume and price of dumped imports from all cumulated countries

---

[78] We will discuss the obligation of an IA to look for factors other than those mentioned in the body of Art. 3.4 AD, and examine their impact in the context of our discussion on the causality requirement, *infra*.

together. The AB justified its approach by looking at the rationale for cumulation (§§116–17).[79]

Note that there is no provision in the AD Agreement allowing for sampling in the context of injury analysis. Yet, as briefly discussed *supra*, this is what happened in an EU investigation: in *EU—Footwear (China)*, the Panel held that the absence of a specific provision does not per se outlaw sampling; the sampled companies must be representative of the whole and, in this vein, volume of production is a relevant but should not be the sole criterion. The Panel, alas, did not identify other criteria (§§7.368ff and especially 7.381ff).[80]

2.2.5 *Threat of Injury*

Art. 3.7 AD sets forth the requirements that an IA has to comply with in the case of a threat of injury examination:

(a) A determination of threat of injury must be based on facts, and not merely on allegations, conjecture, or a remote possibility;

(b) The expected injury must be imminent and clearly foreseen;[81]

(c) A certain number of factors be considered by the authority concerning

  a. whether dumped imports have been increasing at a significant rate which indicates the likelihood of substantially increased importation;

  b. whether there is sufficiently freely disposable or an imminent substantial increase in the capacity of the exporter indicating a likelihood of substantially increased dumped exports;

  c. whether the prices of the dumped imports are such that they have a significant price-depressing or suppressing effect on domestic prices and would therefore likely increase demand for further imports; and

  d. the state of the inventories of the subject product.[82]

The totality of these factors must lead to the conclusion that further dumped exports are imminent and that, unless protective action is taken, material injury would occur. According to the Panel on *US—Softwood Lumber VI*, an IA is required to consider these factors, in the same way as it is required to consider

---

[79] See also the Panel report on *EU—Footwear (China)* at §§7.404ff.

[80] See also the Panel report on *EC—Salmon* at §§7.125ff.

[81] According to the Panel on *US—Softwood Lumber VI*, the change in circumstances that would give rise to a situation in which injury would occur encompasses a single event, or a series of events, or developments in the situation of the industry, and/or concerning the dumped or subsidized imports, which lead to the conclusion that injury which has not yet occurred can be predicted to occur imminently (§7.57).

[82] Because the AD Agreement uses the term 'should' in the context of the factors listed in Art. 3.7 AD, the Panel on *US—Softwood Lumber VI* was of the view that, unlike the situation under Art. 3.4 AD, consideration of each of the factors listed in Art. 3.7 AD is not mandatory. According to this Panel, whether a violation of Art. 3.7 AD exists would depend on the particular facts of the case, in light of the totality of the factors considered and the explanations given; see §7.68.

the volume and price effects of dumped imports in Art. 3.2 AD (§7.67). The Panel on *Mexico—Corn Syrup* held that the factors listed in Art. 3.7 AD relate specifically to the question of the likelihood of increased imports, and do not relate to the consequent impact of the dumped imports on the domestic industry. An examination of the factors listed in Art. 3.7 AD only does not, consequently, suffice to reach a threat determination. In this construction, Art. 3.7 AD sets out factors that must be considered in a threat case, but does not eliminate the obligation to consider the impact of dumped imports on the domestic industry in accordance with the requirements of Art. 3.4 AD (§7.126). This Panel summarized the relationship between Arts. 3.1, 3.4 and 3.7 AD in the following manner (§§7.131–2):

> In sum, we consider that Article 3.7 requires a determination whether material injury would occur, Article 3.1 requires that a determination of injury, including threat of injury, involve an examination of the impact of imports, and Article 3.4 sets out the factors that must be considered, among other relevant factors, in the examination of the impact of imports on the domestic industry. Thus, in our view, the text of the AD Agreement requires consideration of the Article 3.4 factors in a threat determination. Article 3.7 sets out additional factors that must be considered in a threat case, but does not eliminate the obligation to consider the impact of dumped imports on the domestic industry in accordance with the requirements of Article 3.4.
>
> . . . an investigating authority cannot come to a reasoned conclusion, based on an unbiased and objective evaluation of the facts, without taking into account the Article 3.4 factors relating to the impact of imports on the domestic industry. These factors all relate to an evaluation of the general condition and operations of the domestic industry—sales, profits, output, market share, productivity, return on investments, utilization of capacity, factors affecting domestic prices, cash flow, inventories, employment, wages, growth, ability to raise capital. Consideration of these factors is, in our view, necessary in order to establish a background against which the investigating authority can evaluate whether imminent further dumped imports will affect the industry's condition in such a manner that material injury would occur in the absence of protective action, as required by Article 3.7.

The Panel on *US—Softwood Lumber VI* agreed with this view, but did not consider that an IA, once it had examined and evaluated the factors mentioned in Art. 3.4 AD, was required to make projections as to the likely impact of future dumped imports on each of these factors (§7.105). Nor would it be necessary, according to this Panel, for an IA to re-examine the factors mentioned in Art. 3.2 AD concerning volume and price effect of dumped imports in a predictive context in making a threat of material injury determination (§7.111). In sum, it suffices for an IA to conduct an injury examination on the basis of Arts. 3.2 and 3.4 AD, and to consider in addition some or all of the factors mentioned in Art. 3.7 AD in order to be able to conclude that further dumped imports are imminent and that, unless protective action is taken, material injury would occur.

The term 'threat of injury' per construction suggests the future, as opposed to actual, occurrence of an event. As with all future events, some degree of uncertainty is unavoidable. Art. 3.7 AD makes it clear, nevertheless, that a determination of threat of injury should not be based on pure conjecture or remote possibility; it should be based on facts. The AB, in its report on *Mexico—Corn Syrup (Article 21.5—US)*, provided its understanding as to the applicable standard of review (§136):

> In our view, the 'establishment' of facts by investigating authorities includes both affirmative findings of events that took place during the period of investigation as well as assumptions relating to such events made by those authorities in the course of their analyses. In determining the existence of a threat of material injury, the investigating authorities will necessarily have to make assumptions relating to 'the 'occurrence of future events' since such *future* events 'can never be definitively proven by facts". Notwithstanding this intrinsic uncertainty, a 'proper establishment' of facts in a determination of threat of material injury must be based on events that, although they have not yet occurred, must be 'clearly foreseen and imminent', in accordance with Article 3.7 of the *Antidumping Agreement.* (italics and emphasis in the original)

Consequently, the AB takes the view that an IA can lawfully have recourse to threat of injury in order to justify imposition of AD duties, only if the injury is imminent in the short run and not an event which could, speculatively, occur in the distant future. According to the Panel on *US—Softwood Lumber VI*, this implies that (§7.33):

> a degree of attention over and above that required of investigating authorities in all antidumping and countervailing duty injury cases is required in the context of cases involving threat of material injury.

In the same vein, the AB on *US—Softwood Lumber VI (Article 21.5—Canada)* held that any conclusion that there is a greater likelihood that a Panel will uphold a threat of injury determination rather than a determination of current material injury, when those determinations rest on the same level of evidence, would be erroneous (§110). In its view, a Panel, when reviewing the factual basis for a threat of injury determination, must determine (§98):

> whether the investigating authority has provided 'a reasoned and adequate explanation' of:
> (a) how individual pieces of evidence can be reasonably relied on in support of particular inferences, and how the evidence in the record supports its factual findings;
> (b) how the facts in the record, rather than allegation, conjecture, or remote possibility, support and provide a basis for the overall threat of injury determination;
> (c) how its projections and assumptions show a high degree of likelihood that the anticipated injury will materialize in the near future; and
> (d) how it examined alternative explanations and interpretations of the evidence and why it chose to reject or discount such alternatives in coming to its conclusions.

2.2.6 Public Interest Clause

Art. 6.12 AD reads:

> The authorities shall provide opportunities for industrial users of the product under investigation, and for representative consumer organizations in cases where the product is commonly sold at the retail level, to provide information which is relevant to the investigation regarding dumping, injury and causality.

Consumers, of course, have antithetical interests to those of producers regarding the reaction to dumping. Industrial users should also be on the side of consumers (unless otherwise linked to domestic producers). Hence, an IA will in all likelihood be providing enemies of antidumping action with a forum. Still, one should not read too much in this provision, which does not at all put into question the injury-to-competitors standard: all an IA has to do is invite their opinions; it is under no obligation whatsoever to take them on board.

Some WTO Members go a bit further, in particular, the EU[83] and Canada: they have imposed an additional requirement on themselves to examine whether the imposition of duties would not be against the public interest. The public-interest test, or the Community-interest test as it used to be called in the EU, requires the IA to examine whether the negative effects of an AD duty on consumers would not be disproportionate to the advantage of the protection offered to the domestic industry. In practice, nevertheless, it has been not proved effective at halting antidumping actions; the main reason for this outcome is that the Court (ECJ) has adopted a deferential standard of review regarding the Commission definition of public interest and will not disturb similar findings except in the most egregious violations of EU law. The most representative cases concern instances where the interests of industrial users, rather than consumers at large, were at stake. For example, Hoekman and Mavroidis (1996a) discuss the *Extramet* jurisprudence, where the Court overturned an imposition of AD duties because the Commission had overlooked the interests of an industrial user.[84] The EU market for the downstream good was a duopoly, while one of the two companies involved (Péchiney) was also producing the basic input (calcium metal) for the downstream good (pure calcium, mainly used in the metallurgical industry). It refused to sell calcium metal to its competitor (Extramet), which was forced to import it from China. At the request of Péchiney, the Commission of the EU investigated Chinese exports of calcium metal, found them to be dumped, and, as a result of dumping, that Péchiney had been injured. The imposition of AD duties had nefarious effects on Extramet. Extramet initiated proceedings against Péchiney, accusing it of abuse of dominant position, and also against the EU Council for imposing AD duties without properly taking into account that

---

[83] Hoekman and Mavroidis (1996a) discuss the EU practice in detail.
[84] C-358/89, Judgment of the Court of 11 June 1992, ECJ Reports I-3843ff.

Péchiney, by its refusal to sell calcium metal, had contributed to the injury it subsequently suffered. The Court held that, in this case, the EU Council had not properly controlled for the reasons behind the injury suffered by Péchiney and annulled the AD duties imposed.[85] There are no reported cases where consumer organizations managed to undo the imposition of an AD order in the name of the public interest, though.

2.2.7 *The Causality Requirement*

Classic legal analysis would ask the question whether dumped imports are a sufficient cause (*causa adequata*), or whether absent dumped imports, there would be no injury (*conditio sine qua non*). The former test involves some value judgment; the latter is reminiscent of the 'but for' approach, used in economics, although it does not capture the full economics test since it is limited to asking the question whether there was a break in the causality chain or not. Economists would proceed to establish causality, either through direct estimation, or through establishing the counterfactual ('but for' approach). The most common method used for direct estimation purposes is regression analysis, where one estimates the relationship between a dependent and a series of independent (explanatory) variables. As Sapir and Trachtman (2008) have noted, the intuition behind the counterfactual (but for) approach is the close association which is being made between a cause of an event and a *sine qua non* condition of its occurrence. Here a cause is the condition 'but for' which the effect would not have occurred.

The key issue here is how to construct the counterfactual. economists either use trend analysis, where it is assumed that today's world is a continuation of yesterday's world, or empirical models. There are two categories of such models: econometric models, which use statistical techniques to test their validity, and calibration models (simulation) which take them for granted. Their differences, nevertheless, should not be exaggerated since (some of) the assumptions of calibration models are based on econometric estimations.[86] Grossman (1986), for example, uses an econometric model, the multivariate analysis, in order to analyse the true causes of injury in the US steel industry. His purpose is to control for a third factor, i.e. to see whether the variables still move together when the influence of other variables has been removed.[87]

In contingent protection cases, economists will often have recourse to *Granger* causality, whereby they will test whether one variable consistently precedes another. This method requires many observations of both the dependent and

---

[85] This case is one of the few cases where imports are treated as endogenous and not exogenous, and the Court tries to understand what drives imports instead of demonizing them. This is something that WTO courts do not do when deciding on causality as we will see *infra* in this chapter.

[86] See, on this score, Kelly (1988) and Irwin (2003).

[87] See Greene (1993) at pp. 486–507, and for a practical application, see Grossman (1986). The manner in which the model is constructed is the key, however.

the independent variables, otherwise it might not be statistically reliable. It could thus be used in the context of AD, where, usually,[88] many transactions are observed, but not in the context of subsidization. So, instead of asking if A caused B, we try to show that if A had not occurred, B would not have occurred either.[89] Granger tests could also be used to check both directions (e.g., A->B, or B->A). One lesson from Grossman's paper cited above is that we really need to know if there is a third variable (say, C) which causes both A and B. Now, from an economic perspective, this point is correct and the question arises whether that is the case from a legal perspective as well. In other words, is there a legal statutory requirement to treat imports as endogenous? Consider the following example. Suppose we know that bad union contracts are weakening the steel industry and that, as a result, the unions make the domestic industry unprofitable and inefficient. The contracts make it hard for the firms to upgrade their technology (perhaps because they cannot lay off workers). The union contracts also result in 'import pull' as consumers turn to foreign countries for more technologically advanced steel. As a result, policy-makers see both negative profits and higher imports. By themselves, imports are not sufficient to cause injury. But, absent imports, the industry might seek out a small profit. Does the law require the investigating authorities to consider that imports are endogenous? The correct response seems to be negative, as we shall see in what immediately follows.

The causality obligation is embedded in Art. 3.5 AD which imposes a dual obligation on an IA to show that injury is:

(a) Attributed to dumped imports; and
(b) Not attributed to factors other than dumped imports.

The requirement under (b) is often referred to as non-attribution. Under this requirement, an IA will be required to examine the impact of all 'known factors', other than dumped imports, on the state of the domestic industry, and must ensure that injury caused by such factors is not attributed to dumped imports. The last sentence of Art. 3.5 AD contains an indicative list of factors that may appropriately be taken into account in the context of this exercise:

> Factors which may be relevant in this respect include, *inter alia*, the volume and prices of imports not sold at dumping prices, contraction in demand or changes in the patterns of consumption, trade restrictive practices of and competition between the foreign and domestic producers, developments in technology and the export performance and productivity of the domestic industry. (italics in the original)

---

[88] Its relevance in the context of targeted dumping, that is, in cases, for example, of dumped seasonal goods, might be questionable. In such cases, we might be observing one or very few export transactions.

[89] There are limits to the usefulness of this method if three or more variables are at stake.

Case law has confirmed that this list is of an indicative character.[90] Case law has also clarified that a factor is known as soon as it has been raised by a party.[91] In its report on *EC into question—Tube or Pipe Fittings*, the AB added that it is irrelevant if an interested party has raised a factor at one stage of the investigation only and not consistently throughout the investigation. What matters is whether a factor was raised or not (§178). Case law has, consequently, limited the ambit of 'known factors' to factors produced by interested parties during the investigation process, thus limiting the duty of an IA to search for information. This could on occasion be problematic since exporters might not have access to key information. The IA is thus construed as an arbiter between divergent interests and not as a public prosecutor aiming to unearth the truth. Note, nonetheless, that in *US—Wheat Gluten*, a safeguard case as we shall see *infra* in this chapter, the AB suggested that an IA cannot remain passive and rely only on evidence produced by the parties to the dispute. The reason why we do not confidently state here that the same standard should apply to AD investigations (as much as we would like this to be the case) has to do with the difference in wording across the two agreements. Whereas the Safeguard (SG) Agreement requests from an IA to evaluate all relevant factors; the AD Agreement imposes a requirement to examine known factors only.

According to the AB report on *US—Hot-Rolled Steel*, the non-attribution obligation requires from an IA to separate and distinguish the effects of dumped imports from the effects of any other factor on the domestic industry producing the like product (§223). This implies that the nature and extent of the injurious effects of the other known factors need to be identified (§227).[92] The AB conceded that the discipline imposed is quite demanding for any bureaucracy (§228). The next question naturally deals with the methodology to use in order to separate and distinguish the effects from various factors. Where an IA is facing a situation where more than one factor is simultaneously (potentially) influencing an outcome, the AB (*US—Hot-Rolled Steel*, §224) was of the view that an IA can choose any methodology it deems useful in order to disentangle the effects of the various factors causing injury.[93] Next, the AB had to face the question whether the impact of factors other than dumped imports should be examined both individually and collectively. The AB addressed this issue in its report on *EC—Tube or Pipe Fittings*. In the AB's view, an affirmative response to this question would depend on the circumstances of the case. In other words, an assessment of the collective effects of other causal factors is not necessarily required in every case, but it might be necessary in order to honour the non-attribution obligation depending on the

---

[90] Panel report on *EC—Tube or Pipe Fittings* at §7.359.

[91] *EC—Tube or Pipe Fittings*, Panel report at §7.359.

[92] Implicitly, the agreement requests economic and not statistical significance; on the difference between the two terms, see McCloskey and Ziliak (1996).

[93] In this vein, see also the Panel report on *EC—Tube or Pipe Fittings* at §7.366.

facts of the case. The AB did not provide any examples of circumstances that would make such an evaluation a compulsory requirement (§§191–2).[94]

Art. 3.2 AD does not set forth any particular methodology for conducting a price analysis and deciding whether price undercutting, price depression or suppression has been caused by dumped imports either. Panels have, thus, rejected arguments that the analysis is to take place at a particular level of trade (*Egypt—Steel Rebar* (§7.73)), on a quarterly basis (*Thailand—H-Beams* (§7.168)), or over a particular period of time (*Guatemala—Cement II* (§8.266)). More specifically, with regard to the price effect analysis, the Panel on *EC—Tube or Pipe Fittings* rejected the suggestion that an IA must base its price-undercutting analysis on a methodology that offsets undercutting prices with overcutting prices, and calculate one single margin of undercutting based on an examination of every transaction involving the product concerned and the like product. According to the Panel, to do so would have the result of requiring from the IA to conclude that no price undercutting existed when, in fact, there might be a considerable number of sales at prices which might have had an adverse effect on the domestic industry (§7.276). This would not have been in line with the purpose of the price-undercutting analysis (§7.277).

At the end of the day, as dozens of reports have confirmed, what matters is whether there is a genuine and substantial relationship of cause and effect between dumping and injury. Once injury has been shown to have been caused, at least partially, by dumped imports, the whole injury analysis becomes moot for the remaining part of the process: AD duties, as will be shown *infra*, will be imposed to counteract the dumping margin and not the resulting injury for the domestic industry producing the like product. So, although the obligation to disentangle effects of various factors might seem onerous, once dumping has been shown to cause some injury, the AD authority can leave the injury analysis behind it and concentrate on counteracting the established dumping margin.

2.2.8 Lesser Duty Rule

WTO Members at the end of the investigation and upon satisfaction of the substantive requirements mentioned above can impose definitive AD duties. The level of AD duties can, but does not have to be, equal to the established dumping margin; it can be lower, if a lower duty can adequately take care of the injury caused by dumping.

The possibility of a lesser duty (that is, a duty which would be less than the full dumping margin, but enough to counteract the resulting injury) exists in the AD Agreement (Art. 9.1 of the AD). It is, however, a best endeavours clause, that is, there is no obligation to observe the lesser duty rule:

---

[94] On EC AD practice in this respect, see Vermulst (1996).

It is *desirable* that the imposition be permissive in the territory of all Members, and that the duty be less than the margin if such lesser duty would be adequate to remove the injury to the domestic industry. (emphasis added)

The decision to impose a lesser duty than the dumping margin depends solely on the investigating authority. The idea is that, to the extent a lesser duty (than the established dumping margin) suffices to take care of the injury suffered, WTO Members should (but must not) impose a duty at this level and avoid making use of their right to impose a higher duty (and thus disturb even more trade flows). The lesser duty role is thus a consequence of the fact that dumping is not illegal but simply unfair, and it should not always be punished as such as long as its nefarious consequences (injury) have been eliminated.

Although not a matter of legal compulsion under WTO law, some jurisdictions, and most prominently the EU, have adhered to this rule and consistently observe it in their antidumping practice.[95]

2.2.9 Provisional Duties (Provisional Measures)

WTO Members can, when the following conditions included in Art. 7 AD have been met, impose provisional measures:

(a) No provisional duties can be imposed sooner than 60 days from the date of initiation of the investigation (Art. 7.3 AD);
(b) Parties must have had an opportunity to present their views during the course of the investigation up to that stage (Art. 7.1(i) AD);
(c) An affirmative preliminary determination of dumping and consequent injury to the industry has been made (Art. 7.1(ii)AD). Note that there is no absolute requirement to make preliminary determinations, but absent preliminary determinations, provisional duties cannot be lawfully applied;
(d) Preliminary duties are judged necessary to prevent injury caused during the investigation (Art. 7.1(iii)AD);

The duties imposed should preferably be in the form of security (cash deposit or bond), although additional customs duties remain a possibility (Art. 7.2 AD). The level of such duties shall not be higher than the provisionally estimated margin of dumping. Art. 7.4 AD regulates the period for provisional duties in the following manner and limits its application to, in principle, four months, and, assuming a request by exporters representing a significant percentage of the trade involved, up to six months. The Panel on *Mexico—Corn Syrup*[96] found that the application of provisional measures by Mexico for more than six months was inconsistent with Art. 7.4 AD (§7.183).

---

[95] On EU practice on this score, see Vermulst and Waer (1997). A proposal has been tabled in the Doha round in favour of mandatory application of the lesser duty rule; see WTO Doc. TN/RL/GEN/99 of 3 March 2006. The US issued a negative reaction; see WTO Doc. TN/RL/GEN/58.
[96] Howse and Neven (2007b) discuss this report in detail.

2.2.10 *Price Undertakings*

Instead of imposing AD duties, WTO Members can request and/or accept price undertakings from willing exporters (Art. 8 AD): through a price undertaking, an exporter agrees to raise prices up to the level of the dumping margin, or up to the level established in application of the lesser duty rule, if the investigating authority agrees to this latter level. Price undertakings may not be offered to exporters until a preliminary affirmative determination of dumping, injury, and the causal link has been made. There is no obligation to offer price undertakings nor is there an obligation to accept such undertakings when offered by exporters, if the authorities consider their acceptance impractical, or for other reasons including reasons of general policy. The Panel on *US—Offset Act (Byrd Amendment)* emphasized the freedom of the IA to accept or reject price undertakings, holding that an IA is not required to examine a proposed price undertaking in an objective manner (§7.81). The Panel thus rejected the argument that the incentive provided through the so-called 'Byrd payments',[97] combined with the important role given to the US domestic industry in accepting an undertaking from exporters, in tandem violated Art. 8 AD (§7.80). It follows that both the IA and the exporters/producers concerned are completely free to propose, accept, or reject price undertakings.

The acceptance of a price undertaking puts an end to the investigation with respect to the exporter concerned, unless this exporter wants the IA to continue with the investigation. In case of continuation, if the investigation ultimately leads to a negative finding of dumping or injury, the undertaking shall automatically lapse, except in cases where a negative determination is in large part due to the price undertaking itself, in which case the undertaking may be maintained for a reasonable period of time.

Art. 8.6 AD provides for a monitoring device and allows an IA to request exporters to provide information periodically relevant to the fulfilment of the undertaking, thus permitting verification. In case of a violation of an agreed undertaking, the IA is entitled to take expeditious actions, which may include the immediate application of provisional measures using best information available. Definitive duties may be levied retroactively up to 90 days before the application of such provisional measures. No duties may be levied on imports pre-dating the violation.

Price undertakings operate like a voluntary export restraint (VER): by raising prices, exporters will limit, other things equal, the volume of exports. We discuss the incentives for exporters to accept VERs *infra* in this chapter when we discuss safeguards.

---

[97] We discuss the incentive in more detail *infra*. Suffice to state here that, according to the challenged measure, only US companies supporting a petition to impose AD duties would subsequently profit from disbursement of duties if the end of the process were to lead to the imposition of AD duties.

2.2.11 *Definitive Duties*

A duty becomes definitive when the IA issues its final determination (*Mexico—Antidumping Measures on Rice*, AB, §345). As the AB noted in the same report (§346):

> the [AD and SCM] Agreements use the term 'definitive' to distinguish duties imposed after a final determination (following an investigation) from 'provisional' duties that may be imposed under certain conditions during the course of an investigation, namely, after a preliminary determination.

A product will be subjected to an AD duty as soon as the investigation has been concluded, and a final determination has been made to the effect that AD duties are imposed (*Mexico—Antidumping Measures on Rice*, AB, §347). Duties cannot, of course, be imposed, unless the requirements for lawful imposition have been met. Art. 9.1 AD pertinently reads to this effect:

> The decision whether or not to impose an antidumping duty in cases where all requirements for the imposition have been fulfilled, and the decision whether the amount of the antidumping duty to be imposed shall be the full margin of dumping or less, are decisions to be made by the authorities of the importing Member.[98]

In practice, many WTO Members apply a prospective assessment of duties: once the dumping margin has been calculated (and assuming that it has been established that dumping has caused injury), all dumped imports in the market will be burdened with the applicable AD duty. Affected parties shall be promptly refunded for any duty paid in excess of the actual margin of dumping. In other words, if it can be shown that the products were sold at prices such that the margin of dumping following imposition was less than the margin of dumping on which the original duty was calculated, the importer is entitled to a refund of the difference. For the future, however, the original duty will remain in place. The US only applies a system calling for retrospective assessment of duties:[99] once an AD order has been imposed on a product, the importer will have to pay a provisional duty[100] based on the rate calculated during the investigation. The products that enter the US market during the first year that the AD order is in place are not 'liquidated' until a final duty has been paid. This final duty will be calculated on the basis of the export price of the product during the year following the imposition of the AD order. In the course of a duty assessment review or (in

---

[98] As we saw *supra*, some WTO members, in particular, the EU and Canada, have imposed an additional requirement on themselves to examine whether the imposition of duties would not be against the public interest. Observing similar clauses, nevertheless, is not a matter of legal compulsion under WTO law.

[99] See for the AB description of this system in its report on *US—Zeroing (EC)*, §109. Bagwell and Mavroidis (2007) discuss the US system *in extenso*.

[100] Not to be confused with provisional duties under Art. 7 AD.

US parlance) administrative review,[101] the US authority will compare the export prices of the goods over that year, and re-calculate the dumping margin that it will be applying on a definitive basis for all imports to its market (retrospective assessment). The definitive duty may be higher than the provisional duty, in case the dumping margin during the first year exceeds that found during the initial investigation, or lower (in the opposite case). Consequently, this may lead to either an additional bill for the importer or to reimbursement. Only upon payment of the definitive duty will goods be considered to have been liquidated. It is this newly calculated rate which will then form the basis for the provisional duties to be paid the following year, and the process described above will start all over again.[102]

In both cases, a refund is mandated where an importer has paid duties in excess of the margin of dumping and the importer requests a refund. As the AB clearly stated in its report on *Mexico—Antidumping Measures on Rice* (§312):

> The refund of duties is conditioned solely on (i) the request being made by an importer of the product subject to the antidumping duty; and (ii) the request having been 'duly supported by evidence'. Other than these requirements, we see no basis for an investigating authority to decline to affect the mandated refund. Indeed, failure to do so would result in the importer having paid a duty in excess of the dumping margin, contrary to Article 9.3.

In a nutshell, the difference between the US duty assessment and a prospective assessment of duties is that:

(a) In the prospective system, the importer pays a duty, whereas in the US system the provisional duty may take the form of a cash deposit or guarantee;

(b) In the US system, the administration itself will automatically review the duties in light of prices observed the preceding year, whereas in the prospective system the interested parties have to submit a request for reimbursement (in case duties imposed do not correspond to margins any more).[103]

Prospective imposition, however, should be distinguished from retroactive imposition of AD duties. Irrespective of the system followed (prospective, retrospective), AD duties cannot be imposed retroactively except under the very limited

---

[101] Not to be confused with administrative reviews or changed circumstances reviews under Art. 11 AD, which we discuss *infra*.

[102] Although the level of dumping might vary, there is no requirement to conduct a new injury analysis, unless there is a specific request to this effect. The fear of eventual higher definitive duties thus imposes a pricing discipline on exporters to the US market.

[103] A proposal has been made during the Doha round to do away with this request requirement, making it mandatory for the authorities to refund any excessive duties collected. Linked to this is the proposed amendment of Art. 9.3 AD introducing a requirement to establish, upon request, the margin of dumping based upon normal values contemporaneous with the export transactions; see WTO Doc. TN/RL/GEN/131.

conditions provided for in Art. 10 AD. Hence, AD duties have, in principle, an *ex nunc* effect (Art. 10.1 AD). Two exceptions are possible:

(a) Duties can be imposed retroactively up to the moment when provisional measures had been imposed, if, following a finding of injury, provisional duties had been imposed; or, following a finding of threat of injury and a demonstration that in the absence of provisional measures, injury would have materialized, provisional measures had been imposed (Art. 10.2 AD);[104]

(b) Duties can be imposed retroactively until 90 days prior to the imposition of provisional measures, but in no case prior to the initiation of investigation,[105] if there is a history of dumping and injury or if the importer was aware of dumping practices, and, in either case, the injury was caused by 'massive dumped imports' in a short period which, because of, *inter alia*, the timing and volume of the dumped imports, are likely to seriously undermine the remedial effects that AD duties might have (Art. 10.6 AD).[106]

In order to be able to collect duties retroactively to the period preceding the application of provisional measures, the Agreement provides in Art. 10.7 AD that the authorities may, after initiation, take such measures as the withholding of appraisement or assessment as may be necessary for that purpose. The one condition is that the authorities must have sufficient evidence that the conditions for such extended retroactive application are satisfied. The Panel on *US—Hot-Rolled Steel* tried to square the requirements of Art. 10.7 AD with the role it is to play in an investigation when holding that (§7.163):

> Article 10.7 measures serve the same purpose as an order at the beginning of a lawsuit to preserve the *status quo*—they ensure that at the end of the process, effective measures can be put in place should the circumstances warrant.

The Panel discussed in considerable detail the 'massive dumped imports' requirement. Recourse to retroactive measures could be appropriate in order to avoid the remedial effect of the duty being undermined by massive dumped imports in a short period of time. A retroactive application of the duty up to the moment of initiation can only serve that purpose if the massive dumped imports take place between initiation and the application of provisional measures. The dumper uses this window to quickly dump his product on the market before leaving it. The Panel considered

---

104 The retroactive application is actually only a partial retroactivity: if the definitive antidumping duty is higher than the provisional duty paid, the difference shall not be collected, but if the definitive duty is lower, the difference shall be reimbursed (Art. 10.3 AD). In the case of a determination of threat of injury without the additional demonstration of the preventive effect of the measure, the provisional duties paid shall be refunded and any bonds released in an expeditious manner (Art. 10.4 AD). It goes without saying that, were a negative final determination to be made, any cash deposits made during the period of provisional measures shall be refunded and any bonds released (Art. 10.5 AD).

105 As per Art. 7.3 AD, provisional measures may be applied as of 60 days following initiation.

106 The rationale for this provision is to address cases where exporters quickly dump their exports after the initiation of an investigation and stop exporting thereafter.

that, at least in so far as the possibility of taking conservatory measures under Art. 10.7 AD was concerned, an authority is entitled to take into account an earlier short period of time. The Panel agreed with the approach of the US authority to compare a period prior to the reference data with data for the period following it (§§7.166–7). While the Panel appeared to limit its statements to the question of conservatory measures under Art. 10.7 AD, it did at the same time seem to suggest that the massive dumped imports of Art. 10.6 AD could be assessed on the basis of a period of time prior to initiation, if such imports were not made *in tempore non suspectu*. In any case, the requirements for an actual retroactive application of definitive duties up until the moment of initiation remain unclear. It needs to be added that such retroactive application to initiation is highly exceptional in practice.

Art. 9.2 AD states that, once imposed, AD duties shall be collected on a non-discriminatory basis on imports from all sources found to be dumped and causing injury, unless price undertakings have been accepted. This duty, however, is limited to imposition of duties.[107]

AD duties can take various forms. In the case of a fixed duty, imports will be subject to an additional (to the bound or applied) duty of, for example, €10/litre (or any other unit of account). An *ad valorem* duty will be expressed in percentage terms of the value, such as a duty of 10 per cent. In the case of a variable duty, a minimum export price, or reference normal value, will be determined, and a duty will be imposed, based on a comparison between the actual export price and this reference price. The Panel on *Argentina—Poultry Antidumping Duties* confirmed that duties can be *ad valorem*, fixed or variable (§7.364):

> the variable antidumping duties at issue are not inconsistent with Article 9.3 simply because they are collected by reference to a margin of dumping established at the time of collection (i.e., the difference between a 'minimum export price', or reference normal value, and actual export price).

The Panel noted that nothing in the AD Agreement explicitly identifies the form that AD duties must take, and that nothing in the AD Agreement explicitly prohibits the use of variable duties (§7.355).

2.2.12 *Who are Duties Imposed Against?*

The AD Agreement mentions four categories of exporters against which AD duties will be imposed:

(a) Known exporters;
(b) Sampled exporters;

---

[107] Arguably, even the initiation of an investigation is covered by the MFN clause, which states that *any* advantage comes under its purview. It will be an insurmountable evidentiary task, however, to demonstrate that, in presence of information that companies from two different countries were dumping in a third market, the latter chose to attack only one of them. A number of distinguishing factors could cast doubt on a discrimination-based legal challenge.

(c) Non-sampled exporters;

(d) New shippers.

We will discuss later that practice has revealed that national IAs have imposed duties on unknown exporters as well, that is, exporters who were not known to the IA when the AD order was imposed, for which the AD Agreement contains no legal discipline. The consistency of similar national practices with the WTO has been discussed in case law. The Agreement is further silent on the treatment of new shippers before their pricing practices have been scrutinized by the competent IA.

The taxonomy above is very much the natural consequence of the fact that AD duties are, in practice, imposed on a country-wide basis. So although dumping is a business practice, and individual dumping margins must be calculated for each exporter, there is a presumption that all producers originating in a particular country are dumping, even if they were not investigated during the original investigation. This is, however, at least questionable, if not faulty altogether.[108]

Dumping, we recall, is a pricing strategy whereby producers in one country charge lower prices in foreign markets than in their home market: it is practised by firms, not countries. Yet, Art. 2 AD defines dumping in terms of countries with no reference to individual firms. This definition would seem to imply that the pricing strategy of all exporting firms of a particular product is identical, with the same price differential between the home market and the importing country for all relevant firms. This, obviously, makes little or no economic sense. There is no a priori reason to believe that two (or more) firms behave identically in terms of their pricing in different markets simply because they happen to produce the same product in the same country—unless they operate under perfect competition in both the home- and in the importing-country markets. If, nevertheless, perfect competition prevailed, it would be hard to understand how dumping could occur in the first place. Since dumping is a form of price discrimination, it requires that firms be able to set prices in the different markets rather than take them as given, as is the case under perfect competition. If markets were perfectly competitive, the 'law of one price' would prevail and all identical products would have only one price—at least within the same geographical or national market. However, perfect competition is clearly an extreme case that is unlikely to prevail in many circumstances, and therefore, as Varian (1980, p. 651) states, 'the "law of one price" is no law at all'.

There are essentially two reasons why the 'law of one price' does not hold. The trivial reason is that products may not be identical either because they are differentiated or because differences in the services offered by competing firms might lead them to charge different prices for the same product. But even if products are truly homogeneous, price dispersion is likely to be the rule rather than

---

108 The analysis here borrows heavily from Mavroidis and Sapir (2008).

the exception to the 'law of one price'. As Stigler (1961) argued 50 years ago, price dispersion is related to the existence of imperfect information and search costs of consumers. Product differentiation and imperfect information imply that firms might be able to exert some degree of market power and hence to price discriminate. Moreover, different firms can be expected to face different circumstances and to have different capabilities that result in different costs and therefore different prices—unless they operate under perfect competition, in which case prices have to be the same for all firms and the different costs simply translate into different profits. The AD Agreement actually recognizes in two places that firms which produce the same product in the same country do not necessarily behave identically. The first acknowledgement of this comes in Art. 5 AD on antidumping initiations and investigations, where the Agreement states that applications to national authorities by the domestic industry in the importing country for antidumping measures must contain: a complete description of the allegedly dumped product, the names of the country or countries of origin or export in question, the identity of each known exporter or foreign producer, and a list of known persons importing the product in question. Furthermore, Art. 6.10 AD on evidence in antidumping investigations states that:

> The authorities shall, as a rule, determine an individual margin of dumping for each known exporter or producer concerned of the product under investigation.

In other words, the Agreement makes it clear that each 'known exporter or foreign producer' must be identified and that the national authorities must determine individual dumping margins for each of them. There is no question of lumping them all together and assuming that they behave identically.

Against this background, it is remarkable that the interpretation chosen by the Agreement implies that all firms producing the allegedly dumped product in the country in question engage in injurious dumping, unless proven otherwise. It puts, therefore, the burden of proving innocence on all exporters, both those who are 'known' and those who are 'unknown'. Whatever the exact legal basis for the interpretation chosen by the Agreement, the fact of the matter is that it runs counter to economic rationality. The correct economic interpretation would have been that firms producing the same product in the same country will typically behave differently because they face different economic conditions and because perfect competition does not hold. Such an interpretation would have implied that investigating authorities should not presume that all firms engage in injurious dumping simply because some might or even do. This leads us to conclude that the Agreement is internally inconsistent from an economic viewpoint. On the one hand, the Agreement supposes that all exporters or producers of an allegedly dumped product who produce in the country in question are potentially guilty of injurious dumping in the importing country. On the other, it recognizes that different exporters or producers may behave differently and should therefore be subject to different treatment in terms of AD duties. Hence, with respect to the fundamental question of the burden of proof and, ultimately, whether it is countries or firms that should be held responsible for dumping, nothing short of a revision of the AD Agreement itself can be satisfactory from an economic viewpoint.

Against this background, an IA must calculate a dumping margin for each individual exporter/producer, that is, for each known exporter or producer concerned (Art. 6.10 AD). The term 'known exporter' has been interpreted by the AB as referring to all exporters that have been identified in the petition, as well as those who have voluntarily appeared before the IA (*Mexico—Antidumping Measures on Rice*). The Panel on *EC—Salmon (Norway)* held that it was legitimate for an IA to exclude non-producing exporters (§7.167). The Panel on *Korea— Certain Paper* addressed the question whether the practice of 'collapsing' is consistent with the clear obligation in Art. 6.10 AD Agreement to calculate an individual margin of dumping for each known exporter or producer concerned: in this case, Korea had calculated a single margin of dumping for three legally independent Indonesian companies which it considered to constitute one entity for the purposes of its antidumping investigation (collapsing); collapsing is intended to ensure the efficiency of the antidumping measure. The fear is that, if separate companies are sufficiently closely linked, they may be able to start selling through the company for which the lowest duty has been calculated, once the duty has been put in place. In other words, collapsing functions as a sort of pre-emptive anti-circumvention device. The Panel was of the view that Art. 6.10 AD does not define the term 'exporter' or 'producer', but that, when read in context, Art. 6.10 AD does not necessarily preclude treating distinct legal entities as a single exporter or producer for purposes of dumping determinations in AD investigations (§7.161). The Panel added, however, that (§7.161):

> in order to properly treat multiple companies as a single exporter or producer in the context of its dumping determinations in an investigation, the IA has to determine that these companies are in a relationship close enough to support that treatment.

In other words, according to the Panel, only when the (§7.162):

> structural and commercial relationship between the companies in question is sufficiently close to be considered as a single exporter or producer

could collapsing be permissible. In the case at hand, the Panel accepted Korea's decision to treat the three independent Indonesian exporters as a single exporter and calculate a single margin of dumping for them in light of the following factors:

(a) The commonality of management and shareholding;
(b) The use of the same trading company by all three exporters; and
(c) The existence of cross-sales of the subject product among the three companies,

which, according to the Panel, evidenced (§7.168):

the ability and willingness of the three companies to shift products among themselves.

Recall, from our discussion *supra*, that the AD Agreement provides for the possibility to sample exporters: an individually calculated duty will be imposed on sampled exporters, and the question arises what is the level of duty that will be imposed on non-sampled exporters (since duties are imposed on a country-wide basis). Art. 9.4 AD explains that the maximum permissible AD duty that an IA can apply to non-sampled exporters or producers when it has sampled in accordance with Art. 6.10 AD:

> When the authorities have limited their examination in accordance with the second sentence of paragraph 10 of Article 6, any antidumping duty applied to imports from exporters or producers not included in the examination shall not exceed:
> (i) the weighted average margin of dumping established with respect to the selected exporters or producers or,
> (ii) where the liability for payment of antidumping duties is calculated on the basis of a prospective normal value, the difference between the weighted average normal value of the selected exporters or producers and the export prices of exporters or producers not individually examined,
> provided that the authorities shall disregard for the purpose of this paragraph any zero and de minimis margins and margins established under the circumstances referred to in paragraph 8 of Article 6. The authorities shall apply individual duties or normal values to imports from any exporter or producer not included in the examination who has provided the necessary information during the course of the investigation, as provided for in subparagraph 10.2 of Article 6.

Consequently, an IA will calculate individual dumping margins for all exporters that have been sampled, and will apply, at most, the WA to all other known exporters. An individual exporter who has not been included in the investigation can, under Art. 6.10.2 AD, submit evidence and request that the IA apply an individually calculated duty on his exports, if practicable. Importantly, when calculating the maximum duty for non-sampled producers or exporters, an IA must disregard *de minimis* and zero dumping margins, and cannot base itself on margins established through recourse to the facts-available provision of Art. 6.8 AD.[109] The extent of this latter requirement, to exclude facts-available margins, led to disagreements as to the exact scope of the obligation assumed. The AB, in its report on *US—Hot-Rolled Steel*, held that, whenever recourse was made to Art. 9.4 AD, an IA could not include in the average the results of a margin based, even in part, on facts available, that is, through recourse to Art. 6.8 AD (§122).

Art. 9.5 AD allows exporters who did not export any products during the period of investigation (or, who simply did not produce at all during the same period) to

---

[109] We discuss recourse to best information available *infra*. Suffice to say here that, when facing non-cooperative behaviour on behalf of exporters, an IA can, assuming certain statutory conditions have been met, disregard submitted evidence and make its own assessment regarding the dumping margin.

request from the IA to calculate an individual margin of dumping in order to determine their duty rate: these are the so-called *new shippers*. Art. 9.5 AD provides for them as follows:

> If a product is subject to antidumping duties in an importing Member, the authorities shall promptly carry out a review for the purpose of determining individual margins of dumping for any exporters or producers in the exporting country in question who have not exported the product to the importing Member during the period of investigation, provided that these exporters or producers can show that they are not related to any of the exporters or producers in the exporting country who are subject to the antidumping duties on the product. Such a review shall be initiated and carried out on an accelerated basis, compared to normal duty assessment and review proceedings in the importing Member. No antidumping duties shall be levied on imports from such exporters or producers while the review is being carried out. The authorities may, however, withhold appraisement and/or request guarantees to ensure that, should such a review result in a determination of dumping in respect of such producers or exporters, antidumping duties can be levied retroactively to the date of the initiation of the review.

There is no dispute that it is the exporter who must take the initiative and identify itself, and the exporter who must also show that it has no (business) relation to producers already subjected to AD duties: the reason for this latter requirement is to prevent 'new' companies circumventing the duty order in place. The AD Agreement is not explicit as to what type of business relationship should be addressed: presumably, what is meant is that the new shipper is an independent exporter who does not have to follow the pricing policies of another exporter already subjected to AD duties. But the absence of a definition of the term 'related', which appears in Art. 9.5 AD, poses problems and may lead to independent new exporters with some degree of relationship to old exporters being denied the right to an individual duty calculation. At the same time, an exporter whose products are burdened with a high AD duty may simply start exporting through a related company to avoid these high duties. This 'new' exporter could then sell at a high export price for a while, and get a 0 per cent margin in an expedited review, so that no duties will have to be paid. Art. 9.5 AD aims at preventing similar circumvention.

A review has to be carried out promptly, but should be sufficiently long to allow for a proper basis to compare normal value with export price. The Panel and the AB, in their reports on *Mexico—Antidumping Measures on Rice*, held that Art. 9.5 AD:

> clearly does not subject the right to an expedited new shipper review to a showing of a 'representative' volume of export sales.[110]

---

[110] §7.266 of the Panel report and §323 of the AB report.

While this may well be true, it appears that, inevitably, a new exporter will have to wait before it can ask for an expedited review so as to allow a certain period of export sales to provide the basis for a determination of information on normal value and export price.[111] Two major interpretative issues arise:

(a) The first sentence of Art. 9.5 AD seems to suggest that new shipments are at least suspected of being dumped. At the same time, it is unclear as to whether such shipments will be burdened with duties anyway or, conversely, whether this will be the case only after the new shipper investigation has ended. The first sentence suggests that new shippers pay duties, as a duty is imposed on a particular product from a particular country. The third sentence of Art. 9.5 AD, though, states that no duties are levied pending the outcome of the investigation. Should one infer that duties will not be in place unless, following an individual calculation, a positive dumping margin has been established? If yes, then point (b) below is moot. Conversely, Art. 9.5 AD could be interpreted as follows: new shipments will be burdened with duties; if no request for an expedited review has been submitted, duties will be in place. Assuming a request has been submitted, there will be a truce: duties will not be imposed during the investigation and, pending its outcome, they might be imposed retroactively, that is, as of the date of the initiation of the new shipper review investigation. What should be done with the duties that were levied prior to the initiation of the review is unclear; probably they will remain collected;

(b) Assuming that the second interpretation is correct, and indeed this is what practice suggests, we have no information at all as to the level of duties to be imposed on new shipments prior to the calculation of the individual dumping margin during a review. Should it be the WA as per Art. 9.4 AD? Or should it be some other rate? At the heart of this discussion is the legal relationship between Art. 9.4 and Art. 9.5 AD, an issue that has been largely unresolved in the case law. In practice, most IAs impose a residual duty at the level of the WA of individually calculated dumping margins.

Practice reveals the existence of another category of exporters, not foreseen in the AD agreement: the so-called unknown exporters that were not identified as such by the authorities at the time of the investigation. Exporters could be unknown because they managed to hide (let us call this, uncooperative behaviour) or because the authority did not take any reasonable efforts to identify them (for example, they continued to export and were never requested to appear before the authority) or for other reasons. With respect to unknown exporters, the AD Agreement is silent as to whether they should pay a duty at all, and if yes, how much. There is

---

[111] This is one reason why allowing the imposition of a high duty to be applied prior to the request for review is really unfair on the new exporter.

nothing in the Agreement expressly dealing with this situation. It is practice that suggests that a residual rate is calculated and imposed on their exports.

The practice of WTO Members regarding the amount of residual duty that should be applied to unknown exporters is disparate. The US, for example, applies the duty that it applies to non-sampled exporters, the so-called all others' duty (or all others' rate). This is the WA of the individually calculated dumping margins for sampled exporters. EU practice[112] suggests another residual rate, which applies to imports from unknown exporters, that is, exporters that are not new shippers, and that kept quiet during the investigation, or exporters that remained unknown during the investigation, the reasonable efforts of the EU authority to identify them notwithstanding. Assume that the EU authority has sampled three exporters who ship equal volumes to the EU market and that their dumping margin is respectively 20 per cent, 40 per cent, and 60 per cent. The EU authority will impose:

(a) The duties mentioned above on the three investigated exporters;
(b) A 40 per cent (WA) duty on all identified exporters; and
(c) A 60 per cent (residual) rate on non-identified exporters as well as on new shipments.

In *Mexico—Antidumping Measures on Rice*, the WTO adjudicating bodies had the opportunity to pronounce on the consistency of some national practice in this respect. The Mexican IA (Economía) imposed on unknown exporters duties equalling the amount of the highest individual dumping margin. The question raised by the US claim was whether the AD Agreement imposes any limits on the amount of the residual duty. In US practice, the residual rate (WA) found in the context of an Art. 9.4 AD determination must be applied to new shipments as well as other unknown exporters. The US put forward a claim that, consistent with its own practice, Mexico had to impose on new shipments, prior to the expedited review, a maximum AD duty which should not exceed the WA of duties imposed. In other words, the residual rate should equal the *all others' rate*, calculated in accordance with Art. 9.4 AD for exporters not included in the sample. The Panel was not convinced by this argument, as it considered that Art. 9.4 AD provided a specific methodology with regard to the calculation of the duty for those interested parties that did not form part of the sample, but that there existed no requirement to apply that methodology in a case which did not involve sampling (§7.158). We quote from §7.159:

> The US argument that the placement of this provision immediately preceding Article 9.5 of the *AD Agreement* dealing with new shipper reviews implies that its rules also apply to non-shipping exporters is not convincing, as we do not find that anything can be deduced in and of itself from the sequence of provisions in the

---

112 See Vermulst and Waer (1997).

Agreement, particularly when the provision in question relates to an exceptional situation, while the subsequent provision does not. The United States also argues that the non-sampled interested parties and the new shippers dealt with by Article 9.5 are in a similar position and that by analogy the same Article 9.4 methodology for the calculation of a residual duty rate should apply. We are not convinced that the text of the *Agreement* supports this view. In this respect, we find particularly relevant the absence of any cross-referencing in Article 9.5 of the *AD Agreement* dealing with new shippers to the calculation methodology of Article 9.4 of the *AD Agreement*. This absence of cross-referencing is particularly conspicuous if one were to accept, arguendo, the analogous situation of non-sampled and non-shipping exporters. Indeed, especially in such a situation, one would expect the drafters to have explicitly referred to Article 9.4 of the *AD Agreement*. As on other occasions, where the drafters intended to see obligations apply in similar circumstances, they explicitly provided for such cross-referencing. We recall in this respect that the AB also found that the absence of such cross-referencing to obligations contained in other provisions is revealing of the absence of such an obligation. We find that Article 9.4 of the *AD Agreement* does not refer to non-shipping exporters outside a sampling situation, and that there was therefore no obligation for the Mexican authorities to calculate a residual duty margin for Producers Rice based on the 'neutral' methodology set forth in Article 9.4 of the *AD Agreement*. We therefore reject the US claim in this respect. (italics in the original)

The AB, on appeal, did not uphold this Panel finding and, instead, went on to state that an authority is not permitted to impose a residual duty rate based on facts available. According to the AB, an authority which imposes a duty on unidentified exporters based on facts available, including facts from the petition, is acting in violation of Art. 6.8 AD, and Annex II, (§§259–60). According to the AB, putting exporters on notice that facts available will be used is a precondition for the use of facts available: for obvious reasons, this can never be met in the case of unidentified exporters. The AB did not, however, establish the maximum amount of duty to be imposed in similar cases. To conclude on this score, there is undeniably a problem with the lack of precision of the AD Agreement and the imperfect 'completion' of the contract through case law in this respect. Had the Panel report on *Mexico—Antidumping Measures on Rice* been upheld by the AB, this category would probably be insignificant: this report imposed the duty to identify exporters on the shoulders of the IA, leaving little room for unknown exporters. Unfortunately, this was not the case.

2.2.13 Administrative Reviews of AD Duties

During the five-year period that AD duties are in place, an administrative review (sometimes referred to as 'changed circumstances review') might take place, either on the initiative of the IA (usually referred to as a 'self-initiated' or *ex officio* review), or upon request (Art. 11.2 AD). The former will take place when warranted, but the latter only after a reasonable lapse of time has passed. An IA, when conducting an administrative review, must (Art. 11.2 AD):

examine whether the continued imposition of the duty is necessary to offset dumping, whether the injury would be likely to continue or recur if the duty were removed or varied, or both.

The term 'reasonable period of time' has not been interpreted by Panels so far. Panels have been busy discussing disputes among WTO Members as to the conditions under which an *ex officio* review is warranted. We will return to this discussion *infra*. Let us note first that the rationale for this provision has to do with the awareness that, for various reasons, the pricing policies of exporters might change over time, and their resulting impact on the domestic industry producing the like product might, consequently, change as well. A review is meant to address similar issues.

The ambit of an administrative review can vary and has concrete consequences: recall that it suffices, as the Panel on *US—DRAMS* underscored (§6.28), that the IA has shown continuation or recurrence of one of the two elements (dumping, injury), the review of continuation or recurrence of both elements being an option, but not an obligation. The extent of the review has, nevertheless, important repercussions for the remaining life of the AD duties in place:

(a) If a narrow review (continuation or recurrence of either dumping or injury) takes place, and no sunset review takes place,[113] duties will remain in place for a maximum period of five years counting from the date of the original imposition;

(b) If a comprehensive review (continuation or recurrence of both dumping and injury) takes place, duties will remain in place for five years counting from the end of the administrative review. In this case, the administrative review entails the same consequences as a sunset review.

Various Panels have discussed the conditions under which it is warranted to conduct an administrative review *ex officio*. In *US—Antidumping Measures on OCTG*, the Panel discussed the consistency of a US law which imposed, in Mexico's view, stringent conditions for the initiation of an administrative review. As the Panel explained, under the US system, a request for a 'changed circumstances' review can be based on the general review provisions or on the basis of no dumping for three years. In the latter case, a company seeking revocation on the basis of no dumping for three years must demonstrate that it had made sales in the US market in commercial quantities during that period. The Panel held that a company which did not satisfy the additional requirements for revocation on the basis of no dumping was nonetheless entitled to seek revocation of the antidumping duty order as applied to it under the general changed circumstances provision, provided it could supply information substantiating the need for review, in

---

[113] As we explain in more detail *infra*, unless a sunset review takes place, AD duties lapse five years after their imposition.

accordance with Art. 11.2 AD (§§7.164–5). Both in this case (§§7.173–4), as well as in *US—DRAMS* (§§6.58–9),[114] WTO Panels have held that absence of dumping for a period of three years and six months did not in and of itself mandate a self-initiated review. This is probably too much of a sweeping statement: duties are imposed if dumping causes injury for five years. If review is not warranted after 70 per cent of the lifetime of duties has lapsed and no dumping has occurred, then one might legitimately wonder whether a review, in the Panels' understanding, is warranted only in cases where the health of the industry has improved. Recall, however, that no AD duties can be imposed in the first place if injury is the outcome of factors other than dumping.

The AB, in its report on *Mexico—Antidumping Measures on Rice*, agreed with the Panel that to require that a 'representative volume of export sales' has taken place as a condition for conducting a changed circumstances review was inconsistent with the Agreement (§316):

> Article 68 of the Act requires as a rule that each time an interested party is unable to show that volume of exports during the review period was representative, such a review is to be denied.... The change in circumstances is unrelated to the export side of the equation. An interested party is entitled to a changed circumstances review under Article 11.2 of the *AD Agreement* and 21.2 of the *SCM Agreement*, if it submits positive information substantiating the need for a review. What such positive information relates to will depend from case to case, and such positive information does not, in our view, necessarily include that a representative number of exports sales were made. We consider that, by requiring the authority to reject a review each time the volume of export sales was not representative, even in cases where the change in circumstances is unrelated to the export price, Article 68 of the Act requires the authority to reject reviews in a manner which is inconsistent with Article 11.2 of the *AD Agreement*. (italics in the original)

The Panel, in its report on *EC–Tube or Pipe Fittings*, dealt, *inter alia*, with the argument by Brazil over whether the devaluation of Brazil's national currency (which time-wise coincided with the last weeks of the investigation) was, in and of itself, a reason for the EU to launch on its own initiative a review of the necessity to keep in place the antidumping duties. The Panel responded in the negative (§7.116) and concluded as follows (§7.118):

> The findings of the panel in US—DRAMS are relevant here. In examining the nature of a review conducted under Article 11.2 AD, that panel rejected the view that Article 11.2 'requires revocation as soon as an exporter is found to have ceased dumping, and that the continuation of an antidumping duty is precluded a priori in any circumstances other than where there is present dumping'. This reasoning would suggest to us that the *Antidumping Agreement* does not require a decision to be made by the investigating authorities after the end of the IP not to impose duties, nor to review the imposition of a duty immediately after it is imposed based on events

---

[114] See Francois and Palmeter (2008).

between the end of the IP and the time of imposition, much less on the basis of events occurring before the end of the IP. (italics in the original)

In the same case, the Panel had also rejected a claim by Brazil to the effect that the determination could not have been made on the basis of positive evidence as the data from before the devaluation were not informative of the situation that prevailed at the time the duties were imposed, that is, when the devaluation occurred. The Panel rejected this argument, holding that these types of changes could be dealt with in subsequent reviews of the measure (§7.106).

Although there is not much case law regarding the standard of review that WTO adjudicating bodies will apply in cases concerning the administrative review, it seems plausible to argue that some deference might be warranted. In this vein, the Panel on *US–DRAMS* probably had the right reflex when holding that, since the subject-matter of an administrative review was a forward-looking analysis, which necessarily entailed uncertainty, one could not require mathematical certainty from an IA when formulating its conclusions. Some degree of imprecision would thus be unavoidable and permissible (§6.43). Howse and Staiger (2007) have for good reasons taken issue with the attitude of WTO adjudicating bodies in this respect. In their view, they have been applying a mechanical instead of a functional test by paying too much attention to the words in the body of Art. 11.2 AD and overlooking its main purpose. The main purpose, as stated above, is whether with time something has changed that would make a review, not a revocation necessarily, warranted. The conditions for reviewing duties should thus be distinguished from the conditions for revoking them, in the sense that less evidence would be required for the former and more for the latter exercise. In this vein, in deciding whether revocation is warranted, an IA should ask whether a change in competitive conditions did occur, and whether because of it a change of action on its behalf were required as a result.[115]

Finally, as per Art. 12.3 AD, a public notice must be issued any time a review is initiated.

2.2.14 *Sunset Reviews*

One of the major innovations of the Uruguay round AD Agreement was the introduction of 'sunset clauses': AD duties would last for five years, in principle, unless the IA determined as per Art. 11.3 AD:

in a review initiated before that date on their own initiative or upon a duly substantiated request made by or on behalf of the domestic industry within a reasonable period of time prior to that date, that the expiry of the duty would be likely to lead to continuation or recurrence of dumping and injury. The duty may remain in force pending the outcome of such a review.

---

[115] A similar critique has been expressed by Grossman and Wauters (2008) and Bown and Wauters (2008).

The five-year period counts from:

(a) The date of the original imposition; or
(b) From the date of the most recent administrative review under Art. 11.2 AD, if the review at hand covered both dumping and injury; or
(c) From the date of the most recent sunset review.

Since duties can stay in place after the five year-period only following a review, it is inferred that, absent such a review, any AD duties imposed will have to be eliminated. In the words of the AB in *US—Carbon Steel*,[116] dealing with the sunset provision in the SCM Agreement (which is identical to that of the AD Agreement (§88)):

> An automatic time-bound termination of countervailing duties that have been in place for five years from the original investigation or a subsequent comprehensive review is at the heart of this provision. Termination of a countervailing duty is the rule and its continuation is the exception.

The introduction of sunset clauses was a major victory for the negotiators of South East Asian countries who were quite frequently the targets of AD activity.[117] Before their introduction, AD duties could be imposed for long periods and the only hope for exporters was the initiation of an administrative review (a possibility in the Tokyo round AD agreement as well). De facto, the only possibility was a requested administrative review, since case law adopted a very deferential attitude towards *ex officio* reviews. In *US—Swedish Steel Plate*, a GATT Panel ruled that the US was not obliged to *ex officio* initiate a review to evaluate the need to keep 20-year-old AD duties in place. Although 20 years had passed since the original imposition, Sweden had signed an FTA with the EU and was exporting massively to European countries, and the company involved (Avesta) had invested in the US, procuring a steel mill in the Midwest, where close to 98 per cent of its total sales to the US market was originating. A request for review entails, of course, costs for the exporter, a new round of acrimonies with the IA, and there is no guarantee regarding its outcome. The introduction of sunset reviews put an end to all this.

The agreement does not exclude the possibility that duties stay in place for long periods: to this effect, nevertheless, successive sunset reviews must take place and they all must support the necessity for keeping AD duties in place. The standard of review that WTO adjudicating bodies have applied when dealing with sunset reviews becomes thus the key to understanding. A sunset review may be initiated either *ex officio*, or upon a duly substantiated request. When the latter occurs, the request must be deposited within a reasonable period of time prior to the expiry of

---

[116] Grossman and Mavroidis (2007b) discuss in detail and underscore the consequences of automaticity in this respect.

[117] Stewart et al. (1993) discuss this point and the quid pro quos.

the five-year period. The last sentence of Art. 11.3 AD clarifies that duties will remain in place during the review process.

The AD Agreement does not impose an obligation to start *ex officio* sunset reviews on a specific date. As a result, WTO Members retain some discretion on this score. Since the imposed duties will remain in place while the review is going ahead, there is a risk that WTO Members might keep duties in place for a period longer than the statutory five-year period, by starting a review at as late a stage as possible. This risk is somewhat addressed through the discipline included in Art. 11.4 AD which stipulates that a review should normally be completed within 12 months. US law provides for an automatic initiation of sunset reviews. In other words, it is never the case that duties will lapse absent sunset review in the US, since a review will always be initiated. The statutory requirements of the US law in this respect were clarified as follows by the AB in its report on *US—Carbon Steel* (§101):[118]

> Section 751(c)(2) of the Tariff Act directs USDOC to publish a notice of initiation of a sunset review no later than 30 days before, inter alia, the fifth anniversary of the date of publication of a countervailing duty order. Section 351.218(b) of Title 19 of the Regulations confirms that USDOC will conduct a sunset review of each counter-vailing duty order. Both the Sunset Policy Bulletin and the SAA describe the initiation of sunset reviews by USDOC as '*automatic*'. (emphasis in the original)

The AB held that this law was not inconsistent with the requirements of the SCM Agreement (§118). Confirmation that this interpretation is good law in the antidumping context as well came with the Panel report on *US—Corrosion-Resistant Steel Sunset Review*. Facing the same issue, the Panel held that automatic self-initiation procedures in the context of a sunset review were not inconsistent with the AD Agreement, because they did not necessarily[119] result in continuation of the duties in place (§7.55). The Panel declined to rule on a related argument made by Japan to the effect that an automatic sunset review takes away the discretionary authority to initiate a sunset review that is implied by the terms 'on its own initiative', as this claim was not, according to the Panel, properly before it (§§7.46–54).

For an IA to lawfully keep the duties in place, it will have to demonstrate at the sunset-review stage that revocation of AD duties would be likely to lead to continuation or recurrence of dumping and injury (Art. 11.3 AD). The terms 'continuation' and 'recurrence' appearing in the body of this provision refer to two different factual situations: the first term presupposes that dumping and/or injury have not ceased to exist during the period of imposition of AD duties; the latter presupposes that the opposite has happened during the same period. Continuation or recurrence should be 'likely', and this term has been understood by the AB as

---

[118] This case concerned a sunset review of CVDs.
[119] See the analysis of Howse and Staiger (2007) on this score.

equivalent to the term 'probable' (*US—Corrosion-Resistant Steel Sunset Review*, §111). As a result, the ensuing standard of review applied by WTO adjudicating bodies cannot be overly demanding in this respect. The methodology used to demonstrate the likelihood of continuation or recurrence is not prejudged by the AD Agreement: in this regard, Art. 11.3 AD imposes an obligation of result, rather than of specific conduct (and thus leaves discretion in the hands of the IA, with the ensuing consequence for the standard of review). The Panel, in its report on *US—Corrosion-Resistant Steel Sunset Review*, dealt with the consistency of a US statute, which expressed the likelihood standard in negative formulation: duties would be removed, only if it was unlikely that their removal would lead to recurrence or continuation of dumping and injury. It did not find the US statute to be inconsistent with Art. 11.3 AD (§§7.227–8) and the AB did not disturb this finding either. In *US—OCTG Sunset Reviews*, the AB, while agreeing with Argentina that the IA's likelihood determinations under Art. 11.3 AD must be based on positive evidence, made it clear that, since a review is by definition a forward-looking exercise, some speculation about future events cannot be avoided. In other words, the requirement to show likelihood on positive evidence should not be understood as a requirement to completely eliminate uncertainty about the course of future events (§§340–1).

The AB, in its report on *US—OCTG Sunset Reviews*, addressed, *inter alia*, an argument by the complainant (Argentina) to the effect that an IA is obliged, by virtue of Art. 11.3 AD, to establish a precise time frame within which continuation or recurrence of dumping and injury would likely occur. The US statute did not specify the time horizon within which the likelihood of recurrence or continuation should occur, and in Argentina's view, this was unlawful since Art. 11.3 AD imposes a temporal limitation which must be imminent (§358). The AB rejected Argentina's argument. It underscored the Panel's finding that likelihood should be evaluated within the reasonably foreseeable future (with no further precision being required), and cautioned that an assessment whether injury is likely to recur that focuses too far in the future would be highly speculative and hence unhelpful for the purposes of sunset reviews (§360).[120] In its view, a determination of injury can be properly reasoned and rest on a sufficient factual basis even though the time frame for the injury determination is not explicitly mentioned (AB, *US—OCTG Sunset Reviews*, §364).

The likelihood of continuation or recurrence of dumping and/or injury must be determined by the IA. The term 'determine' appearing in the body of Art. 11.3 AD has been interpreted in case law as dictating a standard that obliges authorities to reach their conclusions on positive evidence, and to justify them as well (AB, *US—OCTG Sunset Reviews*, §§179–80). To understand what the 'positive-evidence' standard entails, we refer to the measures challenged in *US—OCTG*

---

[120] Grossman and Wauters (2008) concur, offering other reasons to support this conclusion.

Sunset Reviews, which offers a very appropriate illustration to this effect. The US law on sunset reviews contained two types of waivers:

(a) Those applicable in situations where an interested party (exporter) has provided incomplete information to questions asked by the IA during the review process (in US parlance, *deemed waiver*); and

(b) Those applicable in situations where the exporter has declared that it will not participate in the proceedings (*affirmative waiver*).

Where an interested party waives its right to participate in the review process (either through affirmative or deemed waiver), the US IA will presume likelihood of continuation or recurrence of dumping, without having to investigate to what extent this has actually been the case. The Panel, in its report on *US—OCTG Sunset Reviews*, had found both types of waivers to be WTO-inconsistent (§§7.91–9). On appeal, the US argued that the Panel erred since it had not sufficiently taken into account the process followed by US authorities: waivers were used when a company-specific review was being conducted; company-specific reviews, however, were only the first leg of the sunset review. Subsequent to this exercise, the US IA would examine the likelihood of recurrence or continuation of dumping on an order-wide basis.[121] The AB rejected the US argument and confirmed the Panel in this respect. In its view, even though reviews were order-wide, the input to the final determination was flawed by virtue of the fact that a determination was based on waivers, that is, not on positive evidence. We quote from §234 of the AB report:

> We agree with the Panel's analysis of the impact of the waiver provisions on order-wide determinations. Because the waiver provisions require the USDOC to arrive at affirmative company-specific determinations without regard to any evidence on record, these determinations are merely assumptions made by the agency, rather than findings supported by evidence. The United States contends that respondents waiving the right to participate in a sunset review do so 'intentionally', with full knowledge that, as a result of their failure to submit evidence, the evidence placed on the record by the domestic industry is likely to result in an unfavourable determination on an order-wide basis. In these circumstances, we see no fault in making an unfavourable order-wide determination by taking into account evidence provided by the domestic industry in support thereof. However, the USDOC also takes into account, in such circumstances, statutorily-mandated assumptions. Thus, even assuming that the USDOC takes into account the totality of record evidence in making its order-wide determination, it is clear that, as a result of the operation of the waiver provisions, certain order-wide likelihood determinations made by the USDOC will be based, at least in part, on statutorily-mandated assumptions about a company's likelihood of dumping. In our view, this result is inconsistent with the obligation of an investigating authority under Article 11.3 to 'arrive at a reasoned conclusion' on the basis of 'positive evidence'.

---

[121] This term refers to all companies investigated and, in practice, is synonymous with country-wide determinations.

The AB, in its report on *US—OCTG Sunset Reviews*, specified that, when conducting its review, an IA could use information from the record of the original investigation or subsequent reviews, provided that it took a fresh look at it. The AB did not specifically address the question raised by the complainant (Argentina), whether an IA could base its conclusions solely on already used information, as it considered that this was not what the US had done in the case at hand. The AB did, however, agree with the views expressed by another AB Division[122] in the countervailing duty case, *US—Carbon Steel*, that mere reliance on the determination made in the original investigation would not be sufficient (§328). In the same report, the AB also clarified that a decision to continue the imposition of duties could be based on limited observations: in the case at hand, Argentina complained that the US IA did not base its decision on positive evidence since, following the imposition of AD duties, there were only a few transactions between Argentina and the United States. The AB, upholding the Panel's view in this respect, held that the small volume of export sales to the US market was not an impediment towards a finding that dumping would continue to occur were the duties in place to be revoked (§346).[123] Consequently, limited observations, in the sense of a small volume of export sales, might suffice for the purposes of conducting a lawful review; moreover, facts that have already been evaluated in the original investigation can be re-evaluated at the review stage. It appears, however, that a fresh determination, based on credible evidence will be necessary to establish that the continuation of the duty is warranted.[124]

Art. 11.4 AD provides that the provisions of Art. 6 AD (regarding evidence and certain procedural requirements) shall apply to sunset reviews: reviews shall be carried out expeditiously, and shall, normally, be concluded within 12 months of initiation of the review. The due process rights of interested parties must be respected also in the context of a sunset review. With respect to the applicability of the basic due process provisions (Arts. 6.1 and 6.2 AD), the AB, in its reports on *US—Corrosion Resistant Steel Sunset Reviews* and *US—OCTG Sunset Reviews*, stated that these procedural rules clearly applied to sunset reviews because of the cross-reference in Art. 11.4 AD and that it was, therefore, very important to allow, also in a sunset review, interested parties to present evidence and defend their case. In the words of the AB in its report on *US—Corrosion Resistant Steel Sunset Reviews* (§152):

> Article 6 requires all interested parties to have a full opportunity to defend their interests. In particular, Article 6.1 requires authorities to give all interested parties notice of the information required and ample opportunity to present in writing evidence that those parties consider relevant. Articles 6.2, 6.4 and 6.9 provide other examples of the kind of opportunities that investigating authorities must give each

---

[122] This term refers to the three (out of seven) AB members who adjudicate a particular dispute.
[123] See also the Panel report on *US—OCTG Sunset Reviews* at §7.303.
[124] See the AB report on *US—Carbon Steel* at §88.

interested party. . . They therefore confirm that investigating authorities have certain specific obligations towards each exporter or producer in a sunset review.

So far, we have discussed case law regarding the procedural obligations that an IA should apply when performing a sunset review, as well as the standard of review that WTO adjudicating bodies will apply on national determinations to this effect. We now turn to the heart of the issue, namely, the substantive requirements. The question we will be asking here is how case law understood what needs to be shown for AD duties to remain in place longer than the initial five years. Recall that, when discussing the same issue in the context of administrative reviews, we concurred with Howse and Staiger (2007) who deplore the fact that WTO adjudicating bodies have not managed to introduce a meaningful test here where the response to keeping duties in place would be a function of the response to the question whether competitive conditions have changed so as to justify removal of duties. Is the situation any different in the context of sunset reviews?

We start with the question of whether the standards applied during the original investigation are relevant at the review stage as well. This is important since, assuming an affirmative response, the case law regarding original investigations could be exported 'lock, stock, and barrel' to the sunset context as well. In a nutshell, the answer by Panels and the AB has been that, since sunset reviews and original investigations are distinct processes with different purposes, the disciplines applicable to original investigations cannot be automatically imported into review processes.[125] This is a very basic finding in case law and the source for designing the test regarding substantive requirements that must be met at the sunset stage in a different manner.

In this vein, the Panel on *US—Corrosion-Resistant Steel Sunset Review* held that the *de minimis* thresholds applicable during the original investigation, in the absence of explicit language or cross-referencing to this effect, are not applicable in the context of a review (§§7.70–1). The Panel concluded (§7.85):

> On the basis of this textual analysis of the relevant provisions of the *Antidumping Agreement*, we conclude that the 2 per cent *de minimis* standard of Article 5.8 does not apply in the context of sunset reviews. In this context, we again observe that, in light of the qualitative differences between sunset reviews and investigations, it is unsurprising that the obligations applying to these two distinct processes are not identical. (italics in the original)[126]

The AB, in its report on *US—OCTG Sunset Reviews*, went on to find that, when it comes to establishing injury, an IA does not have to respect the standards included

---

[125] See the AB reports on *US—Corrosion-Resistant Steel Sunset Review* at §§106–7, *US—Carbon Steel* at §87, and *US—OCTG Sunset Reviews* at §359.

[126] The AB reached a similar conclusion in the countervailing duty context in its report on *US—Carbon Steel* (§§81–4).

in Art. 3 AD (§280).[127] The AB did not go the full nine yards and establish what exactly needs to be observed for an injury determination at the sunset-stage to be WTO-consistent.[128] The AB did add, on the other hand, that an IA may, without being obliged to do so, borrow from its analysis under Art. 3 AD (the original investigation), when conducting its review analysis (§284). However, in this case, if the injury analysis is inconsistent with Art. 3 AD, it will be deemed inconsistent with Art. 11.3 AD as well. The Panel report on *EU—Footwear (China)* held as much (§§7.337ff). This finding does not seem to totally square with the finding in the AB report on *US—OCTG Sunset Reviews* that the injury standard is not the same in the original investigation and the sunset review. Eventually it is only through clarifications as to what exactly the injury standard entails at the sunset-review stage that inconsistencies in case law will be avoided.

The Panel, in its report on *US—OCTG Sunset Reviews*, faced, *inter alia*, a claim that, in the absence of specific language to this effect, cumulation was not permissible. Consequently, the US, by cumulating imports from various sources, was acting inconsistently with its obligations under the AD Agreement. The Panel, based on textual and contextual arguments, held that various provisions in the AD Agreement made it clear that cumulation was permissible throughout the investigation and the review processes, but that the standards regarding cumulation during the original investigation reflected in Art. 3.3 AD were not applicable in the context of reviews (§§7.323–36).[129] The AB confirmed this finding (§§300–2).[130] In *US—Antidumping Measures on OCTG*, the AB confirmed its view that Art. 3.3 AD did not apply to sunset reviews, but emphasized that on occasion a cumulative assessment might be inappropriate in light of the conditions of competition in the marketplace (§171).

With respect to the calculation of dumping duties at the review stage, the obligations imposed on an IA have also been interpreted to be less stringent than the corresponding obligations during the original investigation. The Panel on *US—Corrosion-Resistant Steel Sunset Review* held that, during the review, an IA need not calculate in precise manner the dumping margins which would result in case it removed the duties in place. Rather, because uncertainty is inherent in any forward-looking study, some reasonableness standard was warranted and, consequently, an IA should not be requested to make a determination of dumping

---

[127] The same findings are reported in the Panel report on *EU—Footwear (China)* at §§7.330ff. Note, however, that the opposite is true in EU law: in *Euroalliages*, T-188/99 (2001), the Tribunal found that the standards applicable in the original investigation are applicable at the sunset stage as well; in C-422/02, *Europe Chemi Com* (2005), the Court confirmed the Tribunal's case law, invoking the EU interest as justification for its decision.

[128] Also see the Panel report on *US—Antidumping Measures on OCTG* at §7.117. In this case, the Panel went on to examine whether the USITC determination of the likely volume of dumped imports, their likely price effects, and their likely impact was that of an unbiased and objective investigating authority (§§7.122–43).

[129] See also the Panel report on *US—Corrosion-Resistant Steel Sunset Review* at §7.102.

[130] See also the Panel report on *US—Antidumping Measures on OCTG* at §§7.147–51.

in the sense of Art. 2 AD, or provide a precise amount of dumping margins (§§7.162–80). This did not mean, according to the Panel, that evidence of dumping was not relevant for a likelihood of recurrence or continuation of dumping determination (§7.180). On appeal, the AB confirmed this view (§§123–4). However, the AB did make one important clarification and overturned the Panel's ruling in this respect. The AB stated that, where a WTO Member goes ahead and does calculate dumping margins—although no such requirement exists in the AD Agreement—it should do so only in accordance with Art. 2 AD (§§127–8). The same Panel faced the question whether an IA would be required, by analogy with the obligation included in Art. 6.10 AD, to calculate an individual margin of dumping for each exporter or producer investigated, and to make a determination of likelihood of recurrence or continuation of dumping and injury for each exporter or producer under review. The Panel considered that no such company-specific likelihood determination was required, and a determination could thus be made on an order-wide basis (§§7.207–8). The AB confirmed this view. It acknowledged that Art. 11.4 AD contained an explicit cross-reference to the provisions of Art. 6 AD (regarding evidence and procedure), making these rules applicable to review situations. However, Art. 6.10, requiring the IA to calculate individual margins of dumping, could not apply in a review because, according to the AB, in a review, an IA was not required under Art. 11.3 AD to calculate dumping margins in the first place. Hence, the requirement to make an individual company-specific determination as set forth in Art. 6.10 AD cannot apply in a review situation (§155). This finding has, of course, the important consequence that a company can remain subject to an antidumping order even though it is no longer dumping, and its sales will continue to be monitored and remain under threat of antidumping action for another five years.

The single most important case law contribution in this respect concerns the absence of necessity to demonstrate a causal link between future dumping and future injury. The AB held that Art. 11.3 AD requires from an IA to make a determination concerning the likelihood of dumping and injury but not of a causal link between the two: in *US—Antidumping Measures on OCTG*,[131] the AB first confirmed that a causal link between dumping and injury was fundamental to the imposition and maintenance of an antidumping duty under the AD Agreement. The AB was of the view, however, that, because the review contemplated in Art. 11.3 AD was a distinct process with a 'different' purpose (than the original investigation), a causal link between dumping and injury did not need to be established anew. We quote from §§123–4:

> Therefore, what is essential for an affirmative determination under Article 11.3 is proof of likelihood of continuation or recurrence of dumping and injury, if the duty expires. The nature and extent of the evidence required for such proof will vary with

---

[131] Bown and Wauters (2008) critically discuss this case.

the facts and circumstances of the case under review. Furthermore, as the Appellate Body has emphasized previously, determinations under Article 11.3 must rest on a 'sufficient factual basis' that allows the investigating authority to draw 'reasoned and adequate conclusions'. These being the requirements for a sunset review under Article 11.3, we do not see that the requirement of establishing a causal link between likely dumping and likely injury flows into that Article from other provisions of the GATT 1994 and the *Antidumping Agreement*. Indeed, adding such a requirement would have the effect of converting the sunset review into an original investigation, which cannot be justified.

Our conclusion that the establishment of a causal link between likely dumping and likely injury is not required in a sunset review determination does not imply that the causal link between dumping and injury envisaged by Article VI of the GATT 1994 and the *Antidumping Agreement* is severed in a sunset review. It only means that re-establishing such a link is not required, as a matter of legal obligation, in a sunset review. (italics in the original)

The AB can be credited with many cryptic passages, but this must be one of the highlights. What message exactly is the last quoted paragraph supposed to convey? That any recurrence of dumping will unavoidably lead to injury anew? And what if, because of an exogenous shock (say, a technological innovation), domestic industry is so much more productive now that dumping cannot guarantee exporters a foot in the market? This is not only a cryptic passage, but poor economics as well. Be it as it may, the AB through this decision made compliance with the legal requirements a banality for IAs performing sunset reviews.

One would expect that, because of the rather deferential standard[132] that WTO adjudicating bodies have adopted when discussing disputes regarding sunset reviews, WTO Members interested in extending the life of AD duties would find it rather easy to do so. Cadot et al. (2006) examine data from 1979–2005 and conclude that, since the advent of sunset clauses, the majority of AD duties imposed do not stay in place beyond the five-year period. The authors, nevertheless, conclude that one should not readily attribute this success story to the WTO: the agreement itself may be endogenous to autonomous political forces in member countries, precisely those forces that made the agreement possible. They observe that the five-year deadline did not change much with respect to EU practice: duties are rarely imposed for more than five years running, whereas,[133] when the EU

---

[132] We discuss *infra* under a separate heading the statutory standard of review in the AD context and the manner in which it has been understood and applied in WTO case law.

[133] In the last few years, the EU has adopted practice whereby duties will be imposed for periods considerable shorter than the statutory five years. Dordi (2010) discusses prominent EU cases where duties have been imposed for two years, following the advent of new legislation (e.g. Council Regulation (EC) 1472/2006 of 5 October 2006 imposing a definitive antidumping duty and collecting the provisional duty imposed on imports of certain footwear with uppers of leather originating in the People's Republic of China and Vietnam (2006) OJ L275/1), and cases where, following a sunset review, duties have been reimposed for two years only (Council Regulation (EC) 1583/2006 of 23 October 2006 imposing a definitive antidumping duty on imports of ethanolamines originating in the United States of America (2006) OJ L294/2).

imposes price undertakings, they run out after five years anyway. US practice, according to the results in Cadot et al. (2006), tells a different story: it continues to keep most duties in place after reviewing them at the sunset stage.[134] US practice is thus probably aided by the applicable standard of review, although this is not necessarily the only reason: Bloningen and Park (2004) show why reverse causation might also explain why some duties stay in place in the US after the review stage: under incomplete pass-through, the exporter will have to reduce the normal value in order to absorb part of the imposed AD duties. Under the US system of annual reviews, this practice will raise the dumping margin measured by the DOC (Department of Commerce) and will lead to an upward revision of duties.

At any rate, the deferential standard of review certainly facilitates and does not impede the extension of the life of AD duties.

2.2.15 Remedies against Illegally Imposed AD Duties

The question of remedies against illegal imposition of antidumping duties has provoked a series of discussions in GATT/WTO.[135] In the GATT era, a series of Panels, inspired by the standard of compensation in case of the commission of an illegal act in customary international law, had recommended that, in the case of illegally imposed (antidumping and countervailing) duties, the GATT contracting party imposing such duties has the obligation to reimburse the injured exporter.[136] This is how it works: a court's judgment that an illegality has been committed has declaratory but not constitutive effect; a judicial decision acknowledges that an illegal act was committed when the act occurred. An illegal act cannot produce legal effects (*ex injuria non oritur jus*); hence, all consequences of an illegal act must be wiped out. Since it is practically impossible to recreate the world from the moment an AD order was illegally imposed, one should, at the very least, eliminate those consequences that it is feasible to eliminate: AD duties are the immediate consequence of an AD order, and all duties paid must be reimbursed to the concerned exporters. Reimbursement of duties does not necessarily exhaust the damage done, but *restitutio in integrum* (redo in its totality the anterior situation) is practically a fallacy that the legal standard for compensation tries to approximate. Reimbursement of duties in many cases will not take care of the damage done, but it will contribute towards full compensation; moreover, in knowledge that duties might have to be reimbursed, IAs will be more careful when imposing duties in the first place.

---

134 Thus, Cadot et al. (2006, p. 6) do not question the results obtained in Moore (2004) on this score.

135 We do not deal here with refunds of duties in case, for example, the original calculation overshot the dumping margin. This and similar issues are resolved in the AD Agreement that discusses refunds explicitly. Here, we deal with remedies against illegally perceived duties after their definitive calculation has taken place.

136 On GATT practice in this context, see Petersmann (1993), and Mavroidis (1993, 2000a).

The GATT Panels that opted for similar solutions did not have statutory language to rely upon, since the GATT did not explicitly address the issue of reimbursement of illegally perceived AD duties; they constructed the GATT (implicitly at the very least) as an international contract that must respect customary international law. The situation in this respect did not change with the advent of the WTO: the contract remains silent on the issue whether retroactive (*ex tunc*) remedies are permitted or excluded in WTO law. This is why we should turn to practice to see whether GATT practice continues to be of relevance. The Panel on *Guatemala—Cement II*, facing a specific request by Mexico to suggest reimbursement of illegally imposed antidumping duties, acknowledged that in the specific circumstances of the case, a request for reimbursement might be justifiable. However, ultimately, the Panel refused to pronounce on this score (§§9.6–7):

> We have determined that Guatemala has acted inconsistently with its obligations under the *AD Agreement* in its imposition of antidumping duties on imports of grey portland cement from Mexico. We have found these violations to be of a fundamental nature and pervasive. Indeed, in general terms we have found that:
>
> a) An unbiased and objective investigating authority could not properly have determined, based on the evidence and information available at the time of initiation, that there was sufficient evidence to justify initiation of the antidumping investigation;
>
> b) Guatemala conducted the antidumping investigation in a manner inconsistent with its obligations under various provisions of the *AD Agreement*;
>
> c) An unbiased and objective investigating authority could not properly have determined that the imports under investigation were being dumped, that the domestic producer of cement in Guatemala was being injured and that the imports were the cause of that injury.
>
> In light of the nature and extent of the violations in this case, we do not perceive how Guatemala could properly implement our recommendation without revoking the antidumping measure at issue in this dispute. Accordingly, we suggest that Guatemala revoke its antidumping measure on imports of grey portland cement from Mexico. In respect of Mexico's request that we suggest that Guatemala refund the antidumping duties collected, we note that Guatemala has now maintained a WTO-inconsistent antidumping measure in place for a period of three and a half years. Thus, we fully understand Mexico's desire to see the antidumping duties repaid and consider that repayment might be justifiable in circumstances such as these. We recall however that suggestions under Article 19.1 relate to ways in which a Member could implement a recommendation to bring a measure into conformity with a covered agreement. Mexico's request raises important systemic issues regarding the nature of the actions necessary to implement a recommendation under Article 19.1 of the DSU, issues which have not been fully explored in this dispute. Thus, we decline Mexico's request to suggest that Guatemala refund the antidumping duties collected. (italics in the original)

On more or less the same wavelength, the Panel on *Australia—Automotive Leather II* held that the DSU did not exclude the possibility for retroactive remedies. These two Panel reports, nonetheless, are outliers: no other report went so far and typically a finding that duties have been illegally imposed will be accompanied by a statement that the WTO Member concerned should bring its measure into compliance. Although as a matter of domestic law, WTO Members can still go ahead and reimburse illegally perceived duties, there is no compulsion to this effect as a matter of WTO law and hence, typically WTO Members that have illegally imposed duties will simply stop doing so in the future (that is after the end of the reasonable period of time defined in Art. 21 DSU within which they must bring their measures into compliance with their obligations).

2.2.16 *The Standard of Review*

WTO adjudicating bodies have to observe the generic standard of review included in Art. 11 DSU. The AD Agreement is the only covered agreement with its own standard of review (Art. 17.6 AD):

> In examining the matter referred to in paragraph 5:
> (i) in its assessment of the facts of the matter, the panel shall determine whether the authorities' establishment of the facts was proper and whether their evaluation of those facts was unbiased and objective. If the establishment of the facts was proper and the evaluation was unbiased and objective, even though the panel might have reached a different conclusion, the evaluation shall not be overturned;
> (ii) the panel shall interpret the relevant provisions of the Agreement in accordance with customary rules of interpretation of public international law. Where the panel finds that a relevant provision of the Agreement admits of more than one permissible interpretation, the panel shall find the authorities' measure to be in conformity with the Agreement if it rests upon one of those permissible interpretations.

WTO adjudicating bodies will consequently evaluate whether facts were properly established and evaluated in an unbiased manner (Art. 17.6(i)), and whether the overall conclusion reached rests on a permissible interpretation of the AD Agreement (Art. 17.6(ii)). This standard has been consistently applied also in cases dealing with other instruments of contingent protection.[137]

Art. 17.6(i) has been understood in case law as a statutory requirement not to engage in a *de novo* review. There is nothing like a statutory definition of the term; indeed the term itself is an invention of GATT Panels. By *de novo* review, GATT and WTO adjudicating bodies have understood a certain degree of deference towards the establishment and evaluation of facts by an IA: they can, of course, sanction WTO Members for not properly establishing the record and can find that conclusions reached by them are inconsistent with the requirements of the AD Agreement; they will refrain, however, from substituting their own judgment for that of the IA.

There are some definitions of the *de novo* standard which are usually uninformative (*EC—Tube or Pipe Fittings*, Panel report, §7.6). Panels have also cautioned

---

[137] See, for example, the AB report on *US—Countervailing Duty Investigation on DRAMS* at §§182–90. On this issue, see Francois and Palmeter (2008).

that absence of *de novo* review should not be equated with total deference to the opinion of the IA. Yet again, what does total deference mean? It seems that total deference and *de novo* review are the two ends of the spectrum, and the question is at what point in the continuum will WTO adjudicating bodies intervene? Case law has provided some clarifications in this respect.

First, it is by now clear that (*US—Lamb*, AB report, §§106–7) that absence of reasoned and adequate explanation of the decision is fatal for the order. *US—Lamb* dealt with a dispute under the SG Agreement. Its standard of review, however, soon found application in cases coming under other contingent protection instruments. In its report on *US—Softwood Lumber VI (Article 21.5—Canada)*, the AB went one step further and held that it was not the mere existence of plausible alternatives that rendered the IA's determination implausible: a Panel must examine the IA's determination in light of these plausible alternatives rather than in the abstract. This did not imply, according to the AB (§117, and footnote 176), that Panels must reject the IA's explanation, if it did not in its view rebut the alternatives: what is important is that the IA has taken account of and responded to plausible alternative explanations that were raised before it and that, having done so, the explanations provided by it in support of its determination remain 'reasoned and adequate'.

In this vein, the Panel on *US—Softwood Lumber VI (Article 21.5—Canada)* faced a re-determination by the USITC of a threat of injury determination that had been found to be inconsistent with the AD Agreement by the original Panel.[138] The Panel emphasized that the fact that an alternative explanation of the data was possible did not *ipso facto* lead to the conclusion that the USITC had committed a violation. Canada had offered an alternative explanation but, in the eyes of the Panel, had failed to also demonstrate that an unbiased and objective IA could not have reached the conclusions reached by the USITC (§§7.35ff and especially §7.56). In this Panel's view, hence, successful complainants must not only provide an alternative explanation; they must also demonstrate that the explanation offered by the IA is not reasonable. On appeal, the AB reversed the Panel in this respect. In the AB's view, the Panel had shown total deference to the IA in this case. After explaining what it considered to be the Panel's obligation when reviewing a determination of an IA (§106), the AB went on to hold the Panel had failed to abide by the proper standard of review for the following reasons (§138):

> In sum, the Panel's analysis, viewed as a whole, reveals a number of serious infirmities in the standard of review that it articulated and applied in assessing the

---

[138] In this volume, we do not discuss the DSU. Suffice to state here that a compliance Panel is the judicial entity that might be entrusted, in case of disagreement between complainant and defendant, with the question of whether the latter has complied with the findings of the original Panel (assuming of course that the original Panel had accepted the original complaint); see Palmeter and Mavroidis (2004).

consistency of the Section 129 Determination with Articles 3.5 and 3.7 of the *Antidumping Agreement* and Articles 15.5 and 15.7 of the *SCM Agreement*. First, the Panel's repeated reliance on the test that Canada had not demonstrated that an objective and unbiased authority 'could not' have reached the conclusion that the USITC did, is at odds with the standard of review that has been articulated by the Appellate Body in previous reports. As we noted earlier, the standard applied by the Panel imposes an undue burden on the complaining party. Secondly, the 'not unreasonable' standard employed by the Panel at various reprises is also inconsistent with the standard of review that has been articulated by the Appellate Body in previous reports, and it is even more so for ultimate findings as opposed to interme- diate inferences made from particular pieces of evidence. Thirdly, the Panel did not conduct a critical and searching analysis of the USITC's findings in order to test whether they were properly supported by evidence on the record and were 'reasoned and adequate' in the light of alternative explanations of that evidence. Fourthly, the Panel failed to conduct an analysis of whether the totality of the factors and evidence considered by the USITC supported the ultimate finding of a threat of material injury. (italics in the original)

There is thus an obligation imposed on Panels to examine the explanation offered by the IA in light of alternative explanations offered by the complaining party.

Second, Panels cannot take into consideration evidence that was not submitted to the IA or that was not appropriately submitted to the IA, and which the IA had refused to take into account (*Egypt—Steel Rebar*, Panel report, §7.21). In the words of the Panel on *US—Hot-Rolled Steel* (§7.6):

> Thus, for example, in examining the USITC's determination of injury under Article 3 of the *AD Agreement*, we would not consider any evidence concerning the price effects of imports that was not made available to the USITC under the appropriate US procedures. (italics in the original)

The question of what constitutes new facts and evidence was comprehensively addressed in the Panel report on *EC—Bed Linen*[139] in the following manner (§6.43):

> Article 17.5(ii) of the *AD Agreement* provides that a panel shall consider a dispute under the *AD Agreement* 'based upon: . . . the facts made available in conformity with appropriate domestic procedures to the authorities of the importing Member'. It does not require, however, that a panel consider those facts exclusively in the format in which they were originally available to the investigating authority. Indeed, the very purpose of the submissions of the parties to the Panel is to marshal the relevant facts in an organized and comprehensible fashion in support of their arguments and to elucidate the parties' positions. Based on our review of the information that was before the European Communities at the time it made its decision, in particular that presented by India in its Exhibits, the parties' extensive argument regarding this evidence, and our findings with respect to India's claim under Article 5.4, we conclude that the Exhibit in question does not contain new evidence. Thus, we

---

[139] Janow and Staiger (2007) discuss this issue in detail and raise critical remarks regarding the internal consistency of WTO case law.

conclude that the form of the document (that is, a new document) does not preclude us from considering its substance, which comprises facts made available to the investigating authority during the investigation. There is in our view no basis for excluding the document from consideration in this proceeding, and we therefore deny India's request. (italics in the original)

Subsequent Panels have adopted a similar distinction, but not always with consistent results: the Panel on *US—Softwood Lumber V*, for example, excluded a regression analysis based on data that were before the IA, because it considered that such an analysis constituted new evidence that went beyond a mere mechanical reformatting of appropriately submitted facts (§§7.40–1). The same Panel accepted, nonetheless, charts which were not before the IA, since they only (§7.168):

display in graphical form data which was before DOC during the course of the investigation.

Still, both the regression analysis and the graph were based on evidence that had already been submitted to the IA so some additional explanation for the differential treatment would be warranted in this case: to quote the Panel report on *EC—Bed Linen* discussed above, it seems there is a thin line between evidence which is merely marshalling the already submitted evidence and, hence, can be taken into account by a Panel and evidence which constitutes 'a manipulation of already submitted facts and evidence', on which the Panel would not be allowed to base its review if it wants to avoid a *de novo* review; and it is this distinction that probably provides the rationale for the attitude of Panels in the two cases cited here. It is probably the Panel on *US—Steel Plate* that made this point clearer than any other Panel before. This Panel considered that an affidavit based on data that were before the IA at the time of the investigation was acceptable as it did not constitute new information (§7.13):

What the affidavits do is present the information submitted in a different manner than originally submitted, and adjust and sort it in various ways.

This criterion is what distinguishes acceptable from unacceptable evidence. There is one more twist in this story: in accordance with Art. 12 AD, an IA will be required to make public only the essential elements of the investigation which led it to its decision. As a result, it could be the case that an IA disseminates less than the information that it used to reach its conclusions. The question may arise whether such non-disclosed information should be considered as being part of the record and, if so, under what conditions. Following inconsistent case law on this issue, the Panel on *EC—Tube or Pipe Fittings* made the following distinction: facts which have not been submitted to the IA are not properly before the Panel. However, facts which have not been disclosed by the IA, but on which the authority has relied to reach its decision, can (and should) be reviewed by a

WTO Panel (§§7.35 and 7.45). On appeal, the AB upheld the Panel's approach (§§125ff, and especially §133).[140]

A Panel will review whether an IA has properly established the factual record before it. In practice, this amounts to examining whether the IA has diligently assembled the facts. It is against this background that Panels will evaluate whether the IA's appreciation was unbiased and objective. It is worth recalling that this latter test should not lead Panels to re-open the investigation process and re-do the whole procedure, substituting their judgment for that of the IA. The Panel in *US—Hot-Rolled Steel* expressed the requirement to examine whether the facts were properly established and evaluated in an unbiased and objective manner as required by Art. 17.6(i) AD, in the following manner (§7.26):

> The question of whether the establishment of facts was proper does not, in our view, involve the question whether all relevant facts were considered including those that might detract from an affirmative determination. Whether the facts were properly established involves determining whether the investigating authorities collected relevant and reliable information concerning the issue to be decided—it essentially goes to the investigative process. Then, assuming that the establishment of the facts with regard to a particular claim was proper, we consider whether, based on the evidence before the US investigating authorities at the time of the determination, an unbiased and objective investigating authority evaluating that evidence could have reached the conclusions that the US investigating authorities reached on the matter in question. In this context, we consider whether all the evidence was considered, including facts which might detract from the decision actually reached by the investigating authorities.

The relationship between Art. 11 DSU (the default standard of review applied to all cases) and Art. 17.6(ii) AD (the idiosyncratic standard of review applied in antidumping litigation) is the question that has occupied most of the case law. The argument is often made that the AD standard of review is more deferential (than Art. 11 DSU) towards WTO Members.[141] This argument is meritorious: indeed, why would negotiators spend time and effort if it were to reproduce the letter and the spirit of Art. 11 DSU?[142] Practice shows that typically Panels have preferred to apply simultaneously the two standards of review, that is, they see no contradiction between them. For example, the Panel on *US—Corrosion-Resistant Steel Sunset Review* held that the standard of review applicable in the context of sunset reviews would require it to apply both Art. 11 DSU and Art. 17.6 AD to the factual and legal issues before it (§§7.4–7.5). The Panel on *US—Softwood Lumber VI* reflects its understanding of the relationship between the generic and the AD standard of review in the following manner (§7.22):

---

[140] Horn and Mavroidis (2005b) find this distinction useful but point to evidentiary problems that might arise in this context.

[141] See, on this score, Croley and Jackson (1996), and Palmeter (1995).

[142] Mavroidis (2009) discusses this point in more detail. Stewart et al. (1993) point to evidence that its proponents had a deferential standard in mind.

Thus, it is clear to us that, under the *AD Agreement*, a panel is to follow the same rules of treaty interpretation as in any other dispute. The difference is that if a panel finds more than one permissible interpretation of a provision of the *AD Agreement*, it may uphold a measure that rests on one of those interpretations. It is not clear whether the same result could be reached under Articles 3.2 and 11 of the DSU. However, it seems to us that there might well be cases in which the application of the Vienna Convention principles together with the additional provisions of Article 17.6 of the *AD Agreement* could result in a different conclusion being reached in a dispute under the *AD Agreement* than under the *SCM Agreement*. In this case, it has not been necessary for us to resolve this question, as we did not find any instances where the question of violation turned on the question whether there was more than one permissible interpretation of the text of the relevant Agreements. (italics in the original)

Art. 3.2 DSU, as we saw in Chapter 1, requests from WTO adjudicating bodies to apply customary rules of interpretation when called to adjudicate disputes. And it is worth recalling that from its first decision onwards (*US—Gasoline*) the AB has held that it is the VCLT that codifies customary rules of interpretation. So the question arises whether recourse to the VCLT will always lead to one interpretation or, conversely, whether this is impossible. If the latter, then of course the quoted statement above is totally wrong. The Panel on *US—Hot-Rolled Steel* rejected this point of view when holding that, in order to evaluate whether the interpretation reached was a permissible one, the starting point of its analysis should be the VCLT (§7.27). On appeal, the AB confirmed the Panel's position: to reach a conclusion whether more than one interpretation could be permissible, exhaustion of the interpretative elements reflected in the VCLT was the necessary first step (§§59–60):

> This second sentence of Article 17.6(ii) *presupposes* that application of the rules of treaty interpretation in Articles 31 and 32 of the *Vienna Convention* could give rise to, at least, two interpretations of some provisions of the *Antidumping Agreement*, which, under that Convention, would both be 'permissible interpretations'. In that event, a measure is deemed to be in conformity with the *Antidumping Agreement* 'if it rests upon one of those permissible interpretations'.
>
> It follows that, under Article 17.6(ii) of the *Antidumping Agreement*, panels are obliged to determine whether a measure rests upon an interpretation of the relevant provisions of the *Antidumping Agreement* which is *permissible under the rules of treaty interpretation* in Articles 31 and 32 of the *Vienna Convention*. In other words, a permissible interpretation is one which is found to be appropriate after application of the pertinent rules of the *Vienna Convention*. We observe that the rules of treaty interpretation in Articles 31 and 32 of the *Vienna Convention* apply to any treaty, in any field of public international law, and not just to the WTO agreements. These rules of treaty interpretation impose certain common disciplines upon treaty interpreters, irrespective of the content of the treaty provision being examined and irrespective of the field of international law concerned. (italics and emphasis in the original)

So far, there is little evidence of 'permissible interpretations'. The Panel on *Argentina—Poultry Antidumping Duties* was requested to judge whether

46 per cent of all domestic producers should be considered as a major proportion of the total domestic production, in accordance with Art. 4.1 AD. Without delving too much into a thorough discussion of this issue, the Panel accepted that this was indeed a permissible interpretation of the term (§7.341). This is probably the only case where a Panel insinuated that this was one of a range of permissible interpretations and, since it was in the range, it was acceptable.

The relationship between Arts. 11 DSU and 17.6(ii) AD was debated in the AB report on *US—Hot-Rolled Steel* (§62):

> Finally, although the second sentence of Article 17.6(ii) of the *Antidumping Agreement* imposes obligations on panels which are not found in the DSU, we see Article 17.6(ii) as supplementing, rather than replacing, the DSU, and Article 11 in particular. Article 11 requires panels to make an 'objective assessment of the matter' as a whole. Thus, under the DSU, in examining claims, panels must make an 'objective assessment' of the legal provisions at issue, their 'applicability' to the dispute, and the 'conformity' of the measures at issue with the covered agreements. Nothing in Article 17.6(ii) of the *Antidumping Agreement* suggests that panels examining claims under that Agreement should not conduct an 'objective assessment' of the legal provisions of the Agreement, their applicability to the dispute, and the conformity of the measures at issue with the Agreement. Article 17.6(ii) simply adds that a panel shall find that a measure is in conformity with the *Antidumping Agreement* if it rests upon one permissible interpretation of that Agreement.' (italics and emphasis in the original)

Here the AB explicitly suggests that permissible interpretations could be the outcome of an objective assessment of the matter before a Panel. But if this is the case, then what is the value added of this provision other than to state the obvious? In other words, if a Panel assessing objectively the matter before it can anyway reach more than one permissible interpretation, then Art. 11 DSU has already dealt with the issue and there should be no need for Art. 17.6(ii) AD. There are good reasons to support the argument that the negotiating intent for this provision was more deference towards IAs dealing with antidumping than at least with IAs dealing with other instruments of contingent protection.[143] It is quite telling that a similar standard of review was not included in either the SCM or the SG Agreement. On the other hand, it is difficult to measure the impact that this provision has had on the interpretation of the various provisions of the AD Agreement. The interpretation of the causality requirement as well as legal discipline regarding sunset reviews detailed *supra* offer the best examples of a deferential approach by WTO adjudicating bodies.[144]

---

[143] Palmeter (1995); Stewart et al. (1993).

[144] The degree of deference is difficult to measure since there is a lot of room for discretion between the two self-imposed ends of the spectrum (no total deference, no *de novo*). Still, in the view of commentators, there are some notable discrepancies: Howse and Neven (2007b and 2007c) discuss *Mexico—Corn Syrup* and *Argentina—Ceramic Tiles* and conclude that the two Panels did not apply an internally coherent standard of review across the two cases.

2.3 Procedural Requirements

2.3.1 Standing

An AD investigation can be launched either *ex officio* or upon request. The former is highly exceptional and anyway the only interesting issue there is under what evidentiary requirements an investigation can be lawfully launched, an issue to which we return in the next subsection. For now, we concentrate on investigations launched upon request. Art. 5.4 AD lays down the standing requirements that the domestic industry filing an application must fulfil: this provision is meant to prevent WTO Members from initiating an investigation unless a certain percentage of the domestic industry producing the like product supports the application; if this is not the case, the application cannot be considered to have been made 'by or on behalf of the domestic industry'. The inclusion of this provision was intended as guarantee that initiations of investigations will not take place on flimsy grounds.[145] This is so since an initiation of investigation can have nefarious effects on exporters because of the resulting uncertainty regarding transaction costs for the products under investigation. Prusa (1992) looks at a wide sample of cases that includes cases where a petition has been withdrawn. His data shows that these withdrawn cases have at least as great an effect on trade as cases which resulted in duties. What he terms 'nuisance suits', that is, petitions with a low probability of success, can confer large gains on the domestic industry supporting the petition.[146] Actually, an effect on the market might exist from the moment an announcement of a petition is made public. Rutkowski (2007) examines 45 such withdrawals in EU practice (between 1992 and 2004) and tests this hypothesis with similar results. Art. 5.4 AD goes some way towards restricting access to the 'petitioners market'.[147]

There are two thresholds that must be met simultaneously according to this provision for standing to be conferred, a 50 per cent and a 25 per cent support threshold. First, the application needs to be supported by those producers whose collective output is more than 50 per cent of the total production of that portion of the domestic producers expressing an opinion in favour or against the initiation.[148]

---

[145] Palmeter (1995).

[146] Staiger and Wolak (1994) also find that the mere filing of a complaint aiming to open up an AD investigation can significantly reduce trade flows during the period of investigation even though no duties are in place during this period. Their explanation rests on legitimate expectations of exporters as to the outcome of investigation.

[147] The timing of the filing might have something to say about the chances of succeeding: Feinberg (2005) and Knetter and Prusa (2003) discuss how business-cycle effects might affect the chance of prevailing when filing for antidumping duties. Feinberg (2005), using financial health of the domestic industry as proxy for (lack of) injury, showed why in a booming market it will be hard to demonstrate that injury has occurred as a result of dumping.

[148] The Agreement does not explicitly require individual producers' support and appears to allow the authority to consider as sufficient the support expressed by a producers' association on behalf of its members. Support expressed by associations is usually considered as equivalent to support

So assume that A, B, C, and D are the only companies in the US and they are producing 10 tons, 20 tons, 50 tons, and 20 tons, respectively of a certain commodity. A and B support the initiation, C is opposed to initiation, and D remains idle. The joint production of A and B is 30 tons, which is less than 50 per cent of the total production of the producers expressing an opinion (A, B, and C, which together produce 80 tons). If C had remained idle, and it had been D who had voiced opposition to the idea of an initiation, A and B would have met the first threshold as together they produce 30 tons, which is more than 50 per cent of the 50 tons which is produced by A, B, and D. Second, the producers expressly supporting the initiation need to represent at least 25 per cent of total production, that is, not less than 25 per cent of the production of all domestic producers whether expressing an opinion on the initiation or not. In the above example, A and B together produce 30 tons which is more than 25 per cent of the total production of the domestic industry (A, B, C, and D) which amounts to 100 tons.

The Panel on *US—Offset Act* (*Byrd Amendment*) faced the following situation: the US administration promised all US companies that actively backed a petition to impose AD duties a redistribution of proceeds from (the eventually imposed) AD duties, the notorious 'Byrd payments'. The Panel found this measure to be inconsistent with the terms of Art. 5.4 AD since, in its view, it violated the principle of good faith (bona fides): by providing operators with an incentive to support an application, the US authority reduced a statutory requirement (Art. 5.4 AD) to redundancy. The Panel noted that Art. 5.4 AD had been introduced, *inter alia*, in response to the controversial US practice of presuming that an application was made by or on behalf of the domestic industry, unless a major proportion of the domestic industry expressed active opposition to the petition. It considered that the Offset Act undermined the value of the standing requirement (§§7.59–65). On appeal, the AB reversed the Panel's conclusions in this respect (§283):

> A textual examination of Article 5.4 of the Antidumping Agreement and Article 11.4 of the SCM Agreement reveals that those provisions contain no requirement that an investigating authority examine the motives of domestic producers that elect to support an investigation. Nor do they contain any explicit requirement that support be based on certain motives, rather than on others. The use of the terms 'expressing support' and 'expressly supporting' clarify that Articles 5.4 and 11.4 require only that authorities 'determine' that support has been 'expressed' by a sufficient number of domestic producers. Thus, in our view, an 'examination' of the 'degree' of support, and not the 'nature' of support is required. In other words, it is the 'quantity', rather than the 'quality', of support that is the issue.

expressed by all producers represented by this association, even though the association perhaps only supported the application following a small majority vote within the association. It has, therefore, been suggested that the Agreement be clarified in this respect, by requiring that the standing determination be based on the positions expressed by individual domestic producers, and that representation by trade associations should not be counted collectively when such determinations are being made; see WTO Docs. TN/RL/GEN/23; TN/RL/GEN/69.

Consequently, in the AB's view, Art. 5.4 AD imposed a mere formal requirement to ensure that a certain percentage of the domestic industry supported an application. This, however, cannot be correct. There is a reason appearing in the preparatory work for introducing Art. 5.4 AD in the Agreement and this reason was explored by the Panel; the AB did not even pay lip service to it. A WTO Member that manipulates the standing requirements opens the door to 'flimsy' requests, since companies might support a filing, not necessarily because they will eventually receive Byrd payments, but because of the costs they shift to their competitors through the petition, as Prusa (1992) and Rutkowski (2007) show. Instead the AB chose to respond to the claim that Byrd payments might lead to more initiations (§292):

> The Panel found that the CDSOA 'will result' in more applications having the required level of support from domestic industry than would have been the case without the CDSOA and stated that 'given the low costs of supporting a petition, and the strong likelihood that all producers will feel obliged to keep open their eligibility for offset payments for reasons of competitive parity', it 'could conclude that the *majority of petitions will achieve the levels of support required* under AD Article 5.4/SCM Article 11.4'. The evidence contained in the Panel record, however, does not support the overreaching conclusion that 'the majority of petitions will achieve the levels of support required' under Articles 5.4 and 11.4 as a result of the CDSOA. Indeed, we note that, in its first written submission to the Panel, the United States explained that 'it is rare for domestic producers in the United States not to have sufficient industry support in filing antidumping or countervailing duty petitions.' In support of its statement, the United States submitted to the Panel a survey that shows, for example, that during the year prior to the enactment of the CDSOA, all of the applications that were filed met the legal thresholds for support. (italics and emphasis in the original)

This is not the reason why Art. 5.4 AD was enacted in the first place, and the AB missed the boat on this occasion.

2.3.2 Duties can be Imposed only Following an Investigation

An investigation will be initiated if the IA decides that the evidence submitted through the application of the domestic industry is adequate and justifies the initiation of the process. Art. 5.2 AD reflects the elements that an application must contain:

> An application under paragraph 1 shall include evidence of (a) dumping, (b) injury within the meaning of Article VI of GATT 1994 as interpreted by this Agreement and (c) a causal link between the dumped imports and the alleged injury. Simple assertion, unsubstantiated by relevant evidence, cannot be considered sufficient to meet the requirements of this paragraph.

Art. 5.2 AD further specifies that 'the application shall contain such information as is reasonably available to the applicant' concerning the domestic industry, the allegedly dumped product and the alleged dumpers, the normal value and export price, the volume and price effect of the imports, and their consequent impact on the domestic industry.

The term 'simple assertion' denotes that what must be avoided is unsubstantiated information. On the other side of the spectrum, the term 'evidence', used in Art. 5.2 AD, should not be equated to full proof, or proof beyond reasonable doubt: the Panel on *Mexico—Corn Syrup* clarified that the application need not contain information on all of the injury-related factors listed in Art. 3.4 AD (§7.73). In the same vein, the Panel on *Thailand—H-Beams* held that (§7.77):

> raw numerical data would constitute 'relevant evidence' than merely a 'simple assertion' within the meaning of this provision.

More generally, according to the panel on *Mexico—Corn Syrup* (§7.76):

> ...Article 5.2 does not require an application to contain analysis, but rather to contain information, in the sense of evidence, in support of allegations. While we recognize that some analysis linking the information and the allegations would be helpful in assessing the merits of an application, we cannot read the text of Article 5.2 as requiring such an analysis in the application itself.

Similarly, the Panel on *US—Softwood Lumber V* rejected the argument that the 'reasonably available' language included in Art. 5.2 AD is there to toughen the obligation to provide evidence in the application. The opposite, in its view, is the case (§7.54).

When presented with an application (petition), an IA is not obliged to initiate an investigation; it retains discretion to this effect: Art. 5.3 AD provides that, even in cases where the application contains evidence on dumping, injury, and the casual link as required by Art. 5.2 AD, no investigation may be initiated unless the IA has examined the record and verified the accuracy and adequacy of the information contained therein. When the IA is persuaded as to the accuracy of the information provided and the well-founded nature of the allegations, it may decide to launch a formal investigation. In other words, a petitioner that has satisfied the requirements embedded in Art. 5.2 AD is not guaranteed an investigation. It is political economy that will usually decide whether the IA will decide to go ahead and initiate or call a halt. Before doing that, nonetheless, an IA has a duty to actively check the accuracy and adequacy of the information submitted under Art. 5.2 AD. The Panel on *US—Softwood Lumber V* held as much (§§7.74ff). Now what does this duty specifically entail? The Panel on *Guatemala—Cement II* (§8.31), as well as the Panel on *Argentina—Poultry Antidumping Duties* (§7.60) were of the view that, while the accuracy and adequacy of the evidence are relevant to the authorities' determination whether there is sufficient evidence to justify initiation:

> it is however the sufficiency of the evidence, and not its adequacy and accuracy per se, which represents the legal standard to be applied in the case of a determination whether to initiate an investigation.

Art. 5.3 AD does not expressly provide that the evidence in question should relate to the questions of dumping, injury, and the casual link, but Panels, reading Art. 5.3 AD in the context of Art. 5.2 AD, have consistently held that such is the kind of evidence required to justify initiation.[149] In order to determine whether there is sufficient evidence of dumping and injury, an IA cannot entirely disregard the elements that configure the existence of that practice as outlined in Arts. 2 and 3 AD.[150] In other words, even though the various provisions of Art. 2 AD relating to normal value and export price do not apply, as such, to the initiation determination, they are certainly relevant to the authorities' determination regarding the sufficiency of evidence.[151] According to the Panel on *US—Softwood Lumber V* (§7.80):

> this does not, of course, mean that an investigating authority must perform a full-blown determination of dumping in order to initiate an investigation. Rather, it means simply that an investigating authority should take into account the general parameters as to what dumping is when inquiring about the sufficiency of the evidence. The requirement is that the evidence must be such that an unbiased and objective investigating authority could determine that there was sufficient evidence of dumping within the meaning of Article 2 to justify initiation of an investigation.

So less than full proof suffices for an investigation to be lawfully initiated, but how much less? Practice provides some responses in this respect. In *Guatemala—Cement II*, the Panel held that the Guatemalan IA was not justified in initiating an investigation based on an application which presented data for normal value and export price at different levels of trade, and with important differences in the sales quantities, without examining the possible effects of such differences on price comparability (§§8.37ff). The Panel on *Mexico—Steel Pipes and Tubes* held that the information contained in a request for initiation was not sufficient if the information regarding normal value presented therein consisted of one invoice and one price quote which did not even pertain to the known exporter but to a distributor, related only to a small subset of the product under investigation, and concerned one single day. By contrast, the export price information reflected the full spectrum of products imported by Mexico from Guatemala over the entire period of investigation, at the level of the Guatemalan producer or exporter. The Panel found that differences of this kind typically lead to a distortion of the normal value vis-à-vis the export price and thus, if not adjusted, could give rise to apparent margins of dumping where no dumping in fact exists (§7.42). The Panel on *US—Softwood Lumber V* held that the following information was sufficient:

---

[149] See, for example, the Panel report on *Guatemala—Cement II* at §8.35.
[150] Ibid.
[151] Ibid. at §8.36.

(a) Cost-related evidence from smaller surrogate domestic producers (as a proxy for cost data from the exporters/producers allegedly dumping) satisfies the requirements of Art. 5.3 AD (§7.95);

(b) Cost allocation to specific products can legitimately not take place at this stage, and hence absence of evidence concerning such cost allocation is not at odds with the requirements of Art. 5.3 AD (§7.97);

(c) If cost data from various surrogate companies covers the whole year and cost data from one company covers the whole period, Art. 5.3 AD has not been violated (§7.99);

(d) The fact that evidence of dumping is found only with respect to some categories of the product among those for which an initiation of investigation has been requested is not at odds with the requirements of Art. 5.3 AD (§7.101);

(e) Prices for domestic sales (home market) can legitimately be taken from a specialized magazine, even though it reflects a number of sales and is not related to a specific sale (§7.105);

(f) An affidavit which reflects deleted (confidential) information can legitimately be taken into account (§7.120);

(g) Price information on only two out of seven categories of lumber products under investigation suffices to meet the requirements of Art. 5.3 AD, as long as the evidence concerns more than an insignificant subset of the imported product (§7.123);

(h) Freight cost information which related to truck freight only does not violate Art. 5.3 AD as nothing before the authority indicated that only rail was used to transport lumber or even that rail was mostly used (§7.126).

In *Argentina—Poultry Antidumping Duties*, the Panel held that the Argentine IA had not justifiably initiated an investigation, even though the application contained evidence on at least a number of transactions that were dumped: since not all comparable export transactions had been included in the preliminary dumping analysis, the Panel considered that there was not sufficient evidence for initiation. Similarly, in *Guatemala—Cement II*, the IA was faulted for initiating an investigation involving a claim of threat of injury which contained information on dumping, injury, and the causal link, but did not provide information on the additional threat factors of Art. 3.7 AD. The Panel on *Mexico—Steel Pipes and Tubes* held that the Mexican IA could not have initiated an investigation on the basis of the volume of import data at the tariff line level without any breakdown of such data at the specific product level. Interestingly, the Mexican IA had acknowledged this problem, and stated, at the time of initiation, that this was one of the issues it was going to investigate in the course of the investigation in order to determine the exact trend in the volume of imports of the subject product as part of its injury analysis. Actually, the investigation confirmed that the subject product constituted a substantial portion of the imports under this more general tariff line, thus confirming the reliability of the data. The Panel did not consider any of this to be relevant in its assessment of whether, at the time of initiation, the Mexican IA was in possession of information sufficient to justify the investigation (§§7.58–60). The Panel on *US—Softwood Lumber V* is an outlier in this respect since it seems to be of the view that the complexity of the case lowers the evidentiary threshold for initiation (§7.95). This Panel appeared to give an IA the benefit of the doubt in complex cases, even where the complexity was, as in this case, largely self-imposed by the applicants. Tension regarding the standard of review exists between the deferential approach of the Panel on *US—Softwood Lumber V* and the rather demanding approach of Panels in all other cases discussed *supra*.

An IA which is not persuaded by the record before it can go ahead and complete it and, using the additional information it has gathered, initiate an investigation; it has, however, no obligation to do so: the Panel held as much in its report on *US—Softwood Lumber V* (§7.75). Consequently, the decision whether to initiate an investigation can be taken on the basis of information submitted by the applicants and completed *ex officio* by the IA. According to the Panel on *Guatemala—Cement II* (§8.62), this is one of the consequences of the difference between Art. 5.2 AD (where the reasonably available standard refers to the applicant) and Art. 5.3 AD (where the sufficiency of evidence standard is applicable to the IA). It is important to point out that the exporters or producers alleged to have been dumping the product are not involved at all in this pre-initiation phase. Art. 5.5 AD expressly provides that the IA shall avoid publicizing the application for initiation of an investigation, unless a decision has been made to initiate an investigation. The only obligation that exists is to notify the government of the exporting country of the receipt of a properly documented application prior to initiation of the investigation. The reason for this is to avoid the chilling effect on trade, which even the submission of an application may have, given the likelihood that it may lead to the initiation of an investigation and subsequent imposition of AD duties.

Art. 5.7 AD further requires from the IA that:

> The evidence of both dumping and injury shall be considered simultaneously *(a)* in the decision whether or not to initiate an investigation, and *(b)* thereafter, during the course of the investigation, starting on a date not later than the earliest date on which in accordance with the provisions of this Agreement provisional measures may be applied.

It is noteworthy that the few cases in which Panels have called for revocation of the antidumping measures following a successful challenge of such measures before the WTO have all involved disputes in which, *inter alia*, the determination of initiation under Art. 5.3 AD was considered flawed.[152] It appears that Panels are of the view that in cases of a flawed initiation, there can be no justification for

---

[152] See, for example, the Panel reports on *Guatemala—Cement II* at §9.6; *Argentina—Poultry* at §§8.6–7; *Mexico—Steel Pipes and Tubes* at §§8.9–13.

maintaining antidumping measures that were based on an investigation that should not even have taken place. This has certainly added to the bite of Art. 5 AD.

Assuming that the decision is taken to initiate an investigation, the IA investigating authority will have to issue a public notice to this effect. When issuing this notice, the IA concerned will have to observe the requirements reflected in Art. 12.1 AD.

The authorities must of course during the course of the investigation satisfy themselves as to the accuracy of the supplied information upon which their findings will be based (Art. 6.6 AD). This may imply an on-the-spot verification of the information, although there certainly does not appear to exist any obligation on the authorities to conduct such (an often costly) verification. In the view of the Panel on *US—DRAMS*, the authorities (§6.78):

> could 'satisfy themselves as to the accuracy of the information' in a number of ways without proceeding to some type of formal verification, including for example reliance on the reputation of the original source of the information.[153]

The Panel on *EC—Tube or Pipe Fittings* even seemed to consider on-site verification as the exception rather than the rule. According to this Panel, verification is an essentially documentary exercise that may be supplemented by an actual on-site visit (§§7.191–2). The authorities must inform the exporters/foreign producers of the information required for verification purposes (*Argentina—Ceramic Tiles*, Panel report, §6.57).[154] On-the-spot verification may only take place in cases where the firms to be verified agree, and the authorities of the exporting Member have been notified and have not objected to their conduct (Art.6.7 AD). Annex I of the Agreement contains further details relating to on-the-spot verifications. Although the Agreement does not prescribe the conduct that must be followed in case of objections by the firm or the government in question, it appears that the best information available can be used (Art. 6.8 AD) in case a company objects; it is not clear how to treat government objection and there is lack of relevant practice in this respect.

Verification is not limited to information submitted prior to the visit, but may also include information to be provided during the course of verification: the Panel on *Guatemala—Cement II* ruled as much (§8.203). Note, in this vein, that the Panel on *EC—Salmon (Norway)* held that recourse to facts available could not be justified solely on the basis that information provided at the time of the on-the-spot verification was not verifiable (§7.360).

The results of verification must be made available to the verified firms as well as to the applicants. The Panel on *Korea—Certain Paper* held that this disclosure does not necessarily have to be made in writing (§7.188). This holding is not

---

[153] See also the Panel report on *Argentina—Ceramic Tiles* at footnote 65; and the Panel report on *Egypt—Steel Rebar* at §§7.326–7.

[154] Howse and Neven (2007c) discuss these requirements in detail.

totally unproblematic in light of evidentiary problems in case of challenge regarding whether disclosure occurred or not.

Art. 6.7 AD deals with foreign exporter-related verification. The obligation to disclose the results of the verification is intended to ensure that exporters can structure their cases for the rest of the investigation in light of those results. The Panel on *Korea—Certain Paper* held that such disclosure must contain adequate information regarding all aspects of the verification, including a description of the information which was not verified, as well as of the information that was successfully verified, since both could be relevant to the presentation of the interested parties' case (§7.192). It is not clear whether an obligation to make the results of verification available to the exporters exists in cases where verification takes place with respect to the domestic industry's questionnaire responses.

The first act of the IA wishing to initiate an investigation is to send out questionnaires to the domestic industry (requesting information on the injury) and the exporters (requesting information regarding the dumping margin). The AD Agreement does not provide for a definition or a mandatory table of contents for questionnaires. The AB in *EC—Fasteners (China)* rejected the idea that an EU formulary requesting information regarding the market-economy status of individual exporters was a questionnaire, because of its limited scope. It provided in brief its understanding of the term 'questionnaire' (§613):

> Based on these considerations, we conclude that the meaning and scope of the term 'questionnaires' in Article 6.1.1 of the *Anti-Dumping Agreement*, and its application to specific kinds of documents, must reflect a balance between the due process requirement to provide parties with an 'ample opportunity' to submit all information they consider responsive to a questionnaire request in an anti-dumping investigation, and the overall timeframe imposed on the investigation under Article 5.10, along with the need for authorities to proceed expeditiously as contemplated in Article 6.14. We therefore find that the 'questionnaires' referred to in Article 6.1.1 are a particular type of document containing substantial requests for information, distributed early in an investigation, and through which the investigating authority solicits a substantial amount of information relating to the key aspects of the investigation that is to be conducted by the authority (that is, dumping, injury, and causation). While in many investigations one 'questionnaire' may be employed to solicit such information on these aspects of the investigation, we consider that, depending on how different Members organize the conduct of the investigation process, a party may receive several substantial requests soliciting such comprehensive information that are 'questionnaires' within the meaning of Article 6.1.1. (italics in the original)

2.3.3 The Period of Investigation

The importance of the choice of period of investigation (POI) cannot be overstated. The Panel on *Mexico—Antidumping Measures on Rice* summed it up very well at §7.56:

The choice of the period of investigation is obviously crucial in this investigative process as it determines the data that will form the basis for the assessment of dumping, injury and the causal relationship between dumped imports and the injury to the domestic industry.

The POI refers to the period for which dumping and injury related data are collected and analysed. This period normally precedes the initiation of the investigation. The investigation itself normally runs for a period of 12 to a maximum 18 months (Art. 5.10 AD). Strangely enough, the AD Agreement does not expressly discuss the POI for which the data with respect to dumping and injury should be collected, although, as the Panel on *EC—Tube or Pipe Fittings* acknowledged (footnote 116):

> The concept of a set period of investigation to examine the existence of dumping has been present in the GATT system for over 40 years. Indeed, a 1960 Report by a Group of Experts concerning antidumping and countervailing duties considered the use of a 'pre-selection system'. See Group of Experts, Second Report on Antidumping and Countervailing Duties, adopted on 27 May 1960 (L/1141) BISD 9S, 194.

The WTO Antidumping Committee (ADP Committee) adopted a Recommendation Concerning the Periods of Data Collection for Antidumping Investigations (hereinafter, the 'POI Recommendation'), which regulates the period of the POI. In the words of the Panel on *Guatemala—Cement II* (§8.266):

> this recommendation reflects the common practice of Members.

The POI Recommendation[155] distinguishes between periods of data collection for dumping and injury investigations, and provides, *inter alia*, that:

(a) The period of data collection for dumping investigations normally should be twelve months, and in any case no less than six months;

(b) This period should end as close to the date of initiation as is practicable;

(c) The period of data collection for injury investigations should normally be at least three years, unless a party from whom data is being gathered has existed for a lesser period; and

(d) The period of data collection for injury investigations should include the entirety of the period of data collection for the dumping investigation.

The ADP Committee stated in the POI Recommendation that it was merely issuing guidelines, which should not preclude an IA from choosing a different POI. In such cases, an IA should include in public notices, or in separate reports, an explanation of the reason for the selection of a particular period for data collection. There is, thus, no legal compulsion imposed on WTO Members to follow the POI Recommendation verbatim. Moreover, an IA is by no means

---

155 WTO Doc. G/ADP/6, adopted by the ADP Committee on 5 May 2000. On its legal value, see Mavroidis (2008).

obliged to accept the applicants' point of view on this score. The Panel on *US—Hot-Rolled Steel*, based on discussions in the ADP Committee concerning the nature of Committee recommendations, held that the POI Recommendation was a non-binding instrument. Accordingly, in the Panel's view, all obligations imposed on an IA with respect to the length of the POI have to be found in the AD Agreement itself (footnote 152 of the report).[156] Subsequent Panels, nevertheless, have shown considerable deference to the substantive part of the POI Recommendation, its non-binding nature notwithstanding. In its report on *Argentina—Poultry Antidumping Duties*, the Panel held (§7.287):

> Furthermore, we note that the issue of periods of review has been examined by the Antidumping Committee. It has issued a recommendation to the effect that, as a general rule, 'the period of data collection for injury investigations normally should be at least three years, unless a party from whom data is being gathered has existed for a lesser period, and should include the entirety of the period of data collection for the dumping investigation'. It would appear, therefore, that the period of review for injury need only 'include' the entirety of the period of review for dumping. There is nothing in the Antidumping Committee's recommendation to suggest that it should not exceed (in the sense of including more recent data) the period of review for dumping.

The Panel on *Mexico—Antidumping Measures on Rice*, while recognizing its non-binding nature, uses the POI Recommendation as support for its findings (§7.62). On appeal, its approach was upheld in its totality by the AB (§169):

> It appears to us that the Panel referred to the Recommendation, not as a legal basis for its findings, but simply to show that the Recommendation's content was not inconsistent with its own reasoning. Doing so does not constitute an error of law.

By now it is safe to argue that de facto Panels have adhered to the prescriptions of the POI Recommendation.

The Panel on *EC—Tube or Pipe Fittings* explained the rationale for using a POI which ends before the initiation of the investigation in the following terms (§7.101):

> There are practical reasons for using an investigation period, the termination date of which precedes the date of initiation of the investigation. This ensures that the data that will form the basis for the eventual determination are not affected in any way by the initiation of the investigation and any subsequent actions of exporters/importers. The rationale is thus to acquire a finite data set unaffected by the process of the investigation. This can form the basis for an objective and unbiased determination by the investigating authority. The period of investigation terminates as close as possible to the date of initiation of the investigation in order to ensure that the data pertaining to the investigation period, while historical, nevertheless refers to the recent past. The use of a sufficiently long period of investigation is critical in order to ensure that any dumping identified is sustained rather than sporadic.

---

[156] A similar view has been expressed in the Panel report on *Guatemala—Cement II* at §8.266.

In *Mexico—Antidumping Measures on Rice*, the US claimed that the Mexican authority had violated the AD Agreement by selecting a POI for injury which had ended more than 15 months prior to the initiation of the investigation, and analysed only that part of the POI for which data had been gathered. The US contended that this was in violation of the obligation included in Art. 3.1 AD to conduct an objective examination based on positive evidence in order to determine injury and, consequently, the Mexican practice also constituted violation of Arts. 3.2, 3.4, and 3.5 AD. The Panel followed the US in its reasoning. In *US—Hot-Rolled Steel*, the Panel considered whether an injury analysis which revolved around an evaluation of two years of data would be inconsistent with the requirement to conduct an objective examination based on positive evidence. In this case, the US IA had gathered data for a three-year period and acknowledged that this was required for injury purposes. The US did not compare the data, and argued that the reason the authority did not compare data for 1996 with that for 1998 was that 'changes created a new economic context for the performance of the industry'. The US did not explain why it considered the data no longer relevant in light of the changed economic circumstances. Nevertheless, the Panel did not consider it inappropriate for the IA to examine only data from two years, as such data related to the most recent period and included the period of alleged dumped imports (§7.234). The Panel emphasized that no end-point-to-end-point comparison was required and that, in certain circumstances, it would be reasonable for an IA to examine only part of the data covering a two-year period. As long as three years of data were gathered, and such three-year data have at least in part been used, the authority would seem to be able to get away with the fact that it did not analyse part of the data for certain of the factors mentioned in Art. 3.4 AD.

In *Guatemala—Cement II*, the Panel rejected the idea that the use of a one-year period of data collection would be a priori inconsistent with the requirement of Art. 3.2 AD (to consider whether there has been a significant increase in the volume of dumped imports). Recall that the examination of whether a significant increase has occurred is part of the injury analysis for which the POI Recommendation considered that a three-year period of data collection was the norm. The Panel considered that no provision in the Agreement specified the precise duration of the period of data collection. In this case, Guatemala argued that the reason for the short period of data collection was that exports by the Mexican producer, Cruz Azul, did not become significant until the year of data collection, a conclusion supported by the record of the investigation. Under these circumstances, while the Panel was of the view that a longer data collection period might have been preferable, it was unable to find that the use by Guatemala of a one-year data collection period was inconsistent with Guatemala's obligation under Art. 3.2 AD (§8.266).

In *Mexico—Antidumping Measures on Rice*, the US claimed that the AD Agreement had been violated because the Mexican IA had analysed data pertaining to only six months for each of the three years of data collection. Mexico asserted that it was necessary to examine these particular six months of every year, instead of the full year, in order to ensure that the period of injury analysis paralleled the six-month period chosen for the analysis of dumping, so as to avoid any distortions. The Panel saw no a priori reason why the period of investigation for the injury analysis should be chosen to fit the period of investigation for the dumping analysis, in case the latter covers a period of less than 12 months. The Panel considered that the choice of the POI was crucial, as it determined the data that would form the basis for the assessment of the impact of dumping, and that an examination or investigation could only be objective if it was based on data which provided an accurate and unbiased picture of what it was that one was examining. The Panel thus reached the following conclusion (§7.86):

> In sum, we find that the injury analysis of the Mexican investigating authority in the rice investigation, which was based on data covering only six months of each of the three years examined, is inconsistent with Article 3.1 of the AD Agreement as it is not based on positive evidence and does not allow for an objective examination, as it necessarily, and without any proper justification, provides only a part of the picture of the situation. In addition, we find that the particular choice of the limited period of investigation in this case was not that of an unbiased and objective investigating authority as the authority was aware of, and accepted, the fact that the period chosen reflected the highest import penetration, thus ignoring data from a period in which it can be expected that the domestic industry was faring better.

Similarly, the Panel on *EC—Tube or Pipe Fittings* was of the view that an IA is precluded from limiting its dumping analysis to a selective subset of data from only a temporal subsegment of the POI. The Panel relied on the requirement of Art. 2.4.2 AD, which generally calls for a comparison of a WA normal value with a WA of prices of all comparable export transactions, or for a comparison of normal value and export prices on a T-T basis. According to the Panel, these methodologies would generally seem to require that data throughout the entire investigation period would necessarily be consistently taken into account.

In *Argentina—Poultry Antidumping Duties*, the use of different periods for different injury factors was found to be inconsistent with the requirement to conduct an objective examination (§7.283). To examine only a part or a segment of the domestic industry was also considered to be inconsistent with the requirement to conduct an objective examination. The AB stated in its report on *US—Hot-Rolled Steel* that, where an IA undertakes an examination of one part of a domestic industry, it should, in principle, examine, in a like manner, all other parts that make up the industry, as well as the industry as a whole. A partial examination of the domestic industry could make it easier to find injury. This led the AB to conclude that such a practice was inconsistent with the AD Agreement (§204). We can conclude from the above:

(a) The mere fact that the injury POI does not cover a three-year period is not alone sufficient to conclude that the authorities failed to examine injury in an objective manner and based on positive evidence;

(b) The data from the POI should allow the authorities to have an accurate and unbiased picture of the state of the domestic industry.

The requirement that the POI for injury purposes at least include the POI for dumping purposes was discussed by the Panel in its report on *Argentina—Poultry Antidumping Duties*. This Panel rejected the argument that the POI for dumping and the POI for injury should also end at the same time. Brazil had argued that such an identity was required in order to be able to establish a causal link between dumped imports and injury to the domestic industry as required by Art. 3.5 AD. According to the Panel, there was nothing in the POI Recommendation to suggest that the POI for injury should not exceed (in the sense of including more recent data) the period of review for dumping. The Panel added that there may be a time lag between the entry of dumped imports and the injury caused by them, and that it may, therefore, not be appropriate to use identical periods of review for the dumping and injury analyses in all cases (§7.287).

In *Mexico—Antidumping Measures on Rice*, the US challenged the decision by the Mexican IA to use a POI for injury which ended more than 15 months prior to the initiation of the investigation. The Panel considered that, while the AD Agreement does not contain any specific and express rules concerning the period to be used for data collection in an antidumping investigation, this does not mean that the authorities' discretion in using a certain period of investigation is boundless (§7.57). The Panel was of the view that there was necessarily an inherent real-time link between the investigation leading to the imposition of measures, and the data on which the investigation was based. In spite of the fact that an antidumping investigation out of necessity relies on historical data gathered during a past POI, such information should be the most recent information reasonably available (§§7.58ff). The Panel considered that a 15-month gap between the end of the period of investigation and the initiation of the investigation was sufficiently long as to impugn the reliability of the evidence. In the Panel's view, Mexico had thus failed to use data that met the criterion of positive evidence pursuant to Art. 3.1 AD (§7.64). The AB fully upheld the reasoning of the Panel (§§163–72). It emphasized that the determination of whether injury exists should be based on data that provides indications of the situation prevailing when the investigation takes place, because the conditions to impose an antidumping duty are to be assessed with respect to the current situation (§165). The Panel on *Mexico—Steel Pipes and Tubes* agreed with the statements of the Panel and AB in their respective reports on *Mexico—Antidumping Measures on Rice*, concerning the real-time link between the POI and the imposition of measures, but considered that an eight-month gap between the end of the POI and the initiation of the investigation was reasonable. It acknowledged that this eight-month gap implied that the IA did not have 'the most pertinent, credible and reliable information', but considered that 'practical time constraints inherent in the production of data that must then be collected and analyzed by the applicant (in order to be relied upon and submitted in the application), and then analyzed by the investigating authority', and the fact that 'the investigation occurred within the overall time constraints envisaged by the Agreement', were sufficient reasons to conclude that the temporal gap did not preclude the authority from making a determination of injury based on positive evidence and which involved an objective examination (§7.239).

The Panel on *EC—Tube or Pipe Fittings* rejected the argument that the POI would need to be adjusted in the case of important developments, such as a devaluation occurring towards the end of the POI. In other words, the Panel was of the view that, once an appropriate POI was chosen, i.e. a POI which relates to the recent past, there was no need to re-examine the issue (§7.102).

2.3.4 The Duty of Even-Handedness Imposed on IAs

AD duties will be imposed following an investigation. IAs are national administrative entities and for this reason very much an integral part of the domestic political economy constellation. The framers of the AD Agreement, mindful of the potential influence that domestic constituencies might exercise on IAs, opted for institutional guarantees that would reduce similar risks. This is where the requirement for even-handedness imposed on IAs kicks in. It is a multifaceted requirement since IAs must observe this requirement at different stages of the investigation process: since exporters and domestic industry have antithetical interests, they must be afforded 'equal' chances to present their views. Recall that domestic consumers' associations, the natural allies of foreign exporters, have limited rights of participation by virtue of Art. 6.12 AD.

In this vein, interested parties are to be given timely opportunities to see all information that is:

(a) Relevant to the presentation of their cases;
(b) Not confidential;[157] and
(c) Used by the investigating authorities.

Interested parties must be allowed to prepare presentations on the basis of this information and authorities must keep a public record of the investigation to serve this duty (Art. 6.4 AD). For example, in the case of a constructed normal value, the actual figures for cost of manufacture, SG&A expenses, or profits used in the calculation of the constructed normal value are to be disclosed to the interested

---

[157] As the Panel on *Korea—Certain Paper* noted, however, Art. 6.4 AD cannot be interpreted as denying an interested party access to its own confidential information, used, for example, in the calculation of a constructed normal value (§7.201). In this sense, disclosure under Art. 6.4 AD differs clearly from the public notice requirements under Art. 12 AD, which do not allow the disclosure of any confidential information (§7.208).

party requesting such information.[158] This provision thus relates to information submitted by other interested parties, as well as information from other sources or documents prepared by the authorities. It is sometimes referred to as the access-to-file obligation, although an IA can ensure compliance with Art. 6.4 AD through means other than by providing access to the file as well.[159]

During antidumping investigations, a substantial amount of information requested (and often submitted) is of a confidential nature. To provide interested parties with the incentives to submit such information, the AD Agreement guarantees that it will be disclosed only with the permission of the party submitting it (Art. 6.5 AD). According to the Agreement, there are two types of confidential information:

(a) Information which is confidential by nature; and
(b) Information which is confidential because confidential treatment has been requested by the party supplying the information.

Panels (*Guatemala—Cement II*; *Korea—Certain Paper*) have held that, in both cases, good cause must be shown for confidential treatment to be granted by the IA. These Panels found that good cause must be shown by the interested party submitting the confidential information at issue, and not by the IA itself.[160] When confidential information has been submitted, a non-confidential summary will be requested and, in principle, disclosed. The summary should be sufficiently detailed to permit a reasonable understanding of the substance of the information submitted in confidence. The Panel on *Argentina—Ceramic Tiles* held that the purpose of non-confidential summaries was to inform interested parties of the information provided, and to enable them to defend their interests. An IA is, therefore, not allowed to reject an exporters' response, simply because the summary was not sufficiently informative to allow the calculation of normal value, export price, and the margin of dumping (§6.39). If, however, in exceptional circumstances, parties indicate that the information provided cannot be summarized, they will be requested to justify their opinion (Art. 6.5.1 AD).[161] Failure by the IA to request

---

[158] See the Panel report on *Korea—Certain Paper* at §7.199.
[159] See the Panel report on *Guatemala—Cement II* at §8.133.
[160] See the Panel report on *Guatemala—Cement II* at §§8.219–20; the Panel report on *Korea—Certain Paper* at §7.335. The *Korea—Certain Paper* Panel did add that, in its view, while some showing of good cause is necessary for both categories of confidential information, the degree of that requirement may, however, depend on the type of information concerned (§7.335). The Panel on *Mexico—Steel Pipes and Tubes* agreed with such conclusions and added that (§7.378):

> a showing of 'good cause' for information that is 'by nature confidential' may consist of establishing that the information fits into the Article 6.5 (chapeau) description of such information: 'for example, because its disclosure would be of significant competitive advantage to a competitor or because its disclosure would have a significantly adverse effect upon a person supplying the information or upon a person from whom that person acquired the information'.

[161] See the Panel report on *Guatemala—Cement II* at §8.213.

from those providing confidential information to also explain why it is impossible to supply a non-confidential summary amounts to a violation of Art. 6.5.1 AD: the AB found this to be the case in *EC—Fasteners (China)* at §§556ff. Investigating authorities retain discretion and they can refuse to adhere to a request to treat some information as confidential. In similar cases, they can disregard the information, unless it has been demonstrated that it is correct (Art. 6.5.2 AD). Interestingly, the Panel, in its report on *Mexico—Steel Pipes and Tubes*, found that an IA is complying with Art. 6.5 AD where it accepts without any explanation or analysis a request for confidentiality which is accompanied by a statement that a non-confidential summary is not possible for certain reasons. The Panel based its view on the fact that Art. 6.5 AD does not explain exactly how an IA should evaluate a request for confidential treatment; how it should indicate the manner and the extent to which it assessed an applicant's assertion to conclude that a good cause existed for the information to be treated as confidential within the meaning of Art. 6.5 AD; or the extent to which it assessed an assertion that summarization was not possible within the meaning of Art. 6.5.1 AD.[162] In other words, where an IA accepts a request for confidentiality, no justification is required under Art. 6.5 AD (§7.380):

> We see that that Article 6.5.1 strikes a balance between the interests of the interested parties submitting confidential information to have that confidentiality maintained during the investigation and the interests of the rest of the interested parties to be reasonably informed about the substance of that information in order to be able to defend their interests. We are aware that the designation of information as 'confidential' might affect the ability of interested parties to have full access to that information, and therefore might affect their ability to defend their interests in the course of an antidumping investigation. We are further aware of the potential for abuse of the possibility to designate information as confidential so as to consciously place other interested parties at a disadvantage in the investigation. We consider that the conditions set out in Article 6.5, chapeau, and 6.5.1 are of critical importance in preserving the balance between the interests of confidentiality and the ability of another interested party to defend its rights throughout an antidumping investigation. For precisely this reason, we consider it paramount for an investigating authority to ensure that the conditions in these provisions are fulfilled. We consider it equally important for a WTO Panel called upon to review an investigating authority's treatment of confidential information strictly to enforce these conditions, while remaining cognizant of the applicable standard of review.

It appears that this Panel ultimately adopted a deferential standard of review, conceding that the IA had lawfully accepted important aspects of the information submitted by the domestic industry as confidential information, even though it had not examined whether good cause existed, or whether it was indeed not possible to provide a non-confidential summary as alleged by the applicant.

---

[162] See the Panel report on *Mexico—Steel Pipes and Tubes* at § 7.393.

2.3.5 Duties of Parties to Cooperate: Recourse to Best Information Available

Interested parties are under a duty to cooperate with the IA. If this is not the case, though, an IA can, when facing uncooperative behaviour by the addressee of its request for information, base its findings on the facts available, or, as is widely known, the best information available (BIA): Art. 6.8 AD and Annex II provide the legal basis for recourse to BIA and enables the IA to continue with the investigation in spite of the lack of cooperation from an interested party. The AD Agreement does not explain in a detailed manner what the duty to cooperate in an antidumping investigation actually means, except for the reference to BIA in Art. 6.8 AD, and in Annex II, §7:

> It is clear, however, that if an interested party does not cooperate and thus relevant information is being withheld from the authorities, this situation could lead to a result which is less favourable to the party than if the party did cooperate.

The AB, in its report on *US—Hot Rolled Steel*, held that a duty to cooperate exists: an IA is entitled to expect a very significant degree of effort—to the 'best of their abilities'—from investigated exporters (§102). Based on this finding, the Panel on *EC—Countervailing Measures on DRAM Chips* (a case dealing with the application of Art. 12.7 SCM),[163] considered that a duty to cooperate exists in the SCM context as well. This Panel went on to find that an authority can draw adverse inferences, in case interested parties fail to cooperate (§§7.60–1). The Agreement addresses two issues:

(a) What are the conditions for resorting to BIA? and
(b) What information can be used when resorting to BIA?

Recourse to BIA is permissible under Art. 6.8 AD when the requested party:

(a) Refuses access to necessary information; or
(b) Fails to provide necessary information within a reasonable period of time; or
(c) Significantly impedes the investigation.

Point (a): The Agreement does not specify what is meant by 'necessary information'. It is now clear from the case law that, if an IA has not clearly requested certain information, the failure to submit such information cannot automatically be considered to be a failure to provide necessary information. This would be the case only if the IA has first sufficiently specified the kind of information it is after. The Panel on *Argentina—Ceramic Tiles* noted to this effect (§6.55):

> Thus, the first sentence of paragraph 1 [of Annex II] requires the investigating authority to 'specify in detail the information required', while the second sentence requires it to inform interested parties that, if information is not supplied within a

---

[163] This is the corresponding provision in the SCM Agreement dealing with recourse to best information available.

reasonable time, the authorities may make determinations on the basis of the facts available. In our view, the inclusion, in an Annex relating specifically to the use of best information available under Article 6.8, of a requirement to specify in detail the information required, strongly implies that investigating authorities are not entitled to resort to best information available in a situation where a party does not provide certain information if the authorities failed to specify in detail the information which was required.

But does the mere fact that information was requested or required by the authorities suffice to label such information as necessary? This seems to have been the view of the Panel on *Egypt—Steel Rebar* (§7.155). A similar view was held by the Panel on *Korea—Certain Paper*: a certain percentage of the domestic sales of two exporters was made through a related company (called CMI), and the IA, for this reason, had considered that it needed the financial statements of CMI for the purposes of verifying the completeness of the normal value data submitted. In spite of the fact that the two exporting companies and CMI submitted all of their domestic sales data, the IA considered that the failure to provide CMI's financial statements implied that necessary information had not been provided (§7.51). On this basis, the IA decided to reject all of the domestic sales data submitted. Deferring to the IA, the Panel upheld this approach. In this particular case, it was the IA's decision to base its normal value determination on the prices charged by the related company (CMI) to independent buyers which gave prominence to the financial statements of CMI. The Panel expressed the view that necessary information included information which was important in verifying information actually submitted and was not limited to the actual data needed to calculate normal value and export price (§§7.43–4). A legitimate question can be raised here as to whether supporting evidence (like that requested from CMI) actually constitutes necessary information, and hence whether facts available may be used simply because no, or no sufficient, supporting documents have been provided when requested. The Panel on *Argentina—Ceramic Tiles* did not address this issue head on, but linked it to the duty of an IA to specify the information requested (§6.66). One would expect nonetheless that recourse to BIA should not be a matter of discretion when irrelevant or auxiliary information is requested and not provided. Problems might arise in similar cases (assuming a challenge before the WTO), because they might invite borderline *de novo* review by Panels.

Point (b): The Agreement cannot provide for a time limit that must be observed in all circumstances, for it might prove to be draconian on some occasions and too generous on others. Hence, it calls for a 'reasonable period of time' that must be set by the IA. This term is flexible and hence easy to abuse. The Panel on *US—Hot-Rolled Steel* dealt with a challenge by Japan against a US decision to reject submitted information: the US authority (DOC) had rejected information by NSC (a Japanese company) because it was submitted after the deadline it (DOC) had unilaterally fixed. NSC did not respect the deadline, but still sent its responses to the DOC before the initiation of the verification process. In the Panel's view, what mattered was not the respecting of unilateral deadlines, but rather whether the process had suffered as a result of NSC's behaviour. In its view, this was not the case, since there was ample time to verify the submitted information (§7.57). On appeal, the AB confirmed the Panel's finding, and explained in some detail how the term 'reasonable period of time' (within which information must be provided) should be understood (§85):

> In considering whether information is submitted within a reasonable period of time, investigating authorities should consider, in the context of a particular case, factors such as (i) the nature and quantity of the information submitted; (ii) the difficulties encountered by an investigated exporter in obtaining the information; (iii) the verifiability of the information and the ease with which it can be used by the investigating authorities in making their determination; (iv) whether other interested parties are likely to be prejudiced if the information is used; (v) whether acceptance of the information would compromise the ability of the investigating authorities to conduct the investigation expeditiously; and (vi) the numbers of days by which the investigated exporter missed the applicable time-limit.

The Panel on *Korea—Certain Paper* first examined whether information was provided within the deadline set by the IA, and then whether it was nevertheless submitted within a reasonable period by applying the criteria set forth by the AB in the above quoted *US—Hot-Rolled Steel* report (§§7.48–55). This approach has become standing case law.

Note that the effort made by the requested party does not necessarily matter, in the sense that requested parties might in good faith try to supply information and still fall short of the expectations of the IA. Information which was not verifiable or not appropriately submitted does not have to be taken into consideration if the party submitting it acted to the best of its abilities. The Panel on *Egypt—Steel Rebar* noted to this effect that (§7.242):

> . . . an interested party's level of effort to submit certain information does not necessarily have anything to do with the substantive quality of the information submitted and thus the fact of acting to the best of one's ability by itself does not preclude the investigating authority from resorting to facts available in respect of the requested information.

Annex II provides in its §5 that an IA is not justified in disregarding all submitted information simply because there is no absolute overlap between what was requested and what was eventually supplied by a party acting in due diligence.[164]

Point (c): according to the Panel on *Korea—Certain Paper*, Annex II, §6 should not be understood as the means to provide the interested party with a second chance to submit information (§7.85).

The Panel on *Guatemala—Cement II* considered that a failure to cooperate with a verification visit due to a disagreement concerning the composition of the

---

[164] See the AB report on *US—Hot-Rolled Steel* at §81.

verification team and the presence of non-governmental experts with a possible conflict of interest did not necessarily constitute a significant impediment of the investigation within the meaning of the Agreement. According to the Panel, the Agreement 'does not require cooperation by interested parties at any cost' (§8.251). Annex II further provides in its §3:

> All information which is verifiable, which is appropriately submitted so that it can be used in the investigation without undue difficulties, which is supplied in a timely fashion, and, where applicable, which is supplied in a medium or computer language requested by the authorities, should be taken into account when determinations are made. If a party does not respond in the preferred medium or computer language but the authorities find that the circumstances set out in paragraph 2 have been satisfied, the failure to respond in the preferred medium or computer language should not be considered to significantly impede the investigation.

According to the Panel on *US—Steel Plate*, an IA is only required to take into account information which satisfies all of the applicable criteria of §3 of Annex II (§7.57). According to this Panel (§7.71), information is verifiable if the:

> accuracy and reliability of the information can be assessed by an objective process of examination.

The fact that verifiable information was not actually verified is irrelevant in this respect (*Guatemala—Cement II*, Panel report, §8.252). The Panel on *EC—Salmon* (*Norway*) added that merely because information was not provided at the time of the on-the-spot verification does not imply that such information is not verifiable (§7.360).

Information which has not been submitted in accordance with a WTO Member's domestic laws is not appropriately submitted (*Argentina—Poultry Antidumping Duties*, Panel report, §7.191): this Panel held that the information submitted by Brazilian exporters without respecting the Argentine accreditation requirements was not appropriately submitted.

Submitted information does not necessarily have to be used even if it is verifiable. This would be the case when the use of the submitted information cannot be done without undue difficulties, hardly a self-interpreting term. The Panel on *US—Steel Plate* held that it is not possible to determine in the abstract whether information can be used without undue difficulties (§7.74):

> We consider the question of whether information submitted can be used in the investigation 'without undue difficulties' is a highly fact-specific issue. Thus, we consider that it is imperative that the investigating authority explain, as required by paragraph 6 of Annex II, the basis of a conclusion that information which is verifiable and timely submitted cannot be used in the investigation without undue difficulties.

Even where the authority is entitled or forced to make determinations on the basis of the facts available, it is not entirely free to make its determinations on whatever basis it chooses: the determination should still be based on facts, not merely on assumptions or conjecture. The Agreement imposes two distinct obligations in this respect:

(a) First, in light of the requirements set forth in §§3 and 5 of Annex II, an IA must use as much as possible the information submitted by the interested parties. There is a caveat here: as acknowledged by the Panel on *US—Steel Plate*, for certain parts of the information requested, the failure to provide such information may have ramifications beyond that particular item. For example, in the absence of cost of production data, the IA will not be able to determine whether sales were made in the ordinary course of trade (§7.60);

(b) Second, Annex II, §7 requires the IA to use 'special circumspection' when basing its determination on secondary sources of information: it should check the information it receives from independent sources at their disposal (such as published price lists, official import statistics and customs returns), and from other interested parties. If the IA uses information from the petitioner without verifying its accuracy, it will be running foul of its obligations under Annex II (*Mexico—Steel Pipes and Tubes*, Panel report, §7.193). On the other hand, an IA cannot claim that it does not need to verify the information it receives simply because it verified it at a prior stage of the investigation in order to comply with Art. 5.3 AD. The Panel on *Korea—Certain Paper* underscored this point in §7.124 of its report. In *US—Hot-Rolled Steel*, the AB warns IAs against confusing wilful non-cooperation that could allow an IA to use adverse inferences with cases of genuine difficulty in procuring the requested information (§§99–100). Therefore, the AB concludes (§104):

> if the investigating authorities fail to 'take due account' of genuine 'difficulties' experienced by interested parties, and made known to the investigating authorities, they cannot . . . fault the interested parties concerned for a lack of cooperation.

The Panel on *Mexico—Antidumping Measures on Rice* faulted Mexico for having legislation in place which required its IA to always apply the highest (facts-available) margin in case of non-cooperation: according to Mexican laws, the IA would always apply the highest margin (assuming a range of margins) based on facts available to all those exporters that refused to cooperate with it. The Panel held that this law was based on a misunderstanding of Art. 6.8 AD, which was not aimed at punishing non-cooperative parties; in fact, in the Panel's view, case law made it clear that, even when presented with imperfect responses, an IA must always try to make good use of them (§7.238). The AB agreed with the explanation of the Panel concerning the term 'best information available': in its view, this term required an evaluative, comparative assessment in order to determine which facts are best suited to fill in the missing information (§297):

The use of the term 'best information' means that information has to be not simply correct or useful per se, but the most fitting or 'most appropriate' information available in the case at hand. Determining that something is 'best' inevitably requires, in our view, an evaluative, comparative assessment as the term 'best' can only be properly applied where an unambiguously superlative status obtains. It means that, for the conditions of Article 6.8 of the *AD Agreement* and Annex II to be complied with, there can be no better information available to be used in the particular circumstances. Clearly, an investigating authority can only be in a position to make that judgment correctly if it has made an inherently comparative evaluation of the 'evidence available'. (italics in the original)

The AB, in its report on *Mexico—Antidumping Measures on Rice* held that an IA must not use data from secondary sources without ascertaining for itself the reliability and accuracy of such information; it must check it, where practicable, against information obtained from other independent sources at its disposal, including material submitted by interested parties (§289). Note, however, in this context, that the Panel on *Korea—Certain Paper* upheld the Korean authorities' decision to construct NV based on facts available because of a failure by the related third party to provide the necessary information. According to the Panel, without this information from the related party, the authority could not possibly determine whether the sales made were in the ordinary course of trade. As a consequence, the authority was entitled to assume that they were not. In addition, the constructed NV did not simply consist of the exporters' cost of production plus the exporters' SG&A expenses and profits, but also included the constructed SG&A expenses for the trading company, since the decision had been made to determine NV on the basis of the trading company's resale price (§7.94). It appears that the authority never examined whether the remainder of the exporters' domestic sales which were not made through the related trading company were of sufficient volume to allow for a proper comparison.

2.3.6 Transparency Requirements

Before making a final determination, IAs must inform all interested parties of the 'essential facts' which formed the basis for the decision to apply AD measures. This disclosure should take place in sufficient time for the parties to defend their interests (Art. 6.9 AD). Case law reveals that the duty to inform embedded in Art. 6.9 AD does not imply that the IA is required to inform the parties of their legal determinations during the course of an investigation, or of the reasons for accepting or rejecting certain arguments:[165] the disclosure obligation under Art. 6.9 AD, as is the case under Arts. 6.1 and 6.2 AD for that matter, relates only to factual information. Thus, the Panel on *Guatemala—Cement II* rejected Mexico's claim that the Guatemalan IA had violated Art. 6.9 AD by changing its injury determination from a preliminary determination of threat of material injury to a

---

[165] See the Panel report on *Argentina—Poultry Antidumping Duties* at §7.225.

final determination of actual material injury during the course of the investigation, without informing Cruz Azul, the Mexican producer, of that change (§§8.238–9).

Unlike the access-to-file obligation included in Art. 6.4 AD, the disclosure obligation in Art. 6.9 AD requires an IA to identify the facts that it considers essential.[166] Art. 6.9 AD imposes an obligation of result on IAs; the aim of disclosure is to allow interested parties to defend their interests and it is in light of this aim that the means of disclosure may be examined, the modalities of performing disclosure being left to the discretion of IAs (*Argentina—Ceramic Tiles,* Panel report, §6.125).

What should be considered essential facts? In *Argentina—Poultry Antidumping Duties* (§7.224), certain export price and normal value data, which had been supplied by one of the parties but had not been used by the IA, was not considered by the Panel to be an essential fact that should have been disclosed to the interested party. Note, nonetheless, that the Panel on *Argentina—Ceramic Tiles* held that exporters should have been informed of the fact that their information, as submitted, was not going to be used for the final determination (§6.129).

Art. 12.2 AD requests an IA to make public any preliminary or final determination or acceptance of price undertakings. Art. 12.2.1–3 AD reflects the elements that should figure in the public notice.

2.4 Institutional Issues: The ADP Committee

A Committee on Antidumping Practices (ADP Committee) is established, by virtue of Art. 16 AD. WTO Members must, by virtue of Art. 18.5 AD, notify the Committee of any changes in their laws. In *US–Customs Bond Directive*, the Panel found that the US, by not notifying the Committee of its new legislation, had acted inconsistently with its obligations under this provision (§7.285). The ADP Committee is not simply a depository of national AD-related initiatives. Recall that the ADP Committee has produced recommendations, like the one on the duration of the POI, that WTO adjudicating bodies have used in case law.

---

166 See the Panel report on *Guatemala—Cement II* at §§8.229–30.

8

SUBSIDIES

1. The Legal Discipline and its Rationale

The SCM Agreement addresses three issues:

(a) It imposes obligations on WTO Members with respect to subsidization, namely to avoid using two types of prohibited subsidies (local content; export);

(b) It requests from WTO Members to avoid causing adverse effects to their WTO Members through subsidies other than the two prohibited types;[1] and

---

[1] The Agreement on Trade in Civil Aircraft also imposes disciplines on WTO Members with respect to financial support on civil aircraft (it also eliminates duties in civil aircraft and provides for conditions regarding procurement decisions). It numbers 31 Members today. We will not be discussing it in detail in this volume since its disciplines overlap with those of the GATT (Art. II),

(c) It regulates the imposition of countervailing duties (CVDs) in case recourse to them is being made in order to counteract subsidization.

Art. 32.1 SCM makes it clear that the above exhausts the possibility for counteracting subsidies:

> No specific action against a subsidy of another Member can be taken except in accordance with the provisions of GATT 1994, as interpreted by this Agreement.

The interpretation of this provision was the core subject-matter of the dispute between the US and a host of WTO Members regarding the US Continued Dumping and Subsidy Offset Act of 2000 (CDSOA), the notorious 'Byrd Amendment' that we discussed *supra* in Chapter 7. Recall that, according to this law, the US had promised to disburse the monetary equivalent of all perceived AD/CVDs to those US economic operators that had supported a petition to initiate an investigation. Both the Panel and the AB held that the Byrd Amendment, by doing this, was violating Art. 32.1 SCM. On appeal, the AB upheld the Panel's findings (§256).

In a subsequent case (*EC—Commercial Vessels*), the Panel faced an argument by Korea to the effect that the EU TDM (Temporary Defence Mechanism) Regulation violated Art. 32.1 SCM. Korea and the EU had reached an agreement on subsidization of their respective shipyards whereby they had agreed to stop similar practices: through the TDM, the EU had deviated from its commitments and granted subsidies to the shipbuilding sector. In the EU's view, the TDM was necessary since Korea had not respected its own commitments in this regard either.[2] The Panel agreed with the view that the TDM was a specific action relating to subsidization, but distanced itself from the view that it was an instrument conceived to counteract subsidization (§§7.154–74). In its view, a counter-subsidy (like the TDM) is not, in and of itself, an instrument aimed at curbing subsidization. For the Panel, a scheme counteracts subsidy, in the sense of Art. 32.1 SCM, if it contains some element additional to the potential impact on competition (§§7.160ff). Without saying so, the 'spirit' of this Panel report seems to suggest that a measure runs foul of Art. 32.1 SCM not simply because an effect on subsidization is an 'ancillary' by-product of its operation, but rather because it is its main thrust. This Panel thus did not repeat the ruling of the AB with respect to Byrd payments, where the potential disbursement of CVDs to US economic operators sufficed for the measure to be judged WTO-inconsistent. It is thus difficult to reconcile the two reports. The Panel report is later in time, but it is only a Panel report, and, in theory, the AB could very well reverse it. Whether this will be the case remains to be seen.

---

the SCM Agreement discussed here, as well as the Agreement on Government Procurement discussed in Chapter 12.

[2] The TDM Regulation is described in detail in § 7.43 of the Panel report.

The negotiating history of the SCM Agreement[3] supports the conclusion that the Agreement was made possible because of the rapprochement between the EU and the US administrations regarding their attitude towards subsidies.[4] The US was in the 1980s quite hostile to the idea of government intervention in the life of business; it was emerging from its biggest deregulatory experience ever. Many still remember how, in dramatic fashion, in 1982, President Reagan, ordered the dismantlement of the national telecoms carrier, AT&T, which, following this act, was limited to international services, leaving the US market to other firms ('baby bells'). Deregulation, a process that started earlier under the presidency of Jimmy Carter, was of course not limited to telecoms.[5] This is how the US delegate to the GATT described the motives behind deregulation:

> The motive behind deregulation in a number of sectors in the United States had been the feeling that there was not enough competition, nor enough companies. As could be seen from the situation in coastal shipping, the degree of free competition needed was also an issue in his country. On the other hand, the dynamism that may have resulted from deregulation, say in telecommunications, could be attributed to management styles rather than to global trade trends, and of course some dominant firms remained in the market.[6]

In 1992, President Clinton comes to power and with him in his advisors' groups proponents of a different philosophy regarding subsidies as a means of industrial policy: some of them see, under certain conditions, the merits of subsidization, especially in globalized markets where other participants routinely subsidize.[7] It is this change in US attitude that facilitated the advent of the SCM Agreement.

This is not the only case of change in outlook towards subsidies: back in 1971 the US wanted the following to be a prohibited export subsidy:[8]

> special government measures to offset, in whole or in part, the price disadvantages on exports that result from its own or other countries' exchange rate adjustment.

1971 is of course the year the US had unilaterally decided to throw the Bretton Woods system of fixed parities into the dustbin of history by simply pressing the 'delete' function. The US has defended the exact opposite position in recent years following the, in its view, wilful undervaluation of renminbi, the Chinese currency. There are undeniably, some genuine definitional issues regarding the

---

[3] Croome (1995); McDonough (1993); Hoekman and Mavroidis (1996b); Wouters and Coppens (2010).

[4] Horlick and Clark (1994).

[5] The Airlines (1978), Trucking (1980), Railroads (late 1970s and 1980), Telecommunications (1977 and, as mentioned, 1982), Cable Television (late 1970s and 1984), Brokerage (1975), Banking (1980 and 1982), Petroleum (1979), and Natural Gas Industry (1978) were liberalized in that period.

[6] GATT Doc. MDF/10 of 21 May 1985.

[7] D'Andrea Tyson (1992).

[8] Proposal by the US, Supplementary List of Practices that Constitute an Export Subsidy, INT (73)58, 26 June 1973.

understanding of subsidies and we will be looking into them *infra*; the example here is meant to serve as an illustration of how politics have added a new dimension to this discussion.

The Agreement was meant, through the various disciplines imposed, to remove the incentive to purposefully confer an artificial advantage on a specific class of producers through subsidization. Grossman and Mavroidis (2007a) examined thoroughly the various mechanisms established by the the the SCM Agreement and argued that it was negotiated as an instrument meant to discourage governments from taking unilateral actions that would harm their trading partners. And this is how their argument goes in more detail: the presumption in international relations is that governments can do as they choose with regard to policies whose effects are confined within their borders. But many policies—domestic as well as trade policies—impinge upon the interests of foreign citizens and corporations. In the absence of any agreements, governments might have little reason to take these international externalities into account when setting their national policies. Policies that are set without regard to their potentially adverse effects abroad are bound to be globally inefficient, in the sense that an alternative set of policies could be found that all governments would agree is preferable to the chosen ones. To further global efficiency, a trade agreement makes it costly for a government to choose policies that inflict harm on trading partners.[9]

So, against this background, we can ask the question: in what ways might a subsidy inflict 'harm' on another country? The answer to this question depends, of course, on the interpretation of the word 'harm'. One possibility would be to associate harm with a loss of aggregate economic welfare. An interpretation of the SCM Agreement that associates harm with a loss in aggregate economic welfare cannot, however, be sustained in the light of the manner in which the Agreement was structured.[10] If product and factor markets are competitive and well-functioning, then a foreign subsidy of production of a good cannot reduce aggregate welfare in an importing country. A subsidy typically encourages production in the subsidizing country. Thus, at each price, local firms are willing to produce more output when subsidized than otherwise. The effect of the subsidy is to reduce the world price of the subsidized good. If markets were competitive and well-functioning in the importing countries and governments were concerned only about aggregate

---

9 Janow and Staiger (2003 and 2007) reach similar conclusions when discussing the reports on *Canada—Dairy*, and *US—Export Restraints*.

10 Goetz et al. (1986) and Diamond (1989) consider the rationale for countervailing duty law and conclude that these laws are best understood as a means to protect an entitlement of domestic producers to be immune to the harmful effects of foreign subsidies rather than as a means to promote global economic efficiency. Our understanding of the SCM Agreement is quite similar. We do not mean to imply, however, that a welfare standard for injury tests would be the wrong standard to use. To the contrary, we believe that an alternative injury test that looked for harm to aggregate welfare would better serve the objective of promoting international efficiency than the test required in the SCM Agreement as it now stands.

economic welfare, then importing countries would be thankful when a trading partner introduced a subsidy, and would have no reason to discourage such subsidies with the threat of countervailing actions. Of course, it is not true that a subsidy always enhances aggregate welfare in all Member countries. It is simple to see, for example, that a subsidy will reduce welfare in a country that exports products that compete with the subsidized good. Aggregate welfare losses might sometimes occur in an importing country as well. A foreign subsidy can also reduce aggregate welfare in an importing country when a few large firms dominate the industry. In such circumstances, the firms (foreign and domestic) may exploit their market power by charging prices in excess of marginal production costs. As Brander and Spencer (1985) have shown, subsidies can have strategic effects on firm behaviour in markets with imperfect competition. If a subsidy causes foreign firms to sell more output than otherwise, the optimal response of competitors in the importing country may be to reduce the volume of their own sales. But this will spell a loss of monopoly profits for the domestic firms, which will offset and perhaps outweigh the net benefit.[11] Thus, the effect of a subsidy on aggregate welfare in another Member country is a priori ambiguous. Therefore, if the Members had intended the SCM Agreement to discourage actions that would inflict welfare losses on others, they would have directed the 'test' for actionable subsidies toward identifying conditions where aggregate loss is most likely to occur. For example, an external welfare loss is more likely to occur when a government subsidizes firms that sell in an imperfectly competitive market. Similarly, a welfare loss is more likely when wages are sticky in the importing country than when they are flexible; so the Agreement might have made reference to the labour-market conditions there. The Agreement might also have allowed for countervailing measures in Member countries that export goods in competition with the subsidized good, inasmuch as these countries are quite likely to suffer welfare losses as a result of a foreign subsidy. In fact, the SCM Agreement does not confine the use of CVDs to situations in which an importing country has established the presumption of a welfare loss. The Agreement makes no reference to labour-market conditions, to market structure, or even to consumer welfare. And the Agreement makes no allowance for countervailing measures in countries that export the subsidized good, where the presumption of welfare losses surely exists.[12] Rather, countervailing measures are permitted only when there has been (or threatens to be) injury to a domestic industry in an importing country.

---

[11] A predatory subsidy is an extreme example of a strategic subsidy. The intent of such a policy is more than just to induce firms outside the subsidizing country to cede market share, but actually to drive them from the market. Like strategic subsidies, predatory subsidies can reduce aggregate welfare in an importing country, both because the local producers that leave the industry forfeit their prospective profits, and because the consumer price may rise once the local competitors exit.

[12] Although, as we will see in more detail *infra*, the Agreement recognizes the possibility of serious prejudice to the interests of another Member that may arise due to the displacement of exports of a like product to the market of the subsidizing member or to a third-country market, it

Evidently, the signatories meant to discourage certain policy actions that would harm competing producer interests. This objective is understandable in the light of recent literature on the political economy of trade policy, which has emphasized that governments often set their trade policies with objectives other than the maximization of aggregate economic welfare in mind.[13] The policies that are chosen typically reflect a compromise among competing constituent interests. Moreover, some interests—especially those that are relatively concentrated—receive more weight in the political process than others. Less concentrated groups are not so successful in the political arena, in part because they have difficulty in overcoming the free-rider problems that plague collective political action (Olson 1965). Thus, governments often are induced by political pressures to give more weight to producer interests than to consumer welfare when making their decisions about trade policy.

The interpretation that the main objective of the SCM Agreement is to discourage subsidies that might harm producers in importing countries finds support in many other provisions of the Agreement. For example, Art. 12.9 SCM specifies that the domestic producers of a like product must be invited by the investigating authority to offer their views about an alleged subsidy and proposed countervailing measures, whereas the authority has discretion to decide whether or not to allow consumers of the subsidized good to do so. Art. 15.1 SCM requires that:

> a determination of injury . . . shall be based on positive evidence and involve an objective examination of both (a) the volume of the subsidized imports and the effect of the subsidized imports on prices in the domestic market for like products and (b) the consequent impact of these imports on the domestic producers of such products.

And Arts. 14 and 19 SCM require the size of the CVD to be set so as to just offset the adverse effects of the subsidy on conditions in the domestic industry. This latter provision can only be understood as an attempt to restore competitive conditions in the industry to what they would have been absent the subsidy. The various provisions of the Agreement should hence be interpreted in light of this overarching objective, which is very similar, if not altogether identical, to that permeating the AD Agreement.

The negotiating objective is not necessarily an economist's dream: economists would prefer to look at economy-wide effects. Subsidies are viewed by economists as an instrument whereby governments, at least in a perfect competition

---

does not allow serious prejudice to exporting interests to be a basis for countervailing action. Rather, in such cases, the Agreement calls for consultations between the Member that is granting or maintaining a subsidy and the Complaining Member, followed by a Panel review in the event that consultations do not result in a mutually agreed solution. Only after a report by a Panel or AB has been adopted, in which it is determined that a subsidy has resulted in adverse effects to the interests of another Member and the subsidizing Member has failed to take appropriate steps to remove the adverse effects of the subsidy, may the complaining Member take such countermeasures as have been authorized by the Dispute Settlement Body (see Arts. 7.8 and 7.9 of the SCM Agreement).

[13] See, *inter alia*, Grossman and Helpman (1995 and 2001).

model,[14] subsidize foreign consumers: a reduction in the marginal cost of foreign firms (which may be the consequence of a subsidy) in general reduces prices for the domestic firms. Hence, many economists have made the point that instead of imposing countervailing measures to offset subsidization, governments affected by foreign subsidies should be sending a 'thank-you note' to the subsidizing government.[15] Fundamentally, if the purpose of trade agreements is to address negative external effects stemming from the unilateral definition and exercise of trade policies, then one might wonder whether the treatment of subsidies fits this idea: subsidies produce both positive and negative external effects; foreign consumers would be the first to write a thank-you note to subsidizers, whereas foreign producers of competing goods (and not producers in the downstream industry using the subsidized good as input for the production of their final product) would be, in principle, hurt. Should not then the SCM Agreement reflect on both effects and recommend anti-subsidy action accordingly?

Perfect competition, nevertheless, is an unrealistic scenario. It is a logical construct that helps analysts understand the workings of an economy. In practice, subsidies do occur for a variety of reasons. They often, for example, constitute the preferred instrument of industrial policy in most jurisdictions.[16] Strategic trade theory in the 1980s has been interpreted by some policy-makers as a recommendation for active subsidization in order to induce enhanced productivity.[17] It could also be that market failures or distortions may require some collective action. For instance, firms unable to take into account the social benefits associated with their production produce less than they should do. In such a case, a production subsidy could be a solution. This literature offers support for the view that the rationale for subsidies matters. It is, thus, puzzling why the SCM Agreement equates all subsidies and does not ask what the subsidy is meant to address. Assuming market failure, a subsidy might on occasion be a first-best instrument to respond to it.[18] To be fair to the drafters, the original Agreement did try to distinguish the treatment of subsidies depending on whether a distortion is being addressed. To this effect, 'green' subsidies aimed at addressing environmental hazards would remain unanswered. In the same vein, the Agreement on Agriculture that we will

---

[14] It bears emphasizing here that in non-perfect competition markets subsidies granted by governments to monopolies may not necessarily benefit consumers wherever they may be, as the beneficiary-monopolist may use the subsidy (perversely and rationally at the same time) to maximize its profit by setting the price somewhere between the market price and the reservation price (i.e. monopoly price). Ostensibly, even when there are few industries competing on the world stage, these firms may still have incentives to price their products above the market price without entering into any tacit or explicit agreement.

[15] In the absence of any other distortion and if—and this is a big if—such a subsidy will reduce welfare in the two countries combined. The foreign country may lose or gain; the domestic economy may also lose or gain. It all depends on their strategic interaction.

[16] Grossman and Helpman (2001).

[17] Krugman (1983); D'Andrea Tyson (1992).

[18] Coppens (2012) extensively discusses the economic rationale for the SCM Agreement.

be discussing in Chapter 11 contains a provision allowing for farm subsidies to remain unanswered if they are oriented towards net food-importing countries which cannot afford to pay the world price for the good at hand. At the moment of writing, though, this is the only similar example: the current SCM Agreement makes no room for some subsidies depending on their rationale.

It is, of course, difficult to understand why some subsidies are outlawed when tariffs are not. Subsidies are not as distorting as tariffs because they affect only the producers' side of the market, not the consumers' side (consumers may continue to buy the product at the world price, if there is no tariff on the product in question). Subsidies affect one margin of trade (i.e. producers), whereas tariffs have an impact on two margins (i.e. producers and consumers). In this vein, Bagwell and Mavroidis (2010) ask why is it that some subsidies are prohibited when they arguably expand trade, when instruments that reduce trade (such as tariffs) are not outright illegal? Additionally, one might also ask what is the reason for treating export subsidies worse than domestic subsidies, when it is easy to construct examples where the latter are worse for producer welfare (which is, as argued above, what negotiators want to maximize anyway). Indeed, it could very well be the case that on occasion the US, say, cares more about its immense domestic market than about export markets. In a similar vein, Sykes (2003a) pertinently asks why local content schemes should be outlawed—when the same is not done with respect to production subsidies—while the two subsidy schemes can have similar effects on the market.[19] There are some counter-arguments here: Potipiti (2006) offers one example where banning export subsidies might be the sensible thing to do. She shows how, in a world where trade and transportation costs decrease over time, export sectors grow while import-competing sectors decline. Consequently, export sectors attract new entrants and investment that erodes the protection rent associated with export subsidies. It follows that the government rent from paying export subsidies declines as well, and under similar conditions governments might opt to ban export subsidies. Potipiti's point is well taken, yet it is clear that the author makes no case for an agreement to ban subsidies, much as Brou and Ruta (2011) do not make this case: they describe unilateral behaviour.

Over-disciplining subsidies in the WTO context might make WTO Members reluctant to make tariff commitments in the first place, as Bagwell and Staiger (2002) and (2006) note. Moreover, there is a policy-substitution argument that is relevant here. If subsidies become costly (say because of retaliation), then WTO Members might have an incentive to say impose high non-discriminatory taxes. This could be the case, for example, when governments, because they cannot use subsidies to address climate change issues, have recourse to high sales taxes

---

[19] Of course, local content and production subsidies can have different effects: a production subsidy could, for example, lead to exports only, without any effect on domestic goods, whereas local content subsidies will increase demand for domestic goods. They could also, nonetheless, have very similar effects and this is the reason why Sykes's remark is pertinent.

imposed on goods, creating similar problems. Brou and Ruta (2011) respond to the policy-substitution problem by arguing that, relative to an agreement that only commits a government to free trade by disciplining tariffs, a government is better off under an agreement that also imposes rules on subsidies so that it can credibly avoid the policy-substitution problem (where it will be using subsidies instead of tariffs etc.). This is sensible but does not totally respond to the issue raised by Bagwell and Staiger: by disciplining both instruments, trading nations might have even less of an incentive to liberalize since they can use neither of them.

And we should also note that there are definitional problems which have prompted Sykes (2003a) at least to recommend no action since we might be shooting at some of the target while leaving the rest intact. Take, for example, a case where a company wants to raise capital and offers its stocks for sale at the stock exchange for $1,000/share. What if no private party buys a share at this price and the state steps in and buys at this price after 5, 35, or 135 days? Has a subsidy has been granted in all three cases? What if the state pays $800/share after 5, 35, or 135 days? What if the state pays $1,000/share after individuals have (massively or moderately) purchased stocks for $900/share? The response to whether a subsidy has been granted in many of the scenarios above comes close to a quixotic test.[20] The undeniable problems of definition notwithstanding, Bagwell and Mavroidis (2010) distance themselves from this view, arguing that unless action is taken against schemes that anyway qualify as subsidies, the incentive to continue exchanging concessions might be reduced. It is the value of concessions itself that it is being reduced through subsidization. This view has undeniable merits but does not solve the underlying issue that it is on occasion very difficult to understand as to whether a subsidy has been granted. It is also puzzling why a plethora of terms that we will be visiting *infra* (adverse effects, price suppression, price depression, price undercutting, etc.) have been used and, in principle, they all must have a different meaning although they all address more or less the same issue.

With the notable exception of predatory subsidization,[21] economists generally caution against far-reaching disciplines on subsidies. For all these reasons, one might legitimately wonder whether it was sensible to move away from the benign attitude that the GATT had espoused towards subsidies to today's more binding context. Yet, this is what happened over the years, although a 'tightening' of the screws had started to take place already in the GATT years as we shall see *infra* in our discussion of export subsidies. With this in mind, we will be approaching the SCM Agreement as an instrument aimed at removing (or reducing the incentive for providing) schemes that have nefarious effects on individual WTO Members' producers' welfare. Tables 8.1 and 8.1 demonstrate how many actions have been taken to this effect in the first 15 years of the WTO.

---

[20] We will discuss the legal definition of subsidy *infra*.

[21] Theoretically, it could be the case that subsidies are predatory and thus hurt competition, and not just competitors. In the real world, this looks like a highly unlikely scenario.

Table 8.1 Countervailing initiations: by reporting Member, 1 January 1995–30 June 2010

Reporting Member	1995	1996	1997	1998	1999	2000	2001	2002	2003	2004	2005	2006	2007	2008	2009	2010	Total
Argentina	27	22	14	8	23	43	28	14	1	12	12	11	8	19	28	7	277
Australia	5	17	44	13	24	15	23	16	8	9	7	10	2	6	9	4	212
Brazil	5	18	11	18	16	11	17	8	4	8	6	12	13	23	9	5	184
Bulgaria								1									1
Canada	11	5	14	8	18	21	25	5	15	11	1	7	1	3	6	1	152
Chile	4	3		2		5						1	1	1	1	1	19
China				3	2	11	14	30	22	27	24	10	4	14	17	4	182
Colombia	4	1	1	6	2	3	6			2	2	9	1	6	5	2	50
Costa Rica		4	1	1							1	1			2		10
Czech Republic				2	1												3
Ecuador				1													1
Egypt			7	14	7	3	7	3	1		12	9	2		2		67
European Union	33	25	41	22	65	32	28	20	7	30	25	35	9	19	15	8	414
Guatemala		1															1
India	6	21	13	28	64	41	79	81	46	21	28	35	47	55	31	17	613
Indonesia		11	5	8	8	3	4	4	12	5		5	1	7	7	3	83
Israel	5	6	3	7			4	1		1	4			1	6	5	43
Jamaica						1	1	1	1						1	1	6
Japan							2						4				6
Jordan												1					1
Korea, Republic of	4	13	15	3	6	2	4	9	18	3	4	7	15	5		3	111
Latvia							1	6									7
Lithuania					1	6											7
Malaysia	3	2	8	1	2		1	5	6	3	4	8					43
Mexico	4	4	6	12	11	6	6	10	14	6	6	6	3	1	2	1	98
New Zealand	10	4	5	1	4	9	1	2	5	5		1	6				53
Nicaragua				2													2
Pakistan								1	3	3	13	4		3	26		53

(Continued)

Table 8.1 *Continued*

Reporting Member	1995	1996	1997	1998	1999	2000	2001	2002	2003	2004	2005	2006	2007	2008	2009	2010	Total
Panama															4		6
Paraguay																	2
Peru	2	8	2	3	8	1	8	13	4	7	4	3	2		4		69
Philippines	1	1	2	3	6	2		1	1						1		18
Poland			1		7			3	1								12
Slovenia					1												1
South Africa	16	34	23	41	16	21	6	4	8	6	23	3	5	3	3		212
Taipei, Chinese			1	6		4	3	2	2			5			1	1	23
Thailand		1	3				3	21	3	3		3	2	1	1	2	43
Trinidad and Tobago		1		4	3	1	1	2	2								12
Turkey			4	1	8	7	15	18	11	25	12	8	6	23	6	1	145
Ukraine							2	3	2	6	2	1	5	7	2	1	31
United States	14	22	15	36	47	47	77	35	37	26	12	8	28	16	20	2	442
Uruguay			1			1	4										6
Venezuela, Bolivarian Republic of	3	2	6	10	7	1	1	1									31
Total	157	226	246	266	358	298	371	315	234	220	202	203	165	213	209	69	3752

Source: <http://www.wto.org>.

Table 8.2 Countervailing measures: by reporting Member, 01 January 1995–30 June 2010

Reporting Member	1995	1996	1997	1998	1999	2000	2001	2002	2003	2004	2005	2006	2007	2008	2009	2010	Total
Argentina		2		2													4
Australia													1	1			2
Brazil	5								1	1							7
Canada	1					5	1			1	2		1	3	1	1	16
Chile						2											2
China																1	1
Costa Rica										1							1
European Union			1	2	3	10		2	3	2	1				1		25
Japan												1					1
Mexico	7	1															8
New Zealand			2	1			1										4
Peru	1						2										3
South Africa						2		2			1						5
Turkey															1		1
United States	5	2		1	11	2	10	10	2	2		2		7	6	2	62
Venezuela, Bolivarian Republic of										1							1
Total	19	5	3	6	14	21	14	14	6	8	4	3	2	11	9	4	143

Source: <http://www.wto.org>.

2. Coverage of the Legal Discipline: Actionable Subsidies

A WTO Member should not, through subsidies, cause adverse effects to its trading partners. But what is a subsidy? Various GATT provisions, such as Arts. III.8, VI, or XVI, deal with subsidies, but do not provide a definition of the term. While the 1979 Agreement on Interpretation and Application of Articles VI, XVI, and XXIII of the General Agreement on Tariffs and Trade (the Tokyo Round Subsidies Code) elaborated rules on the use of subsidies as well as on protective responses to them, it, too, failed to include a definition of the term 'subsidy'. One of the most important innovations of the WTO SCM Agreement is that it provides, for the first time, a definition of a subsidy as follows:

(a) A financial contribution by a government;
(b) Which confers a benefit;
(c) To a specific recipient.

The first two elements are included in Art. 1 SCM,[22] whereas the latter is in Art. 2 SCM. These elements are relevant for the definition of actionable subsidies: the SCM Agreement distinguishes between two types of subsidies, actionable and prohibited subsidies. A third category, non-actionable subsidies, was originally included in the SCM Agreement on a provisional basis. Failure to renew this category, as we shall see *infra*, led to its extinction. WTO Members can react against both actionable and prohibited subsidies by imposing CVDs and/or by introducing a complaint before the WTO requesting that the subsidy is brought to an end. The latter action is more time consuming than the former, but warranted when effects extend beyond the market of the Member reacting to subsidization.

We will start with a discussion of actionable subsidies before reverting to a discussion of the other types of subsidies. To this effect, we will discuss the three elements of the subsidy definition briefly mentioned *supra*.

2.1 Financial Contribution by Government

The SCM Agreement considers that a financial contribution is provided by the government in three cases (Art. 1.1 SCM):

(a) In case of direct transfer of funds (such as grants, loans, and equity infusions), or potential direct transfer of funds or liabilities (e.g. loan guarantee);
(b) When government revenue that is otherwise due is foregone or not collected (such as fiscal incentives in the form of tax credits); or
(c) Where the government provides goods or services other than general infrastructure, or when it purchases goods;

---

[22] The negotiating history of Art. 1 SCM is described in §§8.64–74 of the Panel report on *US—Export Restraints*. See, on this score, Janow and Staiger (2003) and Rubini (2010).

(d) The government entrusts a private body to do the activities mentioned above;

(e) Or, there is any other form of income support as spelled out in Art. XVI GATT.

The wording of this provision makes it clear that it deals in an exhaustive manner with the types of government involvement that constitute financial contribution. The Panel on *US—Export Restraints* (§8.69) underscored this point. The financial contribution envisaged in the SCM Agreement does not have to be restricted to a transfer of monetary resources: the AB, in its report on *US—Softwood Lumber IV*, held that (§51):

> the concept of subsidy defined in Article 1 of the SCM Agreement captures situations in which something of economic value is transferred by a government to the advantage of a recipient.

'Something of economic value' thus needs to be transferred and this need not be monetary resources. The Panel on *US—Softwood Lumber III* held that in-kind transfers of resources, such as goods or services which can be valued and which represent a value to the recipient, can qualify as subsidies in the SCM sense of the term as well (§7.24).

One would be ill-advised nevertheless to rush to sweeping understandings of the term 'financial contribution' in the sense that anything that can have an economic value is *ipso facto* a subsidy. Take the case, for example, of a law that exempts companies in the steel industry from certain environmental regulations, such as certain pollution standards. By doing so, it may well be providing a benefit to the domestic industry, as it will allow these firms to save an important amount of money. As this does not entail the government foregoing revenue, however, such an exemption will not constitute a financial contribution under the SCM.[23] Similarly, the imposition by the government of an export restraint or an export tax may benefit domestic downstream producers as the suppliers of the taxed product may be inclined to sell their products to domestic downstream producers rather than exporting the product. As the government is not providing funds, or foregoing revenue which is due, or providing a good or service, an export ban or tax does not amount to a financial contribution in the sense of the SCM Agreement, and there will therefore be no subsidy to the downstream producers.[24] It is of relevance that the Panel on *US—Export Restraints* noted that (§7.83):

> the introduction of the two-part definition of subsidy, consisting of 'financial contribution' and 'benefit', was intended specifically to prevent the countervailing of benefits from any sort of (formal, enforceable) government measures, by restricting to a finite list the kinds of government measures that would, if they conferred benefits, constitute subsidies.

---

23 Although, depending on the circumstances, it could qualify as a violation of Art. III.4 GATT; see the relevant discussion in Chapter 4.

24 An export restraint could, of course, violate Art. XI GATT.

This Panel went on to conclude that, even if a government measure has an effect which is equivalent to that of a financial contribution as defined in Art. 1 SCM, it will not be considered a subsidy unless the measure takes the form of a financial contribution as defined in Art. 1.1(a) SCM (§§8.73–4).

A financial contribution also exists when a government does not collect, or foregoes, revenue which is otherwise due. The key term is 'otherwise due' and the question is what the legal benchmark to address this question should be. The WTO Agreement with respect to taxation is a negative integration contract, as we saw in Chapter 4: it does not impose on WTO Members a particular taxation system; WTO Members are free to design their own national tax schemes. In *US—FSC*,[25] the AB held that the basis for the comparison must be the tax rules applied by the Member in question. In this case, the EU had challenged the consistency of US tax practices with the SCM Agreement. In this long-standing dispute between the two transatlantic partners, the EU argued that the US system (the Foreign Sales Corporation Act, FSC), under which companies earning income outside the US were exempted from the obligation to pay US taxes, constituted an export subsidy: this was so since, absent enactment of the FSC, those companies would have been obliged to pay taxes for income made both in the US and outside the US market. The Panel and the AB agreed with the complainant, arguing that it was national law that would serve as the benchmark to decide whether income was otherwise due (§§90ff and especially 98). In *US—FSC (Article 21.5—EC)*, the AB confirmed (§§86, 91–2) that the benchmark to establish whether income was otherwise due was national law.[26] It is thus immaterial if the rationale behind the US law was to re-establish competitive conditions among companies of different national origin: EU companies do not have to pay taxes on income made outside the EU and can thus profit when selling in markets with lower than EU taxation; US companies cannot profit in similar circumstances (where the taxation level is lower abroad than in the US), and FSC was the means to equalize conditions of competition between EU and US companies.[27] In *Canada—Autos*, an import duty exemption granted to certain cars was considered to be revenue otherwise due: this exemption implied that the

---

[25] See the excellent presentation of this case in Howse and Neven (2007d).

[26] This was a compliance Panel which dealt with the legality of the so-called ETI (Extra-territorial Income), a measure the US had enacted in order to conform with the findings of the original Panel. The AB concluded that there appeared to be a marked contrast between the 'other rules' of taxation applicable to foreign-source income and the rules of taxation applicable to foreign source income as qualified in the FSC/ETI measure, the so-called Qualified Foreign Trade Income (QFTI): for US citizens and residents, all foreign-source income (subject to permissible deductions) was taxed; under the ETI measure, QFTI was definitively excluded from US taxation. This, together with the fact that taxpayers could elect to have their income treated more favourably as QFTI or see the normal rules for foreign source income applied to them, led the AB to conclude that the US forewent revenue on QFTI which was otherwise due (§105).

[27] In other words, the net impact of a measure is immaterial when it comes to qualifying it as subsidy.

normal MFN import duty of 6.1 per cent would not have to be paid and consequently, the Canadian government had, in the eyes of the AB, foregone revenue it otherwise would have raised (§91).

Footnote 1 and Annexes I–III to the SCM Agreement identify certain situations when revenue foregone will not confer a benefit and thereby will not result in subsidization. Footnote 1 to the SCM Agreement explains that exempting exported domestic goods from say consumption taxes is not a financial contribution by a government in the sense of foregone income otherwise due.[28] Instruments aimed at avoiding double taxation, an issue to which we will turn in more detail *infra*, constitute another instance of income foregone that is not considered to be a financial contribution by a WTO Member (Annex I). So are some drawback schemes (remission of import charges levied on inputs consumed in the production of exported goods; Annexes II, and III).

The SCM Agreement explicitly deals with the issue of double taxation only to make the point that instruments aimed at avoiding a transaction being taxed twice by two different jurisdictions will not be assimilated to financial contributions by governments even though in similar instances income is foregone. The same transaction can be taxed twice, assuming that one country imposes taxes by virtue of the nationality of the economic operator and another by virtue of the territoriality principle (where a transaction is taxed where it takes place irrespective of the nationality of the parties involved). To avoid this, a number of WTO Members have signed treaties aimed at avoiding double taxation. It is the Illustrative List of Export Subsidies (Annex 1 to the SCM) that discusses the treatment of double taxation; paragraph (e) of that list reads as follows:

> The full or partial exemption, remission, or deferral specifically related to exports, of direct taxes or social welfare charges paid or payable by industrial or commercial enterprises.

Footnote 59 explicitly excludes measures taken to avoid double taxation from the scope of this paragraph.[29] It pertinently reads:

> Paragraph (e) is not intended to limit a Member from taking measures to avoid the double taxation of foreign-source income earned by its enterprises or the enterprises of another Member.

Consequently, remission of taxes in order to avoid double taxation should not be understood to be an export subsidy in the SCM sense of the term. The rationale for excluding double taxation from the realm of the SCM Agreement is unclear in the negotiating history. It must have to do with the acknowledgement that similar schemes do not aim at foregoing income, in the sense of Art. 1.1(a)(1)(ii) SCM, but, in principle, aim at avoiding the penalization of economic operators who

---

[28] Recall our discussion about the Working Party on Border Tax Adjustments in Chapter 4.

[29] For an excellent discussion on tax issues in trade agreements, see Avi-Yonah and Slemrod (2002).

might be dissuaded from trading. It could be that the ensuing contraction of trade (since, by definition, when trading, more than one jurisdictions will be involved and double taxation might disincentivize traders to trade) must have influenced the framers' thinking. If the latter was a genuine concern, though, the SCM Agreement would have a different content altogether, since subsidies typically expand trade. For this reason alone, the fairness argument is the likelier explanation for the treatment of double taxation. The fact that there were numerous agreements dealing with double taxation that would have to be abolished, as a result of the advent of an SCM agreement without provision for exemption, must also have played a role. The AB on *US—FSC (Article 21.5—EC)*[30] held that a measure falls under footnote 59 if it exempts from taxation only foreign-source income. If it further exempts other (than foreign-source) income, then it cannot benefit from this provision (§§184–6).

A government provision of goods or services other than general infrastructure or purchase of goods can constitute a financial contribution (Art. 1.1(a)(1)(iii) SCM). In *US—Softwood Lumber III*,[31] as well as in *US—Softwood Lumber IV*, the question before the WTO adjudicating bodies was whether the Canadian stumpage arrangements amounted to a provision of goods in the sense of the SCM Agreement. Through these arrangements, Canadian harvesters of timber would rent land at less than market value. As a result, their exported products would benefit from a substantial cost advantage vis-à-vis the corresponding US products, since US harvesters had to pay a market price for renting land where they would harvest timber. The AB concluded that, since the Canadian stumpage arrangements gave tenure holders the right to enter onto government lands, cut standing timber, and enjoy exclusive rights over the timber that was harvested, such arrangements represented a situation in which provincial governments provided standing timber to harvesters. It disagreed with Canada's argument that the granting of an intangible right to harvest standing timber could not be equated with the act of providing that standing timber. According to the AB, by granting a right to harvest, the provincial governments put particular stands of timber at the disposal of timber harvesters and allowed those enterprises alone to make use of those resources. The stumpage programmes, thus, amounted to the provision of goods or services other than general infrastructure (§75).

Paragraphs (a)–(c) of Art. 1 SCM deal with practices by government entities, whereas there is a change of focus in (d), which focuses on cases where a government acts through another (non-state) entity. With respect to the class of cases envisaged in (a)–(c), case law has held that these are per se financial contributions, that is, they qualify as such only because they have been committed by a state entity.

---

30 See, on this score, the analysis by Howse and Neven (2007d).
31 See the analysis by Horn and Mavroidis (2007b).

Case law has clarified that:

(a) An act by a government entity does not have to be in the exercise of governmental authority for it to constitute a financial contribution; at the same time, as we shall see in our discussion of the term 'benefit' *infra*, it is not necessarily the case that all government acts must be considered as financial contributions, since government entities might act in accordance with commercial considerations;

(b) A control criterion seems to emerge as the dominant criterion in deciding whether an act has been committed by a public body or a private entity. According to this criterion, a body is public if it is controlled by the government.

It is probably worth mentioning at the outset that the term 'government', which appears in Art. 1 SCM, refers, in the absence of additional information, to all types and layers of government within a country, whether they are acting at the federal, state, or provincial level. Recall, however, that under Art. XXIV.12 GATT:

> Each contracting party shall take such reasonable measures as may be available to it to ensure observance of the provisions of this Agreement by the regional and local governments and authorities within its territories.

The Panel on *Korea—Commercial Vessels* had to entertain an argument by Korea to the effect that a public body can only make a financial contribution, if such contribution takes place within normal government practice: this implied, in Korea's view, that the exercise of government authority is a *sine qua non* for deciding whether a government entity has made a financial contribution. In this vein, Korea argued that KEXIM, the Korean public body in question, was set up for the specific purpose of meeting needs of an industrial or commercial nature, i.e. activities involving the extension of financing facilities in markets where it competes with other public or private operators based on market-oriented principles. Korea argued that, in extending financing facilities, KEXIM was operating in a traditional banking capacity, performing functions normally performed by banks, not by governments. According to the Panel in this case, the term 'government practice' is used to denote the author of the action, rather than the nature of the action, and thus covers all acts of governments or public bodies, irrespective of whether or not they involve the exercise of regulatory powers or taxation authority (§§7.26ff and especially §7.29). This Panel accepted that a public body might operate in accordance with commercial considerations; hence actions by public bodies should not be equated with subsidies simply because they have been operated by public bodies. It went on to propose a control-based criterion to distinguish private from public bodies (§7.44). In this Panel's view, any action by an entity controlled by the government (or other public bodies) was *ipso facto* attributable to the government (§7.50).

537

Case law has addressed the issue whether 100 per cent state ownership in and of itself confers upon an entity the status of a public body: there is state practice to the effect that entities owned 100 per cent by the state are not *ipso facto* considered public bodies. Absent demonstration of control by government, ownership in and of itself in state practice does not necessarily lead an IA to the conclusion that the entity at hand is a public body. Both the US and the EU in their respective countervailing duty examinations into imports of DRAMs[32] from Korea did not consider to be public bodies a number of Korean banks which were 100 per cent, 80 per cent, or government-owned in large proportion. Instead, their national IAs examined whether these entities had been entrusted or directed by the government to provide various financial contributions. The Panel on *US—Countervailing Duty Investigation on DRAMs* seems to side with this view, although in its view 100 per cent ownership will be a factor that will weigh heavily when deciding if the body is public (footnote 29):

> Depending on the circumstances, 100 per cent government ownership might well have justified the treatment of such creditors as public bodies but that on the basis of the criteria provided for in US law, however, the DOC treated these 100 per cent owned Group B creditors as private bodies.[33]

Similarly, the Panel on *EC—Countervailing Measures on DRAM Chips* stated that it did not (footnote 129):

> wish to imply that it would not be possible or justified to treat a 100 per cent government owned entity as a public body, depending on the circumstances.

If ownership is not the decisive criterion (and, consequently, it should most probably be understood as a contributing factor), then what else should Panels be looking at when discussing this issue? The EU, the complainant in *Korea—Commercial Vessels*, had suggested two criteria that should be decisive in determining what a public body is in the SCM sense of the term (that is, a government entity): the public policy objective pursued and access to state resources (§7.32). The Panel dismissed the relevance of the public policy objective (§7.55) and did not express an opinion on whether access to state resources should be a relevant criterion.

The term 'public body' is defined elsewhere in the WTO Agreement. Footnote 48 to Art. 16 SCM, concerning the 'Definition of the Domestic Industry', provides that:

> one shall be deemed to control another when the former is legally or operationally in a position to exercise restraint or direction over the latter.

---

[32] 'DRAM' is an acronym that stands for dynamic random access memory. A DRAM microchip gives memory to a computer.

[33] See also footnote 80 in the same report.

Paragraph 5(c)(i) of the GATS Annex on Financial Services defines a public entity as:

> a government, a central bank or a monetary authority, of a Member, or an entity owned or controlled by a Member, that is principally engaged in carrying out governmental functions or activities for governmental purposes, not including an entity principally engaged in supplying financial services on commercial terms.

The Panel on *Korea—Commercial Vessels* questioned the relevance of the GATS Annex on Financial Services to the interpretation of Art. 1.1(a)(1) SCM, but still went on to construe a test that would decide whether a body is public if it was controlled by government (§7.47). It focused on the fact that the Korean government controlled some of the main appointments and enjoyed extensive control over the mandate that KEXIM should observe (§7.53). In its view, the combination of these two factors sufficed for the entity to be considered a public body. In *US—Antidumping and Countervailing Duties (China)*, the AB continued in this vein and held that the Panel had mistakenly characterized Chinese SOEs (state owned enterprises) as public bodies by essentially equating government ownership with government control (§320).[34] In its view, the Panel should have examined other factors as well, such as those that the USDOC used to examine (but did not in the instant case), to which it referred in §343 of its report:

> The five factors that the USDOC had examined in the past are: (i) government ownership; (ii) government presence on the board of directors; (iii) government control over activities; (iv) pursuit of governmental policies or interests; and (v) whether the entity was created by statute.

Ownership in and of itself does not confer the status of public body. Conversely, the AB found that there was nothing wrong with the treatment of Chinese SOCBs (state owned commercial banks) as public bodies by the USDOC. In this case, the US authority had examined extensively evidence (other than ownership) pointing to meaningful control of those entities by the US government and, consequently, in the AB's view, the examined entities qualified as public bodies (§355).

Financial contribution can of course exist even if channelled by a government entity through a private party: Art. 1.1(a)(1)(iv) SCM provides that there is financial contribution by the government, in cases where the government 'entrusts' or 'directs' a private body to provide a financial contribution in the sense of subparagraphs (i) to (iii) of Art. 1 SCM. The AB noted in its report on *US—Countervailing Duty Investigation on DRAMs* that the purpose of this provision was to act as an anti-circumvention device (§113):

> Paragraph (iv), in particular, is intended to ensure that governments do not evade their obligations under the SCM Agreement by using private bodies to take actions

---

34 Compare Lin and Milhaupt (2011) who maintain that Chinese SOEs are still a black box that has not been penetrated.

that would otherwise fall within Article 1.1(a)(1), were they to be taken by the government itself. In other words, Article 1.1(a)(1)(iv) is, in essence, an anti-circumvention provision.

The Panel on *EC—Countervailing Measures on DRAM Chips* held that, for the 'entrust' or 'direct' test to be met, an entity must be acting on behalf of a government, since purely private actions escape the purview of the WTO Agreement (§§7.52–3). Hence, this test is a quest to decide whether an activity can be attributed to a government. In the words of the AB on *US—Countervailing Duty Investigation on DRAMs* (§108):

> identify the instances where seemingly private conduct may be attributable to a government for purposes of determining whether there has been a financial contribution within the meaning of the SCM Agreement.

Echoing the case law on *Japan—Semiconductors*,[35] the AB held in the same case that it is not necessary that the government threatens sanctions in case of non-compliance with its wishes; it suffices that it provides private parties with sufficient incentives to act in a particular way. The AB did not go so far as to establish a 'but for' test here (e.g. ask the question whether an activity would have taken place even absent government involvement), but went a considerable way in this direction (§116).

Evidence of entrustment or direction does not have to be beyond reasonable doubt. The Panel on *EC—Countervailing Measures on DRAM Chips* stated in this vein that it did not (§7.109):

> want to be seen as requiring an investigating authority to come up with the smoking gun in the sense of a written order by the government to a private body to provide a financial contribution. We understand that, in most cases, the authority will have to base its decision on a number of arguments and pieces of evidence which perhaps when considered in combination may all point in the direction of government entrustment or direction, especially in cases where the level of cooperation by the interested parties is low.

The AB on *US—Countervailing Duty Investigation on DRAMs* confirmed this point when it held that, for a finding that financial contribution has been made (§§175ff), there was no need for compelling evidence. A lesser standard sufficed. As things stand, there is uncertainty as to how much less will suffice.

In *EC—Countervailing Measures on DRAM Chips*, the EU IA had relied on circumstantial evidence to reach the conclusion that the government of Korea was entrusting or directing private bodies to participate in the restructuring of a failing Korean DRAMs producer: alleged non-commercial behaviour and government ownership were two factors that weighed heavily in the IA's decision and the Panel found this approach reasonable. This Panel also held that, even if an IA decides not

---

[35] See the relevant discussion in Chapter 2.

to treat as a public body an entity with important government control, this does not imply that government control or shareholding become irrelevant—quite the contrary: government shareholding in a private body may lower the evidentiary threshold for establishing that the government exercised its shareholding power. The Panel also expressed the view that a significant degree of cooperation is to be expected of interested parties in a countervailing duty investigation. In the absence of any subpoena or other evidence-gathering powers, the possibility of resorting to the facts available and also the possibility of drawing certain inferences from the failure to cooperate can play a crucial role in inducing interested parties to provide the necessary information to the authority (§§7.60–1). This Panel report was not appealed. However, in the appeal concerning the parallel[36] proceedings (*US—Countervailing Duty Investigation on DRAMs*), the AB reversed the Panel's ruling regarding the impact of circumstantial evidence, since the Panel had examined pieces of evidence in isolation, rather than in their totality as the IA had indeed done. The AB emphasized the importance of a holistic approach in countervailing duty cases, as the only way in which important circumstantial evidence could be appropriately taken into consideration by an IA (§150). The AB noted that this approach was particularly relevant in cases of entrustment or direction under Art. 1.1(a)(1)(iv) SCM, where much of the evidence that is publicly available, and therefore readily accessible to interested parties and the IA, would likely be of a circumstantial nature (footnote 277). The AB (*US—Countervailing Duty Investigation on DRAMs*) added that Panels cannot base their findings on evidence that was not reasonably before the IA. In its words, Panels would be violating the standard of review embedded in Art. 11 DSU if they operated with the 'benefit of hindsight' (§175).

Art. 1.1(a)(2) SCM provides that, apart from a financial contribution by the government, any form of 'income or price support' which confers a benefit may also be considered a subsidy. This term is taken directly from the first paragraph of Art. XVI GATT. Income or price support mechanisms play an important role in farm goods, and commodities in general.[37]

2.2 Benefit to Recipient

A finding that financial contribution has occurred as explained above is only the first step towards a finding that a subsidy has been granted. Crucially, making a financial contribution should not be equated with conferring a benefit: the AB has consistently made clear that the two are distinct requirements. We quote, for example, from its report on *Canada—Aircraft*, (§157):

---

[36] These two cases are quasi-identical: the US and the EU countervailed the same Korean practice.
[37] We discuss this issue in more detail in Chapter 11.

the issues—and the respective definitions—of a 'financial contribution' and a 'benefit' as two separate legal elements in Article 1.1 of the SCM Agreement, which together determine whether a subsidy exists.

In this vein, the Panel on *EC—Countervailing Measures on DRAM Chips* clarified that, whereas the requirement to show that a financial contribution has been made is a question that needs to be addressed from the perspective of the donor, the response to the question whether a benefit has indeed been conferred needs to be assessed from the perspective of the recipient (§§7.212ff and especially §7.175). There is, however, a sequence between financial contribution and benefit. As the AB stated in its report on *US—Countervailing Duty Investigation on DRAMs*, if no contribution took place, no benefit can result either (§205).

Art. 1 SCM does not state that the financial contribution must confer a benefit on a recipient: the AB, though, in its report on *Canada—Aircraft* held that a benefit (§154):

> does not exist in the abstract, but must be received and enjoyed by a beneficiary or a recipient. Logically, a 'benefit' can be said to arise only if a person, natural or legal, or a group of persons, has in fact received something. The term 'benefit', therefore, implies that there must be a recipient.

The SCM Agreement does not define the term 'benefit'. Art. 14 SCM, which deals with the calculation of the amount of a subsidy bestowed, states that this term refers to benefit to recipient, and uses market prices as the benchmark for determining the existence and amount of benefit.[38] We will be returning to the question whether this provision contains an exhaustive list of benchmarks *infra*.[39]

Inspired by this provision, in *Canada—Aircraft*,[40] the AB set out its understanding of the term 'benefit' that has since been reproduced in subsequent Panel[41] and AB reports (§§157–8):

> We also believe that the word 'benefit', as used in Article 1.1(b), implies some kind of comparison. This must be so, for there can be no 'benefit' to the recipient unless the 'financial contribution' makes the recipient 'better off' than it would otherwise have been, absent that contribution. In our view, the marketplace provides an appropriate basis for comparison in determining whether a 'benefit' has been

---

[38] Francois (2010).

[39] In the case of alleged subsidization by China (whether in a countervailing context or in the context of a multilateral challenge), China's Accession Protocol provides that WTO Members may deviate from the methodology set forth in Article 14 for determining benefit, if there are special difficulties in its application. The importing WTO Member may then use methodologies for identifying and measuring the benefit which take into account the possibility that prevailing terms and conditions in China may not always be available as appropriate benchmarks. In applying such methodologies, where practicable, the importing WTO Member should adjust such prevailing terms and conditions before considering the use of terms and conditions prevailing outside China. Such methodologies have to be notified to the SCM Committee.

[40] See the discussion of Howse and Neven (2007e).

[41] See, for example, the Arbitrators' report on *Canada—Aircraft Credits and Guarantees* (*Article 22.6—Canada*) at §3.60).

'conferred', because the trade-distorting potential of a 'financial contribution' can be identified by determining whether the recipient has received a 'financial contribution' on terms more favourable than those available to the recipient in the market.

Article 14, which we have said is relevant context in interpreting Article 1.1(b), supports our view that the marketplace is an appropriate basis for comparison. The guidelines set forth in Article 14 relate to equity investments, loans, loan guarantees, the provision of goods or services by a government, and the purchase of goods by a government. A 'benefit' arises under each of the guidelines if the recipient has received a 'financial contribution' on terms more favourable than those available to the recipient in the market.

This is standard case law: with the exception of two cases so far (*Canada—Dairy*,[42] and *EC—Export Subsidies on Sugar*[43]), which both concerned farm subsidies and were adjudicated under the WTO Agreement on Agriculture, case law has consistently used the comparison between the actual situation and that normally prevailing under market conditions (e.g. where no financial contribution had occurred, or where it had occurred but probably was of a different level) in order to decide whether a benefit had indeed occurred: this is the notorious private-investor test to decide whether a benefit has been conferred.

Sometimes the benefit is quite obvious and requires little further examination: for example, in the case where the financial contribution consists of revenue foregone or not collected, there is an obvious benefit to the recipient. The Panel, in its report on *US—FSC*, came to the following conclusion regarding the benefit resulting from tax exemptions granted to foreign sales corporations (§7.103):

> Having found that the various tax exemptions under the FSC scheme give rise to a financial contribution, our next task is to consider whether a benefit is thereby conferred. In our view, the financial contribution clearly confers a benefit, in as much as both FSCs and their parents need not pay certain taxes that would otherwise be due. Further, that benefit can be quite substantial: according to the US Department of Commerce, 'the tax exemption can be as great as 15 to 30 per cent on gross income from exporting'. We note that the United States has raised no contrary argument with respect to the issue of benefit.[44]

This is so because the market-benchmark simply does not make sense in a situation where a government foregoes revenue. On other occasions, for example in cases where public bodies make an investment, the issue before the Panel can be substantially more complicated. Indeed, all sorts of issues can arise: a capital infusion by a public body, for example, does not necessarily confer a benefit upon a recipient, if the company is creditworthy, and the public body acts as private investor. If not, again all sorts of issues can arise when it comes to allocating

---

[42] See, on this score, Janow and Staiger (2007).
[43] See the analysis by Hoekman and Howse (2008).
[44] For a similar finding, see the Panel report on *Canada—Autos* at §10.165.

the subsidy benefits over time: issues such as the average useful life of the physical depreciable assets. The un-adopted GATT Panel report on *US—Lead and Bismuth I* discussed many of these issues, which came back to the WTO through the case law concerning the so-called pass through of financial contributions. A stylized description of the usual facts would want a government to provide an economic operator with a capital infusion; subsequently, the company that benefited from the infusion would be privatized at arm's length (usually through auction); and then, in case the original subsidization had been countervailed, the new owners would initiate a dispute before a WTO Panel in order to decide whether the original contribution had 'passed through' to the new owners. The problem here is that, whether the recipient of the benefit is the firm itself (as an independent legal person), the firm's owners, or the firm's productive assets is not made clear in law. This issue had arisen in *US—Lead and Bismuth I* in the GATT years and it concerned the subsidization of the German (Saarstahl), the French (Usinor Sacilor), and the British (British Steel) steel industries: all were eventually privatized through arm's length sales (where arguably a fair market value for them had been paid) to private owners, but the US continued to impose CVDs against exports of their products to the US market. It arose again under very similar circumstances (since the original Panel report was never adopted and the US continued to impose CVDs) in the WTO era, in *US—Lead and Bismuth II* and in *US—Countervailing Measures on Certain EC Products.*[45]

The US considered that, even following privatization at arm's length, it was still entitled to impose CVDs on the products of these companies, since the subsidies bestowed on them pre-privatization had not been exhausted through the sale at arm's length. In a changed circumstances review under Art. 21.2 SCM,[46] the US had determined that the subsidy continued to exist but the amount paid was much less than the original amount granted to them; the benefit to the productive operations of the company from the original financial contribution continued to exist, albeit reduced. The EU considered that the CVDs were no longer justified, as the new owner of the firm had paid a fair market value in order to acquire the firm and could, therefore, not be considered to have received a benefit. In other words, in the EU's view, payment of market price in and of itself exhausts any subsidy granted before (since the market price paid, so goes the argument, will reflect the subsidy paid as well).

The Panel and the AB sided with the EU: applying the benefit to recipient test, and having established that the recipient must be a natural or legal person (AB, *US—Lead and Bismuth II*, §58), concluded that, by paying a market price for the

---

[45] These two cases are comprehensively discussed in Grossman and Mavroidis (2007) and (2007c).

[46] This is an administrative review operated by the IA and aimed at establishing whether withdrawal of CVDs would lead to recurrence of subsidization and/or injury, as explained in more detail *infra* in this chapter.

company, the new owner was not better off than it would have been otherwise (AB, *US—Lead and Bismuth II*, §68): no benefit was conferred by the financial contribution to the new owner of the privatized firm, so held the AB. Important to the AB's consideration was the fact that the marketplace serves as the benchmark for determining the existence of a benefit, and it is, therefore, not the utility value of the assets of the firm which is important, but rather, their market value. If a market price has been paid for the firm and its assets, there can be no benefit.

In a subsequent case, the AB nuanced this position, holding that payment of fair market value does not in and of itself exhaust previously bestowed benefits. We quote from the AB report on *US—Countervailing Measures on Certain EC Products* (§103):

> We agree with the United States that, irrespective of the price paid by the new private owner, privatization does not *remove* the equipment that a state-owned enterprise may have acquired (or received) with a financial contribution and that, consequently, the same firm may 'continue' to make the same products on the same equipment. However, this observation serves only to illustrate that, following privatization, the *utility value* of equipment acquired as a result of a financial contribution is not extinguished, because it is transferred to the newly-privatized firm. But, the utility value of such equipment to the newly-privatized firm is legally irrelevant for purposes of determining the continued existence of a 'benefit' under the *SCM Agreement*. As we found in *Canada—Aircraft*, the value of the 'benefit' under the *SCM Agreement* is to be assessed using the marketplace as the basis for comparison. It follows, therefore, that once a fair market price is paid for the equipment, its *market value* is redeemed, regardless of the utility the firm may derive from the equipment. Accordingly, it is the market value of the equipment that is the focal point of analysis, and not the equipment's utility value to the privatized firm. (emphasis and italics in the original)

The AB disagreed in this respect with the Panel that had argued that there is an irrebuttable presumption to the effect that every time a fair market value has been paid, the benefit disappears. The AB held that the presumption is rebuttable even in case of payment of the market value and that the facts of the case will reveal whether a benefit continues to exist post-privatization (§§121–4). In other words, according to the AB, even if the privatization has taken place at arm's length, it would still be possible to rebut the presumption that no benefit has been bestowed, if it could be demonstrated that the market price paid by the new owner was not a fair market value, because of particular circumstances that surrounded the privatization. The AB gave no indication at all regarding the nature of circumstances that can successfully rebut a similar presumption.

Grossman and Mavroidis (2007a and 2007d) have taken issue with the decisions of the AB in the privatization cases. In their view, the price paid is simply irrelevant when it comes to deciding whether a benefit continues to exist: at the heart of their disagreement with the AB's decision lies their understanding of the term 'benefit'; they argue that the only interpretation consistent with the aims and objectives of those who drafted the Agreement is one that attributes benefit whenever a firm's competitive position is advantaged relative to what it would have been but for the government's financial contribution (an understanding consistent with the negotiating history and the overall context of the SCM Agreement, as we saw above). To achieve this objective, it makes no sense to interpret 'benefit' in terms of the financial wealth of the owners of a firm. Rather, the potentially adverse effects of a subsidy on producers in an importing country can be avoided only if a subsidy is deemed to exist whenever a government's financial contribution impacts the competitive situation in an industry. And the price at which a change in ownership takes place has no bearing on the subsequent competitive conditions. Consequently, no presumption that the benefit has passed through is legitimate either. It is through an investigation that national authorities will determine whether pass through of subsidies has indeed been the case. Events that occur subsequent to the payment of a subsidy may render infra-marginal an investment that was formerly unprofitable. If an investment becomes infra-marginal, it is impossible to argue that the subsidy is the cause of ongoing injury. In such circumstances, the injury would be present even if the subsidy had never been paid. This is the test that WTO adjudicating bodies should apply to determine whether pass through has occurred or not.

In *US—Softwood Lumber III* and *US—Softwood Lumber IV*, WTO adjudicating bodies faced a related question: is it possible to impose CVDs on products, if their current producers did not themselves receive a financial contribution? The US had imposed CVDs on imports of softwood lumber from Canada, based on a determination of subsidization of the lumber producers through the stumpage programmes discussed *supra*. Recall that, through these programmes, a good (standing timber) was provided to the tenured timber harvesters at less than market price. The timber harvesters sold the trees to the log producers, who sold logs to lumber producers, who turned them into lumber products. It was neither the trees, nor the logs, which were exported or countervailed, but only the lumber products. The question before the Panel was thus whether the lumber producer nevertheless benefited from the cheap trees that were provided by the government to the harvester/log producers. In other words, did the benefit pass through to the lumber producer? The key question for the WTO Panel and the AB was whether a fair market price had been paid by the downstream producer to the upstream producer for the allegedly subsidized input. This was the view of the Panels and the AB dealing with this question. We quote from §144 of the AB report on *US—Softwood Lumber IV*:

> Thus, for a potentially countervailable subsidy to exist, there must be a financial contribution by the government that confers a benefit on a recipient. Where a subsidy is conferred on input products, and the countervailing duty is imposed on processed products, the initial recipient of the subsidy and the producer of the eventually countervailed product, may not be the same. In such a case, there is a direct recipient of the benefit—the producer of the input product. When the input is subsequently processed, the producer of the processed product is an indirect

recipient of the benefit—provided it can be established that the benefit flowing from the input subsidy is passed through, at least in part, to the processed product. Where the input producers and producers of the processed products operate at arm's length, the pass-through of input subsidy benefits from the direct recipients to the indirect recipients downstream cannot simply be presumed; it must be established by the investigating authority. In the absence of such analysis, it cannot be shown that the essential elements of the subsidy definition in Article 1 are present in respect of the processed product.

The Agreement on Agriculture (AG) does not define 'subsidy'; by virtue of case law, the definition provided in the SCM Agreement applies to farm subsidies as well. The AG Agreement provides that certain payments on the export of farm products that are government financed are export subsidies for which reduction commitments have been undertaken. In *Canada—Dairy*, the AB held that the term 'payments' refers to a transfer of economic resources and, thus, equated such payments to financial contributions in the context of the SCM Agreement. Drawing on the case law under the SCM Agreement, the AB held that, for a subsidy to exist, a benefit needs to be conferred by similar payments (§87). The AB suggested a market benchmark for determining whether a benefit had been granted, as it considered that (§113):

> if goods or services are supplied to an enterprise, or a group of enterprises, at reduced rates (that is, at below market-rates), 'payments' are, in effect, made to the recipient of the portion of the price that is not charged.[47]

In the AG Agreement, the terms 'payments' and 'subsidies' seem to have been used interchangeably. In turn, the term 'payment' covers not only the term 'financial contribution', but also the term 'benefit' appearing in the SCM Agreement. The AB endorsed this reading in §§73–4 of its report on *Canada—Dairy* (*Article 21.5—New Zealand and US*). Consequently, according to the AB, there is payment, if the product is supplied at less than its proper (market) value. The AB rejected both the domestic and the world market price as appropriate benchmarks for determining the proper value of the good provided: the former, because it was not a market but an administered price (§81). With regard to the world price, the AB was of the view that it provided one possible measure of the value of the milk to the producer, but that it gave no indication on the key question, namely, whether Canadian export production had been provided with an advantage (§84):

> However, world market prices do not provide a valid basis for determining whether there are 'payments', under Article 9.1(c) of the *Agreement on Agriculture*, for, it remains possible that the reason CEM can be sold at prices competitive with world market prices is precisely because sales of CEM involve subsidies that make it competitive. Thus, a comparison between CEM prices and world market prices

---

[47] Janow and Staiger (2007) discuss this point in detail.

gives no indication on the crucial question, namely, whether Canadian export production has been given an advantage. Furthermore, if the basis for comparison were world market prices, it would be possible for WTO Members to subsidize domestic inputs for export processing, while taking care to maintain the price of these inputs to the processors at a level which equalled or marginally exceeded world market prices. There would then be no 'payments' under Article 9.1(c) of the *Agreement on Agriculture* and WTO Members could easily defeat the export subsidy commitments that they have undertaken in Article 3 of the *Agreement on Agriculture*. (italics in the original)

The AB then decided that the total cost of production offered a more appropriate benchmark for comparison: the average total cost of production (fixed and variable costs of producing milk) whether destined for domestic or export markets would be divided by the total number of units of milk produced in order to define the amount of subsidization per unit of production (§§87–96). The AB explicitly relied on items (j) and (k) of Annex I to the SCM Agreement as contextual support for its interpretation of the AG Agreement (§93).

The cost-of-production test was applied in a subsequent case by the Panel on *EC—Export Subsidies on Sugar*.[48] The facts of the case are reflected in §2 of the AB report:

> EC Regulation 1260/2001 is valid for the marketing years 2001/2002 to 2005/2006 and establishes, *inter alia*: quotas for sugar production; an intervention price for raw and white sugar, respectively; a basic price and a minimum price for beet for quota sugar production; quota (that is, 'A' and 'B') sugar as well as non-quota (that is, 'C') sugar; import and export licensing requirements; producer levies; and preferential import arrangements. Furthermore, the EC sugar regime provides 'export refunds' to its sugar exporters for certain quantities of sugar, other than C sugar. These 'refunds', which are direct export subsidies, cover the difference between the European Communities' internal market price and the prevailing world market price for sugar. Non-quota sugar (that is, C sugar) must be exported, unless it is carried forward, but no 'export refunds' are provided for such exports. (italics in the original)

The Panel was of the view that (§7.264):

> in the present dispute the total cost of production of C beet is an appropriate benchmark for determining whether the sales of C beet to C sugar producers provide a 'payment' to the producers of C sugar within the meaning of Article 9.1(c) of the *Agreement on Agriculture*. (italics in the original)

It follows that this test has been confined so far to cases involving farm subsidies. Note, nevertheless, that it is potentially at odds with the private-investor test, which calls for considerations beyond the cost of production.[49]

---

[48] Hoekman and Howse (2008) offer an in-depth analysis of this case.

[49] One final point is warranted here: Horn and Mavroidis (2005a) alert us to the fact that, in theory, absence of benefit does not necessarily amount to a no-subsidy benchmark: the latter is not necessarily a situation where the subsidy has been removed and nothing else has changed. For it could very well be the case that removal of the subsidy equals its replacement by another lawful

2.3 Specificity

A financial contribution which confers a benefit must do so to a specific recipient, otherwise it is not considered a subsidy in the SCM Agreement sense of the term. The rationale for the specificity requirement reflects the view that only specific financial contributions can lead to inefficient resource allocation, and, eventually, to trade distortions: if a subsidy is generally available, then all productive units in a country can benefit from it, and there will be no diversion of resources to certain enterprises which would not otherwise have attracted such resources. In the words of the Panel on *US—Upland Cotton*, subsidies will not be specific if they are (§7.1142):

> sufficiently broadly available throughout an economy as not to benefit a particular limited group of producers of certain products.

For two types of subsidies, export and local content subsidies, there is no need to satisfy the specificity requirement, as they are considered specific per se (Art. 2.3 SCM). The Panel on *US—Upland Cotton* underscored this point (§7.1153). In similar vein, subsidies limited to certain enterprises located within a designated geographical region are specific by virtue of Art. 2.2 SCM. In contrast, two government activities are considered non-specific:

(a) The setting or change of generally applicable tax rates by all levels of government (Art. 2.2 SCM);
(b) The granting of subsidies according to objective criteria or conditions (Art. 2.1(b) SCM).

The former is the natural consequence of the fact that the WTO Agreement does not prescribe common tax policies. The latter is defined in footnote 2 to the SCM Agreement as follows:

> Objective criteria or conditions, as used herein, mean criteria or conditions which are neutral, which do not favour certain enterprises over others, and which are economic

---

measure. We quote the relevant passage: 'consider the following highly stylized illustration. A government has two instruments, an actionable specific subsidy of s and a non-actionable lawful instrument with effects equivalent to a smaller specific subsidy r. The government's preferred rate of subsidization is equal to s. Its first choice would therefore be to use the actionable subsidy, but when unable to do so, it uses the other instrument, and provides a subsidy equal to r. Now let the CVD equal the difference in price with and without the subsidy. How large will it be? If the no-subsidy benchmark were taken to be the situation where neither of the instruments is used, then the CVD would equal s, this being the difference in price between the two situations. But if instead the no-subsidy benchmark is meant to capture the situation as it would be absent the actionable subsidy, the difference in price would be s − r, which is potentially a much smaller number than s. Differently put, the effect of the actionable subsidy is not to change the subsidy with the amount s but with s − r.' The authors concede, however, that these problems may or may not prove to be important in practice. On the other hand, although probably theoretically sound, the evidentiary standards associated with this approach are very demanding. There are good reasons to avoid going down this road, especially if the likelihood of a counterfactual where a legal avenue is privileged over a subsidy (as opposed to no action at all) is quite small.

in nature and horizontal in application, such as number of employees or size of enterprise.

Nonetheless, it could be that, the presence of objective criteria or conditions notwithstanding, a subsidy is still specific. To determine whether a subsidy is specific to an 'industry' or 'enterprise' or a group of enterprises, an IA must review whether the challenged scheme is (Art. 2.1(c) SCM):

(a) Used by a limited number of certain enterprises;
(b) Predominantly used by certain enterprises;
(c) Disproportionately large amounts are granted to certain enterprises;
(d) Specific because of the manner in which discretion has been exercised by the granting authority in the decision to grant a subsidy.

There is no obligation to examine in each case all four factors, as the Panel on *US—Softwood Lumber IV* made clear (§7.123). In this case, Canada had argued that the Canadian government had never intentionally limited access to the stumpage programmes to lumber producers. In its view, the predominant use of the stumpage programmes by lumber producers could be explained by the fact that the alleged financial contribution consisted of the provision of trees, which, thanks to inherent characteristics, are of interest mainly to a limited number of log and lumber producers. The Panel was of the view that there was no need to show intent in order to satisfy the de facto specificity requirement, although deliberate action by the government might be revealing (§7.116). What matters is that one (at least) of the four criteria mentioned in Art. 2.1(c) SCM has been met.[50]

A subsidy will be deemed specific, if it is granted to an enterprise, or a group of enterprises, or to an industry, or a group of industries, within the jurisdiction of the granting authority (Art. 2.1 SCM). Subsidies are specific either de jure (because they are by law limited to a group of industries and/or enterprises) or de facto (because, although by law generally available, their use is in fact confined to a group of industries and/or enterprises).

The Panel on *EC and Certain Member States—Large Civil Aircraft* understood the term 'explicitly limits' appearing in Art. 2.1(a) SCM as equivalent to the establishment of the existence of a limitation that expressly and unambiguously restricts the availability of a subsidy to certain enterprises and thereby does not make the subsidy sufficiently broadly available throughout an economy. The AB confirmed (§949). In similar vein, in *US—Large Civil Aircraft*, the Panel held that (§7.190):

> The express limitation can be found either in the legislation by which the granting authority operates, or in other statements or means by which the granting authority expresses its will.

---

[50] Note, nonetheless, that an IA is not precluded from examining all four criteria, as the Panel on *EC—Countervailing Measures on DRAM Chips* confirmed.

In *US—Antidumping and Countervailing Duties (China)*, the AB held that a subsidy will be specific if access is limited to either the financial contribution or the benefit (§378).

The SCM Agreement does not define 'industry' in a particular way. The Panel on *US—Softwood Lumber IV* rejected the argument that the term 'industry' should be defined with reference to a particular and specifically defined product. The subsidy may be specific to an industry such as the steel industry or, in the case in question, the lumber industry, even when this industry produces a wide variety of slightly different products. In this case, Canada had argued that more than 200 separate products are manufactured by companies holding harvesting rights, together forming about 23 separate industries. In Canada's view, the wooden door and window industry should, for example, be distinguished from the wooden kitchen cabinet and bathroom vanity industry. A subsidy that is being granted to all those different industries was hardly, in Canada's view, being granted to a limited number of industries. Rejecting Canada's approach, the Panel expressed the view that specificity under Art. 2 SCM must be determined at the enterprise or industry level, and not at the product level: the text of Art. 2 SCM did not require a detailed analysis of the end-products produced by the enterprises involved; nor did Art. 2.1(c) SCM provide that only a limited number of products should benefit from the subsidy (§§7.120–1).

The question nevertheless remains: how big can an industry be? Is, for example, a subsidy specific if it is limited to the farm industry or should it be confined say to wheat producers only? The Panel on *US—Upland Cotton*[51] avoided answering this question head on. It held that the breadth of industry may depend on several factors. In its view, the breadth or narrowness of specificity is not susceptible to rigid quantitative definition (§7.1142). It, thus, came to the following conclusion (§7.1151):

> In our view, the industry represented by a portion of United States agricultural production that is growing and producing certain agricultural crops (and certain livestock in certain regions under restricted conditions) is a sufficiently discrete segment of the United States economy in order to qualify as 'specific' within the meaning of Article 2 of the *SCM Agreement*. (italics in the original)

The Panel on *EC and Certain Member States—Large Civil Aircraft* addressed, *inter alia*, the question of regional subsidies: should a subsidy be deemed specific if it is restricted to a certain region? Or, as the EU had argued, should it be specific only if it is also specific to certain enterprises within that region? The Panel refuted the EU argument (§§7.974ff and especially 7.1223). This is not an unproblematic statement: what if a region replicates the properties of the whole nation when it

---

[51] Sapir and Trachtman (2008) note that the specificity requirement can be met when a scheme is limited to use by specific industries and/or enterprises, and the narrower the list of beneficiaries, the likelier that the requirement will be met.

comes to productive diversification, except that its per capita income is substantially lower than that of the average income in the subsidizing WTO Member? That was probably the reason why regional subsidies were deemed non-actionable in the original WTO setting. This and similar shortcomings point to the need to eventually establish a genuine-intent test, and ask the question whether the regulator's intent was to target specific industries. The statutory proxies discussed *supra* are helpful indeed, but do not constitute a perfect substitute for an intent test.[52]

2.4 Calculating the Amount of Benefit

Art. 14 SCM reflects a list of benchmarks that can be used in order to calculate the amount of benefit. The calculation of the amount of benefit bestowed serves two purposes:

(a) It provides the maximum amount of CVDs;
(b) It also provides the maximum amount of countermeasures.

The question of the calculation of a benefit is separate and distinct from the question whether a benefit exists:[53] a benefit will be calculated only after a Panel has satisfied itself that the three elements of the subsidy definition (financial contribution, benefit, and specificity) are present. The Panel on *EC–Countervailing Measures on DRAM Chips* underscored this point (§§7.187–9). The same Panel emphasized the importance of approaching the question from the perspective of the recipient, rather than from that of the provider of the financial contribution (§§7.211–12).

---

[52] In EU law, the term 'selectivity' is used instead of 'specificity' and the legal test adopted in case law goes some way towards establishing an intent test: a measure is selective if it is such as to 'favour certain undertakings or the production of certain goods' in comparison with other undertakings which are in a legal and factual situation that is comparable in the light of the objective pursued by the measure in question. The Court explicitly laid down this test in C-143/99, *Adria-WienPipeline and Wietersdorfer & Peggauer Zementwerke* (2001) ECR I-8365, §41; subsequently this test has been repeated in many judgments, including the following: Case C-409/00, *Spain v Commission* (2003) ECR I-1487, §47; Case C-88/03, *Portugal v Commission (Azores)* (2006) ECR I-7115, §54; C-172/03, *Heiser* (2005) ECR I-1627, §40, and Joined Cases C-428/06 to C-434/06, *UGT-Rioja and Others* (2008) ECR I-0000, §46.

[53] Of course, the title of Art. 14 SCM suggests that this provision deals with the calculation of the amount of the subsidy in terms of benefit to the recipient, and it deals with the method for calculating the benefit to the recipient as becomes clear from the *chapeau* of Art. 14 SCM. However, the guidelines set forth in paragraphs (a)–(d), with which the calculation methodology has to comply, also clearly deal with the existence or non-existence of a benefit. Whether it is the provision of equity capital, a loan, a loan guarantee, or a good or service, each of the paragraphs provides that the financial contribution shall not be considered as conferring a benefit, unless one of the contingencies mentioned therein happens. Only in the case of loans and loan guarantees (Art. 14(b) and (c) SCM) does the text actually state what the amount of the benefit is. So, Art. 14 SCM, on its face, seems to be as much about the existence of a benefit as it is about the calculation of the amount of the benefit.

Case law has struggled with the question whether the list provided in this provision is of an exhaustive character or not. The wording of Art. 14 SCM provides unambiguous support for the view that benchmarks for calculating a benefit are exhaustively provided in this provision. Yet, case law followed the opposite route. The Panels on *US—Softwood Lumber III* and *US—Softwood Lumber IV* examined the DOC calculation of the benefit conferred on the lumber producers by the Canadian government. The US had used US prices, since, in its view, none of the benchmarks mentioned in the body of Art. 14 SCM was reasonable. The US claimed that it would be meaningless to use Art. 14(d) SCM (which refers to the 'prevailing market conditions' in the subsidizing country), since there were not market conditions at all in Canada with respect to the lumber market: the price of land was heavily subsidized. The Panel disagreed and held that the US should have used the price for trees on private land prevailing in Canada as a benchmark for the calculation of benefit. The Panel's analysis was based on the language of Art. 14 SCM (§7.45). It concluded that (§7.60):

> as long as there are prices determined by independent operators following the principle of supply and demand, even if supply or demand are affected by the government's presence in the market, there is a 'market' in the sense of Article 14(d) [of the] *SCM Agreement*. (italics in the original)

Remarkably, the Panel explicitly acknowledged that, as a matter of economic logic, the US argument was on strong grounds. However, in the Panel's view, its role was not to amend the clear content of a provision, a role reserved to the WTO Membership, even if it was itself not persuaded by the logic of it (§§7.58–60). The AB overturned the Panel's decision, stating that no market may form the appropriate benchmark for measuring benefit and that it could well be the case that a market is so distorted by the government's financial contribution that taking the distorted market as the benchmark would not reveal the true trade distortion caused by the subsidies. According to the AB, it suffices that the benchmark relates to the prevailing market conditions in the country of provision. The AB held that, while market prices will generally represent an appropriate measure of the adequacy of remuneration for the provision of goods, this may not always be the case (§90):

> investigating authorities may use a benchmark other than private prices in the country of provision under Article 14(d), if it is first established that private prices in that country are distorted because of the government's predominant role in providing those goods.

Only this interpretation was, in the eyes of the AB, consistent with the objective of Art. 14(d) SCM, which is to establish whether the recipient is better off than it would have been absent the government financial contribution (§93):

Under the approach advocated by the Panel (that is, private prices in the country of provision must be used whenever they exist), however, there may be situations in which there is no way of telling whether the recipient is 'better off' absent the financial contribution. This is because the government's role in providing the financial contribution is so predominant that it effectively determines the price at which private suppliers sell the same or similar goods, so that the comparison contemplated by Article 14 would become circular.

Thus, the AB considered that the Panel's interpretation frustrated the object and purpose of the SCM Agreement, which disciplines the use of subsidies, while, at the same time, enabling WTO Members whose domestic industries are harmed by subsidized imports to institute countervailing measures (§95). In sum, the AB concluded that the Canadian market was too distorted to be used as a benchmark and, more generally, that it would not be possible to use in-country market prices to calculate the benefit where the government's participation in the market as a provider of the same or similar goods is so predominant that private suppliers will align their prices with those of the government-provided goods (§101). The AB added, nevertheless, a caveat to the effect that determination of whether private prices are distorted because of the government's predominant role in the market, as a provider of certain goods, must be made on a case-by-case basis, according to the particular facts underlying each countervailing duty investigation (§102).

Without explicitly saying so, the AB adopted a teleological interpretation of Art. 14 SCM and privileged the attainment of the objective pursued by the SCM Agreement over the unambiguous wording of this provision. The Panel on *EC—Countervailing Measures on DRAM Chips*, in line with the AB in this respect, held that, when facing problems with the prescribed methodology, an IA is entitled to considerable leeway in adopting a reasonable methodology (§7.213).

In *US—Antidumping and Countervailing Duties (China)*, the US IA refused to use Chinese interest rates as a benchmark to examine whether loans by SOCBs were subsidized (§470):

> ...because of pervasive government intervention in the banking sector, which created significant distortions, restricting and influencing even foreign banks within China. Having rejected interest rates in China as benchmarks, the USDOC resorted to an external benchmark. Specifically, the USDOC constructed, using a regression-based methodology, an interest rate benchmark based on inflation-adjusted interest rates of a group of countries with a gross national income ('GNI') similar to that of China.

The AB explained that the government being a significant supplier of a commodity does not necessarily lead to the conclusion that prices in the exporting market are unreliable and hence recourse to another benchmark is warranted. In its words (§441):

> We read that Appellate Body report as indicating that, if the government is a significant supplier, this fact alone cannot justify a finding that prices are distorted. Instead, where the government is the predominant supplier, it is *likely* that private prices will be distorted, but a case-by-case analysis is still required. (emphasis in the original)

In this case, the Chinese state company possessed a 96.1 per cent market share and 3 per cent of total imports. In the AB's view, this information was enough for it to find that the US IA had the right to move away from the four corners of Art. 14 SCM and use another standard to calculate the benefit granted to the Chinese companies (§§455ff). Remarkably, the AB did not engage in any barriers-to-entry analysis to verify whether the high market share actually corresponded to market power: in an uninformed manner, it equated the two concepts which no sophisticated antitrust authority ever does. The AB went on to examine whether the US had exercised its discretion in a reasonable manner. To do that, the external loan chosen should be comparable to that investigated (§476):

> Thus, a benchmark loan under Article 14(b) should have as many elements as possible in common with the investigated loan to be comparable. The Panel noted that, ideally, an investigating authority should use as a benchmark a loan to the same borrower that has been established around the same time, has the same structure as, and similar maturity to, the government loan, is about the same size, and is denominated in the same currency. The Panel, however, also considered that, in practice, the existence of such an ideal benchmark loan would be extremely rare, and that a comparison should also be possible with other loans that present a lesser degree of similarity.[54] We agree with both of these observations by the Panel.

It went on to state that loans do not lose their character as 'commercial' loans simply because they have been provided by a government; an IA must show how government presence altered the commercial character of the loan (§479). In establishing whether a loan is not 'commercial', the IA must show how because of government presence the loan provided is at odds with market reality (§480).

2.5 Adverse Effects (Injury Analysis)

A scheme that consists of the elements mentioned above is an actionable subsidy. The term 'actionable' implies that action can be taken against similar schemes. Yet, no action can be taken unless a subsidy causes adverse effects to the interests of other WTO Members. Affected WTO Members can have recourse to CVDs, assuming that the conditions of the SCM Agreement concerning lawful imposition of CVDs have been complied with. Through imposition of CVDs, a WTO Member can counteract injury to its domestic producers (resulting from subsidization) in its domestic market. We will return to this discussion *infra*. Through CVDs, a WTO Member cannot address injury that its producers suffered in the subsidizer's market or in third-country markets. To this effect, an affected WTO Member must challenge the consistency of an actionable subsidy with the WTO rules before the WTO adjudicating bodies: this course of action is particularly

---

[54] Panel Report, §10.115.

warranted when most of the damage suffered is not in its import market, but in a third market.[55] Assuming litigation, a WTO Member will have to demonstrate that the subsidy has caused adverse effects. Art. 5 SCM includes the three types of adverse effects:

(a) Injury to the domestic industry;[56]
(b) Nullification or impairment of benefits; and
(c) Serious prejudice.

Art. 5(b) SCM states that adverse effects can take the form of nullification or impairment of benefits accruing either directly or indirectly to other WTO Members, in particular, the benefits of concessions bound under Art. II GATT. A footnote to this provision explains that the term 'nullification or impairment' should be understood as synonymous with the term included in Art. XXIII.1(b) GATT 1994. There is, nonetheless, an important difference regarding the evidence of nullification and impairment under the GATT and in the SCM context. The Panel, in its report on *US—Offset Act* (*Byrd Amendment*), held that, whereas nullification or impairment of benefits may be presumed under the GATT (since any violation of a provision presumably leads to nullification of benefits according to standing case law), no similar presumption exists in the SCM Agreement, where nullification must be proven (§7.119). The Panel held that three elements must be established in order to uphold a claim to this effect (§7.120):

(a) The existence of a benefit accruing under the applicable agreement;
(b) The application of a measure by a WTO Member;
(c) The nullification or impairment of a benefit as a result of the application of a measure.

The GATT Panel on *EEC—Oilseeds* considered that nullification or impairment would arise when the effect of a tariff concession is systematically offset or counteracted by a subsidy programme. The Panel on *US—Offset Act* (*Byrd Amendment*) confirmed this approach (§7.127).

Serious prejudice is defined in Art. 6 SCM. Art. 6.1 SCM reads:

Serious prejudice in the sense of paragraph (c) of Article 5 shall be deemed to exist in the case of:

(a) the total ad valorem subsidization of a product exceeding 5 per cent;
(b) subsidies to cover operating losses sustained by an industry;

---

[55] WTO Members that have small internal markets should almost always fall into this category and this fact also helps explain why Singapore, Hong Kong, China, etc. almost never impose CVDs.
[56] Footnote 11 to Art. 5 SCM states that the term 'injury' is used here in the same way as it is used in the CVD context. Hence, we refer the reader to our discussion of the term *infra*, in the section concerning lawful imposition of CVDs.

(c) subsidies to cover operating losses sustained by an enterprise, other than one-time measures which are non-recurrent and cannot be repeated for that enterprise and which are given merely to provide time for the development of long-term solutions and to avoid acute social problems;

(d) direct forgiveness of debt, i.e. forgiveness of government-held debt, and grants to cover debt repayment.

A footnote to the text (footnote 16) reads:

Members recognize that where royalty-based financing for a civil aircraft programme is not being fully repaid due to the level of actual sales falling below the level of forecast sales, this does not in itself constitute serious prejudice for the purposes of this subparagraph.

Art. 6.1 SCM provides the complainant with an important evidentiary advantage, since it is relieved of the difficult burden of demonstrating the prejudicial effects of a subsidy.[57] As this provision was enacted to serve on a provisional basis, and since WTO Members could not agree on its extension, it has been repealed by virtue of Art. 31 SCM. This does not mean that it is totally irrelevant nowadays: the Panel on *US—Upland Cotton* took the view that it could still provide useful guidance in interpreting serious prejudice (footnote 1487 of the report), even if the evidentiary advantage has ceased. The Panel on *Korea—Commercial Vessels* evidences a similar attitude (§7.583). Its legal relevance, however, should not be overstated since it is now up to individual Panels to draw inspiration from Art. 6.1 SCM. Art. 6.3 SCM is now the forum to decide on serious prejudice. This provision identifies the following situations of serious prejudice:

(a) The effect of the subsidy is to displace from or impede in the market of the subsidizing Member the exports of a like product originating in another Member;

(b) The effect of the subsidy is to displace from or impede in a third-country market the exports of a like product originating in another Member;

(c) The effect of the subsidy is a significant price undercutting or significant price suppression, price depression, or lost sales in the same market;

(d) The effect of the subsidy is an increase in the world market share of the subsidizing Member in a particular subsidized primary product or commodity as compared to the average share it had during the previous period of three years and this increase follows a consistent trend over a period when subsidies have been granted.[58]

---

[57] Messerlin (1995) takes issue with Art. 6.1 SCM, which uses, in his view, a wrong benchmark (a percentage of the subsidy paid, instead of its trade effects) to define serious prejudice.

[58] Art. 6.3(b) SCM is further detailed in Art. 6.4 SCM (change in relative shares of the market to the disadvantage of the non-subsidized like product); Art. 6.3(c) SCM is further detailed in Art. 6.5 SCM (comparison of prices between subsidized and non-subsidized goods at the same level of trade to quantify the size of price undercutting). Annex V SCM, entitled 'Procedures for Developing Information Concerning Serious Prejudice', includes a special procedure for assisting parties involved in dispute settlement in obtaining information and evidence concerning serious prejudice claims. Art. 27.9 SCM contains special rules for determining serious prejudice in case of subsidies provided by developing countries.

The Panel on *Korea—Commercial Vessels* held that the use of the words 'may arise' in the *chapeau* of Art. 6.3 SCM is an indication that the list in this provision is not exhaustive (§7.601). The list appearing in Art. 6.3 SCM nevertheless covers a wide array of cases. The same Panel rejected the argument that, to demonstrate the existence of serious prejudice, the SCM Agreement requires additional elements beyond those referred to in Art. 6 SCM: the importance of that industry to the overall interests of the complaining party was thus judged irrelevant for the purposes of demonstrating serious prejudice (§§7.578–9).[59] The words 'serious prejudice to the interest of another Member' appearing in the body of this provision do not go so far as to allow a WTO Member to claim serious prejudice based on effects felt by a company of that WTO Member but with regard to products not originating in the complaining WTO Member; the Panel on *Indonesia—Autos* (§14.201) held as much.

Arts. 6.3(a) and 6.3(b) SCM provide that a subsidy has an adverse effect if it has the effect of displacing or impeding imports into the market of the subsidizing WTO Member or a third-country market. The Panel on *Indonesia—Autos* examined claims relating to both displacement and impediment of car exports to the Indonesian market, in particular with respect to cars from Japan, the EU, and the US, due to subsidization of the Indonesian carmaker (producing the 'Timor'). To decide whether displacement had occurred, the Panel reviewed data concerning market share and sales. It appeared that, while market share of the European cars had fallen, sales volume in absolute figures did not go down (§14.210). The explanation was that the size of the Indonesian market expanded after the introduction of the Indonesian Timor (§§14.216–17). The data regarding the question of whether sales of EU models in absolute terms would have been higher than the actual had the Indonesian model not been introduced,were inconclusive; as a result, the Panel rejected the claim of displacement (§14.220), since, in its view, serious prejudice must be demonstrated on positive evidence (§14.222). The same Panel understood the term 'impediment' as follows (§14. 218):

> the question before us is therefore whether the market share and sales data above would support a view that, *but for* the introduction of the subsidized Timor, sales of EC C Segment passenger cars *would have been greater* than they were while impedance relates to a situation where sales which otherwise would have occurred were impeded. (emphasis added)

The Panel considered that it had to review the information concerning plans to introduce new EU models in the Indonesian market and to what extent their non-introduction was due to the Indonesian subsidization of its motor industry (§14.227). Once again, the Panel was of the view that the complainants failed to adduce sufficient positive evidence (§14.236). The Panel gave an indication of the kind of evidence it was expecting (§14.234):

---

[59] See also the Panel report on *US—Upland Cotton* at §§7.1370–1.

We do not mean to suggest that in WTO dispute settlement there are any rigid evidentiary rules regarding the admissibility of newspaper reports or the need to demonstrate factual assertions through contemporaneous source information. However, we are concerned that the complainants are asking us to resolve core issues relating to adverse trade effects on the basis of little more than general assertions. This situation is particularly disturbing, given that the affected companies certainly had at their disposal copious evidence in support of the claims of the complainants, such as the actual business plans relating to the new models, government documentation indicating approval for such plans (assuming the 'approval' referred to by the complainants with respect to the Optima means approval by the Indonesian government), and corporate minutes or internal decision memoranda relating both to the initial approval, and the subsequent abandonment, of the plans in question.

In *US—Large Civil Aircraft* (2nd complaint), the AB underscored that trends must be indentified for claims of displacement to be successful (§1126).

Art. 6.3(d) SCM states that, with respect to primary products or commodities, the subsidy has an adverse effect if it leads to an increase in world market share of this commodity as compared to the average share it had had during a previous period of three years. It adds that this increase has to follow a consistent trend over a period when subsidies had been granted. The Panel on *US—Upland Cotton* held that the term 'world market share' (§7.1464):

> refers to share of the world market supplied by the subsidizing Member of the product concerned.

The Panel defined world market as the global geographical area of economic activity, in which buyers and sellers come together and the forces of supply and demand affect prices. It saw no force in the argument that this term would necessarily not include the domestic market of the subsidizing WTO Member (§§7.1431–2). It consequently rejected Brazil's argument that world market share refers to the world market share of exports only (§§7.1434–5).

Art. 6.3(c) SCM lists price suppression, price depression, and price undercutting as three forms of adverse effects.[60] Information regarding these issues typically involves a fact-finding process in the subsidizing country, the complaining WTO Member, as well as third countries. To this effect, Annex V of the SCM Agreement organizes the fact-finding process and even makes room for the participation of a DSB representative to serve the function of facilitating the information-gathering process: Art. 6.8 SCM indicates that the existence of serious prejudice, pursuant to Arts. 5(c) and 6.3(c) SCM, is to be determined on the basis

---

60 There are both price (suppression, depression) and quantity effects in the definition of Art. 6.3 SCM for good reason: quantity effects will be observed irrespective of whether it is a large or a small country subsidizing since, other things equal, subsidies might lead to displacement of imports; price effects, however, will be observed only when large countries subsidize, that is, countries that can affect terms of trade. Hence, in cases of serious prejudice, Panels, when dealing with price effects, should at the outset establish whether the world price has been affected. This is not necessarily what has happened so far.

of information submitted to or obtained by the Panel, including information submitted in accordance with Annex V.

The differences in content across the three terms are not obvious. In case law, price undercutting is equated with selling below a certain price. Price suppression refers to the situation where prices are either prevented or inhibited from rising (that is, they do not increase when they otherwise would have done, or they do actually increase, but the increase is less than it otherwise would have been). Price depression refers to the situation where prices are pressed down or reduced (AB, *US—Upland Cotton*, §423). Yet all three terms refer to effects on the pricing policy of the non-subsidized traders, and one might question the wisdom of using three terms for essentially the same purpose.

Price undercutting must occur in the same market; the Panel on *Indonesia— Autos* ruled as much (§14.239). Art. 6.3(c) SCM, however, does not specify any further which market that is. In *Indonesia—Autos*, the Panel did not have to address this issue any further, since the Panel could anyway reject the US claim because of the fact that the US and the Indonesian product were not competing in the same geographic market. In *US—Upland Cotton*, the AB agreed with the Panel that, in the absence of specification in Art. 6.3(c) SCM, the market in question could be any national, regional, or other market, including the world market (§406). The market could, consequently, be the world market, if it can be demonstrated that the subsidized product and the other product compete in it (AB, *US—Upland Cotton*, §409). A geographic product market is, of course, one where the same conditions of competition prevail. The Panel and the AB on *US—Upland Cotton* accepted as much (AB, §408, referring to §7.1237 of the Panel report):

> the scope of the 'market', for determining the area of competition between two products, may depend on several factors such as the nature of the product, the homogeneity of the conditions of competition, and transport costs.

For some products (say airplanes), this is indeed the world market; for other products, conditions of competition might be affected, notably through trade barriers, and a narrower definition might be appropriate.

For two products to be considered to be in the same market, they must engage in actual or potential competition in that market, even if they are not necessarily sold at the same time and in the same place or country (AB, *US—Upland Cotton*, § 408): the subsidized product and the other product necessarily have to be directly competitive products in order to be able to be in the same market. Whether they have to be like products as well was a question that the AB felt it did not need to resolve. The Panel on *Korea—Commercial Vessels* was more outspoken on this issue. It concluded (§7.553):

> that 'like product' as defined in footnote 46 to Article 15 of the *SCM Agreement* is not a legal requirement for claims of price suppression/price depression pursuant to Article 6.3(c). (italics in the original)

This Panel was dealing with a case of price suppression/depression. It based this conclusion on the absence of an explicit reference to like products for claims concerning price suppression/depression in Art. 6.3(c) SCM. The same provision, nevertheless, requests that the effects of price undercutting must be on the like product (§§7.545–53). This is probably clumsy shorthand on the part of the framers: the three phenomena (undercutting, suppression, depression) refer to essentially the same issue, and it would be odd to accept that the net is cast wider for the latter two. This is probably an issue that could easily be resolved at the negotiating table, unless, of course, WTO adjudicating bodies resolve it first by adopting the (non-commendable) attitude that they did when interpreting Art. 14 SCM in the softwood lumber litigation discussed *supra*.

Interestingly, the AB, in its report on *US—Upland Cotton*, siding with the Panel, held that a suppression effect on the world price for cotton sufficed for making a determination of price suppression, and that it was not necessary to also determine whether prices of Brazilian cotton, the like product in this case, had been suppressed as a consequence of US subsidies. In its view, if world prices had been suppressed, so would Brazilian cotton prices (§417).

Price undercutting (like price suppression and depression) must be significant, otherwise it is not punished. The Panel on *Indonesia—Autos* upheld a claim that the subsidized Indonesian car, the Timor, significantly undercut the prices of EU products in the Indonesian market, because the level of undercutting was 42–54 per cent (§§14.251–4). A quantification is certainly helpful, although, it appears, not strictly necessary. In *US—Upland Cotton*, the Panel understood the term 'significant price depression or suppression' as (§7.1326):

important, notable or consequential.[61]

The same Panel added that (§7.1330):

a relatively small decrease or suppression of prices could be significant because, for example, profit margins may ordinarily be narrow, product homogeneity means that sales are price sensitive or because of the sheer size of the market in terms of the amount of revenue involved in large volumes traded on the markets experiencing the price suppression.

The Panel had found that price suppression indeed existed, based on three factors (§7.1280):

(a) The relative magnitude of the US production and exports in the world upland cotton market;
(b) General price trends (in the world market); and
(c) The nature of the subsidies at issue, and in particular, the fact that they had discernible price suppressive effects.

---

[61] See also the Panel report on *Korea—Commercial Vessels* (§7.571).

The Panel did not consider it necessary to quantify the suppression to conclude that it was significant. Rather, these three factors, as well as the readily available evidence of the order of magnitude of the subsidies, led the Panel to the conclusion that the price suppression in question was indeed significant (§ 7.1333). The AB upheld all of the Panel's conclusions and pointed to the relevance of such factors as the general price trends, the nature of the subsidies, and the relative magnitude of the subsidized product share of the market (§434):

> In the absence of explicit guidance on assessing significant price suppression in the text of Article 6.3(c), we have no reason to reject the relevance of these factors for the Panel's assessment in the present case. An assessment of 'general price trends' is clearly relevant to significant price suppression (although, as the Panel itself recognized, price trends alone are not conclusive). The two other factors—the nature of the subsidies and the relative magnitude of the United States' production and exports of upland cotton—are also relevant for this assessment.

When examining price suppression, the effects of recurring subsidies may be allocated over time and are not limited to the year in which the subsidy was granted. The AB held as much in its report on *US—Upland Cotton* (§482):

> we are not persuaded by the United States' contention that the effect of annually paid subsidies must be 'allocated' or 'expensed' solely to the year in which they are paid and that, therefore, the effect of such subsidies cannot be significant price suppression in any subsequent year. We do not agree with the proposition that, if subsidies are paid annually, their effects are also necessarily extinguished annually.

In *US—Large Civil Aircraft* (2nd complaint), the AB distinguished 'technology effects' from price effects and held that they are adverse effects since, because of subsidies paid, new products were produced faster than otherwise (§§16ff).

Art. 6.3 SCM states that serious prejudice must be the effect of the subsidy. There must be, in other words, a causal relationship between the subsidy and its effects. The term 'price suppression/depression' appeared in the Tokyo round AD Agreement as well. During the GATT era, Panels equated price depression to serious prejudice: the Panels on *EC—Sugar Exports (Australia)* (§4.26), and on *EC—Sugar Exports (Brazil)* (§§4.14–15) can serve as illustrations here. WTO Panels have used a finding of price suppression or depression (as the case may be) as determinative that serious prejudice has occurred. This has been the case in *Indonesia—Autos* (§14.238) and in *US—Upland Cotton* as well, where the Panel stated (§7.1390):

> the Article 6.3(c) examination is determinative . . . for a finding of serious prejudice under Article 5(c). That is, an affirmative conclusion that the effects-based situation in Article 6.3(c) exists is sufficient basis for an affirmative conclusion that 'serious prejudice' exists for the purposes of Article 5(c) of the SCM Agreement.

In this vein, both the Panel on *Korea—Commercial Vessels* (§7.534), and the AB on *US—Upland Cotton* found that price suppression contains some sort of built-in causation requirement, and the factors that lead to a determination of the existence of price suppression may also be relevant to the question regarding its cause: in other words, it may be difficult to separate the existence of any suppression from its cause. There is also an example in the opposite direction, though: the Panel on *US—Upland Cotton*. On appeal, the AB noted the problems inherent in the Panel's approach (§433):

> However, the ordinary meaning of the transitive verb 'suppress' implies the existence of a subject (the challenged subsidies) and an object (in this case, prices in the world market for upland cotton). This suggests that it would be difficult to make a judgment on significant price suppression without taking into account the effect of the subsidies. The Panel's definition of price suppression, explained above, reflects this problem; it includes the notion that prices 'do not increase when they otherwise would have' or 'they do actually increase, but the increase is less than it otherwise would have been'. The word 'otherwise' in this context refers to the hypothetical situation in which the challenged subsidies are absent.

Irrespective, however, of the question regarding the stage when the causation analysis must take place, it is clear that it must take place anyway. The Panel on *Korea—Commercial Vessels* found that the text of Art. 6.3 SCM implies a 'but for' approach to causation and would thus require a Panel to examine the counterfactual (§7.612): the complainant should demonstrate that, but for the subsidy, it could have expected to participate in a growing market (in case of displacement of its shipments from a particular market); or in the case of impeding exports, that, but for the subsidies, its sales and/or market share would have increased, or would have increased more than they actually did. This framework of analysis requires an evaluation of the various factors contributing to the particular market situation forming the subject of the complaint, that is, supply and demand factors, production costs, relative efficiency of the market actors, etc. (§7.615). By way of example, we refer to the Panel's decision on *US—Upland Cotton*. In this case, the Panel found that there was a causal link between price-contingent subsidies and significant price suppression for four reasons (§§7.1347–55):

(a) The US had exerted substantial influence on the world upland cotton market;
(b) The price-contingent subsidies were directly linked to world prices for upland cotton, thereby insulating US producers from low prices;
(c) There was a discernible temporal coincidence of suppressed world market prices, on the one hand, and the price-contingent US subsidies, on the other; and, finally,
(d) Credible evidence on the record concerning the divergence between US producers' total costs of production, and revenue from sales of upland cotton since 1997 supported the proposition that US upland cotton producers would not have been economically capable of remaining in the production of upland cotton, had it not been for the US subsidies, and that the effect of the subsidies was to allow US producers to sell upland cotton at a price lower than would otherwise have been necessary to cover their total costs.

The AB upheld the Panel's reliance on these factors (§§449–53): it emphasized that the nature of the subsidies, as well as the magnitude of the subsidy, played an important role in establishing price suppression, but that, ultimately, all relevant factors had to be taken into consideration (§461):

> However, in assessing whether 'the effect of the subsidy is ... significant price suppression', and ultimately serious prejudice, a panel will need to consider the effects of the subsidy on prices. The magnitude of the subsidy is an important factor in this analysis. A large subsidy that is closely linked to prices of the relevant product is likely to have a greater impact on prices than a small subsidy that is less closely linked to prices. All other things being equal, the smaller the subsidy for a given product, the smaller the degree to which it will affect the costs or revenue of the recipient, and the smaller its likely impact on the prices charged by the recipient for the product. However, the size of a subsidy is only one of the factors that may be relevant to the determination of the effects of a challenged subsidy. A panel needs to assess the effect of the subsidy taking into account all relevant factors.

Art. 6.3 SCM does not, on its face, impose a non-attribution requirement as in the CVD context (Art. 15.5 SCM). Nevertheless, two Panels (*US—Upland Cotton*, §7.1344, and *Korea—Commercial Vessels*, §7.618) considered it logical and appropriate to analyse other possible factors, with a view to determining whether such factors would have had the effect of attenuating the causal link or of rendering insignificant the effect of the subsidy. In its report on *US—Upland Cotton*, the Panel concluded that the condition of a causal link requires a Panel to ensure that the significant price suppression is the effect of the subsidy, within the meaning of Art. 6.3(c) SCM. In the Panel's view, this requirement calls for an examination of US subsidies within the context of other possible causal factors; otherwise an appropriate attribution of causality cannot take place (§7.1344). The AB endorsed this approach (§§436–7):

> As the Panel pointed out, 'Articles 5 and 6.3 ... do not contain the more elaborate and precise "causation" and non-attribution language' found in the trade remedy provisions of the *SCM Agreement*. Part V of the *SCM Agreement*, which relates to the imposition of countervailing duties, requires, inter alia, an examination of 'any known factors other than the subsidized imports which at the same time are injuring the domestic industry'. However, such causation requirements have not been expressly prescribed for an examination of serious prejudice under Article 5(c) and Article 6.3(c) in Part III of the *SCM Agreement*. This suggests that a panel has a certain degree of discretion in selecting an appropriate methodology for determining whether the 'effect' of a subsidy is significant price suppression under Article 6.3(c).
>
> Nevertheless, we agree with the Panel that it is necessary to ensure that the effects of other factors on prices are not improperly attributed to the challenged subsidies. Pursuant to Article 6.3(c) of the *SCM Agreement*, '[s]erious prejudice in the sense of paragraph (c) of Article 5 may arise' when 'the effect of the subsidy is ... significant price suppression'. If the significant price suppression found in the world market for upland cotton were caused by factors other than the challenged subsidies, then that price suppression would not be 'the effect of' the challenged subsidies in the sense of Article 6.3(c). Therefore, we do not find fault with the Panel's approach of 'examin [ing] whether or not 'the effect of the subsidy' is the significant price suppression which [it had] found to exist in the same world market' and separately 'consider[ing] the role of other alleged causal factors in the record before [it] which may affect [the]

analysis of the causal link between the United States subsidies and the significant price suppression'. (italics in the original)

The Panel on *US—Upland Cotton* examined other factors (§7.1363) and held that they had contributed to the price suppression, but, in its view, the challenged subsidy schemes, even in the presence of these factors, still had had a significant price-suppressing effect. The AB found no legal error in the Panel's causation analysis, although it expressed its disappointment about the fact that, in its reasoning, the Panel did not offer a detailed enough analysis (§458). The key here is that, as long as subsidies have caused significant price suppression, it is irrelevant if other factors have added to this effect.

Any time serious prejudice has been caused as a result of subsidization, and WTO Members cannot find a mutually agreed solution, the matter can be referred to a Panel (Art. 7.4 SCM). Following a request to the DSB, recourse can be made to the procedures established in Annex V to the SCM: §2 of Annex V reads:

> In cases where matters are referred to the DSB under paragraph 4 of Article 7, the DSB shall, upon request, initiate the procedure to obtain such information from the government of the subsidizing Member as necessary to establish the existence and amount of subsidization, the value of total sales of the subsidized firms, as well as information necessary to analyze the adverse effects caused by the subsidized product.

The Panel on *US—Large Civil Aircraft* (2nd complaint) held that the DSB will decide on a negative consensus whether to initiate this procedure; hence, the request by the WTO Member interested in initiating this procedure suffices. Nevertheless, total inaction by the DSB entails as sole consequence that the procedure has not been initiated (§§721ff). The AB disagreed and held that the DSB should have initiated the procedure at the time of the Panel's establishment, since the request suffices for initiation of this procedure to occur (§§ 511, 524).

Annex V regulates the manner in which the information-gathering process will take place. A representative is appointed by the Panel, the so-called 'Designated Representative' (DR), who will be in charge of the process and ensure it is completed in a timely manner (Annex V, §5). This process cannot last more than 60 days (Annex V, §6). The Panel will decide based on the information gathered and may even draw inferences in case of non-cooperation (Annex V, §7). No recourse to BIA is permissible, unless the DR's opinion on the reasonableness of the requested information has been heard, as well as the reasons why the requested information could not have been supplied (Annex V, §8). The Panel remains free to seek information additional to that gathered through this process (Annex V, §9). The Panel on *Korea—Commercial Vessels* had recourse to this procedure.[62]

---

[62] See Attachment 1 to the Panel report where it is made clear that the DR retains discretion on issues not explicitly covered in Annex V. See also pp. 159–64 of the Panel report on *Korea—Commercial Vessels*, where the Working Procedures for the Designated Representative are explained.

Art. 7.8 SCM requires from the WTO Member causing adverse effects through its subsidies

> to remove the adverse effects or ... withdraw the subsidy.

So, irrespective of whether adverse effects result in serious prejudice, nullification, and impairment or injury, a WTO Member that has proved their existence can request from a Panel to recommend that the subsidizing WTO Member removes the effects or withdraws the subsidy altogether (Art. 7.8 SCM). In case of non-compliance, the affected WTO Member can take countermeasures commensurate with the degree and nature of the adverse effects determined to exist. Art. 7.9 SCM reads in this respect:

> In the event the Member has not taken appropriate steps to remove the adverse effects of the subsidy or withdraw the subsidy within six months from the date when the DSB adopts the panel report or the Appellate Body Report, and in the absence of agreement on compensation, the DSB shall grant authorization to the complaining Member to take countermeasures, commensurate with the degree and nature of the adverse effects determined to exist, unless the DSB decides by consensus to reject the request.

In case of disagreement between the parties as to whether the proposed counter-measures are indeed commensurate, recourse will be made to an Arbitrator, who will define their level (Art. 7.10 SCM). There has been no practice so far in the context of Art. 7.9 SCM. There are good arguments to construe the term 'commensurate' in parallel with the term 'equivalent', which appears in Art. 22.4 DSU.[63] Thus, the benchmark for calculation should be the injury suffered by the affected party.

3. Non-actionable Subsidies

A third category of subsidies was foreseen in the SCM Agreement, the so-called non-actionable subsidies (Art. 8 SCM). Three types of subsidies were deemed non-actionable: regional aid, environmental subsidies, and subsidies for research and development (R&D) purposes. They were initially contracted for a five-year provisional period. In the absence of agreement to keep this category in place, non-actionable subsidies ceased to exist as of 1 January 2000 (Art. 31 SCM). Consequently, a scheme which qualifies as a subsidy under the SCM Agreement is, nowadays, either a prohibited or an actionable subsidy.

Both Howse (2010) and Rubini (2010) have voiced their concerns over the deletion of non-actionable subsidies from the SCM Agreement: in the current

---

For a first application of this institutional facility, see §§1.17–19 of the Panel report on *Indonesia—Autos*. Information gathering under Annex V was also initiated in *US—Upland Cotton* (see §1.3 of the Panel report).

[63] As stated *supra*, the purpose of the SCM Agreement is to re-establish the balance across producers that would have existed absent subsidization.

fight against climate change, their usefulness, so goes the argument, should not be underestimated. Rubini (2010) argues that, in case there is no agreement to reinstate non-actionable subsidies in the SCM Agreement, Art. XX GATT could be an acceptable second-best since it will allow for subsidies ostensibly justified on environmental grounds to become de facto non-actionable.[64] At the heart of similar claims lies the frustration of trade experts with the absence of recognition in the SCM context of the reason for subsidization. As discussed *supra*, subsidies might be a very appropriate instrument to deal with market distortions and, as the saying goes, 'markets work well when it comes to ice cream, but not necessarily so when it comes to clean air'. Alas, as things stand, similar voices have not been heard by those around the table negotiating the WTO agreements. Still, it is not all doom and gloom in this department since many of the schemes (e.g. environmental subsidies) will typically be non-specific; hence they will escape the purview of the SCM Agreement.

4. Prohibited Subsidies

4.1 The Legal Discipline and its Rationale

Local content and export subsidies are the two forms of prohibited subsidies. Local content measures have been outlawed since the inception of the GATT (Art. III.5); hence, outlawing subsidies conditional upon the use of domestic value added should not come as a surprise. The attitude of the world trading system towards export subsidies has evolved remarkably since the inception of the GATT. The GATT initially followed a much more lenient approach than the current SCM approach.[65] Art. VI GATT implicitly recognized that subsidies may be a legitimate instrument of domestic public policy by specifying that countervailing duties to offset the subsidy can only be imposed if the effect of subsidization has resulted in material injury to a domestic industry. In its original formulation, Art. XVI GATT did not ban export subsidies. As discussed in Chapter 4, it was in the context of the 1955 Review Session of the GATT that trading nations agreed to amend Art. XVI: they introduced §4 (Section B) which banned export subsidies on manufactured goods; export subsidies on farm goods were not banned. From the moment of the GATT Review Session onwards, the US toughened its stance towards export subsidies. The Working Party on Subsidies (1960) aimed, *inter alia*, at ensuring faithful implementation of Art. XVI.4 GATT.[66] §5 of this Working Party reflected an agreed list of illegal subsidies,

---

[64] See the discussion of this issue in Chapter 5, where we explained why it is hard for similar arguments to win the day.

[65] Sykes (2003b); Janow and Staiger (2003); Trebilcock and Howse (2005).

[66] GATT Doc. L/1381 at para. 5, adopted on 19 November 1960, GATT Doc. BISD 9S/185.

namely, illegal currency restriction, direct subsidies, remission of direct taxes, exemption of charges in connection with imports or exports other than indirect taxes, charging of prices below world prices for delivery by governments of raw materials, export credit guarantees at manifestly inadequate rates, export credits at non-market rates, and government-borne costs for obtaining credit. The list was comprehensive, non-exhaustive, and yet the US was not happy with the fact that some export refunds were not outlawed as well.[67] GATT contracting parties accepted a 'Declaration Giving Effect to Provisions of Art. XVI.4' promising action within set deadlines.[68] The last US attempt in the GATT years to tighten the screws on export subsidies even further came with the establishment of the Working Party report on BTAs which, as we saw in Chapter 4, ended with a result that was not what the US had expected.

Art. XVI GATT imposes two obligations: to notify exports subsidies and to limit them, in order to address the concerns of affected trading partners. Art. 3 SCM outlaws two types of subsidies that must be removed with immediate effect: export subsidies and local content requirements.

There are voices arguing in favour of the current legal discipline on export subsidies: Green and Trebilcock (2010) and Coppens (2012) have argued that it is sensible to treat export subsidies differently from domestic subsidies, since the former can and often do upset world markets. Yet proponents of this hard line towards export subsidies have not responded to the arguments that we advanced *supra*, namely: does it make sense to introduce a blanket prohibition against export subsidies (and not domestic subsidies) when it is fairly easy to construct scenarios where domestic subsidies can be more distorting? And why should an instrument that expands trade be treated more harshly than one that restricts it (tariffs)? Few would argue with a prohibition on predatory subsidization, but this is not what the agreement outlaws.

4.2 Coverage of the Legal Discipline

The term 'export subsidy' is quite open-ended. In an effort at clarification, Annex I of the SCM Agreement contains 12 types of export subsidies in an Illustrative List. The AB report on *Brazil—Aircraft* (*Art 21.5—Canada*) held that a scheme that falls under the purview of the Illustrative List is *ipso facto* prohibited: there is no additional requirement to demonstrate that it is contingent upon export performance under Art. 3.1(c) SCM. Assuming a scheme is not reflected in the Illustrative List, the complainant must demonstrate that it is either de jure or de facto an export subsidy: the letter of Art. 3.1 SCM ('either in law or in fact') leaves no doubt that this is the correct conclusion. A case where the law conditions the

---

[67] Hemmendinger (1969) at p. 206; Stewart et al. (2007) reflect in detail the US dissatisfaction with the results of the Working Party on Subsidies as well as the planning of the next steps.

[68] Seventeen GATT contracting parties adhered; see GATT Doc. MTN.GNG/NG10/W/4 of 28 September 1987.

payment of a subsidy upon exportation would amount to de jure export subsidy. De facto export contingency operates as an anti-circumvention provision against attempts by WTO Members to link benefits to exports without explicitly stating that this has indeed been the case. Yet, as much as opening to de facto export subsidies seems to be the correct move, the opening itself to this category of subsidies presents us with serious interpretative issues.[69] One thing is for sure: for the reasons mentioned in Chapters 2 and 4 it cannot be that the evidence required to demonstrate an export subsidy can be the same for de jure and de facto cases. The AB in its report on *Canada—Aircraft* accepted this premise and discussed the different evidentiary standards required to demonstrate the existence of a de jure or a de facto subsidy. It explained why, in its view, the latter was a more demanding standard in the following terms (§167):

> In our view, the legal standard expressed by the word 'contingent' is the same for both *de jure* and *de facto* contingency. There is a difference, however, in what evidence may be employed to prove that a subsidy is export contingent. *De jure* export contingency is demonstrated on the basis of the words of the relevant legislation, regulation or legal instrument. Proving *de facto* export contingency is a much more difficult task. There is no single legal document which will demonstrate, on its face, that a subsidy is 'contingent ... in fact .... Upon export performance.' Instead, the existence of this relationship of contingency, between the subsidy and the export performance, must be inferred from the total configuration of the facts constituting and surrounding the granting of the subsidy, none of which on its own is likely to be decisive in any given case .... We note that satisfaction of the standard for determining *de facto* export contingency set out in footnote 4 requires proof of three different substantive elements: first, 'the granting of a subsidy'; second, 'is ... tied to ...'; and third, 'actual or anticipated exportation or export earnings.' (italics in the original)

In *EC and Certain Member States—Large Civil Aircraft*,[70] the AB explained that, for a scheme to be judged a de facto export subsidy, it must incentivize producers towards exporting rather than selling in the domestic market even though similar behaviour does not correspond to the market conditions of supply and demand (§1102):

> We find that the factual equivalent of *de jure* conditionality between the granting of a subsidy and anticipated exportation can be established where the granting of the subsidy is geared to induce the promotion of future export performance of the recipient. The standard for *de facto* export contingency under Article 3.1(a) and footnote 4 of the *SCM Agreement* would be met when the subsidy is granted so as to provide an incentive to the recipient to export in a way that is not simply reflective of the conditions of supply and demand in the domestic and export markets undistorted by the granting of the subsidy. (italics in the original)

---

[69] As does the opening to de facto import and/or export quotas (Chapter 2), as well as de facto discrimination (Chapter 4).

[70] Compare Slot (2010) and Wu (2010) on this issue.

It follows that inducement suffices for a subsidy to be considered an export subsidy and it is not necessary to impose a legally binding obligation to export. The AB explained its understanding of the evidentiary standard associated with proof of de jure export subsidy in §112 of its report on *US—FSC (Article 21.5—EC)*:

> ...a subsidy is contingent 'in law' upon export performance when the existence of that condition can be demonstrated on the basis of the very words of the relevant legislation, regulation or other legal instrument constituting the measure....[F]or a subsidy to be *de jure* export contingent, the underlying legal instrument does not always have to provide *expressis verbis* that the subsidy is available only upon fulfilment of the condition of export performance. Such conditionality can also be derived by necessary implication from the words actually used in the measure. (italics in the original)

The evidentiary standard associated with a demonstration of de facto export subsidy was discussed in the Panel report on *Australia—Automotive Leather II* (§§9.36–66). In this case, the Panel found that a subsidy was de facto an export subsidy based on the following factors:

(a) Australia had agreed to pay Howe (a private economic operator) 30 million Australian dollars in three instalments, if Howe were to meet certain sales and investment targets;

(b) The terms of the contract between Australia and Howe did not require Howe to export, though it provided the latter with incentives to do so;

(c) The government's awareness, at the time the contract was concluded, that Howe earned the majority of its income from exports was crucial in the Panel's evaluation;

(d) For Howe to meet the targets set, exporting was *passage obligé*, since the Australian market was too small to absorb its production.

This Panel concluded that an export subsidy had been paid based on the totality of the evidence before it. A subsequent report clarified that at least one of the factors mentioned in *Australia—Automotive Leather II* by itself had no probative value that an export subsidy has been paid: the AB in *Canada—Aircraft* was dealing with a subsidy paid by TPC (a Canadian entity) to Canadian aircraft producers. The AB paid particular attention to footnote 4 to Art. 3.1 SCM, and held that mere knowledge that the beneficiary is exporting does not suffice for the de facto threshold to be met. Something more is required. Footnote 4, which interprets the term 'subsidies contingent [. . .] in fact', reads:

> This standard is met when the facts demonstrate that the granting of a subsidy, without having been made legally contingent upon export performance, is in fact tied to actual or anticipated exportation or export earnings. The mere fact that a subsidy is granted to enterprises which export shall not for that reason alone be considered to be an export subsidy within the meaning of this provision.

We quote from §§172–4 of the report:

> The second substantive element in footnote 4 is 'tied to'. The ordinary meaning of 'tied to' confirms the linkage of 'contingency' with 'conditionality' in Article 3.1(a). Among the many meanings of the verb 'tie', we believe that, in this instance, because the word 'tie' is immediately followed by the word 'to' in footnote 4, the relevant ordinary meaning of 'tie' must be to 'limit or restrict as to...conditions'. This element of the standard set forth in footnote 4, therefore, emphasizes that a relationship of conditionality or dependence must be demonstrated. The second substantive element is at the very heart of the legal standard in footnote 4 and cannot be overlooked. In any given case, the facts must 'demonstrate' that the granting of a subsidy is *tied to* or *contingent upon* actual or anticipated exports. It does *not* suffice to demonstrate solely that a government granting a subsidy *anticipated* that exports would result. The prohibition in Article 3.1(a) applies to subsidies that are *contingent* upon export performance.
>
> We turn now to the third substantive element provided in footnote 4. The dictionary meaning of the word 'anticipated' is 'expected'. The use of this word, however, does *not* transform the standard for 'contingent...in fact' into a standard merely for ascertaining 'expectations' of exports on the part of the granting authority. Whether exports were anticipated or 'expected' is to be gleaned from an examination of objective evidence. This examination is quite separate from, *and should not be confused with*, the examination of whether a subsidy is 'tied to' actual or anticipated exports. A subsidy may well be granted in the knowledge, or with the anticipation, that exports will result. Yet, that alone is not sufficient, because that alone is not proof that the granting of the subsidy is *tied to* the anticipation of exportation.
>
> There is a logical relationship between the second sentence of footnote 4 and the 'tied to' requirement set forth in the first sentence of that footnote. The second sentence of footnote 4 precludes a panel from making a finding of *de facto* export contingency for the sole reason that the subsidy is 'granted to enterprises which export'. In our view, merely knowing that a recipient's sales are export-oriented does not demonstrate, without more, that the granting of a subsidy is tied to actual or anticipated exports. The second sentence of footnote 4 is, therefore, a specific expression of the requirement in the first sentence to demonstrate the 'tied to' requirement. We agree with the Panel that, under the second sentence of footnote 4, the export orientation of a recipient may be taken into account as *a* relevant fact, provided that it is one of several facts which are considered and is not the only fact supporting a finding. (emphasis in the original)

Unfortunately, the AB did not complete its analysis in this respect. As a result, we now know that awareness per se is not enough to establish de facto export contingency, but we are in the dark as to what else is required. Although the AB has insisted that this is not the case, this case law looks as if an intent test has already been introduced: assuming the complainant can demonstrate that the government intended the challenged scheme to be an export subsidy, it will be quite hard for the defendant to refute proof of violation of Art. 3 SCM.

Panels can request the help of the Permanent Group of Experts (PGE), established in order to evaluate whether a scheme is a prohibited subsidy. The PGE comprises trade experts and, if requested to pronounce on a case, its opinion binds the Panel (Art. 4.5 SCM). So far, Panels have refused to make use of this institutional facility.

4.3 Counteracting Prohibited Subsidies

Assuming the complainant has prevailed, the Panel and/or the AB will recommend that the subsidy be withdrawn without delay (Art. 4.7 SCM).[71] Panels that are asked to pronounce on this issue are requested, in contrast to their usual procedures, to reach a speedy judgment within 90 days (Art. 4.6 SCM). In case of refusal to implement the recommendation, the injured party can have recourse to appropriate countermeasures (Art. 4.10 SCM). A footnote to Art. 4.10 SCM explains that 'appropriate' means not disproportionate (sic).[72] Recall that Art. 7.9 SCM provides that in case of actionable subsidies, commensurate countermeasures, that is, countermeasures commensurate with the degree and nature of the adverse effects determined to exist, may be authorized. The choice of words prima facie cannot be accidental.

Based on the fact that the case of prohibited subsidies is the only instance where the WTO Agreement not only explicitly outlaws a practice (whereas, in all other cases, outlawing a practice is the privilege of the WTO adjudicating body), but also modifies the substantive content of a Panel's recommendation, WTO adjudicating bodies have held that the punishment of prohibited subsidies through countermeasures should be harder than the punishment of any other breach of the WTO Agreement. The report on *Brazil—Aircraft* (*Art. 22.6—Brazil*) was the first that had the opportunity to clarify the ambit of the term 'appropriate' and explain the relationship between Art. 4.10 SCM and Art. 22.4 DSU.[73] This case (and its 'twin' dispute, *Canada—Aircraft*) concerned (export) subsidization by Canada and Brazil of their respective national aircraft producers. A duopoly producing regional jets (that is, short to medium haul: Embraer for Brazil, Bombardier for Canada) was in place whereby both parties, confirming Brander and Spencer's predictions, saw an interest in subsidizing their domestic producer. To base its finding that the quantification of appropriate countermeasures should be linked to a benchmark other than the damage suffered by the complainant (as is the case under Art. 7.9 SCM), the Arbitrators first explained the difference they saw in the function of the remedy against a prohibited subsidy, as opposed to remedies to address any other nullification or impairment of WTO Members' rights. Important to their

---

[71] This is the only case where the content of a Panel recommendation is specific; normally, WTO adjudicating bodies will recommend that the concerned party bring its measures into compliance, leaving addressees thus with substantial discretion as to the implementing activities (Art. 19 DSU).

[72] Footnotes 9 and 10 provide as follows with respect to the term 'appropriate countermeasures': 'This expression is not meant to allow countermeasures that are disproportionate in light of the fact that the subsidies dealt with under these provisions are prohibited'.

[73] Report of the Arbitrators, *Brazil—Aircraft* (*Art. 22.6—Brazil*), §§3.42–60.

reasoning was the fact that they considered that the purpose of Art. 4 SCM is to achieve the withdrawal of the prohibited subsidy (§3.48):

> . . . the purpose of Article 4 is to achieve the withdrawal of the prohibited subsidy. In this respect, we consider that the requirement to withdraw a prohibited subsidy is of a different nature than removal of the specific nullification or impairment caused to a Member by the measure. The former aims at removing a measure which is presumed under the WTO Agreement to cause negative trade effects, irrespective of who suffers those trade effects and to what extent. The latter aims at eliminating the effects of a measure on the trade of a given Member; the fact that nullification or impairment is established with respect to a measure does not necessarily mean that, in the presence of an obligation to withdraw that measure, the level of appropriate countermeasures should be based only on the level of nullification or impairment suffered by the Member requesting the authorisation to take countermeasures.[74]

The focal point of the exercise for the Arbitrators was thus not the injury suffered by the payment of an illegal subsidy. They consequently rejected arguments by Brazil to the effect that their proposed benchmark (the amount of the subsidy) was not reasonable. The Arbitrators argued that anyway the subsidy benchmark was not too onerous since, in all likelihood, Brazil gained much more from its subsidies than it had actually invested. They also rejected an argument to the effect that their benchmark amounted to punitive damages. We quote from §§3.54 and 3.55:

> Our interpretation of the scope of the term 'appropriate countermeasures' in Article 4 of the SCM Agreement above shows that this would not be the case. Indeed, the level of countermeasures simply corresponds to the amount of subsidy which has to be withdrawn. Actually, given that export subsidies usually operate with a multiplying effect (a given amount allows a company to make a number of sales, thus gaining a foothold in a given market with the possibility to expand and gain market shares), we are of the view that a calculation based on the level of nullification or impairment would, as suggested by the calculation of Canada based on the harm caused to its industry, produce higher figures than one based exclusively on the amount of the subsidy. On the other hand, if the actual level of nullification or impairment is substantially lower than the subsidy, a countermeasure based on the actual level of nullification or impairment will have less or no inducement effect and the subsidizing country may not withdraw the measure at issue.
>
> Brazil also claimed that countermeasures based on the full amount of the subsidy would be highly punitive. We understand the term 'punitive' within the meaning given to it in the Draft Articles. A countermeasure becomes punitive when it is not only intended to ensure that the State in breach of its obligations bring its conduct into conformity with its international obligations, but contains an additional dimension meant to sanction the action of that State. Since we do not find a calculation of the appropriate countermeasures based on the amount of the subsidy granted to be disproportionate, we conclude that, a fortiori, it cannot be punitive.[75]

---

[74] Report of the Arbitrators, *Brazil—Aircraft (Art. 22.6—Brazil)*, at §3.48. Similar issues were raised in the Panel and AB reports on *EC and Certain Members States—Large Civil Aircraft*, the dispute concerning the subsidization of Airbus; see the analysis of Slot (2010) and Wu (2010).

[75] Report of the Arbitrators, *Brazil—Aircraft (Art. 22.6—Brazil)*, §§3.54–3.55.

The same logic was followed in the Arbitrators' report on *US—FSC (Art. 22.6—US)*. The Arbitrators, extensively referring to public international law and the International Law Commission (ILC) reports on state responsibility,[76] held that the EU (complainant) should be authorized to adopt countermeasures up to US $4,043 million, that is, the amount of subsidies paid by the US to its national producers (beneficiaries under the Foreign Sales Corporation (FSC) scheme).[77] One should, however, add a caveat here: the Arbitrators claimed that, had they used an injury to EU standard as benchmark (trade effects), they would have ended up anyway with a similar number.[78] The Arbitrators clarified that trade effects are not a priori ruled out as a benchmark. They were simply of the view that Art. 4.10 SCM does not require a trade-effects test.[79]

To allow one complaining member to take countermeasures of an amount equal to the full amount of the subsidy may prove problematic in cases of sequential enforcement, where more than one WTO Member decides to challenge the same measure in subsequent WTO proceedings. In *US—FSC (Art. 22.6—US)*, the Arbitrators added a few words to address the (hypothetical) situation where, subsequent to the EU challenge, another WTO Member decided to attack the same US measure (the FSC scheme):

> Understandably, it would be our expectation that this determination will have the practical effect of facilitating prompt compliance by the United States. On any hypothesis that there would be a future complainant, we can only observe that this would give rise inevitably to a different situation for assessment. To the extent that the basis sought for countermeasures was purely and simply that of countering the initial measure (as opposed to, e.g., the trade effects on the Member concerned) it is conceivable that the allocation issue would arise (although due regard should be given to the point made in footnote 84 above). We take note, on this point, of the statement by the European Communities:
>
> . . . it may well be that the European Communities would be happy to share the task of applying countermeasures against the United States with another member and voluntarily agree to remove some of its countermeasures so as to provide more scope for another WTO member to be authorized to do the same. This will be another fact that future arbitrators could take into consideration.[80]

---

[76] Report of the Arbitrators, *US—FSC (Art. 22.6—US)*, §§5.30–5.62.

[77] Report of the Arbitrators, *US—FSC (Art. 22.6—US)*, §§6.1–6.30. With respect to the term 'not disproportionate', the arbitrators considered that 'the entitlement to countermeasures is to be assessed in light of the legal status of the wrongful act and the manner in which the breach of that obligation has upset the balance of rights and obligations as between Members. It is from that perspective that the judgment as to whether countermeasures are disproportionate is to be made'; Arbitrator, *US—FSC (Art. 22.6—US)*, §5.24.

[78] Report of the Arbitrators, *US—FSC (Art. 22.6—US)*, §6.57.

[79] Report of the Arbitrators, *US—FSC (Art. 22.6—US)*, §§6.33–6.34.

[80] Report of the Arbitrators, *US—FSC (Art. 22.6—US)*, §§6.28–9. The Arbitrators' claim that they would have ended up with the same amount, had they used trade effects as a benchmark to quantify the appropriateness of countermeasures, and this passage seem hard to reconcile. The Arbitrators calculated total trade effects (something which is discernible from the report): if their calculation is correct, this is a case where (total) trade effects yield a number as high as the amount of

Interestingly, the Arbitrators in *Canada—Aircraft Credits and Guarantees* (*Art. 22.6—Canada*) saw force in the argument that there was need to induce Canada to comply, in light of its statements before the panel that it did not intend to do so. The Arbitrators used the amount of the subsidy as the benchmark[81] and calculated the amount of countermeasures to be US$206,497,305.[82] They then continued, however, to examine whether adjustments needed to be made to this amount to make it 'an appropriate level of countermeasures'. In their view, an upward adjustment of this amount was justified in order to induce compliance, in light of Canada's statements that it would not withdraw the subsidy.[83] So the Arbitrators added 20 per cent to the level of the countermeasures in order to induce compliance:

> Recalling Canada's current position to maintain the subsidy at issue and having regard to the role of countermeasures in inducing compliance, we have decided to adjust the level of countermeasures calculated on the basis of the total amount of the subsidy by an amount which we deem reasonably meaningful to cause Canada to reconsider its current position to maintain the subsidy at issue in breach of its obligations. We consequently adjust the level of countermeasures by an amount corresponding to 20 per cent of the amount of the subsidy as calculated in Section III.E above, i.e.: US$206,497,305 x 20% (US$41,299,461) = US $247,796,766.
>
> As we have noted in paragraph 3.120, adjustments such as the one we are making cannot be precisely calibrated. There is no scientifically based formula that we could use to calculate this adjustment. In that sense, the adjustment might be viewed as a symbolic one. Even so, we are convinced that it is a justified adjustment in light of the circumstances of this case and, in particular, the need to induce compliance with WTO obligations. Without such an adjustment, we would not be satisfied that an appropriate level of countermeasures had been established in this case.[84]

This is the only genuine case of punitive damages, that is, damages dissociated from the legal wrong that has been recommended in WTO case law. But then a sea change occurred: in *US—Upland Cotton* (*Art. 22.6—US*), the Arbitrators abandoned the subsidy benchmark and decided that it was appropriate to use trade effects as a benchmark when calculating countermeasures for refusal to withdraw a prohibited subsidy. We quote the relevant passage (§4.114):

---

subsidy paid. However, since the number chosen is a number within a range of possibilities, we simply do not know if the EU injury is within the lower or the higher part of the range. In other words, the EU might have been over- or under-compensated depending on the location of its injury within the range calculated in the Arbitrators' report. Be it as it may though, Esserman and Howse (2004) voiced their dissatisfaction with this report, arguing that the ultimate remedy was clearly disproportionate, in violation of the standard enshrined in Art. 4.10 SCM.

[81] Report of the Arbitrators, *Canada—Aircraft Credits and Guarantees* (*Art. 22.6—Canada*), §3.51. The amount of the subsidy was calculated on the basis of the benefit to the recipient, that is, the benefit conferred by the loan, rather than the amount of the loan as such. Ibid., §3.60.

[82] Ibid., §3.90.

[83] Ibid., §3.107.

[84] Ibid., §§3.121–2.

In conclusion, we have found that the terms 'appropriate countermeasures', as informed by footnote 9 of the *SCM Agreement*, entitle the complaining party to countermeasures that are suited to the circumstances of the case. This can lead to a countermeasure being authorized at a level that is within the range of the trade-distorting impact that can fairly be said to arise for the complaining Member from the failure to withdraw the illegal measure. We have also determined that footnote 9 further invites us to ensure that the countermeasures to be authorized are not excessive, having regard to the extent to which the trade of the complaining party has been affected, and taking into account also the prohibited nature of the subsidy. (italics in the original)

Paying only lip service to prior case law, this report introduced the trade-effects test as benchmark to calculate appropriate countermeasures and as a result equated the level of appropriate with that of commensurate countermeasures. To defend their choice, the Arbitrators argued that otherwise WTO Members that could have suffered little injury would have been compensated as much as those who had suffered substantially more (§4.60). From a pure legal perspective, it is difficult to accept the idea that the framers used two terms (appropriate, commensurate) in the same provision to describe the same concept. From a policy perspective, though, this is a welcome innovation for the reasons arguing against over-disciplining subsidies.

5. The Coverage of the Legal Discipline: Countervailing Duties (CVDs)

A WTO Member wishing to impose CVDs has to demonstrate that:

(a) A subsidy
(b) Is causing injury
(c) To the domestic industry producing the like product.

CVDs thus have a function very similar to that of AD duties, the difference being that whereas the former address a government act, the latter aim to counteract private practice. It should come as no surprise then that many of the provisions of the SCM Agreement are very similar to those of the AD Agreement. Case law reveals that Panels and the AB consider that the interpretations of AD provisions provide good guidance for the interpretation of similar provisions in the SCM Agreement, and vice versa. The Panel report on *US—Countervailing Duty Investigation on DRAMs* is an appropriate illustration to this effect (§7.351):

The non-attribution requirement in antidumping investigations has been addressed by the Appellate Body in several recent cases. Although it has not been specifically considered in a countervailing duty case, given that the relevant provisions in the two Agreements are identical, and in light of the 'need for the consistent resolution of disputes arising from antidumping and countervailing duty measures' (Ministerial

Declaration on Dispute Settlement Pursuant to the Agreement on Implementation of Article VI of the General Agreement on Tariffs and Trade 1994 or Part V of the Agreement on Subsidies and Countervailing Measures), it is clear to us that the requirement is the same in the context of both antidumping and countervailing duty investigations.

This approach is consistent with the 'Ministerial Declaration on Dispute Settlement Pursuant to the Agreement on Implementation of Article VI of the General Agreement on Tariffs and Trade 1994 or Part V of the Agreement on Subsidies and Countervailing Measures' adopted at Marrakesh at the conclusion of the Uruguay Round which recognized the need for a consistent resolution of disputes arising from antidumping and countervailing duty measures.

5.1 Subsidy

Our discussion *supra* regarding the content of this term finds application here as well.

5.2 Injury

The demonstration of injury is addressed in Art. 15 SCM. As in the AD context, the term 'injury' is used to refer to a situation of 'material injury', 'threat of material injury', or 'material retardation' in the establishment of an industry. The latter situation knows of no practice so far. Arts. 15.1–6 SCM deal with injury in general, while Arts. 15.7 and 15.8 SCM contain special additional obligations in cases of threat of injury. For injury to be shown, a WTO Member must conduct an objective examination based on positive evidence regarding (Art. 15.1 SCM):

(a) The volume of the subsidized imports;
(b) Their effect on prices in the domestic market for like products; as well as
(c) The consequent impact of these imports on the domestic producers of such like products.

Art 15.3 SCM provides that an injury analysis may be conducted on a cumulative basis under the following conditions:

(a) Imports of a product from more than one country are simultaneously subject to CVD investigations;
(b) The amount of subsidization established in relation to the imports from each country is more than *de minimis* as defined in Art. 11.9 SCM;
(c) The volume of imports from each country is not negligible; and
(d) A cumulative assessment of the effects of the imports is appropriate in light of the conditions of competition between the imported products and the conditions of competition between the imported products and the like domestic product.

This is quite similar to Art. 3.3 AD. The amount of subsidy is *de minimis*, if it is less than 1 per cent *ad valorem* (Art. 11.9 SCM). For developing countries, this threshold is set at 2 per cent, and for least developed countries and so-called Annex VII countries, at 3 per cent. There is no definition of the term 'negligible' volumes. Art. 27.10 SCM does so for imports originating in developing countries only: if subsidized (by developing countries) imports are less than 4 per cent of total imports, they are negligible; if subsidized imports from developing countries whose individual shares represent less than 4 per cent and collectively account for less than 9 per cent of total imports, they are negligible as well.

A finding that injury has occurred must be based on positive evidence following an objective examination by the IA. The Panel on *US—Softwood Lumber VI* dealt, *inter alia*, with the interpretation of the terms 'positive evidence' and 'objective examination'. It quoted verbatim §114 of the AB report on *EC—Bed Linen (Article 21.5—India)*, which dealt with an AD investigation (§7.28):

> The term 'positive evidence' relates, in our view, to the quality of the evidence that authorities may rely upon in making a determination. The word 'positive' means, to us, that the evidence must be of an *affirmative, objective* and *verifiable* character, and that it must be *credible*.
>
> The Appellate Body has defined an 'objective examination':
>
> The term 'objective examination' aims at a different aspect of the investigating authorities' determination. While the term 'positive evidence' focuses on the facts underpinning and justifying the injury determination, the term 'objective examination' is concerned with the investigative process itself. The word 'examination' relates, in our view, to the way in which the evidence is gathered, inquired into and, subsequently, evaluated; that is, it relates to the conduct of the investigation generally. The word 'objective', which qualifies the word 'examination', indicates essentially that the 'examination' process must conform to the dictates of the basic principles of good faith and fundamental fairness.
>
> The Appellate Body summed up the requirement to conduct an 'objective examination' as follows:
>
> In short, an 'objective examination' requires that the domestic industry, and the effects of dumped imports, be investigated in an *unbiased* manner, *without favouring the interests of any interested party*, or group of interested parties, in the investigation. The duty of the investigating authorities to conduct an 'objective examination' recognizes that the determination will be influenced by the objectivity, or any lack thereof, of the investigative process. (emphasis in the original)[85]

An evaluation of the volume of imports requires an IA to consider whether there has been a significant increase in subsidized imports, either in absolute terms, or relative to production or consumption in the importing Member. No number

---

[85] See also the Panel report on *US—Countervailing Duty Investigation on DRAMs* (§7.218). Panels have consistently considered that Art. 15.1 SCM is a provision which informs the more detailed obligations set forth in the remainder of Art. 15 SCM; see e.g. the Panel report on *EC—Countervailing Measures on DRAM Chips* at §7.275, quoting from §106 of the AB report on *Thailand—H-Beams*. For that reason, Panels have first examined the consistency of the measures with the specific obligations contained in Arts. 15.2–5 SCM. See the Panel report on *US—Countervailing Duty Investigation on DRAMs* at §7.217; Panel report on *US—Softwood Lumber VI*, at §7.26.

quantifying significance is nevertheless provided and Panels have avoided doing so: a typical illustration is offered by the Panel report on *EC—Countervailing Measures on DRAM Chips*, where the Panel held that the ordinary meaning of the term 'significant', encompasses 'important', 'notable', 'major', as well as 'consequential', which all suggest something more than just a nominal or marginal movement but are not at all precise (§7.307). The evaluation of the volume of subsidized imports is not, by itself, determinative in an injury determination, but forms part of an overall assessment (§7.290 of the Panel report on *EC—Countervailing Measures on DRAM Chips*). The Panel on *US—Countervailing Duty Investigation on DRAMs* held (§7.233) that Art. 15.2 SCM included three alternative ways in which an IA could comply with this provision, suggesting that it sufficed for an IA to consider:

(a) Either an absolute increase;
(b) Or an increase relative to production;
(c) Or an increase relative to consumption.

Panels have not been required, so far, to rule on a determination by an IA which did not look at both an absolute increase and a relative increase in imports. So it remains to be seen whether Panels would be really willing to accept a determination based on an absolute increase without examining the volume in relative terms, for example where demand elasticities are substantial.

The term 'subsidized imports' refers to all imports from a source found to have been subsidized above the *de minimis* level: the Panel on *EC—Countervailing Measures on DRAM Chips* approvingly referred to findings by Panels and the AB in the AD context and, in particular, to §113 of the AB report on *EC—Bed Linen (Article 21.5—India)*, and held as much (§7.298 and footnote 227). In other words, imports from exporters not found to have been receiving subsidies are to be excluded from a determination. In fact, the level of such non-subsidized imports will be one of the other factors that will need to be examined in the context of the causation and non-attribution analysis under Art. 15.5 SCM. The fact that imports from subsidized and non-subsidized sources are discussed side by side by the authority is not inconsistent with the Agreement; what matters is the use made of the data, and whether the consideration required by Art. 15.2 SCM was made on the basis of data concerning imports found to have been subsidized (Panel report on *EC—Countervailing Measures on DRAM Chips*, at §7.298). Neither is it relevant under Art. 15.2 SCM that subsidized imports decreased in relative terms compared to non-subsidized imports, since this is not the focus of the volume determination under this provision (Panel report on *US—Countervailing Duty Investigation on DRAMs*, at §7.243).

The Panel on *US—Countervailing Duty Investigation on DRAMs* found that the fact that the greatest increase in subject imports took place prior to the provision of subsidies was not considered determinative, since (§7.245):

Article 15.2 does not require an investigating authority to demonstrate that all of the subject imports covered by the period of injury investigation are subsidized.

An evaluation of the effects of the subsidized imports on prices requires an IA to consider whether there has been significant price undercutting, depression, or suppression. The SCM Agreement makes clear that the overall evaluation can be based on one or several factors. Art. 15.2 SCM does not impose any particular methodology for analysing prices. What is important is that the methodology chosen is reasonable and objective (§§7.334–6 of the Panel report on *EC—Countervailing Measures on DRAM Chips*).

Art. 15.4 SCM requires that the examination of the impact of the subsidized imports on the domestic industry includes an evaluation of all relevant economic factors and indices having a bearing on the state of the industry, including actual and potential decline in output, sales, market share, profits, productivity, return on investments, or utilization of capacity, factors affecting domestic prices, actual and potential negative effects on cash flow, inventories, employment, wages, growth, ability to raise capital or investments, and, in the case of agriculture, whether there has been an increased burden on government support programmes.[86] It adds that this list is not exhaustive nor can one or several of these factors necessarily give decisive guidance. The SCM Agreement, thus, reflects an indicative list of proxies, recourse to which should demonstrate injury. Case law makes it clear that all factors mentioned in the body of Art. 15.4 SCM *must* be evaluated by the IA (§7.356 of the Panel report on *EC—Countervailing Measures on DRAM Chips*). The obligation of evaluation imposed by Art. 15.4 SCM is not confined to these listed factors, however, but extends to all relevant economic factors. Whether a factor is relevant depends, *inter alia*, on the nature of the industry being examined (§7.363 of the Panel report on *EC—Countervailing Measures on DRAM Chips*). The Panel on *EC—Countervailing Measures on DRAM Chips* stated that relevant economic factors are not to be confused with other causal factors, such as the general economic downturn or the export performance of the domestic industry, which are to be examined as part of the causation and non-attribution analysis of Art. 15.5 SCM (§7.365). What is ultimately required is that these various factors be examined in their overall context. It is not required that each and every factor shows a negative trend. A proper evaluation of the impact of the subsidized imports on the domestic industry is dynamic in nature and should take account of changes in the market that determine the current state of the industry (§7.372 of the Panel report on *EC—Countervailing Measures on DRAM Chips*).

With respect to the period of data collection, the Panel on *EC—Countervailing Measures on DRAM Chips* rejected the argument that a pricing analysis must include the most recent period prior to initiation: the data on which the injury analysis is based should be sufficiently recent in order for these data to be relevant

---

[86] This list is very similar, although not identical to the list included in Art. 3.4 AD.

and probative such as to constitute positive evidence. The Panel considered that, since the EU had gathered data which covered three years, including the last full year for accounting purposes prior to the initiation, its analysis was clearly based on the recent past (§7.341). The Panel on *Mexico—Olive Oil* faced a claim by the EU to the effect that Mexico had been acting inconsistently with its obligations under Art. 15.5 SCM, by using data from some months every year only (April–December) and for the whole 12 months of the years under investigation. The Panel agreed with the complainant that Mexico was indeed running afoul its obligations, since it offered no explanation for its approach (§§7.273ff, and especially 7.289).

If CVDs are imposed on 'threat of injury', the SCM Agreement requires that a demonstration that a threat of injury exists be based on facts and not merely on allegation, conjecture, or remote possibility. In addition, the change in circumstances which would create a situation in which the subsidy would cause injury must be clearly foreseen and imminent (Art. 15.7 SCM). In making a determination regarding the existence of a threat of material injury, the IA should consider, *inter alia*, such factors as:

(a) The nature of the subsidy or subsidies in question and the trade effects likely to arise therefrom;
(b) A significant rate of increase of subsidized imports into the domestic market indicating the likelihood of substantially increased importation;
(c) Sufficient freely disposable or an imminent substantial increase in capacity of the exporter indicating the likelihood of substantially increased subsidized exports to the importing WTO Member's market, taking into account the availability of other export markets to absorb any additional exports;
(d) Whether imports are entering at prices that will have a significant depressing or suppressing effect on domestic prices, and would likely increase demand for further imports; and
(e) Inventories of the product being investigated.

The Agreement adds that not one of these factors by itself can necessarily give decisive guidance, but that the totality of the factors considered must lead to the conclusion that further subsidized exports are imminent and that, unless protective action is taken, material injury would occur. In a threat-of-injury situation, the application of CVDs must be considered and decided with special care (Art. 15.8 SCM).[87] The Panel on *US—Softwood Lumber VI* held that the authorities do not have to go so far as to specify one particular event that will cause injury in the future; indicating a progression of circumstances by and large suffices to meet the requirements of the SCM Agreement in this respect (§7.60). This Panel agreed with the views expressed by the Panel on *Mexico—Corn Syrup* that, in every case in

---

[87] On the special care requirement, see the Panel report on *US—Softwood Lumber VI* at §§7.33–7.

which threat of injury is found, it is necessary to proceed to an evaluation of the condition of the industry in light of the factors included in Art. 15.4 SCM to establish the background against which the impact of future dumped/subsidized imports must be assessed, in addition to an assessment of the specific threat factors (§7.105). But the same Panel added that this requirement should not be interpreted as if a second predictive injury analysis is required (§§7.105, 111).

With regard to the factors that must be examined in order to show threat of injury (Art. 15.7 SCM), the Panel on *US—Softwood Lumber VI* found that the IA has an obligation to consider these factors, but is not obliged to make a finding or determination with respect to the factors considered (§7.67). Moreover, the failure to consider a factor, or to adequately consider a particular factor, would not necessarily demonstrate a violation of this provision; all will depend on the particular facts of the case, the totality of the factors considered, and the explanations given (§7.68).

The Panel on *US—Softwood Lumber VI* (*Article 21.5–Canada*) discussed the applicable standard of review in threat-of-injury cases, and held that it would be more deferential to the IA when examining a threat of injury determination compared to a material injury determination (§7.13):

> The possible range of reasonable predictions of the future that may be drawn based on the observed events of the period of investigation may be broader than the range of reasonable conclusions concerning the present that might be drawn based on those same facts. That is to say, while a determination of threat of material injury must be based on the facts, and not merely on allegation, conjecture, or remote possibility, predictions based on the observed facts may be less susceptible to being found, on review by a panel, to be outside the range of conclusions that might be reached by an unbiased and objective decision maker on the basis of the facts and in light of the explanations given.

This finding is questionable. While it is true that it is more difficult to interfere with predictions than with facts, threat-of-injury determinations should not become an avenue for relaxed imposition of AD/CVD duties. After all, in similar cases injury is threatened, it has not yet happened, and the measures taken are meant to protect an otherwise healthy domestic industry.

Injury (or threat of injury) must be caused to the domestic industry producing the like product. In perfect symmetry with the AD Agreement, the SCM Agreement provides that the term 'domestic industry' refers to the domestic producers as a whole of the like products, or to those of them whose collective output of the products constitutes a major proportion of the total domestic production of those products. In cases where producers are 'related' to the exporters or importers, or are themselves importers of the allegedly subsidized product or a like product from other countries, such producers may be excluded (Art. 16.1 SCM). The term 'related' is explained in footnote 48 to Art. 16.1 SCM:

> producers shall be deemed to be related to exporters or importers only if (a) one of them directly or indirectly controls the other; or (b) both of them are directly or

indirectly controlled by a third person; or (c) together they directly or indirectly control a third person, provided that there are grounds for believing or suspecting that the effect of the relationship is such as to cause the producer concerned to behave differently from non-related producers. For the purpose of this paragraph, one shall be deemed to control another when the former is legally or operationally in a position to exercise restraint or direction over the latter.

The term 'like product' is defined in footnote 46 to the SCM Agreement:

Throughout this Agreement the term 'like product' ('produit similaire') shall be interpreted to mean a product which is identical, i.e. alike in all respects to the product under consideration, or in the absence of such a product, another product which, although not alike in all respects, has characteristics closely resembling those of the product under consideration.

This definition is identical to that provided for in the AD Agreement, and evidences a statutory preference for a narrow definition of the term. The Panel on *Indonesia—Autos* established a parallelism between Art. III.2 GATT, first sentence, and the SCM Agreement and held that the following criteria should be pertinent in evaluating likeness (§14.173):

In our view, the analysis as to which cars have 'characteristics closely resembling' those of the Timor logically must include as an important element the physical characteristics of the cars in question. This is especially the case because many of the other possible criteria identified by the parties are closely related to the physical characteristics of the cars in question. Thus, factors such as brand loyalty, brand image/reputation, status and resale value reflect, at least in part, an assessment by purchasers of the physical characteristics of the cars being purchased. Although it is possible that products that are physically very different can be put to the same uses, differences in uses generally arise out of, and assist in assessing the importance of, different physical characteristics of products. Similarly, the extent to which products are substitutable may also be determined in substantial part by their physical characteristics. Price differences also may (but will not necessarily) reflect physical differences in products. An analysis of tariff classification principles may be useful because it provides guidance as to which physical distinctions between products were considered significant by Customs experts. However, we do not see that the SCM Agreement precludes us from looking at criteria other than physical characteristics, where relevant to the like product analysis. The term 'characteristics closely resem-bling' in its ordinary meaning includes but is not limited to physical characteristics, and we see nothing in the context or object and purpose of the SCM Agreement that would dictate a different conclusion.

This Panel went on to find that a kit car is a like product to a finished car (§14.197). This definition could be an unreasonable constraint when it comes to injury suffered not by the like product, but by the upstream or downstream product. For example, assume imports of subsidized wine; actually assume that it is production of foreign grapes that has been subsidized and not the final product (itself). Could in this case domestic wine producers successfully argue that they have been injured as a result of subsidization of foreign grapes? The Panels on

US—Softwood Lumber III and *US—Softwood Lumber IV*[88] acknowledged that subsidies to an input (upstream subsidies) can result in benefits for the final product (downstream benefits). As a result, an IA can lawfully impose CVDs on the final product, even though such product might not be considered a like product to one of its inputs that has benefited from the subsidy. The rationale for this approach is that subsidies can, as discussed *supra*, on occasion pass through and lead to injury, and hence CVDs, freeing the way for legitimate imposition of CVDs.[89]

But what if domestic wine producers are able to withstand the competition from imported subsidized wine by passing the costs on to the domestic grape producers, who have to accept lower prices for their grapes? Here it is the domestic grape producers who actually suffer injury caused by the subsidies provided to wine. As grapes are not a like product to wine, the domestic industry producing grapes will not be the industry that is the subject of the injury examination. In similar cases, can the upstream producers successfully complain before the WTO? The appropriate response in similar cases should be negative since it is the behaviour of domestic wine producers that at least contributes to the injury suffered by producers of grapes. Still, in the absence of case law dealing head on with this issue, there is no definitive response to this question.[90]

5.3 Causation

The general requirement to establish a causal link between the subsidized imports and injury is expressed in Art. 15.5 SCM.[91] It contains two obligations:

(a) A positive obligation to demonstrate that it is the subsidized imports which are causing the injury; and, in addition,
(b) It sets forth a negative obligation, namely, not to attribute to subsidy injury caused by factors other than subsidized imports (non-attribution).

In this respect, Art. 15.5 SCM requires from an IA to examine any known factors, other than subsidized imports, which are injuring the domestic industry:

> Factors which may be relevant in this respect include, inter alia, the volumes and prices of nonsubsidized imports of the product in question, contraction in demand or changes in the patterns of consumption, trade restrictive practices of and

---

[88] Horn and Mavroidis (2005a, 2007) discuss these two reports.

[89] See, for example, §163 of the AB report on *US—Softwood Lumber IV*. Note also that the Panel on *Mexico—Olive Oil* held that there is no requirement that a particular producer be producing the like product at the moment an application is filed. This view (voiced by the EU) could lead to absurd results, since, if accepted, it could, for example, exclude operators that had exited the market because of the subsidies from filing a petition (§§7.188ff, and especially 7.203).

[90] For the rest, recall our discussion *supra* on like products in the AD context.

[91] There are specific rules as well: for example, Art. 15.2 SCM requires from an IA to establish what caused the price undercutting; the Panel on *EC—Countervailing Measures on DRAM Chips* acknowledged that (§7.338).

competition between the foreign and domestic producers, developments in technology and the export performance and productivity of the domestic industry.

The Panel on *US—Softwood Lumber VI* held that wrong facts, assumptions, and absence of any discussion of specific factors appearing in the body of this provision are fatal; a WTO Member committing such errors is deemed not to have respected the causality requirement (§7.122).

A causal link may be established between subsidized imports and the injury to the domestic industry, even in the absence of any increase in subsidized imports. Increased imports are not a condition for imposition of a CVD measure but merely an element in the overall assessment of injury and causation. This led the Panels on *EC—Countervailing Measures on DRAM Chips* (§7.320), and *US—Countervailing Duty Investigation on DRAMs* (§7.399) to find that there is no generalized requirement to establish a temporal correlation between increased subsidized imports and injury in the context of a countervail investigation. According to the Panel on *EC—Countervailing Measures on DRAM Chips* (§7.399, footnote 277):

> the absence of a temporal correlation certainly raises a flag, but it is not an absolute barrier to a finding of injury.

The Panel on *US—Softwood Lumber VI* dealt with the issue of other factors, that is, factors not mentioned in the body of Art. 15.5 SCM and which could be causing injury. The question before it was whether and if so, under what conditions, an IA should examine them. The Panel condemned the fact that the IA had itself acknowledged the relevance of one other factor (future effects of subsidization on the domestic supplies of lumber) and yet failed to evaluate its impact. In the Panel's view, this failure was a glaring omission and constituted a breach of the obligation to respect non-attribution. (§§7.135–7). Recall that case law in the context of anti-dumping supports the view that the treatment of other factors should not be equated with an obligation to look beyond the list of Art. 15.5 SCM. Factors brought to the attention of the authority during the investigation process, and factors otherwise explicitly acknowledged by the authority (as was the case here), must be analysed though; the Panels on *US—Countervailing Duty Investigation on DRAMs* (§§7.351–3) and *EC—Countervailing Measures on DRAM Chips* (§7.404) are illustrations to this effect. According to the latter Panel, while the AB had not provided guidance as to how an IA should examine other known factors, it was of the view that an IA must do more than simply list other known factors, and then dismiss their role with bare qualitative assertions such as: 'the factor did not contribute in any significant way to the injury'. In the Panel's view (§7.405):

> an investigating authority must make a better effort to quantify the impact of other known factors, relative to subsidized imports, preferably using elementary economic constructs or models.

It thus faulted the EU IA for acknowledging the negative impact on the industry of certain other factors, such as the economic downturn in the market, overcapacity of the domestic industry, and other non-subsidized imports, without examining the extent of this negative impact. The Panel was of the view that a mere assertion that the effect was not such as to break the causal link between subsidized imports and injury without any quantitative or thorough qualitative support did not suffice to separate and distinguish the injury that might have been caused by the subsidized imports (§§ 7.408, 413, 420, 427, 434). How much more is required, we do not know.

Recall our discussion in the antidumping context on the causality requirement and its treatment in case law. To a large extent, the same discussion could be reproduced here, since here as well Panels will typically tick boxes and see whether factors indicating injury have been examined irrespective of the quality of the examination. And yet, it is not that Panels are constrained by law to behave this way; indeed the law, its shortcomings notwithstanding,[92] is quite open-ended. Panels could go ahead and perform meaningful causality analysis. Now, of course, a meaningful causality analysis inspired by economic theory, as briefly discussed in the section on antidumping, has important implications for the agency design as well: it could not be the case that amateur panelists[93] with little if any expertise in similar issues be requested to perform a similar exercise. Moreover, recourse to expertise becomes all the more necessary since in *US—Upland Cotton*, the AB, confirming the Panel in this respect, held that, when dealing with the causation requirement, an IA must ensure that it does not attribute injury to subsidies when this has not been the case; the absence of explicit non-attribution language in the SCM Agreement was no obstacle to the Panel first, and the AB subsequently, in reaching this finding. We quote from §§436–7 of the AB report:

> As the Panel pointed out, 'Articles 5 and 6.3 . . . do not contain the more elaborate and precise "causation" and non-attribution language' found in the trade remedy provisions of the *SCM Agreement*. Part V of the *SCM Agreement*, which relates to the imposition of countervailing duties, requires, *inter alia*, an examination of 'any known factors other than the subsidized imports which at the same time are injuring the domestic industry'. However, such causation requirements have not been expressly prescribed for an examination of *serious prejudice* under Articles 5(c) and Article 6.3(c) in Part III of the *SCM Agreement*. This suggests that a panel has a certain degree of discretion in selecting an appropriate methodology for determining whether the 'effect' of a subsidy is significant price suppression under Article 6.3(c).
>
> Nevertheless, we agree with the Panel that it is necessary to ensure that the effects of other factors on prices are not improperly attributed to the challenged subsidies. Pursuant to Article 6.3(c) of the *SCM Agreement*, '[s]erious prejudice in the sense of paragraph (c) of Article 5 may arise' when 'the effect of *the subsidy* is . . . significant price suppression'. If the significant price suppression found in the world market for upland cotton were caused by factors other than the challenged subsidies, then that

---

[92] The legislative instruction that it is not necessarily the case that one or more of these factors provide decisive guidance could prove misleading (and has been used as fig leaf by Panels to restrict causality analysis to some sort of review whether formal requirements have been met).

[93] Horn et al. (2011) have compiled data suggesting that a large proportion of all Panelists since 1995 are one-timers and not necessarily experts in this field.

price suppression would not be 'the effect of' the challenged subsidies in the sense of Article 6.3(c). Therefore, we do not find fault with the Panel's approach of 'examin [ing] whether or not "the effect of the subsidy" is the significant price suppression which [it had] found to exist in the same world market' and separately 'consider[ing] the role of other alleged causal factors in the record before [it] which may affect [the] analysis of the causal link between the United States subsidies and the significant price suppression.' (italics and emphasis in the original)

Non-attribution complicates the analysis by Panels as well, and yet this is precisely what the AB has requested them to do. In §357 of its report on *US—Upland Cotton (Art. 21.5—US)*, it noted:

> The relative complexity of a model and its parameters is not a reason for a panel to remain agnostic about them. Like other categories of evidence, a panel should reach conclusions with respect to the probative value it accords to economic simulations or models presented to it. This kind of assessment falls within the panel's authority as the initial trier of facts in a serious prejudice case.

In *US—Large Civil Aircraft* (2nd complaint), the AB added that a subsidy does not have to be the only cause of injury, it does not even have to be a substantial cause of injury; attribution however, must take place (§914). The injury standard was first heavily negotiated during the Tokyo round. Before the advent of the Tokyo round SCM Agreement, the US would impose CVDs any time an expert report benefited from a grant irrespective of whether injury had been caused as a result, Graham (1979) pp. 162ff.

5.4 Provisional CVDs

Art. 17 SCM allows for the possibility of imposing provisional measures when the IA judges it necessary to prevent injury being caused during the investigation. These measures may only be imposed after a preliminary affirmative determination has been made that a subsidy exists, and that there is injury to a domestic industry caused by subsidized imports. The SCM Agreement provides that provisional measures are not to be applied sooner than 60 days from the date of initiation of the investigation (Art. 17.3 SCM), and can be lawfully imposed for a period not extending beyond four months (Art. 17.4 SCM). The four-month period does not refer to the period during which cash deposits or bonds are taken, but to the period during which the affected imports enter for consumption. The Panel on *US— Softwood Lumber III* faulted the US for having imposed provisional measures less than 60 days after initiation and for a period of more than four months (§7.101).

5.5 Price Undertakings

The investigation may come temporarily or permanently to a halt, an affirmative preliminary determination of subsidization and injury caused by such subsidization notwithstanding, if satisfactory voluntary undertakings have been received (Art. 18.1 SCM). Art. 18.4 SCM provides that the investigation may be continued at the request of the exporting WTO Member, or simply when the importing WTO Member so decides, in spite of the acceptance of any voluntary undertakings:

> If an undertaking is accepted, the investigation of subsidization and injury shall nevertheless be completed if the exporting Member so desires or the importing Member so decides. In such a case, if a negative determination of subsidization or injury is made, the undertaking shall automatically lapse, except in cases where such a determination is due in large part to the existence of an undertaking. In such cases, the authorities concerned may require that an undertaking be maintained for a reasonable period consistent with the provisions of this Agreement. In the event that an affirmative determination of subsidization and injury is made, the undertaking shall continue consistent with its terms and the provisions of this Agreement.

The undertaking may originate in the exporting country government which undertakes to eliminate or limit the subsidy or take other measures concerning its effects. But it may also concern a commitment by one or more of the exporters under investigation to revise prices so that the investigating authorities are satisfied that the injurious effect of the subsidy has been eliminated: exporter undertakings require the prior consent of the exporting Member, however. The Agreement caps the price increase as it caps the amount of a countervailing duty. The price increases shall not be higher than necessary to eliminate the amount of the subsidy, and it is desirable that the price increases be less than the amount of the subsidy if such increases would be adequate to remove the injury to the domestic industry. Once accepted, compliance with an undertaking may be monitored, and any government or exporter who made an undertaking may be requested to provide periodically information relevant to its fulfilment and to permit verification of pertinent data. Art. 18.6 SCM provides that, in the case of a violation of an undertaking, the authorities of the importing WTO Member may take expeditious actions such as immediate application of provisional measures using the best information available. In addition, definitive duties may be levied retroactively up to 90 days before the application of such provisional measures, except that any such retroactive assessment shall not apply to imports before the violation of the undertaking.

Undertakings are completely voluntary both when the initiative is that of the exporters or exporting Members, and when it is that of the importing country's authorities. Not offering or not agreeing to an undertaking cannot be held against the exporter, nor can the IA be forced to accept undertakings (Art. 18.5 SCM). The IA may refuse to accept undertakings, because of their impracticality: for example, if the number of actual or potential exporters is too great, or for other reasons, including reasons of general policy. Where practicable, the IA should provide the reasons for rejecting an offered undertaking, and, to the extent possible, give the exporter an opportunity to comment (Art. 18.3 SCM).

5.6 Imposition and Collection of Definitive CVDs

Art. 19 SCM provides that, upon completion of an investigation, and where a final determination is made confirming the existence and amount of the subsidy causing injury, CVDs may be imposed (Art. 19.2 SCM). The maximum amount of CVDs is the amount of the subsidy found to exist, calculated in terms of subsidization per unit of the subsidized and exported product. The SCM Agreement also contains a 'lesser duty rule', providing that it is desirable that the duty be less than the total amount of the subsidy, if such a lesser duty would be adequate to remove the injury to the domestic industry. Two provisions deal with the calculation of the amount of the subsidy:

(a) Art. 14 SCM concerns the calculation of the subsidy in terms of benefit to the recipient;
(b) Annex IV deals with the calculation of the total *ad valorem* subsidization (Art.6.1(a) SCM), and is based on a cost-to-government approach.

There is no legislative preference for one or the other method: Annex IV explicitly refers to Art. 6 SCM (serious prejudice), while Art. 14 SCM expressly refers to any calculation of the amount of benefit in Part V (CVD); this seems to suggest that the latter has a wider application. Neither of the two provisions addresses difficult calculation questions concerning, for example, allocation of subsidies over productive assets and/or over time or the difficulties in calculating the subsidy amount in the case of non-recurring subsidies. A report by the Informal Group of Experts (IGE) to the Committee on Subsidies and Countervailing Measures (SCM Committee) discusses the various technical problems relating to the calculation of the amount of the subsidy.[94] It distinguishes between non-recurring subsidies, the benefits of which may have to be allocated over time, and recurring subsidies which are fully expanded in the course of the year of receipt. It makes a number of recommendations concerning, *inter alia*, the average useful life of the physical depreciable assets that could be used as a basis for allocating the subsidy benefits;[95] the time value of money; the need to take account of inflation, and so on.[96]

The SCM Agreement also contains a public-interest test in providing that it is desirable that procedures be established which would allow the IA to take due account of representations made by domestic interested parties, including consumers, and industrial users of the imported product subject to investigation (Art. 19.2 SCM and footnote 50).

The SCM Agreement does not set forth an express obligation to calculate individual duties for each exporter, as Art. 6.10 AD does. Still, it appears that, as the amount of subsidization will be different for each exporter, an individual duty will normally be imposed. In *EC—Countervailing Duty on DRAM Chips*, for example, the EU IA calculated individual margins and ended up imposing duties on Hynix, but not on Samsung (the two Korean companies subject to

---

[94] WTO Doc. G/SCM/W/415/Rev. 2 of 15 May 1998.
[95] The un-adopted GATT Panel report on *US—Lead and Bismuth I* discussed this issue.
[96] The recommendations made by the IGE have formed the basis for a number of proposals that were made in the course of the negotiations to introduce technical guidelines on subsidy calculations.

investigation).[97] While exceptional in practice, Art. 19.3 SCM allows WTO Members to impose duties on an aggregate basis; that is, all imports originating in a country found to be granting subsidies will be burdened with CVDs, irrespective of whether all individual exporters have benefited from subsidies. In this case, individual non-investigated exporters have the right to request an expedited review to establish their rate (if any) of subsidies received (AB, *US— Softwood Lumber IV*, §§152–3). An application of duties on an aggregate basis does not imply that there is no longer any need to establish the basic conditions for the imposition of CVDs, that is, subsidy, injury to the domestic industry, and causation. In case of subsidies to upstream producers, this implies that it must in any case first be established that the subsidy was passed through to the downstream producers (AB, *US—Softwood Lumber IV*, §154).

In principle, CVDs, whether provisional or final, may not be imposed retro-actively, and apply *ex tunc*. This means that where the final determination is negative, any provisional duties shall be refunded and any bonds released in an expeditious manner (Art. 20.5 SCM). There are two exceptions to this general principle, which are similar to the corresponding provisions in the AD context:

(a) Definitive CVDs may be levied retroactively back to the date of application of provisional measures in case of a finding of current material injury: the Panel on *US—Softwood Lumber III* underscored that the possibility to impose retroactive duties exists only with respect to definitive, and not provisional, duties (§§7.93–4). In case a determination is made of threat of injury, duties may be applied retroactively if it can be shown that the provisional measures prevented the injury from materializing; final duties may in such circum-stances be applied retroactively for the period for which provisional measures, if any, have been applied. Retroactivity is therefore limited by the period of application of provisional measures, and by the amount collected as provi-sional duties. Indeed, the SCM Agreement provides that, if the definitive CVDs are higher than the amount guaranteed by the cash deposit or bond, the difference shall not be collected. Moreover, if the definitive duty is less, the excess amount shall be reimbursed, or the bond released in an expeditious manner. It is clear that, if no provisional measures had been applied to start with, the definitive duties may not be applied retroactively;

(b) Art. 20.6 SCM allows for the retroactive application beyond the period of application of provisional measures, in certain critical circumstances where the authorities find that injury which is difficult to repair is caused by massive imports in a relatively short period of a product benefiting from subsidies paid

---

[97] A proposal has been tabled by the EU to introduce a requirement to calculate an individual duty in the CVD context as well, with the possibility of sampling. The level of the duty to be paid by non-sampled exporters would, as in the AD context, be the weighted average of the duty of the sampled exporters; see WTO Docs. TN/RL/GEN/93 and TN/RL/GEN/96.

or bestowed inconsistently with the provisions of SCM and GATT. When the IA deems it necessary, the definitive CVDs may, in order to preclude the recurrence of such injury, be assessed on imports which were entered for consumption up to 90 days prior to the date of application of provisional measures. The SCM Agreement does not, unlike the AD Agreement, explicitly allow WTO Members to take such measures as the withholding of appraisement, or assessment. Nevertheless, it appears that a WTO Member is de facto entitled to take such measures. This has been the view of at least one Panel (*US—Softwood Lumber III*) which held (§7.95):

> We agree with the United States that a Member is allowed to take measures which are necessary to preserve the right to later apply definitive duties retroactively. In our view, an effective interpretation of the right to apply definitive duties retroactively requires that a Member be allowed to take such steps as are necessary to preserve the possibility of exercising that right. What kind of measures may thus be taken by the Member concerned will have to be determined on a case-by-case basis.[98]

5.7 Duration of CVDs

Art. 21.1 SCM states that CVDs can remain in place as long as and to the extent necessary to counteract injurious subsidization. Two types of review, as in the AD Agreement, are provided for in the SCM system:

(a) Administrative review (Art. 21.2 SCM).[99]
(b) Sunset review (Art. 21.3 SCM).

Both types can put an end to the continued imposition of CVDs.

5.8 Administrative Reviews (Changed Circumstances Reviews)

Art. 21.2 SCM makes provision for an administrative review to examine whether the continued imposition of the duty is necessary. It can be initiated:

(a) *Ex officio*, provided that a reasonable time has passed since the imposition of the CVD; or

---

[98] In § 7.98 of its report, this Panel held that requiring the posting of a bond or cash deposit went beyond necessary conservatory measures.

[99] An explanation is warranted here in order to avoid creating confusion: the term administrative review should not be confused with its homonym in US practice. In US practice, this term aims to capture the review undertaken in order to liquidate entries. As we explained *supra*, in the US system, goods that have been found to be subsidized will be burdened with a provisional deposit pending definitive calculation at the end of the year. Then, in the context of a US administrative review, or duty assessment review, the goods concerned will either have to be further burdened or the opposite. What we have here termed administrative review is sometimes referred to as 'changed circumstances review'. In the absence of an official term for the procedure under Art. 21.2 SCM, various nominations compete for prominence.

(b) Upon request by an interested party, at any time following the original imposition, provided that the interested party submits positive information substantiating the need for a review.

If, as a result of a review, the IA determines that CVDs are no longer warranted, their imposition shall be terminated immediately. The subject-matter of an administrative review does not necessarily overlap with that of a sunset review. Irrespective of whether it has been initiated *ex officio* or upon request, an IA could investigate whether:

(a) The continued imposition of duties is necessary to offset subsidization; or
(b) Whether the injury would be likely to recur if the duty in place were removed or varied; or
(c) Whether subsidization resulting in injury will continue/recur, assuming that the duties in place were to be varied or removed.

From the three options listed above only (c) corresponds to the subject-matter of a sunset review. Where a review covers both subsidization and injury, it may form the basis for extension of the measure for another five years.

In its report on *US—Carbon Steel*, the AB held that, whereas in the context of an administrative review the submission of positive evidence is a threshold issue to initiate the review at the request of an interested party, an *ex officio* initiation does not know of a similar requirement (§108).

There is no case law concerning administrative reviews in the SCM context. Recall, however, that in the AD context, the Panel on *US—DRAMs* had held that a period of three years of no dumping did not, in and of itself, warrant an *ex officio* review (§6.60). This finding supports the view that WTO adjudicating bodies will not disturb the discretion of IAs even in case the decision not to initiate a review is borderline by any reasonable benchmark.

In an original investigation, the IA must establish that all conditions set out in the SCM Agreement for the imposition of CVD have been fulfilled; in an administrative review, however, the IA only need address those issues which have been raised before it by the interested parties or, in the case of an investigation conducted on its own initiative, those issues which warranted the examination: the AB held as much in its report on *US—Lead and Bismuth II* (§63). This case concerned the decision by the US IA to continue with the imposition of duties imposed on economic operators which had previously (for example, pre-privatization) benefited from non-recurring subsidies. The AB, in its report, made a distinction between the obligation of WTO Members to show the existence of a benefit conferred by a subsidy during the original investigation and in subsequent reviews. It concluded that, in the context of an administrative review under Art. 21.2 SCM, an IA need not always establish the existence of a benefit during the period of review. Rather, an IA might legitimately presume that a benefit continues to flow from an untied, non-recurring financial contribution. However, this presumption is not irrebuttable. In a case of change of ownership, as the case before it, an IA should review whether a benefit would continue to exist (§§61–2):

> We have already stated that in a case involving countervailing duties imposed as a result of an administrative review, Articles 21.1 and 21.2 of the *SCM Agreement* are relevant. As discussed above, Article 21.1 allows Members to apply countervailing duties 'only as long as and to the extent necessary to counteract subsidization . . .'. Article 21.2 sets out a review mechanism to ensure that Members comply with this rule. In an administrative review pursuant to Article 21.2, the investigating authority may be presented with 'positive information' that the 'financial contribution' has been repaid or withdrawn and/or that the 'benefit' no longer accrues. On the basis of its assessment of the information presented to it by interested parties, as well as of other evidence before it relating to the period of review, the investigating authority must determine whether there is a continuing need for the application of counter-vailing duties. The investigating authority is not free to ignore such information. If it were free to ignore this information, the review mechanism under Article 21.2 would have no purpose.
>
> Therefore, we agree with the Panel that while an investigating authority may presume, in the context of an administrative review under Article 21.2, that a 'benefit' continues to flow from an untied, non-recurring 'financial contribution', this presumption can never be 'irrebuttable'. In this case, given the changes in ownership leading to the creation of UES and BSplc/BSES, the USDOC was required under Article 21.2 to examine, on the basis of the information before it relating to these changes, whether a 'benefit' accrued to UES and BSplc/BSES. (italics in the original)[100]

There are nevertheless, limits to the exercise of discretion by IAs in this context and the deferential standards that WTO adjudicating bodies have adopted in this respect. In *US—Countervailing Measures on Certain EC Products*, WTO adjudicating bodies had to deal with the so-called 'same person methodology' applied by the US when reviewing the need for continued imposition of CVDs following privatization of a previously subsidized firm. The factual aspects of the method are described in detail in §145 of the report and there it is made clear that the US was having recourse to irrebuttable presumptions that affected parties could challenge under no circumstances. The review was thus not based on facts but on fiction. In §146, the AB explained that this method was inconsistent with US obligations under Art. 21.2 SCM: according to the AB, Art. 21.2 SCM sets forth an obligation to take into account positive information substantiating the need for a review (§§145–6):

> The Panel stated, and the United States agreed before the Panel and on appeal, that the 'same person' method requires the USDOC to 'consider'[] that the benefit attributed to the state-owned producer can be automatically attributed to the privatized producer without any examination of the condition of the transaction when the agency determines the post-privatization entity is not a new legal person.

---

[100] See also the AB report on *US—Countervailing Measures on Certain EC Products* at §141.

It is only if the USDOC finds that a new legal person has been created that the agency will make a determination of whether a benefit exists, and, in such cases, the inquiry will be limited to the subject of whether a new subsidy has been provided to the new owners.

Thus, under the 'same person' method, when the USDOC determines that no new legal person is created as a result of privatization, the USDOC will conclude from this determination, without any further analysis, and irrespective of the price paid by the new owners for the newly-privatized enterprise, that the newly-privatized enterprise continues to receive the benefit of a previous financial contribution. This approach is contrary to the obligation in Article 21.2 of the *SCM Agreement* that the investigating authority must take into account in an administrative review 'positive information substantiating the need for a review'. Such information could relate to developments with respect to the subsidy, privatization at arm's length and for fair market value, or some other information. The 'same person' method impedes the USDOC from complying with its obligation to examine whether a countervailable 'benefit' continues to exist in a firm subsequent to that firm's change in ownership. Therefore, we find that the 'same person' method, as such, is inconsistent with the obligations relating to administrative reviews under Article 21.2 of the *SCM Agreement*. (italics in the original)

In other words, as the US IA would never be in a position in the context of an administrative review, or a sunset review for that matter, to examine whether a benefit continued to exist, even if presented with evidence to this effect, what should be a rebuttable presumption becomes an irrebuttable presumption in US law. This is why the AB found that the US legislation at hand violated Art. 21.2 SCM as well as Art. 1 SCM (§147):

In our view, this finding, relating to administrative reviews, leads inevitably to the conclusion that the 'same person' method, as such, is also inconsistent with the obligations of the *SCM Agreement* relating to original investigations. In an original investigation, an investigating authority must establish all conditions set out in the *SCM Agreement* for the imposition of countervailing duties. Those obligations, identified in Article 19.1 of the *SCM Agreement*, read in conjunction with Article 1, include a determination of the existence of a 'benefit'. As in the administrative reviews, the 'same person' method necessarily precludes a proper determination as to the existence of a 'benefit' in original investigations where the pre- and post-privatization entity are the same legal person. Instead, in such cases, the 'same person' method establishes an irrebuttable presumption that the pre-privatization 'benefit' continues to exist after the change in ownership. Because it does not permit the investigating authority to satisfy all the prerequisites stated in the *SCM Agreement* before the imposition of countervailing duties, particularly the identification of a 'benefit', we find that the 'same person' method, as such, is inconsistent with the WTO obligations that apply to the conduct of original investigations. (italics in the original)

Recall that the AB, in its report on *US—Carbon Steel*, underscored the non-applicability of a *de minimis* standard in sunset or administrative reviews (§71). The US legislation governing reviews imposed a 0.5 per cent *ad valorem* threshold for a subsidy to be countervailable. The Panel had agreed with the complainants that the *de minimis* threshold (1 per cent *ad valorem*) applicable to the original imposition of CVDs was legally relevant for reviews as well. The US appealed this finding, arguing that legislative silence had to mean that a *de minimis* standard did not apply. The AB concurred with the US and reversed the Panel's findings on this score (§§88–9).

5.9 Sunset Reviews

All CVDs must be withdrawn five years after their imposition, unless the WTO Member has conducted a review, and has concluded that the expiry of the duty would be likely to lead to continuation or recurrence of subsidization and injury (Art. 21.3 SCM). The AB, in its report on *US—Carbon Steel*, underlined that (§88): 'termination of a countervailing duty is the rule and its continuation is the exception'. In other words, absent a sunset review, all CVDs in place must immediately be withdrawn (§63). The starting point for counting the five-year period is not necessarily that of the original imposition: Art. 21.3 SCM makes it clear that:

(a) If an administrative review has taken place, and
(b) If this review covered both subsidization and injury, then the date when such a review took place becomes the starting point to count the five-year period.

The Agreement notes that the mere fact that the last duty assessment review (as used in retrospective systems) led to the conclusion that no duty should be levied, does not necessarily require from the authorities to terminate the definitive duty (Art. 21.3 SCM, footnote 52). The Agreement does not seem to require the termination of the duty after the subsidy allocation period has ended either: in other words, it seems possible that, although an IA allocated the subsidy over a four-year period of time, CVDs could remain in place for the full five-year period (Art. 21.3 SCM).

A sunset review may be initiated:

(a) On the importing Member's own initiative before the five-year deadline; or
(b) Upon a duly substantiated request made by or on behalf of the domestic industry within a reasonable period of time before the five-year deadline expires.

There are no specific evidentiary requirements for sunset reviews: unlike the original investigation, where Art. 11.6 SCM requires from the IA to have sufficient evidence of subsidization, injury, and a causal link to justify initiation of an investigation, sunset reviews may be automatically initiated every five years (AB, *US—Carbon Steel*, §§103, 116). If, in the context of the sunset review, an IA has demonstrated that withdrawal of CVDs would be likely to lead to continuation or recurrence of subsidization and injury, then the CVDs may remain in place. The Agreement does not set forth any precise methodology for making such a determination of likelihood of continuation or recurrence of subsidization and injury. The Panel on *US—Carbon Steel* considered that such a determination, although inherently prospective, must nevertheless rest on a sufficient factual basis (§§8.95–96). In this case, the US IA had taken the CVD rate established in the original investigation as a starting point, and then subtracted from that rate the share of two subsidy programmes that had been terminated after the imposition. In other words, the factual basis of the DOC determination was limited to the original rate of subsidization and the fact that two of the original subsidy programmes were terminated after the imposition of the original CVD order (§ 8.116). The Panel found that the DOC determination, which did not go beyond simple arithmetic calculation, lacked sufficient factual basis, in particular because the DOC refused to accept information that would have been relevant to the assessment of the likelihood of subsidization (§8.117). In particular, the DOC declined the request made by the German exporters that a calculation memorandum from the original investigation be placed on the record of the sunset review, on the grounds that the submission was untimely, while it concerned information that was actually in the IA's possession and which was clearly relevant to the likelihood determination.

In *US—Carbon Steel*, the AB considered that the mere fact that a review leads to a rate of subsidization below the *de minimis* level, as set forth in Art. 11.9 SCM (applicable to original investigations), does not require an IA to terminate the measure. The AB came to this conclusion on the basis of the absence of any *de minimis* standard in the text of Art. 21 SCM in general and Art. 21.3 SCM in particular, as well as the fact that original investigations and sunset reviews are distinct processes with different purposes, and thus different rules may well apply in these circumstances (§§87–8). The AB added, however, that this does not imply that a likelihood determination should not be based on sufficient factual evidence (§88).

5.10 Standard of Review

The AB, in its report on *US—Lead and Bismuth II*, was confronted with the issue of whether the standard of review in the context of the SCM Agreement should be identical to that practised in the WTO AD (Art. 17.6 AD) or, conversely, whether the generic standard of review enshrined in Art. 11 DSU was applicable in the context of the SCM Agreement as well. The AB ruled that, in the absence of specific language mandating an exception (similar to that embedded in Art. 17.6 AD), the generic standard of review was applicable in the SCM Agreement context as well (§§44–51).

Note, however, that, in a subsequent case, the Panel on *US—Softwood Lumber VI* did not consider it (§7.17): 'either necessary or appropriate to conduct separate analyses of the USITC determination', involving a single injury determination with respect to both subsidized and dumped imports, under the two Agreements. The Panel indicated that, given the similarity of the CVD and the AD processes, inconsistent results should be avoided. In other words, the standard of review should be the same when examining an injury determination in a CVD case and an AD case (§7.18):

> We consider this result appropriate in view of the guidance in the Declaration of Ministers relating to Dispute Settlement under the AD and SCM Agreements. While the Appellate Body has clearly stated that the Ministerial Declaration does not require the application of the Article 17.6 standard of review in countervailing duty investigations, it nonetheless seems to us that in a case such as this one, involving a single injury determination with respect to both subsidized and dumped imports, and where most of Canada's claims involve identical or almost identical provisions of the AD and SCM Agreements, we should seek to avoid inconsistent conclusions.

So far, this case remains an isolated incident and is quite idiosyncratic anyway because of the single injury determination that was performed by the IA for both dumped and subsidized imports.

5.11 Investigation

The procedural obligations included in the SCM Agreement concerning initiation and conduct of the investigation are very similar and, on occasions, identical to those included in the AD Agreement. Art. 11 SCM deals with the initiation of an investigation: except in special circumstances, an investigation to determine the existence, degree, and effect of any alleged subsidy shall be initiated upon a written application by or on behalf of the domestic industry. An application shall include sufficient evidence of the existence of:

(a) A subsidy and, if possible, its amount;
(b) Injury; and
(c) A causal link between the subsidized imports and the alleged injury.

The application shall contain information as is reasonably available to the applicant on (Art. 11.2 SCM):

(a) The identity of the applicant;
(b) The description of the allegedly subsidized product;
(c) The existence, amount, and nature of the subsidy in question; and
(d) The injury to a domestic industry caused by subsidized imports.

A special feature of a CVD investigation is the requirement to enter into consultations with the exporting government (Art. 13 SCM). Consultations should be held as soon as possible after an application has been accepted, and in any event before the initiation of any investigation. The aim is to clarify the situation as to the matters referred to in the application and to arrive at a mutually agreed solution, if possible. Furthermore, throughout the period of investigation, WTO Members, the products of which are the subject of the investigation, are to be afforded a reasonable opportunity to continue consultations. The Agreement emphasizes that no affirmative determination, whether preliminary or final, may be made without reasonable opportunity for consultations (Art. 13.2 SCM and footnote 44). The Agreement adds that the provisions regarding consultations are not intended to prevent the authorities of a WTO Member from proceeding expeditiously with regard to initiating the investigation, reaching preliminary or final determinations, whether affirmative or negative, or from applying provisional or final measures in accordance with the provisions of this Agreement.

The Agreement clarifies that simple assertion, unsubstantiated by relevant evidence, cannot be considered sufficient to meet its requirements. The IA shall review the accuracy and adequacy of the evidence provided in the application to determine whether the evidence is sufficient to justify the initiation of an investigation. If, in special circumstances, the IA decides to initiate an investigation without having received a written application by or on behalf of a domestic industry for the initiation of such investigation, it shall proceed only if it has sufficient evidence of the existence of a subsidy, injury, and causal link to justify the initiation of an investigation.

In case of initiation at the request of the domestic industry, the IA will also need to examine whether the domestic industry filing the application had standing to do so. An investigation shall not be initiated unless the authorities have determined that the application was supported by those domestic producers whose collective output constitutes more than 50 per cent of the total production of the like product produced by that portion of the domestic industry expressing either support for or opposition to the application. In addition, a second threshold needs to be met: the Agreement provides that no investigation shall be initiated when domestic producers expressly supporting the application account for less than 25 per cent of total production of the like product produced by the domestic industry (Art. 11.4 SCM). Investigations shall, except in special circumstances, be concluded within one year. Art. 11.11 SCM states that an investigation shall in no case take more than 18 months from its initiation.

In its report on *Mexico—Olive Oil*, the Panel addressed some of the issues concerning initiation. In this case, there was a dispute between the two parties regarding the timing of the initiation: the EU held the view that the investigation had been initiated when the competent authority had signed the document initiating the process, whereas Mexico submitted that, according to its own law, an investigation is not initiated before the signed act has been published. The Panel agreed with Mexico that municipal law should be the criterion for deciding this issue (§§7.21ff and especially 7.30). The same Panel dismissed a challenge by the EU to the effect that Mexico had not allowed sufficient time to consult (in the Panel's calculation, there were only 13 days between the invitation for consultations and the initiation of investigation, §7.42), arguing that no obligation (to allow sufficient time) existed in the SCM Agreement. Finally, the Panel found that Mexico had violated its obligations under Art. 11.11 SCM by extending the investigation beyond the 18-month period prescribed in the SCM Agreement (§7.123).

5.12 Due Process Obligations

The language of Art. 12 SCM is almost verbatim that of Art. 6 AD. The noteworthy difference is the involvement of the interested member, the subsidizing government: a CVD investigation does not simply relate to private parties' behaviour, but inevitably also involves an examination of the practices of another WTO Member government. This makes the investigation politically more sensitive. The quintessential requirement imposed on an IA is to ensure even-handedness (due process) when performing its tasks, since, during the investigation process, different interests will be represented: on the one hand, the foreign exporters and domestic consumers and, on the other, the domestic industry. For example, an IA is required, by virtue of Art. 15.1 SCM, to perform an objective examination of the matter before it. In its report on *EC—Countervailing Measures on DRAM Chips*, the Panel quoted (§§7.271–6) from a report issued in the area of antidumping. In *US—Hot-Rolled Steel*, the AB provided its understanding of the term 'objective examination', as we saw *supra* (§193):

> The term 'objective examination' aims at a different aspect of the investigating authorities' determination. While the term 'positive evidence' focuses on the facts underpinning and justifying the injury determination, the term 'objective examination' is concerned with the investigative process itself. The word 'examination' relates, in our view, to the way in which the evidence is gathered, inquired into and, subsequently, evaluated; that is, it relates to the conduct of the investigation generally. The word 'objective', which qualifies the word 'examination', indicates essentially that the 'examination' process must conform to the dictates of the basic principles of good faith and fundamental fairness. In short, an 'objective examination' requires that the domestic industry, and the effects of dumped imports, be investigated in an unbiased manner, without favouring the interests of any interested party, or group of interested parties, in the investigation. The duty of the investigating authorities to conduct an 'objective examination' recognizes that the determination will be influenced by the objectivity, or any lack thereof, of the investigative process.

This is not the only due process clause in the SCM Agreement. WTO Members investigating the necessity to impose CVDs have to respect due process in numerous other instances: interested members and all other interested parties (e.g. the exporter, the domestic industry) must be given notice of the information which the authorities require, and ample opportunity to present in writing all evidence which they consider relevant in respect of the investigation in question. Subject to the requirement to protect confidential information, evidence presented in writing by one party shall be made available promptly to the others. Interested members and interested parties also shall have the right, upon justification, to present information orally. Thus, the authorities shall whenever practicable provide timely opportunities for all interested members and interested parties to see all information that is:

(a) Relevant to the presentation of their cases, that is
(b) Not confidential, and that is
(c) Used by the authorities in a CVD investigation, and to prepare presentations on the basis of this information.

Decisions by the IA can only be based on the written record. Except in the case of a determination based on facts available, the authorities have to satisfy themselves as to the accuracy of the information supplied by interested members or interested parties upon which their findings are based. This may be done through on-the-spot verifications or through investigations on the premises of a company of its records if:

(a) The company so agrees; and
(b) The WTO Member in question is notified and does not object.

Subject to the requirement to protect confidential information, the IA shall make the results of any such investigations available or shall provide disclosure thereof to the firms to which they pertain and may make such results available to the applicants. The Panel on *US—Countervailing Duty Investigation on DRAMs* took the view that an interested member should either object to the verification taking place on its soil, or not, but that it cannot be considered to have objected to the verification if it simply expressed concerns about certain aspects of the conduct of the verification. The Panel found that the right of objection cannot be extended to encompass a right to dictate the specific procedures to be followed during the investigation proceedings. The Panel further disagreed that an outright refusal to allow for a verification visit to take place leads to the application of facts available: whether that is so, will actually depend as much on the IA, and whether it has itself acted in a reasonable, objective, and impartial manner (§§ 7.404–7).

The authorities shall, before a final determination is made, inform all interested members and interested parties of the essential facts under consideration which form the basis for the decision whether to apply definitive measures: the disclosure should take place in sufficient time for the parties to defend their interests (Art. 12.8 SCM).

Any information which is by nature confidential (for example, because its disclosure would provide a competitor with significant competitive advantage, or because its disclosure would have a significantly adverse effect upon a person supplying the information or upon a person from whom the supplier acquired the information), or which is provided on a confidential basis by parties to an investigation shall, upon 'good cause' shown, be treated as such by the authorities (Art. 12.4 SCM). A non-confidential summary of confidential information must be furnished, unless, exceptionally, a summary is not possible (Art. 12.4.1

SCM).[101] Confidential information shall not be disclosed without specific permission of the party submitting it. If the IA finds that a request for confidentiality is not warranted, and if the supplier of the information is either unwilling to make the information public or to authorize its disclosure in generalized or summary form, the IA may disregard such information, unless it can be demonstrated to its satisfaction from appropriate sources that the information is correct (Art. 12.4.2 SCM). Requests for confidentiality should not be arbitrarily rejected. The IA may request the waiving of confidentiality only regarding information relevant to the proceedings.

Panels will, typically, adopt specific procedures to deal with the provision and dissemination of business confidential information (BCI) in a particular case. For example, the Panel on *Korea—Commercial Vessels* set out in a detailed attachment how the panel would deal with BCI in this case.

5.13 Duty to Cooperate and Recourse to Facts Available

Art. 12.7 SCM allows the IA to make determinations on the basis of the facts available in case any interested member or interested party refuses access to, or otherwise does not provide, necessary information within a reasonable period or significantly impedes the investigation. It is interesting to note that, although the language is identical to that of the AD Agreement (Art. 6.8), the SCM Agreement does not contain an annex similar to Annex II to the AD Agreement. Nevertheless, in *EC—Countervailing Measures on DRAM Chips*, the Panel was of the view that an IA is entitled to expect a high degree of cooperation from interested parties, to the best of their abilities, and would be entitled to draw adverse inferences from a refusal to cooperate with the authorities, even in the absence of a provision equivalent to Annex II AD, §7. It concluded that (§7.245):

> Article 12.7 identifies the circumstances in which investigating authorities may overcome a lack of information, in the response of the interested parties, by using 'facts' which are otherwise 'available' to the investigating authority.

This report distinguishes between questions relating to the weight given to various pieces of information and evidence in general, on the one hand, and a situation in which information that was requested was not provided and other information available had to be used, on the other. The Panel rejected Korea's argument that the EU had given undue weight to the documents, and that its reading of these documents was improperly coloured by the alleged failure of Korea to provide

---

[101] The Panel on *Mexico—Olive Oil* found that Mexico had violated its obligations under Art. 12.4.1 SCM by not requesting a non-confidential summary from the party that had supplied confidential information (§§7.100–1).

these documents itself (§7.249). This report reveals two instances where recourse to Art. 12.7 SCM is legitimate:

(a) If the requested party provides false information. In the case at hand, Korea had denied that high-level government officials took part in a meeting, and subsequently, full proof that the meeting took place and was attended by such high-level people became available. In the eyes of the Panel, the EU had had legitimate recourse to Art. 12.7 SCM, and looked for information from secondary sources, since necessary information had not been disclosed (§7.254);

(b) If the requested party provides insufficient information, and no information at all when subsequently requested: in the case at hand, Korea provided the EU IA with a one-page excerpt from a 200-page report. The EU took the view that the report was quite relevant to the investigation, and requested additional information, but did not obtain any information (additional to the one-page excerpt). The Panel took the view that, in light of Korea's response, the EU could legitimately have had recourse to information from secondary sources (§7.259).

6. No Double Dipping: CVDs *or* Countermeasures

CVDs are discussed in Part III of the SCM Agreement, and countermeasures in Part II. Footnote 35 to the SCM Agreement reads:

> The provisions of Part II or III may be invoked in parallel with the provisions of Part V; however, with regard to the effects of a particular subsidy in the domestic market of the importing Member, only one form of relief (either a countervailing duty, if the requirements of Part V are met, or a countermeasure under Articles 4 or 7) shall be available. The provisions of Parts III and V shall not be invoked regarding measures considered non-actionable in accordance with the provisions of Part IV. However, measures referred to in paragraph 1(a) of Article 8 may be investigated in order to determine whether or not they are specific within the meaning of Article 2. In addition, in the case of a subsidy referred to in paragraph 2 of Article 8 conferred pursuant to a programme which has not been notified in accordance with paragraph 3 of Article 8, the provisions of Part III or V may be invoked, but such subsidy shall be treated as non-actionable if it is found to conform to the standards set forth in paragraph 2 of Article 8.

It follows that a WTO Member can initiate a CVD investigation and impose CVDs and at the same time request from a Panel to find that it has suffered adverse effects as a result of an actionable subsidy (and/or that a prohibited subsidy had been bestowed). In that case, if the subsidizer refuses to withdraw the adverse effects or the prohibited subsidy, it might (assuming a request to this effect) be authorized to impose countermeasures. When doing so, it must deduct the amount of CVDs already in place. In other words, the SCM Agreement does not allow for double dipping.[102]

CVDs are a form of unilateral relief, much like antidumping measures. While the unilateral nature of the remedy has obvious advantages, it also presents some shortcomings in dealing with subsidies:

(a) CVDs may protect the domestic industry of country A from injury suffered in its domestic market due to subsidized imports from country B, but it does not provide any relief in cases where the subsidies are distorting a third-country market (country C) in which the domestic industry has an export interest. Neither can CVDs address the negative effects of the subsidies (from the point of view of the domestic industry) in the market of the subsidizing Member (the market of country B);

(b) A CVD investigation is a complicated, time- and resource-consuming enterprise. Since a CVD investigation concerns the subsidization practice of another government and not a private company's practice, as is the case in antidumping, it may prove to be particularly difficult and delicate. Moreover, the end-result of the investigation may at best be the imposition of a CVD. While a duty may offset the effects of the subsidy, it does not imply that the product in question is no longer subsidized. The imposition of a CVD may protect the domestic industry at home, but maybe at the expense of the domestic industry's export performance, as the subsidized products move to other markets. Because of this likely trade-diverting effect (of CVDs), the problem may not be solved but simply moved to another market in which the domestic industry was also present and will also feel the effects of the subsidies;

(c) It is not an easy task to calculate the amount of subsidization so that the duty will effectively offset the subsidy bestowed on the imported product. The SCM Agreement does not provide much guidance. It allows for the calculation of the amount of the subsidy in terms of benefit to the recipient. But on other occasions, the Agreement also talks about the cost to government as the starting-point for calculating the amount. When the benefit to the recipient is the starting-point, Art. 14 SCM provides for specific market benchmarks which appear easy to apply in theory, but which present many practical problems. Even determining the amount of benefit by using the benefit to the recipient as the starting-point is not a straightforward exercise. Art. 14 SCM refers to a market benchmark, but is not very detailed or specific as to the way in which such a market benchmark is to be determined. And what if there is no private market for the product, or the market would not have provided the financial contribution in question, how does one determine the existence and amount of benefit? Art. 14 SCM does not provide a clear answer to such questions.

---

[102] Bhagwati and Mavroidis (2004).

Still, CVDs are widely practised. One could go one step further and argue that CVDs are a powerful weapon in the hands of Members with a substantial internal market: they will not have to await a multilateral ruling to provide their domestic industry with adequate relief since it is highly likely that most of the injury will be felt in their domestic market. Conversely, Members with small internal markets cannot get much out of the threat of CVDs: the size of their domestic market takes a lot of wind out of their sails, and their only hope is multilateral action. Whereas CVDs can be imposed within short time limits, they will have to wait close to four years in some cases before they can react in case they have raised a complaint before the WTO. And then, it is questionable how much of a threat their counter-measures might be.[103]

7. Institutional Issues

The Committee on Subsidies and Countervailing Measures (SCM Committee) is established by virtue of Art. 24 SCM. Its tasks are described in this provision and include the establishment of a Permanent Group of Experts (PGE) to assist a Panel, if requested, under Art. 4(5) SCM with regard to whether the measure in question is a prohibited subsidy, and to provide advisory opinions on the existence and nature of any subsidy if so requested by the Committee or a Member in relation to its own subsidy. To date, the PGE has never been requested to intervene in the context of a dispute concerning the provision of a prohibited subsidy.

---

[103] In Schelling's framework of analysis, a threat, unlike a promise, is credible if it does not have to be exercised.

9

SAFEGUARDS

1. Safeguards

1.1 The Legal Discipline and its Rationale

Safeguards (also referred to as the 'escape clause') in the form of tariffs, quotas, or tariff quotas can be lawfully imposed by WTO Members if they can show that, as a result of unforeseen developments, imports have risen and caused injury to the domestic industry producing the like product. Actually, the unforeseen-developments requirement does not figure anywhere in the WTO SG Agreement; it is reflected in Art. XIX GATT only. It is the AB that introduced it by holding that the sources of law with respect to imposing safeguards are reflected in Art. XIX GATT and the SG Agreement.[1] We quote from its report on *Argentina—Footwear* (§81):

---

[1] Wauters (2010) provides an excellent overview of the Agreement.

Therefore, the provisions of Article XIX of the GATT 1994 *and* the provisions of the *Agreement on Safeguards* are *all* provisions of one treaty, the *WTO Agreement*. They entered into force as part of that treaty at the same time. They apply equally and are equally binding on all WTO Members. And, as these provisions relate to the same thing, namely the application by Members of safeguard measures, the Panel was correct in saying that 'Article XIX of GATT and the Safeguards Agreement must *a fortiori* be read as representing an *inseparable package* of rights and disciplines which have to be considered in conjunction.' Yet a treaty interpreter must read all applicable provisions of a treaty in a way that gives meaning to *all* of them, harmoniously. And, an appropriate reading of this 'inseparable package of rights and disciplines' must, accordingly, be one that gives meaning to *all* the relevant provisions of these two equally binding agreements. (emphasis and italics in the original)

According to Maruyama (1989), the first formal safeguard mechanism was included in the 1942 US-Mexico Reciprocal Trade Agreement.[2] The GATT safeguard clause was modelled on this clause and reproduced it almost verbatim.[3] It should thus not come as a surprise that it was the US that introduced the escape clause in the original GATT. The basic premise for the clause was for the US to be allowed to pull back if US negotiators excessively reduced tariffs:

> The 'escape clause' is aimed at providing temporary relief for an industry suffering from serious injury, or the threat thereof, so that the industry will have sufficient time to adjust to the freer international competition.[4]

The first GATT Panel that dealt with this issue, the Hatters' Fur Sales,[5] echoed this rationale for the safeguard clause when it held that Art. XIX was not meant to protect infant industry as does Art. XVIII GATT: its function was distinct and it was mainly to provide temporary relief and not to help develop an industry.[6]

Over the years, the US adopted a series of initiatives that made its own national safeguard clause, the notorious US Section 201 (of the US Trade Act), even more flexible. First, the US Congress eliminated the causality factor with respect to unforeseen developments, introducing §6(a), where it was made clear that it was only in whole or in part causality resulting from tariff concessions that mattered.[7]

---

[2] US Stat. 833 (1943).

[3] Bronckers (1985); Jackson (1969); Stewart and Brilliant (1993).

[4] S. Rep. No. 1298, 93rd Cong., 2nd Sess. 119 (1974). Or to borrow from Segal (2011): trade produces winners and losers, as capital and labour get reallocated to the sectors in which countries excel. Since the winners win more than the losers lose, openness is to the nation's overall benefit— even though the autoworker in Ohio who was put out of work after his factory closed may not share in that benefit. Safeguards are about the autoworker in Ohio. Whether this is sound policy is something that we will be discussing in what follows.

[5] GATT Doc. No. GATT/551-3 at p. 21.

[6] By the same token, Art. XIX GATT serves a different purpose than Art. XXVIII GATT: this latter provision is not meant to provide relief limited in time. As we will see *infra*, the advent of the SG Agreement specified the time limits within which safeguards can be lawfully imposed, in line with the original idea underlying Art. XIX GATT, which did not, however, contain specific time limits as does Art. 8 SG.

[7] Pub. L. No. 82-50, Stat. 73–74 (1951) Trade Agreements Extension Act of 1951.

Then, the Trade Act of 1974[8] amended the requirement that the resulting injury be 'substantial' and adopted instead a different, less stringent standard: imports should be a 'major' cause of injury. One could argue that words like those mentioned here could be amenable to various interpretations; yet, the change must signal something and major is definitely a lesser standard than 'substantial'.

Eventually, grey area measures, the notorious VERs (voluntary export restraints),[9] saw the light of the day and started proliferating: through these measures an exporter, at the (informal) request of another trading nation, would agree to cap its volume of exports or raise their price.[10] VERs were of dubious GATT consistency, if not outright illegal, yet for a number of reasons that we explore *infra* exporters adhered to them. The SG Agreement was meant to be a reaction to the consistent loosening of the safeguard discipline. Whether it was a warranted or unwarranted response is the subject-matter of this section.

There were no corresponding changes in the GATT safeguard clause. Indeed, negotiators over the years aimed at 'tightening' rather than 'loosening' the screws. Before we move on to examine the legislative framework in detail, it is worth delving a bit more into the role that a safeguard clause is called to play in a trade agreement.

The basic purpose[11] of the safeguard clause is to provide an effective safety valve for industries suffering or threatened with serious injury caused by increased imports in the wake of trade liberalization. This legal institution has sound logical underpinnings. The economic environment is constantly changing: new products and production technologies are discovered, consumer tastes change, governments come and go, there are wars, investments are made, new firms see the light of day, and so on.[12] For a trade agreement to be fully efficient, it would need to adapt to all these changes. This adaptation could be fully achieved only under two circumstances: if the parties could perfectly foresee the path of events, then they could specify an agreement (contract) at the outset that would identify how the agreement terms would change along this path. Alternatively, in the absence of perfect information, the parties may want to renegotiate the agreement any time a change occurs, and write a fully state-contingent contract specifying commitments for each possible outcome of the underlying economic environment. It would, under either of these circumstances, be possible to specify a trade agreement that *ex post* ensures the desirable levels of trade. If desirable, this agreement could ensure a gradual adjustment to the changed environment. Hence, in neither case would there be a role for any provision that allowed for an *ex post* change in tariff bindings.

---

8 Trade Act 1974 S. Rep. No. 1298, 93rd Cong., 2nd Sess. 119 (1974).
9 As well as the VIEs (voluntary import expansions).
10 *Japan—Semiconductors*, discussed in Chapter 2, could qualify as VER.
11 This section draws on Horn and Mavroidis (2007b).
12 Bagwell and Staiger (2002); Finger (1993).

Tariff bindings in actual trade agreements are typically not conditioned on external events, however. There is, therefore, a need for instruments that allow *ex post* adjustment of effective levels of bindings (that is, for escape clauses) and the GATT includes several provisions to this effect. Some of them are remedies for problems that are not related to specific industries: Arts. XII and XVIII(b) GATT allow for protective measures in response to economy-wide, macroeconomic (balance of payments) disturbances; Art. XXVIII GATT could address problems in specific industries, since it permits renegotiation with other contracting parties of particular bindings. It might thus allow for more long-run, but also presumably more time-consuming, solutions to problems of *ex post* inefficient tariff bindings. What, then, is the role of Art. XIX GATT and the SG Agreement in this arsenal of escape clauses? Safeguard measures can be unilaterally imposed and might for this reason be a quicker response to changes in the economic environment in particular industries (depending on the administrative requirements imposed on safeguard investigations) than, for instance, a renegotiation under Art. XXVIII GATT.

Art. XIX GATT and the SG Agreement are not the only measures that can be unilaterally imposed—both AD and CVD can be imposed without negotiation with the exporting country. However, safeguards differ from these measures in two important ways: first, safeguards recognize that the problem flows from the failure of the domestic import-competing industry that has been unable to face an import surge from the foreign exporters without being exposed to 'unfair' competition; second, and this is a logical consequence of the first point, safeguards are temporary measures. They are meant to temporarily slow the pace of adjustment to changes in the external economic environment, whereas AD and CVD measures can be in place for as long as the dumping or subsidization continues: by contrast, as we shall see *infra*, there is a *dynamic use constraint* embedded in the SG Agreement whereby imposition of safeguard measures must be followed by an equal period of trade peace.

Both aspects make central the notion of adjustment costs, and the use of the safeguard measures in practice is frequently tied to this notion. The question then arises whether such an instrument can be defended from an economic point of view, in the sense that it might enhance the efficiency of the trade agreement, that is, increase the size of the pie the parties to the contract share through the agreement. The economic notion of adjustment costs is amorphous. The interpretation we have in mind refers to the cost accruing, owing to the transition from one equilibrium to another (and, thus, does not involve a comparison of the final outcome with the initial situation). To define more precisely similar costs, we need to agree on the criterion according to which costs are evaluated. We start by considering adjustment costs from the point of view of social welfare maximization: consider an import-competing domestic industry (lamb meat production, say) that has suffered a severe negative shock: foreign capacity has permanently expanded and prices have fallen significantly as a result. As matters stand, the industry has to shed 12,000 jobs. Suppose first that former employees could all immediately find employment in the beef meat industry, but at lower wages. This lowering of the wage would (ideally adjusted by the price decreases generated by cheaper imports) obviously be costly to workers. But it would not be considered as an adjustment cost, since it would simply reflect differences between two full capacity equilibria, with no transitional period in between: the lowering of the wage is not a cost incurred during the transition from one employment situation to another. Suppose, now, that it takes each worker six months to search for new employment, no matter what, and during this period the worker has to remain unproductive. This would be a social adjustment cost: during the transition period the economy is temporarily producing at less than its long-run full capacity. But this cost does not depend on the speed of adjustment, since each worker by assumption has to be unemployed for six months, no matter what. This period of reduced output is, essentially, an unavoidable investment in a more efficient production pattern. It would, hence, not provide a rationale for imposing a safeguard measure that gradually moved workers into the beef industry, since such a measure would not affect the total magnitude of adjustment costs, but would just cause a costly delay in the necessary adjustment. As a third possibility, assume that each quarter 6,000 vacancies come up in the beef meat industry. A fine-tuned safeguard that gradually reduced the workforce in the lamb meat industry could then ensure that 6,000 workers were reallocated during the first quarter, and another 6,000 the next, without anyone having to be temporarily unemployed. By contrast, if all 12,000 workers had to leave the lamb meat industry immediately, 6,000 of them would be unemployed for a quarter. The speed at which the adjustment takes place, thus, affects the aggregate adjustment costs, and there is a case for a safeguard. This provides an efficiency-enhancing rationale for safeguards: to reduce temporarily the pace of adjustment in order to reduce adjustment costs. This example deserves several remarks:

(a) The example presumes that the alternative to the safeguard is that all 12,000 workers immediately leave the industry. But why do the 6,000 workers not remain in the lamb industry during the first quarter and offer to work at sufficiently low wages for the industry to want to retain them? If wages were reduced this way, there would be no unnecessary loss of output during the transition and, hence, no case for a safeguard (or at least a weaker case). The reason must be some form of inflexibility in the wage, arising from, for instance, labour union resistance to wage cuts or minimum wage legislation. More generally, in order for government intervention to have an efficiency-enhancing role to play, the privately perceived incentives to cope with adjustment must be imperfect from a social point of view (or from a government point of view). If the private sector puts the same emphasis on these costs as the government, and has access to the same (possibly imperfect) information about the future evolution of the economy, and the economy is not distorted in other respects, it does not suffice that there are adjustment costs that depend on the pace of adjustment, for a role for safeguards to exist. For instance, in the example above, the implicitly assumed wage rigidity implied that the cost of labour perceived by the lamb meat industry exceeded the true social cost of this labour, which should reflect the opportunity cost of workers;

(b) The example presumes that the shock to international prices is permanent and the economy will, therefore, eventually have to adapt to the new circumstances. If the shock were temporary, a safeguard could, under certain circumstances, serve a slightly different role, by preventing adjustment costs arising from resources first moving out and then back into the industry. Again, for such a role to arise, it must be that the owners of these resources do not have the right incentives, as perceived from a social point of view, to avoid these adjustment costs by letting resources remain in the industry during the temporary slump;

(c) The examples above presume, for simplicity's sake, that the government has full information about relevant aspects of the future. In practice, there is, of course, often considerable uncertainty about whether negative shocks are transitory or permanent, and this uncertainty may influence the appropriate length and magnitude of a safeguard measure. But this uncertainty does not in and of itself consitute a reason for a government intervention in the form of a safeguard, as long as the government is not better informed than the private sector;

(d) In the examples above, the adjustment costs stemmed from the reallocation of labour. But one can tell similar stories in relation to the reallocation of other factors of production: machinery, for instance.

The reasoning has so far identified two desirable properties of safeguards which contribute to enhance the efficiency of a trade contract. In their capacity to provide an escape from inflexible contract terms, they may increase the efficiency of the contract after external shocks (even in the absence of adjustment costs that depend on the speed of adjustment); but they also have a separate role to play: to reduce temporarily the rate of adjustment in order to reduce the total amount of adjustment costs. There may be a related, additional source of efficiency gains from safeguards, a source that is often emphasized in the policy debate: safeguards may induce countries to liberalize further *ex ante*.[13] Consequently, the combined effect of the induced liberalization, as well as the possibility of increasing tariffs *ex post*, may result in a fall in the average level of protection. Another version of this argument, based more on a public-choice approach, where governments are driven at least partly by motives other than social welfare maximization, is discussed by Sykes (1991). The argument is that governments may, after trade negotiations, face strong pressure for protection in certain industries. A safeguard mechanism

---

[13] Compare the analysis in Bagwell and Staiger (2002).

makes it possible to give in to such pressures and, thus, to avoid political setbacks from engaging in trade liberalization. As a result, governments are more prone to liberalize *ex ante*. While this is not a unique feature of safeguards (it is shared with other escape clause mechanisms), the potential of safeguards to avoid adjustment costs might serve as an additional motive for governments to liberalize.

Some of the problems (and virtues) associated with safeguard actions are illuminated by viewing them as insurance mechanisms, an inexact but useful analogy. An essential character of both trade agreements and insurance contracts is that one side in the contractual relationship may be subject to an adverse shock after the signing of the agreement. In an insurance contract, there is a net transfer of resources from the insurance company to the insured party. Similarly, Art. XIX GATT allows a WTO Member that is exposed to a sufficiently severe negative shock, to increase a trade barrier—that is, to hedge against the possibility that certain unforeseen events occur. Formally, the WTO Member had to provide, on occasion, substantially equivalent compensation to its trading partners, but it seems likely that trading partners will not achieve full compensation: they would have to go through a possibly lengthy and costly dispute procedure to obtain the compensation, which would serve to reduce their incentives to insist on full compensation. Moreover, as we will see *infra*, depending on its duration, a safeguard does not need to be accompanied by payment of compensation. The similarity between safeguards and insurance schemes does not stop here, however. Just as regular insurance contracts seek to limit the possibility of abuse through complex restrictions on their applicability, many of the features of Art. XIX GATT and the SG Agreement can be seen as attempts to limit such problems. For instance, a basic problem in the case of regular insurance contracts is the conflict between 'risk sharing' and 'moral hazard': on the one hand, it is desirable to reduce the risk that a risk-averse party is exposed to by letting a less risk-averse party carry more of the risk. The fact that this is efficiency enhancing (yields gains from trade) is evidenced by the insured party's willingness to pay an insurance premium to be relieved of the risk. On the other hand, the insurance may adversely affect the insured party's incentives to avoid risk—it may cause a moral hazard problem. It is easy to identify potential moral hazard problems in the context of safeguards: in particular, countries could be tempted to refrain from undertaking measures that would prepare the economy for shocks that might occur in a liberalized trade environment in the expectation of being able to rely on safeguards should a problem arise. A number of the requirements in Art. XIX GATT and in the SG Agreement are naturally seen as a means to limit such negative incentives. For instance, a safeguard can only be invoked in the case where the injury, *inter alia*, stems from increased imports. A first-best risk-sharing contract (the optimal contract in a situation without moral hazard problems and so on) would not restrict the insurance to injury from increased imports. But if any domestic negative shock could, to a significant extent, be passed on to trading partners, the incentive for countries to pursue reasonable policies would be diminished. On the other hand, when disturbances emanate from abroad, it is less likely that they are the result of negligence or beggar-thy-neighbour behaviour by the importing country. Furthermore, in order to verify that increased imports are really the source of injury, WTO Members are required to establish a causal link between the two, just like regular insurance contracts require the insured party to verify any claims. Another defence against moral hazard is the requirement that the safeguard solves a problem that could not have been prevented through diligent behaviour—the import surge must be unforeseen.

The notion of unforeseen developments is central to safeguard as an insurance scheme, and the use of the safeguard measures in practice is frequently tied to this notion. In this context, three remarks are useful:

(a) First, for how long can an event be said to be unforeseen? From an economic perspective, it would seem appropriate to relate unforeseen developments to recent concessions. However, most WTO Members do not share this view, and routinely relate unforeseen events to concessions granted many years ago;

(b) Second, could unforeseen events include macroeconomic events, such as financial crises or currency variations? From an economic point of view, a positive answer to this question seems far-fetched or unbalanced, because, if macroeconomic events may reduce the expected gains from a given trade concession, they may, at the same time, increase the gains expected from other concessions. However, WTO Members routinely tend to focus on the first impact and to ignore the second one;

(c) Third, could a safeguard measure taken by a WTO Member constitute an unforeseen development for other WTO Members and hence constitute a basis for adopting safeguard actions? This question is crucial since it has the capability to trigger a cascade of safeguards, as indeed occurred in the steel industry in the early 2000s. WTO Members tend to see a safeguard measure taken by one WTO Member as an unforeseen development to the extent that it may generate fluctuations in the terms of trade and change trade flows. Such an approach relies on a crude perception of the potentially diverted trade flows that ignores factors which could reduce, or even counterbalance, the initial trade diversion. For instance, the trade diversion predicted by the European Commission following the US (2002) safeguard measures on steel did not materialize.

Another generic problem facing the design of an insurance contract arises when the outcome is not perfectly observable. For instance, theft is often by its very nature hard to verify, and an insurance company largely has to trust that reported theft has actually occurred (even though it is also aided by laws against fraudulent insurance claims). When certain outcomes are not observable to the party providing the insurance, the contract needs to be designed so as to guarantee that the insured party has incentives not to over-report, or such that it is only based on circumstances that are verifiable by the insurer. A very similar problem may arise in the context of safeguards in trade agreements, where there is a need to prevent WTO Members from claiming injury that has not occurred. In response, a country wanting to impose safeguards has to provide evidence that its industry is suffering serious injury or facing an imminent threat to do so. Both the distribution of the burden of proof, as well as the fact that the injury must be serious, tend to ease the observability problem.

We have so far painted a rather rosy picture of safeguards (and escape clauses more generally). This picture requires several crucial caveats:

(a) First, it helps to identify circumstances under which a safeguard might improve matters relative to a situation where nothing is done. It has not been argued, however, that an import restriction would be the best way of coping with the problem. For instance, if the source of the wage rigidity cannot be removed, it might still be preferable to use employment subsidies, or even production subsidies, since these do not distort consumer prices to the same extent;

(b) Second, we have neglected any impact that the safeguard may have on the incentives eventually to move out of the industry, by implicitly assuming away any form of strategic interaction between the private sector and the government at a later stage. In practice, firms and workers often remain in the protected industry with the rational expectation that the government will continue to adopt adjustment measures in the future. There is a notable body of economic literature exploring various aspects of this essential point. For instance, it has been shown that tariffs or quotas that remain in place until a firm adopts a new technology (in such a case, adjustment is defined as the need for a domestic firm to catch up with foreign technology) always delay the timing of the firm's technology adoption decision. Indeed, as pointed out by Bown (2005), the targeting principle (one instrument for one problem)[14] suggests that it is not possible for a single restricting safeguard policy to be the most efficient instrument at inducing both resource entry (as in the above catching-up case) and resource exit (as in the above lamb meat example);

(c) Third, the reasoning above showed how social adjustment costs might provide a rationale for social welfare-maximizing governments to include a safeguard provision in a trade agreement. But similar costs should also be of concern to governments that are more sensitive to the influence of special interest groups.

---

[14] See the excellent analysis of Bhagwati and Ramaswami (1963) on this score.

The weight that such a government puts on these costs may depend on who bears them, but the fact that the economy's productive capacity is reduced from a rapid rate of adjustment should reasonably be of concern to a broad range of governments. In this respect, it is worth noting that the economic literature, taking into account the interactions between industry adjustment, lobbying, and the political response, suggests that the use of safeguard measures can raise future protection to the extent that it reduces adjustment, hence that it fails to reduce future lobbying efforts;

(d) Fourth, very little is empirically known about the magnitude of social adjustment costs. Economists often dismiss these as being small and swamped by the gains from trade liberalization, even though it is acknowledged that they typically fall upon a few individuals, while the benefits from trade liberalization are spread over many more. Even less is known empirically about the extent to which adjustment costs depend on the speed of trade liberalization. But, for what it is worth, our intuition suggests that the speed of adjustment can indeed often importantly affect aggregate adjustment costs;

(e) Last, but not least, attention should be paid to the true impact of the non-discrimination clause.[15] There are two main different ways for safeguard measures to incorporate a discriminatory dimension. On the one hand, there are exceptions for partners in preferential trade agreements and for small developing countries and, as expected, these exceptions tend to allow the exporters from the exempted countries to gain market share at the expense of the non-exempted countries. On the other hand, non-discrimination can be channelled through the type of safeguard measures taken. Safeguards based on quantitative restrictions preserve existing market shares better than tariff-based safeguards and hence discriminate against exporters whose market share has recently been growing. Finally, safeguards tend to cause bigger decreases in market shares for fast-growing exporters and new entrants.[16]

Yet, these caveats notwithstanding, there are good arguments in favour of introducing a safeguard clause, but not necessarily the one that has actually been included in the WTO, in a trade agreement. And yet, compared to antidumping, there is scarce use of this instrument as Tables 9.1 and 9.2 show. We will examine the reasons for this phenomenon *infra*.

---

[15] We discuss the legal issues involved *infra*. Suffice to state here that in principle safeguards must be non-discriminatory.

[16] Sykes (1990, 1991) discusses the role of safeguards in trade agreements, in particular, as viewed from the perspective of public choice theory. See also Deardorff (1987), and his treatment of the role of tariff and non-tariff safeguards when social preferences are represented by a Corden 'conservative social welfare function' (where losses are valued more than potential gains).

Table 9.1 Safeguard initiations by reporting Member—29 March 1995–31 2010

Reporting Member	1995	1996	1997	1998	1999	2000	2001	2002	2003	2004	2005	2006	2007	2008	2009	2010	Total
Argentina	0	0	1	1	0	1	1	0	0	1	0	1	0	0	0	0	6
Australia	0	0	0	1	0	0	0	0	0	0	0	0	1	0	0	0	2
Brazil	0	1	0	0	0	0	1	0	0	0	0	0	0	1	0	0	3
Bulgaria*	0	0	0	0	0	1	1	3	1	0	0	0	0	0	0	0	6
Canada	0	0	0	0	0	0	0	1	0	0	2	0	0	0	0	0	3
Chile	0	0	0	0	2	3	2	2	1	1	0	1	0	0	1	0	12
China, P.R.	0	0	0	0	0	0	0	1	0	0	0	0	0	0	0	0	1
Colombia	0	0	0	0	1	0	0	0	0	2	0	0	0	0	0	0	3
Costa Rica	0	0	0	0	0	0	0	1	0	0	0	0	0	0	0	0	1
Croatia	0	0	0	0	0	0	0	0	0	0	0	0	0	0	1	0	1
Czech Republic*	0	0	0	0	1	2	1	5	0	0	0	0	0	0	0	0	9
Dominican Republic	0	0	0	0	0	0	0	0	0	0	0	0	0	0	3	2	5
Ecuador	0	0	0	1	2	1	0	1	4	0	0	0	0	0	0	0	8
Egypt	0	0	0	1	1	0	0	0	0	0	0	0	1	1	0	0	4
El Salvador	0	0	0	0	0	3	0	0	0	0	0	0	0	0	0	0	3
Estonia*	0	0	0	0	0	0	0	0	1	0	0	0	0	0	0	0	1
European Union*	0	0	0	0	0	0	0	1	1	1	1	0	0	0	1	0	5
Hungary*	0	0	0	0	0	2	0	1	1	0	0	0	0	0	0	0	3
India	0	0	1	5	3	2	0	1	1	1	0	1	1	1	10	0	26
Indonesia	0	0	0	0	0	0	0	0	0	0	0	1	2	2	0	7	12
Israel	0	0	0	0	0	0	0	0	1	0	0	0	0	0	0	0	1
Jamaica	0	0	0	0	0	0	0	0	1	0	0	0	0	0	0	0	1
Japan	0	0	0	0	0	1	0	0	0	0	0	0	0	0	0	0	1
Jordan	0	0	0	0	0	1	0	8	0	0	1	1	1	2	0	1	15
Korea, Rep. of	0	2	0	0	0	0	0	0	0	0	0	0	0	0	2	0	4
Kyrgyz Rep.	0	0	0	0	1	0	0	0	0	0	0	0	0	0	2	0	3
Latvia*	0	0	0	0	1	0	0	1	0	0	0	0	0	0	0	0	2
Lithuania*	0	0	0	0	0	0	1	0	0	0	0	0	0	0	0	0	1

(Continued)

Table 9.1 *Continued*

Reporting Member	1995	1996	1997	1998	1999	2000	2001	2002	2003	2004	2005	2006	2007	2008	2009	2010	Total
Mexico	0	0	0	0	0	0	0	1	0	0	0	0	0	0	0	1	2
Moldova	0	0	0	0	0	0	0	0	1	1	0	0	0	0	0	0	2
Morocco	0	0	0	0	0	2	0	0	0	0	1	0	0	0	1	1	5
Pakistan	0	0	0	0	0	0	0	0	0	0	1	0	0	0	0	0	1
Panama	0	0	0	0	0	0	0	0	0	0	1	0	0	0	0	0	1
Peru	0	0	0	0	0	0	0	0	0	1	0	0	0	0	1	0	2
Philippines	0	0	0	0	0	0	3	0	3	0	0	1	0	1	1	0	9
Poland*	0	0	0	0	0	1	0	4	0	0	0	0	0	0	0	0	5
Slovak Republic*	0	0	0	0	0	1	1	1	0	0	0	0	0	0	0	0	3
Slovenia*	0	0	0	1	0	0	0	0	0	0	0	0	0	0	0	0	1
South Africa	0	0	0	0	0	0	0	0	0	0	0	0	1	0	0	0	1
Tunisia	0	0	0	0	0	0	0	0	0	0	0	2	0	0	0	0	2
Turkey	0	0	0	0	0	0	0	0	0	5	0	5	3	1	1	0	15
Ukraine	0	0	1	0	2	2	0	0	0	0	0	0	2	1	2	0	8
United States	1	2	0	1	2	2	1	0	0	0	0	0	0	0	3	0	10
Venezuela	0	0	0	0	0	4	1	1	0	0	0	0	0	0	0	0	6
Totals	2	5	3	10	15	25	12	34	15	14	7	13	8	10	25	18	216

Note: The EU enlarged its membership on 1 May 2004 and on 1 January 2007. The newly acceded countries still appear in the tables in this database as individual WTO Members. All figures pertaining to the EU are counted: (a) on a 15-Member basis for the period between 1 January 1995–30 April 2004; (b) on a 25-Member basis for the period between 1 May 2004–31 December 2006; and (c) on a 27-Member basis for the period after 1 January 2007.

Table 9.2 Safeguard measures by reporting Member—29 March 1995–31 October 2010

Reporting Member	1996	1997	1998	1999	2000	2001	2002	2003	2004	2005	2006	2007	2008	2009	2010	Total
Argentina	0	1	0	0	0	2	0	0	0	0	0	1	0	0	0	4
Brazil	0	1	0	0	0	0	1	0	0	0	0	0	0	0	0	2
Bulgaria*	0	0	0	0	0	0	2	0	0	0	0	0	0	0	0	2
Chile	0	0	0	0	2	1	2	0	0	1	1	0	0	0	0	7
China, P.R.	0	0	0	0	0	0	1	0	0	0	0	0	0	0	0	1
Croatia	0	0	0	0	0	0	0	0	0	0	0	0	0	1	0	1
Czech Republic*	0	0	0	1	0	1	1	2	0	0	0	0	0	0	0	5
Dominican Republic	0	0	0	0	0	0	0	0	0	0	0	0	0	0	1	1
Ecuador	0	0	0	0	0	1	0	1	1	0	0	0	0	0	0	3
Egypt	0	0	0	1	1	1	0	0	0	0	0	0	1	0	0	4
European Union*	0	0	0	0	0	0	1	0	1	1	0	0	0	0	0	3
Hungary*	0	0	0	0	0	0	0	3	0	0	0	0	0	0	0	3
India	0	0	4	1	1	0	2	0	0	1	0	0	0	3	0	12
Indonesia	0	0	0	0	0	0	0	0	0	0	1	0	0	2	0	3
Jordan	0	0	0	0	0	1	1	2	0	1	0	1	0	0	1	7
Korea, Rep. of	0	1	0	0	1	0	0	0	0	0	0	0	0	0	0	2
Kyrgyz Rep.	0	0	0	0	0	0	0	0	0	0	0	0	0	1	0	1
Latvia*	0	0	0	1	0	0	0	1	0	0	0	0	0	0	0	2
Lithuania*	0	0	0	0	0	0	1	0	0	0	0	0	0	0	0	1
Moldova	0	0	0	0	0	0	0	0	1	0	0	0	0	0	0	1
Morocco	0	0	0	0	0	1	0	0	0	0	1	0	0	0	0	2
Panama	0	0	0	0	0	0	0	0	0	0	0	1	0	0	0	1
Philippines	0	0	0	0	0	0	1	1	3	0	0	0	0	1	0	6
Poland*	0	0	0	0	0	0	0	4	0	0	0	0	0	0	0	4
Slovak Republic*	0	0	0	0	0	1	0	0	0	0	0	1	0	0	0	2
South Africa	0	0	0	0	0	0	0	1	0	0	0	0	0	0	0	1
Turkey	0	0	0	0	0	0	0	0	0	2	4	1	4	1	0	12
Ukraine	0	0	0	0	0	0	0	0	0	0	0	0	1	1	0	2
United States	1	0	1	1	2	0	1	0	0	0	0	0	0	0	0	6
Total	1	3	5	5	7	9	14	15	6	6	7	5	6	10	2	101

Note. See note to Table 9.1.

1.2 The Coverage of the Legal Discipline

1.2.1 A Typology of Safeguard Measures

There is no exhaustive or even indicative list of safeguards provided in the SG Agreement or the GATT, yet there are hints as to the type of measures envisaged all over the SG Agreement. Art. 5.1 SG *in fine* states that WTO Members should choose measures most suitable for the achievement of their relevant objectives; the same provision contemplates the obligations of a WTO Member in case a QR has been privileged as a safeguard measure. Art. XIX GATT provides that, under certain circumstances, a WTO Member may be free 'to suspend the obligation in whole or in part or to withdraw or modify the concession.' Art. 7 SG provides that provisional safeguard measures should take the form of tariff increases. In principle, thus, WTO Members are free to choose any measure they deem appropriate be it a tariff, a QR, or even a tariff quota (TRQ).

Based on the notifications by WTO Members to the Safeguards Committee, it appears that *ad valorem* tariff increases are the most widely used safeguards instrument. Almost as popular are tariff quotas. Specific tariff increases are third in the ranking. Quantitative restrictions are a distant fourth only.[17]

What is also clear is that 'voluntary export restraints' (VERs) are now officially illegal under the SG Agreement: VERs in practice take the form of either a price increase (à la *Japan—Semiconductors*) or a cap on the volume of exports. Irrespective of their form, though, they are plainly illegal (Art. 11.2 SG).

> The phasing out of measures referred to in paragraph 1(b) shall be carried out according to timetables to be presented to the Committee on Safeguards by the Members concerned not later than 180 days after the date of entry into force of the WTO Agreement. These timetables shall provide for all measures referred to in paragraph 1 to be phased out or brought into conformity with this Agreement within a period not exceeding four years after the date of entry into force of the WTO Agreement, subject to not more than one specific measure per importing Member, the duration of which shall not extend beyond 31 December 1999.

Paragraph 1(b) explicitly refers to VERs. Here is how we were led to this provision: in literature one often comes across the idea that safeguards must be non-discriminatory. In fact, for many analysts it is this aspect of safeguards that makes them unattractive and has turned national bureaucracies towards active use of the antidumping mechanism. Yet, there is no mention of an obligation to impose safeguards on a non-discriminatory basis anywhere in the body of Art. XIX GATT. In contrast, there is no doubt that the Havana Charter (ITO) contained a similar requirement.[18] Probably because of this provision, practice initially

---

[17] WTO Doc. G/L/936 of 29 October 2010.
[18] Art. 40 of the Havana Charter; see GATT Doc. L/4679.

developed whereby safeguards would be imposed on non-discriminatory terms. Neither the EU nor the US liked the idea of non-discriminatory safeguards though: the notorious Leutwiler report[19] makes references to intense negotiations during the Tokyo round on this score, where the EU and the US tried in vain to persuade the rest of the membership to explicitly provide for country-specific safeguards.[20] In the absence of formal agreement, a practice parallel to (non-discriminatory) safeguards developed: some GATT contracting parties, upon request, would 'voluntarily' agree to limit their exports towards particular destinations.[21] The name VER is probably due to the fact that no formal treaty would be signed to this effect; VERs amounted to unilateral reductions of exports. Even when a consideration was paid for a VER, it was hardly ever observable.

The legality of VERs was never formally tested by a GATT Panel.[22] There were admittedly few, if any, incentives to mount a legal challenge against them: the requesting state would not normally attack a practice it had requested; and the country limiting its exports was, at the very least, adjusting itself to a comfortable second-best. Smith and Venables (1991) have demonstrated that, in the absence of an expectation of capturing the totality of a market, exporting countries that have agreed to a VER will raise the price of their exported goods to that of the competition and will pocket 'monopoly rents'.[23] This could be the outcome of a mere rise in the price of goods exported, or because exporters might have an incentive to 'trade up', that is, to move from low- to high-value goods and increase product differentiation. Empirical work suggests that it is consumers in the importing market that will be burdened with paying higher prices, and consumers have no standing before the WTO.[24] The absence of a formal condemnation notwithstanding, a series of good arguments could be advanced in support of the view that VERs violate Art. XI GATT (since they effectively amount to a quantitative restriction), assuming of course that they could be attributed to a government.

---

[19] A report prepared by experts at the request of the GATT named after the Chairman of the group; see Trade Policies for a Better Future: Proposals for Action, 'The Leutwiler Report', 1985, The GATT: Geneva, at pp. 42ff; see also Stewart et al. (1993) at pp. 1761ff.

[20] This issue is now settled: by virtue of Art. 2.2 SG, safeguards must be non-discriminatory. See also the Panel report on *Dominican Republic—Safeguard Measures* (§7.67).

[21] Sometimes referred to as voluntary restraint agreements (VRA), or even, orderly marketing arrangement (OMA).

[22] AB, *US—Wheat Gluten*, §98. In an effort to increase the probability of litigation, Mattoo and Mavroidis (1995) discuss the possibility of invoking EU competition laws to challenge the consistency of the VER on cars concluded between Japan and the EU. They conclude that, in all likelihood, Japanese producers could hide behind a *foreign sovereign compulsion* defence, with good prospects of thwarting a legal challenge against them: this defence is not the end of the road in EU antitrust litigation, for the EU judge could weigh the EU interest to be of higher importance than that of the foreign sovereign. This is not something that happens routinely though.

[23] The (safe) assumption here is that the country requesting the VER is less competitive and hence the price of its goods is higher than that of the goods of the country agreeing to limit its exports.

[24] Berry et al. (1999); Kostecki (1987); Hindley (1980).

During the Uruguay round, a number of exporting nations requested that the practice of VER be explicitly outlawed. Two provisions mark that their view won the day: indirectly, Art. 2.2 SG makes it legally impossible to have recourse to VERs nowadays, since:

> Safeguard measures shall be applied to a product being imported irrespective of its source.

More directly, Art. 11.1(b) SG explicitly outlaws recourse to VER. It reads:

> Furthermore, a Member shall not seek, take or maintain any voluntary export restraints, orderly marketing arrangements or any other similar measures on the export or the import side. These include actions taken by a single Member as well as actions under agreements, arrangements and understandings entered into by two or more Members. Any such measure in effect on the date of entry into force of the WTO Agreement shall be brought into conformity with this Agreement or phased out in accordance with paragraph 2.

A footnote to this provision reads:

> An import quota applied as a safeguard measure in conformity with the relevant provisions of GATT 1994 and this Agreement may, by mutual agreement, be administered by the exporting Member.

Consequently, a safeguard measure in the form of a QR, which is administered by the exporter, is lawful. Although similar QRs look like a VER, there are important differences between the two schemes:

(a) First, only QRs in conformity with the SG Agreement will, if at all, be administered by the exporter. VERs are not in conformity with the SG Agreement;

(b) Second, the term 'administered' could mean that the exporting country is simply entrusted with the duty to ensure that no more than the quantities unilaterally defined by the WTO Member taking the safeguard action will be exported; it does not necessarily mean that the rents will stay with the exporter. The rents could, theoretically at least, stay with the importer.

1.2.2 Who Can Impose Safeguard Measures?

A CU[25] may impose safeguard measures, either as a single unit or on behalf of one of its members. The AB has acknowledged this possibility in its report on *Argentina—Footwear (EC)* (§108). When a CU imposes a measure on behalf of one of its members, footnote 1 specifies that all the requirements for the determination of serious injury or threat thereof shall be based on the conditions existing in that member and the measure shall be limited to that member as well.

---

[25] Art. 2 SG, footnote 1. FTAs have no common external trade policy; hence, its members will continue to apply safeguards individually.

The question arises whether, when safeguards are imposed at the CU level on behalf of a single member of the CU, restrictions on imports from CU partners will be imposed as well. A parallel question is whether members of an FTA can include imports from their FTA partners when imposing safeguards. This question has been addressed in case law in instances involving safeguards imposed by Argentina (a member of MERCOSUR, a CU), and the US (a member of NAFTA, an FTA). Both Argentina and the US had excluded from the scope of their safeguards measures imports from the other CU/FTA partners. Before we proceed to the case law responses, recall that the last sentence of footnote 1 to the SG Agreement provides that:

> Nothing in this Agreement prejudges the interpretation of the relationship between Article XIX and paragraph 8 of Article XXIV of GATT 1994.

Both Argentina and the US had included in their examination of increased imports goods originating in their CU/FTA partners, correspondingly. In so doing, Argentina and the US were not allowed, in the AB's view, to subsequently exclude their PTA partners from the safeguard measure that they introduced. In other words, a parallelism between the origin of imports examined and the origin of countries against which safeguards are imposed must exist whenever safeguards are imposed (AB, *Argentina—Footwear (EC)*, §§ 112–13; AB, *US—Wheat Gluten*, §96). The AB underscored, however, that it did not want to prejudge the relationship between Art. XXIV.8 GATT and Art. XIX GATT through its case law. It stated in §114 of its report on *Argentina—Footwear (EC)*:

> we wish to underscore that, as the issue is not raised in this appeal, we make no ruling on whether, as a general principle, a member of a customs union can exclude other members of that customs union from the application of a safeguard measure.

It seems reasonable to assume under the circumstances though that, in situations where imports from PTA partners were part of the analysis regarding the increased imports requirement, safeguards against PTA partners can lawfully be imposed.[26] This may be concluded on the basis of the fact that in *US—Wheat Gluten*, *US—Line Pipe*, and *US—Steel Safeguards*,[27] the AB examined whether a reasoned and adequate explanation had been provided by the US IA, to the effect that imports other than those from NAFTA partners were causing serious injury to the domestic industry (*US—Line Pipe*, §188). The AB summarized its case law in its report on *US—Steel Safeguards* in the following manner (§§441–2):

> Thus, where, for purposes of applying a safeguard measure, a Member has conducted an investigation considering imports from all sources (that is, including any members

---

[26] This is why in Chapter 2 we held that the AB has de facto prejudged the question whether a member of a PTA can impose safeguards against its preferential partners, its pronouncements to the contrary notwithstanding; see also Grossman and Mavroidis (2007e).

[27] Grossman and Sykes (2007b).

of a free-trade area), that Member may not, subsequently, without any further analysis, exclude imports from free-trade area partners from the application of the resulting safeguard measure. As we stated in *US—Line Pipe*, if a Member were to do so, there would be a 'gap' between, on the one hand, imports covered by the investigation and, on the other hand, imports falling within the scope of the safeguard measure. In clarifying the obligations of WTO Members under the 'parallel' requirements of the first and second paragraphs of Article 2 of the *Agreement on Safeguards*, we explained in *US—Line Pipe* that such a 'gap' can be justified under the *Agreement on Safeguards* only if the Member establishes:

> ... 'explicitly' that imports from sources covered by the measure satisf[y] the conditions for the application of a safeguard measure, as set out in Article 2.1 and elaborated in Article 4.2 of the *Agreement on Safeguards*.

We further explained, in that same appeal, that, in order to fulfil this obligation in Article 2, 'establish[ing] explicitly' signifies that a competent authority must provide a 'reasoned and adequate explanation of how the facts support their determination', adding that '[t]o be explicit, a statement must express distinctly all that is meant; it must leave nothing merely implied or suggested; it must be clear and unambiguous. (italics in the original)

It follows that case law has in fact opened the door to the possibility of members of an FTA or a CU imposing safeguards against each other.

Irrespective whether safeguards have been imposed by an individual WTO Member, on behalf of an individual WTO Member by a CU, or at a CU level, two conditions must be cumulatively met for their lawful imposition (Art. 2 SG):

(a) A product must be imported in increased quantities;
(b) So as to cause serious injury to the domestic industry producing the like or directly competitive product.

Case law, as mentioned above, has added another condition: the increased imports have to be the result of unforeseen developments.[28]

The AB, in its report on *US—Line Pipe*, advanced a distinction between:

(a) The right to impose a safeguard; and
(b) The lawful application of a safeguard.

For a right to exist, a WTO Member must ensure that it has met all of the requirements mentioned above; for an application to be lawful, the safeguard measure may be applied only to the extent necessary to counteract the resulting damage (§§83–4):

> A WTO Member seeking to apply a safeguard measure will argue, correctly, that the right to apply such measures must be respected in order to maintain the domestic momentum and motivation for ongoing trade liberalization. In turn, a WTO

---

[28] This is the outcome of the cited AB report on *Argentina—Footwear (EC)*, where the AB held that the regulatory framework applicable to impositions of safeguards is not only the SG Agreement, but Art. XIX GATT as well. It is the latter provision that contains the 'unforeseen developments' requirement.

Member whose trade is affected by a safeguard measure will argue, correctly, that the application of such measures must be limited in order to maintain the multilateral integrity of ongoing trade concessions. The balance struck by the WTO Members in reconciling this natural tension relating to safeguard measures is found in the provisions of the *Agreement on Safeguards*.

This natural tension is likewise inherent in two basic inquiries that are conducted in interpreting the *Agreement on Safeguards*. These two basic inquiries are: first, is there a right to apply a safeguard measure? And, second, if so, has that right been exercised, through the application of such a measure, within the limits set out in the treaty? These two inquiries are separate and distinct. They must not be confused by the treaty interpreter. One necessarily precedes and leads to the other. First, the interpreter must inquire whether there is a right, under the circumstances of a particular case, to apply a safeguard measure. For this right to exist, the WTO Member in question must have determined, as required by Article 2.1 of the *Agreement on Safeguards* and pursuant to the provisions of Articles 3 and 4 of the *Agreement on Safeguards*, that a product is being imported into its territory in such increased quantities and under such conditions as to cause or threaten to cause serious injury to the domestic industry. Second, if this first inquiry leads to the conclusion that there is a right to apply a safeguard measure in that particular case, then the interpreter must next consider whether the Member has applied that safeguard measure 'only to the extent necessary to prevent or remedy serious injury and to facilitate adjustment', as required by Article 5.1, first sentence, of the *Agreement on Safeguards*. Thus, the right to apply a safeguard measure—even where it has been found to exist in a particular case and thus can be exercised—is not unlimited. Even when a Member has fulfilled the treaty requirements that establish the right to apply a safeguard measure in a particular case, it must do so only to the extent necessary . . . (italics in the original)

This distinction has been faithfully (indeed, sometimes verbatim) reproduced in subsequent case law. The lawful application of safeguards is regulated in Art. 5SG and we will be discussing it in detail *infra*.

1.2.3 Unforeseen Developments

The AB on *Argentina—Footwear (EC)* held that the legal basis for adding 'unforeseen developments' to the statutory requirements for lawfully imposing safeguards was provided by the letter of Art. 1 SG, which states that safeguard measures will be understood to be the measures provided for in Art. XIX GATT (§§83, 84, 93, and 94).[29]

The term 'unforeseen developments' has been the subject-matter of many discussions before adjudicating bodies, without, however, any one of them coming to a meaningful interpretation. Saggi (2010) has convincingly argued why a similar requirement, its definitional weaknesses notwithstanding, is needed in the SG Agreement: in his view, any time tariff concessions have been made, other things

---

[29] This is probably a legal error since the title of this provision makes it clear that it refers to the types of measures that can be used as safeguards. In contrast, Art. 2 SG, which discusses the conditions for lawful imposition, does not mention the 'unforeseen developments' requirement.

equal, the quantity of imports will increase. Hence, absent the 'unforeseen developments' requirement, WTO Members will be taking with one hand what they will be giving with the other, since they will (almost) always be in a position to satisfy the increased imports requirement. This argument is reinforced by an empirical paper authored by Crowley (2010), who concludes that those who undertook larger tariff reductions also undertook the highest number of SG investigations. So something more than increased imports is required. The 'unforeseen developments' requirement was meant to fill this gap, but has given rise to so much acrimony that one wonders whether the candle was worth the flame after all.

The GATT Panel on *Hatters' Fur Sales*, cited above, held that (p. 10):

> the term 'unforeseen development' should be interpreted to mean developments occurring after the negotiation of the relevant tariff concession which it would not be reasonable to expect that the negotiators of the country making the concession could and should have foreseen at the time when the concession was negotiated.

This report suggests that developments should be unforeseen at the time concessions were made, a point that has been confirmed in subsequent case law: both the Panel on *Argentina—Preserved Peaches* (§§7.26–8) and the Panel on *Dominican Republic—Safeguard Measures* (§7.130) adopted this approach.

This case really states that it is not so much the development that has to be unforeseen (in this case, the change in fashion), but rather the damaging effect on the domestic industry of such a change. This case related to the withdrawal of a concession by the US on women's fur hats and hat bodies. The members of the Working Party agreed that the fact that hat styles had changed did not constitute an unforeseen development within the meaning of Art. XIX GATT, but that the effects of this development (§12):

> particularly the degree to which the change in fashion affected the competitive situation, could not reasonably be expected to have been foreseen by the United States authorities in 1947, and that the condition of Article XIX that the increase in imports must be due to unforeseen developments and to the effect of the tariff concessions can therefore be considered to have been fulfilled.

In *Argentina—Footwear (EC)*, the AB considered unforeseen developments to be (§92): 'a circumstance which must be demonstrated as a matter of fact'. Case law confirms that what needs to be demonstrated is not merely the existence of unforeseen developments, but rather the existence of a logical link between the unforeseen developments and the resulting increase in imports for each of the products subject to the safeguard measure. This was clearly stated by the AB in its report on *US—Steel Safeguards* (§§318–19, 322). Unforeseen developments and increased imports are, nevertheless, two distinct matters, as was clearly stated in the Panel report on *Argentina—Preserved Peaches* (§§7.17–18).

In its report on *Korea—Dairy*, the AB held that 'unforeseen' should be read as synonymous with 'unexpected', as opposed to 'unpredictable', which would be synonymous with 'unforeseeable' (§84). So a distinction should be drawn between unforeseen and unforeseeable.

The AB, in its report on *US—Lamb*, saw a procedural requirement to the effect that an IA must explain in the order imposing safeguard measures how it has observed the unforeseen-developments requirement. Failure to demonstrate this is fatal (§§72–3). The Panel on *US—Steel Safeguards* held that, in case of a multi-stage review (in the present case the US IA first issued a report imposing safeguards, and then added its findings on unforeseen developments), there is no violation of WTO rules, if the IA adds its findings on unforeseen developments at a later stage, provided that such findings precede the application of the safeguard measure (§10.58).

The Panel on *Argentina—Preserved Peaches* found that demonstration of unforeseen developments required a reasoned explanation as to why such developments were unforeseen. In its words (§7.33):

> A mere phrase in a conclusion, without supporting analysis of the existence of unforeseen developments, is not a substitute for a demonstration of fact. The failure of the competent authorities to demonstrate that certain alleged developments were unforeseen in the foregoing section of their report is not cured by the concluding phrase.

The AB, in its report on *US—Steel Safeguards*, held that an IA must lay out a reasoned and adequate explanation supporting the view that a development was unforeseen (§279): it did not suffice that a WTO Member considered data which could be relevant; it must also explain how such data satisfied the unforeseen-developments requirement (§329). The Panel on *US—Steel Safeguards* concluded that, whether an explanation is sufficient and adequate will depend on the circumstances of the case (§10.115); in this case, the US IA had prepared a special report (referred to as the 'Second Supplementary Report' in the Panel report) which focused on unforeseen developments (§10.116). Still, the measure was judged to be WTO-inconsistent, since, in the eyes of the Panel, the IA had failed to provide a sufficient, adequate, and reasoned explanation linking the possible unforeseen developments to the specific increase in imports of the products covered by the measure (§10.122). The Panel found that the US IA had referred to a plausible set of circumstances concerned with the Asian and Russian financial crises at the end of the 1990s, and the strong US dollar and economy (§10.121). It had not examined the actual circumstances in the case at hand that could have given rise to unforeseen developments and this is why the US, in the Panel's view, had acted inconsistently with the requirements of the SG Agreement. Had the US managed, in other words, to connect increased imports in the US market to the financial crises abroad and the strong US dollar, it would have prevailed; it did not, and it lost. Still, because of this report, we know that financial crises abroad can, in principle, qualify as unforeseen developments.[30] In similar vein, the Panel in its report on *Dominican Republic—Safeguard Measures* (§§7.132–44) held that a mere assertion to the effect that imposition of safeguards was necessary because of the accession of China does not suffice to satisfy the unforeseen-developments requirement, which requests a reasoned explanation for why this has been the case.

The inescapable conclusion stemming from the discussion above is that case law has still some way to go before providing a response to the question what are unforeseen developments: we know it must be demonstrated, we also know that unforeseen should be distinguished from unforeseeable (assuming this distinction is of any functional use), and we know that an IA cannot refer to a mere plausible set of circumstances but rather to the actual situation that gave rise to the imposition of safeguards. Against this background, Sykes (2003a) questions whether this requirement should be maintained at all. As he explains, in light of the variables that might influence a potential trade outcome, it is simply impossible to reasonably request from a WTO Member to foresee events that will occur in the not immediate future. To make matters worse, it could, theoretically at least, be the case that the time span is quite long: what if a WTO Member did not make any bindings after the Kennedy or the Tokyo round? Should it still be held liable for not having foreseen events occurring 30 years later? Moreover, the capacity to foresee is highly endogenous since various administrative authorities have asymmetric endowments and capacities: what is unforeseen for some might not be for all. Saggi (2010) got it right when he argued that we need something more than tariff concessions to justify safeguards as a result of increased imports. The unforeseen-developments criterion has proved a stumbling block though, and one might legitimately wonder whether it would be more appropriate to replace it by an easier to use rule of thumb, even if a similar tool might be prone to occasional abuses. We will get back to this issue in Section 2 *infra*.

1.2.4 Increased Quantities of Imports

Art. 2.1 SG provides that, for safeguards to be imposed, a product must be imported in such increased quantities, absolute or relative to domestic production, as to cause serious injury.[31] Note the difference between the SG and the AD Agreements in this respect: in the safeguards context, increased imports constitute an independent condition for imposition of a measure, similar to a finding of

---

[30] The AB upheld; see §330 of its report.

[31] Economic theory suggests that imports per se can never be a cause of injury, for they represent the difference between consumption and domestic production at a given price level: imports thus, are a proximate and not the ultimate cause of injury. Sykes (2003a) has correctly criticized the SG Agreement for being economically naïve in this respect. One possible way to avoid this issue is to interpret the term increased imports as a pure procedural requirement, and also require IAs to investigate why imports have risen. Such an approach has been advanced by Grossman and Mavroidis (2007e). This understanding of the term has not been accepted in case law as we shall discover in our discussion of the increased-imports requirement.

dumping or subsidization in the AD context. Without an increase in imports, there can be no safeguard measure. In the AD context, the requirement to demonstrate increased (dumped) imports is not an independent condition, but rather forms part of the overall injury analysis. Recall also that, as Art. 3.2 AD clearly indicates, and as Panels and the AB have consistently emphasized, no one factor or group of factors can necessarily give decisive guidance. In short, AD measures may be imposed even in the absence of an increase in imports, something that can never happen in the SG context.

There are two additional, albeit less important, differences:

(a) The increase in imports in the SG context must be determined in absolute terms, or in terms of imports relative to production, rather than relative to production or consumption as is the case in the AD context;

(b) While the increase in imports in the SG context is not qualified as necessarily having to be significant (as in the AD context), the increase has to be of such a kind that it is capable of causing serious injury.

The term 'increased quantities' has been interpreted by the AB in many reports. In its report on *Argentina—Footwear (EC)*, it ruled that Panels should look at trends instead of isolated transactions or absolute numbers based on an end-point to end-point comparison (§129). It used the term 'trend', probably to denote an effort to collect information and attempt to spot a pattern.[32] In the same report, the AB emphasized that not just any increase over a period of time will do: for example, if *an increase* occurred early on in the presented data and was followed by a decrease, then the increased-imports requirement might not be satisfied; it is necessary for the competent authorities to focus on recent imports (§130). The AB held that trends of imports should be 'recent, sudden, sharp and significant' enough, both quantitatively and qualitatively, so as to cause serious injury (§131):

> We recall here our reasoning and conclusions above on the meaning of the phrase 'as a result of unforeseen developments' in Article XIX:1(a) of the GATT 1994. We concluded there that the increased quantities of imports should have been 'unforeseen' or 'unexpected'. We also believe that the phrase 'in such increased quantities' in Article 2.1 of the *Agreement on Safeguards* and Article XIX:1(a) of the GATT 1994 is meaningful to this determination. In our view, the determination of whether the requirement of imports 'in such increased quantities' is met is not a merely mathematical or technical determination. In other words, it is not enough for an investigation to show simply that imports of the product this year were more than last year— or five years ago. Again, and it bears repeating, not just *any* increased quantities of imports will suffice. There must be '*such* increased quantities' as to cause or threaten to cause serious injury to the domestic industry in order to fulfil this requirement for applying a safeguard measure. And this language in both Article 2.1 of the *Agreement*

---

[32] In statistics, trend analysis would be employed to detect behaviour that would otherwise be hidden by noise (irrelevant information) in a time series. This is probably not what the AB had in mind here.

on Safeguards and Article XIX:1(a) of the GATT 1994, we believe, requires that the increase in imports must have been recent enough, sudden enough, sharp enough, and significant enough, both quantitatively and qualitatively, to cause or threaten to cause 'serious injury'. (italics and emphasis in the original)

The AB in its report on *US—Steel Safeguards*, in an effort to underscore that trends matter, held that even a decrease at the end of the investigating period cannot detract from a finding that increased imports occurred if this is what the overall picture suggests (§367):

> We agree with the United States that Article 2.1 does not require that imports need to be increasing at the time of the determination. Rather, the plain meaning of the phrase 'is being imported in such increased quantities' suggests merely that imports must have increased, and that the relevant products continue 'being imported' in (such) increased quantities. We also do not believe that a decrease in imports at the end of the period of investigation would necessarily prevent an investigating authority from finding that, nevertheless, products continue to be imported 'in such increased quantities'.

According to the AB view expressed in the same report, what is important in such a case is the explanation to be provided by the IA as to why in the presence of a recent decrease in imports, the increased-imports condition has nevertheless been met (§§368, 370). The Panel on *Argentina—Preserved Peaches* was of the view that an overall *decrease* of imports (not examined in terms of the relative changes in domestic production) between the start and the end of the reference period implies that the increased-imports requirement is not satisfied, unless an adequate and reasoned explanation to the contrary has been provided to this effect (§§7.60–1). The Panel on *US—Steel Safeguards* held that an absolute increase in imports, provided that it is recent, sudden, sharp, and significant enough so as to cause injury, satisfies the requirements of Art. 2.1 SG, even if the increase has not been examined in relative terms (§10.234). This conclusion will not be disturbed by a finding that an increase in absolute terms has been accompanied by an equally strong, or stronger, increase in domestic production and a flourishing domestic industry, in which case there would be no relative increase, and there may not be any causation of serious injury (§10.234). Similarly, the Panel was of the view that (§10.218):

> as a legal matter, a decrease in absolute terms does not invalidate the sufficiency of a relative increase.

The Panel on *US—Steel Safeguards* understood 'sudden' to be synonymous with some sort of emergency and a complement to the unforeseen-developments requirement: together they underline the highly exceptional character of safeguards (§10.166). The same Panel provided in its report graphic illustrations of trends in imports that were considered to satisfy and not satisfy the requirements of Art. 2.1 SG. Figure 9.1 (reflected in §10.179 of the Panel report) and Figure 9.2 (§10.202) are instances where, in the Panel's view, the graphic representation of

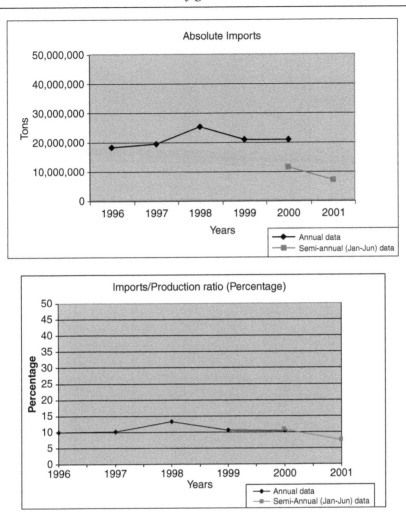

Figure 9.1 Instances in which, in the Panel's view, the graphic representation of imports does not satisfy the requirements of Art. 2.1 SG

imports does not satisfy the requirements of Art. 2.1 SG, essentially because the most recent events had not been taken into account (§§10.183, 10.209). Figure 9.3 (§10.212) and Figure 9.4 (§10.222) are instances where, in the Panel's view, the graphic representation does satisfy the requirements of Art. 2.1 SG.

The SG Agreement does not provide for the length of the investigation period, a fact noted by the Panel on *Argentina—Preserved Peaches* (§7.50). In the absence of legislative guidance, the AB has stepped in and provided some clarifications. In its report on *Argentina—Footwear (EC)*, it held that the investigation period should end not only in the recent past, but in the very recent past (§130). The Panel on *US—Line Pipe* concluded that a five-year period of investigation was justified (§7.201). In practice, the period of investigation for examining increased imports

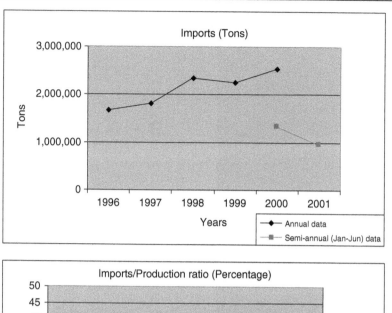

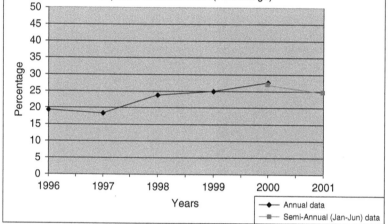

Figure 9.2 Instances in which, in the Panel's view, the graphic representation of imports does not satisfy the requirements of Art. 2.1 SG

tends to be the same as that for examining serious injury. This is different from the practice in a dumping or subsidization context, where the period of investigation for dumping or subsidization is generally shorter (normally one year) than the period for determining material injury (normally three years). The Panel on *US—Line Pipe* explained and justified this different practice in the safeguards context in the following manner (§7.209):

> We are of the view that one of the reasons behind this difference is that, as found by the Appellate Body in *Argentina—Footwear Safeguard*, 'the determination of whether the requirement of imports 'in such increased quantities' is met is not a merely mathematical or technical determination'. The Appellate Body noted that when it comes to a determination of increased imports 'the competent authorities are

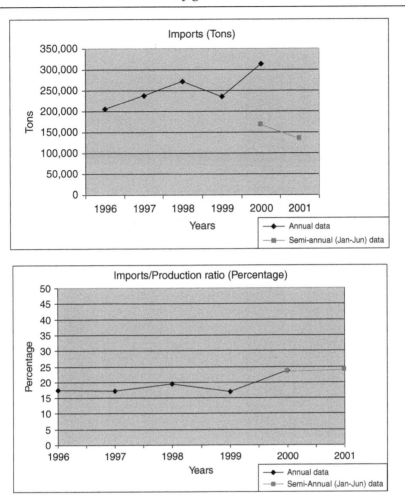

Figure 9.3 Instances in which, in the Panel's view, the graphic representation does satisfy the requirements of Art. 2.1 SG

required to consider the trends in imports over the period of investigation'. The evaluation of trends in imports, as with the evaluation of trends in the factors relevant for determination of serious injury to the domestic industry, can only be carried out over a period of time. Therefore, we conclude that the considerations that the Appellate Body has expressed with respect to the period relevant to an injury determination also apply to an increased imports determination. (italics in the original)

1.2.5 Injury to the Domestic Industry Producing the Like Product

The SG Agreement allows for the imposition of safeguard measures if a WTO Member has shown either serious injury or threat of (serious) injury. Serious injury is defined in Art. 4.1 SG as:

a significant overall impairment in the position of the domestic industry.

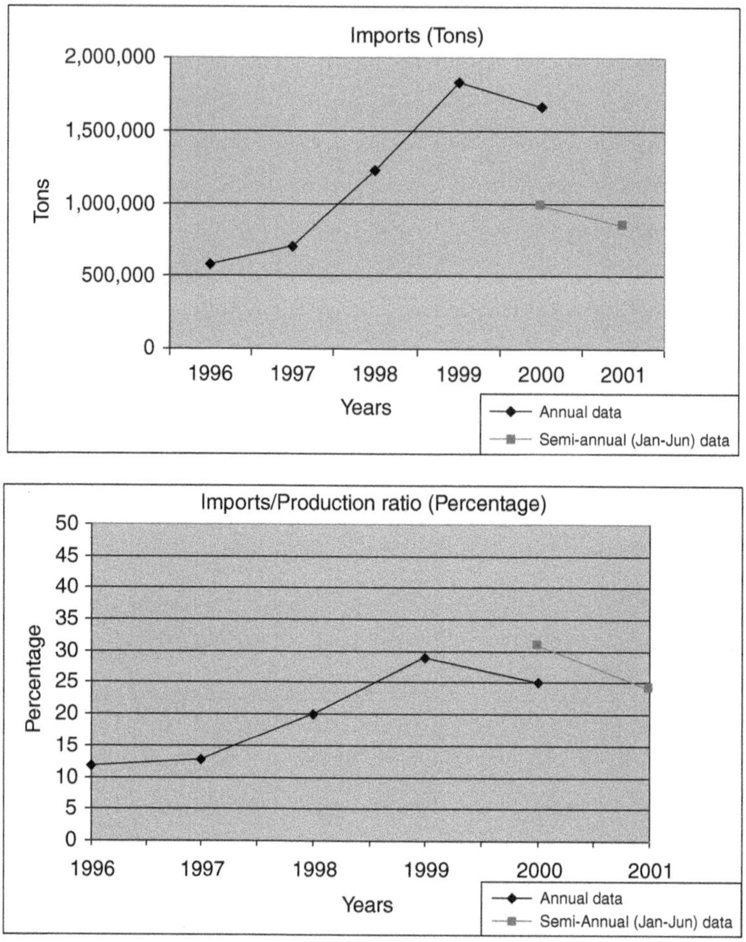

Figure 9.4 Instances in which, in the Panel's view, the graphic representation does satisfy the requirements of Art. 2.1 SG

The regulation of safeguards has triggered a lively debate on how to define the two key terms of 'injury' and 'causal relation'. Imposing a safeguard measure requires proving the existence of serious injury, rather than the weaker, prima facie, material-injury standard[33] required in antidumping investigations. This reading is probably warranted because safeguards are not a response to unfair trade, but rather provide a breather because of the (unexpected) failure of the domestic industry to face foreign competition, the causal link between import surge and injury. The higher statutory injury threshold has been perceived as requiring more

---

[33] We say 'weaker' because serious injury seems to be a more demanding standard than material injury. Recall that there is no definition of the term 'material injury' in the AD or the SCM context. It is all a matter of case law.

elaborate evaluation methods than the mere recourse to trends and descriptive data used in antidumping.[34]

The same provision (Art. 4.1 SG) states that threat of serious injury shall be understood to mean serious injury that is clearly imminent, adding that a determination of the existence of a threat shall be based on facts, and not merely on allegation, conjecture, or remote possibility (Art. 4.1(b) SG). The SG Agreement contains a definition of threat of serious injury:

> Threat of serious injury shall be understood to mean serious injury that is clearly imminent, in accordance with the provisions of paragraph 2. A determination of the existence of a threat of serious injury shall be based on facts and not merely on allegation, conjecture or remote possibility.

The AB, in its report on *US—Lamb*, provided its understanding of the terms 'injury' and 'threat of injury' and the difference between them in the following terms (§§124–5):

> The standard of 'serious injury' set forth in Article 4.1(a) is, on its face, very high. Indeed, in *United States—Wheat Gluten Safeguard*, we referred to this standard as 'exacting'. Further, in this respect, we note that the word 'injury' is qualified by the adjective 'serious', which, in our view, underscores the extent and degree of 'significant overall impairment' that the domestic industry must be suffering, or must be about to suffer, for the standard to be met. We are fortified in our view that the standard of 'serious injury' in the *Agreement on Safeguards* is a very high one when we contrast this standard with the standard of 'material injury' envisaged under the *Antidumping Agreement*, the *Agreement on Subsidies and Countervailing Measures* (the '*SCM Agreement*') and the GATT 1994. We believe that the word 'serious' connotes a much higher standard of injury than the word 'material'.
>
> Moreover, we submit that it accords with the object and purpose of the Agreement on Safeguards that the injury standard for the application of a safeguard measure should be higher than the injury standard for antidumping or countervailing measures, since, as we have observed previously:
>
> [t]he application of a safeguard measure does not depend upon 'unfair' trade actions, as is the case with antidumping or countervailing measures. Thus, the import restrictions that are imposed on products of exporting Members when a safeguard action is taken must be seen, as we have said, as extraordinary. And, when construing the prerequisites for taking such actions, their extraordinary nature must be taken into account.
>
> Returning now to the term 'threat of serious injury', we note that this term is concerned with 'serious injury' which has not yet occurred, but remains a future event whose actual materialization cannot, in fact, be assured with certainty. We note, too, that Article 4.1(b) builds on the definition of 'serious injury' by providing that, in order to constitute a 'threat', the serious injury must be 'clearly imminent'. The word 'imminent' relates to the moment in time when the 'threat' is likely to

---

[34] The original US regulations on safeguards (Section 201 of the 1974 Trade Act) specified that imports must be a more (or no less) important source of injury than any other factor for it to constitute a substantial cause: this standard required listing the potential sources of injury, separating them, and quantifying their respective impact before permitting trade relief.

materialize. The use of this word implies that the anticipated 'serious injury' must be on the very verge of occurring. Moreover, we see the word 'clearly', which qualifies the word 'imminent', as an indication that there must be a high degree of likelihood that the anticipated serious injury will materialize in the very near future. We also note that Article 4.1(b) provides that any determination of a threat of serious injury 'shall be based on facts and not merely on allegation, conjecture or remote possibility'. To us, the word 'clearly' relates also to the factual demonstration of the existence of the 'threat'. Thus, the phrase 'clearly imminent' indicates that, as a matter of fact, it must be manifest that the domestic industry is on the brink of suffering serious injury. (italics in the original)

So, 'serious' is a higher standard than 'material,' but, recall that there is no legislative definition of the term material injury. If at all, this passage suggests that the AB will require definitions of injury that are, at the very least, as rigorous as those that have passed the test of consistency with the AD Agreement. Panels have consistently examined whether an adequate, reasoned and reasonable explanation has been provided by the authorities for their findings of a significant overall impairment of the industry concerned. In *US–Lamb*, the AB highlighted the need to examine the adequacy of the IA's explanation and reasoning in light of some alternative plausible explanation of the facts (§106):

> Panels must, therefore, review whether the competent authorities' explanation fully addresses the nature, and, especially, the complexities, of the data, and responds to other plausible interpretations of that data. A panel must find, in particular, that an explanation is not reasoned, or is not adequate, if some alternative explanation of the facts is plausible, and if the competent authorities' explanation does not seem adequate in the light of that alternative explanation. Thus, in making an 'objective assessment' of a claim under Article 4.2(a), panels must be open to the possibility that the explanation given by the competent authorities is not reasoned or adequate.

What matters is hence that an IA examines whether on the basis of the evidence before it injury has been caused by imports and that the merits of this assessment are discussed in light of alternative hypotheses. In this vein, the Panel on *Argentina—Preserved Peaches* considered the temporal focus of the competent authorities' evaluation of the data in making their determination of a threat of serious injury, and inquired into whether the explanation was adequate in the light of any plausible alternative explanation of the facts (§7.104). The failure of the Argentine IA to discuss alternative explanations led to the condemnation of its practices (§§7.116–17).

To reach the conclusion whether injury has occurred, the SG Agreement requires from an IA to evaluate all relevant factors that it specifically mentions, namely (Art. 4.2(a) SG):

(a) The rate and amount of the increase in imports of the product concerned in absolute and relative terms;

(b) The share of the domestic market taken by increased imports;

(c) Changes in the level of sales;

(d) Production by the domestic industry;

(e) Its productivity;

(f) Its capacity utilization;

(g) Its profits and losses; and

(h) The situation regarding employment.

Note the absence of a sentence equivalent to that included in Art. 3.4 AD and Art. 15.4 SCM, to the effect that no single relevant factor can be accorded decisive importance in the SG context. The AB on *US—Lamb* held in similar vein that no decisive importance should be accorded to one factor, even if this factor is profits, which could be quite telling for the state of health of the domestic industry:

> [P]rofits are simply one of the relevant factors mentioned in Article 4.2(a) and to accord that factor decisive importance would be to disregard the other relevant factors . . .

Although it did acknowledge in the same report that:

> it will be a rare case, indeed, where the relevant factors as a whole indicate that there is a threat of serious injury, even though the 'majority of firms in the industry' is not facing declining profitability.[35]

Similar to the interpretation given by Panels and the AB with respect to the obligation to examine the 15 and 16 factors enumerated in Arts. 3.4 AD and 15.4 SCM Agreement respectively, the AB considered that an IA is required to always examine and evaluate, at the very least, these eight factors (§136). In addition, in the AB's view, Art. 4.2(a) SG requires an IA to evaluate all other objective and quantifiable factors that are relevant to the situation of the industry concerned (§136). The AB, in its report on *Argentina—Footwear (EC)*, emphasized that, in addition to a technical examination regarding the impact of all the listed factors and any other relevant factors, an IA must also examine the overall position of the domestic industry (§139). In marked difference to its jurisprudence in the AD and SCM contexts, the AB, in its report on *US—Wheat Gluten*, made it clear that an IA cannot remain passive and rely on the interested parties to raise a factor other than the eight listed factors as relevant (§§55–6):

> However, in our view, that does not mean that the competent authorities may limit their evaluation of 'all relevant factors', under Article 4.2(a) of the *Agreement on Safeguards*, to the factors which the interested parties have raised as relevant. The competent authorities must, in every case, carry out a full investigation to enable them to conduct a proper evaluation of all of the relevant factors expressly mentioned in Article 4.2(a) of the *Agreement on Safeguards*. Moreover, Article 4.2(a) requires the competent authorities—and not the interested parties—to evaluate fully the relevance, if any, of 'other factors'. If the competent authorities consider that a particular 'other factor' may be relevant to the situation of the domestic industry, under Article

---

[35] *US—Lamb*, footnote 99.

4.2(a), their duties of investigation and evaluation preclude them from remaining passive in the face of possible short-comings in the evidence submitted, and views expressed, by the interested parties. In such cases, where the competent authorities do not have sufficient information before them to evaluate the possible relevance of such an 'other factor', they must investigate fully that 'other factor', so that they can fulfil their obligations of evaluation under Article 4.2(a).

Thus, we disagree with the Panel's finding that the competent authorities need only examine 'other factors' which were 'clearly raised before them as relevant by the interested parties in the domestic investigation'. However, as is clear from the preceding paragraph of this Report, we also reject the European Communities' argument that the competent authorities have an open-ended and unlimited duty to investigate all available facts that might possibly be relevant. (italics in the original)

Whereas, in the AD/CVD context,[36] price analysis (in the sense of comparison of prices between imported and domestic goods) is required as part of the injury analysis, no similar requirement exists in the safeguards context. Instead, a more general evaluation of the conditions under which foreign goods are being imported is required. Indeed, price is not mentioned as a relevant factor among the list of factors appearing in Art. 4.2(a) SG. The Panel on *Korea—Dairy* explicitly rejected the argument that the requirement to conduct price analysis was implied by Art. 2.1 SG in order to establish that increased imports entered the country under such conditions as to cause serious injury (§§7.51–2). What exactly this means is difficult to decipher. Most likely, the Panel wanted to signal that if the final order imposing safeguards is reasonable overall, absence of price analysis will not detract from its solidity. While no price analysis is required for a safeguard to be imposed lawfully, this does not imply that price effects of the imports may be ignored altogether. The Panel on *US—Wheat Gluten* found that price may be a relevant factor that needs to be examined, and may even be quite important in a causation analysis as part of the conditions of competition (§8.109).

An IA invoking threat of injury is required to demonstrate that, absent safeguards, injury will happen imminently, that is, in the very near future. A demonstration that injury is clearly imminent must be based on facts and not merely on allegation, conjecture, or remote possibility (Art. 4.1(b) SG). The AB, in its report on *US—Lamb,* understood this requirement to mean that it must be manifest that the domestic industry is on the brink of suffering serious injury (§125):

...The word 'imminent' relates to the moment in time when the 'threat' is likely to materialize. The use of this word implies that the anticipated 'serious injury' must be on the very verge of occurring. Moreover, we see the word 'clearly', which qualifies the word 'imminent', as an indication that there must be a high degree of likelihood that the anticipated serious injury will materialize in the very near future. We also note that Article 4.1(b) provides that any determination of a threat of serious injury 'shall be based on facts and not merely on allegation, conjecture or remote

---

[36] See Art. 3 AD and Art. 15 SCM.

possibility'. To us, the word 'clearly' relates also to the factual demonstration of the existence of the 'threat'. Thus, the phrase 'clearly imminent' indicates that, as a matter of fact, it must be manifest that the domestic industry is on the brink of suffering serious injury.

The disciplines regarding demonstration of threat of injury have posed numerous interpretative issues. The Panel on *Argentina—Preserved Peaches* found that an IA must demonstrate at least a 'projection' that there is strong likelihood that injury will happen; otherwise, it will not have met the requirements of the SG Agreement with respect to the threat-of-serious-injury standard. The capacity of imports to cause serious injury, which the authorities found to exist, was not, in this Panel's view, enough (§7.122). In other words, serious injury must not simply be the possible consequence of increased imports; it must be the likely consequence. What is, consequently, required from an IA is to perform a fact-based assessment of the likelihood of imports increasing and a projection of what is about to occur.

There is, of course, an unavoidable tension between requesting a future-oriented study (similar to that required for threat of injury to be determined) and, at the same time, obliging the IA to come up with hard data, hence the established-likelihood standard. This is the reason why all that is requested from an IA is to provide adequate justification for its final findings. To do that, it should, in the AB's view (*US—Lamb*, §137) examine recent data, since:

> data relating to the most recent past will provide competent authorities with an essential, and, usually, the most reliable, basis for a determination of a threat of serious injury.[37]

As was emphasized by the AB, recent data should not be examined in isolation from the data for the entire period of investigation, but, rather, in its context (§§136–8).

The AB, in its report on *US—Line Pipe*, addressed the question whether an IA can, using the same set of facts, show serious injury or threat of serious injury. It was addressing a claim to the effect that a discrete finding of either injury or threat of injury was required for a lawful imposition of safeguard measures. The Panel had taken the view that a discrete finding was necessary, since, in its view, the same set of facts could not simultaneously support a finding of injury and a finding of threat of injury. Adopting a textual interpretation, the AB reversed the Panel in this respect and held that a discrete finding was not required by the Agreement. In doing so, the AB took the view that the threat-of-injury standard was a lower threshold than the serious-injury standard. What was important, in the AB's view, for the right to impose a safeguard measure to exist is that at least a

---

[37] As we emphasized before and worth repeating, the question regarding the type of data on which the threat of injury should be based must be dissociated from the standard of review of Panels dealing with similar issues: if on top of 'soft' data Panels adopt a deferential standard, then recourse to similar measures becomes too easy for investigating authorities around the world.

threat of injury be established (§§169–72). In its words, 'serious injury is the realization of threat of injury' (§169).

Injury or threat of injury must be suffered by the domestic industry producing the like product. Art. 4.1(c) SG provides that, in determining injury, a domestic industry shall be understood to mean the producers as a whole of the 'like or directly competitive products' operating within the territory of a member, or those whose collective output of the like or directly competitive products constitutes a major proportion of the total domestic production of those products. While the AD and SCM Agreements contain a definition of the term 'like product', the SG Agreement does not. The term 'directly competitive products' in the GATT context refers to a wider (than like) group of products. This term has not been interpreted in the context of a dispute concerning the SG Agreement. However, the AB did express its views on this term in a safeguards dispute in the context of the now defunct Agreement on Textiles and Clothing (ATC). *US—Cotton Yarn* concerned the conditions under which safeguards could be imposed. The AB found that two products were competitive if they were commercially interchangeable, or if they offered alternative ways of satisfying the same consumer demand. They do not actually have to be presently competing with one another for these two products to be competitive products. It is the capacity of products to compete in the same market which is important (§96). Because of the qualifier 'directly' appearing before the term 'competitive products', the AB was of the view that (§98):

> a safeguard action will not extend to protecting a domestic industry that produces unlike products which have only a remote or tenuous competitive relationship with the imported product.

A similar emphasis on consumer preferences, both actual and potential, as well as on substitutability, in the consideration of two products as directly competitive can be deduced from Art. III GATT.[38] The Panel on *US—Lamb* went so far as to state that (§7.117):

> This being said, it is clear on the face of the *Safeguards Agreement* that the product coverage of a safeguard investigation can potentially be broader than in an anti-dumping or countervail case, to the extent that 'directly competitive' products are involved. In our view, this apparent additional latitude that exists under the *Safeguards Agreement* may be related to the basic purpose of the *Safeguards Agreement* and GATT Article XIX, namely to provide an effective safety valve for industries that are suffering or are threatened with serious injury caused by increased imports in the wake of trade liberalization. (italics in the original)

The AB, in its report on *US—Cotton Yarn,* explained that the term 'domestic industry of the like or directly competitive product' should be interpreted in a

---

[38] In fact, the AB, in its report on *US—Cotton Yarn*, referred explicitly (§91) to its report on *Korea—Alcoholic Beverages*, which had been adjudicated under Art. III GATT.

product-oriented (as opposed to producer-oriented) manner. It thus expressed its preference for demand-side criteria and relegated the relevance of supply-side considerations (§86). In its report on *US—Lamb*, the AB confirmed this point (§94). The fact that there is a high degree of vertical integration between an input producer and a producer of the final like product is not relevant in defining the domestic industry producing the like product (AB, *US—Lamb*, §94). In this case, the US had argued that producers of the input (live lambs) may under certain circumstances be considered part of the domestic industry producing the final product (lamb meat) investigated. It had, accordingly, included in its safeguards investigation of imports of lamb meat not only the domestic producers of lamb meat (the breakers and packers) but also the growers and feeders of live lamb in the US. The US IA had considered that this approach was justified (§89). The AB, like the Panel before it (§§7.71–7, 7.118), in no unclear terms rejected this argument, concluding that it is not permitted to include input producers as part of the industry producing the like product under Art. 4.1(c) SG (§90). The AB, thus, concluded that, by expanding the scope of the domestic industry so as to include producers of other products, namely, live lambs, the USITC had defined its domestic industry inconsistently with Art. 4.1(c) SG: it should have limited it only to packers and breakers of lamb meat (§§95–6).

The Panel on *US—Steel Safeguards* held that the product definition must be such that it allows for the possibility to conduct a meaningful causation analysis. In this case, the US IA had relied on data that sometimes referred to the wider CCFRS (certain carbon flat rolled steel products) category, and sometimes not (§10.358). On its own admittance, reliance on combined data could sometimes involve double-counting. The improper product definition led the Panel to find that the US had acted inconsistently with its obligations to demonstrate causality under Art. 4.2(b) SG (§§10.416–17). In other words, if the product definition is too broad, no meaningful analysis of the conditions of competition is possible and the causation requirement cannot be met. More to the point, the Panel on *Argentina—Footwear* (*EC*) observed that in case of a broad definition (§8.261):[39]

> the statistics for the industry and the imports as a whole will only show averages, and therefore will not be able to provide sufficiently specific information on the locus of competition in the market.

Recall that the domestic industry covers the domestic producers as a whole or those whose collective output constitutes a major proportion of the total domestic product (Art. 4.1(c) SG). In *US—Lamb*, the AB held that the data used had to be sufficiently representative of the domestic industry so as to allow factually accurate determinations about that industry (§131). The AB has also held that it is not

---

[39] On this issue, see also the Panel report on *US—Steel Safeguards* at §10.378.

necessary for an IA to gather data from the whole of the industry producing the like or directly competitive product; it suffices that it has before it data from a statistically valid sample so that they are sufficiently representative to give a true picture of the particular domestic industry in question. Absent such data, the findings risk being found inconsistent with the SG Agreement (§132).

A determination that increased imports caused or are threatening to cause serious injury may only be made where the investigation demonstrates the existence of causal link between the increased imports and serious injury: Art 4.2(b) SG makes it clear that, when factors other than increased imports are causing injury to the domestic industry, injury not caused by increased imports shall not be attributed to them. There is an important body of WTO case law on this issue under the AD and SCM Agreements which contain very similar provisions and its relevance for the SG context has been explicitly acknowledged by the AB in its report on *US—Line Pipe* (§214). Recall that case law stands for the proposition that, under the non-attribution requirement, an IA must separate and distinguish the effects of increased imports from the effects that other factors might have had on the state of its domestic industry producing the like or directly competitive product. It is only after having complied with this requirement that the causal link between increased imports and injury can be established.

In its report on *US—Wheat Gluten*, the AB rejected the argument that an IA must establish that increased imports alone are the cause of serious injury (§79); rather, the obligation to impose safeguard measures so as to counteract only that part of injury caused by increased imports is, in the AB's view, an obligation resulting from Art. 5.1 SG which concerns the application of safeguards (and not the right, as such, to impose them). The AB has made clear that there is a logical/temporal sequence between the two sentences of Art. 4.2 SG, in the sense that one cannot reach the conclusion that serious injury has been caused by imports unless one has first complied with the non-attribution requirement. In its report on *US—Lamb*, the AB pertinently ruled to this effect (§180):

> the 'causal link' between increased imports and serious injury can only be made after the effects of increased imports have been properly assessed, and this assessment, in turn, follows the separation of the effects caused by all the different causal factors.[40]

Two questions arise with respect to the non-attribution requirement:

(a) How will separation occur? and
(b) What happens post-separation?

The first question was addressed by the AB in its report on *US—Lamb* (§181):

> We emphasize that the method and approach WTO Members choose to carry out in the process of separating the effects of the other causal factors is not specified by the

---

[40] See also the AB reports on *US—Wheat Gluten* at §70, and *US—Line Pipe* at §215.

Agreement on Safeguards. What the Agreement requires is simply that the obligation in Article 4.2 must be respected when a safeguard measure is applied. (italics in the original)

The Panel on *US—Steel Safeguards* observed that quantification of the portion of the injury caused by specific factors might on occasion be desirable (§10.336). The same Panel went on to consider that, in certain circumstances, quantification may even be necessary in order to establish non-attribution explicitly on the basis of a reasoned and adequate explanation without, however, explaining when this should be the case (§§10.340–2).

It follows that the methodology to separate the effects of various factors is not prejudged by the Agreement[41] and quantification of their impact might on (undefined) occasions be necessary.

Two Panels (*US—Wheat Gluten* and *US—Lamb*) discussed the second question, namely what should be done post-separation. They took the view that, once the effects of other factors had been separated and distinguished from the effects of the imports, an IA was required to determine that the imports, in and of themselves, were responsible for the serious injury. The AB, in its report on *US—Wheat Gluten*, summarized the Panel's approach in §66 and rejected it in §79. We quote:

> It seems to us that the Panel arrived at this interpretation through the following steps of reasoning: first, under the first sentence of Article 4.2(b), there must be a 'causal link' between increased imports and serious injury; second, the non-'attribution' language of the last sentence of Article 4.2(b) means that the effects caused by increased imports must be distinguished from the effects caused by other factors; third, the effects caused by other factors must, therefore, be excluded totally from the determination of serious injury so as to ensure that these effects are not 'attributed' to the increased imports; fourth, the effects caused by increased imports alone, excluding the effects caused by other factors, must, therefore, be capable of causing serious injury.
>
> . . .
>
> For these reasons, we agree with the first and second steps we identified in the Panel's reasoning; however, we see no support in the text of the *Agreement on Safeguards* for the third and fourth steps of the Panel's reasoning. (italics in the original)

All this might seem quite complicated, especially since the AB has left unresolved the question whether imports, post-separation, must in and of themselves cause serious injury. It seems, though, that the need to provide an adequate and reasoned explanation as to the impact of other factors on the state of the domestic industry emerges as the prime obligation of the IA. The AB held as much, in its report on

---

[41] Although the methodology is not prejudged by legislative fiat, it is difficult to see how separation can happen without recourse to economics. We briefly discuss at the end of this section how regression simulation and, discussed in some detail, the decomposition approach can help in this respect, referring to the work of Kelly (1988), Irwin (2003), and Grossman (1986).

US—Line Pipe (§217). In this vein, in *US—Wheat Gluten*, the AB found that the US had failed to respect Art. 4.2(b) SG by not properly accounting for the increased (US) industry capacity, as the data revealed that this factor may have played a very important role in the deteriorating state of the industry (§89). According to the AB, the US IA had not adequately evaluated the complexities of this issue, in particular, whether the increases in average capacity during the investigative period were causing injury to the domestic industry simultaneously with increased imports (§§90–1). Similarly, in *US—Lamb*, the AB was of the view that, in the absence of any meaningful explanation of the nature and extent of the injurious effect of other factors, the US IA had failed to ensure that it had not attributed to increased imports injury which had actually been caused by other factors (§186). A failure to provide a reasoned and adequate explanation demonstrating that a causal link existed between increased imports and serious injury was also the basis for the Panel finding in *US—Steel Safeguards* (§§10.418ff) that the US order imposing safeguards on nine product categories was inconsistent with Art. 4.2(b) SG.

So imports must not be in and of themselves the sole cause for injury and what matters is whether a reasoned statement concerning causality has been provided by the IA. Nevertheless, a causal link between imports and serious injury must anyway be established post-separation. In §68 of its report on *US—Wheat Gluten*, the AB took the view that a causal link referred to a relationship of cause and effect, such that increased imports contributed to bringing about, producing, or inducing the serious injury (§68). It went on to state that a genuine and substantial relationship between cause and effect must exist for the causality requirement to be met (§69):

> Article 4.2(b) presupposes, therefore, as a first step in the competent authorities' examination of causation, that the injurious effects caused to the domestic industry by increased imports *are distinguished from* the injurious effects caused by other factors. The competent authorities can then, as a second step in their examination, attribute to increased imports, on the one hand, and, by implication, to other relevant factors, on the other hand, 'injury' caused by all of these different factors, including increased imports. Through this two stage process, the competent authorities comply with Article 4.2(b) by ensuring that any injury to the domestic industry that was *actually* caused by factors other than increased imports is not 'attributed' to increased imports and is, therefore, not treated as if it were injury caused by increased imports, when it is not. In this way, the competent authorities determine, as a final step, whether 'the causal link' exists between increased imports and serious injury, and whether this causal link involves a genuine and substantial relationship of cause and effect between these two elements, as required by the *Agreement on Safeguards*. (italics and emphasis in the original)

The US domestic legislation has espoused the substantial-cause standard,[42] the consistency of which with the WTO has been tangentially only discussed in case

---

[42] The decision of 23 December 1977 (97–1077) by the US Court of Appeals for the Federal Circuit (CAFC) re: *Gerald Metals Inc.* described as follows the substantial-cause standard which is reflected in US statutes: '... the statute requires the injury to occur "by reason of" the LTFV (less

law so far. The US causation analysis in all cases challenged so far has been found to be WTO-inconsistent. In addition, certain statements by the AB and the Panel in their respective reports on *US—Lamb* and *US—Line Pipe* suggest that, if challenged as such, the substantial-cause standard will be found wanting. In *US—Lamb*, the AB observed (§184):

> Although an examination of the relative causal importance of the different causal factors may satisfy the requirements of United States law, such an examination does not, for that reason, satisfy the requirements of the Agreement on Safeguards.

In its report on *US—Line Pipe*, the Panel reached the following conclusion (§7.289):

> We do not consider that such an analysis allows an investigating authority to determine whether there is 'a genuine and substantial relationship of cause and effect' between the serious injury and the increased imports.

But what does an authority need to do in order to establish a genuine and substantial relationship? In its report on *Argentina—Footwear (EC)*, the AB agreed with the following analysis by the Panel, as to what was required to comply with the causation requirement of Article 4.2(b) SG (§145):

> ... we will consider whether Argentina's causation analysis meets these requirements on the basis of (i) whether an upward trend in imports coincides with downward trends in the injury factors, and if not, whether a reasoned explanation is provided as to why nevertheless the data show causation; (ii) whether the conditions of competition in the Argentine footwear market between imported and domestic footwear as analysed demonstrate, on the basis of objective evidence, a causal link of the imports to any injury; and (iii) whether other relevant factors have been analysed and whether it is established that injury caused by factors other than imports has not been attributed to imports.

In other words, in the AB's view, a causation analysis involves a three-step analysis of:

(a) Correlation in trends;
(b) The conditions of competition between the imports and domestic like products, and
(c) The effects of other factors on the domestic industry.

---

than fair value) imports. This language does not suggest that an importer of LTFV imports goods can escape countervailing duties by finding some tangential or minor cause unrelated to the LTFV goods that contributed to the harmful effects on domestic market prices. By the same token, this language does not suggest that the Government satisfies its burden of proof by showing that the LTFV goods themselves contributed only minimally or tangentially to the material harm .... Hence, the statute requires adequate evidence to show that the harm occurred "by reason of" the LTFV imports, not by reason of a minimal or tangential contribution to material harm caused by LTFV goods.' (pp. 9–10 of the decision: LTFV stands for 'less than fair value').

Correlation is not causality, but absence of correlation could be fatal to causality analysis: in its report on *Argentina—Footwear* (*EC*), the AB referred with approval to the following statement by the Panel establishing a negative presumption in case of an absence of correlation (§144):

> While such a coincidence [between an increase in imports and a decline in the relevant injury factors] by itself cannot prove causation (because, inter alia, Article 3 requires an explanation—i.e., 'findings and reasoned conclusions'), its absence would create serious doubts as to the existence of a causal link, and would require a very compelling analysis of why causation still is present.

In this vein, the Panel on *US—Steel Safeguards* distinguishes between instances where there is coincidence between increased imports and injury, and instances where this has not been the case: the Panel accepts, in this latter context, that there may be a time lag between the increase in imports and the manifestation of their effects on the domestic industry (§10.310). The Panel was, however, of the view that there are temporal limits to the extent of this time lag, depending on the industry (§10.312):

> Generally speaking, the more rigid the market structure associated with a particular industry, the more likely a lag in effects would exist, at least in relation to some factors. Conversely, the more competitive the market structure, the less tenable it is that lagged effects could be expected.

The same Panel considered that an additional explanation from the IA was required when there was no time coincidence between increased imports and injury (§10.303). The Panel on *Argentina—Footwear* (*EC*) held that, in addition to a trends/correlation analysis, a causation analysis required an examination of the conditions of competition between the imported products and the like or directly competitive products (§8.250). While this may imply a price analysis, this was not necessarily so, in this Panel's view, as much depended on the product in question (§8.251):

> We note in this regard that there are different ways in which products can compete. Sales price clearly is one of these, but it is certainly not the only one, and indeed may be irrelevant or only marginally relevant in any given case. Other bases on which products may compete include physical characteristics (e.g., technical standards or other performance-related aspects, appearance, style or fashion), quality, service, delivery, technological developments consumer tastes, and other supply and demand factors in the market. In any given case, other factors that affect the conditions of competition between the imported and domestic products may be relevant as well. It is these sorts of factors that must be analysed on the basis of objective evidence in a causation analysis to establish the effect of the imports on the domestic industry.[43]

To conclude, assuming that an investigating authority has:

---

[43] Note, however, that the Panel on *US—Steel Safeguards* considered that price was an important, if not the most important, factor when analysing conditions of competition (§10.320).

(a) Examined all relevant factors that might be causing injury;

(b) Separated and distinguished the effects caused by increased imports from those caused by other factors; and

(c) Has found that there exists a causal link between increased imports and serious injury or threat thereof,

it has complied with its substantive obligations under the causality requirement, and can lawfully impose safeguards.

We mentioned above *en passant* that case law does not impose a particular methodology that must be used in order to separate effects from various factors affecting simultaneously the domestic industry. Yet, it seems that recourse to economic analysis is necessary here, since this is the only field that provides for a separation methodology. Economic analysis provides two broad frameworks, making it possible to assess injury with some rigour, and to give a precise operational meaning to the causality condition. Regression simulation, first, is a demanding (data-wise) method trying to attribute imports to particular causes: the IA will be asking whether the state of domestic industry (dependent variable) has been affected by a series of factors (independent variable) and by changing the independent variable each time it proceeds to investigate the cause, while controlling for factors that may be influencing both variables simultaneously.[44]

The 'decomposition' approach seems to be the most in tune with the safeguard instrument because it focuses on quantities—be it the surge of imports or the higher threshold of injury, which can be first expressed in terms of declining domestic production.[45] It is based on the three basic components (curves) which define an open market, namely: domestic demand, domestic supply, and foreign supply (imports). Any equilibrium in this market is jointly determined by these three components, and this equilibrium can be disturbed by shifts in one or two of these components, or in all of them. It is useful to assume, first, that only one of the three components is shifting at a given time. In this case, the resulting equilibrium change is easy to derive. For instance, a shift in foreign supply, mirroring, say, more efficient foreign producers (one leaves aside the debate about whether this increased efficiency should be seen as an unforeseen event, or not), reduces the domestic price in the importing country. In turn, this lower price increases domestic consumption and reduces domestic production, and these two changes generate larger imports. In this first scenario, injury has occurred (domestic production has decreased) and its cause is clearly the increased efficiency of the foreign suppliers. Let us now examine a second scenario consisting in an increase in domestic demand. If domestic and foreign supply are unchanged (once again, one component shifts at a given time), the domestic price increases, triggering an increase in imports and domestic production. This second scenario

---

[44] Grossman (1986).
[45] See Kelly (1988) and Irwin (2003).

describes a prima-facie, no-injury situation, since domestic production increases, even though domestic petitioners may argue that they do not get all the benefits of the increased domestic demand since imports also increase. A third scenario consists in examining the case of a decline in domestic demand, with (now) unchanged domestic and foreign supply. Such a decline reduces the domestic price, hence domestic production—an injury situation. But imports cannot be seen as a source of injury because the decline of the domestic price also reduces foreign supply (imports). All these scenarios, with only one of the three market components shifting at a time, lead to relatively straightforward conclusions about the existence (or not) of injury, and the causal relation between injury and imports.

Reaching such clear assessments becomes much more complex when all three components are shifting simultaneously; unfortunately, this is what often happens in the real world. In this situation, there is a need to isolate the impact of the various shifts and to have a quantitative breakdown of their relative importance. To achieve these goals, the decomposition approach establishes four relations (equations):

(a) The demand relation that domestic demand is a decreasing function of the price;

(b) The production relation that domestic supply is an increasing function of the price;

(c) The import relation that foreign supply is an increasing function of the price,

(d) The fourth relation imposes the condition that the market should be cleared by stating that domestic demand is equal to the sum of domestic and foreign supply.

Simple calculations based on these four relations allow us to express (decompose) any change in domestic supply, as the combined result of three independent changes (in demand, supply, and importation) weighted by the appropriate price elasticities of demand, supply, and importation (Irwin 2003). Such a quantitative decomposition of the observed change in domestic production into three distinguishable changes (related to demand, importation, and production) provides an answer to the legal question of whether imports constitute a substantial cause to the observed injury or not. For instance, the fact that the import change is negative, and of (at least) the same magnitude as the production change, is evidence that imports may be a substantial cause of the domestic injury. This simple decomposition method has a crucial advantage from an operational point of view: it does not impose heavy requirements in terms of data; data about the pre-shock and post-shock market equilibria are provided by the investigation itself, and estimates of elasticities can be drawn from available sources. That said, this method has its limits: the most important one is that it does not show much more than can be seen from the quantity and price trends, since the decomposition calculations are fundamentally based on the observed values of the prices and quantities. Another limit is that the decomposition approach makes use of elasticities, which are rarely specifically estimated for the case examined and, hence, represent some risk of errors.

1.2.6 Provisional Safeguards

Provisional measures can be imposed in accordance with Art. 6 SG:

(a) In cases where delay would cause damage difficult to repair;
(b) A preliminary determination has been made to the effect that there is clear evidence that increased imports have caused, or are threatening to cause, serious injury;
(c) For a period of no more than 200 days; and
(d) In the form of tariff increases.

The period of application of provisional safeguard measures shall be counted as part of the period of application of the final measures. Unlike the AD/CVD context, the SG Agreement does not contain any minimum period of time between initiation of the investigation and imposition of provisional measures.

1.2.7 Application of Definitive Safeguards

Application of safeguards comports two distinct issues: how much of the injury can be addressed through safeguards? Against whom can safeguards be lawfully imposed? Art. 5.1 SG requires from WTO Members to:

> apply safeguard measures only to the extent necessary to prevent or remedy serious injury and to facilitate adjustment.

In its report on *US—Line Pipe*, the AB held that, by virtue of this provision, an IA, following separation of the effects caused by imports from those caused by other factors, can apply the safeguard only up to the level necessary to address the part of injury caused by increased imports. Assume, for example, that it can be shown that increased imports account for 20 per cent of the total injury suffered, a WTO Member, by virtue of Art. 5.1 SG, can impose safeguards to counteract the 20 per cent and not the total amount of injury suffered. The facts in *US—Line Pipe* were as follows: when imposing safeguards, the USITC had identified six factors, other than increased imports, as possible causes contributing to serious injury. The USITC further found that one of the six factors, namely, declining demand in the oil and gas sector, had actually contributed to serious injury. However, since increased imports had a greater impact on injury than this factor, the USITC, in application of the substantial-cause standard, imposed safeguards to counteract all of the injury caused to the US domestic industry (AB, *US—Line Pipe*, §§203, 207). This USITC determination was judged inconsistent with the US's obligation under Art 5.1 SG. In reaching this conclusion, the AB began by explaining that its prior rulings on the obligation to separate the effects of various factors simultaneously causing injury were pertinent only to address the issue whether a right to impose a safeguard exists (§§242–3). The AB then went on to explain why, post-separation, a WTO Member must apply safeguards only to the extent necessary to remedy the part of injury caused by increased imports; that is, separation of effects also in a way serves to highlight the ceiling that safeguards cannot violate.[46] In its view, textual reasons (the wording of Art. 5.1 SG), contextual reasons (the wording of other SG provisions closely related to the subject-matter of Art. 5.1 SG), as well as the object and purpose of the SG Agreement supported this view (§§249–50, 252, 257–8). The AB thus concluded that Art. 5.1 SG required WTO Members to impose safeguards only to the extent necessary to counteract injury caused by increased imports (§260). Yet, absent quantification of the contribution to injury, it will be hard to imagine how the necessity requirement will be respected in practice.

Recall that safeguards must now be imposed on a non-discriminatory basis (Art. 2.2 SG). Recall also our discussion regarding VERs *supra* and the wish of framers to outlaw discriminatory safeguards. VERs are outlawed, but, unless we are in a scenario similar to that encountered in *Japan—Semiconductors* (where the importing country had an interest in importing cheap and some transparency surrounds the VER), it is difficult to imagine how a VER can be litigated. In other words, outlawing a VER does not necessarily lead to their extermination since the incentives to conclude similar schemes have not been addressed in the SG Agreement. The only exception to this statement is the provision for *quota modulation* provided for in Art. 5.2(b) SG. To understand how quota modulation works a short detour into the overarching discipline embedded in Art. 5 SG is necessary. Art. 5.1 SG deals with safeguards in the form of QRs and reads:

> such a measure shall not reduce the quantity of imports below the level of a recent period which shall be the average of imports in the last three representative years for which statistics are available, unless clear justification is given that a different level is necessary to prevent or remedy serious injury.

If imports increased during the last three years from say 100, to 150 in year two, to 200 tons in year three, at least 150 tons should be allowed to enter the country after imposition of a safeguard. There is of course a question about the meaning of the term 'representative'; it could be argued that, in the case of a sudden and sharp increase in imports in the last year of the period of investigation, this last year was not representative of normal import volumes, but rather the result of some unforeseen developments. Excluding this last year from the representative period would of course entail serious implications for the minimum amount of allowable imports. Restricting imports by imposing a QR which lowers the amount of imports to below the average of the last three representative years (in our example, anything below 150 tons) is possible if justification is given that such a different

---

[46] One can, of course, only wonder how this can happen without quantification of the contribution of at least increased imports in the total injury suffered. Recall that case law has so far held that quantification is not necessary.

level is necessary to prevent or remedy serious injury (Art. 5.1 SG). The need for justification in this particular situation led the AB to conclude, in its reports on *Korea—Dairy* (§§99, 103) and *US—Line Pipe* (§234), that in all other situations (that is, cases where the safeguard measures do not take the form of QRs, or in the case of QRs, respect the average-level requirement), there is no need for an authority to provide an explanation of why the level of the measure is actually necessary to prevent or remedy serious injury (§99). So, while there is a substantive obligation to ensure compliance with the necessity requirement, there is no procedural obligation to demonstrate that compliance has indeed occurred. The AB underscored this point in its report on *US—Line Pipe* (§234). In the same report, the AB added that a justification of the measure, while not required as such, would in any case be the incidental effect of the required reasoned and adequate explanation of causal-link analysis under Art. 3.1 SG and Art. 4.2(b) SG (§236).

When safeguard measures are imposed in the form of QRs, they shall, by virtue of Art. 5.2 SG, be allocated to supplying WTO Members by reference to their share in the import market during a previous representative period. Article 5.2(a) SG does not specify the representative period. Case law has not discussed this point either. Consequently, when a quota is privileged, trade within the quota will not be conducted on an MFN basis, but in respect of historic market shares, as is the case under Art. XIII GATT.

Moreover, WTO Members can depart from the obligation to respect historic market shares in their import market and target the relatively more efficient sources of supply (the 'mavericks'), by allocating to them quotas which are less than their historic market share. They can, thus, target those WTO Members which have increased their market share more rapidly: this is what 'quota modulation' under 5.2(b) SG amounts to. According to this provision, quota modulation can take place where a clear demonstration has been given to the Committee on Safeguards that:

(a) Imports from certain WTO Members have increased in disproportionate percentage in relation to the total increase of imports of the product concerned during the representative period;
(b) The reasons for the departure from the historic patterns have been justified; and
(c) The conditions of such departure are equitable to all suppliers of the product concerned.

The duration of any such measure shall not extend beyond the initial period of four years. Such targeted safeguard measures may only be used in case of a finding of current serious injury and not in the case of a threat of serious injury. It is noteworthy that the SG Agreement does not provide that the Committee has to authorize such a departure from historical patterns; it must merely be informed.

The obligations discussed above only apply in cases where the safeguard measure takes the form of a QR. They do not apply in case a safeguard measure takes the form of tariff increases. In its report on *US—Line Pipe*, the Panel rejected the argument by Korea that tariff quotas are a form of quota/quantitative restriction and could thus benefit from this regime (§7.69).

Art. 9.1 SG requests from WTO Members not to apply safeguard measures against imports originating in developing countries if their share does not exceed 3 per cent of the import market, provided that collectively developing countries do not account for 9 per cent of the import market. The Panel report on *Dominican Republic—Safeguard Measures* held that this obligation in fact reflects an obligation not to discriminate (§§7.398–402): the WTO Member imposing safeguards must exclude from imposition all developing countries which meet the statutory requirements. The decision by the Dominican Republic not to exclude Thailand allegedly because it had not exported to it at all in 2009 was inconsistent with this obligation since other WTO Members that also had not exported to it during the same calendar year (e.g. Panama) had nonetheless been excluded.

1.2.8 The Duration of Safeguards

A safeguard measure can be imposed for an initial period of up to four years (Art. 7.1 SG). It can be extended for a maximum four years more if it has been determined that:

(a) The safeguard measure continues to be necessary to prevent or remedy serious injury; and
(b) There is evidence that the industry is adjusting.

Such an extended measure may not be more restrictive than it was at the end of the initial period (Art. 7.4 SG *in fine*). Eight years is the maximum period for a safeguard measure (Art. 7.3 SG), an exception being made for developing countries: a safeguard measure imposed by a developing country is allowed to stay in place for a maximum period of ten years (Art. 9.2 SG). During this time, the measure must be progressively liberalized at regular intervals, unless the measure has been imposed for a period not exceeding one year (Art. 7.4 SG). The SG Agreement provides for a mandatory review of any safeguard measure which has been in place for more than three years, at the latest before the mid-term of this measure. If appropriate, the measure is to be withdrawn or the pace of liberalization increased.

The imposition of a safeguard measure must be followed by no imposition of safeguards in the same product market for an equal time period; this is the 'dynamic use constraint' imposed by Art. 7.5 SG. For example, if country A takes safeguard action in the area of cars for eight years, it has to desist from a safeguard action with respect to cars for the eight years following the expiry of the original safeguard measure. This period is halved for developing countries (Art. 9.2 SG). This grace period shall in any case not be shorter than two years, even if the measure itself was applied for a shorter period of time, except in the case of very short safeguard measures of less than six months (up to 180 days), provided the conditions in Art 7.6 SG have been met. Bagwell and Staiger (2005) note that, because of the dynamic use constraint imposed in the SG Agreement, WTO Members will have an incentive to strategically choose the sectors where they will take protective action. This point is well taken and very true in a world where safeguards are the only way to protect a market. In practice, however, it could be the case that a WTO Member sequences the imposition of safeguards by an imposition of AD duties in the same market.

One might find it counter-intuitive that safeguard measures will be imposed for a period longer than three years given that after this time period compensation must be offered, as we discuss immediately *infra*. However, earlier notifications of safeguard measures to the Safeguards Committee reveal that, in fact, a large number of safeguard measures are imposed for a period exceeding three years.[47]

1.2.9 Compensation

Art. 8 SG provides that, before imposing safeguard measures, WTO Members must enter into negotiations with the affected Members, the object of which is to compensate them for damage suffered as a result of the imposition of safeguards (Art. 8.1 SG). Assuming that there is no agreement within 30 days, the affected Member(s) can withdraw substantially equivalent concessions or other obligations, unless the Council for Trade in Goods (CTG) disapproves of such action; withdrawal should occur at the latest 90 days following imposition of the safeguard, and the CTG should be given at least 30 days to react (Art. 8.2 SG). It is highly unlikely that the CTG would disapprove such action, since the affected WTO Member(s) would likely block a consensus to this effect.

The term 'affected parties', appearing in Art. 8.1 SG, is not specified any further in the SG Agreement. There is, however, a link between Art. 8.1 SG and Art. 12.3 SG, which refers to consultations with those WTO Members having a substantial interest as exporters of the product concerned: the Panel (§8.206) and the AB report (§ 146) on *US—Wheat Gluten* explicitly referred to the link between these two provisions. In light of their approach on this issue, it seems safe to conclude that the term 'affected parties' should cover the WTO Members having a substantial interest as exporters of the product. Consequently, only a subset of the WTO Membership will be entitled to suspend concessions in case of disagreement as to the adequate means of trade compensation to be paid.[48]

The obligation to compensate can be avoided if a WTO Member proposes a safeguard action, the maximum duration of which will not exceed three years, if two conditions have been met (Art. 8.3 SG):

---

[47] See, for example, WTO Docs. G/SG/N/8/EEC/2, G/SG/N/10/EEC/2, and G/SG/N/11/EEC/2/Suppl. 1 of 16 March 2004.

[48] Although the term 'substantial interest' is not defined any further, one could plausibly make arguments to the effect that it should be constructed in a manner consistent with the term 'principal supplying interest' appearing in Art. XXVIII GATT.

(a) The measure has been taken as a result of an absolute increase in imports; *and*
(b) The measure was taken in conformity with the provisions of the SG Agreement.

The question is, of course, who determines whether the measure conforms with the provisions of the SG Agreement? The law does not explicitly decide this issue. In *US—Steel Safeguards*, the EU first published a list of products on which additional duties were going to be levied as of the third birthday of the US safeguard measure, or the fifth day following the date of a decision by the WTO DSB that the measure is incompatible with the WTO Agreement, if that is earlier.[49] In this case, the US repealed the steel safeguard shortly after the AB had issued its report, and even before the DSB had had a chance to adopt the report. The EU countermeasures announced were abandoned shortly thereafter.

1.2.10 Special Safeguard Regime with Respect to China

The accession of China to the WTO introduced a special country-specific safeguards regime for imports of Chinese products. Three types of 'safeguards' measures may be imposed on products from China:[50]

(a) A normal MFN safeguard measure taken under the SG Agreement (an ordinary safeguard). The rules of the SG Agreement apply;
(b) A special China-specific transitional safeguard measure (a transitional safeguard). The provisions governing such a transitional safeguard are set forth in China's Accession Protocol[51] and the Report of the Working Party on the Accession of China;[52]
(c) A textile safeguard measure specific to textile products from China (a textile safeguard). The rules governing such textile safeguards are set forth in the Report of the Working Party on the Accession of China.[53]

WTO Members are not allowed to impose simultaneously a textile and a transitional safeguard.[54] On the other hand, simultaneous application of an ordinary- and a specific or transitional safeguard is not explicitly outlawed: the EU notified the initiation of such a double China-specific and ordinary safeguard investigation on mandarins from China. In the end, only an ordinary safeguard was imposed, with a China-specific quota.[55]

The transitional period during which this regime is applicable is 12 years, that is, until 10 December 2013.[56] The transitional safeguard measure is not imposed

---

[49] See Council Regulation (EC) No.131/2002 of 13 June 2002.
[50] On this issue, see Bown (2010).
[51] See WTO Doc. WT/L/432 at p. 9, §§1–9.
[52] See WTO Doc. WT/MIN (01)/3, section 13, §§245–50.
[53] Idem at §§241–2.
[54] See §242(g) of the Report of the Working Party on the Accession of China.
[55] See WTO Docs. G/SG/N/6/EEC/2 and G/SG/N/8/EEC/Suppl.1.
[56] China's Accession Protocol, section 16, §9.

on an MFN basis, but targets only Chinese products. A transitional safeguard may be imposed:

> in cases where products of Chinese origin are being imported into the territory of any WTO Member in such increased quantities or under such conditions as to cause or threaten to cause market disruption to the domestic producers of like or directly competitive products.[57]

The conditions of increased imports, market disruption, causation, and domestic producers of like or directly competitive products are very similar to those set forth in Art. 2 SG. At first sight, it appears that the important difference is the use of the term 'market disruption', instead of serious injury. China's Accession Protocol seems to equate market disruption with material injury, which can be demonstrated by examining the volume of imports, their price effects, and the effect on the state of the domestic industry:[58]

> Market disruption shall exist whenever imports of an article, like or directly competitive with an article produced by the domestic industry, are increasing rapidly, either absolutely or relatively, so as to be a significant cause of material injury, or threat of material injury to the domestic industry. In determining if market disruption exists, the affected WTO Member shall consider objective factors, including the volume of imports, the effect of imports on prices for like or directly competitive articles, and the effect of such imports on the domestic industry producing like or directly competitive products.

The term 'are increasing' is notably different from the corresponding term appearing in the SG Agreement: trends will not suffice to satisfy this criterion; the Panel on *US—Tyres (China)* found that imports must continue to be increasing at the moment the investigation takes place and the AB upheld this finding (§134):

> The use of the present continuous tense 'are increasing' also suggests that imports follow an upward trend, in that they have increased in the past and continue to increase at present.

China appealed the Panel finding that the requirement above would be satisfied when imports have been increasing in the five year-period preceding the investigation; in China's view, the investigation should focus only on the most recent period. The AB saw nothing in the Chinese Protocol of Accession (Arts. 16§1 and 16§4) to support this argument. It consequently upheld the Panel finding in this respect (§149): it follows that imports must be increasing when the investigation is being conducted, but the increase could be relative to the beginning of the investigation period. Moreover, there is no need for sharp, rapid increases as the AB noted (§158). In fact, even if the rate of increase is dropping, the requirements for imposing a safeguard will have been met as long as imports are increasing in

---

[57] Idem, §1.
[58] Idem, §4.

absolute terms (§167). The AB further held that the term 'material injury' appearing in 16§4 of the Chinese Protocol of Accession is a lower standard than the term 'serious injury' appearing in the SG Agreement without specifying how much lower (§183). The Panel had, however, explained in detail the US standard which in a nutshell required from Chinese imports to have contributed significantly to the injury of the US domestic industry. We quote from §7.150 of the report:

> To determine whether the Section 421 causation standard is inconsistent with the United States' WTO obligations, we must establish what that causation standard actually means. It is well established that, when ascertaining the meaning of domestic legislation, a panel might refer to evidence of the consistent application of that law. In its defence, the United States has produced evidence to the effect that the 'contributes significantly' definition is equivalent to the Protocol's 'significant cause' standard because of consistent USITC practice requiring the demonstration of a 'direct and significant causal link' between the rapidly increasing imports and the market disruption. In particular, the United States refers to the following extract from the USITC Report in the *Tyres* case:
> The third statutory criterion for finding market disruption is whether the rapidly increasing imports are a significant cause of material injury or threat of material injury. The term 'significant cause' is defined in section 421(c)(2) of the Trade Act of 1974 to mean 'a cause which contributes significantly to the material injury of the domestic industry, but need not be equal to or greater than any other cause.' The legislative history of section 406 describes the significant cause standard as follows:
> Under this standard, the imports subject to investigation need not be the leading or most important cause of injury or more important than (or even equal to) any other cause, so long as a direct and significant causal link exists. Thus, if the ITC finds that there are several causes of the material injury, it should seek to determine whether the imports subject to investigation are a significant contributing cause of the injury or are such a subordinate, subsidiary or unimportant cause as to eliminate a direct and significant causal relationship. (italics in the original)

Both the Panel (§§7.160ff) as well as the AB (§§200ff) found the US standard consistent with the US WTO obligations in this respect. The AB, upholding the Panel's findings in this respect, held that the non-attribution language included in Art. 4.2 SG should find application here as well, the absence of specific language to this effect in the Chinese Protocol of Accession notwithstanding (§200).

Transitional safeguards may only be imposed for such period of time as may be necessary to prevent or remedy market disruption, but no maximum time period is provided for.[59] Similarly, the measure may be applied only to the extent necessary to prevent or remedy market disruption.[60] Note that none of the specific disciplines concerning quantitative restrictions as set forth in Art. 5 SG are explicitly

---

[59] Idem, §6.
[60] Idem, §3.

mentioned. The Report of the Working Party on the Accession of China adds in §246(g) that, except for good cause, a grace period of one year has to be respected following the completion of a previous investigation. It appears that this rule does not prohibit the initiation of a new investigation at the time of expiration of the measure.

Provisional measures may be applied in critical circumstances, where delay would cause damage which would be difficult to repair, following a preliminary determination of increased imports, market disruption, and a causal link. The maximum period of time for the application of provisional measures is 200 days.[61] As is the case for ordinary safeguards, a WTO Member imposing a transitional safeguard will have to compensate China, by allowing it to suspend an equivalent level of concessions. But China is not entitled to exercise that right during the first two years of the measure, in cases where the measure was adopted following a finding of relative increase of imports, and during the first three years, in case of a finding of an absolute increase in imports.[62] There is no requirement that the measure has to have been taken in a WTO-consistent manner in order to be able to enjoy a free ride for three years, as was the case in the SG Agreement. Moreover, under the SG Agreement, a relative increase would not have sufficed to escape payment, as only in case of an absolute increase, and a measure taken in conformity with the provisions of the SG Agreement, can the right to compensation be suspended for three years.

From a procedural point of view, a consultation phase precedes the adoption of safeguard measures. It may lead to a bilateral agreement and, accordingly, China might agree to exercise self-restraint and take action to prevent or remedy the market disruption.[63] If bilateral consultations do not lead to an agreement within 60 days, a WTO Member may withdraw concessions or simply limit imports of the Chinese product in question. The Committee on Safeguards has to be notified of any request for consultations and of the decision to impose measures. Before taking action, a WTO Member must conduct an investigation pursuant to procedures previously established and made available to the public.[64] Due process rights, such as public notice, an adequate opportunity for interested parties to submit their views and evidence, including through a public hearing, are respected; moreover, a written notice setting forth the reasons for the measure, its scope, and duration, must be provided by the WTO Member taking the measure.[65]

In *US—Tyres* (*China*), the Panel reproduced the standard of review applicable in safeguard cases and added what in its view were idiosyncratic elements that it

[61] Idem, §7.
[62] Idem, §6.
[63] Idem, §2.
[64] See §246(a) of the Report of the Working Party on the Accession of China.
[65] China's Accession Protocol, section 16, §5.

had to take account of when dealing with a China-specific safeguard. The AB reproduced in §§123–4 of its report and upheld it as well:

> In *US—Lamb*, the Appellate Body provided guidance on how panels should assess the conclusions of national investigating authorities under Article 4.2(a) of the *Agreement on Safeguards*:
>
> A panel must find, in particular, that an explanation is not reasoned, or is not adequate, if some *alternative explanation* of the facts is plausible, and if the competent authorities' explanation does not seem adequate in the light of that alternative explanation. Thus, in making an 'objective assessment' of a claim under Article 4.2 (a), panels must be open to the possibility that the explanation given by the competent authorities is not reasoned or adequate. (emphasis in the original)
>
> In articulating the standard of review that it applied in this dispute, the Panel referred to, and quoted from, the above guidance of the Appellate Body, and made certain additional statements. Importantly, the Panel recalled that the standard of review to be applied by a panel in a given case is also a function of the substantive provisions of the specific covered agreement that is at issue in the dispute, and thus 'must be understood in the light of the obligations of the particular covered agreement at issue'. The Panel noted that, under Paragraph 16.4 of China's Accession Protocol, an investigating authority is required to 'consider objective factors' in determining whether market disruption exists, and that, under Paragraph 16.5, the importing Member 'shall provide written notice of the decision to apply a measure, including the reasons for such measure'. The Panel further observed that 'a panel's standard of review is necessarily distinct from the substantive and procedural obligations of the investigating authority.' On this basis, the Panel considered that, in order to review whether the reasoning of the USITC was adequate, the Panel was required to 'assess whether the reasoning provided by the USITC in its determination seem[ed] adequate in light of plausible alternative explanations of the record evidence or data advanced by China in this proceeding.' The USITC made an affirmative determination that certain passenger vehicle and light truck tyres from China are being imported into the United States in such increased quantities or under such conditions as to cause market disruption. In the present case, the Panel was therefore required to assess whether the USITC provided a reasoned and adequate explanation to support this determination. (italics and emphasis in the original)

A second type of transitional safeguard is the safeguard against the effects of another WTO Member's safeguards action against China: in case of significant trade diversion, caused by the imposition of a transitional safeguard by a WTO Member on a particular type of product originating in China, a third WTO Member may withdraw concessions or otherwise limit imports from China, only to the extent necessary to prevent or remedy such diversions.[66] The Report of the Working Party on China's Accession clarifies (§248) the criteria that would have to be examined in order to determine trade diversion caused by another WTO Member's transitional safeguard, *inter alia*:

---

[66] Idem, §8.

(a) The increase in market share of imports from China;

(b) The nature or extent of the action taken or proposed;

(c) The increase in volume of imports from China due to the action taken;

(d) Conditions of demand and supply in the importing WTO Member for the products at issue; and

(e) The volume of exports from China to the WTO Member imposing the original transitional safeguard.

The trade-diversion safeguard is closely linked to the original transitional safeguard, as it has to be reviewed in case of a change to the original transitional safeguard, and must be terminated at the latest 30 days following expiration of the original transitional safeguard (§§249–50). There is no obligation to compensate.

The textile safeguard is a product-cum-country-specific safeguard: only Chinese textile products come under its purview. The Report of the Working Party on China's Accession contains the rules governing this type of safeguard (§242). The textile safeguard regime remains applicable until 31 December 2008. The products covered, textiles and apparel, are essentially those that were previously covered by the now defunct ATC. The textile safeguards mechanism is a two-stage process and combines a sort of voluntary export restraint by China, with the possibility of imposing a safeguard in case China does not comply with this restraint. A WTO Member may request consultations with China, if it believes that Chinese textile imports were threatening to impede the orderly development of trade. It would need to provide China with a detailed factual statement of reasons and justifications, supported by current data on:

(a) The existence or threat of market disruption; and

(b) The extent to which products of Chinese origin have provoked the market disruption.

Consultations should be held within 30 days, and a mutually satisfactory solution should be reached within 90 days following the request. Immediately following the request for consultations, China is required to hold its shipments of the textile products in question to the WTO Member (requesting consultations) to a level no greater than 7.5 per cent (6 per cent for wool product categories) above the amount entered during the first 12 months of the most recent 14 months preceding the month in which the request for consultations was made. So the request for consultations triggers a self-imposed restraint on exports. If the consultations do not lead to a solution after 90 days, the voluntary restraint may be turned into a safeguard measure by the importing WTO Member, limiting imports of the Chinese textile products in question to the same level (7.5 per cent). This safeguard measure can stay in place for a maximum period of one year, but there are no rules prohibiting the re-application of a new measure on the same products at the end of this period (§242(e), (f)). No investigation is required nor is there any obligation to notify any WTO body of these textile safeguards.

1.2.11 Special and Differential Treatment for Developing Countries

A safeguard measure is not to be applied against imports from developing countries where their share of imports does not exceed 3 per cent of the total in the importing market (or 9 per cent cumulatively, that is, where products originate in various developing countries): this is what Art. 9 SG dictates. If imports from developing countries have been excluded, on the basis of Art. 9 SG, an IA must establish in a clear manner that imports from sources other than the excluded developing countries fulfilled all the conditions for the imposition of a measure (AB, *US—Steel Safeguards*, §472).

1.2.12 Standard of Review

The SG Agreement does not contain a specific provision dealing with the standard of review that is applicable to cases coming under its aegis. Consequently, the generic standard of review included in Art. 11 DSU is applicable. The AB accepted as much in its report on *US—Cotton Yarn* (§74). The term 'objective assessment' is far from being clear. Indeed, could anyone imagine a WTO provision calling for 'subjective assessment'?[67] The AB, in its report on *US—Lamb*, explained that, in order to make an objective assessment of the matter before it, a Panel must satisfy itself that an IA has evaluated all relevant facts before it and has provided an adequate and reasoned explanation for its overall findings (§§103–7). In this vein, the AB, in its report on *US—Cotton Yarn*, added that Panels cannot base their determination on evidence which did not exist when the investigation took place. If they do, they violate *ipso facto* Art. 11 DSU (§78). This is a natural consequence of the fact that, when faced with a decision by an IA (irrespective of whether in the AD, the SCM, or the SG context), a Panel must abstain from conducting a *de novo* review, that is, behave as if it was the IA and start the fact-finding process all over again. In *US—Lamb*, the AB explained that the impossibility of performing a *de novo* review should not be understood by Panels as equivalent to total deference to the findings by an IA. To the contrary, they must actively review the determinations by an IA (§§106–7):

> We wish to emphasize that, although panels are not entitled to conduct a *de novo* review of the evidence, or to substitute their own conclusions for those of the competent authorities, this does not mean that panels must simply accept the conclusions of the competent authorities. To the contrary, in our view, in examining a claim under Article 4.2(a), a panel can assess whether the competent authorities' explanation for its determination is reasoned and adequate only if the panel critically

---

[67] Of course, at the end of the day, judicial assessment is by definition subjective since it is humans—subjective entities—that perform them. The term 'subjective assessment', though, is prone to be understood as biased assessment or something to this effect; hence the legislative preference embedded in Art. 11 DSU. Although Art. 11 DSU refers to the standard of review employed by Panels only, the AB has espoused the same standard in its case law; see Palmeter and Mavroidis (2004).

examines that explanation, in depth, and in the light of the facts before the panel. Panels must, therefore, review whether the competent authorities' explanation fully addresses the nature, and, especially, the complexities, of the data, and responds to other plausible interpretations of those data. A panel must find, in particular, that an explanation is not reasoned, or is not adequate, if some alternative explanation of the facts is plausible, and if the competent authorities' explanation does not seem adequate in the light of that alternative explanation. Thus, in making an 'objective assessment' of a claim under Article 4.2(a), panels must be open to the possibility that the explanation given by the competent authorities is not reasoned or adequate.

In this respect, the phrase '*de novo* review' should not be used loosely. If a panel concludes that the competent authorities, in a particular case, have not provided a reasoned or adequate explanation for their determination, that panel has not, thereby, engaged in a de novo review. Nor has that panel substituted its own conclusions for those of the competent authorities. Rather, the panel has, consistent with its obligations under the DSU, simply reached a conclusion that the determination made by the competent authorities is inconsistent with the specific requirements of Article 4.2 of the *Agreement on Safeguards*. (italics in the original)

The Panel on *US—Steel Safeguards* drew a distinction between the standard of review to be applied by Panels when evaluating the right to apply a safeguard measure and the standard to be applied when evaluating the application of the measure itself. In its view, in the latter case, a Panel's examination can be more intrusive than in the former (§§10.25–7):

The Panel is of the view that the standard of review applicable in the present dispute must be seen in light of the distinction between the first and second enquiry that the Panel must perform when assessing a Member's compliance with the requirements of the *Agreement on Safeguards* and Article XIX of GATT 1994. When assessing a Member's compliance with its obligations pursuant to Articles 2, 3 and 4 of the *Agreement on Safeguards* and Article XIX of GATT, the Panel is not the initial fact finder. Rather, the role of the Panel is to 'review' determinations and demonstrations made and reported by an investigating authority.

The situation is different in the context of the second enquiry when assessing whether the measures were applied only to the extent necessary to prevent the serious injury caused by increased imports. In that situation, it is before the Panel, during the WTO dispute settlement process, that the importing Member is forced for the first time to respond to allegations relating to the level and extent of its safeguard measures. For us, this is clear from the following statement of the Appellate Body in *US—Line Pipe*:

[I]t is clear, therefore, that [. . .] Article 5.1, including the first sentence, does not oblige a Member to justify, at the time of application, that the safeguard measure at issue is applied 'only to the extent necessary'.

Article 5.1 does not establish a general procedural obligation to demonstrate compliance with Article 5.1, first sentence, at the time a measure is applied.

In that second enquiry, the Panel is thus reviewing whether the measures 'as applied' comply with the requirements of Articles 5, 7, 8 and 9 of the *Agreement on Safeguards* on the basis of the evidence and arguments put forward by the parties during the WTO dispute settlement process. (italics in the original)

1.3 The Investigation Process

A WTO Member may apply a safeguard measure only following an investigation by its IA pursuant to procedures previously established and made public (Art. 3.1 SG). Art. 3.1 SG requires an IA of a WTO Member to provide public notice to all interested parties regarding the initiation of investigation, to provide all such parties with the opportunity to present evidence and their views, and to respond to the presentations of other parties. There is no express provision guaranteeing interested parties 'access to the file' apart from the very general need to provide reasonable public notice to all interested parties. Nor does the SG Agreement contain any disclosure obligations (compare Arts. 6.4 and 6.9 AD). The AB has used the general nature of the obligations as a basis for introducing the essential aspects of practically all of the procedural aspects of the more detailed AD and CVD provisions into the SG Agreement. We quote from the report on *US—Wheat Gluten* (§§53–5):

> We turn, therefore, for context, to Article 3.1 of *Agreement on Safeguards*, which is entitled 'Investigation'. Article 3.1 provides that 'A Member may apply a safeguard measure only following an investigation by the competent authorities of that Member...'. The ordinary meaning of the word 'investigation' suggests that the competent authorities should carry out a 'systematic inquiry' or a 'careful study' into the matter before them. The word, therefore, suggests a proper degree of activity on the part of the competent authorities because authorities charged with conducting an inquiry or a study—to use the treaty language, an 'investigation'—must actively seek out pertinent information.
>
> The nature of the 'investigation' required by the *Agreement on Safeguards* is elaborated further in the remainder of Article 3.1, which sets forth certain investigative steps that the competent authorities 'shall include' in order to seek out pertinent information. The focus of the investigative steps mentioned in Article 3.1 is on 'interested parties', who must be notified of the investigation, and who must be given an opportunity to submit 'evidence', as well as their 'views', to the competent authorities. The interested parties are also to be given an opportunity to 'respond to the presentations of other parties'. The *Agreement on Safeguards*, therefore, envisages that the interested parties play a central role in the investigation and that they will be a primary source of information for the competent authorities.
>
> ...
>
> In that respect, we note that the competent authorities' 'investigation' under Article 3.1 is not limited to the investigative steps mentioned in that provision, but must simply 'include' these steps. Therefore, the competent authorities must undertake additional investigative steps, when the circumstances so require, in order to fulfil their obligation to evaluate all relevant factors. (italics in the original)

Art. 3.2 SG incorporates the requirement to protect confidential information, much as Arts. 6.5 AD and 12.4 SCM do: it may not be disclosed without the permission of the party submitting it.

The IA must further publish a report setting out findings and reasoned conclusions reached on all pertinent issues of fact and law. The Panel on *US—Steel*

Safeguards, took the view that Art. 3.1 SG does not require from an IA to send draft findings to interested parties (§10.64–5). The absence of an explicit, in the sense of a clear and unambiguous, explanation of the pertinent issues of fact and law was considered WTO-inconsistent by the AB. The complainant (EU) argued that the US had not fully justified how it had met the unforeseen-developments requirement. On appeal, the AB took the view that, for compliance with Art. 3.1 SG to be achieved, a WTO Member must set forth findings and reasoned conclusions on all pertinent issues of facts and law, since this was the only basis (along with requirements under Art. 4 SG) upon which Panels could base their findings (§299). The US had argued that failure to explain a pertinent issue of fact or law, in its order imposing safeguards, should not amount to a Panel finding that no investigation of this particular issue had been conducted at all. The AB disagreed, and held that such a finding was appropriate, in light of the absence of a reasoned explanation in conformity with Art. 3.1 SG. It should be added here that the disagreement among the parties to the dispute concerned the demonstration of the unforeseen-developments requirement, a quintessential element absent demonstration of which no safeguards can be lawfully imposed. The AB finding is hence very much in line with the legislative directive to explain all 'pertinent' issues of fact and law, for the unforeseen-developments requirement is definitely one of them.

Finally, the IA must conduct the investigation in accordance with procedures previously established and made public.

1.3.1 Initiation

The SG Agreement is silent on the initiation phase and does not subject the decision to initiate an investigation to any procedural or substantive conditions. Unlike other contingent protection instruments, no distinction is drawn between self-initiated (*ex officio*) investigations and investigations upon the request of a private party; the legislative requirements are the same either way. What is clear is that, contrary to the AD and SCM Agreements, there are no standing requirements reflected in the SG Agreement, and no other threshold conditions that must be met for an investigation to be lawfully launched. It could be, for example, the case that one economic operator, representing a minor proportion of the domestic industry, requests initiation of investigation: an investigation could be launched, assuming that the IA agrees to it. There is no need to show some preliminary evidence of increased imports resulting from unforeseen developments nor that imports might be causing injury to the domestic industry. It suffices that the IA has decided to initiate the process. Surprisingly, therefore, an instrument that is supposed, in the words of the AB, to combat fair trade, and which should be used in extraordinary circumstances only, is not associated with a legal framework that imposes stringent conditions on WTO Members wishing to avail themselves of this possibility. The 'start-up' costs are quite low.[68]

1.3.2 Publication and Notification

The SG Agreement does not impose any detailed publication requirements: while Arts. 12 AD and 22 SCM contain specific obligations concerning public notice of the initiation of the investigation and the measures taken, both provisional and final, all that Art. 3.1 SG requires is that the investigation includes reasonable public notice to all interested parties and that the authorities publish a report setting forth their findings and reasoned conclusions on all pertinent issues of fact and law. This obligation is not specified any further.

A separate notification requirement is included in Art. 12 SG: it requires that the WTO Safeguards Committee be duly notified, in timely manner, of decisions to initiate a safeguard investigation (Art. 12.1(a) SG). The same duty exists with respect to the decision to impose provisional measures, impose or extend definitive measures, as well as all findings of injury or threat thereof caused by increased imports (Art. 12.1(b) SG and Art. 12.1(c) SG). The duty to notify is accompanied by the obligation to do so immediately upon making such a finding or taking such a decision. The AB, in its report on *US—Wheat Gluten*, held that the ordinary meaning of the term 'immediately' implies a certain urgency (§§105–6). The requirement of Art. 12.2 SG to provide the Safeguards Committee with all pertinent information on a number of matters has been considered to be different and less demanding than the requirement of Art. 3.1 SG *in fine* to publish a report setting forth an IA's findings and reasoned conclusions on all pertinent issues of fact and law (Panel, *Korea—Dairy*, §7.125). According to the AB (*Korea—Dairy*), a notification which does not set forth the findings with regard to all of the injury factors mentioned in Art. 4.2 SG does not include all pertinent information on serious injury (§109).

Arts. 12.2 and 12.3 SG explain the kind of information that should be included in notifications: a WTO Member which is about to apply or extend a safeguard measure shall provide the WTO Safeguards Committee with all pertinent information including, *inter alia*, evidence of injury, or threat thereof, and information on the proposed measure and its expected duration (Art. 12.2 SG). At the same time, it shall provide all interested WTO Members with the possibility to engage in consultations prior to the imposition of the safeguard measure (Art. 12.3 SG). The aim of these consultations is to allow affected WTO Members to review the notified information, exchange views on the measure proposed, and reach an understanding on the ways to maintain a substantially equivalent level of concessions or adequate trade compensation (Art. 12.3 SG). The AB, in its report on

---

[68] There are of course other costs associated with flimsy initiations both for the IA as well as for the exporters.

Korea—Dairy, agreed with the view of the Panel that the notification serves, essentially, a transparency and information purpose (§111):

> We think that the notification serves essentially a transparency and information purpose. In ensuring transparency, Article 12 allows Members through the Committee on Safeguards to review the measures. Another purpose of the notification of the finding of serious injury and of the proposed measure is to inform Members of the circumstances of the case and the conclusions of the investigation together with the importing country's particular intentions. This allows any interested Member to decide whether to request consultations with the importing country which may lead to modification of the proposed measure(s) and/or compensation.

Notifications under Art. 12.2 SG, concerning findings of injury or threat thereof, and of the decision to take a measure as a result, have to be made prior to the application of the measure and in sufficient time before its application in order to allow for meaningful consultations. The AB, in its report on *US—Line Pipe*, confirmed that WTO Members must provide interested parties with enough time so as to ensure that consultations will be meaningful. In the case at hand, the AB held that the US, by providing Korea with less than 20 days for consultations, violated its obligations under Art. 12.3 SG (§§107 and 111–13).

With respect to a notification concerning the initiation of an investigation, the AB held in *US—Wheat Gluten* that a delay of 16 days was not consistent with the requirements of the SG Agreement. With respect to notification concerning findings of injury caused by increased imports, the AB held that a delay of 26 days was not consistent with the requirements of the SG Agreement either (§§111, 112, and 116). In both cases, the limited content of the notification was an important element in considering that the notification could have been made sooner. On the other hand, with respect to notifications concerning a decision to apply or extend a safeguard, the AB held that the passage of five days between the date when a decision was taken and its notification was not in contravention of the SG Agreement (§129). Similarly, the Panel on *Korea—Dairy* found that a delay of 14 days for the limited notification of the initiation of an investigation, 40 days for notifying the injury finding, and 24 days for the decision to apply a measure was inconsistent with Art. 12.1 SG (§§7.134, 7.136, and 7.145).

The AB, in its report on *US—Line Pipe*, made clear that a violation of the duty to notify a proposed safeguard measure and provide adequate time for consultations to affected parties (under Art. 12 SG) *ipso facto* amounted to a violation of the obligation included in Art. 8.1 SG. It thus read Arts. 8.1 and 12.3 SG together (§§ 116–19).

1.3.3 The Period of Investigation (POI)

The SG Agreement does not provide any guidance on the POI to be used when evaluating serious injury. According to the Panel on *US—Wheat Gluten*, any determination of serious injury must pertain to the recent past (§8.81).

1.4 Institutional Issues

A Committee on Safeguards is established, and its tasks are described, in Art. 13 SG. WTO Members will notify this committee of their safeguard measures and the latter can assist them with all matters regarding imposition of safeguards. This committee performs a transparency function since it is the depository of safeguards and periodically issues documents reporting on the status of notifications, measures in place, etc.

2. Contingent Protection Revisited

There are (at least) two basic normative questions stemming from the discussion in this and the previous two chapters:

(a) What should be the response to subsidization?
(b) What kind of safeguard should we include in the WTO?

With respect to the first question, we have already hinted that, the definitional issues notwithstanding, a response to subsidization is required; otherwise the incentive to make concessions might be eviscerated because of the concession erosion resulting from subsidization. Since the objective of the agreement is to remove the competitive advantage conferred through subsidization, a response should be confined to just that. In this sense, the Arbitrators in *US—Upland Cotton (Art. 22.6—US)* got it right when they deviated from prior case law and provided for the same response to prohibited and actionable subsidies in case of non-compliance with adverse Panel (AB) rulings. It remains to remove the provision for illegal subsidies, especially since there is no a priori reason to think that they are more harmful than domestic subsidies.[69]

Then there is the twin question whether we should account for the rationale for subsidization. Recall that subsidies might on occasion be the first-best instrument to address a market distortion. In a way the SCM Agreement does, or better, did, take account of the rationale for subsidization: Art. 8 SCM provided for an exhaustive list of non-actionable subsidies. Now the problem with this approach is that other, equally innocent (or guilty) subsidies have not been reflected in the list for a myriad of good or bad reasons. The problems notwithstanding, it is probably warranted to reintroduce a similar list rather than try to negotiate a test that will leave ample discretion in the hands of the WTO adjudicating bodies.

---

[69] Occasionally the argument is heard that the distinction between prohibited and actionable subsidies is also supported by the fact that in the latter case a WTO Member behaves within its jurisdiction, whereas in the former this is not the case. It is questionable whether this argument holds in light of increasingly liberalized investment and the continuous questioning of the basis for conferring nationality.

There have been voices arguing along these lines.[70] A number of similar government interventions (say aiming at providing a public good) will anyway be exonerated from prosecution if they are not specific (Art. 2 SCM). Still, the lack of clarity as to the contours of the specificity test makes a negotiation along these lines a candidate for future law-making activities at the WTO level: measures aiming to address climate change multiply and governments will inevitably seek legal certainty in this respect.

The second question is even trickier. Our discussion on antidumping reveals that there is nothing inherently unfair about dumping: indeed traders could be pricing their goods above their average variable cost (a perfectly rational practice) and still find themselves subjected to AD duties. So it is all about introducing a safeguard in the WTO regime and the issue is whether the safeguard can be imposed bilaterally or must always be imposed on a multilateral basis. Many scholars have studied the proliferation of AD duties and the reasons behind this phenomenon, and they almost all support the view that this is a political-economy-driven instrument aimed at providing the domestic industry with breathing space rather than a response to unfair trading.[71] Prusa (2001 and 2005) offers a very comprehensive look at this issue. Finger (1993) concludes that antidumping is best explained through political-economy arguments. The same is true for Bloningen and Prusa (2003). Even closer to what we suggest here comes the study of Finger and Nogues (2006) who have studied antidumping practice in seven Latin American countries (Argentina, Brazil, Chile, Colombia, Costa Rica, Mexico, and Peru). They confirm that the use of antidumping has increased substantially over the years. In their view, however, such use is a necessity, since otherwise the countries examined would have had no way to make the adjustments they needed to, in light of the liberalization commitments they have undertaken since the Uruguay round. In other words, the countries examined view recourse to antidumping as a safeguard rather than as a response to an unfair practice.

Practice and theory, as suggested *supra*, make the case for a safeguard. And it is probably high time the trade community reflected on the type of safeguard that should be introduced: we should eventually do away with the mess of AD duties and the unworkability of the current safeguard clause.

Spence (2011, p. 73) elegantly describes the fallacy of safeguards when stating that their basis is that they protect people by protecting their jobs, whereas they should be protecting people and not jobs.[72] Art. XIX GATT has not been invoked all that often as Tables 9.1 and 9.2 show. Many of these cases were lodged between 1975 and 1978, that is, just before the GATT contracting parties had fully realized the potential of the antidumping instrument, triggering the 'antidumping boom'

---

[70] Howse (2010); Rubini (2010).

[71] There are of course papers like that of Knetter and Prusa (2003), who point to other factors such as the importance of currency exchange. Terms of trade cannot explain antidumping.

[72] Very similar views have been voiced by Dunoff (2010) and Sykes (2003a).

of the 1980s and 1990s which continues at a similar pace nowadays. The initial unpopularity of the safeguard mechanism was due to many factors, but two features stand out:

(a) A safeguard measure should be non-discriminatory among trading partners,[73]
(b) It was subjected to compensation (and, eventually, retaliation if there was a disagreement on the level of compensation between the country imposing a safeguard and its trading partners).

The first condition clearly put any country initiating a safeguard at odds with the coalition of all the existing and potential exporters of the product concerned.[74] The second condition is tantamount to imposing an *ex ante* unknown price on the measure envisaged: indeed, nothing in the SG Agreement requires absolute equivalence between the two actions (imposing safeguards, amount of compensation).[75]

None of these conditions was anyway relevant in the case of VERs. And none of these conditions was required by antidumping procedures, the preferred instrument since the early 1980s. The Uruguay round negotiators were very conscious of the substitutability between the various instruments of contingent protection. As a result, they (at least some of them) tried to make the use of safeguard measures more attractive, in the hope of reducing the use of antidumping measures and ensuring the implementation of the ban on voluntary export restraints and other grey measures. In particular, the Uruguay round SG Agreement specified, as we saw *supra*, that compensation could not be requested for the first three years that a safeguard measure is in effect. Despite such changes, safeguards remain relatively unpopular, compared with antidumping. There have been more safeguard investigations initiated between 1995 and 2005, but their number remains relatively modest, as Tables 9.1 and 9.2 show. However, a word of caution may be necessary here. Looking at the mere number of cases does not fully reflect the renewed importance of safeguard measures compared with antidumping. This is because a safeguard action tends to have coverage systematically wider than an antidumping action, for two reasons. First, its non-discriminatory feature means that a safeguard action covers all the countries in the world; second, the coverage in terms of goods of a safeguard action may be much greater than the coverage of an antidumping

---

[73] Recall our discussion above: there has been a clear legislative imperative to this effect only as of 1995, but practice had developed in this direction before that.

[74] With one caveat: in the presence of mavericks, some exporters will welcome a safeguard (as they welcome any QR) since it will help them preserve their historic quotas which could be under threat as a result of the fast rise of the maverick's export volume. A number of textile-producing countries were behaving along similar lines in order to fend off the challenges posed by China's extraordinary rise in the textiles market.

[75] Hoda (2001) shows that there were few if any cases of disagreement regarding the amount of compensation to be paid. Ethier (2001) made a similar argument to explain why WTO Members have opted for weak rather than strong remedies in the context of dispute settlement.

action (recall our discussion on the definition of the domestic industry in the AD and the SG context). There is no systematic measure of how much greater, on average, the coverage is, in terms of countries and products of a safeguard action, compared with the coverage of an antidumping action. The last decade has also witnessed the emergence of new provisions closely resembling Art. XIX GATT: specific safeguards in the Uruguay round Agreement on Agriculture (Art. 5); in the GATS (Art. X); in the ATC Agreement (Art. 6); and a specific safeguard associated with acceding countries (particularly targeted at China). There have been hundreds of safeguard restrictions taken under the separate provisions on agriculture and textiles.

With this caveat, it seems that it is the non-discriminatory character of safeguards that tilts the balance towards the use of AD measures. The Uruguay round went some way towards addressing this issue by introducing quota modulation. Assuming the time span on which we base our observations (1995–2011) does not suffer from sample bias, this move does not seem to be sufficient. On the other hand, the unforeseen-developments requirement looks to be insurmountable in practice.

Against this background, further simplification[76] of the conditions for lawfully imposing safeguards is probably warranted. There is nothing like a magic recipe though, since over-simplification might lead to moral hazard-type of problems. The case for one instead of two safeguards is persuasive (since de facto this is what antidumping is). Additional thinking is required to design a workable safeguard.

---

[76] This is probably not what trade lawyers would like.

10

TECHNICAL BARRIERS TO TRADE

Sanitary and Phyto-sanitary Measures

1. GATT, TBT, and SPS

The Agreement on Technical Barriers to Trade (TBT) and the Agreement on Sanitary and Phyto-sanitary Measures (SPS) deal with domestic instruments aimed at pursuing various objectives. An indicative list included in Art. 2.2 TBT mentions national security, the prevention of deceptive practices, protection of human health or safety, animal or plant life or health, or the environment. SPS typically covers measures taken in order to address food safety, animal health, the entry and/or spread of pests. Since the TBT and the SPS Agreements cover a subset of all domestic instruments coming under the purview of Art. III GATT, a transaction can, in principle, be subjected to the disciplines of either the GATT or the TBT or the SPS Agreement. If the legal discipline across the three agreements was identical, there would be no need to prolong this discussion any further since it would be totally immaterial whether a particular transaction was subjected to one or the other agreement. The three agreements, though, do not reflect the same legal test for evaluation of the consistency of national policies with their rules: both the TBT and the SPS Agreements are negative integration instruments, as we shall see in more detail *infra*, and for all practical purposes request from WTO Members to adopt non-discriminatory policies without, however, prejudging the level of protection sought. The test to establish non-discrimination, nevertheless, is much more elaborate in the two agreements when compared to the test embedded in Art. III GATT. A measure coming under the aegis of Art. III GATT must observe non-discrimination as explained in Chapter 4; were the same measure to be subjected to the SPS rules and disciplines, it would in principle have to be based on science, necessary to achieve the stated objective, and also be part of a class of measures that exhibit consistently homogeneous levels of protection. Recall that, as we argued in Chapter 4, science, consistency, necessity are all proxies that can be appropriately used to detect whether a measure is protectionist or not. Instead of leaving it to the judge to construct a non-discrimination in light of similar proxies, these agreements pre-empt judicial discretion by supplying a more elaborate test to detect whether a particular behaviour is protectionist. The unanswered question is why similar proxies have been confined to TBT and SPS measures.[1]

From a pure legal perspective, it is thus imperative to first determine which agreement takes precedence, in light of the different legal benchmarks that they employ in order to evaluate the consistency of challenged measures with the WTO.[2] The TBT and the SPS Agreements are Annex 1A agreements and their relationship with the GATT is addressed in the General Interpretative Note to Annex 1A. As we saw, the General Interpretative Note to Annex 1A has not always been interpreted consistently. In *EC—Asbestos*, nevertheless, the AB, reversing the Panel in this respect, concluded that a measure which revealed the characteristics of a technical regulation and thus simultaneously fell under the TBT and the GATT should have been reviewed under the TBT Agreement, and not under the GATT (as the Panel had originally done). The subsequent Panel report on *EC—Sardines* contains an even more explicit reflection of this approach (§§7.14–16):

> ... If we were to determine that the EC Regulation is not inconsistent with the provisions of the TBT Agreement invoked by Peru, it requests that we examine its claims in respect of Article III: 4 of the GATT 1994.
>
> In addressing the issue of the order of analysis, we have taken into account earlier considerations of this question. We recall the AB's statement in EC—Bananas III which stated that the panel 'should' have applied the Licensing Agreement first

---

[1] Scott (2009).

[2] On this issue, see Marceau and Trachtman (2002).

because this agreement deals 'specifically, and in detail' with the administration of import licensing procedures. The AB noted that if the panel had examined the measure under the Licensing Agreement first, there would have been no need to address the alleged inconsistency with Article X:3 of the GATT 1994. The AB suggests that where two agreements apply simultaneously, a panel should normally consider the more specific agreement before the more general agreement.

Arguably, the TBT Agreement deals 'specifically, and in detail' with technical regulations. If the AB's statement in EC—Bananas III is a guide, it suggests that if the EC Regulation is a technical regulation, then the analysis under the TBT Agreement would precede any examination under the GATT 1994. Moreover, Peru, as the complaining party, requested that we first examine its claim under Article 2.4 of the TBT Agreement followed by Article 2.2 if we find that the EC Regulation is consistent with Article 2.4. And similarly, only if we were to find that the EC Regulation is consistent with Article 2.2 does Peru ask us to consider its claim under Article 2.1. In the event that we were to find that the EC Regulation is consistent with the TBT Agreement, Peru requests that we examine its claim under Article III:4 of the GATT 1994. We note that the European Communities did not contest Peru's request regarding this sequencing analysis.

On appeal, the AB did not reverse the order of analysis. Subsequent Panel reports (*US—Tuna II (Mexico)*; *US—Clove Cigarettes*) have followed this order of analysis and it is now commonplace that Panels will start reviewing claims under the TBT Agreement and eventually, if need be, review them under the GATT as well. A measure is covered by TBT if it is a 'technical regulation', a 'standard', or a 'conformity assessment' procedure and we will be discussing the content of these terms *infra*.

The relationship between TBT and SPS is regulated in Art. 1.5 TBT, which clearly states that SPS takes precedence over TBT: in practice, a measure that falls under the ambit of both agreements will be discussed under TBT, unless it concerns a disease, a toxin, or a contaminant.[3] It follows that the complete sentence should be that SPS takes precedence over TBT which takes precedence over GATT.

2. The TBT Agreement

2.1 The Legal Discipline and its Rationale

The TBT Agreement requests from WTO Members to follow relevant international standards when enacting 'technical regulations' and/or 'standards', assuming that such exist and are appropriate in light of the objectives pursued; if this is not the case, they can have recourse to unilateral measures provided that their interventions (in the form of technical regulations and/or standards) are applied in

---

[3] We will, of course, be discussing these notions in more detail *infra*.

a non-discriminatory manner and respect the necessity principle. The TBT Agreement thus, provides, beyond what the GATT does, a twofold insurance policy to safeguard cost-shifting to foreign nations: the necessity requirement will request from WTO Members not to impose an undue burden on their trading partners through the enactment of technical regulations and standards. The incorporation of the necessity requirement can lead to outlawing beggar-thy-neighbour policies in addition to those outlawed by the GATT (Art. III). A non-discriminatory sales embargo, for example, would never run foul of Art. III GATT even if it constitutes a highly restrictive option. If the sales embargo is imposed through a technical regulation, though, it would still have to satisfy the necessity requirement. If not, it would be outlawed, its non-discriminatory character notwithstanding. As we saw in Chapter 5, though, this is an imperfect instrument since the choice of means depends on the formulation of the ends which cannot be put into question by the WTO Membership or the judge. If ends have been formulated in very restrictive terms, then the choice with respect to means will be limited, quite severely so on occasion. And then the TBT Agreement provides for an obligation in principle to use international standards.[4]

The WTO TBT Agreement is not the first multilateral regulatory intervention in this area. During the Tokyo round, a Code on Technical Barriers to Trade had been agreed, calling for avoidance of using unnecessary standards; participation in the Code was optional. The lowering of duties during the Tokyo round made the impact of standards more visible to the world trading community: Baldwin's drainage of the swamp works here as well. This phenomenon, combined with the sheer rise in the number of technical regulations and standards worldwide (and especially in Europe where consumer protection provided the impetus for strict regulation of its industry),[5] persuaded negotiators in the Uruguay round that the time had come to add a binding multilateral agreement to the existing rules. Public health and environmental and consumer protection are the most frequent reasons for imposing technical regulations and standards at the national level. These are areas the regulation of which has, at least in some parts of the world, been heavily influenced by scientific progress.

Why move away from non-discrimination? Non-discrimination is not a guarantee for market access; in fact, the WTO Member with the higher protection

---

[4] To avoid misunderstandings here: the TBT Agreement makes it more onerous (than in a GATT scenario) for regulators to comply with the law since, beyond non-discrimination, they must also comply with the necessity requirement. The latter is, in theory, a proxy for detecting protectionist behaviour; in the TBT setting, though, it is an additional legal requirement that all WTO Members adopting measures coming under the purview of this agreement must meet. The same is true for the SPS Agreement that we discuss in Section 3 *infra*, where, besides the necessity requirement, regulators must in principle base their interventions on science and must adopt consistent policies as well. Other things equal, the requirement to cumulatively respect all these obligations would provoke more of a chilling effect on potential regulators than if similar transactions were subjected to the classic GATT test that we saw in Chapter 4.

[5] Vogel (2003); Graham (1979) pp. 166ff.

(e.g. higher environmental standards) can behave in a perfectly GATT-consistent manner by keeping all products originating in countries with lower environmental standards outside its market. On occasion, it might even have the incentive to enact prohibitively high standards that impose substantial adjustment costs on its trading partners. Employing the terms-of-trade framework for the modelling of trade agreements, Staiger and Sykes (2011) show how 'large' nations may have an incentive to impose discriminatory product standards against imported goods once border instruments are constrained and how inefficiently stringent standards may emerge under certain circumstances even if regulatory discrimination is prohibited.[6] It follows that economic operators established in large, lucrative markets will, other things equal, enjoy an advantage that those exporting to their market will have to pay for.[7]

One might argue that this is not such a bad thing after all since the community of trading nations will be engaging in a race to the top. Note, nevertheless, that political-economy considerations might weigh heavily in this context.[8] Regulation at the national level is not always immune to political-economy-type considerations and, as a result, there is no guarantee that the end product will be a first-best regulatory response to an existing distortion.[9] Linking regulation to standards such as 'scientific validity' prima facie immunizes the regulatory process against capture. And yet, even in this constellation, there are issues to discuss: why be more demanding (in terms of requesting scientific expertise) in one and not in another area? Or, is it really necessary to be very risk averse when regulating a particular transaction? And then very often regulation in the TBT context is only superficially or not at all science-informed. In this context, the discussion on social preferences becomes more fuzzy and unpredictable. These are debatable issues in

---

[6] The authors then assess the WTO legal framework in light of their results, arguing that it does a reasonably thorough job of policing regulatory discrimination, but that it does relatively little to address excessive non-discriminatory regulations, a point we also made in our discussion of national treatment in Chapter 4.

[7] A 2000 OECD study, prepared by Spencer Henson and Rupert Loader in collaboration with Akira Kawamoto and Anthony Kleitz, entitled 'An Assessment of the Costs for International Trade in Meeting Regulatory Requirements' (OECD Doc. TD/TC/WP(99)8/FINAL of 28 February 2000, hereinafter 'OECD 2000') provides empirical support for the conclusion that big companies enjoy an advantage over small companies when it comes to meeting divergent standards across export markets: in short, big companies have either subsidiaries or joint companies overseas, which are used extensively in order to obtain information about standards, and this provides them with an advantage over small companies when it comes to developing or re-designing goods that fit the standards; see OECD (2000, pp. 36ff).

[8] Mansfield and Busch (1995).

[9] Kono (2006), for example, observes that it is democracies that typically create non-tariff barriers (NTBs). In his analysis, by increasing the transparency of some policies relative to others, democracy induces politicians to replace transparent trade barriers (such as tariffs) with less transparent ones (such as NTBs). He tests his hypothesis using a sample of 75 countries and concludes that democracy leads to lower tariffs, higher core NTBs, and even higher quality NTBs. In his view, democracy promotes optimal obfuscation, which allows politicians to protect their markets while maintaining a veneer of liberalization. Compare Milner (1988).

a domestic setting and it is domestic political economy that will decide on the outcome. Büthe and Mattli (2011, p. 135) offer the following example of regulatory capture by domestic lobbies:

> A Japanese product standard ... adopted in 1986 by the Consumer Product Safety Association (CPSA) at the request of the nascent Japanese ski manufacturing industry, required that skis sold in Japan would have to comply with particular product design specifications in order to get a consumer safety seal. None of the major foreign manufacturers met the standard. The CPSA sought to justify the introduction of the ski standard by arguing that Japanese snow is 'different' from snow in other (ski-exporting) countries.

What snow did for the Japanese, something else might have done for others. There is an unavoidable international dimension in this discussion: in the absence of coordination, traders have been increasingly facing obstacles resulting from similar barriers, especially because societies are not symmetrically risk averse, or simply because they have different preferences, which could be the outcome of endogenous factors (culture, religion, level of development, etc.). As a result, if business is required to comply with different regulations in an export market than those in the home market, it will be facing additional costs that will reduce its competitiveness vis-à-vis domestic suppliers in that home market. At any rate, diverse standards can and often do undermine economies of scale for export-oriented companies and oblige exporters to bear costs in gathering information about regulation in export markets and eventually incur unnecessary adjustments costs (that they pass on to consumers).[10] Additional costs may also be imposed as a result of differing conformity assessment and testing procedures. These costs have negative implications for market access, trade, and economic growth. To quote but one similar example, that has been discussed in the TBT Committee:

> One example from EU-US trade in the automotive sector helps illustrate the economic rationale for regulatory cooperation. It has been argued that diversity between the two markets in standards and conformity testing requirements for automotive parts such as headlights, wiper blades, seatbelts, and crash standards persist despite any measurable differences in safety benefits. For instance, in order to market a domestically successful model in the other market, one manufacturer reportedly invested USD 40 million and utilized 100 unique additional parts to develop a model that would satisfy the requirements of the other market. However, the safety and emissions performance of this export model was identical to that of the domestic model. This example illustrates an instance of unnecessary regulatory diversity; the standards and testing procedures of the two markets could be better harmonized without compromising the objective of the measures, while

---

[10] Nor should one overlook the possibility that harmonization of standards might favour one trading group over another: Büthe and Mattli (2011) provide ample support for the thesis that many international standards are not a compromise between various national attempts to standardize a market, but the victory of one national standard over another.

saving exporters significant cost and permitting economies of scale, as well as promoting trade, market access and economic growth. Naturally, some diversity may be necessary between Members' automotive standards, for instance in the cases of differences in geographic and climatic conditions. In such a case, regulatory cooperation can also help reduce costs of compliance by lowering information costs and reducing uncertainty.[11]

Perhaps, the following statement by Gerald Ritterbusch, director of standards and regulations for the US firm Caterpillar before the Committee on Science of the US House of Representatives quoted by Büthe and Mattli (2011, p. 9) captures best the problems posed for international traders by unilateral standard-setting:

> How do standards impact our ability to compete internationally?...When we have domestic standards that are different from international standards, everybody loses. We lose domestically because we must build a product that is different from products we sell internationally. That raises...costs, hurting American consumers...causing for us unfavourable opportunities in foreign markets. What is needed is that our domestic standards experts aggressively participate in international standards developments to get domestic standards accepted...

Are these costs substantial? There are two approaches that are used to measure costs for compliance: the macro approach, where costs are measured by estimating the variations of standards across different countries, and the micro approach, where costs are measured by estimating the costs directly borne by business asked to meet divergent requirements. The former is used more widely, although it is difficult to totally isolate the impact of standards from other explanatory variables.[12] There are dozens of measurements of costs stemming from different standards: according to the WTO World Trade Report (2009), one-third of global trade in goods (estimated in $15.8 trillion in 2008) was affected by standards that often differ across national jurisdictions; the same report estimates that harmonization of standards would be equivalent to tariff reductions across the globe of several percentage points.[13] Kawamoto et al. (1997) estimate that national differences in product standards result in losses for the US alone of between $20–40 billion per year. Keep in mind that it is difficult to measure all costs in a precise manner: negotiation of and eventually adherence to international standards will, for example, increase lobbying costs, since lobbyists will now have to persuade more than one agent.

---

[11] WTO Doc. G/TBT/W/340.

[12] Cecchini (1988) provides estimates on the impact of standards on European firms, but nothing on costs for firms engaging in cross-border operations. Some authors went ahead and provided estimations; see, for example, de Melo and Tarr (1992) who calculated the tariff-equivalent for US standards in the automotive sector to be 49 per cent. The calculation rests of course on some assumptions. Baldwin (1991) provides a macro and Henson (1996) a series of micro estimations of costs of compliance.

[13] WTO, World Trade Report, 2009, pp. 4ff.

In order to avoid rent-seeking behaviour from domestic lobbies, a certain degree of cooperation might be warranted.[14] There is a great deal of discussion in economic theory regarding whether and under what circumstances harmonization (international standards) is welfare enhancing. The answer is far from clear.[15] There are, for example, solid arguments advanced to the effect that standardization of production at the international level is a better guarantee for market access in regulated sectors. Many will argue that, in the case of network externalities, enacting compatibility standards can have positive welfare implications.[16] In this case, however, the market might reach this outcome anyway. Some economists[17] will further agree that harmonization definitely makes sense in the presence of global externalities, such as environmental pollution, and in the presence of network externalities, since, in such instances, governments tend to under-regulate.[18] Hundreds of standards are being negotiated every day in various fora: Kawamato et al. (1997) calculate the share of US exports affected by foreign product standards rose from 10 per cent in 1970 to 65 per cent in 1993.

---

[14] Sykes (2000); Pelkmans (2003). Deardorff and Stern (1998) have shown the measurement of technical barriers to trade is not a simple task even for the most gifted econometricians (the 'tariffication' of NTBs is, in other words, a demanding enterprise). However, Kee et al. (2009) offer a quantification of NTBs in a sample of 78 countries and conclude their *ad valorem* equivalent is higher than the duties in place in these countries. Still, even in the absence of precise measurement, one should not conclude that it is impossible to measure more or less the resulting welfare implications: Wilson and Otsuki (2004) conclude that, in the sectors they examined (289 firms from 25 industries), the negative implications of unilateral standard-setting, especially for developing countries, should not be underestimated. The WTO, in partnership with other organizations, delivers technical cooperation to LDCs and other low income countries through the Standards and Trade Development Facility (STDF): in 2010 and 2011, a total of 27 projects were approved. They are meant to improve the capacity in developing countries to meet international SPS standards and thus, their ability to trade in food and farm goods. See WTO Doc. WT/MIN(11)/5 of 18 November 2011 at pp. 9ff. It is remarkable that developing countries have not invested more negotiating recources in this area, probably because, as Büthe (2008) argues, they overestimated how much they could achieve through the special and differential provisions included in the SPS Agreement.

[15] Drabek (2005). See also the discussion in various parts of the World Trade Report (2005, pp. 29ff).

[16] Katz and Shapiro (1985). The literature offers numerous examples, some more 'classic' than others (computers and plugs, hardware and software, etc.). The argument is that standard-setting is preferable to the use of adaptors which come at a cost anyway.

[17] See the discussion in the World Trade Report (2005, pp. 53ff).

[18] What is, however, the counterfactual? Take the case of the negotiations on the Kyoto Protocol which deals with an admittedly global environmental issue. One reading of the situation is that (some) states, either because they will not be directly affected by their own pollution or because there is a problem of collective action, might prefer not to intervene at all or to intervene in an un-costly and probably ineffective manner. Another reading suggested by Gollier et al. (2000) is that some states believe that no intervention is required on an issue like climate change until more about the hazard is known. Assuming this view is correct, states might be under-regulating for fear that by doing so they might be doing more harm than good. One should, thus, not necessarily impose a negative value on under-regulation. It is not suggested here that action in accordance with the Kyoto Protocol is unnecessary. It is merely suggested that under-regulation could be a value judgement.

This literature falls short of establishing when and under what circumstances the 'optimal regulatory area' should cover the world. Indeed, would the Kyoto Protocol suffer if an islet in the Pacific decided not to join? Regulatory cooperation can under certain assumptions be beneficial, but, as alluded to above, the tough question is what is the optimal number of participants in the cooperation scheme? When should one go for a bilateral mutual recognition agreement (MRA), when should similar agreements be extended to some and when to all partners? This is a far from easy question to answer since a number of variables might affect the outcome and it is not by simply ticking boxes that one is led to the correct answer, assuming there is one. In practice, the starting-point for mutual recognition is that trading partners have more or less similar levels of protection in, for example, safety, health, environment, and consumer protection. In this case, full harmonization is no longer necessary and cross-border trade is facilitated.[19] Theory[20] predicts that recognition agreements would occur across countries that trust each other's regulatory regime. Trust is necessary since through recognition a party accepts another country's regime as equivalent to its own:[21] crucially, it cannot at all influence the shaping of the regime it accepts as equivalent. Trust, however, is hard to quantify. Recourse to proxies is thus necessary to establish whether trust exists. A number of proxies have been identified in the literature, such as language, geographic proximity, similarity across legal regimes, religion, etc. There is, of course, no guarantee at all that tomorrow's policies will be judged equivalent to yesterday's by all parties to the original contract. Breaking from the contract might be costly.[22] Negotiating costs would suggest narrower rather than more expansive agreements; arguments regarding gains from innovation would argue in favour of MRAs. On the other hand, negative external effects for all from unilateral definition of policies would suggest wider participation and this is the case when global concerns are in place, with the caveats mentioned above. Moreover, although empirical evidence to this effect across sectors is less persuasive than before, one cannot exclude a race to the bottom or, even, as Vogel (1997) shows, an unnecessary race to the top.

---

[19] Beviglia-Zampetti (2000a and 2000b); Nicolaidis (2000); Nicolaidis and Trachtman (2000); Piermartini (2005); Vogel (1997). The 'depth' of integration influences perceptions regarding similarities and differences can be exacerbated depending on the context: the differences between say the new EU members and the original members are minimal compared to the differences between LDCs and the most advanced WTO Members and yet they are consistently highlighted in literature precisely because the EU integration process is more demanding than the WTO; see Maduro (2007).

[20] Guiso et al. (2009).

[21] For a number of good reasons, equivalence can of course (some of them discussed *infra*) be an elusive concept. Hence, in practice, trading nations opt for equivalence of conformity assessment results in order to facilitate trade between them.

[22] Which probably explains why MRAs are typically signed between players in frequent interaction (repeat players), between whom some element of 'trust' exists.

Against this background, the TBT Agreement imposes an obligation in principle to observe appropriate international standards, and allows for bilateral deals on recognition, provided that they will be extended to all meeting the requisite criteria. The multilateral character of the WTO contract is thus preserved, but only just: terms of trade, as we noted in Chapter 4, can be affected through domestic instruments as well. Non-discrimination, as Staiger and Sykes (2011) and Saggi and Nese (2008) have argued, favours those who can affect terms of trade, since market access will be guaranteed only for those that can meet their regulatory requirements. There is by now ample empirical support to the effect that those who can affect terms of trade are those with the 'higher' so to speak regulatory standards.[23] So why then would these players wish to curtail their bargaining power? They undeniably do so when, next to non-discrimination, they add prerequisites for regulatory intervention such as that regulations must be science-based, consistent, necessary etc. But why? The discussion so far points to extra costs for (export) companies that have to comply with different standards. US companies might legitimately have thought that their Food and Drugs Authority (FDA) was strict enough, only to be surprised by the EU regulations on hormone-treated beef and GMOs (genetically modified organisms). In comparable vein, EU car producers might legitimately have thought that they were taking enough care of passengers safety only to realize that their cars need new bumpers to be allowed market access to the US. The transatlantic divergence definitely justified a dialogue (which had already started in various fora such as the international standardizing bodies and was thus easily exported to the WTO). They had an interest in trying to understand each other's standards and it is not by accident that most of the negotiating history of the SPS Agreement is a negotiation between the two (then) superpowers. It is of course difficult to explain reciprocity in this context (as indeed is the case any time a negotiation on regulatory standards takes place), and consequently we still lack a terms-of-trade explanation for these agreements: still, the negotiating history points to a bargain between two symmetric players. And what about the rest of the world? They would profit, in principle, from the efforts to curtail each other's bargaining power. And, yes, this could be in line with the Hullian idea that MFN is the contribution of the superpowers to peace. But how much do they profit? As we shall see *infra*, bilateral recognition schemes are not easily multilateralized. Internationalization of standards is probably the best avenue for those with good ideas and little bargaining power to advance their point of view. The recent work by Büthe and Mattli (2011) suggests that for the time being this is a process largely dominated by the big players.[24]

---

[23] Various contributions in Wilson and Abiola (2003) make this point.

[24] The EU and the US are not uni-dimensional actors: they both have competitive domestic markets (in the overwhelming majority of goods produced) and there is a cause and effect between the rivalry in their domestic markets and their representation in standardizing bodies.

The TBT Agreement (and the SPS as we shall see *infra* in this chapter) provides the best regulatory paradigm we have (and hopefully this will be shown in the following pages) to distinguish the wheat from the chaff in the realm of domestic instruments: the proxies established are highly appropriate and as a result the WTO judge dealing with similar cases is in a better position than when dealing with GATT cases. They are, alas, also knowledge-demanding and thus represent a challenge for the current agency design for dispute adjudication at the WTO: the judge, as we shall see *infra*, will frequently be confronted with issues regarding the scientific validity of regulatory propositions, or difficult judgments regarding the regulatory consistency of trading nations. Recourse to expertise is not necessarily a panacea since ultimately the judge will be asked to evaluate (often) contradictory expertise.

2.2 The Coverage of the Discipline

2.2.1 The Instruments Coming under the Purview of TBT

The TBT Agreement regulates three instruments: technical regulations, standards, and international standards. Since, in principle, WTO Members must use international standards if appropriate, we start the discussion here.[25]

2.2.2 International Standards

Recourse to international standards is compulsory under Art. 2.4 TBT:[26]

> Where technical regulations are required and relevant international standards exist or their completion is imminent, Members shall use them, or the relevant parts of them, as a basis for their technical regulations except when such international standards or relevant parts would be an ineffective or inappropriate means for the fulfillment of the legitimate objectives pursued, for instance because of fundamental climatic or geographical factors or fundamental technological problems.[27]

There is thus no obligation for WTO Members to adopt international standards every time they are concluded: they must do so only if they unilaterally decide to intervene in an area covered by an international standard. If not, Art. 2.4 TBT is irrelevant. The TBT Agreement should, for this reason alone, not be construed as an instrument mandating positive integration. The term 'international standard' is not defined at all, except for a reference in Annex 1 to the effect that:

> Standards prepared by the international standardization community are based on consensus. This Agreement covers also documents that are not based on consensus.

---

[25] Sykes (1995 and 1999) discusses the various legal disciplines.

[26] International standardization is one of the objectives of the TBT Agreement, prominently featuring in its Preamble.

[27] Gormann (2009) shows that standards are adopted for a variety of reasons: for example, Brazil, China, and India often adopt ISO/IEC standards lock, stock, and barrel in an effort to avoid becoming the dumping ground for products non-compliant with international standards.

The international standardization community is not defined either: in its Annexes, though, the TBT Agreement makes references to the ISO (International Organization for Standardization). For the rest, in case of disagreement it will be up to Panels to decide whether a document can be considered as standard. In principle, even an ISO standard would have to be accepted as an international standard by a Panel, since nowhere does the Agreement give Panels discretion to this effect. And yet few institutions are responsible for the majority of standards issued: besides the International Accounting Standards Board (IASB), which deals with financial rule-making, two private regulators stand out: the ISO and the International Electro-technical Commission (IEC) which jointly account for about 85 per cent of all international product standards.[28] These are neither pure governmental nor totally private entities, but in the words of Büthe and Mattli (2011, p. 5), they are best described as:

> ...centrally coordinated global networks comprising hundreds of technical committees from all over the world and involving tens to thousands of experts representing industries and other groups in developing and regularly maintaining technical standards.

There is an increasing political-economy literature discussing standard-setting in similar bodies. Domestic standard-setting institutions will try to influence standard-setting at the international level and promote national choices. Büthe and Mattli (2011, pp. 11ff) probably got it right when they argued that technical expertise is a necessary but not sufficient condition in the quest for pre-eminence in international standard-setting bodies; it is 'timely information and effective representation of domestic interest that confer the critical advantage in these regulatory processes, determining who wins and who loses'.[29]

The IEC and the ISO[30] became household names in the trade community thanks to Art. 2.4 TBT. Not all international standards carry the same legitimacy as far as the TBT Agreement is concerned: only those standards that are appropriate and/or effective means to achieve a stated objective must, in principle, be used by WTO Members. The WTO does not condition the relevance of standards in any other way: the Explanatory Note in Annex 1 to the TBT states that the TBT Agreement covers 'documents' that are not based on consensus,[31] thus

---

[28] Büthe and Mattli (2011) at p. 5.

[29] Büthe and Mattli (2011) at pp. 12–13.

[30] On the advent and the history of these two institutions, see Büthe and Mattli (2011) at pp. 128ff.

[31] The Explanatory Note in Annex 1 of the TBT Agreement reads: 'The terms as defined in ISO/IEC Guide 2 cover products, processes and services. This Agreement deals only with technical regulations, standards and conformity assessment procedures related to products or processes and production methods. Standards as defined by ISO/IEC Guide 2 may be mandatory or voluntary. For the purpose of this Agreement standards are defined as voluntary and technical regulations as mandatory documents. Standards prepared by the international standardization community are based on consensus. This Agreement covers also documents that are not based on consensus'.

undermining, prima facie at least, the representativeness (legitimacy) of standards incorporated in the TBT Agreement.[32]

In this vein, in *EC—Sardines* (§225),[33] the AB rejected an argument advanced by the EU that only standards adopted by unanimity are international standards: at stake was a standard adopted by the ISO/IEC. Noting that the ISO/IEC Guide accepts only consensus-based standards as international standards,[34] the AB went on to state that the deviation included in the Explanatory Note in Annex 1 of the TBT Agreement, according to which even standards adopted without consensus are recognized as international standards, must have been voluntary. It thus held that an international standard adopted without a unanimity vote can still qualify as standard under Art. 2.4 TBT Agreement. The Panel and the AB accepted in this dispute that a standard adopted by the Codex Alimentarius Commission relating to the species that can lawfully carry the name 'sardine' was an international standard in the TBT sense of the term.

Remarkably, the Panel and the AB did not even pay lip service to the 2000 TBT Committee Decision,[35] which included six principles that should be observed when international standards are elaborated. §1 of the Decision reads:

> The following principles and procedures should be observed, when international standards, guides and recommendations (as mentioned under Articles 2, 5 and Annex 3 of the TBT Agreement for the preparation of mandatory technical regulations, conformity assessment procedures and voluntary standards) are elaborated, to ensure transparency, openness, impartiality and consensus, effectiveness and relevance, coherence, and to address the concerns of developing countries.

§8 of the Decision explains in more detail how it understand the 'consensus' principle:

> All relevant bodies of WTO Members should be provided with meaningful opportunities to contribute to the elaboration of an international standard so that the standard development process will not give privilege to, or favour the interests of, a particular supplier/s, country/ies or region/s. Consensus procedures should be

---

[32] See, on this issue, the very interesting account with respect to the hormones standards provided in Abdel Motaal (2004). Büthe and Mattli (2011, pp. 140ff) discuss the structure and voting procedures in ISO/IEC and explain why it is the US and the EU that dominate the process there.

[33] Horn and Weiler (2007); in *EC—Sardines*, the AB, upholding the Panel's findings in this respect, confirmed that the definition of 'standard' in §2 of Annex 1 to the TBT is relevant not only for domestic (that is, non-compulsory), but for international standards as well (§220).

[34] Nevertheless, as Büthe and Mattli (2011, pp. 145–6) note, 'consensus' in the ISO/IEC context does not see eye to eye with the commonplace understanding of the term: it means something akin to striving for the greatest feasible agreement among the technical preferences of the member countries that have taken a position on a draft standard; it can also entail that negative opinions without justification will be discarded.

[35] Decision by the Committee on Principles for the Development of International Standards, Guides and Recommendations in Relation to Articles 2, 5 and Annex 3 of the Agreement, WTO Doc. G/TBT/9 of 13 November 2000.

established that seek to take into account the views of all parties concerned and to reconcile any conflicting arguments.

Now this principle seems to restrict the ambit of the Explanatory Note. The WTO Membership (since all Members participate in the TBT Committee), post-Uruguay round, seems to hold the view that at least opportunities should be given to all WTO Members (and their relevant bodies) to express themselves when elaborating international standards. The wording is unclear as to whether the six principles also apply to standards adopted before 2000 (the advent of the Decision). Good arguments could be advanced against its retroactive relevance. Assuming WTO adjudicating bodies will recognize the legal relevance of this Decision,[36] then one should expect that it becomes relevant for standards adopted after it was enacted.

WTO Members will have to base their regulatory interventions on international standards, only to the extent that the latter are relevant to the objective they are pursuing. In *EC—Sardines*,[37] the EU had argued that, since the product coverage between the international standard and the EU technical regulation was not identical, the former was not relevant for the latter: the international standard covered the marketing of 21 fish species, while the EU technical regulation only covered the marketing of one of them. The AB rejected this argument: since the EU technical regulation had legal implications for the marketing of the other 20 species covered by the international standard, the AB held that the international standard was relevant for the EU technical regulation (§§222ff). This seems an eminently reasonable conclusion: if one were to accept the EU argument, circumvention of international standards would become a simple act of acknowledging the rights of only a sub-part of the right-holders in an international standard context.

International standards or the relevant parts of them must be used as the basis for the adoption of technical regulations (Art. 2.4 TBT). The AB, in its report on *EC—Sardines*, understood the term 'basis' as at least entailing that a technical regulation should not be contradictory to the relevant international standard. The AB also pointed out that all relevant parts of an international standard, not only some of them, must form the basis of a technical regulation (§§248 and 250).

WTO Members can deviate from an international standard, if it is ineffective or inappropriate for the attainment of a sought objective. In *EC—Sardines*, Peru complained that the EU had unjustifiably deviated from the international standard reflecting the denomination of sardines. The facts of the case[38] are as follows: the dispute concerned the name under which certain species of fish could be marketed

---

[36] As they have done on other occasions, recall our discussion in Chapter 7 on the relevance of a recommendation by the AD committee on the duration of the period of investigation. On the legal relevance of secondary law in WTO adjudication, see Mavroidis (2008).

[37] We discuss the facts in detail *infra*.

[38] For a more detailed description, see §§2–8 of the AB report.

in the EU. An EU Council Regulation[39] set forth common marketing standards for preserved sardines, allowing only products conforming to the following four requirements to carry the name 'sardine' commercially:

(a) They must be covered by CN codes 1604 13 10 and ex 1604 20 50;
(b) They must be prepared exclusively from fish of the species '*Sardina pilchardus Walbaum*';
(c) They must be pre-packaged with any appropriate covering medium in a hermetically sealed container; and, finally,
(d) They must be sterilized by appropriate treatment.

Sardina pilchardus Walbaum ('*Sardina pilchardus*'), is found mainly around the coasts of the eastern North Atlantic Ocean, in the Mediterranean Sea, and in the Black Sea, that is, the area where EU fishermen normally fish. In 1978, the Codex Alimentarius Commission of the United Nations Food and Agriculture Organization (FAO) and the World Health Organization (WHO) adopted a worldwide standard for preserved sardines and sardine-type products, which regulates matters such as presentation, essential composition and quality factors, food additives, hygiene and handling, labelling, sampling, examination and analyses, defects and lot acceptance. This standard (CODEX STAN 94–1981, Rev.1–1995) covers preserved sardines or sardine-type products prepared from 21 fish species, and among them *Sardina pilchardus* and *Sardinops sagax*. Section 6.1.1 of CODEX STAN 94–1981, Rev.1–1995 regulated the name that the 21 mentioned species could legitimately carry in the following manner:

(a) 'Sardines' to be reserved exclusively for *Sardina pilchardus* (*Walbaum*); or
(b) 'X sardines' of a country, a geographic area, the species, or the common name of the species in accordance with the law and custom of the country in which the product is sold, and in a manner not to mislead the consumer.

Peru exported preserved products prepared from *Sardinops sagax*. This species is found mainly in the eastern Pacific Ocean, along the coasts of Peru and Chile. Peru was prohibited, pursuant to the EU regulation, from exporting its product under the name 'sardine', and feared that marketing its exports under a different name would adversely affect its interests. It thus requested the establishment of a WTO Panel to examine the consistency of the EU regulation with the TBT disciplines. The proceedings were facilitated by the fact that there was no dispute among the parties that the EU had deviated from the international standard. The AB first had to decide the meaning of the term 'ineffective or inappropriate' (§285):

---

[39] (EEC) 2136/89 of 21 June 1989 laying down common marketing standards for preserved sardines, 1989, OJ L212/79.

...we noted earlier the Panel's view that the term 'ineffective or inappropriate means' refers to two questions—the question of the *effectiveness* of the measure and the question of the *appropriateness* of the measure—and that these two questions, although closely related, are different in nature. The Panel pointed out that the term 'ineffective' 'refers to something which is not 'having the function of accomplishing', 'having a result', or 'brought to bear', whereas [the term] 'inappropriate' refers to something which is not 'specially suitable', 'proper', or 'fitting' '. The Panel also stated that:

Thus, in the context of Article 2.4, an ineffective means is a means which does not have the function of accomplishing the legitimate objective pursued, whereas an inappropriate means is a means which is not specially suitable for the fulfillment of the legitimate objective pursued ... The question of effectiveness bears upon the *results* of the means employed, whereas the question of appropriateness relates more to the *nature* of the means employed.

We agree with the Panel's interpretation. (emphasis in the original)[40]

The AB then had to respond to the question who carries the burden of proof to show whether, in case of deviation from an international standard, deviation has been TBT-consistent because the standard at hand was ineffective or inappropriate. The AB reversed the Panel in this respect: it concluded that the burden stays with the complaining party to prove that the international standard is appropriate and effective and, consequently, the defendant could have reached its objectives staying within its four corners (§282). In the AB's view, the complainant was not placed at disadvantage through its allocation of the burden of proof: it could easily acquire the necessary information regarding the EU standard through the various transparency obligations embedded in the TBT Agreement, and critically through the enquiry points that the TBT Agreement requires from WTO to establish in order to inform traders about their standards (Art. 10 TBT); but even if this was not enough, Peru anyway became accustomed to the EU standard, in the AB's view, through the litigation process. The AB also referred to its case law under the SPS (*EC—Hormones*), where it had decided this issue in a similar manner, and saw no reason to decide otherwise in the context of the TBT Agreement. Curiously, though, although it reversed the Panel, it still found in favour of Peru, based on evidence that Peru had submitted before the Panel where the allocation of burden of proof had been different (§290).

Horn and Weiler (2007) have, validly in our view, criticized the approach of the AB. They question whether, in light of the current allocation of the burden of proof, traders will have an incentive to be forthcoming when it comes to providing information regarding their standards; arguably, they will have an incentive to be

---

[40] In *US—Tuna II (Mexico)*, the Panel addressed an argument by Mexico to the effect that the US had violated its obligations under the TBT by deviating from an international standard (the AIDCP standard, discussed in more detail below). The Panel held that the invoked standard was not as effective as the US chosen means, since it did not address both of the concerns advanced by the US as the underlying rationale for adoption of its measure (§§7.721ff and especially 7.726).

circumspect. In this vein, they question whether it is possible at all for the complainant to know why the defendant took the view that the international standard was ineffective or inappropriate. This could be a classic case of private information and, in light of the incentives described above, could remain private for some time. Curiously though, the AB's construction of Art. 2.4 TBT does not bring into question the legitimacy of international standards: the very low burden of persuasion imposed on Peru is the reason. Quoting from Horn and Weiler (2007):

> In the dispute Peru submitted evidence suggesting that 'sardines' by itself or combined with the name of a country or region is a common name for *Sardinops sagax* in the EC. Peru here referred to three dictionaries/publications, two of which produced in cooperation with, or with support by, the European Commission, and one prepared by the OECD. But it should be noted that this evidence does not directly show that consumers would not confuse *Sarinops sagax*, if labeled as 'Peruvian Sardines', with *Sardina pilchardus*. On the contrary, it might perhaps be argued that the existence of these lexica suggests that the classification of fish is not a simple matter, and that consequently there are reasons to suspect that consumers might be confused about the different species of fish. Hence, it is strictly speaking not clear what these publications say about consumer perceptions.

Still, on that evidence, Peru prevailed. Remarkably, the AB, a body that usually adopts literal interpretations,[41] chose to pay lip service only to the term 'except' prominently featured in Art. 2.4 TBT, and held that there was nothing exceptional about deviations from international standards. In its view, this provision refers to two equally frequent or infrequent circumstances: when international standards exist and when not. This was the basis for the allocation of the burden of proof in the manner described above. But, of course, this is not what the provision suggests. The term 'except' was inserted because the framers wanted to underline the primacy of international standards; the AB tried to undo this construction but it probably failed, if Horn and Weiler (2007) are proved right and the AB continues to be relaxed when it comes to the burden of persuasion in future cases.

2.2.3 Technical Regulations

A WTO Member deviating from an international standard, or a WTO Member wishing to intervene in the absence of international standard, will have to abide by the TBT Agreement if it adopts a technical regulation or a standard (or a conformity assessment procedure). Whereas compliance with the former is compulsory otherwise market access will be denied in the regulating WTO Member, compliance with the latter is not a precondition for market access. The term 'technical regulation' is defined in Annex 1, §1 of the TBT Agreement as follows:

> Document which lays down product characteristics or their related processes and production methods, including the applicable administrative provisions, with which

---

[41] The *Oxford English Dictionary* is cited in almost all its reports.

compliance is mandatory. It may also include or deal exclusively with terminology, symbols, packaging, marking or labeling requirements as they apply to a product, process or production method.

Reviewing its prior jurisprudence on the issue (§§67–72, *EC—Asbestos*), the AB defined technical regulation in its report on *EC—Sardines* in the following manner (§§175–6):

> In doing so, we set out *three criteria* that a document must meet to fall within the definition of 'technical regulation' in the *TBT Agreement*. *First*, the document must apply to an identifiable product or group of products. The *identifiable* product or group of products need not, however, be expressly *identified* in the document. *Second*, the document must lay down one or more characteristics of the product. These product characteristics may be intrinsic, or they may be related to the product. They may be prescribed or imposed in either a positive or a negative form. *Third*, compliance with the product characteristics must be mandatory. (emphasis in the original)[42]

The wording used will decide whether we are in presence of a technical regulation. Words like 'shall', 'must', etc. denote binding nature, that is, unless compliance with the substantive content of the relevant document has been demonstrated, market access will be denied. In *EC—Asbestos*, however, the AB held that even when the words used in a document are of a hortatory nature, we could still be in presence of a technical regulation if the latter (§68):

> has the *effect* of prescribing or imposing one or more 'characteristics'—'features', 'qualities', 'attributes', or other 'distinguishing mark. (emphasis in the original)

In this vein, the Panel on *US—COOL* went on to examine whether a letter sent by US Secretary of Agriculture Vilsack which contained unambiguously hortatory language could be considered as technical regulation. In this case, Canada and Mexico had challenged a US measure imposing compulsory labelling indicating the origin of imported goods (such as bovine meat and pork).[43] The US measure established four categories: category A referring to say beef wholly produced and slaughtered in the US, whereas category D covered beef produced and slaughtered abroad. There were two in-between categories, B and C, the functionality of which is explained in §7.697 of the report:

---

[42] See also the Panel report on *US—COOL* at §7.147. In *US—Tuna II (Mexico)*, the Panel held that US legislation which did not impose the label 'dolphin safe' on imports of tuna but which conditioned its lawful use upon meeting certain criteria was a technical regulation and not a standard (§§7.100ff and especially 7.120 and 7.131). This would be a wrong understanding of what a standard is because, if the Panel's view is eventually upheld by the AB, standards would become totally unenforceable. A separate opinion issued by one member of the Panel got it right when it stressed that what is relevant for the qualification of the measure was ultimately whether imports had to or could choose whether to carry the label 'dolphin safe' and, consequently, that the measure at hand was a standard (§§7.146ff).

[43] For detailed description of the goods concerned, see §7.78 of the Panel report.

We recall that meat falling within the scope of categories B and C is required to carry labels indicating 'product of the US, Country X' (Label B) and 'product of Country X, the US' (Label C). As described above in Section VII.C.1(b)(i), Label B refers to meat derived from animals born in Country X, and raised and slaughtered in the United States, whereas Label C refers to meat derived from animals imported for immediate slaughter (i.e. animals born and raised outside the United States). Labels B and C are therefore differentiated by the order of country names indicated on the label.

Secretary Thomas J. Vilsack issued a letter aiming at the implementation of the US statute, which in part read as follows (§7.123):

> I am suggesting...that the industry *voluntarily* adopt the following practices to ensure that consumers are adequately informed about the source of food products: ...processors should *voluntarily* include information about what production steps occurred in each country when multiple countries appear on each label....Even if products [that are otherwise exempt] are subject to curing, smoking, broiling, grilling, or steaming, *voluntary* labeling would be appropriate....(emphasis in the original)

The Panel went ahead and examined whether, its language notwithstanding, this letter could be considered as technical regulation; it concluded in the negative since it found no empirical evidence suggesting it operated as such (§§7.188ff).

Usually, a technical regulation defines specific product characteristics, such as size, shape, design, functions, performance, labelling, or packaging, as well as related process and production standards. The AB, interpreting the identification requirement, has emphasized that there is no obligation that a particular product be explicitly mentioned in the body of the technical regulation; it suffices that a product can be identified. Therefore, omissions are not fatal (*EC—Sardines*, §§ 180, 183): in that case, although the challenged regulation did not explicitly identify *sardinops sagax* as one of the types of sardines that was covered, it was quite clear, in the AB's view, that the scope of the regulation covered this type of sardines as well; in its view, what matters is whether a means of identification of a product has been provided (§§190–1).

Technical regulations must respect three disciplines:

(a) They must be non-discriminatory;
(b) They must be necessary to achieve a particular objective; and
(c) They must be pursuing a legitimate objective.

These three disciplines must be cumulatively met (Arts 2.1 and 2.2 TBT). WTO Members must, by virtue of the non-discrimination discipline, not afford imported goods less favourable treatment than that afforded to domestic like products. The term 'like product' remained for years un-interpreted, and was first interpreted in two Panel reports issued in 2011. In *US—Tuna II (Mexico)* and *US—Clove Cigarettes*, two Panels were requested to provide their understanding of the term. The first case concerned a challenge by Indonesia against the US's

Family Smoking Prevention Tobacco Control Act of 2009 that banned clove cigarettes. Indonesia alleged that Section 907 of this law prohibited the production or sale in the US of cigarettes containing certain additives, including clove, but would continue to permit the production and sale of other cigarettes, including cigarettes containing menthol. Indonesia alleged that Section 907 was inconsistent with Art. 2 TBT. The question arose whether clove and menthol cigarettes were like products. In the second case, Mexico challenged a series of US measures (the US Code, Title 16, Section 1385, 'Dolphin Protection Consumer Information Act'; the US Code of Federal Regulations, Title 50, Section 216.91, 'Dolphin-safe labeling standards', and Section 216.92, 'Dolphin-safe requirements for tuna harvested in the Eastern Tropical Pacific Ocean by large purse seine vessels'; and the ruling by a US Court in *Earth Island Institute v Hogarth*, 494 F.3d 757 (9th Cir. 2007)). In Mexico's view, the measures at issue, which established the conditions for use of a 'dolphin-safe' label on tuna products and conditioned the access to the US Department of Commerce official dolphin-safe label upon bringing certain documentary evidence that varied depending on the area where tuna contained in the tuna product had been harvested and the fishing method by which it had been harvested, were inconsistent with Art. 2.1 TBT. The Panel here had to pronounce on the likeness of two tuna products harvested in different geographic locations.

In *US—Tuna II (Mexico)*, the Panel held that (§§7.225–6):

> The TBT Agreement applies to a limited set of measures, and our understanding of its terms, including the terms 'like products' must be informed by this context. As expressed in the preamble of the TBT Agreement, this Agreement reflects the intention of the negotiators to:
>
>> '[E]nsure that technical regulations and standards, including packaging, marking and labelling requirements, and procedures for assessment of conformity with technical regulations and standards do not create unnecessary obstacles to trade.'
>
> To the extent that Article 2.1 contributes to avoiding 'unnecessary obstacles to trade' arising from undue discrimination with respect to technical regulations, it seeks to preserve the competitive opportunities of products originating in any Member, in relation to technical regulations. Thus, the term 'like products' under Article 2.1 of the TBT Agreement may be similarly understood as relating to 'the nature and extent of a competitive relationship' between and among products.
>
> We further note, as the Appellate Body did in relation to Article III:4 of the GATT 1994, that this does not necessarily imply that Members may not draw any regulatory distinctions, under Article 2.1 of the TBT Agreement, between products that have been determined to be like products. The question of the treatment to be given to products that are like is addressed separately in the requirement of not affording treatment less favourable, which we consider in the next Section of our Report.

In *US—Clove Cigarettes*, the Panel held that (§§7.244–7):

> As we have explained, we believe that such legitimate objective must permeate and inform our likeness analysis. In the weighing of these criteria, we have therefore

carefully considered the relevance of those traits that are significant for the public health objective of Section 907(a)(1)(A), i.e., to reduce youth smoking.

We consider that our basic approach to 'likeness' in this case is consistent with a very helpful hypothetical presented by the United States at the second meeting of the Panel, and reiterated in response to a question from the Panel:

> 'Certain products may be considered like in certain contexts but not in others. For example, as the United States noted at the Second Substantive Meeting with Panel, cups made from paper, plastic and aluminum might be considered "like" products regardless of these physical differences with respect to a tax or other fiscal measure. They all serve the same end-use of holding liquids, and may be viewed as interchangeable by consumers in this context. The different materials used in the cups may be considered to be less important in the like product analysis in this situation. However, the same cups might not be considered "like" with respect to a measure regulating products that can be used safely in microwave ovens. In that case, the different materials used to make the cups would be more relevant, as aluminum may not be safely used in a microwave. This difference would effect whether consumers viewed each cup as suitable for use in a microwave and would be relevant to measures regulating which cups could be used in microwaves. In this context, the different materials used would be significant differences among the cups. The particular measure at issue is relevant to whether the different physical properties of the cup mean that one cup is not "like" another cup.'

We think that clove cigarettes and menthol cigarettes may be considered 'like' in certain contexts but not in others. For example, these two kinds of cigarettes might not be considered 'like' in the context of a hypothetical measure regulating products on the basis of characteristics that clove cigarettes and menthol cigarettes do not have in common, for example whether they contain eugenol (clove cigarettes do, and most menthol cigarettes do not). Along the same lines, they might not be considered 'like' in the context of a hypothetical tax or fiscal measure based on the type of tobacco they contain (clove cigarettes tend to contain Java sun-cured tobacco, menthol cigarettes do not). However, these same two types of cigarettes might be considered 'like' in the context of other measures that regulate products on the basis of characteristics that clove and menthol cigarettes do have in common, for example a hypothetical measure distinguishing between various tobacco products on the basis of whether or not those products are carcinogenic (which clove cigarettes and menthol cigarettes both are).

The measure at issue in this case plainly regulates cigarettes on the basis of a characteristic that clove cigarettes and menthol cigarettes have in common, which in the words of Section 907(a)(1)(A), is the shared characteristic that they 'contain, as a constituent . . . or additive, an artificial or natural flavor . . . or an herb or spice . . . that is a characterizing flavor'. In the context of this particular measure, which regulates tobacco products on the basis of this particular characteristic—which may be regarded as perhaps the defining feature of each type of product—we find it very difficult to see how clove cigarettes and menthol cigarettes would not be considered to be 'like'. As discussed in our findings, we are aware that there are certain differences between clove cigarettes and menthol cigarettes. These differences may well lead to the conclusion that these two products are not 'like' in the context of different measures. However, in the context of the measure at issue in this dispute, these differences are less significant, and less relevant. In other words, contrary to what the United States argues, those differences do not relate to the public health objective of the measure at issue and therefore, are not relevant to the like product analysis in this case. In our view, the similarities related to the public health objective of Section 907(a)(1)(A) are highly relevant to the like product analysis in the circumstances of this case.

The two reports are hard to reconcile: the former suggests that likeness will be a matter of competitive relationship, implying that it is the market that will decide this point. The latter suggests that an inquiry into the aims of the challenged measure is appropriate in order to conclude whether two goods are like or not. In a way, this latter approach reminds us of the 'aims and effects' test discussed in Chapter 4. On its face, this discrepancy looks irreconcilable. The AB on *US—Clove Cigarettes* held that likeness will be defined by consumers' reactions and informed by health risks. Unfortunately, it is unclear if by health risks they referred to regulatory objectives or consumers' reactions. Deciding on likeness is the first step towards establishing violation of the non-discrimination principle. The second, decisive step calls for a demonstration that Less favourable treatment (LFT) has been afforded to imported like goods. This is where the two Panel reports see eye to eye in that they espouse the test established in *Dominican Republic—Import and Sale of Cigarettes*. In *US—Clove Cigarettes*, the Panel made it clear that it was (§7.269):

> ... required to consider whether the detrimental effect(s) can be explained by factors or circumstances *unrelated to the foreign origin of the product*... (emphasis in the original)[44]

So, if a government enacts a technical regulation for a reason unrelated to the origin of the good, the question for the Panel ultimately will be for what purpose will it use the submitted information regarding the objective pursued: will it do it in order to decide on likeness of the goods, as *US—Clove Cigarettes* dictates, or will it use it in order to decide on whether LFT has been afforded to imported like goods, as the Panel on *US—Tuna II (Mexico)* decided? The AB upheld the finding by the Panel on *US—Clove Cigarettes* so this discussion at least seems settled (§175 ff.).

In *US—COOL*, the Panel evaluated econometric evidence in order to reach the conclusion that de facto discrimination had been afforded to imported goods, for example, that imported goods were granted LFT than domestic like goods in contravention of Art. 2.1 TBT. The question before the Panel was whether certain country of origin labelling requirements on meat and meat products[45] imposed additional costs on imports. An econometrics study (by Informa Economics, a consultancy) had been submitted to the Panel and this study had found that costs were indeed being imposed on foreign goods that did not have to be borne by domestic goods: this was the case because, in the Panel's view, imported goods had to face higher segregation costs (corresponding to costs associated with verification of the origin of the various stage of production of beef). The Panel refused to accept the reliability of the study, since in its words it (§7.499):

---

[44] The same attitude is evidenced in the Panel report on *US—Tuna II (Mexico)* at §7.375, as well as in *US—COOL* §7.313: this report went so far as to explicitly state that Art. III.4 GATT was the legal context for the interpretation of the LFT requirement under the TBT Agreement, §§7.234ff.

[45] COOL stands for 'Country Of Origin Labeling'.

is silent on its methodology and the sample considered.

The complainants submitted another study, this time prepared by Prof. Sumner (University of California at Davis). Sumner had compared Canadian meat prices and market shares in two scenarios: one where COOL requirements were present and one where they were not. He found that US retailers were willing to pay significantly less for Canadian meat in the first scenario, simply because of the ensuing compliance costs with the COOL requirements. In his view, this was the reason why the market share for Canadian meat had been reduced. There were also other studies submitted estimating the impact of the COOL requirements on imports by both the US (Department of Agriculture) and Canada (Sumner): these studies reached opposite results. The Panel made it clear that it was going to limit its review of the case to the econometrics expertise already supplied, and that it was not going to request its own expertise as it could have done by virtue of Art. 13 DSU. In this vein, the Panel held that that the study prepared by Sumner made a prima-facie case that the request to comply with the COOL requirements resulted in de facto discrimination. In its words, the study (§7.542):

> makes a prima facie case that the COOL measure negatively and significantly affected the import shares and price basis of Canadian livestock.

In its view, the study submitted by the US was not sufficiently robust and as a result did not refute the prima-facie case established by Sumner's study (§7.543–5):

> In fact, the 13 estimated equations for the cattle analysis do not show sufficient consistency to reach a robust conclusion. According to the USDA Econometric study, the COOL variable and its impact are never significant. However, the impact of economic recession is only negative and significant in a limited number of specifications and even in those cases only at a relatively low level of precision, i.e. at a 90% instead of the usual 95% level of confidence. This means that the USDA Econometric Study does not provide a sufficiently robust explanation that any negative impact is attributable to economic recession rather than to the COOL measure. In addition, any finding of the USDA Econometric Study with regard to the economic recession variable and its impact is called into question by potential multicollinearity, which the study failed to address.
>
> As regards hogs, the USDA Econometric Study merely refers to certain features of the hog market, i.e. US-based pricing and Canadian hog's inventory decline, but this cannot substitute for a proper and robust econometric analysis.
>
> Hence, the USDA Econometric Study does not rebut the prima facie case for a negative and significant COOL impact established by the Sumner Econometric Study.

There are good arguments, nonetheless, to suggest that the discussion above might prove if not redundant, at least only partially relevant in future practice.[46] Once

---

[46] The discussion here is equally applicable to technical regulations as well as standards.

a technical regulation has been enacted, the question before a national authority will be to what extent an imported good meets the requirements included in it, that is, to what extent the regulating state is pursuing a legitimate objective and has employed the least restrictive means while doing so. If yes, then the only remaining question would be whether both imported and domestic goods meet the regulatory requirements: if yes, then the measure should be applied in even-handed manner to both and if no, those failing to meet the standards will be lawfully denied market access. To ensure that imported goods meet the standards (assume domestic goods do so), the TBT Agreement requests from WTO Members to perform a conformity assessment. In other words, assuming lawfulness of the requirements included in a technical regulation, the question whether the imported good is a like good to the domestic good (which, we assume is in conformity with the technical regulation) will directly depend on the response to the question whether it meets the criteria set in the technical regulation. Consequently, there will be no need to examine consumers' perceptions etc. In other words, the focus in the TBT Agreement is different than the GATT focus:

(a) In TBT, consumers' perceptions are immaterial since the Agreement kicks in (so to speak) once a legitimate objective has been identified and applied. In other words, the case for regulation is very much a prerequisite for the applicability of the TBT Agreement;

(b) The LFT requirement is reduced to a simple yes or no answer, assuming the statutory requirements have been met: can the imported good access the market in case a technical regulation has been enacted? Can it carry say the same label in case a standard has been issued?

(c) Hence, the discussion in the TBT context should focus on whether the necessity requirement has been complied with when technical regulations and/or standards are being issued.[47]

What we are advancing as methodology to address future TBT litigation is a two-step procedure, whereby Panels should first inquire into whether the challenged technical regulation observes the necessity requirement, before discussing non-discrimination. We discuss necessity in more detail in what immediately follows; suffice to say in order to clarify the argument here that case law has understood the necessity requirement in the TBT context to be symmetric with the same requirement as we know it from Art. XX GATT. If this is the case indeed, then already some discussion regarding non-discrimination will take place within the four corners of the necessity test. In *US—Section 337*, a GATT Panel held (§5.26):

> By the same token, in cases where a measure consistent with other GATT provisions is not reasonably available, a contracting party is bound to use, among the measures

---

[47] Non-discrimination could be an issue in case of equivalence too, but we discuss this point *infra*.

reasonably available to it, that which entails the least degree of inconsistency with other GATT provisions.

In similar vein, the GATT Panel on *Thailand—Cigarettes* held in §75:

> The Panel concluded from the above that the import restrictions imposed by Thailand could be considered to be 'necessary' in terms of Article XX(b) only if there were no alternative measure consistent with the General Agreement, or less inconsistent with it, which Thailand could reasonably be expected to employ to achieve its health policy objectives.

This Panel subsequently went on to examine whether, instead of having recourse to GATT-inconsistent import restrictions, a series of GATT-consistent options would have allowed Thailand to reach its objective, namely, to protect human health (§§76ff). Of course, and it begs repetition, consistency with the necessity requirement is not the end but the beginning of the road: all the more so, since, in the TBT context, the non-discrimination obligation is a substantive obligation, whereas under Art. XX GATT compliance with the *chapeau* (which reflects an obligation of even-handedness as we saw in Chapter 5) concerns only the application and not the substantive conformity of a measure with the GATT. Assuming, thus, that the necessity requirement has been met, Panels could then review whether the measure also meets Art. 2.1 TBT: doing it the other way round though, can lead to difficult, if not altogether untenable, constructions of the TBT Agreement.

The TBT Agreement requests from WTO Members to ensure that technical regulations should not be enacted unless necessary and, if enacted, they should not be more trade restrictive than necessary to achieve the stated regulatory objective. The necessity requirement thus cuts two ways: first, the legislator invites an analysis of the risks in case no regulatory intervention takes place; second, if intervention is judged necessary, the chosen means must not be more restrictive than necessary to reach the stated legitimate objective.

Interventions based on international standards are, by virtue of Art. 2.5 TBT, presumed necessary to achieve a legitimate objective.[48]

Case law has evolved since the GATT years (*US—Section 337*) and it is probably not mere semantics that nowadays a 'significantly' less restrictive (as well as equally efficient) option must be reasonably available to the regulating state, otherwise no violation of the necessity requirement will be established.[49] In light of the allocation of the burden of proof,[50] the complainant must thus point not to a

---

[48] The Panel on *US—Clove Cigarettes* held that this provision (Art. 2.5 TBT) creates a rebuttable presumption (§7.331).

[49] AB, *Australia—Apples* at §363. We discuss this case in detail *infra* in this chapter. It is an SPS dispute; nevertheless the Panel report on *US—COOL* opted for a coherent interpretation of the necessity requirement across the GATT, the SPS, and the TBT: for this reason, it is of legal relevance here.

[50] *US—Gambling*, as discussed in Chapter 5.

marginally, but to a significantly, less restrictive option for the regulating state to be found in violation of its obligations under Art. 2.2 TBT.

In *US—Tuna II* (*Mexico*), the Panel underscored that the appropriate level of protection is the exclusive privilege of WTO Members who are solely responsible to define it, Panels being reduced to controlling the means employed to reach the objectives (§7.622). In the same report, the Panel held that the US had violated the necessity requirement by insisting on its 'dolphin safe' label and not allowing for the AIDCP standard to be also marketed in the US. The AIDCP (Agreement on International Dolphin Conservation Program) is a multilateral convention which has been quite successful in drastically reducing dolphin mortality. Its standard is less restrictive than the US standard, and by not allowing it, the US had violated Art. 2.2 TBT (§§7.601ff).

In *US—COOL*, the Panel found that the US measure was violating the necessity requirement since it did not clearly convey the message it was supposed to convey in the first place: consumers could be quite confused regarding which step of production was undertaken in which country in case different stages of production had taken place in different countries; in other words, because it was disservicing the objective pursued, the Panel was led to find that the US measure was unnecessary (§§7.684ff and especially 7.697 and 7.708ff). The same report held that the fact that the requirement to demonstrate origin was imposed on some of the products that could be characterized as DCS did not make the measure unnecessary; that is, the consistency requirement is not an integral part of the necessity test in the eyes of this Panel (§§7.682–3). Finally, this report held that, in interpreting the necessity requirement in the TBT context, it would be inspired by the case law interpretation of the same term in the GATT and the SPS context (§§7.667ff).

The TBT includes an illustrative list of legitimate objectives: national security requirements; the prevention of deceptive practices; protection of human health or safety, animal or plant life or health, or the environment. Panels, when assessing such risks, can take into account available scientific and technical information, related processing technology, or the intended end-uses of products. WTO Members have of course the right to determine for themselves the legitimate policies they want to pursue, and this is but an indicative list. It is worth bringing here the following quote from p. 29 of the AB report on *US—Gasoline*:

> WTO Members have a large measure of autonomy to determine their own policies on the environment (including its relationship with trade), their environmental objectives and the environmental legislation they enact and implement. So far as concerns the WTO, that autonomy is circumscribed only by the need to respect the requirements of the *General Agreement* and the other covered agreements. (italics in the original)[51]

---

[51] In *US—Clove Cigarettes*, the Panel held that banning clove cigarettes on allegedly public health grounds (reducing smoking by youth) should be upheld; it cautioned the complainant (Indonesia) that

A similarly deferential (towards the regulating WTO Member) attitude is evidenced in the Panel report on *US—COOL*: in this case, nevertheless, the Panel did impose a limit, marking thus the extent of its review when finding that the regulating state cannot be self-contradictory when pursuing objectives that it can unilaterally decide (§§7.611ff).

WTO Members are, by virtue of Art. 2.3 TBT, obliged to set aside technical regulations where the circumstances that gave rise to their adoption no longer exist.

Technical regulations should, whenever feasible, be drafted in terms of performance requirements (Art. 2.8 TBT). Requiring WTO Members to draft their technical regulations in terms of performance requirements, whenever feasible, reduces the risk of interventions aiming to favour domestic production by imposing adjustment costs on international competition. For instance, enacting a regulation which states that fire-proof doors must be made from X or Y material does not meet the test of Art. 2.8 TBT (assuming it is feasible to enact such a regulation in terms of performance requirements); conversely, a regulation which states that fire-proof doors should be able to resist for 15 minutes when exposed to fire (assuming a certain measurement of temperature), irrespective of their production process, would meet this test.[52]

The TBT Agreement also imposes certain procedural obligations on WTO Members enacting technical regulations. Except for cases of urgency, WTO Members are required to respect both *ex ante* and *ex post* transparency requirements when enacting technical regulations:

(a) Art. 2.5 TBT, and Art. 2.9 TBT impose on WTO Members an *ex ante* transparency obligation, namely a duty to notify the WTO of their upcoming technical regulations and, upon request, provide a justification for them;[53]

(b) Art. 2.12 TBT requests from WTO Members to allow a 'reasonable interval' between notification of their proposed technical regulation and its entry into force. In *US—Clove Cigarettes*, the Panel found that a US decision to allow for an interval of three months only was in violation of this provision (§§7.563 ff): to reach this conclusion, the Panel based itself on a Decision by the TBT Committee[54] which had incorporated §5.2 of the Doha Ministerial Decision

---

claims to the effect that the defendant acted in bad faith (enacted the law on grounds other than those invoked) are associated with a very demanding burden of persuasion (§§7.335ff). In *US—Tuna II (Mexico)*, the Panel held that protection of animal life is not limited to endangered species only, but extends to any animal irrespective of whether it qualifies as an endangered species or not (§7.437).

[52] In *US—Clove Cigarettes*, the Panel dismissed an argument by Indonesia to the effect that Art. 2.8 TBT required from WTO Members to provide a certain level of specificity. In its view, the only requirement there is to opt for performance requirements if appropriate (§§7.473ff).

[53] Failure to notify the list of products covered by a technical regulation by the US led the Panel on *US—Clove Cigarettes* to conclude that it had violated its obligations under Art. 2.9.2 TBT (§7.550).

[54] WTO Doc. G/TBT/1/Rev. 8 of 23 May 2002. On appeal the AB upheld this finding stating that the Doha Ministerial Decision is subsequent agreement in the sense of Art. 31.3(a) VCLT.

which pertinently read in part: '...the phrase "reasonable interval" shall be understood to mean normally a period of not less than 6 months, except when this would be ineffective in fulfilling the legitimate objectives pursued'; in this Panel's view, the Doha Ministerial Decision was in line with art. IX.2 of the Agreement Establishing the WTO, in that it helped fill a gap in the original text, and hence, should be taken into account. The notification requirement is less burdensome with respect to technical regulations adopted at the local government-level or by non-governmental bodies (Art. 3.2 TBT): no notification is required if the content is substantially the same as that of previous notifications of the central authority;[55]

(c) Art. 10 TBT obliges WTO Members to establish enquiry points, through which interested parties can request information about the upcoming or already in force technical regulations;

(d) Finally, Art. 2.11 TBT imposes a publication requirement for all technical regulations adopted.

2.2.4 Standards

The term 'standard' is defined in Annex A to the TBT Agreement in the following manner:

> Document approved by a recognized body, that provides, for common and repeated use, rules, guidelines or characteristics for products or related processes and production methods, with which compliance is not mandatory. It may also include or deal exclusively with terminology, symbols, packaging, marking or labeling requirements as they apply to a product, process or production method.

The natural question to ask is why should the TBT Agreement address measures that are not mandatory, compliance with which is not the precondition for market access? The simple answer is because standards do have market impact, and sometimes it is quite strong.[56] Depending on the good that is being 'standardized', for example, the impact of the standard will vary: one would intuitively expect more of an impact if it is credence goods that are being standardized, where consumers, even after consumption, might not be in a position to fully assess the quality of the good; less so if it is an experience good that is standardized; and even less so if it is a search good. Still, consumers' choices will be affected even with respect to the latter if the standardizing body is in their view a 'trustworthy' entity:

---

[55] In exceptional circumstances, Art. 2.10 TBT explicitly exempts WTO Members from their obligations under Art. 2.9. In *US—Clove Cigarettes*, the Panel held that Art. 2.10 TBT can only be invoked as justification for deviations from obligations under Art. 2.9 TBT, since, and we quote, 'we see no situation in which a WTO Member's actions would fall within the scope of both obligations at the same time' (§7.502).

[56] Sykes (1995); Busch (2011); Ganslandt and Markusen (2001) show how standards harm especially smaller economies. OECD (2000) provides empirical support for this point and goes so far as to conclude that 'meeting non-mandatory technical standards was seen [by those interviewed] as much, if not more, of an issue than meeting, mandatory technical requirements' (p. 7).

many producers of say toothbrushes would long for endorsement by the American Dental Association.

There is nowadays a variety of standards in various fields from toothbrushes to sustainable forest management.[57] Standards can be national, or regional.[58] Marx (2011) discusses the significant increase in recent years in standard-setting, which, as mentioned *supra*, covers a sizeable part of world trade. Standards are set by standardizing bodies at different levels of government (federal, local etc.) and even by non-governmental bodies. Art. 4.1 TBT states that WTO Members must ensure that their central government standardizing bodies are bound by the disciplines included in the Code of Good Practices which appears in Annex 3 of the TBT Agreement, and to take all reasonable measures to ensure that local and/or non-governmental standardizing bodies adhere to it as well.[59]

Compliance with the Code of Good Practices amounts *ipso facto* to compliance with the principles of the TBT Agreement (Art. 4.2 TBT): anyway, §D of the Code of Good Practices explicitly includes an MFN plus NT clause. Except for §D, the Code of Good Practices imposes the following obligations:

§E: standards must respect the necessity requirement;

§F: WTO Members must use international standards when appropriate (this provision corresponds to Art. 2.4 TBT);

§G: to further harmonization among nationally defined standards, (national) standardizing bodies are encouraged to participate in the work of international standardizing bodies;

§H: national standardizing bodies should avoid duplication of the work done at the international level;

§I: standards should be drafted in terms of performance requirements, when feasible;

§J: standardizing bodies should publish at least once every six months their work programme;

§K: standardizing bodies should join the ISONET (the ISO information network);

---

[57] Marx and Cuypers (2010).

[58] In the EU, for example, ETSI (European Telecommunications Standards Institute), CEN (Committee for Standardization), CENELEC (European Committee for Electrotechnical Standardization) elaborate standards that can be converted to common technical requirements by the EU Commission after consultations with the EU Member States in the context of the Approvals Committee for Technical Equipment (ACTE). In the US, it is, for example, the US Federal Communications Commission (FCC) that establishes requirements for the certification of telecoms equipment.

[59] Standards are of course set by the market as well as, for example, the Microsoft experience has amply demonstrated; see Gandal (2001).

§L: WTO Members should allow 60 days, if possible, to lapse between adoption and entry into force of the standard;

§M: *ex ante* transparency is required in the sense that draft standards must be made available to interested parties to comment upon;

§N: comments received on draft standards should be, if appropriate, taken into account when drafting the final text;

§O: all standards must be published.

§P: standardizing authorities should provide, if requested, information about their work programme.

Standards can be issued as briefly mentioned above not only by recognized (governmental, at some level) bodies, but also by private entities and in the latter case we talk of 'private standards'. The question arises whether similar entities would have to respect (any of) the obligations embedded in the TBT Agreement. The question is highly relevant nowadays in light of the proliferation of private standards.[60] Recall that under Art. 4.1 TBT, WTO Members:

> ...shall take such reasonable measures as may be available to them to ensure that local government and non-governmental standardizing bodies within their terri-tories, as well as regional standardizing bodies of which they or one or more bodies within their territories are members, accept and comply with this Code of Good Practices. In addition, Members shall not take measures which have the effect of, directly or indirectly, requiring or encouraging such standardizing bodies to act in a manner inconsistent with the Code of Good Practice. The obligations of Members with respect to compliance of standardizing bodies with the provisions of the Code of Good Practice shall apply irrespective of whether or not a standardizing body has accepted the Code of Good Practice

The reasonableness standard thus established provides the benchmark for state responsibility in this area. During the Fifth Triennial Review, many WTO Members expressed their concern regarding the emergence of private standards and the ensuing obstacles to international trade and the plea for effective compli-ance with the Code of Good Practices was reiterated.[61] Yet, not much more was achieved, since not much more can be achieved; the WTO after all is a govern-ment-to-government contract and the only way available to enhance the current level of implementation of the legal principles embedded in the Code of Good Practices is to transform it into domestic law. Then, by virtue of domestic (and not WTO) law, the elaboration of private standards would have to respect the agreed principles.

As things stand, there are many initiatives to at least shed light in the world of many, sometimes overlapping and sometimes divergent private standards, and two

---

[60] Schepel (2005) provides a very comprehensive account: compare Marx (2011).
[61] WTO Doc. G/TBT/13 at §25.

initiatives are worth mentioning here: the UN Industrial Development Organization (UNIDO) issued in 2008 a booklet aptly entitled 'Making Private Standard Work for You', aiming to familiarize traders with standards worldwide; in similar vein, the International Trade Centre (ITC) has issued its 'Standards Map', which is an online tool that enables traders and all other interested parties to analyse and compare private standards.

2.2.5 Conformity Assessment

Conformity assessment is defined in §3 of Annex 1 to the TBT Agreement as follows:

> Any procedure used, directly or indirectly, to determine that relevant requirements in technical regulations or standards are fulfilled.
>
> *Explanatory note*
>
> Conformity assessment procedures include, *inter alia*, procedures for sampling, testing and inspection; evaluation, verification and assurance of conformity; registration, accreditation and approval as well as their combinations.

Arts. 5–7 TBT contain the basic obligations that must be assumed by 'central government bodies' which must be applied to 'local government bodies', 'non-governmental bodies', and 'international and regional systems', by virtue of Arts. 7–9 TBT. All these terms are defined in Annex 1 to the TBT as follows:

§4 International body or system

Body or system whose membership is open to the relevant bodies of at least all Members.

§5 Regional body or system

Body or system whose membership is open to the relevant bodies of only some of the Members.

§6 Central government body

Central government, its ministries and departments, or any body subject to the control of the central government in respect of the activity in question.

> Explanatory note:
>
> In the case of the European Communities the provisions governing central government bodies apply. However, regional bodies or conformity assessment systems may be established within the European Communities, and in such cases would be subject to the provisions of this Agreement on regional bodies or conformity assessment systems.

§7 Local government body

Government other than a central government (e.g. states, provinces, Länder, cantons, municipalities, etc.), its ministries or departments, or any body subject to the control of such a government in respect of the activity in question.

698

§8 Non-governmental body

Body other than a central government body or a local government body, including a non-governmental body which has legal power to enforce a technical regulation.

Whereas WTO Members must ensure that central government bodies behave in accordance with the TBT Agreement described above when performing conformity assessment (Art. 6 TBT), they are expected to only take reasonable measures available to them in order to ensure that local and non-government bodies behave in a similar manner: Art. 22.9 DSU is clear in this respect.

WTO Members are free to design their own conformity-assessment procedures, which must respect the necessity requirement, in the sense that they should not be more trade-restrictive than what is required to achieve their objective (Art. 5.1.2 TBT); they must further be published (Art. 5.8 TBT), and explained in detail to interested parties (Art. 5.2 and 5.6 TBT). Once they have enacted their conformity-assessment procedures, they must provide interested WTO Members with access to them: Art. 5.1.1 TBT reads:

> WTO Members are obliged to give access to foreign suppliers to their facilities, under the same conditions applied to domestic producers, to have the conformity of their products with the technical regulation or standard at hand assessed.[62]

Conformity assessment can be performed in relation to specific products, or in relation to the activity of conformity assessment. Products will typically be tested in laboratories, inspected by inspection bodies, and certified by certification bodies. It is metrological and accreditation bodies that will review the activities performed by laboratories, inspection, and certification bodies. The ISO/IEC have developed a glossary of the various procedures in relation to the conformity assessment of products as well as in relation to the activity of conformity assessment: the working groups of the ISO Committee on Conformity Assessment (CASCO)[63] and the ISO/IEC Guide 2 (1991) are the two relevant documents.

With respect to products, the ISO/IEC Guide 2 distinguishes between 'sampling' (the procedure whereby a sample of the whole that will form the subject-matter of conformity assessment will be put together: of course, the sample must reflect the properties of the whole, otherwise one risks running into sample bias); 'testing' (determining technical characteristics of the product); 'inspection' (where the conformity of the product will be evaluated); 'evaluation of conformity' (intimately linked to inspection, but here the examination of conformity is systematic, aiming to establish the extent to which a particular product meets the requested properties); 'verification of conformity' (looking at the evidence, the entity entrusted with verification will confirm conformity); 'assurance of

---

[62] In practice, reference is also made to 'legal metrology', that is, the regulatory requirements for measurements and measuring instruments: it aims to ensure the appropriate quality and credibility of measurements related to official controls in the areas of health, safety, and the environment; see Lesser (2007).

[63] ISO/IEC 17000, International Standard, ISO 2004, Geneva.

conformity' (this should be the last step or the consequence of verification of conformity and is usually a statement of confidence that a particular product meets the requested standards); 'certification' (assurance by a certification body that the product meets the requested standards); 'supplier's declaration of conformity' (the supplier provides assurance that its products meet the requested standards); 'approval' (permission granted to a product to be marketed under the conditions imposed by the approving entity); 'registration' (a body indicates in a publicly available document that a product meets the requested standards).

Conformity assessment for products can be performed by the producer itself (called 'first-party assessment'), the purchaser or a conformity assessment body on its behalf ('second-party assessment'), or a body independent from both the producer and the purchaser ('third-party assessment'). The incentives of each of the entities involved in assessing products are different of course and so is the ensuing market confidence in the procedures followed.

When it comes to procedures in relation to the activity of conformity assessment, the ISO/IEC Guide 2 distinguishes between 'accreditation' (whereby an entity entrusted with this function recognizes that another entity can carry tasks relating to conformity assessment); 'registration' (an entity reflects in a publicly available document that a product or another entity meets specific requested standards); 'metrology' (science of measurement). This last point deserves some additional explanation: in fact, all sorts of issues can affect conformity assessment and some are counter-intuitive, like the expression say of weight in kilograms and pounds.[64] This is why the Convention du Mètre established the 'Bureau International des Poids et des Mesures' (International Bureau of Weights and Measures), an intergovernmental organization counting nowadays 55 members and 34 associate members, the mandate of which is to provide the basis for a single, coherent system of measurements throughout the world.

The need for cooperation in this area is evident, but then again cooperation requires some sort of acceptance of each other's standard: there is a specific provision dealing with recognition (and we discuss it in the next subsection). Beyond recognition, the TBT Agreement aims to contribute to increasing the quality of standards worldwide and also the technical capacity regarding conformity-assessment procedures. The TBT Committee has organized a number of events aimed at developing technical capacity in this area, especially among those in need of expertise.[65] Moreover, the TBT Agreement specifically refers to 'accreditation' as a means to verify the competence of entities entrusted with conformity assessment in the exporting WTO Member (Art. 6.1.1). Assuming this can be achieved, transaction costs regarding conformity assessment are substantially reduced. Similar agreements, however, are usually signed across WTO

---

[64] De Bièvre et al. (2011).

[65] See, for example, WTO Docs. G/TBT/9 of 13 November 2000; G/TBT/M/33/Add.1 of 21 October 2004; G/TBT/35 of 24 May 2005; and G/TBT/38/Add. 1 of 6 June 2006.

Members of a similar development level. Accreditation bodies are working towards harmonizing international practices in this context. WTO Members are, more generally, encouraged to participate in the work of international bodies aiming at harmonizing conformity-assessment procedures (Art. 5.5 TBT), or to opt for recognition, which we discuss immediately after. WTO Members must also use relevant guides and recommendations issued by international standardizing bodies as a basis for the elaboration of their conformity-assessment procedures (Art. 5.4 TBT). This obligation kicks in if positive assurance is required that products conform with technical regulations or standards and relevant guides or recommendations by international standardizing bodies exist. There is justifiable deviation from this obligation if the guides or recommendations are 'inappropriate'. The last sentence of this provision (Art. 5.4 TBT) includes an indicative list of what might constitute an 'inappropriate' guide or recommendation: if prevention of deceptive practices is sought; protection of the environment; national security; protection of human health or safety; fundamental problems regarding infrastructure; climatic factors; technological problems. This list will be completed over the years through the notifications system established through the TBT Agreement. WTO members notifying a conformity-assessment procedure must indicate the objective sought as well as the rationale for it (Arts. 5.62 and 5.7.1 TBT). Eventually, thanks to similar notifications, the WTO Membership will have a more complete picture regarding instances where guides and recommendations issued by standardizing bodies are considered 'inappropriate'.[66]

Over the years, conformity-assessment procedures have been streamlined: OECD (2000) concludes that deregulation of the approval process has led to increasing competition across approving agencies and, thus, to decreasing costs of approvals. The contribution by the TBT Committee in this respect should not be underestimated here: through its forum on 'good regulatory practice' it has significantly promoted rational behaviour when it comes to regulating areas coming under the mandate of the TBT Agreement.[67]

Finally, conformity assessment can be greatly facilitated through an essentially unilateral action, the SDoC (Supplier's Declaration of Conformity). The SDoC at the very least identifies the supplier who makes the declaration, the relevant standard or technical regulation that its products meet, and, of course, the product(s) covered. This definition corresponds to the ISO/IEC Guide 2 definition (since the SDoC is not mentioned in the TBT Agreement):

---

[66] The TBT Committee established in 1996 a 'Technical Working Group on ISO/IEC Guides Relating to Articles 5 and 6 of the Agreement' (WTO Doc. G/TBT/M/6 of 6 December 1996 at §14); it met three times in 1998 and the basic conclusions were compiled in a document (WTO Doc. G/TBT/W/43). The work and relevance of the ISO/IEC Guides has been discussed in every Triennial Review so far; see, for example WTO Doc. G/TBT/26 of 13 November 2009.

[67] We discuss all this *infra*, under 'Institutional Issues'.

13.5.1 Supplier's declaration: procedure by which a supplier gives written assurance that a product, process or service conforms to specified requirements.

SDoC as a means to ease conformity assessment has been discussed in the TBT Committee: during the Third Triennial Review, it was observed that for SDoC to be effective, it would have to be accompanied at least by effective product liability laws, and penalties for false or misleading declarations of conformity assessment by the supplier.[68] During the same review, it was added in this discussion that use of international standards could help make the SDoC more transparent and extend its use and usefulness.[69]

2.2.6 Recognition

WTO Members are encouraged to recognize each other's technical regulations as equivalent (Art. 2.7 TBT). Recognition could be unilateral, or two (or more) WTO Members could sign an MRA regarding the manner in which conformity with technical regulations can be assessed.[70] In fact, WTO Members are encouraged to sign MRAs (Art. 6.3 TBT).

Entering into an MRA usually entails that the products of the exporting state do not have to undergo conformity assessment in the importing state in order to ensure that they meet the relevant regulatory requirements. Any time an MRA has been agreed, any WTO Member which takes the view that it can comply with its requirements can legitimately request that it benefits from its extension: it will, of course, have to assume the burden of proving equivalence between its own regulation and that of the MRA partners. WTO Members must provide recognition if they are satisfied that conformity with applicable technical regulations and/ or standards in another WTO Member is equivalent to their own (Art. 6.1 TBT): this provision deals only with recognition by central government bodies, and mentions 'equivalence' not 'equation'; hence, what matters is not absolute identity between two procedures but whether, as a result of using either, conformity has been achieved to the satisfaction of the recognizing WTO Member. WTO Members are encouraged to enter into consultations in order to achieve equivalence (Art. 6.1.1 TBT).

The WTO must be notified of all MRAs (Art. 10.7 TBT). One hundred and seven agreements have been notified so far and they must all observe MFN, although it is difficult for outsiders to make a persuasive case to this effect: agreements are typically signed between WTO Members because of properties endogenous to partners which are not necessarily shared by all trading partners.[71] Hence, it should not come as a surprise that there are few MRAs thus far, and that they are in any event confined to more or less 'homogeneous' contractual

---

[68] WTO Doc. G/TBT/13 at §§32ff.
[69] WTO Doc. G/TBT/13 at §32.
[70] Baller (2007) provides a classification for different types of MRAs.
[71] See, on this score, Messerlin and Palmeter (2000) and Beviglia-Zampetti (2000a).

partners.[72] The TBT Committee, in its Fourth Triennial Review, discussed some of the many reasons why agreements are being signed almost exclusively across 'like-minded' countries, and identified the following grounds to this effect: differences in development levels across WTO Members is a concern and an explanation for lack of agreements across the WTO Membership; so is the (opportunity) cost of negotiating similar agreements, etc.[73]

Recognition can also take place on voluntary basis. In this vein, Art. 9.2 TBT is relevant; it reads:

> Members shall take such reasonable measures as may be available to them to ensure that international and regional systems for conformity assessment in which relevant bodies within their territories are members or participants comply with the provisions of Articles 5 and 6. In addition, Members shall not take any measures which have the effect of, directly or indirectly, requiring or encouraging such systems to act in a manner inconsistent with any of the provisions of Articles 5 and 6.

There are now agreements among accreditation bodies or even individual laboratories, whereby networks of conformity assessment are established on which members can rely. For example, 'CB Test Certificates' are issued by laboratories participating in the IECEE-CB Scheme, an agreement among IEC members which allows participating certification institutions to issue similar certificates that confirm that electrical products are in conformity with IEC standards. A manufacturer possessing a CB Test Certificate can, with this document alone, obtain certification in all countries participating in the IECEE-CB Scheme. And certification is not the only area where similar agreements occur; accreditation is another. The International Laboratory Accreditation Cooperation (ILAC) has developed a recognition agreement among its 65 members: the 'ILAC Arrangement', as is well-known, is based on results of an evaluation by peers ('peer assessment'). Each body signatory must ensure conformity with ISO/IEC 17011 and 17025; the ILAC Arrangement builds on existing regional arrangements which are required to maintain the necessary 'confidence' in accreditation bodies from their region.[74]

2.2.7 Special and Differential Treatment for Developing Countries

Recall the empirical studies mentioned above regarding the welfare implications of standards for developing countries. The TBT Agreement does not address this issue at all but contains a provision aimed at obliging developed WTO Members

---

[72] Nicolaidis (2000) has characterized non-discriminatory MRA as an oxymoron.

[73] WTO Doc. G/TBT/19 at §39.

[74] The European Cooperation for Accreditation (EA), the Asia Pacific Laboratory Accreditation Cooperation (APLAC), and the Inter-American Accreditation Cooperation (IAAC) are the current ILAC-recognized regions with acceptable mutual recognition arrangements (MRAs) and evaluation procedures. The Southern African Development Community in Accreditation (SADCA) is currently developing their MRA evaluation processes before requesting recognition and approval by ILAC.

to account for the relative difficulty of developing countries to set and abide by their standards. To this effect, developed WTO Members must:

(a) By virtue of Art. 11 TBT assist developing countries in the preparation of technical regulations, standards etc.;

(b) By virtue of Art. 12 TBT take account of the special development, financial, and trade needs of developing country Members when enacting technical regulations, standards, and conformity assessment procedures, with a view to ensuring that they do not create unnecessary obstacles to the exports of developing countries. The same Article explains that WTO Members should not expect developing countries to base their own technical regulations or standards on international standards, if the latter are not necessarily conducive to their development needs.

The second point is relatively speaking of more importance at the early stages of the game when developed countries have an abundance of standards and developing countries' exports will be negatively affected unless they conform to these standards. Many of the standards, as suggested above, reflect measurement, so scientific involvement is quintessential. This is an area where typically developing countries, and especially LDCs, lag behind. The provision does not go any further than requesting from WTO Members to reflect on the necessity of a particular conformity assessment: necessity is more demanding than pure non-discrimination since the former excludes unnecessary non-discriminatory measures (the latter does not). But not much is required from WTO Members in this respect: in *US— Clove Cigarettes*, the Panel held that the fact that Indonesia had raised its concerns about adopting a technical regulation before the US authorities, and the fact that key officials in the US government had debated the concerns raised, was enough for the US to be deemed in compliance with its obligations under this provision, even though in the end it did not endorse any of them (§§7.644ff).

2.3 Institutional Issues

A TBT Committee is established and entrusted with the responsibility of overseeing the operation of the Agreement (Art. 13 TBT). The TBT Committee is quite unique among WTO Committees in some respects: participation in the Committee is often entrusted to technical experts (often with scientific expertise) and not to typical trade delegates. In this respect, it resembles the SPS Committee that we discuss *infra*. Its mandate extends to a variety of issues; it has been quite successful both in advancing the 'law-making' agenda, as well as in settling disputes.[75] In the context of the TBT, initiatives have been taken to reduce the

---

[75] Horn et al. (2012). WTO Doc. G/TBT/1/Rev. 10 of 9 June 2011 contains all decisions by the TBT Committee since 1995.

problems posed on international trade as a result of regulatory diversity across WTO Members.

Pursuant to Art. 15.3 TBT, it has been conducting annual reviews discussing implementation of transparency provisions (notifications), technical assistance, and disputes involving the TBT Agreement. As of the end of the first three years, and at the end of every following three year-period, it has been conducting a review with the aim of proposing any necessary adjustments to the TBT Agreement. These are the Triennial Reviews, with a view to (Art. 15.4 TBT):

> Recommending an adjustment of the rights and obligations of this Agreement where necessary to ensure mutual economic advantage and balance of rights and obligations, without prejudice to the provisions of Article 12.[76]

The TBT Committee, in its Fourth Triennial Review of the Operation and Implementation of the TBT Agreement, issued a report[77] where, *inter alia*, it advanced the following priorities:

(a) Good regulatory practice (in the sense that a decision whether there is need to regulate should always precede a decision to regulate) must be encouraged;

(b) The use of Supplier's Declaration of Conformity (SDoC) should also be encouraged in order to avoid unnecessary costs with respect to conformity assessment;

(c) Unilateral recognition of results of foreign conformity assessment (Art. 6.1 TBT) should also take place more frequently, if possible, as should participation of foreign conformity assessment bodies in domestic conformity assessment procedures (Art. 6.4 TBT); finally,

(d) The document supports the conclusion of MRAs, and notes the conclusion of voluntary MRAs between domestic and foreign conformity assessment bodies (individual laboratories, certification and inspection bodies).

Discussions on good regulatory practice continued in the Fifth Triennial Review,[78] while discussions have been initiated regarding 'regulatory cooperation' across WTO Members defined as follows:

> Regulatory cooperation between Members is, in essence, about reducing *unnecessary* regulatory diversity; it is also about limiting the costs associated with *necessary* regulatory diversity. Regulatory cooperation is premised on the notion that it is possible to remove unnecessary regulatory diversity without preventing Members from achieving their legitimate policy objectives. When fruitful, cooperation between Members—in various forms and configurations—can contribute to the reduction of unnecessary barriers to trade. (emphasis in the original)[79]

---

[76] Recall that this provision deals with special and differential treatment for developing countries.

[77] WTO Doc. G/TBT/19 of 14 November 2006. For a more recent report on this score, see WTO Doc. G/TBT/26.

[78] WTO Doc. G/TBT/13 of 13 November 2009.

[79] WTO Doc. G/TBT/W/340.

Regulatory cooperation is actively promoted by the WTO TBT Committee. Some of it, of course, already exists embedded in various TBT provisions such as international standards, equivalence, conformity assessment, etc. Some already takes place at regional level such as the FTA between China and New Zealand, or the regulatory cooperation schemes between Australia and New Zealand, and between the EU and the US. The latter has already been discussed extensively in the TBT Committee[80] and focuses on three issues: the 'Regulatory Cooperation Roadmap' (sector-specific agreements on a series of goods such as autos, drugs, and medical devices); the US Office of Management and Budget (OMB) and EU Commission dialogue on good regulatory practices (transparency, impact assessment, etc.); and the Regulatory Cooperation Forum (senior-level meetings on issues such as new technology, safety of goods, etc.). The discussions take place under the aegis of the Transatlantic Economic Council (TEC), a body established to direct economic cooperation between the EU and the US.

On the other hand, a number of disputes, aptly named 'specific trade concerns' (STCs), are routinely submitted to the TBT Committee; there have been over 300 so far.[81] The majority of STCs are requests for further clarification, followed by claims that the necessity requirement has not been complied with, transparency-related claims, the use of international standards, etc. Technical regulations are the most often challenged instrument, followed by conformity-assessment procedures. Roughly two-thirds of all STCs have been raised once or twice before the TBT Committee, a quarter of them have been raised three-to-five times, whereas 12 per cent have been raised more than five times. Public health, environmental protection, and prevention of deceptive practices are the three stated objectives of the instruments most often challenged; 39 per cent of all measures challenged originate in Asia-Pacific, a quarter in the EU, 16 per cent in Latin America, 15 per cent in North America, 11.4 per cent in Middle East, and 3 per cent in Africa.[82] The fact that only a handful of the submitted STCs have reached the Panel stage is a testimony to the good work at the Committee level, which has managed to resolve the majority of them.[83]

The WTO Secretariat has, in concert with WTO Members, taken active steps to provide much-needed transparency with respect to measures coming under the purview of the TBT Agreement. Most notable is the establishment of the TBT Information Management System (TBT IMS),[84] which allows users to obtain

---

[80] WTO Doc. G/TBT/W/287 of 11 March 2008.

[81] The TBT Committee will periodically issue documents that refer to all of them; see, for example, WTO Doc. G/TBT/29 of 8 March 2011.

[82] WTO Doc. G/TBT/GEN/74/Rev. 8 of 1 June 2011.

[83] Horn et al. (2012) discuss in detail the record in this respect. Lang and Scott (2009) discuss the works of the TBT Committee in a more comprehensive manner, and not simply its activities relating to settlement of disputes.

[84] Available at <http://tbtims.wto.org>.

information on measures notified to the TBT Committee, on conformity-assessment procedures, enquiry points etc.

A Panel adjudicating a dispute coming under the TBT Agreement may, at the request of a party or on its own initiative, establish an expert group to assist it on issues of a technical nature (Art. 14.2 TBT). Annex 2 to the TBT Agreement sets out in detail the procedure to be followed on this score. The mandate of TBT experts is thus limited to questions of a technical nature only. Moreover, note that, contrary to what is the case under Art. 13 DSU, where Panels only have the right to appoint experts, TBT experts can be appointed either at the request of parties or on the Panel's own initiative. One would expect scientific expertise to be on occasion very much an issue in this context.[85] So far, nevertheless, Panels have not made use of this opportunity.

3. The SPS

3.1 The Legal Discipline and its Rationale

The Agreement on Sanitary and Phyto-sanitary Measures (SPS) deals with SPS measures; Annex A to the SPS Agreement defines SPS measures as follows:
   Any measure applied:

(a) to protect animal or plant life or health within the territory of the Member from risks arising from the entry, establishment or spread of pests, diseases, disease-carrying organisms or disease-causing organisms;

(b) to protect human or animal life or health within the territory of the Member from risks arising from additives, contaminants, toxins or disease-causing organisms in foods, beverages or feedstuffs;

(c) to protect human life or health within the territory of the Member from risks arising from diseases carried by animals, plants or products thereof, or from the entry, establishment or spread of pests; or

(d) to prevent or limit other damage within the territory of the Member from the entry, establishment or spread of pests.

Sanitary or phytosanitary measures include all relevant laws, decrees, regulations, requirements and procedures including, *inter alia*, end product criteria; processes and production methods; testing, inspection, certification and approval procedures; quarantine treatments including relevant requirements associated with the transport of animals or plants, or with the materials necessary for their survival during transport; provisions on relevant statistical methods, sampling procedures and methods of risk assessment; and packaging and labelling requirements directly related to food safety.

---

[85] Pauwelyn (1998, 1999).

In *Australia—Apples*, the AB was facing a challenge by New Zealand against an Australian measure aimed to protect apples from 'fire blight and apple leafcurling midge' (ALCM). It discussed at the outset whether the Australian measure was suitably understood as an SPS measure and held to this effect that (§173):

> Whether a measure is 'applied . . . to protect' in the sense of Annex A(1)(a) must be ascertained not only from the objectives of the measure as expressed by the respond-ing party, but also from the text and structure of the relevant measure, its surround-ing regulatory context, and the way in which it is designed and applied. For any given measure to fall within the scope of Annex A(1)(a), scrutiny of such circum-stances must reveal a clear and objective relationship between that measure and the specific purposes enumerated in Annex A(1)(a).

Measures, thus, aimed at addressing pests, diseases, dealing with risks arising from additives, contaminants, and/or toxins come under the purview of the SPS Agreement: broadly speaking, SPS measures can protect humans and animals from food-borne health risks, and humans, animals, and plants alike from pests and diseases. The SPS Agreement requires that measures coming under its purview are not only non-discriminatory and necessary to achieve their stated objective, but also consistent and based on scientific evidence. Thus, this agreement innovates, in comparison to Art. III GATT, in two important ways:

(1) It incorporates a more elaborate test to detect whether a measure operates so as to afford protection to domestic production.[86] The SPS Agreement includes a series of proxies, such as necessity, scientific evidence, consistency, interna-tional standards, which will help distinguish beggar-thy-neighbour behaviour from policies genuinely aiming at protecting legitimate objectives (such as health, environment, etc.);

(2) The second innovation has to do with the class of beggar-thy-neighbour policies outlawed. Recall that Art. III GATT imposes nothing beyond non-discrimination. Let us assume that a WTO Member does not produce product A and wants to exclude it from its market, because, in its view, it is associated with adverse health implications. A trade embargo would never run foul of Art. III GATT, since there is no discrimination issue here (assume no DCS products are involved). It might, however, be caught by the disciplines included in the SPS Agreement, if the measure is not necessary to achieve the stated regulatory objective, if it is not based on scientific evidence, or if it is not consistent; it is irrelevant if it affords no advantage to the competing domestic production. In other words, through this agreement, domestic measures which affect solely imported products can still be found to be WTO-inconsistent. This agreement, thus, outlaws beggar-thy-neighbour policies in addition to those outlawed by the GATT.[87]

---

[86] Melloni (2005).
[87] In this situation, potential national production must be prohibited as well.

Our discussion *supra* in the TBT context regarding the reasons for harmonizing regulations on a multilateral or more restricted basis finds application here as well. There are two additions though: public health and environment are areas where, at least in some parts of the world, the regulatory process has been heavily influenced by scientific progress; the US FDA (Food and Drugs Authority), as well as the EU EFSA (European Food Safety Authority) are notorious examples to this effect.[88] Scientific evidence at the domestic level can serve as some sort of buffer against political-economy-type pressure.[89] On the international plane, it can help distinguish legitimate from protectionist regulations and this is why it has been included as an in principle requirement, upon which SPS measures must be based.[90] Consistency in the formulation of, say, public health policies is another proxy to infer the regulatory intent: a WTO Member which consistently aims at high public health protection cannot be easily accused of a protectionist agenda when doing so in a particular sector.

3.2 The Coverage of the Legal Discipline

3.2.1 What is an SPS Measure?

Recall the definition of SPS measures reflected *supra*.[91] The Panel on *EC— Approval and Marketing of Biotech Products*[92] held that the purpose of an SPS measure can be expressed in terms of requirement, or in terms of a procedure that should be followed (§7.149).

3.2.2 The Measures Covered

As is the case under the TBT Agreement, WTO Members can either use international standards or proceed unilaterally and enact their own SPS measures. Unlike the TBT Agreement, no distinction exists between technical regulations and standards: all measures coming under the purview of the SPS Agreement are legally binding on their addressees, in the sense that foreign products might be denied market access, unless they meet the established requirements.

---

[88] And it is the EU and the US that were the arch negotiators of the SPS Agreement; see Alemanno (2007).

[89] But, on occasion, it can also serve as means for pressure when the holder of scientific evidence requests regulation in accordance with say its patent.

[90] In the TBT context, available scientific information is relevant in assessing the risk resulting from non-fulfilment of a legitimate objective mentioned in Art. 2.2 TBT; there is, nevertheless, no obligation to base technical regulations or standards on science.

[91] For a comprehensive discussion of the SPS, see Iynedjan (2002) and Scott (2009).

[92] This case dealt with an EU moratorium that would severely hamper, if not prohibit altogether, the marketing and commercialization of genetically modified organisms (GMOs) in the EU market. It did not contain any revelations regarding the construction of case law, but did manage to occupy literature because of the manner in which it understood the relationship between WTO and public international law. See the contributions by Broude (2007), Conrad (2007), Davies (2007), Footer (2007), Howse and Horn (2009), and Perez (2007).

As is the case with the GATT, only measures attributable to a government can come under the purview of the SPS Agreement. WTO Members are required to take reasonable measures to ensure that bodies other than governmental bodies will also observe the SPS Agreement (Art. 13 SPS). This provision is reminiscent of the federal clause embedded in Art. XXIV.12 GATT. Assuming the case law there applies here, *mutatis mutandis*, one should expect that WTO Members will be acting in accordance with this provision by adhering to their constitutional powers.

3.2.3 *International Standards*

As is the case under the TBT Agreement, WTO Members must use an international standard, assuming it is effective and appropriate and will thus help them reach their objectives. Art. 3.1 SPS reads to this effect:

> Members shall base their sanitary or phytosanitary measures on international standards, guidelines or recommendations, where they exist, except as otherwise provided for in this Agreement, and in particular in paragraph 3.

Art. 3.3 SPS, to which reference is made in the body of this provision, reads:

> Members may introduce or maintain sanitary or phytosanitary measures which result in a higher level of sanitary or phytosanitary protection than would be achieved by measures based on the relevant international standards, guidelines or recommendations, if there is a scientific justification, or as a consequence of the level of sanitary or phytosanitary protection a Member determines to be appropriate in accordance with the relevant provisions of paragraphs 1 through 8 of Article 5. Notwithstanding the above, all measures which result in a level of sanitary or phytosanitary protection different from that which would be achieved by measures based on international standards, guidelines or recommendations shall not be inconsistent with any other provision of this Agreement.

A footnote to this provision reads:

> For the purposes of paragraph 3 of Article 3, there is a scientific justification if, on the basis of an examination and evaluation of available scientific information in conformity with the relevant provisions of this Agreement, a Member determines that the relevant international standards, guidelines or recommendations are not sufficient to achieve its appropriate level of sanitary or phytosanitary protection.

The SPS Agreement, in parallel with the TBT Agreement, does not define which standards are acknowledged as international standards. In contrast to the TBT Agreement, the SPS Agreement identifies several standard-setting institutions; consequently, standards prepared by the explicitly mentioned institutions (Codex Alimentarius Commission, International Office of Epozootics, International Plant Protection Convention) are international standards in the SPS sense of the term (Art. 3.4 SPS). The list is indicative: standards originating in institutions other than those mentioned in Art. 3.4 SPS can be recognized as international standards as well. Annex A, §3 SPS pertinently reads:

(a) For food safety, the standards, guidelines and recommendations established by the Codex Alimentarius Commission relating to food additives, veterinary drug and pesticide residues, contaminants, methods of analysis and sampling, and codes and guidelines of hygienic practice;

(b) For animal health and zoonoses, the standards, guidelines and recommendations developed under the auspices of the International Office of Epizootics;

(c) For plant health, the international standards, guidelines and recommendations developed under the auspices of the Secretariat of the International Plant Protection Convention in cooperation with regional organizations operating within the framework of the International Plant Protection Convention; and

(d) For matters not covered by the above organizations, appropriate standards, guidelines and recommendations promulgated by other relevant international organizations open for membership to all Members, as identified by the Committee.

The SPS Committee can also identify which other standards of which institutions are relevant.[93]

The AB in *EC—Hormones (US)*[94] had the opportunity to explain its understanding of the *ratio legis* for Art. 3.1 SPS (§177):

> ...In generalized terms, the object and purpose of Article 3 is to promote the harmonization of the SPS measures of Members on as wide a basis as possible, while recognizing and safeguarding, at the same time, the right and duty of Members to protect the life and health of their people. The ultimate goal of the harmonization of SPS measures is to prevent the use of such measures for arbitrary or unjustifiable discrimination between Members or as a disguised restriction on international trade, without preventing Members from adopting or enforcing measures which are both 'necessary to protect' human life or health and 'based on scientific principles', and without requiring them to change their appropriate level of protection.

In the same case, the AB held that the term 'based on', appearing in Art. 3.1 SPS, does not impose on WTO Members a requirement of absolute conformity between the regulatory intervention and the relevant international standard; rather, WTO Members, when basing their interventions on an international standard, still retain the discretion to use some (and not use other) elements included in it. The EU in that case had banned the sale of hormone-treated beef (both domestic and imported) on the ground that such beef was dangerous to human health. However, the EU regulation contravened a relevant international standard that had been adopted to this effect. The AB had to address the extent to

---

93 At the time of writing, no other institution has been identified by the SPS Committee. The door is, of course, always open. Eventually, one could see, for example, the International Health Regulations of the WHO or the Cartagena Protocol coming under the purview of Annex A §3(d). Panels as well, in the absence of action by the WTO SPS committee, have the inherent power to identify institutions in this context.

94 This case concerned a sales ban on hormone-treated beef imposed by the EU which affected largely US exports of beef where cows are often subjected to growth hormones.

which the EU was required to shape its SPS measure in absolute conformity with the relevant international standard. It disagreed with the Panel which had held that absolute conformity was required (§177). In reaching this conclusion, the AB took the view that the intention of the parties (the framers of the SPS Agreement) was not to vest international standards with broad powers such as to require absolute conformity between them, on the one hand, and national SPS measures, on the other (§165). The AB nevertheless did not cite any preparatory work to support its view.

There is a statutory presumption that international standards respect the necessity requirement (Art. 3.2 SPS).[95] In *EC—Hormones* (*US*), the AB specified that the presumption of conformity established by Art. 3.2 SPS is rebuttable (§170). There is no case so far where this presumption has been defeated.

Deviation from international standards is possible in the SPS context as well, assuming the conditions of Art. 3.3 SPS quoted above have been met. In short:

(a) WTO Members may choose a level of sanitary or phyto-sanitary protection higher than that provided for in the international standard if there is scientific justification to this effect; or

(b) Following risk assessment (Art. 5 SPS), a WTO Member decides on its appropriate level of protection and this is different from that provided for in the international standard.

Whereas Art. 3.3 SPS clearly indicates that a WTO Member must comply with Art. 5 SPS whenever it has recourse to option (b), no similar obligation is imposed when recourse to option (a) is made. However, the last sentence of Art. 3.3 SPS requires that in case of deviation from an international standard, irrespective of whether recourse is made to option (a) or (b), WTO Members must ensure consistency with the other provisions of the SPS Agreement. The question arose in *EC—Hormones* (*US*) whether a WTO Member still needed to perform a risk assessment when choosing option (a). The AB responded in the affirmative (§§ 175 and 177).

The question who bears the burden of proof where the regulating state has deviated from an international standard was first discussed in the SPS context and it is this case law that inspired the ruling in *EC—Sardines*. The Panel on *EC—Hormones* (*US*) had originally found that the burden rested with the deviating party (the EU) to prove that its deviation from the relevant international standard was justified under the SPS (§§8.86ff). The AB disagreed and reversed this finding. In its view, WTO Members that choose not to use an international standard should not be penalized for their decision to do so (§102). Therefore, it held, it is up to the complainant to establish that the regulating Member could have attained

---

[95] See, on this issue, the analysis by Luff (2004).

its objectives by sticking to the international standard and that, consequently, no need for deviation was warranted (§§104 and 172).

If a WTO Member decides to deviate from an international standard, or if no international standard exists, then it can adopt a unilateral SPS measure. SPS must, in principle, be:

(a) Non-discriminatory;
(b) Based on scientific evidence;
(c) Necessary to achieve the stated objective; and
(d) Consistent (with other SPS measures adopted by the same WTO Member).

These requirements must be cumulatively met, and failing to meet one of them will lead to pronouncing the SPS measure suffering from this defect to be WTO-inconsistent. We will examine all these requirements one by one in what follows.

3.2.4 Non-discrimination

WTO Members must, by virtue of Art. 2.3 SPS, respect non-discrimination when adopting SPS measures:

> Members shall ensure that their sanitary and phytosanitary measures do not arbitrarily or unjustifiably discriminate between Members where identical or similar conditions prevail, including between their own territory and that of other Members. Sanitary and phytosanitary measures shall not be applied in a manner which would constitute a disguised restriction on international trade.

The terms 'like product' or 'less favourable treatment' that we have encountered in numerous provisions regarding non-discrimination are missing here. This provision is reminiscent of the *chapeau* of Art. XX GATT and a similar test should apply here as well. This point of view is strengthened by the fact that Art. 2.4 SPS makes explicit reference to Art. XX(b) GATT: it states that SPS measures conforming to the SPS Agreement shall be deemed to be in accordance with Art. XX(b) GATT as well. Although case law has not developed this point any further, the presumption of legality established here seems to be irrebuttable.

3.2.5 Scientific Evidence[96]

Art. 2.2 SPS reads:

> Members shall ensure that any sanitary or phytosanitary measure is applied only to the extent necessary to protect human, animal or plant life or health, is based on scientific principles and is not maintained without sufficient scientific evidence, except as provided for in paragraph 7 of Article 5.[97]

---

[96] See the excellent analysis of earlier WTO case law on this score by Trebilcock and Soloway (2002) and Sykes (2006a).

[97] This paragraph reflects the 'precautionary principle', which we discuss *infra*.

In *EC—Hormones* (*US*), the AB held that this provision must be read in tandem with Art. 5.1 SPS, which provides for the obligation to ensure that SPS measures are based on risk assessment (§250). These two provisions, according to the AB, aim to strike the appropriate balance between the interest to promote world trade, and the interest to protect life and the health of humans (*Australia—Salmon*, §177).[98] The AB has explicitly acknowledged, in its report on *Australia—Salmon* that Art. 5.1 SPS is *lex specialis* to Art. 2.2 SPS (§180):

> ...the Panel considered that Article 5.1 may be viewed as a specific application of the basic obligations contained in Article 2.2 of the *SPS Agreement*...We agree with this general consideration and would also stress that Articles 2.2 and 5.1 should constantly be read together. Article 2.2 informs Article 5.1: the elements that define the basic obligation set out in Article 2.2 impart meaning to Article 5.1.

The AB added in the same report that a violation of Art 2.2 of the SPS amounted *ipso facto* to a violation of Art 5.1 and vice versa (§138).

Both provisions request that SPS measures be 'based' on scientific evidence: in its report on *EC—Hormones* (*US*),[99] the AB explained that the term 'based' suggests that there must be a rational connection between the (science-based) risk assessment and the SPS measure eventually adopted, in the sense that the former must reasonably support the latter (§193):

> ...We believe that Article 5.1, when contextually read as it should be, in conjunction with and as informed by Article 2.2 of the *SPS Agreement*, requires that the results of the risk assessment must sufficiently warrant—that is to say, reasonably support—the SPS measure at stake. The requirement that an SPS measure be 'based

---

[98] Garcia (2006) offers a comprehensive analysis of this dispute.

[99] There are already two WTO disputes recorded on this issue (*EC—Hormones* (*US*); *US—Suspended Concession*). The original dispute dates back to the 1980s and the narrative has been reflected in the excellent account by Meng (1990). In the late 1970s and early 1980s, EU Member States did not have a common attitude towards hormones but to different degrees worried about (some) hormones because of the so-called 'hormone scandals'. In 1981 the first ban on use of some hormones at EU-wide basis was promulgated and covered thyrostatics and stilbenes, but there was no agreement with respect to all other hormones. Between 1981–4 additional research was conducted, the result of which was that natural hormones did not represent any risk to human health; the need to continue examining synthetic hormones was underlined. In 1985 formal rules of control were adopted. In the same year, a ban on all hormones was also adopted (the results of scientific studies notwithstanding): the Commission chose Art. 43 of the Treaty as an appropriate legal basis; this provision allowed for the adoption of legal instruments on a qualified majority (e.g. dissenting votes notwithstanding). The UK and Denmark dissented (Éire abstained); the US introduced a legal complaint before the ECJ (85/469/EEC). It partly prevailed and the Court declared the legal instrument null and void but accepted the legal basis. The ban on hormones was re-enacted (by 'healing' the vice observed this time) in 1988 and the ban on all hormones was reimposed. The US requested the establishment of a technical experts group to examine the consistency of the EU measure under the provisions of the Tokyo round TBT Code. The EU refused the US request (this was at a time when trading nations could still block the establishment of a Panel and this is the only recorded case where a refusal was expressed), and the US imposed countermeasures as a result, without, however, prior authorization by the GATT CONTRACTING PARTIES. The EU agreed to a GATT Panel, but only in order to examine the consistency of the US countermeasures with the GATT. The result of the disagreement was that no Panel was ever established in the GATT era.

on' a risk assessment is a substantive requirement that there be a rational relationship between the measure and the risk assessment. (italics in the original)[100]

Scientific evidence will need to point to a 'risk' and, consequently, a risk assessment must take place. Before we discuss the understanding of the term 'risk assessment', though, it is probably warranted to explain how the WTO adjudicating bodies have understood the terms 'risk', 'scientific evidence', and the requirement to 'base' risk assessment on scientific evidence. The AB, in *EC—Hormones (US)*, explained that the risk must be identifiable, and not a mere hypothetical possibility (§186):

> In one part of its Reports, the Panel opposes a requirement of an 'identifiable risk' to the uncertainty that theoretically always remains since science can *never* provide *absolute* certainty that a given substance will not *ever* have adverse health effects. We agree with the Panel that this theoretical uncertainty is not the kind of risk which, under Article 5.1, is to be assessed. (emphasis in the original).

This statement is almost impossible to understand: a hypothetical possibility presupposes as a matter of logic an identification process, that is, some sort of quantification of the probability that a risk will occur. When reference is made to risk assessment, one often knows the distribution of probabilities: there is, thus, certainty as to the probability that a risk might occur say 30 per cent of the time that a certain action takes place (although uncertainty regarding at which precise times the risk will occur). Based on similar assessments and a function of their aversion towards risk, societies will decide whether to intervene at all, and if yes, what kind of intervention they will adopt. Societies wanting to take measures, when there is uncertainty as to whether a risk might occur, are not risk-averse, but ambiguity-averse societies. The two concepts are related but are not identical. In an elaborate document prepared for the European Scientific Technology Observatory (ESTO), Stirling (2001) argues that precaution should be a response to a distinct concept, ignorance. Ignorance is but one element in a wider context. The starting-point is a distinction between knowledge about likelihoods and knowledge about outcomes. The former is further distinguished between firm, shaky, and no basis for probabilities; the latter consists in a continuum of outcomes, ranging from the set of discrete outcomes to outcomes poorly defined. Depending on the combination between the various elements of the two variables, we can end up with a state of uncertainty, ambiguity, or ignorance. Uncertainty is the state where there is a continuum of outcomes, but we have no basis for probabilities; ambiguity is the state where outcomes are poorly defined, but we have a firm or, at the very least, a basis for probabilities; finally, ignorance is the state where we have

---

[100] This view has been repeatedly confirmed in case law. The AB, for example, in its report on *Japan—Agricultural Products II* held that, as per Art 5.2 SPS, a legal requirement is imposed on WTO Members to provide a rational relationship between the SPS measure enacted and the available scientific evidence that exists (§84). See the relevant analysis by Dunoff (1999 and 2006).

no basis for probabilities and outcomes are poorly defined. In epistemic terms, scenario analysis is recommended in cases of uncertainty, sensitivity analysis in cases of ambiguity, and precaution in cases of ignorance. Precaution emerges as the scientific approach to address incommensurability, that is, the situation where one compares apples to oranges. Should precaution in WTO parlance be confined to cases of ignorance and incommensurability only? Or should we understand precaution as an antidote to uncertainty and ambiguity as well? It seems reasonable to assume that the latter should be the case. Recall that sensitivity and scenario analyses are scientific, not regulatory responses. The view of precaution as an antidote to both uncertainty and ambiguity is very much in line with the idea that there is no firewall between science and no science; that science is an ever-evolving construct; and that regulatory responses might be warranted irrespective of the degree of certainty about scientific evidence. Ultimately, regulation is the privilege of the statesman. One should be able to distinguish between scientifically informed and scientifically dependent regulation: in the very famous and oft-quoted words of Churchill, 'science should be on tap, not on top'.[101] This is probably what the AB wanted to capture in the first place and simply chose the wrong words. The fact that the AB in the immediately following paragraph of the same report (*EC—Hormones (US)*) held that the risk envisaged in the SPS Agreement is not just a laboratory risk but a real-life risk that takes into account behavioural factors lends support to the thesis advanced here. In an oft-quoted passage, it stated (§187):

> It is essential to bear in mind that the risk that is to be evaluated in a risk assessment under Article 5.1 is not only risk ascertainable in a science laboratory operating under strictly controlled conditions, but also risk in human societies as they actually exist, in other words, the actual potential for adverse effects on human health in the real world where people live and work and die.[102]

Now this is of course an equally problematic passage. One extreme reading of this paragraph would suggest that, unless scientific experiments take place in real-life scenarios, they will not be taken into account by the AB. Surely this cannot be what the AB meant for, if true, it would lead to doing away with almost all scientific evidence. Yet, both statements point in the direction of an improbable, if not an impossible risk altogether and this is probably how they should be understood. In the same case, the AB held that SPS measures need not be based solely on the prevailing opinion in the relevant scientific field in order to satisfy the statutory requirements included in Arts. 2.2 and 5.1 SPS: SPS measures based on minority scientific opinions could very well be WTO-consistent (§194). In *US—*

---

[101] On this issue, see Gollier et al. (2000), Kuhn (1962, and 1996), and also Sunstein (2002).
[102] In this vein, the Panel in its report on *Japan—Apples (Art. 21.5—US)* dismissed the relevance of two studies presented to it because they did not correspond to natural conditions (§§8.65 and 8.140ff).

Suspended Concession,[103] the AB held that evidence will be considered scientific if it respects the standards of the relevant scientific community (§591). In *Australia— Apples*, the AB held that this standard is further divided into two steps (§215):

> Thus, in its discussion of the standard of review that applies to a panel reviewing a risk assessment under Article 5.1 of the *SPS Agreement*, the Appellate Body identified two aspects of a panel's scrutiny of a risk assessment, namely, scrutiny of the underlying scientific basis and scrutiny of the reasoning of the risk assessor based upon such underlying science. (italics in the original)

It went on to hold that the first step was particularly pertinent whenever regulation was based on minority scientific opinions (§221):

> We note that the first aspect, the panel's review of the scientific basis of the risk assessment, may be particularly relevant in cases where the importing Member has relied on minority scientific opinions in conducting a risk assessment. In such cases, the question whether such opinions constitute 'legitimate' science from respected and qualified sources according to the standards of the relevant scientific community may have greater prominence.

This pronouncement makes a lot of sense and comes very close to the *Daubert* standard of the US Supreme Court.[104] In *Daubert,*[105] the Supreme Court embraced 'reliability' as the primary criterion for admitting expert evidence. Lianos (2010) got it right when arguing that the Court here collapsed two different concepts: the scientific standard of reliability (does the principle support what it aims to show?) and validity (does application of the principle produce consistent results?) into one legal standard of reliability: evidentiary reliability. In the words of the Court, in order to qualify as scientific knowledge,

> an inference or assertion must be derived by the scientific method.[106]

The term 'risk assessment' is defined in Annex A §4 to the SPS Agreement:

---

[103] This is the sequel to *EC—Hormones (US)*. Following the condemnation of its practices, the EU did not change its conduct and did not implement the findings of the WTO adjudicating bodies. The US was authorized to impose countermeasures (suspension of tariff concessions according to Art. 22.6 DSU) against the EU, which it did. Years later, the EU initiated a new Panel against the US, arguing that it had subsequently complied with the rulings and hence that the US should withdraw its countermeasures as a result. An astonishing Panel report found that the EU was right and that, while the disagreement between the two parties persisted as to whether implementation had occurred, the US should stop imposing countermeasures immediately; according to this Panel, if it wanted to resurrect the imposition of countermeasures, the US would have to initiate a new dispute. Luckily, the Panel was totally overturned by the AB in the case discussed here: the AB held that countermeasures lawfully remain in place until either the parties to the dispute have agreed that implementation has indeed occurred, or a multilateral ruling to this effect has been issued. The unilateral declaration of the party interested in seeing measures against it removed does not suffice, as the AB quite correctly held. Compare the analysis by Hoekman and Trachtman (2010).

[104] On this issue, see the excellent analysis and the critical remarks of Lianos (2010).

[105] *Daubert v Merrell Dow Pharm, Inc.,* 509 US 579, 588–9 (1993). See also Sykes (2006a).

[106] P. 590.

> *Risk assessment*—The evaluation of the likelihood of entry, establishment or spread of a pest or disease within the territory of an importing Member according to the sanitary or phytosanitary measures which might be applied, and of the associated potential biological and economic consequences; or the evaluation of the potential for adverse effects on human or animal health arising from the presence of additives, contaminants, toxins or disease-causing organisms in food, beverages or feedstuffs. (italics in the original)

There are, thus, two kinds of risk assessment:[107] all risks arising from the presence of additives, contaminants, toxins or disease-causing organisms in food, beverages or feedstuffs, must be assessed and their potential effects on human or animal life evaluated (Risk assessment I). On the other hand, as far as pests or diseases are concerned, the SPS Agreement provides for assessment of the likelihood of a pest or disease entering, establishing, and spreading, and the associated potential biological and economic consequences (Risk assessment II). Whereas it is the potential effects that must be assessed in Risk assessment I, it is the likelihood of a pest entering a particular market that must be assessed in Risk assessment II. There are different evidentiary standards associated with the two terms (potential, likelihood) and, thus, with the two types of risk assessment. In *EC—Hormones (US)*, the AB had articulated its understanding of the term 'likelihood' and 'potential' (§§123–4) and determined that 'likelihood' was a more demanding standard than 'potential' (§§183–4):

> Interpreting [paragraph 4 of Annex A of the SPS Agreement], the Panel elaborates risk assessment as a two-step process that 'should (i) *identify* the *adverse effects* on human health (if any) arising from the presence of the hormones at issue when used as growth promoters *in meat* . . . , and (ii) if any such adverse effects exist, *evaluate* the *potential* or probability of occurrence of such effects'.
> . . . Although the utility of a two-step analysis may be debated, it does not appear to us to be substantially wrong. What needs to be pointed out at this stage is that the Panel's use of 'probability' as an alternative term for 'potential' creates a significant concern. The ordinary meaning of 'potential' relates to 'possibility' and is different from the ordinary meaning of 'probability'. 'Probability' implies a higher degree or a threshold of potentiality or possibility. It thus appears that here the Panel introduces a quantitative dimension to the notion of risk. (emphasis in the original)

Consequently, the standard with respect to Risk assessment II is more demanding.

In its report on *Australia—Salmon*, the AB provided its understanding of the duty to perform a risk assessment in the following terms (§121):

> . . . a risk assessment within the meaning of Article 5.1 must:

> (1) *identify* the diseases whose entry, establishment or spread a Member wants to prevent within its territory, as well as the potential biological and economic

---

[107] Gruszczynski (2010) offers a very comprehensive discussion of WTO case law regarding risk assessment.

consequences associated with the entry, establishment or spread of these diseases;

(2) *evaluate the likelihood* of entry, establishment or spread of these diseases, as well as the associated potential biological and economic consequences; and

(3) evaluate the likelihood of entry, establishment or spread of these diseases *according to the SPS measures which might be applied.* (emphasis in the original)

In *US—Suspended Concession*, the AB explained the sequential steps that Panels should take whenever they face a challenge against the legality of a risk assessment (§598):

> Looking at the Panel's analysis of whether the European Communities specifically assessed the risks arising from the consumption of meat from cattle treated with oestradiol-17β, we note that a significant portion of the Panel's reasoning consists of summaries of the responses of the experts. It is only after summarizing the experts' responses that the Panel describes some of the issues discussed in the 1999 Opinion. Given the applicable standard of review and the role of the Panel that is determined by it, the Panel's analysis should have proceeded differently. The Panel should have first looked at the European Communities' risk assessment. It should then have determined whether the scientific basis relied upon in that risk assessment came from a respected and qualified source. The Panel should have sought assistance from the scientific experts in confirming that it had properly identified the scientific basis underlying the European Communities' risk assessment or to determine whether that scientific basis originated in a respected and qualified source. The Panel should also have sought the experts' assistance in determining whether the reasoning articulated by the European Communities on the basis of the scientific evidence is objective and coherent, so that the conclusions reached in the risk assessment sufficiently warrant the SPS measure. Instead, the Panel seems to have conducted a survey of the advice presented by the scientific experts and based its decisions on whether the majority of the experts, or the opinion that was most thoroughly reasoned or specific to the question at issue, agreed with the conclusion drawn in the European Communities' risk assessment. This approach is not consistent with the applicable standard of review under the *SPS Agreement.* (italics in the original)

In *US—Suspended Concession*, the AB faced the following facts (§536):

> Before we proceed to examine the European Communities' claims, we briefly summarize some of the relevant facts of this case. We note that Codex has adopted an international standard for oestradiol-17β, based on evaluations carried out by JECFA [the Joint FAO/WHO Expert Committee on Food Additives]. The European Communities asserts that it has determined a higher level of protection than that which would be achieved under Codex's standard. According to the European Communities, its level of protection is 'no (avoidable) risk, that is a level of protection that does not allow any unnecessary addition from exposure to genotoxic chemical substances that are intended to be added deliberately to food.' The European Communities also notes that it has performed a risk assessment for meat from cattle treated with oestradiol-17β for growth-promotion purposes. This risk assessment consists of the 1999, 2000, and 2002 Opinions, as supported by 17 studies conducted between 1998 and 2001. The European Communities further explains that its SPS measure—that is, the import and marketing ban applied

pursuant to Directive 2003/74/EC—was taken in the light of the higher level of protection that it determined for itself and is properly based on its risk assessment.

In its risk assessment, the EU had assessed not only the risk from growth hormones, but also the risk resulting from abuse or misuse in the administration of hormones; such risk apparently exists when 'good veterinary practices' are not observed. The Panel had summarily dismissed the relevance of this assessment and the AB, in total disagreement with the Panel in this respect, reversed its findings: in its view, the risk originating in the administration of hormones can, of course, be included (§545ff and especially §§553–5). It added that, in case various factors contribute to a risk, there is no obligation to disentangle their effects (§562).

In *Japan—Apples*, the issue was whether the SPS Agreement prejudges the methodology that should be used in the context of risk assessment. The AB found that the agreement does not impose a particular methodology to this effect (§204). In the same report, the AB, confirming prior case law on this issue, held that the obligation to base measures on risk assessment entails that the WTO Member wishing to enact an SPS measure cannot carry out a risk assessment in a manner that precludes phyto-sanitary measures, other than the one already in place, from being considered. The AB found (§209) that Japan had violated its obligations under the SPS Agreement by conducting a risk assessment justifying the measure it had in place, without, however, inquiring into the possibility of other, potentially applicable, measures. In this regard, the AB concluded that, although the SPS Agreement does not require a particular methodology to be applied, it does require that the chosen methodology be specific to (in close connection with) the factual situation investigated.

The AB explained in its report on *EC—Hormones (US)* that a WTO Member can base its measures on a risk assessment performed either by another WTO Member or by an international organization (§190). This is a very sensible judgment, since developing countries which typically do not possess scientific expertise in a number of areas can still enact SPS measures, 'borrowing' from the expertise of those who possess it.

In the same report, the AB reversed a finding by the Panel to the effect that Arts. 2.2 and 5.1 SPS impose a minimum procedural requirement, in the sense that a WTO Member adopting an SPS measure must provide evidence that it did base its measure on scientific evidence at the time when the measures had been originally adopted. In this case, the Panel had found no evidence in the body of the EC regulation (reflecting the SPS measure), or in its preamble, that the EU had indeed based its measure on science and, consequently, held that it had violated its obligations under the SPS. The AB disagreed (§§188–90): in its view, no such obligation can be discerned in the SPS Agreement.

The AB's reasoning does pose some problems. It is true that a textual reading of the relevant provisions (Arts. 2.2 and 5.1 SPS) does not lead to the conclusion that they impose a similar requirement; and yet, from an evidentiary perspective, it is almost impossible for uninformed parties to discern the basis of an SPS measure unless some evidence is provided.[108] The Agreement imposes transparency obligations, that much is for sure, and maybe the AB held that these requirements in and of themselves suffice; WTO Members must, pursuant to §1 of Annex B to the SPS Agreement, ensure:

> that all sanitary and phytosanitary regulations which have been adopted are published promptly in such a manner as to enable interested Members to become acquainted with them.

§3 of the same Annex further requires from WTO Members to introduce 'enquiry points' whereby interested parties can request (and obtain) information regarding the SPS measures. Consequently, even in the absence of procedural requirement, WTO Members will be violating their obligations (§3 of the Annex) if they do not provide adequate information regarding the basis of their measures: were one to take the view that WTO Members have complied with this provision by providing say meaningless or unhelpful information, it would deprive §3 of the Annex of its *effet utile*. If WTO Members play fair in this respect, then the AB holding regarding the minimum procedural requirement will be a minor issue. As we shall see in more detail in Chapter 13, SPS notifications rank high and this is one area where transparency has largely been observed.

Assuming the existence of risk, it is for WTO Members, depending on their risk aversion, to decide whether to intervene or not. WTO adjudicating bodies cannot prejudge the level of risk aversion that a given society unilaterally sets. In the WTO era, the AB reaffirmed this point in the most unambiguous terms in *EC—Hormones (US)* (§186):

> To the extent that the Panel purported to require a risk assessment to establish a minimum magnitude of risk, we must note that imposition of such a quantitative requirement finds no basis in the SPS Agreement. A panel is authorized only to determine whether a given SPS measure is 'based on' risk assessment.

In order to reach this finding, the AB went through a rather convoluted reasoning, dissociating (for no apparent reason) the notion of 'risk assessment' from that of 'risk management': the latter is often used to denote the level of risk that a given society is prepared to live with; risk management naturally follows risk assessment, in the sense that, assuming knowledge as to the distribution or probabilities that an event might occur, a given society, depending on its risk aversion, will define the level of protection that it deems appropriate. It is following this logic that the Panel on *EC—Hormones (US)* accepted the distinction between risk management and risk assessment. The AB, however, back to its textualist best, on formal grounds (lack of explicit reference to risk management in the SPS Agreement), dismissed its

---

[108] Davey (2006) advances a series of arguments on this score regarding the reversal of the Panel finding.

relevance altogether (§181). And yet, a few paragraphs further down, as we saw *supra*, the AB accepted (§186) that WTO Members can unilaterally set their appropriate level of protection that Panels cannot disturb:[109] but is not this paragraph effectively admitting that risk management is the privilege of WTO Members? We believe it does.

The discretion of WTO Members to set their appropriate level of protection has been respected in all but one case: *Japan—Apples*.[110] Japan imposed a series of measures to ban trade of apples originating in the US, fearing that some of them might suffer from 'fire blight'. The measure challenged by the US consisted of nine prohibitions or requirements (§§8.5ff). Among these measures was a prohibition on importing apples from US states other than Oregon and Washington, certification requirements, and the prohibition of exports if fire blight had been detected in a neighbouring geographical area. According to the Japanese regulator, in the absence of a total embargo on imports, the risk that the disease would spread was very much alive. Fire blight affects apples, and not human life. There was no evidence that apples infected with fire blight had been exported to Japan, although there was evidence of a shipment of infected apples to the separate customs territory of Taiwan, Penghu, Kinmen, and Matsu.[111] However, the apples shipped to Taiwan, Penghu, Kinmen, and Matsu had not been infected with fire blight, but rather by another disease ('codling moth'). Japan claimed that it possessed sufficient scientific evidence that risk did exist: the record shows that apples infected with fire blight had been exported to New Zealand in the early twentieth century, to the United Kingdom in the 1950s, and to Egypt a little later. Scientific evidence showed (with a considerable degree of confidence) that the disease had been transmitted because of the nature of the trade involved (trade in root stocks, that is, in apple trees and not in apples). The trade involved in the *Japan—Apples* dispute concerned apples and not apple trees. The expertise provided to the Panel suggested that the risk of completing the pathway (and thus, transmitting the disease) was negligible. The Panel rejected the US argument that it was required to confine its review only to mature, symptom-less apples, since only such apples were being exported to Japan; the Panel held that the risk (because of human error) that immature, symptom-full apples be exported to Japan should also be taken into account. In the experts' view, however, even if this were the case, the risk would still be negligible, because the disease could only be transmitted through birds flying from infected apples to uninfected apple trees. Relying on the guidance of the experts on this point, the Panel explicitly accepted that there was negligible risk. It still went ahead, nevertheless, and found that there was no rational or objective relationship between the measure and the relevant scientific

---

[109] The AB went so far as to accept that WTO Members can opt for zero risk (though it is doubtful if it ever exists).

[110] Neven and Weiler (2006) have provided an excellent, critical account of this dispute.

[111] See §160 of the AB report and footnote 289.

evidence: in light of the negligible risk identified on the basis of the scientific evidence and the nature of elements composing the measure, the Panel concluded that the Japanese measure was clearly disproportionate (§§8.198–9). Note that the Panel did not reach its finding in this respect based on Art. 5.6 SPS (which reflects the necessity requirement). It decided to exercise judicial economy in this respect. It held that the measure was inconsistent with Art. 2.2 SPS, since there was no scientific evidence to support it, although it accepted that risk, albeit negligible, did exist. The AB endorsed the idea that, in light of the negligible risk, the challenged measure was disproportionate (§§160 and 163ff) and was, thus, in violation of Art. 2.2 SPS.

This is a remarkable finding: zero risk was accepted in *EC—Hormones (US)* and negligible risk, for sure higher than zero risk, was not enough to base SPS measures in *Japan—Apples*. This unfortunate AB report flies against the letter and the spirit of the SPS Agreement. In Annex A entitled 'Definitions', §5 reads:

> *Appropriate level of sanitary or phytosanitary protection*—The level of protection deemed appropriate by the Member establishing a sanitary or phytosanitary measure to protect human, animal or plant life or health within its territory. (italics in the original)

The Preamble to the SPS Agreement in relevant part reads:

> without requiring Members to change their appropriate level of protection of human, animal or plant life or health

Indeed, although the expression chosen is imprecise, this is probably what the AB aimed to capture when it held, in *EC—Hormones (US)* first, and repeated in *Australia—Salmon* later, that zero risk is acceptable if this is the will of the regulating WTO Member.[112]

The finding would have probably been acceptable had it been made within the context of an examination under the necessity requirement. This, alas, was not the case. The finding in *Japan—Apples* is indefensible. In the words of Neven and Weiler (2006), it is one bad apple that should not be repeated in the future.

3.2.6 The Necessity Requirement

The necessity requirement is set out in Art. 5.6 SPS:

> ...Members shall ensure that such measures are not more trade-restrictive than required to achieve their appropriate level of sanitary or phytosanitary protection, taking into account technical and economic feasibility.

A footnote to Art. 5.6 SPS further specifies:

> For purposes of paragraph 6 of Article 5, a measure is not more trade-restrictive than required unless there is another measure, reasonably available taking into account

---

[112] See the relevant discussion *infra*.

technical and economic feasibility, that achieves the appropriate level of sanitary or phytosanitary protection and is significantly less restrictive to trade.

This provision crystallizes into GATT case law on the necessity requirement. In parallel with the TBT Agreement, international standards are presumed to be in conformity with the necessity requirement (Art. 3.2 SPS).

In *Australia—Salmon*, the question was whether an Australian measure banning on health grounds imports of salmon not treated in a particular manner was consistent with various provisions of the SPS Agreement and, *inter alia*, whether it was necessary in the sense of Art. 5.6 SPS.[113] The AB provided the test that should be applied by WTO adjudicating bodies in order to establish a violation of Art. 5.6 SPS in the following terms (§194):

> We agree with the Panel that Article 5.6 and, in particular, the footnote to this provision, clearly provides a three-pronged test to establish a violation of Article 5.6. As already noted, the three elements of this test under Article 5.6 are that there is an SPS measure which:
>
> (1) is reasonably available taking into account technical and economic feasibility;
> (2) achieves the Member's appropriate level of sanitary or phytosanitary protection; and
> (3) is significantly less restrictive to trade than the SPS measure contested.
>
> These three elements are cumulative in the sense that, to establish consistency with Article 5.6, all of them have to be met. If any of these elements is not fulfilled, the measure in dispute would be inconsistent with Article 5.6.[114]

In *Australia—Apples*, the AB explained that its quest for a reasonably available significantly less restrictive measure was meant to be an intellectual exercise aimed at establishing whether the necessity requirement had been adhered to (§363):

> Compliance with this requirement is tested through a comparison of the measure at issue to possible alternative measures. Such alternatives, however, are mere conceptual tools for the purpose of the Article 5.6 analysis. A demonstration that an alternative measure meets the relevant Member's appropriate level of protection, is reasonably available, and is significantly less trade restrictive than the existing measure suffices to prove that the measure at issue is more trade restrictive than necessary. Yet this does not imply that the importing Member must adopt that alternative measure or that the alternative measure is the only option that would achieve the desired level of protection

The judicial review is limited to an evaluation of the means that are employed to reach ends that cannot be put into question. Recall our discussion above on *Japan—Apples* and the appropriate level of protection: the case law discussed immediately after leaves no doubt that *Japan—Apples* was an outlier. There is, of course, a logical link between the instrument chosen and the level of protection

---

[113] Garcia (2006) discusses this case extensively.
[114] See also the AB report on *Japan—Agricultural Products II* (§95), and §8.162 of the Panel report on *Japan—Apples* (*Art. 21.5—US*).

desired: assuming the level chosen is quite strict, a regulator might not have the luxury to select from a plethora of instruments in order to reach the targeted level.[115]

In *EC—Hormones* (*US*), the AB held that WTO Members can unilaterally define the level of risk by which they are prepared to abide. In *Australia—Salmon*, the AB confirmed this impression. Dealing with the interpretation of the term 'appropriate level of protection', quoted *supra*, the AB held that the choice of the level of protection logically precedes the choice of the instrument that will eventually be used: a WTO Member first defines its appropriate level of protection and only then will choose the instrument to achieve the level sought (§§200, 201, 203). In §199 it went so far as to state:

> We do not believe that Article 11 of the DSU, or any other provision of the DSU or of the *SPS Agreement*, entitles the Panel or the AB, for the purpose of applying Article 5.6 in the present case, to substitute its own reasoning about the implied level of protection for that expressed consistently by Australia. The determination of the appropriate level of protection, a notion defined in paragraph 5 of Annex A, as 'the level of protection deemed appropriate by the Member establishing a sanitary... measure', is a *prerogative* of the Member concerned and not of a panel or of the AB.

Repeating prior case law, it went on to say that a WTO Member could therefore decide to accept zero risk when defining its policies:

> ... As stated in our Report in *European Communities—Hormones*, the 'risk' evaluated in a risk assessment must be an ascertainable risk; theoretical uncertainty is 'not the kind of risk which, under Article 5.1, is to be assessed.' This does not mean, however, that a Member cannot determine its own appropriate level of protection to be 'zero risk'. (italics in the original)

In the same report, the AB explains that WTO Members have no obligation to express their appropriate level of protection in quantitative terms. However, some degree of precision is required, otherwise it will be impossible to determine whether they have complied with other relevant provisions of the SPS Agreement: unless expressed in precise enough terms, the quest for the relationship between the measure chosen and the level of protection sought will be severely hindered and, consequently, a WTO adjudicating body, facing a claim under Art. 5.6 SPS, might find it impossible to carry out its task. To avoid this, WTO Members are required to define with precision (albeit, not necessarily in quantitative terms) their level of protection (§206):

> We thus believe that the *SPS Agreement* contains an implicit obligation to determine the appropriate level of protection. We do not believe that there is an obligation to determine the appropriate level of protection in quantitative terms. This does not mean, however, that an importing Member is free to determine its level of protection

---

[115] Recall that the AB has discussed the allocation of the burden of proof in the context of the necessity requirement in *US—Gambling* (see Chapter 5).

with such vagueness or equivocation that the application of the relevant provisions of the *SPS Agreement*, such as Article 5.6, becomes impossible. It would obviously be wrong to interpret the *SPS Agreement* in a way that would render nugatory entire articles or paragraphs of articles of this Agreement and allow Members to escape from their obligations under this Agreement. (italics in the original)

In the same report, the AB held that, if a WTO Member fails to determine the appropriate level of protection (or when it does so with insufficient precision), Panels might on occasion be in a position to fill the gap: a review of the SPS measure employed will help them to establish the appropriate level of protection (§207). In other words, absence of definition of the level of protection, or insufficient precision, is not fatal for the regulating state.

3.2.7 Consistency

Art. 5.5 SPS reflects the consistency requirement:

> ...each Member shall avoid arbitrary or unjustifiable distinctions in the levels it considers to be appropriate in different situations, if such distinctions result in discrimination or a disguised restriction on international trade.

The rationale for this provision is obvious: WTO Members will not be allowed to pick and choose the sectors where they will be demanding and the sectors where they will not, and as a result will reduce the potential for beggar-thy-neighbour policies à la carte.[116] The key question here has to do with the extent of the consistency requirement: at one end of the spectrum, it should be confined to the relevant product market, the DCS category of goods as defined in Chapter 4 on the other, it should extend to cover all comparable risks irrespective of whether related to DCS goods or not.

WTO case law (AB, *EC—Hormones (US)*, §§212, 238) has established that this provision should be read together with Art. 2.3 SPS, which, as we saw *supra*, requires non-discriminatory behaviour across WTO Members. In *Australia—Salmon*, the AB went one step further and explained that a violation of Art. 5.5 SPS *ipso facto* entails a violation of Art. 2.3 SPS as well (§252).[117] Whereas the latter part (across WTO Members) seems easier to grasp, the former part (across situations) is far from being a walk in the park for the adjudicator. A benchmark is required in order to establish comparability across situations. Case law has contributed some clarifications on this score.

The AB held in *EC—Hormones (US)* that, for a violation of Art. 5.5 SPS to be established, a complaining party must satisfy a three-prong test (§§214–15):

---

[116] Pienaar (2003).

[117] Note, however, that, by virtue of Art. 6 SPS, WTO Members do not need to apply their SPS measures against all exports when a pest or a disease has surfaced which necessitated the adoption of the SPS measure. Pest- and disease-free areas can legitimately be excluded. The terms 'pest- or disease-free area' and 'area of low pest or disease' are further detailed in §§6 and 7 of Annex A to the SPS Agreement.

Close inspection of Article 5.5 indicates that a complaint of violation of this Article must show the presence of three distinct elements. The first element is that the Member imposing the measure complained of has adopted its own appropriate levels of sanitary protection against risks to human life or health in several different situations. The second element to be shown is that those *levels of protection* exhibit arbitrary or unjustifiable differences ('distinctions' in the language of Article 5.5) in their treatment of different situations. The last element requires that the arbitrary or unjustifiable differences result in discrimination or a disguised restriction of international trade. We understand the last element to be referring to the *measure* embodying or implementing a particular level of protection as resulting, in its application, in discrimination or a disguised restriction on international trade.

We consider the above three elements of Article 5.5 to be cumulative in nature; all of them must be demonstrated to be present if violation of Article 5.5 is to be found. In particular, both the second and third elements must be found. The second element alone would not suffice. The third element must also be demonstrably present: the implementing measure must be shown to be applied in such a manner as to result in discrimination or a disguised restriction on international trade. The presence of the second element—the arbitrary or unjustifiable character of differences in *levels of protection* considered by a Member as appropriate in differing situations—may in practical effect operate as a 'warning' signal that the implementing *measure* in its application *might* be a discriminatory measure or *might* be a restriction on international trade disguised as an SPS measure for the protection of human life or health. Nevertheless, the measure itself needs to be examined and appraised and, in the context of the differing levels of protection, shown to result in discrimination or a disguised restriction on international trade. (emphasis in the original)

To perform this test, the complaining party needs to first establish comparability across situations. In §§217ff of its report on *EC—Hormones* (*US*), the AB, applying this test, held that the EU had violated Art. 5.5 SPS by banning sales of hormone-treated beef, and not banning sales of hormone-treated pork. Nevertheless, the only element of comparability was that pork and beef are probably DCS goods in the EU market. The AB did not deem it necessary to also examine whether risks from consumption of hormone-treated beef are comparable to those presented by hormone-treated chicken. This is quite problematic since, assuming that risks are asymmetric, and in light of the fact that it is the EU prerogative to define its appropriate level of protection, it could very well have chosen to address one (the higher) and not the other (the lower). Alas, we will never know what the actual risk was. This report, on the other hand, implicitly establishes that the DCS relationship is an element of comparability.[118] The AB explained in the same report that the letter and the spirit of Art. 5.5 SPS does not require WTO Members to guarantee an absolute uniformity across the various appropriate levels of protection that they pursue. In its view, Art. 5.5 SPS should be

---

[118] Horn and Mavroidis (2003).

properly understood as a legal prohibition of arbitrary or unjustifiable discrimination (§213):

> The objective of Article 5.5 is formulated as the 'achieving [of] consistency in the application of the concept of appropriate level of sanitary or phytosanitary protection'. Clearly, the desired consistency is defined as a goal to be achieved in the future.... Thus, we agree with the Panel's view that the statement of that goal does not establish a *legal obligation* of consistency of appropriate levels of protection. We think, too, that the goal set is not absolute or perfect consistency, since governments establish their appropriate levels of protection frequently on an *ad hoc* basis and over time, as different risks present themselves at different times. It is only arbitrary or unjustifiable inconsistencies that are to be avoided. (italics and emphasis in the original)

Subsequently, in *Australia—Salmon*, the AB offered another benchmark for comparability (§§146 and 152):

> the Panel was correct in stating that situations can be compared under Article 5.5 if these situations involve *either* a risk of entry, establishment or spread of the same or a similar disease, *or* a risk of the same or similar 'associated potential biological and economic consequences'....
>
> we believe that for situations to be comparable under Article 5.5, it is sufficient for these situations to have in common a risk of entry, establishment or spread of *one* disease of concern. There is no need for these situations to have in common a risk of entry, establishment or spread of *all* diseases of concern. (emphasis in the original)

Therefore, similarity of the disease or of the associated risk also provides a comparability element. The question, nonetheless, remains whether the test should be confined to the DCS category of goods or not. In *Australia—Salmon*, the AB introduced the term 'warning signals', which refers to elements or properties of particular SPS measures that could be relevant in establishing a violation of Art. 5.5 SPS. The quantity and quality of such warning signals will ultimately prove to be the decisive factor in determining whether Art. 5.5 SPS has been violated: substantial difference in the level of protection across two comparable situations (§164), and/or violation of Art. 5.1 SPS (§ 166), could serve as warning signals.[119]

Case law, thus, has made some advance on this issue but the big questions still lie ahead. The WTO Members adopted on 22 June 2000[120] Guidelines which provide some clarification on the scope of the obligation assumed under Art 5.5 of the SPS Agreement: WTO Members must, in order to observe their consistency obligation, indicate the level of protection which they consider appropriate and also indicate if there is a difference in the level of protection under consideration and levels already determined by the regulating WTO Member in different

---

[119] Evidence of this attitude can also be detected in §240 of the AB's report on *EC—Hormones* (*US*).

[120] WTO Doc G/SPS/15 of 18 July 2000.

situations. WTO Members must further compare the level of protection now being sought with that already considered in previous situations which contain sufficient common elements so as to render the two situations comparable.[121]

In Horn and Mavroidis (2003), we had argued that the test for consistency should be confined within the DCS category of goods.[122] After all, the SPS is part of a wider trade agreement, the Agreement Establishing the WTO, the purpose of which is to combat protectionism: a presumption that protectionism has been sought is much stronger when the test of Art 5.5 SPS is confined within a relevant product market. Moreover, casting the net too wide has one important consequence: WTO Panels and the AB become the arbiters of consistency in the formulation of national health policies. The risk of false positives by the WTO adjudicating bodies in the field of health-related matters is not comparable, both from a human and from an institutional perspective, to the risk of false positives say in the field of AD. Restricting the test, for the purposes of Art 5.5 SPS analysis, to an examination of national (health, environmental) policies within the relevant product market under consideration is consistent with different criteria, some of them explicitly and some of them implicitly mentioned in the Guidelines as well. Comparability of the risk distribution is such an element; so is comparability of the disease (similar disease, in the Guidelines lingo). At least these factors should be evaluated cumulatively. Were one to isolate, for example, comparability of risk distribution, one might end up with results that would hardly make sense in the context of a trade agreement. Assume, for example, that a consumer smoking a fixed number of cigarettes and consuming a fixed amount of hormone-treated beef incurs the same probability to suffer the same disease. Assume further that a country bans hormone-treated beef, but simply taxes sales of cigarettes. Has this country violated Art 5.5 SPS? Yes, if comparability of risk distribution and/or disease is viewed as the only relevant criterion to decide on the consistency requirement; no, were one to control for the purpose of signing the SPS. It is highly unlikely, if not implausible altogether, that consumers of hormone-treated beef will start smoking more as a result of the ban on beef. Moreover, the tax on cigarettes will be borne by both domestic and foreign producers. By the same token, adjustment costs have been imposed on both domestic and foreign beef producers. This is hardly a case of discrimination, if by this term, in a trade context, we understand a ban on protectionism. An illustration is definitely helpful in this context. Take the *EC—Hormones* case, for example, and the manner in which the AB treated the fact that the defendant had not imposed a similar measure on hormone-treated pork (as it did with respect to hormone-treated beef). The EU must, by virtue of Art 2.3 SPS, ban sales of hormone-treated beef irrespective of its origin: Art 2.3 of the SPS, in other words, covers only the

---

121 See p. 3 of the Guidelines, op. cit. under A4.
122 Compare Scott (2009).

identical product market and not the relevant product market.[123] Art 5.5 SPS extends this obligation to the relevant product market: the EU must, by virtue of this provision, examine whether a ban on hormone-treated products, which are substitutable for beef, and, provided that at least the comparability factors mentioned above have been satisfactorily met, is warranted. In this vein, the obligation reflected in Art 5.5 SPS cements the obligation reflected in Art 2.3 SPS; it serves as an anti-circumvention provision: WTO Members will not arbitrarily choose levels of protection when faced with comparable risks stemming from comparable diseases within a relevant product market and thus confer an advantage upon domestic (equally hazardous) production.

In Horn and Mavroidis (2003), we probably offered too narrow a coverage for the consistency requirement. Take, for example, the case where a disease imported through whatever channel affects two fields producing goods which are not in a DCS relationship. Assume further that the damage done is symmetric. Assume also that there is science which points to comparable risk: say both fields will be equally affected. To give a concrete example, Home allows production of GMO corn but not GMO strawberries. Should similar cases be tolerated because the products concerned are not in a DCS relationship? After all, beggar-thy-neighbour policies can and do occur through instruments affecting distinct markets. Here, intuitively, one would want to respond in the affirmative, and the Guidelines mentioned above leave ample room for an affirmative response. We read on p. 4 of the Guidelines:

> What a Member is comparing are the levels of protection against the risks posed . . .
>   Characterizing risks as 'similar' must include a comparison of both the relevant likelihood and the corresponding consequences.

And probably this is the right response. One word of caution though: as we move away from the DCS category, the presumption of protectionism fades away. In similar cases, the judge should feel confident regarding the comparability across transactions and persuade him/herself that cost-shifting takes place from the regulating to the affected state: elements such as those mentioned above (comparability of risk level, scientific evidence to this effect, etc.) could be useful input in similar exercises.

3.2.8 Measures Adopted on Precaution

WTO Members can, in accordance with Art. 5.7 SPS, provisionally adopt SPS measures on the basis of available information, even in the absence of scientific

---

[123] The argument here is that a very narrow construction of the obligation included in Art. 2.3 SPS is warranted. This is probably not always the correct level of disaggregation: if, for example, growth hormones might have a differential effect on an animal (and thus present a different risk for human health) depending on the age at which it is injected (the growth hormone), then a WTO member should legitimately control for such differences without risking a panel finding that it has violated its obligations under Art 2.3 SPS.

backing. In this case, however, they are under an obligation to collect information that will enable them to perform a risk assessment within a reasonable period of time. Although Art. 5.7 SPS does not explicitly refer to the 'precautionary principle', WTO adjudicating bodies have held that this provision reflects it. In *EC—Hormones (US)*,[124] the AB offered its understanding of this principle in public international law and summarized its relevance in the WTO legal order (§§ 123–5):

(a) The precautionary principle is reflected in Art. 5.7 SPS, but is also reflected in other SPS provisions such as the preamble and Art. 3.3 SPS. Hence, the precautionary principle is not exhaustively reflected in Art. 5.7 SPS;
(b) The status of precautionary principle under customary international law is unclear;[125]
(c) WTO Panels should keep precautionary principle in mind when interpreting the SPS; but
(d) The precautionary principle does not override the explicit wording of specific SPS provisions.

The relationship between Art. 5.7 SPS, on one hand, and Art. 2.2 SPS (the obligation to base measures on scientific evidence), on the other, was addressed by various AB reports, and not always in a consistent manner. In *Japan—Agricultural Products II*,[126] the AB held (§80):

> . . . Article 5.7 allows Members to adopt provisional SPS measures '[I]n cases where relevant scientific evidence is insufficient' and certain other requirements are fulfilled. Article 5.7 operates as a *qualified* exemption from the obligation under Article 2.2 not to maintain SPS measures without sufficient scientific evidence. An overly broad and flexible interpretation of that obligation would render Article 5.7 meaningless. (emphasis in the original)

In its report, the AB went probably too far too fast: why is recourse to precaution a qualified exemption from the obligation to base SPS measures on science? Is it because there is scientific evidence about most issues that we care to regulate? Or is it because, absent science, the SPS Agreement should be construed as a preference to restrain regulation? We submit that a negative response is due to both questions: it is impossible to respond to the first question even if we give a time value to scientific proof and discount totally the possibility that new science will overturn the existing paradigm and hence all existing science should be viewed with scepticism; the whole idea of precautionary measures is to avoid imminent harm

---

[124] Mercurio and Shao (2010) offer an analysis of this dispute as well as of all the WTO case law on precaution.
[125] In *EC—Approval and Marketing of Biotech Products*, the Panel, when dealing with the EU regime for approval of genetically modified organisms (GMOs), even cited the International Tribunal of the Law of the Sea (ITLOS) as support for its finding that the precautionary principle had an uncertain status under customary international law (§7.89).
[126] See Dunoff (2006) for an excellent account of this dispute.

and allow regulators to intervene until proof (one way or the other) exists as to the merits of the regulatory intervention. The AB here provided a rather unfortunate construction of the SPS Agreement.

Still, in *Japan—Apples*, the AB went one step further: in its view, if science is well settled on an issue, recourse to precaution is unwarranted. In a sense, the AB sees a firewall between scientific evidence and precaution (§184):

> The application of Article 5.7 is triggered not by the existence of scientific uncertainty, but rather by the insufficiency of scientific evidence. The text of Article 5.7 is clear: it refers to 'cases where relevant scientific evidence is insufficient', not to 'scientific uncertainty'. The two concepts are not interchangeable. Therefore, we are unable to endorse Japan's approach of interpreting Article 5.7 through the prism of 'scientific uncertainty'.[127]

It follows that, in the early cases discussed by the AB, a measure can either be based on science or on Art. 5.7 SPS, and that recourse to the latter is appropriate in cases of scientific insufficiency, but not of scientific uncertainty. Where precisely one should draw the line between these two concepts is a mystery.[128] In *US—Suspended Concession*, the AB revisited its prior case law, distanced itself from it, and adopted a more coherent approach on this issue. In this case, an international standard for growth hormones existed, from which the EU had deviated in seeking higher protection. The AB implicitly held that there should be no firewall between science and precaution, since science normally proceeds incrementally, and only rarely do we experience paradigm shifts (§703). In its view, nothing should stop WTO Members from challenging the orthodoxy of an accepted scientific *acquis*. In this vein, the presence of an international standard is no presumption that recourse to Art. 5.7 SPS is impossible. It could very well be the case, as indeed was the case in this particular dispute, that the regulating state seeks a level of protection higher than that achieved by the international standard in place (§§627ff and in particular §697). Moreover, distancing itself from a Panel ruling to this effect, the AB held that there is no need to demonstrate a critical mass of evidence to support a measure based on Art. 5.7 SPS, when an international standard exists. In its words (§725):

> In concluding that it is 'not convinced' that the ultra-sensitive assay study referred to by the European Communities 'call[s] into question the fundamental precepts of previous knowledge' in relation to the effect of the five hormones on pre-pubertal children, the Panel applied an excessively high threshold in relation to the new scientific evidence which is required to render previously sufficient scientific evidence 'insufficient' within the meaning of Article 5.7. Irrespective of whether the Panel was itself persuaded by the Klein study, the Panel erred to the extent that it considered that a paradigmatic shift in the scientific knowledge was required in order

---

[127] See also §188 of this report.
[128] Popper (1992) would have regarded this distinction and the whole idea that there is a firewall between science and precaution with some consternation.

to render the scientific evidence relied by JECFA now 'insufficient' within the meaning of Article 5.7. The 'insufficiency' requirement in Article 5.7 does not imply that new scientific evidence must entirely displace the scientific evidence upon which an international standard relies. It suffices that new scientific developments call into question whether the body of scientific evidence still permits of a sufficiently objective assessment of risk.

WTO case law has also dealt with the mechanics of the compliance with Art. 5.7 SPS.[129] The AB, in its report on *Japan—Agricultural Products II* established a four-prong test that must be met in its entirety for a measure to be deemed consistent with Art. 5.7 SPS (§89):

> Article 5.7 of the *SPS Agreement* sets out four requirements which must be met in order to adopt and maintain a provisional SPS measure. Pursuant to the first sentence of Article 5.7, a Member may provisionally adopt an SPS measure if this measure is:
>
> (1) imposed in respect of a situation where 'relevant scientific information is insufficient'; and
> (2) adopted 'on the basis of available pertinent information'.
>
> Pursuant to the second sentence of Article 5.7, such a provisional measure may not be maintained unless the Member which adopted the measure:
>
> (1) 'seek[s] to obtain the additional information necessary for a more objective assessment of risk'; and
> (2) 'review[s] the ... measure accordingly within a reasonable period of time.
>
> These four requirements are clearly cumulative in nature and are equally important for the purpose of determining consistency with this provision. Whenever *one* of these four requirements is not met, the measure at issue is inconsistent with Article 5.7. (emphasis in the original)

The term 'reasonable period of time' was discussed in the AB report on *Japan— Agricultural Products II*. There, the AB held that this term will have to be interpreted on a case-by-case basis. In this particular case, four years of inaction by Japan subsequent to the adoption of a measure under Art. 5.7 SPS was deemed to be unreasonable (§93). In the same dispute, the AB held that the additional information sought during the reasonable period of time must be germane in conducting a risk assessment (§92). Case law has so far not addressed the question of whether precautionary measures must still observe the non-discrimination obligation (Art. 2.3 SPS), the consistency requirement (Art. 5.5 SPS), and the necessity requirement (Art. 5.6 SPS). The text of Art. 5.7 SPS does not absolve

---

129 Foster (2011) offers a construction not espoused by case law and discusses how allocation of the burden of proof (reversal of the burden of production of proof) can help reduce the potential for error when adjudicating disputes regarding the application of the precautionary principle. Compare with the current understanding in case law of the allocation of burden of proof as explained in Grando (2009).

WTO Members from the obligation to observe the three obligations, but does not compel them to observe them either. The *travaux préparatoires* unfortunately do not shed enough light on this issue: some of the negotiating history of this provision[130] suggests that it was drafted to deal with emergency situations, such as an outbreak of a disease. This is by now water under the bridge: the AB, in its report on *EC—Hormones (US)*, extended Art. 5.7 SPS to cover precautionary measures which do not necessarily have to be taken as a matter of urgency. Subsequently, the EU circulated a proposal inviting the WTO Membership to think further about the content of the precautionary principle.[131] In its view, measures based on precaution must be proportional to the chosen level of protection, non-discriminatory in their application, and also consistent with past practice (assuming, of course, that comparability across transactions has been established).[132] The EU proposal echoed EU law: one of the leading cases in EU law in this area is *Commission v Netherlands*,[133] where the Court outlawed a Dutch measure banning marketing of foodstuffs to which nutrients had been added. The Court first made it clear that the proportionality requirement (adopting the least restrictive trade measure) should be observed in cases where the precautionary principle has been invoked as well (§46). It then moved on to provide its understanding that the precautionary principle should not be dissociated completely from scientific evidence. The court understands precaution as one point along a continuum that might lead to scientific proof:

> A proper application of the precautionary principle requires, in the first place, the identification of the potentially negative consequences for health of the proposed addition of nutrients, and, secondly, a comprehensive assessment of the risk for health based on the most reliable scientific data available and the most recent results of international research. (*Commission v Denmark*, §51).
>
> Where it proves to be impossible to determine with certainty the existence or extent of the alleged risk because of the insufficiency, inconclusiveness or imprecision of the results of studies conducted, but the likelihood of real harm to public health persists should the risk materialise, the precautionary principle justifies the adoption of restrictive measures. (*Commission v Denmark*, §§52 and 53).

The unanswered question so far is what exactly 'pertinent information' means? At one end of the spectrum, we could imagine cases where risk assessment has not provided us with responses either way, but where the scientific process is well under way; at the other end of the spectrum, we could conceive of cases where

---

[130] GATT Docs. MTN.GNG/NG5/WGSP/7 of 20 November 1990, and MTN.GNG/NG5/WGSP/17 of 30 April 1990.

[131] WTO Doc. G/SPS/GEN/168 of 14 March 2000.

[132] See also the European Council Resolution on the Precautionary Principle, WTO Doc. G/SPS/GEN/225 of 2 February 2001, and the Communication from the Commission on the Precautionary Principle, COM (2000) 1 final, 2 February 2000.

[133] C-41/02, *Commission of the European Communities v Kingdom of the Netherlands* [2004] ECR I-11375.

there is public anxiety even if it is caused by flimsy reasons, such as dissemination of irresponsible information through the mass media, and, even worse, sometimes in order to advance domestic producers' interests. There should be no doubt that the former end of the spectrum should be covered, but how far down the road should we go towards the latter? This issue is highly debated by scholars from different disciplines, and it is hard to come up with the 'correct' response, assuming there is one. Slovic (2000), an eminent psychologist, states for example:

> Human beings have invented the concept of 'risk' to help them understand and cope with the dangers and uncertainties of life. Although these dangers are real, there is no such thing as 'real risk' or 'objective risk'.

The affect heuristic certainly simplifies our life. Quoting from Kahneman (2011, p. 140):

> ... people who had received a message extolling the benefits of a technology also changed their beliefs about its risks. Although they had received no relevant evidence, the technology they now liked more than before was also perceived as less risky.

In the words of Haidt (2001), 'the emotional tail wags the rational dog'. On the other hand, Sunstein (2003) and Kuran and Sunstein (1999) warn against populist excesses: they term 'availability cascade' a chain of events which might originate in media and lead up to public panic. Kuran and Sunstein (1999) discuss a couple of incidents where regulation was totally baseless and unfounded and might have also done public health a disservice. They criticize public intervention absent serious scrutiny of the legitimacy of public anxiety. Kahneman (2011) takes a seemingly conciliatory attitude here but de facto sides with Slovic when he states (p. 144):

> I share Sunstein's discomfort with the influence of irrational fears and availability cascades on public policy in the domain of risk. However, I also share Slovic's belief that widespread fears, even if they are unreasonable, should not be ignored by policy makers. Rational or not, fear is painful and debilitating, and policy makers must endeavor to protect the public from fear, not only from real dangers.

This is quite reasonable. And at any rate, as far as the trade effect of similar interventions is concerned, one should always keep in mind that there are some safety valves in the WTO in the sense that precautionary measures must at the very least be non-discriminatory (the difficulties in establishing discrimination being an issue). These are highly complicated issues and probably the best response is to avoid false positives: a cautious attitude by WTO adjudicating bodies is, thus, highly to be recommended.

3.2.9 Control Procedures

Art. 8 SPS reads:

> Members shall observe the provisions of Annex C in the operation of control, inspection and approval procedures, including national systems for approving the

use of additives or for establishing tolerances for contaminants in foods, beverages or feedstuffs, and otherwise ensure that their procedures are not inconsistent with the provisions of this Agreement.

Annex C requires that any procedure to check the fulfilment of SPS measures be undertaken and completed without undue delay and in no less favourable manner for imported products than for like domestic products; that the procedure is published and communicated upon request; that confidentiality requirements will observe NT; that control requirements will be limited to what is reasonable and necessary; that equitable fees will be imposed on inspected products, if at all; and, finally,that procedures for complaints shall be introduced.

The SPS Agreement encourages WTO Members to conclude MRAs between themselves which must nevertheless respect the non-discrimination obligation, as reflected in Art. 4 SPS: WTO Members not party to an MRA can request that the MRA be extended to them, if they can establish that their regulatory framework is equivalent to those of the MRA partners. An SPS Committee Decision sheds some light on Art. 4 SPS.[134] This decision makes it clear that equivalence can be accepted for measures relating to a specific product or categories of products or a system-wide basis, hence the coverage can be quite extensive; that a reliable communication channel must be established between the exporting (requesting equivalence) and the importing WTO Member: the latter should provide information regarding its level of protection, justification of its SPS measures, and the former should cooperate in supplying information regarding its scientific capacity, the product-related infrastructure. etc. Trade should not be interrupted only because a request for equivalence has been tabled. WTO Members should participate in the ongoing work of international institutions harmonizing standards, such as the Codex Alimentarius Commission, in equivalence-related work by the World Organization for Animal Health, and in the framework of the International Plant Protection Convention. It does not detail any further how the MFN requirement will be complied with in presence of equivalence (unilateral or MRA), but does mention the word 'confidence' a number of times: this word is unquantifiable and this property in and of itself makes the MFN requirement a tough test for outsiders to meet (as is the case in the TBT Agreement).

Art. 7 SPS (which is further detailed in Annex B to the SPS Agreement) reads:

Members shall notify changes in their sanitary or phytosanitary measures and shall provide information on their sanitary or phytosanitary measures in accordance with the provisions of Annex B.

To this effect, §1 of Annex B requires that all SPS measures be published. The AB held, in its report on *Japan—Agricultural Products II*, that the term 'laws, decrees or ordinances' (appearing in §1 of Annex B) should be interpreted broadly, so that

---

[134] WTO Doc. G/SPS/19/Rev. 2 of 23 July 2004.

all SPS measures are covered, and not just those that can formally be characterized as such. In its view, what matters is the objective sought through this provision, that is, to ensure that all SPS measures are published, irrespective of their qualification under domestic law (§§105–6).

3.2.10 *Special and Differential Treatment for Developing Countries*

Art. 10 SPS contains the special and differential treatment provision of the Agreement and essentially follows the TBT recipe in this respect. By the same token, the Doha Ministerial Declaration discussed *supra* calls for the passage of a certain period of time between the enactment of a measure and its entry into force so that foreign producers can adjust to the new regulatory reality and not be caught off guard.

3.3 Expertise in SPS-related Dispute Adjudication

Since SPS measures must, in principle, be based on scientific evidence, it is to be expected that scientific experts might be called upon to explain regulatory interventions if need be before WTO adjudicating bodies. Since scientific disagreements are not uncommon, judges might be called to resolve similar disagreements.[135] The question, of course, is how judges (who typically are not trained scientists) can do so.

Art. 11.2 SPS urges Panels to have recourse to experts when dealing with SPS issues, stating in relevant part that:

a panel should seek advice from experts.

This expression is in slight contrast to the formulation privileged in Art. 13.2 DSU which reflects the generic provision regarding recourse to expertise:

Panels [. . .] may consult.

Although the wording of Art.11.2 SPS suggests a slightly more imperative tone, it is nonetheless within the discretion of a Panel to decide whether or not to have recourse to experts. If they do opt to have recourse to expertise, then Panels must respect Art. 11.2 SPS:

In a dispute under this Agreement involving scientific or technical issues, a panel should seek advice from experts chosen by the panel in consultation with the parties to the dispute. To this end, the panel may, when it deems it appropriate, establish an advisory technical experts group, or consult the relevant international organizations, at the request of either party to the dispute or on its own initiative.

---

135 Horn and Mavroidis (2003) set out a scenario in which a Panel selects two economists which are experts in the field of industrial organization, where one is an 'antitrust hawk' and the other an 'antitrust dove'.

Two issues have occupied case law so far: first, what are the contours within which expertise can be lawfully submitted and taken into account. In *Japan—Agricultural Products II*, the question arose whether an expert opinion extending beyond an argument[136] advanced by one of the parties could still be of legal relevance to the Panel. More precisely, the US had claimed that Japan's measures had violated the necessity requirement. In support of its claim, the US had argued that Japan could have used another measure that was less restrictive than the one that had actually been used. Experts confirmed the US point of view. In doing so, however, they pointed to an alternative measure, other than that advanced by the US, which, in their view, constituted an even less restrictive option. The US had advanced the argument that Japan should have used 'testing by product' instead of the measure privileged by Japan; the experts argued that Japan should have used 'sorption levels', a measure that had not been discussed at all by the US in its pleadings. The Panel accepted the claim by the US and held that Japan had not complied with its obligations under Art. 5.6 SPS. The AB reversed this finding on the ground that, in the absence of an argument by the US to this effect, the Panel did not have the legal authority to find against Japan for an argument advanced by the experts only (§§125ff). The AB probably equated the expertise regarding sorption levels as a claim that had not been lawfully introduced by the US; in this case, even if the US had endorsed the supplied expertise, it would have run foul of its obligations under Art. 6.2 DSU since the claim was introduced after the establishment of the Panel. Had the AB taken the view that this was an argument in support of a wider claim regarding the inconsistency of an SPS measure, it would have ruled to the contrary. There are good reasons that Pauwelyn (1999) has developed in detail to believe that this will be the case in the future.

Second, case law has dealt with the selection of experts. Expertise has been routinely sought by Panels dealing with challenges against SPS measures. Panels privilege experts affiliated with the institutions explicitly mentioned in the SPS Agreement (Office International des Epizooties, International Plant Protection Convention, Codex Alimentarius Commission). In *Australia—Salmon*, the Panel selected four experts after consultations with the Office International des Epizooties (§§6.1ff). In *Japan—Agricultural Products II*, the Panel chose three experts after soliciting suggestions from the Secretariat of the International Plant Protection Convention (§§6.1ff).

In *EC—Hormones (US)*, the Panel initially requested the parties to the dispute to name one expert each. It then named two experts (from a list prepared by the

---

[136] A claim consists of a statement to the effect that particular practice is WTO-inconsistent (factual matter) as well as the legal basis that is allegedly being violated (legal matter). Arguments are (logical) constructions aiming to substantiate a claim. WTO Members, when litigating, are required to present all their claims at the moment they request the establishment of a Panel (Art. 6.2 DSU). They can add arguments to support their claims during the Panel proceedings; see Palmeter and Mavroidis (2004).

Codex Alimentarius Commission and the International Agency for Research on Cancer) and one additional expert in the area of the carcinogenic effects of hormones (§§6.1ff). The EU appealed the fact that one of the experts was a national of a third party and had ties with the pharmaceutical industry. The AB dismissed the EU argument and held that (§148):

> once the panel has decided to request the opinion of individual scientific experts, there is no legal obstacle to the panel drawing up, in consultation with the parties to the dispute, ad hoc rules for those particular proceedings.

Until *US—Suspended Concession*, there had never been a case when experts had been selected against the will of one of the parties to the dispute; but, in this case, the EU objected to the appointment of two experts on the grounds that they had real or perceived conflicts of interest that should have disqualified them from assisting the panel, in particular, because (§§416–24):

(a) They were both affiliated with JEFCA, the institution that had elaborated the international standard that the EU had criticized and from which it had deviated;
(b) One of them had taken a position on the issue in the dispute, and the other had received research money from the pharmaceutical industry.

The AB established for the first time that due process considerations should guide the selection of panelists (§436); it further recalled the disclosure obligations that selected experts must observe in order to ensure that due process has been complied with (§438). It went on to confirm the Panel's rejection of the EU claims regarding point (b) above (§455). The AB, however, found that the Panel should not have selected the two experts because of their institutional affiliation with JEFCA, the standard of which the EU had been criticizing (§469). The AB went on to find that the Panel had violated the EU's due process rights, and in doing so, failed to perform an objective assessment of the matter before it as it is required to do by virtue of Art. 11 DSU (§§481–2). It added that all subsequent findings by the Panel could be invalidated because of this choice, but still went on and examined them one by one (§484). The AB's decision in this respect is sensible: the Panel should have appointed experts with some distance from the facts of the case. Participation in the preparation of the contested standard legitimately casts doubt on the appropriateness of the selected experts. This point is particularly underscored by the fact that, at the moment that this Panel had been established, there had never been a case where a Panel had openly disagreed with the testimony of the Panel-appointed expert. Panels are not bound by law by the opinion of experts in the SPS-context. There are other instances in the WTO system where the expert's opinion binds Panels: Art. 4.5 SCM provides for the possibility to establish an expert group in order to decide whether a subsidy granted is prohibited in the SCM sense of the term; the opinion of the expert group is binding on the Panel that sought it. There is no corresponding provision in the SPS Agreement; hence, Panels might be as deferential towards expertise as they deem appropriate. In practice, though, Panels have been quite deferential towards court-appointed experts.

With the decision to apply due process in experts' selection, the WTO took its first steps towards rationalizing a process that comports many dangers. Recall the original setting here, that is, a classic situation of asymmetry of information (where experts know and judges typically do not), and where those possessing information have a strong incentive to manipulate those that do not. We might have avoided disasters so far, but recall that the WTO SPS Agreement is only 15 years old. True, the adversarial system can take care of some of the issues since it is often the case that the parties in the dispute are participating in a zero-sum game. Still, the possibility of collusion cannot be outright excluded, just as the possibility of making an error cannot be discarded either. To minimize similar risks, the WTO could be inspired by other legal orders that have had more experience of dealing with expertise. The US Ninth circuit, for example, held on remand in the cited *Daubert* litigation that expert testimony should not merely be relevant, but that it should fit the requirements of the litigation where it has been offered. The fit requirement is 'higher than bare relevance' but 'lower than the standard of correctness'.[137] Thus, courts will not be deprived of useful information, while ensuring that they will not be lost in useless, confusing details either. In this vein, *Daubert* requires a thorough analysis of the expert's economic model, which should not be admitted if it does not apply to the specific facts of the case. 'Relevant evidence' is defined in Rule 401 of the Federal Rules of Evidence (US) as:

> evidence having any tendency to make the existence of any fact that is of consequence to the determination of the action more probable or less probable.

This seems like a sensible approach and the WTO Panel would profit from a similar rule. Yet, in the absence of a developed procedural law applicable in WTO litigation, it is for Panels to take the initiative and move in this direction.

US Courts further examine the qualifications of the experts.[138] In *Berlyn, Inc v Gazette*, for example, a district court excluded the testimony of an expert, who was an experienced newspaper executive, on the relevant market in question, for the simple reason that he was not an economist or an attorney and had never published anything related to economics or antitrust:

---

[137] 364 *Daubert v Merrell Dow Pharmaceuticals, Inc.*, 43 F.3d 1311, 1321 (9th Cir. 1995); see also, *re Linerboard Antitrust Litigation*, 497 F.Supp.2d 666, 673 (E.D.Pa 2007); *United States v Ford*, 481 F.3d 215, 220 n. 6 (3d Cir. 2007); 365 *re Linerboard Antitrust Litigation*, at 673; *United States v Williams*, 2007 WL 1643197, 3 (3d Cir., 7 June 2007).
[138] *Paoli R.R. Yard PCB Litig.*, 35 F.3d 717 (3d Cir. 1994); *Raskin v Wyatt Co*, 125 F.3d 55, 66 (2d Cir. 1997).

general business experience unrelated to antitrust economics does not render a witness qualified to offer an opinion on complicated antitrust issues such as defining relevant markets.[139]

It is highly unlikely that Panels will behave in similar manner, yet they would be greatly facilitating their task if they did. It is beyond the scope of this volume to delve into detail on this issue. Suffice to state here that, unless the current design of Panels changes and professional judges replace the current ad hoc Panellists, one should legitimately expect a passive rather than an active attitude in this respect.[140]

Finally, note that a Panel does not need to explicitly refer to all expertise received by experts to observe its duty to perform an objective assessment of the matter before it (Art. DSU). In *Australia—Apples*, the AB pertinently held (§275):

> Regarding the Panel's treatment of the evidence, we consider that its role as the trier of facts requires it to review and consider all the evidence that it receives from the parties or that it seeks pursuant to Article 13 of the DSU. Nonetheless, as the Appellate Body explained in *EC—Hormones*, a panel cannot be expected to refer to all the statements made by the experts it consulted. To reproduce every statement made by the experts in the report is neither a necessary nor a sufficient condition for a panel to perform its function in accordance with Article 11 of the DSU. Article 11 requires a panel, in its reasoning on a given issue, to weigh and balance all the relevant evidence, including testimony by the experts. A panel may reproduce the relevant statements by the experts, but still fail to make an objective assessment of the facts under Article 11 if it then fails to properly assess the significance of these statements in its reasoning, as the Appellate Body found in *US/Canada—Continued Suspension*. Conversely, a panel that does not expressly reproduce certain statements of its appointed experts may still act consistently with Article 11, especially when the panel's reasoning reveals that it has nevertheless assessed the significance of these statements or that these statements are manifestly not relevant to the panel's objective assessment of the facts and issues before it. (italics in the original)

3.4 Standard of Review[141]

The AB, in *EC—Hormones (US)*, held that WTO adjudicating bodies, when dealing with cases coming under the purview of the SPS Agreement, must apply the standard of review set out in Art. 11 DSU and are not required to follow any

---

[139] *Berlyn Inc. v Gazette Newspapers, Inc.*, 214 F.Supp. 2d 530, 536 (D.Md. 2002).

[140] Posner (1999a and 1999b) has suggested that the publication of expertise provided to the court might provide such an incentive, since the author might suffer reputation costs and, as a result (which could, eventually, make him/her a non-repeat player), might have an incentive to come up with the 'truth' in the first place. Stein (1996) contemplates how strategic allocation of the burden of proof might be of assistance in this context. Stein (2008), looking at practice in US courts, uses Carl Ginet's concept of 'disinterested justification' to pronounce on the boundaries of the epistemic authority of courts. He claims that courts exercise this authority in the 'interest-free' zone, in which their determinations of disputed facts' probabilities can be made solely on epistemic grounds. In the 'interest-laden' domain, where courts allocate risks of error under uncertainty, this is not the case. In this domain, courts will rely on risk-allocating evidentiary rules (burden of proof, corroboration, hearsay, opinion, character, etc.). To a large extent, his analysis echoes WTO practice as well.

[141] On this issue, see the excellent analysis in Åhman (2012) at pp. 222ff, 242ff, and 256ff.

other particular standard of review (§§131ff). Recall, nevertheless, that in *EC—Asbestos* and in case law regarding the interpretation of Art. XX GATT, the AB has held that a more deferential standard is warranted if the objective is protection of human health.[142] One would expect a similar attitude towards at least those SPS measures that aim to protect public health. Case law so far has definitely not been internally consistent with respect to all SPS measures: recall the AB findings in *Japan—Apples* where negligible risk was not a sufficient basis for an SPS measure, and which offers an approach hardly reconcilable with that in other reports (like *EC—Hormones* (*US*) or *Australia—Salmon*). Is acceptance of zero risk the first evidence of a (more) deferential standard of review when public health is at stake? It is hard to respond to this question since we are still awaiting clarifications by the AB in this respect. In our view, this should not be the case, for the appropriate level of protection should be the absolute privilege of trading nations. The standard of review should be more or less deferential towards the regulating entity in light of the chosen level of protection and not in spite of it.[143]

3.5 Institutional Issues

An SPS Committee is established which provides a regular forum for consultations among WTO Members and, in general, is in charge of the administration of the SPS Agreement. It aims to provide transparency regarding national SPS measures, provide clarifications of the SPS Agreement (like the Decision on Art. 4 and the Guidelines regarding Art. 5.5 SPS), promote regulatory cooperation across WTO Members and international harmonization, and also, if possible, resolve disputes.

In parallel with the TBT Agreement, it has established an online forum providing detailed information regarding national measures.[144] The SPS Notification Submission System (NSS) was recently launched. It enabled WTO Members to fill out and submit notifications online. The online submission system was designed to ensure that notifications would become more complete and accurate. Since the WTO was set up 16 years ago, governments have shared with each other, in the context of the SPS Committee, information on over 10,000 SPS measures that they have implemented on food safety and animal and plant health.[145]

---

[142] By adding to the evidence required to demonstrate a violation of the WTO in similar cases, the WTO judge de facto reduces the potential for regulatory chill, while increasing the deterrence-factor vis-à-vis potential complainants; see Kaplow (2012).

[143] Palmeter (2006) has provided thoughts in a similar vein.

[144] <http://spsims.wto.org>.

[145] <http://www.wto.org/english/news_e/news11_e/sps_19oct11_e.htm>.

11

AGREEMENT ON AGRICULTURE; AGREEMENT ON TEXTILES AND CLOTHING

1. In the Shadow of the GATT

Farm and textiles trade remained either partially (in the case of farm trade) or totally (textiles) outside the GATT disciplines until the end of the Uruguay round. The reasons for their exclusion from the coverage are idiosyncratic to each one of them and we will discuss them in the corresponding sections of this chapter. The end result is quite similar though: farm and textiles trade has been impeded over the years because of high tariffs and the various non-tariff measures that have been applied to (farm and textile) goods, especially by the two main hubs, the EU and the US. Indeed, the Uruguay round was largely a quest to address the twin tariff peaks and open up trade in the two sectors.

Relatively speaking, the Uruguay round agreements achieved more in the context of textiles trade, where all protection is now in the form of tariffs. Giant steps were taken as well in an effort to equate protection of farm goods with that of any other good coming under the aegis of the GATT, but there are still some areas (e.g. export subsidies) where farm goods do not have to totally abide by the existing disciplines imposed on all other goods.

2. The Agreement on Agriculture

2.1 The Legal Discipline and its Rationale

The Agreement imposes distinct disciplines on border measures, domestic support, and export subsidies. Its objective is to reduce and eventually eliminate import tariffs and export subsidies while regulating domestic support. To understand this 'trichotomy', we need to look briefly into the history of farm trade.

The GATT did not regulate goods by sector: instead, as we saw in the previous chapters, disciplines were imposed on all goods that qualified as such.[1] Tariff concessions on farm goods could, of course, be exchanged during the GATT years in the context of the various trade rounds, but they were of rather secondary importance for the reasons we discuss below. Some specific GATT provisions addressed farm trade: Art. XI.1 GATT prohibits quantitative restrictions, but Art. XI.2 GATT reflects an exception for farm products.[2] As the Executive Secretary of the GATT once observed, though Art. XI.2 GATT was:

> largely tailor-made to United States requirements [...] the tailors cut the cloth too fine.[3]

In similar vein, Art. XVI.3 GATT regulates export subsidies for primary (farm) products: this provision aims at discouraging the subsidization of primary goods, and allows subsidization only to the extent that the subsidizing GATT contracting party does not end up with more than an 'equitable share of the world market'. Beyond these two provisions, there is no other GATT provision that deals specifically with trade in agricultural goods.

---

[1] The HS is the source for tariff commitments.
[2] See the relevant discussion in Chapter 2.
[3] Eric Wyndham-White, quoted in Dam (1970, p. 260).

The question naturally arises why specific references to farm trade were warranted in the GATT. It is difficult to point to one dominant explanation, but in a nutshell farm trade was one area where influential GATT contracting parties opted to take exemptions from or to outright disregard free trade.

Following the traumatic experience in WWII many countries assigned themselves the objective of becoming self-sufficient in food production and adopted corresponding farm policies. The US was not one of them, since it requested and obtained a waiver in 1955[4] in order to address the surplus of many farm products. The applicable US legislation at that time (Section 22 of the US Agricultural Adjustment Act of 1933) provided for specific and often GATT-inconsistent action and, consequently, a waiver was necessary for it to avoid challenges of its practices by its trading partners. The waiver was of unlimited duration, but subject to annual review. Through this waiver, the US was essentially free to control imports in order to be able to heavily subsidize its farm production.[5]

Following the US example, other GATT contracting parties also managed to keep their farm policies immune from legal challenges, either through waivers (Belgium and Luxembourg) or through special clauses in their protocol of accession (Switzerland). Besides quantitative restrictions and high tariffs on imports, public policy in most developed countries included price and supply management tools, seen as appropriate and necessary to maintain the viability of rural and agrarian communities and ensure an adequate food supply. For some agricultural products (e.g. rice in Japan), market access for imports was effectively non-existent.

The result was that many import farm markets became highly insulated. It is consumers of course that paid the price of fragmentation, but as the classic analysis of Olson (1965) suggests, consumers have little influence in the shaping of national trade policies anyway. Recall our discussion in Chapter 3 about the Haberler report: the well-known Harvard economist had concluded that one reason why the rate of exports of farm goods did not match that of industrial goods was farm protectionism.[6] Well, this was very much the outcome of the

---

[4] GATT Doc. BISD 3S/32 ff. In fact, in 1953 the first request by the US was turned down and the US went so far as to threaten to quit the GATT unless the waiver was granted; see Jackson (1969) at pp. 548ff; Dam (1970) at pp. 260ff. See also the more general discussion in Brewster (2009, pp. 246ff).

[5] Over the years, the US reduced subsidization and became a hawk in farm talks, famously adopting a zero protection on farm trade policy during the Uruguay round. 'Deficiency payments' (that is, support from the federal government tied to prices and the production of specific crops) were replaced by direct payments in 1996; the US Food, Conservation and Energy Act (FCE) of 2008 guaranteed a stream of income to farmers (decoupled from production) until 2012, and the Average Crop Revenue Election (ACRE) programme of the same year ensured cash flows irrespective of price volatility; see Gardner (2002, 2009), Orden (2009), and Blandford and Orden (2011).

[6] Brink (2011) offers a discussion on this score. He perceptively points to the fact that the current structure in the AG Agreement corresponds to Haberler's distinction between measures aimed at discouraging imports, measures aimed at encouraging exports, and those aimed at encouraging domestic production as well.

various waivers and special clauses that governments of developed countries requested and obtained.

The EU originally assigned itself the objective to become self-sufficient in farm goods.[7] This was the paramount objective of the then newly established Common Agricultural Policy, the notorious CAP. It used a system of variable levies, which varied inversely with world prices in the sense that the higher the world price, the lower the levy (and correspondingly, the lower the world price, the higher the levy).[8] In other words, farm goods, when imported into the EU market, would pay not a fixed, but a variable levy, which would ensure that the price of such goods to EU consumers becomes equal to the price of domestic (EU) farm goods. The EU farm market thus became impenetrable: the term 'Fortress Europe' is largely due to the segmentation of the EU farm market.[9] Alongside this scheme, the EU practised a system of export subsidies since, otherwise, EU farm goods could not find buyers in world markets (where prices were consistently lower than EU prices). Josling and Swinbank (2011) correctly deduce that the combination of variable levies and export subsidies made the need for domestic support mechanisms redundant.

Variable import levies were present in many relevant farm product markets. The consistency of this scheme with the GATT was, at the very least, questionable. There were ongoing discussions among the GATT contracting parties on farm protectionism in general. During the 19th session, for example, Committee II (discussing agricultural protection) issued a document calling for moderation of the protection, but which stopped short of making specific proposals.[10] Negotiated solutions, though, stopped short of fully addressing this issue, so why did not we see any formal legal challenges then? The EU could, of course, have rebuffed requests to establish a Panel and this possibility in and of itself could have presented potential complainants with a disincentive to introduce a complaint in the first place.[11] Josling et al. (1996, pp. 71ff) have argued that the

---

[7] The EU is not alone in this, India is doing the same; see Gopinath (2011). One might legitimately cast doubt on the wisdom of similar policies in light of the multitude of sources of farm supplies around the world and the impossibility of facing cartelized practices. There are other justifications for regulation of farm trade often heard in policy circles, such as the unusual price instability, preservation of lifestyle, or the cost for farmers in LDCs. While the latter is hard to resist, the validity of the other two grounds is questionable. If it is lifestyle we care about, why not simply adopt decoupled income payments? Price instability becomes less of a concern with scientific progress. At the end of the day, a lot of intervention is purely the outcome of political-economy factors.

[8] Some variable duties were as high as 480 per cent *ad valorem*; see p. 84 in Committee on Finance, United States Finance, Summary and Analysis of H.R. 10710—The Trade Reform Act of 26 February 1973, US Government Printing Office, Washington, DC, 1974, states US exports to the world grew twice as much as towards the EU between 1961–70.

[9] Balassa (1975) offers a most useful discussion on farm protectionism in Europe.

[10] GATT Doc. BISD 10s/135ff.

[11] On the other hand, of course, a refusal to concede to the establishment of a Panel in a world of de facto compulsory third-party adjudication, the GATT world before the advent of the WTO, as Hudec (1993a) helped us understand, would have been quite damaging to the EU reputation. In

political importance of European integration and the central role that the CAP played in that process made the US, at least initially, reluctant to request the establishment of a GATT Panel to challenge the legality of the CAP. Similar challenges, in the authors' view, would have jeopardized the goal of European integration itself, something the US would not have dared to bring into question. The unwillingness of the US to destabilize the European integration process thus probably explains why EU farm policy remained unchallenged: if the US did not take the first step, who would?[12] The response is very few.

The most dramatic challenge was the complaint launched by Uruguay in 1962 against 15 GATT contracting parties,[13] whereby Uruguay challenged, *inter alia*, the consistency of variable import levies with the GATT rules. The Panel's deliberations were inconclusive in this respect (§17):

> The Panel was faced with a particular difficulty in considering the status of variable import levies or charges. It noted the discussion which took place at the nineteenth session of the CONTRACTING PARTIES on this subject during which it was pointed out that such measures raised serious questions which had not been resolved. In these circumstances the Panel has not considered it appropriate to examine the consistency or otherwise of these measures under the General Agreement.[14]

Consequently, the Panel did not make any recommendations regarding the consistency of variable import levies with the GATT rules. It did, nonetheless, acknowledge their detrimental effect on the export interests of Uruguay. We read, for example, at pp. 135–6 of the report where the Panel discusses the complaint against the Netherlands:

> However, in respect of the *variable import levies*, the Panel considers that, having regard to the nature of the measures and the interest which Uruguay has in the products in question, there are *a priori* grounds for assuming that those measures could have an adverse effect on Uruguayan exports. (italics in the original)

The US eventually did submit some complaints in the 1980s attacking various aspects of the CAP, probably because it could not resolve its differences with the EU on the negotiating table preceding and during the Uruguay round. The reports remained un-adopted though and thus of limited legal value. At any rate, by refusing to adopt them, the EU showed its will to continue to protect its farmers.

---

similar vein, the US could have scored a moral victory had it prevailed before the Panel, but the EU could always have blocked adoption of the report and thus minimized the negative impact.

[12] The same scenario could have led to different outcomes in today's world, with the emergence of other WTO Members to prominence.

[13] *Uruguayan Request to Article XXIII*, Report adopted on 16 November 1962, GATT Doc. BISD 11s/95ff.

[14] Some later GATT discussions, though, reveal that variable duties that exceeded the level of bound duties would be deemed illegal; see GATT Doc AG/M/3, p. 63 (1984).

The very high percentage that farm protection represented in the EU budget, the dissatisfaction of other EU lobbies who were not prepared to see gains from trade evade them in the name of EU farm protectionism,[15] and the resolve of foreign traders to open up the lucrative EU market are the most important reasons that pushed Europe towards a reform of the CAP.[16] And there was also the question of who profits from the CAP. Is it the small farmer that benefits from the CAP? No, suggests Baldwin (2005), and we quote (p. 3):

> The gigantic farms account for only 2 tenths of one per cent of all EU farms; the average payment to these farms is €780,000 per year.
>
> The 1.5% biggest farms get 27% of the money; the payment-per-farm averaged over all farms in this group is €70,000 per year.
>
> The top 6% of the farms by size get half the money (53%); the payment-per-farm averaged over all farms in this group is €30,000 per year.
>
> The 52% smallest farms share only 4% of the CAP money among themselves; the payment-per-farm averaged over all farms in this group is €425 per year.

Non-farm lobbies could thus point not only to the opportunity cost of farm protectionism but further to the unfairness of the whole endeavour.

In the Uruguay round, a coalition of exporters of agricultural products countries—the so-called 'Cairns group'[17]—provided the necessary stimulus to push for a worldwide liberalization of agricultural trade. The US was no longer isolated in pursuing its aggressive policy towards the EU, and the diverse membership of the group provided attacks on CAP with legitimacy in the eyes of neutral observers. Although it is probably an overstatement to credit the Cairns group with the successful completion of the negotiations on agricultural trade, it did nonetheless play a decisive role in getting the item on the agenda, in making farm liberalization one of the priorities of the Uruguay round, and eventually in making it a round-breaker so to speak (in the sense that it became common knowledge that, absent some sort of an agreement on farm trade, the whole round risked being left in limbo).[18]

---

[15] In Marchetti and Mavroidis (2011), we provided some evidence to the effect that the EU services lobby was not prepared to sit back and postpone services liberalization in the name of EU farm protectionism, although key political European figures thought otherwise. Compare Swinbank (2009).

[16] Various contributions in Swinnen (2008) discuss the most recent reforms in the EU farm policy, whereas Swinnen (2009) discusses the evolution in farm protection in the Europe in the nineteenth and twentieth centuries.

[17] The Cairns group comprised 19 agricultural exporting countries and borrowed its name from the Australian city where the original founders first met. The group was originally composed of Argentina, Australia, Brazil, Canada, Chile, Colombia, Fiji, Hungary, Indonesia, Malaysia, New Zealand, the Philippines, Thailand, and Uruguay. Later Hungary and Fiji left the group and Bolivia, Costa Rica, Guatemala, Paraguay, South Africa, Pakistan, and Peru joined. See Breene (1993).

[18] On the negotiation of the agreement on agriculture, see Olsen (2005). For an excellent survey of the WTO AG, see McMahon (2006).

The EU underwent changes in its CAP.[19] As Messerlin (2001, pp. 95ff) states, though material change started only after the conclusion of the Uruguay round, the seeds of change were, nevertheless, sown during the Uruguay round. By the end of the round, the EU enlargement to Austria, Finland, and Sweden had been completed and the enlargement towards the ex-communist European countries (many of them important farming countries) was well on track. First, the MacSharry reforms (1992–4), which introduced direct payments to farmers to address price cuts in cereals and beef, were agreed. These reforms were discussed between the EU and the US at Blair House (November 1992). This meeting signalled the untying of the Gordian knot that had denied the conclusion of the Uruguay round.[20] The Berlin decisions (1999 Berlin Council) went some way towards reversing the tide inside the EU. Importantly, through these decisions:

(1) The risk of overcompensation of EU farmers was reduced;
(2) The CAP budget was stabilized in absolute monetary amounts;
(3) Roll-back of existing aid was not excluded; and
(4) A reduction of all direct subsidies by 20 per cent at most was called for.

Following these decisions, Agenda 2000 was decided and it included an extra 20 per cent cut of the guaranteed prices for cereals, 30 per cent for beef, and 15 per cent for dairy products (without touching upon 'thorny' issues such as sugar and olive oil). In Messerlin's (2001) view:

> More important, the whole debate revealed increasingly stronger forces in favour of further reforms for *domestic* reasons—the need to reallocate scarce funds to other purposes than agriculture, the necessity of preparing for the accession of Central European countries (some of them having substantial capacities in agriculture in the long run) and last but not least consumers' interests in getting cheaper products (...). In particular, the debate began to clarify the merits of 'renationalizing' EC farm subsidies (co-financing, in EC parlance) in comparison with 'modulating' (reducing) them. (emphasis in the original)

Then came the Fischler reform, named after the then (2003) EU Commissioner for Agriculture, that introduced single payment schemes unrelated to current production, and finally the 2008 CAP Health Check that introduced further decoupling between payments and production.[21] The passage to the EU-27 signalled even less price support and even more payments unrelated to domestic production.[22]

---

[19] Various contributions in Anderson (2009) discuss these points.

[20] The subject-matter of these reforms coincides with what is now known as the 'blue box', which we discuss *infra*.

[21] Josling and Swinbank (2011) at pp. 64ff; Swinnen (2008).

[22] Swinbank and Tanner (1996) argue that the eventual accession of the ten new EU Member States (and most notably, Poland, a large farming country), with its resulting implications for the EU budget, proved to be a decisive factor in favour of rationalization of the CAP.

The change in the EU policy facilitated the conclusion of the Uruguay round, since farm talks and the ensuing opening of the EU market was the 'holy grail' of the talks.[23] The AG Agreement was a milestone in that finally farm goods would come under the purview of the multilateral rules. And yet, unlike for example what happened in ATC, the subjection of farm goods to the multilateral disciplines would not happen by a fixed deadline: upon conclusion,[24] negotiators clarified that this was the start of the liberalization process and that future negotiations would be needed to further liberalize agricultural trade. Art. 20 AG addresses this point:

> Recognizing that the long-term objective of substantial progressive reductions in support and protection resulting in fundamental reform is an ongoing process, Members agree that negotiations for continuing the process will be initiated one year before the end of the implementation period, taking into account:
>
> (a) the experience to that date from implementing the reduction commitments;
>
> (b) the effects of the reduction commitments on world trade in agriculture;
>
> (c) non-trade concerns, special and differential treatment to developing country Members, and the objective to establish a fair and market-oriented agricultural trading system, and the other objectives and concerns mentioned in the preamble to this Agreement; and
>
> (d) what further commitments are necessary to achieve the above mentioned long-term objectives.[25]

Yeutter (1998, p. 73) sums it up perfectly when quoting Carole Brookins, a prominent agricultural economist:

> The Agreement was a remarkable achievement, bringing agricultural trade under the rules and disciplines of the GATT for the first time. No one should underestimate the value of full tariffication, nor the initial steps made towards eliminating export subsidies. In fact, the great tragedy for the agricultural sector and for the whole world economy is the nearly half century of time lost in getting this job started. If we had begun this process in 1947 when the GATT began its work in reducing industrial tariffs, we would have a 50 year 'adjustment' period to transition down to full open markets in agriculture by 1997. And what a difference that would have made.

---

[23] One should not equate farm protectionism to CAP. Except for the 'usual suspects' (Korea and Japan and their price stabilization schemes, Canada and its marketing boards), others have also kept farm markets hermetically shut to imports: citing abundant evidence, Gopinath (2011) explains how India, in the name of the balance of payments, managed to keep QRs on 96 per cent of all tariff lines (until its practices were condemned by the AB in *India—Quantitative Restrictions*); Trebilcock (2011, p. 101) cites evidence to the effect that farm protection to non-farm households in Europe, the US, and Japan averaged $1,400 per year in 1992, and Messerlin (2001) cites similar evidence regarding Europe only. Government intervention, on the other hand, did not necessarily lead to protectionism as Cheng (2011) explains in his brief history of farm trade regulation in China.

[24] For a concise description, see O'Connor (2005).

[25] In *Canada—Dairy* (§§7.25 and 7.26), the Panel accepted as much, arguing that this agreement was a framework for further liberalization.

2.2 The Coverage of the Legal Discipline

The legal disciplines imposed by the AG Agreement could be described in a nutshell as follows:

(a) Art. 4 AG requests from WTO Members to convert all non-tariff border measures (such as import quotas or variable levies) into tariffs. This is the notorious 'tariffication' process of border farm protection.[26] A six-year implementation period was established and WTO Members undertook to have reduced their overall tariff protection (following tariffication) by 36 per cent by the end of that period. While WTO Members retain some discretion as to the sectors which will suffer more and which less tariff reductions, the AG Agreement is that a minimum of 15 per cent tariff reduction be implemented for each product category. Tariffs would be the only form of protection of farm goods as WTO Members cannot introduce new non-tariff measures following the advent of the WTO. WTO Members also agreed to allow foreign producers to gain at least 3 per cent of their import markets (to increase to 5 per cent by the end of the implementation period) as a result of the reduction in border protection;

(b) Domestic support would be curbed. A common metric, the Aggregate Measurement of Support (AMS),[27] was devised and a base period for its calculation agreed (1986–8). WTO Members were requested to reduce their support by 20 per cent from the established baseline (Arts. 1(a), 6 AG, and Annex 3 to the AG Agreement). WTO Members enjoy flexibility and can decide to decrease protection in one agricultural commodity, while increasing it somewhere else, as long as they abide by the 20 per cent reduction obligation. All forms of domestic support are classified in three categories ('boxes'): the green, the blue, and the yellow (or amber) boxes. Each WTO Member must notify its programmes that come under each of the three boxes. Although the agreement contains fairly detailed criteria for notification, disagreements might arise across members as to the designation of a particular national programme.[28] The green box (Annex 2) includes programmes that are not at all, or that are minimally distorting, such as agricultural research, and these are exempted from reduction commitments. Blue box schemes include production-limiting support for either crop or livestock production and are not subject to reduction commitments as long as they meet the criteria of Art.

---

[26] The Illustrative list of measures that must be converted to tariffs includes variable import levies and minimum import prices (Art. 4.2 AG); see Panagariya (2005).

[27] The AMS was based, but does not entirely correspond to, the OECD Producer Subsidy Equivalent (PSE), which we discuss in more detail *infra*.

[28] As a result, disputes might be initiated before the WTO: in *US—Upland Cotton*, for example, Brazil successfully challenged the US designation of production flexibility contract (PFC) as fully decoupled, and therefore, green box-consistent.

6.5 AG. The amber box includes measures that do not come under the exempted categories (blue box, green box): these are capped and must be reduced by 20 per cent at the end of the implementation period;

(c) With respect to export subsidies,[29] WTO Members undertake product-specific (or group of product-specific) commitments, in the form of budgetary-outlay reduction commitments and export-quantity reduction commitments. WTO Members must reduce export subsidies over a six-year period by 21 per cent in terms of the volume of products that receive subsidies, and 36 per cent in terms of the cash value of these subsidies (Arts. 8–10 AG);

(d) Under the *de minimis* provisions (Art. 6.4 AG), WTO Members are allowed to use subsidies up to 5 per cent (10 per cent for developing countries) of the total value of domestic agricultural production;

(e) WTO Members undertake some other specific obligations (such as time-limited due restraint, export prohibition, transparency requirements, and obligations vis-à-vis net food-importing developing countries).

2.2.1 The Relationship between the AG and the SCM Agreements

As we saw in Chapter 8, export subsidies are illegal. Yet, export farm subsidies can be tolerated as long as they respect the agreed caps. Hence, the relationship between the SCM and the AG Agreements is key to understanding the extent of the exception. Art 21.1 AG reads:

> The provisions of GATT 1994 and of other Multilateral Trade Agreements in Annex 1A to the WTO Agreement shall apply subject to the provisions of this Agreement.

This provision gives precedence to the AG Agreement, but does not use the term 'conflict', as, for example the General Interpretative Note does, which, as we saw, regulates the relationship between the GATT and the other Annex 1A agreements. There is thus, an issue whether the terms 'subject to' should be understood as equivalent to the term 'conflict'. The Panel on *Canada—Dairy* had to deal with this issue. In this case, the question was whether the Canadian Special Milk Classes Scheme constituted a subsidy or not. The parties also disagreed over whether Canada had exceeded its commitments on exports of milk, assuming the scheme was viewed by the panel as an export subsidy. To respond to the question asked, the Panel had, *inter alia*, to discuss the relationship between AG and SCM (§§7.20ff). It held that WTO Members must observe both the AG and

---

[29] Hoekman and Messerlin (2006) estimate that the EU accounted for $4.95 billion of export subsidies; Switzerland, for $292 million; and the US, for $147 million. The same figures for 1999 were $2.6 billion for the EU and $80 million for the US. The numbers are substantially smaller for domestic subsidies (see WTO Doc. TN/AG/S/1). Hart and Beghin (2006) show how the EU has moved a lot of its programmes from the amber box (which includes subsidies that should be eliminated) to the green box (which includes subsidies that are tolerated).

the SCM disciplines, since the former does not constitute a 'safe harbour' for measures inconsistent with the SCM.

This point was made even clearer by the AB in its report on *US—Upland Cotton*. The AB faced, *inter alia*, an appeal by the US concerning the Panel's findings on the consistency of the so-called Step 2 payments with the AG and SCM (§514):

> Under the program, marketing certificates or cash payments (collectively referred to by the Panel as 'user marketing (Step 2) payments') are issued to eligible domestic users and exporters of eligible upland cotton when certain market conditions exist such that United States cotton pricing benchmarks are exceeded. 'Eligible upland cotton' is defined as 'domestically produced baled upland cotton which bale is opened by an eligible domestic user...or exported by an eligible exporter'. An 'eligible domestic user' of upland cotton is defined under the regulations as:
> A person regularly engaged in the business of opening bales of eligible upland cotton for the purpose of manufacturing such cotton into cotton products in the United States (domestic user), who has entered into an agreement with CCC to participate in the upland cotton user marketing certificate program.

Brazil did not contest that the US was in compliance with its obligations under Art. 6.3 AG (which imposes a cap on total spending). It contested, nevertheless, the consistency of the US payments with the SCM, arguing that such payments, which amounted to local content subsidies, were inconsistent with Art. 3.1(b) SCM. The AB agreed with the Panel that Art. 21.1 AG applies in three situations (§532):

> where, for example, the domestic support provisions of the *Agreement on Agriculture* would prevail in the event that an explicit carve-out or exemption from the disciplines in Article 3.1(b) of the *SCM Agreement* existed in the *text* of the *Agreement on Agriculture*. Another situation would be where it would be impossible for a Member to comply with its domestic support obligations under the *Agreement on Agriculture* and the Article 3.1(b) prohibition simultaneously. Another situation might be where there is an explicit authorization in the text of the *Agreement on Agriculture* that would authorize a measure that, in the absence of such an express authorization, would be prohibited by Article 3.1(b) of the *SCM Agreement*. (italics in the original)

The AB took the view that the situation before it was different from all three described above, and then concluded that (§550):

> In providing such domestic support, however, WTO Members must be mindful of their other WTO obligations, including the prohibition in Article 3.1(b) of the *SCM Agreement* on the provision of subsidies that are contingent on the use of domestic over imported goods. (italics in the original)

Consequently, whenever it is possible for a WTO Member to simultaneously comply with both the AG and the SCM Agreements, it should do so. As a result, the AB outlawed the US Step 2 payments (§552).[30]

---

[30] Eventually the US settled the case by agreeing to pay a lump sum to Brazil for technical-capacity purposes, and subsequently the payments stopped; Brink (2011) at pp. 38ff.

2.2.2 Product Coverage and Schedules of Concessions

Art. 2 AG states that this Agreement applies to all products included in Annex 1. This Annex provides a list of the products coming under the purview of AG Agreement: it covers HS Chapters 1–24, except for fish and fish products, plus a number of other more detailed headings which are not exhaustively mentioned in Annex 1. The schedule of concessions is based on the list of products mentioned in Annex 1, annexed to the AG Agreement (Annex 1) and form an integral part thereof (Art. 21.2 AG). The AB, in its report on *EC—Export Subsidies on Sugar*, confirmed that the WTO Members' schedules of concession have to adhere to the disciplines included in the AG Agreement (§§224–6). This is a facts-intensive case and it is warranted to reproduce the factual basis as understood by the AB (§§159–61):

> The export subsidy commitments made by the European Communities with respect to sugar, as specified in Section II, Part IV of the European Communities' Schedule, are as follows: (i) the 'base quantity level' (the average of the quantity of subsidized exports of sugar during the base period 1986–1990) was 1,612,000 tonnes, and this quantity level would be progressively reduced to 1,273,500 tonnes in the year 2000 as the 'final quantity commitment level' for sugar; and (ii) the 'base outlay level' (the average of the budgetary outlay on subsidized exports of sugar during the base period 1986–1990) was €779.9 million, and this budgetary outlay level would be progressively reduced to €499.1 million in the year 2000 as the 'final [budgetary] outlay commitment level' for sugar. There is no dispute in this case regarding these figures pertaining to quantity and budgetary outlay commitment levels for sugar as specified in the European Communities' Schedule.
>
> According to the European Communities, these export subsidy commitments are 'further elaborated' in Footnote 1 to the European Communities' Schedule, which states:
>
> Does not include exports of sugar of ACP and Indian origin on which the Community is not making any reduction commitments. The average of export in the period 1986 to 1990 amounted to 1,6 mio t.
>
> At issue in this dispute is the meaning of Footnote 1, its conformity with the European Communities' obligations under the *Agreement on Agriculture*, and its implications for the European Communities' export subsidy reduction commitments for sugar. (italics in the original)

The AB, repeating its *EC—Bananas III* findings that we saw in Chapter 2, held that footnote 1 of the EU schedule should not be regarded as a commitment: assuming *arguendo*, however, that one took the opposite view, it would still run foul of the specific obligations embedded in AG Agreement. It, thus, rejected the EU arguments and upheld the Panel's findings (§224):

> For all these reasons, we find that, even assuming that Footnote 1 constitutes a 'commitment' expressing a limitation on export subsidization of ACP/India equivalent sugar, Footnote 1 does not contain *both quantity and budgetary commitments* and is, therefore, inconsistent with Article 3.3 of the *Agreement on Agriculture*. In addition, Footnote 1 is inconsistent with Article 9.1 of the *Agreement on*

Agriculture, because exports of ACP/India equivalent sugar are not subject to *reduction commitments*. As Footnote 1 is inconsistent with the provisions of Articles 3.3 and 9.1, it follows that Footnote 1 is also inconsistent with Article 8 of the Agreement. (italics and emphasis in the original)

2.2.3 Border Measures: Tariffication

Arts. 4.1 and 4.2 AG request from WTO Members to express all their pre-Uruguay round border farm protection in tariffs. Footnote 1 (to Art. 4.2 AG) includes an indicative list of measures that come under the purview of this provision:

> These measures include quantitative import restrictions, variable import levies, minimum import prices, discretionary import licensing, non-tariff measures maintained through state-trading enterprises, voluntary export restraints, and similar border measures other than ordinary customs duties, whether or not the measures are maintained under country-specific derogations from the provisions of GATT 1947, but not measures maintained under balance-of-payments provisions or under other general, non-agriculture-specific provisions of GATT 1994 or of the other Multilateral Trade Agreements in Annex 1A to the WTO Agreement.

WTO Members often use specific duties to protect their own farm production (see Table 11.1).

In *Chile—Price Band*,[31] WTO adjudicating bodies contributed some important clarifications regarding the interpretation of the discipline included in Art. 4.2 AG. The case concerned a Chilean measure which operated as a buffer between

Table 11.1 Specific and *ad valorem* duties on farm goods

Members with non-*ad valorem* bindings accounting for less than 20% of all bound agricultural tariffs	Members with non-*ad valorem* bindings accounting for 20 to 50% of all bound agricultural tariffs	Members with non-*ad valorem* bindings accounting for more than 50% of all bound agricultural tariffs
Australia	Canada	Malta
Brunei Darussalam	Cyprus	Norway
Bulgaria	EU	Switzerland
Egypt	Iceland	
India	Poland	
Israel	Slovenia	
Japan	Thailand	
Korea	US	
Malaysia		
Mexico		
New Zealand		
Papua New Guinea		
Singapore		
Solomon Islands		

Note: Bulgaria, Cyprus, Malta, Poland, and Slovenia have since joined the EU.

Source: WTO Secretariat, Market Access Unfinished Business: Post-Uruguay round Inventory (2001).

---

[31] Bagwell and Sykes (2007a) discuss the case.

domestic and international prices, aiming to ensure some margin of fluctuation between the two. The duty imposed on imports was divided into two parts: the *ad valorem* duty and a specific duty (the price band), which was the outcome of a calculation where a reference price would be compared to the upper or lower threshold of the band. The bands were annually determined. The question was whether a similar scheme which had not been explicitly included in footnote 1 should still be the subject of tariffication. The Panel held that the obligation to tariffy includes, but is not limited to, quantitative restrictions (§7.29), variable import levies, and minimum import prices (§§7.36, 7.41, 7.46, and 7.48–65); the AB confirmed the Panel's finding in this respect (§262) and added that measures that should have been converted and were not, cannot be maintained after the WTO Agreement entered into force (§207). They thus requested from Chile to tariff the price band.[32] There are, nevertheless, two exceptions to this rule:

(a) First, in accordance with the procedures of Art. 5 AG, a WTO Member can adopt a provisional safeguard provision (called a 'special safeguard provision');
(b) Second, WTO Members can continue to apply non-tariff measures with respect to the so-called 'special treatment' cases referred to in Annex 5.

WTO Members must denote in their schedule of concessions the products that will benefit from the special safeguard provision with the acronym 'SSG'. A WTO Member can levy an additional duty until the end of the year in which it has been imposed (which cannot exceed one-third of the duty applied during the year when safeguard action is taken; Art. 5.4 AG) if the volume of imports exceeds a trigger level (calculated in accordance with Art. 5.4 AG) or if the price of the good concerned falls below a trigger price equal to the average 1986–8 reference price (CIF: cost, insurance, freight unit value of the product concerned): Art. 5.1 (b) AG says as much. So, contrary to what is the case for other goods, safeguards on farm goods may be imposed automatically if WTO Members have *ex ante* reserved their right to make use of this possibility. Thirty-nine WTO Members have indicated that they will be making use special safeguards on 6,156 products (see Table 11.2).[33]

The duration of the special safeguard clause is unclear. Art. 5.9 AG states that it will last as long as the reform process included in Art. 20 AG, the end of which is nowhere specified. At any rate, though, the generic safeguards clause that we discussed in Chapter 9 is anyway applicable to farm products as well. If at all, the special safeguard clause is additional protection, with an easier to meet standard for compliance.

---

[32] Bagwell and Sykes (2007a) question the solidity of this approach since the band could lead to lower duties as well. Compare McMahon (2011).
[33] Finger (2010) discusses the special safeguard clause in detail.

Table 11.2 WTO Members making use of special safeguards

Australia (10)	Indonesia (13)	Poland (144)
Barbados (37)	Israel (41)	Romania (175)
Botswana (161)	Japan (121)	Slovak Republic (114)
Bulgaria (21)	Korea (111)	South Africa (166)
Canada (150)	Malaysia (72)	Swaziland (166)
Colombia (56)	Mexico (293)	Switzerland-Liechtenstein (961)
Costa Rica (87)	Morocco (374)	Chinese Taipei (84)
Czech Republic (236)	Namibia (166)	Thailand (52)
Ecuador (7)	New Zealand (4)	Tunisia (32)
El Salvador (84)	Nicaragua (21)	United States (189)
EU (539)	Norway (581)	Uruguay (2)
Guatemala (107)	Panama (6)	Venezuela (76)
Hungary (117)	Philippines (118)	
Iceland (462)		

Source: <http://www.wto.org>.

Additional protection can be imposed on 'special treatment' cases as well. WTO Members can do that with respect to 'designated products',[34] if the following conditions have been cumulatively met:

(a) Imports of the designated products comprised less than 3 per cent of the domestic consumption during the agreed base *period* (1986–8);
(b) No export subsidies have been provided to the designated products since the beginning of the agreed base period;
(c) Effective production-restricting measures are applied to the primary agricultural product;
(d) Minimum access opportunities corresponding to 4 per cent of the base period domestic consumption and increasing by 0.8 per cent per year for the remainder of the implementation period shall be afforded.[35]

Special treatment can extend beyond the end of the tenth year following the beginning of the implementation period,[36] if successful negotiations have been undertaken to this effect and have been completed during this time period (Annex 5, §§8–10). Korea and the Philippines have negotiated to this effect for rice. When special treatment ceases to exist, the applied protection must be tariffied and will be subjected to reduction commitments provided for in Annex 5, §6. Following the tariffication process, WTO Members will enter into their Schedules of

---

[34] These products are designated with the symbol ST—Annex 5 in Section I-B of Part I of a Member's Schedule.

[35] They would be guaranteed through TRQs, the utilization rate of which was, however, disappointing due probably to the high in-quota rate: see Abbott and Morse (2004), Ingco and Winters (2004), and Laborde and Martin (2011).

[36] Art. 1(f) AG states that the implementation period 'means the six-year period commencing in the year 1995, except that, for the purposes of Article 13, it means the nine-year period commencing in 1995.

Concessions their commitments, which they are bound not to exceed (Art. 4.1 AG). Recall that developed countries agreed to average tariff reductions of 36 per cent (with a minimum of 15 per cent per product) over a period of six years; developing countries agreed to average tariff reductions of 24 per cent (with a minimum of 10 per cent) over a period of ten years; LDCs were not required to undertake reduction commitments.

2.2.4 Domestic Subsidies: AMS

Recall that negotiators were looking for a common metric in which to express all domestic support and, on this basis, to decide on their commitments. The common metric is the AMS (Art. 6.1 AG), which is further expressed as Annual and Final Bound Commitment Levels. WTO Members must calculate their Total AMS[37] (Art. 1(h) AG, which should be distinguished from product-specific AMS), and reduction commitments will be based on this calculation. Recall that WTO Members can raise product-specific AMS and still be within the bounds of their contractual obligations, provided that their Total AMS has been reduced by the agreed amount (20 per cent by the end of the implementation period).

The AMS, as we mentioned above, is based on the PSE, the producer subsidy equivalent, an index of domestic farm protection elaborated by the OECD. In 1982, the OECD Ministerial Council decided that farm policies should be reformed and that farm trade should be integrated into the multilateral disciplines. Farm protection was quite asymmetric across OECD members and, worse, it was polymorphous. OECD members were, consequently, in search of a common metric, a common base for their policy dialogue, a consistent and comparable method to evaluate the incidence of farm policies. This is where and why the PSE was born. The notion of subsidy-equivalent stems from economic theory in the 1970s and aims to evaluate the effects of tariffs. The subsidy-equivalent of a given policy instrument is the payment per unit of output that a government would have to pay domestic producers in order to generate the same impact on production as that measure, say an import tariff.[38] The OECD used the PSE initially defined as:

> the payment that would be required to compensate farmers for the loss of income resulting from the removal of a given policy measure.[39]

Since the original definition did not control for problems arising at the implementation stage, the PSE was redefined in 1990 as:

> The annual monetary value of gross transfers from consumers and taxpayers to agricultural producers, measured at the farm-gate level, arising from policy measures

---

[37] During the Doha round negotiations, the term Final Bound Total AMS (FBTAMS) was privileged.

[38] For a comprehensive analysis of this concept, see Corden (1971).

[39] OECD's Producer Support Estimate and Related Indicators of Agricultural Support, Concepts, Calculations, Interpretation and Use (The PSE Manual), September 2010, OECD: Paris, France at p. 21.

that support agriculture, regardless of their nature, objectives or impact on farm production or income.[40]

It was eventually renamed as the Producer Support Estimate (which allowed it to keep the acronym PSE), without however changing the above definition.

Annex 3 explains the specifics for the calculation of the AMS. The AMS covers the so-called amber (or yellow) box. This box has no specified content: it covers whatever is not included in the other two boxes and exceptions mentioned in the AG Agreement. There are four categories of payments that are excluded from the calculation of the AMS:

(a) Payments relating to development needs available to developing countries only (Art. 6.2 AG);
(b) *De minimis* payments (Art. 6.4 AG);
(c) Direct payments for production-limiting programmes (blue box) (Art. 6.5 AG);
(d) Green Box (Annex 2).

Development subsidies: this exemption is available only for developing countries. Three types of payments are excluded: investment subsidies that are generally available; agricultural input subsidies, which are generally available to low-income or resource-poor producers; support to encourage diversification away from growing illicit narcotic crops.[41] Orden et al. (2011a) cite evidence of the wide use of this possibility: India, for example, has included under this heading subsidies on fertilizer, electricity, and irrigation.

De minimis payments: the Agreement distinguishes between product-specific and non-product-specific support. With respect to the former, payments below 5 per cent of the relevant WTO Member's total value of production of a 'basic agricultural product' during the relevant year[42] is exempted. Art. 1(b) AG defines basic agricultural product, as:

> the product as close as practicable to the point of first sale as specified in a Member's Schedule and in related supporting material.

With respect to non-product-specific support, WTO Members can exempt from the calculation of AMS payments up to 5 per cent of the value of their total farm production. Art. 6.4(b) AG makes it clear that the figures are adjusted to 10 per cent (for both categories) for developing countries which are WTO Members.

---

[40] Idem at p. 22.
[41] This category is often referred to in the literature as the 'development box'; Brink (2011) at pp. 29ff.
[42] Throughout the Agreement, the term 'year', in relation to specific commitments of a Member, refers to the calendar, financial or marketing year specified in the Schedule relating to that Member (Art. 1(i) AG).

Direct payments for production-limiting programmes (*blue box*): Art. 6.5 AG identifies three situations where a WTO Member can legitimately exempt direct payments under production-limiting programmes from the calculation of its AMS: payments are based on fixed area and yields; or payments are made on 85 per cent or less of the base level of production; or in the case of livestock payments which are made on a fixed number of head.

Green Box: this is the largest category of exemptions. Annex 2 exempts from the calculation of AMS 12 measures of support funded through a government programme which does not have the effect of price support (§1).[43] The rationale for the exclusion of 12 government services included in Annex 2 is that they have no, or minimal, trade-distorting effects.[44] To avoid any misunderstandings as to the exhaustive character of programmes featured in Annex 2, Art. 7.2 AG makes it clear that any programme which does not satisfy the criteria specified in Annex 2 must be included in the calculation of the total AMS. Art. 7.1 AG, moreover, requests from WTO Members to ensure that their measures that are initially characterized as green box continue to satisfy the criteria for exclusion from AMS in the future as well. The schemes excluded from the calculation of the AMS come under the following headings:

(a) General Services: payments relating to research, pest and disease control, inspection (health, safety, standardization), marketing, infrastructure are covered. Direct payments to producers are not covered.
(b) Food Security: for payments to be excluded under this heading, the volume and accumulation of stocks must be predetermined.
(c) Food Aid: direct provisions to those concerned are excluded from the calculation of the AMS.
(d) Direct Payments: payments cannot be exempted unless they meet the general criteria (government funded and not, or minimally, trade-distorting), and the criteria included under the various headings dealing with specific categories of direct payments that follow in (v)–(xii). An example is appropriate: while a pest control service can be provided under the heading 'General Services', a direct payment to compensate the producer for anything culled to control pests comes under this 'Direct Payments' heading. Consequently, the cost of supplying the service to the farmer comes under the heading 'General

---

[43] There is no workable definition of what is a non-distorting subsidy and this is (probably) the reason why negotiators felt that an indicative list would better reflect their intentions; compare Brink (2011) at pp. 31ff.

[44] Stancanelli (2009, p. 32) mentions that, during the negotiations, the EU insisted on including hectare and cattle herd payments in the 'green box', since this was very much a measure at the core of the CAP reform. It seems that the extent of the green box was influenced by similar concerns. Stancanelli (2009) discusses the various proposals regarding the green box entries of the key players during the Uruguay round at pp. 27ff.

Services', whereas the direct payment to producer would come under this and the following headings and have to comply with them in order to be excluded from the calculation of AMS. Decoupled Income Payments are one of the categories of direct payments that deserves particular attention in light of the relevant practice in this context. Eligibility for such payments can be established on clear criteria, such as income, status as producer or landowner, production level etc. Payments should not be related to production, factors of production, or prices. The AB in its report on *US—Upland Cotton* provided some clarifications regarding the disciplines imposed on decoupled income payments. The report reflects a brief but very informative presentation of the legal framework applicable to decoupled income payments as reflected in Annex 2 (§325):

> Paragraph 6 of Annex 2, entitled '[d]ecoupled income support', seeks to decouple or de-link direct payments to producers from various aspects of their production decisions and thus aims at neutrality in this regard. Subparagraph (b) decouples the payments from production; subparagraph (c) decouples payments from prices; and subparagraph (d) decouples payments from factors of production. Subparagraph (e) completes the process by making it clear that no production shall be required in order to receive such payments. Decoupling of payments from production under paragraph 6(b) can only be ensured if the payments are not related to, or based upon, either a positive requirement to produce certain crops or a negative requirement not to produce certain crops or a combination of both positive and negative requirements on production of crops.

The AB was called upon to review the Panel's finding that the US production flexibility contract payments were inconsistent with Annex 2, §6(b). The AB describes the contentious US law as follows (§311):

> The production flexibility contract program dispensed with the requirement that producers continue to plant upland cotton in order to receive payments; instead, payments would generally be made regardless of what the producer chose to grow, and whether or not the producer chose to produce anything at all. However, there were limits to this planting flexibility. Specifically, payments were reduced or eliminated if fruits and vegetables (other than lentils, mung beans, and dry peas) were planted on upland cotton base acres, subject to certain other exceptions.

The AB formulated the issue before it in the following manner (§312):

> The question before us in this appeal thus concerns a measure with a partial exclusion combining planting flexibility and payments with the reduction or elimination of the payments when the excluded crops are produced, while providing payments even when no crops are produced at all.

The Panel had originally found that the US measure at hand was not a decoupled income payment pursuant to Annex 2, §6(b). The AB upheld the Panel's findings in this respect for the following reasons (§329):

We agree with the Panel that a partial exclusion of some crops from payments has the potential to channel production towards the production of crops that remain eligible for payments. In contrast to a total production ban, the channelling of production that may follow from a partial exclusion of some crops from payments will have *positive* production effects as regards crops eligible for payments. The extent of this will depend on the scope of the exclusion. We note in this regard that the Panel found, as a matter of fact, that planting flexibility limitations at issue in this case 'significantly constrain production choices available to PFC and DP payment recipients and effectively eliminate a significant proportion of them'. The fact that farmers may continue to receive payments if they produce nothing at all does not detract from this assessment because, according to the Panel, it is not the option preferred by the 'overwhelming majority' of farmers, who continue to produce some type of permitted crop. In the light of these findings by the Panel, we are unable to agree with the United States' argument that the planting flexibility limitations only negatively affect the production of crops that are excluded. (emphasis in the original)

Note that the US had not required production of any kind in order to make the decoupled income payments; when reading §§329–31, one is left with the impression that the decision to produce was a private decision by US farmers. It seems that the AB was led to this conclusion in light of the extent of the partial exclusion: the US scheme required producers not to produce fruits and vegetables, but did not impose an absolute ban on production of farm goods. Because, in its view, the exclusion was not substantial, the AB was led to believe that:

because the opportunity for farmers to receive payments for producing crops, while less or no such payments are made to farmers who produce excluded crops, provides an incentive to switch from producing excluding crops to producing eligible for payments. (§331 *in fine*)

In the AB's view, hence, these payments were not sufficiently decoupled. This is a rather odd finding though. It is quite surprising that the AB was persuaded by the argument (and jumped to the conclusion) that partial exclusion leads by definition to production. As rational individuals, farmers might choose not to produce at all if, through the decoupled income payments received, they can have higher returns by, for example, investing the sums received. Or, what if US producers had found it more profitable to make cash deposits in a bank because of the interest associated with their deposit? They will produce only if, in their view, this is a rational decision. Hence, at the end of the day, it is a private decision to produce which has little, if anything to do with the US-imposed partial exclusion. By punishing such private decisions, the AB cast the net too wide.

(e) Income Safety Net: these payments aim at compensating farmers for losses of income. They can legitimately be excluded from the calculation of AMS, if the loss corresponds to at least 30 per cent of the income (made during a reference period), and provided that the compensation does not exceed 70 per cent of the income lost.

(f) Natural Disasters: these are payments aiming at compensating farmers for natural disasters (including disease outbreaks, pest manifestations, nuclear accidents, and war). Assuming that production loss is at least 30 per cent of the production during a reference period, and provided that the compensation aims to cover losses only, such payments can legitimately be excluded from the calculation of the AMS.

(g) Producer Retirement: such payments are legitimately exempted, if they are conditioned upon the total and permanent retirement of the beneficiaries.

(h) Resource Retirement: these payments are legitimately exempted, provided that the land will be set aside for three years at least.

(i) Investment Aids: these payments can be exempted if farmers suffer from objectively demonstrated structural disadvantages which are not based on the type/volume of production, are not related to prices, and provided that they take place only as long as necessary to overcome the mentioned disadvantages.

(j) Environmental Programmes: these payments are exempted to the extent that they are limited to the cost of compliance with the government programme.[45]

(k) Regional Assistance: these payments are exempted, if they are generally available to all producers in a disadvantaged region, and are limited to the costs that the producer must undertake because of the location of its production.

Green box schemes have been increasing over the years, but not in all countries: Brazil and Japan, for example, report no increase in this respect. Orden et al. (2011b, pp. 408ff) calculate that they represent 20 per cent of the value of production in the EU and the US (2008) and 40 per cent for the same period in Brazil, China, and India. Developing countries have not made much use of developing countries, essentially because the areas where they are most interested in (extension services, research, soil conservation, pest and disease control) come under the green box but only up to limits which they find hard to cope with.[46]

All remaining domestic protection comes under the AMS. Annex 3 explains how the AMS will be calculated:[47]

---

[45] Steenblik and Tsai (2009) discuss the environmental impact of all schemes coming under the green box category and report mixed results: while items such as agri-environmental subsidies and inspection services might have a positive impact on environment, entries such as research might have either a positive or a negative impact (depending on the technologies that they give rise to), whereas direct payments, especially to smaller firms, might have a negative impact.

[46] Compare in this respect the experiences of India, China, and African countries discussed in Dhar (2009), Xie (2009), and Oduro (2009) respectively.

[47] As can be seen, the WTO and the OECD definitions are not identical. Critically, the OECD definition uses an evolving market benchmark to calculate the subsidy-equivalent, whereas the WTO AMS uses a defined, static base period. For a comprehensive discussion in the differences, see Diakosavvas (2002).

(a) The AMS covers both product-specific and non-product-specific payments;

(b) Product-specific payments cover market price support, non-exempt direct payments, and any other subsidy, except, of course, for those that are explicitly exempted (§1 of the Annex). Payments at both the national and the sub-national level will be taken into account (§3). Payments by farmers will be deducted (§4);

(c) Non-product-specific payments will be expressed in one (non-product-specific) AMS in monetary terms (§1);

(d) Market price support will be calculated by multiplying the quantities of products eligible to receive it by the difference between the fixed external reference price and the applied administered price. Items such as storage costs will not be part of the calculation (§8). The base period (reference period) for the calculation will be 1986–8, and, for net exporting countries, it is the FOB (free on board) price that matters, whereas, for net importing countries, it is the CIF (cost, insurance, freight) price that will be used (§9);

(e) Non-exempt direct payments will be calculated, either in the same manner as market price support, or by using budgetary outlays (§10). Art. 1(c) AG makes it clear that the term 'budgetary outlays' covers revenue foregone as well. If non-exempt direct payments have been based on non-price factors, then they will be measured by reference to budgetary outlays only (§12);

(f) Product-specific AMS will be expressed in monetary terms (§6), as close as possible to the first point of sale (§7).

When the calculation of AMS is impracticable, support to producers will be calculated through recourse to the Equivalent Measurement of Support (EMS), which is defined in Art. 1(d) AG:

> 'Equivalent Measurement of Support' means the annual level of support, expressed in monetary terms, provided to producers of a basic agricultural product through the application of one or more measures, the calculation of which in accordance with the AMS methodology is impracticable, other than support provided under programmes that qualify as exempt from reduction under Annex 2 to this Agreement, and which is:
>
>   (i) with respect to support provided during the base period, specified in the relevant tables of supporting material incorporated by reference in Part IV of a Member's Schedule; and
>
> (ii) with respect to support provided during any year of the implementation period and thereafter, calculated in accordance with the provisions of Annex 4 of this Agreement and taking into account the constituent data and methodology used in the tables of supporting material incorporated by reference in Part IV of the Member's Schedule.

Recourse to EMS was made in a very limited number of cases only. Calculation of AMS is to be made in accordance with Art. 1 AG, and Annex 3, but in some instances the 1986–8 external reference price for the supported product was not available in the constituent data and methodology (that is, in the supporting tables, the so-called 'AGST Tables', included for reference in Part VI of each Member's Schedule of Concessions). One explanation was that a product was not traded by that particular country during that particular reference period; hence no external reference price was recorded. In such instances, the notifying Member used the proxy approach (i.e. the EMS) in order to evaluate the level of support granted to the product, for notification purposes. Argentina, for example, used EMS for the calculation of its support on tobacco.[48]

Annex 4 explains the calculation of EMS: in parallel with the AMS, product-specific EMS will be derived from a multiplication of the applied administered price by the quantities eligible for budgetary outlays, and will be calculated as close as possible to the first point of sale. Non-exempt direct payments will be calculated in the same manner as in AMS. An example may be of help in this context: in the EU, a system of minimum import prices was in place for beef and cereals. Such prices depended on various factors, such as:

(a) Tariff protection;
(b) Production controls;
(c) The EU intervention price (a price decided by the EU ministers for agriculture normally on a yearly basis, which corresponds to the applied administered price as indicated in §8 of Annex 3); and
(d) Export subsidies.

The system of minimum import prices aimed at restricting supply to the domestic (EU) market, thus keeping domestic prices higher than the world price. The AMS calculation for beef and cereals was estimated to be the value of support for the volume of production multiplied by the difference between the EU intervention price and the world price (for the base period between 1986 and 1988). Assuming, for example, that the intervention price for wheat is €200 per tonne, the world price is €100 per tonne, and the total wheat production in the EU is 1,000,000 tones, the EU AMS for wheat is €10,000,000.[49] Developed countries have agreed to reduce their total AMS by 20 per cent by the end of a period of six years; developing countries have agreed to reduce their total AMS by 13.3 per cent by the end of a period of ten years; LDCs must bind their AMS support level (if applicable), but were not required to make any reduction commitments.

2.2.5 Export Subsidies

The original GATT contained no provisions on export subsidies for farm goods. In the 1955 Review Session, Art. XVI.3 GATT sanctioned export subsidies that led to the subsidizing country obtaining more than an equitable share of the world market, but stopped short of outlawing export subsidies. In the GATT era, the

---

[48] WTO Doc. G/AG/N/ARG/24 of 25 April 2006.
[49] For a concrete application, see the AB report on *Korea—Various Measures on Beef* (§§90ff).

Panel on *EC—Refunds on Exports of Sugar* held that a reference period of the last three years could be appropriately used to decide on the size of the share of the subsidizing state and the extent to which it was inconsistent with Art. XVI.3 GATT. The situation changed, of course, with the entry into force of the SCM Agreement and the outright ban on export subsidies. The AG Agreement constitutes an exception from this ban.

The term 'export subsidy' is defined in Art. 1(e) AG:

> export subsidies refers to subsidies contingent upon export performance, including the export subsidies listed in Article 9 of this Agreement.

Art. 9.1 AG contains a list of export subsidies to which reduction commitments are to be applied:

> (a) the provision by governments or their agencies of direct subsidies, including payments-in-kind, to a firm, to an industry, to producers of an agricultural product, to a cooperative or other association of such producers, or to a marketing board, contingent on export performance;
> (b) the sale or disposal for export by governments or their agencies of non-commercial stocks of agricultural products at a price lower than the comparable price charged for the like product to buyers in the domestic market;
> (c) payments on the export of an agricultural product that are financed by virtue of governmental action, whether or not a charge on the public account is involved, including payments that are financed from the proceeds of a levy imposed on the agricultural product concerned or on an agricultural product from which the exported product is derived;
> (d) the provision of subsidies to reduce the costs of marketing exports of agricultural products (other than widely available export promotion and advisory services) including handling, upgrading and other processing costs, and the costs of international transport and freight;
> (e) internal transport and freight charges on export shipments, provided or mandated by governments, on terms more favourable than for domestic shipments;
> (f) subsidies on agricultural products contingent on their incorporation in exported products.

In *Canada—Dairy*, the AB held that the cost of production could serve as a benchmark to determine whether a payment has in fact been made within the meaning of Art. 9.1(c) AG. In *EC—Export Subsidies on Sugar*, the AB clarified its understanding of the terms 'financed' and 'by virtue of governmental action' that appear in Art. 9.1(c) AG (§§236–7):

> Addressing the word 'financed', the AB held that this word generally refers to the 'mechanism' or 'process' by which financial resources are provided, such that payments are made. Article 9.1(c), by stating 'whether or not a charge on the public account is involved', expressly provides that the government itself need not provide the resources for producers to make payments. Instead, payments may be made and funded by private parties.
>
> With respect to the words 'by virtue of', the AB has previously held that there must be a 'nexus' or 'demonstrable link' between the governmental action at issue

and the financing of payments. The AB clarified that not every governmental action will have the requisite 'nexus' to the financing of payments. For instance, the AB held that the 'demonstrable link' between 'governmental action' and the 'financing' of payments would not exist in a scenario in which 'governmental action . . . establish [es] a regulatory framework merely *enabling* a third person freely to make and finance "payments".' In this situation, the link between the governmental action and the financing of payments would be 'too tenuous', such that the 'payments' could not be regarded as 'financed by virtue of governmental action' within the meaning of Article 9.1(c). Rather, according to the AB, there must be a 'tighter nexus' between the mechanism or process by which the payments are financed (even if by a third person) and governmental action. In this respect, the AB clarified that, although governmental action is essential, Article 9.1(c) contemplates that 'payments may be financed by virtue of governmental action even though significant aspects of the financing might not involve government.' Thus, even if government does not fund the payments itself, it must play a sufficiently important part in the process by which a private party funds 'payments', such that the requisite nexus exists between 'governmental action' and the 'financing'. The alleged link must be examined on a case-by-case basis, taking account of the particular character of the governmental action at issue and its relationship to the payments made. (emphasis in the original)

It follows that the form of financing is immaterial; a tight nexus must be established between the government action and the financing of the payments. It is not the case that any nexus will do: a framework that merely enables third persons to make payments is not enough, in the AB's view, for the scheme to be subjected to the disciplines of Art. 9.1 AG. This case law is reminiscent of our discussions regarding attribution of a practice to government that we considered in Chapter 2 when discussing *Japan—Semiconductors*. The same logic would suggest that, although legal compulsion is not necessary, a practice will not be attributed to a government unless the latter has provided individuals with incentives to act in a particular way. Unfortunately, this test suffers from the imprecisions that we discussed already in Chapter 2. The AB went on to apply this test to the growers of 'C Sugar' in its report on *EC—Export Subsidies on Sugar*, where it used the term 'incentives' as a criterion to attribute behaviour to the EU. The facts of the case are reflected in §2 of the report:

EC Regulation 1260/2001 is valid for the marketing years 2001/2002 to 2005/2006 and establishes, *inter alia*: quotas for sugar production; an intervention price for raw and white sugar, respectively; a basic price and a minimum price for beet for quota sugar production; quota (that is, 'A' and 'B') sugar as well as non-quota (that is, 'C') sugar; import and export licensing requirements; producer levies; and preferential import arrangements. Furthermore, the EC sugar regime provides 'export refunds' to its sugar exporters for certain quantities of sugar, other than C sugar. These 'refunds', which are direct export subsidies, cover the difference between the European Communities' internal market price and the prevailing world market price for sugar. Non-quota sugar (that is, C sugar) must be exported, unless it is carried forward, but no 'export refunds' are provided for such exports. (italics in the original)

The AB upheld the Panel's finding that the EU regime be considered an export subsidy in the sense of Art. 9.1(c) AG (§§238–9):

> Turning to the specific circumstances of the present dispute, we note that, in its finding that 'payments' in the form of sales of C beet below its total cost of production are 'financed by virtue of governmental action', the Panel relied on a number of aspects of the EC sugar regime. The Panel considered, *inter alia*, that: the EC sugar regime regulates prices of A and B beet and establishes a framework for the contractual relationships between beet growers and sugar producers with a view to ensuring a stable and adequate income for beet growers; C beet is invariably produced together with A and B beet in one single line of production; a significant percentage of beet growers are likely to finance sales of C beet below the total cost of production as a result of participation in the domestic market by making 'highly remunerative' sales of A and B beet; the European Communities 'controls virtually every aspect of domestic beet and sugar supply and management', including through financial penalties imposed on sugar producers that divert C sugar into the domestic market; the European Communities' Sugar Management Committee 'overviews, supervises and protects the [European Communities'] domestic sugar through, *inter alia*, supply management'; the growing of C beet is not 'incidental', but rather an 'integral' part of the governmental regulation of the sugar market; and C sugar producers '*have incentives* to produce C sugar so as to maintain their share of the A and B quotas', while C beet growers 'have an incentive to supply as much as is requested by C sugar producers with a view to receiving the high prices for A and B beet and their allocated amount of...C beet'.
>
> We agree with the Panel that, in the circumstances of the present case, all of these aspects of the EC sugar regime have a direct bearing on whether below-cost sales of C beet are financed by virtue of governmental action. As a result, we are unable to agree with the European Communities' first argument on appeal, namely, that the Panel applied a test under which an Article 9.1(c) subsidy was deemed to exist 'simply because [governmental] action "enabled" the beet growers to finance and make payments'. Rather, we believe that the Panel relied on aspects of the EC sugar regime that go far beyond merely 'enabling' or 'permitting' beet growers to make payments to sugar producers. Indeed, in our view, there is a tight nexus between the European Communities' 'governmental action' and the financing of payments in the case before us. We have no doubt that, without the highly remunerative prices guaranteed by the EC sugar regime for A and B beet, sales of C beet could not take place profitably at a price below the total cost of production. (italics and emphasis in the original)

Art. 3.3 AG reads:

> Subject to the provisions of paragraphs 2(b) and 4 of Article 9, a Member shall not provide export subsidies listed in paragraph 1 of Article 9 in respect of the agricultural products or groups of products specified in Section II of Part IV of its Schedule in excess of the budgetary outlay and quantity commitment levels specified therein and shall not provide such subsidies in respect of any agricultural product not specified in that Section of its Schedule.

This obligation is compounded by Art. 8 AG which reads:

Each Member undertakes not to provide export subsidies otherwise than in conformity with this Agreement and with the commitments as specified in that Member's Schedule.

It is thus clear from the text of Art. 3.3 AG that WTO Members have accepted disciplines with respect to both scheduled goods (that is, goods that they have included in their schedules of concessions) and unscheduled goods (that is, goods that they have not included in their schedules of concessions). There is a difference though:

(a) With respect to the former, they have entered commitments with respect to both the volume of exports, and the maximum subsidization: developed countries agreed to a reduction by 21 per cent of the volume of exports, and 36 per cent of budgetary outlays over a period of six years, and for incorporated/processed products, they agreed to a reduction of only budgetary outlays by 36 per cent (Art. 11 AG); developing countries agreed to a reduction equalling two-thirds of the reduction required by developed countries, over a period of ten years, and, by virtue of Art. 9.4 AG, they have been granted an exception during the implementation period with respect to certain marketing and internal transportation services. No commitments have been requested by LDCs.

(b) With respect to unscheduled goods, WTO Members cannot provide any export subsidy.[50]

It follows that WTO Members had an incentive to schedule goods if subsidization was practised in the base period of 1986–90, and if they intended to subsidize them. All commitments are product-specific. The AB, in *US—FSC*, held (§§151–2) that the nature of commitments assumed with respect to scheduled goods is some sort of limited authorization, which will instantly turn into a prohibition when the thresholds established in the relevant schedule of concessions have been met.

Art. 10 AG is the anti-circumvention provision included in the Agreement. It contains four paragraphs, each of them dealing with a specific subject-matter: Art. 10.1 AG reflects the general rule that export subsidy commitments should not be circumvented; Art. 10.2 AG reflects the willingness of WTO Members to eventually develop international disciplines on export credits, export credit guarantees, and insurance programmes; Art. 10.3 AG deals with the allocation of burden of proof in cases where a WTO Member claims that its exports exceeding its commitments have not been subsidized; finally, Art. 10.4 AG deals with

---

[50] The AB held as much in its report on *US—FSC* at §§145–6. In *EC—Export Subsidies on Sugar*, it confirmed that, pursuant to Art. 9 AG, WTO Members are required to make both budgetary-outlay and quantity-reduction commitments (§193).

international food aid: it provides that aid must not be tied to commercial exports of farm products and must be carried out in accordance with international standards, namely, the 'Principles of Surplus Disposal and Consultative Obligations', including, where appropriate, the system of Usual Marketing Requirements (URM) established by the FAO (Food Agricultural Organization). In *US— Upland Cotton*, the AB had to decide on the relationship between the general prohibition of circumvention (Art. 10.1 AG) and the more specific provision regarding export credits (and guarantees) included in Art. 10.2 AG. Art. 10.2 AG reads:

> Members undertake to work toward the development of internationally agreed disciplines to govern the provision of export credits, export credit guarantees or insurance programmes and, after agreement on such disciplines, to provide export credits, export credit guarantees or insurance programmes only in conformity therewith.

The US and Brazil presented divergent arguments regarding the interpretation of this provision. The former contended that, in light of the wording of Art. 10.1 AG, export credit guarantees were 'carved out' from the discipline included in Art. 10.1 AG. The latter claimed that this should not be the case. The three-member division of the AB deciding the dispute could not agree on this issue. The majority sided with Brazil and held that, until disciplines have been elaborated, export credit guarantees must observe the existing discipline included in Art. 10.1 AG (§§607ff and especially 616, 626–7). One member of the AB expressed a minority opinion: in its view, Art. 10.2 AG should be regarded as a carve-out from the obligation included in Art. 10.1 AG. Until disciplines have been worked out, WTO Members incur, on this view, no obligation with respect to export credits, export credit guarantees, and insurance programmes (§§631–41). The best arguments lie with the minority opinion: both the wording and the negotiating history[51] of this provision suggest that export credit guarantees were not meant to be covered by the outright ban embedded in Art. 10.1 AG. If export credits came under the purview of Art. 10.1 AG, why would negotiators spend negotiating effort on introducing Art. 10.2? Did they want to signal that they were prepared to exclude export credits from the disciplines of the Agreement through future action? This is a highly unlikely outcome, since the whole negotiation was meant to discipline instruments and not the opposite. Alas, this is by now water under the bridge.

Case law has also dealt with the interpretation of Art. 10.3 AG: WTO Members exporting beyond the committed quantity must establish that the surplus exports have not benefited from export subsidies. The AB has consistently held (*Canada— Dairy*, §75; *US—Upland Cotton*, §645) that all the complaining party needs to establish is the quantitative part of its claim, i.e. that the subsidizing state has

---

[51] Breene (1993).

exported quantities beyond its export quantity-reduction commitments. The burden of proof will then shift to the subsidizing state to demonstrate that its exports have not benefited from subsidies mentioned in Art. 9.1 AG. In *US—Upland Cotton*, the AB distanced itself from the Panel's findings in this respect, and held that Art. 10.3 AG does not apply to unscheduled goods (§652):

> We disagree with the Panel's view that Article 10.3 applies to *unscheduled* products. Under the Panel's approach, the only thing a complainant would have to do to meet its burden of proof when bringing a claim against an *unscheduled* product is to demonstrate that the respondent has exported that product. Once that has been established, the respondent would have to demonstrate that it has not provided an export subsidy. This seems to us an extreme result. In effect, it would mean that any export of an unscheduled product is *presumed* to be subsidized. In our view, the presumption of subsidization when exported quantities exceed the reduction commitments makes sense in respect of a *scheduled* product because, by including it in its schedule, a WTO Member is reserving for itself the right to apply export subsidies to that product, within the limits in its schedule. In the case of *unscheduled* products, however, such a presumption appears inappropriate. Export subsidies for both unscheduled agricultural products and industrial products are completely prohibited under the *Agreement on Agriculture* and under the *SCM Agreement*, respectively. The Panel's interpretation implies that the burden of proof with regard to the same issue would apply differently, however, under each Agreement: it would be on the respondent under the *Agreement on Agriculture*, while it would be on the complainant under the *SCM Agreement*. (italics and emphasis in the original)

Referring to prior case law, the AB held in *US—Upland Cotton* that not only actual, but also threat of, circumvention might suffice for a violation of Art. 10 AG. Nevertheless, the mere possibility that circumvention might occur at some point in the future as a result of government behaviour does not fall within the meaning of threat of circumvention; the AB held that a likelihood-standard that an event might occur must be complied with (§§704, 710, and 713).

This discussion concludes our discussion regarding the three major commitments that WTO Members undertook with respect to farm protection. Although notifications of measures are judged inadequate by many in the literature, there is widespread agreement in the literature that the established carve-outs have greatly contributed towards the objectives sought, that is, that WTO Members meet the commitments entered upon signing the AG Agreement.[52]

2.2.6 Peace Clause

During the implementation period WTO Members have agreed that compliance with the obligations imposed under the green box, the blue box, and Arts. 8–10 AG would mean *ipso facto* compliance with the WTO and, hence, no CVDs can be imposed against similar measures nor can NVCs be raised against them (Art. 13

---

[52] Orden et al. (2011b, pp. 402ff), in general, and Nassar (2011, pp. 223ff) with respect to Brazil.

AG).[53] As we saw in *US—Upland Cotton*, following the end of the implementation period, export subsidies must comply not only with the AG, but also with the SCM requirements: this is so because it is Art. 21 AG that governs the relationship between the two agreements. Consequently, the peace clause provision (Art. 13 AG) is best understood as a time-bound exception to Art. 21 AG.[54]

2.2.7 Net Food-Importing Developing Countries

The commitments under the Agreement, and the export commitments in particular, might have a negative impact on net food-importing countries, since they will not be in a position to procure farm goods on favourable (i.e. subsidized) terms. Two provisions aim at addressing the situation. First, Art. 16 AG requires that developed countries take action in accordance with the 'Decision on Measures Concerning the Possible Negative Effects of the Reform Programme on Least Developed and Net Food Importing Developing Countries'. This Decision aims to ensure that LDCs and net food-importing developing countries will not be negatively affected by the commitments undertaken as a result of the successful conclusion of the Uruguay round. More specifically, it calls for a review of the level of food aid established periodically by the Committee on Food Aid under the Food Aid Convention; the initiation of negotiations in order to establish a level of food aid commitments sufficient to meet the needs of net food importers; the adoption of guidelines to ensure that increasing proportions of basic foodstuffs will be provided as a grant; an agreement by developed countries to help, through technical advice, increase the productivity in net food-importing countries.[55] The Committee on Agriculture has established a list of countries that will benefit from such initiatives: it comprises all LDCs, plus originally 19 developing countries, namely, Barbados, Botswana, Cuba, Côte d'Ivoire, Dominican Republic, Egypt, Honduras, Jamaica, Kenya, Mauritius, Morocco, Pakistan, Peru, Saint Lucia, Senegal, Sri Lanka, Trinidad and Tobago, Tunisia, and Venezuela. The list has been updated and there are now 29 countries that figure on this list. The ten new developing countries are: Dominica, Gabon, Grenada, Jordan, Maldives, Mongolia, Namibia, Saint Kitts and Nevis, Saint Vincent and the Grenadines, and Swaziland.[56] Second, Art. 12 AG requests WTO Members that have had lawful recourse to export restrictions (Art. XI.2(a) GATT) to pay due consideration to importing Members' food security; to this effect, the WTO Member restricting exports must notify the Committee on Agriculture of similar measures, and consult, if requested, with those negatively affected.

---

[53] Chambovay (2002), Delcros (2000), and Morgan and Goh (2003) offer different perspectives on this score.

[54] Similar conclusions are reported by Bown and Meagher (2010).

[55] Schoenbaum (2011) offers a very persuasive explanation of why changing circumstances matter here more than elsewhere.

[56] WTO Doc. G/AG/5/Rev. 9 of 6 April 2011.

2.2.8 The Cotton Initiative

Four WTO Members, namely, Benin, Burkina Faso, Chad, and Mali, tabled a proposal in 2003 to the WTO General Council, arguing that they must be compensated for damages suffered by subsidies paid by developed WTO Members on production of cotton, and also requested that cotton subsidies be withdrawn. Given the very high dependence of these poor African economies on cotton exports, it was agreed that cotton was a special issue. The WTO General Council decision of 1 August 2004 (reflecting the so-called 'July package') contained a specific reference to this issue and called for action:

> the General Council reaffirms the importance of the Sectoral Initiative on Cotton and takes note of the parameters set out in Annex A within which the trade-related aspects of this issue will be pursued in the agriculture negotiations. The General Council also attaches importance to the development aspects of the Cotton Initiative and wishes to stress the complementarity between the trade and development aspects. The Council takes note of the recent Workshop on Cotton in Cotonou on 23–24 March 2004 organized by the WTO Secretariat, and other bilateral and multilateral efforts to make progress on the development assistance aspects and instructs the Secretariat to continue to work with the development community and to provide the Council with periodic reports on relevant developments.
>
> Members should work on related issues of development multilaterally with the international financial institutions, continue their bilateral programmes, and all developed countries are urged to participate. In this regard, the General Council instructs the Director General to consult with the relevant international organizations, including the Bretton Woods Institutions, the Food and Agriculture Organization and the International Trade Centre to direct effectively existing programmes and any additional resources towards development of the economies where cotton has vital importance.

The Cotton Sub-Committee was established on 19 November 2004, with a mandate to focus on cotton as a specific issue in the wider negotiations on liberalization of trade in farm goods. WTO Members, as well as countries that have observer status in the WTO, were welcome to participate. This organ operates in close cooperation with the WTO General Council, the Trade Negotiations Committee (TNC), and the Ministerial Conference.

This initiative raises the question whether similar arrangements are foreseeable and even warranted with respect to other farm goods where concerns of this or a comparable order can be raised. Panagariya (2005) has adequately explained why cotton is an outlier, and that the whole institutional arrangement dealing with trade in cotton should be viewed as idiosyncratic: it is the only (or one of the very few) known sector-specific case where subsidization by developed countries has seriously jeopardized the interests of developing countries.[57]

---

[57] Compare Francois (2005).

2.2.9 Transparency Requirements

WTO Members undertake, by virtue of Art. 18 AG, to promptly notify the Committee on Agriculture of all matters of interest to the reform programme: that is, WTO Members must notify everything of interest to their commitment with respect to tariffication, domestic and export subsidies. Brink (2011, p. 37) reflects the common view in this respect, arguing that notifications of measures regarding commitments and, more generally, farm-protecting measures, have been inadequate. Recall that with respect to subsidies characterized as green box, for example, WTO Members must ensure that their measures remain during their lifetime within the parameters of Annex 2; absent transparency regarding eventual changes, it is impossible to monitor effectively the respect of this obligation at the multilateral level. Information costs when trying to detect the specifics of similar measures might be quite high. It is the combination of lack of transparency and high information costs that probably explains the low volume of disputes in Brink's (2011) view: there have been only two genuine farm trade disputes reported before 2007, and a handful since.

2.3 Institutional Issues

The Committee on Agriculture has been established and it is responsible for the administration of the AG Agreement. All WTO Members, as well as observers to the WTO, participate therein. It meets four times a year, but (additional) special sessions can be arranged. This committee has been overseeing the reform programme, that is, the implementation of commitments undertaken during the Uruguay round.

2.4 State Trading

A substantial amount of farm trade takes place through marketing boards, that is, state trading entities, and not between private traders. For historic and other reasons, even mainstream market economies, like Canada, keep in place similar entities that administer trade for a number of commodities. State trading companies must respect the disciplines of Art. XVII GATT. This provision covers entities that do not necessarily engage in farm trade; hence its disciplines are relevant for a wider category of transactions.

2.4.1 The Legal Discipline and its Rationale

State trading enterprises (STEs) operating within WTO Members must, by virtue of Art. XVII GATT, respect non-discrimination: to the extent that an STE is acting as an importer only, respecting the non-discrimination principle is tantamount to respecting MFN and it should, consequently, not discriminate across products because of their origin; to the extent, however, that an STE acts as a distributor as well, it must not only observe MFN, but also NT. The leading case is *Korea—Various Measures on Beef*, where, following a quota on beef imposed (the justification being balance of payments), Korea had established a producer-controlled import monopoly for the importation and distribution of beef: the monopoly was the sole importer and distributor of beef, at a time when the price of imported beef was substantially lower than that of domestic beef. The Korean measure was under attack for various reasons, one of them being its alleged inconsistency with Art. XVII GATT. The Panel held that the legal obligation not to discriminate included in Art. XVII.1 GATT covered both MFN and NT, since the Korean monopoly operated not only on the importation, but also on the distribution, of beef (§7.53):

> Article XVII.1(a) establishes the general obligation on state trading enterprises to undertake their activities in accordance with the GATT principles of non-discrimination. The panel considers that this principle of non-discrimination includes at least the provisions of Articles I and III of the GATT.

To understand the rationale for disciplining STEs, we need to briefly check the historical record. As Irwin et al. (2008) report, the inclusion of a provision on STEs was very much a request by the UK government, which, *inter alia*, aimed at preserving the role of the state within a context of liberal trade policy. Negotiators feared that, unless disciplined, STEs could be used in order to circumvent concessions (concession erosion), since they might have little incentive to act in accordance with commercial considerations and might be used instead to advance, for example, national industrial policy goals. This led them to negotiate Art. XVII GATT.

The AB, in its report on *Canada—Wheat Exports and Grain Imports*,[58] confirmed that the rationale for this provision is to operate as an anti-circumvention device in the following terms (§85):

> Subparagraph (a) seeks to ensure that a Member cannot, through the creation or maintenance of a State enterprise or the grant of exclusive or special privileges to any enterprise, engage in or facilitate conduct that would be condemned as discriminatory under the GATT 1994 if such conduct were undertaken directly by the Member itself. In other words, subparagraph (a) is an 'anti-circumvention' provision.

2.4.2 The Coverage of the Legal Discipline

Art. XVII GATT does not contain a definition of STEs. It merely states that it applies to STEs, and to enterprises which have been granted formally or in effect exclusive or special privileges: the coverage of the legal discipline will be affected by the manner in which the term 'in effect' is understood, since there should be little doubt as to what a de jure STE is. The Interpretative Note ad Art. XVII GATT provides two clarifications:

---

[58] Hoekman and Trachtman (2008) discuss this case in detail.

(a) Marketing Boards are covered;

(b) Standards aimed at ensuring quality or efficiency, or privileges granted for the exploitation of natural resources, but which do not empower the government to exercise control over the trading activities of the enterprise in question, do not constitute exclusive or special privileges.

Art. XVII.2 GATT reflects a caveat which is critical for the understanding of the term 'STE': the legal obligations assumed do not concern government procurement. Hence, STEs must be entities which buy and resell, and not entities which buy for governmental use.[59]

The Understanding on the Interpretation of Art. XVII GATT, adopted during the Uruguay Round, provides some additional clarification. §1 reads:

> governmental and non-governmental enterprises, including marketing boards, which have been granted exclusive or special rights or privileges, including statutory or constitutional powers, in the exercise of which they influence through their purchases or sales the level or direction of imports or exports.

The added value here is that it suffices that STEs influence (as opposed to regulate) the level or direction of imports and exports and that the form regarding their establishment is not prejudged at the WTO level.

Adjudication has confirmed that some egregious cases of state intervention in the trading of particular commodities should be regarded as STEs: the GATT Panel on *Korea—Beef (US)* held that, a producer-controlled import monopoly for beef should be subjected to the discipline of Art. XVII GATT. By the same token, the Canadian Wheat Board, entrusted with the exclusive right to purchase and sell western Canadian wheat for export and human consumption, was considered to be an STE by a WTO Panel (*Canada—Wheat Exports and Grain Imports*). That much nevertheless should be clear since monopolies by definition influence the level or direction of exports and/or imports.

The WTO webpage which reproduces notified entities mentions the following types of STEs:

(a) Statutory marketing boards (also referred to as statutory marketing authorities, or control boards): quite common in the agricultural sector, they often combine a monopoly in international trade and management of domestic production and distribution;

(b) Export marketing boards: these are enterprises which manage exports of domestic goods;

(c) Regulatory marketing boards: they look like statutory marketing boards, except that they do not participate in the conduct of international trade operations;

---

[59] See, on this issue, Blank and Marceau (1997).

(d) Fiscal monopolies: they cover trade in goods for which domestic demand is (relatively speaking) price-inelastic and foreign demand is (relatively speaking) price-elastic, and with respect to which the government has an active public health policy in place (e.g. tobacco, matches, etc.);

(e) Canalizing agencies: developing countries use them in order to channel specific goods particularly to domestic producers;

(f) Foreign trade enterprises: non-market economies (NMEs) often use this term instead of STEs to denote entities entrusted with state trading;

(g) Boards of nationalized industries: to the extent that they get involved in the production/trade of goods, they come under the purview of Art. XVII GATT.

The Working Party on State Trading Enterprises is currently developing a more elaborate (hopefully) illustrative list of STEs. In case of disagreement between two WTO Members as to whether a particular entity should be regarded as STE, it is ultimately WTO adjudicating bodies that will decide on this issue.[60]

Art. XVII.2 GATT requests WTO Members to ensure that their STEs:

(a) Observe the obligation not to discriminate;

(b) Behave in accordance with commercial considerations; and

(c) Afford companies (with respect to their purchases or sales) adequate opportunities to compete.

The question arose in dispute settlement practice, whether obligations (b) and (c) are mere illustrations of the non-discrimination obligation, or, conversely, whether they should be understood as obligations additional to the obligation not to discriminate. This issue was discussed in several Panel reports. The Panel on *Canada—FIRA* held that the obligations embedded in Art. XVII.1(b) GATT are a mere illustration of the non-discrimination obligation (§5.16). As a result, STEs do not incur any obligations additional to the obligation not to discriminate. The Panel on *Korea—Various Measures on Beef* contained a statement that seemed to cast doubt on this view (§7.57):

> A conclusion that the principle of non-discrimination was violated would suffice to prove a violation of Article XVII; similarly, a conclusion that a decision to purchase or buy was not based on 'commercial considerations', would also suffice to show a violation of Article XVII.

Any doubts, however, on this score were put to rest by the AB: in its report on *Canada—Wheat Exports and Grain Imports*, the AB held that the two obligations

---

[60] Indicative lists here are very appropriate since the term 'special privileges' is prone not only to use but also to abuse: would you consider, for example, two economic operators who have received a clearance by a domestic antitrust authority (e.g. their joint venture is cleared, its anti-competitive effects notwithstanding, because it is expected to yield technological advances) as enterprises with special privileges? What if similar practice contravenes all prior practice in this respect? One can reasonably assume that such was not the intent of the drafters, and yet one cannot outright exclude similar transactions from entering the equation.

reflected in Art. XVII.1(b) GATT are a mere illustration of the obligation not to discriminate (§§89–106). As a result, the AB was unwilling to extend its review to any issues beyond claims of discriminatory behaviour (§145):

> The disciplines of Article XVII:1 are aimed at preventing certain types of discriminatory behaviour. We see no basis for interpreting that provision as imposing comprehensive competition-law-type obligations on STEs, as the United States would have us do.[61]

The Panel on *Canada—Wheat Exports and Grain Imports* added that the obligation to not discriminate entails the two distinct obligations to act in accordance with commercial considerations, and to afford adequate opportunities to enterprises of other WTO Members (§6.60); this trend can be traced back to the GATT Panel on *Belgian Family Allowances* (§4):

> As regards the exception contained in paragraph 2 of Article XVII, it would appear that it referred only to the principle set forth in paragraph 1 of that Article, i.e., the obligation to make purchases in accordance with commercial considerations and did not extend to matters dealt with in Article III.[62]

The Interpretative Note ad Art. XVII GATT provides an illustration of a practice that should be considered consonant with the obligation to act solely on commercial considerations:

> A country receiving a 'tied loan' is free to take this loan into account as a 'commercial consideration' when purchasing requirements abroad.

The Panel on *Canada—Wheat Exports and Grain Imports* dealt with a number of claims by the US to the effect that a Canadian STE was not acting in accordance with commercial considerations: the US had claimed that the law required from the relevant Canadian STE (the Canadian Wheat Board) not to sell with the objective of maximizing sales, but with the objective of maximizing profits. Although the first type of behaviour might be viewed as rational, to the US, it was not per se a commercial consideration. Continuing this line of thinking, the US also claimed that Canada should not allow its STE to use its privileges in order to maximize sales. The privileges of the Canadian Wheat Board were:

(a) The exclusive right to purchase and sell western Canadian wheat for export and domestic human consumption;

---

[61] Hoekman and Trachtman (2008) discuss this litigation: in their view, it is not unthinkable that private operators could behave in similar manner to the Canadian STE.

[62] There were a fair number of cases dealing with Art. XVII GATT in the GATT years. Very often, though, Panels had condemned challenged measures under other provisions of the GATT and, exercising judicial economy, did not pronounce on claims under Art. XVII GATT; see, for example, *Canada—FIRA* at §5.16 and *Canada—Provincial Liquor Boards* (*EEC*) at §4.27.

(b) The right to set, subject to government approval, the initial price payable for western Canadian wheat destined for export or domestic human consumption;

(c) The government guarantee of the initial payment to producers of western Canadian wheat;

(d) The government guarantee of its borrowing; and

(e) government guarantees of certain of its credit sales to foreign buyers.

The US added two more claims: the Canadian Wheat Board was acting inconsistently with its obligations because, when selling, it should not be discriminating across markets, and it should not be selling below market rates anyway; the Canadian STE's behaviour was GATT-inconsistent, since it was seeking to maximize revenue and not profit and was, hence, not acting like a private grain trader (a profit-maximizing firm).

The Panel rejected all US claims and arguments in this respect. It took the view that the STE at hand could legitimately use its privilege to the disadvantage of commercial actors (§6.106), that selling below market prices was perfectly legitimate as well (§6.129), and that not selling for its own profit should not be equated with acting without respecting commercial considerations (§6.133). In the view of the Panel (§6.60):

> In our view, the circumstance that STEs are not inherently 'commercial actors' does not necessarily lead to the conclusion that the 'commercial considerations' requirement is intended to make STEs behave like 'commercial' actors. Indeed, we think it should lead to a different conclusion, namely that the requirement in question is simply intended to prevent STEs from behaving like 'political' actors.

And in a footnote it added:

> We use the term 'political actors' here merely to contrast our understanding of the first clause with that of the United States. Non-commercial considerations include, but are not limited to, political considerations.

Following an appeal by the US, the AB had the chance to explain its own understanding of the term 'commercial considerations'. Stating, first, the Panel's understanding of the term (§140), it went on to state that, as long as they do not discriminate, STEs can be deemed to have acted in accordance with commercial considerations and, thus, can make use of their privileges which they do not have to undo in order to be deemed to be acting consistently with Art. XVII GATT (§§146–51).[63]

One can hardly find fault with the AB's analysis, in the sense that it would be rather cavalier to read Art. XVII GATT as requesting from STEs to prepare their own demise. And, yet, something is missing in this picture: making use of the

---

[63] The corresponding provision in EU law is more demanding and is discussed in Mavroidis and Messerlin (1998).

privileges could for example, lead to abusive behaviour; in the absence of world competition law punishing monopolization, similar behaviour could undermine tariff negotiations. The only legal instrument that affected parties can lean on to address similar concerns is NVCs, associated nevertheless with an important burden of persuasion for the complaining parties.[64]

An un-appealed finding of the same Panel (*Canada—Wheat Exports and Grain Imports*) concerns the interpretation of the term 'solely': in the Panel's view, were an STE to make purchases or sales on the following considerations:

(a) The nationality of potential buyers or sellers;
(b) The policies pursued;
(c) Or the national (economic or political) interest of the Member maintaining the STE,

it would not be acting solely in accordance with commercial considerations (§6.88).

In *Canada—Wheat Exports and Grain Imports*, the US had also complained about the practices of the Canadian STE vis-à-vis other enterprises, arguing that it did not afford other companies adequate opportunities to compete and was, thus, in violation of the second clause embedded in Art. XVII.1(b) GATT. The US was arguing that the obligation to afford adequate opportunities to other enterprises to compete extended to cover enterprises in competition with an STE, that is, enterprises which could substitute the STE, as a purchaser or a seller. The Panel had already rejected this claim, and the AB confirmed this finding (§157):

> In other words, the second clause of subparagraph (b) refers to purchases and sales transactions where: (i) one of the parties involved in the transaction is an STE; and (ii) the transaction involves imports to or exports from the Member maintaining the STE. Thus, the requirement to afford an adequate opportunity to compete for participation (*i.e.*, taking part with others) in 'such' purchases and sales (import or export transactions involving an STE) must refer to the opportunity to become the STE's counterpart in the transaction, *not* to an opportunity to replace the STE as a participant in the transaction. If it were otherwise, the transaction would no longer be the type of transaction described by the phrase '*such* purchases or sales' in the second clause of Article XVII:1(b), because it would not involve an STE as a party. Thus, in transactions involving two parties, one of whom is an STE seller, the word 'enterprises' in the second clause of Article XVII:1(b) can refer *only* to buyers. (italics and emphasis in the original)

In §161 it added:

> the panel's findings that the terms 'enterprises of the other Members' in the second clause of paragraph (b) of Article XVII:1 includes 'enterprises interested in buying the products offered for sale by an export STE' but not 'enterprises selling the same

---

64 Petersmann (1991); Bagwell and Staiger (2002).

product as that offered for sale by the export STE in question' (i.e., the competitors of the export STE).

This is probably a warranted interpretation; the question still arises, though, whether the AB's understanding has any teeth: it could, for example, be understood as a mere obligation to make sure that STEs and others participate in a competition, but that the rules of the competition can always favour the STE. This and similar gaps can of course be filled through domestic law, but recall that with respect to domestic instruments the GATT is an instrument of negative integration. There are no signs of STEs fading away and similar concerns will, unavoidably, continue to surface.[65]

The Interpretative Note ad Arts. XI, XII, XIII, XIV, and XVII GATT suggests that STEs should not be used as conduit to circumvent the obligation to impose QRs:

> Throughout Articles XI, XII, XIII, XIV and XVII, the terms 'import restrictions' or 'export restrictions' include restrictions made effective through state-trading operations.

The WTO website (<http://www.wto.org/english/tratop_e/statra_e/statra_e. htm>) mentions one example of a law that would run foul of this provision:

> a law which granted a state trading enterprise exclusive import rights in a certain product, and a decision by that enterprise to refuse to import at all, would appear to be a violation of article XI.

Although it is neither a WTO statute nor a Panel/AB finding,[66] the inclusion of this example on the WTO website strongly supports the view that similar practices would be judged illegal in case of litigation by WTO adjudicating bodies.

The Interpretative Note ad Art. XVII.3 GATT includes a reference to Art. II.4 GATT: this provision requires from WTO Members to ensure that any monopoly in the importation of a product will not result in protection which is on the average in excess of the amount of protection provided for in the relevant schedule of concessions. Art. XVII.4 GATT deals with import monopolies on products which are not subject to concessions in accordance with Art. II GATT: it provides that the WTO Member concerned shall, upon request, provide information on the import mark-up for any given product coming under its purview during a previous representative period.[67]

---

[65] Petersmann (1998) believes that additional regulation is necessary and his proposals are inspired by the corresponding EU regime.

[66] The WTO website is compiled by the WTO Secretariat and its content does not bind subsequent panels. It is, nonetheless, the official WTO website and represents the WTO Secretariat point of view.

[67] Drebentsov and Michalopoulos (1998) discusses STEs in Russia; Wood (1998), STEs in the United States; Sapir (1998b), STEs in the European Union; Matsushita (1998), STEs in Japan; Martin and Bach (1998M), STEs in China; Howse (1998), STEs in Canada. Davey (1998) raises

2.4.3 *Justifying Deviations*

Art. XX(d) GATT explicitly mentions STEs and states that nothing in the GATT shall prevent the adoption of measures necessary to secure compliance, *inter alia*, with laws or regulations relating to the enforcement of STEs.

2.4.4 *Transparency Requirements*

All STEs must be notified to the WTO. But in light of the uncertainty regarding the definition of the term, it is highly likely that (some) notifications are deficient. The Understanding on the Interpretation of Art. XVII GATT (§4) allows for the possibility to cross-notify STEs, but there is no record of cross-notifications so far. To facilitate notifications, the Council for Trade in Goods (CTG) has adopted a series of decisions relating to the periodic notifications requirement that WTO Members must observe.[68]

Further, a Working Party on State Trading Enterprises has been established following the advent of the Understanding on the Interpretation of Art. XVII GATT (§5). This body will review all notifications (and updating of notifications) of STEs; it will meet, at the very least, once a year, and reports to the CTG. It has revised the 1960 Questionnaire (that has been used for notification purposes) and, as stated above, is in the process of elaborating an Illustrative List of STEs. Updating notifications for 1999 and 2000 were received from 47 and 44 Members, respectively. New and full notifications were received from 54 Members for the year 2001 and updating notifications for 2002 and 2003 were received from 42 and 33 Members, respectively. New and full notifications for 2004 and 2006 were received from 34 and 22 Members, respectively.[69] Participation is open to all WTO Members.[70]

3. The Agreement on Textiles and Clothing

3.1 The Legal Discipline and its Rationale

Trade in textiles is now governed by the disciplines discussed in the previous chapters and there is nothing special about it other than that textiles are one of the tariff peaks (goods with high import tariffs). This has not always been the case

---

questions regarding the adequacy of the current disciplines to deal with Chinese and eventually Russian STEs. China has entered the WTO since his paper appeared and the consistency of Chinese STEs with the multilateral rules has been challenged in the SCM context as we saw in Chapter 8. Petersmann (1998) has advanced a very comprehensive set of proposals aimed at disciplining STEs and obliging them to behave like all other economic operators in a given market.

[68] WTO Docs. G/C/M/1, G/STR/N/1, and all subsequent numbers in this series.

[69] WTO Doc. G/L/829 of 10 October 2007. An Annex to this document contains information about all STEs notified so far.

[70] The most recent notifications appear in WTO Doc. G/L/223/Rev. 18 of 9 March 2011 at pp. 66–7.

though: textiles were brought into the multilateral trading system through the WTO Agreement on Textiles and Clothing (ATC), a transitional arrangement aimed at breaking with the past. In previous years, trade in textiles took place outside the GATT disciplines. A separate, textiles-specific agreement was in place, which regulated international trade in textiles and clothing: textile and clothing quotas were negotiated bilaterally and governed by the rules of the Multi-fibre Arrangement, the notorious MFA.[71] The MFA was signed in 1974 between some developed and 31 developing countries, and essentially imposed a worldwide system of bilateral quotas. In fact, even before, that is since 1961, international trade in textiles and clothing had been virtually excluded from the normal rules and disciplines of the GATT. It was governed by a system of discriminatory restrictions, which deviated from the basic GATT principles. The system was first incorporated in a so-called Short-Term Cotton Arrangement (STA), concluded in 1961 for one year, followed by a Long-Term Arrangement (LTA) which was in force from 1962–73. The MFA is the successor arrangement to the LTA.[72] Bagchi (2001) attributes the advent of the MFA to an alliance that Richard Nixon, then candidate for the US Presidency, struck with the US textiles lobby. He quotes (p. 73) the following 1968 speech by candidate Nixon:

> As President my policy will be . . . to assure prompt action to effectively administer the existing Long Term Cotton Textile Agreement. Also, I will promptly take the steps necessary to extend the concept of international trade agreement to all other textile articles involving wool, manmade fibres and blends.

He definitely delivered on his electoral promise. The MFA continued until the WTO Agreements came into effect on 1 January 1995: in fact, the MFA was a four-year arrangement which was renewed at the end in the sense that MFA I was in force from 1974–8, MFA II, 1978–82, etc. MFA IV was supposed to lapse by 1991. However, the impossibility of concluding the Uruguay round by that time led trading partners to renew it so as to ensure a time-wise coincidence between the end of the MFA and the advent of the WTO. It was negotiated because of concerns in developed countries over rising imports.[73] Art. 1 MFA states:

> To achieve the expansion of trade, the reduction of barriers to such trade and the progressive liberalization of world trade in textile products, while at the same time ensuring the orderly and equitable development of this trade and avoidance of disruptive effects in individual markets and on individual lines of production of both importing and exporting countries.

---

[71] For a comprehensive account on the history of MFA, see the very informative discussion in Trebilcock and Howse (2005, pp. 482ff).

[72] Tang (1998) pp. 176ff.

[73] US ITC, The History and Current Status of Multifiber Arrangement, USITC Pub. No. 850 (1978).

The world was divided into textiles-exporting (usually developing) and textiles-importing (usually developed) countries, and it was agreed that the former would be exporting a certain amount of textiles and clothing products to the latter.

The Arrangement could be summarily described as follows: a Textiles Surveillance Body (TSB) was established (Art. 11), composed of a Chairman and eight members (an equal number of delegates from textile-importing and textile-exporting countries). Participants were textiles experts from countries participating in the Arrangement and, consequently, one could legitimately raise doubts as to their impartiality when administering the MFA:[74] the expectation probably was that by appointing delegates from countries with divergent interests, useful and legitimate (e.g. representative) compromises could be reached. The TSB received notifications of all existing QRs, which, if not notified, were deemed contrary to the Arrangement (Art. 2). Notified QRs had to be eliminated, unless, through bilateral negotiations (and agreements), parties agreed to limit trade so as to avoid the risk of market disruption, as defined in Annex A to the Arrangement (sharp increase of imported products offered at prices substantially below those of comparable domestic goods). Agreements had to include 'base levels' and 'growth rates'. It was through similar bilateral agreements that a quota system was imposed on textiles trade. Participants agreed to refrain from introducing new restrictions, unless such action could be justified through recourse to Art. 3: if imports caused market disruption. There was nonetheless no need for injury determination in order to determine whether market disruption existed; contrary to the standard GATT safeguard clause, restrictions could be placed in the presence of difference across domestic prices and prices of imported goods, irrespective of whether the domestic industry was injured at all, never mind the reasons for injury.[75]

A best-endeavours clause was included, to the effect that the interests of developing countries would be taken into account (Art. 6).[76] Disputes regarding the operation of the Arrangement would be brought to the TSB. Participants were free to subsequently take their dispute further and request the establishment of a GATT Panel. In such case, however, the Panel would have to take into account the conclusions of the TSB (Art. 11.10). The TSB would report to the Textiles Committee. The Textiles Committee was established and all participants in the Arrangement had a representative therein. It would receive an annual report from the TSB and oversee the operation of the MFA. The MFA entered into force on 1 January 1974. Gradually, some liberalization occurred: estimates based on 1990 data indicate that close to 11 per cent of world trade in textiles and 35 per cent of world trade in clothing were covered by the MFA. On 1 November 1994, the

[74] Tang (1998) at pp. 180ff.
[75] Low (1993) at pp. 108ff.
[76] The International Textiles and Clothing Bureau (ITCB) was established in the mid-1980s to serve as an antechamber where developing countries could meet and coordinate their policies; see Dickerson (1995) at pp. 379ff.

MFA counted 39 participants, eight of which should be described as 'importers', and of these Austria, Canada, the EU, Finland, Norway, and the US continued to apply restrictions, Japan and Switzerland having dropped them in the meantime.[77] The MFA was a worldwide cartel, where consumers' interests were not represented at all.[78]

Hence, the MFA was, on its face, inconsistent with various GATT rules (including, Art. XI, Art. XIX, and Art. I GATT, since, in practice, the quotas were country-specific). The inconsistency however, was healed by the fact that it benefited from a de facto waiver.[79] The Arrangement Regarding International Trade in Textiles (as is the official title of the MFA) was adopted and published in the BISD Series (21S/3): although no formal waiver was ever requested, GATT contracting parties behaved as if the Arrangement amounted to a de facto waiver, and never challenged its consistency with the multilateral rules.

The MFA was a costly instrument, since consumers were deprived of cheap goods and forced to purchase domestic, expensive substitutes. Cline's (1987, p. 15) estimation of the costs for the US were:

> Total consumer cost of protection amount to $7.6 billion annually in apparel and $2.8 billion in textiles. Total protection preserves 214,200 direct jobs in apparel and 20,700 jobs in textiles.... The consumer cost per job saved is approximately $82,000 in apparel and $135,000 in textiles.

Similar studies saw the light of the day. De Melo and Tarr (1992), for example, estimated that the US could have enjoyed a welfare gain of between $7–15 billion by removing all textiles and apparel quotas. Kathuria et al. (2003) discuss welfare implications for exporters and especially India: it is true that India could capture monopoly rents as a result of the passage of the MFA; gains from export rents though were offset by losses in exports to unrestricted markets and efficiency losses resulting from inability to put resources to their best uses.[80] The economic

---

[77] The Results of the Uruguay Round of Multilateral Trade Negotiations, Market Access for Goods and services: Overview of the Results, The GATT: Geneva, 1994.

[78] Dickerson (1995) at pp. 490ff.

[79] Actually, even the MFA was on occasion judged insufficient by some importing countries: Dickerson (1995, pp. 87ff) discusses the US attempts to move to an even more restrictive regime with the discussion of the 'Jenkins Bill'.

[80] The World Bank has produced a number of studies concerning the welfare implications of the MFA and published them in a series entitled Policy Research Working Papers (2001). The OECD did the same with a collection of papers edited by Navaretti, Faini, and Silberston (1995). Faini et al. (1995) and Faini (1995) start from the premise that it is generally agreed that the arrangements that have regulated trade in textiles and clothing have slowed the natural shift in comparative advantage from industrial countries to developing countries. But there is quite a bit of disagreement about how restrictive the Multi-fibre Agreements (MFA) were. The authors address the potential sources of allocative inefficiency occasioned by the MFA and search for evidence that the MFA indeed led to such inefficiency. In a theoretical section, they identify five sources of inefficiency relating to allocations across countries, across consumers, and among firms within constrained countries. In the empirical part of the paper, they first provide evidence of the restrictiveness of the quota arrangements from trends in import shares for aggregate categories of textiles and clothing, before

evidence and the ensuing case against the MFA is thus overwhelming. Wolf et al. (1984, p. 136) captured it best when they stated:

> The MFA is a monument to diplomatic compromise, political appeasement and bureaucratic obfuscation. A defence can hardly be made in economic terms.

The MFA was eventually replaced in 1995 by the ATC. The ATC[81] was signed along with the other Uruguay round agreements, and replaced the MFA. It was, as explained in more detail *infra*, a transitional agreement aimed at the elimination of existing quotas and the introduction of trade in textiles and clothing into the GATT disciplines. Its basic objective was thus to integrate textiles trade into the multilateral disciplines. During the Uruguay round, in the TNC meeting of April 1989, a decision was taken to this effect. It relevantly read in §2:[82]

> Substantive negotiations will begin in April 1989 in order to reach agreement within the time-frame of the Uruguay Round on modalities for the integration of this sector into GATT, in accordance with the negotiating objective; . . . such modalities for the process of integration into GATT on the basis of strengthened GATT rules and disciplines should inter alia cover the phasing out of restrictions under the Multi-fibre Arrangement

It follows that the objective sought through the enactment of the ATC was to undo the restrictions imposed by the MFA. Art. 1.1 ATC captures this point:

> This Agreement sets out provisions to be applied by Members during a transition period for the integration of the textiles and clothing sector into GATT 1994.

The Panel on *US—Underwear* stated in similar vein (§7.19):

> the overall purpose of the ATC is to integrate the textiles and clothing sector into GATT 1994. Article 1 of the ATC makes this point clear. To this effect, the ATC

---

and during the MFA. They then provide evidence from a detailed examination of quota utilization rates and price differentials among EC importing countries. Among their findings: relatively high utilization rates across exporters suggest a relatively high degree (and stability) of quota bindingness across exporters; overshipment was highest for the most important (by shipment value) products; there is concentration among a few leading exporters (China, Hong Kong, Taiwan, and Thailand) and a few importers (Benelux, Germany, and the United Kingdom). The data suggest a positive correlation between the coefficients of variation in prices and quota utilization rates for China, Hong Kong, and Korea, suggesting that prices are related, as one would expect, to the degree of bindingness; and the data suggest that binding quotas would be associated with higher import prices. Martin and Winters (2001) estimated the gains from the elimination of MFA to be up to $25 billion/year for the European Community and the United States by 2005, but only $2 billion/year for China. In their view, exporting countries might lose, since quotas raise prices that exporters receive, and their elimination would undoubtedly make some exporters worse off. The countries that would lose from the elimination of the MFA were, in the authors' view, those that were allotted larger quotas than they should have been in accordance with their comparative advantage, and those that moved into the production of textiles because of the guaranteed market access through the MFA and not because of their comparative production in producing textiles.

[81] The drafting history of this agreement is explained in detail in Bagchi (2001, pp. 224ff) and Raffaelli and Jenkins (1995); see also Croome (1995).

[82] Raffaelli and Jenkins (1995).

requires notification of all existing quantitative restrictions (Article 2 of the ATC) and provides that they will have to be terminated by the year 2004 (Article 9 of the ATC). The ATC allows adoption of new restrictions in addition to those notified under Article 2 of the ATC for products not yet integrated into GATT 1994 pursuant to Article 2.6 to 2.8 of the ATC only exceptionally and in accordance with the relevant provisions of the ATC or in accordance with the relevant provisions of GATT 1994.[83]

WTO Members agreed to notify the newly established Textiles Monitoring Body (TMB) of their quotas and abolish them within ten years, that is, by 1 January 2005. Art. 9 ATC underscores the transitional character of the TMB, which has also ceased to exist as of 1 January 2005. After that date, it is only through tariffs that textiles goods are protected.[84]

3.2 The Coverage of the Legal Discipline

3.2.1 Product Coverage

Art. 1.7 ATC explains that the product coverage of the ATC is elaborated in the Annex to the Agreement. The Annex includes the relevant HS classifications at the six-digit level (Chapters 51–63, and some products in Chapters 30–49 and 64–96), and also states a list of products on which no transitional safeguard can be imposed.

3.2.2 The ATC in a Nutshell

The ATC imposes two main obligations:

(a) To integrate textiles trade into the multilateral rules within a predefined calendar; and
(b) To avoid introducing any new restrictions, unless by respecting the strict conditions embedded in Art. 6 ATC.

Besides these two obligations, the ATC:

(a) Requests from exporting WTO Members to continue to administer their restrictions;
(b) Includes anti-circumvention provisions; and
(c) Assigns to the TMB the responsibility to administer the Agreement.

3.2.3 Integrating Textiles Trade into the Multilateral Disciplines

The integration process is explained in Art. 2 ATC: WTO Members must integrate the products listed in the Annex into the rules of GATT over a ten-year period.

---

[83] The AB in this case, as well as the Panel on *US—Cotton Yarn* (§7.73), went so far as to state that the MFA was not a legal context, in the VCLT sense of the term, for the interpretation of the ATC.

[84] Deardorff and Stern (1998, pp. 20ff) attempt a quantification of the barriers resulting from MFA and show how high protection was during the MFA years.

This will be carried out progressively in three periods. All covered products must have been integrated into the GATT rules at the end of the ten-year period.[85]

The first period began on 1 January 1995, with the integration of products representing not less than 16 per cent of Members' total 1990 imports (of all products included in the product coverage appearing in the Annex); the second period began on 1 January 1998, and WTO Members undertook the obligation to integrate a further 17 per cent (of the same total); the third period started on 1 January 2002, and a further 18 per cent (of the same total) was integrated. On 1 January 2005, all remaining products (amounting to 49 per cent of the same total) were integrated, and the ATC, as a result, ceased to exist. WTO Members enjoyed substantial discretion with respect to the products that they would be integrating in each of the three periods. All existing restrictions had to be notified, however; otherwise they could not benefit from the transitional regime included in the ATC. The restrictions notified were assumed to correspond to the totality of existing restrictions: Art. 2.4 ATC made clear that WTO Members could not enter any new restrictions, unless in conformity with the multilateral rules (essentially, by invoking the safeguard mechanism included in Art. 6 ATC). The Panel on *Turkey—Textiles* explicitly acknowledged this understanding of the integration process (§§9.68–9). In this vein, it held that, since Turkey had notified no restrictions, it could not introduce any new ones, unless in conformity with the ATC and other relevant GATT provisions. Turkey thus could either invoke Art. 6 ATC or another appropriate GATT provision, like Art. XXIV, to this effect, though it would have to comply with the requirements included in this provision (§9.78).

The MFA growth rates were increased on 1 January 1995 by a factor of 16 per cent for the first period, and the new growth rate was applied annually. The growth rate for the first period was then increased by 25 per cent for the second period (starting on 1 January 1998), and was further increased by 27 per cent for the third, and last, period, beginning on 1 January 2002.

3.2.4 Special Transitional Safeguard Mechanism

Art. 6 ATC protects a WTO Member against surges in imports during the transition period from products which had not yet been integrated into GATT and which were not already under quota, if, as a result of a surge, its domestic industry producing the like product had been damaged. A WTO Member wishing to invoke this provision had to:

(a) Determine that total imports of a specific product were causing serious damage, or actual threat thereof, to its domestic industry; and
(b) Decide to which individual Member(s) this serious damage could be attributed.

---

[85] Das (2001, pp. 104ff) offers a concise description of the ATC.

The purpose of the special transitional safeguard mechanism was explained in the Panel report on *US—Underwear* (§§7.23–4):

> The overall purpose of Article 6 of the ATC is to give Members the possibility to adopt new restrictions on products not already integrated into GATT 1994 pursuant to Article 2.6 to 2.8 of the ATC and not under existing restrictions, i.e., not notified under Article 2.1 of the ATC. Article 6 of the ATC, in our view, establishes a three-step approach which has to be followed for a new restriction to be imposed.

The interested WTO Member had then to seek consultations with the exporting Member(s). Safeguard measures could be applied on a selective, country-by-country basis, irrespective of whether or not an agreement had been reached (between the importing and the exporting Members) within a 60-day consultation process. The quota imposed could not be lower than the actual level of imports for the exporting country during a recent reference period (12 months); safeguard measures could remain in place for up to three years. If, however, a safeguard measure was in place for over a year, the growth rate should be at least 6 per cent. WTO Members were required to notify the TMB if they wished to retain the right to use the special transitional safeguard mechanism (Art. 6.1 ATC). Fifty-five WTO Members chose to retain this right and most of them provided lists of products for integration. Nine WTO Members, namely, Australia, Brunei Darussalam, Chile, Cuba, Hong Kong, Iceland, Macau, New Zealand, and Singapore decided not to maintain the right to use the special transitional safeguard mechanism. The special safeguard was invoked on 24 occasions in 1995 (all of them by the US); eight times in 1996 (seven times by Brazil, once by the US); twice in 1997 (both times by the US); and ten times in 1998 (nine times by Colombia , once by the US).

Safeguard measures could be invoked because an import surge had caused, or because it threatened to cause, damage. The Panel on *US—Underwear* explained that the two notions were distinct, and that consequently a separate type of analysis was required in order to demonstrate damage or threat of damage. The facts of the case were as follows: on 27 March 1995, the US had requested consultations with Costa Rica on trade in cotton and man-made fibre underwear under Art. 6.7 ATC. At the same time, the US provided Costa Rica with a Statement of Serious Damage, dated March 1995 (the 'March Statement'), on the basis of which it had proposed the introduction of a restraint on imports of underwear from Costa Rica. Notice of the request for consultations, the proposed restraint, and the proposed restraint level was published in the US Federal Register on 21 April 1995. Consultations were held, but the US and Costa Rica failed to negotiate a mutually acceptable settlement. The US subsequently invoked Art. 6.10 ATC and introduced a transitional safeguard measure in respect of cotton and man-made fibre underwear imports from Costa Rica on 23 June 1995. The measure was, by its terms, to be valid for a period of 12 months, effective from 27 March 1995 (i.e. the date of the request for consultations). The TMB found that the US had failed to demonstrate serious damage to its domestic industry: it did not reach consensus on the existence of an actual threat of serious damage though, and similarly (because of lack of consensus), the TMB also failed to make public its findings on the effective date of application of the US restraint. Accordingly, the TMB recommended that the US and Costa Rica hold further consultations with a view to resolving the matter. In the absence of any settlement, the parties reverted to the TMB, which confirmed its earlier findings and considered its review of the matter complete. Although further consultations took place between the US and Costa Rica in November 1995, no agreement was reached. In December 1995, Costa Rica invoked the dispute settlement provisions. One of the questions before the Panel was whether a separate analysis was required for a finding of damage and/or threat of damage. The Panel rejected the US argument that no separate analysis was required (§7.55).[86] The Panel further rejected the US argument that it had acted consistently with its obligations under the ATC, when it established that damage had indeed occurred. In its view, the US analysis suffered from serious weaknesses, since it was predicated on a review of the situation of:

> only one or two companies of indeterminate size or market share out of an industry consisting of 395 establishments. (§7.45).

However, the Panel refrained from making a finding on this point of law. It found that the factors listed in Art. 6.3 ATC did not provide sufficient and exclusive guidance and the Panel was therefore not in a position to conclude that the US had failed to demonstrate serious damage or actual threat thereof.

Damage or threat of damage has to be suffered by the domestic industry producing the like and/or directly competitive product (Art. 6.2 ATC). The interpretation of the term 'like and/or directly competitive product' was discussed in the Panel and AB report on *US—Cotton Yarn*. On 24 December 1998, the US filed a request for bilateral consultations with Pakistan, pursuant to Art. 6.7 ATC, on its proposed safeguard measure. The US attached to this request its Report of Investigation and Statement of Serious Damage or Actual Threat Thereof: Combed Cotton Yarn for Sale: Category 301 (December 1998) (the 'Market Statement'), which formed the basis for the proposed safeguard measure. The Market Statement set out the results of the investigation of the conditions prevailing in the US market for yarn. It defined the domestic industry and concluded that increased imports had caused serious damage, and actual threat thereof, to the domestic industry, and that this damage and threat were attributable to Pakistan. The US held bilateral consultations with Pakistan in February

---

[86] Recall, however, our discussions in Chapter 7 that subsequently, in the case law concerning contingent protection, WTO adjudicating bodies adopted the opposite point of view, that is, that the same facts can be used to support findings of threat of injury and also of injury, without imposing a requirement for separate analysis.

1999, which did not result in a mutually agreed solution. Subsequently, the US imposed the transitional safeguard measure at issue in this dispute in the form of a quantitative restriction on Category 301 imports of yarn from Pakistan. The safeguard measure was made effective for one year as of 17 March 1999, and was extended twice, each time for one further year, effective 17 March 2000 and 17 March 2001, respectively. The TMB reviewed the matter, pursuant to Arts. 6.10 and 8.10 ATC, in April and June 1999. The TMB concluded on both occasions that the US had not demonstrated successfully that yarn was being imported into its territory in such increased quantities as to cause serious damage, or actual threat thereof, to its domestic industry producing the like and/or directly competitive product. Accordingly, the TMB recommended that the safeguard measure introduced by the US on imports of yarn from Pakistan be rescinded. On 6 August 1999, the US informed the TMB that it believed its action was justified under the provisions of Art. 6 ATC, and that it would maintain the safeguard measure. The US and Pakistan held a further round of consultations in November 1999, but failed to reach a mutually agreed solution. On 3 April 2000, Pakistan requested the establishment of a Panel. One of the questions before the Panel was whether captive consumption should be excluded from the definition of the industry producing the like product, as the US had argued. The AB rejected the US argument, while explaining at the same time its understanding of the like product analysis (§§99–101):

> We will now examine whether, in this case, yarn produced by the vertically integrated fabric producers of the United States for their own captive consumption is directly competitive with the imported yarn for the purposes of Article 6.2 of the *ATC*. The United States argues that such yarn is not directly competitive because it is not offered for sale on the market except when the captive production is 'out of balance', and even then only in *de minimis* quantities. In addition, vertically integrated fabric producers are not dependent on the merchant market for meeting any of their requirements of yarn except to a *de minimis* extent. In the United States' view, these factors are clearly reflected in the very low and stable rate of yarn sold or purchased by vertically integrated fabric producers to or from the merchant market over the last several years.
>
> We are unable to subscribe to this static view which makes the competitive relationship between yarn sold on the merchant market and yarn used for internal consumption by vertically integrated producers dependent on what they choose to do at a particular point in time.
>
> If the competitive relationship between the two products is properly considered, it will be clear that they are 'directly competitive' within the meaning of that term in Article 6.2. (italics in the original)

The attribution of damage to a particular country (Art. 6.4 ATC) is the last step for lawful imposition of transitional safeguard under the ATC: it requires an assessment that an import surge caused injury to the domestic industry producing the like product. The AB held as much in its report on *US—Cotton Yarn* (§§112–15). Total damage (or threat thereof) must be attributed proportionately to the exporting WTO Member, that is, in accordance with the damage caused by its exports to a given (importing) market (AB, *US—Cotton Yarn*, §119). The AB acknowledged that the attribution analysis could be done in various ways. Art. 6.4 ATC provided some information concerning the elements (levels of imports, market share, prices, etc.) that had to be taken into account in the context of this analysis. For the rest, case law added that the investigating authority of the importing state must perform a comparative analysis, whereby it would compare the effects of imports from various sources (§§122–3, *US—Cotton Yarn*, AB). The requirement to perform comparative analysis was echoed by the Panel on *US—Underwear* (§7.49).

The WTO Member proposing to take safeguard action had to request consultations with the affected Members, informing them about the results of its investigation (Art. 6.7 ATC). The request for consultations (as well as all relevant factual information regarding the investigation process) had to be communicated to the Chairman of the TMB. If parties reached an agreement, they had to communicate it to the TMB (Art. 6.8 ATC). Details of the agreement had to be communicated to the TMB (Art. 6.9 ATC); even in the absence of an agreement, though, a WTO Member could, nonetheless, go ahead and apply a safeguard (Art. 6.10 ATC). In this case, either the importing or the affected Member(s) could refer the matter to the TMB and request that it reviews the matter. The TMB should promptly examine the matter and make appropriate recommendations to the Members concerned (Art. 6.11 ATC).

Art. 6.10 ATC allowed WTO Members to impose safeguards within 30 days following the 60-day consultation period. Art. 3.5(i) MFA states that the restraint could be instituted:

> for the twelve-month period beginning on the day when the request was received by the participating exporting country or countries.

The question arose whether the importing state could retroactively impose safeguards at that stage: Costa Rica argued that the US had retroactively applied restrictions in violation of Art. 6.10 ATC; restrictions were introduced on 23 June 1995 for a period of 12 months starting on 27 March 1995, which was the date of the request for consultations under Art. 6.7 ATC. Thus, the question before the Panel was whether the ATC should be interpreted as prohibiting a practice which was explicitly recognized under the MFA, and if so, what should be the appropriate date from which the restraint period is to be calculated under the ATC. The AB, having dismissed the relevance of MFA as a context for the ATC as we saw *supra*, held in its report on *US—Underwear* that WTO Members should not be imposing safeguards in retroactive manner (p. 14):

> we believe that, in the absence of an express authorization in Article 6.10, *ATC*, to backdate the effectivity of a safeguard restraint measure, a presumption arises from the very text of Article 6.10 that such a measure may be applied only prospectively.

The Panel on *US—Underwear* held that a violation of Art. 6 ATC amounted *ipso facto* to a violation of Art. 2.4 ATC (§7.71).

3.2.5 Obligations of WTO Members during the Transition Period

The ATC entrusted exporting WTO Members with the responsibility to administer the restrictions during the transition period. Any changes in practices, rules, or procedures were subject to consultations with a view to reaching mutually acceptable solutions (Art. 4 ATC). Art. 5 ATC contained the rules and procedures concerning circumvention of the quotas through trans-shipment, re-routing, false declaration of origin, or falsification of official documents. WTO Members should establish the necessary legal provisions and/or administrative procedures to address and take action against circumvention. When sufficient evidence was available, possible recourse might have included the denial of entry of goods.

3.2.6 Institutional Arrangements: The TMB

The TMB was the successor to the TSB. It was composed of delegates from both exporting and importing countries and had the power to recommend ways to end disputes brought to its attention (Arts 8.8–10 of the ATC).[87]

The TMB was established to supervise the implementation of the ATC and to examine all measures taken under it, to ensure that they were in conformity with the rules. It was a quasi-judicial, standing body, and consisted of a Chairman and ten members, discharging their function on an *ad personam* basis, and taking all decisions by consensus: participation in the TMB was a function of criteria similar to those guiding participation in the TSB: representativeness of the WTO Membership; proportionate participation of textiles-importing as well as of textiles-exporting WTO Members.

Recall that the TMB would be notified of all restrictions and requested to pronounce on their consistency with the ATC. The question arose in practice whether Panels were bound by the TMB recommendations or whether they were free to decide the issue: in its report on *Turkey—Textiles*, the Panel held that some deference to the TMB was appropriate, but underlined that it was not bound by its recommendations (§§9.85):

> We consider, based on the interpretation by the Appellate Body in *Guatemala—Cement* with regard to the relationship between the DSU and the Antidumping Agreement, that the provisions of the ATC (providing jurisdiction to the TMB to examine measures applied pursuant to the ATC) and the provisions of the DSU (providing jurisdiction for panels to interpret any covered agreement, including the ATC) may both apply together. Therefore even if the TMB has jurisdiction to determine what constitutes a 'new' measure in the sense of the ATC and whether a violation of the ATC has taken place, we remain convinced that a panel is entitled to interpret the ATC to the extent necessary to ascertain whether Turkey benefits from

---

[87] Tang (1998) at pp. 187ff.

a defence to India's claims under Articles XI and XIII of GATT based on the provisions of the ATC.

The TMB ceased to exist at the end of the transitional period envisaged in the ATC, that is, as of 1 January 2005.

4. Beyond the Uruguay Round

Agriculture: At the end of the Uruguay round, the WTO Secretariat prepared a study where the results of the Uruguay round were reported.[88] Tables 11.3 and 11.4 are based on information included in this study. Table 11.3 presents the average bound duty on farm goods in selected WTO Members and the percentage of all tariff lines that are considered tariff peaks: there is nothing like a standard definition of this term, but according to this study, bound tariffs beyond 15 per cent are considered tariff peaks. Table 11.4 reflects the tariff peaks in the EU and US and presents information regarding the number of tariff lines that are subjected to bound duties between 15–25 per cent, 25–50 per cent, 50–100 per cent, and more than 100 per cent.

Against this background, it is easier to grasp why there is an observed low utilization rate of TRQs in farm goods, and consequently why minimum market access opportunities have not proved very meaningful: the in-quota rate is on many occasions high.

Table 11.3 Level of bound duties on farm products

	Average bound rate	Percentage of tariff peaks
Brazil	35.2%	96%
EU	20%	33.9%
India	101%	99.4%
Switzerland	46.9%	16.5%
US	9%	2.6%

Table 11.4 EU and US tariff peaks

	15–25%	25–50%	50–100%	<100%
EU	10.8%	8.9%	4.1%	0.8%
US	3.4%	1.6%	0.3%	0.5%

[88] Market Access Unfinished Business, Post Uruguay Round Inventory, the WTO: Geneva (2001).

Intervention in the farm sector has been justified on various grounds, and we referred to some of these *supra*.[89] Some of them, like self-sufficiency, are hard to justify in a world where farm production exists everywhere in the world and the chances for cartelized practices are negligible if not totally non-existent. Other claims are more meritorious: price volatility has been raised as a reason for intervention and the introduction of stabilization schemes that take the form of reference or intervention prices. The validity of these claims depends on various issues: 'wealthy' farmers in the North would suffer less from price volatility than their counterparts in the developing world; the social safety net in other words can absorb part if not the totality of the shock. Gilbert (2006) goes one step further: he checks the historic record on price volatility of farm commodities and concludes that the emerging picture is not as straightforward as it often appears in literature. True, there are cases where volatility can be established (even high volatility), but the time span of the observation might have a lot do with the end conclusions. He does stress, however, that vulnerability for producers of weak economies is not necessarily a function of volatility. In his view, there should be less talk of the volatility issue and more about the fact that some countries have not managed to move to production of other more remunerative activities. This type of argument, though, leads to a wider discussion regarding economic policy which escapes the narrow framework of a trade agreement.

Then there is the argument that farm production is multifunctional and, hence, any negotiation should control for this characteristic. It is difficult to establish that this is an idiosyncratic feature of farm production: for instance, why do we need farm production to keep farmers in the countryside and not another form of production, say a car plant? And at any rate, if the objective is to protect the environment, then subsidies would be decoupled, and normally come under the blue box.

During the Doha round negotiations, some of these arguments resurfaced and were renegotiated.[90] At the moment of writing, and in light of the overall uncertainty regarding the future of the round,[91] it is impossible to predict the end result. It is nevertheless quite clear that the overall structure of the AG Agreement will not undergo changes and, consequently, that farm trade will continue to be liberalized along the lines agreed in 1994.

Textiles: At the end of the Uruguay round, tariff protection replaced the previously existing quotas. Negotiations were held across the trading partners and, following initial offers, they managed to agree on the level of binding for their

---

[89] Trebilcock (2011, pp. 100ff) offers a brief and concise discussion on this issue.
[90] McMahon (2011) offers a very comprehensive analysis of all these issues.
[91] WTO Doc. WT/MIN(11)/5 of 18 November 2011.

Table 11.5 EU and US average and maximum bound tariffs on textiles goods

	Average	Maximum
EU	6.5%	12%
US	7.9%	40%

Table 11.6 Bound and applied duties on textiles products (2006)

	Bound (average)	Applied (average)
China	9.7%	9.7%
EU	6.6%	6.6%
Pakistan	23.3%	16.4%
India	31.4%	20.2%
US	7.9%	7.9%

Source: The World Tariff Profiles 2006: the WTO, Geneva.

tariffs, while doing away with existing quantitative restrictions.[92] Compared to other goods, textiles' tariffs can be characterized as peaks. Table 11.5 is based on information extracted from the 2001 WTO Study referred to above.

The transitional period has by now lapsed, and the ATC no longer exists. WTO Members have unilaterally liberalized tariff protection (by applying duties lower than their bound rates) and are in the process of negotiating lower tariff protection in the Doha round. The average bound and applied tariffs for all textiles products in 2006 for China, the EU, Pakistan, India, and the US are as shown in Table 11.6.

According to the 2007 World Trade Report (WTO: Geneva), the (volume) share of world textiles exports for the EU fell from 35.6 per cent in 2000 to 32.6 per cent in 2006, but the EU continued to be the world's largest textiles exporter. The numbers for China were: 4.6 per cent (1980), 6.9 per cent (1990), 10.2 per cent (2000), and 22.3 per cent (2006). The numbers for the US were: 6.8 per cent (1980), 4.8 per cent (1990), 6.9 per cent (2000), and 5.8 per cent (2006). The numbers for India were: 2.4 per cent (1980), 2.1 per cent (1990), 3.8 per cent (2000), and 4.3 per cent (2006). Finally, the numbers for Pakistan for the same period were: 1.6 per cent, 2.6 per cent, 2.9 per cent, and 3.4 per cent. On the import side, the numbers for the EU were 32.9 per cent (2000) and 30.7 per cent (2006), its enlargement from 15 to 25 countries during that period notwithstanding. The numbers for the US were: 4.2 per cent (1980), 6.2 per cent (1990), 9.5 per cent (2000), and 10.2 per cent (2006). For the same period, the numbers for

---

[92] See, for example, the offer from Finland, GATT Doc. MTN.GNG/NG1/W/53 of 17 October 1990; Israel, GATT Doc. MTN.GNG/NG1/W/65 of 30 November 1990; Norway, GATT Doc. MTN.GNG/NG1/W/57 of 23 October 1990; Sweden, GATT Doc. MTN.GNG/NG1/W/49 of 17 October 1990.

China were: 1.9 per cent, 4.9 per cent, 7.6 per cent, 7.1 per cent; for India: 0.1 per cent, 0.2 per cent, 0.3 per cent, 0.9 per cent.

World trade in textiles is thus changing drastically, with China becoming a major force. Note that China joined the WTO in 2001. It is the remarkable ascension of China in the textiles market that prompted other textiles exporters to rethink their strategy, which was in favour of total dismantlement of the MFA.[93] Nevertheless, as things stand, they cannot block Chinese exports to third markets, but only to their own: textiles trade has now been fully integrated into the multilateral disciplines and those affected by the rise in Chinese export trade can have recourse to contingent protection only.

---

[93] Raffaelli (1998) had the prescience to suggest that maybe some exporting nations would be requiring separate negotiation to address issues posed by the growth of Chinese textiles exports.

12

GOVERNMENT PROCUREMENT

1. The Legal Discipline and its Rationale

The signatories to the Agreement on Government Procurement (GPA) commit that certain (governmental, non-governmental) entities, which they have included in their lists of concessions, will purchase on a non-discriminatory basis from suppliers originating in other signatories: the GPA covers cases where governments buy, but not with the intention to resell. Accordingly, the GPA should be distinguished from state trading (Art. XVII GATT).

There are undisputed gains from trade liberalization in the government procurement market: although the importance of the government procurement market tends to be overstated sometimes,[1] it is far from negligible, as various contributions in Hoekman and Mavroidis (1997) demonstrate.[2] A 2001 OECD

---

[1] According to the WTO DG, the new GPA package agreed in the Doha round would result in gains in market access of between $80–100 billion annually, but this of course depends on a number of parameters that are unknown or relatively little known at this moment. It is, of course, only natural that the DG should opt for a high number in an effort to persuade trading nations to join the GPA; see WTO Doc. WT/MIN(11)/5 of 18 November 2011 at p. 6.

[2] See, for example, Francois et al. (1997), who calculate the welfare implications of liberalization in the GP market for the US.

study[3] shows that, on average, the size of the government procurement market (besides defence-related spending and compensation to employees) for all OECD Members is roughly 7.57 per cent of their national incomes. The WTO webpage calculates it at $1.6 trillion for 2008.

Why, then, did countries not liberalize unilaterally before the advent of the GPA? Evenett and Hoekman (2007) have pointed to the prevalence in the late 1940s of the Keynesian idea that an increase in national income due to a rise in government expenditure was greater, the smaller the share of goods produced outside the country. Thus, it was originally decided that government procurement would not be part of the GATT disciplines.[4]

Over the years, government procurement became a formidable weapon at the disposal of national industrial policy. It is remarkable that even serious integration initiatives, such as the EU, could not easily tame the will of governments to restrict this market to local suppliers only. Messerlin's study (2001) of the EU market (see Table 12.1) shows that in the wake of the great expansion of the EU from 15 to 25 and then to 27 Member States, its government procurement market was largely

Table 12.1 Government procurement in EU countries (EU-15)

Country	€bn
Austria	17.6
Belgium-Luxembourg	8.8
United Kingdom	97.3
Denmark	9.8
Finland	8.8
France	85.9
Germany	179.8
Greece	4.9
Ireland	3.0
Italy	56.4
Netherlands	16.6
Portugal	6.3
Spain	29.5
Sweden	22.7
EU-15	547.4

Source: Messerlin (2001).

---

[3] OECD (2001), 'The Size of Government Procurement Markets', the OECD, Paris, available at <http://www.oecd.org/dataoecd/34/14/18845927.pdf>. Note that the OECD study refers to the contestable market, that is, the part of the government procurement market that is open to foreign bidders and not to the overall market which could be substantially higher.

[4] We still lack a theoretical paper that discusses the possibility of understanding commitments under the GPA through the lens of the terms of trade. And yet there are some reasons to believe that this could be the case: the two main procurement markets negotiating in the context of the GPA (EU, US) are quite symmetric, and reciprocity of market access commitments is an important consideration in the negotiations. On this last point, see Anderson (2011), and WTO Committee on Government Procurement, Modalities for the Negotiations on Extension of Coverage and Elimination of Discriminatory Measures and Practices, WTO Doc. WT/GPA/79 of 19 July 2004.

segmented, with national champions dominating national markets. In similar vein, the 'Buy American Act' included formal margins of preference in favour of domestic suppliers.[*]

Anderson et al. (2011c) have estimated that the accession of the five BRICS countries (Brazil, China, India, Russia, and South Africa) to the GPA would, by itself, add in the range of $233–596 billion annually to the current value of the government procurement market.[5] The gains from participation in the GPA are not limited though to simply the price gap between procuring goods from a productive foreign company as opposed to procuring them from an unproductive domestic company. Anderson (2007) correctly holds that:

> work on public procurement in the WTO—particularly, the Agreement on Government Procurement—is consistent with, and reinforces, the objectives of national reforms aimed at promoting competition, transparency and enhanced value for money in national procurement regimes. In this regard, the contribution of the GPA should not be seen solely in terms of facilitating international market access; the Agreement can also make an important contribution to good governance.

Eventually, first in the Tokyo round and then in a more meaningful way in the Uruguay round, trading nations agreed to take the first steps towards liberalization of their procurement markets.[6] The main discipline imposed through the GPA is non-discrimination when committed entities purchase goods. Absent the GPA, discrimination was of course legally possible: by virtue of Art. III.8 GATT, Members are not bound by the NT obligation with respect to government purchasing. By the same token, Art. XIII GATS excludes national treatment from government procurement in the services sector. Signatories to the GPA, consequently, have brought, with respect to their list of covered entities, government procurement back into the realm of national treatment. There were questions asked regarding the legal relevance of MFN in the GP context: the issue is whether, in the absence of a paragraph equivalent to Art. III.8 GATT in the body of Art. I GATT, WTO Members should still observe MFN with respect to public purchasing. Assuming an affirmative response to this question, any time a WTO Member granted an advantage to a GPA signatory, it would have to extend it to all WTO Members, irrespective of whether they were GPA signatories or not. The Panel on *EC—Commercial Vessels* held that this should not be the case. Looking into the negotiating history of the relevant legal instruments, it concluded that, with respect to government procurement, GATT contracting parties aimed to introduce a caveat from both the MFN obligation as well as the national treatment obligation (§§7.85–7):

---

[*] 41 USC §§10a–10c (1976). The regulations which implemented the federal Buy American Act established a 6 per cent margin of preference, 41 CFR §1–1.18–603–1 (1977); see also Graham (1979).

[5] In the same vein, see the results in Chen and Whalley (2011).

[6] Arrowsmith (2002).

In support of its reading of 'all matters referred to in paragraphs 2 and 4 of Article III', Korea argues that this phrase was inserted during the Geneva Session of the ITO Preparatory Committee in 1947 in order to extend the grant of MFN treatment to all matters dealt with in those paragraphs regardless of whether national treatment is provided for in respect of such matters. We note in this respect that during that session of the ITO Preparatory Committee the United States made a proposal to amend the text of what was then draft Article 14 (general most-favoured-nation treatment) of the ITO Charter by replacing the phrase 'with respect to all matters in regard to which national treatment is provided for in Article 15' (national treatment) with 'with respect to all matters referred to in paragraphs 1,2,3, and 4 of Article 15'.

... At the time the United States made this proposal, paragraph 5 of Article 15, which eventually became paragraph 8 of Article 18 of the Havana Charter and of Article III of the GATT, provided that the national treatment obligations would not apply to government procurement.... Therefore, we fail to see how this... can support the position taken by Korea in this dispute that a measure expressly removed from the scope of the national treatment obligation in Article III can nevertheless be among the 'matters referred to in paragraphs 2 and 4 of Article III'.

It is noteworthy in this regard that in a discussion on draft Article 18.8(a) of the Havana Charter corresponding to Article III:8(a), it was observed at a meeting in February 1948 that:

'... the Sub-Committee had considered that the language of paragraph 8 would except from the scope of Article 18 [national treatment] and hence from Article 16 [MFN treatment], laws, regulations and requirements governing purchases effected for governmental purposes where resale was only incidental ...'.

This clearly suggests that negotiators understood that the reference to government procurement in Article 18.8(a) would also apply in the context of the MFN clause (Article 16).

Thus the relevant drafting history that we are aware of shows that the exclusion of government procurement from the national treatment article would also apply to the MFN clause. (emphasis in the original)

2. The Coverage of the Legal Discipline

2.1 A Plurilateral Agreement

The GPA is one of the four original plurilateral agreements. As a result, the GPA is binding only upon those WTO Members which have adhered to it. The WTO GPA is not the first agreement in this area; it is a successor agreement to the Tokyo round GPA.[7] According to the Agreement Establishing the WTO (Art. XII.3), participation in a plurilateral agreement shall be governed by the provisions of each such agreement. Art. XXIV.2 GPA reserves the right to participate in the GPA to WTO Members only. The modalities of the accession procedures are reflected in a WTO document prepared to this effect:[8] a Working Party will be established

---

[7] On the history of GPA, see Blank and Marceau (1997).
[8] WTO Doc. WTO/GPA/1, Annex 2.

where all signatories will participate and discuss the terms of accession for the acceding country; at the end of negotiations, a (final) report will be submitted to the GPA Committee,[9] which will decide by consensus on the request for accession.

2.2 The GPA Membership

The following WTO Members are signatories to the GPA: Armenia,[10] Canada, Chinese Taipei,[11] the EU,[12] Hong Kong, China, Iceland, Israel, Japan, Korea, Liechtenstein, Netherlands with respect to Aruba, Norway, Singapore, Switzerland, the US. The GPA is dominated by developed countries. Armenia and Chinese Taipei emerge as the only developing countries that have joined the GPA so far. This much was probably anticipated by the framers of the WTO, and this is probably why, to encourage participation by developing countries, Art. V.3 GPA provides:

> With a view to ensuring that developing countries are able to adhere to this Agreement on terms consistent with their development, financial and trade needs, the objectives listed in paragraph 1 shall be duly taken into account in the course of negotiations with respect to the procurement of developing countries to be covered by the provisions of this Agreement. Developed countries, in the preparation of their coverage lists under the provisions of this Agreement, shall endeavour to include entities procuring products and services of export interest to developing countries.

There are other provisions as well which are meant to encourage participation of developing countries to the GPA: Art. V (Special and Differential Treatment), for example, contains a number of best-endeavours clauses calling on GPA signatories to take into account the need of developing countries to safeguard their balance-of-payments position; to promote the establishment of domestic industries; to support their industrial units; and to encourage their development through arrangements among developing countries. Mattoo (1997) advances a series of good reasons explaining why developing countries have so far refused to join: many of them might, on occasion, be requested to pay supra-competitive prices since, because of the 'smallness' of their market, they might not be attracting enough competitors when issuing tenders and those participating might have a strong incentive to collude. It is true that participation in the GPA, under certain assumptions, might help WTO Members to induce pro-competitive behaviour; it

---

[9] Each signatory has a delegate participating in the GPA Committee. An indicative time frame for accession negotiations has been agreed (WTO Doc. GPA/W/109/Rev. 2). The GPA Committee has also agreed on a checklist of issues for the provision of information by the applicant governments (WTO Doc. GPA/35).

[10] Armenia joined the GPA on 15 September 2011.

[11] On 9 December 2008, the Committee on Government Procurement adopted a decision inviting Chinese Taipei to accede to the plurilateral agreement—ending their accession negotiations. Chinese Taipei finally joined the GPA on 15 July 2009.

[12] On the enlargement of the EU from 15 to 25 and the corresponding accession of its ten new Members to the GPA, see WTO Doc. GPA/78 of 4 May 2004; on the enlargement of the EU from 25 to 27 (accession of Bulgaria and Romania to the GPA), see WTO Doc. GPA/90 of 11 December 2006.

should not, nevertheless, be considered to be a perfect substitute for effective competition laws.[13] The reasons for not joining are not necessarily the same across WTO Members. Wang (2011), for example, goes so far as to suggest lack of political momentum in China in favour of accession to the WTO in light of the difficulty in measuring the pros and the cons, the commitment to join in the Chinese Protocol of Accession notwithstanding. Chakravarthy and Dawar (2011) argue that political economy explains India's reluctance.

Albania, China, Georgia, Jordan, the Kyrgyz Republic, Moldova, Oman, and Panama are formally in the process of acceding to the GPA. None of them, nonetheless, has, at the moment of writing (April 2012), acceded to the GPA. A further six WTO Members have provisions in their respective Protocols of Accession to the WTO regarding accession to the GPA: Armenia, Croatia, the Former Yugoslav Republic of Macedonia, Mongolia, and Saudi Arabia.[14] Twenty-one WTO Members have observer status in the GPA Committee: Albania, Argentina, Australia, Bahrain, Cameroon, Chile, China, Colombia, Croatia, Georgia, Jordan, the Kyrgyz Republic, Moldova, Mongolia, New Zealand, Oman, Panama, Saudi Arabia, Sri Lanka, Turkey, and Ukraine. Observer status is sometimes the antechamber before participation, yet this has not been the case so far in the context of the GPA. Four intergovernmental organizations also have observer status: the IMF, International Trade Centre (ITC), OECD, and UNCTAD.

2.3 The Entities Covered

WTO Members joining the GPA can decide on how much they want to liberalize their procurement markets: Art. I GPA makes it clear that the GPA disciplines apply only to entities committed by the signatories and inscribed to this effect in an appendix to the GPA:

> This Agreement applies to any law, regulation, procedure or practice regarding any procurement by entities covered by this Agreement, as specified in Appendix 1.

Appendix 1, which forms an integral part of the GPA, is divided into five Annexes and reflects the commitments of each GPA signatory with respect to:

(a) Central government entities (Annex 1);
(b) Sub-central government entities (Annex 2);
(c) All other entities that procure in accordance with the provisions of this Agreement (Annex 3);
(d) Entities procuring services (Annex 4);
(e) Entities procuring construction services (Annex 5).

---

[13] Anderson et al. (2011a); Georgopoulos (2000); Wood (1997). Similar results are reported in the empirical study regarding the government procurement provisions in the EC-CARIFORUM agreement by Dawar and Evenett (2011).

[14] WTO Doc. GPA/92 of 13 December 2007.

Whereas the first three Annexes refer to covered entities, the last two refer to types of contracts that the covered entities can sign. Each GPA signatory will select the entities for which it agrees to abide by the GPA obligations. Hence, the GPA covers entities procuring both goods and services, albeit the latter in limited manner.[15] A parallel process aiming to liberalize procurement in the services markets is under way, but has not as yet led to a fruitful conclusion: under Art. XIII.1 GATS, procurement of services is subject neither to MFN (Art. I GATS) nor to specific commitments (Arts. XVI and XVII GATS). Art. XIII.2 GATS explains that multilateral negotiations should take place within two years of the entry into force of the Agreement Establishing the WTO, with the aim of liberalizing the government procurement market for services. In March 1995, the GATS Rules Working Party was established and it has been in place ever since. According to the Guidelines and Procedures for the Negotiations on Trade in Services (established in WTO Doc. S/L/93), WTO Members should, *inter alia*, complete negotiations under Art. XIII GATS before negotiating specific commitments. The mandate was reaffirmed in the Hong Kong Ministerial Declaration (2005).[16] The EU has taken the initiative and proposed the elements of an agreement;[17] so far, however, negotiations have been inconclusive.[18] So, with the exception Annexes 4 and 5 to the GPA, there are no multilateral disciplines regarding government procurement in the services market.

It is not the case that any purchasing by the entities covered will *ipso facto* have to respect the disciplines included in the GPA. WTO Members will specify in each Annex the relevant threshold value: contracts worth a value above the established threshold value will have to respect the GPA disciplines. Art. I.4 GPA reads in this respect:

> this Agreement applies to any procurement contract of a value of not less than the relevant threshold specified in Appendix I.[19]

The GPA does not provide for one valuation method to be used by all GPA signatories at all times. It rather provides for criteria to be used when establishing the valuation method. As a result, some discretion is left to the signatories.

---

[15] Low et al. (1997) and Bronckers (1997). At the 1996 Singapore Ministerial Conference, another multilateral track aiming at the liberalization of the government procurement market was established: the Working Group on Transparency in Government Procurement. It has been inactive following a decision to this effect at the Cancun meeting, that is, the mid-term review of the Doha round (2004).

[16] See Annex C of the Declaration.

[17] See WTO Doc. S/WPGR/M/54 of 20 June 2006.

[18] See S/WPGR/17 of 16 November 2007, and WTO Doc. S/WPGR/M/60 of 17 January 2008.

[19] The usual threshold values used are 130,000 SDRs (special drawing rights) for goods and services, and 5,000,000 SDR for construction services procured by Annex 1 entities. Higher thresholds have been used for some entities covered by Annexes 2 and 3.

To cement the obligation reflected in Art. I.4 GPA, Art. II.3 GPA relevantly provides that:

> the selection of the valuation method by the entity shall not be used, nor shall any procurement requirement be divided, with the intention of avoiding the application of this Agreement.

2.4 Non-discrimination

Art. III GPA reflects the non-discrimination obligation; it requires GPA signatories to treat foreign suppliers no less favourably than they treat their domestic suppliers in the context of government purchasing:

> With respect to all laws, regulations, procedures and practices regarding government procurement covered by this Agreement, each Party shall provide immediately and unconditionally to the products, services and suppliers of other Parties offering products and services of the Parties, treatment no less favourable than:
>
> (a) that accorded to domestic producers, services and suppliers; and
> (b) that accorded to products, services and suppliers of any other Party.[20]

Art. III.3 GPA clarifies that:

> the provisions of paragraphs 1 and 2 shall not apply to customs duties and charges of any kind imposed on or in connection with importation, the method of levying such duties and charges, other import regulations and formalities, and measures affecting trade in services other than laws, regulations, procedures and practices regarding government procurement covered by this Agreement.

This clarification is necessary in order to leave no doubt that imported goods will have to pay the import duty that has been agreed through negotiations.[21]

Each WTO Member is free to unilaterally define the origin of the supplier, and apply its definition in a manner consistent with the NT obligation. Art. IV.2 GPA requests, when the negotiations on the WTO Agreement on Rules of Origin are completed, to:

> take the results of that work programme and those negotiations into account in amending paragraph 1 as appropriate.[22]

As is the case in both the GATT and the GATS, the GPA contains a list of exceptions to the Agreement, set out in Art. XXIII. Art. XXIII.1 GPA refers to national security, while Art. XXIII.2 GPA sets out the list of general exceptions.[23]

---

[20] Domestic laws, on the other hand, will regulate the behaviour of suppliers. As Wood (1997) points out, antitrust might have an important role to play in this respect. Recall, nonetheless, that there is nothing like a world competition law, so regulation in this respect could be asymmetric across countries.

[21] Reich (1999).

[22] As we saw in Chapter 3 though, the end is nowhere near at this stage.

[23] See the discussion in Chapter 5.

The schedules of concessions under the GPA often contain General Notes at the end which might provide for a number of additional exceptions, including from the obligation not to discriminate; this practice has developed, although the GPA nowhere mentions that signatories can legitimately introduce such clauses in their schedules.[24] For example, Israel entered a General Note in its schedule to reduce by 1 January 2005 its offsets to 20 per cent of the value of the contract. During the debate in the GPA Committee, following inconclusive discussions on the legal basis of General Notes, it was agreed that Israel should refer to Art. XXIV.6 GPA. This provision is of a merely procedural character, however, and covers modifications and/or rectifications to schedules, not substantive deviations from it.[25] Still, practice has now developed in this way.

Modifications of schedules are possible by virtue of Art. XXIV.6 GPA: to this effect, the Member requesting modification will notify its new concession and, assuming no objection has been raised within 30 days, the concession will be modified accordingly.[26]

2.5 Awarding a Contract

2.5.1 *The Procedure*

The GPA distinguishes between four different modes, following which a decision to award a contract will be taken:

(a) Open tendering procedures, whereby, by virtue of Art. VII.3(a) GPA, any interested party may apply and participate in a competition to win a government procurement contract;

(b) Selective tendering procedures, whereby only a few suppliers are invited by the procuring entity to participate (provided that Art. X GPA and Art. VII.3 (b) GPA have been respected). To ensure that these procedures will not serve as a gateway to protectionist behaviour, the procuring entities are required to invite the maximum number of entities to submit a tender. Art. VIII GPA includes safeguards to ensure that conditions for qualification do not discriminate against foreign suppliers. Moreover, by virtue of Art. IX.9 GPA, procuring entities are required to publish on a yearly basis the list of suppliers that qualify for these procedures, as well as the criteria that new suppliers are required to meet for their inclusion in the list. The selective procedure allows for a stage for negotiations with suppliers even after the submission of bids, provided that this intent is clearly mentioned in the invitation to participate.

---

[24] A signatory can, of course, assuming the relevant conditions have been met, take exemption from the obligation not to discriminate for health, national security etc. reasons. A General Note does not serve this purpose though.

[25] WTO Doc. GPA/83.

[26] Objections are raised not infrequently; see, for example, objections to Canada's modifications in WTO Doc. GPA/92 of 13 December 2007.

This is important because it makes the GPA more flexible in comparison with other regimes (for example, the EU Public Sector Procurement Directive) and more comparable to the EU Utilities Directive and the Defence and Security Directive;

(c) Limited tendering procedures, whereby an entity may, by virtue of Art. VII.3 (c) GPA, contact suppliers individually provided that the conditions included in Art. XV GPA have been respected. Art. XV GPA reserves this possibility for cases of urgency, or cases where no response to an open and/or selective procedure has been registered, or cases where the product or service purchased can only be purchased from one supplier;

(d) Negotiations between the procuring entity and economic operators under the strict conditions expressed in Art. XIV GPA (for example, when it is clear that no one tender is the most advantageous and subject to the non-discrimination discipline).

2.5.2 *Kicking the Process Off: The Invitation to Submit*

Covered entities wishing to procure must, according to Art. IX.1 GPA, publish an invitation to participate for all cases of intended procurement which are covered by the GPA ('tender notice'): through this document, they will inform all GPA signatories of the imminent procurement. The tender notice must reflect all elements referred to in Art. IX.6 GPA:

(a) The nature and quantity of the procurement as well as an estimate of timing;
(b) Whether the procedure is open, selective, or whether it will involve negotiation;
(c) Date for starting delivery;
(d) Address and deadline for submission;
(e) Address of the entity awarding the contract;
(f) Economic and technical requirements;
(g) The amount and terms of payment;
(h) Whether offers concern purchase, lease etc.

A summary of the notice of initiation must be published in one of the official languages of the WTO, that is, English, French, or Spanish (Art. IX.8 GPA). In the 'tender documentation' (Art. XII GPA), the procuring entity will be further required to provide all information necessary to the suppliers in order to prepare their proposals: this includes technical specifications (if applicable), as well as the criteria under which the contract will be awarded. Parties to the GPA are requested, by virtue of Art. VI GPA, when drawing up technical specifications reflecting the characteristics of the products or services to be procured (such as quality, performance, safety and dimensions, packaging, etc.) to ensure that their requirements:

shall not be prepared, adopted or applied with a view to, or with the effect of, creating unnecessary obstacles to trade.

In the same vein, Art. VI.2 GPA reads:

Technical specifications prescribed by procuring entities shall, where appropriate:
(a) be in terms of performance rather than design or descriptive characteristics; and
(b) be based on international standards, where such exist . . .

2.5.3 *Awarding the Contract*

Art. XVIII.1 GPA obliges GPA signatories to publish, within 72 days of the award of a contract, a statement where they indicate, *inter alia*, the winning supplier. They do not necessarily have to award the contract to the lowest bidder; they could very well award it to the supplier who, in their judgment, tabled the most advantageous offer: consequently, procuring entities retain substantial authority when deciding on the winning party and their decisions can hardly, assuming no arbitrariness is involved, be put into question. In the absence of case law on this specific issue, we can safely presume that WTO adjudicating bodies will adopt a standard similar to that adopted in contingent protection instruments, that is, neither *de novo* review nor total deference.

There is no obligation imposed on procuring entities to include the rationale for the award of the contract in their decision;[27] only if requested by an unsuccessful supplier must an entity provide the reasons that led it to award the contract to a particular supplier (Art. XVIII.2 GPA).

2.6 Transparency Requirements

Besides the transparency-requirements with respect to the announcing and the award of contracts, WTO Members of the GPA must, by virtue of Art. XIX.5 GPA, collect and provide, on an annual basis, statistics on their procurements covered by the GPA.[28]

Recall that a Working Group on Transparency in Government Procurement was established in 1996 and produced some interesting work regarding transparency in this context regarding for example, the scope of procurement, the various procurement methods etc.[29] As mentioned, this group has been inactive since 2004 following the decision taken to this effect in Cancun (2003).

---

[27] Arrowsmith (2005) provides an authoritative explanation of this issue.

[28] See, for example, Norway's notification for 2006 (WTO Doc. GPA/88/Add. 1 of 12 March 2007), and Hong Kong, China's for the same year (WTO Doc. GPA/91 of 9 October 2007).

[29] See WTO doc. WT/WGTGP/W/32 of 23 May 2002, a compilation of the various discussion topics by the WTO Secretariat.

2.7 Enforcing the GPA: The Challenge Procedures

Art. XX GPA reflects the obligation to establish a forum to entertain disputes between private parties and the entities concerned. The rationale behind this provision has to do with the general feeling of uneasiness that surrounded the remedy recommended in the Trondheim dispute (*Norway—Trondheim Roll Ring*) in the GATT years, and the resolve to ensure that effective remedies against violations would be provided for in the WTO GPA. An adequate summary of the facts of the case can be found in §4.1 of the report:

> The basic facts of the case before the Panel are that in March 1991 the Norwegian Public Roads Administration awarded a contract relating to electronic toll collection equipment for a toll system around the city of Trondheim to a Norwegian company, Micro Design, after single tendering the procurement with that company. The central point of difference between the two parties to the dispute was whether, in single tendering the procurement, Norway had met the requirements of Article V:16 (e) of the Agreement. Norway maintained that the single tendering of the contract was justifiable under these provisions, since the contract was for research and development and the part of the contract which it considered was covered by the Agreement was for the procurement of prototypes which had been developed in the course of and for that research and development contract. Furthermore, Norway contended that it had complied with the requirements in the headnote to Article V:16. The United States maintained that Article V:16(e) was not applicable since, in its view, the objective of the contract was not research and development but the procurement of toll collection equipment. Moreover, the United States disputed that research and/or development had been required to produce these products, that the products could justifiably be characterised as prototypes and that Norway had met the requirements in the headnote to Article V:16.

The US complained that Norway, by not publishing the tender document, had violated its obligations under the GPA and hence for this reason alone had wrongfully awarded the contract to the Norwegian company. It was a rather obvious violation (since the contract concerned the construction of the toll ring system and not research and development) and the Panel had no problem establishing that Norway had indeed violated its obligations under the GPA (§§4.14ff) But then came the question what should the consequence be for Norway, in what way should it bring its measures into compliance? The US had requested that it be allowed to negotiate compensation with Norway based on lost opportunities. One thing was clear: it would be next to impossible to calculate precise compensation since, in the absence of transparency regarding the tender, any company by any GPA signatory could in principle have won.[30] The Panel, against this background,

---

[30] This is probably an exaggeration since not all companies have identical endowments. It is, however, probably true for a smaller segment of all potential candidates, assuming competition in the relevant market. See, on this score, Mavroidis (1993).

decided to request from Norway to promise that it would never commit a similar sin and left it there[31] (§§4.26ff):

> In the light of the above, the Panel did not consider that it would be appropriate for it to recommend that Norway negotiate a mutually satisfactory solution with the United States that took into account the lost opportunities of United States companies in the procurement or that, in the event that such a negotiation did not yield a mutually satisfactory result, the Committee be prepared to authorise the United States to withdraw benefits under the Agreement from Norway with respect to opportunities to bid of equal value to the Trondheim contract. The Panel had recognised, however, that nothing prevented the United States from pursuing these matters further in the Committee or from seeking to negotiate with Norway a mutually satisfactory solution provided that it was consistent with the provisions of this and other GATT agreements.
>
> ...
>
> On the basis of the findings set out above, the Panel <u>concluded</u> that Norway had not complied with its obligations under the Agreement on Government Procurement in its conduct of the procurement of toll collection equipment for the city of Trondheim in that the single tendering of this procurement could not be justified under Article V:16(e) or under other provisions of the Agreement.
>
> The Panel <u>recommends</u> that the Committee request Norway to take the measures necessary to ensure that the entities listed in the Norwegian Annex to the Agreement conduct government procurement in accordance with the above findings. (emphasis in the original)

Now this remedy was not much consolation for the US, but what else could be done? Recall that, in principle at least, an unidentified number of companies originating in any GPA signatory could have won the contract. As a result, it is almost impossible to identify the eventual winner (had the contract been awarded in GPA-consistent manner); consequently, it is also almost impossible to quantify the extent of damages (opportunity cost) suffered by each potential participant in the tendering procedure. In Mavroidis (1993), we advanced the argument that in similar cases a fine (some form of lump-sum payment) should be paid by the author of the illegal act: depending on the sums involved, a system of fines could disincentivize potential violators from committing similar illegalities. Similar schemes, however, do not fly in the 'pragmatic' WTO world that has de facto settled for prospective remedies when a violation has been committed.[32]

Against this background, and probably out of fear that a system of fines might find sympathetic voices in agreements beyond the GPA, it is not surprising

---

[31] What in public international law parlance is known as 'guarantees of non-repetition'; see Mavroidis (1993).

[32] Mavroidis (2000a), Pauwelyn (2000), and Petersmann (1993) all discuss remedies in GATT/WTO practice.

that GPA signatories settled for a different solution:[33] yes, something needed to be done against similar behaviour, and the GPA framers attempted to reduce the potential for similar events. This is where the GPA 'challenge procedures' come in. They are meant to provide:

> non-discriminatory, timely, transparent and effective procedures enabling suppliers to challenge alleged breaches of the Agreement arising in the context of procurements in which they have, or have had, an interest. (Art. XX.2 GPA)

Consequently, private parties will have direct access to the national fora established to adjudicate GPA-related disputes. Private parties must exercise their rights within relatively short deadlines (no less than ten days from the time when the basis of the complaint is known or reasonably should be known, according to Art. XX.5 GPA). Complaints shall be heard 'by a court or by an impartial and independent review body' (Art. XX.6 GPA). Art. XX.7 GPA regulates the *remedies* that should be recommended, if a challenge procedure has been successfully invoked by a private party:

> Challenge procedures shall provide for:
>
> (a) rapid interim measures to correct breaches of the Agreement and to preserve commercial opportunities. Such action may result in suspension of the procurement process. However, procedures may provide that overriding adverse consequences for the interests concerned, including the public interest, may be taken into account in deciding whether such measures should be applied. In such circumstances, just cause for not acting shall be provided in writing;
> (b) an assessment and a possibility for a decision on the justification of the challenge;
> (c) correction of the breach of the Agreement or compensation for the loss of damages suffered, which may be limited to costs for tender preparation or protest.

Although the GPA does not set a limit for the completion of the procedures, it does request (Art. XX.8 GPA) that 'the challenge procedure shall normally be completed in a timely fashion'.[34] The GPA challenge procedures leave substantial discretion to signatories to 'flesh out' the various steps involved.[35] In this respect, WTO Members might find it useful to be inspired by the UNCITRAL Model Law which discusses in substantial detail various elements such as the remedy of suspension, the review of decision, etc.[36]

---

[33] Moreover, a system of fines is, of course, an imperfect remedy since there it offers no response to the possible scenario where a WTO Member with substantial bargaining power refuses to pay; see Limão and Saggi (2008).

[34] Galli et al. (2007) discuss the Swiss experience with respect to challenge procedures; Georgopoulos (2005) discusses Greece's experience of enforcing government procurement.

[35] The EU Remedies Directive, for example, the EU domestic instrument to this effect, provides for a mandatory standstill period and an automatic suspension; see Priess and Friton (2011).

[36] There are inconsistencies across the two instruments and, consequently, 'lock, stock and barrel' transpositions should be avoided; see Zhang (2011) for a comprehensive analysis of this issue.

Art. XXII GPA also makes it clear that, in principle, the DSU is applicable for disputes arising in the GPA context as well: of course, as briefly discussed in Chapter 1, the WTO dispute settlement is a state-to-state forum where private parties have no standing. One should, consequently, expect to see here disputes that do not concern the types of issues that could come under challenge procedures. Art. XXII.4 GPA contains the standard terms of reference to be used by interested parties, unless of course they agree to special terms. Interestingly, and in contradiction with the DSU rules, Art. XXII.7 GPA does not allow for cross-retaliation: a GPA signatory suspending concessions following non-implementation of rulings in the context of GATT, GATS, or TRIPs cannot retaliate by withdrawing concessions under the GPA; by the same token, a WTO Member winning a GPA dispute cannot withdraw benefits under the GATT, GATS, or TRIPs against the recalcitrant state. Disputes under the GPA are, thus, self-contained.

Practice reveals only a few cases where recourse to the WTO dispute settlement procedures was judged necessary:

(a) In *Japan—Procurement of a Navigation Satellite*, the EU requested consultations, arguing that tender specifications by a Japanese entity contravened various GPA rules. The Japanese Ministry of Transportation, an entity covered by the GPA, wanted to purchase a satellite and the technical specifications issued to this effect explicitly referred to a US system used for air traffic management. During consultations, an arrangement was reached between the complainant and the defendant whereby the latter agreed to establish a cooperative arrangement between the Ministry and an EU agency, guaranteeing the interoperability of the two (the European and the US) systems;[37]

(b) In *US—Massachusetts State Law Prohibiting Contracts with Firms doing Business with or in Myanmar*, the EU and Japan challenged the consistency of a US state law prohibiting covered entities from awarding contracts to companies originating in states doing business with Myanmar. This measure was designed to ban companies doing business with a regime which, in the eyes of the Massachusetts government, was in violation of the most fundamental human rights. Following unsuccessful consultations, a panel was established at the request of the complainants. However, shortly thereafter, a US court set aside the law. The Panel was suspended and since no party to the dispute requested, within in a year, that it be reconvened, its authority under Art. 12.12 DSU lapsed;[38]

(c) In *Korea—Procurement*, the US claimed that Korea had not respected its obligations under the GPA when constructing the Inchon International Airport. Following unsuccessful consultations, the dispute was submitted to

---

[37] WTO Doc. GPA/M/8.
[38] WTO Docs. WT/DS88/5, WT/DS95/5, and WT/DSB/M/49. See Linarelli (2011).

a panel which ruled that the Korean procuring entity was not covered by the GPA disciplines. No appeal against the Panel report was launched.

There are reasons to believe that the GPA acted as a shield against recourse to protectionism during the recent financial crisis: although it is difficult to quantify its impact, it is probably the case that it was a contributing factor. For example, the 2009 US Recovery and Reinvestment Act (the stimulus package) contained a 'buy American' provision, but made room to apply it in conformity with the GPA when stating that the Act would be applied in a manner consistent with US obligations under international agreements.[39]

3. Institutional Issues

A GPA Committee has been established, where each signatory is represented. This body discusses all issues coming under the purview of the GPA, as well as accessions/withdrawals from the GPA (Art. XXI GPA). It issues an annual report pursuant to Art. XXIV.7(a) GPA.

4. A New GPA(?)

The negotiations on a new GPA were de-linked from the Doha round package. The negotiators managed to agree on a new text in 2006,[40] which has not, however, entered into force. The reason for its non-entry into force until December 2011 has to do with an informal agreement struck by the parties in December 2006, under which the revised GPA text could not come into force until there was also a mutually satisfactory conclusion in the coverage negotiations. It was agreed during the Ministerial Conference of the WTO that the new GPA enter into force.[41]

The GPA has not been much of a success when it comes to inducing participation, as membership remains essentially limited to the OECD countries (and Chinese Taipei). The new revised GPA contains four additional elements aimed at streamlining special and differential treatment and ensuring that developing countries can benefit from market liberalization, that enough room is made to recognize idiosyncratic elements due to their current level of development, but also that their deviations from obligations will not become a permanent theme. To this effect, a series of provisional—that is, time-bound measures, such as price

---

[39] Report of the WTO Committee on Government Procurement, WTO Doc. WT/GPA/103 of 12 November 2009.

[40] WTO Doc. GPA/W/297 of 11 December 2006.

[41] WTO Doc. GP/112 of 16 December 2011.

preferences, are at the disposal of developing countries. These are intended to facilitate their accession to the GPA;[42] they will not find themselves in the twilight zone between active participation. Recourse to similar measures can take place provided that there is prior demonstration that they correspond to specific development needs; reciprocity (across commitments by developed and developing countries) is the key in negotiating similar measures.[43]

This is of course tomorrow's music, and it is impossible at this stage to quantify the impact that similar measures might have. It is, thus, important to ask why the GPA, as it stands, has not attracted more participation by developing countries, given the presumption that its rules of the game are beneficial; at least this is presumably the case given that the OECD has committed to apply them. There are many hypotheses, including a lack of direct benefits because developing countries are pursuing procurement reform unilaterally, perhaps with assistance from donors; they may not see any export interests; the administrative costs associated with compliance—notification, reporting, procedures, etc.—may be perceived to be too high; and governments may want to use procurement policies as an instrument of industrial and redistributive policy—a way that governments can promote the interests of domestic firms, disadvantaged ethnic or religious groups, minorities, or regions within the country.

The lack of interest on the part of developing countries in acceding to the GPA led to a shift in focus at the WTO to transparency and away from efforts to reduce the incidence of/scope for discriminatory procurement policy. The focus on transparency also reflected the US interest in combating corruption and extending the US Foreign Corrupt Practices Act to the rest of the OECD. The WTO Working Group on Transparency in Procurement did not result in agreement on negotiating disciplines in this sub-area of procurement policy. One reason for this was a perception that market access would be (was) on the agenda, no matter what was said by OECD countries. Another was uncertainty as to what the implications of the rules would be. A third was a sense that there would be no 'mercantilist' payoff to transparency—this was essentially an agenda that revolved around domestic policies, and might be beneficial, but would not generate more exports. Research has demonstrated that transparency is unambiguously good for national (and global) welfare, but that it is not necessarily good for market access: more transparency can lead to more domestic sourcing.

The failure at the WTO has not implied writing off the use of trade agreements—increasingly, bilateral and regional agreements are being negotiated that

---

42 Mattoo (1997), borrowing from theoretical work in this area, identified the absence of price preferences as one of the reasons why developing countries might legitimately want to abstain from joining the GPA: absent a scheme to this effect, bidding companies might have an incentive to collude in the absence of meaningful competition from local companies.

43 For an extensive discussion of the new GPA provisions dealing with special and differential treatment, see Müller (2011).

cover procurement: CAFTA (Central American Free Trade Agreement) is a recent example for the US, while the EU ACP negotiations and the European Neighbourhood Policy (ENP) are examples on the EU side. These agreements include WTO + rules.[44] Why there and not in WTO? Is it because there is more on the table—preferential access to the EU/US market? Or is it because there is an aid dimension to the agreements that is not part of the WTO discussion? Whatever the reasons, and there is no reason why they should be the same across the various PTAs, opening up the government procurement market on a preferential basis could be, as Anderson et al. (2011b) conclude in their study on this score, a test bed for those wishing to join the WTO GPA.

There is an increasingly widely held perception that trade agreements are not enough and that 'one size does not fit all'. Even if there is a case for common rules (harmonization), trade commitments can and should be complemented by what is coming to be called aid for trade. That is, there are arguments for linking procurement reform to aid, perhaps using the WTO as both a commitment device for policy reforms and aid, as well as a monitoring mechanism. Monitoring could comprise what donors do to support needed institutional improvements in developing countries and what governments of these countries do in terms of taking action and implementation of reforms.

---

[44] Horn et al. (2010).

13

TRANSPARENCY

1. Transparency in the WTO

In the preceding chapters, we discussed many transparency disciplines which are specific to individual agreements. To a large extent, it is through notifications by the WTO Members possessing the requisite information that transparency is served. Transparency is the first step towards enforcing the various WTO obligations, and sometimes it is not simply a necessary but also a sufficient condition for enforcing them. This is probably what Bhagwati wants to capture whenever he uses his inimitable expression that transparency should be likened to the 'Dracula principle': by throwing light on it, the problem might disappear. This is, of course, a rather exceptional case since, for many good reasons, facts might be interpreted in different ways and disagreements might arise as to their legal qualification and GATT consistency. Knowledge about facts is at any rate the necessary first step towards establishing (un)lawful behaviour.

Knowledge about facts is not costless, however: it is associated with (sometimes) important costs. In a world with uneven spending power, those with the means to spend could profit from lack of transparency since they would be favoured in a scenario where they could spend to buy information when others cannot.[1] Transparency obligations, thus, in a sense subsidize those who cannot or cannot easily procure information, those for whom spending on similar issues is associated with a high opportunity cost.

One should not be oblivious to the possibility of reducing if not altogether eliminating, disputes through adequate notification: it is the various WTO Committees that provide the forum for transparency-related notifications and this is where the notifications supplied are first discussed. The SPS Committee, the forum which is by any reasonable account the host of the most far-reaching (in both quantity and quality of supplied information) notification record, is also the forum where most (potential) disputes are being resolved. Although technically speaking a specific trade concern (STC) raised in the SPS Committee is not a dispute (in the sense of Art. 1 DSU), it is a disagreement about policies that could give rise to a dispute. The overwhelming majority of STCs are resolved at the SPS Committee level.[2]

There are various factors influencing the extent of notifications: the subject-matter of notification in and of itself influences the incentive to notify. A government typically looks good when it adopts a measure against the ozone layer, but not so good when it favours one segment of society (and in extreme cases, one particular economic operator) over another, since (at least in a democratic society) its popularity increases when it provides and safeguards public goods and decreases when it cherry-picks beneficiaries. Moreover, in the case of subsidies notifications, providing information is self-incriminating since similar information amounts to acknowledging that a benefit has been provided which is at least countervailable, as we saw in Chapter 8.

But even if incentives are present, some WTO Members, for reasons of lack of capacity (especially when facing high administrative costs), might be notifying the WTO in a suboptimal manner. Take the example of notifications under TBT/SPS and under ILA. They both contain provisions providing for transparency. Quoting from Arts. 10.1 and 10.10 TBT:

> Each Member shall ensure that an enquiry point exists which is able to answer all reasonable enquiries from other Members and interested parties in other Members as well as to provide the relevant documents regarding . . .
>
> . . .
>
> Members shall designate a single central government authority that is responsible for the implementation on the national level of the provisions concerning notification procedures under this Agreement except those included in Annex 3.[3]

---

[1] Horn et al. (2005a) mention the uneven distribution of information concerning illegal trade barriers as one of the possible causes explaining participation in the WTO dispute settlement system.

[2] Horn et al. (2012).

[3] The corresponding SPS provisions are §§3 and 10 in Annex B.

So, through the TBT regime, WTO Members reduce notification costs for domestic producers at home through the central government authority established (the one-stop shop), while providing an information service to all interested parties. There are no corresponding provisions in ILA; as a result, it is quite costly for WTO Members to gather information regarding import licensing and the natural consequence is suboptimal notifications, while, on the other hand, traders and consumers will know little if anything about the quotas in place.[4]

All these factors contribute (probably unevenly) to the picture we see: the record regarding unilateral notifications is not judged satisfactory. Collins-Williams and Wolfe (2010) conducted an extensive research of notifications in various WTO Committees; their analysis shows that, with notable exceptions such as the TBT and SPS Committees, the record of notifications to the WTO is no reason to celebrate and, in fact, on occasion (notifications to the SCM Committee), the record is quite abysmal.[5] A WTO Secretariat document[6] reflects similar conclusions: only 15 WTO Members have submitted notifications under the ILA (§§153ff); only 56 WTO Members have submitted their responses to questions regarding the function of the CV Agreement (§§155ff); but, on the other hand, we are now beyond 10,000 notifications in the SPS context. Since there is nothing idiosyncratic about notification requirements in the SPS Agreement, there is at least a presumption that the subject-matter of notifications must have something to do with the amount and quality of notified material.[7] The Overview Secretariat Document contains information regarding the number of notifications received between 1995–2010 (see Figure 13.1).

WTO Members have to observe 176 distinct obligations when notifying information to the WTO, 42 of which are recurring obligations, that is, semi-annual, annual, bi-annual, triennial, etc. (see Table 13.1).

Hence, from a regulatory perspective, the issue becomes whether it makes sense to keep the same subject for notifications across transactions irrespective of the subject-matter or whether a common agent should, on occasion, be entrusted with the task of unearthing and notifying information. The WTO regime is a mix. But how did we end up here?

---

[4] Of course, WTO Members can on their own initiative provide for similar one-stop shops in the ILA context as well, but here we tackle again the question of incentives. This is not to say that by addressing the costliness of gathering information through the establishment of one-stop shops the problem disappears. But at least if this happens (a rather non-costly option), we know better what the problem is and how to tackle the (eventually) missing incentives to notify the WTO of import licencing schemes.

[5] Horn et al. (2011) reflect similar conclusions regarding notifications of mutually agreed solutions to the Dispute Settlement Body (DSB).

[6] WTO Doc. WT/TPR/OV/14, Overview of Developments for the International Trading Environment, 21 November 2011 (hereinafter the 'Overview Secretariat Document').

[7] It is of course a daunting task to pronounce in an informed manner about all notifications in the WTO. And this is an area where views are quite divergent across WTO Members, as well as in the literature.

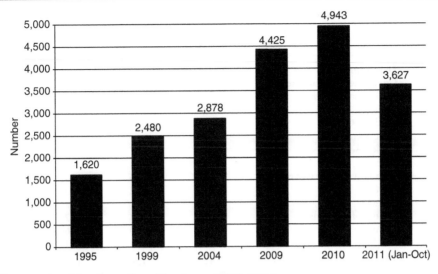

Figure 13.1 Number of notifications, 1995–2011
Source: Overview Secretariat Document, WTO: Geneva, 21 November 2011 at p. 52.

Originally, that is, in the GATT era, there were obligations to publish trade-related information and notify the GATT of measures coming under its purview: this is what the Overview Secretariat Document terms 'the first generation transparency provisions' (pp. 50ff). During the Tokyo round, the right to request information became a legal possibility ('second generation transparency provisions'). To this effect the Tokyo round Understanding Regarding Notification, Consultation, Dispute Settlement and Surveillance mentions (§3):

> Contracting parties which have reasons to believe that such trade measures have been adopted by another contracting party may seek information on such measures bilaterally, from the contracting party concerned.

During the Uruguay round, the arguably third-generation transparency provisions were agreed and came into effect: cross-notifications became widely used, and the role of the WTO Secretariat was upgraded significantly. For example, recently the US cross-notified the WTO of dozens of (alleged) Chinese and Indian subsidy schemes that China and India had failed to notify the WTO about. With respect to Chinese schemes, the US notified the WTO of 42 green technology schemes, 92 export subsidies, and 52 other schemes belonging to various categories.[8] It further notified the WTO of 23 Indian schemes.[9] Most of the activity regarding cross-notifications is in the subsidies context, as should be expected in light of the corresponding (dis)incentives to notify.

---

[8] WTO Doc. G/SCM/Q2/CHN/42 of 11 October 2011.
[9] WTO Doc. G/SCM/Q2/IND/20 of 10 October 2011.

Table 13.1 Notification Obligations in the WTO

	Regular	Ad hoc	Total
Development		7	7
Government Procurement	3	8	11
Intellectual Property	3	23	26
Services	3	11	14
Trade in Goods			
Agriculture	8	7	15
Market Access	9	27	36
Rules	7	34	41
Technical Barriers to Trade	1	13	14
TRIMs	1	2	3
General			
Balance of payments	1	1	2
RTAs	6	0	6
TPRM	0	1	1
Total	**42**	**134**	**176**

Source: Overview Secretariat Document, WTO: Geneva, 21 November 2011 at p. 51.

The WTO Secretariat saw an increase in its powers to become an international 'watchdog', monitoring transparency obligations but also itself unearthing information and making it public. Sometimes acting on a clear mandate provided by its Members (TPRM, Working Group on Notifications of Obligations and Procedures) and sometimes adopting a proactive attitude, the shaky legal basis for it notwithstanding (initiatives post-financial crisis), the WTO Secretariat has emerged as a central component in the quest for transparency.

Already in the 1980s there were voices arguing for a more proactive attitude in order to enhance the then level of transparency: the Leutwiler report first underscored that transparency could be key in mobilizing domestic constituencies in favour of trade liberalization.[10] In similar vein, the former GATT DG, Olivier Long, suggested in a report he co-authored that transparency obligations had to be rethought since the efficiency of the multilateral edifice relied very much on the robustness of the information that it received.[11] The TPRM was established during the Uruguay round, providing the WTO Secretariat with a clear mandate to monitor and report on trade policies by all WTO Members. A Decision on Notification Procedures was adopted during the Uruguay round which underlined the general obligation to notify, assigned to the Council for Trade in Goods the authority to monitor notifications, provided in its Annex an indicative list of notifiable measures, and established the Central Registry of Notifications (CRN), with the following mandate:

---

[10] Trade Policies for a Better Future, Proposals for Action, 'The Leutwiler Report', 1985, The GATT: Geneva.
[11] Long (1989).

A central registry of notifications shall be established under the responsibility of the Secretariat. While Members will continue to follow existing notification procedures, the Secretariat shall ensure that the central registry records such elements of the information provided on the measure by the Member concerned as its purpose, its trade coverage, and the requirement under which it has been notified. The central registry shall cross-reference its records of notifications by Member and obligation.

The central registry shall inform each Member annually of the regular notification obligations to which that Member will be expected to respond in the course of the following year.

The central registry shall draw the attention of individual Members to regular notification requirements which remain unfulfilled.

Information in the central registry regarding individual notifications shall be made available on request to any Member entitled to receive the notification concerned.

Transparency-related obligations multiplied as a result of the many agreements signed during the Uruguay round and the CRN was a first response towards streamlining notifications. A second response came through the establishment of the Working Party on Notifications Obligations and Procedures which was established in order to streamline the various transparency obligations: its final report is the first clear statement on where the WTO stood on this issue following the many agreements signed during the Uruguay round.[12] This report contained an Annex (Annex III) which reflected the type of information that should be included in notifications by WTO Members, an issue to which we shall return below, as well as a mandate to review at the multilateral level the consistency of notified information.

And this was not the end of the road: following lengthy negotiations, the Integrated Database (IDB) was established in 1997 through a decision by the General Council which requested from WTO Members to notify information relevant to tariffs and import trade.[13] Following practice judged unsatisfactory, the WTO Members adopted a decision in 2009 which enabled the WTO Secretariat to gather information on its own initiative on the issues covered by the original decisions.[14]

The most recent initiative in the ongoing strengthening of the WTO Secretariat powers in this respect came with the discussions on financial crisis and the role of the WTO in this context. The question arose whether nations would have had recourse to protectionism as a response to the financial crisis and various mechanisms were established to monitor the situation.[15] The G 20, at their 2 April 2009 meeting, called on the WTO to adopt monitoring mechanisms regarding

---

[12] Report of the Working Party on Notifications Obligations and Procedures, WTO Doc. G/L/112, 7 October 1996.

[13] WTO Doc. WT/L/225 of 18 July 1997, and WTO Doc. G/MA/IDB/1/Rev. 1 of 27 June 1997 which explains the modalities and operation of the IDB and the kind of information requested.

[14] WTO Doc. G/MA/239 of 4 September 2009.

[15] The record is difficult to interpret since many of the reported barriers are probably unrelated to the financial crisis, but the overall emerging picture is not as bleak as those drawing parallels with the

trade measures. There was no official WTO reaction to this effect other than a communication by a group of 13 WTO Members which, *inter alia*, included a plea to avoid recourse to protectionist measures in response to the financial crisis and a

> call to the DG to continue to monitor and report publicly on our adherence to these undertakings on a quarterly basis.[16]

This proved enough for the DG to instruct the WTO Secretariat to embark on the exercise and start reporting periodically on dozens of trade barriers. The Overview Secretariat Document also cites §G of the TPRM as an appropriate legal basis:

> G. *Overview of Developments in the International Trading Environment*
> An annual overview of developments in the international trading environment which are having an impact on the multilateral trading system shall also be undertaken by the TPRB. The overview is to be assisted by an annual report by the Director-General setting out major activities of the WTO and highlighting significant policy issues affecting the trading system.

True this provision does confer wide powers on the Secretariat, but why did not the WTO make use of it in the pre-2008 period as well? Moreover, this provision calls for annual not quarterly review. It seems that the lack of an appropriate legal basis notwithstanding, the legitimacy of the exercise is down to the acquiescence of the WTO Membership. In fact, the Decision of 17 December 2011 regarding TPRM, adopted during the Ministerial Conference held in Geneva, is simultaneously proof of acquiescence and the legal basis needed to continue reporting on this score. It reads in part:

> We therefore invite the Director-General to continue presenting his trade monitoring reports on a regular basis, and ask the TPRB to consider these monitoring reports in addition to its meeting to undertake the Annual Overview of Developments in the International Trading Environment.[17]

The WTO Secretariat started issuing a series of documents concerning the manner in which WTO Members had been complying with their obligations to notify the WTO in accordance with the substantive content of Annex III that we saw *supra*. It started issuing G/L/223 documents, where it would 'name and shame' the WTO Members that had been neglecting their notification obligations. Entitled 'Updating of the Listing of Notification Obligations and the Compliance Therewith as Set Out in Annex III of the Report of the Working Group on Notification Obligation and Procedures', documents in these series have been reflecting the manner in which WTO Members have been complying over the years with their

---

1929 crisis might have originally anticipated. On the other hand, it is probably too optimistic to give all the credit to the WTO for this outcome; see the various contributions in Bown (2011).

[16] WTO Doc. WT/GC/W/604 of 22 May 2009.
[17] WTO Doc. WT/L/848 of 19 December 2011.

obligation to notify under the various agreements that come under the aegis of the WTO.[18]

There is, thus, an arsenal of legal instruments aimed at increasing transparency and the move towards increasing the role of the common agent (the WTO Secretariat) is the (implicit) response to the failure to submit notifications by WTO Members. There is only so much that a Secretariat can do though: it too faces search costs and its powers of naming and shaming are limited. There are notorious cases that emerge when going through the G/L/223 series of WTO Members repeatedly refusing to notify requested information. It is also true, however, that there is a lot more information available in both absolute and relative terms than there ever was before. There are, of course, still cases where information is scarce (recall our discussion regarding notifications under the AG and SCM Agreements); but some decisive steps have been taken towards addressing missing information and the gradual change from WTO Members being exclusively competent to notify the GATT/WTO to increasing the powers of the disinterested (in domestic political-economy matters) agent, the WTO Secretariat, surely has a lot do with it.

In what follows we will move to a more general discussion regarding transparency in the WTO. This chapter is divided into three Sections:

(a) The general transparency obligation embedded in the GATT (Art. X);
(b) The WTO Trade Policy Review Mechanism (TPRM);
(c) The WTO Secretariat initiatives to gather and classify information regarding trade barriers following the world financial crisis (2008).

2. The General Transparency Obligation in the GATT (Art. X)

2.1 The Legal Discipline and its Rationale

Art. X GATT imposes the following obligations:

(a) All laws, administrative and judicial decisions of general application affecting trade must be published (Art. X.1 GATT);
(b) State acts covered by the aforementioned legal discipline will not be enforced before their publication if they represent a new or more burdensome requirement on imports (Art. X.2 GATT);
(c) State acts coming under the purview of Art. X.1 GATT must be administered in 'uniform, reasonable, and impartial' manner and a (national) forum must be provided where claims regarding the administration of customs laws can be adjudicated (Art. X.3 GATT).

---

[18] See, for example, WTO Doc. G/L/223/Rev. 18 of 9 March 2011.

Laws of general application cover an, in principle, unidentified number of commercial transactions, and consequently are of significant value to traders; on the other hand, it is to be expected that transaction-specific regulations are to be communicated to the interested parties anyway. Similar laws often allow for (some) discretion: for example, a requirement that the customs authority randomly inspects shipments to ensure that imports do not represent a health risk for domestic consumers would require the importing state to perform this task in a manner that does not violate MFN. The obligation to administer such laws in uniform, impartial, and reasonable manner corresponds to this logic. In this vein, the AB, in its report on *US—Underwear*, understood the transparency obligation embedded in Art. X GATT as a due process obligation (p. 21).[19]

In *EC—IT Products*, the Panel found that the EU had violated its obligations by publishing documents ten months after they had been made effective (§7.1076).

2.2 The Coverage of the Legal Discipline

2.2.1 Laws and Other Acts of General Application

A number of WTO reports have dealt with the interpretation of the term 'general application' appearing in Art. X GATT. The Panel on *US—Underwear* held that a safeguard imposed by the US on imports of cotton was a measure of general application. The relevant criterion in the Panel's view was that the measure at hand applied to an, in principle, unidentified number of economic operators and not to specific shipments. We quote from §7.65:

> The mere fact that the restraint at issue was an administrative order does not prevent us from concluding that the restraint was a measure of general application. Nor does the fact that it was a country-specific measure exclude the possibility of it being a measure of general application. If, for instance, the restraint was addressed to a specific company or applied to a specific shipment, it would not have qualified as a measure of general application. However, to the extent that the restraint affects an unidentified number of economic operators, including domestic and foreign producers, we find it to be a measure of general application.

On appeal, the AB upheld this finding (p. 21). The AB, in its report on *EC—Poultry*, provided the explicit confirmation to this effect: it was facing an appeal against a Panel finding to the effect that import licences issued by the EU to specific companies interested in importing poultry products and/or import licences applied to specific shipments (poultry products) to the EU were not measures of general application and, thus, not justiciable under Art. X GATT. The AB upheld the Panel's findings in this respect in the following terms (§113):

---

[19] See also in this respect the Panel report on *Argentina—Hides and Leather* (§11.76).

We agree with the Panel that 'conversely, licences issued to a specific company or applied to a specific shipment cannot be considered to be a measure "of general application"' within the meaning of Article X.[20]

The form that a measure coming under the purview of Art. X GATT must revert to is a separate issue. Recall that Art. X GATT mentions four categories only: laws; regulations; judicial decisions; and administrative rulings. Now these are supposed to be generic terms that should apply across the various denominations employed by WTO Members and disagreements regarding the coverage of this provision can naturally arise. The Panel on *Dominican Republic—Importation and Sale of Cigarettes* faced the following situation: the Central Bank of the defendant (Dominican Republic) was publishing price surveys for imported cigarettes. In the Panel's view, these surveys could not, in principle, come under any of the categories envisaged by Art. X.1 GATT. However, they constituted an essential input to the final determination of the duty imposed on imported cigarettes: duties are of course measures of general application by any reasonable standard. Consequently, although price surveys lacked, in the Panel's view, the formal characteristics of the categories envisaged by Art. X GATT, because they functioned as input to a measure of general application, they should come under Art. X.1 GATT anyway (§§7.404–8).

In *US—COOL*, the Panel held that (§7.840):

The act of providing guidance on the meaning of specific requirements under a measure, for instance by publishing 'frequently asked questions', is an act of administering such measure within the meaning of Art. X:3(a).

The same report held that a letter by the US Secretary of Agriculture, Thomas J. Vilsack (quoted in §7.123 of the Panel report), providing details regarding the implementation of a US statute regarding the origin of goods,[21] also qualifies as a measure covered by Art. X GATT (§7.840).

In *Thailand—Cigarettes (Philippines)*, the AB confirmed the Panel's finding to the effect that providing a guarantee in order to release goods through customs was a measure covered by Art. X GATT (§§215–16). In *EC—IT Products*, the Panel faced a claim to the effect that 'CNEN' should be considered as measures covered by this provision: a CNEN is an Explanatory Note to an EU Council Regulation.[22] It held that a measure does not have to be binding to be covered by Art. X GATT; it suffices that it is 'authoritative'. In its view, CNEN were authoritative because they were issued by the Commission and were meant to help the EU Member States to achieve uniformity with the EU Council Regulation (§§7.1023ff and especially 7.1027).

---

[20] See also the Panel report on *Argentina—Hides and Leather* at §§11.73ff.

[21] See the relevant discussion in Chapter 10.

[22] The Council Regulation 2658/87 of 23 July 1987 on Tariffs and Statistical Nomenclature and on the Common Customs Tariff, OJ L256/1, 7 September 1987.

2.2.2 Uniform, Reasonable, and Impartial Administration of Laws

In *US—Shrimp*, the AB had to address claims by a host of trading nations regarding the certification procedures practised by the US. Recall that, as we saw in Chapter 5, certification regarding the (accidental) rate of sea turtle mortality was required by the US authorities for shrimps to be lawfully imported in the US market. The claim by the complainants was that non-transparent, internal governmental procedures applied by the competent officials in the US Office of Marine Conservation, the US Department of State, and the US National Marine Fisheries Service throughout the certification processes under Section 609, as well as the fact that countries whose applications are denied do not receive formal notice of such denial, nor of the reasons for the denial, and the fact, too, that there is no formal legal procedure for review of, or appeal from, a denial of an application were all measures inconsistent with Art. X.3 GATT. The AB went on to state that Art. X GATT should be understood as imposing minimum transparency requirements, implying that WTO Members must anyway respect its letter and spirit while being free to go beyond the established standards, provided of course that their actions are otherwise GATT-consistent. We quote from §§182–3:

> The provisions of Article X:3 of the GATT 1994 bear upon this matter. In our view, Section 609 falls within the 'laws, regulations, judicial decisions and administrative rulings of general application' described in Article X:1. Inasmuch as there are due process requirements generally for measures that are otherwise imposed in compliance with WTO obligations, it is only reasonable that rigorous compliance with the fundamental requirements of due process should be required in the application and administration of a measure which purports to be an exception to the treaty obligations of the Member imposing the measure and which effectively results in a suspension *pro hac vice* of the treaty rights of other Members.
>
> It is also clear to us that Article X:3 of the GATT 1994 establishes certain minimum standards for transparency and procedural fairness in the administration of trade regulations which, in our view, are not met here. The non-transparent and *ex parte* nature of the internal governmental procedures applied by the competent officials in the Office of Marine Conservation, the Department of State, and the United States National Marine Fisheries Service throughout the certification processes under Section 609, as well as the fact that countries whose applications are denied do not receive formal notice of such denial, nor of the reasons for the denial, and the fact, too, that there is no formal legal procedure for review of, or appeal from, a denial of an application, are all contrary to the spirit, if not the letter, of Article X:3 of the GATT 1994.

The Panel on *Argentina—Hides and Leather* held that the obligation to administer laws in a uniform, reasonable, and impartial manner included three distinct requirements that would have to be interpreted separately (§11.86). The natural conclusion emerging from this finding is that WTO Members must satisfy all three separate requirements to be consistent with their obligations under the GATT.

Uniform Administration: The Panel on *Argentina—Hides and Leather* discussed, as we saw in Chapter 2, the consistency of an Argentine measure allowing
for representatives of the Argentine producers of leather products to be present
during customs clearance of hides with the multilateral rules. Recall that Argentina
had enacted Resolution 2235/96 which, *inter alia*, made it possible for representatives of the Argentine tanning industry (Association of Industrial Producers of
Leather, Leather Manufactures and Related Products, or ADICMA) to be present
during customs clearing procedures concerning exports of bovine hides. In the
view of the EU, the presence of ADICMA representatives amounted to a de facto
export restriction prohibited by Art. XI GATT (since ADICMA representatives
would have had an interest in keeping bovine hides in the Argentine market and
would, thus, have had an incentive to affect the total volume of exports). The bulk
of the complaint by the EU focused on the inconsistency of the said practice with
Art. XI GATT, as already discussed in Chapter 2. The claim under Art. X GATT
focused on the administration of Resolution 2235/96. More specifically, the EU
claimed that, in administering Resolution 2235/96 in an unreasonable, impartial,
and not uniform manner, Argentina was violating its obligations under Art. X.3
GATT. We quote the EU claim as reproduced in the AB report (§11.58):

> The European Communities argues that the presence of 'partial and interested'
> representatives of the tanning industry makes an impartial application of the relevant
> customs rules impossible. The European Communities also considers that it is
> not 'reasonable' within the meaning of Article X:3(a) that the interested industry is
> informed of all attempts at exports by those from whom they wish to obtain
> the exclusive right to purchase hides. The European Communities argued that the
> Argentinean administration of its laws also was not 'uniform'. According to the
> European Communities it was improper for Argentina to construct a special set
> of procedures for administering its export laws for only one type of product. Other
> products are subject to export duties or are eligible for export 'refunds'. In light of
> this, hides should not be singled out.

The EU claimed that the Argentine measure was not uniformly administered and,
thus, was in contradiction with Art. X.3 GATT, because it was applied to bovine
hides only and not to other products. The Panel dismissed this claim. In its view,
what mattered when reviewing the consistency of the challenged measure with Art.
X.3 GATT was not whether the measure was discriminatory or not, but whether it
provided traders with predictability as to future transactions. We quote from §§
11.83–5:

> It is obvious from these uses of the terms that it is meant that Customs laws should
> not vary, that every exporter and importer should be able to expect treatment of the
> same kind, in the same manner both over time and in different places and with
> respect to other persons. Uniform administration requires that Members ensure that
> their laws are applied consistently and predictably and is not limited, for instance, to
> ensuring equal treatment with respect to WTO Members. That would be a substan-
> tive violation properly addressed under Article I. This is a requirement of uniform

administration of Customs laws and procedures between individual shippers and even with respect to the same person at different times and different places.

We are of the view that this provision should not be read as a broad anti-discrimination provision. We do not think this provision should be interpreted to require all products be treated identically. That would be reading far too much into this paragraph which focuses on the day to day application of Customs laws, rules and regulations. There are many variations in products which might require differential treatment and we do not think this provision should be read as a general invitation for a panel to make such distinctions.

In our view, there is no evidence that Argentina has applied Resolution 2235 in a non-uniform manner with respect to hides. All hides exports are uniformly subject to the possibility of ADICMA representatives being present. Indeed, the European Communities' complaints are about Resolution 2235's application across the board. The difficulties of Argentina's administration of its Customs laws pursuant to Resolution 2235 are adequately dealt with under the other provisions of Article X:3(a).

So, uniformity should not be confused with non-discriminatory treatment across products. The request for uniform administration of laws is, in the Panel's eyes, tantamount to the obligation to provide predictability as to the treatment of future transactions and nothing beyond that. The Panel on *EC—Selected Customs Matters* held that the obligation for uniformity covers, *inter alia*, geographic uniformity.[23] This Panel held that the EU was in violation of Art. X GATT, because identical products within its sovereignty were subjected to different customs treatment (§§7.135 ff). By the same token, the same Panel found that differential customs administration of LCD monitors (Liquid Crystal Display) within the EU was tantamount to a violation of Art. X GATT (§7.305).[24] In this Panel's view, 'uniformity' should not be confused with 'identity'. Some differentiation might be appropriate, and the degree of uniformity should be determined on a case-by-case basis: the narrower the challenge (that is, the more specific the aspects of the administrative action complained about), the higher the degree of uniformity required (and, consequently, the lower the burden for the complainant to make a prima-facie case). More specifically, with respect to the tariff classification of LCD monitors with a digital video interface (hereinafter, LCD monitors), the situation was as follows: video monitors were classified under tariff heading 8528 and were subjected to a 14 per cent import duty in the EU market, whereas computer monitors were classified under tariff heading 8471 and paid 0 per cent import duty. The Netherlands classified LCD monitors under tariff heading 8528, whereas other EU Member States classified them under 8471. As a result, there was a discrepancy as to the import duty that LCD monitors exported to the EU market were subjected to, depending on whether the destination was the

---

[23] Hoekman and Mavroidis (2009) approvingly discuss this issue in more detail.

[24] In a rather cryptic passage, the precedence value of which can legitimately be brought into question, the Panel held that Art. XXIV.12 GATT is not an exception to Art. X.3(a) GATT.

Netherlands or another EU Member State. The Panel had originally found that this discrepancy amounted to non-uniform application and, consequently, run foul of Art. X.3(a) GATT, and the EU appealed this finding. It did not contest that divergence indeed existed across the various EU Member States; it did argue, however, that it had taken action since 2004 to address this phenomenon (§246, AB report). It submitted that the adoption of EC Reg. 2171/2005, combined with the withdrawal of the Dutch measure (classifying LCD monitors under 8528), were two measures that amply demonstrated that it had addressed the discrepancy and regretted that the Panel did not take either into account. The Panel had refused to take such evidence into account because it had been submitted belatedly, that is, after the interim review stage. The EU believed that the Panel's handling of this evidence was DSU-inconsistent, since the evidence submitted directly related to the interim report that had been circulated to the parties to the dispute (§248, AB report). Additionally, in the eyes of the EU, the Panel had violated its duty under Art. 11 DSU to make an objective assessment, since it took into account actions (the classification of LCD monitors by the Dutch authorities) that post-dated its establishment (§249, AB report). The AB was, thus, confronted with two issues:

(a) Can the Panel rely on evidence that post-dates its establishment?
(b) Was the Panel's decision not to take into account the evidence submitted by the EU at the interim review stage correct?

The AB responded affirmatively to the first question. In its view, the Panel could legitimately rely on data which post-dates its establishment in order to understand how a measure, which was in place when the Panel was established, was being administered. The AB found support for this conclusion in the fact that the EU did not point to any evidence that pre-dated the establishment of the Panel which could contradict the evidence on which the Panel relied (§254, AB report). Hence, absence of uniform administration can be established using data that post-dates the establishment of the Panel. The AB responded affirmatively to the second question as well. In prior case law, the AB had established that evidence submitted for the first time at the interim review stage is legitimately rejected (§259, AB report).

The requirement for uniformity has, consequently, been interpreted so far as tantamount to a requirement to ensure predictability (for the handling of future transactions), and a requirement for geographic uniformity.

Reasonable Administration: In its report on *Dominican Republic—Importation and Sale of Cigarettes*, the Panel found that not only positive actions, but also omissions can come under scrutiny in the context of the review regarding the consistency of a specific law, regulation etc. with Art. X.3 GATT (§7.379). In the case at hand, Honduras challenged the practice by Dominican Republic of avoiding calculating the imposition of a tax on imported cigarettes based on one of the three methods reflected in the Dominican law (§7.387). Instead, the Dominican Republic, on its own admission, was calculating the amount of imposition based on variables other than those published in the relevant generally applicable law. That is, the Dominican Republic had not included in its publication of laws variables used for the calculation of the imposition in this respect. Such an omission constituted, in the Panel's view, an unreasonable administration of its laws (§7.388).

The Panel on *Argentina—Hides and Leather* addressed, *inter alia*, a claim by the EU to the effect that the Argentine measure was in breach of Art. X.3 GATT, since it provided representatives of ADICMA with the possibility of access to confidential business information: namely, they could learn the names of the exporters and their pricing schemes. In the Panel's view, similar information could then be used to confer an advantage on the Argentine tanning industry, when negotiating with the upstream segment of this market. To reach its conclusion, the Panel first turned to the objective of the challenged Argentine law (§§11.90):

> In considering this requirement, we first turn to the stated objective for Resolution 2235 offered by Argentina. Argentina stated that it required assistance in the classification of bovine hides when exported in order to ensure there were no mistakes or fraud regarding the proper payment of export duties and awarding of export 'refunds'. While a manifestly WTO-inconsistent measure cannot be justified by assertions of good intentions, we consider it reasonable in this instance to accept for purposes of analysis the proffered explanation in light of all the facts of the dispute.

It subsequently concluded that an administration of laws which allowed for this possibility to occur was unreasonable and, thus, in contradiction with Art. X GATT, since it allowed for the dissemination of business confidential information which could be used to the commercial advantage of the Argentine producers of leather goods (§§11.92–4):

> To provide some specific examples, ADICMA representatives should not be able to see the pricing information of the suppliers to ADICMA's members. This is information which ADICMA members could use to their commercial advantage in negotiations with the *frigoríficos*. We should note in this regard that Argentina bases its export duties on prices of hides quoted in the United States. Thus, even if we were to consider it reasonable for the tanners to be involved in the export clearance process, there would be no reason whatever for them to see the prices as these would be irrelevant to the assessment of export duties. We also see no need for them to be made aware of the destination or quantities involved as these data are irrelevant to the tasks ADICMA representatives are involved in.
>
> We think it is particularly important for the reasonable administration of Argentina's export laws that the tanners not be provided the name of exporters. Argentina claims that this is no longer possible. However, as it was part of the European Communities' claims and was unarguably possible as recently as May of 1999 that such written information was supplied to ADICMA, we consider it necessary to specifically find that it is unreasonable for such information to be provided to

ADICMA or its members. However, this question goes beyond just supply of the name in writing. Argentina has stressed in its arguments under all three conditions of Article X:3(a) that the process is balanced because the exporters may be present during the Customs process. However, it necessarily follows that exercising this right would reveal the identity of the exporter. While it could be argued that the exporter could send a representative or agent and may thereby conceal his identity, imposing such a burden with respect to an exporter's own products would be unreasonable.

Therefore, we must conclude that a process aimed at assuring the proper classification of products, but which inherently contains the possibility of revealing confidential business information, is an unreasonable manner of administering the laws, regulations and rules identified in Article X:1 and therefore is inconsistent with Article X:3(a). (italics in the original)

It follows that, so far, the requirement for reasonable administration has been understood as a requirement not to confer a commercial advantage on domestic producers.

Impartial Administration: The Panel on *EC—Selected Customs Matters* held that the requirement for impartiality meant that the reviewing agency (tribunal) should be independent from the agency the acts of which were being challenged (§7. 519). In *Argentina—Hides and Leather*, the EU had argued that the Argentine measure was not being administered in an impartial manner, since there was absolutely no legitimate reason why ADICMA representatives should be present during customs clearance of bovine hides. Moreover, information obtained by their mere presence could potentially be used to their own advantage (as already discussed *supra*). Hence, there was at least potentially a case of conflict of interest. The Panel upheld this claim, since it agreed that the mere possibility that the Argentine industry present in customs clearance could use confidential information to its own advantage amounted *ipso facto* to a violation of the impartial administration requirement embedded in Art. X GATT (§§11.99–102):

> The only private parties that have a contractual legal interest in the product and transaction are the exporter (and his agent) and the foreign buyer. The government also has a relevant legal interest in the transaction based on the sovereign right to regulate and tax exports. In contrast with this, the ADICMA representatives have, outside of the measure in question itself, no legal relationship with either the products or the sales contract. ADICMA, in fact, represents an adverse commercial interest in that the exports are not in its members' interests as such exports potentially drive up the costs of hides. Furthermore, ADICMA members are competitors of the foreign buyers of the hides.
>
> Much as we are concerned in general about the presence of private parties with conflicting commercial interests in the Customs process, in our view the requirement of impartial administration in this dispute is not a matter of mere presence of ADICMA representatives in such processes. It all depends on what that person is permitted to do. In our view, the answer to this question is related directly to the question of access to information as part of the product classification process as discussed in the previous Section. Our concern here is focused on the need for safeguards to prevent the inappropriate flow of one private person's confidential

information to another as a result of the administration of the Customs laws, in this case the implementing Resolution 2235.

Whenever a party with a contrary commercial interest, but no relevant legal interest, is allowed to participate in an export transaction such as this, there is an inherent danger that the Customs laws, regulations and rules will be applied in a partial manner so as to permit persons with adverse commercial interests to obtain confidential information to which they have no right.

While this situation could be remedied by adequate safeguards, we do not consider that such safeguards presently are in place. Therefore, Resolution 2235 cannot be considered an impartial administration of the Customs laws, regulations and rules described in Article X:1 and, thus, is inconsistent with Article X:3(a) of the GATT 1994.

A very demanding standard was thus established and WTO Members, following this case law, will have to ensure adherence to it.

2.3 The Obligation to Maintain Independent Tribunals

WTO Members must, by virtue of Art. X.3(b) GATT, establish (judicial, arbitral, administrative) tribunals (or procedures) that will be independent from the agency the acts of which they will be reviewing. Traders should have recourse to such tribunals or procedures. The Panel on *EC—Selected Customs Matters* underscored this requirement for impartiality of tribunals (§7. 519). In this report, the Panel dealt with the question to what extent a decision should govern the practice of all agencies entrusted with administrative enforcement throughout the territory of the WTO Member concerned. The Panel held that reading Art. X3(b) GATT in this way was unwarranted. It based its finding on its understanding that tribunals mentioned in Art. X.3(b) GATT were in all likelihood first instance tribunals and requiring similar effect of their decisions could raise public order-type concerns: in the Panel's view, the courts viewed by this provision should be typically first instance courts and, as such, it is only normal that in some national jurisdictions they might have been assigned a specific territorial scope.[25] The US appealed this finding (that WTO Members need not, by virtue of the obligation included in Art. X.3(b) GATT, establish courts which will have the authority to bind all agencies entrusted with administrative enforcement throughout the territory of a WTO Member). The US had recourse to predominantly textual arguments. In its view, the Panel had not paid sufficient attention to the term 'agencies' appearing in Art. X.3(b) GATT, which, unless understood to cover all administrative agencies throughout the territory of a WTO Member, could not guarantee uniform application of laws as required by this provision. The AB was thus presented with the opportunity to clarify its understanding of the obligation included in Art. X.3(b) GATT. The AB upheld the Panel's finding to the effect that the tribunals envisaged in the first sentence of this provision are first instance tribunals (§294).

---

[25] See the analysis leading to the final ruling in §7.539.

Based on textual and contextual arguments (first instance courts do not extend their jurisdiction throughout the territory of a WTO Member; the existence of second instance courts supports this thesis), it sided with the Panel (§§298–9). It then went on to find that the obligation is limited to first instance courts and not all administrative agencies as the US had argued, upholding the Panel's findings on this score in the following terms (§303):

> For these reasons, we are of the view that Article X:3(b) of the GATT 1994 requires a WTO Member to establish and maintain independent mechanisms for prompt review and correction of administrative action in the area of customs administration. However, neither text nor context nor the object and purpose of this Article require that the decisions emanating from such first instance review must govern the practice of *all* agencies entrusted with administrative enforcement *throughout the territory* of a particular WTO Member. (emphasis in the original)

2.4 Standard of Review

WTO adjudicating bodies must, by virtue of Art. 11 DSU, make an objective assessment of the factual record before them; case law has clarified that, with respect to disputes coming under the purview of Art. X GATT, this duty will, more specifically, entail that they:

(a) Are satisfied that a violation has occurred in cases where there is likely impact on the competitive situation across domestic and foreign products, due to the unreasonableness, lack of uniformity, and/or partiality in the administration of a law;

(b) Will not be questioning the substantive consistency of a law with the multi-lateral rules; rather, their review should be confined to the consistency in the administration of laws in accordance with the obligations included in Art. X GATT.

In *Argentina—Hides and Leather*, one of the questions before the Panel was to what extent, in order to observe its burden of proof, the EU had to show actual effects (of trade damage) for its producers and traders, as a result of the administration of the contested legislation. The Panel dismissed this thesis; in its view, it sufficed that the EU demonstrated the likelihood that the interests of traders would be negatively affected, as a result of the administration of Resolution 2235/96, and no actual trade damage had to be shown. We quote from §11.77:

> Thus, it can be seen that Article X:3(a) requires an examination of the real effect that a measure might have on traders operating in the commercial world. This, of course, does not require a showing of trade damage, as that is generally not a requirement with respect to violations of the GATT 1994. But it can involve an examination of whether there is a possible impact on the competitive situation due to alleged

partiality, unreasonableness or lack of uniformity in the application of customs rules, regulations, decisions, etc.[26]

How much examination is required to observe the standard of review under Art. X GATT thus established is to be decided on a case-by-case basis. The AB in its report on *US—OCTG Sunset Reviews* confirmed that some explanation is necessary for a claim to succeed and that a mere submission of data, which could be interpreted in more than one way, is not sufficient. In this case, Argentina argued that the US had not been administering its sunset reviews of antidumping duties in a reasonable manner, since the domestic industry recorded 223 wins in 223 cases, that is, there was no case where the exporters prevailed (§ 218). The AB refused to accept the Argentine claim in this respect since, in its view, for a claim under Art. X.3 GATT to be successful, solid evidence was required. Mere statistical evidence which could be interpreted in various ways did not suffice (§§217–19). It follows that Argentina should have demonstrated that the outcome was due to unreasonable, or non-uniform, or partial administration of laws.

Art. X GATT is not concerned with the substantive consistency of a particular act with the GATT rules either. This is the subject-matter of other GATT provisions. Art. X GATT is concerned with the administration of laws. The AB held as much in its report on *EC—Bananas III* (§200):

> The context of Article X:3(a) within Article X, which is entitled 'Publication and Administration of Trade Regulations', and a reading of the other paragraphs of Article X, make it clear that Article X applies to the *administration* of laws, regulations, decisions and rulings. To the extent that the laws, regulations, decisions and rulings themselves are discriminatory, they can be examined for their consistency with the relevant provisions of the GATT 1994.

In the same vein, the AB reached a similar conclusion in its report on *EC—Poultry*. The AB entertained a claim by Brazil to the effect that an EU measure relating to imports of frozen poultry meat did not allow Brazilian traders to know whether a particular shipment would be subjected to the rules governing in-quota trade or to rules relating to out-of-quota trade. Brazil maintained that this was a violation of Art. X GATT. The AB held the view that, in part, this claim concerned the substantive consistency of the EU measure at hand with the pertinent GATT rules and that this part of the claim lay outside the coverage of Art. X GATT. It stated in §115:

> Thus, to the extent that Brazil's appeal relates to the *substantive content* of the EC rules themselves, and not to their *publication* or *administration*, that appeal falls outside the scope of Article X of the GATT 1994. The WTO-consistency of such

---

[26] The potential for non-uniform administration of laws sufficed for the Panel to find against the EU in its report on *EC—Selected Customs Matters*. In this case, the Panel held that the defendant was in breach of its WTO obligations because of the possibility that blackout drapery lining was treated in German customs differently than it was in other EU customs (§§7.276ff).

substantive content must be determined by reference to provisions of the covered agreements other than Article X of the GATT 1994. (emphasis in the original)[27]

The Panel on *Argentina—Hides and Leather* reached a similar conclusion (§§11.60):

> The context of Article X:3(a) within Article X, which is entitled 'Publication and Administration of Trade Regulations', and a reading of the other paragraphs of Article X, make it clear that Article X applies to the *administration* of laws, regulations, decisions and rulings. To the extent that the laws, regulations, decisions and rulings themselves are discriminatory, they can be examined for their consistency with the relevant provisions of the GATT 1994.

In *EC—Selected Customs Matters*, the AB provided a noteworthy precision: the substantive content of the instrument that regulates administration of a measure can of course be challenged. It is the substantive content of instruments being administered that cannot be challenged (§§200–1):

> The statements of the Appellate Body in *EC—Bananas III* and *EC—Poultry* do not exclude, however, the possibility of challenging under Article X:3(a) the substantive content of a legal instrument that regulates the administration of a legal instrument of the kind described in Article X:1. Under Article X:3(a), a distinction must be made between the legal instrument being administered and the legal instrument that regulates the application or implementation of that instrument. While the substantive content of the legal instrument being administered is not challengeable under Article X:3(a), we see no reason why a legal instrument that regulates the application or implementation of that instrument cannot be examined under Article X:3(a) if it is alleged to lead to a lack of uniform, impartial, or reasonable administration of that legal instrument.
>
> This distinction has of course implications with respect to the type of evidence that the complainant must submit to support a claim of a violation of Article X:3(a) GATT. If a WTO Member challenges, under Article X:3(a) GATT, the substantive content of a legal instrument that regulates the administration of a legal instrument of the kind described in Article X:1, it will have to prove that this instrument *necessarily* leads to a lack of uniform, impartial, or reasonable administration. It is not sufficient for the complainant merely to cite the provisions of that legal instrument. The complainant must discharge the burden of substantiating how and why those provisions necessarily lead to impermissible administration of the legal instrument of the kind described in Article X:1.

This might be a laudable clarification but, by attempting to place the procedural and substantive aspects of the law into hermetically sealed boxes so to speak, the relevant WTO body may end up with a problematic interpretation: for instance, the manner in which a law is administered should pay due regard to its substantive nature. In essence, it is surely impractical to strike down administrative procedures without at least inquiring into the rationale behind the law in question. This is not meant to support the thesis that a WTO Panel should, when entertaining a

---

[27] For additional confirmation, see §7.113 of the Panel report on *EC—Selected Customs Matters*.

complaint that Art. X GATT has been violated, take the liberty to pronounce on the substantive consistency of a law with another GATT provision. Nevertheless, an inquiry into the rationale of the law might occasionally prove a useful stepping stone in constructing its findings with respect to the consistency of the challenged measure with Art. X GATT. This is probably what the drafters of this Panel report had in mind when performing the distinction mentioned above.

3. The Trade Policy Review Mechanism (TPRM)

The Trade Policy Review Mechanism (TPRM) was established in 1989 on a provisional basis, and became a permanent feature of the multilateral trading system pursuant to Annex 3 WTO Agreement. The WTO Agreement required that the operation of the TPRM was to be evaluated by the Trade Policy Review Body (TPRB, the WTO body administering the TPRM) in 1999. The evaluation concluded that the TPRM functions effectively, and as a consequence, the TPRM has become a permanent feature of the WTO legal edifice.[28] In accordance with Annex 3 of the WTO Agreement, the objectives of the TPRM are:

> to contribute to improved adherence by all Members to rules, disciplines and commitments made under the Multilateral Trade Agreements and, where applicable, the Plurilateral Trade Agreements, and hence to the smoother functioning of the multilateral trading system, by achieving greater transparency in, and understanding of, the trade policies and practices of Members.

To this effect, the WTO Secretariat, which is entrusted with the responsibility to prepare the reports, is required to periodically review the trade policies and practices of all WTO Members. The reports are prepared by the WTO Secretariat (by a special unit called the Trade Policy Review Mechanism Division). Over the years, the special unit has had more and more recourse to in-house expertise: members of other specialized divisions of the WTO have been participating in the drafting of reports which have thus been enriched.[29] Occasionally, the WTO Secretariat reports are prepared with the help of outside consultants (this has been the case for the reviews of the Maldives, Niger, Senegal, and the Southern African Customs Union). The WTO Secretariat's reports are written in close consultation with the authorities of the Member under review. Since the WTO Secretariat does not have the authority to interpret the covered agreements, a TPRM report on the trade policies and practices of a Member does not provide an assessment as to the legal consistency of particular policies with the multilateral agreements; it is a mere

---

[28] WTO Doc. WT/MIN(99)/2 of 8 October 1999.
[29] WTO Doc. WT/TPR/OV/14 of 21 November 2011 at §181.

exercise in transparency. A WTO document[30] reflecting the record of the TPRM as of mid-2003 concluded that:

> while each review highlights the specific issues and measures concerning the individual Member, certain common themes emerged during the course of the reviews conducted in the period January–July 2003. These included:
>
> transparency in policy-making and implementation; economic environment and trade liberalization; implementation of the WTO Agreements; regional trade agreements and their relationship with the multilateral trading system; tariff issues, including peaks, escalation, preferences, rationalization and the difference between applied and bound rates; customs clearance procedures; import and export restrictions and licensing procedures; the use of contingency measures such as anti-dumping and countervailing duties; technical and sanitary measures and market access; standards and their equivalence with international norms; intellectual property rights legislation and enforcement; government procurement policies and practices; state involvement in the economy and privatization programmes; trade-related competition and investment policy issues; incentive measures such as subsidies and tax forgone; sectoral trade-policy issues, particularly liberalization in agriculture and certain services sectors; GATS commitments; special and differential treatment, including market access and implementation, particularly for customs valuation, TRIPS and TRIMs; small-island and small land-locked Members; and technical assistance in implementing the WTO Agreements and the experience with the Integrated Framework.

By the end of 2011, 338 reviews had been conducted since the establishment of the TPRB: the reviews covered 141 of 153 Members, representing some 89 per cent of world trade and 96 per cent of the trade of Members.[31] All but three WTO Members (namely, Cuba, Guinea Bissau, and Myanmar) will have been reviewed by February 2012.[32] Not all WTO Members are reviewed with similar frequency. The periodicity of the reviews depends on the relative weight that WTO Members have in world trade. Annex 3 of the WTO Agreement, where the decision to establish the TPRM has been included, pertinently reads at item C:

> The trade policies and practices of all Members shall be subject to periodic review. The impact of individual Members on the functioning of the multilateral trading system, defined in terms of their share of world trade in a recent representative period, will be the determining factor in deciding on the frequency of reviews. The first four trading entities so identified (counting the European Communities as one) shall be subject to review every two years. The next 16 shall be reviewed every four years. Other Members shall be reviewed every six years, except that a longer period may be fixed for least-developed country Members.

This feature of the TPRM has been criticized by many in the literature, the crux of the argument being that it is LDCs and developing countries in general that

---

[30] WTO Doc. WT/TPR/134 of 27 June 2003.
[31] WTO Doc. WT/TPR/287 of 15 November 2011.
[32] WTO Doc. WT/TPR/OV/14 of 21 November 2011 at p. 59.

should be reviewed more frequently rather than the other way round. After all, one of the aims of the TPRM is to make the WTO a policy-relevant option for domestic legislature and the need in this respect is far greater among LDCs and developing countries. Over the years TPRM has become more responsive to this type of arguments and indeed 29 out of 32 LDCs have by now been reviewed, the frequency of reviews being, alas, still an issue.[33]

Still the TPRM continues to face criticism: among the most representative critics, Ghosh (2010) argued that the TPRM does not provide the kind of information that developing countries would be interested in and, thus, its usefulness in this respect is limited and should not be exaggerated. This is a valid point in the sense that reports are not tailor-made to correspond to the needs of developing countries, which might need to undertake additional effort in order to familiarize themselves with policy options taken by their trading partners that affect them most. Zahrnt (2009) would like to see reports that discuss the costs of protectionism; otherwise their contribution towards shaping domestic policies will be limited, if not irrelevant altogether. Quantifying the costs of protectionism would definitely help improve the quality of domestic dialogue regarding the type of trade policies that should be pursued. Yet, one would need to first agree on a different function for the TPRM, which, according to its item A, should pursue the following:

> The purpose of the Trade Policy Review Mechanism ('TPRM') is to contribute to improved adherence by all Members to rules, disciplines and commitments made under the Multilateral Trade Agreements and, where applicable, the Plurilateral Trade Agreements, and hence to the smoother functioning of the multilateral trading system, by achieving greater transparency in, and understanding of, the trade policies and practices of Members.

The current disciplines contain clearly protectionist instruments, such as the AD Agreement, that the TPRM must help to be implemented.

4. WTO Secretariat Initiatives

As discussed above, since the outbreak of the 2008 financial crisis, the WTO Secretariat, along with the OECD and UNCTAD secretariats, has prepared regular reports on G 20 trade and investment measures adopted during the crisis.[34] These reports are issued as TPR documents, that is, under the aegis of TPRM, but they differ in that they are issued frequently and reflect trade-obstructing measures irrespective of their *raison d'être*.

---

[33] WTO Doc. WT/TPR/287 of 15 November 2011 at §7.
[34] WTO Doc. WT/MIN(11)/5 of 18 November 2011 at p. 6.

At this stage, it is difficult to predict how this initiative will shape up in the future: it was clearly linked to the financial crisis and one would expect that, were the crisis to be eventually addressed, the mandate will lapse. And yet, the argument for a common agent is quite strong in the transparency context, where, as stated above, the incentives to notify might be missing. Recall our discussion above: the subject-matter of notification influences the incentive to notify; those with the power to purchase information are disadvantaged when information becomes free for all. These two are probably the strongest reasons why the record of notifications has not been satisfactory across the board. Assigning competence to the WTO Secretariat avoids the problems posed by the missing incentives to notify and strengthen the transparency obligations.[35]

The WTO is no bottleneck when it comes to securing information regarding trade barriers: there are many initiatives in this context. For example, the Global Trade Alert (<http://www.globaltradealert.org>) has emerged as a databank with information regarding measures taken in response to the financial crisis. The authors probably consciously decided to err on the supply side by including all measures adopted during the crisis, even though some (many) of them were adopted for reasons unrelated to the crisis itself. They, thus, provided the WTO and trading nations with invaluable information, while placing the onus on the trading nations adopting similar measures to explain their rationale. In similar vein, the World Bank has established a databank with information regarding contingent protection instruments, namely, antidumping, countervailing duties, safeguards, and the China special safeguard clause (<http://econ.worldbank.org/ttbd/>). Collins-Williams and Wolfe (2010) have argued in favour of making similar information available through official WTO channels by, for example, allowing for cross-notifications by NGOs[36] and/or other international organizations. These arguments are definitely worth taking on board, for there is no reason for the WTO to close its eyes to reliable and useful information, assuming it has satisfied itself that this is indeed the case.

---

[35] Similar thoughts have been expressed in Hoekman and Mavroidis (2000).

[36] For example the Global Subsidies Initiative, an NGO specializing in gathering information about all types of subsidies, is very critical of subsidies notifications to the WTO (<http://www.globalsubsidies.org>) and could be instrumental in providing information regarding missing notifications.

CONCLUSIONS

1. What Explains the GATT?

We started this volume by asking what drives international agreements like the GATT. In this volume, we took the view that trading nations signed the GATT in order to avoid (reduce) cost-shifting by other trading nations to them. We referred repeatedly to the work of Bagwell and Staiger (2002) and Grossman et al. (2012), who have attempted to understand the various GATT disciplines through these lenses. The differences between the studies notwithstanding, they share one fundamental core feature: it is international externalities that trade agreements aim to resolve and not domestic issues. In doing that, we discarded commitment theory as an explanation for the GATT: individual trading nations might wish to commit to the international level, but their wish in and of itself does not explain why a domestic issue should become the foundation of an international agreement.

2. Gaps in the Contract

The GATT framers must be credited with a remarkable agreement that has successfully withstood the test of time. They devised a pragmatic, flexible contract that provided the forum for remarkable trade liberalization in the second part of the twentieth century. Dam (1970, p.80) put it very succinctly:

> Because of the economic nature of tariff concessions and the domestic sensitivity involved in trade issues, a system that made withdrawals of concessions impossible would tend to discourage the making of concessions in the first place. It is better, for example, that 100 commitments should be made and that 10 should be withdrawn than that only 50 commitments should be made and that all of them should be kept.

The GATT contract nevertheless, remarkable as it is, is not perfect. For the reasons explained in Chapter 4, the WTO contract is 'incomplete'. Since it is not a renegotiation-proof contract, it was (and is) always possible to add to the original content. And, indeed, the high costs of renegotiation (because of the consensus rule applicable to the decision-making process) notwithstanding, some renegotiation has taken place, especially regarding the disciplining of domestic instruments. The problem is that, for the reasons developed in Horn et al. (2010a), it is virtually impossible to write a complete state-contingent contract, the amount of effort notwithstanding. Take the example of the SPS: compared to the GATT, it is a net improvement when it comes to drawing an anti-protectionism test; and yet, terms such as 'based on scientific evidence', 'consistency', 'international standard', 'appropriate' have been understood in different ways by different WTO Members and have given rise to disputes. Contractual incompleteness is a source of legitimate disputes, not to mention that some disputes could originate in bad faith. As we have no theory to distinguish between good- and bad-faith disputes, though, the WTO rationally does not distinguish either. The point here is that, in the presence of contractual incompleteness and in light of the high negotiating costs, the role of the WTO judge becomes crucial.

3. Settling Disputes in the WTO: The Crown Jewel of the System?

There have been numerous accounts of the WTO dispute settlement system[1] and its workings, and the purpose of these concluding remarks is definitely not to delve into the details of dispute adjudication. It has been hailed by many as the crown jewel of the WTO system, the most effective dispute settlement system in international relations.[2] And yet, as we have attempted to show in this volume, with few exceptions the law that the WTO framers have put in place is reasonable; it is case law that falters.

The WTO is a rarity in international relations in that it is a system of compulsory third-party adjudication. Largely due to the GATT pragmatism in resolving disputes, as the monumental study by Hudec (1993a) has shown, the framers of the DSU decided to judicialize the process even further.[3] The WTO has evolved into the busiest state-to-state court in international relations, dwarfing other tribunals in numbers of disputes adjudicated.[4] To be sure, many of the disputes are solved in the pre-Panel phase, as the work of Busch and Reinhardt (2001, 2002, 2003, and 2005), and Guzman and Simmons (2005) shows. But then again, consultations are part of the WTO dispute settlement system and the WTO should be credited with the remarkable success in solving almost two-thirds of all submitted disputes at the consultations stage.

Roughly one-third of all disputes go to the Panel stage. It is here where the judge acts as the entity that 'completes' the contract, providing the additional

---

[1] Abbott (1996); Davey (1987); Horn and Mavroidis (2007); Hudec (1990); Palmeter and Mavroidis (2004); Trachtman (1998).

[2] Guzman (2004) echoes the view of many in this respect.

[3] von Bogdandy (2003); Ehlermann (2004); Ehlermann and Lockhart (2004).

[4] As Koremenos (2007) has shown, the fact that half the PTAs do not have their own dispute settlement system has helped (compare Levy and Srinivasan (1996) in this respect); as has the fact that countries like Mexico would rather litigate disputes with their NAFTA partners before the WTO rather than before a NAFTA Panel, as evidenced by the work by Huerta Goldman (2009).

information (missing in the original contract) and clarifying the rule of law. The judge must respect the statutory limits of discretion, and cannot undo the balance of rights and obligations struck by the framers of the WTO. It is an agent, not a principal; the judge is in an unenviable position, since it must interpret one incomplete contract (GATT and Annex 1A Agreements as we saw in this volume) through another (the VCLT). The judge risks the wrath of the Membership even when not at fault: the WTO is a self-enforcing contract and, at the end of the day (on occasion at least), implementation is not a function of the persuasiveness of the findings, but of the relative bargaining power of the parties to the dispute. Against this background, the judge must prepare for its own demise in the sense that it must make the law so predictable that recourse to it will become unnecessary. The judge, in other words, is no substitute for consultations. There all sorts of arguments and reasons that will dictate the outcome; before the judge it must be the rule of law as understood through the lens of the VCLT.

Critical voices have been raised regarding the functioning of WTO dispute settlement. Some are totally unrelated to the role of the judge: Shaffer (2003) and Nordström (2007; and Nordström and Shaffer 2007) point to the lack of capacity by developing countries to effectively participate in the WTO Committees and the dispute settlement system in light of the associated costs. Some of the critique, which has recently been translated into concrete negotiating proposals in the context of the DSU Review, has to do with the system of remedies: some, (probably) inspired by Becker (1968) and Schelling (1960), have argued that the system as it stands has no credible institutional threat against potential violators; others, like Goh and Ziegler (2003), Mavroidis (2000a), and Pauwelyn (2000 and 2003), have noted the discrepancy between remedies in public international law and the WTO system and tried to understand what best explains the difference.[5]

There is critique that has to do with agency design (and not necessarily with the quality of the output, although one cannot exclude that it is the critical evaluation of the output that is at the heart of the critique): Bourgeois (2005), Cottier (2004), Davey (2004), Kessie (2004), and various contributions in Weiss (2000) have argued in favour of permanent (instead of ad hoc) Panellists; Nordström (2007), on the other hand, has called for the role of the Secretariat to be curtailed.

And then there are those who directly criticize the output, chief among them the ALI (American Law Institute) edited annual volumes: 65 reports, discussing the case law since 2000, have already been published and close to 60 per cent of them criticize the output for incoherence or for the total absence of methodology. Indeed, even perusing some of the chapters in this volume will persuade the reader

---

[5] In our view, Ethier (2001) offered the best explanation when he argued that the uncertainty regarding the identity of defendants and losers is what prompted the framers to avoid introducing hard remedies in the system. Still, Esserman and Howse (2004) took the view that remedies in the *US—FSC* litigation were excessive, while Schwarz and Sykes (1998) would have preferred more drastic remedies.

that case law has found it impossible to adopt meaningful interpretations of even the most basic concepts. Ask yourself what the outcome will be if the *EC—Asbestos* methodology is applied in the next case dealing with like products. Can anyone with certainty predict the outcome? The problem lies in the fact that the whole judgment hinges on the 'reasonable consumer' test, an arbitrary concept which, like an accordion (another invention of the AB), can accommodate more or less goods depending on unknown (to the users of the system) circumstances. One could run the same example by asking what is a reasonable benchmark for calculating the benefit resulting from a subsidy: how can we predict the outcome when all we know is that the benchmark must be reasonable? And so on and so forth. It is methodology that matters in a system like the WTO and not the final outcome. Outcomes are transaction-specific and of no intrinsic value in predicting the resolution of the marginal transaction. It is no use knowing that asbestos-containing construction material is not a like product to asbestos-free construction material; it is of use to know how we ended up with that outcome.

Moreover, there are cases—and there are quite a few of them (we have discussed them in this volume)—where Panels have expressed contradictory opinions: the cases regarding zeroing, the cases regarding likeness, etc. Recently (2011), three disputes were adjudicated under the TBT and reports were issued within two months of each other; they do not see eye to eye on any of the issues discussed. If at all, they point to a problem of coordination and the question arises whether the AB as it now stands can solve similar problems. The answer, based on the record so far, is sometimes yes (e.g. the zeroing cases), sometimes no (e.g. the privatization cases), and sometimes we simply do not know since the methodology for resolving an issue has not been revealed (e.g. the likeness cases).

Since, as argued above, the judge has substantial discretion in light of contract incompleteness, it is time for the WTO to rethink the agency design in priority terms. It is, for example, unwarranted to assume that tough economic issues (like the causality requirement; the definition of the relevant product market, etc.) are entrusted to members of the WTO Secretariat with no training at all in economics. It is surprising that, while economic analysis of law has managed to become so influential in antitrust, it still lags behind when it comes to trade law, the fact that the two fields of law share quintessential elements notwithstanding. Or that the majority of appointed Panellists are delegates in Geneva who represent national interests (sometimes, in similar cases); or that the members of the AB dealing at last resort with issues such as the subsidization of Airbus and Boeing, the subsidization of the EU steel industry, and the consistency of anti-GMO legislation with the multilateral rules are part-timers who cannot (by reason of the agency design) spend the time needed to discuss similar issues with the attention they undeniably deserve.

Some will argue that no disaster has occurred and there is no problem to fix. Of course, it is all a matter of opinion and if by 'disaster' we understand a WTO Member walking out in protest, or refusal to comply because of the poor quality of reports, or collective action against a judgment,[6] then disaster has not happened as yet. But there is absolutely no need to wait for a disaster before fixing a problem, for if a problem does happen, then it may be too late to fix it anyway. There is still hope, at the moment of writing, that agency design will find its way to the ongoing Doha round: in this respect, the non-conclusion of the round is probably a blessing.

4. Trade in Goods in Context

The WTO regime for trade in goods is facing serious challenges and it is not because of the difficulties in concluding the Doha round that this is the case. Serious problems are being posed to the current design.

Without at all pretending that what follows is an exhaustive, or even an absolute priority, list, we illustrate three issues. First, the gradual reduction in tariff protection, and especially their eventual elimination, raises the veil behind which tomorrow's trade negotiations will have to take place. What place is there for reciprocity in trade negotiations regarding, for all practical purposes, domestic instruments of a non-fiscal nature? Yes, regulations are implicit taxes, but how will equivalence across regulations aiming at totally different objectives ever be established? This is probably not the first issue to address in tomorrow's world since we are still some way off eliminating tariff protection altogether, but it is something that we should all start thinking about.

More pressing are two other issues: the success of the GATT in liberalizing trade (as well as the unilateral liberalization of investment) has opened the road to very substantial free mobility of factors of production around the world. Supply chains that span the world are the natural outcome of this phenomenon, as markets become increasingly competitive and delocalization of (parts of) production becomes inevitable in order to respond to competitive pressures. We pointed for example in Chapter 3 to the problems that internationalization of production poses for rules of origin. We could add its influence on the domestic political economy: will US lobbies push for AD duties against imports of LeNovo computers when a high percentage of the value added is American and only a small percentage Chinese? But most important for our discussion here is the challenges that internationalization of supply chains poses to the current design of negative integration. Tolerance of anti-competitive practices in one part of the world can now have very substantial effects on intra-firm trade and Antras and Staiger (forthcoming) are right to point to this issue and its eventual implications for the design of tomorrow's multilateral trading system.

---

[6] We came close to this, though, in the aftermath of the reports on the possibility of an *amicus curiae* to communicate its views to a WTO adjudicating body; see Mavroidis (2004a).

Finally, PTAs seem to be running away with the trade agenda. President Obama was celebrating the integration of the Pacific in Honolulu days before the Ministerial Conference was pronouncing the impossibility of concluding the Doha round in Geneva. There is a stark contrast here.

In the coming months and years, the WTO will have to rethink its attitude towards PTAs and towards its own agenda, and the two are not unrelated. There are no magic solutions and the WTO is a negotiating forum and not a think tank. But these are serious issues that have to be confronted, for the future existence and success of the multilateral trading system will largely depend on the responses provided to these questions. The WTO might not be functioning to perfection, but it is a powerful mechanism signalling that multilateral cooperation, the genuine contribution to peace, exists.

REFERENCES

Aaronson, Susan Ariel. 1999. *Who Decides? Congress and the Debate over Trade Policy in 1934 and 1974*, Council of Foreign Relations: New York, NY.

Abbott, Fred. 2000. The NAFTA and the Legalization of World Politics, *International Organization*, 54: 519–50.

Abbott, Kenneth W. 1996. Defensive Unfairness: The Normative Structure of Section 301, pp. 415–71 in Jagdish Bhagwati and Robert Hudec (eds.), *Fair Trade And Harmonization*, MIT Press: Cambridge, Mass.

Abbott, Philip, and B. Adair Morse. 2004. How Developing Countries are Implementing Tariff Rate Quotas, pp. 74–100 in Merlinda D. Ingco and L. Alan Winters (eds.), *Agriculture and the New Trade Agenda*, Cambridge University Press: Cambridge, UK.

Abdel Motaal, Dooa. 2004. The 'Multilateral Scientific Consensus' and the World Trade Organization, *Journal of World Trade*, 38: 855–76.

Acharya, Rohini, Jo-Ann Crawford, Maryla Maliszewska, and Christelle Rernard. 2011. Landscape, pp. 37–68 in Jean-Pierre Chauffour and Jean-Christophe Maur (eds.), *Preferential Trade Agreement Policies for Development: A Handbook*, World Bank Group: Washington, DC.

Acheson, Dean. 1969. Present at the Creation: My Years in the State Department. W. W. Norton: New York, NY.

Acheson, Keith, and Christopher Maule. 2001. *Much Ado about Culture*, University of Michigan Press: Ann Arbor, Mich.

Åhman, Joachim. 2012. *Trade Liberalisation, Health Protection, and the Burden of Proof in WTO Law*, Kluwer Law: The Netherlands.

Alemanno, Alberto. 2007. *Trade in Food: Regulatory and Judicial Approaches in EC and the WTO*, Cameron May: London, UK.

Alvarez, Jose. 1994. Positivism Regained, Nihilism Postponed, *Michigan Journal of International Law*, 15: 747–81.

Anderson, James E., and Eric van Wincoop. 2003. Gravity with Gravitas: A Solution to the Border Puzzle, *American Economic Review*, 93: 170–92.

Anderson, Kym. 2009. *Distortions to Agricultural Incentives: A Global Perspective 1995–2007*, Palgrave Macmillan and the World Bank Group: London, UK and Washington, DC.

Anderson, Robert. 2007. Reviewing the WTO Agreement on Government Procurement, Progress to Date and Ongoing Negotiations, *Public Procurement Law Review*, 4: 255–73.

Anderson, Robert D. 2011. Reflections on Bagwell and Staiger in Light of the Revised WTO Agreement on Government Procurement. Mimeo.

—— and Sue Arrowsmith. 2011. The WTO Regime on Government Procurement pp. 3–58 in Sue Arrowsmith and Robert D. Anderson (eds.), *The WTO Regime on Government Procurement: Challenge and Reform*, Cambridge University Press: Cambridge, UK.

—— William Kovacic, and Anna Caroline Müller. 2011a. Ensuring Integrity and Competition in Public Procurement Markets: a Dual Challenge for Good Governance, pp. 681–718 in Sue Arrowsmith and Robert D. Anderson (eds.), *The WTO Regime on Government Procurement: Challenge and Reform*, Cambridge University Press: Cambridge, UK.

—— Anna Caroline Müller, Kodjo Osei-Lah, Josefita Pardo De Leon, and Philippe Pelletier. 2011b. Government Procurement Provisions in Regional Trade Agreements: A Stepping Stone to WTO Accession? pp. 561–656 in Sue Arrowsmith and Robert D. Anderson (eds.), *The WTO Regime on Government Procurement: Challenge and Reform*, Cambridge University Press: Cambridge, UK.

—— Philippe Pelletier, Kodjo Osei-Lah, and Anna Caroline Müller. 2011c. Assessing the Value of Future Accessions to the WTO Agreement on Government Procurement (GPA): Some New Data Sources, Provisional Estimates, and an Evaluative Framework for Individual WTO Members Considering Accession, WTO Staff Working Paper, ERSD-2011–15, The WTO: Geneva.

Antras, Pol, and Robert W. Staiger. Forthcoming. Offshoring and the Role of Trade Agreements, *American Economic Review*.

Arrow, Kenneth. J. 1962. Economic Welfare and the Allocation of Resources for Inventions, pp. 609–35 in R.R Nelson (ed.), *The Rate and Direction of Inventive Activity: Economic and Social Factors*, Princeton University Press: Princeton, NJ.

Arrowsmith, Sue. 2002. *Government Procurement in the WTO*, Kluwer: The Hague.

—— 2005. *The Law of Public and Utilities Procurement,* Sweet and Maxwell: London.

Avi-Yonah, Reuben, and J. B. Slemrod. 2002. (How) Should Trade Agreements Deal with Income Tax Issues? *Taxation Law Review*, 55: 533–54.

Axelrod, Robert. 1984. *The Evolution of Cooperation*, Basic Books: New York City, NY.

Bagchi, Sanjoy. 2001. *International Trade Policy in Textiles, Fifty Years of Protectionism*, ITCB: Geneva.

Bagwell, Kyle. 2008. Remedies in the WTO: An Economics Perspective, pp. 733–70 in Merit E. Janow, Victoria J. Donaldson, and Alan Yanovich (eds.), *The WTO Governance, Dispute Settlement and Developing Countries*, Juris Publishing: Huntington, New York.

—— and Petros C. Mavroidis. 2007. US-Section 129: Beating around (the) Bush, pp. 315–38 in Henrik Horn and Petros C. Mavroidis (eds.), *The WTO Case-Law of 2001–3: The American Law Institute Reporters' Studies*, Cambridge University Press: Cambridge, UK.

—— —— 2010. Too Much, Too Little, . . . Too Late? pp. 168–71 in Kyle W. Bagwell, George A. Bermann, and Petros C. Mavroidis (eds.), *Law and Economics of Contingent Protection in International Trade*, Cambridge University Press: Cambridge, UK.

—— —— and Robert W. Staiger. 2002. It is All About Market Access, *American Journal of International Law*, 96: 56–76.

—— —— —— 2005. The Case for Tradable Remedies in the WTO, pp. 395–414 in Simon Evenett and Bernard Hoekman (eds.), *Economic Development and Multilateral Trade Cooperation*, Palgrave Macmillan and the World Bank: Washington, DC.

—— and Robert W. Staiger. 1990. A Theory of Managed Trade, *American Economic Review*, 80: 779–95.

—— —— 1995. Protection and the Business Cycle, NBER Discussion Paper 5168.

—— —— 2002. *The Economics of the World Trading System*, MIT Press: Cambridge, MA.

—— —— 2005. Enforcement, Private Political Pressures and the GATT/WTO Escape Clause, *Journal of Legal Studies,* 34: 471–513.

—— —— 2006. Will International Rules on Subsidies Disrupt the World Trading System? *American Economic Review,* 96: 877–95.

Bagwell, Kyle. 2011a. What Do Trade Negotiators Negotiate About? Empirical Evidence from the World Trade Organization, *American Economic Review*, 101: 1238–73.

—— —— 2011b. Can the Doha Round Be a Development Round? Setting a Place at the Table. Mimeo.

—— and Alan O. Sykes. 2007a. Chile-Price Band, pp.436–60 in Henrik Horn and Petros C. Mavroidis (eds.), *The WTO Case-Law of 2001–3: The American Law Institute Reporters' Studies*, Cambridge University Press: Cambridge, UK.

—— —— 2007b. India-Measures Affecting the Automobile Sector, pp. 461–81 in Henrik Horn and Petros C. Mavroidis (eds.), *The WTO Case-Law of 2001–3: The American Law Institute Reporters' Studies*, Cambridge University Press: Cambridge, UK.

Balassa, Bela. 1966. Tariff Reductions and Trade in Manufactures among the Industrial Countries, *American Economic Review*, 56: 466–73.

—— 1967. Trade Creation and Trade Diversion in the European Common Market, *Economic Journal*, 77: 1–21.

—— 1975. *European Economic Integration*, North Holland: Amsterdam: The Netherlands.

Baldwin, Robert E. 1970. *Non-tariff Distortions in International Trade*, Brookings Institution: Washington, DC.

—— 1991. Measuring the Effects of Non-tariff Trade-Distorting Policies, pp. 25–43 in Jaime de Melo and André Sapir (eds.), *Trade Theory and Economic Reform*, Blackwell: Cambridge, Mass.

—— 1992. Measurable Dynamic Gains from Trade, *Journal of Political Economy*, 100: 162–74.

—— 1993. On the Measurement of Dynamic Effects of Integration, *Empirica*, 20: 129–45.

—— 1995. A Domino Theory of Regionalism, pp. 25–48 in Richard E. Baldwin, Pertti Haaparanta, and Jiakko Kiander (eds.), *Expanding Membership of the European Union*, Cambridge University Press: New York City, NY.

—— 1997. The Causes of Regionalism, *The World Economy*, 20: 865–88.

—— 2005. Who Finances the Queen's CAP Payments? CEPS Policy Brief, No. 88, Centre for Economic Policy Studies: Brussels, Belgium.

—— 2006. Multilateralising Regionalism, Spaghetti Bowls as Building Blocks on the Path to Global Free Trade, *The World Economy*, 29: 1451–518.

—— 2008. Sequencing and Depth of Regional Economic Integration: Lessons for the Americas from Europe, *The World Economy*, 31: 5–30.

—— and Elena Seghezza. 2010. Are Trade Blocs Building or Stumbling Blocs? *Journal of Economic Integration*, 25: 276–97.

—— and Anthony J. Venables. 1995. Regional Economic Integration, pp. 1597–644 in Gene M. Grossman and Kenneth Rogoff (eds.), *Handbook of International Economics, vol. 3*, Elsevier-North Holland: Amsterdam, New York, and Oxford.

Baller, Silja. 2007. *Trade Effects of Regional Standards Liberalisation: A Heterogeneous Firm Approach*, World Bank: Washington, DC.

Baltagi, Badi H., Peter Egger, and Michael Pfaffermayr. 2008. Estimating Regional Trade Agreement Effects on FDI in an Interdependent World, *Journal of Econometrics*, 145: 194–208.

Banerjee, Abhijit V., and Esther Duflo. 2011. *Poor Economics: A Radical Rethinking on the Way to Fight Global Poverty*, Public Affairs: New York City, NY.

Barfield, Claude. 2001. *Free Trade, Sovereignty, Democracy: The Future of the World Trade Organization*, American Enterprise Institute: Washington, DC.

Bartels, Lorand. 2002. Article XX of the GATT and the Problem of Extraterritorial Jurisdiction, *Journal of World Trade*, 36: 353–403.

—— 2005. *Human Rights' Conditionality in the EU's International Agreements*, Oxford University Press: Oxford, UK.

—— 2009. Trade and Human Rights, pp. 571–96 in Daniel Bethlehem, Donald McRae, Rodney Neufeld, and Isabelle Van Damme (eds.), *The Oxford Handbook of International Trade Law*, Oxford University Press: Oxford, UK.

—— and Federico Ortino (eds.) 2006. *Regional Trade Agreements and the WTO Legal System*, Oxford University Press: Oxford, UK.

Basdevant, Suzanne. 1929. *La Clause de la nation la plus favorisée*, Lapradelle et Nipdoyet: Paris.

Battigalli, Pierpaolo, and Giovanni Maggi. 2002. Rigidity, Discretion and the Costs of Writing Contracts, *American Economic Review*, 92(4): 798–817.

Baye, Michael, John Morgan, and Patrick Scholten. 2006. Information, Search, and Price Dispersion, pp. 323–76 in Terry Hendershott (ed.), *Handbook of Economics and Information Systems*, Elsevier Science: Amsterdam, the Netherlands.

Becker, Gary S. 1968. Crime and Punishment, *Journal of Political Economy*, 76: 169–217.

Benedek, Wolfgang. 1991. *Das GATT aus völkerrecthlicher Sicht*, Springer Verlag: Heidelberg.

Bermann, George, Roger Goebel, William J. Davey, and Eleanor Fox. 2002. *European Community Law*, West Publishing: Eagan, Minn.

Berry, Steve, Jim Levinsohn, and Ariel Pakes. 1999. Voluntary Export Restraints on Automobiles: Evaluating a Trade Policy, *American Economic Review*, 89: 400–30.

Beviglia-Zampetti, Americo. 2000a. Market Access through Mutual Recognition, pp. 283–306 in Pierre Sauvé and Robert Stern (eds.), *The GATS 2000, New Directions in Services Trade Liberalization*, Brookings: Washington, D.C.

—— 2000b. Mutual Recognition in the Transatlantic Context: Some Reflections on Future Negotiations, pp. 303–28 in Thomas Cottier and Petros C. Mavroidis (eds.), *Regulatory Barriers and the Principle of Non-discrimination in World Trade Law*, University of Michigan Press: Ann Arbor, Mich.

—— 2006. *Fairness in the The World Economy: US Perspectives on International Trade Relations*, Edward Elgar: Cheltenham, UK.

Bhagwati, Jagdish. 1965. On the Equivalence of Tariffs and Quotas, pp. 53–67 in Robert E. Baldwin et al. (eds.), *Trade, Growth, and the Balance of Payments*, Rand McNally: Chicago, Ill.

—— 1988. *Protectionism*. MIT Press: Cambridge, Mass.

—— 1998. The Damages of Selective Safeguards, pp. 109–12 in Jagdish Bhagwati, *A Stream of Windows*, MIT Press: Cambridge, Mass.

—— 2002. The Unilateral Freeing of Trade versus Reciprocity, pp. 1–30 in Jagdish Bhagwati (ed.), *Going Alone: The Case for Relaxed Reciprocity in Freeing Trade*, MIT Press: Cambridge, Mass.

—— 2008. *Termites in the World Trading System*, Oxford University Press: New York, NY.

—— R. A. Brecher, E. Dinopoulos, and T. N. Srinivasan. 1987. Quid pro quo, Foreign Investment and Welfare: A Political Economy Theoretic Approach, *Journal of Development Economics*, 27: 127–38.

—— and Robert E. Hudec (eds.) 1996. *Fair Trade and Harmonization*, Cambridge University Press: Cambridge, MA.

—— and Petros C. Mavroidis. 2004. Killing the Byrd Amendment with the Right Stone, *The World Trade Review*, 3: 1–9.

Bhagwati, Jagdish., and Arvid Panagariya. 1999. Preferential Trading Areas and Multilateralism—Strangers, Friends, or Foes, pp. 33–100 in Jagdish Bhagwati, Pravin Krishna, and Arvind Panagariya, *Trading Blocs: Alternative Approaches to Analyzing Preferential Trade Agreements*, MIT Press: Cambridge, Mass.

—— and V.K. Ramaswami. 1963. Domestic Distortions, Tariffs, and the Theory of Optimum Subsidy, *Journal of Political Economy*, 71: 44–50.

Bhala, Raj. 2004. Saudi Arabia, the WTO, and American Trade Law and Policy, *The International Lawyer*, 34: 741–812.

Bickerdike, Charles F. 1907. Review of AC Pigou's Protective and Preferential Import Duties, *Economic Journal*, 17: 98–108.

Bidwell, Percy W. 1932. Trade, Tariffs, the Depression, *Foreign Affairs*, 10: 391–401.

Blackhurst, Richard, and David Hartridge. 2005. Improving the Capacity of WTO Institutions to Fulfil their Mandate, pp. 455–67 in Ernst-Ulrich Petersmann (ed.), *Reforming the World Trading System*, Oxford University Press: Oxford, UK.

Blandford, David, and David Orden. 2011. United States, pp. 97–152 in David Orden, David Blandford, and Tim Josling (eds.), *WTO Disciplines on Agricultural Support: Seeking a Fair Basis for Trade*, Cambridge University Press: New York City, NY.

Blank, Annet, and Gabrielle Marceau. 1997. A History of Multilateral Negotiations on Procurement: From ITO to WTO', pp. 31–56 in Bernard M. Hoekman and Petros C. Mavroidis (eds.), *Law and Policy in Public Purchasing*, University of Michigan Press: Ann Arbor, Mich.

Bloningen, Bruce, and Jee Hyeong Park. 2004. Dynamic Pricing in the Presence of Antidumping Policy: Theory and Evidence, *American Economic Review*, 94: 134–54.

—— and Thomas J. Prusa. 2003. Antidumping, pp. 251–86 in E. Kwan Choi and James Harrigan (eds.), *Handbook of International Trade*, Blackwell: Malden, Mass.

Bogdandy von, Armin. 2003. Legitimacy of International Economic Governance: Interpretative Approaches to WTO Law and the Prospects of its Proceduralization, pp. 103–48 in S. Griller (ed.), *International Economic Governance and Non-economic Concerns*, Springer Verlag: Vienna and New York.

Boltuck, Richard. 1991. Assessing the Effects on the Domestic Industry of Price Dumping, pp. 99–141 in P. K. M. Tharakan (ed.), *Policy Implications of Antidumping Measures*, North Holland: Amsterdam, the Netherlands.

—— and Robert E. Litan. 1991. *Down in the Dumps, Administration of the Unfair Trade Laws*, Brookings: Washington, DC.

Bourgeois, Jacques. 2005. Some Reflections on the WTO Dispute Settlement System from a Practitioner's Perspective, pp. 39–50 in J. H. J. Bourgeois, *Trade Law Experienced: Pottering about in the GATT and the WTO*, Cameron May: London, UK.

Bown, Chad P. 2002. Why are Safeguards under the WTO so Unpopular?' *The World Trade Review*, 1: 47–62.

—— 2005. Global Antidumping Database, World Bank Policy Research Paper No. 3737 (available at <http://people.brandeis.edu/~cbown/global_ad/research.html>)

—— 2010. China's WTO Entry: Antidumping, Safeguards, and Dispute Settlement, pp. 281–337 in Robert C. Feenstra, and Shang-Jin Wei (eds.), *China's Growing Role in World Trade*, University of Chicago Press: Chicago, Ill.

—— (ed.) 2011. *The Great Recession and Import Protection*, CEPR and the World Bank Group: Washington, DC.

—— and Bernard Hoekman. 2005. WTO Dispute Settlement and the Missing Developing Country Cases: Engaging the Private Sector, *Journal of International Economic Law*, 8: 861–90.

—— —— and C. Ozden. 2004. Developing Countries and U.S. Antidumping: The Path from Initial Filing to WTO Dispute Settlement, *The World Trade Review*, 2: 349–71.

—— and Rachel McCulloch. 2003. Nondiscrimination and the WTO Agreement on Safeguards, *The World Trade Review*, 2: 327–48.

—— and Niall Meagher. 2010. Mexico-Olive Oil: Remedy without a Cause? pp. 85–116 in Henrik Horn and Petros C. Mavroidis (eds.), *The WTO Case-Law of 2008: The American Law Institute Reporters' Studies*, Cambridge University Press: Cambridge, UK.

—— and Alan O. Sykes. 2008. The Zeroing Issue: a Critical Analysis of US—Softwood Lumber V, pp. 121–42 in Henrik Horn and Petros C. Mavroidis (eds.), *The WTO Case-Law of 2004–5: The American Law Institute Reporters' Studies*, Cambridge University Press: Cambridge, UK.

—— and Joel P. Trachtman. 2009. Brazil-Measures Affecting Imports of Retreaded Tyres: A Balancing Act, pp. 85–136 in Henrik Horn and Petros C. Mavroidis (eds.), *The WTO Case-Law of 2006–7: The American Law Institute Reporters' Studies*, Cambridge University Press: Cambridge, UK.

—— and Jasper M. Wauters. 2008. US—AD Measures on OCTG of Mexico: a Legal-Economic Assessment of Sunset Reviews, pp. 269–98 in Henrik Horn and Petros C. Mavroidis (eds.), *The WTO Case-Law of 2004–5: The American Law Institute Reporters' Studies*, Cambridge University Press: Cambridge, UK.

Brainard, S. Lael, and Thierry Verdier. 1994. Lobbying and Adjustment in Declining Industries, *European Economic Review*, 38: 586–95.

Brander, James, and Barbara Spencer. 1985. Export Subsidies and International Market Share Rivalry, *Journal of International Economics*, 18: 83–100.

Breene, John. 1993. Agriculture, pp. 123–254 in Terence P. Stewart (ed.), *The GATT Uruguay Round: A Negotiating History (1986–1992)*, Kluwer Law: Deventer, the Netherlands and Boston, Mass.

Brenton, Paul. 2003. Integrating the Least Developed Countries into the World Trading System: The Current Impact of EU Preferences under Everything but Arms, *Journal of World Trade*, 37: 623–46.

—— and Miriam Manchin. 2003. Making EU Trade Agreements Work: The Role of Rules of Origin, *The World Economy*, 26: 755–69.

Brewster, Rachel. 2009. Unpacking the State's Reputation, *Harvard Journal of International Law*, 50: 231–69.

Brink, Lars. 2011. The WTO Disciplines on Domestic Support, pp. 23–60 in David Orden, David Blandford, and Tim Josling (eds.), *WTO Disciplines on Agricultural Support: Seeking a Fair Basis for Trade*, Cambridge University Press: New York City, NY.

Broda, Christian, Nuno Limão and David E. Weinstein. 2008. Optimal Tariffs and Market Power: The Evidence, *American Economic Review*, 98: 2031–65.

—— and David E. Weinstein. 2006. Globalization and the Gains from Variety, *Quarterly Journal of Economics*, 121: 541–85.

Bronckers, Marco C. E. J. 1985. *Selective Safeguard Measures in Multilateral Trade Relations*, Springer: New York.

—— 1987. A Legal Analysis of Protectionist Measures Affecting Japanese Imports into the European Community—Revisited, pp. 57–120 in E. L. M. Völker (ed.), *Protectionism and the European Community*, Kluwer: Deventer, the Netherlands.

—— 1997. Priviatized Utilities under the WTO and the EU Procurement Rules, pp. 243–60 in Bernard M. Hoekman and Petros C. Mavroidis (eds.) *Law and Policy in Public Purchasing*, University of Michigan Press: Ann Arbor, Mich.

Bronckers, Marco C. E. J. 2004. The Special Safeguard Clause in Respect of China: (How) Will it Work? pp. 39–50 in M. Matsushita and H. Ahn (eds.), *WTO and Asia: New Perspectives*, Cameron May: London.

—— and Natalie McNelis. 2000. Fact and Law in Pleadings before the WTO Appellate Body, pp. 321–33 in Friedl Weiss (ed.), *Improving WTO Dispute Settlement Procedures: Issues and Lessons from the Practice of Other International Courts and Tribunals*, Cameron May: London.

—— and Naboth van den Broek. 2005. Financial Compensation in the WTO: Improving Remedies in WTO Dispute Settlement, *Journal of International Economic Law*, 8: 101–26.

Brou, Daniel, and Michele Ruta. 2011. A Commitment Theory of Subsidies Agreements. Mimeo.

Broude, Tomer. 2007. Genetically Modified Rules: An Awkward Rule-Exception-Right Distinction in EC-Biotech, *The World Trade Review*, 6: 215–32.

Brown, Drusilla K. 1987. General Equilibrium Effects of the US GSP, *Southern Economic Journal*, 54: 27–47.

—— 1989. Trade and Welfare Effects of the European Schemes of the GSP, *Economic Development and Cultural Change*, 40: 532–44.

Brown, Winthrop. 1950. *The United States and the Restoration of World Trade: An Analysis and Appraisal of the ITO Charter and the General Agreement on Tariffs and Trade*, Brookings Institution: Washington, DC.

Busch, Lawrence. 2011. *Standards, Recipes for Reality*, MIT Press: Cambridge, Mass.

Busch, Marc L., and Eric Reinhardt. 2001. Bargaining in the Shadow of the Law: Early Settlement in GATT/WTO Disputes, *Fordham International Law Journal*, 24: 158–72.

—— —— 2002. Testing International Trade Law: Empirical Studies of GATT/WTO Dispute Settlement, pp. 457–81 in Daniel M. Kennedy and James D. Southwick (eds.), *The Political Economy of International Trade Law: Essays in Honor of Robert Hudec*, Cambridge University Press: Cambridge, Mass.

—— —— 2003. Developing Countries and GATT/WTO Dispute Settlement, *Journal of World Trade*, 37(4): 719–35.

—— —— 2005. Three's a Crowd: The Influence of Third Parties on GATT/WTO Dispute Settlement. Mimeo. Georgetown University.

Büthe, Tim. 2008. The Globalization of Health and Safety Standards: Delegation of Regulatory Authority in the SPS Agreement of the 1994 Agreement Establishing the World Trade Organization, *Law and Contemporary Problems*, 71: 219–55.

—— and Walter Mattli. 2011. *The New Global Rulers*, Princeton University Press: Princeton, NJ.

Cadot, Olivier, Céline Carrère, Jaime de Melo, and Bolormaa Tumurchudur. 2005. Product-Specific Rules of Origin in EU and US Preferential Trading Arrangements: An Assessment, *The World Trade Review*, 25: 199–224.

—— and Jaime de Melo. 2008. Why OECD Countries Should Reform Rules of Origin, *The World Bank Research Observer*, 33: 77–105.

—— —— and Bolormaa Tumurchudur. 2006. AD Sunset Reviews: Did the WTO Agreement Make any Difference? Mimeo.

Caliendo, Lorenzo, and Fernando Parro. 2009. Estimates of the Trade and Welfare Effects of NAFTA. Mimeo. University of Chicago: Chicago, Ill.

Candau, Fabie, and Sébastien Jean. 2009. What are European Union Trade Preferences Worth for Sub-Saharan African and Other Developing Countries? pp. 65–102 in Bernard M. Hoekman, Will Martin, and Carlos A. Primo Braga (eds.), *Trade Preference*

Erosion, Measurement and Policy Response, Palgrave Macmillan and the World Bank: Washington, DC.

Capling, Ann. 2001. *Australia and the Global Trade System: From Havana to Seattle,* Cambridge University Press: New York, NY.

Carriere, C., and J. de Melo. 2006. Are Different Rules of Origin Equally Costly? Estimates from NAFTA, pp. 191–213 in O. Cadot, A. Estevadeordal, A Suwa-Eisenmann, and T. Verdier (eds.), *The Origin of Goods, Rules of Origin in Regional Trade Agreements,* Oxford University Press: Oxford, UK.

Cecchini, Paolo. 1988. *The European Challenge: The Benefits of a Single Market,* Gower: Surrey, UK.

Chakravarthy, S., and Kamala Dawar. 2011. India's Possible Accession to the Agreement on Government Procurement: What are the Pros and Cons? pp. 117–39 in Sue Arrowsmith and Robert D. Anderson (eds.), *The WTO Regime on Government Procurement: Challenge and Reform,* Cambridge University Press: Cambridge, UK.

Chambovay, Didier. 2002. How the Expiry of the Peace Clause (Article 13 of the WTO Agreement on Agriculture) Might Alter Disciplines on Agricultural Subsidies in the WTO Framework, *Journal of World Trade,* 36: 305–52.

Chang, Howard. 1995. An Economic Analysis of Trade Measures to Protect the Global Environment, *Georgetown Law Journal,* 83: 2131–60.

Charnovitz, Steve. 1991. Exploring the Environmental Exceptions in GATT Article XX. *Journal of World Trade,* 25: 37–55.

—— 1995. Promoting Higher Labour Standards, *The Washington Quarterly,* 18: 167–90.

—— 1996. New WTO Adjudication and its Implications for the Environment, *BNA International Environmental Reporter,* 18 September: 851–62

—— 1998. The Moral Exception in Trade Policy, *Virginia Journal of International Law,* 38: 689–732.

—— 2002. The Law of Environmental PPMs in the WTO: Debunking the Myth of Illegality, *Yale Journal of International Law,* 27: 59–109.

—— 2006. Exploring the Law of WTO Accession. Mimeo.

Chase, Kerry A. 2006. Multilateralism Compromised: The Mysterious Origins of GATT Article XXIV, *The World Trade Review,* 5: 1–30.

Chen, Hejing, and John Whalley. 2011. The WTO Government Procurement Agreement and its Impacts on Trade, Working Paper 17365, US National Bureau of Economic Research (NBER).

Chen, Maggie Xiaoyang, and Aaditya Mattoo. 2008. Regionalism in Standards: Good or Bad for Trade? *Canadian Journal of Economics,* 41: 838–63.

Cheng, Fuzhi. 2011. China, pp. 310–52 in David Orden, David Blandford, and Tim Josling (eds.), *WTO Disciplines on Agricultural Support: Seeking a Fair Basis for Trade,* Cambridge University Press: New York City, NY.

Choi, Wong Mong. 2003. *Like Products in International Trade Law,* Oxford University Press: Oxford, UK.

Clerc, Evelyne. 2000. La Mondialisation et les Marchés Publics: Bilan et Perspective de l'Accord de l'OMC sur les Marchés Publics, pp. 141–94 in D. Batselé et al. (eds.), *Les marchés publics à L'aube du XXI siècle,* Bruylant: Brussels.

Cline, William R. 1987. *The Future of World Trade in Textiles and Apparel,* Institute of International Economics: Washington, DC.

Collier, Paul. 2007. *The Bottom Billion,* Oxford University Press: Oxford, UK.

Collins-Williams, Terry, and Robert Wolfe. 2010. Transparency as Trade Policy Tool: The WTO's Cloudy Windows, *The World Trade Review,* 9: 551–81.

Conconi, Paola, and Robert L. Howse. 2012. Panel Report on EC-IT, *The World Trade Review*, 11: 223–56.

—— and Joost Pauwelyn. 2011. Trading Cultures: Appellate Body Report on China-Audiovisuals, pp. 93–118 in Henrik Horn and Petros C. Mavroidis (eds.), *The WTO Case-Law of 2009: The American Law Institute Reporters' Studies*, Cambridge University Press: Cambridge, UK.

—— and Jan Wouters. 2010. India—Additional and Extra-Additional Duties on Imports from the US, pp. 239–64 in Henrik Horn and Petros C. Mavroidis (eds), *The WTO Case-Law of 2008, The American Law Institute Reporters' Studies*, Cambridge University Press: Cambridge, UK.

Conrad, Christiane R. 2007. The EC-Biotech Dispute and Applicability of the SPS Agreement: Are the Panel's Findings Built on Shaky Ground? *The World Trade Review*, 6: 233–48.

—— 2011. *Processes and Production Methods (PPMs) in WTO Law, Interfacing Trade and Social Goods*, Cambridge University Press: Cambridge, UK.

Coppens, Dominique. 2012. *WTO Disciplines on Subsidies and Countervailing Measures: Balancing Policy Space and Legal Constraints in International Law*, Cambridge University Press: Cambridge, UK.

Corden, Max W. 1971. *The Theory of Protection*, Oxford University Press: London, UK.

Cottier, Thomas. 2004. Proposals for Moving from *ad hoc* Panels to Permanent WTO Panelists, pp. 31–40 in F. Ortino and E.-U. Petersmann (eds.), *The WTO Dispute Settlement System 1995–2003*, Kluwer: The Hague.

Crandall, Samuel B. 1913. The American Construction of the Most-Favored-Nation Clause, *American Journal of International Law*, 7: 709–10.

Cremona, Marise. 2010. The European Union and Regional Trade Agreements, pp. 245–68 in Christoph Hermann and Philipp Terhechte (eds.), *The European Yearbook of International Economic Law*, Springer Verlag: Berlin and London, UK.

Croley, Steve, and John H. Jackson. 1996. WTO Dispute Procedures, Standard of Review, and Deference to National Governance, *American Journal of International Law*, 90: 193–213.

Croome, John. 1995. *Reshaping the World Trading System*, The World Trade Organization: Geneva.

Crowley, Meredith. 2005. Do Antidumping Duties and Safeguard Tariffs Open or Close Technology Gaps? *Journal of International Economics*, 68: 469–84.

—— 2010. Why are Safeguards Needed in a Trade Agreement?, pp. 379–400 in Kyle W. Bagwell, George A. Bermann, and Petros C. Mavroidis (eds.), *Law and Economics of Contingent Protection in International Trade*, Cambridge University Press: New York City, NY.

—— and Robert L. Howse. 2010. US-Stainless Steel (Mexico), pp. 117–50 in Henrik Horn and Petros C. Mavroidis (eds.), *The WTO Case-Law of 2008: The American Law Institute Reporters' Studies*, Cambridge University Press: Cambridge, UK.

—— and David Palmeter. 2009. US—Countervailing Duties on Dynamic Random Access Memories from Korea, pp. 259–72 in Henrik Horn and Petros C. Mavroidis (eds.), *The WTO Case-Law of 2006–7: The American Law Institute Reporters' Studies*, Cambridge University Press: Cambridge, UK.

Czako, Judith, Johan Human, and Jorge Miranda. 2003. *A Handbook on Anti-Dumping Investigations*, Cambridge University Press: Cambridge, UK.

Daly, Michael. 1998. Investment Incentives and the Multilateral Agreement on Investment, *Journal of World Trade*, 32: 5–41.

Dam, Kenneth W. 1963. Regional Economic Arrangements and the GATT: The Legacy of Misconception, *University of Chicago Law Review*, 30: 615–65.

—— 1970. *The GATT: Law and International Economic Organization*, University of Chicago Press: Chicago, Ill.

—— 1977. 'The American Fiscal Constitution', *University of Chicago Law Review*, 44: 271–96.

—— 2001. *The Rules of the Global Game*. University of Chicago Press: Chicago, Ill.

—— 2004. Cordell Hull, The Reciprocal Trade Agreement Act, and the WTO. Mimeo.

D' Andrea Tyson, Laura. 1992. *Who's Bashing Whom? Trade Conflict in High-Technology Industries*, Institute for International Economics: Washington, DC.

Das, Dilip K. 2001. *Global Trading System at the Cross-roads*, Routledge: London, UK.

Davey, William, J. 1987. Dispute Settlement in GATT, *Fordham International Law Journal*, 11: 51–99.

—— 1998. Article XVII GATT: An Overview, pp. 17–36 in Thomas Cottier and Petros C. Mavroidis (eds.), *State Trading in the Twenty-First Century*, University of Michigan Press: Ann Arbor, Mich.

—— 2004. Proposals for Improving the Working Procedures of WTO Dispute Settlement Panels, pp. 19–30 in Federico Ortino and Ernst-Ulrich Petersmann (eds.), *The WTO Dispute Settlement System 1995–2003*: Kluwer: The Hague.

—— 2006. Reflections in the Appellate Body Decision in the Hormones Case and the Meaning of the SPS Agreement, pp. 118–32 in George A. Bermann and Petros C. Mavroidis (eds.), *Trade and Human Health and Safety*, Cambridge University Press: New York City, NY.

—— 2011. A Model Article XXIV: Are There Realistic Possibilities to Improve it?, pp. 233–61 in Kyle W. Bagwell and Petros C. Mavroidis (eds.), *Preferential Trade Agreements: A Law and Economics Analysis*, Cambridge University Press: New York.

—— and Joost Pauwelyn. 2000. MFN Unconditionality: A Legal Analysis of the Concept in View of its Evolution in the GATT/WTO Jurisprudence with Particular Reference to the Issue of 'Like Products', pp. 13–50 in Thomas Cottier and Petros C. Mavroidis (eds.), *Regulatory Barriers and the Principle of Non-discrimination in World Trade Law*, University of Michigan Press: Ann Arbor, Mich.

—— and André Sapir. 2009. The Soft Drinks Case: The WTO and Regional Agreements, pp. 5–24 in Henrik Horn and Petros C. Mavroidis (eds.), *The WTO Case-Law of 2006–7: The American Law Institute Reporters' Studies*, Cambridge University Press: Cambridge, UK.

—— —— 2010. US—Subsidies on Upland Cotton Recourse to Article 21.5 by Brazil, pp.181–200 in Henrik Horn and Petros C. Mavroidis (eds.), *The WTO Case-Law of 2008: The American Law Institute Reporters' Studies*, Cambridge University Press: Cambridge, UK.

Davies, Gareth. 2007. Morality Clauses and Decision-Making in Situations of Scientific Uncertainty: The Case of GMOs, *The World Trade Review*, 6: 249–64.

Dawar, Kamala, and Simon Evenett. 2011. A Case Study of Regionalism: the EC-CARIFORUM Economic Partnership, pp. 657–78 in Sue Arrowsmith and Robert D. Anderson (eds.), *The WTO Regime on Government Procurement: Challenge and Reform*, Cambridge University Press: Cambridge, UK.

Dean, Judith M., and John Wainio. 2009. Quantifying the Value of US Tariff Preferences for Developing Countries, pp. 29–64 in Bernard M. Hoekman, Will Martin, and Carlos A. Primo Braga (eds.), *Trade Preference Erosion, Measurement and Policy Response*, Palgrave Macmillan and the World Bank: Washington, DC.

Deardorff, Alan V. 1980. The General Validity of the Law of Comparative Advantage, *Journal of Political Economy*, 88: 941–57.

—— 1987. Safeguards Policy and the Conservative Social Welfare Function, in Henryk Kierzkowski (ed.), *Protection and Competition in International Trade: Essays in Honor of W.M. Corden*, Blackwell: Oxford, UK.

—— and Robert M. Stern. 1998. *Measurement of Non-tariff Barriers*, University of Michigan Press: Ann Arbor, Mich.

De Bièvre, Paul, R. Dybkaer, A. Fajgelj, and B. Hibbert. 2011. Metrological Traceability of Measurement Results in Chemistry—Concepts and Implementation. Mimeo.

De Jong, David N., and Maria Ripoli. 2006. Tariffs and Growth: An Empirical Exploration of Contingent Relationships, *The Review of Economic Statistics*, 88: 625–40.

Delcros, Fabien. 2002. The Legal Status of Agriculture in the World Trade Organization, *Journal of World Trade*, 36: 219–54.

Delpeuch, Claire, Marie-Agnès Jouanjean, Alexandre Le Vernoy, Patrick Messerlin, and Thomas Orliac. 2011. Aid for Trade: A Meta-evaluation. Mimeo.

Démaret, Paul, and R. Stewardson. 1994. Border Tax Adjustments under GATT and EC Law and General Implications for Environmental Taxes, *Journal of World Trade*, 28: 5–65.

de Melo, Jaime. 2007. Regionalism and Developing Countries: A Primer, *Journal of World Trade*, 41: 347–66.

—— and David Tarr. 1992. A *General Equilibrium Analysis of US Foreign Trade Policy*, MIT Press: Cambridge, Mass.

Dennis, Allen, and Ben Shepherd. 2011. Trade Facilitation and Export Diversification, *The World Economy*, 34: 101–22.

Desmedt, Axel G. 1998. Hormones: Objective Assessment and (or as) Standard of Review, *Journal of International Economic Law*, 1: 695–8.

Dewatripont, Mathias, André Sapir, and Khalid Sekkat. 1999. Labour Market Effects of Trade with LLDCs in Europe, pp. 60–78 in Mathias Dewatripont, André Sapir and Khalid Sekkat (eds.), *Trade and Jobs in Europe: Much Ado about Nothing?*, Oxford University Press: Oxford, UK.

Dhar, Bisjwajit. 2009. Use of Green Box Measures by Developing Countries: An Assessment, pp. 369–98 in Ricardo Melendez-Ortiz, Christophe Bellmann, and Jonathan Hepburn (eds.), *Agricultural Subsidies in the WTO Green Box*, Cambridge University Press: New York City, NY.

Diakantoni, Antonia, and H. Eskaith. 2009. Mapping the Tariff Waters, WTO Working Paper Series, ERSD: 2009–13.

Diakosavvas, Dimitrios. 2002. How to Measure the Level of Agricultural Support: Comparison of the Methodologies Applied by the OECD and WTO, pp. 217–45 in OECD, *Agricultural Policies in China after WTO Accession*, OECD: Paris, France.

Diamond, Richard. 1989. Economic Foundations of Countervailing Duty Law. *Virginia Journal of International Law*, 29: 767–812.

Dickerson, Kitty G. 1995. *Textiles and Apparel in the Global Economy*, 2nd edn., Merrill: Englewood Cliffs, NJ.

Diebold, William Jr 1952. *The End of the ITO*, Essays in International Finance, No. 16, Princeton International Finance Section, Princeton University: Princeton, NJ.

—— 1993. Reflections on the International Trade Organization, *Northern Illinois University Law Review*, 14: 335–46.

Di Mascio, Nicholas, and Joost Pauwelyn. 2008. Non Discrimination in Trade and Investment Treaties: Worlds Apart or Two Sides of the Same Coin? *American Journal of International Law*, 102: 48–89.

Dordi, Claudio. 2010. The Appellate Body Interpretation of Sunset Reviews Provisions of Antidumping and Countervailing Measures Agreements: A Critical Analysis, pp. 309–27 in Kyle W. Bagwell, George A. Bermann, and Petros C. Mavroidis (eds.), *Law and Economics of Contingent Protection in International Trade,* Cambridge University Press: New York City, NY.

Douglas, Roger. 1987. *Toward Prosperity,* David Bateman Ltd: Auckland, New Zealand.

Downs, George, and David Rocke. 1997. *Optimal Imperfection? Domestic Uncertainty and Institutions in International Relations,* Princeton University Press: Princeton, NJ.

Drabek, Zdenek. 2005. Limits to Harmonization of Domestic Regulation. Mimeo.

Drache, Daniel. 2003. ITO: When Labour and Investment Standards Almost Mattered: A Putative History Lesson in Trade Politics that Ought Not to be Forgotten, pp. 9–28 in James Busumtwi-Sam et al. (eds.), *Global Instability: Uncertainty and New Visions in Political Economy,* Kluwer: Amsterdam, the Netherlands.

Drebentsov, Vladimir, and Constantine Michalopoulos. 1998. State Trading in Russia, pp. 303–18 in Thomas Cottier and Petros C. Mavroidis (eds.), *State Trading in the Twenty-First Century,* University of Michigan Press: Ann Arbor, Mich.

Dunoff, Jeffrey.1999. The Death of the Trade Regime, *European Journal of International Law,* 10: 733–60.

—— 2006. Lotus Eaters: The Varietals Dispute, the SPS Agreement, and WTO Dispute Resolution, pp. 153–89 in George Bermann and Petros C. Mavroidis (eds.), *Trade and Health in the WTO,* Cambridge University Press: Cambridge, UK.

—— 2009. Linking International Markets and Global Justice, *Michigan Law Review,* 107: 1039–58.

—— 2010. How Not to Think about Safeguards, pp. 401–12 in Kyle W. Bagwell, George A. Bermann, and Petros C. Mavroidis (eds.), *Law and Economics of Contingent Protection in International Trade,* Cambridge University Press: New York City, NY.

Easterly, William. 2001. *The Elusive Quest for Growth: Economists' Adventures and Misadventures in the Topics,* MIT Press: Cambridge, Mass.

Edgeworth, F.Y. 1894. The Theory of International Values, *Economic Journal,* 4: 35–50.

Eeckhout, Piet. 2010. The Scales of Trade Reflections on the Growth and Functions of the WTO, *Journal of International Economic Law,* 13: 3–26.

Ehlermann, Claus-Dieter. 2004. Reflections on the Process of Clarification and Improvement of the DSU, pp. 105–14 in F. Ortino and E.-U. Petersmann (eds), *The WTO Dispute Settlement System 1995–2003,* Kluwer: The Hague.

—— and Nicolas Lockhart. 2004. Standard of Review in WTO Law, *Journal of International Economic Law,* 7: 491–521.

Ehring, Lothar. 2002. De Facto Discrimination in World Trade Law: National and Most Favoured Nation Treatment—or Equal Treatment, *Journal of World Trade,* 36: 921–77.

—— 2011. Article IV of the GATT: An Obsolete Provision or Still a Basis for Cultural Policy?, pp. 96–118 in Inge Govaere, Reinhard Quick, and Marco Bronckers (eds.), *Trade and Competition Law in the EU and Beyond,* Edward Elgar: Cheltenham, UK.

Eichengreen, Barry. 2006. *The European Economy since 1945: Coordinated Capitalism and Beyond,* Princeton University Press: Princeton, NJ.

—— 2011. *Exorbitant Privilege,* Oxford University Press: New York City, NY.

Epps, Tracey. 2008. *International Trade and Health Protection: A Critical Assessment of the WTO's SPS Agreement,* Edward Elgar: Cheltenham, UK.

Esserman, Susan, and Robert Howse. 2004. Trade Disputes Require Fairer Arbitration, *The Financial Times,* 12 September (available at <http://www.ft.com>).

Estevadeordal, Antoni, and L. J. Garay. 1996. Protection, Preferential Tariffs, and Rules of Origin in America, *Integration and Trade*, 1: 2–25.

—— C. Freund, and E. Ornelas. 2008. Does Regionalism Affect Trade Liberalization towards Non-members?, *The Quarterly Journal of Economics*, 123: 1531–75.

Ethier, Wilfred J. 1982. National and International Returns to Scale in the Modern Theory of International Trade, *American Economic Review*, 72: 389–405.

—— 1998. Regionalism in a Multilateral World, *Journal of Political Economy*, 106: 1214–45.

—— 2001. *Punishments and Dispute Settlement in Trade Agreements*, Copenhagen: EPRU.

—— 2002. Unilateralism in a Multilateral World, *Economic Journal*, 112: 266–92.

—— 2004. Political Externalities, Non-discrimination and a Multilateral World, *Review of International Economics*, 12: 303–20.

Evenett, Simon, and Bernard M. Hoekman. 2007. International Disciplines on Public Procurement: Teaching Materials. Mimeo.

Faini, Ricardo. 1995. Demand and Supply Factors in Textile Trade, pp. 45–60 in Giorgio Barba Navaretti, Ricardo Faini, and Aubrey Silberston (eds.), *Beyond the Multifibre Agreement: Third World Competition and Restructuring Europe's Textile Trade*, OECD: Paris.

—— Jaime de Melo, and Wendy Takacs. 1995. A Primer on the MFA Maze, pp. 1–27 in Giorgio Barba Navaretti, Ricardo Faini and Aubrey Silberston (eds.), *Beyond the Multifibre Agreement: Third World Competition and Restructuring Europe's Textile Trade*, OECD: Paris.

Fauchald, Ole Christian. 1998. *Environmental Taxes and Trade Discrimination*, Kluwer: Amsterdam.

Feddersen, Christoph T. 1998. Focusing on Substantive Law in International Economic Relations: The Public Morals of GATT's Article XX(a) and 'Conventional' Rules of Interpretation, *Minnesota Journal of Global Trade*, 7: 75–101.

Feenstra, Robert C. 2004. *Advanced International Trade*, Princeton University Press: Princeton, NJ.

—— Benjamin R. Mandel, Marshall B. Reinsdorf, and Matthew J. Slaughter. 2009. Effects of Terms of Trade and Tariff Changes on the Measurement of US Productivity Growth, NBER Working Paper No. 15592.

Feinberg, Robert. 2005. US Antidumping Enforcement and Macroeconomic Indicators Revisited: Do Petitioners Learn? *Review of World Economics*, 141: 612–22.

Finger, Michael (ed.) 1993. *Antidumping: How It Works And Who Gets Hurt*, University of Michigan Press: Ann Arbor, Mich.

—— 2010. A Special Safeguard Mechanism for Agricultural Products: What Experience with Other GATT/WTO Safeguards Will Tell Us about What Might Work, *The World Trade Review*, 9: 280–318.

—— and Julio J. Nogues. 2006. *Safeguards and Antidumping in Latin American Trading Liberalization: Fighting Fire with Fire*, World Bank: Washington, DC.

—— and Philip Schuler. 2000. Implementation of the Uruguay Round Commitments: The Development Challenge, *The World Economy*, 23: 511–25.

Fink, Carsten, A. Mattoo, and C. I. Neagu. 2002a. Trade in International Maritime Services: How Much Does Policy Matter? *World Economic Review*, 16: 81–108.

—— —— —— 2002b. Assessing the Role of Communication Costs in International Trade, World Bank Working Paper No. 2929, The World Bank: Washington, DC.

Flam, Harry, and Håkan Nordström. 2011. Gravity Estimation of the Intensive and Extensive Margins of Trade: An Alternative Procedure with Alternative Data, CESifo Working Paper Series No. 3387.

Fontagne, Lionel, Thierry Mayer, and Soledad Zignago. 2007. A Re-evaluation of the Impact of Regional Agreements on Trade Patterns. *Integration and Trade Journal*, 26: 31–51.

Footer, Mary E. 2007. Post-Normal Science in the Multilateral trading System: Social Science Expertise and the EC-Biotech Panel, *The World Trade Review*, 6: 281–98.

Foster, Caroline E. 2011. *Science and the Precautionary Principle in International Courts and Tribunals*, Cambridge University Press: Cambridge, UK.

Fox, Eleanor. 1997. Toward World Antitrust and Market Access, *American Journal of International Law*, 91: 1–25.

Francois, Joseph F. 2005. *The Implications of Agricultural Trade Liberalization and Preference Erosion for Developing Countries*, UNIDO: Geneva.

—— 2010. Subsidies and Countervailing Measures: Determining the Benefit of Subsidies, pp. 103–15 in Kyle W. Bagwell, George A. Bermann, and Petros C. Mavroidis (eds.), *Law and Economics of Contingent Protection in International Trade*, Cambridge University Press: New York City, NY.

—— and K. H. Hall 1993. *COMPAS: Commercial Policy Analysis System*, International Trade Commission: Washington, DC.

—— Douglas Nelson, and David Palmeter. 1997. Public Procurement in the United States: A Post-Uruguay Round Perspective, pp. 105–24 in Bernard M. Hoekman and Petros C. Mavroidis (eds.), *Law and Policy in Public Purchasing*, University of Michigan Press: Ann Arbor, Mich.

—— and David Palmeter. 2008. US—Countervailing Duty Investigation on DRAMS, pp. 219–30 in Henrik Horn and Petros C. Mavroidis (eds.), *The WTO Case-Law of 2004–5: The American Law Institute Reporters' Studies*, Cambridge University Press: Cambridge, UK.

Frank, Isaiah. 1987. Import Quotas, the Balance Payments and the GATT, *The World Economy*, 10: 307–18.

Freund, Caroline. 2011. Third Country Effects of Regional Trade Agreements, pp. 40–59 in Kyle W. Bagwell and Petros C. Mavroidis (eds.), *Preferential Trade Agreements: A Law and Economics Analysis*, Cambridge University Press: New York, NY.

Friedman, Thomas. 2005. *The World is Flat: A Brief History of the Twenty-First Century*, Farrar, Straus and Giroux: New York, NY.

Fudenberg, Drew, and Jean Tirole. 1991. *Game Theory*, MIT Press: Cambridge, Mass.

Galli, Peter, André Moser, Elisabeth Lang, and Evelyne Clerc. 2007. *Praxis des öffentlichen Beschaffungsrechts*, Schultess: Basel, Switzerland.

Gamberoni, Elisa, and Richard Newfarmer. 2009. Aid for Trade: Matching Supply and Demand, World Bank Policy Research Working Paper No. 4991.

Gandal, Neil. 2001. Quantifying the Trade Impact of Compatibility Standards and Barriers: An Industrial Organization Perspective, pp. 137–54 in Keith E. Maskus and John S. Wilson (eds.), *Quantifying the Impact of Technical Barriers to Trade: Can it be Done?*, University of Michigan Press: Ann Arbor, Mich.

Ganslandt, Mattias, and James R. Markusen. 2001. Standards and Related Regulations in International Trade: A Modelling Approach, pp. 95–136 in Keith E. Maskus and John S. Wilson (eds.), *Quantifying the Impact of Technical Barriers to Trade: Can it be Done?* University of Michigan Press: Ann Arbor, Mich.

Gantz, David A. 2009. Regional Trade Agreements, pp. 237–68 in Daniel Bethlehem, Donald McRae, Rodney Neufeld, and Isabelle Van Damme (eds.), *The Oxford Handbook of International Trade Law*, Oxford University Press: Oxford, UK.

Gantz, David A. 2011. Commentary on Contingent Protection Rules in Regional Trade Agreements, pp. 101–14 in Kyle W. Bagwell and Petros C. Mavroidis (eds.), *Preferential Trade Agreements: A Law and Economics Analysis*, Cambridge University Press: New York, NY.

—— and Simon Schropp. 2009. Rice Age, pp.145–78 in Henrik Horn and Petros C. Mavroidis (eds.), *The WTO Case-Law of 2006–7: The American Law Institute Reporters' Studies*, Cambridge University Press: Cambridge, UK.

Garcia, Frank J. 2006. The Salmon Case: Evolution of Balancing Mechanisms for Non-trade Values in WTO, pp. 133–52 in George A. Bermann and Petros C. Mavroidis (eds.), *Trade and Human Health and Safety*, Cambridge University Press: New York City, NY.

Gardner, Bruce L. 2002. *American Agriculture in the Twentieth Century: How it Flourished and What it Cost*, Harvard University Press: Cambridge, Mass.

—— 2009. Distortions to Agricultural Incentives in the United States and Canada, pp. 177–220 in Kym Anderson (ed.), *Distortions to Agricultural Incentives: A Global Perspective 1995–2007*, Palgrave Macmillan and the World Bank Group: London, UK and Washington, DC.

Gardner, Richard N. 1956. *Sterling-Dollar Diplomacy*, Columbia University Press: New York City, NY.

Gay, Daniel. 2005. Vanuatu's Suspended Accession Bid: Second Thoughts? pp. 590–606 in Peter Gallagher, Patrick A. Low, and Andrew L. Stoller (eds.), *Managing the Challenges of WTO Participation: 45 Case Studies*, Cambridge University Press: Cambridge, UK.

Genasci, Matthew. 2008. Border Tax Adjustments and Emissions Trading: the Implications of International Trade Law for Policy Design, *Carbon and Climate Law Review*, 2: 33–42.

Georgopoulos, Aris. 2000. The System of Remedies in Enforcing Public Procurement Rules in Greece, *Public Procurement Law Review*, 9: 75–93.

—— 2005. The Impact of Public Procurement on Competition, *Public Procurement Law Review*, 14: 48–50.

Ghosh, Arunabha. 2010. Developing Countries in the WTO Trade Policy Review Mechanism, *The World Trade Review*, 9: 419–55.

Gilbert, Christopher R. 2006. Trends and Volatility in Agricultural Commodity Prices, pp. 31–60 in Alexander Sarris and David Hallam (eds.), *Agricultural Commodity Markets and Trade*, Edward Elgar: Cheltenham, UK.

Giri, Shiva, and Michael Trebilcock. 2005. The National Treatment Principle in International Trade Law, pp. 185–238 in E. Kwan Choi and James C. Hartigan (eds.), *Handbook of International Trade, Vol. II*, Blackwell: Oxford, UK.

Goetz, Charles J., Granet, Lloyd, and Schwartz, Warren F. 1986. The Meaning of 'Subsidy' and 'Injury' in the Countervailing Duty Law, *International Review of Law and Economics*, 6: 17–32.

Goh, Gavin, and Andreas R. Ziegler. 2003. Retrospective Remedies in the WTO after Automotive Leather, *Journal of International Economic Law*, 6: 545–664.

Goldberg, Pinelopi K., and Frank Verboven. 2005. Market Integration and Convergence on the Law of One Price: Evidence from the European Car Market, *Journal of International Economics*, 65: 49–73.

Goldsmith, Jack L., and Eric Posner. 2005. *The Limits of International Law*, Oxford University Press: New York, NY.

Gollier, C., B. Julien, and N. Treich. 2000. Scientific Progress and Irreversibility: An Economic Interpretation of the Precautionary Principle, *Journal of Public Economics*, 75: 229–53.

Gopinath, Munisamy. 2011. India, pp. 277–309 in David Orden, David Blandford, and Tim Josling (eds.), *WTO Disciplines on Agricultural Support: Seeking a Fair Basis for Trade*, Cambridge University Press: New York City, NY.

Gormann, Maryann. 2009. Conformity Assessment, Standards and Trade: An Interview with Ann Weeks of Underwriters Laboratories, *ASTM Standardization News*, 37, March/April.

Graham, Edward D. 2000. *Fighting the Wrong Enemy: Antiglobal Activists and Multinational Enterprises*, Institute for International Economics: Washington, DC.

Graham, Frank. 1948. *The Theory of International Values*, Princeton University Press: Princeton, NJ.

Graham, Thomas J. 1978. The US Generalized System of Preferences for Developing Countries: International Innovation and the Art of the Possible, *American Journal of International Law*, 72: 513–40.

—— 1979. Results of the Tokyo Round, *Georgia Journal of International and Comparative Law*, 9: 153–75.

Grando, Michelle T. 2009. *Evidence, Proof, and Fact-Finding in WTO Dispute Settlement*, Oxford University Press: Oxford, UK.

Green, Andrew, and Michael Trebilcock. 2010. The Enduring Problem of World Trade Organization Export Subsidies Rules, pp. 116–67 in Kyle W. Bagwell, George A. Bermann, and Petros C. Mavroidis (eds.), *Law and Economics of Contingent Protection in International Trade*, Cambridge University Press: New York City, NY.

Greene, William H. 1993. *Econometric Analysis*, 2nd edn., Macmillan: New York, NY.

Grinols, Earl L., and Roberto Perrelli. 2006. The WTO Impact on International Trade Disputes: An Event History Analysis, *The Review of Economics and Statistics*, 88: 613–24.

Grossman, Gene M. 1980. Border Tax Adjustments: Do they Distort Trade? *Journal of International Economics*, 10: 117–28.

—— 1986. Imports as a Cause of Injury: The Case of the US Steel Industry, *Journal of International Economics*, 20: 201–23.

—— and Elhanan Helpman. 1995. The Politics of Free Trade Agreements, *American Economic Review*, 85: 667–90.

—— —— 2001. *Special Interest Politics*, MIT Press: Cambridge, Mass. and London.

—— —— 2002. *Interest Groups and Trade Policy*, Princeton University Press: Princeton, NJ.

—— Henrik Horn, and Petros C. Mavroidis. 2012. *Principles of World Trade Law: National Treatment*, ALI Study, Cambridge University Press: Cambridge, UK.

—— and Petros C. Mavroidis. 2007a. Here Today, Gone Tomorrow? pp. 183–213 in Henrik Horn and Petros C. Mavroidis (eds.), *The American Law Institute Reporters' Studies on WTO Case Law*, Cambridge University Press: New York, NY.

—— —— 2007b. Would've or Should've? Impaired Benefits Due to Copyright Infringement, pp. 294–314 in Henrik Horn and Petros C. Mavroidis (eds.), *The American Law Institute Reporters' Studies on WTO Case Law*, Cambridge University Press: New York, NY.

—— —— 2007c. The Sounds of Silence, pp. 367–80 in Henrik Horn and Petros C. Mavroidis (eds.), *The American Law Institute Reporters' Studies on WTO Case Law*, Cambridge University Press: New York, NY.

—— —— 2007d. Recurring Misunderstandings of Non-Recurring Subsidies, pp. 381–90 in Henrik Horn and Petros C. Mavroidis (eds.), *The American Law Institute Reporters' Studies on WTO Case Law*, Cambridge University Press: New York, NY.

—— —— 2007e. Not for Attribution, pp. 402–35 in Henrik Horn and Petros C. Mavroidis (eds.), *The American Law Institute Reporters' Studies on WTO Case Law*, Cambridge University Press: New York, NY.

—— and Esteban Rossi-Hansberg. 2008. Trading Tasks: A Simple Theory of Offshoring, *American Economic Review*, 98: 1978–97.

—— and Alan Sykes. 2005. A Preference for Development: The Law and Economics of GSP, *The World Trade Review*, 4: 41–68.

Grossman, Gene M. 2007a. EC—Antidumping Duties on Imports of Cotton-Type Bed Linen from India, pp. 581–600 in Henrik Horn and Petros C. Mavroidis (eds.), *The American Law Institute Reporters' Studies on WTO Case Law*, Cambridge University Press: New York, NY.

—— 2007b. US—Definitive Safeguard Measures on Imports of Certain Steel Products, pp. 716–57 in Henrik Horn and Petros C. Mavroidis (eds.), *The American Law Institute Reporters' Studies on WTO Case Law*, Cambridge University Press: New York, NY.

—— 2011. 'Optimal' Retaliation in the WTO—a Commentary on the Upland-Cotton Arbitration, pp.133–64 in Henrik Horn and Petros C. Mavroidis (eds.), *The WTO Case-Law of 2009: The American Law Institute Reporters' Studies*, Cambridge University Press: Cambridge, UK.

—— and Jasper Wauters. 2008. Sunset Reviews of AD Measures on OCTG from Argentina: A Cloudy Sunset, pp.235–64 in Henrik Horn and Petros C. Mavroidis (eds.), *The WTO Case-Law of 2004–5: The American Law Institute Reporters' Studies*, Cambridge University Press: Cambridge, UK.

Grubel, Herbert J., and Peter J. Lloyd. 1975. *Intra-industry Trade: The Theory and Measurement of International Trade in Differentiated Products*, Wiley: New York City, NY.

Gruszczynski, Lukasz. 2010. *Regulating Health and Environmental Risks under WTO Law: A Critical Analysis of the SPS Agreement*, Oxford University Press: New York City, NY.

Guiso, Luigi, Paola Sapienza, and Luigi Zingales. 2009. Cultural Biases in Economic Exchange, *Quarterly Journal of Economics,* 124: 1095–131.

Gupta, Poonam, and Arvind Panagariya. 2006. Injury Investigations in Antidumping and the Super-additivity Effect: A Theoretical Explanation, *Weltwirtschaftliches Archiv/ Review of World Economics*, 142: 151–64.

Guth, Eckart. 2012. The End of the Bananas Saga, *Journal of World Trade*, 46: 1–32.

Guzman, Andrew T. 2004. Global Governance and the WTO, *Harvard Journal of International Law*, 45: 303–36.

—— and Beth Simmons. 2005. Power Plays and Capacity Constraints: The Selection of Defendants in WTO Disputes, *Journal of Legal Studies*, 37: 557–80.

Hafner-Burton, Emilie M. 2005. Trading Human Rights: how Preferential Trade Agreements Influence Government Repression, *International Organization*, 59: 593–629.

Hahn, Michael J. 1991. Vital Interests in the Law of the GATT: An Analysis of the GATT's Security Exception, *Michigan Journal of International Law*, 12: 558–84.

Haidt, Jonathan. 2001. The Emotional Dog and its Rational Tail: A Social Intuitionist Approach to Moral Judgment, *Psychological Review*, 108: 814–34.

Hansen, Wendy L., and Thomas J. Prusa. 1996. Cumulation and ITC Decision-Making: The Sum of the Parts is Greater than the Whole, *Economic Inquiry*, 34: 746–69.

Hart, Chad E., and John C. Beghin. 2006. Rethinking Agricultural Domestic Support under the WTO, chapter 8 in Kym Anderson and Will Martin (eds.), *Agricultural Trade and Doha Development Agenda*, World Bank: Washington, DC.

Hart, Michael. 1998. *Fifty Years of Canadian Statecraft: Canada in the GATT 1947–1997*, Centre for Trade Policy and Law: Ottawa.

—— 2002. *A Trading Nation: Canadian Trade Policy from Colonialism to Globalization*, University of British Columbia Press: Vancouver.

Hawkins, Harry C. 1951. *Commercial Treaties and Agreement Principles and Practice*, Rinehart & Co: New York, NY.

Helpman, Elhanan. 2006. Trade, FDI, and the Organization of Firms, *Journal of Economic Literature*, XLIV: 589–630.

—— 2011. *Understanding Global Trade*, The Belknap Press of Harvard University Press: Cambridge, Mass.

Hemmendinger, Noel. 1969. Non-tariff Trade Barriers, *American Society of International Law Proceedings*, 63: 204–11.

Henson, Spencer. 1996. *The Costs of Compliance with Food Regulations in the UK*, Department of Agricultural and Food Economics, The University of Reading: Reading, UK.

Hindley, Brian. 1980. Voluntary Export Restraints and the GATT's Main Escape Clause, *The World Economy*, 3: 313–41.

Hirsch, Moshe. 2002. International Trade Law, Political Economy and Rules of Origin— a Plea for Reform of the WTO Regime on Rules of Origin, *Journal of World Trade*, 36: 171–90.

Hoda, Anwarul. 2001. *Tariff Negotiations and Renegotiations under the GATT and the WTO*, Cambridge University Press: Cambridge, UK.

Hoekman, Bernard M. 2005. Operationalizing the Concept of Policy Space in the WTO: Beyond Special and Differential Treatment, *Journal of International Economic Law*, 8: 405–24.

—— and Robert L. Howse. 2008. EC-Sugar, pp.149–78 in Henrik Horn and Petros C. Mavroidis (eds.), *The WTO Case-Law of 2004–5: The American Law Institute Reporters' Studies*, Cambridge University Press: Cambridge, UK.

—— and Michel Kostecki. 2009. *The Political Economy of the World Trading System*, 3rd edn., Oxford University Press: Oxford.

—— and Petros C. Mavroidis. 1994. Competition, Competition Policy and the GATT, *The World Economy*, 17: 121–50.

—— —— 1996a. Dumping, Antidumping and Antitrust, *Journal of World Trade*, 30: 27–42.

—— —— 1996b. Policy Externalities and High-Tech Rivalry, Competition and Multilateral Cooperation beyond the WTO, *Leiden Journal of International Law*, 9: 273–318.

—— —— (eds.) 1997. *Law and Policy in Public Purchasing*, University of Michigan Press: Ann Arbor, Mich.

—— —— 2000. WTO Dispute Settlement, Transparency and Surveillance, *The World Economy*, 23: 527–42.

—— —— 2009. Nothing Dramatic (. . . Regarding Administration of Customs Laws), pp.31–44 in Henrik Horn and Petros C. Mavroidis (eds.), *The WTO Case-Law of 2006–7: The American Law Institute Reporters' Studies*, Cambridge University Press: Cambridge, UK.

—— and Patrick Messerlin. 2006. Removing the Exception of Agricultural Export Subsidies, chapter 7 in Kym Anderson and Will Martin (eds.), *Agricultural Trade and Doha Development Agenda*, World Bank: Washington, DC.

—— C. Michalopoulos, and L. Alan Winters. 2004. More Favorable and Differential Treatment of Developing Countries: Towards a New Approach in the WTO, *The World Economy*, 27(4): 481–506.

—— Francis Ng and Marcelo Olarreaga. 2001. Eliminating Excessive Tariffs on Exports of Least Developed Countries, World Bank Policy Research Working Paper 2604, The World Bank Group: Washington, DC.

—— and A. Nicita. 2010. Assessing the Doha Round: Market Access, Transaction Costs and Aid for Trade Facilitation, *Journal of International Trade and Economic Development*, 19: 65–80.

—— and Susan Prowse. 2009. Economic Policy Responses to Preference Erosion: From Trade as Aid to Aid for Trade, pp. 425–48 in Bernard M. Hoekman, Will Martin, and Carlos A. Primo Braga (eds.), *Trade Preference Erosion, Measurement and Policy Response,* Palgrave Macmillan and the World Bank: Washington, DC.

—— and Joel P. Trachtman. 2008. Canada-Wheat: Discrimination, Non-commercial Considerations, and the Right to Regulate State Trading Enterprises, pp. 45–66 in Henrik Horn and Petros C. Mavroidis (eds.), *The WTO Case-Law of 2004–5: The American Law Institute Reporters' Studies*, Cambridge University Press: Cambridge, UK.

—— —— 2010. Continued Suspense: EC-Hormones and WTO Disciplines on Discrimination and Domestic Regulation, pp. 151–80 in Henrik Horn and Petros C. Mavroidis (eds.), *The WTO Case-Law of 2008: The American Law Institute Reporters' Studies*, Cambridge University Press: Cambridge, UK.

—— and Jasper Wauters. 2011. US Compliance with WTO Rulings on Zeroing in Antidumping, pp. 5–44 in Henrik Horn and Petros C. Mavroidis (eds.), *The WTO Case-Law of 2009: The American Law Institute Reporters' Studies*, Cambridge University Press: Cambridge, UK.

Horlick, Gary. 1993. How the GATT Became Protectionist: An Analysis of the Uruguay round Draft Final Antidumping Code, *Journal of World Trade*, 27: 5–17.

—— 2002. Problems with the Compliance Structure of the WTO Dispute Resolution Process, pp. 636–45 in Dan Kennedy and James Southwick (eds.), *The Political Economy of the International Trade Law: Essays in Honour of Robert E. Hudec,* Cambridge University Press: Cambridge, UK.

—— and Peggy Clark. 1994. The 1994 WTO Subsidies Agreement, *World Competition*, 17: 41–54.

Horn, Henrik. 2006. National Treatment in Trade Agreements, *American Economic Review*, 96: 394–404.

—— and Robert L. Howse. 2008. EC-Customs Classification on Frozen Boneless Chicken Cuts, pp. 9–38 in Henrik Horn and Petros C. Mavroidis (eds.), *The WTO Case-Law of 2004–5: The American Law Institute Reporters' Studies*, Cambridge University Press: Cambridge, UK.

—— Louise Johannesson, and Petros C. Mavroidis. 2011. The WTO Dispute Settlement System (1995–2010): Some Descriptive Statistics, *Journal of World Trade*, 45: 1107–38.

—— Giovanni Maggi, and Robert W. Staiger. 2010. Trade Agreements as Endogenously Incomplete Contracts, *American Economic Review*, 100: 394–419.

—— and Petros C. Mavroidis. 2001. Legal and Economic Aspects of MFN, *European Journal of Political Economy*, 17: 233–79.

—— —— 2003. US—Lamb, pp. 52–86 pp. 72–114 in Henrik Horn and Petros C. Mavroidis (eds.), *The WTO Case-Law of 2001: The American Law Institute Reporters' Studies*, Cambridge University Press: Cambridge, UK.

—— —— 2004. Still Hazy after All These Years: The Interpretation of National Treatment in the GATT/WTO Case-Law on Tax Discrimination, *European Journal of International Law*, 15: 39–69.

—— —— 2005a. A Comment on US—Offset Act (Byrd Amendment), pp. 52–86 in Henrik Horn and Petros C. Mavroidis (eds.), *The WTO Case-Law of 2003: The American Law Institute Reports' Studies*, Cambridge University Press: Cambridge.

—— —— 2005b. What is a Subsidy?' pp. 220–47 in Henrik Horn and Petros C. Mavroidis (eds), *The WTO Case-Law of 2002, The American Law Institute Reporters' Studies*, Cambridge University Press: Cambridge.

——— 2007a. International Trade: Dispute Settlement, pp. 177–210 in Andrew Guzman and Alan O. Sykes (eds.), *Handbook on International Trade*, Edward Elgar: Cheltenham, UK.

——— 2007b. US—Final Determination with Respect to Certain Softwood Lumber from Canada, pp. 700–15 in Henrik Horn and Petros C. Mavroidis (eds.), *The American Law Institute Reporters' Studies on WTO Case Law*, Cambridge University Press: New York.

——— 2007c. US—Lamb, pp. 85–127 in Henrik Horn and Petros C. Mavroidis (eds.), *The American Law Institute Reporters' Studies on WTO Case Law*, Cambridge University Press: New York.

—— —— 2008. The Permissible Reach of National Environmental Policies, *The Journal of World Trade*, 42: 1107–78.

—— —— 2009. Non-Discrimination, pp. 833–9 in Kenneth A. Reinert, R. S. Rajan, A. J. Glass, and L. S. Davis (eds.), Princeton Encyclopedia of the World Economy, Princeton University Press: Princeton, NJ.

—— —— 2010. Climate Change and the WTO: Legal Issues Concerning Border Tax Adjustments, *Japanese Yearbook of International Law*, 53: 19–40.

—— —— 2012. MEAs in the WTO: Silence Speaks Volumes. Mimeo.

—— —— and Håkan Nordström. 2005. Is the Use of the WTO Dispute Settlement System Biased? pp. 454–86 in Petros C. Mavroidis and Alan O. Sykes (eds.), *The WTO and International Trade Law Dispute Settlement*, Edward Elgar: Cheltenham, UK.

—— —— and André Sapir. 2010b. Beyond the WTO: An Anatomy of the EU and US Preferential Trade Agreements, *The World Economy*, 33: 1565–88.

—— —— and Erik Wijkström. 2012. Adjudicated and Negotiated Resolution of Environmental Disputes in the WTO. Mimeo.

—— and Joseph H. H. Weiler. 2003. European Communities—Measures Affecting Asbestos and Asbestos-Containing Products, pp. 14–40 in Henrik Horn and Petros C. Mavroidis (eds.), *The WTO Case-Law of 2001: The American Law Institute Reports' Studies*, Cambridge University Press: Cambridge, UK.

—— —— 2007. EC-Trade Description of Sardines: Textualism and its Discontent, pp. 551–78 in Henrik Horn and Petros C. Mavroidis (eds.), *The WTO Case-Law of 2001–3: The American Law Institute Reporters' Studies*, Cambridge University Press: Cambridge, UK.

Hovenkamp, Herbert. 2011. *Federal Antitrust Policy: The Law of Competition and its Practice*, Thomson, West: St Paul, Minn.

Howse, Robert. 1998. State Trading Enterprises and Multilateral Trade Rules: The Canadian Experience, pp. 181–210 in Thomas Cottier and Petros C. Mavroidis (eds.), *State Trading in the Twenty-First Century*, University of Michigan Press: Ann Arbor, Mich.

—— 2000. Democracy, Science, and Free Trade: Risk Regulation on Trial at the World Trade Organization, *Michigan Law Review* 98, 7: 2329–57.

—— 2002. The Appellate Body Rulings in the Shrimp/Turtle Case: A New Legal Baseline for the Trade and Environmental Debate (Symposium: Trade, Sustainability and Global Governance), *Columbia Journal of Environmental Law*, 27: 491–521.

—— 2003. India's WTO Challenge to Drug Enforcement Conditions in the European Community GSP: A Little Known Case with Major Repercussions for 'Political' Conditionality in US Trade Policy, *Chicago Journal of International Law*, 4: 385–405.

—— 2010. Do the World Trade Organization Disciplines on Domestic Subsidies Make Sense? The Case for Legalizing Some Subsidies, pp. 85–102 in Kyle W. Bagwell, George A. Bermann, and Petros C. Mavroidis (eds.), *Law and Economics of Contingent Protection in International Trade*, Cambridge University Press: New York City, NY.

—— and Antonia Eliason. 2009. Domestic and International Strategies to Address Climate Change: An Overview of the WTO Legal Issues, pp. 48–94 in Thomas Cottier, Olga Nartova, and Sadeq Z. Bigdeli (eds.), *International Trade Regulation and the Mitigation of Climate Change*, Cambridge University Press: Cambridge, UK.

—— and Henrik Horn. 2009. EC-Measures Affecting the Approval and Marketing of Biotech Products, pp. 49–84 in Henrik Horn and Petros C. Mavroidis (eds.), *The WTO Case-Law of 2006–7: The American Law Institute Reporters' Studies*, Cambridge University Press: Cambridge, UK.

—— and Damien J. Neven. 2007a. US-Shrimp Recourse to Article 21.5 of the DSU by Malaysia, pp. 54–84 in Henrik Horn and Petros C. Mavroidis (eds.), *The WTO Case-Law of 2001–3: The American Law Institute Reporters' Studies*, Cambridge University Press: Cambridge, UK.

—— —— 2007b. Mexico-Corn Syrup, pp. 153–67 in Henrik Horn and Petros C. Mavroidis (eds.), *The WTO Case-Law of 2001–3: The American Law Institute Reporters' Studies*, Cambridge University Press: Cambridge, UK.

—— —— 2007c. Argentina-Ceramic Tiles, pp. 168–82 in Henrik Horn and Petros C. Mavroidis (eds.), *The WTO Case-Law of 2001–3: The American Law Institute Reporters' Studies*, Cambridge University Press: Cambridge, UK.

—— —— 2007d. US-Tax Treatment for FSC Recourse to Arbitration by the US under Article 22.6 of the DSU and Article 4.11 of the SCM Agreement, pp. 339–66 in Henrik Horn and Petros C. Mavroidis (eds.), *The WTO Case-Law of 2001–3: The American Law Institute Reporters' Studies*, Cambridge University Press: Cambridge, UK.

—— —— 2007e. Canada-Export Credits and Loan Guarantees for Regional Aircraft, pp. 391–401 in Henrik Horn and Petros C. Mavroidis (eds.), *The WTO Case-Law of 2001–3: The American Law Institute Reporters' Studies*, Cambridge University Press: Cambridge, UK.

—— —— 2007f. US-Section 211 Omnibus Appropriations Act of 1998, pp. 472–522 in Henrik Horn and Petros C. Mavroidis (eds.), *The WTO Case-Law of 2001–3: The American Law Institute Reporters' Studies*, Cambridge University Press: Cambridge, UK.

—— and Don Regan. 2000. The Product/Process Distinction—An Illusory Basis for Disciplining 'Unilateralism' in Trade Policy, *European Journal of International Law*, 11: 249–89.

—— and Robert W. Staiger. 2006. United States—Anti-Dumping Act of 1916 (Original Complaint by the European Communities)—Recourse to Arbitration by the United States under 22.6 of the DSU, WT/DS136/ARB, 24 February 2004: A Legal and Economic Analysis, *The World Trade Review*, 4: 295–316.

—— —— 2007. US-Sunset Reviews of AD Duties on Corrosion-Resistant Carbon Steel Flat Products from Japan, pp. 601–21 in Henrik Horn and Petros C. Mavroidis (eds.), *The WTO Case-Law of 2001–3: The American Law Institute Reporters' Studies*, Cambridge University Press: Cambridge, UK.

—— and E. Türk. 2001. The WTO Impact on Internal Regulations—A Case Study of the Canada-EC Asbestos Dispute, pp. 283–328 in G. de Búrca and J. Scott, *The EU and the WTO: Legal and Constitutional Issues*, Hart Publishing: Oxford.

Hudec, Robert E. 1972. GATT or GABB? The Future Design of the General Agreement on Tariffs and Trade, *The Yale Law Journal*, 80: 1299–386.

—— 1975. *The GATT Legal System and the World Trade Diplomacy*, Praeger: New York, NY.

—— 1987. *Developing Countries in the GATT Legal System*, Gower Publishing Company: Aldershot, UK.

—— 1988. Tiger, Tiger in the House: A Critical Evaluation of the Case against Discriminatory Trade Measures, pp. 165–96 in Ernst-Ulrich Petersmann and Meinhard Hilf (eds.), *The New GATT Round of Multilateral Trade Negotiations: Legal and Economic Problems*, Kluwer: Deventer.

—— 1990. *The GATT Legal System and the World Trade Diplomacy*, Butterworth Legal Publishers: Salem.

—— 1993a. *Enforcing International Trade Law*, Butterworths: London.

—— 1993b. GATT's Influence on Regional Agreements: A Comment, pp. 151–5 in Jaime de Melo and Arvind Panagariya (eds.), *New Dimensions in Regional Integration*, CEPR, Cambridge University Press: Cambridge, Mass.

—— 1998. GATT/WTO Constraints on National Regulation: Requiem for an 'Aims and Effect' Test, *International Lawyer*, 32: 619.

—— 2000. 'Like Product': The Differences in Meaning in GATT Articles I and III, pp. 101–23 in Thomas Cottier and Petros C. Mavroidis, *Regulatory Barriers and the Principle of Non-discrimination in World Trade Law*, University of Michigan Press: Ann Arbor, Mich.

Huerta Goldman, Jorge Alberto. 2009. *Mexico in the WTO and NAFTA: Litigating International Trade Disputes*, Kluwer: Amsterdam, the Netherlands.

Hufbauer, Clyde, Steve Charnovitz, and Jisun Kim. 2009. *Global Warming and the World Trading System*, Peterson Institute for International Economics and World Resources Institute: Washington, DC.

Hull, Cordell. 1948. *The Memoirs of Cordell Hull, volumes I and II*, Macmillan: New York, NY.

Hummels, D. 2001. Time as a Trade Barrier, Mimeo, Department of Economics, Purdue University: Indiana.

Huner, Jan. 1998. Environmental Regulation and International Investment Agreements: Lessons from the MAI, Introduction, Seminar Trade, Investment and the Environment, Royal Institute of International Affairs, Chatham House: United Kingdom.

Imam, Abid Hussain. 2011. What the MFN Means, *DAWN*, 7 November 2011, Lahore, Pakistan.

Inama, Stefano. 2003. Trade Preferences and the WTO Negotiations on Market Access: Battling for Compensation of Erosion of GSP, ACP and Other Trade Preferences or Assessing and Improving their Utilization and Value by Addressing Rules of Origin and Graduation, *Journal of World Trade*, 37: 959–76.

—— 2009. *Rules of Origin in International Trade*, Cambridge University Press: Cambridge, UK.

—— and Edwin Vermulst. 2010. Non-preferential Origin Rules in Antidumping Law and Practice, pp. 276–305 in Kyle W. Bagwell, George A. Bermann, and Petros C. Mavroidis (eds.), *Law and Economics of Contingent Protection in International Trade*, Cambridge University Press: New York City, NY.

Ingco, Merlinda D., and L. Alan Winters. 2004. Agriculture and the Trade Negotiations: A Synopsis, pp. 16–36 in Merlinda D. Ingco, and L. Alan Winters (eds.), *Agriculture and the New Trade Agenda*, Cambridge University Press: Cambridge, UK.

Irwin, Douglas A. 1995. The GATT in Historical Perspective, *American Economic Review*, 85: 323–8.

—— 1996. *Against the Tide*, Princeton University Press: Princeton, NJ.

—— 1998a. Changes in US Tariffs: The Role of Import Prices and Commercial Policies, *American Economic Review*, 88: 1015–26.

—— 1998b. The Smoot-Hawley Tariff: A Quantitative Assessment, *Review of Economics and Statistics*, 80: 326–34.

Irwin, Douglas A. 2002. Reciprocity and the Origins of US Trade Liberalization, pp. 61–84 in Jagdish Bhagwati (ed.), *Going Alone: The Case for Relaxed Reciprocity in Freeing Trade*, MIT Press: Cambridge, Mass.

—— 2003. Causing Problems? The WTO Review of Causation and Injury Attribution in U.S. Section 201 Cases, *The World Trade Review*, 2: 297–325.

—— 2005. *Free Trade under Fire*, 2nd edn., Princeton University Press: Princeton, NJ.

—— 2011. *Peddling Protectionism*, Princeton University Press: Princeton, NJ.

—— 2012. *Trade Policy Disaster*, MIT Press: Cambridge, Mass.

—— Petros C. Mavroidis, and Alan O. Sykes. 2008. *The Genesis of the GATT*, Cambridge University Press: New York City, NY.

Iynedjan, Marc. 2002. *L'Accord de l'Organisation mondiale du commerce sur l'application des mesures sanitaires et phytosanitaires: Une analyse juridique*, LGDJ: Paris.

Jackson, John H. 1969. *World Trade and the Law of the GATT*, Bobbs-Merrill: Indianapolis, Ind.

—— 1989. National Treatment Obligations and Non-tariff Barriers, *Michigan Journal of International Law*, 10: 198–222.

—— 1997. *The World Trading System: Law and Policy of International Economic Relations*, 2nd edn., Cambridge University Press: Cambridge, UK.

—— 1998. *The World Trade Organization: Constitution and Jurisprudence*. Chatham House Papers, Royal Institute of International Affairs: London, UK.

—— 2006. *Sovereignty, the WTO, and Changing Fundamentals of International Law*, Cambridge University Press: Cambridge, UK.

—— and Grant Aldonas. 2003. The WTO: Domestic Regulation and the Challenge of Shaping Trade, *The International Lawyer*, 37: 809–13.

—— William J. Davey and Alan O. Sykes. 2002. *Legal Problems of International Economic Relations*, WEST Group: St Paul, Minn.

Janow, Merit, and Robert W. Staiger. 2003. Canada-Measures Affecting the Importation of Dairy Products and the Exportation of Milk, pp. 236–80 in Henrik Horn and Petros C. Mavroidis (eds.), *The WTO Case-Law of 2001: The American Law Institute Reporters' Studies*, Cambridge University Press: Cambridge, UK.

—— —— 2007. US-Export Restraints, pp. 214–48 in Henrik Horn and Petros C. Mavroidis (eds.), *The WTO Case-Law of 2001–3: The American Law Institute Reporters' Studies*, Cambridge University Press: Cambridge, UK.

Jansen, Marion, and Eddie Lee. 2007. *Trade and Employment: Challenges for Policy Research*, ILO and WTO joint publication: Geneva.

Jawara, Fatoumata, and Aileen Kwa. 2003. *Behind the Scenes at the WTO: The Real World of International Negotiations*, Zed Books: London, UK.

Jimenez de Arréchaga, Eduardo. 1978. International Law in the Past Third of the Century, *Recueil des Cours*, 159, Brill Academic Publishers: The Hague, Netherlands.

Johnson, H. G. 1953–4. Optimum Tariffs and Retaliation, *Review of Economic Studies*, 1: 142–53.

—— 1976. Trade Negotiations and the New International Monetary System, in G. Curzon and V. Curzon (eds.), *Commercial Policy Issues*, A. W. Sijthoff: Leiden, the Netherlands.

—— and Mel Krauss. 1970. Border Taxes, Border Tax Adjustments, Comparative Advantage, and the Balance of Payments, *Canadian Journal of Economics*, 3(4): 595–602.

Joshi, Vivek. 2011. Preferential Tariff Formation: The Case of the European Union, *Journal of World Trade*, 45: 901–52.

Josling, Timothy E., and Alan Swinbank. 2011. European Union, pp. 61–96 in David Orden, David Blandford, and Tim Josling (eds.), *WTO Disciplines on Agricultural Support: Seeking a Fair Basis for Trade*, Cambridge University Press: New York City, NY.

—— Stefan Tangerman, and T. K. Warley. 1996. *Agriculture in the GATT*, Macmillan: Basingstoke.

Kahneman, Daniel. 2011. *Thinking Fast and Slow*, Farrar, Straus and Giroux: New York City, NY.

Kaplow, Louis. 2012. Burden of Proof, *The Yale Law Journal*, 121: 738–839.

Karacaovali, Baybars, and Nuno Limão. 2008. The Clash of Liberalizations: Preferential vs. Multilateral Trade Liberalization in the European Union, *Journal of International Economics*, 74: 299–327.

Karl, Joachim. 1998. Das multilaterale Investitionsabkommen, *Recht der internationalen Wirtschaft*, 44: 432–56.

Karsenty, Guy, and Sam Laird. 1986. The GSP: A Quantitative Assessment of the Direct Trade Effects and of Policy Options, UNCTAD Discussion Paper 18, UNCTAD: Geneva.

Kathuria, Sanjay, Will J. Martin, and Anjali Bhardwaj. 2003. Implications of Multifibre Arrangement Abolition for India and South Asia, pp. 47–66 in Aaditya Mattoo and Robert M. Stern (eds.), *India and the WTO*, Oxford University Press and the World Bank Group: Washington, DC.

Katz, M. L., and C. Shapiro. 1985. Network Externalities, Competition and Compatibility, *American Economic Review*, 75: 424–40.

Kawamoto, Akira, Scott Jacobs, Sveinbjorn Blondal, and Bernard J. Phillips. 1997. Product Standards, Conformity Assessment, and Regulatory reform, pp. 275–328 in *OECD Report on Regulatory Reform*, OECD: Paris.

Keck, Alexander, and Patrick Low. 2003. Special and Differential Treatment in the WTO: Why, When and How? Mimeo.

Kee, Hiau Looi, Alessandro Nicita, and Marcelo Olarreaga. 2009. Estimating Trade Restrictiveness Indices, *The Economic Journal*, 119: 172–99.

Kelly, Kenneth. 1988. The Analysis of Causality in Escape Clause Cases, *Journal of Industrial Economics*, 37: 187–207.

Kennedy, Matthew. 2010. When Will the Protocol Amending the TRIPs Agreement Enter into Force? *Journal of International Economic Law*, 13: 459–74.

Kenner, Jeff. 2011. Labour Clauses in EU Preferential Trade Agreements—An Analysis of the Cotonou Partnership Agreement, pp. 180–209 in Kyle W. Bagwell and Petros C. Mavroidis (eds.), *Preferential Trade Agreements: A Law and Economics Analysis*, Cambridge University Press: New York, NY.

Keohane, Robert O., and Joseph S. Nye. 1974. Transgovernmental Relations and International Organizations, *World Politics*, 27: 1–41.

Kessie, Edwini. 2004. The Early Harvest Negotiations in 2003, pp. 115–50 in Federico Ortino and Ernst-Ulrich Petersmann (eds.), *The WTO Dispute Settlement System 1995–2003*, Kluwer: The Hague, Netherlands.

—— 2007. The Legal Status of Special and Differential Treatment Provisions under the WTO Agreements, pp. 12–35 in George A. Bermann, and Petros C. Mavroidis (eds.), *WTO Law and Developing Countries*, Cambridge University Press: New York City, NY.

Khorana, Sangeeta, May T. Yeung, William A. Kerr, and Nick Perdikis. 2012. The Battle over the EU's Proposed Humanitarian Trade Preferences of Pakistan: A Case Study in Multifaceted Protectionism, *Journal of World Trade*, 46: 33–60.

Kim, Jong Bum. 2011. WTO Legality of Discriminatory Liberalization of Internal Regulations: Role of RTA National Treatment, *The World Trade Review*, 10: 473–96.

Kindleberger, Charles P. 1984. *Multinational Excursions*, MIT Press: Cambridge, Mass.

—— 1986. International Public Goods without International Government, *American Economic Review*, 76: 1–13.

Knetter, Michael and Tom Prusa. 2003. Macroeconomic Factors and Antidumping Filings: Evidence from Four Countries, *Journal of International Economics*, 61: 1–17.

Komuro, Norio. 2009. Japan's Generalized System of Preferences, pp. 103–30 in Bernard M. Hoekman, Will Martin, and Carlos A. Primo Braga (eds.), *Trade Preference Erosion, Measurement and Policy Response*, Palgrave Macmillan and the World Bank: Washington, DC.

Kono, Daniel Y. 2006. Optimal Obfuscation: Democracy and Trade Policy Transparency, *American Political Science Review*, 100: 369–84.

Koremenos, Barbara. 2007. If Only Half of International Agreements Have Dispute Resolution Provisions, Which Half Needs Explaining? *Journal of Legal Studies*, 36: 189–221.

Kostecki, Michel. 1987. Export Restraint Arrangements and Trade Liberalization, *The World Economy*, 10: 425–53.

Kotschwar, Barbara. 2010. Mapping Investment Provisions in Regional Trade Agreements: Towards an International Investment Regime?, pp. 365–417 in Antoni Estevadeordal, Kati Suominen, and Robert Teh (eds.), *Regional Rules in the Global Trading System*, Cambridge University Press: Cambridge, UK.

Koulen, Mark. 2001. Foreign Investment in the WTO, pp. 181–203 in E. C. Nieuwenhuys and M. M. T. A. Brus (eds.), *Multilateral Regulation of Investment*, Kluwer: Deventer.

Kovacic, William E. 2010. Price Differentiation in Antitrust and Trade Instruments, pp. 264–75 in Kyle W. Bagwell, George A. Bermann, and Petros C. Mavroidis (eds.), *Law and Economics of Contingent Protection in International Trade*, Cambridge University Press: New York City, NY.

Kowalczyk, Carsten. 1990. Welfare and Customs Union, NBER Working Paper No 3476.

Kowalski, Przemyslaw. 2009. The Canadian Preferential Tariff Regime and Potential Economic Impacts of its Erosion, pp. 131–72 in Bernard M. Hoekman, Will Martin, and Carlos A. Primo Braga (eds.), *Trade Preference Erosion, Measurement and Policy Response*, Palgrave Macmillan and the World Bank: Washington, DC.

Kramer, Larry. 1995. Extra-territorial Application of Antitrust Law after the *Insurance Antitrust Case*: A Reply to Professors Lowenfeld and Trimble, *American Journal of International Law*, 89: 750–8.

Krishna, Kala. 2005. Understanding Rules of Origin, NBER Working Paper No. 11150.

Krishna, Pravin. 1998. Regionalism and Multilateralism: A Political Economy Approach, *Quarterly Journal of Economics*, 113: 227–51.

—— 2005. *Trade Blocs: Economics and Politics*, Cambridge University Press: New York, NY.

Krueger, Anne O. 1964. The Political Economy of Rent Seeking Society, *American Economic Review*, 64: 291–303.

—— 1997. Free Trade Areas vs. Customs Unions, *Journal of Development Economics*, 54: 169–87.

—— 2007. Free Trade Agreements as Protectionist Devices: Rules of Origin, pp. 91–102 in Kym Anderson and Bernard M. Hoekman (eds.), *Critical Perspectives on the Global Trading System and the WTO*, Routledge: London, UK.

Krugman, Paul. 1979. Increasing Returns, Monopolistic Competition, and International Trade, *Journal of International Economics*, 9: 469–79.

—— 1980. Scale Economies, Product Differentiation, and the Pattern of Trade, *American Economic Review*, 70: 950–9.

—— 1983. Targeted Industrial Policies: Theory and Evidence, pp. 123–55 in *Industrial Change and Public Policy*, Kansas City: Federal Reserve Bank: Kansas, KS.

—— 1991. The Move Toward Free Trade Zones, *Economic Review*, 35: 1–24.

—— 1995. Growing World Trade: Causes and Consequences, *Brooking Papers on Economic Activity*, 1: 327–62.

—— 1997. What Should Trade Negotiators Negotiate About? *Journal of Economic Literature*, 35: 113–20.

—— and Maurice Obstfeld. 1997. *International Economics*, 4th edn., Addison-Wesley: New York, NY.

—— and Robin Wells. 2005. *Microeconomics*, Worth Publishers: New York, NY.

Kucik, Jeffrey, and Eric Reinhardt. 2007. Does Flexibility Promote Cooperation? 'Efficient Breach' in the Global Trade Regime. Mimeo, available at <http://user-www.service.emory.edu/~herein/>.

Kuhn, Thomas. 1962. *The Structure of Scientific Revolutions*, Harvard University Press: Cambridge, Mass.

—— 1996. *The Road since Structure*, Harvard University Press: Cambridge, Mass.

Kuran, Timur, and Cass Sunstein. 1999. Availability Cascades and Risk Regulation, *Stanford Law Review*, 51: 683–768.

Laborde, David and Will Martin. 2011. Agricultural Market Access, pp. 35–54 in Will Martin and Aaditya Mattoo (eds.), *Unfinished Business? The WTO's Doha Agenda*, The World Bank Group: Washington, DC.

Laird, Sam and Alexander Yeats. 1990. *Quantitative Methods for Trade Barriers Analysis*, NYU Press: New York City, NY.

Lal, Deepak. 2000. *The Poverty of Development Economics*, MIT Press: Cambridge, Mass.

Lang, Andrew, and Joanne Scott. 2009. The Hidden World of WTO Governance, *European Journal of International Law*, 20: 575–614.

Lawrence, Robert. 2003. *Crimes and Punishment: Retaliation under the WTO*, Institute for International Economics: Washington, DC.

Leddy, John. 1958. GATT: A Cohesive Influence in the Free World, *Journal of Farm Economics*, 40: 228–37.

Lee, Yong-Shik. 2005. *Safeguard Measures in World Trade: The Legal Analysis*, 2nd edn., Kluwer: The Hague.

Lesser, Caroline. 2007. Do Bilateral and Regional Approaches for Reducing Technical Barriers to Trade Converge Towards the Multilateral Trading System? OECD Trade Policy Working Papers No. 58, OECD: Paris.

Lester, Simon. 2011. The Problem of Subsidies as a Means of Protectionism: Lessons from the WTO EC-Aircraft Case, *Melbourne Journal of International Law*, 12: 1–28.

Levy, Philip, and T. N. Srinivasan. 1996. Regionalism and the (Dis)advantage of Dispute-Settlement Access, *American Economic Association Papers and Proceedings*, 86(2): 93–8.

Li, Changying and Keith E. Maskus. 2006. The Impact of Parallel Imports on Cost-Reducing Research and Development, *Journal of International Economics*, 68: 443–55.

Liang, Margaret. 2011. Antidumping Negotiations in the Uruguay Round: Reflections of a Singapore Negotiator, pp. 59–101 in C.I. Lim and Margaret Liang (eds.), *Economic Diplomacy, Essays and Reflections by Singapore's Negotiators*, Lee Kuan Yew School of Public Policy: Singapore.

Lianos, Ioannis. 2010. Judging Economists: Economic Expertise in Competition Law Litigation—A European View, pp. 185–322 in Ioannis Lianos and Ioannis Kokkoris (eds.), *New Challenges in EC Competition Law Enforcement*, Kluwer: Amsterdam, the Netherlands.

Limão, Nuno. 2006a. Preferential Trade Agreements as Stumbling Blocks for Multilateral Trade Liberalization: Evidence for the U.S., *American Economic* Review, 96: 896–914.

—— 2006b. Preferential vs. Multilateral Trade Liberalization: Evidence and Open Questions, *The World Trade Review*, 5: 155–76.

—— 2006c. Trade Preferences to Small Developing Countries and the Welfare Costs of Lost Multilateral Liberalization, *World Bank Economic Review*, 20: 217–40.

—— 2011. Comments on 'Beyond the WTO? Coverage and Legal Inflation in EU and US Preferential Trade Agreements, pp. 175–9 in Kyle W. Bagwell and Petros C. Mavroidis (eds.), *Preferential Trade Agreements: A Law and Economics Analysis*, Cambridge University Press: New York, NY.

—— and Kamal Saggi. 2008. Tariff Retaliation versus Financial Compensation in the Enforcement of International Trade Agreements, *Journal of International Economics*, 76: 48–60.

Lin, Li-Wen and Curtis Milhaupt. 2011. We Are the (National) Champions: Understanding the Mechanics of State Capitalism in China, Columbia Law and Economics Working Paper Series No. 409.

Linarelli, John. 2011. Global Procurement Law in Times of Crisis: New Buy American Policies and Option in the WTO Legal Systems, pp. 444–58 in Sue Arrowsmith and Robert D. Anderson (eds.), *The WTO Regime on Government Procurement: Challenge and Reform*, Cambridge University Press: Cambridge, UK.

Lippoldt, Douglas. 2009. The Australian Preferential Tariff Regime, pp. 173–218 in Bernard M. Hoekman, Will Martin, and Carlos A. Primo Braga (eds.), *Trade Preference Erosion, Measurement and Policy Response*, Palgrave Macmillan and the World Bank: Washington, DC.

Lloyd, Peter. 1993. A Tariff Substitute for Rules of Origin in Free Trade Areas, *The World Economy*, 16: 691–712.

Long, Olivier. 1989. *Public Scrutiny of Protection, Domestic Policy, Transparency, and Trade Liberalization*, Trade Policy Research Centre: London, UK.

Low, Patrick A. 1993. *Trading Free*. Twentieth Century Fund: New York City, NY.

—— 1995. Pre-shipment Inspection Services, World Bank Discussion Paper No. 278, World Bank: Washington, DC.

—— 2007. Is the WTO Doing Enough for Developing Countries? pp. 324–57 in George A. Bermann and Petros C. Mavroidis (eds.), *WTO Law and Developing Countries*, Cambridge University Press: New York City, NY.

—— Aaditya Mattoo, and Arvind Subramanian. 1997. Government Procurement in Services, pp. 225–42 in Bernard M. Hoekman and Petros C. Mavroidis (eds.), *Law and Policy in Public Purchasing*, University of Michigan Press: Ann Arbor, Mich.

Lowenfeld, Andreas F. 1995. Conflict, Balancing of Interests, and the Exercise of Jurisdiction to Prescribe: Reflections on the *Insurance Antitrust Case*, *American Journal of International Law*, 89: 42–53.

Lucas, Robert, E. 1988. On the Mechanism of Economic Development, *Journal of Monetary Economics*, 22: 3–42.

Ludema, Rodney, 1991. International Trade Bargaining and the Most-Favored-Nation Clause, *Economics and Politics*, 3: 1–20.

Luff, David. 2004. *Le droit de l'OMC: analyse critique*, Bruylant, LGDJ: Brussels.

Lydgate, Emily Barrett. 2011. Consumer Preferences and the National Treatment Principle: Emerging Environmental Regulations Prompt a New Look at an Old Problem, *The World Trade Review*, 10: 165–88.

MacPhee, Craig R., and Victor Iwuagwu Oguledo. 1991. The Trade Effects of the US GSP, *Atlantic Economic Journal*, 19: 19–26.

Maduro, Miguel. 2007. So Close and Yet So Far: The Paradoxes of Mutual Recognition, *Journal of European Public Policy*, 14: 814–25.

Maggi, Giovanni. 1999. The Value of Commitment with Imperfect Observability and Private Information, *The Rand Journal of Economics*, 30: 555–74.

—— and Andres Rodriguez-Clare. 1998. The Value of Trade Agreements in the Presence of Political Pressures, *Journal of Political Economy*, 106: 574–601.

—— —— 2007. A Political Economy Theory of Trade Agreements, *American Economic Review*, 97: 1374–406.

—— and Robert W. Staiger. 2011. The Role of Dispute Settlement Procedures in International Trade Agreements, *The Quarterly Journal of Economics*, 126: 475–515.

Mansfield, Edward D., and Marc L. Busch. 1995. The Political Economy of Non-tariff Barriers: A Cross-National Analysis, *International Organization*, 49: 723–49.

Marceau, Gabrielle, and Joel Trachtman. 2002. The TBT, the SPS and the GATT: A Map of the WTO Law of Domestic Regulation of Goods, *Journal of World Trade*, 36: 811–82.

Marchetti, Juan A., and Petros C. Mavroidis. 2011. The Genesis of GATS, *European Journal of International Law*, 2011(22): 1–33.

Martin, Alberto, and Wouter Vergote. 2008. On the Role of Retaliation in Trade Agreements, *Journal of International Economics*, 76: 61–77.

Martin, William, and Christian Bach. 1998. State Trading in China, pp. 287 302 in Thomas Cottier and Petros C. Mavroidis (eds.), *State Trading in the Twenty-First Century*, University of Michigan Press: Ann Arbor, Mich.

Martin, Will J., and L. Alan Winters. 2001. The Uruguay Round: A Milestone for Developing Countries, pp. 1–30 in Will J. Martin and L. Alan Winters (eds.), *The Uruguay Round and the Developing Countries*, Cambridge University Press: Cambridge.

Maruyama, Warren H. 1989. The Evolution of Escape Clause Section 201 of the Tariff Act of 1974 as Amended by the Omnibus Trade and Competitiveness Act of 1988, *Brigham Young University Law Review*: 393–430.

Marx, Axel. 2011. Global Governance and the Certification Revolution, pp. 590–603 in D. Levi-Faur (ed.), *Handbook of the Politics of Regulation*, Edward Elgar: Cheltenham, UK.

—— and D. Cuypers. 2010. Forest Certification as a Global Environmental Governance Tool: What is the Macro-impact of the Forest Stewardship Council? *Regulation and Governance*, 4: 408–34.

Maskin, Eric, and Jean Tirole. 1999. Unforeseen Developments and Incomplete Contracts, *Review of Economic Studies*, 66: 83–114.

Maskus, Keith E., Tsunehiro Otsuki, and John S. Wilson. 2001. An Empirical Frame-work for Analyzing Technical Regulations and Trade, pp. 29–58 in Keith E. Maskus, and John S. Wilson (eds.), *Quantifying the Impact of Technical Barriers to Trade: Can it be Done?*, University of Michigan Press: Ann Arbor, Mich.

Mathis, James H. 2002. *Regional Trade Agreements in the GATT/WTO, Article XXIV and the Internal Trade Requirement*, TMC Asser Press: The Hague.

—— 2006. Regional Trade Agreements and Domestic Regulation: What Reach for 'Other Restrictive Regulations of Commerce'? pp. 79–108 in Lorand Bartels and Federico Ortino (eds.), *Regional Trade Agreements and the WTO Legal System*, Oxford University Press: Oxford, UK.

—— 2011. The Legalization of GATT Article XXIV—Can Foes Become Friends? pp. 31–9 in Kyle W. Bagwell and Petros C. Mavroidis (eds.), *Preferential Trade Agreements: A Law and Economics Analysis*, Cambridge University Press: New York.

Matsushita, Mitsuo. 1998. State Trading in Japan, pp. 245–68 in Thomas Cottier and Petros C. Mavroidis (eds.), *State Trading in the Twenty-First Century*, University of Michigan Press: Ann Arbor, Mich.

—— Thomas J. Schonbaum, and Petros C. Mavroidis. 2006. *The World Trade Organization, Law Practice, and Policy*, 2nd edn., Oxford University Press: Oxford.

Mattli, Walter. 1999. *The Logic of Regional Integration: Europe and Beyond*, Cambridge University Press: Cambridge, UK.

Mattoo, Aaditya. 1997. Economic Theory and the Procurement Agreement, pp. 57–72 in Bernard M. Hoekman and Petros C. Mavroidis (eds.), *Law and Policy in Public Purchasing*, University of Michigan Press: Ann Arbor, Mich.

—— and Petros C. Mavroidis. 1995. The EEC/Japan Consensus on Cars: Interaction between Trade and Competition Policies, *The World Economy*, 18: 347–66.

—— —— 1997. Trade, Environment and the WTO: The Dispute Settlement Practice Relating to Art. XX of the GATT, pp. 325–44 in Ernst Ulrich Petersmann (ed.), *International Trade Law and the GATT/WTO Dispute Settlement System*, Kluwer: Amsterdam, the Netherlands.

—— Devesh Roy and Arvind Subramanian. 2003. The Africa Growth and Opportunity Act and its Rules of Origin: Generosity Undermined? *The World Economy*, 26: 829–51.

—— and Arvind Subramanian. 1998. Regulatory Autonomy and Multilateral Disciplines: The Dilemma and Possible Resolution, *Journal of International Economic Law*, 1: 303–24.

—— —— 2009. Currency Undervaluation and Sovereign Wealth Fund: A New Role for the World Trade Organization, *The World Economy*, 32: 1135–64.

Mavroidis, Petros C. 1993. Government Procurement Agreement; The Trondheim Case: The Remedies Issue, *Aussenwirtschaft*, 48: 77–94.

—— 2000a. Remedies in the WTO Legal System: Between a Rock and a Hard Place, *European Journal of International Law*, 11: 763–813.

—— 2000b. Trade and Environment after the Shrimps-Turtles Litigation, *Journal of World Trade*, 34: 73–88.

—— 2002. Judicial Supremacy, Judicial Restraint and the Issue of Consistency of Preferential Trade Agreements with the WTO: The Apple in the Picture, pp. 583–601 in Dan Kennedy and James Southwick (eds.), *The Political Economy of the International Trade Law: Essays in Honour of Robert E. Hudec*, Cambridge University Press: Cambridge, Mass.

—— 2004a. *Amicus curiae* Briefs before the WTO: Much Ado about Nothing, pp. 317–30 in Armin von Bogdandy, Petros C. Mavroidis, and Yves Meny (eds.), *In Honour of Claus-Dieter Ehlermann*, Kluwer: Amsterdam, the Netherlands.

—— 2004b. The Need to Micro-manage Regulatory Diversity, pp. 314–25 in K. Basu, H. Horn, L. Roman, and J. Shapiro (eds.), *International Labour Standards*, Blackwell Publishing: Oxford, UK.

—— 2005. Do not Ask too Many Questions: The Institutional Arrangements for Accommodating Regional Integration within the WTO, pp. 239–78 in E. Kwan Choi and James C. Hartigan (eds.), *Handbook of International Trade, volume II: Economic and Legal Analysis of Trade Policy Institutions*, Blackwell Publishing: Malden, Mass.

—— 2006. If I Don't Do it, Somebody Else Will (or Won't), *Journal of World Trade*, 40: 187–214.

—— 2008. No Outsourcing of Law? WTO Law as Practised by WTO Courts, *American Journal of International Law*, 102: 421–74.

—— 2009. Crisis? What Crisis? Is the WTO Appellate Body Coming of Age? pp. 173–83 in Terence P. Stewart (ed.), *Opportunities and Obligations: New Perspectives on Global and US Trade Policy*, Kluwer: Amsterdam, The Netherlands.

—— 2011. Always Look at the Bright Side of Non-delivery: WTO and Preferential Trade Agreements, Yesterday and Today, *The World Trade Review*, 10: 375–87.

—— George A. Bermann, and Mark Wu. 2010. *The Law of the WTO: Documents, Cases, and Analysis*, West Publishing: Egan, Minn.

—— and Patrick Messerlin. 1998. Has Art. 90 ECT Prejudiced the Status of Property Ownership? pp 345–60 in Thomas Cottier and Petros C. Mavroidis (eds.), *State-Trading in the 21st Century*, The University of Michigan Press: Ann Arbor, Mich.

—— —— and Jasper M. Wauters. 2008. *The Law and Economics of Contingent Protection*, Edward Elgar: Cheltenham, UK.

—— and Damien J. Neven. 1999. Some Reflections on Extraterritoriality in International Economic Law: A Law and Economic Analysis, pp. 1297–325 in *Mélanges en homage de Michel Waelbroeck*, Bruylant: Bruxelles.

—— and André Sapir. 2008. Mexico—AD Measures on Rice: Don't Ask Me No Questions and I Won't Tell You No Lies, pp. 305–24 in Henrik Horn and Petros C. Mavroidis (eds.), *The WTO Case-Law of 2004–5: The American Law Institute Reporters' Studies*, Cambridge University Press: Cambridge, UK.

McCloskey, Deirdre N., and Stephan T. Ziliak. 1996. The Standard Error of Regressions, *Journal of Economic Literature*, 34: 97–114.

McDonough, Patrick J. 1993. Subsidies and Countervailing Measures, pp. 803–1008 in Terence P. Stewart (ed.), *The GATT Uruguay Round: A Negotiating History (1986–1992)*, Kluwer Law: Deventer, the Netherlands and Boston, Mass.

McMahon, Joseph. 2006. *The WTO Agreement on Agriculture: A Commentary*, Oxford University Press: Oxford, UK.

—— 2011. *The Negotiations for a New Agreement on Agriculture*, Martinus Nijhoff: Leiden, the Netherlands.

Meade, James. 1942. *The Economic Basis of Durable Peace*, G. Allen and Unwin Ltd: London.

—— 1955. *The Theory of Customs Unions*, North Holland: Amsterdam, the Netherlands.

—— 1974. A Note on Border-Tax Adjustments, *Journal of Political Economy*, 82: 1013–15.

—— 1990. *The Collected Papers of James Meade*, edited by Susan Howson and Donald Moggridge, vol. IV: The Cabinet Office Diary 1944–1946, Unwin Hyman: London, UK.

Meagher, Niall. 2007. Representing Developing Countries in WTO Dispute Settlement Proceedings, pp. 213–26 in George A. Bermann and Petros C. Mavroidis (eds.), *WTO Law and Developing Countries*, Cambridge University Press: New York City, NY.

—— 2008. A Comment on EC-Customs Classification on Frozen Boneless Chicken Cuts, pp. 39–44 in Henrik Horn and Petros C. Mavroidis (eds.), *The WTO Case-Law of 2004–5: The American Law Institute Reporters' Studies*, Cambridge University Press: Cambridge, UK.

Meessen, Karl M. 1996. *Extraterritorial Jurisdiction in Theory and Practice*, Kluwer: London, UK.

Melitz, Marc. 2003. The Impact of Trade on Intra-industry Reallocations and Aggregate Industry Productivity, *Econometrica*, 71: 1695–725.

Melloni, Mattia. 2005. *The Principle of National Treatment in the GATT*, Bruylant: Brussels.

Meng, Werner P. 1990. The Hormones Conflict between the EEC and the United States within the Context of GATT, *Michigan Journal of International Law*, 11: 819–39.

Mercurio, Bryan, and Dianna Shao. 2010. A Precautionary Approach to Decision Making: the Evolving Jurisprudence on Article 5.7 of the SPS Agreement, *Trade, Law and Development*, II: 195–223.

Messerlin, Patrick. 1995. *La nouvelle OMC*, Dunant: Paris.

—— 2001. *Measuring the Cost of Protection in Europe*, Institute Of International Economics: Washington, DC.

—— and David Palmeter. 2000. Technical Regulations and Industry Standards (TRIS), pp. 245–60 in Thomas Cottier and Petros C. Mavroidis (eds.), *Regulatory Barriers and the Principle of Non-discrimination in World Trade Law*, University of Michigan Press: Ann Arbor, Mich.

Michalopoulos, Constantine. 2001. *Developing Countries in the WTO*, Palgrave: Basingstoke.

Miller, James N. 2000. Origins of the GATT: British Resistance to American Multilateralism, Cambridge University, Jerome Levy Economics Institute at Bard College, Working Paper No. 318.

Milner, Helen V. 1988. *Resisting Protectionism: Global Industries and the Politics of International Trade*, Princeton University Press, Princeton, NJ.

Moore, Michael O. 2002. Commerce Department Antidumping Sunset Reviews: A First Assessment, *Journal of World Trade*, 36: 675–98.

—— 2004. Can the US Dump Antidumping? Evidence from Past Reforms. Mimeo.

Morgan, David, and Gavin Goh. 2003. Peace in our Time? An Analysis of Article 13 of the Agreement on Agriculture, *Journal of World Trade*, 37: 977–92.

Morkre, Morris E., and Harold E. Kruth. 1989. Determining Whether Dumped or Subsidized Imports Injure Domestic Industries: International Trade Commission Approach, *Contemporary Economic Policy*, 7: 78–95.

Mostashari, Shalam. 2010. Trade Growth, the Extensive Margin, and Vertical Specialization, Ph.D. Dissertation, University of Texas: Austin, Texas.

Müller, Anna Caroline. 2011. Special and Differential Treatment and Other Special Measures for Developing Countries under the Agreement on Government Procurement: The Current Text and the New Provisions, pp. 339–76 in Sue Arrowsmith and Robert D. Anderson (eds.), *The WTO Regime on Government Procurement: Challenge and Reform*, Cambridge University Press: Cambridge, UK.

Musgrave, Richard. 1959. *The Theory of Public Finance: A Study in Public Economy*, McGraw-Hill: New York City, NY.

Narlikar, Amrita, and John S. Odell. 2006. The Strict Distributive Strategy for a Bargaining Coalition: The Like Minded Group in the World Trade Organization, pp. 115–44 in John S. Odell (ed.), *Negotiating Trade, Developing Countries in the WTO and NAFTA*, Cambridge University Press: Cambridge, UK.

Nassar, André. 2011. Brazil, pp. 223–76 in David Orden, David Blandford, and Tim Josling (eds.), *WTO Disciplines on Agricultural Support: Seeking a Fair Basis for Trade*, Cambridge University Press: New York City, NY.

Navaretti, Giorgio Barba, Ricardo Faini, and Aubrey Silberston (eds.) (1995), *Beyond the Multifibre Agreement: Third World Competition and Restructuring Europe's Textile Trade*, OECD: Paris.

Navarro Varona, Edurne. 1994. Rules of Origin in the GATT, pp. 355–92 in Edwin Vermulst, Paul Waer, and Jacques Bourgeois (eds.), *Rules of Origin in International Trade*, University of Michigan Press: Ann Arbor, Mich.

Neven, Damien J. 2001. How Should Protection be Evaluated in Article III GATT Disputes? *European Journal of Political Economy*, 17: 421–44.

—— and Joseph H. H. Weiler. 2006. Japan—Measures Affecting the Importation of Apples: One Bad Apple? pp. 280–310 in Henrik Horn and Petros C. Mavroidis (eds.), *The WTO Case Law of 2003: The ALI Reporters' Studies*, Cambridge University Press: Cambridge, UK.

Neyman, Jerzy, and Egon S. Pearson. 1933. On the Problem of the Most Efficient Tests of Statistical Hypotheses, *Philosophical Transactions of the Royal Society*, 231: 289–337.

Nicolaidis, Kalypso. 2000. Non-discriminatory Mutual Recognition: An Oxymoron in the New WTO Lexicon?, pp. 267–301 in Thomas Cottier and Petros C. Mavroidis (eds.), *Regulatory Barriers and the Principle of Non-discrimination in World Trade Law*, University of Michigan Press: Ann Arbor, Mich.

—— and Joel Trachtman. 2000. From Policed Regulation to Managed Recognition in GATS, pp. 241–82 in Pierre Sauvé, and Robert Stern (eds.), *The GATS 2000, New Directions in Services Trade Liberalization*, Brookings: Washington, DC.

Nolde, Boris Baron. 1932. La Clause de la Nation la Plus Favorisée et les Tariffs Préférentiels, *Recueil des cours* 39(35), Hague Academy of International Law: The Hague.

Nordström, Håkan. 2005. The WTO Secretariat in a Changing World, *Journal of World Trade*, 39: 819–53.

—— 2007. Participation of Developing Countries in the WTO—New Evidence Based on the 2003 Official Records, pp. 146–85 in George A. Bermann and Petros C. Mavroidis (eds.), *WTO Law and Developing Countries*, Cambridge University Press: New York City, NY.

—— and Gregory C. Shaffer. 2007. Access to Justice in the World Trade Organization: A Case for a Small Claims Procedure, SSNR, available at <http://works.bepress.com/gregory_shaffer/14>.

O'Connor, Bernard. 2005. The Structure of the Agreement on Agriculture, pp. 83–90 in Bernard O'Connor (ed.), *Agriculture in WTO Law*, Cameron May: London, UK.

Odell, John. 2005. Chairing a WTO Negotiation, *Journal of International Economic Law*, 8: 425–48.

—— and Barry Eichengreen. 1998. The United States, the ITO and the WTO: Exit Options, Agent Slack, and Presidential Leadership, pp. 181–209 in Anne O. Krueger (ed.), *The WTO as an International Organization*, University of Chicago Press: Chicago, Ill.

877

Oduro, Abena. 2009. African Countries and the Green Box, pp. 412–24 in Ricardo Melendez-Ortiz, Christophe Bellmann, and Jonathan Hepburn (eds.), *Agricultural Subsidies in the WTO Green Box*, Cambridge University Press: New York City, NY.

Oesch, Matthias. 2003. *Standards of Review in WTO Dispute Resolution*, Oxford University Press: Oxford and New York, NY.

Olsen, Sven. 2005. The Negotiation of the Agreement on Agriculture, pp. 43–82 in Bernard O'Connor (ed.), *Agriculture in WTO Law*, Cameron May: London.

Olson, Moncur. 1965. *The Logic of Collective Action*, Harvard University Press: Cambridge, Mass.

Orden, David. 2009. Farm Policy Reform in the United States: Past Progress and Future Direction, pp. 86–120 in Ricardo Melendez-Ortiz, Christophe Bellmann and Jonathan Hepburn (eds.), *Agricultural Subsidies in the WTO Green Box*, Cambridge University Press: New York City, NY.

—— David Blandford, and Tim Josling. 2011a. Introduction, pp. 3–22 in David Orden, David Blandford, and Tim Josling (eds.), *WTO Disciplines on Agricultural Support: Seeking a Fair Basis for Trade*, Cambridge University Press: New York City, NY.

—— —— —— 2011b. The Difficult Task of Disciplining Domestic Support, pp. 389–432 in David Orden, David Blandford, and Tim Josling (eds.), *WTO Disciplines on Agricultural Support: Seeking a Fair Basis for Trade*, Cambridge University Press: New York City, NY.

Ortino, Federico. 2003. *Basic Legal Instruments for the Liberalisation of Trade: A Comparative Analysis of EC and WTO Law*, Hart Publishing: Oxford.

—— 2009. Non-discriminatory Treatment in Investment Disputes, pp. 344–66 in Pierre-Marie Dupuy, F. Francioni, and E. U. Petersmann (eds.), *Human Rights in International Investment Law and Arbitration*, Oxford University Press: Oxford, UK.

Ossa, Ralph. 2011. A New Trade Theory of GATT/WTO Negotiations, *Journal of Political Economy*, 119: 122–52.

Ostry, Sylvia. 1997. *The Post-Cold War Trading System, Who's on First?* University of Chicago Press: Chicago, Ill.

Özden, Czaglar, and Eric Reinhardt. 2003. The Perversity of Preferences: GSP and Developing Country Trade Policies, 1976–2000, World Bank Working Paper 2955, The World Bank: Washington, DC.

Paemen, Hugo, and Alexandra Bentsch. 1995. *From the GATT to the WTO: The European Community in the Uruguay Round*, Leuven University Press: Leuven, Belgium.

Palmeter, David N. 1987. Rules of Origin or Rules of Restriction? A Commentary on a New Form of Protectionism, *Fordham International Law Journal*, 11: 9–16.

—— 1993. Environment and Trade: Much Ado about Little? *Journal of World Trade*, 27: 55–65.

—— 1995. US Implementation of the Uruguay Round Antidumping Code, *Journal of World Trade*, 29: 39–82

—— 1999. National Sovereignty and the World Trade Organization, *Journal of World Intellectual Property*, 2: 77–94.

—— 2006. The WTO Standard of Review in Health and Safety Disputes, pp. 224–34 in George A. Bermann and Petros C. Mavroidis (eds.), *Trade and Human Health and Safety*, Cambridge University Press: New York City, NY.

—— and Petros C. Mavroidis. 1998. The WTO Legal System: Sources of Law, *American Journal of International Law*, 92: 398–413.

—— —— 2004. *Dispute Settlement in the WTO, Practice and Procedure*, 2nd edn., Cambridge University Press: Cambridge, UK.

Panagariya, Arvind. 2000. Preferential Trade Liberalization: The Traditional Theory and New Developments, *Journal of Economic Literature*, 38: 287–331.

—— 2005. Liberalizing Agriculture, *Foreign Affairs*, 84: 182–202.

Pauwelyn, Joost. 1998. Evidence, Proof and Persuasion in WTO Dispute Settlement: Who Bears the Burden? *Journal of International Economic Law*, 1: 227–58.

—— 1999. The WTO Agreement on Sanitary and Phytosanitary (SPS) Measures as Applied in the First Three SPS Disputes: EC—Hormones, Australia—Salmon, and Japan—Varietals, *Journal of International Economic Law*, 2: 641–64.

—— 2000. Enforcement and Countermeasures in the WTO: Rules are Rules—Toward a More Collective Approach, *American Journal of International Law*, 94: 335–47.

—— 2003. *Conflicts of Norms in Public International Law: How WTO Relates to Other Rules of International Law*, Cambridge University Press: Cambridge, UK.

—— 2007. *US Federal Climate Policy and Competitiveness Concerns: The Limits and Options of International Trade Law*, Nicholas Institute for Environmental Policy Studies: Duke University, NC.

Pelkmans, Jacques. 2003. Mutual Recognition in Goods and Services: An Economic Perspective, Working Paper No. 16, European Network of Economic Policy Research Institutes.

Penrose, Ernest F. 1953. *Economic Planning for Peace*, Princeton University Press: Princeton, NJ.

Perez, Oren. 2007. Anomalies at the Precautionary Kingdom: Reflections on the GMO Panel's Decision, *The World Trade Review*, 6: 265–80.

Petersmann, Ernst-Ulrich. 1991. Non-violation Complaints in Public International Trade Law, *German Yearbook of International Law*, 34: 175–231.

—— 1993. International Competition Rules for the GATT—MTO World Trade and Legal System, *Journal of World Trade*, 27: 35–86.

—— 1998. GATT Law on State Trading Enterprises: Critical Evaluation of Article XVII and Proposals for Reform, pp. 71–96 in Thomas Cottier and Petros C. Mavroidis (eds.), *State Trading in the Twenty-First Century*, University of Michigan Press: Ann Arbor, Mich.

—— 2000. International Trade Law and International Environmental Law: Environmental Taxes and Border Tax Adjustment in WTO Law and EC Law, pp. 127–65 in R. Revesz, P. Sands, and T. Stewart (eds.), *Environmental Law, The Economy and Sustainable Development*, Cambridge University Press: Cambridge, Mass.

—— 2002. Constitutionalism and WTO Law: From a State-Centered Approach towards a Human Rights Approach in International Economic Law, pp. 32–67 in Daniel L. M. Kennedy and James D. Southwick (eds.), *The Political Economy of International Trade Law: Essays in Honor of Robert E. Hudec*, Cambridge University Press: Cambridge, UK.

Pienaar, Natalie. 2003. *Economic Aspects of the Consistency Requirement in the WTO Agreement on the Application of SPS Measures*, The Institute for International Economic Studies: Stockholm.

Piermartini, Roberta. 2005. Harmonization and Mutual Recognition of Product Standards: The Effect on Intra-EU Trade, WTO Discussion Paper, WTO: Geneva.

Plesch, Dan. 2011. *America, Hitler, and the UN*, I.B. Tauris: London, UK.

Popper, Karl. 1992. *The Logic of Scientific Discovery*, Routledge: New York, NY.

Porges, Amelia, and Joel Trachtman. 2003. Robert Hudec and Domestic Regulation: The Resurrection of Aim and Effects, *Journal of World Trade*, 37: 783–99.

Posner, Richard A. 1999a. The Law and Economics of the Economics Expert Witness, *Journal of Economic Perspectives*, 13: 91–9.

—— 1999b. An Economic Approach to Law of Evidence, *Stanford Law Review,* 51: 1477–546.

Potipiti, Tanapong. 2006. *Import Tariffs and Export Subsidies in the WTO: A Small Country Approach,* Proceedings of the 2nd National Conference of Economists: Bangkok, Thailand.

Prahalad, C. K. 2010. *The Fortune at the Bottom of the Pyramid,* Wharton School Publishing: Upper Saddle River, NJ.

Pregg, Ernest H. 1995. *Traders in a Brave New World: The Uruguay Round and the Future of the International Trading System,* University of Chicago Press: Chicago, Ill.

Priess, Hans-Joachim, and Pascal Friton. 2011. Designing Effective Challenge Procedures: The EU's Experience with Remedies, pp. 511–31 in Sue Arrowsmith and Robert D. Anderson (eds.), *The WTO Regime on Government Procurement: Challenge and Reform,* Cambridge University Press: Cambridge, UK.

Prusa, Thomas J. 1992. Why are so Many Antidumping Petitions Withdrawn? *Journal of International Economics,* 33: 1–20.

—— 2001. On the Spread and Impact of Antidumping, *Canadian Journal of Economics,* 34: 591–611.

—— 2005. Anti-dumping: A Growing Problem in International Trade, *The World Economy,* 28(5): 683–700.

—— and David Sharp. 2001. A Simultaneous Equations Approach to Antidumping Injury Investigations, *Journal of Forensic Economics,* 14: 63–78.

—— and Robert Teh. 2011. Contingent Protection Rules in Regional Trade Agreements, pp. 60–100 in Kyle W. Bagwell and Petros C. Mavroidis (eds.), *Preferential Trade Agreements: A Law and Economics Analysis,* Cambridge University Press: New York, NY.

—— and Edwin Vermulst. 2009. A One-Two Punch on Zeroing, pp. 187–242 in Henrik Horn and Petros C. Mavroidis (eds.), *The WTO Case-Law of 2006–7: The American Law Institute Reporters' Studies,* Cambridge University Press: Cambridge, UK.

—— —— 2010. Guilt by Association, pp. 59–84 in Henrik Horn and Petros C. Mavroidis (eds.), *The WTO Case-Law of 2008: The American Law Institute Reporters' Studies,* Cambridge University Press: Cambridge, UK.

—— —— 2011. US-Continued Existence and Application of Zeroing Methodology: The End of Zeroing? pp. 45–62 in Henrik Horn and Petros C. Mavroidis (eds.), *The WTO Case-Law of 2009: The American Law Institute Reporters' Studies,* Cambridge University Press: Cambridge, UK.

Puccio, Laura. 2012. *Building Bridges between Regionalism and Multilateralism: Enquiries on the Ways and Means to Internationally Regulate Preferential Rules of Origin,* EUI: Florence, Italy.

Qureshi, Asif H. 2006. *Interpreting WTO Agreements,* Cambridge University Press: Cambridge, UK.

Raffaelli, Marcelo. 1998. Bringing Textiles into the Multilateral Trading System, pp. 51–60 in Jagdish Bhagwati and Matthias Hirsch (eds.), *The Uruguay Round and Beyond: Essays in Honour of Arthur Dunkel,* The University of Michigan Press: Ann Arbor, Mich.

—— and Tripti Jenkins. 1995. The Drafting History of the Agreement on Textiles and Clothing, ITCB: Geneva.

Raustiala, Kal. 2006. The Evolution of Territoriality: International Relations and American Law, in Miles Khaler and Barbara Walter (eds.), *Territoriality and Conflict in the Age of Globalization,* Cambridge University Press: Cambridge, Mass.

Ray, John, Edward. 1981. The Determinants of Tariffs and Non-tariff Restrictions in the US, *Journal of Political Economy,* 89: 105–21.

Razin, Asaf. 2001. Social Benefits and Losses from FDI, pp. 310–25 in Takatoshi Ito and Anne Krueger (eds.), *Regional and Global Capital Flows*, NBER, The University of Chicago Press: Chicago, Ill.

—— 2004. The Contribution of FDI Flows to Domestic Investment in Capacity, and Vice Versa, p. 149 in Takatoshi Ito and Andrew K. Rose (eds.), *Growth and Productivity in East Asia: NBER-East Asia Seminar on Economics*, vol. 13, University of Chicago Press: Chicago, Ill.

Regan, Donald H. 2002. Regulatory Purpose and 'Like Products' in Article III:4 of the GATT (With Additional Remarks on Article II:2), *Journal of World Trade*, 36: 443–78.

Regan, Donald H. 2003. The Dormant Commerce Clause and the Hormones Problem, pp. 91–117 in Thomas Cottier and Petros C. Mavroidis (eds.), *The Role of the Judge in International Trade Regulation: Experience and Lessons for the WTO*, University of Michigan Press: Ann Arbor, Mich.

—— 2006. What are trade agreements for? Two Conflicting Stories Told by Economists, with a Lesson for Lawyers, *Journal of International Economic Law*, 9: 951–988.

Reich, Arie. 1999. *International Public Procurement Law: The Evolution of International Regimes on Public Purchasing*, Kluwer: The Hague.

Ricardo, David. 1817. On the Principles of Political Economy and Taxation, in P. Sraffa (ed.), *The Works and Correspondence of David Ricardo, 1951*, Cambridge University Press: Cambridge, UK.

Rodriguez, Francisco, and Dani Rodrik. 2001. Trade Policy and Economic Growth: A Skeptic's Guide to the Cross-National Evidence, in Ben S. Bernanke and Kenneth S. Rogoff (eds.), *NBER Macroeconomics Annual 2000*, MIT Press: Cambridge, Mass.

Rodrik, Dani. 1999. *Making Openness Work: The New Global Economy and the Developing Countries*, Overseas Development Council, Washington, DC.

—— 2001. *The Global Governance of Trade as if Development Really Mattered*, UNDP: New York, NY.

—— 2002. What is Wrong with the (Augmented) Washington Consensus? Mimeo (available at <http://www.sopde.org/discussion.htm>).

—— 2011. *The Globalization Paradox*, Norton: New York City, NY.

Roessler, Frieder. 1993. The Relationship between Regional Integration Agreements and the Multilateral Trade Order, pp. 311–25 in Kym Anderson and Richard Blackhurst (eds.), *Regional Integration and the Global Trading System*, Harvester Wheatsheaf: Exeter, UK.

—— 1996. Diverging Domestic Policies and Multilateral Trade Integration, pp. 21–64 in Jagdish Bhagwati, and Robert E. Hudec (eds.), *Fair Trade and Harmonization, vol. 2: Legal Analysis*, Cambridge University Press: Cambridge, Mass.

—— 2000. The Institutional Balance between the Judicial and the Political Organs of the WTO, pp. 325–47 in Marco C. E. J. Bronckers and Reinhard Quick (eds.), *New Directions in International Economic Law—Essays in Honour of John H. Jackson*, Kluwer Law International: The Hague.

—— 2003. Beyond the Ostensible: A Tribute to Professor Robert Hudec's Insights on the Determination of the Likeness of Products under the National Treatment Provisions of the GATT, *Journal of World Trade*, 37: 771–81.

—— 2010. Comment on India-Additional and Extra-Additional Duties on Imports from the US, pp. 265–72 in Henrik Horn and Petros C. Mavroidis (eds.), *The WTO Case-Law of 2008: The American Law Institute Reporters' Studies*, Cambridge University Press: Cambridge, UK.

Rose, Andrew K. 2004. Do We Really Know that the WTO Increases Trade?, *American Economic Review*, 94: 98–114.

Rosendorf, Peter B., and Helen V. Milner. 2001. The Optimal Design of International Trade Institutions: Uncertainty and Escape, *International Organization*, 55: 829–57.

Rosenow, Sheri, and Brian J. O'Shea. 2010. *A Handbook on the WTO Customs Valuation Agreement*, Cambridge University Press: Cambridge, UK.

Rubini, Luca. 2010. *The Definition of Subsidy and State Aid: WTO and EC Law in Comparative Perspective*, Oxford University Press: Oxford, UK.

—— and Ingrid Jegou. 2011. The Allocation of Emission Allowances Free of Charge: Legal and Economic Considerations. Mimeo.

Rutkowski, Aleksander. 2007. Withdrawals of Anti-dumping Complaints in the EU: A Sign of Collusion, *The World Economy*, 30: 470–503.

Sacerdotti, Giorgio. 1997. Bilateral Treaties and Multilateral Instruments on Investment Protection, *Recueil des cours*, 269.

Sachs, Jeffrey D. 2005. *The End of Poverty: Economic Possibilities for our Time*, Penguin Books: New York City, NY.

—— and Andrew M. Warner. 1995. Economic Reform and the Process of Global Integration, *Brookings Papers on Economic Activity*, 1: 1–95.

Saggi, Kamal. 2010. The Agreement on Safeguards: Does it Raise More Questions than it Answers?, pp. 374–8 in Kyle W. Bagwell, George A. Bermann, and Petros C. Mavroidis (eds.), *Law and Economics of Contingent Protection in International Trade*, Cambridge University Press: New York City, NY.

—— and Sara Nese. 2008. National Treatment at the WTO: The Roles of Product and Country Heterogeneity, *International Economic Review*, 49: 1367–96.

—— and Halis Murat Yildiz. 2011. Bilateralism, Multilateralism, and the Quest for Global Free Trade, *Journal of International Economics*, 81: 26–37.

—— and Joel Trachtman. 2011. Incomplete Harmonization Contracts in International Economic Law, pp. 63–86 in Henrik Horn and Petros C. Mavroidis (eds.), *The WTO Case-Law of 2009: The American Law Institute Reporters' Studies*, Cambridge University Press: Cambridge, UK.

—— Alan Woodland, and Halis Murat Yildiz. 2010. On the Relationship between Preferential and Multilateral Trade Liberalization: The Case of Customs Unions. Mimeo.

Sanchirico, Chris. 1997. The Burden of Proof in Civil Litigation: A Simple Model of Mechanism Design, *International Review of Law and Economics*, 17: 431–65.

Santana, Roy. 2012. A Negotiating History of the ITA, Mimeo.

Sapir, André. 1998a. The Political Economy of EC Regionalism, *European Economic Review*, 42: 717–32.

—— 1998b. The Role of Articles 37 and 90 ECT in the Integration of EC Markets: The Case of Utilities, pp. 231–44 in Thomas Cottier and Petros C. Mavroidis (eds.), *State Trading in the Twenty-First Century*, University of Michigan Press: Ann Arbor, Mich.

—— 2000a. EC Regionalism at the Turn of the Millennium: Towards a New Paradigm? *The World Economy*, 23: 1135–48.

—— 2000b. Trade Regionalism in Europe: Towards an Integrated Approach, *Journal of Common Market Studies*, 38: 151–63.

—— 2001. Domino Effects in Western European Regional Trade, 1960–1992, *European Journal of Political Economy*, 17: 377–88.

—— 2011. European Integration at the Crossroads: A Review Essay on the 50th Anniversary of Bela Balassa's Theory of Economic Integration, *Journal of Economic Literature*, 49: 1200–29.

—— and Lars Lundberg. 1984. The US GSP and its Impacts, pp. 195–231 in Robert E. Baldwin and Anne O. Krueger (eds.), *The Structure and Evolution of Recent US Trade Policy*, The University of Chicago Press: Chicago, Ill.

—— and Joel Trachtman. 2008. Subsidization, Price Suppression and Expertise: Causation and Precision in US—Upland Cotton, pp. 183–210 in Henrik Horn and Petros C. Mavroidis (eds.), *The WTO Case-Law of 2004–5: The American Law Institute Reporters' Studies*, Cambridge University Press: Cambridge, UK.

Sauvé, Pierre, and Arvind Subramanian. 2001. Dark Clouds over Geneva? The Troubled Prospects of the Multilateral Trading System, pp. 16–33 in Robert Porter, Pierre Sauvé, Arvind Subramanian, and Americo Beviglia–Zampetti (eds.), *Efficiency, Equity, Legitimacy: The Multilateral Trading System at the Millennium*, Brookings: Washington, DC.

—— and Christopher Wilkie. 2000. Investment Liberalization in GATS, pp. 331–63 in Pierre Sauvé and Robert M. Stern (eds.), *GATS 2000: New Directions in Services Trade Liberalization*, Brookings: Washington, DC.

Schelling, Thomas. 1960. *The Strategy of Conflict*, Harvard University Press: Cambridge, Mass.

—— 1971. National Security Considerations Affecting Trade Policy, pp. 723–37 in *United States International Economic Policy in an Interdependent World*, Commission on International Trade and Investment Policy: Washington, DC.

Schepel, Harm. 2005. *The Constitution of Private Governance*, Hart Publishing: Oxford, UK.

Schiff, Maurice, and L. Alan Winters. 2003. *Regional Integration and Development*, Oxford University Press: Oxford, UK.

Schoenbaum, Thomas J. 2011. Fashioning a New Regime for Agricultural Trade: New Issues and the Global Food Crisis, *Journal of International Economic Law*, 14: 593–612.

Schott, Jeffrey. 1989. More Free Trade Areas?, pp. 1–58 in Jeffrey Schott (ed.), *Free Trade Areas and US Trade Policy*, Institute of International Economics: Washington, DC.

Schropp, Simon. 2005. The Case for Tariff Compensation in WTO Dispute Settlement, *Aussenwirtschaft*, 60: 485–528.

—— and David Palmeter. 2010. Appellate Body Report in EC-Bananas III: Waiver-Thin, or Lock, Stock, and Metric Ton?, pp. 7–58 in Henrik Horn and Petros C. Mavroidis (eds.), *The WTO Case-Law of 2008: The American Law Institute Reporters' Studies*, Cambridge University Press: Cambridge, UK.

Schwarz, Warren F., and Alan O. Sykes. 1998. The Positive Economics of the Most Favored Nation Obligation and its Exceptions in the WTO/GATT System, pp. 43–75 in J. Bhandari and A. Sykes (eds.), *Economic Dimensions in International Law*, Cambridge University Press: Cambridge, Mass.

—— —— 2002. The Economic Structure of Renegotiation and Dispute Resolution in the WTO/GATT System, *Journal of Legal Studies*, 31: 179–204.

Scott, Joanne. 2003. European Regulation of GMOs and the WTO, *Columbia Journal of European Law*, 9: 213–40.

—— 2009. *The WTO Agreement on Sanitary and Phyto-sanitary Measures: A Commentary*, Oxford University Press: New York City, NY.

Scott, Robert E., and Paul B. Stephan. 2006. *The Limits of Leviathan*, Cambridge University Press: New York, NY.

Segal, Adam. 2011. *Advantage*, Norton: New York City, NY.

Sengupta, Nirmal. 2007. *The Economics of Trade Facilitation*, Oxford University Press: New Delhi.

Serra, Jaime, Guillermo Aguilar, Jose Cordoba, Gene Grossman, Carla Hills, John Jackson, Julius Katz, Pedro Noyola, and Michael Wilson. 1997. *Reflections on*

Regionalism; Report of the Study Group on International Trade, Carnegie Endowment for International Peace, The Brookings Institution Press: Washington, DC.

Shaffer, Greg. 2003. *Defending Interests: the Public-Private Partnership in WTO Litigation*, Brookings: Washington, DC.

Slovic, Paul. 2000. *The Perception of Risk*, Earthscan: Sterling, Va.

Slot, Piet-Jan. 2010. The Boeing-Airbus Dispute: A Case for the Application of the European Community State Aid Rules?, pp. 172–84 in Kyle W. Bagwell, George A. Bermann, and Petros C. Mavroidis (eds.), *Law and Economics of Contingent Protection in International Trade*, Cambridge University Press: New York City, NY.

Smith, Alasdair, and Antony Venables. 1991. Counting the Cost of Voluntary Export Restraints in the European Market, pp. 187–220 in E. Helpman and A. Razin (eds.), *International Trade and Trade Policy*, MIT Press: Cambridge, Mass.

Snyder, Francis. 2003. The Gatekeepers: The European Courts and WTO Law, *Common Market Law Review*, 40: 313–67.

Snyder, Richard Carlton. 1948. *The Most-Favored-Nation Clause: Analysis with Particular Reference to Recent Treaty Practice and Tariffs,* Columbia University Press: New York, NY.

Sornarajah, M. 2004. *The International Law on Foreign Investment*, Cambridge University Press: Cambridge, UK.

Spadi, Fabio. 2000. Discriminatory Safeguards in the Light of the Admission of the People's Republic of China to the World Trade Organization, *Journal of International Economic Law*, 5: 421–43.

Spence, Michael. 2011. *The Next Convergence*, Farrar, Straus and Giroux: New York City, NY.

Srinivasan, T. N. 1998. *Developing Countries and the Multilateral Trading System: GATT 1947 to Uruguay Round and Beyond*, Westview Press: Boulder, Colo.

—— 2005. Non-discrimination in GATT/WTO: Was There Anything to Being with and is There Anything Left?' *The World Trade Review*, 4: 69–95.

—— 2011. Comments on 'A Model Article XXIV: Are There Realistic Possibilities to Improve it?', pp. 262–8 in Kyle W. Bagwell and Petros C. Mavroidis (eds.), *Preferential Trade Agreements: A Law and Economics Analysis,* Cambridge University Press: New York City, NY.

Staiger, Robert W. 2011. Non Tariff Measures and the WTO. Mimeo.

—— 2010.Currency Manipulation and World Trade, *The World Trade Review*, 9: 583–628.

—— 2011. International Trade, National Treatment and Domestic Regulation, *The Journal of Legal Studies*, 40: 149–203.

—— and Guido Tabellini. 1987. Discretionary Trade Policy and Excessive Protection, *American Economic Review*, 77: 823–37.

—— —— 1999. Do GATT Rules Help Governments Make Domestic Commitments? *Economics and Politics*, 11: 109–44.

—— and F. Wolak. 1994. Measuring Industry Specific Protection: Antidumping in the United States, *Brookings Papers on Economic Activity: Microeconomics*, Brookings Institution: Washington, DC.

Stancanelli, Nestor. 2009. The Historical Context of the Green Box, pp. 19–35 in Ricardo Melendez-Ortiz, Christophe Bellmann, and Jonathan Hepburn (eds.), *Agricultural Subsidies in the WTO Green Box*, Cambridge University Press: New York City, NY.

Staples, Brian Rankin. 1998. Trade Facilitation. Mimeo.

Steenblik, Ronald, and Charles Tsai. 2009. The Environmental Impact of Green Box Subsidies: Exploring the Linkages, pp. 427–67 in Ricardo Melendez-Ortiz, Christophe

Bellmann, and Jonathan Hepburn (eds.), *Agricultural Subsidies in the WTO Green Box*, Cambridge University Press: New York City, NY.

Stein, Alex. 1996. The Re-foundation of Evidence Law, *The Canadian Journal of Law and Jurisprudence*, 9: 279–342.

—— 2005. *Foundations of Evidence Law*, Oxford University Press: New York City, NY.

—— 2008. On the Epistemic Authority of Courts, *Episteme*: 402–10.

Stevens, Christopher. 2002. The Future of SDT for Developing Countries in the WTO, Mimeo, Institute for Development Studies, Sussex.

Stewart, Terence P., and Myron Brilliant. 1993. Safeguards, pp. 1711–820 in Terence P. Stewart (ed.), *The GATT Uruguay Round: A Negotiating History (1986–1992)*, Kluwer Law: Deventer, the Netherlands and Boston, Mass.

—— and Amy S. Dwyer. 2009. Antidumping: Overview of the Agreement, pp. 197–240 in Kyle W. Bagwell, George A. Bermann, and Petros C. Mavroidis (eds.), *The Law and Economics of Contingent Protection in International Trade*, Cambridge University Press: New York City, NY.

—— Susan G. Markel, and Michael T. Kerwin. 1993. Antidumping, pp. 1383–710 in Terence P. Stewart (ed.), *The GATT Uruguay Round: A Negotiating History (1986–1992)*, Kluwer Law: Deventer, the Netherlands and Boston, Mass.

—— Eric P. Salonen, and Patrick J. McDonough. 2007. *More than 50 Years of Trade Rule Discrimination on Taxation: How Trade with China is Affected*, The Trade Lawyers Advisory Group: Washington, DC.

Stigler, George J. 1961. The Economics of Information, *The Journal of Political Economy*, 69: 213–25.

Stiglitz, Joseph E. 2000. Two Principles for the Next Round or, How to Bring Developing Countries in from the Cold, *The World Economy*, 23: 437–54.

—— 2003. *Globalization and its Discontents*, W.W. Norton: New York and London, UK.

Stirling, Andrew (ed.) 2001. On Science and Precaution in the Management of Technological Risk (<http://www.esto.jrc.es/detailshort:cfm?ID_report = 809>).

Subramanian, Arvind, and Shang Jin Wei. 2007. The WTO Promotes Trade Strongly but Unevenly, *Journal of International Economics*, 72: 151–75.

Summers, Larry. 1991. Regionalism and the World Trading System, pp. 42–65 in *Policy Implications of Trade and Currency Zones*, The Federal Reserve Bank of Kansas City.

Sunstein, Cass. 1999. *One Case at a Time*, Harvard University Press: Cambridge, Mass.

—— 2002. *Risk and Reason*, Harvard University Press: Cambridge, Mass.

—— 2003. Beyond the Precautionary Principle, *University of Pennsylvania Law Review*, 151: 1003–76.

Swinbank, Alan. 2009. The Reform of the EU's Common Agricultural Policy, pp. 70–85 in Ricardo Melendez-Ortiz, Christophe Bellmann, and Jonathan Hepburn (eds.), *Agricultural Subsidies in the WTO Green Box*, Cambridge University Press: New York City, NY.

—— and Carolyn Tanner. 1996. *Farm Policy and Trade Conflict*, University of Michigan Press: Ann Arbor, Mich.

Swinnen, Jo F. M. 2008. *The Perfect Storm: The Political Economy of the Fischler Reports of the Common Agricultural Policy*, Centre for European Policy Studies: Brussels.

—— 2009. The Growth of Agricultural Protection in Europe in the 19th Century, *The World Economy*, 32: 1499–537.

Sykes, Alan O. 1990. GATT Safeguards Reform: The Injury Test, pp. 203–36 in Michael Trebilcock and R. York, *Fair Exchange: Reforming Trade Remedy Laws,* Policy Study 11, C.D. Howe Institute: Toronto.

—— 1991. Protectionism as a 'Safeguard': A Positive Analysis of GATT Article XIX with Normative Speculations, *University of Chicago Law Review*, 58: 255–82.

—— 1995. *Product Standards for Internationally Integrated Goods Markets*, Brookings Institution: Washington, DC.

—— 1999. Regulatory Protectionism and the Law of International Trade, *University of Chicago Law Review*, 66: 1–45.

—— 2000. Regulatory Competition or Regulatory Harmonization? A Silly Question?, *Journal of International Economic Law*, 2: 257–64.

Sykes, Alan O. 2003a. The Safeguards Mess: A Critique of WTO Jurisprudence, *The World Trade Review*, 3: 216–96.

—— 2003b. The Economics of the WTO Rules on Subsidies and Countervailing Measures, John M. Olin Program in Law & Economics Working Papers, No. 186, University of Chicago.

—— 2003c. The Least Restrictive Means, *University of Chicago Law Review*, 70: 403–16.

—— 2006a. *The WTO Agreement on Safeguards: A Commentary*, Oxford University Press: Oxford, UK.

—— 2006b. Domestic Regulation, Sovereignty and Scientific Evidence Requirements: A Pessimistic View, pp. 257–70 in George A. Bermann and Petros C. Mavroidis (eds.), *Trade and Human Health and Safety*, Cambridge University Press: New York City, NY.

Tang, Man Keung, and Shang Jin Wei. 2009. The Value of Making Commitments Externally: Evidence from WTO Accession, *Journal of International Economics*, 78: 216–29.

Tang, Xiaobing. 1998. The Integration of Textiles and Clothing into GATT and WTO Dispute settlement, pp. 171–205 in James Cameron and Karen Campbell (eds.), *Dispute Resolution in the World Trade Organisation*, Cameron May: London, UK.

Tinbergen, Jan. 1962. *Shaping the World Economy*, The Twentieth Century Fund: New York City, NY.

Tokarick, Stephen. 2006. Does Import Protection Discourage Exports? IMF Working Paper WP/06/20, IMF: Washington, DC.

Torrens, Robert. 1815. *An Essay on the External Corn Trade*, J. Hatchard: London, UK.

Toye, Richard. 2003. The Attlee Government, the Imperial Preference System, and the Creation of the GATT, *English Historical Review*, 68: 912–39.

Trachtman, Joel. 1998. Trade and... Problems, Cost-Benefit Analysis and Subsidiarity, *European Journal of International Law*, 9: 32–60.

—— 1999. The Domain of the WTO Dispute Resolution, *Harvard Journal of International Law*, 40: 333–63.

—— 2011. The Limits of PTAs: WTO Legal restrictions on the Use of WTO-Plus Standards Regulation in PTAs, pp. 115–49 in Kyle W. Bagwell and Petros C. Mavroidis (eds.), *Preferential Trade Agreements: A Law and Economics Analysis*, Cambridge University Press: New York.

Trebilcock, Michael J. 2011. *Understanding Trade Law*, Edward Elgar: Cheltenham, UK.

—— and Michael Fishbein. 2007. International Trade: Barriers to Trade, pp. 1–61 in Andrew T. Guzman, and Alan O. Sykes (eds.), *Research Handbook International Economic Law*, Edward Elgar: Cheltenham, UK.

—— and Robert Howse. 2005. *International Trade Regulation*, 3rd edn., Routledge: London.

—— and Julie Soloway. 2002. International Trade Policy and Domestic Food Safety Regulation: The Case for Substantial Deference by the WTO Dispute Settlement Body under the SPS Agreement, pp. 537–74 in Daniel M. Kennedy and James D. Southwick (eds.), *The Political Economy of International Trade Law—Essays in Honor of Robert E. Hudec*, Cambridge University Press: Cambridge, Mass.

Trefler, Daniel. 2004. The Long and Short of the Canada-US Free Trade Agreement, *American Economic Review*, 94: 870–95.

Tumlir, Jan. 1985. *Protectionism: Trade Policy in Democratic Societies*, American Enterprise Institute: Washington, DC.

Tupy, Marian. 2005. Africa's War on Poverty Begins at Home, *The Financial Times*, 19 December (available at <http://www.ft.com>).

Vadcar, Corinne. 1998. Le Projet de l'Accord Multilateral sur l'Investissement: Problématique de l'Adhésion des Pays du Sud, *Journal du droit international*, 125: 9–31.

Vagts, Detlev. 2003. Extra-Territoriality and the Corporate Governance Law, *American Journal of International Law*, 97: 289–94.

Van Damme, Isabelle. 2007. The Interpretation of Schedules of Commitments, *Journal of World Trade*, 41: 1–52.

Van den Bossche, Pieter. 2005. *The WTO, Texts, Cases and Materials*, Cambridge University Press: Cambridge, UK.

van der Mensbrugghe, Dominique. 2009. The Doha Development Agenda and Preference Erosion: Modeling the Impacts, pp. 357–400 in Bernard M. Hoekman, Will Martin, and Carlos A. Primo Braga (eds.), *Trade Preference Erosion, Measurement and Policy Response*, Palgrave Macmillan and the World Bank: Washington, DC.

Varian, Hal R. 1980. A Model of Sales, *American Economic Review*, 70: 651–9.

Verhoosel, Gaetan. 2002. *National Treatment and WTO Dispute Settlement*, Hart Publishing: Oxford, UK.

Vermulst, Edwin. 1992. Rules of Origin as Commercial Policy Instruments—Revisited, *Journal of World Trade*, 26: 61–102.

——— 1995. Rules of Origin in the Future: Selected Issues, pp. 353–60 in Jacques Bourgeois, Frederique Perrod and Eric Gippini Fournier (eds.), *The Uruguay Round Results*, Brussels Inter-university Press: Brussels.

——— 1996. *EC Antidumping Law and Practice*, Sweet & Maxwell: London.

——— and Hiroshi Imagawa. 2005. The Agreement on Rules of Origin, pp. 601–78 in Patrick Macrory, Arthur Appleton, and Michael Plummer (eds.), *The World Trade Organization: Legal, Economic and Political Analysis vol. I*, Springer: New York, NY.

——— and Paul Waer. 1990. European Community Rules of Origin as Commercial Policy Instruments, *Journal of World Trade*, 24: 55–100.

——— ——— 1997. *EC Antidumping Law and Practice*, Sweet & Maxwell: London.

Viner, Jacob. 1922. *Dumping: A Problem in International Trade*, reprinted by Reprints of Economics Classics (1966), Augustus M. Kelley: New York City, NY.

——— 1924. The Most-Favored-Nation Clause in American Commercial Treaties, *Journal of Political Economy*, 32: 126–50.

——— 1950. *The Customs Union Issue*, Carnegie Endowment for International Peace: New York, NY.

Vogel, David. 1997. *Barriers or Benefits? Regulation in Transatlantic Trade*, Brookings Institution: Washington, DC.

——— 2003. The Hare and the Tortoise Revisited: The New Politics of Consumer and Environmental Regulation in Europe, *British Journal of Political Science*, 33: 557–80.

Wälde, Thomas. 1996. *The Energy Charter Treaty: An East-West Gateway for Investment and Trade,* Kluwer: London, UK.

Wang, Ping. 2011. Accession to the Agreement on Government Procurement: The Case of China, pp. 92–116 in Sue Arrowsmith and Robert D. Anderson (eds.), *The WTO*

Regime on Government Procurement: Challenge and Reform, Cambridge University Press: Cambridge, UK.

Wang, Z. K., and L. A. Winters. 2000. Putting 'Humpty' Together Again: Including Developing Countries in a Consensus for the WTO, CEPR Policy Paper No 4.

Wauters, Jasper M. 2010. The Safeguards Agreement—An Overview, pp. 334–66 in Kyle W. Bagwell, George A. Bermann, and Petros C. Mavroidis (eds.), *Law and Economics of Contingent Protection in International Trade*, Cambridge University Press: New York City, NY.

Wauters, Jasper M. and Hylke Vandenbussche. 2010. China-Measures Affecting Imports of Automobile Parts, pp. 201–38 in Henrik Horn and Petros C. Mavroidis (eds.), *The WTO Case-Law of 2008: The American Law Institute Reporters' Studies*, Cambridge University Press: Cambridge, UK.

Weatherill, Stephen. 2002. Preemption, Harmonisation and the Distribution of Competence to Regulate the Internal Market, pp. 41–73 in Catherine Barnard and Joanne Scott (eds.), *The Law of The Single European Market*, Hart Publishing: Oxford, UK.

Weiss, Friedl (ed.) 2000. *Improving WTO Dispute Settlement Procedures: Issues and Lessons from the Practice of Other International Courts and Tribunals*, Cameron May: London, UK.

Weston, Burns, Richard B. Lillich, and David J. Benderman. 1999. *International Claims: Their Settlements by Lump-Sum Agreements*, Transnational Publishers Inc.: Ardsley, NY.

Whalley, John (ed.) 1989. *Developing Countries and the Global Trading System*, University of Michigan Press: Ann Arbor, Mich.

—— 2008. Recent Regional Agreements: Why So Many, Why So Much Variance in Form, Why Coming So Fast, and Where Are They Headed?, *The World Economy*, 31: 517–32.

Wilcox, Clair. 1949. *A Charter for World Trade*, Macmillan: New York, NY.

Williamson, Oliver E. 2005. Why Law, Economics and Organization?, *Annual Review of Law and Social Science*, 1: 369–96.

Wilson, John S., and V. Abiola (eds.) 2003. *Standards and Global Trade: A Voice for Africa*, The World Bank: Washington, DC.

—— Catherine L. Mann, and Tsunehiro Otsuki. 2003. Trade Facilitation and Economic Development: A New Approach to Measuring the Impact, *World Bank Economic Review*, 17: 367–89.

—— —— —— 2005. Assessing the Benefits of Trade Facilitation: A Global Perspective, *The World Economy*, 28: 841–71.

—— and Tsunehiro Otsuki. 2004. *Standard and Technical Regulations and Firms in Developing Countries: New Evidence from a World Bank Technical Barriers to Trade Survey*, The World Bank: Washington, DC.

Wilson, Theodore A. 1991. *The First Summit: Roosevelt and Churchill at Placentia Bay, 1941*, rev. edn, University Press of Kansas: Lawrence, Kan.

Winham, Gilbert R. 1986. *International Trade and the Tokyo Round Negotiations*, Princeton University Press: Princeton, NJ.

Winters, Alan L. 1996. Regionalism versus Multilateralism, Discussion Paper No. 1525, CEPR: London.

—— 2011. Preferential Trading Agreements: Friend or Foe?, pp. 7–30 in Kyle W. Bagwell and Petros C. Mavroidis (eds.), *Preferential Trade Agreements: A Law and Economics Analysis*, Cambridge University Press: New York, NY.

—— and Won Chang. 2000. Regional Integration and Import Prices: An Empirical Investigation, *Journal of International Economics*, 51: 363–77.

—— and Maurice Schiff. 1998. *Regional Integration as Diplomacy*, The World Bank: Washington, DC.

Wolf, Martin, Hans Heinrich Glismann, Joseph Pelzman, and Dean Spinanger. 1984. Costs of Protecting Jobs in Textiles and Clothing, Thames Essay No. 37, Trade Policy Research Centre: London, UK.

Wood, Diane P. 1997. The WTO Agreement on Government Procurement: An Antitrust Perspective, pp. 261–72 in Bernard M. Hoekman and Petros C. Mavroidis (eds.), *Law and Policy in Public Purchasing*, University of Michigan Press: Ann Arbor, Mich.

—— 1998. State Trading in the United States, pp. 211–30 in Thomas Cottier, and Petros C. Mavroidis (eds.), *State Trading in the Twenty-First Century*, University of Michigan Press: Ann Arbor, Mich.

Wouters, Jan, and Dominic Coppens. 2010. An Overview of the Agreement on Subsidies and Countervailing Measures—Including a Discussion of the Agreement on Agriculture, pp. 7–84 in Kyle W. Bagwell, George A. Bermann, and Petros C. Mavroidis (eds.), *Law and Economics of Contingent Protection in International Trade*, Cambridge University Press: New York City, NY.

Wu, Mark. 2008. Free Trade and the Protection of Public Morals: An Analysis of the Newly Emerging Public Morals Clause Doctrine, *Yale Journal of International Law*, 33: 215–51.

—— 2010. Why Not Brussels? European Community State Aid Rules and the Boeing-Airbus Dispute, pp. 185–96 in Kyle W. Bagwell, George A. Bermann, and Petros C. Mavroidis (eds.), *Law and Economics of Contingent Protection in International Trade*, Cambridge University Press: New York City, NY

Xie, Jianmin. 2009. A Chinese Perspective of the Green Box, pp. 399–411 in Ricardo Melendez-Ortiz, Christophe Bellmann, and Jonathan Hepburn (eds.), *Agricultural Subsidies in the WTO Green Box*, Cambridge University Press: New York City, NY.

Yavitz, Laura. 2002. The WTO Appellate Body Report EC—Measures Affecting Asbestos and Asbestos-Containing Products, *Minnesota Journal of Global Trade*, 11: 35–65.

Yeutter, Clayton. 1998. Bringing Agriculture into the Multilateral Trading System, pp. 61–78 in Jagdish Bhagwati and Matthias Hirsch (eds.), *The Uruguay Round and Beyond, Essays in Honour of Arthur Dunkel*, The University of Michigan Press: Ann Arbor, Mich.

Zahrnt, Valentin. 2009. *The WTO's Trade Policy Review Mechanism: How to Create Political Will for Liberalization*, European Centre for International Political Economy (ECIPE): Brussels.

Zanardi, Maurizio. 2004. Antidumping: What are the Numbers to Discuss? *The World Economy*: 403–33.

Zeiler, Thomas W. 1999. *Free Trade, Free World: The Advent of the GATT*, The University of North Carolina Press: Chapel Hill, NC.

Zhang, Xinglin. 2011. Constructing a System of Challenge Procedures to Comply with the Agreement on Government Procurement, pp. 483–510 in Sue Arrowsmith and Robert D. Anderson (eds.), *The WTO Regime on Government Procurement: Challenge and Reform*, Cambridge University Press: Cambridge, UK.

Zhou, Weihuan. 2012. The Role of Regulatory Purpose Under Articles III:2 and 4: Toward Consistency between Negotiating History and WTO Jurisprudence, *The World Trade Review*, 11: 81–118.

INDEX

894

895